# WORLD SCRIPTURE

*A Comparative Anthology of Sacred Texts*

For the Religious Studies Dept of King Alfred College from all of us at IIFWP in London
43, Lancaster Gate London W.2 3NA
020 7 723-0721
(Unification Movement)

Edited by
Andrew Wilson

Foreword by
Ninian Smart

## Editorial Board

# WORLD SCRIPTURE

*A Comparative Anthology of Sacred Texts*

A Project of the International Religious Foundation

PARAGON HOUSE

*St. Paul, Minnesota*

First paperback edition, 1995

Published in the United States by
Paragon House Publishers
2700 University Avenue West
St. Paul, Minnesota 55114



**The International Religious Foundation** is dedicated to the promotion
of world peace through interreligious dialogue and cooperation.
This volume reflects the emerging confluence of religious traditions on the
basis of interreligious, interdisciplinary, and intercultural exchange.



LIBRARY OF CONGRESS CATALOGING-IN-PUBLICATION DATA

World scripture / foreword by Ninian Smart; editor, Andrew Wilson.
Includes bibliographical references and indexes.
ISBN 0-89226-129-3-cloth
ISBN 1-55778-723-9
1. Religions—Quotations, maxims, etc. I. Wilson, Andrew.
BL29.263 1991
291.8—DC20 91-14350
CIP

# *Advisors and Contributors*

Savas C. Agourides
Professor of New Testament
School of Theology
University of Athens
Athens, Greece
(Christianity, Orthodox)

Bhagchandra Jain Bhaskar
Professor and Head
Department of Pali and Prakrit
Nagpur University
Nagpur, India
(Jainism)

Sister Maura Campbell
Professor of Religious Studies
Caldwell College
Caldwell, New Jersey
(Christianity, Roman Catholic)

Dr. Chu-hsien Chen
Hamburg, Germany
(Chinese Religions)

Canon Bernard Rex Davis
Subdean, Lincoln Cathedral
Lincoln, United Kingdom
(Christianity, Protestant)

Dr. Homi B. Dhalla
Lecturer, B.J.P.C. Institute
Bombay, India
(Zoroastrianism)

Dr. Paul B. Fenton
University of Lyon
Lyon, France
(Judaism)

Dr. Betty J. Fisher
General Editor
Baha'i Publishing Trust
Wilmette, Illinois
(Baha'i Faith)

Fung Hu-hsiang
Professor of Philosophy and Dean
College of Liberal Arts
National Central University
Taiwan, Republic of China
(Confucianism)

Rabbi Dr. Emanuel S. Goldsmith
Associate Professor of Jewish Studies
Queens College of the City
University of New York
Flushing, New York
(Judaism)

Rev. Canon Dr. Raymond J. Hammer
Anglican Interfaith Consultants
London, United Kingdom
Former Canon of Kobe Cathedral
Kobe, Japan
(Japanese Religions)

Institute for the Reverend Sun Myung
Moon's Sermons and Speeches
Sung Hwa University
Chonan, Korea
(Unification Church)

Rev. Dr. Frederick Jelly, O.P.
Dean of Studies
Mount St. Mary's Seminary
Emmitsburg, Maryland
(Christianity, Roman Catholic)

Jay E. Jensen
Director, Scriptures Coordination
The Church of Jesus Christ of
Latter-day Saints
Salt Lake City, Utah
(Church of Jesus Christ of Latter-day Saints)

Dr. Inamullah Khan
Secretary General
World Muslim Congress
Karachi, Pakistan
(Islam)

Dr. Maulana Wahiduddin Khan
President, The Islamic Centre
New Delhi, India
(Islam)

Sheikh Dr. Ahmad Kuftaro
Grand Mufti of Syria
Damascus, Syria
(Islam)

Dr. Byong Joo Lee
Chairman, Chung Hyun Seo Wun
Senior Committee Member
Sung Kyun Kwan National Confucian University
Seoul, Korea
(Confucianism)

Prof. Gobind Singh Mansukhani
Sikh Council for Interfaith Relations
London, United Kingdom
(Sikhism)

H. K. Mirza
High Priest of the Parsis
Professor Emeritus of Zoroastrian Studies
Bombay University
Bombay, India
(Zoroastrianism)

Hajime Nakamura
Professor of Religion Emeritus
Tokyo University
Founder-Director
The Eastern Institute
Tokyo, Japan
(Buddhism)

Prof. Kofi Asare Opoku
Institute of African Studies
University of Ghana
Legon, Ghana
(African Traditional Religions)

Dr. Yasar Nuri Ozturk
Faculty of Theology
Marmara University
Religion Commentator
Hurriyet Newspaper
Istanbul, Turkey
(Islam)

Dr. Ryszard Pachocinski
Head, Department of Comparative Education
Institute for Educational Research
Warsaw, Poland
(African Traditional Religions)

Jordan Paper
Associate Professor of Religious Studies
York University
North York, Ontario, Canada
(Native American Religions)

Dr. Pahalawattage Don Premasiri
Department of Philosophy
University of Peradeniya
Peradeniya, Sri Lanka
(Theravada Buddhism)

K. B. Ramakrishna Rao
Professor and Head,
Department of Philosophy
Mysore University
Mysore, India
(Hinduism)

K. L. Seshagiri Rao
Professor of Religious Studies
University of Virginia
Charlottesville, Virginia
(Hinduism)

Gene Reeves
Professor of Theology
Meadville/Lombard Theological School
Chicago, Illinois
(Japanese New Religions)

Ven. Prof. Samdhong L. Tenzin, Rinpoche
Director, Central Institute of Higher Tibetan Studies
Sarnath, Varanasi, India
(Tibetan Buddhism)

Rev. Losang Norbu Shastri
Central Institute of Higher Tibetan Studies
Sarnath, Varanasi, India
(Tibetan Buddhism)

Dr. Shivamurthy Shivacharya, Mahaswamiji
Sri Taralabalu Jagadguru Brihanmath
Sirigere, India
(Lingayat Hinduism)

Monsignor Antonio Silvestrelli
Congregation for the Doctrine of the Faith
Vatican City
(Christianity, Roman Catholic)

Dr. Avtar Singh
Dean, Faculty of Humanities and Religious Studies
Punjabi University
Patiala, India
(Sikhism)

Sant Giani Naranjan Singh
Guru Nanak Ashram
Patiala, India
(Sikhism)

Ninian Smart
J.F. Rowny Professor of Comparative Religions
University of California Santa Barbara
Santa Barbara, California
(General Consultant)

Huston Smith
Thomas J. Watson Professor Emeritus of Religion
Syracuse University
Graduate Theological Union
Berkeley, California
(General Consultant)

Rev. Takahide Takahashi
The Eastern Institute
Tokyo, Japan
(Japanese Buddhism)

Kapil Tiwari
Professor of World Religions
Victoria University
Wellington, New Zealand
(South Pacific Traditional Religions)

Dr. David Manning White
President, Marlborough Publishing House
Richmond, Virginia
(World Spirituality)

❖

# CONTENTS

## *Part Five: Providence, Society, and the Kingdom of Heaven*

# *Foreword*

IT IS OBVIOUS THAT AS WE MOVE TOWARD a world civilization, in which so many cultures and spiritual traditions will impinge on one another, all of us should understand one another. This does not necessarily mean agreement—how could it given the diversity of human values evident in the world? But it can mean growing convergence and complementarity among the faiths, large and small, of our shrinking planet. It is therefore good to have sources of comparison among religious traditions, and one obvious place to look is in the scriptures and sacred writings of the various cultures.

*World Scripture* offers an admirable assemblage of quotations from the holy texts of the world from a broadly theistic angle. Of course, others might prefer a different articulation of the material. As Andrew Wilson rightly points out in his introduction, they should create their own books of world scripture. Our world is surely hospitable to a variety of approaches. This way of treating the great traditions could be paralleled by others. It has some flavor of Unificationism. But I think that the systematic arrangement of themes and texts has provided a logical and orderly way of comparing and contrasting the wide range of material. *World Scripture* therefore provides us with a collection which is illuminating.

This kind of anthology will be of interest in various areas. First, people who have genuine concern for religion and spirituality will be further stimulated by easy access to so many scriptural traditions. Second, many students of the comparative study of religions or the history of religions will be able to use this book in the classroom and beyond. Third, many religious professionals, whether Christian or Muslim or Buddhist or whatever, will find this a good reference book.

After all, in today's world every tradition must take account of the other traditions. What does the Buddhist say about Christian theism? What does the Muslim say about Chinese traditions? What does the theist say about non-theistic religions? These are vital questions, if men and women in the world are to take both their own traditions and those of others seriously. This anthology will help to guide their path and to spark questions. It is compiled in the spirit of reverence for all spiritual paths. Such a spirit is needed if we are to live at peace with one another. That is not always easy; I would not underestimate the tensions which can occur among sisters and brothers of apparently rival faiths. But gradually, as we approach a world culture, we shall overcome such tensions and learn to converse and argue gently with one another. An anthology such as this will help such conversations.

I am therefore very glad that the International Religious Foundation has taken so much trouble in bringing this book to publication. We can all learn from one another.

Ninian Smart
J.F. Rowny Professor of Comparative Religions
University of California, Santa Barbara

# PREFACE

ALL THE GREAT RELIGIONS OF THE WORLD revere sacred scriptures. Such texts include the Dhammapada and Lotus Sutra of Buddhism, the New Testament of Christianity, the Qur'an of Islam, the Vedas and the Bhagavad Gita of Hinduism, the Torah of Judaism, the Confucian Analects, and the Adi Granth of Sikhism. These sacred scriptures contain essential truths. And they have immeasurably great historical significance, for they have influenced the minds, hearts, and practices of billions of people in the past. They continue to exert tremendous impact in the present, and we have every reason to believe that such influence will continue into the future. The words of truth in sacred scriptures form the core beliefs of religion and thus, of civilization.

For this reason, the Reverend Sun Myung Moon, founder of the International Religious Foundation, commissioned this World Scripture project. One purpose is to celebrate and honor the richness and universality of religious truth contained in the world's great scriptures. An additional purpose is to serve the cause of world peace. Peace has been the central focus of all the activities of the International Religious Foundation which is dedicated to "world peace through religious dialogue and harmony." The work of the International Religious Foundation has culminated in the establishment of the Inter-Religious Federation for World Peace (IRFWP), created at the 1990 Assembly of the World's Religions. *World Scripture* is directly related to the quest for peace that is the mission of IRFWP. Although all the great religions speak of peace, a tragic complicity has existed between religion and conflict. In too many instances, religion either fuels division and conflict or it proves unable or unwilling to mediate the solution to division and conflict. We can say that religious power, like any other power, can be used for good or evil. What is needed so desperately in our world today is a mobilization of religious power on behalf of world peace; that is, mobilized to defuse the hatred, the resentments, and the bitter memories that divide even religious people.

While sacred texts have often functioned as the axis of truth, ethics, and identity for religious communities, they have also served as points of exclusivism and separateness among these communities. As long as our world remained divided into discrete spheres of culture with little exchange among regions and cultures, particular scriptures could be affirmed as absolute and unique. Today, however, science and technology have bridged the gaps that previously divided us as cultures, nations, and religions. We are unavoidably interconnected and interrelated. Therefore, each religion can no longer refuse to recognize the spirituality and legitimacy of the truths embodied in other religions' sacred scriptures.

*World Scripture* is designed to underscore the universality within all religions and to demonstrate that there exists a vast sphere of spiritual common ground. This is not to suggest that specific religions lack distinctions or unique aspects, nor is it intended to advocate syncretism. Rather, such a perspective calls attention to the shared insights and vision of all religions. By focusing on these common elements, we can learn from and inherit each other's spiritual foundation and prepare for mutual cooperation.

Unless religious people from all backgrounds can work with one another respectfully and cooperatively, in a spirit of brotherhood and sisterhood, there seems little hope that the enmity that distorts the relations among peoples can be eliminated. Religious people have a great responsibility at this hour in history. As religious people, we should repent for inadequately responding to the world's need, and even more for allowing our religious commitments to become the basis for exclusivity and hatred.

It is my sincere hope that *World Scripture* will make a most significant contribution to world peace by illuminating the shared wisdom and light of the great religious teachers of the world. May this light shine brightly, and may there be peace on earth.

Chung Hwan Kwak
President
International Religious Foundation

# *Introduction*

WE LIVE IN AN ECUMENICAL AGE. The progress in transportation and communication that has brought all the peoples of the world into one global village has also brought the religions of the world into close contact. Just half a century ago, Christians living in North America might never have met a Muslim or a Buddhist throughout their whole lives; in ignorance they could believe that such people were heathen and in dire need of salvation. Muslims in Syria, or Buddhists in Thailand, could as easily hold a similar view of the foreign religions that occasionally intruded upon their lands. But today Western cities teem with immigrants from Asia and Africa bearing their native faiths, and our commercial and political affairs connect us with all nations. A movement for a "wider ecumenism" has begun, bringing together for dialogue leaders and scholars from all the world's religions. Theologians of all faiths are affirming the positive worth of other religions and seeking to overcome the prejudice of an earlier time. It is now widely recognized that humanity's search for God, or for the Ultimate Reality, called by whatever name, is at the root of all religions.

The first step toward appreciating other religions is to understand each on its own terms. Each religion has its own spiritual depth; each gives its own distinctive answers to many of the fundamental questions which trouble human existence. To this end, most religion textbooks treat each major religion in turn, and most anthologies present selections from the world's scriptures religion by religion. However, by treating each religion separately, these texts and anthologies tend to emphasize differences and overlook similarities. They may give the impression that each religion stands alone as an independent system and a different way of knowing and being. Thus the variety of religions would appear to be a testimony to the relativity of human beliefs rather than to the existence of the one Absolute Reality which stands behind all of them.

Interfaith dialogue in our time is going beyond the first step of appreciating other religions to a growing recognition that the religions of the world have much in common. The Christian participant may find something in Islam, for example, that can deepen his or her Christianity, and the Muslim participant may find something instructive from the teachings of Buddhism. The common ground between religions becomes more apparent as the dialogue partners penetrate beneath superficial disagreements in doctrine.

Today the call for a "world theology" has been sounded by many scholars, including Wilfred Cantwell Smith, John Hick, and Raimundo Panikkar. They explain that religions are not tight and consistent philosophical systems. While a particular religion may have certain predominant themes, it must—as the foundation of a culture—be broad enough to inform all aspects of human experience. Hence every religion has, within its own borders, considerable diversity of belief and practice. The variety of ways of being human religiously cut across the religions: the Roman Catholic mystic, the seeker of Brahman through Hindu Vedanta, and the Zen Buddhist monk may have more in common with one another than with the members of the fundamentalist movements of their own traditions, and fundamentalist Christians, Jews, and Muslims may similarly find common ground not shared by their more mystically oriented counterparts.

In addition, historians of religions now recognize that the religious traditions of the world did not grow up in isolation; they have enriched one another in diverse ways at many significant points of contact. Hence it is inadequate to treat religions as discrete and independent entities. We must seek new, holistic models to describe the human religious experience. We may even, like Hick, speak of a coming "Copernican revolution" in religion that recognizes a unity underlying all religions. To discern the shape of this underlying unity is the end towards which *World Scripture* has been compiled.

## *Purpose of World Scripture*

*WORLD SCRIPTURE* GATHERS PASSAGES from the scriptures of the various religious traditions around certain topics. Often these scriptural passages support a common theme; sometimes they illuminate several contrasting positions on the topic. This method of organization allows each topic to be addressed with the resources of many different traditions, often providing a broader and deeper understanding of the topic than would be possible from the resources of a single tradition. Each religion has much value to contribute to humankind's understanding of truth, which transcends any particular expression.

All religions do not teach the same message. The contributors have provided passages which fairly represent the main thrust of each religion's teachings. However, since the tenets of each religion are taken out of their ordinary frame of reference, there is always the danger that they might be misinterpreted. Therefore, it would be a mistake to read *World Scripture* as though it were proclaiming a monolithic, universal teaching of all religions. Rather, the similarities and common themes highlighted in this anthology should be viewed against each religion's distinctive message. The reader is cautioned: Until one takes the first step of understanding each religion in its own distinctiveness, its contribution to the unity of religions is likely to be misinterpreted. Many would also suggest that to truly understand another religion, one should first be deeply committed to one's own faith and its traditions.

Granting the integrity of each religion, it is significant for the believer of one faith to find in other faiths common teachings and common attitudes towards life, death, and ultimate ends. First, there is the discovery that the transcendent Reality that is the ground of life in one's own faith is also grounding the spiritual life of people whose faith stems from different revelations, different revealers. This confirms and testifies to the oneness of God, the Ultimate Reality, who appears in different guises from age to age and culture to culture. Second, the discovery that people of other faiths are leading spiritual lives similar to one's own can promote tolerance of, and respect for, other faiths. By understanding one another's religions in depth and with empathy, people can find peaceful solutions to disputes which might otherwise degenerate into dangerous conflict. Third, the teachings of another tradition may spark new insights into similar issues in one's own life of faith. Indeed, if each religion is but a witness to the Truth that transcends its particular expression, then all of them should contribute valuable insights to our understanding of any question. Fourth, humankind needs to rediscover the spiritual foundations of values in order to overcome the sterile materialist outlooks and philosophies of our day. Despite both the common moral values and the traditional spiritual wisdom found in all religions, persistent squabbles among religions have served to discredit them, making universal values appear to be relative and sectarian. The foundations of a pluralistic society—its cultural expressions, legal system, and public schools—requires values that are grounded in the universal experience of humankind, not just in the doctrines of one particular faith. Necessary to this foundation is testimony to the universality of religious values such as found herein. Finally, *World Scripture* can support a world theology and guide us toward a unity of the world's peoples that is grounded in God.

## *Organization of World Scripture*

THE BULK OF THE MATERIAL found in *World Scripture* comes from the scriptures of the five major living world religious traditions: Christianity, Islam, Buddhism, Hinduism, and Chinese religions (Confucianism and Taoism). There are also a considerable number of texts from the smaller living religions: Judaism, Jainism, Sikhism, Shinto, and Zoroastrianism. Whenever these religions have a word to say about any topic in the anthology, the contributors have provided suitable passages. There are also a limited number of selections from the recorded prayers and proverbs of the traditional religions of Africa, the Americas, Asia, and the South Pacific, and from some of the new religions of the nineteenth and twentieth centuries. Texts from these smaller religions, both traditional and contemporary, are included to acknowledge the diversity of religious expression in the world today. These are all voices which should be heard. However, one group of voices that is sometimes found in anthologies of religion has been omitted: Since *World Scripture* aims to promote harmony among living faiths, it does not include texts from the dead religions of the past such as those of ancient Egypt, Mesopotamia, and pre-Columbian Mesoamerica.

The texts in *World Scripture* have been deliberately restricted, wherever possible, to passages from scripture. This distinguishes it from topical anthologies of religious wisdom which draw on the writings of mystics, saints, and theologians. Scripture may be regarded variously as direct revelation from God or as the distilled insights received by the founder and his disciples. In either case, it posseses a certain authority and priority as the fount of the religion. In scripture we grasp the freshness of the original revelation. Through constant liturgical use, scriptural texts are engraved in the hearts of believers. The laws in scripture provide the standard around which a religion elaborates its cultural norms. It is to scripture that believers turn for inspiration and revival in every age.

The definition of scripture and canon varies from one religion to another; in general each religion's own definition of its canonical scriptures has been accepted as the criterion for this anthology. The selection of a canon reflects both the usage of these texts by the religious community and historical decisions by councils and groups as the religion grappled with its identity and established norms of doctrine and practice. Through history and usage, the community of believers settled on sacred texts which speak with enduring authority.

There are inevitable dissimilarities between the scriptures of religions with a tightly circumscribed canon limited to texts used by the founder and his immediate disciples, e.g., Christianity, Islam, and Sikhism, and the scriptures of religions with an open canon that includes texts of many periods in the religion's history, e.g., Mahayana Buddhism, Hinduism, and Jainism. The scriptures of religions with a narrow canon are limited to one or a few books—the Bible, the Qur'an, the Adi Granth—while the scriptures of religions with an open canon may include hundreds of books: sutras, upanishads, agamas, shastras, puranas, tantras, and commentaries. We have tried to preserve a balance among the number of passages cited for each of the major religions. Fortunately, the various scriptures of religions with an open canon contain considerable repetition, and hence a few representative passages can be culled for each topic.

The term "scripture" is used somewhat loosely for the inspired writings of the new religions which may still live in the presence of the founder or his immediate disciples. Many of them have distinctive texts, but some are too young to have settled on which of them are scripture; the process of establishing a canon takes place only after a religion has had time to define its boundaries and solidify its traditions.

We must further stretch the limits of what is considered scripture in order to include the traditional religions of Africa, Asia, and the Americas, which have no written texts. What makes scripture important is not the fact that it is written but that it is inspired and authoritative. In these traditional religions, an authoritative body of tradition has been passed down from generation to generation through words, symbols, and rituals. This body of tradition fulfills the function of scripture by giving an account of, among other things, the nature of God, the origin of the world, the duty of human beings, and human destiny. All the written scriptures of the major religions began as oral traditions. We consider the enduring oral traditions of the traditional religions as scripture in a broad sense, for they are written in the hearts of the practitioners of these faiths.

Another problem in dealing with scripture is that many of them cannot be adequately translated into English. The manifold nuances of a scripture's original language can never be fully rendered in translation. Furthermore, for those religions, including Judaism, Islam, and Hinduism, which revere the language of their scriptures as sacred, the holiness of their scriptures can be conveyed only in the sacred tongue. We must acknowledge, therefore, that the English translations of scriptures in *World Scripture* are only interpretations which convey a pale reflection of the original. We have sought translations which, whenever possible, satisfy two criteria: The translator should himself or herself be a practitioner of the religion with a spiritual sensitivity to the depth of the tradition, and the translator should have a good command of the English language. In several cases where no English translation was available or where existing translations were judged inadequate, new translations were commissioned. Furthermore, as this book is intended for the general reading public, diacritical marks have been dispensed with, except as sources and terms are identified in the indexes.

In making their selections, the editors have exercised discretion in seeking higher expressions of the spirit and avoiding passages that are mean-spirited and offensive to other religions. The scriptures of most religions contain passages attacking, and often misrepresenting, the doctrines and practices of other religions. This is understandable in light of the conflicts which most religions experienced in their youth against the older dominant religion. Sometimes the older religion was in a corrupt form that was far removed from its own higher expressions. Polemics attacking a priest, brahmin, mullah, or rabbi for hypocrisy should best be understood not as a partisan attack on another religion, but rather as illuminating a universal problem of religious people. But too often they have fostered prejudice and inhibited interreligious understanding. Examples include: New Testament polemics against the Jews and the Mosaic Law, the Qur'an's polemics against the Christian doctrine that Jesus is the Son of God, and the Lotus Sutra's polemics against Theravada Buddhism as an inferior vehicle.

The topics around which the scripture passages are gathered have been selected as broadly comprehensive of the concerns shared by many of the major religions. Certain topics that belong to only one or two religions are omitted in favor of topics that can be construed to include several distinct but related religious ideas. Thus, for example, there is no topic "resurrection," but Christian and Muslim passages on resurrection are included under the broader topics *The Immortal Soul*, *Heaven*, and *Hell* where they stand alongside passages from other religions on the afterlife. While each religion has something to say about more than seventy percent of the topics, certain themes are ignored or even rejected by some religions: for example, Jainism and Buddhism say nothing about a God who is Creator. In those cases, the religion will not show any passages on that topic. Sometimes counterexamples will be given, for example under the topic *Asceticism and Monasticism* are several critiques of the practice. Furthermore, since many passages are relevant to more than one topic, extensive cross-references are given in footnotes, and a few key passages may be duplicated under several headings.

The organization of the topics follows generally the pattern of Christian systematic theology: God and creation, evil and sin, salvation, ethics, and eschatology. But this outline has been broadened by the inclusion of many non-Christian themes in order to include every topic regarded as central by any of the world's religions. Some may object at this point that the *World Scripture* has such a recognizably theistic perspective. Certainly the topics could have been organized differently: for example, according to a Buddhist schema of the Four Noble Truths or a Hindu schema of the several *margas* or paths to Ultimate Reality.[1] There is at present no recognized systematic theology of world religious knowledge. Some particular organizational scheme had to be selected, and, whatever the organization, it would necessarily be more congenial to one religion or another. To those whose religious understanding leads them to take exception to the organizational scheme selected, we can only invite them to write their own world scriptures from their own religious understandings and faith perspectives. By publicizing the enduring worth and common testimonies of the scriptures of other faiths, all such anthologies, whatever their perspectives, will contribute to the broad dialogue among religions that will promote interreligious harmony.

Selecting the topics and assembling the passages for the *World Scripture* has required the efforts of advisors and contributors representing all of the major world religions. Some of them labored long and hard to gather the texts which would best express the unique perspective of their religions. Others gave invaluable reviews of the unfinished manuscript. Through this collaboration, we have sought to ensure that the selection of topics and of scriptural passages will not reflect the viewpoint of any one religion, but will indeed embrace the breadth and variety of religious viewpoints in a balanced manner.

At this point it is worthwhile to introduce the various religions and their scriptures which are included in this anthology. We will proceed, geographically, from West to East.

---

[1] An organizational plan rooted in Hinduism is found in Whitall N. Perry, *A Treasury of Traditional Wisdom* (New York: Harper & Row, 1986). Perry divides his anthology of scriptural texts and mystical passages according to the three paths of karma yoga, (action), bhakti yoga (devotion), and jnana yoga (knowledge), although he does not explicitly acknowledge this indebtedness to the Hindu tradition.

## *The World's Religions and their Scriptures*

JUDAISM AND CHRISTIANITY are two monotheistic, ethical religions which share a part of their scriptures in common; the *Bible* of the Jews is the *Old Testament* of the Christians. These religions share many common beliefs: (1) There is one God, (2) mighty and (3) good, (4) the Creator, (5) who reveals his Word to man, and (6) answers prayers. Both Judaism and Christianity make (7) a positive affirmation of the world as the arena of God's activity, (8) as the place where people have an obligation to act ethically, and (9) which should be redeemed from injustice. Both believe in (10) a future life, as well as a doctrine of resurrection. Finally, both look to (11) a final consummation of history and (12) the realization of God's complete sovereignty on earth, through the coming of a Messiah or, in the case of modern forms of Judaism, a Messianic Age. Besides these similarities of doctrine, Christianity is bound to pay special attention to Judaism because Jesus and his disciples were Jews. They lived as Jews; the Jewish Bible was their scripture, and they criticized Jewish beliefs and practices as reformers from within. Jesus' life and teachings are largely incomprehensible without an understanding of the Judaism of his time.

Although Judaism and Christianity share many common elements in their beliefs, there are also deep differences. First, for Judaism God is one and unique; for Christianity God is one in his nature but there are three Persons constituting the Holy Trinity: Father, Son, and Holy Spirit. Christians believe in Jesus, called Christ, the Messiah, who is the Incarnation of the Second Person of the Trinity: therefore adoration is not given to man but to God who became man. Salvation for mankind is entirely the gift of God, through the sacrifice of the Second Person of the Trinity, who became man and suffered and died in his humanity and became alive again. Christians believe in Christ and in his passion, death, and resurrection; they follow his teachings and example; and after death they expect to share in his glorious resurrection. Judaism, for its part, is no less conscious of God's grace, but it offers sanctification through membership in the Jewish people and by regarding the scriptures as teaching and enjoining a life of holiness. For Jews the Messiah has not yet come, and they still anticipate the coming of the Messiah or Messianic Age. Their future hope is an earthly vision of a world of peace and justice. The Christian future hope is expressed by the doctrine of the Second Coming of Christ, when evil will finally come to an end and the spiritual blessings already accomplished in Jesus Christ will be manifested substantially in the Kingdom of Heaven.

Both Judaism and Christianity no longer practice the scriptural laws of animal sacrifices. But while for Judaism the *mitzvot*, the ethical and ritual commandments of the Bible, remain normative, and are elaborated in the Talmud as the *halakah* or requirements of life, Christianity has regard only for the Bible's ethical teachings—i.e., the Ten Commandments. Christianity emphasizes faith in Jesus Christ, who gives grace, empowerment, and guidance for living the moral life.[1] Judaism teaches a life of holiness through performing mitzvot and emphasizes the importance of

[1] Even within the Christian family, the relative value of faith (the grace of Christ) and works (obedience to the moral law) for salvation has been a source of contention. Most Protestants stress salvation by faith alone, with good works being a consequence of faith. Roman Catholics, Orthodox, and some Protestants (i.e., Anglicans) see faith and works as contributing synergistically to realization of the highest good.

adhering to the Bible's standards of social justice as laid down by the Prophets. The two religions have also diverged on the meaning of the Fall of Man; Christianity affirms a doctrine of Original Sin which is not emphasized in Judaism.

These deep differences extend to the way Judaism and Christianity regard their sacred writings. Judaism regards its sacred books as the complete source for all the teachings which God requires of his people for their welfare. For Christianity, the sacred books of Judaism, called the Old Testament, are taken as a preparation for the final revelation that God would make through Christ—a revelation that is written in the books of the *New Testament.*

Judaism's Bible or *Tanakh* is made up of the *Law* (*Torah*), the *Prophets* (*Nebi'im*), and the *Writings* (*Ketuvim*); its books were written over a period of more than thirteen hundred years of Jewish history, from the time of Moses until several centuries before the common era. The center of this scripture is the Torah, the Five Books of Moses. The book of Genesis contains stories of creation, the Fall of Man, and the lives of the patriarchs Noah, Abraham, Isaac, Jacob, and Joseph. Exodus, Leviticus, Numbers, and Deuteronomy recount the Jews' liberation from slavery in Egypt and the revealing of the Law to Moses on Mount Sinai. The Prophets include the books of Joshua, Judges, Samuel, and Kings recounting the history of Israel in the days when it was guided by its prophets, and Isaiah, Jeremiah, Ezekiel, Amos, Hosea, Micah, Habakkuk, Jonah, Haggai, Zechariah, Malachi, etc., which record the words of individual prophets. Among the Writings are the book of Psalms containing prayers and hymns; Proverbs, Ecclesiastes, and Job containing wise sayings, discourses on wisdom, and meditations on the human condition; Lamentations mourning the destruction of the Temple; Song of Songs, whose love poetry has long been interpreted as describing the mystical relationship between God and Israel or God and man; and Daniel with its stories of faith in the midst of persecution.

In addition to the Tanakh, a tradition of Oral Torah, passed down to the rabbis of the first several centuries of the common era and codified in the *Talmud*, which is constituted by the *Mishnah* and the *Gemara*, is authoritative for the observant Jew. One may regard the role of Talmud as providing the interpretative perspective for a proper understanding of the Bible. While much of the Talmud is devoted to discussions and codifications of law, it also contains passages of universal spiritual and ethical wisdom. The best known collection of the latter is a small tractate of the Mishnah called the *Abot* or *Sayings of the Fathers.*[1] The books of *Midrash*, rabbinic interpretation of scripture, are replete with moral and spiritual lessons and stories. Of equal authority are other rabbinic texts from this period: the *Sifra*, *Sifre Numbers* and *Sifre Deuteronomy*, *Tanhuma*, *Pesikta Rabbati* and *Pesikta Kahana*, and the *Tosefta*. Beyond these, Jewish tradition also hallows the books of statutory prayers. The mystical treatise called the *Zohar* and several other works together constitute the *Kabbalah* or mystical tradition which has canonical status for many Jews. A number of theological works, notably *The Guide for the Perplexed* by Moses Maimonides (1135-1204) and *Shulhan Arukh* by Joseph Caro (16th century) are also held in the highest regard.

The *Christian Bible* includes the *Old* and *New Testaments*. The Old Testament was the scripture of Jesus and his followers who were themselves Jews. It is identical to the Jewish Bible but with its books in a different order. Christians emphasize the prophetic books above all other parts of the Old Testament, for they are seen to announce the advent of Jesus Christ.

[1] Where a scripture is known by more than one name, or by both an English name and a title in the original language, it will be cited by the name which appears first in this introduction.

Roman Catholic and Orthodox Bibles include a number of additional books, called *Deutero-canonical Books*, in the Old Testament. Notable among them are the wisdom books Sirach and the Wisdom of Solomon, the stories of Tobit and Judith, and the history of the Maccabean revolt with its stories glorifying martyrdom in 1-4 Maccabees. These books circulated among Jews during the last two centuries before Christ and were included in the *Septuagint*, the Greek translation of the scriptures. The New Testament is written in Greek; the early Christians largely spoke Greek; and they used the Septuagint as their Old Testament. But these books were not included in the canon of Hebrew scriptures as fixed by the rabbis at Jamnia in 90 A.D. At the time of the Protestant Reformation, when the Reformers returned to the Hebrew rabbinic text as their standard, they omitted these books from their vernacular translations of the Bible—e.g., Luther's Bible and the English King James Version. Thus they are known to Protestants as the *Apocrypha*. The Roman Catholic Church reaffirmed their status as holy scripture at the Council of Trent (1545-1603), and they remain part of the Orthodox scriptures as well. Most modern translations of the Bible now include them.

The New Testament contains the four Gospels: Matthew, Mark, Luke, and John. The first three synoptic Gospels have much in common, recording the life and sayings of Jesus, his death, and resurrection. The Gospel of John provides a life of Christ who is portrayed as the mystical source of salvation. The epistles by the apostles Paul, Peter, James, John, and others discuss matters of theology, doctrine, faith, and morals for the early Church of the first century. Paul was the foremost of the apostles, and his writings include the epistle to the Romans, 1 and 2 Corinthians, Galatians, Philippians, 1 Thessalonians, and Philemon. Other letters attributed to Paul, and which certainly are indebted to his influence, include Ephesians, Colossians, 1 and 2 Timothy, Titus, and Hebrews. Acts of the Apostles is a history of the church from the first Pentecost to the evangelical tours of Peter and Paul. The Revelation gives a vision of the end of the world and the Second Coming of Christ. All the books of the New Testament were written within one hundred years of Jesus' death, although the final decision about which books would be included or excluded from the New Testament canon was not made until the fourth century.

ISLAM IS THE THIRD GREAT monotheistic religion which traces its roots back to Abraham, and its teachings show many continuities with the Jewish and Christian scriptures. Islam proclaims Allah, the one God, the Creator, who is sovereign and good, who answers prayers, and who works with mankind in history by calling prophets to proclaim God's word. There is a positive affirmation of the world as God's creation and the arena where people are obligated to act ethically. Islam offers only two choices for mankind: belief or unbelief, God or Satan, with the result that they will attain either Paradise or the fire of hell.

For Islam, the prophets are God's intermediaries to humanity, and Muhammad (c. 570-632 A.D.) is the Seal of the Prophets. The prophets: Adam, Noah, Abraham, Ishmael, Moses, and many others named and unnamed, delivered God's word to diverse peoples. They each had specific missions, but their messages are ultimately one: submit the self to the will of God. Jesus is one of the prophets; though titled Messiah, he has no distinctive messianic role in the sense that Christians ascribe to him, nor is he in any sense divine. His message and purpose were consistent with those of the prophets before and after him. The revelation to Muhammad is the perfect and accurate record of God's message by the prophets of every age.

Islam is a religion to be practiced, and five obligations are required of every Muslim—called the Five Pillars: (1) confession of faith in God and in Muhammad as God's messenger, (2) daily prayer at the five appointed times, (3) fasting during the month of Ramadan, (4) paying an alms-tax and giving charity to the poor, and (5) pilgrimage to the holy city of Mecca and its sacred shrine, the *Kaaba*. By fulfilling these obligations and remembering God often, the Muslim is assured of God's favor both on earth and at the judgment.

Islam's basic scripture is the *Qur'an*, which was revealed by the angel Gabriel to the prophet Muhammad, who according to tradition was unlettered. Gabriel recited its verses to Muhammad, who in turn taught them to his followers who memorized them and wrote them down on leaves and scraps of paper. They were gathered into the definitive text of the Qur'an within a generation of the prophet's death. The Qur'an has 114 suras, arranged in order of decreasing length.[1] Several interpretations of the Qur'an are available in English, but no true translation: The Qur'an was revealed specifically in Arabic, and a translation into any other language cannot convey the holiness of the Arabic Qur'an.

With regard to the authority of texts beyond the Qur'an, Islam is split into two large sects, *Sunni* and *Shiite*. The many Sufi writings, so popular in the West, are not regarded as having the authority of scripture in Islam.

Sunni Muslims revere the *Sunnah*, the teaching of Muhammad based upon *hadith*, the traditions and sayings of the prophet Muhammad as recollected and transmitted by his Companions. Most of the hadith concern the specifics of Islamic law, but some concern matters of faith, morality, and eschatology. The six great classical compilers of the Sunnah are: Bukhari, Muslim, Abu Dawud, Tirmidhi, an-Nasa'i, and Ibn Majah—with Bukhari and Muslim the most authoritative. These collections are the fruits of *'Ilm al-hadith*, the Science of Tradition, which established criteria for deciding the reliability of traditions, classifying them as "sound," "good," "weak," or "infirm." The compilations by Bukhari and Muslim, and several secondary collections of hadith based upon the six compilations, are available in English translation. Most notable among them is *The Forty Hadith of an-Nawawi*, a slim collection of traditions which continues to inspire with its concise expression of the heart of Islamic spirituality. Another authoritative tradition in Islam which has been excerpted for this anthology is the biography of Muhammad by Ibn Ishaq, the *Sirat Rasul Allah*, which survives only in the version edited by his disciple Ibn Hisham.

The Shiite tradition in Islam has its own collections of hadith which differ only in minor details from the Sunni collections, but these do not have the authority of the Sunnah and are not quoted in this anthology. What most distinguishes Shiite Islam is its reverence for 'Ali (d. 661 A.D.), the son-in-law of Muhammad, who became the fourth Caliph and ruled the Muslim peoples for seven years until his death as a martyr. 'Ali is regarded as the perfect exemplar of Islam, and his sermons and sayings are collected in the *Nahjul Balagha*. For Shiite Muslims the Nahjul Balagha is a sacred scripture second only to the Qur'an.

THE PROPHET ZARATHUSTRA (c. 1000 B.C.) is the founder of Zoroastrianism. Once the major religion of ancient Persia, Zoroastrianism has had considerable influence on the thought of Christianity and Islam. Yet despite its historical importance, today Zoroastrianism exists only as a remnant. After suffering persecution and expulsion from Iran, the community of practicing Zoroastrians has dwindled to less than one hundred thousand Parsees, most of whom live in the vicinity of Bombay, India.

---

[1] There are variations in the versification of the several English renderings of the Qur'an. This anthology has selected the versification employed by M. Pickthall's translation as a standard.

Contemporary Zoroastrians are monotheistic. They worship one God, Ahura Mazda, the Lord of Wisdom, whose various aspects are personified in scripture as the archangels Good Mind, Righteousness, Devotion, Dominion, and others. He is symbolized by the fire, which is at the center of Zoroastrian ritual. Zoroastrianism teaches an ethical dualism; there is a constant battle between a wholly good God and the powers of evil. This struggle occurs within the human breast and necessitates the choice between good and evil. The soul is immortal, and each will receive divine justice according to its deeds in life. But good and evil are not equal: God and Right will ultimately triumph at the end of history. The good life is one of purity, virtue, industry, and benevolence.

The scripture of Zoroastrianism is the *Avesta*. Among its books, the main liturgical text is called the *Yasna*. At the core of the Yasna are the *Gathas*, hymns composed by Zarathustra and his immediate followers, which make up chapters 28-34, 43-51, and 53 of the Yasna. They are at the center of Zoroastrian worship. The other books of the Avesta include the *Videvdad*, a collection of purificatory laws, the *Visparad*, a collection of ritual litanies to all spiritual lords, and the *Yasht*, containing Zoroastrian epic literature. This anthology quotes selections mainly from the Gathas. In selecting suitable translations of their allusive poetry, the editor has favored translations which express their meaning for contemporary believers.

THE HINDU RELIGIOUS TRADITION defies description by any simple list of doctrines and practices. Some branches are monistic and see divinity as pervading all reality, some are largely dualistic and posit reality as the interrelation of the divine Spirit (*Purusha*) and primordial material nature (*prakriti*), some are monotheistic and revere a personal God, and still others worship the Nameless and Formless God with many names and forms. A Hindu may worship God in the form of Krishna or Shiva, or seek unity with the impersonal Brahman, yet he will regard all these as symbols for one Ultimate Reality. Whether a Vedantist who sees Reality as impersonal or a devotee of the Goddess Durga, he finds sanction for his views in the same scriptures. As it is stated in the Rig Veda: "Truth is one, and the learned call it by many names."

If one might hazard a list of common features of Hindu faith and practice, it might include: (1) Brahman or Ultimate Reality is both personal and impersonal and appears in many forms; (2) it is accessible through a variety of paths (*margas*): knowledge (*jnana yoga*), devotion (*bhakti yoga*), and action (*karma yoga*); and (3) it is realized by those sages who have attained union or communion with that Reality. (4) On the other hand, creation and the phenomena of worldly life are temporal and partial; they conceal the total Truth and its realization. (5) Hindus further hold the doctrine of *karma*, which says that each thought, word, and action brings appropriate recompense, thereby upholding the moral government and ultimate justice of the cosmos; and (6) the doctrine of reincarnation, understood as a dreary round of continued suffering or a continuous series of fresh opportunities to improve one's lot. Inequality of endowment and fortune is explained as the working out of karma and not as the result of some discrimination by God. Hindus also uphold (7) the authority of the Vedas; (8) the traditions of family and social life, with its four stages of student, householder, spiritual seeker, and ascetic who renounces all for the sake of spiritual progress and the welfare of all; (9) the four goals of life: righteousness (*dharma*), worldly success (*artha*), pleasure (*kama*), and spiritual freedom (*moksha*); and (10) the validity and viability of the ideal social order and its attendant duties, which have degenerated into the caste system. The many sects of Hinduism, with few exceptions, share these features in common. Those Indian faiths which protested several of these features, such as Jainism, Sikhism, and Buddhism, soon became distinguished from the Hindu fold.

Hinduism's long tradition has produced many sacred works. The most ancient and authoritative are the revealed literature (*shruti*): these are the *Vedas* that include the *Samhitas*, *Brahmanas*, *Aranyakas*, and *Upanishads*.

The four Vedas, the *Rig Veda*, *Sama Veda*, *Yajur Veda*, and *Atharva Veda*, have been transmitted orally from generation to generation for more than three thousand years. They are written in verse and contain hymns, ritual formulae, chants, and prayers. An exact method of traditional vedic chanting has preserved most of the vedic hymns from corruption. Many of the vedic hymns are addressed to deified powers of nature which are understood as manifestations of cosmic truth. Some refer to partaking of Soma and the horse sacrifice, rituals that are rarely practiced by modern Hindus. Nevertheless, a proper understanding of the ancient Vedas shows them to contain all the essential elements of Hindu thought.

The Brahmanas are prose amplifications of the Vedas. Two of them are quoted in this volume: the *Satapatha Brahmana* and the *Tandya Maha Brahmana*.

There are 108 Upanishads, composed at various times (900 B.C. to 200 B.C.); they belong to one or another recension of the Vedas or Aranyakas. Etymologically, upanishad means "sitting near," and the Upanishads record the philosophical and mystical teachings given by the ancient sages as they sat surrounded by their disciples. The commentaries of Shankara (d. 750 A.D.) highlighted eleven principal Upanishads: the *Isha*, *Kena*, *Katha*, *Prasna*, *Mundaka*, *Mandukya*, *Aitareya*, *Taittiriya*, *Chandogya*, *Brihadaranyaka*, and *Svetasvatara*. The *Maitri Upanishad* is also regarded as significent by many authorities. A few Upanishads such as the Svetasvatara may be interpreted in a predominantly monotheistic sense as teaching devotion to a personal God, but the general trend of the Upanishads is to identify Reality as supra-personal Brahman, who is "not this, not that"—beyond any particular description, and who is one with the *Atman* or universal Self residing in the heart of each person. They teach that liberation is to realize the Atman within while transcending the ego-self that is identified with the psycho-physical organism, its actions and desires.

The most widely known Hindu scripture is the *Bhagavad Gita*. Composed several centuries before the beginning of our era, it is but one book of the epic Mahabharata. However, the authority and influence of the Bhagavad Gita is such that it is usually raised to the status of an Upanishad. It has been called "India's favorite Bible," and with its emphasis on selfless service it was a prime source of inspiration for Mahatma Gandhi. Sharing many affinities with the older Upanishads, the Bhagavad Gita sanctions several paths for realizing the highest goal of life. But it is also distinctively monotheistic, teaching that devotion (*bhakti*) is the supreme way to approach God and receive His grace.

Other later Hindu texts, called sacred traditions (*smriti*), are of lesser authority than the *shruti*. These include the great epics, the Ramayana and the Mahabharata. Episodes from these epics are familiar to every Indian school child, and they provide the themes of countless popular dramas and movies. The Ramayana recounts the story of Rama, who is an *avatar* or incarnation of Vishnu, and his wife Sita. It exalts the obligations of family life as superior to claims of rule and wealth. Rama obeys his father even though it means giving up his kingdom and dwelling in the forest. Then, when Sita is abducted by the evil demon-king Ravana, Rama must go through many trials until he can mount an expedition to defeat Ravana and regain his wife. Sita's perfect virtue is manifest as she faithfully goes into exile with Rama and later preserves her chastity during the captivity under Ravana. The Mahabharata recounts the civil war between the clan of the Kauravas, led by the evil Duryodhana and his cohort Karna, against the Pandavas who are championed by Arjuna and Krishna. Krishna is, like Rama, an avatar of Vishnu (the name used by Vaishnavas to designate the One God) under human conditions and limitations, but in the eleventh chapter of the Bhagavad Gita he reveals his transcendental form to Arjuna. Throughout the epic the virtues of courage, devotion to duty, and right living are extolled.

Another group of smriti texts are the collections of *dharma*, duty or law as it relates to members of society. The *Laws of Manu* is the most important of these, and we also include excerpts from the collections of Narada, Vasishtha, Vishnu, and Apastamba. Regarding the laws in these collections, the editors have chosen to avoid those controversial matters relating to the caste system. Despite the vedic origins of *varnashrama dharma*, the degenerate caste system is probably the one feature of Hinduism which is repudiated by most modern Hindu reformers and intellectuals. This is in keeping with the aim of *World Scripture*, to accentuate the positive features of religion.

The *Puranas* are medieval collections of laws, stories, and philosophy which largely reflect the teachings of older scriptures but also illustrate them with concrete stories and examples. They are enormously influential in the popular religious expressions of modern India. The most well-known of these is the *Srimad Bhagavatam* or *Bhagavata Purana*, the scripture of Krishna's life and teachings, his childhood exploits, and his love of the adoring cowherd girls. It is central to the religion of Vaishnavite Hindus. Another Vaishnavite scripture, the *Vishnu Purana*, contains a prophecy about Kalki, a future avatar. The *Shiva Purana*, *Skanda Purana*, and *Linga Purana* are among the scriptures of Shaivism. The *Garuda Purana* and *Matsya Purana* contain descriptions of the afterlife and the effects of karma on a person's destiny. The *Markandeya Purana* contains a story of a king whose compassionate attitude closely resembles that of a bodhisattva, and a description of the victory of the Goddess Durga, a popular Hindu deity. Many other Puranas exist, and more are still being written, adding to the fascinating variety of India's religious landscape.

*Tantras* are manuals of religious practice. Tantrism in both Hinduism and Buddhism uses yogic techniques, symbolic ritual, and the transmutation of ordinary desire in order to transcend all desires by identification with Ultimate Reality. This last feature has given Tantrism a scandalous reputation for purportedly licentious rites, although in theory all genuine Tantric practice requires as a prerequisite mastery over ordinary desires by total ascetic self-control. Hindu Tantrism is represented here by the *Kularnava Tantra*.

Hindu philosophers, saints, and poets have produced a voluminous literature which is largely beyond the scope of an anthology limited to scripture. We mention the sutras, and their commentaries laying out the six orthodox philosophical systems (*darshanas*): Vedanta (the *Brahma Sutra* of Badarayana and commentaries by Shankara, Ramanuja, and Madhva), Yoga (the *Yoga Sutra* of Patanjali), Sankhya, Nyaya, Vaisheshika, and Purva Mimamsa. These texts delve into specialized realms of philosophy; in large measure, the religious content of these systems is already covered by the Vedas and Upanishads upon which they heavily draw.

We also cannot do justice to the literature of the medieval saints who expressed their devotion to Shiva or Vishnu in dance, poems, and love songs in the vernacular languages of the many states of India. In Tamil-nadu the Nayanars adored Shiva and the Alvars sang of Vishnu: Chief among them was Nammalvar who wrote of the devotee as a woman totally immersed in love with her husband Vishnu. Of Hindi poets the foremost was Kabir, whose poetry joining Hindu and Islamic Sufi concepts has become an enduring source of wisdom for all Indians; we meet some of his verses as they have been incorporated in the Sikh scriptures. Others include Tulsidas, who wrote the Hindi version of the Ramayana, and Jayadeva, whose *Gita Govinda*, a poem in Sanskrit describing the love of Radha and Krishna, is widely performed in temple dances. These and countless other saints continue to express the Hindu tradition in forms that are ever new.

Of these devotional movements, the Lingayats of Karnataka province in southwest India are worthy of special mention because of their distinctive beliefs and reforming spirit. The Virashaiva movement, founded by Basavanna (12th century A.D.), rejected the caste system, disputed the authority of the Vedas, opposed image-worship, and taught a personal religion of devotional monotheism that dispensed with temple and priesthood. His *Vacanas* are venerated as scripture.

SIKHISM IS A MONOTHEISTIC religion with about twenty million adherents. It teaches devotion to God and denial of egoism as the basis for the good life. A relatively modern religion, it was born in the fifteenth century in the Punjab in northern India under the inspiration of Guru Nanak (1469-1539 A.D.). He and the four Gurus who followed him sought to cut through the differences between Hindus and Muslims and among castes, teaching that inner intention and purity of devotion, not doctrine or social status, are the measure of a person before God. Each of these Gurus spoke as a reformer within his own community, as a Hindu among Hindus and a Muslim among Muslims; their intention was to reform from within, though now they speak to us as founders of an independent religion. For under the pressure of persecution, Sikhism developed under the last five Gurus into a distinct religious community with its own code of conduct and distinctive forms of dress.

The writings of the first five Gurus were compiled by Guru Arjan Dev, the fifth Guru, into the *Adi Granth*. The tenth Guru, Gobind Singh, ended the succession of Gurus and invested the Adi Granth as the *Guru Granth Sahib*, the eternal living Guru. Since then, the Guru Granth has been the object of ultimate sanctity and the source of sacred inspiration; it is the highest authority for the Sikhs.

The Adi Granth is a collection of verse compositions, grouped together into *ragas*, the musical meters according to which they are sung. The pagination is standardized in the Punjabi text, along with notation indicating which Guru authored the verse: M.1 indicates verses of Guru Nanak; M.2, those of Guru Angad; M.3, those of Guru Amar Das; M.4, those of Guru Ram Das; M.5, those of Guru Arjan Dev; and M.9, of Guru Tegh Bahadur. In line with the expansive spirit of the Gurus, the Adi Granth also contains verses from Hindu and Muslim poets of that age such as Kabir, Ravidas, Surdas, Farid, and Ramanand.

JAINISM IS THE RELIGION of about ten million people in India, with its own distinctive scriptures, history, and a long philosophic tradition. Although a part of the greater Indian culture, Jainism, like Buddhism, is a non-vedic religious tradition, rejecting the authority of the Vedas, Upanishads, and other Hindu scriptures and their deities. Noted for its rigorous asceticism, Jain thought has influenced the greater Indian culture especially through its doctrine of *ahimsa*, non-injury to all living beings. Jainism teaches a strict doctrine of karma, which binds a person to suffer rebirth and retribution for all evil actions. A person must therefore liberate himself or herself from the fetters of karma by taking a vow of asceticism and thenceforth avoiding all violence in deed, in word, and in thought. All passionate desire begets violence, and is itself the result of the karmas of a deluded consciousness which must be eliminated. Jainism does not accept a creator God or personal God; instead each person has within himself or herself the potential to realize perfection and become a *Paramatman*, a soul freed from all karmic fetters and able to reach the highest point in the universe.

Mahavira, born Nataputta Vardhamana (599-527 B.C.), realized this perfection and became a *Tirthankara*, the Fordfinder, who discovered the Path to salvation. A near contemporary of the Buddha, he is twenty-fourth in a long succession of Tirthankaras extending back to Rishabhadeva of the vedic period.[1] Popular Jainism venerates him to the point of worshiping him as a divine source of grace, thus adding a personal, devotional element absent from Jain philosophy.

There are two branches of Jainism, divided over whether a monk may or may not wear clothing: the *Shvetambaras* allow clothes and the *Digambaras* demand total nudity, as they each believe was the practice of Mahavira.

The canon of Jain scriptures (*agamas*) begins with the sermons of Mahavira, written down by his disciples in the ancient language of Ardhamagadhi, called the *Purvas*. The oldest of these, however, have been lost, and thence the two Jain communities reconstructed different canons from the collections of surviving scriptures, now written in Prakrit and Sanskrit.

The scriptures according to the Shvetambara Jains are composed of twelve limbs (*angas*) and 34 subsidiary texts (*angabahya*). The first limb is the *Acarangasutra*, which contains laws for monks and nuns and the most authoritative biography of Mahavira. The *Sutrakritanga* is the second limb and contains Jain doctrines expounded through disputes with other Hindu and early Buddhist teachings. Among the angabahya the best known is the *Uttaradhyayana Sutra*, an anthology of dialogues and teachings believed to be the last sermon of the Mahavira, and the *Kalpa Sutra*, containing biographies of the Jinas. Other scriptures of the Shvetambara canon include the *Upasakadasanga Sutra*, *Dashavaikalika Sutra*, and *Nandi Sutra*.

The Digambara Jains believe that most of the orignal Purvas have been lost and dispute the authenticity of the Shvetambara scriptures. To the small surviving portion of the ancient Purvas they add a large number of scholastic expositions (*anuyoga*). These expositions constitute the scriptures of the Digambara tradition. Among them are the writings of Kundakunda (1st century A.D.): the *Samayasara*, *Niyamasara*, *Pravacanasara*, and *Pancastikaya*; the *Anupreksa* of Kartikeya (2nd century A.D.), and the *Samadhishataka* of Pujyapada (6th century A.D.). The *Tattvarthasutra* of Umasvati (2nd century A.D.) is a systematization of Jain doctrine into concise aphorisms in the style of the Hindu Vedanta Sutras; its Digambara commentaries include the *Sarvarthasiddhi* of Pujyapada, the *Tattvartharajavartika* of Akalanka (8th century A.D.), and the *Tattvarthaslokavartika* of Vidyanandi (9th century A.D.). The Tattvarthasutra is recognized as authoritative, with only minor differences, by both Digambara and Shvetambara sects. Another exposition which is accepted by both sects is the *Sanmatitarka* by Siddhasena (5th century A.D.), a treatise on logic concerned with establishing the simultaneous validity of several viewpoints on reality. Surviving fragments of the Purvas spawned commentaries such as the *Gomattasara* of Nemichandra (950 A.D.) and the *Jayadhavala* by Virasena (820 A.D.). Legends and biographies of saints are found in the *Adipurana* of Jinasena (9th century A.D.); their praises are sung in the *Dvatrimshika* of Siddhasena; while the *Aptamimamsa* of Samantabadhra (5th century A.D.) gives philosophical arguments for the Jina's perfection, omniscience, and purity. The *Mulacara* of Vattakera (2nd century A.D.) contains monastic rules comparable to those in the Acarangasutra, while the *Ratnakarandasravakacara* of Samantabadhra provides ethical instruction for lay people. This listing does not nearly exhaust the selection of anuyoga cited herein. Among the extra-canonical works, we include several passages from the *Nitivakyamrita* of Somadeva (10th century A.D.), a Jain classic on polity.

---

[1] He is attested to by the Rig Veda (10.136), the Srimad Bhagavatam (5.3.20), and the Shiva Purana (7.2.9). Mahavira's predecessor, Parsva, the twenty-third Tirthankara, is mentioned with Mahavira in the Pali Buddhist scriptures.

THE BUDDHA, BORN SIDDHARTHA Gautama (c. 581-501 B.C.),[1] taught in India, where Buddhism flourished for nearly fifteen hundred years and where most of its basic scriptures were written. There Buddhism evolved into many schools, of which two major branches survive: Theravada Buddhism which spread to Sri Lanka and throughout Southeast Asia, and Mahayana Buddhism which spread northward to Tibet, Mongolia, China, Korea, and Japan. Eventually Buddhism would nearly disappear from India, and these two branches thence developed independently until this present ecumenical age.

*Theravada* Buddhism, the Teaching of the elders, claims to preserve the original teaching of the Buddha. It teaches the ideal of the *arahant* (Skt. *arhat*), one who has achieved liberation from all fetters of selfhood and craving. The goal of liberation, *Nibbana* (Skt. *Nirvana*), can be reached through self-purification and proper understanding of the *Dhamma* (Skt. *Dharma*), which is specifically the Four Noble Truths: (1) all existence is suffering (*dukkha*): we must inevitably live with things we dislike and separate from things we like; (2) suffering is due to grasping for existence and craving (*tanha*) for the pleasures of sense and mind; (3) the cessation of suffering comes with giving up all craving and grasping; and (4) the practice that leads to the cessation of suffering is the Noble Eightfold Path. This path to salvation requires constant practice and training; there is no appeal to divine grace.

More important than ascetic practices, which can be counterproductive by promoting a false sense of pride, is the realization that the self has no reality; it is a mirage born of conditioning and is, like the body, impermanent. As there is no self, also there is no God in the sense of a Being with whom one could identify his Self (as in the Hindu Atman). Buddhism demotes the Hindu deities to the level of spirits, conditioned by their own past lives as human beings and hence liable at some time to be reborn; they are not yet liberated.

The path of the monk, who has abandoned ties with worldly life, greatly facilitates progress towards the ultimate goal. Lay people generally pursue the more modest goal of gaining merit by ethical living and contributing to the welfare of the order of monks. Yet the Theravada tradition has its lay saints who achieved the highest meditative states and became wholly enlightened.

The Theravada scriptures are written in Pali, a language formerly of northwestern India; with the advent of Buddhism Pali became the common language among the Buddhist monks of South Asia. The canon of Theravada scriptures is called the *Tipitaka* (Skt. *Tripitaka*) or Three Baskets, and they are divided as follows: the *Vinaya Pitaka*, collections of rules and precepts for the order of monks; the *Sutta Pitaka*, discourses and dialogues of the Buddha; and the *Abhidhamma Pitaka*, scholastic and philosophical treatises. Most of the passages selected from the Tipitaka for this anthology are taken from the books of the second basket, the Sutta Pitaka.

The most well-known and widely quoted scripture among them is the *Dhammapada* or Verses of Righteousness. A book of pithy sayings on Buddhist practice and ethics, it has been called the Buddhist counterpart to the Bhagavaḍ Gita, and it is a basic text for the education of school children in Theravada Buddhist countries. Another basic text is the *Khuddaka Patha* or the Short Section; it is layman's prayer book containing a simple catechism, precepts, and teachings. Three other important books containing material stemming from the Buddha himself are the *Sutta*

[1] The Buddha's chronology is uncertain; the available data has suggested a range of dates for the death of the Buddha from 544 B.C.—the date officially accepted by much of the Buddhist world—to 483 B.C. Evidence suggests that he lived about twenty years after the passing of Mahavira.

*Nipata*, the *Udana*, and the *Itivuttaka*. They contain short, often rational teachings by the Buddha about the way to the liberation, on leading a life of balance and self-control, and condemning prejudice and traditionalism. The *Theragatha* and *Therigatha* are verses describing the experiences of early monks and nuns, and the *Petavatthu* is a book of stories of ghosts and spirits: these are among the 15 books comprising the division (*nikaya*) of the Sutta Pitaka called the *Khuddaka Nikaya*.

The remainder of the Sutta Pitaka contains texts organized by divisions: the *Digha Nikaya*, long, mainly narrative discourses; the *Majjhima Nikaya*, medium length discourses on the application of Buddhist teaching or dhamma; the *Samyutta Nikaya*, prescriptions on Buddhist life connected by subject; and the *Anguttara Nikaya*, numerically arranged discourses.

Beyond the Pali Tipitaka are semi-canonical works of wide acceptance: the *Jataka* stories of Buddha's previous lives, the *Visuddhimagga* or Path of Purification by Buddhaghosa, and the *Questions of King Milinda* where the Greek King Menander (2nd century B.C.) inquires of the Buddhist sage Nagasena. We have made use of the traditional biography of the Buddha, the *Buddhacarita* by Ashvaghosha (c. 100 A.D.). The *Anagatavamsa* predicts the advent of a future Buddha.

*Mahayana* Buddhism, the Great Vehicle, is divided into many schools, each with its own favorite scriptures. These schools concur with most of the fundamental doctrines found in Theravada Buddhism (which it calls *Hinayana* or the lesser vehicle), including the doctrines of no-self and the conditioned nature of worldly reality. But many Mahayana schools identify an eternal, transcendent reality, Suchness (*Tathata)*, the Truth or Law which governs this Universe. For the enlightened, everything is considered as a manifestation of this Truth; within human beings it is present as the Buddha Nature, the pure Mind, which is realized as one develops on the path to Buddhahood. Suchness is by no means a Creator God in the sense of Western religions; from the Buddhist point of view the word "God" is too often loaded with connotations from other traditions to be helpful for understanding Buddhism. Nevertheless, we find that Mahayana Buddhism contains doctrines of Ultimate Reality and grace that are absent from the doctrines of the Theravada school.

In addition, Mahayana Buddhism teaches the ideal of the *bodhisattva*, the man of great compassion who gives himself for the liberation of all beings. The absence of the reality of self means that all things are interrelated and indivisible, hence the salvation of the individual is inseparable from compassion for others. A third distinctive feature of Mahayana Buddhism is that certain great bodhisattvas, which we may regard as the symbolic manifestations of the Buddha's perfections of wisdom, morality, charity, and compassion, are worshipped on the popular level as spiritual benefactors. In popular Buddhism Kuan Yin (Jap. Kannon; Skt. Avalokitesvara), Amitabha Buddha, Samantabhadra, and other Buddhas and bodhisattvas are worshipped and entreated for grace and succor.

The vast Mahayana collections of scriptures are written in Sanskrit and collected in Chinese and Tibetan Tripitakas. Each of the several Mahayana schools of Buddhism venerates certain particular canonical scriptures, supplemented by texts from the founders of the school. Yet despite the proliferation of schools, all of them share a common core of belief and practice, and hence there is much repetition in content among the various scriptures. Most Mahayanists also accept the authority of the texts in the Pali canon.

Among the most beloved of Mahayana scriptures is the *Lotus Sutra* (*Saddharma-pundarika*). It teaches the doctrine of the One Vehicle, which promises that regardless of their particular sect and way of Buddhist practice, all beings will surely attain Buddhahood. It contains the doctrine of the eternal cosmic Buddha, whose abundant and universal grace is the source of this salvation. Furthermore, the Buddha's salvation is available to all through faith in the sutra—the emphasis on faith has led some Christian scholars to liken the Lotus Sutra to the Gospel. This sutra is especially central to the Chinese *T'ien-t'ai* (Jap. *Tendai*) school and the several sects inspired by Nichiren (1222-1282) in Japan.

Buddhists of the Pure Land schools, including in Japan the *Jodo Shu* founded by Honen and the *Jodo Shinshu* founded by Shinran, rely on the grace of Buddha Amitabha (also called Buddha Amitayus), the Buddha of Infinite Light, to bring them into the Western Paradise (*Sukhavati*). Their total reliance on grace, to the exclusion of human efforts which are condemned as a form of self-seeking, is comparable to Lutheran Protestantism. The scriptures of the Pure Land schools include the two *Sukhavativyuha Sutras*, which describe the vows of Buddha Amitabha to lead all people to that Pure Land, and the *Meditation on Buddha Amitayus* (*Amitayur Dhyana Sutra*).

The *Garland Sutra* (*Avatamsaka Sutra*) is the scripture of the Chinese *Hua-yen* (Jap. *Kegon*) school. It is a vast collection full of rich imagery and containing a wide range of teachings. Among them: Buddha is presented as a cosmic principle and a manifestation of that principle, representing Enlightenment itself; all things, all causes, all effects, are interdependent and interpenetrating and should not be regarded from a partial viewpoint; and the career of the bodhisattva is represented as spanning ten stages of ever expanding awareness, inner peace, and compassion for all other beings. The *Gandavyuha Sutra*, the thirty-ninth book of the Garland Sutra, sometimes stands on its own. It describes the journeys of a seeker who travels all over India receiving religious advice from fifty-five teachers from all walks of life and ultimately realizes the highest truth.

The sutras on the perfection of wisdom (*prajnaparamita*) are widely studied. This literature comprises sutras of various lengths: from the short *Heart Sutra* (*Prajnaparamita-hridaya Sutra*), which takes up less than one page, to massive sutras in 18,000, 25,000 and 100,000 verses. The earliest and most formative for all the wisdom schools is the *Perfection of Wisdom in Eight Thousand Lines* (*Astasahasrika Prajnaparamita Sutra*), which deals with the doctrine of Emptiness (*Sunyata*) and the path of the bodhisattva who "courses in perfect wisdom" to realize the six perfections. Perhaps the most famous wisdom sutra is the *Diamond Sutra* (*Vajracchedika Prajnaparamita Sutra*). Its brief and paradoxical utterances which confound ordinary logic lead one to a deeper apprehension of Emptiness.

Out of this tradition arose the meditation (Chin. *Ch'an*, Jap. *Zen*) schools of Buddhism, comprising those which teach a gradual enlightenment—the Japanese *Soto Zen* school—and those which emphasize sudden enlightenment—the *Rinzai* school which was popularized in the West by Daisetz Suzuki. Ch'an was much influenced by Taoist naturalism, and this has shaped Zen practice and the Zen ethos in Japan as well. The classic Chinese expression of Ch'an is the *Sutra of Hui Neng*, also called the *Platform Sutra*, by Hui Neng the Sixth Patriarch (638-713 A.D.) and founder of the school of sudden enlightenment. This sutra's main teaching is the identity of each person's original mind with Buddha nature. Sudden Zen employs the *koan*. It is a pithy and paradoxical statement which teaches emptiness by confounding the intellect, forcing the student back on his or her own direct apprehension of Reality. The student may only gain entry into truth by intuition, never by logic, and thence he may experience insight (Jap. *satori*) corresponding with the Buddha's enlightenment. This anthology includes selections from the collection of koans known as the *Mumonkan* or *Gateless Gate*. It is a commentary on a group of forty-eight koans compiled by Wu-men Hui-k'ai (Jap. Mumon Ekai) of Sung dynasty China. The *Lankavatara Sutra* is a philosophical source for much of Zen doctrine; it teaches that false discriminations of subject and

and object occur because of the seeds of defilement which accumulate in the subconscious mind; in reality all discriminated entities are empty; they are nothing but creations of our mind.

A vast compendium of Buddhist teachings which is little known in the West is the *Mahaparinirvana Sutra*, whose main theme is the Buddha nature which is full of compassion and transcends the impermanent world of activity. Better known is the *Holy Teaching of Vimalakirti*, in which a lay bodhisattva shows himself superior at argument and possessed of more supernatural powers than a congregation of Buddha's greatest disciples. It teaches that one may aspire to Buddhahood while living in the midst of the world—to be in the world but not of the world. This is in accord with Nagarjuna's teaching that equates Samsara and Nirvana. In other words, Nirvana is not a goal in the future but can be actualized in the present. In the *Surangama Sutra* Buddha teaches one disciple who nearly falls into lust the way to control the mind and hence to progress towards Enlightenment. In the *Lion's Roar of Queen Srimala* a woman lay follower evinces deep insight as she teaches about the Original Mind which is inherently free of defilement. The *Golden Light Sutra* (*Suvarnaprabhasottama*), popular in Japan, includes teachings on political theory. The *Sutra of Forty-two Sections* is a popular ethical text inspired by Theravada teachings. The *Sikshasamuccaya*, or Compendium of Training, is a collection of Mahayana sutras compiled by Shantideva.

In Tibet, the great teachers of Mahayana Buddhism: Nagarjuna, Shantideva, Aryadeva, Vasubandhu, Dharmakirti, and others, are venerated as great bodhisattvas, and among Tibetan Buddhists their writings are frequently quoted as scripture. The works of the founders of the four traditions of Tibetan Buddhism: Gyalwa Longchenpa, Sakya Pandita, Milarepa, and Lama Tsong-ka-pa, are also venerated. *World Scripture* includes excerpts from the works of the above authorities which are available wholly or partly translated into English, in particular Nagarjuna's *Mulamadhyamaka Karika* and *Precious Garland* and Shantideva's *Guide to the Bodhisattva's Way of Life* (*Bodhisattvacharyavatara*). Nagarjuna was a formidable logician who gave the foundational philosophical expression to the doctrine of Sunyata and to the identity of Samsara and Nirvana. Shantideva's work expresses the ethic of the aspiring bodhisattva, who lives in the world unattached to self while doing gracious deeds for the sake of others.

Buddhism in Tibet includes both orthodox Mahayana doctrine and esoteric Vajrayana doctrine with its Tantric practices. Tantric practice, as in Hinduism, uses yogic techniques, symbolic ritual, and the transmutation of ordinary desire in order to transcend all desires by identification with Ultimate Reality. The *Hevajra Tantra*, *Kalacakra Tantra*, and *Guhyasamaja Tantra* are excerpted here; also included is the *Tibetan Book of the Dead* (*Bardo Thodol*) which contains instructions for the soul on its journey into the next life.

THE RELIGIOUS WORLD OF CHINA can be described as a complex blending of many currents. The indigenous religion, characterized by reverence for ancestors and striving for harmony with the forces of nature, was elevated on the one side by the ethical ideals of Confucianism and on the other by the mystical ideals of Taoism. With the introduction of Buddhism, which after some conflict, harmonized with the older Chinese traditions, it could be said that the traditional Chinese spirit became a blend of the Three Teachings (*san chiao*): Confucianism in matters of education and ethics; Taoism in regard to personal enlightenment as well as when threatened by sickness or bad fortune; and Buddhism in regard to death and the afterlife—these in addition to the traditional sacrifices offered to the departed of the family and nature spirits. Modern western influences on China, both through Christianity and Communism, have yet to be fully integrated with this rich tradition. Because China's religious traditions are so interwoven in the Chinese soul, it may be misleading to discuss Confucianism or Taoism as independent religions, though this is how they are customarily treated in the West.

Confucianism is a system mainly of ethical relations, defining values of family life and the administration of the state. It also incorporated the traditional Chinese veneration of ancestors and engendered a cult of Confucius as the official patron of education and culture. Confucius (551-479 B.C.) himself was a reformer who sought to lift up the most humane elements in existing traditions of government and social life. He urged his students to pursue an ideal of conduct, which he refered to as the way of the gentleman or the superior man. The superior man is sincere, filial toward his parents, loyal to his lord, adheres to social and religious forms (*li*), practices reciprocity—the Golden Rule, and has a broad knowledge of culture. Most of all, he is humane (*jen*) towards his relations, friends, and associates. Based on the obligations of filial piety and the ethic of humaneness, society is ordered according to the Five Relations: sovereign and subject, father and son, elder brother and younger brother, husband and wife, and friend and friend. These relations are not formal duties; they should be motivated by the flow of deep love.

The ruler especially should be endowed with the virtues of the superior man, and rule by example, rather than by force. A king who governs by raw force does not deserve the name. A government that does not have the support of the people will lose the Mandate of Heaven and will inevitably be overthrown; hence there can be justification for revolution.

Confucius said little about divinity, but Confucianism has a religious side with a deep reverence for Heaven and Earth, whose powers regulate the flow of nature and influence human events. The cosmology of *yin* and *yang* predates both Confucianism and Taoism, and is incorporated into both. The ways of man should conform to the principles of the cosmos, or else they will be frustrated. Therefore the Confucianist may consult the *I Ching*, divining the changes in these natural forces in order to guide his life properly. There is profound respect for nature, for all the myriad things partake of Principle that is also the basis for a sincere mind.

The canonical scriptures of Confucianism are the Five Classics and the Four Books. The Five Classics are, with some exceptions, the ancient sources which Confucius himself studied, from which he drew his teachings, and upon which he left his interpretive stamp. The *Book of Songs* (*Shih Ching*) contains ritual odes, love songs, and songs describing political life of China's ancient rulers from the tenth to seventh century B.C. The *Book of History* (*Shu Ching*) contains speeches and decrees attributed to the early Chou dynasty (1122-722 B.C.), especially surrounding the reigns of the Confucian culture heroes: Kings Wen and Wu and the Duke of Chou. The *Spring and Autumn Annals* (*Ch'un Ch'iu*) are chronicles of the state of Lu. The *Book of Ritual* (*Li Chi*) is a compilation of materials dealing with rites and proper social forms, expressing the conviction that adherence to rules of social and ritual propriety is an outward reflection of inner sincerity and uprightness.

The *I Ching* (*Book of Changes*) is canonical for both Confucianism and Taoism, but of its many ancient recensions only the version with Confucius' commentary survives as one of the Five Classics. As mentioned above, the I Ching is traditionally used for divination; but its commentaries imbue the book's oracles with Confucian values. Its yin-yang cosmology lies at the root of a metaphysics that has been adopted by Confucianists and Taoists alike. Taoist handbooks on the I Ching emphasize its use as a manual for divination, a guide for meditation and spiritual growth, and as the foundation for systems of medicine, painting, and martial arts.

The Four Books were selected by the Neo-Confucianist scholar Ch'eng I (1032-1107 A.D.). Together with the commentary by Chu Hsi (1130-1200 A.D.) they are the standard works of Confucian orthodoxy and the core of traditional Chinese education. They are: the *Analects* (*Lun*

*Yü*), a collection of aphorisms by Confucius himself; the *Great Learning (Ta Hsüeh)*, a foundation text for education; the *Doctrine of the Mean* (*Chung Yung*), a philosophical exposition of Confucian thought;[1] and the *Mencius*, the work of Confucius' greatest successor (372-289 B.C.). In addition to the Five Classics and the Four Books, we have included selections from the *Classic on Filial Piety* and some passages on the life of Confucius from the classic of Chinese historiography, the *Shih Chi* by Ssu-ma Ch'ien (c. 145-85 B.C.).

The Taoist viewpoint stands in a complementary relationship to Confucianism, emphasizing the free and easy original nature of the individual, unsullied by social convention, against Confucianism's strenuous efforts to mold society and its emphasis on social forms and ethical norms. The two traditions have coexisted in a balance, complementing each other like male and female, summer and winter, yang and yin. A Confucianist statesmen could retire to the country and find joy in the natural aesthetic fostered by Taoism.

Taoism teaches that the way to a good society is not through educating man to society's norms, but through stripping them away to arrive at a state of nature. The Taoist sages seek mystical identification with the great pattern of nature, the impersonal *Tao*, through meditation and trance. In attaining union with nature and its Tao, the sage becomes nameless, formless, and simple, yet paradoxically gains *te*, which may be translated "virtue" or "power." By doing nothing (*wu-wei*) he attains everything because he will spontaneously unite with nature and find his own original self. But to cling to human distinctions and to try and force a certain result is to go out of harmony with the Tao and accomplish nothing. The ideal Taoist ruler should do nothing to encourage wealth or power, for that would just lead to thievery and usurpation. Rather he should "empty people's minds and fill their bellies" in a state of primitive simplicity.

The chief scripture of philosophical Taoism is the *Tao Te Ching*. It is attributed to the legendary Taoist founder Lao Tzu, who is traditionally believed to have lived slightly before Confucius. Written in a terse and cryptic style, it is difficult to translate, as the many divergent English translations attest. The second Taoist scripture is the *Chuang Tzu*, whose earliest strata date from the fourth century B.C. Its vivid imagery, in parables and metaphorical tales, contains the essence of early Taoist thought.

A chief emphasis of Taoism is the pursuit of long life. In the popular mind, Taoist sages are thought to have attained longevity and to have become virtually immortal. Institutional Taoism—in contrast to the philosophical Taoism of the texts described above—promoted systems of inner hygiene that have become popular throughout the Orient: Through proper diet and exercise and by regulating breathing one opens the inner channels of the body to nature's vital forces. The achievements of Chinese medicine and the various schools of martial arts are all practical outgrowths of Taoism and rely upon Taoist science and metaphysics. Taoism also includes a vast canon of mystical and ritual texts, most of them unavailable in English. There is a pantheon of Taoist deities, immortals, and ancestors from whom people may seek favors and beseech expiation for their sins. Taoist texts often emphasize divine rewards and punishments which affect both one's lifespan and destiny in the hereafter. In this anthology, popular religious Taoism is represented by two ethical tracts: the *Treatise on Response and Retribution* (*T'ai-Shang Kan-Ying P'ien*) and the *Tract of the Quiet Way* (*Yin Chih Wen*).

SHINTO IS THE INDIGENOUS religion of the Japanese people. It coexists with Confucianism and Buddhism, and the three religions are intertwined, molding Japanese culture, ethics, and atti-

[1] These two books were taken from chapters 39 and 28 of the *Book of Ritual*.

tudes towards life and death. Shinto is centered on the worship of the myriad deities called *kami*. The kami embody what is numenous, or spiritual. They include the spirits embodied in natural objects and phenomena—wind and thunder, sun, mountains, rivers and trees; ancestral and guardian spirits of the nation and of its clans—especially the Imperial family; and the spirits of national heroes and people who have contributed to civilization. Chief among the kami is Amaterasu, the Sun Goddess and patron deity of Japan. In spite of this polymorphism, the kami operate harmoniously for the world's benefit, and hence they are often regarded as a collective whole and may be referred to by some authors as "God." Unlike western religions, there is not a great distinction between man, nature, and the deities; man is endowed with life and spirit from the kami and his ancestors, and finally he becomes a kami. The kami may be revered anywhere, but most worship takes place in shrines, which are usually located in beautiful natural surroundings. Through devotion to the kami, one can be united with them and attain the state of having a bright, clear mind.

Shinto ethics stresses *wa*, "roundedness," which connotes harmony, and *makoto*, or sincerity. The good is found in sincerity of heart, good will, and cooperation. Evil is to possess an evil heart, selfish desire and hatred, and to cause social discord. Thus, ethics is not defined by a code of commandments; instead it is a matter of inner sincerity and harmonious human relations.

The living Shinto faith is mediated by the shrines and the rituals performed there. Every home has its *kamidana*, or god-shelf, which is the focus of daily offerings and worship. The local shrine with its annual festival is the focus of the community. More important shrines are visited on special occasions: weddings, New Year's Day, and public holidays. The *kagura* is danced at the shrines by the *miko*, female attendants who are a survival of an earlier shamanistic heritage. In Shinto outstanding personages, such as the emperors at one time, are regarded as *ikigami*, living kami—meaning that the divine is already manifested in them. It is wrong, however, to equate their status with God in an absolute sense (a mistake that is sometimes made in speaking of the emperor's "divinity").

Shinto is not a religion mediated by written scriptures. Nevertheless, certain writings are central to Shinto and embody its spirit. The classics of Shinto are the *Kojiki* and the *Nihon Shoki*, which contain the mythology of the kami, the founding of Japan and its imperial line, and the records of the early emperors. Shinto ritual texts excerpted include *Engishiki*, litanies of purification, and the *Kagura-uta*, ritual dances. There are a number of oracles associated with Shinto shrines which have wide influence. The *Man'yoshu* is a collection of poetry from the Nara period (700-1150 A.D.).

Later sources of Shinto include poetry and didactic texts by Shinto priests and scholars from the Kamakura period to the present. We include selections of works by Moritake Arakida (c. 1525), Ekken Kaibara (1630-1714), Mochimasa Hikita (ca. 1660), Naokata Nakanishi (1643-1709), Norinaga Motoori (1730-1801), Ieyuki Asai (1688-1736), Kanetomo Yoshida (1435-1511), Masamichi Imbe, Genchi Kato, and others.

THERE ARE MORE THAN one hundred million adherents of the various traditional religions of Africa, North America, South America, Asia, and the South Pacific. While many of these religions are restricted to village and tribal societies, others are vigorous in urban areas, where they offer dimensions of the sacred in the midst of an industrializing society. Some are even expanding to the status of world religions: The Yoruba religion, for example, has more than 30 million adherents and has spread from its homeland in Nigeria to Brazil and the Caribbean where its variants go by the names Candomble and Santeria.

African traditional religion shows belief in a Supreme Being, a transcendent Creator, who is at the same time immanent in his or her involvement in the lives of human beings and as the Sustainer of the universe. African names for God are built on one or another of God's attributes: as Creator he is called *Nzame* (Fang), *Mu'umba* (Swahili), *Chineke* (Igbo), *Ngai* (Kikuyu), and *Imana* (Ruanda-Urundi); as the Supreme Being his name is *Oludumare* (Yoruba), *Mawu* (Ewe), and *Unkulu-Nkulu* (Zulu). As Grandfather or Great Ancestor he is called *Nana* (Akan) and *Ataa Naa Nyonmo* (Ga); among the Kalibari she is *Opu Tamuno*, Great Mother. As *Orise* (Yoruba) he is the Source of All Being; as *Yataa* (Kono) and *Nyinyi* (Bamum) he is everywhere present; *Chukwu* (Igbo) means Great Providence who Determines Destinies; *Onyame* (Akan, Ashanti) means the One Who Gives Fullness. As the Spirit of the universe he is *Molimo* (Bantu); as Heaven or the Spirit of the sky he is called *Nhialic* (Dinka), *Kwoth* (Nuer), *Soko* (Nupe), *Olorun* (Yoruba); and by the Igbo name *Ama-ama-amasi-amasi* he is Who is Never Fully Known. Despite the many names and representations of God which vary from one part of Africa to another, the people recognize that they all refer to one Supreme Being, whose dominion extends through the length and breadth of the universe.

Below the Supreme Being, and more immediately felt as influencing human affairs, is a constellation of subordinate deities and ancestral spirits. Human beings depend upon the intercession and activity of good deities and spirits to protect them from disease and misfortunes which are often caused by malevolent powers and spirits. Prayers, offerings, rituals, and an ethical life help gain God's blessing and the assistance of good deities and ancestors. African traditional religions also place great importance on the community. Members of the same village or community are expected to help each other and share each other's burdens, as social solidarity is the norm. The community is held together by its traditions, as expressed in ritual and handed down by elders, priests, shamans, and gifted spiritual leaders.

Native American religions recognize that the natural world is pervaded by the primary generative spiritual forces. In the Native American world view, all beings are related, both physically and emotionally, and there is no sharp distinction between natural and supernatural entities. This world with its divine powers is symbolized in ritual by the six directions: North, South, East, West, the zenith, and the nadir, and by the living entities which represent them. Hence the zenith is understood as Grandfather (day) Sky, represented by Father Sun and the Thunderbirds; the night sky, especially Grandmother Moon, is understood as female. The nadir is Mother or Grandmother Earth, including all of her aspects which give life and nourishment: Water, Corn Mother, Buffalo Mother, etc. In many modern Native American cultures, the totality of the spiritual forces may be referred to by a single term, examples being *K'che Manitou* in the Ojibwa language of the Algonquin and *Wakan Tanka* in Lakota of the Sioux.

The goal of Native American religions is wholeness, to bring individuals, the community, and all their relations (Earth, plants, animals, spirits) into harmonious balance, to complete the circles of life, to walk in beauty. Native American rituals are oriented toward communal wholeness. Thus, the ritual use of tobacco, unique to the Americas, creates communion both among the participants and with the sacred beings to whom tobacco is offered in the sacred pipe. In many rituals, the participants strip themselves to their essential being in order to approach the spirits with humility and openness. Rituals of the sweat lodge, fasting, the sun dance, the vision quest, and even those using psychoactive substances create the means for direct apprehension and communication with spiritual beings. Thus, individuals develop relationships with spiritual entities that enable them to successfully live their lives for the good of their communities.

Shamanism is widespread in most traditional religions. The shaman is specially gifted with the ability to communicate with the spiritual world. Since the unseen spiritual forces are recognized as in control of many phenomena on earth, a shaman may be called upon to heal physical and mental illness, to ferret out criminals, or to discover the reason for bad luck. The shaman may go into a trance for many hours, accompanied by dancing and the presentation of ritual objects. Other participants may join in the trance as well, as they try to cure the afflicted soul.

The traditional religions of the South Pacific are represented by a tradition from Tahiti and a legend of the Maori of New Zealand. Maori and Polynesian legends celebrate the prowess of those ancestors who bested the elements, explored and settled new islands, and won preeminence over their brethren. These heroes sometimes attained their goals through clever ruses, sometimes were adept at magic, and sometimes showed bravery in war. Some emerged as heroes despite low social status; some were impetuous and had to atone for their own mistakes; many had to deal with strife within their own families. Yet underneath is a deep longing for peace and harmony, even though it is rarely attained.

THE NEW RELIGIONS OF THE nineteenth and twentieth centuries, with an aggregate membership of over 130 million people, comprise the fastest growing segment of the religious life on this planet. They demonstrate the continued vitality and freedom of the spirit, which ever seeks to break out of conventional institutional forms. Most of the new religions may be regarded as offshoots of older religious traditions. Although they are often grouped together on sociological grounds, from the viewpoint of their religious content they resemble their parent religions far more than they resemble each other. Some new religions have been accepted by their parent communities as expressions of orthodoxy; for example, the Hare Krishna movement is accepted by many Hindus, and some of the African independent churches have been reconciled with the leaders of mainline Christianity. Others, like the Church of Jesus Christ of Latter-day Saints, the Jehovah's Witnesses, and the followers of Yogi Bhajan, claim that they are continuous with an established world religion despite conflicts with its leaders and institutions.

We have alluded previously to the problems of defining scriptures for these new religions. In some cases the founder is still alive and giving messages which have yet to be digested into scripture. Many religions which regard themselves as continuous with their parent tradition utilize the parent tradition's scripture in teaching their doctrines. A few have distinctive texts suitable for inclusion in *World Scripture*—be they official scripture, an interpretation of an older scripture, the informal record of new revelations, or a collection of the founder's speeches.

First, there are new sects and movements in Hinduism both in India and the West, for example, the Sri Aurobindo Ashram, the Theosophical Society, Arya Samaj, Brahmo Samaj, Ananda Marga, Transcendental Meditation, the International Society for Krishna Consciousness (Hare Krishna), and movements centering on Meher Baba, Sathya Sai Baba, Bhagwan Rajneesh, and others. Some of these movements are eclectic and controversial in relation to their orthodox traditions, yet to a large extent their teachings are founded upon traditional scriptures which are well represented in *World Scripture*. For example, the International Society for Krishna Consciousness is a sect of Vaishnavite Hinduism which relies upon the Bhagavad Gita and the Srimad Bhagavatam. The same consideration applies to the western missions of Buddhists (Chogyam Trungpa Rinpoche and Hsuan Hua), Sikhs (Yogi Bhajan and Kirpal Singh), and Taoists (George Ohsawa, Macrobiotics).

The rapid industrialization of Japan in the last century brought with it the rise of a number of new religions, many of which have missionary presences around the world. Several Buddhist lay movements are offshoots of the branch of Japanese Buddhism founded by Nichiren (1222-1282 A.D.) and rely upon the Lotus Sutra as their scripture. These include Rissho Kosei Kai, whose leader, Nikkyo Niwano, has been much involved in international peace movements, and Soka

Gakkai, founded by Jozaburo Makiguchi, whose political wing, the Komeito party, is a strong force in the Japanese Diet. Another new religion with Buddhist roots is Agon Shu, which uses the Dhammapada and other Theravada sutras as scripture combined with esoteric Shingon Buddhist practices.

The new religions with Shinto roots have unique scriptures of their own. First among the new religions of Japan was Tenrikyo. Founded by Miki Nakayama (1798-1887), its central scriptures are four collections of her revelations: *Mikagura-uta*, *Ofudesaki*, *Osashizu*, and *Koki*. They teach that God, *Tsukihi*, is the divine Parent who longs for people to purify their minds from defiling "dust" and receive healing power and grace. Tsukihi means Sun and Moon, indicating the union of yin and yang, male and female. The main sanctuary at Tenri is believed to be at the place of the creation of the world, and in the ritual ten couples dance around the central column of this shrine which symbolizes the central pillar of the earth. The millennium is coming when heavenly dew will descend on the shrine at Tenri and enter the planet's omphalos. Tenrikyo encourages voluntary charitable activity and loving deeds to remove the dust that accumulates on one's character.

Other new religions have combined Shinto with ideas from Christianity, Buddhism, and Shamanism. Omoto Kyo, The Great Foundation, was founded by Nao Deguchi in 1892. Internationalist from the beginning (i.e., advocating the use of Esperanto), and for a time suppressed by the government, it teaches that God is the all-pervading Spirit, demanding that people work for unity and universal brotherhood. We include excerpts from its scripture *Michi-no-Shiori*.

Sekai Kyusei Kyo, The Church of World Messianity, was founded by Mokichi Okada (1882-1955), a former staff member of Omoto Kyo who in 1926 received revelations and was empowered to be a channel of God's Healing Light (*jorei*) to remove illness, poverty, and strife from the world and inaugurate a new messianic age. Okada's teaching is represented by the scripture *Johrei*, which has been edited and translated by the Society of Johrei, an offshoot of Okada's movement.

The founder of Mahikari, Yoshikazu Okada (1901-1974), was a member of Sekai Kyusei Kyo before receiving his own revelations in 1959 which have been collected into a scripture called *Goseigen*. The two sects Mahikari and Sukyo Mahikari both practice a nearly identical form of healing called *okiyome*, in which God's Light (jorei) is focused through a pendant worn by the practitioner called the *omitama*.

The doctrines of Seicho-no-Ie, that mind is the sole reality and that the body can be healed through faith and mental purification, bear a marked resemblance to those of Christian Science. The teachings of its founder Masaharu Taniguchi, who had also been a member of Omoto Kyo, are represented by *Nectarean Shower of Holy Doctrines* and *Holy Sutra for Spiritual Healing*.

Perfect Liberty Kyodan, founded by Tokuharu Miki in 1926, combines elements of Shinto and Buddhism. It worships the Supreme Spirit of the universe but also stresses the role of ancestral spirits as part of one's karma. In the slogan "Life is Art," Perfect Liberty Kyodan draws upon the Buddhist teaching of non-self, by which what is truly authentic in a person comes to spontaneous expression. There is emphasis on human creativity, by which we are to beautify and perfect our environment.

Korea, since the 1960s, has seen the emergence of religious movements seeking to rediscover the indigenous Korean religion, that ancient religion which is believed to have prevailed prior to the importation of Confucianism, Buddhism, and Christianity. These movements include the Tan Goon Church, named after Tan Goon, the ancestor of the Korean people; the Tae Jong Church, the Han Il Church, the Chun Do Church, and countless small groups of folk relgionists. The ancient thought of Korea has been preserved in several scriptures, the most important being the

*Chun Boo Kyung*. This scripture is a chart of 81 Chinese characters, arranged in a square of nine rows and nine columns. The chart is quite cryptic, and its characters can be read in every possible combination of rows, columns, and diagonals. Yet it has yielded extensive interpretations revealing the principle of Heaven which governs man and the cosmos and by which life can prosper.

The Baha'i Faith grew out of nineteenth century Islam, and much of its teaching is congruent with traditional Islamic, and especially Sufi, ideas of man's mystic love for and union with God. It departs from Islam, however, with the proclamation that humanity has entered a new age of world unity and that the spiritual impulse for the new age has been given by God's new messenger and messiah, Baha'u'llah. The Baha'i scriptures have been gleaned and assembled from the many letters of Baha'u'llah, his forerunner the Bab, and his first disciples. We have included selections from *Gleanings from the Writings of Baha'u'llah*, the *Book of Certitude* (*Kitab-i-Iqan*), the *Hidden Words of Baha'u'llah*, and *Epistle to the Son of the Wolf*. Now more than five million strong, there are Baha'i communities in most nations of the world.

Among the Christian-based sects and new religions, many retain the Bible as their scripture, although it is given distinctive interpretation through the revelations to their founders. Among them are the Seventh-Day Adventists and the Jehovah's Witnesses, sects born out of nineteenth century American Protestant millennialism which have large missionary presences throughout the world. In the twentieth century, new Christian groups tend to be more charismatic. They include the independent churches in Africa such as the Kimbanguists in Zaire and the Brotherhood of the Cross and Star in Nigeria. The Rastafarians are prominent in the Caribbean.

Other new religions in the Christian family supplement the Bible with their own distinctive scriptural texts. The Church of Jesus Christ of Latter-day Saints, with a membership exceeding seven million, has, in addition to the Bible, three revealed scriptures: *The Book of Mormon*, *Doctrine and Covenants*, and *Pearl of Great Price*. The Book of Mormon is a translation from golden plates received by Joseph Smith after the visitation of the angel Moroni.[1] It tells the story of God's dealings with ancient inhabitants of the Americas and Jesus' appearances among them. Doctrine and Covenants contains revelations, prophecies, and decrees by Joseph Smith, Brigham Young, and other early Latter-day Saint leaders by which the church was constituted. Pearl of Great Price is a selection of revelations and translations, including translations of certain Egyptian papyri containing writings purported to be by Abraham and Moses and an autobiographical account of Joseph Smith's call. These scriptures teach distinctive doctrines concerning the nature of God, salvation, and the hereafter, and instruct on rituals such as the baptism of the dead and eternal Temple marriages which bring people closer to the glory of God's Kingdom.

The Church of Christ, Scientist relies on *Science and Health with Key to the Scriptures* by Mary Baker Eddy. It contains her spiritualized interpretations of biblical texts, where she meditated especially on the healing miracles of Jesus. Christian Science teaches that mind is the sole reality, while belief in the reality of matter is an illusion. Disease and death, being properties of matter, are also illusory, and hence disease can be healed through mental power alone.

The Unification Church, founded in Korea by Sun Myung Moon in 1954, is another new religion in the Christian tradition. Aside from the Bible, which is its basic scripture, it is represented by *Divine Principle*, a doctrinal text, and collections of the founder's sermons.[2] They teach that

[1] On the meaning of "translation," see p. 453n.

[2] Sun Myung Moon's sermons are conventionally identified by date.

human beings were created to fulfill God's ideal of goodness and harmony on this earth, but the Fall of Man destroyed God's ideal by corrupting human love with self-centered, satanic elements. Jesus came as the perfect incarnation of God's love, with the purpose of restoring God's ideal, but because the people failed to unite with him during his lifetime the promise of the Kingdom of God on earth remained unfulfilled. Today people are again called to overcome selfishness, extend themselves sacrificially to love their enemies, and thereby make a new foundation to receive the Messiah, who comes in this age as the True Parents, to restore the universal family of God.

Other new religions take their inspiration from sources outside of the major world religions. These sources include the traditions of Hermetic philosophy, witchcraft, nature religions, spiritualism, astrology, and psychology. In the West there has been a proliferation of New Age and human potential groups, and as a representative we have chosen the Church of Scientology, founded by L. Ron Hubbard. His writings describe a systematic psychological and spiritual technique for purifying the mind from negative influences embedded in the subconscious mind in order to realize a state of Clear and spiritual freedom.

## *Acknowledgments*

COMPILATION OF *WORLD SCRIPTURE* was possible only through the cooperation of a great many scholars and religious thinkers who devoted themselves unselfishly to the massive task of assembling and sifting through countless passages from scripture. The members of the Editorial Board, who materially participated in this task or who kindly reviewed the completed manuscript to assure that their tradition was represented fairly, performed an invaluable service. In addition, we wish to acknowledge the efforts of the many contributors, who offered texts and source material to this project. Words of encouragement and valuable advice came from many sources: from Prof. Wande Abimbola, Dr. M. Darrol Bryant, Rev. Kanake Dhammadina, Jin Seung Eu, Dr. Frank K. Flinn, Prof. Durwood Foster, Rabbi David J. Goldberg, Prof. Naofusa Hiraii, Dr. Emefie Ikenga-Metuh, Prof. David Kalupahana, Dr. Frank Kaufmann, Dr. Quan-tae Kim, Robert Kittel, Acharya Sushil Kumarji Maharaj, Dan May, Dr. Richard Quebedeaux, Thomas Selover, Bishop Krister Stendahl, Dr. Robert Stockman, Dr. Thomas G. Walsh, and from students at the Unification Theological Seminary. Special thanks goes to Dr. Yoshihiko Masuda, who gave many years of devoted service to the project. Robert Brooks, Carroll Ann Brooks, Hal McKenzie, Betty Lancaster, Allan Gonzalez, Robert Selle, Dr. Lewis Ray, Rev. David Hose, Gerry Servito, Christine Hammond, Barry Geller, Floyd Christofferson, Dirk Anthonis, and Thomas Cromwell all worked on the many tasks of production to enable this book to see the light of day. Rev. Chung Hwan Kwak, President of the International Religious Foundation, offered precious spiritual guidance and unstinting financial support.

Behind the efforts of these individuals lies the larger project of interreligious dialogue, which has created the spiritual and intellectual climate which has made this anthology possible. In particular, through the conferences of the International Religious Foundation, where many of the advisors and contributors have sat together to discuss common themes and problems among the religions, we have come to a consciousness of the common ground among religions. These conferences have also fostered a spirit of interreligious alliance, as we have come to recognize that the religious perspective on human life, which begins with acknowledging Ultimate Reality, needs defense and support from religious people everywhere, regardless of tradition or creed. Such interfaith discussions created the spiritual foundation upon which *World Scripture* could be created with the cooperation of many individuals in the spirit of genuine dialogue.

Finally, we wish to give grateful acknowledgment to the Reverend Sun Myung Moon, who first conceived the idea for *World Scripture* and commissioned its preparation. In his address to the first Assembly of the World's Religions in 1985, he called the religious leaders of the world to discover their common purposes and bonds of friendship with which to create an alliance of all the world's religions:

> As far as I know, God is not sectarian. He is not obsessed with minor details of doctrine. We should quickly liberate ourselves from theological conflict which results from blind attachment to doctrines and rituals, and instead focus on living communication with God. I think we urgently need to purify the religious atmosphere into one in which believers can have living faith and every soul can communicate with God. In God's parental heart and His great love, there is no discrimination based on color or nationality. There are no barriers between countries or cultural traditions, between East and West, North and South. Today God is trying to embrace the whole of humankind as His children. Through interreligious dialogue and harmony we should realize one ideal world of peace, which is God's purpose of creation and the common ideal of humankind.

We present *World Scripture* with the hope that it will further this noble goal.

❖

# INVOCATION

WE OPEN WITH REPRESENTATIVE PRAYERS, taken from the scriptures of the world's religions. They invoke, give thanks, and affirm the efficacious influence of Absolute Reality in human life.

OM.
We meditate upon the glorious splendor
Of the Vivifier divine.
May he himself illumine our minds.
OM.

*Hinduism*. Rig Veda 3.62.10: The Gayatri Mantra

Homage to Him, the Exalted One, the Arahant, the All-enlightened One.
To the Buddha I go for refuge.
To the Norm I go for refuge.
To the Order I go for refuge.

*Buddhism*. Khuddaka Patha

In the name of God, the Beneficent, the Merciful.
Praise be to God, Lord of the Worlds,
The Beneficent, the Merciful,
Owner of the Day of Judgment.
Thee alone we worship; Thee alone we ask for help.

**Rig Veda 3.62.10:** The opening syllable OM is regarded as the cosmic sound of Being. When it is chanted it resonates in oneness with the divine Source. Cf. Katha Upanishad 1.2.15-16, p. 597; Mandukya Upanishad, p. 597.

**Khuddaka Patha:** The Three Refuges from this suffering world are the Buddha (the Teacher), the *Dhamma* (the Teaching), and the *Sangha* (the Taught). These three are also called the Three Jewels. See Dhammapada 188-92, p. 483.

Show us the straight path:
The path of those whom Thou hast favored;
not of those who earn Thine anger
nor of those who go astray.

*Islam*. Qur'an 1: The Fatihah

Our Father who art in heaven,
Hallowed be thy name.
Thy kingdom come, thy will be done,
On earth as it is in heaven.
Give us this day our daily bread;
And forgive us our debts,
As we also have forgiven our debtors.
And lead us not into temptation,
But deliver us from evil.

*Christianity*. Matthew 6.9-13: The Lord's Prayer

Glorified and sanctified be God's great name throughout the world which he has created according to his will. May he establish his kingdom in your lifetime and during your days, and within the life of the entire house of Israel, speedily and soon; and say, Amen.

May his great name be blessed forever and to all eternity.

Blessed and praised, glorified and exalted, extolled and honored, adored and lauded be the name of the Holy One, blessed be he, beyond all the blessings and hymns, praises and consolations that are ever spoken in the world; and say, Amen.

May the prayers and supplications of the whole house of Israel be accepted by their Father who is in heaven; and say, Amen.

May there be abundant peace from heaven, and life, for us and for all Israel; and say, Amen.

He who creates peace in his celestial heights, may he create peace for us and for all Israel; and say, Amen.

*Judaism*. Daily Prayer Book: The Kaddish

Our Father, it is thy universe, it is thy will,
Let us be at peace, let the souls of the people be cool.
Thou art our Father; remove all evil from our path.

*African Traditional Religions*. Nuer Prayer (Sudan)

With pleasure of the Wise Lord!
Blessed is the thought, blessed the word,
Blessed is the deed of Holy Zarathustra!

Do I pray with obeisance,
With upstretched hands for this support:
First, O Lord, that I perform all deeds
With Right, of the beneficent Spirit,
With wisdom of Good Thought,
So I may serve the Soul of the Creation!

*Zoroastrianism*. Avesta, Yasna 28.1

I bow to the Arahants, the perfected human beings, Godmen.
I bow to the Siddhas, liberated bodiless souls, God.
I bow to the Acharyas, the masters and heads of congregations.
I bow to the Upadhyayas, the spiritual teachers.
I bow to the spiritual practitioners in the universe, Sadhus.

**Qur'an 1:** The Fatihah is the chief Muslim prayer; it is recited with prostrations five times a day. In honor and in parallel content it is frequently compared to The Lord's Prayer.

**Matthew 6.9-13:** The Lord's Prayer is not only a supplication; it includes a pledge to live up to the ideals of a Christian, specifically to forgive. God only forgives us if we forgive others; see Matthew 18.21-35, p. 702 and 5.23-24, p. 701.

**The Kaddish** is a source for The Lord's Prayer (above), to which it bears much resemblance.

**Nuer Prayer:** This is only one of the African invocations represented in this anthology; cf. Anuak Prayer, p. 54; Dinka Song, p. 73; Shona Prayer, p. 83; Boran Prayer, p. 398; Kikuyu Prayer, p. 550.

**Yasna 28.1:** In modern Zoroastrianism, 'Good Thought' and 'Spirit' are aspects of the one Wise Lord, the only God, Ahura Mazda. Historians have theorized that in earlier ages they were regarded as subordinate deities.

This fivefold obeisance mantra,
Destroys all sins and obstacles,
And of all auspicious repetitions,
Is the first and foremost.

*Jainism*. Namokar Mantra

He is the Sole Supreme Being; of eternal manifestation;
Creator, Immanent Reality; Without Fear, Without Rancor;
Timeless Form; Unincarnated; Self-existent;
Realized by the grace of the Holy Preceptor.

*Sikhism*. Adi Granth, Japuji, p. 1: The Mul Mantra

Hear, O Israel, the Lord our God, the Lord is One. You shall love the Lord your God with all your heart, with all your soul, and with all your might. And these words which I command you this day shall be upon your heart; and you shall teach them diligently to your children, and shall talk of them when you sit in your house, and when you walk by the way, and when you lie down, and when you rise. And you shall bind them as a sign upon your hand, and they shall be as frontlets between your eyes. And you shall write them upon the doorposts of your house and upon your gates.

*Judaism*. Deuteronomy 6.4-9: The Shema

The Sky blesses me, the Earth blesses me;
Up in the Skies I cause to dance the Spirits;
On the Earth, the people I cause to dance.

*Native American Religions*. Cree Round Dance Song

All this is full. All That is full.
From fullness, fullness comes.
When fullness is taken from fullness,
Fullness still remains.
Om. Peace, peace, peace.

*Hinduism*. Isha Upanishad: Peace Chant

From the unreal lead me to the Real!
From darkness lead me to the light!
From death lead me to immortality!
Om.

*Hinduism*. Brihadaranyaka Upanishad 1.3.28

May the Lord bless you and keep you;
May the Lord make his face to shine upon you, and be gracious to you;
May the Lord lift up his countenance upon you, and give you peace.

*Judaism* and *Christianity*. Numbers 6.24-26: The Aaronic Benediction

Our Lord! Lo! We have heard a crier calling unto faith, "Believe in your Lord!" So we believed. Our Lord! Therefore forgive us our sins, and remit from us our evil deeds, and make us die the death of the righteous.

*Islam*. Qur'an 3.193

Let the words of my mouth
and the meditation of my heart
be acceptable in thy sight, O Lord,
my rock and my redeemer.

*Judaism* and *Christianity*. Psalm 19.14

**Namokar Mantra:** English translations cannot do justice to mantras such as this one and the Gayatri (above), which, when recited in the original language, call forth spiritual energies through the very sounds themselves. Invocations and mantras beginning with the words "Obeisance" or "All hail" are exceedingly common; cf. the Shiva Mantra in Black Yajur Veda 6.6, p. 90; the Nichiren Buddhist mantra "Homage to the Lotus Sutra," the Pure Land Buddhist chant "Adoration to Buddha Amitabha," and the Roman Catholic "Hail, Mary," p. 597.

**Deuteronomy 6.4-9:** Cf. Matthew 22.36-40, p. 115.

**Cree Round Dance Song:** This song describes the intercourse between the spiritual and physical realms; cf. Winnebago Invocation at the Sweat Lodge, p. 260-61; Cheyenne Song, p. 205.

**Isha Upanishad:** 'That' is interpreted by both Shankara and Ramanuja as Brahman; 'this' as the individual soul.

In the name of God, the Beneficent, the
Merciful.
Say, I take refuge in the Lord of mankind,
the King of mankind,
the God of mankind,
from the evil of the sneaking whisperer
who whispers in the hearts of mankind,
of the jinn and of mankind.

*Islam.* Qur'an 114

❖

**Qur'an 114:** This is the concluding sura of the Qur'an.

# PROLOGUE

ONE GUIDING PRINCIPLE BEHIND *WORLD SCRIPTURE* is that all religions are connected to the same Ultimate Reality and lead people toward a common goal. This is true even though the various religions make exclusive claims about themselves, sometimes asserting the uniqueness and incomparability of their God or ultimate principle. Nevertheless, in affirming the existence of Ultimate Reality or an ultimate principle, we assume that it can be only one, regardless of the various beliefs which people hold about it—be it described as one or many, impersonal or personal, absolute emptiness or absolute Being, and regardless of the name by which it is called.

Similarly, the goals of spiritual practice for each religion, while not identical, have much in common. Since the ideals imbued in human nature are universal, we may expect to find that people who have reached the goal, be it enlightenment, salvation, sanctification, self-realization, or liberation, indeed manifest the highest human qualities: love, compassion, wisdom, purity, courage, patience, righteousness, strength of character, calmness of mind, and inner joy. Regardless of religious belief, people who have realized such a goal inevitably impress others by their personal virtue. Ultimately, these goals converge and become one, inasmuch as they express the best of our common humanity.

This principle is neither a new idea nor the novel result of the interfaith movement. The scriptures of each religion contain passages which recognize that there are truths in other paths. They recognize that the God(s) worshipped by other faiths may be the same as their own God. They recognize that the teachings and practices of other faiths may be similar in many respects to their own teachings and practices. They also teach toleration and respect for righteous and sincere believers of other faiths. They condemn quarrels over doctrines for displaying egoism and enmity that have no place in the religious life.

# The Truth in Many Paths

PASSAGES FROM DIVERSE SCRIPTURES affirm that others who do not share the faith of that scripture are also following the way of Truth. Thus Hinduism, Jainism, and Buddhism understand the various deities to be expressions of a single Absolute Reality, and the various paths to lead to one Supreme Goal. Judaism has the doctrine of the Noahic laws, God's revelation to all humankind through which non-Jews can be righteous before God. The Christian Bible contains passages affirming that God had intimated himself in the religion of the Greeks. Sikhism affirms the common spiritual origin of Islam and Hinduism. The Islamic scriptures affirm that Jews and Christians are people of the Book who share the same God as the God of Muhammad. Furthermore, many religions teach that a nonbeliever, if he does righteousness, is acceptable before God and will receive a reward.

However, there are limits to such openness. Even if the goal is ultimately one, many interpreters of religion may consider their particular path as the best or only effective path to the goal. For example, although the Qur'an testifies to other scriptures as divinely inspired, a typical Muslim view is to regard them as having suffered corruptions and interpolations; the only accurate witness to those previous revelations is the testimony of the Qur'an itself. Christians may emphasize the uniqueness of God as revealed in Christ, and deny that the revelations of other faiths reach the essence of God's true being, even as they acknowledge that these scriptures have elements of the principles of truth, love, justice, wisdom, and morality common also to Christianity.

Then there is the problem of idolatry: When is another person's god truly the One God, and when is it a false idol? We remark that idolatry—and similarly the question of corrupt scripture—is expressing the negative judgment that certain aspects of religion are false because they are human creations which are elevated incorrectly to the status of absolutes: see *Idolatry*, pp. 286-89. But no genuine religion is entirely man-made. Every religion has led its sincere believers to transcendental knowledge and realization of Ultimate Reality. Could not doctrinal intolerance toward the claims of other religions itself be a form of idolatry, falsely absolutizing the beliefs of one's own group?

As men approach me, so I receive them. All paths, Arjuna, lead to me.

*Hinduism.* Bhagavad Gita 4.11

Confucius said... "In the world there are many different roads but the destination is the same. There are a hundred deliberations but the result is one."

*Confucianism.* I Ching, Appended Remarks 2.5

At any time, in any form and accepted name, if one is shorn of all attachment, that one is you alone. My Lord! You are one although variously appearing.

*Jainism.* Hemachandra, Anyayogavyavacchedika 29

They have called him Indra, Mitra, Varuna, Agni,
And the divine fine-winged Garuda;
They speak of Indra, Yama, Matrarisvan:
The One Being sages call by many names.

*Hinduism.* Rig Veda 1.164.46

The Hindus and the Muslims have but one and the same God,
What can a mullah or a sheikh do?

*Sikhism.* Adi Granth, Bhairo, p. 1158

Sometimes I [the Buddha] spoke of myself, sometimes of others; sometimes I presented myself, sometimes others; sometimes I showed my own actions, sometimes those of others. All my doctrines are true and none are false.

*Buddhism.* Lotus Sutra 16

The Buddha declared to the bodhisattva Aksayamati, "Good man, if there are beings in the land who can be conveyed to deliverance by the body of a Buddha, then the bodhisattva Avalokitesvara preaches the Truth by displaying the body of a Buddha.... To those who can be conveyed to deliverance by the body of Brahma [God the Creator] he preaches the Truth by displaying the body of Brahma. To those who can be conveyed to deliverance by the body of the god Shakra he preaches the Truth by displaying the body of the god Shakra. To those who can be conveyed to deliverance by the body of the god Ishvara [the personal God] he preaches the Truth by displaying the body of the god Ishvara.... To those who can be conveyed to deliverance by the body of an elder... a householder... an official... a woman... a boy or girl... a god, dragon, spirit, angel, demon, garuda-bird, centaur, serpent, human or non-human, he preaches Dharma by displaying the appropriate body.... The bodhisattva Avalokitesvara, by resort to a variety of forms, travels the world, conveying the beings to salvation."

*Buddhism.* Lotus Sutra 25

This is the land of the gods. The people should revere them. In my essence I am the Buddha Vairocana. Let my people understand this and take refuge in the Law of the Buddhas.

*Shinto.* Revelation of Amaterasu to Emperor Shomu

Say, We believe in God, and in what has been revealed to us, and what was revealed to Abraham, Ishmael, Isaac, Jacob, and the Tribes, and in what was given to Moses, Jesus, and the Prophets from their Lord. We make no distinction between any of them, and to God do we submit.

*Islam.* Qur'an 3.84

There can be no doubt that whatever the peoples of the world, of whatever race or religion, they derive their inspiration from one heavenly Source, and are the subjects of one God. The difference between the ordinances under which they abide should be attributed to the varying requirements and exigencies of the age in which they were revealed. All of them, except for a few which are the outcome of human perversity, were ordained of God, and are a reflection of His Will and Purpose.

*Baha'i Faith.* Gleanings from the Writings of Baha'u'llah 111

**Rig Veda 1.164.46:** Cf. Rig Veda 10.63.2, p. 256.

**Lotus Sutra 16:** After revealing the eternity of the Buddha, cf. Lotus Sutra 16, p. 463, Buddha explains that he has assumed various human forms in countless different worlds to guide every possible being to the right path. Similarly, the doctrines preached by the various enlightened sages, inasmuch as they are all manifestations of the same eternal Buddha, are all true teachings. Compare Tattvarthaslokavartika 116, p. 576.

**Revelation of Amaterasu to Emperor Shomu:** Vairocana is the Buddha of the Sun, just as Amaterasu is the Shinto Sun Goddess.

**Qur'an 3.84:** The Qur'an teaches that Muhammad is one of a succession of true prophets who have given God's message to diverse peoples; cf. Qur'an 4.163-65, p. 474, and 19.41-58, p. 475-76.

Rabbi Joshua said, "There are righteous men among the nations who have a share in the world to come."

*Judaism*. Tosefta Sanhedrin 13.2

I look at all the major religions of the world as one big family.

*Unification Church*. Sun Myung Moon, 1-1-87

And I [Jesus] have other sheep, that are not of this fold; I must bring them also, and they will heed my voice. So there shall be one flock, one shepherd.

*Christianity*. John 10.16

And there never was a people, without a warner having lived among them.

*Islam*. Qur'an 35.24

Verily We have sent messengers before you, among them some of those of whom We have told you, and some of whom We have not told you.

*Islam*. Qur'an 40.78

Unto each nation have We given sacred rites which they are to perform; so let them not dispute with you of the matter, but you summon unto your Lord.

*Islam*. Qur'an 22.67

There is not a single place in all the corners of the world where God is absent.

*Omoto Kyo*. Michi-no-Shiori

For from the rising of the sun to its setting my name is great among the nations, and in every place incense is offered to my name, and a pure offering; for my name is great among the nations, says the Lord of hosts.

*Judaism* and *Christianity*. Malachi 1.11

Those who believe in the Qur'an, those who follow the Jewish scriptures, and the Sabeans and the Christians—any who believe in God and the Last Day, and work righteousness—on them shall be no fear, nor shall they grieve.

*Islam*. Qur'an 5.69

Seven precepts were commanded to the children of Noah: social laws [civil justice]; to refrain from blasphemy; idolatry; adultery; bloodshed; robbery; and eating flesh cut from a living animal.

*Judaism*. Talmud, Sanhedrin 56a

Some call on the Lord, "Rama," some cry, "Khuda,"
Some bow to Him as Gosain, some as Allah;
He is called the Ground of Grounds and also the Bountiful,
The Compassionate One and Gracious.
Hindus bathe in holy waters for His sake;
Muslims make the pilgrimage to Mecca.
The Hindus perform puja; others bow their heads in namaz.
There are those who read the Vedas and others—Christians, Jews, Muslims—who read the Semitic scriptures.
Some wear blue, some white robes,
Some call themselves Muslims, others Hindus.
Some aspire to *bahishat* (Muslim heaven), some to *swarga* (Hindu heaven).
Says Nanak, Whoever realizes the will of the Lord,
He will find out the Lord's secrets!

*Sikhism*. Adi Granth, Ramkali, M.5, p. 885

**Qur'an 35.24, 40.78** and **22.67:** Based on these verses, Muslims can respect the founders and teachings of Buddhism, Jainism, Hinduism, Confucianism, etc. which are not mentioned in the Qur'an. Cf. Qur'an 2.115, p. 70; 10.47-49, p. 733; 16.36, p. 286.

**Sanhedrin 56a:** Since the children of Noah are the ancestors of all humankind, the rabbis have traditionally interpreted these laws, given by God to Noah after the flood in Genesis 9.3-7, as moral legislation given by God to all nations. By obeying these laws, a Gentile is accounted righteous before God.

Lo! We did reveal the Torah, wherein is guidance and a light, by which the Prophets who surrendered unto God judged the Jews and the rabbis and the priests, judged by such portion of God's Scripture as they were bidden to observe, and to which they were witnesses. So fear not mankind, but fear Me. And barter not My revelations for a little gain. Whoso judges not by that which God has sent down—such are disbelievers....

And We caused Jesus, son of Mary, to follow in their footsteps, confirming the Torah before him, and We bestowed on him the Gospel, wherein is guidance and a light, confirming that which was revealed before it in the Torah—a guidance and an admonition for those who ward off evil.

Let the People of the Gospel judge by that which God has revealed therein. Whosoever judges not by that which God has revealed—such are those who live in evil.

And unto you We revealed the Scripture with the truth, confirming whatever Scripture was before it, and a watcher over it. So judge between them by that which God has revealed, and follow not their desires apart from the truth which has come unto you. For each We have appointed a divine law and a traced-out way. Had God willed He could have made you one community. But that He may try you by that which He has given you, He made you as you are. So vie one with another in good works. Unto God you will all return, and He will then inform you of that wherein you differ.

*Islam*. Qur'an 5.44-48

So Paul, standing in the middle of the Areopagus, said, "Men of Athens, I perceive that in every way you are very religious. For as I passed along, and observed the objects of your worship, I found also an altar with this inscription, 'To an unknown god.' What therefore you worship as unknown, this I proclaim to you. The God who made the world and everything in it, being Lord of heaven and earth, does not live in shrines made by man, nor is he served by human hands, as though he needed anything, since he himself gives to all men life and breath and everything. And he made from one every nation of men to live on the face of the earth, having determined allotted periods and the boundaries of their habitation, that they should seek God, in the hope that they might feel after him and find him. Yet he is not far from each one of us, for 'In him we live and move and have our being'; as even some of your poets have said, 'For we are indeed his offspring.'"

*Christianity*. Acts 17.22-28

Rabbi Yohanan ben Zakkai said, "Just as the sin-offering atones for Israel, so righteousness atones for the peoples of the world."

*Judaism*. Talmud, Baba Batra 10b

And Peter opened his mouth and said, "Truly I perceive that God shows no partiality, but in every nation any one who fears him and does what is right is acceptable to him."

*Christianity*. Acts 10.34-35

**Qur'an 5.44-48:** The Qur'an states that it is a trustworthy standard of truth, 'a watcher' over other revelations by which their beliefs can be tested and evaluated. Orthodox Islam goes further and regards the path laid down in the Qur'an to be the one sole path. Where the Jewish and Christian scriptures differ from the testimony of the Qur'an, the error is laid to the interpolations made by corrupt Jewish and Christian divines. But this interpretation may go beyond the letter of the Qur'an, which prohibits such disputes between religions. Each is held responsible only to the truth as found in its own scripture. Any contest between religious communities should be carried out on the field of good works. The question of reconciling different doctrines is left to God.

**Acts 17.22-28:** Paul is quoting Greek poets; the first quotation is often attributed to Epimenides; the second is from Aratus' *Phaenomena*.

**Baba Batra 10b:** On what is righteousness, see Sanhedrin 56a, p. 36. Cf. Seder Eliyyahu Rabba 10, p. 191; Sifra 86b, p. 193.

**Acts 10.34-35:** Cf. Romans 2.9-11, p. 190.

Of whatsoever teachings, Gotamid, you can assure yourself thus, "These doctrines conduce to passions, not to dispassion; to bondage, not to detachment; to increase of worldly gains, not to decrease of them; to covetousness, not to frugality; to discontent, and not contentment; to company, not solitude; to sluggishness, not energy; to delight in evil, not delight in good"—of such teachings you may with certainty affirm, Gotamid, "This is not the Norm. This is not the Discipline. This is not the Master's Message."

But of whatsoever teachings you can assure yourself [that they are the opposite of these things that I have told you]—of such teachings you may with certainty affirm, "This is the Norm. This is the Discipline. This is the Master's Message."

*Buddhism.* Vinaya Pitaka ii.10

Let some worship the Truthful One [a Taoist deity], and revere the Northern Constellation, while others bow before the Buddha and recite sutras.

P'an Ch'ung-mou says, "What is to be avoided most in our life is vacillation and frivolity; what is most excellent is a reverential heart. Therefore, we Confucians endeavor to preserve sincerity of heart and consider reverence as most essential. It is needless to say that sincerity and reverence make us companions of heaven and earth, gods and spirits. There is, however, another class of people who adopt Buddhism as their guidance. They bow before the Buddha and recite his sutras, always bent on preserving reverence and awe. They will never relax the vigilant guard over the heart, which will by degrees become pure and bright, free from evil thoughts and ready to do good. This enlightenment is called their most happy land. What is necessary, then, for Buddhists as well as Confucians is to avoid vacillation and frivolity, which will render you unreliable. Keep the heart always restrained by reverence and awe. Otherwise what can be the use of the recitation of sutras or the discourses of Confucius?"

*Taoism.* Tract of the Quiet Way

❖

**Vinaya Pitaka ii.10:** The Buddha is proposing a test that may be applied to determine the truth of any teaching.

**Tract of the Quiet Way:** Religion in China is syncretic, combining the Three Teachings (*san chiao*): Confucianism, Taoism, and Buddhism. Although the Tract of the Quiet Way is a Taoist scripture, the commentator P'an Ch'ung-mou is a Confucian, and he calls for reverence of Buddhist sutras. See Tract of the Quiet Way, p. 723.

## *Tolerance and Respect for All Believers*

THIS SECTION CONTAINS selected passages calling for tolerance and respect for believers of other religions, and for conscientious people generally. Believers are urged to treat everyone with equal respect, not to have a different standard of conduct for people of other faiths than for one's own community. Religious disputes and doctrinal conflicts are condemnable; they are often motivated by egoism disguised as piety, and by displaying enmity they do not give proper witness to one's faith. The polemicist betrays his ignorance: attached to his own partial viewpoint, he cannot see the possible validity of another's. Herein is included the famous parable of the blind men and the elephant. It teaches the folly of regarding any single religious perspective as absolute and complete. Such is also the import of the Jain doctrine of *Anekanta*, which regards all disparate doctrines as complementary parts of a single whole.

There is no compulsion in religion.

*Islam*. Qur'an 2.256

Will you then compel mankind, against their will, to believe? No soul can believe, except by the Will of God.

*Islam*. Qur'an 10.99-100

Those who praise their own doctrines and disparage the doctrines of others do not solve any problem.

*Jainism*. Sutrakritanga 1.1.50

The Buddha says, "To be attached to a certain view and to look down upon other views as inferior—this the wise men call a fetter."

*Buddhism*. Sutta Nipata 798

Truth has many aspects. Infinite truth has infinite expressions. Though the sages speak in divers ways, they express one and the same Truth.

Ignorant is he who says, "What I say and know is true; others are wrong." It is because of this attitude of the ignorant that there have been doubts and misunderstandings about God. This attitude it is that causes dispute among men. But all doubts vanish when one gains self-control and attains tranquillity by realizing the heart of Truth. Thereupon dispute, too, is at an end.

*Hinduism*. Srimad Bhagavatam 11.15

Kapathika: "How should a wise man maintain truth?"

The Buddha: "A man has a faith. If he says 'This is my faith,' so far he maintains truth. But by that he cannot proceed to the absolute conclusion: 'This alone is Truth, and everything else is false.' "

*Buddhism*. Majjhima Nikaya ii.176, Canki Sutta

Comprehend one philosophical view through comprehensive study of another one.

*Jainism*. Acarangasutra 5.113

All the doctrines are right in their own respective spheres—but if they encroach upon the province of other doctrines and try to refute their views, they are wrong. A man who holds the view of the cumulative character of truth

**Qur'an 2.256:** Cf. Analects 12.19, p. 756.
**Qur'an 10.99-100:** Cf. Qur'an 16.125, p. 723.
**Sutta Nipata 798:** Cf. 1 Corinthians 8.1-3, p. 570; Diamond Sutra 21, p. 572.

never says that a particular view is right or that a particular view is wrong.

*Jainism.* Siddhasena, Sanmatitarka 1.28

Like the bee, gathering honey from different flowers, the wise man accepts the essence of different scriptures and sees only the good in all religions.

*Hinduism.* Srimad Bhagavatam 11.3

And nearest to them in love to the believers you will find those who say, "We are Christians," because among them are men devoted to learning and men who have renounced the world, and they are not arrogant. And when they listen to the revelation received by the Apostle, you will see their eyes overflowing with tears, for they recognize the truth. They pray, "Our Lord! we believe; write us down among the witnesses."

*Islam.* Qur'an 5.82-83

A Pharisee in the council named Gamaliel, a teacher of the law, held in honor by all the people, stood up and ordered that [Peter and the apostles] be put outside for a while. And he said to the council, "Men of Israel, take care what you do with these men. For before these days Theudas arose, giving himself out to be somebody, and a number of men, about four hundred, joined him; but he was slain and all who followed him were dispersed and came to nothing. After him Judas the Galilean arose in the days of the census and drew away some of the people after him; he also perished, and all who followed him were scattered. So in the present case I tell you, keep away from these men and let them alone; for if this plan or this undertaking is of men, it will fail; but if it is of God, you will not be able to overthrow them. You might even be found opposing God!"

*Christianity.* Acts 5.34-39

A man among the Muslims and a man among the Jews reviled one another. The Muslim said, "By Him who chose Muhammad above the universe," and the Jew said, "By Him who chose Moses above the universe." Thereupon the Muslim raised his hand and struck the Jew on his face, and the Jew went to the Prophet and told him what had happened between him and the Muslim. The Prophet summoned the Muslim and asked him about that, and when he informed him the Prophet said, "Do not make me superior to Moses, for mankind will swoon on the day of resurrection and I shall swoon along with them. I shall be the first to recover and see Moses seizing the side of the Throne; and I shall not know whether he was among those who had swooned and had recovered before me, or whether he was among those of whom God had made an exception.... Do not make distinctions between the Prophets."

*Islam.* Hadith of Bukhari and Muslim

Suppose you and I have had an argument. If you have beaten me instead of my beating you, then are you necessarily right and am I necessarily wrong? If I have beaten you instead of your beating me, then am I necessarily right and are you necessarily wrong? Is one of us right and the other wrong? Are both of us right or are both of us wrong? If you and I don't know the answer, then other people are bound to be even more in the dark. Whom shall we get to decide what is right? Shall we get someone who agrees with you to decide? But if he already agrees with you, how can he decide

**Sanmatitarka:** Cf. Tattvarthaslokavartika 116, p. 576.

**Qur'an 5.82-83:** Those Christians of the time of Muhammad exemplified an attitude that is ever essential to interreligious understanding: we should be open to recognize the truth in another's religion and rejoice in it.

**Acts 5.34-39:** The liberal attitude of Rabbi Gamaliel swayed the council to allow Peter and the apostles freedom to preach the Christian gospel in Jerusalem. Christians use this passage to argue for toleration of unconventional sects and opinions. Gamaliel's dictum, that undertakings of men will fail but those of God cannot be defeated, is consistent with Jewish teaching: cf. Abot 4.14, p. 763.

fairly? Shall we get someone who agrees with me? But if he already agrees with me, how can he decide? Shall we get someone who disagrees with both of us?...

But waiting for one shifting voice [to decide for] another is the same as waiting for none of them. Harmonize them all with the Heavenly Equality, leave them to their endless changes, and so live out your years. What do I mean by harmonizing them with the Heavenly Equality? Right is not right; so is not so. If right were really right, it would differ so clearly from not right that there would be no need for argument. If so were really so, it would differ so clearly from not so that there would be no need for argument. Forget the years; forget distinctions. Leap into the boundless and make it your home!

*Taoism*. Chuang Tzu 2

A number of disciples went to the Buddha and said, "Sir, there are living here in Savatthi many wandering hermits and scholars who indulge in constant dispute, some saying that the world is infinite and eternal and others that it is finite and not eternal, some saying that the soul dies with the body and others that it lives on forever, and so forth. What, sir, would you say concerning them?"

The Buddha answered, "Once upon a time there was a certain raja who called to his servant and said, 'Come, good fellow, go and gather together in one place all the men of Savatthi who were born blind... and show them an elephant.' 'Very good, sire,' replied the servant, and he did as he was told. He said to the blind men assembled there, 'Here is an elephant,' and to one man he presented the head of the elephant, to another its ears, to another a tusk, to another the trunk, the foot, back, tail, and tuft of the tail, saying to each one that that was the elephant.

"When the blind men had felt the elephant, the raja went to each of them and said to each, 'Well, blind man, have you seen the elephant? Tell me, what sort of thing is an elephant?'

"Thereupon the men who were presented with the head answered, 'Sire, an elephant is like a pot.' And the men who had observed the ear replied, 'An elephant is like a winnowing basket.' Those who had been presented with a tusk said it was a ploughshare. Those who knew only the trunk said it was a plough; others said the body was a grainery; the foot, a pillar; the back, a mortar; the tail, a pestle, the tuft of the tail, a brush.

"Then they began to quarrel, shouting, 'Yes it is!' 'No, it is not!' 'An elephant is not that!' 'Yes, it's like that!' and so on, till they came to blows over the matter.

"Brethren, the raja was delighted with the scene.

"Just so are these preachers and scholars holding various views blind and unseeing.... In their ignorance they are by nature quarrelsome, wrangling, and disputatious, each maintaining reality is thus and thus."

Then the Exalted One rendered this meaning by uttering this verse of uplift,

O how they cling and wrangle, some who
  claim
For preacher and monk the honored name!
For, quarreling, each to his view they cling.
Such folk see only one side of a thing.

*Jainism* and *Buddhism*. Udana 68-69:
Parable of the Blind Men
and the Elephant

Do not break a promise, not that which you contracted with a non-Zoroastrian nor that with a co-religionist. Both are valid.

*Zoroastrianism*. Avesta,
Mihir Yasht 10.2

**Chuang Tzu 2:** Cf. Chuang Tzu 2, p. 120; Tao Te Ching 2, p. 572; also Digha Nikaya i.3, p. 709.

**Udana 68-69:** We give a version of this well-known Indian tale from the Buddhist canon, but some assert it is of Jain origin. It does illustrate well the Jain doctrine of *Anekanta*, the manysidedness of things. Cf. Tattvarthaslokavartika 116, p. 576.

**Mihir Yasht 10.2:** Cf. Analects 15.5, p. 718.

Revile not those unto whom they pray besides God, lest they out of spite revile God through ignorance.

*Islam*. Qur'an 6.108

Maintain good conduct among the Gentiles, so that in case they speak against you as wrongdoers, they may see your good deeds and glorify God on the day of visitation.

*Christianity*. 1 Peter 2.12

Our rabbis have taught, We support the poor of the heathen along with the poor of Israel, visit the sick of the heathen along with the sick of Israel, and bury the [dead] poor of the heathen along with the dead of Israel, in the interests of peace.

*Judaism*. Talmud, Gittin 61a

❖

**1 Peter 2.12:** Cf. 2 Corinthians 6.3-13; Lotus Sutra 14, p. 724.
**Gittin 61a:** Cf. Sota 14a, p. 697; Hadith of Bukhari, p. 686; Gandavyuha Sutra, p. 699.

PART ONE

# *ULTIMATE REALITY AND THE PURPOSE OF HUMAN EXISTENCE*

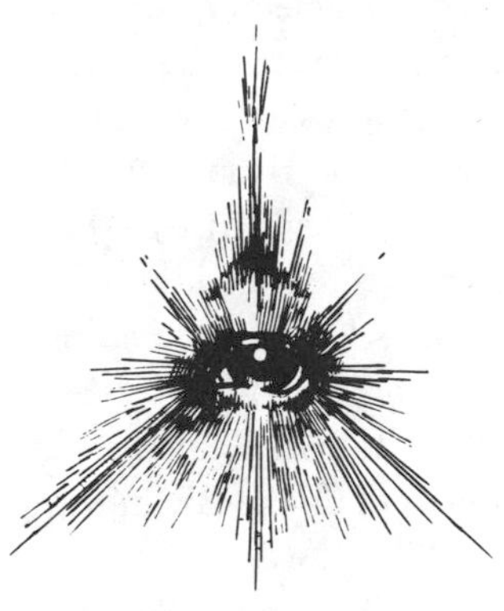

# CHAPTER 1
# ULTIMATE REALITY

THIS CHAPTER CONTAINS selected passages on the nature of God or Ultimate Reality. This Reality is both knowable and mysterious, transcendent and immanent, unchanging and passionate. He or she may be encountered as a personal, loving God, as impersonal Being, or as Truth which is neither being nor non-being. It is a Unity, yet has many manifestations. In many religions, it is credited with the creation of the universe.

Religions denote Ultimate Reality in various ways. If one contrasts the personal God of Christianity, Islam, and Judaism with the impersonal Absolute of Hindu Vedanta, one may infer that each religion has its distinctive way of apprehending the Absolute. However, it is more accurate to consider a variety of images of the Absolute even though important distinctions are to be made between similar images in different religions. A seven-part typology is helpful for understanding how these passages from various scriptures have been put together.

First, we may speak of one image of Ultimate Reality as a personal God; this image is central to Christianity, Islam, Judaism, Sikhism, and to the theistic traditions of Hinduism. Second, there is the image of Ultimate Reality as an impersonal transcendent Being, the ultimate source of all existence: this is Brahman in some Hindu traditions, the Primal Unity or Tao of Chinese tradition, the Christian philosophical image of God as the Unmoved Mover, the Sikh One Without Attributes, the Mahayana Buddhist concept of Suchness (*Tathata*). Third, there is also an image of Ultimate Reality as immanent within each person: this is the Hindu *Atman* which has an eternal substance, the Mahayana Buddhist Enlightening Mind or Buddha Mind (*Bodhi*) or Womb of the Tathagata (*Tathagatagarbha*) which dwells in Liberation and has no substance, and Christian concepts of the indwelling Spirit. Fourth is an image of Ultimate Reality as the ultimate goal or blessed state; here is the Buddhist goal of Liberation (*Nirvana*) and the Jain ideal of the soul in its most purified, divine stage (*Paramatman*). Fifth, religions which recognize many spiritual beings may image Ultimate Reality as their common solidarity which works with a single purpose: the Shinto *kami* and the Taoist deities and the Native American spirits (Sioux *wakan*) may be called Heaven or Divinity in the singular. Yet a sixth image establishes Ultimate Reality based upon the manifestation of the Founder; this is the Buddhist image of the Absolute as the Buddha in his eternal, cosmic manifestation (*Dharmakaya*), the Christian image of the cosmic Christ on his heavenly throne, as in the Book of Revelation, or again the Jain Paramatman as revealed through the *Tirthankara*. Finally, Ultimate Reality may be depicted as eternal law, as Hindu *Dharma* or *Rita*, Taoism's *Tao*, Buddhist *Dhamma*, Christianity's Word (*Logos*), Jewish *Torah*, etc. But as this last type is often recognized to be a subordinate and consequent attribute of Ultimate Reality that is itself beyond any law, we will defer its consideration to a general treatment of divine law in the next chapter.

Although this typology can distinguish the several different ways of imaging Ultimate Reality, in fact the concepts typically overlap. For example, the goodness of God can be understood in any of these seven images: the loving kindness of the personal God, the impersonal beneficence of Heaven, the absolute bliss of Nirvana, the solidarity of the kami for the promotion of beauty and purity, or the compassionate nature of Reality as revealed in the compassion of the Buddha. Therefore, for the sake of finding common ground between religions, we have placed side by side these various expressions of Ultimate Reality as they pertain to common themes. The themes which are distinguished in this chapter are: traces of God's existence in nature and in ourselves; the unity of God; Ultimate Reality as formless, unknowable, or void; Ultimate Reality as transcendent; the sovereignty and power of God; divine omniscience, knowing all secret thoughts and deeds; Ultimate Reality immanent in nature and in the human heart; its unchanging nature in the midst of a world of transience; God the Creator; the goodness of God; and God our divine Parent. Further themes that deal with the nature of Ultimate Reality can be found in sections scattered throughout later chapters.

## *Traces of God's Existence*

HOW CAN HUMAN BEINGS recognize the existence of this transcendent Reality, the invisible God, all-pervasive Truth? Although the vast philosophical literature dealing with proofs for God's existence is beyond the scope of this anthology, there are certain arguments which are put forth in scripture. Although God is invisible, he has left evidence of his reality by which people can know him, if they only look. These include: first, the doorway of contemplation by which God is sensed by the inner self; second, the universality of the moral law, which mirrors the law of nature; third, the evidence of his handiwork in the glories of the creation; and finally, the testimony of the founders of religion. By these means traces of Ultimate Reality can be ascertained in the midst of this relative existence.

Who knows this truly, and who will now declare it, what paths lead together to the gods? Only their lowest aspects of existence are seen, who exist on supreme, mystical planes.

*Hinduism.* Rig Veda 3.54.5

Eye cannot see him, nor words reveal him;
by the senses, austerity, or works he is not known.
When the mind is cleansed by the grace of wisdom,
he is seen by contemplation—the One without parts.

*Hinduism.* Mundaka Upanishad 3.1.8

The door of the Truth is covered by a golden disc. Open it, O Nourisher!
Remove it so that I who have been worshipping the Truth may behold It.

O Nourisher, lone Traveller of the sky! Controller!
O Sun, offspring of Prajapati! Gather your rays;
withdraw your light. I would see, through your grace,
that form of yours which is the fairest.
He, that Person who dwells there—is I myself!

*Hinduism.* Isha Upanishad 15-16

He who looks inwardly at the self revels in the self;
He who revels in the self looks inwardly at the self.

*Jainism.* Acarangasutra 2.173

The thing that is called Tao is eluding and vague.
Vague and eluding, there is in it the form.
Eluding and vague, in it are things.
Deep and obscure, in it is the essence.
The essence is very real; in it are evidences.
From the time of old until now, its manifestations ever remain,
By which we may see the beginnings of all things.
How do I know that the beginnings of all things are so?
Through this.

*Taoism.* Tao Te Ching 21

**Rig Veda 3.54.5:** 'Who knows this?' cf. Rig Veda 10.129, pp. 83-84.

**Isha Upanishad 15-16:** Cf. Bhagavad Gita 15.9-11, p. 148; Milarepa, p. 415; 2 Corinthians 3.18, p. 415.

**Acarangasutra 2.173:** Cf. Chandogya Upanishad 7.25.2, pp. 377-78.

**Tao Te Ching 21:** The word essence (*ching*) also means spirit, intelligence, life force. 'This' in the last line can mean through intuition.

Confucius said, "The power of spiritual forces in the universe—how active it is everywhere! Invisible to the eyes and impalpable to the senses, it is inherent in all things, and nothing can escape its operation."

It is the fact that there are these forces which make men in all countries fast and purify themselves, and with solemnity of dress institute services of sacrifice and religious worship. Like the rush of mighty waters, the presence of unseen Powers is felt; sometimes above us, sometimes around us. In the Book of Songs it is said,

The presence of the Spirit:  
It cannot be surmised,  
How may it be ignored!

Such is the evidence of things invisible that it is impossible to doubt the spiritual nature of man."

*Confucianism.* Doctrine of the Mean 16

There is, monks, a condition where there is neither the element of extension, the element of cohesion, the element of heat, nor the element of motion, nor the sphere of the infinity of space, nor the sphere of the infinity of consciousness, nor the sphere of nothingness, nor the sphere of neither-perception-nor-non-perception; neither this world, nor a world beyond, nor sun and moon.

There, monks, I say, there is neither coming nor going nor staying nor passing away nor arising. Without support or mobility or basis is it. This is indeed the end of suffering.

That which is Selfless, hard it is to see;  
Not easy is it to perceive the Truth.  
But who has ended craving utterly  
Has naught to cling to, he alone can see.

There is, monks, an unborn, a not-become, a not-made, a not-compounded. If, monks, there were not this unborn, not-become, not-made, not-compounded, there would not here be an escape from the born, the become, the made, the compounded. But because there is an unborn, a not-become, a not-made, a not-compounded, therefore there is an escape from the born, the become, the made, the compounded.

*Buddhism.* Udana 80

We shall show then Our signs on the horizons and within themselves until it becomes clear to them that it is the Truth.

*Islam.* Qur'an 41.53

For what can be known about God is plain to [all], because God has showed it to them. Ever since the creation of the world his invisible nature, namely, his eternal power and deity, has been clearly perceived in the things that have been made. So they are without excuse.

*Christianity.* Romans 1.19-20

The Book of Songs says,

The hawk soars to the heavens above;  
Fishes dive to the depths below.

That is to say, there is no place in the highest heavens above nor in the deepest waters below where the moral law is not to be found.

*Confucianism.* Doctrine of the Mean 12

Known by the name of Protectress  
is the Goddess girt by Eternal Law;  
by her beauty are these trees green  
and have put on their green garlands.

*Hinduism.* Atharva Veda 10.8.31

**Doctrine of the Mean 16:** This also refers to evidences of a spiritual world; cf. 2 Corinthians 12.2-4, p. 226.

**Udana 80:** The Buddha only describes this condition negatively; he refuses to speculate on the nature of Being itself. Cf. Diamond Sutra 29, p. 77; 21, p. 572; Majjhima Nikaya i.426-31, pp. 577-78. But elsewhere he calls this unborn condition Nirvana; cf. Sutta Nipata 758, p. 79; Anguttara Nikaya v.322, p. 88. Mahayana Buddhism gives it a positive definition and calls it Suchness; cf. Lankavatara Sutra 83, p. 52; Perfection of Wisdom in Eight Thousand Lines 31.1, p. 81.

**Atharva Veda 10.8.31:** Cf. Rig Veda 10.85.1, p. 99. On beauty as an attribute of God, cf. Rig Veda 5.82.5-7, p. 88.

The deeds which I shall do and those which I
have done ere now,
And the things which are precious to the eye,
through Good Mind,
The light of the sun, the sparkling dawn of the
days,
All this is for your praise, O Wise Lord, as
righteousness!

*Zoroastrianism*. Avesta, Yasna 50.10

The heavens are telling the glory of God;
and the firmament proclaims his handiwork.
Day to day pours forth speech,
and night to night declares knowledge.
There is no speech, nor are there words,
neither is their voice heard;
yet their voice goes out through all the earth,
and their words to the end of the world.

*Judaism* and *Christianity*. Psalm 19.1-4

It is God who splits the grain and the date-stone. He brings forth the living from the dead; He brings forth the dead too from the living. So that then is God; then how are you perverted?

He splits the sky into dawn, and has made the night for a repose, and the sun and moon for a reckoning. That is the ordaining of the All-mighty, the All-knowing.

It is He who has appointed for you the stars, that by them you might be guided in the shadows of land and sea. We have distinguished the signs for a people who know.

It is He who produced you from one living soul, and then a lodging place, and then a repository. We have distinguished the signs for a people who understand. It is He who sent down out of heaven water, and thereby We have brought forth the shoot of every plant. And then We have brought forth the green leaf of it, bringing forth from it close-compounded grain, and out of the palm tree, from the spathe of it, dates thick-clustered, ready to the hand, and gardens of vines, olives, pomegranates, like each to each, and each unlike to each. Look upon their fruits when they fructify and ripen! Surely, in all this are signs for a people who do believe.

*Islam*. Qur'an 6.95-99

And of His signs is that He created you from the dust; now behold you are human beings, ranging widely.

And of His signs is that He created for you, of yourselves, spouses that you might find repose in them, and He has planted love and kindness in your hearts. Surely there are signs in this for people who reflect.

And of His signs is the creation of the heavens and the earth and the variety of your tongues and hues, surely there are signs in this for people who have knowledge.

And of His signs is your slumber by night and day, and your seeking of His bounty. Surely there are signs in this for people who hear.

The lightning which He shows you for fear and hope is yet another of His signs; He sends down water from the sky, thereby reviving the earth after it is dead. Surely in this there are signs for people who understand.

And of His signs is that space and the earth stand firm by His command; then when He calls you, suddenly, from the earth you shall emerge.

*Islam*. Qur'an 30.20-25

**Yasna 50.10:** Zarathustra is equating the beauty of nature and the revelation of God through his prophet—natural revelation and special revelation—as testifying equally to the glory of God.

**Psalm 19.1-4:** There are slight differences in versification among the various Christian and Jewish Bibles. This anthology has adopted the versification of English-language Protestant Christian Bibles. In Catholic and Jewish Bibles, this passage is Psalm 19.2-5.

**Qur'an 6.95-99** and **30.20-25:** It is a cardinal doctrine of Islam that God's signs are to be found everywhere. Recognizing God as the source of these bounties, humans should be thankful; cf. Qur'an 16.10-18, p. 91; 55.5-30, pp. 82-83. In the opening verse, 'splits the grain…' refers to sprouting and new life. Verse 22 grounds the equality of the races in their common source as God's creatures; cf. Qur'an 35.27-28, p. 193.

For each and every form he is the Model;
it is his form that is to be seen everywhere;
Indra moves multiform by his creative charm;
the bay steeds yoked to his car are a thousand.

*Hinduism*. Rig Veda 6.47.18

All things are made to bear record of me, both things which are temporal and things which are spiritual; things which are in the heavens above, and things which are on the earth, and things which are in the earth, and things which are under the earth, both above and beneath: all things bear record of me.

*The Church of Jesus Christ of Latter-day Saints*. Pearl of Great Price, Moses 6.63

Praise be to God, who knows the secrets of all things and proofs of whose existence shine in various phases of nature. No physical eye has and will ever see Him. But those who have not seen Him physically cannot deny His existence, yet the minds of those who have accepted His existence cannot grasp the real essence of Divine Nature. His place is so high that nothing can be imagined higher. He is so near to us that nothing can be nearer. The eminence of His position has not placed Him any further away from His creatures, and His nearness has not brought them on a par with Him. He has not permitted the human mind to grasp the essence of His Being, yet He has not prevented them from realizing His presence. Various aspects of the universe force even atheists to accept Him [as its Grand Architect], yet He is far above the conceptions of those who refuse His existence, and also of those who imagine His attributes in various expressions of nature.

*Islam*. Nahjul Balagha, Sermon 54

No one has ever seen God; the only Son, who is in the bosom of the Father, he has made him known.

*Christianity*. John 1.18

When Abraham saw the sun issuing in the morning from the east, he was first moved to think that that was God, and said, "This is the King that created me," and worshipped it the whole day. In the evening when the sun went down and the moon commenced to shine, he said, "Verily this rules over the orb which I worshipped the whole day, since the latter is darkened before it and does not shine any more." So he served the moon all that night. In the morning when he saw the darkness depart and the east grow light, he said, "Of a surety there is a King who rules over all these orbs and orders them."

*Judaism*. Zohar, Genesis 86a

So also did We show Abraham the power and the laws of the heavens and the earth, that he might have certitude. When the night covered him over, he saw a star; he said, "This is my Lord." But when it set, he said, "I love not those that set." When he saw the moon rising in splendor, he said, "This is my Lord," but when the moon set, he said, "Unless my Lord guide me, I shall surely be among those who go astray." When he saw the sun rising in splendor, he said, "This is my Lord; this is the greatest of all," but when the sun set, he said, "O my people! I am indeed free from your [error] of ascribing partners to God. For me, I have set my face firmly and truly towards Him Who created the heavens and the earth, and never shall I ascribe partners to God."

*Islam*. Qur'an 6.75-79

**John 1.18:** For Christianity, the book of nature and a person's own spiritual experience give only partial knowledge of Ultimate Reality. Only through the special revelation of God in Jesus Christ is the fulness of God's nature made manifest in the world. Cf. John 14.6, p. 450, and comparable passages; Lotus Sutra 2, p. 102.

**Zohar, Genesis 86a:** Cf. Genesis Rabbah 39.1, p. 421.

# *The One*

IN THIS SECTION ARE collected passages describing the unity of God. Absolute Reality is one, unique, and absolute according to many texts. This One is called God in the monotheistic religions, Primal Absolute at the root of phenomena in Confucian and Taoist metaphysical texts, and a reality called Nirvana or Suchness in Mahayana Buddhism which transcends any being, divine or human. Other passages, especially from the Hindu tradition, recognize many deities but understand them to be diverse manifestations of the One that is beyond any name. Or, in the case of Native American religions, the many spiritual forces are one by virtue of their solidarity in action. For related texts on the One God who exists at the root of all religions, see *The Truth in Many Paths*, pp. 34-38.

On the other hand, we also include some representative passages which define the Oneness of God in contradistinction to all other existence. Other divine beings are regarded at best as subordinate to the One God and at worst as illusory or demonic: see *Idolatry*, pp. 286-89.

Hear O Israel: the Lord our God, the Lord is One.

*Judaism* and *Christianity*. Deuteronomy 6.4

I am the Lord, and there is no other,
besides me there is no God.

*Judaism* and *Christianity*. Isaiah 45.5

Say, He is God, the One!
God, the eternally Besought of all!
He neither begets nor was begotten.
And there is none comparable unto Him.

*Islam*. Qur'an 112

He is the one God, hidden in all beings, all-pervading, the Self within all beings, watching over all works, dwelling in all beings, the witness, the perceiver, the only one, free from qualities.

*Hinduism*. Svetasvatara Upanishad 6.11

He is the Sole Supreme Being; of eternal manifestation;
Creator, Immanent Reality; Without Fear, Without Rancor;
Timeless Form; Unincarnated; Self-existent;
Realized by the grace of the Holy Preceptor.

*Sikhism*. Adi Granth, Japuji, p. 1: The Mul Mantra

The sage clasps the Primal Unity,
Testing by it everything under heaven.

*Taoism*. Tao Te Ching 22

**Deuteronomy 6.4:** The opening lines of the Shema, p. 31.

**Qur'an 112:** This sura, which concludes the Qur'an (except for two prayers for protection), has been called the essence of the Qur'an. God's oneness implies that all reality is a unity (*tawhid*): see Qur'an 2.115, p. 70.

**Svetasvatara Upanishad 6.11:** This is a favorite verse of Shankara: see Vedanta Sutra I.1.4; cf. Sama Veda 372, pp. 548-49.

Absolute truth is indestructible. Being indestructible, it is eternal. Being eternal, it is self-existent. Being self-existent, it is infinite. Being infinite, it is vast and deep. Being vast and deep, it is transcendental and intelligent. It is because it is vast and deep that it contains all existence. It is because it is transcendental and intelligent that it embraces all existence. It is because it is infinite and eternal that it fulfils or perfects all existence. In vastness and depth it is like the Earth. In transcendental intelligence it is like Heaven. Infinite and eternal, it is the Infinite itself.

Such being the nature of absolute truth, it manifests itself without being seen; it produces effects without motion; it accomplishes its ends without action.

*Confucianism*. Doctrine of the Mean 26

When appearances and names are put away and all discrimination ceases, that which remains is the true and essential nature of things and, as nothing can be predicated as to the nature of essence, it is called the "Suchness" of Reality. This universal, undifferentiated, inscrutable Suchness is the only Reality, but it is variously characterized as Truth, Mind-essence, Transcendental Intelligence, Perfection of Wisdom, etc. This Dharma of the imagelessness of the Essence-nature of Ultimate Reality is the Dharma which has been proclaimed by all the Buddhas, and when all things are understood in full agreement with it, one is in possession of Perfect Knowledge.

*Buddhism*. Lankavatara Sutra 83

Tathagatas certainly do not come from anywhere, nor do they go anywhere. Because Suchness does not move, and the Tathagata is Suchness. Non-production does not come nor go, and the Tathagata is non-production. One cannot conceive of the coming or going of the reality-limit, and the Tathagata is the reality-limit. The same can be said of emptiness, of what exists in accordance with fact, of dispassion, of stopping, of the element of space. For the Tathagata is not outside these dharmas. The Suchness of these dharmas and the Suchness of all dharmas and the Suchness of the Tathagata are simply this one single Suchness. There is no division within Suchness. Just simply one single is this Suchness, not two, nor three.

*Buddhism*. Perfection of Wisdom in Eight Thousand Lines 31.1

Then Vidagdha, son of Shakala, asked him, "How many gods are there, Yajnavalkya?" Yajnavalkya, ascertaining the number through a group of mantras known as the Nivid, replied, "As many as are mentioned in the Nivid of the gods: three hundred and three, and three thousand and three."

"Very good," said the son of Shakala, "and how many gods are there, Yajnavalkya?"

"Thirty-three."

"Very good, and how many gods are there, Yajnavalkya?"

"Six."

"Very good, and how many gods are there, Yajnavalkya?"

"Three."

"Very good, and how many gods are there, Yajnavalkya?"

**Doctrine of the Mean 26:** Compare descriptions of the Tao and Dharmakaya as a single transcendent principle, e.g., Tao Te Ching 25, pp. 61-62, and Garland Sutra 37, p. 62.

**Lankavatara Sutra 83:** This sutra teaches that the existing world is created by mind. The world of appearances, which is characterized by suffering, is rooted in the seeds of defilements that are accumulated in the subconscious mind. True Reality is what is realized when all defilements have been removed and the mind operates with Perfect Wisdom. The Suchness of existence is thus identical with the essence of Mind.

**Perfection of Wisdom in Eight Thousand Lines 31.1:** This is one of the earliest Mahayana sutras, and the first which used the word Mahayana. The doctrine of Suchness deals with the unchanging truth beyond the limit of phenomenal reality. It is the same as Emptiness—the doctrine that one cannot rely upon any phenomenon, as all are impermanent, relative, and conditioned by other phenomena. It is also the same as the *Tathagata*, that is, the Buddha whose essence is eternity.

"Two."

"Very good, and how many gods are there, Yajnavalkya?"

"One and a half."

"Very good, and how many gods are there, Yajnavalkya?"

"One."

*Hinduism.* Brihadaranyaka Upanishad 3.9.1

There is only one God; all the "gods" are but His ministering angels who are His manifestations.

*Omoto Kyo.* Michi-no-Shiori

Now there are varieties of gifts, but the same Spirit; and there are varieties of service, but the same Lord; and there are varieties of working, but it is the same God who inspires them all in every one. To each is given the manifestation of the Spirit for the common good.

*Christianity.* 1 Corinthians 12.4-7

God said to Israel, "Because you have seen me in many likenesses, there are not therefore many gods. But it is ever the same God: I am the Lord your God." Rabbi Levi said, "God appeared to them like a mirror, in which many faces can be reflected; a thousand people look at it; it looks at all of them." So when God spoke to the Israelites, each one thought that God spoke individually to him.

*Judaism.* Pesikta Kahana 109b-10a

Just as light is diffused from a fire which is confined to one spot, so is this whole universe the diffused energy of the supreme Brahman. And as light shows a difference, greater or less, according to its nearness or distance from the fire, so is there a variation in the energy of the impersonal Brahman. Brahma, Vishnu, and Shiva are his chief energies. The deities are inferior to them; the yakshas, etc., to the deities; men, cattle, wild animals, birds, and reptiles to the yakshas, etc.; and trees and plants are the lowest of all these energies....

Vishnu is the highest and most immediate of all the energies of Brahman, the embodied Brahman, formed of the whole of Brahman. On him this entire universe is woven and interwoven: from him is the world, and the world is in him; and he is the whole universe. Vishnu, the Lord, consisting of what is perishable as well as what is imperishable, sustains everything, both Spirit and Matter, in the form of his ornaments and weapons.

*Hinduism.* Vishnu Purana 1.22

Every object in the world has a spirit, and that spirit is *wakan*. Thus the spirits of the tree or things of that kind, while not like the spirit of man, are also wakan. Wakan comes from the wakan beings. These wakan beings are greater than mankind in the same way that mankind is greater than animals. They are never born and never die. They can do many things that mankind cannot do. Mankind can pray to the wakan beings for help. There are many of these beings but all are of four kinds. The word *Wakan Tanka* means all of the wakan beings because they are all as if one.

*Wakan Tanka Kin* signifies the chief or leading wakan being, which is the Sun. However, the most powerful of the wakan beings is *Nagk Tanka*, the Great Spirit, who is also called *Taku Shanskan*, the Sky....

Mankind is permitted to pray to the wakan beings. If their prayer is directed to all the good wakan beings, they should pray to Wakan Tanka; but if the prayer is offered to only one of these beings, then the one addressed should

**Brihadaranyaka Upanishad 3.9.1:** The infinite number of gods is included in the limited number represented in the Nivid; these are again but manifestations of the Thirty-three, and these are likewise included in the successively more fundamental things down to the One, That, Brahman. Cf. Rig Veda 1.164.46, p. 35.

**Michi-no-Shiori:** Cf. Hebrews 1.14, p. 257.

**Vishnu Purana 1.22:** The first paragraph is a good statement of Pantheism and the theory of creation by emanation. Brahma, Vishnu, and Shiva are sometimes called the Hindu trinity. Cf. Chun Boo Kyung, p. 62.

be named.... Wakan Tanka is like sixteen different persons; but each person is *kan*. Therefore, they are only the same as one.

*Native American Religions*. Sioux Tradition

O God, you are great,
You are the one who created me,
I have no other.
God, you are in the heavens,
You are the only one:
Now my child is sick,
And you will grant me my desire.

*African Traditional Religions*. Anuak Prayer (Sudan)

God has not chosen any son, nor is there any god along with Him; else each god would have surely championed that which he created, and some of them would have overcome others. Glorified be God above all that they allege... exalted be He over all that they ascribe as partners unto Him!

*Islam*. Qur'an 23.91-92

We know that an idol has no real existence, and that there is no God but one. For although there may be so-called gods in heaven or on earth—as indeed there are many "gods" and many "lords"—yet for us there is one God, the Father, from whom are all things and for whom we exist, and one Lord, Jesus Christ, through whom are all things and through whom we exist.

*Christianity*. 1 Corinthians 8.4-6

Only from the unitary and unified Cause, can the unified resultant world be created.

*Unification Church*. Sun Myung Moon, 10-13-72

To Him belong all creatures in the heavens and on the earth: even those who are in His very Presence are not too proud to serve Him, nor are they ever weary. They celebrate His praises night and day, nor do they ever flag or intermit. Or have they taken gods from the earth who can raise the dead? If there were, in the heavens or in the earth, other gods besides God, there would have been confusion in both! But glory to God, the Lord of the Throne; high is He above what they attribute to Him!

*Islam*. Qur'an 21.19-22

**Sioux Tradition:** This is a concise statement of the solidarity of all spiritual forces; see Cree Round Dance Song, p. 31; Zuni Song, p. 206; Sioux Tradition, pp. 258-59; Yanomami Shaman, p. 259; Winnebago Invocation at the Sweat Lodge, pp. 260-61.

**Qur'an 23.91-92:** Cf. Qur'an 18.110, p. 468; 29.41, p. 286; and related passages.

**Qur'an 21.19-22:** Cf. Qur'an 21.26-29, p. 263.

## *Formless, Emptiness, Mystery*

ULTIMATE REALITY IS A MYSTERY, not a thing that can be defined by form or a concept of being. In the monotheistic religions, God is beyond any human concept, hidden, and inscrutable: "My thoughts are not your thoughts, neither are your ways my ways." The prohibition of images is a statement about the utter transcendence of God, for to make an idol to represent God is to reduce the infinite to finitude. Buddhism, Hinduism, Jainism, and Taoism affirm the ineffability of Ultimate Reality in their assertions that no words or intellection can properly convey its nature. It is beyond all duality, e.g., all attempts to think of it as a "thing" separate from other things. Its nature is emptiness.

Emptiness in the eastern religions should never be misunderstood as a cognitive statement about Reality—such a statement or its referent is a "thing" and cannot itself be empty. Rather, as the Buddhist scholar Edward Conze writes,

> Emptiness is not a theory, but a ladder that reaches out into the infinite. A ladder is not there to be discussed, but to be climbed.... It is a practical concept, and it embodies an aspiration, not a view. Its only use is to help us to get rid of this world and of the ignorance which binds us to it. It has not only one meaning, but several, which can unfold themselves on the successive stages of the actual process of transcending the world through wisdom. Not everyone, of course, is meant to understand what emptiness means. In that case it is better to pass on to something else.[1]

Truly thou art a God who hidest thyself.

*Judaism* and *Christianity*. Isaiah 45.15

Invent not similitudes for God; for God knows, and you know not.

*Islam*. Qur'an 16.74

For my thoughts are not your thoughts,
neither are your ways my ways, says the Lord.
For as the heavens are higher than the earth,
so are my ways higher than your ways
and my thoughts than your thoughts.

*Judaism* and *Christianity*. Isaiah 55.8-9

No vision can grasp Him,
but His grasp is over all vision;
He is above all comprehension,
yet is acquainted with all things.

*Islam*. Qur'an 6.103

Can you find out the deep things of God?
Can you find out the limit of the Almighty?
It is higher than heaven—what can you do?
Deeper than Sheol—what can you know?
Its measure is longer than the earth,
and broader than the sea.

*Judaism* and *Christianity*. Job 11.7-9

We raise to degrees of wisdom whom We please; but over all endued with knowledge is One, the All-knowing.

*Islam*. Qur'an 12.76

**Isaiah 55.8-9:** Cf. 1 Corinthians 1.20-25, p. 570.

[1] Conze, *Selected Sayings from the Perfection of Wisdom* (Boulder: Prajna Press, 1978) p. 24.

At this time the World-honored One serenely arose from meditation and addressed Shariputra: "The wisdom of all the Buddhas is infinitely profound and immeasurable. The portal to this wisdom is difficult to understand and difficult to enter. Neither men of learning nor men of realization are able to comprehend it."

*Buddhism.* Lotus Sutra 2

If you think that you know well the truth of Brahman, know that you know little. What you think to be Brahman in your self, or what you think to be Brahman in the gods—that is not Brahman. What is indeed the truth of Brahman you must therefore learn.

I cannot say that I know Brahman fully. Nor can I say that I know him not. He among us knows him best who understands the spirit of the words, "Nor do I know that I know him not."

He truly knows Brahman who knows him as beyond knowledge; he who thinks that he knows, knows not. The ignorant think that Brahman is known, but the wise know him to be beyond knowledge.

*Hinduism.* Kena Upanishad 2.1-3

All praise and glory is due the Lord, whose worth cannot be described even by the greatest rhetoricians of all times... None can fully understand or explain His Being however hard he may try. Reason and sagacity cannot visualize Him. Intelligence, understanding, and attainment cannot attain the depths of knowledge to study and scrutinize the Godhead. Human faculties of conception, perception and learning, and attributes of volition, intuition, and apprehension cannot catch sight of His Person or fathom the extent of His might and glory. His attributes cannot be fixed, limited or defined. There do not exist words in any language to specify or define His qualities, peculiarities, characteristics or singularities.

*Islam.* Nahjul Balagha, Sermon 1

I asked the Messenger of God, "Did you see your Lord?" He said, "He is a Light; how could I see Him?"

*Islam.* Hadith of Muslim

Verily, there exist seventy thousand veils of light and darkness before God. If He were to lift them, the light of the Majesty of His countenance would consume all of creation within sight.

*Islam.* Hadith

God is formless. If you think He is big, He is infinite, and if you think He is small, He is infinitesimal.

*Unification Church.*
Sun Myung Moon, 10-13-70

The eye cannot see it; the mind cannot grasp it.
The deathless Self has neither caste nor race,
Neither eyes nor ears nor hands nor feet.
Sages say this Self is infinite in the great
And in the small, everlasting and changeless,
The source of life.

*Hinduism.* Mundaka Upanishad 1.1.6

In the beginning was God,
Today is God
Tomorrow will be God.
Who can make an image of God?
He has no body.
He is as a word which comes out of your
mouth.

**Lotus Sutra 2:** 'Men of learning' are *shravakas* who rightly understand the Theravada teachings and attain arhatship; 'men of realization' are *pratyekabuddhas* who attain enlightenment through solitary effort and meditation. This sutra was composed in a period of rivalry among the various schools of Buddhism. The Buddha goes on to say that the only way to enter the door is by faith.

**Kena Upanishad 2.1-3:** Cf. 1 Corinthians 8.1-3, p. 570; Diamond Sutra 21, p. 572; Sirach 24.28-29, p. 576.

**Nahjul Balagha, Sermon 1:** Cf. 1 Corinthians 1.20-25, p. 570.

**Hadith:** On the notion that God is the transcendent and veiled center, see also Katha Upanishad 2.3.7-8, p. 60; 3.13, p. 601; Ezekiel 1.3-28, p. 100; Zohar Genesis 19b, pp. 228-29.

That word! It is no more,
It is past, and still it lives!
So is God.

*African Traditional Religions.*
Pygmy Hymn (Zaire)

Moses said, "I pray thee, show me thy glory." And [the Lord] said, "I will make all my goodness pass before you, and will proclaim before you my name 'The Lord'; and I will be gracious to whom I will be gracious, and will show mercy on whom I will show mercy." "But," he said, "you cannot see my face; for man shall not see me and live." And the Lord said, "Behold, there is a place by me where you shall stand upon the rock; and while my glory passes by I will put you in a cleft of the rock, and I will cover you with my hand until I have passed by; then I will take away my hand, and you shall see my back; but my face shall not be seen."

*Judaism* and *Christianity.*
Exodus 33.18-23

Moses said to God, "Show me now thy ways" [Exodus 33.13]. And he showed them to him, as it is said, "He made known his ways unto Moses" [Psalm 103.7]. Then Moses said, "Show me now thy glory" [Exodus 33.18], that is, "the attributes wherewith thou governest the world." Then God said, "You can not comprehend my attributes."

*Judaism.* Midrash Psalms 25.4

The Formless is Attributed and Unattributed,
And gone into absorption in the cosmic Void.
Himself has He made creation; Himself on it meditates.

In the cosmic Void is He absorbed,
Where plays the unstruck mystic music—
Beyond expression is this miraculous wonder.

*Sikhism.* Adi Granth,
Gauri Sukhmani M.5, pp. 290, 293

The way that can be spoken of
Is not the eternal Way;
The name that can be named
Is not the eternal name.
The nameless was the beginning of heaven and earth;
The named was the mother of the myriad creatures.
Hence always rid yourself of desire in order to observe its secrets;
But always allow yourself to have desires in order to observe its manifestations.
These two are the same
But diverge in name as they issue forth.
Being the same they are called mysteries,
Mystery upon mystery—
The gateway of the manifold secrets.

*Taoism.* Tao Te Ching 1

You look at it, but it is not to be seen;
Its name is Formless.
You listen to it, but it is not to be heard;
Its name is Soundless.
You grasp it, but it is not to be held;
Its name is Bodiless.
These three elude all scrutiny,
And hence they blend and become one.
Its upper side is not bright;
Its under side is not dim.
Continuous, unceasing, and unnameable,
It reverts to nothingness.
It is called formless form, thingless image;
It is called the elusive, the evasive.
Confronting it, you do not see its face;
Following it, you do not see its back.
Yet by holding fast to this Way of old,
You can harness the events of the present,
You can know the beginnings of the past—
Here is the essence of the Way.

*Taoism.* Tao Te Ching 14

**Midrash Psalms 25.4:** The true nature of God is beyond any of his attributes as humanly conceived; cf. The Kaddish, p. 30.

**Gauri Sukhmani M.5:** On the music of the spheres, see Qur'an 71.15, p. 229.

**Tao Te Ching 1:** The 'way,' that is, the Tao.

All voices get reflected there in the Supreme Soul (*Paramatman*). There is no reason; the intellect fails to grasp him. He is one and alone, bodiless and the Knower. He is neither long nor short, nor a circle nor a triangle, nor a quadrilateral nor a sphere. He is neither black nor blue nor red nor yellow nor white. He is neither a pleasant smell nor an unpleasant smell. He is neither pungent nor bitter nor astringent nor sour nor sweet. He is neither hard nor soft, neither heavy nor light, neither cold nor hot, neither rough nor smooth. He is bodiless. He is not subject to birth. He is free from attachment. He is neither female nor male nor neuter. He is immaculate knowledge and intuition. There exists no simile to comprehend him. He is formless existence. He is what baffles all terminology. There is no word to comprehend him. He is neither sound nor form nor odor nor taste nor touch. Only so much I say.

*Jainism*. Acarangasutra 5.123-40

The capacity of the mind is as great as that of space. It is infinite, neither round nor square, neither great nor small, neither green nor yellow, neither red nor white, neither above nor below, neither long nor short, neither angry nor happy, neither right nor wrong, neither good nor evil, neither first nor last. All universes are as void as space. Intrinsically our transcendental nature is void and not a single thing can be attained. It is the same with the Essence of Mind, which is a state of Absolute Void.

*Buddhism*. Sutra of Hui Neng 2

Reversion is the action of Tao.
Weakness is the function of Tao.
All things in the world came from being;
And being comes from non-being.

*Taoism*. Tao Te Ching 40

Here, O Shariputra, form is emptiness, and the very emptiness is form; emptiness does not differ from form, form does not differ from emptiness; whatever is form, that is emptiness, whatever is emptiness, that is form. The same is true of feelings, perceptions, impulses, consciousness.

*Buddhism*. Heart Sutra

Vimalakirti: "Manjusri, all worlds are empty."

Manjusri: "What makes them empty?"

"They are empty because [their ultimate reality is] emptiness."

"What is 'empty' about emptiness?"

"Constructions are empty, because of emptiness."

"Can emptiness be conceptually constructed?"

"Even that concept is itself empty, and emptiness cannot construct emptiness."

*Buddhism*. Holy Teaching of Vimalakirti 5

As long as there is duality, one sees "the other," one hears "the other," one smells "the other," one speaks to "the other," one thinks of "the other," one knows "the other"; but when for the illumined soul the all is dissolved in the Self, who is there to be seen by whom, who is there to be smelled by whom, who is there to

**Acarangasutra 5.123-40:** This is the fundamental statement of Mahavira's enlightenment. In Jainism, the Supreme Soul is not God, but rather the condition of the liberated human soul, which in liberation becomes eternal, infinite, blissful, omniscient, and supreme in all the cosmos. Cf. Niyamasara 176-77, p. 153; Pancastikaya 170, p. 131.

**Sutra of Hui Neng 2:** Cf. Mumonkan 33, p. 640.

**Tao Te Ching 40:** Cf. Chuang Tzu 12, pp. 416.

**Heart Sutra:** This famous and enigmatic statement declares that all material phenomena are relative existences. Even emptiness itself is, if considered as a separate thing, a relative existence. At the same time, all material phenomena in their relativity participate in emptiness. The complete sutra is given on p. 598. Cf. Katha Upanishad 2.1.10-11, pp. 415-16.

**Holy Teaching of Vimalakirti 5:** This is a conversation between Vimalakirti, who is a wealthy lay Buddhist well versed in Mahayana teachings, and Manjusri, one of the great bodhisattvas. The doctrine of emptiness (*sunyata*) is too profound for words; to describe it leads only to an infinite regress. This sutra is a favorite of lay Buddhists as Vimalakirti, the layman, excels all the monks in wisdom. Cf. Diamond Sutra 21, p. 572; Lankavatara Sutra 61, pp. 454-55.; Mumonkan 33, p. 640.

be heard by whom, who is there to be spoken to by whom, who is there to be thought of by whom, who is there to be known by whom? Ah, Maitreyi, my beloved, the Intelligence which reveals all—by what shall it be revealed? By whom shall the Knower be known? The Self is described as "not this, not that" (*neti, neti*). It is incomprehensible, for it cannot be comprehended; undecaying, for it never decays; unattached, for it never attaches itself; unbound, for it is never bound. By whom, O my beloved, shall the Knower be known?

*Hinduism.*
Bhrihadaranyaka Upanishad 4.5.15

What is never cast off, seized, interrupted, constant, extinguished, and produced—this is called Nirvana.

Indeed, Nirvana is not strictly in the nature of ordinary existence for, if it were, there would wrongly follow the characteristics of old age and death. For, such an existence cannot be without those characteristics.

If Nirvana is strictly in the nature of ordinary existence, it would be of the created realm. For, no ordinary existence of the uncreated realm ever exists anywhere at all.

If Nirvana is strictly in the nature of ordinary existence, why is it non-appropriating? For, no ordinary existence that is non-appropriating ever exists.

If Nirvana is not strictly in the nature of ordinary existence, how could what is in the nature of non-existence be Nirvana? Where there is no existence, equally so, there can be no non-existence.

If Nirvana is in the nature of non-existence, why is it non-appropriating? For, indeed, a non-appropriating non-existence does not prevail.

The status of the birth-death cycle is due to existential grasping [of the skandhas] and relational condition [of the being]. That which is non-grasping and non-relational is taught as Nirvana.

The Teacher has taught the abandonment of the concepts of being and non-being. Therefore, Nirvana is properly neither [in the realm of] existence nor non-existence.

If Nirvana is [in the realm of] both existence and non-existence, then liberation will also be both. But that is not proper.

If Nirvana is [in the realm of] both existence and non-existence, it will not be non-appropriating. For, both realms are always in the process of appropriating.

How could Nirvana be [in the realm of] both existence and non-existence? Nirvana is of the uncreated realm while existence and non-existence are of the created realm.

How could Nirvana be [in the realm of] both existence and non-existence? Both cannot be together in one place just as the situation is with light and darkness.

The proposition that Nirvana is neither existence nor non-existence could only be valid if and when the realms of existence and non-existence are established.

If indeed Nirvana is asserted to be neither existence nor non-existence, then by what means are the assertions to be known?

It cannot be said that the Blessed One exists after *nirodha* (release from worldly desires). Nor can it be said that He does not exist after nirodha, or both, or neither.

It cannot be said that the Blessed One even exists in the present living process. Nor can it be said that He does not exist in the present living process, or both, or neither.

Samsara is nothing essentially different from Nirvana. Nirvana is nothing essentially different from Samsara.

The limits of Nirvana are the limits of Samsara. Between the two, also, there is not the slightest difference whatsoever.

The various views concerning the status of life after nirodha, the limits of the world, the concept of permanence, etc., are all based on [such concepts as] Nirvana, posterior and anterior states of existence.

**Brihadaranyaka Upanishad 4.5.15:** This is the classic statement of the *via negativa*, as the seeker gradually strips away all relative phenomena, descending ever deeper into darkness. Through such an emptying of the soul, perhaps the Absolute may be found. Cf. Chuang Tzu 2, p. 120.

Since all factors of existence are in the nature of Emptiness, why assert the finite, the infinite, both finite and infinite, and neither finite nor infinite?

Why assert the identity, difference, permanence, impermanence, both permanence and impermanence, or neither permanence nor impermanence?

All acquisitions [i.e., grasping] as well as play of concepts [i.e., symbolic representation] are basically in the nature of cessation and quiescence. Any factor of experience with regards to anyone at any place was never taught by the Buddha.

*Buddhism*. Nagarjuna, Mulamadhyamaka Karika 25

❖

## *Transcendent, All-pervasive Reality*

THIS AND THE FOLLOWING sections describe the various attributes of Ultimate Reality. Passages on the essential nature of Ultimate Reality as transcendent and beyond all phenomenal existence teach, at the same time, that Ultimate Reality is all-pervasive and immanent, the Ground of Being, the Source of the energy within every atom, and the Life in every creature. Yet God's involvement with the world, even his immanence in all things, in no way limits or affects his essential, absolute nature. God's glory fills the world, but the world cannot exhaust God. We conclude with some well-known theophanies which reveal, in a manner far more vivid than is possible through theological conceptions alone, the transcendence of divinity and the all-pervasiveness of Truth.

Beyond the senses is the mind, beyond the mind is the intellect, higher than the intellect is the Great Atman, higher than the Great Atman is the Unmanifest. Beyond the Unmanifest is the Person, all-pervading, and imperceptible.

*Hinduism*. Katha Upanishad 2.3.7-8

God! There is no God but He,
the Living, the Everlasting.
Slumber seizes Him not, neither sleep;
to Him belongs all that is in the heavens and
the earth.
Who is there who shall intercede with Him
save by His leave?

**Mulamadhyamaka Karika 25:** In this well-known passage, Nagarjuna sets forth a logical argument for the identity of *Nirvana* (unconditioned existence) and *Samsara* (the world of changing, relative and interdependent phenomena). Cf. Heart Sutra, pp. 416-17.; Lankavatara Sutra 78, p 121; Milarepa, p. 415.

**Katha Upanishad 2.3.7-8:** The specific meanings of these successive levels of reality are in some dispute. The mind is the seat of emotion, perception, and consciousness. The intellect (*buddhi*) is a finer faculty of enlightened discrimination. The Great Atman is understood by some as the Ego, by others as the collective consciousness of all minds. The Unmanifest is either the undifferentiated consciouness of reality or Brahman in his attribute as the seed of the causal realm. The Person (*Purusha*) may be Brahman or the Supreme Being. For other Upanishadic discussions of four levels of reality, see Katha Upanishad 3.13, p. 601; Mandukya Upanishad, p. 597. Compare the Hadith of the veils, p. 56; the mystical interpretation of Qur'an 24.35, p. 74; and the Zohar's discourse on the nut garden, pp. 228-29.

He knows what lies before them
and what is after them,
and they comprehend not anything of His
knowledge
save such as He wills.
His throne comprises the heavens and earth;
the preserving of them oppresses Him not;
He is the All-high, the All-glorious.

*Islam.* Qur'an 2.255: The Throne Verse

The Self is one. Ever still, the Self is
Swifter than thought, swifter than the senses.
Though motionless, he outruns all pursuit.
Without the Self, never could life exist.

The Self seems to move, but is ever still.
He seems far away, but is ever near.
He is within all, and he transcends all.

The Self is everywhere. Bright is the Self,
Indivisible, untouched by sin, wise,
Immanent and transcendent. He it is
Who holds the cosmos together.

*Hinduism.* Isha Upanishad 4-8

Some sing of His noble attributes and exalted
state.
Some express Him through philosophical
intricacies and ratiocination.
Some tell of His giving life and taking it away.
Some sing of His taking away life and giving it
back.
Some sing of His transcendence;
To some is He ever manifest.
Millions upon millions discourse endlessly of
Him.
Eternally He doles out gifts;
Those receiving them at last can receive no
more.
Infinitely the creation receives from Him
sustenance.
He is the Ordainer;
By His Ordinance the universe He runs.
Says Nanak, Ever is He in bliss,
Ever fulfilled.

*Sikhism.* Adi Granth, Japuji 3, M.1, pp. 1-2

"In what does the Infinite rest?"

"In its own glory—nay, not even in that. In the world it is said that cows and horses, elephants and gold, slaves, wives, fields, and houses are man's glory—but these are poor and finite things. How shall the Infinite rest anywhere but in itself?

"The infinite is below, above, behind, before, to the right, to the left. I am all this. This Infinite is the Self. The Self is below, above, behind, before, to the right, to the left. I am all this. One who knows, meditates upon, and realizes the truth of the Self—such a one delights in the Self, rejoices in the Self. He becomes master of himself, master of all worlds. Slaves are they who know not this truth."

*Hinduism.* Chandogya Upanishad 7.23-25

Caesar said to Rabbi Gamaliel, "You state that whenever ten Israelites are assembled, the *Shechinah* (Divine Presence) is found. How many Shechinahs are there then?" Rabbi Gamaliel summoned the ruler's servant, struck him on the neck, and asked, "Why did you permit the sun to enter the house of your master?" Thereupon the ruler replied, "The sun shines over all the earth." Rabbi Gamaliel then said, "If the sun, which is only one of the hundred million servants of the Lord, can shine over all the earth, how much more would this be true for the Shechinah of the Lord Himself?"

*Judaism.* Talmud, Sanhedrin 39a

There was something undifferentiated and yet
complete,
Which existed before heaven and earth.
Soundless and formless, it depends on nothing
and does not change.
It operates everywhere and is free from danger.
It may be considered the mother of the
universe.
I do not know its name; I call it Tao.
If forced to give it a name, I shall call it Great.

**Isha Upanidhad 4-8:** Vv. 4, 5, 8. Compare Svetasvatara Upanishad 6.11, p. 51, Chandogya Upanishad 7.25.2, pp. 377-78.

**Sanhedrin 39a:** The saying about ten Israelites refers to the *minyan*, the minimum number of men required to start a synagogue. But the holy Spirit (*Shechinah*) can come among even two gathered together in God's name; cf. Abot 3.2, p. 186.

Now being great means functioning everywhere.
Functioning everywhere means far-reaching.
Being far-reaching means returning to the original point.

*Taoism*. Tao Te Ching 25

Any and everything of this universe is all the body of God.

*Tenrikyo*. Ofudesaki 3.40

God's mind is not only in his Word, but also in everything he created. God's mind exists wherever we go in heaven or on earth.

*Unification Church*. Sun Myung Moon, 12-13-59

The one that is visible begins from the invisible. The invisible consists of three ultimates, and their essence is infinite.

*Korean Religions*. Chun Boo Kyung

Divinity is that which was there before the appearance of heaven and earth, and which gives form to them; that which surpasses the yin and the yang, yet has the quality of them. This Divinity is thus the absolute existence, governing the entire universe of heaven and earth, yet at the same time, it dwells within all things, where it is called spirit; omnipresent within human beings, it is called mind.

In other words, human mind communes with the Divinity which is ruler of heaven and earth; mind and Divinity are one and the same. Divinity is the root origin of heaven and earth, the spiritual nature of all things, and the source of human destiny. Itself without form, it is Divinity which nurtures things with form.

*Shinto*. Kanetomo Yoshida, An Outline of Shinto

Buddha abides in the infinite, the unobstructed, ultimate realm of reality, in the realm of space, in the essence of True Thusness, without birth or death, and in ultimate truth, appearing to sentient beings according to the time, sustained by past vows, without ever ceasing, not abandoning all beings, all lands, all phenomena....

How should enlightening beings see the body of Buddha? (*Dharmakaya*) They should see the body of Buddha in infinite places. Why? They should not see Buddha in just one thing, one phenomenon, one body, one land, one being—they should see Buddha everywhere. Just as space is omnipresent, in all places, material or immaterial, yet without either arriving or not arriving there, because space is incorporeal, in the same way Buddha is omnipresent, in all places, in all beings, in all things, in all lands, yet neither arriving nor not arriving there, because Buddha's body is incorporeal, manifesting a body for the sake of sentient beings.

*Buddhism*. Garland Sutra 37

The Tathagata... is the essence which is the reality of matter, but he is not matter. He is the essence which is the reality of sensation, but he is not sensation. He is the essence which is the reality of intellect, but he is not intellect. He is the essence which is the reality of motivation, but he is not motivation. He is the essence which is the reality of consciousness, yet he is not consciousness. Like the element of space, he does not abide in any of the four elements. Transcending the scope of eye, ear, nose, tongue, body, and mind, he is not produced in the six sense media... He abides in ultimate reality, yet there is no relationship between it and him. He is not produced from causes, nor does he depend on conditions. He is not with-

**Tao Te Ching 25:** Cf. Doctrine of the Mean 26, p. 52; I Ching, Great Commentary 1.10.4, p. 77.

**Chun Boo Kyung:** God as the cause is one body, but three in function. These three spirits appear in the world of phenomena as three poles: *sung* (character), *myung* (life), and *chung* (energy). Since the essence of the one is infinite, the three poles are divided and yet undivided. It is everywhere self-existing and omnipresent. Another interpretation: the three ultimate poles are manifest in the invisible world as internal character or mind, external form or substance, and their unity as substantial beings; and they are similarly manifest in the visible world as proton, electron, and neutron. Cf. Vishnu Purana 1, p. 53.

**Garland Sutra 37:** The teachings in this sutra are: (1) all beings equally possess Buddha nature when viewed from the standpoint of the Ultimate Truth; (2) all phenomena come into being due to their interdependence with other phenomena; (3) each experience contains all experience due to their interdependent relationship. Cf. Lion's Roar of Queen Srimala 5, p. 466.

out any characteristic, nor has he any characteristic. He has no single nature nor a diversity of natures. He is not a conception, not a mental construction, nor is he a nonconception. He is neither the other shore, nor this shore, nor that between. He is neither here, nor there, nor anywhere else.

*Buddhism.* Holy Teaching of Vimalakirti 12

This Teacher of mine, this Teacher of mine—he passes judgment on the ten thousand things but he doesn't think himself severe; his bounty extends to ten thousand generations but he doesn't think himself benevolent. He is older than the highest antiquity but he doesn't think himself long-lived; he covers heaven, bears up the earth, carves and fashions countless forms, but he doesn't think himself skilled. It is with him alone I wander.

*Taoism.* Chuang Tzu 6

God is incorporeal, divine, supreme, infinite Mind, Spirit, Soul, Principle, Life, Truth, Love.

Science reveals Spirit, Soul, as not in the body, and God as not in man but as reflected by man. The greater cannot be in the lesser.... We reason imperfectly from effect to cause, when we conclude that matter is the effect of Spirit; but a priori reasoning shows material existence to be enigmatical. Spirit gives the true mental idea. We cannot interpret Spirit, Mind, through matter. Matter neither sees, hears, nor feels.

*Christian Science.* Science and Health, 465, 467

The Supreme Being (*Purusha*) is thousand-headed,
thousand eyed, thousand footed;
and, pervading the earth on all sides,
He exists beyond the ten directions.
The Supreme Being, indeed, is all this,
what has been and what will be,
and the Lord of immortality
as well as of mortal creatures.

Such is His magnificence, but
the Supreme Being is even greater than this;
all beings are a fourth of Him,
three-fourths—His immortality—lie in heaven.

Three-fourths of the Supreme Being ascended;
the fourth part came here again and again,
and, diversified in form, it moved
to the animate and the inanimate world.

*Hinduism.* Rig Veda 10.90.1-4

My material world is eightfold,
divided into earth, water,
fire, air, ether, mind, the faculty of meditation,
and self-awareness.
This is the lower nature. My higher
nature is different.
It is the very life
that sustains the world.
Do not forget that this is the source
of all existence.
I am the genesis and the end
of the entire world.
There is nothing higher than I am,
O Conqueror of Wealth!
The world is strung on me
like pearls on a string.

*Hinduism.* Bhagavad Gita 7.4-7

Thou art the fire
Thou art the sun
Thou art the air
Thou art the moon
Thou art the starry firmament
Thou art Brahman Supreme;
Thou art the waters—Thou, the Creator of all!

Thou art woman, thou art man,
Thou art the youth, thou art the maiden,

**Holy Teaching of Vimalakirti 12:** The transcendence of Buddha is comparable to the Jain doctrine of the Paramatman; see Niyamasara 176-77, p. 153. Cf. Brihadaranyaka Upanishad 4.5.15, pp. 58-59; Mulamadhyamaka Karika 25, pp. 59-60.

**Science and Health:** The capitalized words 'Spirit' and 'Soul' are among the Seven Deific Synonyms for God.

**Rig Veda 10.90.1-4:** Cf. Rig Veda 1.164.45, p. 576; Svetasvatara Upanishad 3.7-10, p. 412.

Thou art the old man tottering with his staff;
Thou facest everywhere.

Thou art the dark butterfly,
Thou art the green parrot with red eyes,
Thou art the thunder cloud, the seasons, the seas.
Without beginning art Thou,
beyond time and space.
Thou art He from whom sprang
the three worlds.

*Hinduism.* Svetasvatara Upanishad 4.2-4

Tung-kuo Tzu asked Chuang Tzu, "What is called Tao—where is it?"

"It is everywhere," replied Chuang Tzu.

Tung-kuo Tzu said, "It will not do unless you are more specific."

"It is in the ant," said Chuang Tzu.

"Why go so low down?"

"It is in the weeds."

"Why even lower?"

"It is in a potsherd."

"Why still lower?"

"It is in the excrement and urine," said Chuang Tzu. Tung-kuo gave no response.

"Sir," said Chuang Tzu, "your question does not touch the essential. When inspector Huo asked the superintendent of markets about the fatness of pigs, the tests were always made in parts less and less likely to be fat. Do not insist on any particular thing. Nothing escapes from Tao. Such is perfect Tao, and so is great speech. The three words, Complete, Entire, and All, differ in name but are the same in actuality. They all designate the One."

*Taoism.* Chuang Tzu 22

In the year that King Uzziah died I saw the Lord sitting upon a throne, high and lifted up; and his train filled the temple. Above him stood the seraphim; each had six wings: with two he covered his face, and with two he covered his feet, and with two he flew. And one called to another and said,

Holy, holy, holy is the Lord of hosts;
the whole earth is full of His glory.

And the foundations of the thresholds shook at the voice of him who called, and the house was filled with smoke. And I said, "Woe is me! For I am lost; for I am a man of unclean lips, and I dwell in the midst of a people of unclean lips; for my eyes have seen the King, the Lord of hosts!"

*Judaism* and *Christianity.* Isaiah 6.1-5

Then the Buddha, wishing to enable all the enlightening beings to realize the spiritual power of the boundless realm of the Enlightened One, emitted a light from between his brows. That light was called the Treasury of the Light of Knowledge of All Enlightening Beings Illuminating the Ten Directions. Its form was like a cloud of lamps with jewellike light. It shone throughout all buddha fields in the ten directions, revealing all the lands and beings therein. It also caused all networks of worlds to tremble. In every single atom it revealed innumerable Buddhas showering the teachings of all the Buddhas of all times, in accord with the differences in character and inclination of the various sentient beings. It clearly showed the Buddha's ocean of transcendent ways, and also rained infinite clouds of various emancipations, causing the sentient beings to forever cross over birth and death. It also showered clouds of the great vows of the Buddhas, and clearly showed, in all worlds in the ten directions, the universally good enlightening beings' congregations at the sites of enlightenment. Having done all this, the

**Svetasvatara Upanishad 4.2-4:** Cf. Rig Veda 6.47.18, p. 50.

**Chuang Tzu 22:** Compare Mumonkan 21: "A man asked Umman, 'What is Buddha?' Umman replied, 'Shit-stick (*Kanshiketsu*)!' " See Mumonkan 18, p. 417.

**Isaiah 6.1-5:** This vision of God's glory in the Temple is the prelude to Isaiah's call to be a prophet.

light swirled around the Buddha, circling to the right, then went in under his feet.

*Buddhism*. Garland Sutra 2

Jacob... came to a certain place, and stayed there that night, because the sun had set. Taking one of the stones of the place, he put it under his head and lay down in that place to sleep. And he dreamed that there was a ladder set up on the earth, and the top of it reached to heaven; and behold, the angels of God were ascending and descending on it! And behold, the Lord stood above it and said, "I am the Lord, the God of Abraham your father and the God of Isaac; the land on which you lie I will give to you and to your descendants; and your descendants shall be like the dust of the earth, and you shall spread abroad to the west and to the east and to the north and to the south; by you and your descendants shall all the families of the earth be blessed. Behold, I am with you and will keep you wherever you go, and will bring you back to this land; for I will not leave you until I have done that of which I have spoken to you." Then Jacob awoke from his sleep and said, "Surely the Lord is in this place; and I did not know it." And he was afraid, and said, "How awesome is this place! This is none other than the house of God, and this is the gate of heaven."

*Judaism* and *Christianity*.
Genesis 28.10-17

I John, your brother, who share with you in Jesus the tribulation and the kingdom and the patient endurance, was on the island called Patmos, [exiled] on account of the word of God and the testimony of Jesus. I was in the Spirit on the Lord's day, and I heard behind me a loud voice like a trumpet... Then I turned to see the voice that was speaking to me, and on turning I saw seven golden lampstands, and in the midst of the lampstands was one like a son of man, clothed with a long robe and with a golden girdle round his breast; his head and his hair were white as white wool, white as snow; his eyes were like a flame of fire, his feet were like burnished bronze, refined as in a furnace, and his voice was like the sound of many waters; in his right hand he held seven stars, from his mouth issued a sharp two-edged sword, and his face was like the sun shining in full strength. When I saw him, I fell at his feet as though dead. But he laid his right hand upon me, saying, "Fear not, I am the first and the last, and the living one; I died, and behold I am alive for evermore, and I have the keys of Death and Hades. Now write what you see, what is and what is to take place hereafter."

*Christianity*. Revelation 1.9-19

The word of the Lord came to Ezekiel the priest, the son of Buzi, in the land of the Chaldeans by the river Chebar; and the hand of the Lord was upon him there.

As I looked, behold, a stormy wind came out of the north, and a great cloud, with brightness round about it, and the fire flashing forth continually, and in the midst of the fire, as it were gleaming bronze. And from the midst of it came the likeness of four living creatures. And this was their appearance: they had the form of men, but each had four faces, and each of them had four wings.... As for the likeness of their faces, each had the face of a man in front, the four had the face of a lion on the right side, the four had the face of an ox on the left side, and the four had the face of an eagle at the back.

**Garland Sutra 2:** In Buddhist scriptures, these visions of the Buddha's transcendent reality generally introduce a sermon or a teaching. Here what follows is the Bodhisattva Samantabhadra explaining the heavenly domain of the Buddha Vairocana. The vision itself vividly depicts the Buddha's grace, as his Light of compassion, the *Sambhogakaya* (see Lion's Roar of Queen Srimala 5, p. 466), shines in all directions revealing the true Reality (*Dharmakaya*). Cf. Udana 49, p. 381, and comparable passages on enlightenment.

**Genesis 28.10-17:** Jacob's vision of a ladder extending to heaven confirmed God's grace upon him as he was about to embark on twenty lonely and burdensome years of exile. It is also the founding legend of the shrine and city of Bethel, 'House of God,' the royal sanctuary of the northern kingdom of Israel.

**Revelation 1.9-19:** This is a spiritual manifestation of the resurrected Jesus. Jesus also appeared transfigured before his disciples in Matthew 17.1-8, p. 467

Such were their faces. And their wings were spread out above; each creature had two wings, each of which touched the wing of another, while two covered their bodies. And each went straight forward; wherever the spirit would go, they went, without turning as they went. In the midst of the living creatures there was something that looked like burning coals of fire, like torches moving to and fro among the living creatures; and the fire was bright, and out of the fire went forth lightning. And the living creatures darted to and fro, like a flash of lightning.

Now as I looked at the living creatures, I saw a wheel upon the earth beside the living creatures, one for each of the four of them. As for the appearance of the wheels and their construction: their appearance was like the gleaming of chrysolite; and the four had the same likeness, their construction being as it were a wheel within a wheel. When they went, they went in any of their four directions without turning as they went. The four wheels had rims and they had spokes; and their rims were full of eyes round about. And when the living creatures went, the wheels went beside them; and when the living creatures rose from the earth, the wheels rose... for the spirit of the living creatures was in the wheels.

Over the heads of the living creatures there was the likeness of a firmament, shining like crystal, spread out above their heads. And under the firmament their wings were stretched out straight, one toward another; and each creature had two wings covering its body. And when they went, I heard the sound of their wings like the sound of many waters, like the thunder of the Almighty, a sound of tumult like the sound of a host....

And above the firmament over their heads there was the likeness of a throne, in appearance like sapphire; and seated on the throne was a likeness as it were of a human form. And upward from what had the appearance of his loins I saw as it were gleaming bronze, like the appearance of fire enclosed round about; and downward from what had the appearance of his loins I saw as it were the appearance of fire, and there was brightness round about him. Like the appearance of the bow that is in the cloud on the day of rain, so was the appearance of the brightness round about.

Such was the appearance of the likeness of the glory of the Lord. And when I saw it, I fell upon my face.

*Judaism* and *Christianity*. Ezekiel 1.3-28

Arjuna:
O Highest Lord, I wish I could see you,
your form as Lord,
just as you yourself say you are,
Supreme Divine Being.
O Lord, if you think it is possible
that I might see you—
then, Lord of mystic power,
show me your changeless self.

The Lord:
Open your eyes and see
my hundreds, my thousands of forms,
in all their variety, heavenly splendor,
in all their colors and semblances.

Look upon the Gods of Heaven, the Radiant Gods,
the Terrifying Gods, the Kind Celestial Twins.
See, Arjuna, countless marvels
never seen before.

Here is my body, in one place, now
the whole world—
all that moves and does not move—
and whatever else you want to see.

Of course, with the ordinary eye
you cannot see me.
I give you divine vision.
Behold my absolute power!

Samjaya:
With these words, Vishnu,

**Ezekiel 1.3-28:** This vision of God's chariot throne has been the inspiration for a school of Jewish mysticism called *merkabah* (chariot) mysticism. It emphasizes the unbridgeable distance between God and man. The mystic journeys ever higher, through heaven after heaven and glory after glory, approaching the divine throne but never reaching even to its footstool. The faces of the four living creatures have become, in Christian tradition, symbols for the four Evangelists.

the great Lord of mystic power,
gave Arjuna the vision
of his highest, absolute form—

His form with many mouths and eyes,
appearing in many miraculous ways,
with many divine ornaments
and divine, unsheathed weapons.

He wore garlands and robes
and ointments of divine fragrance.
He was a wholly wonderful god,
infinite, facing in every direction.

If the light of a thousand suns
should effulge all at once,
it would resemble the radiance
of that god of overpowering reality.

Then and there, Arjuna saw
the entire world unified,
yet divided manifold,
embodied in the God of gods.

Bewildered and enraptured,
Arjuna, the Pursuer of Wealth,
bowed his head to the god,
joined his palms, and said,

Arjuna:
Master! Within you I see the gods,
and all classes of beings,
the Creator
on his lotus seat,
and all seers and divine serpents.

Far and near, I see you
without limit,
reaching, containing everything, and
with innumerable mouths and eyes.
I see no end to you, no middle,
and no beginning—
O universal Lord and form of all!

You, Wearer
of Crown, Mace, and Discus,
you are a deluge of brilliant light
all around.
I see you,
who can hardly be seen,
with the splendor of radiant fires and suns,
immeasurable.

You are the one imperishable
paramount necessary core of knowledge,
the world's ultimate foundation;
you never cease to guard the eternal tradition.
You are the everlasting
Divine Being.

There is no telling what is
beginning, middle, or end in you.
Your power is infinite;
your arms reach infinitely far.
Sun and moon are your eyes.
This is how I see you.
Your mouth is a flaming sacrificial fire.
You burn up the world with your radiance.

For you alone fill the quarters of heaven
and the space between heaven and earth.
The world above,
man's world,
and the world in between
are frightened at the awesome sight of you,
O mighty being!

There I see throngs of gods entering you.
Some are afraid,
they join their palms
and call upon your name.
Throngs of great seers and perfect sages hail
you
with magnificent hymns.

The Terrifying Gods,
the Gods of Heaven, the Radiant Gods,
also the Celestial Spirits,
the All-Gods, the Celestial Twins,
the Storm Gods, and the Ancestors;
multitudes of heavenly musicians,
good sprites, demons, and perfect sages
all look upon you in wonder.

When the worlds see your form
of many mouths and eyes,
of many arms, legs, feet
many torsos, many terrible tusks,
they tremble,
as do I.

For seeing you
ablaze with all the colors of the rainbow,
touching the sky,
with gaping mouths and wide, flaming eyes,
my heart in me is shaken.
O God,
I have lost all certainty, all peace.

Your mouths and their terrible tusks
evoke the world in conflagration.
Looking at them
I can no longer orient myself.
There is no refuge.
O Lord of Gods,
dwelling place of the world,
give me Your grace.

*Hinduism*. Bhagavad Gita 11.3-25

## *Sovereign and Omnipotent*

WE HAVE SELECTED PASSAGES, largely from the monotheistic religions, on God's sovereignty over the affairs of the world. God rules over the affairs of men and women and decides their destinies; humans are therefore subject to the will of God: see *Providence*, pp. 763-72. The teaching that God is omnipotent often includes the belief that God determines everything that happens in this world, be it for good or evil; this relates to the doctrine of *Predestination*, pp. 494-97.

The Lord will reign for ever and ever.

*Judaism* and *Christianity*. Exodus 15.18

Unto God belongs the sovereignty of the heavens and the earth and all that is therein, and it is He who has power over all things.

*Islam*. Qur'an 5.120

The earth is wide, but God is the elder.

*African Traditional Religions*. Akan Proverb (Ghana)

All that are rulers, kings, potentates, lords
chiefs, officials—
All are God's creation.
Their will is subject to God's;
On God are they all dependent.

*Sikhism*. Adi Granth, Bilaval-ki-Var, M.4, p. 851

The Wise One is the most mindful of the
plans,
Which, indeed, were wrought in the past,
By demons and by men,
And which will be wrought hereafter!
He, the Lord, is the sole decider,
So may it be unto us as He wills!

*Zoroastrianism*. Avesta, Yasna 29.4

Revere the anger of Heaven,
And presume not to make sport or be idle.

**Bhagavad Gita 11.3-25** This is the climax of the Bhagavad Gita, when Krishna allows Arjuna a glimpse of his transcendent form. This magnificent theophany continues with a vision of the fate of all the combatants in the Mahabharata War, who rush headlong to destruction into Krishna's multifold gaping jaws or sharp tusks; cf. Bhagavad Gita 11.26-34, pp. 738-39. God is omnipotent and controls all worldly phenomena; thus with the theophany comes insight into the future, and Arjuna can have confidence in victory. But such a theophany is rare, and only given to those who have eyes to see. Once before, in front of Duryodhana and the assembled lords of the Kauravas, Krishna had displayed his transcendental form in an effort to make peace; but they utterly ignored it and showered him with insults (Mahabharata, Udogya Parva 43).

**Akan Proverb:** Cf. Ashanti Verse, p. 204.

Revere the changing moods of Heaven,
And presume not to drive about at your pleasure.
Great Heaven is intelligent,
And is with you in all your goings.
Great Heaven is clear-seeing,
And is with you in your wanderings and indulgences.

*Confucianism*. Book of Songs, Ode 254

I, even I, am he,
and there is no god beside me;
I kill and I make alive;
I wound and I heal;
and there is none that can deliver out of my hand.

*Judaism* and *Christianity*. Deuteronomy 32.39

All that is in the heavens and the earth magnifies God;
He is the All-mighty, the All-wise.
To Him belongs the Kingdom of the heavens and the earth;
He gives life, and He makes to die, and He is powerful over everything.
He is the First and the Last, the Outward and the Inward;
He has knowledge of everything.
It is He that created the heavens and the earth in six days
then seated Himself upon the Throne.
He knows what penetrates into the earth, and what comes forth from it,
what comes down from heaven, and what goes up into it.
He is with you wherever you are; and God sees the things you do.
To Him belongs the Kingdom of the heavens and the earth;
and unto Him all matters are returned.
He makes the night enter into the day
and makes the day enter into the night.
He knows the thoughts within the breasts.

*Islam*. Qur'an 57.1-6

The tree set up by *Imana* (God) cannot be blown down by the wind.

*African Traditional Religions*. Banyarawanda Proverb (Tanzania)

With men it is impossible, but not with God; for all things are possible with God.

*Christianity*. Mark 10.27

If He so will, He can remove you and put in your place a new creation; that is surely no great matter for God.

*Islam*. Qur'an 14.19-20

The Creator of the heavens and the earth; and when He decrees a thing, He but says to it "Be," and it is.

*Islam*. Qur'an 2.117

For I am God, and there is no other;
I am God, and there is none like me,
declaring the end from the beginning
and from ancient times things not yet done,
saying, "My counsel shall stand,
and I will accomplish all my purpose,"
calling a bird of prey from the east,
the man of my counsel from a far country.
I have spoken, and I will bring it to pass;
I have purposed, and I will do it.

*Judaism* and *Christianity*. Isaiah 46.9-11

**Book of Songs, Ode 254:** This is a classic statement of the teaching that rulers must pay regard to the Mandate of Heaven, without which their reign becomes untenable. It is one stanza of a longer poem given on pp. 769-70.

**Banyarawanda Proverb:** Cf. Boran Prayer, p. 398.

**Qur'an 2.117:** Compare Genesis 1.3: "And God said, 'Let there be light'; and there was light," p. 81.

**Isaiah 46.9-11:** The word and judgments of God will inevitably come to pass. The specific historical setting of this verse is the announcement by God through the anonymous prophet deutero-Isaiah concerning the coming of King Cyrus of Persia, the 'bird of prey from the east,' to conquer Babylon. Cf. Habakkuk 2.2-3, p. 738.

## *Omniscient*

GOD'S SOVEREIGNTY OVER HUMAN AFFAIRS includes total knowledge of human thoughts and actions. Nothing is hidden from God. There is no place to hide from him. Hence the believer should be sincere in his thoughts, and he can have confidence in the truthfulness of God's justice. We do not deal here with the question of divine foreknowledge; see *Predestination*, pp. 494-97. In Buddhism, Jainism, and many schools of Hinduism, the functions of omniscience and omnipotence to judge human affairs are not fulfilled through God's agency, but rather through the omnipresent workings of karma; see *Cosmic Justice*, pp. 122-27.

Our Lord! Lo! Thou knowest that which we hide and that which we proclaim. Nothing in the earth or in heaven is hidden from God.

*Islam*. Qur'an 14.38

Thou knowest when I sit down and when I rise up;
thou discernest my thoughts from afar.
Thou searchest out my path and my lying down,
and art acquainted with all my ways.

*Judaism* and *Christianity*. Psalm 139.2-3

Mark well three things and you will not fall into the clutches of sin: Know what is above you—an eye that sees, an ear that hears, and all your actions recorded in the book.

*Judaism*. Mishnah, Abot 2.1

To God belong the East and the West;
whithersoever you turn, there is the Face of God;
God is All-embracing, All-knowing.

*Islam*. Qur'an 2.115

For the word of God is living and active, sharper than any two-edged sword, piercing to the division of soul and spirit, of joints and marrow, and discerning the thoughts and intentions of the heart. And before him no creature is hidden, but all are open and laid bare to the eyes of him with whom we have to do.

*Christianity*. Hebrews 4.12-13

Surely God—He has knowledge of the Hour;
He sends down the rain; He knows what is in the wombs.
No soul knows what it shall earn tomorrow, and
no soul knows in what land it shall die.
Surely God is All-knowing, All-aware.

*Islam*. Qur'an 31.34

The eyes are not prevented [from seeing] by a hedge;
God has nothing hid from him.

*African Traditional Religions*
Ovambo Proverb (Angola)

You who dive down as if under water to steal,
Though no earthly king may have seen you,
The King of heaven sees.

*African Traditional Religions*.
Yoruba Proverb (Nigeria)

**Qur'an 14.38:** Cf. Qur'an 2.284, p. 126; 26.220, p. 538. On angels as God's watchers, see Qur'an 13.10-11, p. 126.

**Abot 2.1:** Cf. Abot 3.20, p. 124.

**Qur'an 2.115:** This has been interpreted by Muslims to mean that God appears to people of every culture and religion, east and west. God, who is one Unity (*tawhid*), embraces every one of his creatures. Cf. Amos 9.2-4, p. 124.

**Hebrews 4.12-13:** For a similar passage in the Hebrew Bible, see 1 Samuel 16.7; cf. Jeremiah 17.10, p. 125.

In the Book of Songs it is said,

In your secret chamber even you are judged;
See you do nothing to blush for,
Though but the ceiling looks down upon
you.

Therefore the moral man, even when he is not doing anything, is serious; and, even when he does not speak, is truthful.

*Confucianism.* Doctrine of the Mean 33

See you not that God knows all that is in the heavens and on earth? There is not a secret consultation between three unless He is their fourth, nor between five unless He is their sixth, nor between fewer or more unless He is in their midst, wheresoever they be.

*Islam.* Qur'an 58.7

The great Ruler of all these worlds,
beholds as if from near at hand
the man who thinks he acts by stealth:
the Gods know all this of him.

When one stands or walks or moves in secret,
or goes to his lying down or uprising,
when two sitting together take secret counsel,
King Varuna knows, being there the Third.

This earth belongs to Varuna, the King,
and the heavens, whose ends are far apart.
Both the oceans are the loins of Varuna,
and He is merged within the small water drop.

If one will go away beyond the heavens,
still he cannot escape King Varuna;
his envoys move about here from the heavens,
and, thousand-eyed, they look upon the earth.

King Varuna observes all that which lies
between heaven and earth and beyond them;
the twinklings of men's eyes have been counted
by him;
as a dicer the dice, he measures everything.

These fatal snares of thine, O Varuna,
that stand stretched seven by seven-and-three-
fold,
let all these catch up the man who tells a lie,
but pass by one who speaks the truth.

With a hundred nooses bind him, Varuna,
let him not who lies escape thee, Looker on
men!
Let the mean fellow sit stretching his belly
like a cask of which the bands have been cut.

Varuna is that which is the warp,
Varuna is that which is the woof,
Varuna is of our own land, he is of foreign
lands.
Varuna is transcendant, he is immanent.

*Hinduism.* Atharva Veda 4.16.1-8

The sun shines and sends its burning rays down
upon us,
The moon rises in its glory.
Rain will come and again the sun will shine,
And over it all passes the eyes of God.
Nothing is hidden from Him.
Whether you be in your home, whether you be
on the water,
Whether you rest in the shade of a tree in the
open,
Here is your Master.

Did you think because you were more powerful
than some poor orphan,
You could covet his wealth and deceive him,
Saying to yourself, "I cannot be seen"?
So then remember that you are always in the
presence of God.

Not today, not today, not today!
But some day He will give you your just reward
For thinking in your heart
That you have but cheated a slave, an orphan.

*African Traditional Religion.* Yoruba Song (Nigeria)

**Doctrine of the Mean 33:** Cf. Great Learning 6.1-4, pp. 516-17.

**Qur'an 58.7:** Cf. Matthew 18.20, p. 186, where a similar image is used to make a different point.

**Atharva Veda 4.16:** Varuna is the vedic god who represents the divine attribute of justice, weighing sins and also forgiving them. Etymologically, he is related to Zoroastrian Ahura Mazda. Cf. Amos 9.2-4, p. 124.

**Yoruba Song:** On the theme of delayed recompense, see Qur'an 3.176-78, Ecclesiastes 8.10-12, p. 124.

## *Immanent and Near At Hand*

THIS SECTION BRINGS TOGETHER passages on God's immanence. God is described in the Qur'an as "nearer than the jugular vein," knowing all a person's thoughts and desires, and abiding within the human heart. In the Bible, God's immanence is expressed in the revelation to Elijah, where instead of a grand manifestation in earthquake or thunder, God's self-revelation is as "a still small voice." Scriptures speak of God coming near or dwelling in the heart only when there is receptivity, humility, and faith. In the scriptures of the Abrahamic religions, while God is near at hand, he is rarely identified with the soul itself; that could be seen as tantamount to idolatry.

Other traditions teach more thoroughgoing notions of divine immanence. Sufis interpret the qur'anic parable of the Lamp as expressing the presence of God in the human heart as a light, illuminating the lamp of the body. In Hinduism, Sikhism, and Jainism the divine immanence is described ontologically: Ultimate Reality *is* the Self (*Atman*). In Buddhism the divine immanence is described psychologically: Essence of Mind or Suchness (*Tathata*) is realized by a mind dwelling in Perfect Wisdom and expressing a mind of Enlightenment (*Bodhi*), Dhamma nature or Buddha nature. But there is no ontological self which could be immanent. These various doctrines of divine immanence avoid a simple identification of God with the individual soul. The ordinary individual soul (*jiva*) is beclouded and deluded by an egoistic sense of self; in contrast, the divine Self within, or Suchness, can only be realized by one dwelling in Enlightenment.

The complete realization of the God within is a potential and an ideal which will be treated more fully in Chapter 3. Yet as many of these texts point out, even the ordinary beclouded mind is intrinsically pure and contains the germ of divinity.

We indeed created man; and We know what his soul whispers within him, and We are nearer to him than the jugular vein.

*Islam*. Qur'an 50.16

Ever is He present with you—think not He is far:
By the Master's teaching recognize Him within yourself.

*Sikhism*. Adi Granth, Majh Ashtpadi, M.3, p. 116

[God] is not far from each one of us, for "In him we live and move and have our being."

*Christianity*. Acts 17.27-28

The Master said, "Is Goodness indeed so far away? If we really wanted Goodness, we should find that it was at our very side."

*Confucianism*. Analects 7.29

Brahman shines forth, vast, self-luminous, inconceivable, subtler than the subtle. He is far beyond what is far, and yet here very near at

**Qur'an 50.16:** Cf. Qur'an 2.186, p. 592.
**Majh Ashtpadi, M.3:** Cf. Gaund, M.5, p. 142; Chandogya Upanishad 6.8.7, p. 140.
**Acts 17.27-28:** Cf. Psalm 145.18, p. 592.
**Analects 7.29:** Cf. Luke 17.20-21, p. 146; Bhagavad Gita 7.21-23, Forty Hadith of an-Nawawi 1, p. 518; Tao Te Ching 23, p. 492.

hand. Verily, He is seen here, dwelling in the cave of the heart of conscious beings.

*Hinduism*, Mundaka Upanishad 3.1.7

For thus says the high and lofty One
who inhabits eternity, whose name is Holy,
"I dwell in the high and holy place,
and also with him who is of a contrite and
humble spirit,
to revive the spirit of the humble,
and to revive the heart of the contrite."

*Judaism* and *Christianity*. Isaiah 57.15

"If I [God] am there, all are there, and if I am not there, who is there?" Hillel also used to say, "To the place where I wish to be, there do my feet bring me. If you come to my house, I will come to your house; if you do not come to my house, I will not come to your house. As it says, In all places where I cause my Name to be mentioned, I will come to you and bless you [Exodus 20.24]."

*Judaism*. Talmud, Sukka 53a

Great Deng is near, and some say far, O
Divinity!
The Creator is near, and some say he has not
reached us!
Do you not hear, O Divinity?
The black bull of the rain has been released
from the moon's byre,
Do you not hear, O Divinity?

*African Traditional Religions*. Dinka Song (Sudan)

Why do you go to the forest in search of God?
He lives in all and is yet ever distinct;
He abides with you, too,
As fragrance dwells in a flower,
And reflection in a mirror;
So does God dwell inside everything;
Seek Him, therefore, in your heart.

*Sikhism*. Adi Granth, Dhanasari, M.9, p. 684

The supreme Self is without a beginning, undifferentiated, deathless. Though it dwells in the body, Arjuna, it neither acts nor is touched by action. As radiation pervades the cosmos but remains unstained, the Self can never be tainted though it dwells in every creature.

*Hinduism*. Bhagavad Gita 13.32

Within our Essence of Mind the *Trikaya* (Three Bodies) of Buddha are to be found, and they are common to everybody. Because the mind labors under delusions, he knows not his own inner nature; and the result is that he ignores the Trikaya within himself, erroneously believing that they are to be sought from without. Within yourself you will find the Trikaya which, being the manifestation of the Essence of Mind, are not to be sought from without.

*Buddhism*. Sutra of Hui Neng 6

As the holy one I recognized thee, O Wise
Lord,
When he came to me as Good Mind;
The Silent Thought taught me the greatest
good
so that I might proclaim it.

*Zoroastrianism*. Avesta, Yasna 45.15

**Mundaka Upanishad 3.1.7:** Cf. Katha Upanishad 1.2.20-22, p. 142; Mundaka Upanishad 2.2.1-2, p. 212; Isha Upanishad 15-16, p. 47.

**Isaiah 57.15:** Cf. Psalm 51.17, p. 642.

**Sukka 53a:** Compare Hadith, p. 492.

**Dinka Song:** The intention of the song in suggesting that 'some say far' is to urge Divinity to come near and help.

**Dhanasari, M.9:** Cf. Suhi, M.5, pp. 282-83.

**Sutra of Hui Neng 6:** 'Essence of Mind' as Hui Neng uses the term denotes the original mind which is intrinsically the same as Buddha nature; cf. other passages from this sutra on pp. 146-47. But 'Essence of Mind' is *Tathata*, which can also be translated Essence of all things. These indeed are not different, as the essence of things can be grasped only by mind; cf. Lankavatara Sutra 61-64, pp. 102-3. For more on the Mahayana doctrine of the *Trikaya*, the Buddha's three bodies, cf. p. 465; Lotus Sutra 16, p. 77; Meditation on Buddha Amitayus 17, p. 462; Lion's Roar of Queen Srimala 5, p. 466.

God said to Elijah... "Go forth, and stand upon the mount before the Lord." And behold, the Lord passed by, and a great and strong wind rent the mountains, and broke in pieces the rocks before the Lord, but the Lord was not in the wind; and after the wind an earthquake, but the Lord was not in the earthquake; and after the earthquake a fire, but the Lord was not in the fire; and after the fire a still small voice.

*Judaism* and *Christianity*.
1 Kings 19.11-12

God is the Light of the heavens and the earth.
The parable of His Light
is as if there were a Niche;
and within it a Lamp;
the Lamp enclosed in Glass;
the glass as it were a brilliant star;
lit from a blessed Tree,
an Olive neither of the East nor of the West,
whose oil is well-nigh luminous,
though fire scarce touched it.
Light upon Light!
God guides whom He will to His Light:
God sets forth parables for men, and God knows all things.

*Islam*. Qur'an 24.35

In the golden city of the heart dwells
The Lord of Love, without parts, without stain.
Know him as the radiant light of lights.
There shines not the sun, neither moon nor star,
Nor flash of lightning, nor fire lit on earth.
The Lord is the light reflected by all.
He shining, everything shines after him.

*Hinduism*.
Mundaka Upanishad 2.2.10-11

Daibai asked Baso, "What is the Buddha?" Baso answered, "This very mind is the Buddha."

*Buddhism*. Mumonkan 30

That mind which gives life
to all the people
in the world:
Such is the very mind
which nourishes me!

*Shinto*. Moritake Arakida,
One Hundred Poems about the World

God is the subject of heart. He has feelings of boundless sorrow and joy.

*Unification Church*.
Sun Myung Moon, 2-12-61

I am the nucleus of every creature, Arjuna; for without me nothing can exist, neither animate nor inanimate.... Wherever you find strength, or beauty, or spiritual power, you may be sure that these have sprung from a spark of my essence.

*Hinduism*. Bhagavad Gita 10.39-41

**1 Kings 19.11-12:** God is manifest in his Word, communicated to the heart. He is not in the storm or the earthquake or other manifestations of power in nature. This is a radical critique of nature-religion as it was practiced by the Canaanites.

**Qur'an 24.35:** Islamic mystics since Ghazzali have interpreted these verses as expressing God's inner illumination of the human soul. The Niche, Glass, Lamp, Tree, and Oil correspond to the five faculties of the soul, namely: (1) the sensory faculty; (2) the imagination; (3) the discriminative intellect; (4) the faculty of ratiocination capable of abstract knowledge, and (5) the transcendent prophetic spirit that may apprehend divine truth. The human soul is thus a graded succession of lights, 'Light upon light,' whose source is God. Cf. Katha Upanishad 2.3.7-8, p. 60.

**Mumonkan 30:** Compare "That art thou," Chandogya Upanishad 6.8.7, p. 140. But Mumonkan 33, p. 640, asserts the seeming opposite!

**Sun Myung Moon, 2-12-61:** 'Heart' is the irrepressible impulse to love others, which is the inner motivation for all God's actions. In humans, heart lies at the root of the mind, motivating intellect, emotion, and will. In prayer one can touch the heart of God and feel its affective aspect: joy when his beloved children respond to him and deep sorrow for those who are lost in sin. Cf. Sun Myung Moon, 10-20-73, p. 94; 6-20-82, p. 94.

**Bhagavad Gita 10.39-41:** Cf. Mundaka Upanishad 1.1.7, p. 85.

At whose behest does the mind think? Who bids the body live? Who makes the tongue speak? Who is that effulgent Being that directs the eye to form and color and the ear to sound?

The Self (*Atman*) is ear of the ear, mind of the mind, speech of speech. He is also breath of the breath, and eye of the eye. Having given up the false identification of the Self with the senses and the mind, and knowing the Self to be Brahman, the wise, on departing this life, become immortal.

*Hinduism*. Kena Upanishad 1.1-2

Lord, the Tathagatagarbha is not born, does not die, does not pass away to become reborn. The Tathagatagarbha excludes the realm with the characteristic of the constructed. The Tathagatagarbha is permanent, steadfast, eternal. Therefore the Tathagatagarbha is the support, the holder, the base of constructed [Buddha natures] that are nondiscrete, not dissociated, and knowing as liberated from the stores of defilement; and furthermore is the support, the holder, the base of external constructed natures that are discrete, dissociated, and knowing as not liberated.

Lord, if there were no Tathagatagarbha, there would be neither aversion toward suffering nor longing, eagerness, and aspiration toward Nirvana. What is the reason? Whatever be these six perceptions [i.e., the five senses plus the mind], and whatever be this other perception [perhaps intellectual cognition], these seven natures are unfixed, momentary, and lack experience of suffering; hence these natures are unfit for aversion toward suffering or for longing, eagerness, and aspiration towards Nirvana. Lord, the Tathagatagarbha has ultimate existence without beginning or end, has an unborn and undying nature, and experiences suffering; hence it is worthy of the Tathagatagarbha to have aversion toward suffering as well as longing, eagerness, and aspiration toward Nirvana.

Lord, the Tathagatagarbha is neither self nor sentient being, nor soul, nor personality .... Lord, this Tathagatagarbha is the embryo of the illustrious Dharmadhatu, the embryo of the Dharmakaya, the embryo of the supramundane Doctrine, the embryo of the intrinsically pure Doctrine.

*Buddhism*.
Lion's Roar of Queen Srimala 13

❖

**Kena Upanishad 1.1-2:** Cf. Atharva Veda 10.8.43-44, pp. 411-12; Chandogya Upanishad 6.8.7, p. 140; Mandukya Upanishad, p. 597; Katha Upanishad 3.13, p. 601; Black Elk, pp. 381-82; Luke 11.34-36, p. 381.

**Lion's Roar of Queen Srimala 13:** In Mahayana scriptures the *Tathagatagarbha*, Embryo of the Tathagata, is the intrinsically pure consciousness pervading all sentient beings which is capable of maturing into Buddhahood.

## *Eternal—in a World of Transience*

ULTIMATE REALITY IS ETERNAL and unchanging. The monotheistic religious claim is that God is absolute, eternal, and unchanging; a similar teaching applies to other religious conceptions of the Absolute: Nirvana, Dhamma, the Dharmakaya, the Tao; and in the I Ching it applies to the ground of Change itself. The complementary assertion, which is central to Buddhism and other Eastern religions but also found in analogous expressions in the monotheistic faiths, is that all beings, things, and phenomena in the world are transient, impermanent, conditioned, and hence less than truly Real. These two doctrines are presented together as the positive and negative poles of a single truth.

Holy, holy, holy, is the Lord God Almighty,
who was and is and is to come!

*Christianity*. Revelation 4.8

"Holy, holy holy"—in heaven, on earth, and to all eternity.

*Judaism*. Targum Jonathan, Isaiah 6.3

The great, unborn Self is undecaying, immortal, undying, fearless, infinite.

*Hinduism*. Brihadaranyaka Upanishad 4.4.25

The spirit of the valley never dies.
It is called the subtle and profound female.
The gate of the subtle and profound female
Is the root of heaven and earth.
It is continuous, and seems to be always existing.
Use it and you will never wear it out.

*Taoism*. Tao Te Ching 6

I am the Alpha and the Omega, the first and the last, the beginning and the end.

*Christianity*. Revelation 22.13

Then did I recognize Thee in mind,
to be the first and the last, O Lord,

*Zoroastrianism*. Avesta, Yasna 31.8

All that is on the earth will perish:
But will abide for ever the face of thy Lord—
full of Majesty, Bounty, and Honor.

*Islam*. Qur'an 55.26-27

In primal time, in all time, was the Creator;
Nothing is real but the Eternal.
Nothing shall last but the Eternal.

*Sikhism*. Adi Granth, Japuji 1, M.1, p. 1

Moses said to God, "If I come to the people of Israel and say to them, 'The God of your fathers has sent me to you,' and they ask me, 'What is his name?' what shall I say to them?" God said to Moses, "I Am Who I Am." And he said, "Say this to the people of Israel, 'I Am' has sent me to you."

*Judaism* and *Christianity*. Exodus 3.13-15

**Revelation 4.8** and **Targum Jonathan:** These two passages illustrate the operation of midrashic exegesis, where each detail in the word of God is plumbed for its meaning. The question, "Why is the word 'holy' repeated three times in Isaiah 6.3?" (p. 64) is answered by a three-fold description of God's range over time and space.

**Brihadaranyaka Upanishad 4.4.25:** Cf. Bhagavad Gita 13.32, p. 73.

**Tao Te Ching 6:** Cf. Tao Te Ching 4, p. 374. This describes the eternal feminine spirit; see pp. 94-95.

**Exodus 3.13-15:** This passage, from Moses' encounter with God at the burning bush, gives the traditional etymology of the name of God, the Tetragrammaton YHWH, as The Eternal, 'I Am.' This verse is also the foundation of Christian and Jewish theological discussion of God's unchangeability and eternity. For another traditional Jewish interpretation of this passage, see Torah Yesharah, p. 361.

The divine Mind maintains all identities, from a blade of grass to a star, as distinct and eternal. Nothing is real and eternal—nothing is Spirit—but God and His idea.

*Christian Science.* Science and Health, 70–71

Nothing can ever destroy the Buddha nature. The nature of self is nothing but the undisclosed storehouse of the Tathagata. Such a storehouse can never be broken, put to fire, or plundered. Though it is not possible to destroy or see it, one can know it when one attains the unsurpassed enlightenment.

*Buddhism.* Mahaparinirvana Sutra 220

There is no changing the words of God; that is the mighty triumph.

*Islam.* Qur'an 10.64

Rites are something created by the vulgar men of the world; the Truth is that which is received from Heaven. By nature it is the way it is and cannot be changed.

*Taoism.* Chuang Tzu 31

Change has neither thought nor action, because it is in the state of absolute quiet and inactivity, and when acted on, it immediately penetrates all things. If it were not the most spirit-like thing in the world, how can it take part in this universal transformation?

*Confucianism.* I Ching, Great Commentary 1.10.4

Jesus Christ is the same yesterday and today and for ever.

*Christianity.* Hebrews 13.8

The *Dharmadhatu* (Absolute Truth) abides forever, whether the Tathagata appears in the world or not.

*Buddhism.* Lankavatara Sutra 61

Subhuti, if anyone should say that the Tathagata comes or goes or sits or reclines, he fails to understand my teaching. Why? Because "Thus Gone" (*Tathagata*) has neither whence nor whither, and therefore he is called "Tathagata."

*Buddhism.* Diamond Sutra 29

Listen each of you to the secret, mysterious, and supernatural power of the Thus Come One. All the worlds of gods, men, and demons declare, "Now has Shakyamuni Buddha, coming forth from the palace of the Shakya clan, and seated at the place of enlightenment, not far from the city of Gaya, attained to Perfect Enlightenment." But, good sons, since in fact I became Buddha, there have passed infinite, boundless, hundreds, thousands, myriads, millions, trillions of eons.... From that time forward I have constantly been preaching and teaching in this universe, and also leading and benefiting the living in other places in hundreds, thousands, myriads, millions, trillions of numberless domains.

*Buddhism.* Lotus Sutra 16

**Mahaparinivana Sutra 220:** Cf. Lion's Roar of Queen Srimala 13, p. 75n.

**Chuang Tzu 31:** Cf. Chuang Tzu 6, p. 101.

**I Ching, Great Commentary 1.10.4:** Cf. Tao Te Ching 14, p. 57; 25, pp. 61-62; Chuang Tzu 6, p. 413.

**Lankavatara Sutra 61:** Part of a longer passage given on p. 155.

**Diamond Sutra 29:** *Tathagata* is a title given to the Buddha. It means "Comes thus far," i.e., the one who has arrived at the goal of enlightenment.

**Lotus Sutra 16:** See also the parallel passages in verse, pp. 463, 791. The thought that there is an historic manifestation of the Eternal Buddha in every eon corresponds to the Hindu doctrine of avatars—see Bhagavad Gita 4.7-8, p. 474. In the doctrine of the *Trikaya* (Three Bodies) of Mahayana Buddhism, the Eternal Buddha of the Lotus Sutra is the *Sambhogakaya* (Glorified Body), while the historical Buddha is the *Nirmanakaya* (Accommodated Body). The Ultimate Buddha, the *Dharmakaya*, is Reality itself; cf. Lion's Roar of Queen Srimala 5, p. 466; Garland Sutra 37, p. 62.

The One who, himself without color, by the manifold application of his power
Distributes many colors in his hidden purpose,
And into whom, its end and its beginning, the whole world dissolves—
He is God!

*Hinduism*. Svestasvatara Upanishad 4.1

Of old thou didst lay the foundation of the earth,
and the heavens are the work of thy hands;
They will perish,
but thou dost endure.
They will all wear out like a garment,
thou changest them like raiment, and they pass away.
But thou art the same,
and thy years have no end.

*Judaism* and *Christianity*. Psalm 102.25-27

Who knows the Eternal's day
and the Eternal's night,
each lasting a thousand ages, truly
knows day and night.
At daybreak all things are disclosed;
they arise from the unmanifest.
At dusk they dissolve into
the very same unmanifest.
Again and again, the whole multitude
of creatures is born, and when night falls,
is dissolved, without their will,
and at daybreak, is born again.
Beyond that unmanifest is
another, everlasting unmanifest
which has no end, although
every creature perish.
This is called the imperishable
unmanifest and the highest goal.
Who reaches it does not return.
It is my supreme abode.

*Hinduism*. Bhagavad Gita 8.17-21

With the Lord one day is as a thousand years, and a thousand years as one day.

*Christianity*. 2 Peter 3.8

The image of The Marrying Maiden.
Thus the superior man
understands the transitory
in the light of the eternity of the end.

*Confucianism*. I Ching 54: The Marrying Maiden

Even ornamented royal chariots wear out. So too the body reaches old age. But the Dhamma of the Good grows not old. Thus do the Good reveal it among the Good.

*Buddhism*. Dhammapada 151

The impermanent [objects of the senses] have no reality; reality lies in the eternal. Those who have seen the boundary between these two have attained the end of all knowledge. Realize that which pervades the universe and is indestructible; no power can affect this unchanging, imperishable reality.

*Hinduism*. Bhagavad Gita 2.16-17

All flesh is grass,
and all its beauty is like the flower of the field.
The grass withers, the flower fades,
when the breath of the Lord blows upon it....
The grass withers, the flower fades,
but the word of our God will stand forever.

*Judaism* and *Christianity*. Isaiah 40.6-8

**Psalm 102.25-27:** Cf. Hebrews 1.10-12.

**Bhagavad Gita 8.17-21:** This is a description of the Day of Brahman, the ever-repeating cycle of cosmic time, measured in myriads of years, between the creation of one universe and its dissolution. In some cosmologies the Day of Brahman is divided into the four *yugas*, of which the Kali Yuga is the final period before the next cosmic dissolution. Cf. Bhagavad Gita 9.4-10, p. 86; Katha Upanishad 1.3.15, p. 411; Laws of Manu 1.81-86, pp. 307-308.

**2 Peter 3.8:** This is a quotation from Psalm 90.4.

**I Ching 54:** Human relationships are likely to be successful only if they are grounded in the perspective of eternity.

**Bhagavad Gita 2.16-17:** Cf. Bhagavad Gita 18.61-62, p. 393.

**Isaiah 40.6-8:** Cf. Ecclesiastes 3.1-8, p. 272.

By detachment from appearances, abide in Real Truth. So I tell you, Thus shall you think of all this fleeting world,

> A star at dawn, a bubble in a stream;
> A flash of lightning in a summer cloud,
> A flickering lamp, a phantom, a dream.

*Buddhism.* Diamond Sutra 32

The wise man looks upon life as a mere dew drop which quivers upon the tip of a blade of kusa grass, to be whisked off or blown away by the breeze at any moment. The life of an unwise, imprudent, and ignorant person is likewise as transient as said dew drop.

*Jainism.* Acarangasutra 5.5

Who comes, finally comes not. Who goes, finally goes not. Why? Who comes is not known to come. Who goes is not known to go. Who appears is finally not to be seen.

*Buddhism.* Holy Teaching of Vimalakirti 5

In the world, inclusive of its gods, substance is seen in what is insubstantial. They are tied to to their psychophysical beings and so they think that there is some substance, some reality in them.

But whatever be the phenomenon through which they think of seeking their self-identity, it turns out to be transitory. It becomes false, for what lasts for a moment is deceptive.

The state that is not deceptive is Nibbana: that is what the men of worth know as being real. With this insight into reality their hunger ends: cessation, total calm.

*Buddhism.* Sutta Nipata 756-58

❖

**Diamond Sutra 32:** This is the fundamental stance of Buddhism towards worldly phenomena. It lies at the heart of Buddhism's ethic of nonattachment and it is comforting counsel to those who are suffering from pain, loss, or bereavement. See the Parable of the Mustard Seed, p. 272.

**Holy Teaching of Vimalakirti 5:** This statement is from an exchange between Manjusri and Vimalakirti when the bodhisattva visits Vimalalakirti on his sick bed. Like any phenomenal existence, they conclude that Vimalakirti's illness is ultimately unreal. This is a general statement of the concept of *sunya,* that all things are empty of any nature that is independent, discrete, and permanent. Also, compare John 14.15-21, p. 462, where the *going* of Jesus is seen as a *coming,* but both the going and coming are resolved in a *presence.*

**Sutta Nipata 756-58:** Cf. Udana 80, p. 48.

# *The Creator*

THIS SECTION GATHERS PASSAGES on God as the Creator. Included are various accounts of the creation of the world, some beginning with a word and some from a desire within the primoridal Absolute. Some teach creation out of nothing (*ex nihilo*), affirming the distinction between creator and creation. Others teach that the world originated and exists as an emanation of the Absolute which nevertheless remains distinct and transcendent—a view termed panentheism. There are no Buddhist or Jain texts in this section because these religions deny a Creator God.[1] Additional Hindu, Native American, Zoroastrian, and Shinto texts on creation by the agency of one or several deities can be found scattered throughout this anthology.[2] The scriptures in this section give accounts of how the universe was created, explain the method of creation, and describe God's continuing creative activity which sustains the cosmos.

This do I ask, O Lord, reveal unto me the truth!
Who is the first begetter, father of the Cosmic Law?
Who assigned orbit to the sun and the stars?
Who causes the moon to wax and again to wane?
Who other than Thee? This and else I wish to know!

Who is the upholder of the earth and of the sky?
Who prevents them from falling down?
Who maintains the waters and also the plants?
Who yoked speed to winds and clouds?
Who is the creator of the creatures?

Who is the architect of light and darkness?
Who created sleep and wakefulness?
By whom exists dawn, mid-day and night,
Which monitor the duties of men?

*Zoroastrianism*. Avesta, Yasna 44.3-5

God it is who created the heavens and the earth,
and that which is between them, in six days.
Then He mounted the throne.
You have not, beside Him, a protecting friend or mediator.
Will you not then remember?
He directs the ordinance from the heaven to the earth;
then it ascends to Him in a Day, whose measure is a thousand years of your reckoning.
Such is the Knower of the invisible and the visible,
the Mighty, the Merciful,

**Yasna 44.3-5:** In this text from the Yasna there is only one true Creator, the Lord Ahura Mazda. Other Zoroastrian texts give dualistic accounts of creation, attributing diseases and other natural evils to the creations of the Evil One; thus Yasna 30.3-5, p. 276; Videvdad 1.3-11, p. 311. 'Who is?' cf. Rig Veda 10.129, pp. 83-84.

[1] The Buddhist dialogue Agganna Sutta (Digha Nikaya iii.84-92), and its Mahayana version Ekottara Agama, p. 305, give an account of the creation of human beings. But there is no creator god, and the theme of the dialogue is the degeneration of humankind. It has biblical parallels with the fall of Adam and Eve. Cf. Surangama Sutra, p. 276.

[2] Rig Veda 10.90.6-16, pp. 621-22, 189; Aitareya Upanishad 1-3, p. 213; Brihadaranyaka Upanishad 1.4.3, p. 174; Vishnu Purana 1, p. 53; Okanogan Creation, p. 207; Mohawk Creation, pp. 311-12; Videvdad 1.3-11, p. 311; Kojiki 4-6, p. 306; Maori Tradition, pp. 216-17a; and others.

Who made all things good which He created.
And He began the creation of man from clay;
then He made his seed from a draught of
despised fluid;
then He fashioned him and breathed into him
of His spirit;
and appointed for you hearing and sight and
hearts.
Small thanks you give!

*Islam.* Qur'an 32.4-9

In the beginning God created the heavens and the earth. The earth was without form and void, and darkness was upon the face of the deep; and the Spirit of God was moving over the face of the waters.

And God said, "Let there be light"; and there was light. And God saw that the light was good; and God separated the light from the darkness. God called the light Day, and the darkness he called Night. And there was evening and there was morning, one day.

And God said, "Let there be a firmament in the midst of the waters, and let it separate the waters from the waters." And God made the firmament and separated the waters which were under the firmament from the waters which were above the firmament. And it was so. And God called the firmament Heaven. And there was evening and there was morning, a second day.

And God said, "Let the waters under the heavens be gathered together into one place, and let the dry land appear." And it was so. God called the dry land Earth, and the waters that were gathered together he called Seas. And God saw that it was good. And God said, "let the earth put forth vegetation, plants yielding seed, and fruit trees bearing fruit in which is their seed, each according to its kind, upon the earth." And it was so. The earth brought forth vegetation, plants yielding seed according to their own kinds, and trees bearing fruit in which is their seed, each according to its kind. And God saw that it was good. And there was evening and there was morning, a third day.

And God said, "Let there be lights in the firmament of the heavens to separate the day from the night; and let them be for signs and for seasons and for days and years, and let them be lights in the firmament of the heavens to give light upon the earth." And it was so. And God made the two great lights, the greater light to rule the day, and the lesser light to rule the night; he made the stars also. And God set them in the firmament of the heavens to give light upon the earth, to rule over the day and over the night, and to separate the light from the darkness. And God saw that it was good. And there was evening and there was morning, a fourth day.

And God said, "Let the waters bring forth swarms of living creatures, and let birds fly above the earth across the firmament of the heavens." So God created the great sea monsters and every living creature that moves, with which the waters swarm, according to their kinds, and every winged bird according to its kind. And God saw that it was good. And God blessed them, saying, "Be fruitful and multiply and fill the waters in the seas, and let birds multiply on the earth." And there was evening and there was morning, a fifth day.

And God said, "Let the earth bring forth living creatures according to their kinds, cattle and creeping things and beasts of the earth according to their kinds." And it was so. And God made the beasts of the earth according to their kinds, and the cattle according to their kinds, and everything that creeps upon the ground according to its kind. And God saw that it was good.

Then God said, "Let us make man in our image, after our likeness; and let them have dominion over the fish of the sea, and over the

**Qur'an 32.4-9:** The Qur'an, like the Bible, affirms that God made all things good. These verses describe God as a craftsman who molds and shapes the things of creation, finishing in six days and then ascending the throne to rest. He then directs the affairs of earth from heaven, and predicts the coming Day of Judgment, when all will be dissolved and return to him. The Qur'an's description of God's creation should elicit thanksgiving, but most people take the existence of the world and of their very bodies and souls as a matter of course.

birds of the air, and over the cattle, and over all the earth, and over every creeping thing that creeps upon the earth." So God created man in his own image, in the image of God he created him; male and female he created them. And God blessed them, and God said to them, "Be fruitful and multiply, and fill the earth and subdue it; and have dominion over the fish of the sea and over the birds of the air and over every living thing that moves upon the earth." And God said, "Behold, I have given you every plant yielding seed which is upon the face of all earth, and every tree with seed in its fruit; you shall have them for food. And to every beast of the earth, and to every bird of the air, and to everything that creeps on the earth, everything that has the breath of life, I have given every green plant for food." And it was so. And God saw everything that he had made, and behold, it was very good. And there was evening and there was morning, a sixth day.

Thus the heavens and the earth were finished, and all the host of them. And on the seventh day God finished his work which he had done. So God blessed the seventh day and hallowed it, because on it God rested from all his work which he had done in creation.

*Judaism* and *Christianity*. Genesis 1.1-2.3

We created man of an extraction of clay,
then We set him, a drop, in a receptacle secure,
then We created of the drop a clot
then We created of the clot a tissue
then We created of the tissue bones
then We garmented the bones in flesh;
thereafter We produced him as another creature.
So blessed be God, the fairest of creators!

*Islam*. Qur'an 23.14

The All-merciful has taught the Qur'an.
He created man
and He taught him the Explanation.

The sun and the moon to a reckoning,
and the stars and the trees bow themselves;
and heaven—He raised it up, and set The Balance.
(Transgress not in the Balance,
and weigh with justice, and skimp not in the Balance.)
And the earth—He set it down for all beings,
therein fruits, and palm-trees with sheaths,
and grain in the blade, and fragrant herbs
O which of your Lord's bounties will you and you deny?

He created man of a clay like a potter's,
and He created the jinn of a smokeless fire.
O which of your Lord's bounties will you and you deny?
Lord of the Two Easts, Lord of the Two Wests
O which of your Lord's bounties will you and you deny?
He set forth the two seas that meet together,
between them a barrier they do not overpass.
O which of your Lord's bounties will you and you deny?
From them come forth the pearl and the coral.
O which of your Lord's bounties will you and you deny?
His too are the ships that run, raised up in the sea like landmarks.
O which of your Lord's bounties will you and you deny?...
Whatsoever is in the heavens and the earth implore Him; every day He is upon some labor.

**Genesis 1:** This is the preeminent creation account in the Western tradition and a source for the accounts in the Qur'an. God creates by his word: 'Let there be...'; compare Qur'an 2.117, p. 69. The six 'days' or stages of creation have been compared to the epochs of geologic time, since "with the Lord a thousand years is as a day," cf. 2 Peter 3.8, p. 78; Qur'an 32.6, pp. 80-81. Thus we have the big bang (first day), the ordering of the cosmos (second day), the solidification of the earth (third day), the clearing of its atmosphere so that the stars can be seen (fourth day), the beginnings of life in the oceans (fifth day), the emergence of land animals, and finally, man (sixth day). Yet even though the general account of the stages of creation may be shown to correspond with the account of creation put forward by modern science, the Bible should not be taken as a source of scientific knowledge. It was revealed to people who held to an ancient cosmology in which the earth was at the center and a solid dome, the firmament, formed the sky above and held back its waters. Compare the account of creation from a cosmic egg in Laws of Manu 1.5-16, below.

O which of your Lord's bounties will you and you deny?

*Islam*. Qur'an 55.5-30

Great Spirit!
Piler-up of the rocks into towering mountains:
When you stamp on the stone
The dust rises and fills the land,
Hardness of the precipice;
Waters of the pool that turn
Into misty rain when stirred.
Vessels overflowing with oil!
Father of Runji,
Who sews the heavens like cloth:
May you knit together that which is below.
Caller-forth of the branching trees:
You bring forth the shoots
That they stand erect.
You have filled the land with mankind,
The dust rises on high, O Lord!
Wonderful One, you live
In the midst of the sheltering rocks,
You give rain to mankind:
We pray to you; hear us, Lord!
Show mercy when we beseech you, Lord.
You are on high with the spirits of the great.
You raise the grass-covered hills
Above the earth, and create the rivers.
Gracious One.

*African Traditional Religions*.
Shona Prayer (Zimbabwe)

He was. Taaroa was his name.
He stood in the void: no earth, no sky, no men.
Taaroa calls the the four corners of the universe; nothing replies.
Alone existing, he changes himself into the universe.
Taaroa is the light, he is the seed, he is the base, he is the incorruptible.
The universe is only the shell of Taaroa.
It is he who puts it in motion and brings forth its harmony.

*Tahitian Traditional Religion*.

At first was neither Being nor Nonbeing.
There was not air nor yet sky beyond.
What was its wrapping? Where? In whose protection?
Was Water there, unfathomable and deep?
There was no death then, nor yet deathlessness;
of night or day there was not any sign.
The One breathed without breath, by its own impulse.
Other than that was nothing else at all.
Darkness was there, all wrapped around by darkness,
and all was Water indiscriminate. Then
that which was hidden by the void, that One, emerging,
stirring, through the power of ardor (*tapas*), came to be.

In the beginning Love arose,
which was the primal germ cell of the mind.
The Seers, searching in their hearts with wisdom,
discovered the connection of Being in Nonbeing.

A crosswise line cut Being from Nonbeing.
What was described above it, what below?
Bearers of seed there were and mighty forces,
thrust from below and forward move above.

Who really knows? Who can presume to tell it?
Whence was it born? Whence issued this creation?
Even the Gods came after its emergence.
Then who can tell from whence it came to be?

**Qur'an 55.5-30:** Vv. 5-25, 29-30. This hymn depicts God's provision for man, connecting his creating the physical world and its laws with his establishing morality and religion: giving the Qur'an and setting 'the Balance.' Each creative act is an act of God's bounty, which should elicit gratitude and submission to the Lord of the Universe—see Qur'an 6.95-99, 30.20-25, p. 49; 16.10-18, p. 91. The 'Two Easts' and 'Two Wests' refer to the northernmost and southernmost points of the sunrise and the sunset at the winter and summer solstices. The sura goes on to give a lengthy description of the joys of paradise.

**Shona Prayer:** Cf. Ashanti Verse, p. 204.

That out of which creation has arisen,
whether it held it firm or it did not,
He who surveys it in the highest heaven,
He surely knows—or maybe He does not!

*Hinduism*. Rig Veda 10.129

This universe existed in the shape of darkness, unperceived, destitute of distinctive marks, unattainable by reasoning, unknowable, wholly immersed, as it were, in deep sleep.

Then the Divine Self-existent, himself indiscernible but making all this, the great elements and the rest, discernible, appeared with irresistible power, dispelling the darkness.

He who can be perceived by the internal organ alone, who is subtle, indiscernible, and eternal, who contains all created beings and is inconceivable, shone forth of his own will.

He, desiring to produce beings of many kinds from his own body, first with a thought created the waters, and placed his seed in them.

That seed became a golden egg, in brilliancy equal to the sun; in that egg he himself was born as Brahma, the progenitor of the whole world....

The Divine One resided in that egg during a whole year, then he himself by his thought divided it into two halves;

And out of those two halves he formed heaven and earth, between them the middle sphere, the eight points of the horizon, and the eternal abode of the waters.

From himself he also drew forth the mind, which is both real and unreal, likewise from the mind ego, which possesses the function of self-consciousness and is lordly.

Moreover, the great one, the soul, and all products affected by the three qualities, and, in their order, the five organs which perceive the objects of sensation.

But, joining minute particles even of those six, which possess measureless power, with particles of himself, he created all beings.

*Hinduism*. Laws of Manu 1.5-16

For millions upon millions, countless years was
  spread darkness,
When existed neither earth nor heaven, but
  only the limitless Divine Ordinance.
Then existed neither day or night, nor sun or
  moon;
As the Creator was absorbed in an unbroken
  trance.
Existed then neither forms of creation, nor of
  speech; neither wind nor water.
Neither was creation or disappearance or transmigration.

Then were not continents, neither regions, the
  seven seas, nor rivers with water flowing.
Existed then neither heaven or the mortal
  world or the nether world;
Neither hell or heaven or time that destroys.
Hell and heaven, birth and death were then
  not—none arrived or departed.
Then were not Brahma, Vishnu or Shiva:
None other than the Sole Lord was visible.
Neither existed then female or male, or caste
  and birth—
None suffering and joy received.

**Rig Veda 10.129:** In this account of the formation of cosmos out of chaos (represented by the Waters), 'that One,' *tad ekam*, is void of reality prior to the creation. The appearance of mind precedes creation; its motive is 'Love,' the desire of the One to find fulfillment with a partner; cf. Brihadaranyaka Upanishad 1.4.17, p. 174. The first act of creation, dividing being from nonbeing, resembles the first creative act in the Genesis account, above. The 'bearers of seed' and 'mighty forces' are the male and female principles—see Prasna Upanishad 1.4-5, pp. 116-17; Rig Veda 1.185, p. 117; Shiva Purana, p. 118. Yet ultimately the miracle of creation remains a mystery: 'who really knows?'—cf. Rig Veda 3.54.5, p. 47. Even the vedic gods are ignorant of their origin, since they emerged after Being differentiated itself.

**Laws of Manu 1.5-16:** This passage describes creation from a cosmic egg. Creation of heaven and earth out of the two halves of the egg echoes the creation myths of Mesopotamia, in which the creator deity slays the dragon of chaos and splits it in two: the top half of the carcass forming heaven and the bottom half forming the earth; compare Maori Tradition, pp. 216-17. The god Brahma, creator of heaven and earth, is only a manifestation of Ultimate Reality, the 'Divine Self-existent,' as with Rig Veda 10.129, above. 'Those six' are understood by traditional commentators to mean the five sense organs and the mind. The idea of creation from an egg has resonances with creation from a woman's body in the Okanogan Creation, p. 207.

Unknowable Himself, was He the source of all
utterance; Himself the unknowable unmanifested.
As it pleased Him, the world He created;
Without a supporting power the expanse He
sustained.
Brahma, Vishnu, and Shiva He created and to
maya-attachment gave increase.
(To a rare one was the Master's Word imparted.)
Himself He made His Ordinance operative and
watched over it:
Creating continents, spheres and nether
worlds, the hidden He made manifest.
Creating the universe Himself, He has
remained unattached.
The compassionate Lord too has made the holy
center [the human being].
Combining air, water, and fire, He created the
citadel of the body.
The Creator fashioned the Nine Abodes [of
sensation];
In the Tenth [the superconscious mind] is
lodged the Lord, unknowable, limitless.
The illimitable Lord in His unattributed state
of void assumed might;
He, the infinite One, remaining detached:
Displaying his power, He himself from the void
created inanimate things.
From the unattributed void were created air
and water.
Raising creation, He dwells as monarch in the
citadel of the body.
Lord! In the fire and water [of the body] exists
Thy light;
In Thy [original] state of void was lodged
[unmanifest] the power of creation.

*Sikhism*. Adi Granth,
Maru Sohale, M.1, pp. 1035-37

As the web issues out of the spider
And is withdrawn, as plants sprout from the
earth,
As hair grows from the body, even so,
The sages say, this universe springs from
The deathless Self, the source of life.

The deathless Self meditated upon
Himself and projected the universe
As evolutionary energy.
From this energy developed life, mind,
The elements, and the world of karma,
Which is enchained by cause and effect.

The deathless Self sees all, knows all. From
him
Springs Brahma, who embodies the process
Of evolution into name and form
By which the One appears to be many.

*Hinduism*. Mundaka Upanishad 1.1.7-9

The Great Primal Beginning (*T'ai chi*) . . . generates the two primary forces (*yang* and *yin*). The two primary forces generate the four images. The four images generate the eight trigrams. The eight trigrams determine good fortune and misfortune. Good fortune and misfortune create the great field of action.

*Confucianism*. I Ching,
Great Commentary 1.11.5-6

**Maru Sohale, M.1:** For Sikhism, God is first formless, without attributes, and thence manifesting attributes as he creates, preserves, and dissolves the universe through his Maya (his 'might'). As the unattributed Supreme Being, God is beyond time and space. In his manifestation god creates and appears to mankind through the Word (*Nam*).

**Mundaka Upanishad 1.1.7-9:** Cf. Bhagavad Gita 10.39-41, p. 74; Rig Veda 10.190.1-3, p. 100; Aitareya Upanishad 1-3, p. 213; Rig Veda 10.90.6-10, pp. 621-22.

**I Ching, Great Commentary:** The creative interaction between the polarities of yin and yang is fundamental to Oriental philosophy; see pp. 117-18. The 'great field of action' includes both the phenomena of the world and the laws discovered by the sages in order to obtain good fortune and to avoid danger.

Tao gave them birth;
The power of Tao reared them,
Shaped them according to their kinds,
Perfected them, giving to each its strength.
Therefore of the ten thousand things there is not one that does not worship Tao and do homage to its power. Yet no mandate ever went forth that accorded to Tao the right to be worshipped, nor to its power the right to receive homage. It was always and of itself so.

*Taoism*. Tao Te Ching 51

Vast indeed is the sublime Creative Principle, the Source of all, co-extensive with the heavens. It causes the clouds to come forth, the rain to bestow its bounty and all objects to flow into their respective forms. Its dazzling brilliance permeates all things from first to last; its activities, symbolized by the component lines [of the hexagram], reach full completion, each at the proper time. [The superior man], mounting them when the time is ripe, is carried heavenwards as though six dragons were his steeds! The Creative Principle functions through Change; accordingly, when we rectify our way of life by conjoining it with the universal harmony, our firm persistence is richly rewarded.

*Confucianism*. I Ching 1: The Creative

My shape is unmanifest, but I
pervade the world.
All beings have their being in me,
but I do not rest in them.
See my sovereign technique:
creatures both in me and not in me.
Supporting beings, my person brings
beings to life, without living in them.
I am omnipresent as the storm wind
which resides in space.
All beings exist in me.
Remember that.
All creatures enter into my nature
at the end of an eon.
In another beginning
I send them forth again.
Establishing my own nature,
time after time I send them forth,
this host of beings, without
their will, by dint of that nature.
This activity does not
imprison me, O Fighter for Wealth!
I appear as an onlooker, detached
in the midst of this work.
Nature gives birth to all moving
and unmoving things. I supervise.
That is how the world keeps turning,
Son of Kunti!

*Hinduism*. Bhagavad Gita 9.4-10

If God removes his hand the world will end.

*African Traditional Religions*. Proverb

Nothing whatsoever exists without me or beyond me. The atoms of the universe may be counted, but not so my manifestations; for eternally I create innumerable worlds.

*Hinduism*.
Srimad Bhagavaṭam 11.10

**Tao Te Ching 51:** The passage continues that humans should act likewise in exercising dominion, whether over nature or over people; see p. 205. 'Power' (*te*) means the force of virtue which arises from unity with cosmic law.

**I Ching 1:** This commentary describes the creative principle in terms of its hexagram *Ch'ien*. The 'six dragons' are the six strong lines of the hexagram. Cf. Chuang Tzu 12, p. 416. In Taoism the creative power of spirit is known as *ch'i* (*qi*); see Chuang Tzu 15, p. 602.

**Bhagavad Gita 9.4-10:** Cf. Rig Veda 6.47-4, p. 50.

**Srimad Bhagavatam 11.10:** Cf. Bhagavad Gita 7.4-7, p. 63; 10.39-41, p. 74; Svetasvatara Upanishad 4.2-4, pp. 63-64; Vishnu Purana 1, p. 53.

## *Goodness and Love*

THE FOLLOWING TWO SECTIONS bring together passages describing some personal attributes of Ultimate Reality. Passages from scripture discussing God's attributes of goodness and love often describe God as good, loving, beautiful, truthful, compassionate, and faithful in personal terms. Theologians have argued that the personality of God is the highest aspect of God's nature, just as the faculties of intellect, emotion, and will make human beings the highest achievement of the created order. In this sense, goodness, compassion, and love are the primary attributes of Ultimate Reality. They are seen in God's gracious provision to human beings, where God's goodness is especially manifest in his help for the poor and downtrodden.

In addition, there are passages which describe the absolute goodness of Ultimate Reality in impersonal terms. Ultimate Reality is above the fetters of human cravings and above relative human judgments of good and evil. This goodness is universal and all-embracing. Common metaphors liken this goodness to the beneficial influences of the rain and the sun to promote growth and abundance to all nature.

The passages in this section focus on the nature of Ultimate Reality itself as loving, merciful, and good. Related themes on various manifestations of divine love and mercy include: *Grace*, pp. 360-65 and *Help and Deliverance*, pp. 396-402. Related topics on human love as a response to divine love include: *True Love*, pp. 159-63; *Husband and Wife*, pp. 174-82; *Devotion and Praise*, pp. 544-48; and *Loving-kindness*, pp. 684-87.

God is love.

*Christianity*. 1 John 4.8

My mercy embraces all things.

*Islam*. Qur'an 7.156

The Great Compassionate Heart is the essence of Buddhahood.

*Buddhism*. Gandavyuha Sutra

To love is to know Me,
My innermost nature,
the truth that I am.

*Hinduism*. Bhagavad Gita 18.55

The hawk says, "All God did is good."

*African Traditional Religions*. Ashanti Proverb (Ghana)

God is All-gentle to His servants, providing for whomsoever He will.

*Islam*. Qur'an 42.19

Tao never acts, yet nothing is left undone.

*Taoism*. Tao Te Ching 37

**Qur'an 7.156:** The mercy and beneficence of God are the foremost of his attributes mentioned in the *Fatihah*, Qur'an 1, pp. 29-30.

**Ashanti Proverb:** cf. Kikuyu Prayer, p. 550.

**Qur'an 42.19:** Cf. Qur'an 2.268-69, p. 361.

**Tao Te Ching 37:** *Wu wei* or Non-action is the Taoist concept comparable to love in Christianity or mercy in Buddhism. It is the essence of Ultimate Reality's way of being and relating to creatures. It is impartial, and wholly beneficent, whereas action, its opposite, is partial and leads to division, inequality, and strife. Cf. Tao Te Ching 34, p. 91.

That which is free from birth, old age, disease, death, grief, pain, and fear, is eternal, blissful, and the nature of pure delight, is called Nirvana.

*Jainism*. Samantabadhra, Ratnakarandasravakacara 131

This is Peace, this is the excellent, namely the calm of all the impulses, the casting out of all "basis," the extinction of craving, dispassion, stopping, Nirvana.

*Buddhism*. Anguttara Nikaya v.322

He, indeed, is the great Purusha, the Lord, who inspires the mind to attain the state of stainlessness. He is the Ruler and the imperishable Light.

*Hinduism*. Svetasvatara Upanishad 3.12

Then did I recognize Thee in mind,
to be the first and the last, O Lord,
Father of good thought,
when I apprehended Thee in my eye,
true creator of Right,
the Lord over the actions of life!

*Zoroastrianism*. Avesta, Yasna 31.8

The Lord is gracious and merciful,
slow to anger and abounding in steadfast love.
The Lord is good to all,
and his compassion is over all that he has
made.

*Judaism* and *Christianity*. Psalm 145.8-9

The Lord and Cherisher of the Worlds—
Who created me, and it is He who guides me;
Who gives me food and drink,
And when I am ill, it is He who cures me;
Who will cause me to die, and then to live
again;
And who, I hope, will forgive me my faults on
the Day of Judgment.

*Islam*. Qur'an 26.77-82

The Dwelling of the Tathagata is the great compassionate heart within all the living. The Robe of the Tathagata is the gentle and forbearing heart. The Seat of the Tathagata is the "spirituality of all existence."

*Buddhism*. Lotus Sutra 10

I have no corporeal existence,
but Universal Benevolence is my divine body.
I have no physical power,
but Uprightness is my strength.
I have no religious clairvoyance beyond what is
bestowed by Wisdom,
I have no power of miracle other than the
attainment of quiet happiness,
I have no tact except the exercise of gentleness.

*Shinto*. Oracle of Sumiyoshi

God is beautiful and loves beauty.

*Islam*. Hadith of Muslim

All that is evil, Savitri, God, send away from
us,
and send us what is good.
Purified, for spiritual might, under God
Savitri's impulsion,
we think of all beautiful things.
The universal God, Lord of goodness, we with
hymns elect today,
Savitri, whose power lies in truth.

*Hinduism*. Rig Veda 5.82.5-7

**Ratnakarandasravakacara 131** and **Anguttara Nikaya v.322:** Nirvana is the Ultimate Good because it is the complete end of all the impulses and passions that produce evil.

**Lotus Sutra 10:** This is another way of asserting the one ultimate which is all-embracing. The twin pillars of Mahayana Buddhism are wisdom (*prajna*) and compassion (*karuna*). At the level of feeling or experience, compassion is that which embraces all things. Wisdom teaches the oneness and interconnectedness of all existence; hence it, too, evokes compassion.

**Hadith of Muslim:** Cf. Atharva Veda 10.8.31, p. 48.

**Rig Veda 5.28.5-7:** God is recognized to be the source of goodness, truth, and beauty.

Love is the firstborn, loftier than the gods, the Fathers and men.
You, O Love, are the eldest of all, altogether mighty.
To you we pay homage!

Greater than the breadth of earth and heaven, or of waters and Fire,
You, O Love, are the eldest of all, altogether mighty.
To you we pay homage!...

In many a form of goodness, O Love, you show your face.
Grant that these forms may penetrate within our hearts.
Send elsewhere all malice!

*Hinduism.* Atharva Veda 9.2.19-25

One attempting to express God's creation and to contemplate it
Shall find it beyond counting and innumerable.
The Bull of Dharma is born of compassion;
Content of mind holds creation together.
Whoever understands this is enlightened;
How great is the load under which this Bull stands!

*Sikhism.* Adi Granth, Japuji 16, M.1, p. 3

O good man! One who acts good is the "true thinking."
The true thinking is compassion.
Compassion is the Tathagata.

O good man! Compassion is the bodhi path;
The bodhi path is the Tathagata.
The Tathagata is compassion.

O good man! Compassion is Great Brahma.
Great Brahma is compassion.
Compassion is the Tathagata.

O good man! Compassion acts as parent to all beings.
The parent is compassion.
Know that compassion is the Tathagata.

O good man! Compassion is the Buddha nature of all beings.
Such a Buddha nature is long overshadowed by illusion.
That is why beings cannot see.
The Buddha nature is Compassion.
Compassion is the Tathagata.

*Buddhism.* Mahaparinirvana Sutra 259

God drives away flies for a cow which has no tail.

*African Traditional Religions.* Yoruba Proverb (Nigeria)

It is the Way of Heaven to show no favoritism.
It is for ever on the side of the good man.

*Taoism.* Tao Te Ching 79

What is God? He/she is an existence that absolutely lives for others.

*Unification Church.* Sun Myung Moon, 4-16-88

**Atharva Veda 9.2.19-25:** *Kama*, translated 'Love,' is often translated Desire. Specifically, it is desire which seeks fulfillment in love, comparable to the Western concept of *eros*. According to the Rig Veda 10.129, pp. 83-84, this love is the creative and generative power for all life. *Kama* appears personified in myth as the enemy of asceticism and spiritual attainment, yet he cannot be destroyed; all life depends upon the working of desire; see Skanda Purana 1.1.21.82-99, p. 297.

**Japuji 16:** The underlying source of the universe within its laws, the 'Bull of Dharma,' is the divine mind, specifically divine compassion. The world's pain and suffering is a heavy burden indeed: cf. pp. 324-27.

**Mahaparinirvana Sutra 259:** Buddhist compassion is closer to the Western concept of *agape* love. It is not desire seeking fulfillment, but rather the unconditional offering of love, like that of parents to their children. Based on his compassion, Buddha is called the Father of the world in the Lotus Sutra 3, p. 93.

**Tao Te Ching 79:** By 'favoritism' is meant the perquisites which the world gives to the rich and powerful. Cf. Bhagavad Gita 9.29 and comparable passages, pp. 190-94.

**Sun Myung Moon, 4-16-88:** Cf. Matthew 5.43-48, p. 705.

For the Lord your God is God of gods and Lord of lords, the great, the mighty and the terrible God, who is not partial and takes no bribe. He executes justice for the fatherless and the widow, and loves the sojourner, giving him food and clothing.

*Judaism* and *Christianity*. Deuteronomy 10.17-18

O Rudra, that form of yours which is benevolent, not fearful, not manifesting the sinful, with that most beneficent form, you who extend happiness to humankind from your mountain abode, reveal yourself to us often. This Rudra of blue neck and red complexion, who glides aside, him the shepherds saw, the servant maids that bring water saw, and even [the lowliest of] all beings saw—may he make us happy.

Obeisance to the God who is benevolent as well as terrible, who destroys beings and is their protector as well. Obeisance to the small and the puny, to the big and the aged. Obeisance to him who is to be lauded with hymns and who is there where hymns do not reach. Obeisance to the redeemer, to the bringer of peace and happiness, to the producer of well-being and joy. Obeisance to him who is auspicious and exceedingly so.

*Hinduism*. Black Yajur Veda 6.6

Lo! We have shown man the way, whether he be grateful or disbelieving.

*Islam*. Qur'an 76.3

He [God] makes his sun rise on the evil and on the good, and sends rain on the just and on the unjust.

*Christianity*. Matthew 5.45

The Tao is the refuge for the myriad creatures.
It is that by which the good man protects,
And that by which the bad is protected.

*Taoism*. Tao Te Ching 62

This world is a garden,
The Lord its gardener,
Cherishing all, none neglected.

*Sikhism*. Adi Granth, Majh Ashtpadi, M.3, p. 118

Abundant is the year, with much millet and much rice;
And we have our high granaries,
With myriads, and hundreds of thousands, and millions [of measures in them];
For spirits and sweet spirits,
To present our ancestors, male and female,
And to supply all our ceremonies.
The blessings sent down on us are of every kind.

*Confucianism*. Book of Songs, Ode 279

The scent of the sakaki leaves is fragrant;
Drawing near, I see countless kinsmen
Assembled all around,
Assembled all around.

On divine-dwelling mountain of sacred altar,
The sakaki leaves have grown thick
In the presence of the kami.
Before the kami
They have grown in profusion.

*Shinto*. Kagura-uta

**Deuteronomy 10.17-18:** God liberated Israel from slavery; the foundational experience of God in the Judeo-Christian tradition is as defender of the poor and powerless. Cf. 1 Samuel 2.4-9, p. 388.

**Black Yajur Veda 6.6:** Rudra is another name for Shiva. The last sentence is the sacred Shiva mantra.

**Qur'an 76.3** and **Matthew 5.45:** Cf. Bhagavad Gita 9.29, p. 190; Romans 2.9-11, p. 190; Sun Myung Moon, p. 361; Vitaragastava 13.1, p. 360.

**Majh Ashtpadi, M.3:** Cf. Kirtan Sohila, M.1 pp. 360-61.

**Kagura-uta:** The branches of the sakaki tree, called *tamagushi*, are sacred in Shinto rites, and worshippers attach to them their offerings of hemp and paper streamers containing the prayers and fortunes of loved ones. The branches symbolize the spirit of the kami bestowing blessings to the world. Shinto worship incorporates ritual dances (*kagura*) which seek to bring about harmony in the universe. In the Kojiki, the kami are themselves seen performing a cosmic dance. Compare the dance of Shiva in Hinduism, which has both a creative and preservative role. Cf. One Hundred Poems on the Jewelled Spear, p. 558.

The great Tao flows everywhere;
It can go left; it can go right.
The myriad things owe their existence to it,
And it does not reject them.
When its work is accomplished,
It does not take possession.
It clothes and feeds all,
But does not pose as their master.
Ever without ambition,
It may be called Small.
All things return to it as their home,
And yet it does not pose as their master,
Therefore it may be called Great.
Because it would never claim greatness,
Therefore its greatness is fully realized.

*Taoism.* Tao Te Ching 34

It is He who sends down to you out of heaven water of which you may drink, and by which [grow] trees, for you to pasture your herds, and thereby He brings forth for you crops, and olives, and palms, and vines, and all manner of fruit. Surely in that is a sign for a people who reflect.

And He subjected for you the night and day, and the sun and moon; and the stars are subjected by His command. Surely in that are signs for a people who understand.

And He has multiplied for you in the earth things of diverse hues. Surely in that is a sign for a people who remember.

It is He who subjected for you the sea, that you may eat of it fresh flesh, and bring forth out of it ornaments for you to wear; and you may see the ships cleaving through it; that you may seek of His bounty, and so haply you will be thankful....

If you count God's blessing, you can never number it; surely God is All-forgiving, All-compassionate.

*Islam.* Qur'an 16.10-18

Know, Kashyapa!
It is like unto a great cloud
Rising above the world,
Covering all things everywhere,
A gracious cloud full of moisture;
Lightning-flames flash and dazzle,
Voice of thunder vibrates afar,
Bringing joy and ease to all.
The sun's rays are veiled,
And the earth is cooled;
The cloud lowers and spreads
As if it might be caught and gathered;
Its rain everywhere equally
Descends on all sides,
Streaming and pouring unstinted,
Permeating the land.
On mountains, by rivers, in valleys,
In hidden recesses, there grow
The plants, trees, and herbs;
Trees, both great and small,
The shoots of the ripening grain,
Grape vine and sugar cane.
Fertilized are these by the rain
And abundantly enriched;
The dry ground is soaked,
Herbs and trees flourish together.
From the one water which
Issued from that cloud,
Plants, trees, thickets, forests,
According to their need receive moisture.
All the various trees,
Lofty, medium, low,
Each according to its size,
Grows and develops
Roots, stalks, branches, leaves,
Blossoms and fruits in their brilliant colors;
Wherever the one rain reaches,
All become fresh and glossy.
According as their bodies, forms
And natures are great or small,
So the enriching rain,
Though it is one and the same,
Yet makes each of them flourish.

In like manner also the Buddha
Appears here in the world,
Like unto a great cloud
Universally covering all things;
And having appeared in the world,
He, for the sake of the living,

**Tao Te Ching 34:** This selfless Tao is the way of the sage; cf. Tao Te Ching 2, p. 667.
**Qur'an 16.10-18:** Cf. Qur'an 6.95-99, p. 49; 30.20-25, p. 49; 55.5-30, pp. 82-83.

Discriminates and proclaims
The truth in regard to all laws.
The Great Holy World-honored One,
Among the gods and men
And among the other beings,
Proclaims abroad this word:
"I am the Tathagata,
The Most Honored among men;
I appear in the world
Like unto this great cloud,
To pour enrichment on all
Parched living beings,
To free them from their misery
To attain the joy of peace,
Joy of the present world,
And joy of Nirvana....

Upon all I ever look
Everywhere impartially,
Without distinction of persons,
Or mind of love or hate.
I have no predilections
Nor any limitations;
Ever to all beings
I preach the Law equally;
As I preach to one person,
So I preach to all.
Ever I proclaim the Law,
Engaged in naught else;
Going, coming, sitting, standing,
Never am I weary of
Pouring it copious on the world,
Like the all-enriching rain.
On honored and humble, high and low,
Law-keepers and law-breakers,
Those of perfect character,
And those of imperfect,
Orthodox and heterodox,
Quick-witted and dull-witted,
Equally I rain the Law-rain
Unwearyingly."

*Buddhism.* Lotus Sutra 5:
Parable of the Rain Cloud

❖

**Lotus Sutra 5:** This Parable of the Rain Cloud describes the impartial and equal care which the Buddha gives to all creatures. In addition, it speaks to the specific issue of this sutra, which is the unity of the various paths (*shravaka*-vehicle, *pratyekabuddha*-vehicle, and *bodhisattva*-vehicle) as stepping stones in the overarching dispensation of the Buddha—the One Vehicle.

## *Divine Father and Mother*

DIVINE LOVE AND COMPASSION is often expressed by the relationship of parent and child. The Jewish and Christian scriptures call God our Heavenly Father; in the Lotus Sutra the Buddha is called Father of the World; and similar statements are found in the Vedas and the Confucian Classics. In many religious traditions Ultimate Reality is also recognized to be our divine Mother. Often God's Fatherhood and Motherhood are identified with Heaven and Earth, which cooperate in the creation and nurturing of humankind and the universe.

We may recognize from these scriptures that Ultimate Reality has the attributes of both Father and Mother. Even religions that restrict the vision of God to a patriarchal image only, or religions like Islam that avoid using the language of parenthood altogether, describe God's love in terms that can be said to encompass both fatherly love—Creator, Teacher, Guide, and Savior—and motherly love—Nurturer, Fount of compassion, and Sustainer.[1]

Our Father who art in heaven, hallowed be thy name.

*Christianity*. Matthew 6.9

God! Give us wisdom as a father gives to his sons.
Guide us, O Much-invoked, in this path.
May we live in light.

*Hinduism*. Rig Veda 7.32.26

I tell you, Shariputra,
I, too, am like this,
Being the Most Venerable among many saints,
The Father of the World....

I tell you, Shariputra,
You men
Are all my children,
And I am your Father.
For age upon age, you
Have been scorched by multitudinous woes,
And I have saved you all.

*Buddhism*. Lotus Sutra 3

Do you thus requite the Lord,
you foolish and senseless people?
Is not he your father, who created you,
who made you and established you?

He found [Israel] in a desert land,
in the howling waste of the wilderness;
he encircled him, he cared for him,
he kept him as the apple of his eye.
Like an eagle that stirs up its nest,
that flutters over its young,
spreading out its wings, catching them,
bearing them on its pinions,
the Lord alone did lead him,
and there was no foreign god with him.

*Judaism* and *Christianity*. Deuteronomy 32.6, 10-12

**Lotus Sutra 3:** This stanza follows the Parable of the Burning House, in which the Buddha, as a compassionate father, rescues his children from the burning house of mundane existence by various means. The image of existence as burning goes back to the Buddha himself; cf. the Fire Sermon, p. 271. The Buddha is our parent by virtue of his limitless compassion—see Mahaparinirvana Sutra 259, p. 89.

[1] Islam's reticence about describing God as Father may be understood in light of its strong rejection of polytheistic religions in which gods beget other gods. Any language which could be suggestive of divine procreation—and the notion of a heavenly father could be misinterpreted to give such a mistaken idea—is avoided in the Qur'an.

You are the children of the Lord your God.

*Judaism* and *Christianity*. Deuteronomy 14.1

For all who are led by the spirit of God are sons of God. For you did not receive the spirit of slavery to fall back into fear, but you have received the spirit of sonship. When we cry, "Abba! Father!" it is the Spirit himself bearing witness that we are the children of God, and if children, then heirs, heirs of God and fellow heirs with Christ, provided that we suffer with him in order that we may also be glorified with him.

*Christianity*. Romans 8.14-17

Anas and 'Abdullah reported God's Messenger as saying, "All [human] creatures are God's children, and those dearest to God are the ones who treat His children kindly."

*Islam*. Hadith of Baihaqi

God Himself told me that the most basic and central truth of the universe is that God is the Father and we are his children. We are all created as children of God. And he said there is nothing closer, nothing deeper, nothing more ultimate than when father and son are one: One in love, one in life, and one in ideal.

*Unification Church*
Sun Myung Moon, 10-20-73

Why did God create the universe? The reason is that God wants to realize the relationship of Father and children centering on love. So we can come to the conclusion that the foundation of the universe is the relationship of Father and children.

*Unification Church*.
Sun Myung Moon, 6-20-82

We are the children of our Maker
And do not fear that he will kill us.
We are the children of God
And do not fear that he will kill.

*African Traditional Religions*.
Dinka Prayer (Sudan)

What father among you, if his son asks for a fish, will instead of a fish give him a serpent; or if he asks for an egg, will give him a scorpion? If you then, who are evil, know how to give good gifts to your children, how much more will the heavenly Father give the Holy Spirit to those who ask him!

*Christianity*. Luke 11.11-13

That breast of Thine which is inexhaustible,
health-giving,
by which Thou nursest all that is noble,
containing treasure, bearing wealth, bestowed
freely;
lay that bare, Sarasvati [divine Mother], for our
nurture.

*Hinduism*. Rig Veda 1.164.49

As one whom his mother comforts,
so will I comfort you;
you shall be comforted in Jerusalem.

*Judaism* and *Christianity*. Isaiah 66.13

**Deuteronomy 14.1:** Some Christians stereotype Judaism as a religion in which man relates to God as a servant to his master, whereas the revelation of Christ opened for the first time the more intimate relationship of a child to his Heavenly Father. This is the negative side of Paul's joyous experience of sonship in Romans 8.14-17. Yet Judaism in its true expression also seeks the intimacy of a parent-child relationship. God already revealed his abiding fatherly love for his people in the Torah of the Jews, in such passages as Isaiah 1.2, 63.16, 64.8, and Jeremiah 3.19; cf. The Kaddish, p. 30.

**Sun Myung Moon, 10-20-73:** Our relationship with God includes the dimension of empathy with the divine heart. It should mirror—in its intimacy and through comparable ethical norms—the natural relation of a child to his or her parent.

**Sun Myung Moon, 6-20-82:** Cf. Sun Myung Moon, 2-12-61, p. 74n.

**Dinka Prayer:** Cf. Tiv Proverb, p. 397.

**Rig Veda 1.164.49:** Cf. Candi Mahatmya 10, p. 401; Sarang, M.1, p. 546. On earth as the divine Mother, see Atharva Veda 12.1, p. 207.

**Isaiah 66.13:** This is one of the many images of the feminine and motherly aspect of God found in the Bible; cf. Hosea 11.1-9, pp. 326-27.

The Valley Spirit never dies.
It is named the Mysterious Female.
And the Doorway of the Mysterious Female
Is the base from which Heaven and Earth
sprang.
It is there within us all the while;
Draw upon it as you will, it never runs dry.

*Taoism.* Tao Te Ching 6

O Mother of Imupa, advocate for the whole
[feminine] world!
What a remarkable Mother I have!
O Mother, a pillar, a refuge!
O Mother, to whom all prostrate in greeting
Before one enters her habitation!
I am justly proud of my Mother.
O Mother who arrives,
Who arrives majestic and offers water to all!

*African Traditional Religions.* Yoruba Prayer (Nigeria)

I am Father and Mother of the world.

*Hinduism.* Bhagavad Gita 9.17

Thou art Father, Mother, Friend, Brother.
With Thee as succorer in all places, what fear
have I?

*Sikhism.* Adi Granth, Majh M.5, p. 103

Love, the divine Principle, is the Father and Mother of the universe, including man.

*Christian Science.* Science and Health, 256

For God, people of the whole world are all My children. All of you equally must understand that I am your Parent.

*Tenrikyo.* Ofudesaki 4.79

Heaven and Earth are the father and mother of the ten thousand things. Men are the sensibility of the ten thousand things.

*Confucianism.* Book of History 5.1.1: The Great Declaration

All ye under the heaven! Regard heaven as your father, earth as your mother, and all things as your brothers and sisters.

*Shinto.* Oracle of Atsuta

Mother Earth have pity on us and give us food
to eat!
Father, the Sun, bless all our children and may
our paths be straight!

*Native American Religions.* Blackfoot Prayer

The Great Principle, the Divine, is my womb;
I cast the seed into it;
There is the origin
of all creatures.
Whatever forms originate
in any wombs
the real womb is the Divine, the Great
Principle.
I am the Father that gives the seed.

*Hinduism.* Bhagavad Gita 14.3-4

**Tao Te Ching 6:** Cf. Tao Te Ching 20, p. 434.

**Yoruba Prayer:** On God worshipped as Father in African traditional religions, we have texts from a Nuer Prayer, p. 30; a Susu Prayer, p. 140, and a Kikuyu Prayer, p. 550.

**Book of History 5.1.1:** The complete passage (see p. 753) states that the ruler is likewise father and mother to the people.

**Oracle of Atsuta:** This notion that people are tied together with the kami and things of nature in one universal family builds a sense of community and respect for nature. Atsuta is a shrine near Nagoya.

**Blackfoot Prayer:** Cf. Cheyenne Song, p. 205; Cree Round Dance Song, p. 31; and Okanogan Creation, p. 207. For a comparable Hindu passage, see Rig Veda 1.185.1-5, p. 117.

## CHAPTER 2

# DIVINE LAW, TRUTH, AND COSMIC PRINCIPLE

ALL RELIGIONS RECOGNIZE A TRANSCENDENT LAW, Truth, or Principle which governs the universe and human affairs. Sometimes this principle is identified with Ultimate Reality itself, but it is more often consequent upon and subordinate to it. We have placed side by side passages on the Word (Greek *Logos*) or Wisdom (Hebrew *Kochma*) of Christianity, Torah of Judaism, Dharma and order (*Rita*) of Hinduism; and Tao and Principle (*Li*) of Chinese Religion. In Buddhism we have passages on several related concepts: Wisdom (*Prajna*), Absolute Truth (*Dharmadhatu*), and Teaching (*Dhamma*). In placing passages on these concepts together, their variety should illuminate the subtle differences among them.

In some religious doctrines, truth or lawfulness is a property inherent in Ultimate Reality. The laws of the universe are the basis of the Absolute—e.g., the Tao of Chinese religion which is the creative principle itself, or the Absolute Truth which is realized by the Buddha. In other traditions—Judaism, Christianity, Islam, and theistic Hinduism—God conceives of Law and then sets it up as the standard or measure for his work of creation. This leads to a question which has engaged theologians: Is God bound by his own laws, or is he free to contravene them to perform miracles, etc? Hindu mythology has no trouble with deities performing all manner of miracles, but in Christianity the tendency has been to assert the consistency of rational principles, and even to seek explanations for the miraculous within the normal functioning of natural law. In Christianity, the Word finds its chief manifestation in Christ, the Word made flesh, the Truth incarnate. This is echoed in Confucian and Buddhist scriptures where the Tao or the Dharma is only completely realized by a perfectly enlightened being. In some traditions, the law is a property of samsaric existence which must ultimately be transcended—e.g., the Hindu and Jain law of karma and the Buddhist doctrine of Dependent Origination. Similarly, in Christianity Paul critiques the law as a form of slavery, unable to save. These are some of the diverse colors which one finds in these passages depicting the Truth or Law or Principle which is at the heart of the cosmos.

Regardless of these differences, these religious viewpoints share a respect for the Law which human beings violate at their peril. The universe is fundamentally moral, an expression of the workings of a divine Principle or natural law in both the realms of nature and of human affairs. Hence human morality is not relative, not explicable as the result of social and cultural conditioning alone. Morality and ethics are rooted in the way things are (ontology); they are as enduring as the laws of physics.

This chapter treats the topic of divine law under six heads. The first section deals with the origins and foundations of law as the eternal, pre-existent and all-pervasive ground of existing reality. The second section discusses divine law as the ground for human ethics and the basis for the path to liberation. The remaining sections treat four general expressions of law. First we have lists of divine commandments. The chief example is the Ten Commandments or Decalogue of Christianity and Judaism, but there are many parallels in other scriptures, for example the Buddhist Eightfold Path. Next is the Golden Rule, or the principle of reciprocity, which is found universally in the scriptures of all religions. This concise principle is often regarded as a summary statement of all ethics. Then in the fifth section we move to a more philosophical plane and treat interdependence and mutuality as a principle at work throughout nature. We include passages on the polarities of *yang* and *yin*, Shiva and Shakti, *Purusha* and *prakriti*, and passages on the relativity and interchangeability of all phenomena. The final section treats the law of cause and effect, karma, and the principle of divine justice through which each person reaps what he or she has sown.

❖

## *Eternal Truth*

THE ETERNAL WORD, TRUTH, WISDOM, OR PRINCIPLE pre-existed the creation of the universe, and continues to function in guiding the creative process. The Word is all-pervasive, and operates through specific physical, moral, and spiritual laws. Some texts assert that Truth or Principle may be grasped by ordinary reason as the impersonal laws which govern the cosmos. Other passages describe the essence of Truth as that which is comprehended only in Christ, or in Buddha, or in the mind of the sage. It does not partake of anything evil or immoral, according to Confucianism, and hence is only accessible to the moral person. Analogously for Christians, the Word is manifested completely only in Christ, the perfect man. Finally, this spiritual Word, according to Buddhism, is hidden from surface phenomena and may be understood only when the external world is not grasped or discriminated. It is Mind-only, a theme that finds echoes in contemporary metaphysical movements such as Christian Science.

He has created the heavens and the earth with truth.

*Islam*. Qur'an 16.3

From the bosom of the sacred Word he brought forth the world. On high, below, he abides in his own laws.

*Hinduism*. Atharva Veda 4.1.3

Righteousness and justice are the foundation of thy throne;
steadfast love and faithfulness go before thee.

*Judaism* and *Christianity*. Psalm 89.14

God moves according to universal law. Universal law does not work for the sake of oneself, but for the public good. Universal law embodies the spirit of sacrifice and service towards others.

*Unification Church*.
Sun Myung Moon, 9-30-79

By Truth is the earth sustained,
and by the sun are the heavens;
by Order (*Rita*) the gods stand
and Soma is set in the sky.

*Hinduism*. Rig Veda 10.85.1

God ordained the measures of the creation fifty thousand years before He created the heavens and the earth, while His throne was on the waters.

*Islam*. Hadith of Muslim

This, [in the beginning] was the only Lord of the Universe. His Word was with him. This Word was his second. He contemplated. He said, "I will deliver this Word so that she will produce and bring into being all this world."

*Hinduism*.
Tandya Maha Brahmana 20.14.2

In the beginning was the Word, and the Word was with God, and the Word was God. He was

**Qur'an 16.3:** Cf. Shabbat 55, p. 717.
**Atharva Veda 4.1.3:** Cf. Brihadaranyaka Upanishad 1.4.14, p. 750.
**Sun Myung Moon, 9-30-79:** Cf. Galatians 6.2, p. 688; Shabbat 31a, p. 115.
**Rig Veda 10.85.1:** Cf. Atharva Veda 10.8.31, p. 48, Brihadaranyaka Upanishad 1.4.14, p. 750.
**Tandya Maha Brahmana 20.14.2:** 'This' signifies the impersonal Absolute; cf. Rig Veda 1.64.45, p. 576.

in the beginning with God; all things were made through him, and without him was not anything made that was made. In him was life, and the life was the light of men.

*Christianity*. John 1.1-4

Universal Order and Truth
were born of blazing spiritual fire,
and thence night was born, and thence
the billowy ocean of space.

From the billowy ocean of space
was born Time—the year
ordaining days and nights,
the ruler of every moment.

In the beginning, as before,
the Creator made the sun,
the moon, the heaven and the earth,
the firmament and the realm of light.

*Hinduism*. Rig Veda 10.190.1-3

The Lord created me at the beginning of his work,
the first of his acts of old.
Ages ago I was set up,
at the first, before the beginning of the earth.
When there were no depths I was brought forth,
when there were no springs abounding with water.
Before the mountains had been shaped,
before the hills, I was brought forth;
before he had made the earth with its fields,
or the first of the dust of the world.
When he established the heavens, I was there,
when he drew a circle on the face of the deep,
when he made firm the skies above,
when he established the fountains of the deep,
when he assigned to the sea its limit,
so that the waters might not transgress his command,
when he marked out the foundations of the earth,
then I was beside him, like a master workman;
and I was daily his delight,
rejoicing before him always,
rejoicing in his inhabited world
and delighting in the sons of men.

*Judaism* and *Christianity*. Proverbs 8.22-31

"Then I was beside Him, as a nursling (*amon*); and I was daily all His delight" [Proverbs 8.30].... '*Amon*' is a workman (*uman*). The Torah thus declares, "I was the working tool of the Holy One, blessed be He." In human practice, when a mortal king builds a palace, he builds it not with his own skill but with the skill of an architect. The architect moreover does not build it out of his head, but employs plans and diagrams to know how to arrange the chambers and the doors. Thus God consulted the Torah and created the world.

*Judaism*. Midrash, Genesis Rabbah 1.1

I pay homage to the Perfection of Wisdom! She is worthy of homage. She is unstained, the entire world cannot stain her. She is a source of light, and from everyone in the triple world she removes darkness, and she leads away from the blinding darkness caused by the defilements

**John 1.1-4:** In Greek philosophy, the Word is the *logos* or plan by which God created the universe. The Bible asserts that Christ is himself the Word, the model and plan for creation; cf. Colossians 1.15-17. The Buddhist doctrine of the *Dharmakaya*, by which the Buddha is one with the eternally abiding reality of the universe, is similar except that there is no creation; cf. Lion's Roar of Queen Srimala 5, p. 466; Samyutta Nikaya iii.120, p. 465.

**Rig Veda 10.190.1-3:** *Tapas*, the 'spiritual fire' harnessed and concentrated through meditation, is regarded as the source of all creative energy; cf. Mundaka Upanishad 1.1.8, p. 85; Prasna Upanishad 1.4-5, pp. 116-17. Truth and Order were the first productions of tapas. In the third stanza, the words 'as before' indicates recurrent creation.

**Proverbs 8.22-31:** Wisdom is personified here and in Proverbs 8.1-11, pp. 565. For Christians wisdom is the preexistent Word that is incarnate in Christ; for Jews wisdom is Torah, as in the following passage, which is a midrash (rabbinic interpretation) on this one. On the pre-existence of wisdom, cf. 1 Corinthians 2.6-7, p. 383. Regarding the term 'master workman,' the Hebrew word '*amon*' is rare, and some translate it 'little child,' which seems better to fit the context. See the next passage.

**Genesis Rabbah 1.1:** See previous note.

and by wrong views. In her we can find shelter. Most excellent are her works. She makes us seek the safety of the wings of Enlightenment. She brings light to the blind, she brings light so that all fear and distress may be forsaken.... She is the mother of the Bodhisattvas, on account of the emptiness of her own marks. As the donor of the jewel of all the Buddha-dharmas she brings about the ten powers [of a Buddha]. She cannot be crushed. She protects the unprotected, with the help of the four grounds of self-confidence. She is the antidote to birth-and-death. She has a clear knowledge of the own-being of all dharmas, for she does not stray away from it. The Pefection of Wisdom of the Buddhas, the Lords, sets in motion the Wheel of the Law.

*Buddhism*. Perfection of Wisdom in Eight Thousand Lines 7.1

The Tao has its reality and its signs but is without action or form. You can hand it down but you cannot receive it; you can get it but you cannot see it. It is its own source, its own root. Before heaven and earth existed it was there, firm from ancient times. It gave spirituality to the spirits and to God; it gave birth to heaven and to earth. It exists beyond the highest point, and yet you cannot call it lofty; it exists beneath the limit of the six directions, and yet you cannot call it deep. It was born before heaven and earth, and yet you cannot say it has been there for long; it is earlier than the earliest time, and yet you cannot call it old.

*Taoism*. Chuang Tzu 6

By Divine Law are all forms manifested;
Inexpressible is the Law.
By Divine Law are beings created;
By Law are some exalted.
By Divine Law are beings marked with nobility
 or ignominy;
By the Law are they visited with bliss or bale.
On some by His Law falls grace;
Others by His Law are whirled around in cycles
 of births and deaths.
All by the Law are governed,
None is exempt.
Says Nanak, Should man realize the power of
 the Law,
He would certainly disclaim his ego.

*Sikhism*. Adi Granth, Japuji 2, M.1, p. 1

The moral law is to be found everywhere, and yet it is a secret.

The simple intelligence of ordinary men and women of the people may understand something of the moral law; but in its utmost reaches there is something which even the wisest and holiest men cannot understand. The ignoble natures of ordinary men and women of the people may be able to carry out the moral law; but in its utmost reaches even the wisest and holiest of men cannot live up to it.

Great as the Universe is, man is yet not always satisfied with it. For there is nothing so great but the mind of the moral man can conceive of something still greater which nothing in the world can hold. There is nothing so small but the mind of the moral man can conceive of something still smaller which nothing in the world can split.

The Book of Songs says,

The hawk soars to the heavens above,
Fishes dive to the depths below.

That is to say, there is no place in the highest heavens above nor in the deepest waters below where the moral law is not to be found. The moral man finds the moral law beginning in the relation between man and woman; but ending in the vast reaches of the universe.

*Confucianism*. Doctrine of the Mean 12

There is no changing the words of God; that is the mighty triumph.

*Islam*. Qur'an 10.64

Falsehood shall be destroyed; truth in the end shall prevail.

*Sikhism*. Adi Granth, Ramkali-ki-Var, M.1, p. 953

**Chuang Tzu 6:** Cf. Chuang Tzu 31, p. 77, I Ching, Great Commentary 1.4.i-iv, pp. 228.
**Japuji 2, M.1:** Cf. Japuji 3, M.1, p. 61.

Truth is victorious, never untruth.
Truth is the way; truth is the goal of life,
Reached by sages who are free from self-will.

*Hinduism.* Mundaka Upanishad 3.1.6

The question as to when the union of soul with karma occured for the first time cannot arise, since this is a beginningless relation like gold and stone.

*Jainism.* Pancadhyayi 2.35-36

The ten thousand things all come from the same seed, and with their different forms they give place to one another. Beginning and end are part of a single ring and no one can comprehend its principle. This is called Heaven the Equalizer.

*Taoism.* Chuang Tzu 27

The world exists because of causal actions, all things are produced by causal actions and all beings are governed and bound by causal actions. They are fixed like the rolling wheel of a cart, fixed by the pin of its axle shaft.

*Buddhism.* Sutta Nipata 654

"What, brethren, is causal happening?"

"Conditioned by rebirth is decay and death."

"Whether, brethren, there be an arising of Tathagatas or whether there be no such arising, this nature of things just stands, this causal status, this causal orderliness, the relatedness of this to that."

*Buddhism.* Samyutta Nikaya ii.25

Jesus said, "I am the way, the truth, and the life; no one comes to the Father, but by me."

*Christianity.* John 14.6

Concerning the prime, rare, hard-to-understand dharmas, only a Buddha and a Buddha can exhaust their reality, namely, the suchness of the dharmas, the suchness of their marks, the suchness of their nature, the suchness of their substance, the suchness of their powers, the suchness of their functions, the suchness of their causes, the suchness of their conditions, the suchness of their effects, the suchness of their retributions, and the absolute identity of their beginning and end.

*Buddhism.* Lotus Sutra 2

In the Book of Songs it is said,

The ordinance of God,
How inscrutable it is and goes on for ever.

That is to say, this is the essence of God. It is again said,

How excellent it is,
The moral perfection of King Wen.

That is to say, this is the essence of the noble character of the Emperor Wen. Moral perfection also never dies.

*Confucianism.* Doctrine of the Mean 26.10

"What is meant by an eternally-abiding reality? The ancient road of reality, Mahamati, has been here all the time, like gold, silver, or pearl preserved in the mine. The *Dharmadhatu* (Absolute Truth) abides forever, whether the Tathagata appears in the world or not. As the Tathagata eternally abides so does the Reason of all things. Reality forever abides, reality keeps its order, like the roads in an ancient city.

**Pancadhyayi 2.35-36:** The principles governing the influx and stopping of karma determine both the laws of cause and effect and the laws of liberation.

**Sutta Nipata 654:** This also refers to the laws of karma; cf. Maitri Upanishad 4.2, p. 499; Dhammapada 127, p. 124, Surangama Sutra, p. 276.

**John 14.6:** Jesus reveals the eternal truth by his own personal example and way of life—the manifestation of God's love and truth. This and the following passages describe the truth as that which is comprehended by the mind of a saint.

**Lotus Sutra 2:** There is one ultimate reality which embraces everything—'Suchness.' This is also expressed through the universality of the Buddha nature and the all-encompassing Dharmakaya which is the Buddha's body. There is nothing real apart from Reality itself.

**Doctrine of the Mean 26.10:** In other words, the truth of Heaven and the moral perfection of the sage are alike; both continue forever.

For instance, a man who is walking in a forest and discovering an ancient city with its orderly streets may enter into the city, and having entered into it, he may have a rest, conduct himself like a citizen, and enjoy all the pleasures accruing therefrom. What do you think, Mahamati? Did this man make the road along which he enters into the city, and the various things in the city?"

"No, Blessed One."

"Just so, what has been realized by myself and the other Tathagatas is this Reality, this eternally-abiding reality, the self-regulating reality, the Suchness of things, the Realness of things, the truth itself."

"The world of the ignorant is observed as the continuation of birth and death, whereby dualisms are nourished, and because of the perversion [the truth] is not perceived.

"There is just one truth, which is Nirvana—it has nothing to do with intellection. The world seen as subject to discrimination resembles a plantain tree, a dream, a mirage."

"The Mind as norm is the abode of self-nature which has nothing to do with the realm of causation; of this norm, which is perfect existence and the highest Absolute, I speak.

"Of neither existence nor non-existence do I speak, but of Mind-only which has nothing to do with existence and non-existence, and which is thus free from intellection.

"Suchness, emptiness, Absolute Truth... these I call Mind-only."

*Buddhism.* Lankavatara Sutra 61, 63, 64

The universe, like man, is to be interpreted by Science from its divine Principle, God, and then it can be understood; but when explained on the basis of physical sense and represented as subject to growth, maturity, and decay, the universe, like man, is, and must continue to be, an enigma.

Adhesion, cohesion, and attraction are properties of Mind. They belong to divine Principle, and support the equipoise of that thought-force, which launched the earth in its orbit and said to the proud wave, "Thus far and no farther."

Spirit is the life, substance and continuity of all things. We tread on forces. Withdraw them, and creation must collapse. Human knowledge calls them forces of matter; but divine Science declares that they belong wholly to divine Mind, are inherent in this Mind, and so restores them to their rightful home and classification.

*Christian Science.*
Science and Health, 124

❖

**Lankavatara Sutra:** See Surangama Sutra, p. 276. The 'highest Absolute' means the reality cleansed of all impure dualistic discriminations. The parable of the ancient city is also found in the Theravada scriptures: see Samyutta Nikaya ii.106, pp. 389. On the difference between truth and intellection, see Garland Sutra 10, p. 571, and related passages.

# *Moral Law*

UNLIKE THE LAWS DESCRIBED by modern science, the immutable divine law is inherently moral, and is the basis for human ethics. The Hindu concept of Dharma, for example, embraces at once the cosmological, ethical, social, and legal principles that provide the basis for belief in an ordered universe and an ordered, prosperous society. Religion, therefore, cannot easily accept the modern distinction between fact and value: There are ethical values in human life that are as absolute as the fact that the earth revolves about the sun. The way to salvation lies in following the divine laws and revealed teachings—e.g., the Tao, the Torah, the eternal Dharma, the guidance of the Qur'an, the Dhamma revealed by the Buddha, or the Word revealed in the Gospel.

The Law applies to all people, though not always equally. Most religions, including Buddhism, Islam, and Christianity, teach a single standard of law that applies to all people. In Hinduism, however, there are different dharmas for people of different social status (*varna*), stage of life (*ashrama*), and quality of inborn nature (*guna*), even though this differentiation should not obscure an underlying unity in the divine principle. Sometimes religions distinguish between the law for believers and the law for unbelievers, for the law of the community of believers is distinctive in that it is covenanted (contracted) with God. Regardless of this tendency to pluralism of laws, we can discern an underlying common ground for the moral law—often called natural law—which transcends religion or social circumstance. This common ground will be explored in the following sections on the *Decalogue* and the *Golden Rule*.

This section begins with passages urging people to follow the divine law or holy teachings. These laws are liberating. They define the Way through which a person sanctifies his life, according to Judaism. They lay out the road to heaven, according to Hinduism and Sikhism, or to Nirvana, according to Buddhism. They are the keys to happiness and success in life, as depicted through the parables of the tree and the rock from the scriptures of Christianity and Islam.

Law or teaching is often an ambiguous concept, for there are laws that fetter as well as teachings that liberate. Christianity, for example, distinguishes the Mosaic Law which educates but confines from the liberating grace available through faith in Christ. Works of law cannot save or liberate, according to passages from the New Testament, the Upanishads, and the Buddhist scriptures. Laws and doctrines are of provisional value, a concession to human sin, according to a text from the Tao Te Ching. These religions look beyond the limitations of law to a higher relationship with the Absolute, what the Christian calls justification by faith, the Hindu experiences as union with Brahman, and the Buddhist experiences as Enlightenment. The concluding passages suggest this limitation of law and works done to fulfill the law.

Liberation comes from living the holy Word.

*Sikhism*. Adi Granth,
Sri Raga Ashtpadi, M.1, p. 62

To him who orders his way aright,
I will show the salvation of God!

*Judaism* and *Christianity*.
Psalm 50.23

**Sri Raga Ashtpadi, M.1:** Cf. Japuji 1, p. 552.

The God of old bids us all abide by his injunctions.
Then shall we get whatever we want,
Be it white or red.

*African Traditional Religion.* Akan Prayer on Talking Drums

He who looks into the perfect law, the law of liberty, and perseveres, being no hearer that forgets but a doer that acts, he shall be blessed in his doing.

*Christianity.* James 1.25

And now, Israel, what does the Lord your God require of you, but to fear the Lord your God, to walk in all his ways, to love him, to serve the Lord your God with all your heart and with all your soul, and to keep the commandments and the statutes of the Lord, which I command you this day for your good?

*Judaism.* Deuteronomy 10.12-13

God has revealed the fairest of statements, a Scripture consistent, [with promises of reward] paired [with threats of punishment], at which creeps the flesh of those who fear their Lord, so that their flesh and their hearts soften to God's reminder. Such is God's guidance, with which He guides whom He will. And him whom God sends astray, for him there is no guide.

*Islam.* Qur'an 39.23

The Holy One desired to make Israel worthy, so He gave them many laws and commandments.

*Judaism.* Mishnah, Makkot 3.16

Truth is victorious, never untruth.
Truth is the way; truth is the goal of life,
Reached by sages who are free from self-will.

*Hinduism.* Mundaka Upanishad 3.1.6

Truth is said to be the one unequalled means of purification of the soul. Truth is the ladder by which man ascends to heaven, as a ferry plies from one bank of a river to another.

*Hinduism.* Narada Dharma Sutra 1.210

Because perfect wisdom tames and transforms him, wrath and conceit he does not increase. Neither enmity nor ill-will take hold of him, nor is there even a tendency towards them. He will be mindful and friendly.... It is wonderful how this perfection of wisdom has been set up for the control and training of the bodhisattvas.

*Buddhism.* Perfection of Wisdom in Eight Thousand Lines 3.51-54

Then do I proclaim what the Most Beneficent spoke to me,
The Words to be heeded, which are best for mortals:
Those who shall give hearing and reverence
Shall attain unto Perfection and Immortality
By the deeds of good spirit of the Lord of Wisdom!

*Zoroastrianism.* Avesta, Yasna 45.5

Sweet blows the breeze for him who lives by Law, rivers for him pour sweets.
So [as we live by Law] may the plants be sweet to us!
Pleasant be our nights, pleasant dawns, and pleasant the dust of the earth!
Pleasant for us be Father Heaven!

*Hinduism.* Rig Veda 1.90.6-7

The law of the Lord is perfect,
reviving the soul;
the testimony of the Lord is sure,
making wise the simple;
the precepts of the Lord are right,
rejoicing the heart;
the commandment of the Lord is pure,
enlightening the eyes;
the fear of the Lord is clean,
enduring for ever;

**James 1.25:** Cf. John 8.32, p. 379.

**Deuteronomy 10.12-13:** Cf. Joshua 1.1-9, p. 745.

**Makkot 3.16:** For Jews, the Law is not a burden—as some interpret Paul in Galatians 3.10-14, p. 108—but a way of sanctification; cf. Abot 6.2, p. 379; Tanhuma Shimeni 15b, p. 612.

**Yasna 45.5:** See Yasna 34.12, p. 552.

the ordinances of the Lord are true,
and righteous altogether.
More to be desired are they than gold,
even much fine gold;
sweeter also than honey
and drippings of the honeycomb.

*Judaism* and *Christianity*. Psalm 19.7-10

Blessed is the man
who walks not in the counsel of the wicked,
nor stands in the way of the sinners,
nor sits in the seat of scoffers;
but his delight is in the law of the Lord,
and on his law he meditates day and night.
He is like a tree
planted by streams of water,
that yields its fruit in its season
and its leaf does not wither.
In all that he does, he prospers.

*Judaism* and *Christianity*. Psalm 1.1-3

Have you not seen how God has struck a similitude?
A good word is as a good tree—
its roots are firm,
and its branches are in heaven;
it gives its produce every season
by the leave of its Lord.
So God strikes similitudes for men;
haply they will remember.
And the likeness of a corrupt word
is as a corrupt tree—
uprooted form the earth,
having no establishment.
God confirms those who believe with the firm word,
in the present life and in the world to come;
and God leads astray the evildoers;
and God does what He will.

*Islam*. Qur'an 14.24-27

What Tao plants cannot be plucked,
What Tao clasps cannot slip.
By its virtue alone can one generation after another carry on the ancestral sacrifice.
Apply it to yourself and by its power you will be freed from dross.
Apply it to your household and your household shall thereby have abundance.
Apply it to the village, and the village will be made secure.
Apply it to the kingdom, and the kingdom shall thereby be made to flourish.
Apply it to an empire, and the empire shall thereby be extended.

*Taoism*. Tao Te Ching 54

Every one then who hears these words of mine and does them will be like a wise man who built his house upon the rock; and the rain fell, and the floods came, and the winds blew and beat upon that house, but it did not fall, because it had been founded on the rock. And every one who hears these words of mine and does not do them will be like a foolish man who built his house upon the sand; and the rain fell, and the floods came, and the winds blew and beat against that house, and it fell; and great was the fall of it.

*Christianity*. Matthew 7.24-27

Whoever lives contemplating pleasant things, with senses unrestrained, in food immoderate, indolent, inactive, him verily Mara overthrows, as the wind blows down a weak tree.

Whoever lives contemplating the impurities of the body, with senses restrained, in food moderate, full of faith, full of sustained energy, him Mara overthrows not, as the wind cannot shake a rocky mountain.

*Buddhism*. Dhammapada 7-8

**Psalm 19.7-10:** See Abot 3.6, p. 551.

**Psalm 1.1-3:** See Joshua 1.1-9, p. 745. This and the following passage from the Qur'an use the image of the Tree of Life to describe the person who lives in accordance with God's Word; cf. Revelation 22.1-5, pp. 795. Likewise, in John 15.4-11, p. 462, and Var Majh, M.1, pp. 462, the Tree of Life symbolizes the founder and those who are united with him.

**Matthew 7.24-27:** Cf. Dhammapada 25, p. 511.

**Dhammapada 7-8:** Cf. Dhammapada 337, pp. 658.

Why, is he better who founds his building upon the fear of God and His good pleasure, or he who founds his building upon the brink of a crumbling bank that will tumble with him into the fire of hell? And God does not guide the people of the evildoers.

The buildings they have built will not cease to be a point of doubt within their hearts, until their hearts are cut to pieces; God is All-knowing, All-wise.

*Islam*. Qur'an 9.109-10

Easily known is the progressive one, easily known the one who declines. He who loves Dhamma progresses, he who hates it declines.

*Buddhism*. Sutta Nipata 92

The night passes; it is never to return again.
The night passes in vain
for one who acts not according to the law.

*Jainism*. Uttaradhyayana Sutra 14.24

Those who live in accordance with the divine laws without complaining, firmly established in faith, are released from karma. Those who violate these laws, criticizing and complaining, are utterly deluded, and are the cause of their own suffering.

*Hinduism*. Bhagavad Gita 3.31-32

Confucius remarked, "The life of the moral man is an exemplification of the universal moral order (*chung yung*). The life of the vulgar person, on the other hand, is a contradiction of the universal moral order.

"The moral man's life is an exemplification of the universal order, because he is a moral person who unceasingly cultivates his true self or moral being. The vulgar person's life is a contradiction of the universal order, because he is a vulgar person who in his heart has no regard for, or fear of, the moral law."

*Confucianism*. Doctrine of the Mean 2

The blessed Buddhas, of virtues endless and limitless, are born of the Law of Righteousness; they dwell in the Law, are fashioned by the Law; they have the Law as their master, the Law as their light, the Law as their field of action, the Law as their refuge...

The Law is equal, equal for all beings. For low or middle or high the Law cares nothing. So I must make my thought like the Law.

The Law has no regard for the pleasant. Impartial is the Law. So I must make my thought like the Law....

The Law does not seek refuge. The refuge of all the world is the Law. So I must make my thought like the Law.

The Law has none who can resist it. Irresistible is the Law. So I must make my thought like the Law.

The Law has no preferences. Without preference is the Law. So I must make my thought like the Law.

The Law has no fear of the terrors of birth-and-death, nor is it lured by Nirvana. Ever without misgiving is the Law. So I must make my thought like the Law.

*Buddhism*. Dharmasangiti Sutra

Now we know that whatever the law says it speaks to those who are under the law, so that every mouth may be stopped, and the whole world may be held accountable to God. For no human being will be justified in his sight by works of the law, since through the law comes knowledge of sin....

What then shall we say? That the law is sin? By no means! Yet, if it had not been for the law, I should not have known sin. I should not have known what it is to covet if the law had not said, "You shall not covet." But sin, finding opportunity in the commandment, wrought in me all kinds of covetousness. Apart from the law sin lies dead. I was once alive apart from

**Qur'an 9.109-10:** Cf. Nahjul Balagha, Sermon 21, p. 750.

**Sutta Nipata 92:** Cf. Diamond Sutra 27, p. 379.

**Bhagavad Gita 3.31-32:** Cf. Bhagavad Gita 5.24, p. 379.

**Doctrine of the Mean 2:** Cf. I Ching 50, p. 551; Book of Ritual 7.2.20, p. 333. 'Chung Yung' is also translated Doctrine of the Mean, which is the title of the scripture.

**Dharmasangiti Sutra:** This is one sutra in a large Mahayana collection of sutras called the Sikshasamuccaya, compiled by Shantideva.

the law, but when the commandment came, sin revived and I died; the very commandment which promised life proved to be death to me. For sin, finding opportunity in the commandment, deceived me and by it killed me.

*Christianity*. Romans 3.19-20 and 7.7-11

For all who rely on works of the law are under a curse, for it is written, "Cursed be every one who does not abide by all things written in the book of the law, and do them." Now it is evident that no man is justified before God by the law; for "He who through faith is righteous shall live"; but the law does not rest on faith, for "He who does them shall live by them." Christ redeemed us from the curse of the law....

Is the law then against the promises of God? Certainly not; for if a law had been given which could make alive, then righteousness would indeed be by the law. But the scripture consigned all things to sin, that what was promised to faith in Jesus Christ might be given to those who believe.

Now before faith came, we were confined under the law, kept under restraint until faith should be revealed. So that the law was our custodian until Christ came, that we might be justified by faith. But now that faith has come, we are no longer under a custodian; for in Christ Jesus you are all sons of God, through faith.

*Christianity*.
Galatians 3.10-13 and 3.21-26

Finite and transient are the fruits of sacrificial rites. The deluded, who regard them as the highest good, remain subject to birth and death.... Attached to works, they know not God. Works lead them only to heaven, whence, to their sorrow, their rewards quickly exhausted, they are flung back to earth. Considering religion to be observance of rituals and performance of acts of charity, the deluded remain ignorant of the highest good. Having enjoyed in heaven the reward of their good works, they enter again into the world of mortals. But wise, self-controlled, and tranquil souls, who are contented in spirit, and who practice austerity and meditation in solitude and silence, are freed from all impurity, and attain by the path of liberation to the immortal, the truly existing, the changeless Self.

*Hinduism*.
Mundaka Upanishad 1.2.7-11

People under delusion accumulate tainted
merits but do not tread the Path.

**Romans 3.19-20:** The traditional Christian evangelical purpose of the Old Testament (the Law) is to reveal the high standards of godly behavior, and thereby to show people how sinful they are, to elicit repentance, and thus to prepare them for the liberating word of the Gospel. But contrast Matthew 5.17-18, p. 474.

**Romans 7.7-11:** This passage presents the psychological paradox that religious commandments often incite to sin. Furthermore the law, by making one conscious of moral obligations, may lead to an oppressive sense of guilt.

**Galatians 3.10-13:** The law becomes oppressive if interpreted in a perfectionistic manner, as though one could not feel justified unless he kept the law punctiliously to its smallest detail. The grace of God in Jesus Christ is a free unconditional gift; it is especially liberating to those who regard the law as a burden which they cannot carry and feel oppressed by guilt for violating it. This of course does not mean that in Christ one can be licentious; he should live in the Spirit of good works; cf. Galatians 5.19-23, p. 331; James 2.14-26, p. 712.

**Galatians 3.21-26:** The argument that 'scripture consigned all things to sin' refers to the fundamental human condition of Original Sin—cf. Romans 3.9-12, p. 273—which persists regardless of one's efforts to follow the law. This sinful condition, the 'death' which resulted from Adam's fall, is only redeemed by faith in Christ, who conquered death; cf. 1 Corinthians 15.21-22, p. 388.

**Mundaka Upanishad 1.2.7-11:** Good works, done to expiate evil karma produce merit according to the law of karma, cannot help a person escape the wheel of rebirth. Only through realizing Brahman is there true liberation.

They are under the impression that to accumulate merits and to tread the Path are one and the same thing.
Though their merits for alms-giving and offerings are infinite
They do not realize that the ultimate source of sin lies in the three poisons within their own mind.

*Buddhism.* Sutra of Hui Neng 6

On a cerain occasion the Exalted One was staying at Uruvela, on the bank of the river Neranjara at the foot of the Bodhi-tree, having just won the highest wisdom. He was seated for seven days in one posture and experienced the bliss of release. Then the Exalted One, after the lapse of those seven days, during the first watch of the night, rousing himself from that concentration of mind, gave close attention to causal uprising in direct order, thus,

> This being, that becomes; by the arising of this, that arises, namely: Conditioned by ignorance, activities; conditioned by activities, consciousness; conditioned by consciousness, mind and body; conditioned by mind and body, the six sense-spheres; conditioned by the six sense-spheres, contact; conditioned by contact, feeling; conditioned by feeling, craving; conditioned by craving, grasping; conditioned by grasping, becoming; conditioned by becoming, birth; conditioned by birth, old age and death, grief, lamentation, suffering, sorrow and despair come into being. Thus is the arising of this mass of Ill.

*Buddhism.* Udana 1.1

Actions (*karma*) resulting from past deeds, productions of causes and conditions, are all unreal and empty, are not self, are not substantial.

*Buddhism.* Garland Sutra 22

The man of superior virtue is not conscious of his virtue,
And in this way he really possesses virtue.
The man of inferior virtue never loses sight of his virtue,
And in this way he loses his virtue....
Therefore, only when Tao is lost does the doctrine of virtue arise.
When virtue is lost, only then does the doctrine of humanity arise.
When humanity is lost, only then does the doctrine of righteousness arise.
When rightousness is lost, only then arise rules of propriety.
Now, propriety is a superficial expression of loyalty and faithfulness, and the beginning of disorder.

*Taoism.* Tao Te Ching 38

**Sutra of Hui Neng 6:** Good works done out of a desire to earn a place in heaven are tainted by selfishness; hence they still produce karma and cannot bring about liberation from bondage.

**Udana 1.1:** This is a typical statement of Dependent Origination (Skt. *Paticcasamuppada*). It is a law which describes the situation of human bondage; cf. Surangama Sutra, p. 276. In that sense it is comparable to the statements by Paul that 'through the law comes knowledge of sin' (Romans 3.20 above). Yet only by a proper knowledge of ill can ill be overcome, by reversing the chain of causation: "If this is not, that does not come to be; from the stopping of this, that is stopped"—Majjhima Nikaya ii.32, p. 389; cf. Samyutta Nikaya xii.90, pp. 389-90.

**Garland Sutra 22:** Mahayana Buddhism teaches that from the vantage point of Enlightenment, when all distinctions of subject and object have been transcended, the laws of cause and effect and Dependent Origination are themselves empty and unreal. Concern with such laws are only provisional teachings—see Mulamadhamaka Karika 24.8-12, pp. 720; Heart Sutra, pp. 416-17.

**Tao Te Ching 38:** Laws and doctrines are only needed for people who deviate from the Tao, and they are poor substitutes for that ideal of oneness. Cf. Tao Te Ching 2, p. 572; 18-19, p. 201; Chuang Tzu 13, p. 148.

## *The Decalogue*

THE MORAL OUTLOOKS of most religions are basically quite similar. Just as the Decalogue, or Ten Commandments, is the basis of Jewish and Christian ethical values, similar lists of ethical principles may be found in one form or another in the scriptures of most religions. The Qur'an contains several passages summarizing proper ethical behavior which have been called Islamic decalogues. In Buddhism, Hinduism, and Jainism we find lists of ten charges or ten precepts for monks and lay people, and there are further condensations into five universal dharmas called *samanya dharma*. Another comparable list is found in the Buddhist Eightfold Path.

The first table of the Decalogue contains positive injunctions for right worship to establish a proper vertical relationship with God, and the second table contains negative injunctions prohibiting criminal behavior in order to foster horizontal relationships of community. These two ethical dimensions, the vertical towards the Absolute and the horizontal towards one's neighbor, are characteristic of such lists in every religion. We may regard the injunctions to renunciation and meditation in the Buddhist Eightfold Path and in Hindu, Buddhist, and Jain lists of dharmas as non-theistic expressions of the vertical dimension. In the horizontal dimension of law, prohibitions against social crimes such as murder, adultery, and stealing are universal. The specific offenses will be taken up again individually in Chapter 9.

And God spoke all these words, saying,

"I am the Lord your God, who brought you out of the land of Egypt, out of the house of bondage.

You shall have no other gods before me.

You shall not make for yourself a graven image, or any likeness of anything that is in heaven above, or that is in the earth beneath, or that is in the water under the earth; you shall not bow down to them or serve them; for I the Lord your God am a jealous God, visiting the iniquity of the fathers upon the children to the third and fourth generation of those who hate me, but showing steadfast love to thousands of those who love me and keep my commandments.

You shall not take the name of the Lord your God in vain: for the Lord will not hold him guiltless who takes his name in vain.

Remember the sabbath day, to keep it holy. Six days you shall labor, and do all your work; but the seventh day is a sabbath to the Lord your God; in it you shall not do any work, you, or your son, or your daughter, your manservant, or your maidservant, or your cattle, or the sojourner who is within your gates; for in six days the Lord made heaven and earth, the sea, and all that is in them, and rested on the seventh day; therefore the Lord blessed the sabbath day and hallowed it.

Honor your father and your mother, that your days may be long in the land which the Lord your God gives you.

You shall not kill.

You shall not commit adultery.

You shall not steal.

You shall not bear false witness against your neighbor.

You shall not covet your neighbor's house; you shall not covet your neighbor's wife, or his manservant, or his maidservant, or his ox, or his ass, or anything that is your neighbor's."

*Judaism* and *Christianity*.
Exodus 20.1-17: The Ten Commandments

**Exodus 20.1-17:** These are the Ten Commandments. There is some variation as to how they should be divided. In the Jewish tradition the verse 'I am the Lord your God, who brought you out of the land of

The second five commandments were intended to be paired off with the first five commandments.

"You shall not murder" corresponds to "I the Lord am your God." The Holy One said, "If you did murder, I hold it against you as though you have diminished the image of God."

"You shall not commit adultery" is paired with "You shall have no other gods." God said, "If you committed adultery, I hold it against you as though you bowed down to another god."

"You shall not steal" is paired with "You shall not swear falsely by the name of the Lord your God."…. If you steal, you will go on to swear falsely, go on to lie, and end up swearing by My name falsely.

"You shall not bear false witness" is paired with "Remember the Sabbath day." God said, "If you bear false witness against your neighbor, I hold it against you as though you bore witness against Me to the effect that I did not create My world in six days and did not rest on the seventh."

"You shall not covet" is paired with "Honor your father and your mother." Clans like Gaius of Gadara and Lucius of Susitha would sneak into each other's homes and cohabit with the wives of the others, the others with the wives of these. In time a quarrel fell out between them, and a man killed his father, unware that it was his father.

*Judaism.* Pesikta Rabbati

Say, Come, I will recite what God has made a sacred duty for you:

Ascribe nothing as equal with Him;

Be good to your parents;

Kill not your children on a plea of want—
We provide sustenance for you and for them;

Approach not lewd behavior whether open or in secret,

Take not life, which God has made sacred, except by way of justice and law. Thus does He command you, that you may learn wisdom.

And approach not the property of the orphan, except to improve it, until he attains the age of maturity.

Give full measure and weight, in justice—
No burden do We place on any soul but that which it can bear.

And if you give your word, do it justice, even if a near relative is concerned; and fulfill your obligations before God. Thus does He command you, that you may remember.

Verily, this is My straight Path: follow it, and do not follow other paths which will separate you from His Path. Thus does He command you, that you may be righteous.

*Islam.* Qur'an 6.151-53

The charge to avoid the taking of life.
The charge to avoid taking what is not given.
The charge to avoid unchastity.
The charge to avoid falsehood.
The charge to avoid fermented liquor, distilled liquor, intoxicants giving rise to sloth.
The charge to avoid unseasonable meals.
The charge to avoid dancing, song, playing music, and seeing shows.
The charge to avoid the use of flowers, scents, and unguents, wearing ornaments and decorations.

Egypt, the house of bondage' is regarded as the first commandment, but Christians regard it as a prologue. Most Protestants and Eastern Orthodox Christians reckon 'You shall have no other gods before me' as the first commandment and the prohibition of images as the second commandment. For Jews the second commandment includes both 'You shall have no other gods' and the prohibition of graven images. Lutherans and Roman Catholics likewise regard 'You shall have no other gods' and the prohibition of graven images as together constituting a single commandment, but reckon it the first commandment; they then divide the verse against covetousness into two commandments to make up the ten. Cf. the short enumerations of the commandments in Psalm 24.3-6, p. 155; Hosea 4.1-3, p. 222; Jeremiah 7.1-15, pp. 768-69.

**Pesikta Rabbati:** Cf. Tosefta Shebuot 3.6, p. 281.

**Qur'an 6.151-53:** See Qur'an 2.177, p. 615; Hadith of Bukhari and Muslim, p. 349; also Qur'an 17.23-38.

The charge to avoid the use of raised beds, of wide beds.
The charge to avoid the accepting of gold and silver.

*Buddhism.* Khuddaka Patha: The Ten Charges

Contentment, forgiveness, self-control, not appropriating anything unrighteously, purification, coercion of the organs, wisdom, knowledge of the Supreme, truthfulness, and abstention from anger: these constitute the tenfold law [for ascetics].

*Hinduism.* Laws of Manu 6.92

Forgiveness, humility, straightforwardness, purity, truthfulness, self-restraint, austerity, renunciation, non-attachment and chastity [with one's spouse] are the ten duties [of lay people].

*Jainism.* Tatthvarthasutra 9.6

Not killing, no longer stealing, forsaking the wives of others, refraining completely from false, divisive, harsh and senseless speech, forsaking covetousness, harmful intent and the views of Nihilists—these are the ten white paths of action, their opposites are black.

*Buddhism.* Nagarjuna, Precious Garland 8-9

The first great vow, sir, runs thus: I renounce all killing of living beings, whether subtle or gross, whether movable or immovable. Nor shall I myself kill living beings [nor cause others to do it, nor consent to it]. As long as I live, I confess and blame, repent and exempt myself of these sins, in the thrice threefold way [i.e., acting, commanding, or consenting, either in the past, present, or future], in mind, speech, and body. There are five clauses....

The second great vow, sir, runs thus: I renounce all vices of lying speech arising from anger or greed or fear or mirth. I shall neither myself speak lies, nor cause others to speak lies, nor consent to the speaking of lies by others. I confess.... There are five clauses....

The third great vow, sir, runs thus: I renounce all taking of anything not given, either in a village or a town or a wood, either of little or much, of small or great, of living or lifeless things. I shall neither take myself what is not given, nor cause others to take it, nor consent to their taking it. As long as I live, I confess.... There are five clauses....

The fourth great vow, sir, runs thus: I renounce all sexual pleasures, either with gods or men or animals. I shall not give way to sensuality, nor cause others to give way to it, nor consent to their giving way to it. As long as I live, I confess.... There are five clauses....

The fifth great vow, sir, runs thus: I renounce all attachments, whether little or much, small or great, living or lifeless; neither shall I myself form such attachments, nor cause others to do so, nor consent to their doing so. As long as I live, I confess.... There are five clauses....

He who is well provided with these great vows and their twenty-five clauses is really homeless if he, according to the sacred teaching, the precepts and the way, correctly practices, follows, executes, explains, establishes and, according to the precept, effects them.

*Jainism.* Acarangasutra 24

Nonviolence, truthfulness, not stealing, purity, control of the senses—this, in brief, says Manu, is the Dharma for all the four castes.

*Hinduism.* Laws of Manu 10.63

**Khuddaka Patha:** These are the rules of training observed by the monks, with the third charge modified as a concession to lay people (a monk would of course take a vow of celibacy). Lay people ordinarily observe the first five charges. Cf. Dhammapada 246-47, p. 329.

**Khuddaka Patha, Laws of Manu 6.92, Tatthvarthasutra 9.6** and **Precious Garland 8-9:** The tradition of ten precepts runs through Hinduism, Buddhism, and Jainism, though elements in the list may vary.

**Laws of Manu 10.63:** This list of universally applicable dharma for all castes and stages of life is called *samanya dharma.* It is the universal foundation upon which are erected the specific dharmas which differentiate the castes. It is a least common denominator by which Hindu society, for all its variety of castes, roles, and traditions, maintains an ethical consensus. Cf. Chandogya Upanishad 5.10.9, p. 330.

The Noble Truth of the Path leading to the cessation of suffering is this Noble Eightfold Path, namely: right view, right aspiration, right speech, right action, right livelihood, right effort, right mindfulness, right concentration.

What is right view? Knowledge of suffering, knowledge of the arising of suffering, knowledge of the cessation of suffering, knowledge of the path leading to the cessation of suffering—this is called right view.

What is right aspiration? Aspiration for renunciation, aspiration for non-malevolence, aspiration for harmlessness—this is called right aspiration.

What is right speech? Refraining from lying speech, refraining from slanderous speech, refraining from harsh speech, refraining from gossip—this is called right speech.

What is right action? Refraining from violence against creatures, refraining from taking what has not been given, refraining from going wrongly among the sense-pleasures, this is called right action.

What is right livelihood? A disciple of the Noble Ones, getting rid of a wrong mode of livelihood, makes his living by a right mode of livelihood. This is called right livelihood.

What is right effort? A monk generates desire, effort, stirs up energy, exerts his mind and strives for the non-arising of evil unskilled states that have not arisen... for the getting rid of evil unskilled states that have arisen... for the arising of skilled states that have not arisen... for the maintenance and completion of skilled states that have arisen. This is called right effort.

What is right mindfulness? A monk fares along contemplating the body in the body... the feelings in the feelings... the mind in the mind... the mental states in the mental states... ardent, clearly conscious of them, mindful of them so as to control the covetousness and dejection in the world. This is called right mindfulness.

And what is right concentration? A monk, aloof from the pleasures of the senses, aloof from unskilled states of mind, enters on and abides in the first meditation which is accompanied by initial thought and discursive thought, is born of aloofness, is rapturous and joyful. By allaying initial thought and discursive thought, with the mind subjectively tranquilized and fixed on one point, he enters on and abides in the second meditation which is devoid of initial thought and discursive thought, is born of concentration, and is rapturous and joyful. By the fading out of rapture... he enters on and abides in the third meditation... the fourth meditation. This is called right concentration.

*Buddhism.* Majjhima Nikaya iii.251-52,
Saccavibhanga Sutta:
The Noble Eightfold Path

❖

## *The Golden Rule*

THE GOLDEN RULE or the ethic of reciprocity is found in the scriptures of nearly every religion. It is often regarded as the most concise and general principle of ethics. It is a condensation in one principle of all longer lists of ordinances such as the Decalogue—see also texts on *Loving-kindness*, pp. 684-87.

You shall love your neighbor as yourself.

*Judaism* and *Christianity*. Leviticus 19.18

Whatever you wish that men would do to you, do so to them.

*Christianity*. Matthew 7.12

Not one of you is a believer until he loves for his brother what he loves for himself.

*Islam*. Forty Hadith of an-Nawawi 13

A man should wander about treating all creatures as he himself would be treated.

*Jainism*. Sutrakritanga 1.11.33

Try your best to treat others as you would wish to be treated yourself, and you will find that this is the shortest way to benevolence.

*Confucianism*. Mencius VII.A.4

One should not behave towards others in a way which is disagreeable to oneself. This is the essence of morality. All other activities are due to selfish desire.

*Hinduism*. Mahabharata, Anusasana Parva 113.8

Tsekung asked, "Is there one word that can serve as a principle of conduct for life?" Confucius replied, "It is the word *shu*—reciprocity: Do not do to others what you do not want them to do to you."

*Confucianism*. Analects 15.23

Comparing oneself to others in such terms as "Just as I am so are they, just as they are so am I," he should neither kill nor cause others to kill.

*Buddhism*. Sutta Nipata 705

One going to take a pointed stick to pinch a baby bird should first try it on himself to feel how it hurts.

*African Traditional Religions*. Yoruba Proverb (Nigeria)

One who you think should be hit is none else but you. One who you think should be governed is none else but you. One who you think should be tortured is none else but you. One who you think should be enslaved is none else but you. One who you think should be killed is none else but you. A sage is ingenuous and leads his life after comprehending the parity of the killed and the killer. Therefore, neither does he cause violence to others nor does he make others do so.

*Jainism*. Acarangasutra 5.101-2

**Leviticus 19.18:** Quoted by Jesus in Matthew 22.36-40 (below).
**Mencius VII.A.4** and **Analects 15.23:** Cf. Analects 6.28.2, p. 688.
**Sutta Nipata 705:** Cf. Dhammapada 129-30, p. 340.
**Acarangasutra 5.101-2:** Cf. Dhammapada 129-30, p. 340.

The Ariyan disciple thus reflects, Here am I, fond of my life, not wanting to die, fond of pleasure and averse from pain. Suppose someone should rob me of my life... it would not be a thing pleasing and delightful to me. If I, in my turn, should rob of his life one fond of his life, not wanting to die, one fond of pleasure and averse to pain, it would not be a thing pleasing or delightful to him. For a state that is not pleasant or delightful to me must also be to him also; and a state that is not pleasing or delightful to me, how could I inflict that upon another?

As a result of such reflection he himself abstains from taking the life of creatures and he encourages others so to abstain, and speaks in praise of so abstaining.

*Buddhism*. Samyutta Nikaya v.353

A certain heathen came to Shammai and said to him, "Make me a proselyte, on condition that you teach me the whole Torah while I stand on one foot." Thereupon he repulsed him with the rod which was in his hand. When he went to Hillel, he said to him, "What is hateful to you, do not do to your neighbor: that is the whole Torah; all the rest of it is commentary; go and learn."

*Judaism*. Talmud, Shabbat 31a

"Teacher, which is the great commandment in the law?" Jesus said to him, "You shall love the Lord your God with all your heart, and with all your soul, and with all your mind. This is the great and first commandment. And a second is like it, You shall love your neighbor as yourself. On these two commandments depend all the law and the prophets."

*Christianity*. Matthew 22.36-40

❖

**Samyutta Nikaya v.353:** The passage gives a similar reflection about abstaining from other types of immoral behavior: theft, adultery, etc. To identify oneself with others is also a corollary to the Mahayana insight that all reality is interdependent and mutually related; cf. Guide to the Bodhisattva's Way of Life 8.112-16, p. 120; Majjhima Nikaya i.415, p. 330.

**Matthew 22.36-40:** Cf. Deuteronomy 6.4-9, p. 31; Leviticus 19.18, p. 114; Luke 10.25-37, pp. 686-87; Galatians 6.2, p. 688; Brihadaranyaka Upanishad 5.2.2, p. 687; Sun Myung Moon, 9-30-79, p. 99.

## *Polarity, Relationality, and Interdependence*

ONE CONSEQUENCE OF THE TRANSCENDENT LAW underlying the cosmos is that the cosmos evidences order, regularity, and mutuality. All existences, great and small, are linked in a web of interdependent relationships. Every relationship has a certain polarity and a certain order, and there is dynamic, mutual movement and exchange between male and female, heaven and earth, mind and matter, subject and object, light and dark, being and non-being, this and that, myself and the other. The movement within and between beings in relationship is the source of generative and creative power. This motion is seen in the regular cycles of nature, the changing seasons. It is sometimes mythically represented by the cosmic union of god and goddess, of male and female principles.

In addition, interdependence is the basis for teachings which deny egoism and acquisitiveness while encouraging compassion and reciprocity. The Buddhist and Taoist understandings of causality link all beings into an interdependent whole of which the individual is but one part, and this is the basis for the attitude of no-self and the ethic of compassion. Each person *is* his neighbor; any distinction between myself as subject and the other as object is illusory.

The Great Primal Beginning (*T'ai chi*) generates the two primary forces (*yang* and *yin*). The two primary forces generate... the great field of action.

*Confucianism*. I Ching, Great Commentary 1.11.5-6

And of everything created We two kinds; haply you will remember.

*Islam*. Qur'an 51.49

Beauty arises from the fusion of extremes into a harmonious oneness.

*Unification Church*. Sun Myung Moon, 9-11-79

All things are twofold, one opposite the other,
and he has made nothing incomplete.
One confirms the good things of the other,
and who can have enough of beholding his
glory?

*Christianity*. Sirach 42.24-25

So God created man in his own image, in the image of God he created him; male and female he created them.

*Judaism* and *Christianity*. Genesis 1.27

The Originator of the heavens and the earth; He has appointed for you of yourselves spouses, and pairs also of the cattle, by means of which He multiplies you.

*Islam*. Qur'an 42.11

All life, all pulsation in creation throbs with the mighty declaration of the biune truth of Shiva-Shakti, the eternal He and the eternal She at play in manifestation.

*Hinduism*. Kularnava Tantra 3

The creator, out of desire to procreate, devoted himself to concentrated ardor (*tapas*). Whilst thus devoted to concentrated ardor, he produced a couple, Matter and Life, saying to himself, "these two will produce all manner

**Sun Myung Moon, 9-11-79:** Cf. Book of Ritual 19, p. 229.
**Kularnava Tantra 3:** In the Tantra this defines a Mantra 'Ham-sa,' identified with the breath, inhaling and exhaling.

of creatures for me." Now Life is the Sun; Matter is the Moon.

*Hinduism*. Prasna Upanishad 1.4-5

The Master said, "Heaven and earth come together, and all things take shape and find form. Male and female mix their seed, and all creatures take shape and are born." In the Changes it is said, 'When three people journey together, their number decreases by one. When one man journeys alone, he finds a companion.' "

*Confucianism*. I Ching, Great Commentary 2.5.13

Observe how all God's creations borrow from each other: day borrows from night and night from day, but they do not go to law one with another as mortals do.... The moon borrows from the stars and the stars from the moon... the sky borrows from the earth and the earth from the sky.... All God's creatures borrow from the other, yet make peace with one another without lawsuits; but if man borrows from his friend, he seeks to swallow him up with usury and robbery.

*Judaism*. Midrash, Exodus Rabbah 31.15

When the sun goes, the moon comes; when the moon goes, the sun comes. Sun and moon alternate; thus light comes into existence. When cold goes, heat comes; when heat goes, cold comes. Cold and heat alternate, and thus the year completes itself. The past contracts. The future expands. Contraction and expansion act upon each other; hereby arises that which furthers.

The measuring worm draws itself together when it wants to stretch out. Dragons and snakes hibernate in order to preserve life. Thus the penetration of germinal thought into the mind promotes the workings of the mind. When this working furthers and brings peace to life, it elevates a man's nature.

*Confucianism*. I Ching, Great Commentary 2.5.2-3

Which of these two came earlier, which came later?
How did they come to birth? Who, O Seers, can discern it?
They contain within them all that has a name,
while days and nights revolve as on a wheel.

You two, though motionless and footless, nurture
a varied offspring having feet and movement.
Like parents clasping children to their bosoms,
O Heaven and Earth, deliver us from evil!

These twin maidens [day and night], like two friendly sisters
nestled close together, rest in their parents' bosom
and kiss together the center of the world.
O Heaven and Earth, deliver us from evil!

*Hinduism*. Rig Veda 1.185.1,2,5

Heaven is high, the earth is low; thus the Creative and the Receptive are determined. In correspondence with this difference between low and high, inferior and superior places are established.

Movement and rest have their definite laws; according to these, firm and yielding lines [of the hexagrams] are differentiated.

Events follow definite trends, each according to its nature. Things are distinguished from one another in definite classes. In this way good

**Prasna Upanishad 1.4-5:** Tradition has speculated on the fact that matter (*rayi*) is feminine and life or energy (*prana*) is masculine. This is another expression of the polarity of Purusha and prakriti, or Shiva and Shakti. Cf. Brihadaranyaka Upanishad 1.4.3, p. 174; Rig Veda 10.129, pp. 83-84; 10.190.1-3, p. 100; Bhagavad Gita. 13.19-26, p. 118; Shiva Purana, p. 118.

**I Ching, Great Commentary 2.5.13:** Cf. I Ching, Great Commentary 1.4.1-4, p. 228.

**I Ching, Great Commentary 2.5.2-3:** The philosophy of the I Ching emphasizes the constant dynamic interchange of yang and yin. Every action engenders its opposite. One who wishes to prosper should understand the principles of change and use them to his advantage; cf. Tao Te Ching 22, pp. 390-91, and Chuang Tzu 27, p. 102. Hence the example: he who wishes to create and expand must first look within and concentrate the self—cf. Chuang Tzu 12, p. 416.

fortune and misfortune come about. In the heavens phenomena take form; on earth shapes take form. In this way change and transformation become manifest.

Therefore the eight trigrams succeed one another by turns, as the firm and the yielding displace each other.

Things are aroused by thunder and lightning; they are fertilized by wind and rain. Sun and moon follow their courses and it is now hot, now cold.

The way of the Creative brings about the male.

The way of the Receptive brings about the female.

The Creative knows the great beginnings.

The Receptive completes the finished things.

*Confucianism.* I Ching, Great Commentary 1.1.1-5

Know that *prakriti* (nature, energy) and *Purusha* (spirit) are both without beginning, and that from prakriti come the *gunas* (qualities of the phenomenal world) and all that changes. Prakriti is the agent, cause, and effect of every action, but it is Purusha that seems to experience pleasure and pain. Purusha, resting in prakriti, witnesses the play of the gunas born of prakriti. But attachment to the gunas leads a person to be born for good or evil. Within the body the supreme Purusha is called the witness, approver, supporter, enjoyer, the supreme Lord, the highest Self... Whatever exists, Arjuna, animate or inanimate, is born through the union of the field and its Knower.

*Hinduism.* Bhagavad Gita 13.19-22, 26

The original Being without a second, with neither beginning nor end... the Supreme Brahman, the all-pervasive and undecaying, vanished. The manifest form of that formless Being is Shiva. Scholars of the ancient and succeeding ages have sung of it as Ishvara.

Ishvara, though alone, then created the physical form Shakti from his body. This Shakti did not affect his body in any way.

Shakti is called by various names: Pradhana, Prakriti, Maya, Gunavati, Para. She is the mother of cosmic intelligence, without modification. That Shakti is matter-energy (*prakriti*), the goddess of all and the prime cause and mother of the three gunas....

The supreme Purusha is Shiva. He has no other lord over Him.... In the form of time (*kala*) together with Shakti, they simultaneously created the holy center called Shivaloka. It is the seat of salvation shining over and above everything. The holy center is of the nature of supreme Bliss inasmuch as the primordial lovers, supremely blissful, made the beautiful holy center their perpetual abode.

*Hinduism.* Shiva Purana, Rudrasamhita 1.16

The deities Izanagi and Izanami descended from Heaven to the island Ono-goro and erected a heavenly pillar and a spacious palace.... "Let us, you and me, walk in a circle around this heavenly pillar and meet and have conjugal intercourse," said Izanagi. "You walk around from the right, and I will walk around from the left and meet you."... They united and gave birth to children, [the eight islands of Japan].

*Shinto.* Kojiki 4-6

**I Ching, Great Commentary 1.1.1-5:** The philosophy of Change finds its concrete form in the system of divination of the I Ching, with its 64 hexagrams, each composed of two trigrams. Each of the six lines of the hexagram may be either yang or yin, firm or yielding. Because these lines change into each other according to rule: firm yang becoming yielding yin, firm yin becoming yielding yang, the hexagrams denote a fortune that is dynamic and has various potentials for change. This passage is a commentary on two paradigmatic hexagrams: the Creative (*Ch'ien*) is composed of all six yang lines and the Receptive (*K'un*) is composed of all six yin lines.

**Bhagavad Gita 13.19-22, 26:** The cosmos is formed by the polarity of *Purusha*—mind, consciousness, divinity—and *prakriti*—matter, energy, the world of nature. However, in monistic Vedanta, the duality of Purusha and prakriti is not at all benign or supportive of enlightenment, it is rather a fetter to be transcended. Cf. Mundaka Upanishad 3.1.1-3, pp. 275-76.

**Kojiki 4-6:** In Shinto, the deities Izanagi and Izanami correspond to the male and female principles. The union of opposites is seen as the source of life, divine and human. However, the deities at first erred in this ritual; the complete text is given on p. 306.

In space
is the triangle;
here meditate.
Thence the circles
in right order,
and the divine forms
appearing in due order.

In the lotus
lies knowledge;
here is union.
Thence bliss
self-experiencing,
which is *bodhicitta*
and is thought of
enlightenment.

Therefore the Innate is twofold, for Wisdom is the woman and Means is the man. Thereafter these both become twofold, distinguished as absolute and relative. In man there is this twofold nature: the thought of enlightenment [relative] and the bliss arising from it [absolute]; in woman too it is the same, the thought of enlightenment and the bliss arising from it.

*Buddhism*. Hevajra Tantra 8.26-29

When ones accumulate to become ten, it becomes a complete being. Heaven is three because positivity and negativity harmonize to produce the neutral. Earth is three because positivity and negativity come together to produce the one. Man is three because man and woman come together to produce the one. The three poles are added together to form six. The processes of life are manifested through the seven, eight, and nine.

The Ultimate One achieves the four by the movement of the three [poles]. The five becomes the seven by a circular movement, and then returns to the one as life flows on mysteriously. Although myriads of things come out from the one, flow, are used, and change, the root is always present in all movement coming and going. It lies in man to highly brighten the core of his mind like the sun.

Heaven is one, earth is one, and they move as one body. The end of a finite being is a return to the endless; the beginning and the end are one.

*Korean Religions*. Chun Boo Kyung

Thirty spokes share one hub to make a wheel.
Through its not-being (*wu*),
There being (*yu*) the use of the carriage.

Mold clay into a vessel.
Through its not-being,
There being the use of the vessel.

Cut out doors and windows to make a house.
Through its not-being
There being the use of the house.

Therefore in the being of a thing,
There lies the benefit;
In the not-being of a thing,
There lies its use.

*Taoism*. Tao Te Ching 11

Every existence has both internal character [mind] and external form [body]; accordingly, its purpose is two-fold. One purpose pertains to internal character and the other to external form. The purpose pertaining to internal character is for the whole, while the purpose per-

**Hevajra Tantra 8.26-29:** This Tantric text advocates the attainment of enlightenment by the union of Wisdom (*prajna*) and Means (*upaya*), the female and male principles. The first column describes the Means, a meditation surrounded by certain geometric symbols, and the second column describes the unfolding of Wisdom. The union of Wisdom and Means can be envisioned abstractly, or, in "secret yoga," it can be enacted in a ritual sexual union. For a Buddhist critique of this Tantric dualism, see Sutra of Forty-two Sections 25, p. 660.

**Chun Boo Kyung:** This cryptic text plays with numbers one to ten but never explains what these numbers mean, leaving much to interpretation. Many see the Chun Boo Kyung as setting forth a theory of generation, movement, and return. The theory of generation states that the three poles, interpreted as mind, life, and energy, or positive, negative, and neutral (see Chun Boo Kyung, p. 62), are generated through the harmony of subject and object. This generates the power of growth through nine stages to maturity, the tenth stage. The theory of movement descibes a circular or spherical motion of the three poles centered on the Ultimate One, thus creating a unified body of four positions. It is said that man should similarly brighten his mind by centering on the Ultimate and participating in this movement. Finally, the theory of return affirms that all things return to their origin and continually change into new forms of existence.

**Tao Te Ching 11:** The usefulness of the wheel, the vessel, and the house is through the empty space, or 'non-being,' contained in them. Utility comes through the recurring process of coming to be and ceasing to be, making a complete circuit of the Tao.

taining to external form is for the individual. These relate to each other as cause and effect, internal and external, and subject and object. Therefore, there cannot be any purpose of the individual apart from the purpose of the whole, nor any purpose of the whole that does not include the purpose of the individual. All the creatures in the entire universe form a vast complex linked together by these dual purposes.

*Unification Church.* Divine Principle I.1.3.1

This world of men, given over to the idea of "I am the agent," bound up with the idea "another is the agent," understand not truly this thing; they have not seen it as a thorn. For one who looks at this thorn with caution, the idea "I am the agent" exists not, the idea "another is the agent" exists not.

*Buddhism.* Udana 70

We are members one of another.

*Christianity.* Ephesians 4.25

Why should I be unable
To regard the bodies of others as "I"?
It is not difficult to see
That my body is also that of others.

In the same way as the hands and so forth
Are regarded as limbs of the body,
Likewise why are embodied creatures
Not regarded as limbs of life?

Only through acquaintance has the thought of "I" arisen
Towards this impersonal body;
So in a similar way, why should it not arise
Towards other living beings?

When I work in this way for the sake of others,
I should not let conceit or [the feeling that I am] wonderful arise.
It is just like feeding myself—
I hope for nothing in return.

*Buddhism.* Shantideva, Guide to the Bodhisattva's Way of Life 8.112-16

Everything has its "that," everything has its "this." From the point of view of "that" you cannot see it, but through understanding you can know it. So I say, "that" comes out of "this" and "this" depends on "that"—which is to say that "this" and "that" give birth to each other. But where there is birth there must be death; where there is death there must be birth. Where there is acceptability there must be unacceptability; where there is unacceptability there must be acceptability. Where there is recognition of right there must be recognition of wrong; where there is recognition of wrong there must be recognition of right. Therefore the sage does not proceed in such a way, but illuminates all in the light of Heaven. He too recognizes a "this", but a "this" which is also "that"; a "that" that is also "this". His "that" has both a right and a wrong in it; his "this" too has both a right and a wrong in it. So, in fact, does he still have a "this" and "that"? Or does he in fact no longer have a "this" and "that"? A state in which "this" and "that" no longer find their opposites is called the Hinge of the Way. When the hinge is fitted into the socket, it can respond endlessly.

*Taoism.* Chuang Tzu 2

**Divine Principle I.1.3.1:** The mind or 'internal character' of human beings is the original mind that pursues transcendent values, ideals, and love. Thus it most essentially relates with beings beyond itself. The body is concerned with gratification of sense-desires and survival. The relationship between them suggested here gives priority to the whole purpose of the 'internal character,' while the individual purpose of the 'external form' is in a supporting role. This interdependent complex linked together by purpose—compare 1 Corinthians 12.12-27, pp. 189-90—is descriptive of nature, which follows God's principle, but prescriptive for humans, who often have their priorities upside-down.

**Guide to the Bodhisattva's Way of Life 8.112-16:** Vv. 112, 114-16. Cf. Samyutta Nikaya v.353, p. 115; Dhammapada 129-30, p. 340; Acarangasutra 5.101-2, p. 114.

**Chuang Tzu 2:** The Taoist ideal is to transcend all distinctions of 'this' and 'that' and live in the free motion of the Tao, in which all things rise and fall, develop and revert to their origin. Cf. Tao Te Ching 2, p. 572; Chuang Tzu 2, pp. 40-41; 7, p. 416. This ideal has resemblances to the *satori* of Zen; cf. Diamond Sutra 22-23, p. 415; Seng Ts'an, pp. 150-51.

The doing away with the notion of cause and condition, the giving up of a causal agency, the establishment of the Mind-only—this I state to be no-birth.

The getting-rid of the idea that things are caused, the removal of the dualism of imagined and imagining, the being liberated from the alternatives of being and non-being—this I state to be no-birth.

No external [separate] existence, no non-existence, not even the grasping of mind; things are like a dream, a hair-net, Maya, a mirage... this is what characterizes no-birth.

It is only in accordance with general convention that a chain of mutual dependence is talked of; birth has no sense when the chain of dependence is severed.

If [someone holds that] there is anything born somewhere apart from concatenation [the chain of mutual relations], he is one who is to be recognized as an advocate of no-causation as he destroys concatenation.

If concatenation worked [from outside] like a lamp revealing all kinds of things, this means the presence of something outside concatenation itself.

All things are devoid of self-nature [separate existence], have never been born, and in their original nature are [transparent] like the sky; things separated from concatenation belong to the discrimination of the ignorant.

When this entire world is regarded as concatenation, as nothing else but concatenation, then the mind gains tranquillity.

*Buddhism.* Lankavatara Sutra 78

❖

**Lankavatara Sutra 78:** All things are interdependent, mutually influencing one another through cause and effect, and hence bound to the realm of birth, suffering, and death. This concatenation must also include the observer; it is an illusion to think that there could exist a separate ego that can stand outside of it. But Buddhist insight can allow one to see the transcendent reality of no-birth, which is established in the mind when it rests in the state of Nirvana. Then discrimination of dualism ceases. Cf. Seng Ts'an, pp. 150-51; Heart Sutra, pp. 416-17; Mulamadhyamaka Karika 25, pp. 59-60; and the traditional statement of Dependent Origination: Samyutta Nikaya xxii.90, pp. 389-90.

# *Cosmic Justice*

THE MAXIM THAT A PERSON REAPS what he has sown, the doctrine of karma, and belief in divine retribution are different expressions of a common principle that the world is governed by justice. Religions give diverse teachings regarding the specific manner in which justice will be vindicated; e.g., through one's fate in this life, through reincarnation into a being of a different status, or through one's fate in the afterlife. For the latter, including beliefs about heaven and hell, see Chapter 6.

The principle of justice bears the same ambiguous relationship to Ultimate Reality as does divine law generally. In Judaism, Christianity, Islam, Sikhism, and African traditional religions it is God who executes judgment to maintain justice, while in Hinduism, Buddhism, and Jainism the principle of justice is inherent in the fabric of the cosmos and is distinguished from and subordinate to the ultimate goal of liberation. In Chinese religion there is both an impersonal Tao or Heaven which gives recompense according to principle and Taoist deities who execute judgment.

More will be said in later chapters about the doctrine of karma, particularly the accumulated *Karma and Inherited Sin*, pp. 498-503, as they impinge on the present. Karma may function to explain a person's life circumstances by attributing them to conditions created in past lives; in that sense the doctrine of karma functions analogously to the doctrine of predestination in theistic religions. Yet the Buddhist scriptures caution against interpreting karma as a deterministic principle, and Hindu texts recognize that it can be blotted out through grace.[1]

This collection of texts begins with passages on the principle of cause and effect, on justice as inherent to the nature of reality. The next group of passages deals with the problem of the frequent delay between actions and the ripening of their fruits. The scriptures affirm that regardless of the delay, recompense is inescapable, sometimes describing it through the metaphor of Heaven's net. One solution to this problem is that recompense occurs in another life; we offer several fundamental texts on karma, the impersonal law by which the deserts of one's deeds are reaped in the next incarnation. The next group of passages gives another solution, which is to envision that sure recompense comes only at the Last Judgment. The final group of passages depicts God, or his angels, as personally deciding and enforcing the judgment for one's deeds.

Do not be deceived; God is not mocked, for whatever a man sows, that he will also reap.

*Christianity*. Galatians 6.7

Suffering is the offspring of violence—realize this and be ever vigilant.

*Jainism*. Acarangasutra 3.13

Whatever affliction may visit you is for what your own hands have earned.

*Islam*. Qur'an 42.30

Our body in Kali Yuga is a field of action:
As a man sows, so is his reward.
Nothing by empty talk is determined:

**Galatians 6.7:** Cf. Ezekiel 18.1-30, pp. 490.
**Qur'an 42.30:** Cf. Qur'an 53.36-42, p. 490.

[1] See p. 498nn.

Anyone swallowing poison must die.
Brother! behold the Creator's justice:
As are a man's actions, so is his recompense.

*Sikhism*. Adi Granth, Gauri Var, M.4, p. 308

All who take the sword will perish by the sword.

*Christianity*. Matthew 26.52

Those who wrongfully kill men are only putting their weapons into the hands of others who will in turn kill them.

*Taoism*. Treatise on Response and Retribution 5

Ashes fly back in the face of him who throws them.

*African Traditional Religions*. Yoruba Proverb (Nigeria)

For they sow the wind, and they shall reap the whirlwind.

*Judaism* and *Christianity*. Hosea 8.7

An ignorant man committing evil deeds does not realize the consequences. The imprudent man is consumed by his own deeds, like one burnt by fire.

*Buddhism*. Dhammapada 136

Men who acquire wealth by evil deeds, by adhering to principles which are wrong, fall into the trap of their own passions and fettered with karma they sink further down.

*Jainism*. Uttaradhyayana Sutra 4.2

A man who has committed one of the deadly sins will never again, until his death, lose the thought of that action; he cannot get rid of it or remove it, but it follows after him until the time of his death.

*Buddhism*. Perfection of Wisdom in Eight Thousand Lines 17.3

I have acted, I have caused others to act, and I have approved of others' actions. One should first comprehend that all such actions taking place in the world are the cause of the influx of karma particles, and then should forswear them.

*Jainism*. Acarangasutra 1.6-7

Unrighteousness, practiced in this world, does not at once produce its fruit; but, like a cow, advancing slowly, it cuts off the roots of him who committed it.

*Hinduism*. Laws of Manu 4.172

Even if they attain to sovereignty, the wicked, engaged in cruel deeds, condemned by all men, do not enjoy it long, but fall like trees whose roots have been severed. O dweller in darkness, as in its proper season the tree puts forth its flowers, so in the course of time evil actions produce bitter fruit.

*Hinduism*. Ramayana, Aranya Kanda 29

Good fortune and misfortune take effect through perseverance. The tao of heaven and earth becomes visible through perseverance. The tao of sun and moon becomes bright through perseverance. All movements under heaven become uniform through perseverance.

*Confucianism*. I Ching, Great Commentary 2.1.5

As sweet as honey is an evil deed, so thinks the fool so long as it ripens not; but when it ripens, then he comes to grief.

Verily, an evil deed committed does not immediately bear fruit, just as milk does not curdle at once; but like a smoldering fire covered with ashes, it remains with the fool until the moment it ignites and burns him.

*Buddhism*. Dhammapada 69, 71

Let not their conduct grieve you, who run easily to disbelief, for lo! they injure God not at all.

**Gauri Var, M.4:** Cf. Maitri Upanishad 4.2, p. 499.

**Dhammapada 136:** Cf. Dhammapada 131-32, p. 340.

**Perfection of Wisdom in Eight Thousand Lines 17.3:** The 'deadly sins' in Buddhism are specifically: (1) to kill one's mother; (2) to kill one's father; (3) to kill an arhat; (4) to cause schism in the Order; and (5) to harm the body of a Buddha.

It is God's will to assign them no portion in the hereafter, and theirs will be an awful doom....

And let not those who disbelieve imagine that the rein We give them bodes good for their souls. We only give them rein that they may grow in sinfulness. And theirs will be a shameful doom.

*Islam.* Qur'an 3.176, 178

Then I saw the wicked buried; they used to go in and out of the holy place, and were praised in the city where they had done such things. Because sentence against an evil deed is not executed speedily, the heart of the sons of men is fully set to do evil. Though a sinner does evil a hundred times and prolongs his life, yet I know that it will be well with those who fear God, because they fear before him.

*Judaism* and *Christianity*. Ecclesiastes 8.10-12

The net of Heaven is cast wide. Though the mesh is not fine, yet nothing ever slips through.

*Taoism.* Tao Te Ching 73

Further, as Heaven and Earth are the greatest of things, it is natural, from the point of view of universal principles, that they have spiritual power. Having spiritual power it is proper that they reward good and punish evil. Nevetheless their expanse is great and their net is wide-meshed. There is not necessarily an immediate response as soon as this net is set in operation.

*Taoism.* Pao-p'u Tzu

Everything is given on pledge, and a net is spread for all the living; the shop is open; and the dealer gives credit; and the ledger lies open; and the hand writes; and whosoever wishes to borrow may come and borrow; but the collectors regularly make their daily round, and exact payment from man whether he be content or not; and they have that whereon they can rely in their demand; and the judgment is a judgment of truth; and everything is prepared for the feast.

*Judaism.* Mishnah, Abot 3.20

Not in the sky, nor in mid-ocean, nor in a mountain cave, is found that place on earth where abiding one may escape from the consequences of one's evil deed.

*Buddhism.* Dhammapada 127

Though they dig into Sheol,
from there shall my hand take them;
though they climb up to heaven,
from there I will bring them down.
Though they hide themselves on the top of Carmel,
from there I will search out and take them;
and though they hide from my sight at the bottom of the sea,
there I will command the serpent, and it shall bite them.
And though they go into captivity before their enemies,
there I will command the sword, and it shall slay them;
and I will set my eyes upon them for evil and not for good.

*Judaism* and *Christianity*. Amos 9.2-4

According as one acts, according as one conducts himself, so does he become. The doer of good becomes good. The doer of evil becomes evil. One becomes virtuous by virtuous action, bad by bad action.

**Qur'an 3.176, 178:** Cf. Qur'an 4.92, p. 339, and 14.42-51, p. 782; also 2 Peter 3.10, p. 781, where the reason for God's slowness is divine forbearance that the wicked might have a chance to repent.

**Ecclesiastes 8.10-12:** Cf. Yoruba Song, p. 71.

**Pao-p'u Tzu:** Written by Ko Hung (253-333 A.D.), the Pao-p'u Tzu is among the most important classics of religious Taoism. It expounds belief in the Taoist Immortals, the doctrine of retribution, and the use of alchemical means to prolong life.

**Abot 3.20:** The image of the ledger is a frequent one; cf. Abot 4.29, p. 243; Qur'an 17.13-14, pp. 242-43; 39.68-75, pp. 244-45; 50.17-19, p. 243; 69.13-37, p. 781; Revelation 20.11-12, p. 243; Ramkali-ki-Var, M.1, p. 243.

**Amos 9.2-4:** Cf. Qur'an 2.115, Atharva Veda 4.16, p. 71.

But people say, "A person is made [not of acts, but] of desires only." [I say,] as his desire, such is his resolve; as is his resolve, such the action he performs; what action he performs, that he procures for himself.

On this point there is this verse:

Where one's mind is attached—the inner self
Goes thereto with action, being attached to it alone.
Obtaining the end of his action,
Whatever he does in this world,
He comes again from that world
To this world of action.

So the mind who desires.

*Hinduism*. Brihadaranyaka Upanishad 4.4.5-6

Action, which springs from the mind, from speech, and from the body, produces either good or evil results; by action are caused the conditions of men, the highest, the middling, and the lowest.

A man obtains the result of a good or evil mental act in his mind; that of a verbal act in his speech; that of a bodily act in his body.

In consequence of sinful acts committed with his body, a man becomes in the next birth an inanimate thing; in consequence of sins committed by speech, he becomes a bird or a beast; in consequence of mental sins he is reborn in a low caste.

*Hinduism*. Laws of Manu 12.3,8,9

According to what deeds are done
Do their resulting consequences come to be;
Yet the doer has no existence:
This is the Buddha's teaching.

Like a clear mirror,
According to what comes before it,
Reflecting forms, each different,
So is the nature of actions.

*Buddhism*. Garland Sutra 10

As you plan for somebody so God plans for you.

*African Traditional Religions*. Igbo Proverb (Nigeria)

All creatures on their actions are judged
In God's court, just and true.

*Sikhism*. Adi Granth, Japuji 34, p. 7

God is not hornless;
He is horned:
He exacts punishment for every deed.

*African Traditional Religions*. Ovambo Proverb (Angola)

I the Lord search the mind
and try the heart,
to give to every man according to his ways,
according to the fruit of his doings.

*Judaism* and *Christianity*. Jeremiah 17.10

Whoever vows to tyrannize over the humble and the meek,
The Supreme Lord burns him in flames.
The Creator dispenses perfect justice
And preserves His devotee.

*Sikhism*. Adi Granth, Gauri, M.5, p. 199

**Brihadaranyaka Upanishad 4.4.5-6:** This classic text describes the principle by which karma determines the site of reincarnation. Cf. Vedanta Sutra 1.2.1, p. 238; Svetasvatara Upanishad 5.11-12, p. 499.

**Laws of Manu 12.1-9:** Cf. Vedanta Sutra 1.2.1, p. 238; Maitri Upanishad 4.2, p. 499.

**Garland Sutra 10:** This passage reconciles karma and voidness. A person is subject to karma only as long as he dwells in the illusion that he exists as a self. Intrinsically empty of self, a person is like a clear mirror whose purity is not affected by the reflections that impinge upon it. Thus the person who courses in enlightenment will not accumulate new karma, though he may still have to work out the effects of past deeds. Cf. Majjhima Nikaya i.389-90, p. 242 and Anguttara Nikaya iii.33, p. 499.

**Ovambo Proverb:** Cf. Yoruba Song, p. 502; Igbo Consecration, p. 550.

**Jeremiah 17.10:** Cf. Hebrews 4.12-13, p. 70.

To God belongs all that is in the heavens and on the earth; and whether you make known what is in your minds or hide it, God will bring you to account for it. He will forgive whom He will and He will punish whom He will. God is able to do all things.

*Islam.* Qur'an 2.284

Never mind if the people are not intimidated
by your [correct] authority.
A mightier Authority will deal with them in
the end.

*Taoism.* Tao Te Ching 72

For the Son of man is to come with his angels in the glory of his Father, and then he will repay every man for what he has done.

*Christianity.* Matthew 16.27

Holy, then, did I recognize Thee, O Wise Lord.
I perceived Thee foremost at the birth of life,
When Thou didst endow acts and words with
retribution:
Bad unto bad, good blessing unto holy,
Through Thy wisdom, at the final goal of life!

*Zoroastrianism.* Avesta, Yasna 43.5

Even if the wrong-doers had all that there is on earth, and as much more, in vain would they offer it for ransom from the pain of the penalty on the Day of Judgment, but something will confront them from God which they could never have counted upon! For the evils of their deeds will confront them, and they will be encircled by that at which they used to mock!

*Islam.* Qur'an 39.47-48

Upon that Day men shall issue in scatterings to
see their works,
And whoso has done an atom's weight of good
shall see it,
And whoso has done an atom's weight of evil
shall see it.

*Islam.* Qur'an 99.6-8

And it is requisite with the justice of God that men should be judged according to their works; and if their works were good in this life, and the desires of their hearts were good, that they should also, in the last day, be restored unto that which is good.

And if their works are evil they shall be restored unto them for evil. Therefore, all things shall be restored to their proper order, every thing to its natural frame—mortality raised to immortality, corruption to incorruption—raised to endless happiness to inherit the kingdom of God, or to endless misery to inherit the kingdom of the devil, the one on one hand, the other on the other.

*Church of Jesus Christ of Latter-day Saints.*
Book of Mormon, Alma 41.3-4

Alike of you is he who conceals his speech, and he who proclaims it, he who hides himself in the night, and he who sallies forth by day; he has attendant angels, before him and behind him, watching over him by God's command.

*Islam.* Qur'an 13.10-11

The Exalted One says, "There are no special doors for calamity and happiness [in men's lot]; they come as men themselves call them. Their recompenses follow good and evil as the shadow follows the substance."

**Qur'an 2.284:** Cf. Qur'an 14.38, p. 70. God's attributes of justice and mercy are often in seeming contradiction; see Abot 3.19, p. 493; Rig Veda 7.86.1-4, p. 643.

**Matthew 16.27:** Cf. Matthew 25.31-46, p. 699; 13.47-50, p. 780.

**Yasna 43.5:** Cf. Yasna 48.4, p. 290. The 'final goal of life' will come at the Last Judgment—see Yasna 30.8-10, pp. 780-81.

**Qur'an 39.47-48:** Cf. Qur'an 69.13-37, pp. 781, and similar passages on the last judgment.

**Qur'an 13.10-11:** Cf. Qur'an 41.30-31, p. 257; 50.17-19, p. 243. Atharva Veda 4.16.4, p. 71, speaks of Varuna's envoys who spy out the doings of men.

Accordingly, in heaven and earth there are spirits that take account of men's transgressions, and, according to the lightness or gravity of their offenses, take away from their term of life. When that term is curtailed, men become poor and reduced, and meet with many sorrows and afflictions. All people hate them; punishments and calamities attend them; good luck and occasions for felicitation shun them; evil stars send down misfortune on them. When their term of life is exhausted they die.

*Taoism.* Treatise on Response and Retribution 1-2

❖

**Treatise on Response and Retribution 1-2:** In popular Chinese religion, the Spirit of the Hearth ascends to Heaven annually to report on the deeds which transpired in that family, at which time a determination is made on each individual's span of life; see Tract of the Quiet Way, p. 243. Compare Qur'an 39.42, p. 235; Igbo Consecration, p. 550.

CHAPTER 3

# THE PURPOSE OF LIFE FOR THE INDIVIDUAL

THE PURPOSE OF HUMAN LIFE IS AN IDEAL which transcends the mundane goals of human existence, for it is based upon the vision of God or Ultimate Reality. The beatific vision, divine joy, and uniting with the divine will or divine nature are some of the ways in which this purpose is expressed. At the same time, since the human being is grounded in this Ultimate, the purpose of life coheres with the essential nature of human beings. The highest and best of human values—love, truth, beauty, goodness, joy, and happiness—are aspirations grounded in the original human nature. Therefore, the purpose of life may also be conceived as the realization of what is most essentially human. That is, true human beings manifest the Ultimate in themselves, through manifesting the perfections of purity, wisdom, impartiality, integrity, and compassion in their own lives. The fulfillment of humanity is also the sanctification of humanity.

The first section in this chapter describes the purpose of life as the desire of all people for happiness and especially inner satisfaction. The beatific vision, divine bliss, Nirvana, and the joys of heaven are incomparably more desirable than the joy that comes with the satisfaction of mundane desires. In the second section, we turn to the purpose of life as determined from its divine source. Especially in monotheistic religions where God is the Creator and humans are creatures, the purpose for human life flows from the purpose for God's creating. We may speak of the purpose to do God's will, to glorify and return joy to God.

In the next three sections the purpose of life is considered from the point of view of the intrinsic nature of the human person. The third section gathers passages on the human being as the image of God or the dwelling place of God. The fourth section discusses humanity's intrinsic goodness: the innocence of a child and the inner compass that is the conscience. The fifth section gathers passages on the original mind, the true Self or Buddha nature; its realization is the goal of the spiritual life. This most essential Self is far from the ordinary egoistic meaning of the self: free of conceptualizations, desires, or egoistic grasping, it may also be characterized as without self or No-mind.

Finally, we turn to the purpose of life understood as the realization of the divine perfections. The sixth section expresses the ideal for human existence as a state of holiness, perfection, or sanctification. The person who attains such a stage of maturity knows at all times an abiding unity with the Absolute. He or she is unaffected by self-centered desires and unmoved by praise or blame from others; the mind is absolutely unified and clear. The final section describes the perfection of human existence as revealed in the person who has deep love and compassion for others. The saint is known for his overflowing love, which has its source in the divine ground of his existence.

The purposes of human life encompass the human being not only as an individual, but also as a social being and as a participant in the web of all life. We find identity, meaning, and fulfillment in relationships of family and community. Thus religions define correct social roles and promote the ideals of social harmony, justice, and peace. Furthermore, human beings have a purpose in relation to nature. We must protect and enhance our environment while at the same time cultivating it and harvesting its riches. Finally, human beings have an ultimate destiny, sometimes expressed in terms of personal immortality and sometimes as a final merging with the Absolute. These additional dimensions of human life and its purposes will be treated in subsequent chapters.

# *Joy and Happiness*

THE SEARCH FOR HAPPINESS is basic to human life, and to the purpose of religion as well. This first section brings together passages dealing with the religious experience of transcendental joy through union with Ultimate Reality or the realization of one's true mind. This state may be characterized as bliss (Skt. *ananda*) or Nirvana; it is a reality beyond any suffering. Scriptures of all religions depict and extol the ultimate goal of the religious journey as a state of intoxicating joy.

The section opens with passages which extol the bliss which is the final goal of the spiritual life. A second group of passages assert how heavenly joys are in every way superior to mundane pleasures, and then various degrees of happiness are discerned, depending upon the level of one's spiritual awareness. The highest level is attained only with the complete cessation of self-centered desires and denial of self in relation to the Absolute. The last group of passages recommend that one live in a state of contentment, joy, and praise, even as one pursues the path to ultimate bliss; a heart filled with bliss is itself a prerequisite for realizing higher, more refined states of divine happiness.

Thou dost show me the path of life;
in thy presence there is fulness of joy,
in thy right hand are pleasures for evermore.

*Judaism* and *Christianity*. Psalm 16.11

No person knows what delights of the eye are kept hidden for them—as a reward for their good deeds.

*Islam*. Qur'an 32.17

No eye has seen, nor ear heard,
nor the heart of man conceived,
what God has prepared for those who love him.

*Christianity*. 1 Corinthians 2.9

I created you human beings because I desired to see you lead a joyous life.

*Tenrikyo*. Ofudesaki 14.25

Those who believe, and whose hearts find satisfaction in the remembrance of God: for without doubt, in the remembrance of God do hearts find satisfaction. For those who believe and work righteousness, is blessedness, and a beautiful place of return.

*Islam*. Qur'an 13.28-29

The soul which is free from the defect of karma gets to the highest point of the universe, knows all and perceives all, and obtains the transcendental bliss everlasting.

*Jainism*. Kundakunda, Pancastikaya 170

And may the sovereign Good be ours!
According as one desires bliss may one receive bliss
Through Thy most far-seeing Spirit, O Lord,
The wonders of the Good Mind which Thou wilt give as righteousness,
With the joy of long life all the days!

*Zoroastrianism*. Avesta, Yasna 43.2

Lao Tan said, "I was letting my mind wander in the beginning of things."

"What does this mean?" asked Confucius....

**Ofudesaki 14.25:** Cf. Sun Myung Moon, 6-20-82, p.94.
**Qur'an 13.28-29:** 'Blessedness' means the state of internal satisfaction and inward joy.
**Pancastikaya 170:** Cf. Acarangasutra 2.173, p. 47; Ratnakarandasravakacara 131, p. 88.

Lao Tan said, "It means to attain Perfect Beauty and Perfect Happiness. He who attains Perfect Beauty and wanders in Perfect Happiness may be called the Perfect Man."

*Taoism*. Chuang Tzu 21

At any one moment, Nirvana has neither the phenomenon of becoming, nor that of cessation, nor even the ceasing of operation of becoming and cessation. It is the manifestation of perfect rest and cessation of changes, but at the time of manifestation there is not even a concept of manifestation; so it is called the Everlasting Joy which has neither enjoyer nor non-enjoyer.

*Buddhism*. Sutra of Hui Neng 7

There is no limit to joy. Happiness has no end. When you are standing in the love of God, every cell in your body jumps for joy. You breathe in and out with the entire universe. In this state, your life is fulfilled. This is how God means us to live, intoxicated in love and joy. And through our joy, God receives his joy. The joy of man is the joy of God; and the joy of God is the joy of man.

*Unification Church*. Sun Myung Moon, 10-20-73

In spontaneous joy is rising the mystic melody;
In the holy Word my heart feels joy and perpetually disports.
In the cave of spontaneous realization is it in trance,
Stationed on a splendid high cushion.
After wandering to my home [true self] have I returned,
And all of my desires have obtained.
Devotees of God! completely fulfilled is my self,
As the Master has granted a vision of the Supreme Being,
realized by mystic illumination.

Himself is He King, Himself the multitude;
Himself the supremely liberated, Himself of joys the Relisher;
With Him seated on the throne of eternal justice,
ended is all wailing and crying.
As I have seen, such vision of Him have I conveyed—
Only those who are initiated into this mystery have its joy.
As light is merged into Divine Light, has joy come:
Nanak, servant of God, has beheld the sole, all-pervading Supreme Being.

*Sikhism*. Adi Granth, Majh, M.5, p. 97

The kingdom of God is not food and drink but righteousness and peace and joy in the Holy Spirit.

*Christianity*. Romans 14.17

You should devote yourselves to find joy in pleasures of the Dharma, and should take no pleasure in desires.

*Buddhism*. Holy Teaching of Vimalakirti 4

**Chuang Tzu 21:** Cf. Chuang Tzu 13, p. 215.

**Sutra of Hui Neng 7:** Cf. Anguttara Nikaya v.322, p. 88.

**Sun Myung Moon, 10-20-73:** Cf. Sun Myung Moon, 9-11-77, p. 415; Sun Myung Moon, 4-25-81, p. 162; Divine Principle I.1.3.1, p. 137. On the intoxication of divine bliss, see Srimad Bhagavatam 11.8, p. 545.

**Majh, M.5:** Cf. Japuji 37, p. 248.

**Romans 14.17:** Cf. Galatians 5.19-23, pp. 331-32; Analects 4.8, p. 392.

**Holy Teaching of Vimalakirti 4:** Vimalakirti goes on to elucidate the 'pleasures of the Dharma.' They are to: (1) have faith in the Buddha; (2) listen to the Dharma; (3) make offerings to the Sangha; (4) leave the five inherent desires; (5) regard the five skandhas as enemies; (6) regard the four basic elements which constitute the body as poisonous snakes; (7) keep the determination to achieve Buddhahood in one's mind; (8) respect one's teachers; (9) accumulate merits, etc. Cf. Dhammapada 290, Katha Upanishad 1.2.2, p. 485.

The Infinite is the source of joy. There is no joy in the finite. Only in the Infinite is there joy. Ask to know the Infinite.

*Hinduism.*
Chandogya Upanishad 7.23

When totally free from outer contacts
a man finds happiness in himself,
he is fully trained in God's discipline
and reaches unending bliss.
The experiences we owe to our sense of touch
are only sources of unpleasantness.
They have a beginning and an end.
A wise man takes no pleasure in them.
That man is disciplined and happy
who can prevail over the turmoil
that springs from desire and anger,
here on earth, before he leaves his body.

*Hinduism.* Bhagavad Gita 5.21-23

Diseases have hunger as their worst. Sufferings have dispositions as their worst. Knowing this in proper perspective, Freedom (*Nibbana*) is the ultimate happiness.

Of all gains, good health is the greatest. Of all wealth, contentment is the greatest. Among kinsmen, the trusty is the greatest. Freedom (*Nibbana*) is the ultimate happiness.

Having imbibed the essence of solitude and the essence of tranquillity, and imbibing the joyous essence of righteousness, one becomes free from anguish and free from evil.

*Buddhism.* Dhammapada 203-5

The bliss of lusts and heaven-world equal not
One sixteenth of the bliss of craving's ending.

*Buddhism.* Udana 11

The felicity that results from the gratification of desire, or that other purer felicity which one enjoys in heaven, does not come to even a sixteenth part of that which arises upon the abandonment of all kinds of thirst!

*Hinduism.* Mahabharata,
Shanti Parva 177

God has promised to believers... beautiful mansions in Gardens of everlasting bliss. But the greatest bliss is the good pleasure of God: that is the supreme felicity.

*Islam.* Qur'an 9.72

From Joy there is some bliss, from Perfect Joy yet more, from the Joy of cessation comes a passionless state, and the Joy of the Innate is finality. The first comes by desire for contact, the second by desire for bliss, the third from the passing of passion, and by this means the fourth is realized.

*Buddhism.* Hevajra Tantra 8.32-33

The Self-existent is the essence of all felicity... Who could live, who could breathe, if that blissful Self dwelt not within the lotus of the heart? He it is that gives joy.

Of what is the nature of joy?

Consider the lot of a young man, noble, well-read, intelligent, strong, healthy, with all the wealth of the world at his command. Assume that he is happy, and measure his joy as one unit.

One hundred times that joy is one unit of the gandharvas; but no less joy than gandharvas has the seer to whom the Self has been revealed, and who is without craving.

One hundred times the joy of the gandharvas is one unit of the joy of celestial gandharvas [angels]; but no less joy than the celestial gandharvas has the sage to whom the Self has been revealed, and who is without craving.

**Chandogya Upanishad 7.23:** Cf. Chandogya Upanishad 7.25.2, pp. 377-78; Srimad Bhagavatam 11.8, p. 545.

**Bhagavad Gita 5.21-23:** Cf. Bhagavad Gita 6.20-22, p. 603; Brihadaranyaka Upanishad 4.4.6-7, p. 658; Dhammapada 89, p. 152.

**Dhammapada 203-5:** The joy of right concentration is also mentioned as the final stage in the Noble Eightfold Path in Majjhima Nikaya iii.251-52, p. 113. This is ecstasy, which, as the word literally indicates, means to turn from the old center—whether selfishness or a dependence on the illusory or temporal—to a new and ultimate center. Cf. Anguttara Nikaya i.137, p. 378; Lotus Sutra 21, p. 137.

**Udana 11:** Cf. Udana 19-20, p. 555.

**Qur'an 9.72:** Cf. Qur'an 56.10-27, p. 248.

One hundred times the joy of the celestial gandharvas is one unit of the joy of the pitris in their paradise... joy of the devas... joy of the devas born out of sacrifice... joy of the ruling devas... joy of Indra... joy of Brihaspati... joy of Prajapati... joy of Brahma, but no less joy than Brahma has the seer to whom the Self has been revealed, and who is without craving.

It is written: He who knows the joy of Brahman, which words cannot express and the mind cannot reach, is free from fear. He is not distressed by the thought, "Why did I not do what is right? Why did I do what is wrong?" He who knows the joy of Brahman, knowing both good and evil, transcends them both.

*Hinduism.* Taittiriya Upanishad 2.7-9

Life is art.
The whole life of man is Self-expression.
The individual is an expression of God.
We suffer if we do not express ourselves.

*Perfect Liberty Kyodan.* Precepts 1-4

The Holy Spirit rests on him only who has a joyous heart.

*Judaism.* Jerusalem Talmud, Sukkat 5.1

Rabbi Baruqa of Huza often went to the marketplace at Lapet. One day, the prophet Elijah appeared to him there, and Rabbi Baruqa asked him, "Is there anyone among all these people who will have a share in the World to Come?" Elijah answered, "There is none." Later, two men came to the marketplace, and Elijah said to Rabbi Baruqa, "Those two will have a share in the World to Come!" Rabbi Baruqa asked the newcomers, "What is your occupation?" They replied, "We are clowns. When we see someone who is sad, we cheer him up. When we see two people quarreling, we try to make peace between them."

*Judaism.* Talmud, Taanit 22a

To seek gladness through righteous persistence is the way to accord with heaven and to respond to men.

*Confucianism.* I Ching 58: Joy

When one obtains happiness then one proceeds to act [perform sacrifice].
No one acts without first obtaining happiness.
Only by obtaining happiness does one act.

*Hinduism.* Chandogya Upanishad 7.22

Mother mine! Bliss have I attained in union with the Divine Master:
Spontaneously has union with the Divine Master come about—
In my mind resounds joyous music.
Fairies of the family of jewel harmony have descended to sing holy songs;
Sing all ye the Lord's song, who have lodged it in heart!
Says Nanak, Bliss have I attained on union with the Divine Master.

*Sikhism.* Ramkali, Anandu, M.3, p. 917

Let us live happily, without hate amongst those who hate. Let us dwell unhating amidst hateful men.

Let us live happily, in good health amongst those who are sick. Let us dwell in good health amidst ailing men.

Let us live happily, without yearning for sensual pleasures amongst those who yearn for them. Let us dwell without yearning amidst those who yearn.

**Taittiriya Upanishad 2.7-9:** On the joys of heaven, see Rig Veda 9.113.8-11, p. 248. On the multiple levels of spiritual realities, cf. 1 Corinthians 15.40-41, p. 226; Doctrine and Covenants 76.54-93, p. 227.

**Taanit 22a:** Cf. Matthew 5.9, p. 394.

**Chandogya Upanishad 7.22:** The proper frame of mind for engaging in worship is one of tranquillity and joy. Cf. Chuang Tzu 23, p. 524; Berakot 5.1, p. 524; Taittiriya Upanishad 1.11.3, p. 620; 2 Corinthians 9.7, p. 620; Sutta Nipata 506, p. 620.

**Ramkali, Anandu M.3:** Cf. Japuji 37, p. 248; Bilaval Chhant 2.1-2, p. 546.

Let us live happily, we who have no impediments. We shall subsist on joy even as the radiant gods.

*Buddhism*. Dhammapada 197-200

Make a joyful noise to the Lord, all the lands!
Serve the Lord with gladness!
Come into his presence with singing!
Know that the Lord is God!
It is he that made us, and we are his;
we are his people, and the sheep of his pasture.
Enter his gates with thanksgiving,
and his courts with praise!
Give thanks to him, bless his name!
For the Lord is good;
his steadfast love endures forever,
and his faithfulness to all generations.

*Judaism* and *Christianity*. Psalm 100

❖

## *For God's Good Pleasure*

AS CREATURES, HUMAN BEINGS are created with a purpose that is determined not by themselves but by their Creator. This understanding is particularly well understood in the monotheistic religions, which recognize that God's purpose for creating human beings is to find those creatures who would recognize, serve, glorify, and love him. Therefore, human beings can find fulfillment in the service of God.

In the Jewish tradition and in some new religions, the loving God himself rejoices when He is glorified and adored by human beings reflecting his image; thus we can speak of the purpose of life as fulfilled in returning joy to God. God's love for humankind blossoms into divine ecstasy as that love is multiplied and happiness spreads thoughout the human race. (On the other side of divine passion, namely God's sorrow over the evil plight of mankind, see *God's Grief*, pp. 324-27.) Analogously, in Mahayana Buddhist texts the Buddha rejoices as sentient beings are enlightened by the Dharma. In Hinduism the embodied Self within stands as the Enjoyer of all phenomena. The joy of God may be recognized as the divine counterpart to the quest for human happiness described in the previous section.

On the other hand, in religious conceptions which lack a personal God, or which stress God's absolute sovereignty, Ultimate Reality is already perfect, beyond desiring, impassible, and without need of anything. In Islam, God is often conceived of as the Sovereign Lord, high above the world and unilaterally enforcing his will on mankind. In Hindu Vedanta, God's apparent motivation for activity in the world and among human beings is *lila*, divine play. Several passages teaching the divine impassibility are given at the conclusion of this section.

I have created the jinn and humankind only that they might serve Me.

*Islam*. Qur'an 51.56

How then to become true to the Creator?
How to demolish the wall of illusion?
Through obedience to His Ordinance and
Will.

*Sikhism*. Adi Granth, Japuji 1, M.1, p. 1

Do not try to develop what is natural to man; develop what is natural to Heaven. He who develops Heaven benefits life; he who develops man injures life.

*Taoism*. Chuang Tzu 19

If it be your wish, O people, to know God and to discover the greatness of His might, look, then, upon Me with My own eyes, and not with the eyes of anyone besides Me. You will, otherwise, be never capable of recognizing Me, though you ponder My Cause as long as My Kingdom endures.

*Baha'i Faith*. Gleanings from the Writings of Baha'u'llah 127

There is one God, the Father, from whom are all things and for whom we exist.

*Christianity*. 1 Corinthians 8.6

All that God created in his world He created only for his glory, as it is said, "All that is called

**Qur'an 51.56:** Cf. Qur'an 9.72, p. 133.
**Japuji 1, M.1:** Cf. Yasna 34.12, p. 552.
**Chuang Tzu 19:** On how developing man injures life, see Chuang Tzu 17, p. 205.
**1 Corinthians 8.6:** Cf. John 6.38, p. 551.

by my name, for my glory I created and fashioned and made it" [Isaiah 43.7].

*Judaism.* Mishnah, Abot 6.11

O Lord of all, hail unto thee!
The Soul of all, causing all acts,
Enjoying all, all life art thou!
Lord of all pleasure and delight!

*Hinduism.* Maitri Upanishad 5.1

I was a secret treasure, and I created the creatures in order that I might be known.

*Islam.* Hadith

God's purpose in creating the universe was to feel happiness when He saw the purpose of goodness fulfilled in the Heavenly Kingdom, which the whole creation, including man, could have established.... The purpose of the universe's existence centered on man is to return joy to God, the Creator.

*Unification Church.* Divine Principle I.1.3.1

O Son of Man! Veiled in My immemorial being and in the ancient eternity of My essence, I knew My love for thee; therefore I created thee, have engraved on thee Mine image, and revealed to thee My beauty.

*Baha'i Faith.* Hidden Words of Baha'u'llah, Arabic 3

Happiness is spiritual, born of Truth and Love. It is unselfish; therefore it cannot exist alone, but requires all mankind to share it.

*Christian Science.* Science and Health, 57

God longs to hear the prayer of the righteous.

*Judaism.* Talmud, Yebamot 64a

When all human beings have accomplished the purification of their minds and come to lead a life full of joy, I, Tsukihi [God], will become cheered up. And when I become cheered up, so will all human beings. When the minds of all the world become cheered up, God and human beings will become altogether cheered up in one accord.

*Tenrikyo.* Ofudesaki 7.109-11

Those who can hold to this scripture
Shall cause me and the emanations of my body,
As well as the Buddha Many Jewels, now
passed into extinction,
All without exception to rejoice.
The Buddhas of the present in all ten quarters,
As well as those of past and future,
They shall both see and shower with offerings,
Enabling them, too, to gain joy.

*Buddhism.* Lotus Sutra 21

You shall no more be termed Forsaken,
and your land shall no more be termed
Desolate;
but you shall be called My Delight is in Her,
and your land Married;
for the Lord delights in you,
and your land shall be married.
For as a young man marries a virgin,
so shall your sons marry you,
and as the bridegroom rejoices over the bride,
so shall your God rejoice over you.

*Judaism* and *Christianity.* Isaiah 62.4-5

Ever is He in bliss, ever fulfilled.

*Sikhism.* Adi Granth, Japuji 3, M.1, p. 2

**Hadith:** Cf. Qur'an 89.27-30, p. 392.

**Divine Principle I.1.3.1:** Cf. Sun Myung Moon 2-12-61, p. 74; 6-20-82, p. 94; 10-20-73, p. 132.

**Hidden Words of Baha'u'llah, Arabic 3:** Cf. Gleanings from the Writings of Baha'u'llah 27, pp. 215-16.

**Science and Health, 57:** Cf. Brihadaranyaka Upanishad 1.4.17 and 1.4.3, p. 174.

**Yebamot 64a:** Cf. Hosea 11.1-9, pp. 326-27; Matthew 23.37, p. 325.

**Ofudesaki 7.109-11:** Cf. Ofudesaki 17.64-70, p. 326.

**Lotus Sutra 21:** The 'Buddha Many Jewels' is the Buddha called Prabhutaratna, who symbolically represents the Dharma. The Buddha and his emanations will enjoy ecstasy, which is an element of the latter stages in the Noble Eightfold Path—cf. Majjhima Nikaya iii.251-52, p. 113.

**Isaiah 62.4-5:** Cf. Revelation 21.1-7, pp. 794-95.

**Japuji 3:** Cf. Majh, M.5, p. 132.

O mankind! It is you that have need of God: but God is the One Free of all wants, worthy of all praise.

*Islam.* Qur'an 35.15

Brahma's creative activity is not undertaken by way of any need on his part, but simply by way of sport.

*Hinduism.* Vedanta Sutra 2.1.32-33

We created not the heaven and the earth and all that is between them in play. If We had wished to find a pastime, We could have found it in Our presence—if We ever did. Nay, but We hurl the true against the false, and it prevails over it, and lo! [the false] vanishes... To Him belongs whosoever is in the heavens and the earth. And those who dwell in His presence are not too proud to worship Him, nor do they weary.

*Islam.* Qur'an 21.16-19

❖

**Vedanta Sutra 2.1.32-33:** Cf. Chandogya Upanishad 7.23-25, p. 61.

## *Image of God and Temple of God*

THE ORIGINAL HUMAN NATURE OR DIVINE SELF within every person is the topic of the next three sections. Some such concept is found universally, yet there are important distinctions and different emphases among the various religions. This section contains passages depicting humans as reflecting the image of God, as temples of God, and as dwelling places of God's Spirit. These include psychological and metaphysical claims of man's likeness to divinity and exhortations to become the image of God as an ideal of holiness.

In Judaism and Christianity, human beings are regarded as created in the image of God (*imago dei*) and meant to be the home for God's indwelling Spirit. Christians disagree, however, on the extent to which the image of God has been damaged by the Fall of Man (the Original Sin); see *Degraded Human Nature*, pp. 321-23. Conservative Protestants in the Calvinist tradition regard the damage as so severe that humans cannot be good or have a relationship with God without the added grace of Christ. Catholic, Orthodox, and liberal Protestant Christians still see vestiges of the imago dei in fallen humanity, giving all people the intuitive ability to judge right from wrong and to know God.

There is wider agreement when the image of God is presented as an ideal of holiness. Confucian, Jewish, Christian, and Shinto scriptures speak of the saint or superior man as one who is like unto Heaven, or a Buddha, or one who manifests the character of God.

In Hindu and Sikh scriptures the *Atman* or Self is the immutable and ever-present manifestation of Ultimate Reality immanent in each person. Most people live in ignorance of the Self, act entirely from the motives of egoism, and are enchained by their karma; hence to realize the true Self is liberation. This is an ontological assertion about what is most essentially human; since humans are essentially Spirit they should not make the error of identifying themselves with matter. The Metaphysical Movement in the nineteenth century spawned new religions which hold a similar view; among them are Christian Science, Seicho-no-Ie, and (with significant differences) the Church of Jesus Christ of Latter-day Saints.

God said, "Let us make man in our image, after our likeness."

*Judaism* and *Christianity*. Genesis 1.26

If we keep unperverted the human heart—which is like unto heaven and received from earth—that is God.

*Shinto*. Revelation to Emperor Seiwa

**Genesis 1.26:** The plural has been variously understood as the persons of the Trinity, God speaking to his angels, or the plural of majesty.

**Revelation to Emperor Seiwa:** Finding kami within is discovering the reality of one's own nature. This quotation shows the influence of the Buddhist concept of Buddha nature. The Shinto flavor comes in the linking of heaven and earth—like the rope which links the shrine (symbol of the divine presence) and the worshipper.

Every being has the Buddha Nature. This is the self.

*Buddhism.* Mahaparinirvana Sutra 214

That which is the finest essence—this whole world has that as its soul. That is Reality. That is the Self. That art thou.

*Hinduism.* Chandogya Upanishad 6.8.7

Conform yourselves to the character of God.

*Islam.* Hadith of Abu Nuaym

Fire blazing from the earth.
The superior man reflects in his person the
glory of [Heaven's] virtue.

*Confucianism.* I Ching 35: Progress

You, therefore, must be perfect, as your heavenly Father is perfect.

*Christianity.* Matthew 5.48

And the Lord said to Moses, "Say to all the congregation of the people of Israel, 'You shall be holy; for I the Lord your God am holy.'"

*Judaism* and *Christianity.* Leviticus 19.1-2

As God is called merciful and gracious, so you be merciful and gracious, offering gifts gratis to all; as the Lord is called righteous and loving, so you be righteous and loving.

*Judaism.* Sifre Deuteronomy 85a

Beloved is man, for he was created in the image of God. But it was by a special love that it was made known to him that he was created in the image of God.

*Judaism.* Mishnah, Abot 3.18

Father, O mighty Force,
That Force which is in everything,
Come down between us, fill us,
Until we become like thee,
Until we become like thee.

*African Traditional Religions.* Susu Prayer (Guinea)

"Now what do you think, Vasettha... is Brahma in possession of wives and wealth, or is he not?"

"He is not, Gotama."

"Is his mind full of anger, or free from anger?"

"Free from anger, Gotama."

"Is his mind full of malice, or free from malice?"

"Free from malice, Gotama."

"Is his mind tarnished, or is it pure?"

"It is pure, Gotama."

"Has he self-mastery, or has he not?"

"He has, Gotama."

"Now what do you think, Vasettha, are the brahmins versed in the Vedas in possession of wives and wealth, or are they not?"

"They are, Gotama."

"Have they anger in their hearts, or have they not?"

"They have, Gotama."

"Do they bear malice, or do they not?"

"They do, Gotama."

"Are they pure in heart, or are they not?"

"They are not, Gotama."

**Mahaparinirvana Sutra 214:** The Buddha nature is not an ontological immanent Being, as in the following passage from the Upanishads, but is rather a quality of thought and action that is pure and participates fully in the Buddha's wisdom and compassion. See the longer passage on p. 147. Compare "This very mind is Buddha," Mumonkan 30, p. 74; also Sutra of Hui Neng 1, p. 146.

**Chandogya Upanishad 6.8.7:** See also Bhagavad Gita 10.41, Kena Upanishad 1.1-2, p. 75.

**I Ching 35:** Cf. I Ching, Great Commentary 1.4.3, p. 153; also Sutra of Forty-two Sections 15, p. 153; Doctrine of the Mean 20.18, p. 154.

**Matthew 5.48:** See Matthew 5.43-48, p. 705; John 1.18, p. 50; Sun Myung Moon, 8-26-86, p. 196; 10-20-73, p. 94.

**Leviticus 19.1-2:** This is a particularly important foundational verse for the Jewish ethic of holiness—to be in the image of God. See the rabbinic passages which follow and Sifra 93d, p. 681.

**Susu Prayer:** Cf. Acts 17.27-28, p. 72.

"Have they self-mastery, or have they not?"

"They have not, Gotama."

"Can there, then, be agreement and likeness between the brahmins with their wives and property, and Brahma, who has none of these things?"

"Certainly not, Gotama!"

"Then that these brahmins versed in the Vedas, who also live married and wealthy, should after death, when the body is dissolved, become united with Brahma, who has none of these things—such a condition of things is impossible!"...

"Now what do you think, Vasettha, will the bhikkhu who lives [according to the Dhamma] be in possession of women and of wealth, or will he not?"

"He will not, Gotama!"

"Will he be full of anger, or free from anger?"

"He will be free from anger, Gotama!"

"Will his mind be full of malice, or free from malice?"

"Free from malice, Gotama!"

"Will his mind be tarnished, or pure?"

"It will be pure, Gotama!"

"Will he have self-mastery, or will he not?"

"Surely he will, Gotama!"

"Then as you say, the bhikkhu is free from household and worldly cares, free from anger, free from malice, pure in mind, and master of himself; and Brahma also is free from household and worldly cares, free from anger, free from malice, pure in mind, and master of himself. Is there then agreement and likeness between the bhikkhu and Brahma?"

"There is, Gotama!"

"Then verily, that the bhikkhu who is free from household cares should after death, when the body is dissolved, become united with Brahma, who is the same—such a condition of things is in every way possible!"

*Buddhism.* Digha Nikaya xiii.31-34, 80
Tevijja Sutta

I have breathed into man of My spirit.

*Islam.* Qur'an 15.29

Let a man always consider himself as if the Holy One dwells within him.

*Judaism.* Talmud, Taanit 11b

I have been crucified with Christ; it is no longer I who live, but Christ who lives in me.

*Christianity.* Galatians 2.20

Do you not know that you are God's temple and that God's Spirit dwells in you?... For God's temple is holy, and that temple you are.

*Christianity.* 1 Corinthians 3.16-17

Just as God fills the whole world, so the soul fills the body. Just as God sees, but is not seen, so the soul sees, but is not itself seen. Just as God feeds the whole world, so the soul feeds the whole body. Just as God is pure, so the soul is pure. Just as God dwells in the innermost precincts [of the Temple], so also the soul dwells in the innermost part of the body.

*Judaism.* Talmud, Berakot 10a

**Tevijja Sutta:** The Buddha did not himself maintain the existence of Brahma as the supreme God; for no supreme God can be found in Emptiness. Yet the principle at issue is affirmed: the arahant is in the image of Ultimate Reality since the arahant in his own being is empty. Cf. Heart Sutra, pp. 416-17. This argument is an example of the Buddha's skill in means, expressing the truth of Buddhism in terms suitable to a Hindu who believes in Brahma.

**Galatians 2.20:** With the coming of Christ, divinity entered humanity and humanity became deified. For Christians of the Orthodox faith, the highest goal is divinization, oneness with Christ. As St. Athanasius taught: in Jesus Christ, God became man that man might be drawn back into the divine harmony. Cf. John 14.15-21, p. 462.

**1 Corinthians 3.16-17:** Every human being is meant to be a holy temple of God. This also applies to the body, which should never suffer defilement; cf. 1 Corinthians 6.13-19, p. 336-37.

The rich build temples to Shiva,
What shall I, a poor man, do?
O my Lord! my legs are the pillars,
My torso, the shrine,
And my head, the golden pinnacle!
Things standing shall fall,
But the moving ever shall stay!

*Hinduism.* Basavanna, Vacana 820

The deity is immanent in man and man is inherent in the deity; there is neither the divine nor the human; there is no difference in essence at all between them.

*Shinto.* Genchi Kato

Smaller than the smallest, greater than the greatest, this Self forever dwells within the hearts of all. When a man is free from desire, his mind and senses purified, he beholds the glory of the Self and is without sorrow.

Though seated, he travels far; though at rest, he moves all things. Who but the purest of the pure can realize this Effulgent Being, who is joy and who is beyond joy.

Formless is he, though inhabiting form. In the midst of the fleeting he abides forever. All-pervading and supreme is the Self. The wise man, knowing him in his true nature, transcends all grief.

*Hinduism.* Katha Upanishad 1.2.20-22

This is a wonderful, unique discourse:
The living self is the image of the Supreme Being.
It is neither old nor a child;
Neither it suffers pain, nor in death's snare is caught;
It is not shattered nor dies;
In all time it is pervasive.
It feels not heat nor cold;
Neither has it friend nor foe;
It feels not joy nor sorrow:
All is its own; to it belongs all might.
It has neither father nor mother;
Beyond the limits of matter has it ever existed.
Of sin and goodness it feels not the touch—
Within the heart of each being it is ever awake.

*Sikhism.* Adi Granth, Gaund, M.5, p. 868

Bright but hidden, the Self dwells in the heart.
Everything that moves, breathes, opens, and closes
Lives in the Self. He is the source of love
And may be known through love but not through thought.
He is the goal of life. Attain this goal!

The shining Self dwells hidden in the heart.
Everything in the cosmos, great and small,
Lives in the Self. He is the source of life,
Truth beyond the transience of this world.
He is the goal of life. Attain this goal!

*Hinduism.* Mundaka Upanishad 2.2.1-2

What is man?
Man is not matter; he is not made up of brain, blood, bones, and other material elements. The Scriptures inform us that man is made in the image and likeness of God. Matter is not that likeness. The likeness of Spirit cannot be so unlike Spirit. Man is spiritual and perfect; and because he is spiritual and perfect, he must be so understood in Christian Science. Man is idea, the image, of Love; he is not physique.

*Christian Science.* Science and Health, 475

Become fully aware of the true image of man:
Man is spirit,
Man is life,
Man is deathless.

God is the light source of man,
And man is the light that came from God.
There is neither light source without light,
Nor light without a light source.

**Vacana 820:** Indian temples are traditionally built in the image of the human body, which is the primordial blueprint of the cosmos. In Lingayat Shaivism, the body itself becomes a temple of Shiva in private worship—see Vacana 743, p. 610. Indeed, to overcome the formalization of temple worship, we should return to the living original temple.

**Katha Upanishad 1.2.20-22:** Cf. Mundaka Upanishad 2.2.10-11, p. 74; Kena Upanishad 1.1-2, p. 75.

Just as light and its light source are one,
So man and God are one.

God is Spirit; therefore, man is also spirit.
God is Love; therefore, man is also love.
God is Wisdom; therefore, man is also wisdom.
Spirit is not material in nature;
Love is not material in nature;
Wisdom is not material in nature.

Therefore, man, who is spirit, love, and wisdom, is in no way related to matter.

*Seicho-no-Ie*. Nectarean Shower of Holy Doctrines 48-49

Man was also in the beginning with God. Intelligence, or the light of truth, was not created or made, neither indeed can be. All truth is independent in that sphere in which God has placed it, to act for itself, as all intelligence also; otherwise there is no existence.

Behold, here is the agency of man, and here is the condemnation of man; because that which was from the beginning is plainly manifest unto them, and they receive not the light. And every man whose spirit receiveth not the light is under condemnation.

For man is spirit. The elements are eternal, and spirit and element, inseparably connected, receive a fulness of joy; and when separated, man cannot receive a fulness of joy. The elements are the tabernacle of God; yea, man is the tabernacle of God, even temples; and whatsoever temple is defiled, God shall destroy that temple.

*Church of Jesus Christ of Latter-day Saints*. Doctrine and Covenants 93.29-35

❖

**Nectarean Shower of Holy Doctrines:** In his expressions Taniguchi, the founder of Seicho-no-Ie, is influenced by Christian terminology. Yet the thought is still rooted in the fusion of Shinto and Buddhist traditions of popular Japanese religion.

**Doctrine and Covenants 93.29-35:** While the human person is essentially spirit or Intelligence, matter and the body also have a positive role. As in the Christian tradition generally, scriptures of the Latter-day Saints teach that Spirit must be enfleshed to produce God's temple and in order that humans may realize their full purpose.

# *Inborn Goodness and Conscience*

WE CONTINUE THE THEME of the original human nature with passages on the essential goodness of human beings. Confucianism, for example, regards the original heart of man as inherently good and characterized by benevolence (*jen*); this is illustrated by the well-known passage from Mencius about people's spontaneous reactions to a child falling into a well. Islam likewise regards human nature as inherently upright, and St. Paul wrote of the human conscience, which allows even those unacquainted with religion or moral teachings to distinguish right from wrong. We begin, however, with a group of passages on the ideal of the little child, whose innocence and purity allows him or her to easily and naturally grasp the truth. On the converse, the innate sinfulness of man, see *Ill*, pp. 270-74.

Every child is born of the nature of purity and submission to God.

*Islam*. Hadith of Bukhari

God needs no pointing out to a child.

*African Traditional Religions*. Akan Proverb (Ghana)

Mencius said, "The great man is he who does not lose his child's heart."

*Confucianism*. Mencius IV.B.12

Every spirit of man was innocent in the beginning; and God having redeemed man from the fall, man became again, in their infant state, innocent before God.

*Church of Jesus Christ of Latter-day Saints*. Doctrine and Covenants 93.38

At that time the disciples came to Jesus, saying, "Who is the greatest in the kingdom of heaven?" And calling to him a child, he put him in the midst of them, and said, "Truly, I say to you, unless you turn and become like children, you will never enter the kingdom of heaven."

*Christianity*. Matthew 18.1-3

Gentleness and goodness are the roots of humanity.

*Confucianism*. Book of Ritual 38.18

Religion is basically virtue, which is grounded ultimately in the spiritual nature of man.

*Jainism*. Kundakunda, Pravacanasara 7

So set your purpose for religion as a man by nature upright—the nature [framed] of God, in which He has created man. There is no altering the laws of God's creation. That is the right religion.

*Islam*. Qur'an 30.30

You may not see yourself growing up, but you definitely know it when you are sinning.

*African Traditional Religions*. Akan Proverb (Ghana)

**Mencius IV.B.12:** Cf. Tao Te Ching 55, p. 156; 20, p. 434.

**Doctrine and Covenants 93.38:** This is an argument against the need for infant baptism. Christ has already redeemed mankind from the original sin, and hence all people start out innocent at birth.

**Matthew 18.1-3:** Christians do not take this text to mean that the original nature of man is innocent. Rather, the child exemplifies an attitude of simplicity and innocence by which one can easily accept the gospel; cf. Luke 18.16-17, p. 648.

**Book of Ritual 38.18:** But the initial goodness is ordinarily corrupted; see Book of Songs, Ode 255, p. 274.

**Pravacanasara 7:** Cf. Gomattasara, pp. 321-22.

**Qur'an 30.30:** See also Qur'an 12.53, p. 273.

Wabisah ibn Ma'bad said, "I went to see the Messenger of God and he said to me, 'You want to question me on the subject of virtue?' 'Yes,' I replied, and he went on, 'Question your heart. Virtue is that by which the soul enjoys repose and the heart tranquillity. Sin is what introduces trouble into the soul and tumult into man's bosom—and this despite the religious advice which men may give you.' "

*Islam*. Forty Hadith of an-Nawawi 27

When Gentiles who have not the Law do by nature what the Law requires, they are a law to themselves, even though they do not have the Law. They show that what the Law requires is written on their hearts, while their conscience also bears witness and their conflicting thoughts accuse or perhaps excuse them on that day when, according to my gospel, God judges the secrets of men by Christ Jesus.

*Christianity*. Romans 2.14-16

We are the pitiful prisoners of sin, totally ignorant of the most precious and intimate being and master whom we would never trade for everything in heaven and earth. That master is one's own conscience. How often has this conscience given us advice, and while we were immersed in sinful thinking day and night it tirelessly helped us to cross the river to safety.

*Unification Church*.
Sun Myung Moon, 3-30-90

Mencius said, "All men have this heart that, when they see another man suffer, they suffer, too. The ancient kings had this heart: when they saw men suffer, they suffered, too. Therefore the former kings ran a government that, when it saw men suffer, it suffered, too. With a heart such as that... they could rule the empire as if it were something they turned in the palm of their hand.

"What do I mean, 'All men have this heart, that when they see another man suffer, they suffer too?' Well, take an example: a man looks out; a child is about to fall into a well. No matter who the man is, his heart will flip-flop, and he will feel the child's predicament; and not because he expects to get something out of it from the child's parents, or because he wants praise from his neighbors, associates, or friends, or because he is afraid of a bad name, or anything like that.

"From this we can see that it is not human not to have a heart that sympathizes with pain. Likewise not to have a heart that is repelled by vice: that is not human, either. Not to have a heart that is willing to defer: that's not human. And not to have a heart that discriminates between true and false is not human, either.

"What is the foundation of natural human feeling for others (*jen*)? The heart that sympathizes with pain. What is the foundation of a commitment to the common good (*i*)? The heart that is repelled by vice. What is the foundation of respect for social and religious forms (*li*)? The heart that is willing to defer. And what is the foundation for a liberal education (*chih*)? The heart that can tell true from false.

"People have these four foundations like they have four limbs. A man who says he cannot practice them is calling himself a criminal. A man who says the ruler cannot practice that is calling the ruler a criminal.

"Everybody has these four foundations in himself. If these four foundations can be filled in on a broad scale, it will be like a fire starting up, it will be like a spring bursting through. If they can be filled in, it will be enough to create and preserve the world order. Leave them unfilled, it will be impossible for a man to take care of his father and mother."

Confucianism. Mencius II.A.6

**Romans 2.14-16:** The conscience is that universal attribute of man that allows everyone to recognize the truth. Yet at the same time, everyone is afflicted by sin; see Romans 3.9-12, p. 273; 1 John 1.8, p. 272.

**Sun Myung Moon, 3-30-90:** Cf. Romans 7.15-24, p. 278; Chandogya Upanishad 8.12.1, p. 275.

**Mencius II.A.6:** Mencius lists the four Confucian virtues: benevolence (*jen*), dutifulness or concern for the public good (*i*), observance of proper social and religious forms (*li*), and education (*chih*). They are all founded upon germs which lie in the heart of every person.

## *Original Mind, No-mind*

THE ORIGINAL MIND OR TRUE SELF of the human being is the proper ground of enlightenment. This intrinsic essence of mind is inherently pure and good, and in Christian terms it can be said to participate in the Kingdom of God. In Eastern traditions it is prior to thought, prior to desire, prior to any conceptualization at all. It is discovered by stripping away all sensation, desire, concepts, intellection, volition, and awareness of "I." It partakes of the Oneness of all. Buddhism calls this mind the Buddha nature, and much of Buddhist practice is aimed at its realization. They also call it No-mind because it is without any grasping at a (selfish) self. Taoists agree, and seek to strip away all intellection and formalism in order to arrive at the spontaneous activity of the natural man who lives at one with the Tao of the universe. Some of the passages here criticize pious attempts to delineate a true nature of man based on doctrinal or formal criteria like Goodness or Benevolence, saying they only increase delusion by imposing artificial obstructions in the way of the functioning of the true self. Instead, all attachments must be stripped away until there is nothing but emptiness. Then the heart can be heard. Cf. *Immanent*, pp. 72-75.

That which is the finest essence—this whole world has that as its soul. That is Reality. That is the Self (*Atman*). That art thou.

*Hinduism*. Chandogya Upanishad 6.8.7

For him who... knows his own mind and sees intuitively his own nature, he is a Hero, a Teacher of gods and men, a Buddha.

*Buddhism*. Sutra of Hui Neng 1

The kingdom of God is not coming with signs to be observed, nor will they say, "Lo, here it is!" or "There!" for behold, the kingdom of God is within you.

*Christianity*. Luke 17.20-21

The Plain of High Heaven is not a specific place localized here or there, but refers rather to a pure state without any anomaly or excess. In terms of the human body, it is a state within the human breast without thought, contemplation, or passions.

*Shinto*. Masamichi Imbe, Secret Oral Tradition of the Book of the Divine Age

One may understand the true nature of the Tirthankara.... One may have interest in and devotion to the scripture. One may have self-control and penance. With all these, if one is not capable of realizing his own true self, to him Nirvana is beyond reach.

*Jainism*. Kundakunda, Pancastikaya 170

**Chandogya Upanishad 6.8.7:** Cf. Isha Upanishad 15-16, p. 47; Mundaka Upanishad 3.1.7, pp. 72-73; Majh Ashtpadi M.3, p. 72.

**Sutra of Hui Neng 1:** Cf. Sutra of Hui Neng 2, p. 381; 6, p. 73; Mumonkan 30, p. 74; Meditation on Buddha Amitayus 17, p. 462.

**Luke 17.20-21:** This passage has been interpreted in various ways by exegetes. The words 'within you' can also be translated 'in the midst of you,' in which case the passage means that the people should regard Jesus and his community which dwells among them as the incipient kingdom. But the more mystical meaning of the passage is that the kingdom is within the minds and hearts of believers.

**Secret Oral Tradition:** Cf. Records of the Enthronement of the Two Imperial Deities at Ise, p. 594.

**Pancastikaya 170:** Cf. Tattvarthasutra 1.19-29, p. 572; Svetasvatara Upanishad 4.8, p. 575.

Ordinary men and ignorant people understand neither the Essence of Mind nor the Pure Land within themselves, so they wish to be born in the East or the West[ern Paradise]. But to the enlightened, everywhere is the same. As the Buddha said, "No matter where they happen to be, they are always happy and comfortable." If your mind is free from evil, the West is not far from here; but difficult indeed it would be for one whose heart is impure to be born there by invoking Amitabha!

*Buddhism*. Sutra of Hui Neng 3

Is it not the fact that there is in the body a clot of blood which, if it is in good condition, the whole body is, too; and if it is in rotten condition, so too is the whole body? Is not this the heart?

*Islam*. Forty Hadith of an-Nawawi 6

Your eye is the lamp of your body; when your eye is sound, your whole body is full of light; but when it is not sound, your body is full of darkness. Therefore be careful lest the light in you be darkness. If then your whole body is full of light, having no part dark, it will be wholly bright, as when a lamp with its rays gives you light.

*Christianity*. Luke 11.34-36

As one not knowing that a golden treasure lies buried beneath his feet may walk over it again and again, yet never find it, so all beings live every moment in the city of Brahman, yet never find him because of the veil of illusion by which he is concealed.

*Hinduism*. Chandogya Upanishad 8.3.2

Every being has the Buddha Nature. This is the self. Such a self is, since the very beginning, under cover of innumerable illusions. That is why a man cannot see it. O good man! There was a poor woman who had gold hidden somewhere in her house, but no one knew where it was. But there was a stranger who, by expediency, speaks to the poor woman, "I shall employ you to weed the lawn." The woman answered, "I cannot do it now, but if you show my son where the gold is hidden, I will work for you." The man says, "I know the way; I will show it to your son." The woman replies, "No one in my house, big or small, knows where the gold is hidden. How can you know?" The man then digs out the hidden gold and shows it to the woman. She is glad, and begins to respect him. O good man! The same is the case with a man's Buddha Nature. No one can see it. It is like the gold which the poor woman possessed and yet could not locate. I now let people see the Buddha Nature which they possess, but which was hidden by illusions. The Tathagata shows all beings the storehouse of enlightenment, which is the cask of true gold—their Buddha Nature.

*Buddhism*. Mahaparinirvana Sutra 214-15: Parable of the Hidden Treasure

The Purpose of the one true God, exalted be His glory, in revealing Himself unto men is to lay bare those gems that lie hidden within the mine of their true and inmost selves.

*Baha'i Faith*. Gleanings from the Writings of Baha'u'llah 132

When you pursue your original mind, you should be able to hear moral laws and see divinity in your mind's eye. You should be able to feel and touch the heart of God with your mind.

*Unification Church*. Sun Myung Moon, 4-14-57

**Sutra of Hui Neng 3:** Here is a criticism of Pure Land Buddhism with its emphasis on salvation by faith in the vow of Amitabha Buddha; cf. Larger Sukhavativyuha Sutra 8.18, p. 457.

**Forty Hadith of an-Nawawi 6:** Cf. Qur'an 22.46, p. 283; Black Elk, pp. 381-82.

**Luke 11.34-36:** Cf. Bhagavad Gita 5.15-16, p. 381.

**Chandogya Upanishad 8.3.2 and Mahaparinirvana Sutra 214-15:** Variations of this parable are found in many Buddhist sutras—see the Parable of a Gem in the Lapel in Lotus Sutra 8, p. 382. On the original (divine) nature buried within, cf. Isha Upanishad 15-16, p. 47; Sutra of Hui Neng 6, p. 73; Mumonkan 30, p. 74; also Kena Upanishad 1.1-2, p. 75; Svetasvatara Upanishad 1.11-12, p. 414; Luke 11.34-36, p. 381.

The Lord takes his stand upon
hearing, sight, touch, taste, smell,
and upon the mind.
He enjoys what mind and senses enjoy.

Deluded men cannot trace his course.
Only the eye of wisdom sees him
clothed in the states of existence, going forth,
being in the body, or taking in experience.
Disciplined men can also make an effort
and see his presence in themselves.

*Hinduism.* Bhagavad Gita 15.9-11

Passions consist of conceptualizations. The ultimate non-existence of these conceptualizations and imaginary fabrications—that is the purity that is the intrinsic nature of the mind. Misapprehensions are passions. The ultimate absence of misapprehensions is the intrinsic nature of mind. The presumption of self is passion. The absence of self is the intrinsic nature of mind.

*Buddhism.* Holy Teaching of Vimalakirti 3

"What is the gist of your teaching?" said Lao Tzu.

"The gist of it," said Confucius, "is benevolence and righteousness."

"May I ask if benevolence and righteousness belong to the inborn nature of man?" asked Lao Tzu.

"Of course," said Confucius. "If the gentleman lacks benevolence, he will get nowhere; if he lacks righteousness, he cannot even stay alive. Benevolence and righteousness are truly the inborn nature of man. What else could they be?"

Lao Tzu said, "May I ask your definition of benevolence and righteousness?"

Confucius said, "To be glad and joyful in mind; to embrace universal love and be without partisanship—this is the true form of benevolence and righteousness."

Lao Tzu said, "Hmm—close—except for the last part. 'Universal love'— that's a rather nebulous ideal, isn't it? And to be without partisanship is already a kind of partisanship. Do you want to keep the world from losing its simplicity? Heaven and earth hold fast to their constant ways, the sun and moon to their brightness, the stars and planets to their ranks, the birds and beasts to their flocks, the trees and shrubs to their stands. You have only to go along with Virtue in your actions, to follow the Way in your journey, and already you will be there. Why these flags of benevolence and righteousness so bravely upraised, as though you were beating a drum and searching for a lost child? Ah, you will bring confusion to the nature of man."

*Taoism.* Chuang Tzu 13

It is like a painter
Spreading the various colors:
Delusion grasps different forms
But the elements have no distinctions.

In the elements there's no form,
And no form in the elements;
Yet apart from the elements
No form can be found.

In the mind is no painting,
In painting there is no mind;
Yet not apart from mind
Is any painting to be found.

That mind never stops,
Manifesting all forms,
Countless, inconceivably many,
Unknown to one another.

Just as a painter
Cannot know his own mind
Yet paints due to his mind,
So is the nature of all things.

Mind is like an artist,
Able to paint the worlds:

**Bhagavad Gita 15.9-11:** Cf. Isha Upanishad 15-16, p. 47; Svetasvatara Upanishad 1.11-12, p. 414; Qur'an 59.19, p. 280; Parable of the Anthill, Majjhima Nikaya i.142-45, p. 659.

**Holy Teaching of Vimalakirti 3:** Cf. Sutta Nipata 1072-76, p. 379; Anguttara Nikaya i.10, p. 322; Hevajra Tantra 8.32-33, p. 133; Sutra of Hui Neng 2, p. 381; 6, p. 283; Perfection of Wisdom in Eight Thousand Lines 12.3, p. 284.

**Chuang Tzu 13:** Cf. Tao Te Ching 2, p. 572; 18-19, p. 201; 38, p. 109; 81, p. 570; Chuang Tzu 10, pp. 571-72; 11, p. 297; 31, p. 516; Sri Raga Ashtpadi, M.3, p. 516; Records of the Divine Wind, p. 516.

The five clusters [aggregates] are born thence;
There is nothing it does not make.

As in the mind, so is the Buddha;
As the Buddha, so living beings:
Know that Buddha and mind
Are in essence inexhaustible.

If people know the actions of mind
Create all the worlds,
They will see the Buddha
And understand Buddha's true nature.

Mind does not stay in the body,
Nor body stay in mind:
Yet it is able to perform Buddha-work
Freely, without precedent.

If people want to really know
All Buddhas of all times,
They should contemplate the nature of the cosmos:
All is but mental construction.

*Buddhism.* Garland Sutra 20

One day the Fifth Patriarch assembled all his disciples and said to them, "Go and seek for Wisdom in your own mind and then write me a stanza about it. He who understands what the Essence of Mind is will be given the Robe and the Dharma, and I shall make him the Sixth Patriarch. Go away quickly. Delay not in writing the stanza, as deliberation is quite unnecessary and of no use. The man who has realized the Essence of Mind can speak of it at once."

Having received this instruction, the disciples withdrew, but none dared to write a stanza, as they all deferred to the head instructor Shen Hsiu... At 12 o'clock that night Shen Hsiu went secretly with a lamp to write his stanza on the wall of the south corridor, so that the Patriarch might know what spiritual insight he had attained. The stanza read,

> Our body is the Bodhi tree,
> And our mind a mirror bright,
> Carefully we wipe them hour by hour,
> And let no dust alight.

...When the Patriarch saw the stanza the next morning, he instructed that it be read and recited by all the disciples, so that they might realize the Essence of Mind. At midnight he sent for Shen Hsiu to come to the hall, and asked him if the stanza was written by him or not. "It was, Sir," replied Shen Hsiu. "I dare not be so vain as to expect to get the Patriarchate, but I wish Your Holiness would kindly tell me whether my stanza shows the least grain of wisdom." "Your stanza," replied the Patriarch, "shows that you have not yet realized the Essence of Mind. So far you have reached the 'door of enlightenment,' but you have not yet entered it. To seek for supreme enlightenment with such an understanding as yours can hardly be successful.... You had better go back to think it over again for a couple of days, and submit to me another stanza."

I [Hui Neng] was pounding rice when I heard a young boy reciting the stanza written by Shen Hsiu... I asked him to lead me to the hall and show me the stanza. A petty officer who happened to be there read it out to me. When he had finished reading, I told him that I had also composed a stanza, and asked him to write it on the wall. "Don't despise a beginner," I said. "You should know that the lowest class may have the sharpest wit, while the highest may be in want of intelligence. If you slight others, you commit a very great sin." I dictated my stanza, which read,

> There is no Bodhi tree,
> Nor stand of a mirror bright.
> Since all is void,
> Where can the dust alight?

When he had written this, the crowd of disciples was overwhelmed with amazement, but the Patriarch rubbed off the stanza with his shoe, lest jealous ones should do me injury. The next night he invited me secretly to his room, and expounded the Diamond Sutra to me. When he came to the sentence, "One should use one's mind in such a way that it will be free from any attachment," I at once became thoroughly enlightened, and realized that all things in the universe are the Essence of Mind itself. "Who would have thought," I said to the Patriarch, "that the Essence of Mind is intrinsically pure!..." Thus, to the knowledge of no one, the Dharma was transmitted to me at midnight, and I became the Sixth Patriarch.

*Buddhism.* Sutra of Hui Neng 1

The Perfect Way is only difficult for those who pick and choose;
Do not like, do not dislike; all will then be clear.
Make a hairbreadth difference, and Heaven and Earth are set apart;
If you want the truth to stand clear before you, never be for or against.
The struggle between "for" and "against" is the mind's worst disease;
While the deep meaning is misunderstood, it is useless to meditate on Rest.
It [the Original Mind] is blank and featureless as space; It has no "too little" or "too much";
Only because we take and reject does it seem to us not to be so.
Do not chase after entanglements as though they were real things,
Do not try to drive pain away by pretending that it is not real;
Pain, if you seek serenity in Oneness, will vanish of its own accord.
Stop all movement in order to get rest, and rest will itself be restless;
Linger over either extreme, and Oneness is forever lost.
Those who cannot attain Oneness in either case will fail;
To banish Reality is to sink deeper into the Real;
Allegiance to the Void implies denial of its voidness.
The more you talk about It, the more you think about It, the further from It you go.
Stop talking, stop thinking, and there is nothing you will not understand.
Return to the Root and you will find the Meaning;
Pursue the Light, and you will lose its source.
Look inward, and in a flash you will conquer the Apparent and the Void.
For the whirligigs of Apparent and Void all come from mistaken views;
There is no need to seek Truth; only stop having views.
Do not accept either position, examine it or pursue it;
At the least thought of "is" or "isn't" there is chaos, and the Mind is lost.
Though the two exist because of the One, do not cling to the One;
Only when no thought arises are the Dharmas without blame.
No blame, no Dharmas, no arising, no thought....
Let things take their own course; know that the Essence
Will neither go nor stay;
Let your nature blend with the Way and wander in it free from care.
Thoughts that are fettered turn from Truth,
Sink into the unwise habit of "not liking."
"Not liking" brings weariness of spirit; estrangements serve no purpose....
In the Dharma there are no separate dharmas [stations in life]; only the foolish cleave
To their own preferences and attachments....
If the mind makes no distinctions all Dharmas become one.
Let the One with its mystery blot out all memory of complications.
Let the thought of the Dharmas as All-one bring you to the So-in-itself....

At the ultimate point, beyond which you can go no further,
You get to where there are no rules, no standards,
To where thought can accept Impartiality,
To where effect of action ceases,
Doubt is washed away, belief has no obstacle.
Nothing is left over, nothing remembered;
Space is bright, but self-illumined; no power of mind is exerted.
Nor indeed could mere thought bring us to such a place.
Nor could sense or feeling comprehend it.
It is the Truly-so, the Transcendent Sphere, where there is neither He nor I.
For swift converse with this sphere use the concept "Not Two";
In the "Not Two" are no separate things, yet all things are included.
The wise throughout the Ten Quarters have had access to this Primal Truth;
For it is not a thing with extension in Time or Space;
A moment and an aeon for it are one.

Whether we see it or fail to see it, it is manifest always and everywhere.
The very small is as the very large when boundaries are forgotten;
The very large is as the very small when its outlines are not seen.
Being is an aspect of Non-being; Non-being is an aspect of Being.
In climes of thought where it is not so the mind does ill to dwell.
The One is none other than the All, the All none other than the One.
Take your stand on this, and the rest will follow of its own accord;
To trust in the Heart is the Not Two, the Not Two is to trust in the Heart.
I have spoken, but in vain; for what can words tell
Of things that have no yesterday, tomorrow, or today?

*Buddhism.* Seng Ts'an, On Trust in the Heart

❖

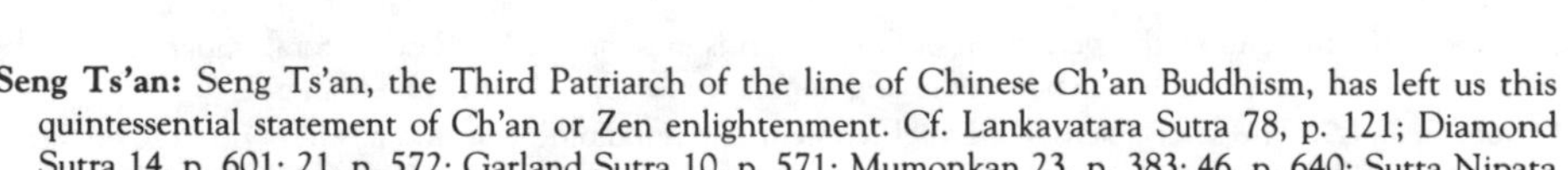
**Seng Ts'an:** Seng Ts'an, the Third Patriarch of the line of Chinese Ch'an Buddhism, has left us this quintessential statement of Ch'an or Zen enlightenment. Cf. Lankavatara Sutra 78, p. 121; Diamond Sutra 14, p. 601; 21, p. 572; Garland Sutra 10, p. 571; Mumonkan 23, p. 383; 46, p. 640; Sutta Nipata 919-20, p. 393; Heart Sutra, pp. 416-17.

## *Perfection*

THE SCRIPTURES DESCRIBE the perfect virtues of the person who is at one with the Absolute, who is firmly established in truth, purity, and integrity, who is without sin or bondage to worldly corruption, who exhibits the fulness of sanctifying grace. Such a person may be called a saint, a sage, an arahant, a siddha, a Buddha, a perfect man, or by other names. There is remarkable unanimity among religions as to what characterizes the realized or perfected human being.

Such a person embodies in himself the perfections of Ultimate Reality. Therefore he is truly in the *Image of God*, pp. 139-43. Furthermore, the saint has overcome selfish desires and is purified of any feelings of lust, greed, or other cravings. He is unfettered by attachment to worldly concerns for wealth, power, or reputation. He is free from bondage to sin and does not have any desire to commit sin: In Augustine's words, he is one who can "love God and do what you will." He is unified within himself and has dominion over himself. He has risen above the world of change and conditions and therefore attains immortality. These characteristics of the saint are described in the passages collected in this section.

You, therefore, must be perfect, as your heavenly Father is perfect.

*Christianity*. Matthew 5.48

Abu Huraira reported God's Messenger as saying, "The believers whose faith is most perfect are those who have the best character."

*Islam*. Hadith of Abu Dawud and Darimi

Whose minds are well perfected in the Factors of Enlightenment, who, without clinging, delight in the giving up of grasping, they, the corruption-free, shining ones, have attained Nibbana even in this world.

*Buddhism*. Dhammapada 89

One should be known as true who in his heart bears truth—
His impurity of falsehood cast off, his person should be washed clean.
One should be known as true who to truth is devoted in love.

*Sikhism*. Adi Granth, Asa-ki-Var, M.1, p. 468

He who has achieved it cannot either be drawn into friendship or repelled,
Cannot be benefited, cannot be harmed,
Cannot either be raised or humbled,
And for that reason is highest of all creatures under heaven.

*Taoism*. Tao Te Ching 56

God the Almighty has said..., "My servant will not approach Me with anything dearer than that which I put on him as an obligation; and he continues presenting Me with works of supererogation, that I may love him. And when I love him, I am his hearing by which he hears, his sight by which he sees, his hand by

**Matthew 5.48:** In context, the perfection of God which is most stressed by Jesus is total impartiality and unconditional love, even to the point of loving one's enemies. See Matthew 5.43-48, p. 705.

**Dhammapada 89:** The seven Factors of Enlightenment are: mindfulness, searching the scriptures, energy, zest, tranquillity, contemplation, and evenmindedness. Cf. Large Sutra on Perfect Wisdom 211-12, p. 469; Bhagavad Gita 5.21-23, p. 133.

which he strikes, and his foot with which he walks."

*Islam.* Forty Hadith of an-Nawawi 38

Yea, come unto Christ, and be perfected in him, and deny yourselves of all ungodliness; and if you shall deny yourselves of all ungodliness; and love God with all your might, mind, and strength, then is his grace sufficient for you, that by his grace you may be perfect in Christ; and if by the grace of God you are perfect in Christ, you can in no way deny the power of God.

*Church of Jesus Christ of Latter-day Saints.* Book of Mormon, Moroni 10.32-33

Rabbi Me'ir said, "Whosoever labors in the Torah for its own sake merits many things; and not only so, but the whole world is indebted to him: he is called friend, beloved, a lover of the All-present, a lover of mankind; it clothes him in meekness and reverence; it fits him to become just, pious, upright, and faithful; it keeps him far from sin, and brings him near to virtue."

*Judaism.* Mishnah, Abot 6.1

In this way [the superior] man comes to resemble heaven and earth; he is not in conflict with them. His wisdom embraces all things, and his Tao brings order into the whole world; therefore he does not err. He is active everywhere but does not let himself be carried away. He rejoices in heaven and has knowledge of fate, therefore he is free of care. He is content with his circumstances and genuine in his kindness, therefore he can practice love.

*Confucianism.* I Ching, Great Commentary 1.4.3

The Supreme Soul (*Paramatman*) is free from birth, old age, and death; he is supreme, pure, and devoid of the eight karmas; he possesses infinite knowledge, intuition, bliss, and potency; he is indivisible, indestructible, and inexhaustible. Besides, he is supersensuous and unparalleled, is free from obstructions, merit, demerit, and rebirth, and is eternal, steady, and independent.

*Jainism.* Kundakunda, Niyamasara 176-77

The Supreme Reality stands revealed in the consciousness of those who have conquered themselves. They live in peace, alike in cold and heat, pleasure and pain, praise and blame.

They are completely filled by spiritual wisdom and have realized the Self. Having conquered their senses, they have climbed to the summit of human consciousness. To such people a clod of dirt, a stone, and gold are the same. They are equally disposed to family, enemies, and friends, to those who support them and those who are hostile, to the good and the evil alike. Because they are impartial, they rise to great heights.

*Hinduism.* Bhagavad Gita 6.7-9

By fulness of leadership,
The Wise Lord shall grant powerful communion
Of perfection and Immortality,
Of Right, Dominion and Good Thought—
To him who is a sworn friend;
To him by spirit and by actions!

Clear are these to the man of insight,
As to a knowing one by mind.
He upholds good Dominion,
And Right by words and by actions.
He, O Lord of Wisdom,
Shall be Thy most helping associate!

*Zoroastrianism.* Avesta, Yasna 31.21-22

None of you truly believes until his inclination is in accordance with what I have brought.

*Islam.* Forty Hadith of an-Nawawi 41

A novice asked the Buddha, "What is goodness and what is greatness?" The Buddha replied, "To follow the Way and hold to what is true is good. When the will is in conformity with the Way, that is greatness."

*Buddhism.* Sutra of Forty-two Sections 15

**Moroni 10.32-33:** Cf. Ephesians 4.7-16, pp. 511.
**Forty Hadith of an-Nawawi 41:** Compare the hadith from Abu Nuaym, p. 140.
**Niyamasara 176-77:** Cf. Acarangasutra 5.123-40, p. 58; Pancasticaya 170, p. 131.

Of the saying, He upon whom neither love of mastery, vanity, resentment, nor covetousness have any hold may be called Good, the Master said, "Such a one has done what is difficult; but whether he should be called Good I do not know."

*Confucianism.* Analects 14.2

Sincerity [Absolute Truth] is the Way of Heaven; the attainment of Sincerity is the Way of man. He who possesses Sincerity achieves what is right without effort, understands without thinking, and naturally and easily is centered on the Way. He is a sage.

*Confucianism.*
Doctrine of the Mean 20.18

The whole world is sustained by God's charity; and the righteous are sustained by their own force.

*Judaism.* Talmud, Berakot 17b

No one born of God commits sin; for God's nature abides in him, and he cannot sin because he is born of God.

*Christianity.* 1 John 3.9

One who is rich in the enlightenment will not indulge in any sinful action, since his conscience is guided by the intellect fully illumined with Truth.

*Jainism.* Acarangasutra i.174

The arahant monk, who has destroyed the cankers, lived the life, done what was to be done, laid town the burden, won the goal, burst the bonds of becoming, and is freed by the fulness of gnosis, cannot transgress nine standards: a monk in whom the cankers are destroyed cannot deliberately take the life of any living thing; cannot, with intention to steal, take what is not given; cannot indulge in carnal intercourse; cannot intentionally tell a lie; cannot enjoy pleasures from memories as of yore when a householder; a monk, in whom the cankers are destroyed, cannot go astray through desire; cannot go astray through hate; cannot go astray through delusion; cannot go astray through fear.

*Buddhism.* Anguttara Nikaya iv.370

Clear: The name of a state achieved through auditing, or an individual who has achieved this state. A Clear is a being who no longer has his own reactive mind. A Clear is an unaberrated person and is rational in that he forms the best possible solutions he can on the data he has and from his viewpoint.

Operating Thetan: It is a state of beingness. It is a being "at cause [can assume responsibility] over matter, energy, space, time, form, and life." Operating comes from "able to operate without dependency on things," and Thetan is [from] the Greek letter theta, which the Greeks used to represent thought....

*Scientology.* L. Ron Hubbard,
Scientology 0-8, The Book of Basics

Undivided I am,
undivided my soul,
undivided my sight,
undivided my hearing;
undivided my in-breathing,
undivided my outbreathing,
undivided my diffusive breath;
undivided the whole of me.

*Hinduism.* Atharva Veda 19.51.1

**Analects 14.2:** Confucius considered goodness to be the loftiest ideal and doubted if any human could attain to it. Cf. Analects 4.6, p. 273; Analects 7.33, pp. 468-69; compare Mark 10.17-18, p. 468.

**Doctrine of the Mean 20.18:** Cf. Mencius II.A.2, p. 527; Chuang Tzu 12, p. 416.

**1 John 3.9:** Cf. Sun Myung Moon, 10-20-73, p. 94.

**Scientology 0-8:** According to Scientology, spiritual attainment is on a graduated scale. The state of Clear is the level where an individual can function optimally, without any negative thoughts or desires—the 'reactive mind'—to confuse his reason. It is achieved through training by a process of instruction called 'auditing.' 'Operating Thetan' is an even higher stage, one of total freedom in the world of being and able to take responsibility for all things.

**Atharva Veda 19.51.1:** The human condition of internal conflict and contradiction—Maitri Upanishad 6.34, p.277; Bhagavad Gita 6.5-6, p. 278—is overcome by one in perfect unity; cf. Mundaka Upanishad

While there are no stirrings of pleasure, anger, sorrow, or joy, the mind may be said to be in a state of equlibrium (*chung*). When those feelings have been stirred, and they act in their due degree, there ensues what may be called the state of harmony (*ho*). This equilibrium is the great root from which grow all the human actings in the world, and this harmony is the universal path which they all should pursue. Let the states of equilibrium and harmony exist in perfection, and a happy order will prevail throughout heaven and earth, and all things will be nourished and flourish.

*Confucianism*. Doctrine of the Mean 1.4-5

Who shall ascend the hill of the Lord?
And who shall stand in his holy place?
He who has clean hands and a pure heart,
who does not lift up his soul to what is false,
and does not swear deceitfully.
He will receive blessing from the Lord,
and vindication from the God of his salvation.
Such is the generation of those who seek him,
who seek the face of the God of Jacob.

*Judaism* and *Christianity*. Psalm 24.3-6

Blessed are the poor in spirit, for theirs is the kingdom of heaven.
Blessed are those who mourn, for they shall be comforted.
Blessed are the meek, for they shall inherit the earth.
Blessed are those who hunger and thirst for righteousness, for they shall be satisfied.
Blessed are the merciful, for they shall obtain mercy.
Blessed are the pure in heart, for they shall see God.
Blessed are the peacemakers, for they shall be called sons of God.
Blessed are those who are persecuted for righteousness' sake, for theirs is the kingdom of heaven.

*Christianity*. Matthew 5.3-10: The Beatitudes

Arjuna:
Tell me of those who live established in wisdom, ever aware of the Self, O Krishna. How do they talk? How sit? How move about?

Lord Krishna:
They live in wisdom who see themselves in all and all in them, who have renounced every selfish desire and sense craving tormenting the heart.

Neither agitated by grief nor hankering after pleasure, they live free from lust and fear and anger. Established in meditation, they are truly wise. Fettered no more by selfish attachments, they are neither elated by good fortune nor depressed by bad. Such are the seers.

Even as a tortoise draws in its limbs, the wise can draw in their senses at will. Aspirants abstain from sense pleasures, but they still

3.1.1-3, pp. 275-76. This verse also refers to the attainment of tranquillity and unity in meditation; cf. Bhagavad Gita 6.10-27, p. 603.

**Doctrine of the Mean 1.4-5:** Cf. Doctrine of the Mean 22, p. 221; Chuang Tzu 12, p. 416.

**Psalm 24.3-6:** The conditions enumerated here correspond to the Decalogue; see Exodus 20.1-17, p. 110. This psalm was sung in ancient Israel by pilgrims as they reached the Temple gates, where they would proclaim their qualifications to enter its holy precincts. Cf. Yasna 60.21, p. 515.

**Matthew 5.3-10:** These are the first eight of the nine Beatitudes. They proclaim God's favor to those who fear him, who have cast off egoism, and who aspire to do his will. 'Poor in spirit' refers to those who recognize their spiritual poverty though they may know countless doctrines and formal teachings—cf. 1 Corinthians 1.18-25, p. 570. 'Those who mourn' expresses the fact that people in the lower classes of society who suffer grief, poverty, and oppression are often less bound by attachments to worldly things and more able to receive God's wisdom—cf. Matthew 19.21-24, p. 666; Luke 18.10-14, p. 642. 'The meek' are not puffed up with pride and do not act arrogantly towards others. They are the little children to whom belongs the Kingdom of Heaven—cf. Luke 18.16-17, p. 648. 'Those who hunger and thirst for righteousness' have a deep sense of empathy with the suffering of others and are not just concerned with their own situation. On the 'pure in heart,' cf. 2 Timothy 2.21-22, p. 520. For Jesus' teachings on mercy, see Matthew 18.21-35, p. 702, and on making peace, see Matthew 5.23-24, p. 701. To willingly accept persecution for God's sake is the highest expression of discipleship—cf. Matthew 16.24-25, p. 625.

crave for them. These cravings all disappear when they see the highest goal. Even of those who tread the path, the stormy senses can sweep off the mind. They live in wisdom who subdue their senses and keep their minds ever absorbed in me.

*Hinduism.* Bhagavad Gita 2.54-61

For him who has completed the journey, for him who is sorrowless, for him who from everything is wholly free, for him who has destroyed all ties, the fever of passion exists not....

He whose corruptions are destroyed, he who is not attached to food, he who has deliverance, which is void [of lust, hate, and ignorance] and signless [without the signs of lust, etc.], as his object—his path, like that of the birds of the air, cannot be traced.

He whose senses are subdued, like steeds well-trained by a charioteer, he whose pride is destroyed and is free from the corruptions—such a steadfast one even the gods hold dear.

Like the earth, a balanced and well-disciplined person resents not.... He is like a pool, unsullied by mud; to such a balanced one, life's wanderings do not arise.

Calm is his mind, calm is his speech, calm is his action, who, rightly knowing, is wholly freed [from defilements], perfectly peaceful and equipoised.

The man who is not credulous but truly understands the Uncreate (*Nibbana*), who has cut off the links, who has put an end to occasion [of good and evil], who has eschewed all desires, he indeed is a supreme man.

*Buddhism.* Dhammapada 90-97

He who possesses virtue in abundance
May be compared to an infant.
Poisonous insects will not sting him.
Fierce beasts will not seize him.
Birds of prey will not strike him.
His bones are weak, his sinews tender, but his grasp is firm.
He does not yet know the union of male and female,
But his organ is aroused.
This means that his essence is at its height.
He may cry all day without becoming hoarse,
This means that his natural harmony is perfect.
To know harmony means to be in accord with the eternal.
To be in accord with the eternal means to be enlightened.

*Taoism.* Tao Te Ching 55

Living beyond the reach of "I" and "mine" and of pleasure and pain, patient, contented, self-controlled, firm in faith, with all his heart and all his mind given to me—with such a one I am in love.

Not frightening the world or by it frightened, he stands above the sway of elation, competition, and fear—he is my beloved.

He is detached, pure, efficient, impartial, never anxious, selfless in all his undertakings—he is my devotee, very dear to me.

Running not after the pleasant or away from the painful, grieving not, lusting not, but letting things come and go as they happen—he is very dear to me.

That devotee who looks upon friend and foe with equal regard, who is not buoyed up by praise nor cast down by blame, alike in heat and cold, pleasure and pain, free from selfish attachments, the same in honor and dishonor, quiet, ever full, in harmony everywhere, firm in faith—such a one is dear to me.

Those who meditate upon this immortal Truth as I have declared it, full of faith and seeking me as life's supreme goal, are truly my devotees, and my love for them is very great.

*Hinduism.* Bhagavad Gita 12.14-20

**Dhammapada 90-97:** Cf. Sutta Nipata 1072-76, p. 379; Anguttara Nikaya ii.37-39, p. 468.

**Tao Te Ching 55:** The little child is totally spontaneous and acts without any artifice. This spontaneity means that the child is fully expressing his original nature; this is the Taoist ideal. Cf. Tao Te Ching 10, p. 601; 20, p. 434; 28, p. 648; Atharva Veda 6.121.4, p. 379.

He who realizes here in this world the destruction of his sorrow, who has laid the burden aside and is emancipated [from defilements]—him I call a brahmin.

He whose knowledge is deep, who is wise, who is skilled in the right and wrong way, and who has reached the Highest Goal—him I call a brahmin.

He who has no longings pertaining to this world or to the next, who is desireless [for himself] and emancipated—him I call a brahmin.

He who has no longings, who, through knowledge, is free from doubts, who has gained a firm footing in the Deathless (*Nibbana*)—him I call a brahmin.

Herein he who has transcended both good and evil, and the Ties [lust, hatred, delusions, pride and false views] as well, who is sorrowless, stainless, and pure—him I call a brahmin.

He who is spotless as the moon, who is pure, serene, and unperturbed, who has destroyed craving for becoming—him I call a brahmin.

He who has passed beyond this quagmire which is difficult to cross, the ocean of life (*samsara*), this delusion, who has crossed over and gone beyond; who is meditative, free from craving and doubts; who, clinging to naught, has attained Nibbana—him I call a brahmin.

The fearless, the noble, the hero, the great sage, the conqueror, the desireless, the cleanser [of defilements], the enlightened—him I call a brahmin.

*Buddhism*. Dhammapada 402-22

Whoever in his self the Supreme Being has lodged,
His name is truly the servant of God:
On his vision has flashed the Lord that is also within the self.
This by utter humility has he obtained.
The servant who ever realizes the Lord to be near,
At the divine Portal finds acceptance.
By divine grace falling on His servant,
Comes to him full realization.
To be with all, yet in his self unattached—
Such a way, says Nanak, to God's servant is known.

One that the Lord's command in mind cherishes,
Is truly to be called *Jivan-mukta* (liberated while living).
To such a one are joy and sorrow alike;
Ever in joy, never feels he sorrow.
Gold and a clod of earth to him are alike,
As also nectar and foul-tasting poison.
To him are honor and dishonor alike;
Alike also pauper and prince.
One that such a way practices,
Says Nanak, a Jivan-mukta may be called.

*Sikhism*. Adi Granth,
Gauri Sukhmani, M.5, p. 275

The servants of the All-merciful are those who walk in the earth modestly and who, when the ignorant address them, say, "Peace";

who pass the night prostrate to their Lord and standing; who say, "Our Lord, turn Thou from us the chastisement of Gehenna; surely its chastisement is torment most terrible; evil it is as a lodging place and an abode";

who, when they expend, are neither prodigal nor parsimonious, but between that is a just stand;

who call not upon another god with God, nor slay the soul God has forbidden except by right, neither fornicate....

And those who bear not false witness and, when they pass by idle talk, pass by with dignity;

who, when they are reminded of the signs of their Lord, fall not down thereat deaf and blind;

who say, "Our Lord, give us refreshment of our wives and seed, and make us a model to the godfearing."

**Dhammapada 402-22:** Vv. 402, 403, 410-414, 422. These verses, taken from the concluding chapter of the Dhammapada, describe the ideal of the arahant—one who has realized the highest goal. But they also make a political statement for the equality of all people regardless of race or caste. Instead of being a brahmin by birth, any person can become a brahmin—one who knows Brahman—by attaining enlightenment through the path laid out by the Buddha. Cf. Dhammapada 393, 396, p. 191.

Those shall be recompensed with the highest heaven, for that they endured patiently, and they shall receive therein a greeting and "Peace." Therein they shall dwell forever; fair is it as a lodging place and an abode.

*Islam.* Qur'an 25.63-76

In order to know Shinto, the people must first be united with the mind of the kami.... Whoever would serve the kami in worship must cast off his polluted mind, and stand with pure, bright mind before the deity both morning and evening, serving the kami warmly and with utmost propriety and awe, in order to accord with the august mind of the divine.

With propriety never ending, the utmost in truth, without a single falsehood, correct and rectified without a single error, pure and without a spot of pollution, without selfish desires, and thus not greedy of personal gain, full of love and affection. Such is the mind of the kami.

With the foremost quality of truth, the mind of the divine is purity and honesty. Since this is so, the emperor, too, has been in accord with these virtues since ancient times to the present. Accordingly, the people as well should follow the emperor's example of purity and honesty, making their own minds earnest, meek, and gallant.

*Shinto.* Ekken Kaibara, Divine Injunctions

Mahamati, when the bodhisattvas face and perceive the happiness of the Samadhi of perfect tranquillization, they are moved with the feeling of love and sympathy owing to their original vows [made for the salvation of all beings, saying, "So long as they do not attain Nirvana, I will not attain it myself"], and they become aware of the part they are to perform as regards the inexhaustible vows. Thus, they do not enter Nirvana. But the fact is that they are already in Nirvana, because in them there is no rising of discrimination. With them the discrimination of grasped and grasping no more takes place; as they recognize that there is nothing in the world but what is seen of the Mind itself, they have done away with the thought of discrimination concerning all things. They have abandoned adhering to and discriminating based upon the faculties of cognition (*citta*), analysis (*manas*), and judgment (*manovijnana*), and external objects, and self-nature. However, they have not given up the things promoting the cause of Buddhism. Because of their attachment to the inner insight which belongs to the stage of Tathagatahood, whatever they do all issues from this transcendental knowledge.

*Buddhism.* Lankavatara Sutra 80

What do I mean by a True Man? The True Man of ancient times did not rebel against want, did not grow proud in plenty, and did not plan his affairs. Being like this, he could commit an error and not regret it, could meet with success and not make a show. Being like this, he could climb the high places and not be frightened, could enter the water and not get wet, could enter the fire and not get burned. His knowledge was able to climb all the way up to the Way like this.

**Qur'an 25.63-76:** Vv. 63-68, 72-76. Cf. Qur'an 6.151-53, p. 111; 8.2-4, p. 537; and 17.23-38.

**Divine Injunctions:** The Emperor of Japan has traditionally been regarded as *ikigami*—a living god. In life he is already manifesting the kami nature, which ordinary people will manifest only after death. Many of the founders of the new religions in Japan are equally seen as ikigami. Their words and actions have inherent authority and ultimacy. On the responsibility of rulers to manifest the most perfect character, see Doctrine of the Mean 33, p. 731; Analects 12.19, Bhagavad Gita 3.20-21, p. 756; Anguttara Nikaya ii.75, p. 757; and related passages.

**Lankavatara Sutra 80:** This describes the bodhisattva who has taken a vow not to enter Nirvana until he has rescued all beings from suffering—cf. Sikshasamuccaya 280-81, p. 692, and Garland Sutra 23, p. 692. His attitude is so totally without self that he is, according to this sutra, already in Nirvana. Thus Nirvana is a state of being that can be lived out in the world; cf. Mulamadhyamaka Karika 25, pp. 59-60; Holy Teaching of Vimalakirti 2, p. 682.

The True Man of ancient times slept without dreaming and woke without care; he ate without savoring and his breath came from deep inside. The True Man breathes with his heels; the mass of men breathe with their throats. They, crushed and bound down, gasp out their words as though they were retching. Deep in their passions and desires, they are shallow in the workings of Heaven.

The True Man of ancient times knew nothing of loving life, knew nothing of hating death. He emerged without delight; he went back in without a fuss. He came briskly, he went briskly, and that was all. He did not forget where he began; he did not try to find out where he would end. He received something and took pleasure in it; he forgot about it and handed it back again. This is what I call not using the mind to repel the Way, not using man to help out Heaven. This is what I call the True Man.

*Taoism.* Chuang Tzu 6

## *True Love*

WHEN THE INDIVIDUAL realizes Truth and fulfills God's purpose for his life, he comes to embody universal love. He delights in the well-being of others and selflessly works for their benefit. Love or compassion, being the core of Ultimate Reality, is manifested by the saint who can rise above self-centered attachments and desires. It is true love, love that is totally committed to the welfare of the other. It is love that is universal, overcoming the ordinary tendency to self-centeredness or favoritism for one's own.

The ideal of love described in this section is rare in the world. Such love requires the foundation of integrity, truthfulness, and unity with the Absolute as described in the previous section on Perfection. Other passages which describe love as an ethic can be found under *Loving-kindness*, pp. 684-87.

Several well-known passages describe human love as grounded in divine love: 1 John 4 and 1 Corinthians 13 of the Christian Bible, from the Bhagavad Gita, and the Buddhist Metta Sutta. Further texts describe divine love as universal, flowing impartially to all beings, insentient to likes and dislikes. The last three passages discuss true love from the standpoint of love in the family. On the one hand, as love for children and love for spouse are the most intense of human loves, such love is the standard that should be universally applied to all. Thus a Buddhist sutra states that the bodhisattva loves everyone as though they were a most-loved only child. On the other hand, even love of family often succumbs to partiality; as the Confucian passage from the Doctrine of the Mean cautions, it is not true love if the personal foundation is not right.

Beloved, let us love one another; for love is of God, and he who loves is born of God and knows God. He who does not love does not know God; for God is love.

No man has ever seen God; if we love one another, God abides in us and his love is perfected in us. By this we know that we abide in him and he in us, because he has given us of his own Spirit.

There is no fear in love, but perfect love casts out fear. For fear has to do with punishment, and he who fears is not perfected in love.

We love, because he first loved us. If anyone says, "I love God," and hates his brother, he is a liar; for he who does not love his brother whom he has seen, cannot love God whom he has not seen.

*Christianity*. 1 John 4.7-20

The infinite joy of touching the Godhead is easily attained by those who are free from the burden of evil and established within themselves. They see the Self in every creature and all creation in the Self. With consciousness unified through meditation, they see everything with an equal eye.

I am ever present into those who have realized me in every creature. Seeing all life as my manifestation, they are never separated from me. They worship me in the hearts of all, and all their actions proceed from me. Wherever they may live, they abide in me.

When a person responds to the joys and sorrows of others as if they were his own, he has attained the highest state of spiritual union.

*Hinduism*. Bhagavad Gita 6.28-32

If I speak in the tongues of men and of angels, but have not love, I am a noisy gong or a clanging cymbal. And if I have prophetic powers, and understand all mysteries and all knowledge, and if I have all faith, so as to remove mountains, but have not love, I am nothing. If I give away all I have, and if I deliver my body to be burned, but have not love, I gain nothing.

Love is patient and kind; love is not jealous or boastful; it is not arrogant or rude. Love does not insist on its own way; it is not irritable or resentful; it does not rejoice at wrong, but rejoices in the right. Love bears all things, believes all things, hopes all things, endures all things.

Love never ends; as for prophecies, they will pass away; as for tongues, they will cease; as for knowledge, it will pass away. For our knowledge is imperfect and our prophecy is imperfect; but when the perfect comes, the imperfect will pass away. When I was a child, I spoke like a child, I thought like a child, I reasoned like a child; when I became a man, I gave up childish ways. For now we see in a mirror dimly, but then face to face. Now I know in part; then I shall understand fully, even as I have been fully understood. So faith, hope, love abide, these three; but the greatest of these is love.

*Christianity*. 1 Corinthians 13

He who is skilled in welfare, who wishes to attain that calm state (*Nibbana*), should act thus: He should be able, upright, perfectly upright, of noble speech, gentle, and humble. Contented, easily supported, with few wants and simple tastes, with senses calmed, discreet, not impudent, not greedily attached to families....

[He should always hold this thought,] "May all beings be happy and secure, may their hearts be wholesome! Whatever living beings there be: feeble or strong, tall, stout or medium, short, small or large, without exception; seen or unseen, those dwelling far or near, those who are born or those yet unborn—may all beings be happy!"

Let none deceive another, nor despise any person whatsoever in any place. Let him not wish any harm to another out of anger or ill-will. Just as a mother would protect her only child at the risk of her own life, even so, let him cultivate a boundless heart towards all beings. Let his thoughts of boundless love pervade the whole world: above, below, and across without any obstruction, without any hatred, without any enmity. Whether he stands, walks,

**1 John 4.7-20:** Cf. Sota 31a, p. 544; John 17.20-21, p. 186.

**Bhagavad Gita 6.28-32:** Cf. Bhagavad Gita 3.15-26, pp. 689-90.

**1 Corinthians 13:** Cf. Abot 2.13; Oracle of Kasuga, p. 685; Precious Garland 283, p. 614; Sun Myung Moon, 4-18-77, p. 248.

sits or lies down, as long as he is awake, he should develop this mindfulness. This, they say, is the noblest living here.

*Buddhism*. Sutta Nipata 143-51, Metta Sutta

Now, I am jealous of no one,
Now that I have attained unto the Society of the Saints:
I am estranged with no one: nor is anyone a stranger to me,
Indeed, I am the friend of all.
All that God does, with that I am pleased;
This is the wisdom I have received from the saints.
Yea, the One God pervades all: and, seeing Him,
I am wholly in bloom.

*Sikhism*. Adi Granth, Kanara, M.5, p. 1299

Compassion is a mind that savors only
Mercy and love for all sentient beings.

*Buddhism*. Nagarjuna, Precious Garland 437

That one I love who is incapable of ill will, who is friendly and compassionate.

*Hinduism*. Bhagavad Gita 12.13

If, like a cracked gong, you silence yourself, you have already attained Nibbana: no vindictiveness will be found in you.

*Buddhism*. Dhammapada 134

A man is a true Muslim when no other Muslim has to fear anything from either his tongue or his hand.

*Islam*. Hadith of Bukhari

To the addict, nothing is like his dope;
To the fish, nothing is like water:
But those immersed in the love of God feel love for all things.

*Sikhism*. Adi Granth, Wadhans, M.1, p. 557

Then that do we choose, O Lord of Wisdom, O beautiful Truth, that do we think, do we speak, and do we practice, which shall be best of the actions of living ones for both worlds!

*Zoroastrianism*. Avesta, Yasna 35.3

Hillel said, "Be of the disciples of Aaron—one that loves peace, that loves mankind, and brings them nigh to the Law."

*Judaism*. Mishnah, Abot 1.12

Have benevolence towards all living beings, joy at the sight of the virtuous, compassion and sympathy for the afflicted, and tolerance toward the indolent and ill-behaved.

*Jainism*. Tattvarthasutra 7.11

Of the adage, Only a Good man knows how to like people, knows how to dislike them, Confucius said, "He whose heart is in the smallest degree set upon Goodness will dislike no one."

*Confucianism*. Analects 4.3-4

Strong One, make me strong.
May all beings look on me with the eye of friend!
May I look on all beings with the eye of friend!
May we look on one another with the eye of friend!

*Hinduism*. Yajur Veda 36.18

He lets his mind pervade one quarter of the world with thoughts of love, and so the second, and so the third, and so the fourth. And thus the whole wide world, above, below, around, and everywhere, does he continue to pervade with the heart of love, far-reaching, exalted,

**Metta Sutta:** This is the classic Buddhist passage on loving-kindness. Cf. Dhammapada 368, p. 685; Perfection of Wisdom in Eight Thousand Lines 321-22, p. 686; Garland Sutra 23, p. 705-6; 23, p. 692; Sikshasamuccaya 280-81, pp. 692.

**Wadhans 1.1:** This is a good test of whether an emotion is godly love or ordinary love. Godly love is all-embracing, while ordinary love focuses on one object exclusively, thereby inciting jealousy. Godly love seeks to benefit others, while ordinary love is tinged with selfish desire. Cf. Asa-ki-Var, M.2, p. 706; Sun Myung Moon, 9-11-77, p. 189.

beyond measure. Just as a mighty trumpeter makes himself heard—and that without difficulty—in all the four directions; even so of all things that have the shape of life there is not one that he passes by or leaves aside, but regards them all with mind set free, and deep-felt love. Verily this is the way to a state of union with Brahma.

*Buddhism.* Digha Nikaya xiii.76-77, Tevijja Sutta

All humanity should walk the path of love. True peace and a world of joy cannot be realized without love. Happiness is the same. Can you feel happiness alone? You can only feel true happiness when you are able to have a reciprocal relationship of love with another.

Freedom is the same. You cannot experience freedom alone; it can only be achieved through love and within love. You don't feel tired in the place of true love. No matter how exhausted you are, if you are intoxicated with love and you burst into tears out of love then your tiredness will suddenly disappear. When you feel true love you don't feel hungry or tired. Also you do not feel afraid of death.

*Unification Church.* Sun Myung Moon, 4-25-81

What is meant by saying that the regulation of the family depends on the cultivation of the personal life is this: Men are partial toward those for whom they have affection and whom they love, partial toward those whom they despise and dislike, partial toward those whom they fear and revere, partial toward those whom they pity and for whom they have compassion, and partial toward those whom they do not respect. Therefore there are few people in the world who know what is bad in those whom they love and what is good in those whom they dislike. Hence it is said, People do not know the faults of their sons and do not know [are not satisfied with] the bigness of their seedlings. This is what is meant by saying that if the personal life is not cultivated, one cannot regulate his family.

*Confucianism.* Great Learning 8

If you step on a stranger's foot in the marketplace, you apologize at length for your carelessness. If you step on your older brother's foot, you give him an affectionate pat, and if you step on your parent's foot, you know you are already forgiven. So it is said, Perfect ritual makes no distinction of persons; perfect righteousness takes no account of things [wealth]; perfect knowledge does not scheme; perfect benevolence knows no [partiality in] affection; perfect trust dispenses with gold.

*Taoism.* Chuang Tzu 23

The bodhisattva, the great being, having practiced compassion, sympathy, and joy, attains the stage of the best-loved only son. For example, the father and mother greatly rejoice as they see their son at peace. The same is the case with the bodhisattva who abides in this stage: he sees all beings just as the parents see their only son. Seeing him practicing good, he greatly rejoices. So we call this stage the best-loved.

For example, the father and mother are worried at heart as they see their son ill. Commiseration poisons their heart; the mind cannot part with the illness. So it is with the bodhisattva, the great being, who abides in this stage. As he sees beings bound up in the illness of illusion, his heart aches. He is worried as in the case of an only son. Blood comes out from

**Great Learning 8:** Confucianism teaches that one should be partial toward one's own family and relatives—yet only as the starting point for a social ethic which is an expansion of family relations—cf. Mencius I.A.7, p. 686. To counter the tendency of partiality to become corrupt, another aspect to Confucian teaching is the search for a univeral objective basis for action in the world: the cultivation of personal virtue. Each person should have a foundation of benevolence within himself or herself in order that love—both to family and to strangers—may be correct. Cf. Mencius II.A.6, p. 145; Mencius VII.B.1 6, p. 684.

**Chuang Tzu 23:** Perfect action is spontaneous, heartfelt, trusting, and intimate; it dispenses with formalities. It can only exist where there is true love. Cf. Tao Te Ching 49, p. 706.

all pores of the skin. That is why we call this stage as that of an only son.

A child picks up earth, dirty things, tiles, stones, old bones, pieces of wood and puts them into his mouth, at which the father and mother, apprehensive of the harms that might arise thereby, take the child with the left hand and with the right take these out. The same goes with the bodhisattva: he sees that all beings are not grown up to the stage of law body and that non-good is done in body, speech, and mind. The bodhisattva sees, and with the hand of wisdom has it extracted. He does not wish that man should repeat birth and death, receiving thereby sorrow and worry.

When a father and mother part with their beloved son as the son dies, their hearts so ache that they feel that they themselves should die together with him. The same is the case with the bodhisattva: as he sees a benighted person fall into hell, he himself desires to be born there, too. [He thinks,] "Perhaps the man, as he experiences the pain, may gain a moment of repentance where I can speak to him of the Law in various ways and enable him to gain a thought of good."

For the father and mother of an only son, in sleep or while awake, or while walking, standing, sitting, or reclining, their minds always think of the son. If he does wrong, they give kindly advice and lead the boy that he does not do evil any more. The same is the case of the bodhisattva: as he sees beings fall into the realms of hell, hungry ghosts and animals, or sees them doing good and evil in the world of man and in heaven, his mind is ever upon them and not apart from them. He may see them doing all evil, yet he does not become angry or punish with evil intent.

*Buddhism.*
Mahaparinirvana Sutra 470-71

❖

**Mahaparinirvana Sutra 470-71:** The love of a mother for her only child, as developed in this Mahayana text as the way of the bodhisattva, is similar to the Theravada concept of compassion as set forth in the Metta Sutta (above). Cf. Holy Teaching of Vimalakirti 5, p. 325; Perfection of Wisdom in Eight Thousand Lines 402-3, p. 724. The 'stage of law body' is the complete realization of Buddhahood, when one is totally identical with Reality, the *Dharmakaya*.

# CHAPTER 4
# THE PURPOSE OF LIFE IN THE FAMILY AND SOCIETY

IN ADDITION TO A VISION OF HOLINESS or perfection for the individual, all religions recognize that individuals are nurtured and in turn give of themselves within the context of family and community. To participate in the family, fulfilling the roles of parent and child, husband and wife, grandparent, cousin, etc., is, many would say, essential to being human. The same can be said of the social roles and responsibilities which people undertake as they constitute communities, nations, and even the family of all humankind.

In considering the social dimension of the purpose of life, we are informed by the Confucian doctrine of the Five Relations—between ruler and subject, father and son, husband and wife, elder and younger brothers, and between friends. Summarized in the all-encompassing virtue of filial piety, this ideal finds support in most religious traditions. We are also informed by the first three of the Four Ends of Man (*Purushartha*) in Hinduism: social ethics (*dharma*), material gain (*artha*), and pleasure (*kama*). We find principles of family and social life at the center of the Law given to Moses and the Shariah of Islam.

These expressions of social morality do not simply sanctify existing customs and norms. At their best, they teach a spiritual ideal by which the family and society may prosper and be upheld in divine grace. In addition, they contain teachings which promote equality beyond race, class, gender, or creed, and affirm the dignity of all members of society. We can even find in them a common vision of the family of humankind. Thus the world's religions have been and continue to be wellsprings for humanity's perennial hopes for world peace.

❖

# The Family

WE MAY REGARD THE FAMILY as having two axes: a vertical axis running through the generations from grandparents to parents to children, and a horizontal axis including members of the same generation: husband and wife, brothers and sisters. Furthermore, the ultimate vertical axis is the relation between the family and Ultimate Reality, recognizing God as the Ultimate Parent. Happiness and harmony in the family are thus directly related to the good character, truthfulness, and God-directedness of the individual: of the parents first and also of other family members. Good family relations, in turn, are productive of good citizens who are able to apply the lessons of family relations to relations with their elders and superiors, co-workers, and subordinates, in school, business, government, and community affairs. The passages in this section deal with the various relations in the family all together. The following two sections gather passages on the vertical axis of parents and children and the horizontal axis of husband and wife.

Supporting one's father and mother, cherishing wife and children and a peaceful occupation; this is the greatest blessing.

*Buddhism*. Sutta Nipata 262

Lord, give us joy in our wives and children, and make us models for the God-fearing.

*Islam*. Qur'an 25.74

May in this family discipline overcome indiscipline, peace discord, charity miserliness, devotion arrogance, the truth-spoken word the false spoken word which destroys the holy order.

*Zoroastrianism*. Avesta, Yasna 60.5

There are five relations of utmost importance under Heaven... between prince and minister; between father and son; between husband and wife; between elder and younger brothers; and between friends.

*Confucianism*. Doctrine of the Mean 20.8

What are "the things which men consider right"? Kindness on the part of the father, and filial duty on that of the son; gentleness on the part of the elder brother, and obedience on that of the younger; righteousness on the part of the husband, and submission on that of the wife; kindness on the part of elders, and deference on that of juniors; with benevolence on the part of the ruler, and loyalty on that of the minister;—these ten are the things which men consider to be right.

*Confucianism*. Book of Ritual 7.2.19

Natural mildness should be there in the family. Observance of the vows leads to mildness.... Right belief should there be amongst family members. Crookedness and deception cause unhappiness in the family. Straightforwardness and honesty in one's body, speech, and mental activities lead the family to an auspicious path. Purity, reverence, ceaseless pursuit of knowledge, charity, removal of obstacles that threaten equanimity, service to others—these make the family happy.

*Jainism*. Tattvarthasutra 6.18-24

The moral life of man may be likened to traveling to a distant place: one must start from the

**Doctrine of the Mean 20.8:** These are the Confucian Five Relations. They are further explicated in the following passage.

**Book of Ritual 7.2.19:** Cf. I Ching 37, p. 180.

**Tattvarthasutra 6.18.24:** Cf. Acarangasutra 1.35-37, p. 527; Tattvarthasutra 9.6, p. 112.

nearest stage. It may also be likened to ascending a height [of public responsibility]: one must begin from the lowest step [one's family]. The Book of Songs says,

> When wives and children and their sires are one,
> 'Tis like the harp and lute in unison.
> When brothers live in concord and at peace
> The strain of harmony shall never cease.
> The lamp of happy union lights the home,
> And bright days follow when the children come.

Confucius, commenting on the above, remarked, "In such a state of things what more satisfaction can parents have?"

*Confucianism.*
Doctrine of the Mean 15.2-3

Thus I have heard: The Buddha was once staying near Rajagaha in the Bamboo Wood at the Squirrels' Feeding Ground. Now at this time young Sigala, a householder's son, rising betimes, went forth from Rajagaha, and with wet hair and wet garments and clasped hands uplifted, paid worship to the several quarters of the earth and sky: to the east, south, west, and north, to the nadir and the zenith.

And the Exalted One early that morning dressed himself, took bowl and robe and entered Rajagaha seeking alms. Now he saw young Sigala worshipping and spoke to him thus:

"Why, young householder, do you worship the several quarters of earth and sky?"

"Sir, my father, when he was dying, said to me: 'Dear son, you should worship the quarters of the earth and sky.' So I, sir, honoring my father's word, rise and worship in this way."

"But in the religion of an educated man, the six quarters should not be worshipped thus."

"How then, sir, in the religion of an educated man, should the six quarters be worshipped? It would be an excellent thing if the Exalted One would so teach me the correct way..."

"How, O young householder, does the educated man serve the six quarters? The following should be looked upon as the six quarters: parents as the east, teachers as the south, wife and children as the west, friends and companions as the north, servants as the nadir, and religious leaders as the zenith.

"In five ways should a child minister to his parents as the eastern quarter: 'Once supported by them, I will now be their support; I will perform duties incumbent on them; I will keep up the lineage and tradition of my family; I will make myself worthy of my heritage.'

"In five ways parents thus ministered to, as the eastern quarter, by their child, show their love for him: They restrain him from vice, they exhort him to virtue, they train him to a profession, they contract a suitable marriage for him, and in due time they hand over to him his inheritance.

"Thus is the eastern quarter protected by him and made safe and secure.

"In five ways should pupils minister to their teachers as the southern quarter: by respectfully greeting them, by waiting upon them, by eagerness to learn, by personal service, and by attentiveness to their teaching.

"In five ways do teachers, thus ministered to as the southern quarter by their pupils, love their pupil: They train him in what they have been trained; they make him hold fast to moral precepts; they thoroughly instruct him in the lore of every subject; they speak well of him among his friends and companions; they counsel him for his safety and benefit.

"Thus is the southern quarter protected by him and made safe and secure.

"In five ways should a wife as western quarter be ministered to by her husband: by respect, by courtesy, by faithfulness, by handing over authority to her, by providing her with adornment.

"In five ways does the wife, ministered to by her husband as the western quarter, love him: Her duties are well performed, she is hospitable to their relatives, she is faithful, she watches over the wages and goods which he brings home, she discharges all her business with skill and industry.

"Thus is the western quarter protected by him and made safe and secure.

"In five ways should one minister to his friends and companions as the northern quarter: by generosity, courtesy, and benevolence, by treating them as he treats himself, and by being as good as his word.

"In five ways do his friends and familiars, thus ministered to as the northern quarter, love him: They protect him when he is off his guard, and on occasions guard his property; they become a refuge in danger; they do not forsake him in his troubles; and they show consideration for his family.

"Thus is the northern quarter protected by him and made safe and secure.

"In five ways does a noble master minister to his servants and employees as the nadir: by assigning them work according to their strength, by supplying them with food and wages, by tending them in sickness, by sharing with them unusual delicacies, by granting them leave at times.

"In five ways, thus ministered to by their master, do servants and employees love him: They rise before him, they lie down to rest after him, they are content with their wages, they do their work well, and they carry about his praise and good fame.

"Thus is the nadir by him protected and made safe and secure.

"In five ways should the layman minister to saints, priests, and religious leaders as the zenith: by affection in act and speech and mind, by keeping open house to them, and by supplying their temporal needs.

"Ministered to as the zenith, monks, priests, and religious leaders show their love for the layman in six ways: They restrain him from evil, they exhort him to good, they love him with kindly thoughts, they teach him what he has not heard, they correct and purify what he has heard, they reveal to him the way of heaven.

"Thus by him is the zenith protected and made safe and secure."

*Buddhism*. Digha Nikaya iii.185-91,
Sigalovada Sutta

❖

## *Parents and Children*

IN A FAMILY, parents are responsible for the welfare of the children and offer the children an embracing, unconditional love that overlooks and compensates for their weaknesses. Through their example, they teach their children the basic values and attitudes which they will carry throughout life. The children, in turn, respect their parents as the source of their very being, as their teachers, and as the ones who have labored and sacrificed for their sakes. When they are grown, they should be responsible to care for their parents in their old age. These relative responsibilites should not be undertaken only as a matter of duty; ideally they emerge from the spontaneous promptings of parental love and the children's gratitude and respect. This is the vertical axis defining relations of love and respect between people of unequal status and different responsibilites.

Train up a child in the way he should go,
and when he is old he will not depart from it.

*Judaism* and *Christianity*. Proverbs 22.6

He who spares the rod hates his son,
but he who loves him is diligent to discipline him.

*Judaism* and *Christianity*. Proverbs 13.24

You can only coil a fish when it is fresh.

*African Traditional Religions*. Nupe Proverb (Nigeria)

And remember when Luqman said to his son by way of instruction, "O my dear son! Establish worship and enjoin kindness and forbid iniquity, and persevere, whatever may befall you. Lo! that is the steadfast heart of things."

*Islam*. Qur'an 31.17

As the child, according to its natural disposition, commits thousands of faults,
The father instructs and slights, but again hugs him to his bosom.

*Sikhism*. Adi Granth, Sorath, M.5

Attend strictly to the commands of your parents and the instructions of your teachers. Serve your leader with diligence; be upright of heart; eschew falsehood; and be diligent in study; that you may conform to the wishes of the heavenly spirit.

*Shinto*. Oracle of Temmangu

Children are the clothes of a man.

*African Traditional Religions*. Yoruba Proverb (Nigeria)

He established a testimony in Jacob,
and appointed a law in Israel,
which he commanded our fathers
to teach to their children;
that the next generation might know them,
the children yet unborn,
and arise and tell them to their children,

**Nupe Proverb:** In other words, you must train a child from infancy when his character is pliable; as an adult his character is already set.

**Oracle of Temmangu:** Temmangu is a shrine in Osaka. Its patron deity, Tenjin, who was in life the scholar Michizane Sugawara (845-903), is venerated as a god of education and literature. Schoolchildren will buy amulets of Tenjin for luck at the time of school entrance examinations.

**Yoruba Proverb:** This means that a man is assessed by the character of his children.

so that they should set their hope in God,
and not forget the works of God,
but keep his commandments.

*Judaism* and *Christianity*. Psalm 78.5-7

Do not despise the breath of your fathers,
But draw it into your body.
That our roads may reach to where the life-giving road of our sun father comes out,
That, clasping one another tight,
Holding one another fast,
We may finish our roads together;
That this may be, I add to your breath now.
To this end:
May my father bless you with life;
May your road reach to Dawn Lake,
May your road be fulfilled.

*Native American Religions*. Zuni Prayer

Brethren, a new child is born.
While in the uterus it was the woman's thing;
Safely delivered, it is everybody's child, a native of Nibo, a Nigerian.

He shall grow under the care of his parents;
When mature he will look after his parents.
He shall listen to the good advice of his parents,
He ought not to obey wrong things.

We want truly good children, not any thing at all:
He will grow up industrious, imitating father, mother, and other relations.

No evil child!
Instead of a thief, may it pass away through miscarriage.
The name of the baby is "Chinenye."

*African Traditional Religions*.
Igbo Naming Ceremony (Nigeria)

There was always, too, a Pipe-child—a girl, unless the keeper had no daughters....

"When I was the Pipe-child, whenever my mother took the Pipe bundle outside of the lodge, I took the tripod out after her. I was told how to set the tripod when the camp was about to move, with two of the legs close together and the third far out. Whenever my father made smudge with pine needles, he would give me some and I would chew them and would hold my hands over the smudge. Then I would rub my left palm up to my right arm, my right palm up to my left arm, and then both palms from the top of my head down the sides of my neck and down my breast...

Whenever while I was the Pipe-child I got sick my father would put pine needles on me, and then he would take down the bundle and put it on my parents' bed, and would say to me, "Put your arms around your brother [the Pipe] and pray to your brother so you may get well." [My father] the Pipe-keeper and his wife claim the Feathered Pipe as their son and tell their children that the Pipe is their brother.... Of course the Pipe was not human, but because I was a baby when my father got it I grew up with it and thought just as much of it as of my own blood relatives.

When my father transferred the Pipe to Sitting High I was outside playing. When I was coming home I saw the bundle at Sitting High's door, and when I saw it I started to cry, and when I saw my father I said to him, "Why did you give my Pipe away?" It was just like a person leaving. I was lonesome for it, and felt just as if I had lost a relative or friend. All through my life I have felt the same toward it. All through my life I have made it a point to be present at any Feathered Pipe ceremony.

**Psalm 78.5-7:** Cf. Yebamot 62, p. 178.

**Zuni Prayer:** This prayer is spoken at the close of the novice's initiation.

**Igbo Naming Ceremony:** This prayer was uttered by an elder from the village of Nibo at the naming of his grandson, Chinenye. Notice the phrase 'it is everybody's child,' which indicates that raising children is a community responsibility.

And whenever I went to any ceremony, I would bring something for it....

My father used to tell me, "This Pipe was given by the Supreme Being through Bha'a; the Supreme Being is the father of the Pipe."

*Native American Religions.*
Gros Ventres Tradition of the Pipe Child

This I ask Thee. Tell me truly, Lord.
Who fashioned esteemed piety in addition to rule?
Who made a son respectful in his attentiveness to his father?

*Zoroastrianism.* Avesta, Yasna 44.7

The gentleman works upon the trunk. When that is firmly set up, the Way grows. And surely proper behavior towards parents and elder brothers is the trunk of Goodness?

*Confucianism.* Analects 1.2

In the Kingdom of Heaven, true love is fulfilled centered on parental love.... The family is the original base [of true love] and the foundation of eternity.

*Unification Church.*
Sun Myung Moon, 9-30-69

Honor your father and your mother, that your days may be long in the land which the Lord your God gives you.

*Judaism* and *Christianity.* Exodus 20.12

There are three partners in man, God, father, and mother. When a man honors his father and mother, God says, "I regard it as though I had dwelt among them and they had honored me."

*Judaism.* Talmud, Kiddushin 30b

"Do not neglect the [sacrificial] works due to the gods and the fathers! Let your mother be to you like unto a god! Let your father be to you like unto a god! Let your teacher be to you like unto a god!"

*Hinduism.*
Taittiriya Upanishad 1.11.2

Those who wish to be born in [the Pure Land] of Buddha... should act filially towards their parents and support them, and should serve and respect their teachers and elders.

*Buddhism.*
Meditation on Buddha Amitayus 27

Thy Lord has decreed... that you be kind to parents. Whether one or both of them attain old age in your lifetime, do not say to them a word of contempt, nor repel them, but address them in terms of honor. And, out of kindness, lower to them the wing of humility, and say, "My Lord! bestow on them Thy mercy even as they cherished me in childhood."

*Islam.* Qur'an 17.23

One Companion asked, "O Apostle of God! Who is the person worthiest of my consideration?" He replied, "Your mother." He asked again, "And second to my mother?" The Prophet said, "Your mother." The companion insisted, "And then?" The Messenger of God said, "After your mother, your father."

*Islam.* Hadith of Bukhari and Muslim

Now filial piety is the root of all virtue, and the stem out of which grows all moral teaching.... Our bodies—to every hair and bit of skin—are received by us from our parents, and we must not presume to injure or wound them: this is the beginning of filial piety. When we have established our character by the practice of the filial course, so as to make our name famous in future ages, and thereby glorify our parents: this is the end of filial piety. It commences with the

**Gros Ventres Tradition of the Pipe Child:** This testimony is an example of how, in traditional societies, religious education of the young is integral to daily life.

**Analects 1.2:** Cf. Book of History 5.9, pp. 331-32.

service of parents; it proceeds to the service of the ruler; it is completed by the establishment of [good] character.

*Confucianism*. Classic on Filial Piety 1

Son, why do you quarrel with your father,
Due to him you have grown to this age?
It is a sin to argue with him.

*Sikhism*. Adi Granth, Sarang, M.4, p. 1200

Rama: "How can I transgress this command of my mother and my father? It is for you to occupy the throne in Ayodhya, the throne that all revere, and for me to live in the Dandaka Forest, wearing robes of bark! Having spoken thus, the great King Dasharatha made this division of duties in the presence of the people and then ascended to heaven. The word of that virtuous monarch is our law! It is for you to enjoy the kingdom given you by our sire, and, taking refuge in the Dandaka Forest for fourteen years, I shall carry out the part assigned to me by my magnanimous sire. That which my high-souled father... has directed me to do, I regard as my supreme felicity, not the dominion of all the worlds."

*Hinduism*. Ramayana, Ayodhya Kanda 101

We have enjoined on man kindness to his parents: In pain did his mother bear him, and in pain did she give him birth. The carrying of the child to his weaning is thirty months. At length, when he reaches the age of full strength and attains forty years, he says, "O my Lord! Grant me that I may be grateful for Your favor which You have bestowed upon me, and upon both my parents, and that I may work righteousness such as You may approve; and be gracious to me in my issue. Truly have I turned to You and truly do I bow to You in Islam."

Such are they from whom We shall accept the best of their deeds and pass by their ill deeds: they shall be among the Companions of the Garden: a promise of truth, which was made to them.

*Islam*. Qur'an 46.15-16

Brethren, one can never repay two persons, I declare. What two? Mother and father.

Even if one should carry about his mother on one shoulder and his father on the other, and so doing should live a hundred years; and if he should support them, anointing them with unguents, kneading and rubbing their limbs, and they meanwhile should even void their excrements upon him—even so could he not repay his parents. Moreover, if he should establish his parents in supreme authority, in the absolute rule over this mighty earth abounding in the seven treasures—not even thus could he repay his parents. Why not? Brethren, parents do much for their children; they bring them up, they nourish them, they introduce them to this world.

However, brethren, whoso incites his unbelieving parents, settles and establishes them in the faith; whoso incites his immoral parents, settles and establishes them in morality; whoso incites his stingy parents, settles and establishes them in liberality; whoso incites his foolish parents, settles and establishes them in wisdom—such a one, just by so doing, does repay, does more than repay what is due to his parents.

*Buddhism*. Anguttara Nikaya i.61

My father, thank you for petting me;
My mother, thank you for making me comfortable;
Thank you for robing me with wisdom, which is more important than robing me with clothes.

**Ramayana:** At the insistence of Rama's stepmother, his father the king decreed that upon his death, Rama the heir apparent would be exiled to wander in the forest for fourteen years while his stepbrother Bharata was to rule as king. Though Bharata himself, along with all the populace, implored Rama to take his rightful place as king, Rama refused out of filial loyalty to his departed father. Cf. Ramayana, Ayodhya Kanda 109, pp. 506-7.

Slaves will minister unto you;
Servants will be your helpers.
Children which I shall bear will minister unto
you.

*African Traditional Religions.*
Yoruba Nuptial Chant (Nigeria)

If your parents take care of you up to the time you cut your teeth, you take care of them when they lose theirs.

*African Traditional Religions.*
Akan Proverb (Ghana)

You shall rise up before the hoary head, and honor the face of an old man, and you shall fear your God: I am the Lord.

*Judaism* and *Christianity*. Leviticus 19.32

My father sent for me; I saw he was dying. I buried him in that beautiful valley of winding waters. I love that land more than all the rest of the world. A man who would not love his father's grave is worse than a wild animal.

*Native American Religions.*
Nez Perce Tradition

❖

**Nez Perce Tradition:** Veneration of parents' graves and the spirits of ancestors is an important expression of a son's or daughter's abiding love for their parents. Cf. Winnebago Invocation at the Sweat Lodge, pp. 260-61; Igbo Invocation at a Trial, p. 260; Khuddaka Patha, p. 261; Nihon Shoki 3, p. 259; One Hundred Poems on the Jeweled Spear, p. 558.

# *Husband and Wife*

THE HORIZONTAL AXIS of family life is manifested primarily in the mutual love between husband and wife. The bond of marriage is regarded as divinely ordained in most religious traditions. As such, it carries with it the promise of God's blessing, and should be full of love and joy.

But love is not merely a matter of unfettered emotion. Subsequent passages spell out some of the responsibilites of marriage for both the husband and wife. The husband should honor his wife, never oppress or mistreat her, and always be faithful—and the wife should do likewise. The scriptures of all religions also distinguish between roles of the husband and wife: the husband as the head of the household protects and supports his wife, yet defers to her in domestic affairs. The wife is obedient to her husband, serves him with kindness, and takes primary responsibility for raising the children. While of late these traditional roles have been questioned, they have served to strengthen the bonds of family through every generation. Finally, we include several passages on the subject of the good wife.

Not those are true husband and wife that with each other [merely] consort:
Truly wedded are those that in two frames, are as one light.

*Sikhism*. Adi Granth, Var Suhi, M.3, p. 788

I am He, you are She;
I am Song, you are Verse,
I am Heaven, you are Earth.
We two shall here together dwell,
becoming parents of children.

*Hinduism*. Atharva Veda 14.2.71

Sweet be the glances we exchange,
our faces showing true concord.
Enshrine me in your heart and let
one spirit dwell within us.

I wrap around you this my robe
which came to me from Manu,
so that you may be wholly mine
and never seek another.

*Hinduism*. Atharva Veda 7.36-37

Representing heaven and earth, I have created husband and wife. This is the beginning of the world.

*Tenrikyo*. Mikagura-uta

In the beginning there was only the Self, one only. He desired, "May I have a wife in order to have offspring; may I have wealth in order to perform a work!"—for desire reaches this far. Even if one wishes, one cannot obtain more than this. As long as one does not attain each of these [desires], he thinks himself to be incomplete.

He found no joy; so even today, one who is all alone finds no joy. He yearned for a second. He became as large as a man and a woman locked in close embrace. This self he split into two; hence arose husband and wife. Therefore, as Yajnavalkya used to observe, "Oneself is like half of a split pea." That is why this void is filled by woman. He was united with her, and thence were born human beings.

*Hinduism*. Brihadaranyaka Upanishad 1.4.17 and 1.4.3

**Atharva Veda 7.36-37:** The ceremonial exchange of glances is part of the marriage ritual; in certain parts of India a cloth is thrown over the bride and bridegroom.

**Brihadaranyaka Upanishad 1.4.17 and 1.4.3:** This is an account of the creation of pairs from the primordial Androgyne. Cf. Prasna Upanishad 1.4-5, p. 116-17; Maori Tradition, pp. 216-17; Mahabharata, Adi Parva 220, p. 673.

Then the Lord God said, "It is not good that the man should be alone; I will make him a helper fit for him." So out of the ground the Lord God formed every beast of the field and every bird of the air, and brought them to the man to see what he would call them; and whatever the man called every living creature, that was its name. The man gave names to all cattle, and to the birds of the air, and to every beast of the field; but for the man there was not found a helper fit for him. So the Lord God caused a deep sleep to fall upon the man, and while he slept took one of his ribs and closed up its place with flesh; and the rib which the Lord God had taken from the man he made into a woman and brought her to the man. Then the man said, "This at last is bone of my bones and flesh of my flesh; she shall be called Woman, because she was taken out of Man." Therefore a man leaves his father and his mother and cleaves to his wife, and they become one flesh.

*Judaism* and *Christianity*. Genesis 2.18-24

The verse, "And Isaac brought her into his mother Sarah's tent" [Genesis 24.67], our masters have interpreted to mean that the Divine Presence came into Isaac's house along with Rebecca. According to the secret doctrine, the supernal Mother is together with the male only when the house is in readiness and at the time the male and female are conjoined. At such time blessings are showered forth by the supernal Mother upon them.

*Judaism*. Zohar, Genesis 101b

The moral man finds the moral law beginning in the relation between man and woman, but ending in the vast reaches of the universe.

*Confucianism*. Doctrine of the Mean 12

The point at which Adam and Eve join into one body as husband and wife is also the point at which God, the subject of love, and man, the object of beauty, become one union, thus establishing the center of goodness. Here, for the first time, the purpose of creation is accomplished. God, our Parent, is able to abide with perfected men as His children, and peacefully rest for eternity. At that time, this center would become the object of God's eternal love, and through this, God would be stimulated with happiness for eternity. Here God's Word would be physically incarnated for the first time in human history.... However, the universe lost this center when man fell.

*Unification Church*. Divine Principle I.1.2.3.4

Blessed art Thou, O Lord our God, King of the universe, who has created all things to his glory.

Blessed art Thou, O Lord our God, King of the universe, Creator of humankind.

Blessed art Thou, O Lord our God, King of the universe, who created humankind in his image, in the image of the likeness of his form, and has prepared for him from his very own person an eternal building. Blessed art Thou, O Lord, Creator of man.

May you be glad and exultant, O barren one, when her children are gathered to her with joy. Blessed art Thou, O Lord, who makes Zion joyful through her children.

May Thou make joyful these beloved companions, just as Thou gladdened Thy creatures in the Garden of Eden in primordial times. Blessed art Thou, O Lord, who makes bridegroom and bride to rejoice.

Blessed art Thou, O Lord, King of the universe, who created mirth and joy, bridegroom and bride, gladness, jubilation, dancing and delight, love and brotherhood, peace and fellowship. Quickly, O Lord our God, may the

**Genesis 2.18-24:** These verses give divine sanction to marriage. Jesus used them to declare that divorce was not acceptable to God—see Mark 10.2-12, p. 338.

**Doctrine of the Mean 12:** Cf. I Ching 54, p. 78.

**Divine Principle I.1.2.3.4:** The Blessing, or holy wedding, is the chief sacrament in the Unification Church. Blessed marriages are for eternity. Cf. Divine Principle I.2.2.2, pp. 304-5; Sun Myung Moon, 8-20-89, p. 408.

sound of mirth and joy be heard in the streets of Judah and Jerusalem, the voice of bridegroom and bride, jubilant voices of bridegrooms from their canopies and youths from the feasts of song. Blessed art Thou, O Lord, who makes the bridegroom rejoice with the bride.

*Judaism.* Talmud, Ketubot 8a

In the celestial glory there are three heavens or degrees; and in order to obtain the highest, a man must enter into this order of the priesthood (meaning the new and everlasting covenant of marriage); and if he does not, he cannot obtain it.

And again, verily I say unto you, if a man marry a wife by my word, which is my law, and by the new and everlasting covenant, and is sealed unto them by the Holy Spirit of promise, by him who is anointed, unto whom I have appointed this power and the keys of this priesthood; and it shall be said unto them—Ye shall come forth in the first resurrection... and shall inherit thrones, kingdoms, principalities, and powers, dominions, all heights and depths—then shall it be written in the Lamb's Book of Life... and shall be of full force when they are out of the world; and they shall pass by the angels, and the gods, which are set there, to their exaltation and glory in all things, as hath been sealed upon their heads, which glory shall be a fulness and a continuation of the seeds forever and ever.

*Church of Jesus Christ of Latter-day Saints.* Doctrine and Covenants 131.1-3 and 132.19

Among His signs is that He created spouses for you among yourselves that you may console yourselves with them. He has planted affection and mercy between you.

*Islam.* Qur'an 30.21

Set me as a seal upon your heart,
as a seal upon your arm;
for love is strong as death,
jealousy is cruel as the grave.
Its flashes are flashes of fire,
a most vehement flame.
Many waters cannot quench love,
neither can floods drown it.
If a man offered for love
all the wealth of his house,
it would be utterly scorned.

*Judaism* and *Christianity.* Song of Solomon 8.6-7

Kwan-kwan go the ospreys,
On the islet in the river.
The modest, retiring, virtuous, young lady—
For our prince a good mate is she.

Here long, there short, is the duckweed,
To the left, to the right, borne about by the current.
The modest, retiring, virtuous, young lady—
Waking and sleeping, he sought her.

He sought her and found her not,
And waking and sleeping he thought about her.
Long he thought; oh! long and anxiously;
On his side, on his back, he turned, and back again.

Here long, there short, is the duckweed;
On the left, on the right, we gather it.
The modest, retiring, virtuous, young lady—
With lutes, small and large, let us give her friendly welcome.

Here long, there short, is the duckweed;
On the left, on the right, we cook and present it.

**Ketubot 8a:** These six benedictions are recited at the wedding ceremony. The 'building' refers to the creation of Eve from Adam's rib, as well as the household of the family. The reference to God as the Creator of humankind denotes that marriage is God's design for the perpetuation of the human race, which began with the blessing to Adam and Eve in Eden. The last benediction connects the joy of the newlyweds with the eschatological joy at the fulfillment of God's kingdom in Jerusalem. Bridal 'canopies' are used at all Jewish weddings.

**Doctrine and Covenants 131.1-3 and 132.19:** Latter-day Saints of pure faith, who are members of the priesthood, may enter into Temple Marriage, which establishes an eternal, indissoluble bond.

The modest, retiring, virtuous, young lady—
With bells and drums let us show delight in
her.

*Confucianism.* Book of Songs, Ode 1

Kaen-kwan went the axle ends of my carriage,
As I thought of the young beauty, and went to
fetch her.
It was not that I was hungry or thirsty,
But I longed for one of such virtuous fame to
come and be with me.
Although no good friends be with us, we will
feast and be glad.

Dense is that forest in the plain,
And there sit the long-tailed pheasants.
In her proper season that well-grown lady,
With her admirable virtue, is come to instruct
me.
We will feast, and I will praise her.
"I love you, and will never be weary of you."

Although I have no good spirits,
We will drink, and perhaps be satisfied.
Although I have no good viands,
We will eat, and perhaps be satisfied.
Although I have no virtue to impart to you,
We will sing and dance.

I ascend that lofty ridge,
And split the branches of the oaks for firewood.
I split the branches of the oaks for firewood
Amid the luxuriance of their leaves.
I see you whose match is seldom to be seen,
And my whole heart is satisfied.

The high hill is seen above;
The great road is easy to travel,
My four steeds advanced without stopping;
The six reins [make music] in my hands like
lute-strings.
I see you, my bride,
To the comfort of my heart.

*Confucianism.* Book of Songs, Ode 218

The union of hearts and minds
and freedom from hate I'll bring you.
Love one another as the cow
loves the calf that she has borne.

Let son be loyal to father,
and of one mind with his mother;
let wife speak to husband words
that are honey-sweet and gentle.

Let not a brother hate a brother,
nor a sister hate a sister,
unanimous, united in aims,
speak you words with friendliness.

I will make the prayer for that
concord among men at home
by which the gods do not separate,
nor ever hate one another.

Be not parted—growing old, taking thought,
thriving together, moving under a common
yoke,
come speaking sweetly to one another;
I'll make you have one aim and be of one
mind.

Common be your water-store, common your
share of food;
I bind you together to a common yoke.
United, gather round the sacrificial fire
like spokes around the nave of a wheel.

With your common desire I'll make you all
have one aim, be of one mind, following one
leader,
like the gods who preserve their immortality.
Morn and eve may there be the loving heart in
you.

*Hinduism.* Atharva Veda 3.30

Behold the comely forms of Surya!
her border-cloth and her headwear,
and her garment triply parted,
these the priest has sanctified.

**Book of Songs, Ode 1:** This ode begins by describing a lover's anxiety as he awaits his bride, and ends with the joy of friends and family at their wedding. Many interpret the ode as describing the virtue of a bride of King Wen, as shown by her modest disposition and retiring manner. The king's anxiety and long quest to obtain his bride is often remarked. The sound of male and female ospreys answering each other at a distance alludes to the distance between the lovers; the soft duckweed gathered and presented as an offering alludes to their union. Confucius cites this ode, see Analects 3.20, p. 654, as a model of restrained pleasure, of joy not carried to extremes. Cf. Song of Solomon 3:1-5, p. 546.

**Atharva Veda 3.30:** This hymn sets forth the ideal of the Hindu family. Cf. Rig Veda 10.191.2-4, p. 187.

I take your hand for good fortune, that you
may attain old age with me, your husband. The
solar deities—
Bhaga, Aryaman, Savitri, Purandhi—
have given you to me to be mistress of my
household.

Pushan, arouse her, the most blissful one;
through whom a new generation will spring to
life.
She, in the ardor of her love, will meet me,
and I, ardently loving, will meet her....

Live you two here, be not parted,
enjoy the full length of life,
sporting with your sons and grandsons,
rejoicing in your own abode.

May Prajapati bring forth children of us, may
Aryaman unite us together till old age,
Not inauspicious, enter your husband's house,
be gracious to our people and animals.

Come, not with fierce looks, not harming your
husband,
good to animals, kind-hearted and glorious,
a mother of heroes, loving the gods,
pleasant, gracious to humans and to animals.

Make her, thou bounteous Indra,
a good mother of sons; grant her
good fortune; give her ten sons
and make her husband the eleventh.

Be a queen to your father-in-law,
a queen to your mother-in-law,
a queen to your husband's sisters,
and a queen to your husband's brothers.

May the universal Devas
and Apas join our hearts together;
so may Matarisvan, Dhatri,
and Dveshtri unite us both.

*Hinduism*. Rig Veda 10.85.35-47

A man is forbidden to compel his wife to her marital duty.

*Judaism*. Talmud, Erubin 100b

"Your wife has rights over you," said the Prophet, according to Abu Juhaifa.

*Islam*. Hadith of Bukhari

Your wives are as a tilth to you: so approach your tilth when or how you will; but do some good act for your souls beforehand, and fear God.

*Islam*. Qur'an 2.223

He who loves his wife as himself; who honors her more than himself; who rears his children in the right path, and who marries them off at the proper time of their life, concerning him it is written: "And you will know that your home is at peace."

*Judaism*. Talmud, Yebamot 62

Do not abuse your wife. Women are sacred. If you make your wife suffer, you will die in a short time. Our grandmother, Earth, is a woman, and in abusing your wife you are abusing her. By thus abusing our grandmother, who takes care of us, by your action you will be practically killing yourself.

*Native American Religions*.
A Winnebago Father's Precepts

When women are honored, there the gods are pleased; but where they are not honored, no sacred rite yields rewards.

When the female relations live in grief, the family soon wholly perishes; but that family where they are not unhappy ever prospers.

*Hinduism*. Laws of Manu 3.56-57

From woman is man born, inside her he is
conceived;
To woman man is engaged, and woman he
marries.
With woman is man's companionship.
From woman originate new generations.
Should woman die, is another sought;

**Rig Veda 10.85.35-47:** Vv. 35-37, 42-47. This is the traditional Hindu marriage vow and blessings. The bride is Surya, daughter of the solar deity Savitri; she is the prototype of all brides. 'Her husband the eleventh' means the wife will mother her husband in his old age; 'queen' describes the wife's status as the central authority at home.

By woman's help is man kept in restraint.
Why revile her of whom are born great ones of the earth?

*Sikhism.* Adi Granth, Asa-ki-Var, M.1, p. 473

It is well for a man not to touch a woman. But because of the temptation to immorality, each man should have his own wife and each woman her own husband. The husband should give to his wife her conjugal rights, and likewise the wife to her husband. For the wife does not rule over her own body, but the husband does; likewise the husband does not rule over his body, but the wife does. Do not refuse one another except perhaps by agreement for a season, that you may devote yourselves to prayer; but then come together again, lest Satan tempt you through lack of self-control.

To the unmarried and the widows I say that it is well for them to remain single as I do. But if they cannot exercise self-control, they should marry. For it is better to marry than to be aflame with passion.

*Christianity.* 1 Corinthians 7.1-9

Each one of you has ties to others, so marry them with their family's consent and give them their marriage portions decently as matrons rather than taking them on as mistresses, nor having [any secret affairs with] them as girlfriends.... That goes for any of you who worries lest he may not control his impulses; however it is better for you to discipline yourselves.

*Islam.* Qur'an 4.25

A virtuous wife who, after the death of her husband, constantly remains chaste even though she have no son, will reach heaven just as do men living a life of renunciation.

*Hinduism.* Laws of Manu 5.160

It floats about, that boat of cypress wood,
There in the middle of the Ho.
With his two tufts of hair falling over his forehead,
He was my mate;
And I swear that till death I will have no other.
O mother, O Heaven,
Why will you not understand me?

It floats about, that boat of cypress wood,
There by the side of the Ho.
With his two tufts of hair falling over his forehead,
He was my only one;
And I swear that till death I will not do the evil thing.
O mother, O Heaven,
Why will you not understand me?

*Confucianism.* Book of Songs, Ode 45

The possession of many wives undermines a man's moral nature.

*Hinduism.* Srimad Bhagavatam 11.3

You will not be able to deal equally between your wives, however much you wish to do so.

*Islam.* Qur'an 4.129

Whoever has many wives will have troubles in surfeit.
He will be deceitful, he will lie, he will betray [some of them] to have them together;
It is not certain that he can have peace to pray well.

*African Tradional Religions.* Yoruba Poem (Nigeria)

Men are the protectors and maintainers of women, because God has given the one more strength than the other, and because they support them from their means. Therefore the

**Laws of Manu 5.160:** According to Hindu tradition, a virtuous widow will remain chaste and not remarry. However noble this ethic may be, it leaves widows destitute if their relatives or society do not take on the responsibility of supporting them. Cf. Mencius I.B.5, p. 754.

**Book of Songs, Ode 45:** This poem was sung by Kung Chiang, the widow of Prince Kung-po of Wei. Her mother wanted to force her into a second marriage, and she protests. The Chinese have always considered the refusal of a widow to marry again to be a great virtue. Cf. I Ching 54, p. 78.

**Qur'an 4.129:** The Qur'an sanctions a man to support as many as four wives, but this was expressly a concession in time of war, when many widows and orphans needed to be supported (Qur'an 4.3). But it declares that monogamy is the only equitable arrangement.

righteous women are devoutly obedient, and guard in the husband's absence what God would have them guard.

*Islam.* Qur'an 4.34

All of you are guardians and are responsible for your wards. The ruler is a guardian; the man is a guardian of his family; the lady is a guardian and is responsible for her husband's house and his offspring; and so all of you are guardians and are responsible for your wards.

*Islam.* Hadith of Bukhari

In the family women's appropriate place is within; men's, without. When men and women keep their proper places they act in accord with Heaven's great norm. Among the members of the family are the dignified master and mistress whom we term father and mother. When father, mother, sons, elder and younger brothers all act in a manner suited to their various positions within the family, when husbands play their proper role and wives are truly wifely, the way of that family runs straight. It is by the proper regulation of each family that the whole world is stabilized.

*Confucianism.* I Ching 37: The Family

My dear sisters the women, you have had a hard life to live in this world, yet without you this world would not be what it is. Wakan Tanka intends that you should bear much sorrow—comfort others in time of sorrow. By your hands the family moves.

*Native American Religions.* Sioux Tradition of the Sacred Pipe

The whole future of the race depends upon its attitude toward children; and a race which specializes in women for "menial purposes" or which believes that the contest of the sexes in the spheres of business and politics is a worthier endeavor than the creation of tomorrow's generation, is a race which is dying.

*Scientology.* L. Ron Hubbard, Science of Survival

Woman, before decking yourself, make yourself
acceptable to your Lord,
Lest He should visit not your couch, and your
make-up be gone to waste.
In the woman finding acceptance with her
Lord, lies beauty of her make-up.
Should her make-up be acceptable, shall she
have love of her Lord.
Let her deck herself in fear of the Lord, joy in
God her perfume,
Love her sustenance.
Dedicating body and mind to her Lord, let her
in love to Him be united.

*Sikhism.* Adi Granth, Var Suhi, M.3, p. 788

You wives, be submissive to your husbands, so that some, though they do not obey the Word, may be won without a word by the behavior of their wives, when they see your reverent and chaste behavior. Let not yours be the outward adorning with braiding of hair, decoration of gold, and wearing of fine clothing, but let it be the hidden person of the heart with the imperishable jewel of a gentle and quiet spirit, which in God's sight is very precious. So once the holy women who hoped in God used to adorn themselves and were submissive to their husbands, as Sarah obeyed Abraham, calling him lord. And you are now her children if you do right and let nothing terrify you.

*Christianity.* 1 Peter 3.1-6

Be subject to one another out of reverence for Christ. Wives, be subject to your husbands, as to the Lord. For the husband is the head of the wife as Christ is the head of the church, his body, and is himself its Savior. As the church is subject to Christ, so let wives also be subject in everything to their husbands. Husbands, love your wives, as Christ loved the church and gave himself up for her, the he might sanctify her, having cleansed her by the washing of water with the word, that he might present the church to himself in splendor, without spot or wrinkle or any such thing, that she might be

**I Ching 37:** Cf. the Five Relations as set forth in Doctrine of the Mean 20.8, p. 166.

**1 Peter 3.1-6:** The matriarch Sarah, wife of Abraham, is the model for later generations of women; cf. Isaiah 51.1-2, p. 585; Hebrews 11.11, pp. 539-40.

holy and without blemish. Even so husbands should love their wives as their own bodies. He who loves his wife loves himself. For no man ever hates his own flesh, but nourishes it and cherishes it, as Christ does the church, because we are members of his body. "For this reason a man shall leave his father and mother and be joined to his wife, and the two shall become one flesh." This mystery is a profound one, and I am saying that it refers to Christ and the church; however, let each one of you love his wife as himself, and let the wife see that she respects her husband.

*Christianity*. Ephesians 5.21-33

The husband who wedded her with sacred texts always gives happiness to his wife, both in season or out of season.

Though he may be destitute of virtue, or seek his pleasure elsewhere, or devoid of good qualities, yet a husband must be constantly revered as a god by a faithful wife.

Women need perform no sacrifice, no vow, no fast; if she obeys her husband, she will for that reason alone be exalted in heaven.

A faithful wife, who desires to dwell after death with her husband, must never do anything that might displease him who took her hand, whether he be alive or dead....

She who, controlling her thoughts, words, and deeds, never slights her lord, resides after death with her husband in heaven, and is called a virtuous wife.

*Hinduism*. Laws of Manu 5.153-65

Sujata, the young wife of an eldest son of a rich merchant, Anathapindika, was arrogant, did not respect others and did not listen to the instruction of her husband and his parents. Consequently, some discord arose in the family. One day the Blessed One came to visit Anathapindika and noticed this state of affairs. He called the young wife, Sujata, to him and spoke to her kindly, saying, "Sujata, there are seven types of wives:

A wife who is pitiless, corrupt in mind,
Neglecting husband and unamiable,
Inflamed by other men, a prostitute bent on murder,
Call that wife a slayer!

A wife who would rob her husband of his gains—
Though little be the profit that he makes,
Whether by craftsmanship, or from his trade, or by the plough—
Call that wife a robber!

The slothful glutton, bent on doing nothing,
A gossip and a shrew with strident voice,
Who brings to low account her husband's zeal and industry—
Call that wife a master!

Who with loving sympathy,
Just as a mother for her only son,
For husband cares, and over his stored-up wealth keeps watch and ward—
Call that wife a mother!

Who holds her husband in the same regard
As younger sister holds the elder born,
The meek in heart, who in his every wish her husband serves—
Call that wife a sister!

And she who is as glad her lord to see
As boon companions long apart to meet,
A gracious character of gentle birth, a fond helpmate—
Call that wife a friend!

If fearless of the lash and stick, unmoved,
All things enduring, calm, and pure in heart,
She bear obedience to her husband's word, from anger free—
Call that wife a handmaid!

Now she who's called: a mistress, slayer, thief,
Who's harsh, immoral, lacking in respect, when death comes—
Will wander in the miseries of hell.

**Ephesians 5.21-33:** On this metaphor of the Church as the Bride of Christ, cf. Revelation 21.1-7, pp. 794-95; also Isaiah 62.4-5, p. 137; Exodus Rabbah 49.1, p. 195.

But mother, sister or companion, slave,
In precept long established and restrained,
when death comes—
Will wander in the happy heaven world.

These, Sujata, are the seven kinds of wives a man may have; and which of them are you?" "Lord," said Sujata, "let the Exalted One think of me as a handmaid from this day forth."

*Buddhism.* Anguttara Nikaya iv.91, Sujata Sutta

She gathers the white southernwood,
By the ponds, on the islets.
She employs it,
In the business of our prince.

She gathers the white southernwood,
Along the streams in the valleys.
She employs it,
In the temple of our prince.

With headdress reverently rising aloft,
Early, while yet it is night, she is in the prince's temple.
In her headdress, slowly retiring,
She returns [to her own apartments].

*Confucianism.* Book of Songs, Ode 13

A good wife who can find?
She is far more precious than jewels.
The heart of her husband trusts in her,
and he will have no lack of gain.
She does him good, and not harm,
all the days of her life.
She seeks wool and flax,
and works with willing hands.
She is like the ships of the merchant,
she brings her food from afar.
She rises while it is yet night
and provides food for her household
and tasks for her maidens.
She considers a field and buys it;
with the fruit of her hands she plants a vineyard.
She girds her loins with strength
and makes her arms strong.
She perceives that her merchandise is profitable.
Her lamp does not go out at night.
She puts her hands to the distaff,
and her hands hold the spindle....

She opens her mouth with wisdom,
and the teaching of kindness is on her tongue.
She looks well to the ways of her household,
and does not eat the bread of idleness.
Her children rise up and call her blessed;
her husband also, and he praises her,
"Many women have done excellently,
but you surpass them all."
Charm is deceitful, and beauty is vain,
but a woman who fears the Lord is to be praised.
Give her of the fruit of her hands,
and let her works praise her in the gates.

*Judaism* and *Christianity.* Proverbs 31.10-31

**Book of Songs, Ode 13:** This song praising the dutiful wife may be describing how she gathers wood for nurturing silkworms. But the word 'temple,' although it could mean any large public building, rather suggests that she is engaged in religious duties at a royal shrine. Chinese moralists have long referred to this piece to show how even the most trivial things are accepted in sacrifice, when presented with reverence and sincerity.

## *Friendship*

BEYOND THE CIRCLE OF THE FAMILY, a person seeks friends who will be honest, faithful, and true. The scriptures uphold the ideal of the true friend, while admonishing people to choose their friends carefully, lest they be misled or find themselves abandoned in adversity.

Greater love has no man than this, that a man lay down his life for his friends.

*Christianity*. John 15.13

And the believers, men and women, are protecting friends one of another; they enjoin the right and forbid the wrong, and they establish worship and pay the poor-due, and they obey God and His messenger.

*Islam*. Qur'an 9.71

I am distressed for you, my brother Jonathan;
very pleasant have you been to me;
your love to me was wonderful,
passing the love of women.

*Judaism* and *Christianity*. 2 Samuel 1.26

Only two virtues are enough;
Why should the good stand in need of many?
Anger lived like a lightning flash
And friendship enduring like a line inscribed on a rock.

*Jainism*. Vajjalagam 42

Men bound in fellowship first weep and lament,
But afterward they laugh. [Hexagram 13: Fellowship with Men]

The Master said,
"Life leads the thoughtful man on a path of many windings.
Now the course is checked, now it runs straight again.
Here winged thoughts may pour freely forth in words,
There the heavy burden of knowledge must be shut away in silence.
But when two people are at one in their inmost hearts,
They shatter even the strength of iron or of bronze.
And when two people understand each other in their inmost hearts,
Their words are sweet and strong, like the fragrance of orchids."

*Confucianism*. I Ching, Great Commentary 1.8.6

There are friends who pretend to be friends, but there is a friend who sticks closer than a brother.

*Judaism* and *Christianity*. Proverbs 18.24

He who entreats aid for his comrade, though he himself is in need, is answered first.

*Judaism*. Talmud, Baba Kamma 92a

The dog says, "If you fall down, and I fall down, the play will be enjoyable."

*African Traditional Religions*. Nupe Proverb (Nigeria)

**John 15.13:** Cf. Galatians 6.2, p. 688, and related passages.

**Qur'an 9.71:** Cf. Qur'an 49.10, p. 186, and Hadith of Bukhari, p. 688.

**2 Samuel 1.26:** The story of David and Jonathan is a tale of an exemplary friendship. Jonathan, the son of King Saul (and heir apparent), risked his life to help David flee his father's wrath. David sings this verse in an eulogy for his friend, on hearing of his death in battle.

**I Ching, Great Commentary 1.8.6:** Cf. Book of Songs, Ode 64, p. 696.

**Nupe Proverb:** Good friends should share each other's feelings.

Offend me and I will question you—this is the medicine for friendship.

*African Traditional Religions*. Yoruba Proverb (Nigeria)

Only few people act in our interest in our absence,
When we are not around.
But in our presence, every Dick and Harry, slaves and freeborn,
Display their love for us.

*African Traditional Religions*. Yoruba Verse (Nigeria)

Confucius said, "There are three sorts of friend that are profitable, and three sorts that are harmful. Friendship with the upright, with the true-to-death, and with those who have heard much is profitable. Friendship with the obsequious, friendship with those who are good at accommodating their principles, friendship with those who are clever at talk is harmful."

*Confucianism*. Analects 16.4

It is by dealing with a man that his virtue is to be known, and that too after a long time; not by one who gives it a passing thought or no thought at all; by a wise man, not by a fool. It is by association that a man's integrity is to be known... It is in times of trouble that his fortitude is to be known... It is by conversing with him, that a man's wisdom is to be known, and that too after a long time; not by one who gives it a passing thought or no thought at all; by a wise man, not by a fool.

*Buddhism*. Udana 65-66

When you gain a friend, gain him through testing,
and do not trust him hastily.
For there is a friend who is such at his own convenience,
but will not stand by you in your day of trouble.
And there is a friend who changes into an enemy,
and will disclose a quarrel to your disgrace.
And there is a friend who is a table companion,
but will not stand by you in your day of trouble.
In your prosperity he will make himself your equal,
and be bold with your servants;
but if you are brought low he will turn against you,
and will hide himself from your presence.

A faithful friend is a sturdy shelter:
he that has found one has found a treasure.
There is nothing so precious as a faithful friend,
and no scales can measure his excellence.
A faithful friend is an elixir of life;
and those who fear the Lord will find him.
Whoever fears the Lord directs his friendship aright,
for as he is, so is his neighbor also.

*Christianity*. Sirach 6.7-17

The friend who always seeks his benefit,
The friend whose words are other than his deeds,
The friend who flatters just to make you pleased,
The friend who keeps you company in wrong,
These four the wise regard as enemies:
Shun them from afar as paths of danger.

The friend who is a helper all the time,
The friend in happiness and sorrow both,
The friend who gives advice that's always good,
The friend who has full sympathy with you,
These four the wise see as good-hearted friends
And with devotion cherish such as these
As does a mother cherish her own child.

*Buddhism*. Digha Nikaya iii.187, Sigalovada Sutta

**Yoruba Verse:** Cf. Yoruba Song, p. 675; Analects 1.4, p. 718.
**Udana 65-66:** Cf. Majjhima Nikaya i.123-24, pp. 333-34.
**Sirach 6.7-17:** Cf. Micah 7:5-7, p. 674; Analects 13.25, p. 332.

What is attached to the defiled will be defiled; and what is attached to the pure will be pure.

*Judaism.* Mishnah, Kelim 12.2

Those that are good, seek for friends; that will help you to practice virtue with body and soul. Those that are wicked, keep at a distance; it will prevent evil from approaching you.

*Taoism.* Tract of the Quiet Way

Friend! listen to the benefits of holy company:
Thereby is cast off impurity, vanished are millions of sins,
And purified is the mind.

*Sikhism.* Adi Granth, Bilaval, M.5, p. 809

Sit in the assembly of the honest; join with those that are good and virtuous; nay, seek out a noble enemy where enmity cannot be helped and have nothing to do with the wicked and the unrighteous. Even in bondage you should live with the virtuous, the erudite, and the truthful; but not for a kingdom should you stay with the wicked and the malicious.

*Hinduism.* Garuda Purana 112

As the man one makes his friend,
As the one he follows,
Such does he himself become;
he is like unto his mate.
Follower and following,
Toucher and touched alike,
As a shaft with poison smeared
Poisons all the bunch unsmeared,
Both are fouled. A man inspired
In the fear of being soiled
Should not company with rogues.

If a man string putrid flesh
On a blade of kusha grass,
That same grass will smell putrid.
So with him who follows fools.
If a man wrap frankincense
In a leaf, that leaf smells sweet.
So with those who follow sages.
Mindful of that leaf-basket,
Knowing what will him befall,
The prudent man should company
With the good, not with the bad.
Bad men lead to purgatory;
The good bring to the happy bourn.

*Buddhism.* Itivuttaka 68-69

❖

**Bilaval, M.5:** Cf. Kanara, M.5, p. 195.
**Garuda Purana 112:** Cf. 1 Corinthians 5.9-13, p. 681.

## *Unity and Community*

INDIVIDUALS AND FAMILIES function within the context of a community, which in turn functions within a larger society, nation, and world. The individual's and family's well-being is bound up with the community's well-being, and likewise its well-being is inseparable from the peace and prosperity of the society, the nation, and ultimately, the world. Religious precepts undergird community by teaching the virtues of cooperation, friendship, justice, and public-mindedness. These create the spirit of unity by which community can thrive and prosper.

This section deals specifically with the theme of unity. The opening texts indicate that unity is first of all a gift of grace—a manifestation of the oneness of Ultimate Reality—reconciling those who would otherwise be enemies. The passages that follow call for unity among all members of the community—even to the unity of all humanity—and condemn divisions. The section concludes with passages which use the metaphors of a building and of the human body to depict the varieties of tasks and social roles which should mutually support each other to build a united community.

Israel's reconciliation with God can be achieved only when they are all one brotherhood.

*Judaism.* Talmud, Menahot 27a

The believers indeed are brothers; so set things right between your two brothers, and fear God; haply so you will find mercy.

*Islam.* Qur'an 49.10

Happy is the unity of the Sangha.
Happy is the discipline of the united ones.

*Buddhism.* Dhammapada 194

I do not pray for these [my disciples] only, but also for those who believe in me through their word, that they may all be one; even as thou, Father, art in me, and I in thee, that they also may be in us, so that the world may believe that thou hast sent me.

*Christianity.* John 17.20-21

Again I say to you, if two of you agree on earth about anything they ask, it will be done for them by my Father in heaven. For where two or three are gathered in my name, there am I in the midst of them.

*Christianity.* Matthew 18.19-20

If two sit together and the words between them are of Torah, then the Shechinah is in their midst.

*Judaism.* Mishnah, Abot 3.2

And when a company meets together in one of the houses of God to pore over the Book of God and to study it together among themselves, the Shechinah comes down to them and mercy overshadows them, the angels surround them, and God remembers them among them that are His.

*Islam.* Forty Hadith of an-Nawawi 36

**John 17.20-21:** This is Jesus' prayer for the church to be united, as a testimony to the world of God's presence in him. Cf. 1 John 4.12-13, pp. 159-60; Pesikta Kahana 102b, p. 196.

**Matthew 18.19-20:** Compare Qur'an 58.7, p. 71, where the same image is used to describe God's omniscience, a third party to every secret consultation.

Behold, how good and pleasant it is
when brothers dwell in unity!
It is like the precious oil upon the head,
running down upon the beard,
upon the beard of Aaron,
running down on the collar of his robes!
It is like the dew of Hermon,
which falls on the mountains of Zion!
For there the Lord has commanded the blessing,
life for evermore.

*Judaism* and *Christianity*. Psalm 133

Hold fast, all together, to God's rope, and be not divided among yourselves. Remember with gratitude God's favor on you, for you were enemies and He joined your hearts in love, so that by His grace you became brethren. You were on the brink of the fiery Pit, and He saved you from it. Thus does God make His signs clear to you, that you may be guided.

Let there arise out of you one community, inviting to all that is good, enjoining what is right, and forbidding what is wrong: those will be prosperous. Be not like those who are divided amongst themselves and fall into disputations after receiving clear signs: for them is a dreadful penalty.

*Islam*. Qur'an 3.103-5

It is because one antelope will blow the dust from the other's eye that two antelopes walk together.

*African Traditional Religions*. Akan Proverb (Ghana)

Meet together, speak together,
let your minds be of one accord,
as the Gods of old, being of one mind,
accepted their share of the sacrifice.

May your counsel be common, your assembly common,
common the mind, and the thoughts of these united.
A common purpose do I lay before you,
and worship with your common oblation.

Let your aims be common,
and your hearts of one accord,
and all of you be of one mind,
so you may live well together.

*Hinduism*. Rig Veda 10.191.2-4

Abruptly he [King Hsiang] asked me, "Through what can the Empire be settled?"

"Through unity," I said.

"Who can unite it?"

"One who is not fond of killing can unite it," I said.

*Confucianism*. Mencius I.A.6

Let us have concord with our own people,
and concord with people who are strangers to us;
the divine Twins create between us and the strangers
a unity of hearts.

May we unite in our minds, unite in our purposes,
and not fight against the divine spirit within us.
Let not the battle-cry arise amidst many slain,
nor the arrows of the War-god fall with the break of day.

*Hinduism*. Atharva Veda 7.52.1-2

My children, war, fear, and disunity have brought you from your villages to this sacred council fire. Facing a common danger, and fear-

**Psalm 133:** Cf. Pearl of Great Price, Moses 7.18, p. 196.

**Qur'an 3.103-5:** God is one unity, and humankind should similarly be united; this reconciliation comes through submission to God. The unity of God, the unity of spirit and body within the individual, the unity of society, and the ideal unity of all reality (cf. Qur'an 2.115, p. 70), are encompassed in the Islamic concept of *tawhid*.

**Akan Proverb:** Doing good to each other is the basis of societal unity.

**Rig Veda 10.191.2-4:** Cf. Atharva Veda 3.30, p. 177.

**Atharva Veda 7.52.1-2:** The Asvins, or divine Twins, symbolize perfect unity of two. Cf. Rig Veda 2.39.

ing for the lives of your families, you have yet drifted apart, each tribe thinking and acting only for itself. Remember how I took you from one small band and nursed you into many nations. You must reunite now and act as one. No tribe alone can withstand our savage enemies, who care nothing about the eternal law, who sweep upon us like the storms of winter, spreading death and destruction everywhere.

My children, listen well. Remember that you are brothers, that the downfall of one means the downfall of all. You must have one fire, one pipe, one war club.

*Native American Religions.* Hiawatha, Onondaga Tradition

Separate not yourself from the community.

*Judaism.* Mishnah, Abot 2.4

Maintain religion, and do not stir up any divisions within it.

*Islam.* Qur'an 42.13

Every kingdom divided against itself is laid waste, and no city or house divided against itself will stand.

*Christianity.* Matthew 12.25

One thing, when it comes to pass, does so to the loss, to the unhappiness of many folk... to the misery of the gods and humankind. What is that one thing? Schism in the order of monks. When the order is broken there are mutual quarrels, mutual abuse, mutual exclusiveness, and mutual betrayals. Thereupon those who are at variance are not reconciled, and between some of those who were at one there arises some difference.

*Buddhism.* Itivuttaka 11

Let all mankind be thy sect.

*Sikhism.* Adi Granth, Japuji 28, M.1, p. 6

Consider the family of humankind one.

*Jainism.* Jinasena, Adipurana

My house shall be called a house of prayer for all peoples.

*Judaism* and *Christianity*. Isaiah 56.7

All ye under the heaven! Regard heaven as your father, earth as your mother, and all things as your brothers and sisters.

*Shinto.* Oracle of Atsuta

There is neither Jew nor Greek, there is neither slave nor free, there is neither male nor female; for you are all one in Christ Jesus.

*Christianity.* Galatians 3.28

O contending peoples and kindreds of the earth! Set your faces toward unity, and let the radiance of its light shine upon you. Gather ye together, and for the sake of God resolve to root out whatever is the source of contention among you. Then will the effulgence of the world's great Luminary envelop the whole earth, and its inhabitants become the citizens of one city, and the occupants of one and the same throne.

*Baha'i Faith.* Gleanings from the Writings of Baha'u'llah 111

**Hiawatha:** Hiawatha (Tekanawita, c. 1450), the legendary chief of the Onondaga tribe, unified the Five Nations of the Iroquois. The Iroquois League became the most prosperous and powerful of the Native American nations in what is now the eastern United States.

**Qur'an 42.13:** Cf. Qur'an 30.31-32, p. 318.

**Matthew 12.25:** Hence for the sake of unity, members who are immoral and rebellious may be expelled; see 1 Corinthians 5.9-13, p. 681.

**Itivuttaka 11:** See Udana 55, pp. 681-82, and Vinaya Pitaka 2.184-98, pp. 318-20, the story of the schismatic Devadatta. To make a schism in the Sangha is regarded as one of the Five Deadly Sins—see p. 123n.

**Oracle of Atsuta:** This notion that people are tied together with the kami and things of nature in one universal family builds a sense of community and respect for nature. Atsuta is a shrine in Nagoya.

**Galatians 3.28:** Cf. Ephesians 2.14, p. 394.

**Gleanings from the Writings of Baha'u'llah 111:** Cf. Gleanings from the Writings of Baha'u'llah 115, p. 367.

To accomplish the gigantic historical task [of unification], you must discover the extraordinary power of love, love that does not become the circumstantial victim of society. Supreme love transcends every national, racial, and cultural barrier. People have always talked about love, but human love alone will never accomplish the task of universal unity. Therefore, we rally around one love—the love and heart of God.... The East and West are meeting here today, not merely because we want to see each other for personal reasons, but because the heart of God is linking us into one.

*Unification Church.*
Sun Myung Moon, 9-11-77

The pebbles are the strength of the wall.

*African Traditional Religions.*
Buji Proverb (Nigeria)

Abu Musa reported the Prophet as saying, "Believers are to one another like a building whose parts support one another." He then interlaced his fingers.

*Islam.* Hadith of Bukhari and Muslim

Beware lest the desires of the flesh and of a corrupt inclination provoke divisions among you. Be ye as the fingers of one hand, the members of one body. Thus counsels you the Pen of Revelation, if ye be of them that believe.

*Baha'i Faith.* Gleanings from the Writings of Baha'u'llah 72

When one finger is sore you do not cut it off.

*African Traditional Religions.*
Njak Proverb (Nigeria)

When they divided the Supreme Being,
how many portions did they make?
What did they call his mouth? What his arms?
and what his thighs and his feet?

The Brahmin was his mouth, and
his arms were made the Kshatriya,
his thighs became the Vaishya, and
from his feet was the Sudra born.

*Hinduism.* Rig Veda 10.90.11-12

Just as the body is one and has many members, and all the members of the body, though many, are one body, so it is with Christ. For by one Spirit we were all baptized into one body—Jews or Greeks, slaves or free—and all were made to drink of one Spirit.

For the body does not consist of one member but of many. If the foot should say, "Because I am not a hand, I do not belong to the body," that would not make it any less a part of the body. And if the ear should say, "Because I am not an eye, I do not belong to the body," that would not make it any less a part of the body. If the whole body were an eye, where would be the hearing? If the whole body were an ear, where would be the sense of smell? But as it is, God arranged the organs in the body, each one of them, as he chose. If all were a single organ, where would the body be? As it is, there are many parts, yet one body. The eye cannot say to the hand, "I have no need of you," nor again the head to the feet, "I have no need of you." On the contrary, the parts of the body which seem to be weaker are indispensable, and those parts of the body which we think less honorable we invest with the greater honor, and our unpresentable parts are treated with greater

**Sun Myung Moon, 9-11-77:** Cf. Sun Myung Moon, 10-20-73, p. 94; Wadhans, M.1, p. 161; Ephesians 2.14, p. 394.

**Njak Proverb:** Dependent, unsuccessful relatives and friends are still part of the community to be protected. Cf. Mencius IV.B.7, pp. 691-92; Romans 15.1-3, p. 691.

**Rig Veda 10.90.11-12:** This famous passage is the chief vedic foundation for the caste system. It sanctions the distinctions between castes as having originated with the creation itself. Hence a person's caste, being defined by birth, is immutable. Some contemporary Hindu thinkers would prefer to interpret this passage to establish only a functional differentiation of social roles (as in 1 Corinthians 12, below). In that case, the various roles could be filled by people regardless of their birth or parentage. More of this hymn is found on pp. 621-22.

modesty, which are more presentable parts do not require. But God has so adjusted the body, giving the greater honor to the inferior part, that there may be no discord in the body, but that the members may have the same care for one another. If one member suffers, all suffer together; if one member is honored, all rejoice together. Now you are the body of Christ and individually members of it.

*Christianity*. 1 Corinthians 12.12-27

❖

# *Equality*

THE EQUALITY OF ALL PERSONS, male and female, rich and poor, of any race, class, or caste, is proclaimed in the scriptures of all faiths. This is true despite the conventions of many cultures that discriminate between people on the basis of caste, class, race, or sex. Regrettably, such discrimination is also on occasion supported by certain conventional interpretations of passages from sacred texts. Yet with the development of a more refined religious consciousness, all forms of discrimination are being overcome, and interpretations of religious texts which have traditionally undergirded discriminatory attitudes and practices are being shown to be erroneous.

The essential equality of all people is supported by the doctrines of the monotheistic faiths, that God is the Parent of all humanity and that all human beings are descended from one pair of original ancestors, Adam and Eve. In Buddhism, Jainism, Hinduism, and Confucianism, this equality is grounded in the fact that Enlightenment, unity with the Absolute, or the realization of Goodness is available to all universally. Distinctions among people, therefore, should be based only on their conduct, morality, level of (spiritual) education, and attainment.

The passages below are grouped under the following themes: (1) equality is grounded in the One Absolute; (2) a person's value is determined by his education and attainments, not by birth; and (3) there are no distinctions of class or caste, (4) nationality, (5) race, or (6) sex. For further relevant passages on the equality of people of different creeds, *The Truth in Many Paths*, pp. 34-38.

Have we not all one father? Has not one God created us?

*Judaism* and *Christianity*. Malachi 2.10

I look upon all creatures equally; none are less dear to me and none more dear.

*Hinduism*. Bhagavad Gita 9.29

There will be tribulation and distress for every human being who does evil, the Jew first and also the Greek, but glory and honor and peace for every one who does good, the Jew first and also the Greek. For God shows no partiality.

*Christianity*. Romans 2.9-11

**1 Corinthians 12.12-27:** Cf. Ephesians 2.19-22, p. 196.
**Bhagavad Gita 9.29:** Cf. Tao Te Ching 79, p. 139; Qur'an 76.3, p. 90.
**Romans 2.9-11:** Cf. Acts 10.34-35, p. 37.

There is neither Jew nor Greek, there is neither slave nor free, there is neither male nor female, for you are all one in Christ Jesus.

*Christianity*. Galatians 3.28

I call heaven and earth to witness: whether Jew or Gentile, whether man or woman, whether servant or freeman, they are all equal in this: that the Holy Spirit rests upon them in accordance with their deeds!

*Judaism*. Seder Eliyyahu Rabbah 10

The Law is that which leads to welfare and salvation. It forms conduct and character distinguished by the sense of equality among all beings.

*Jainism*. Somadeva, Nitivakyamrita 1.1

But a single man [Adam] was created for the sake of peace among mankind, that none should say to his fellow, "My father was greater than your father."

*Judaism*. Mishnah, Sanhedrin 4.5

O mankind! We created you from a single pair of a male and a female and made you into nations and tribes, that you might know each other [not that you might despise each other]. Verily the most honored among you in the sight of God is he who is the most righteous.

*Islam*. Qur'an 49.13

All the people of the whole world are equally brothers and sisters. There is no one who is an utter stranger. There is no one who has known the truth of this origin. It is the very cause of the regret of God. The souls of all people are equal, whether they live on the high mountains or at the bottoms of the valleys.

*Tenrikyo*. Ofudesaki 13.43-45

Confucius said, "By nature men are pretty much alike; it is learning and practice that set them apart."

*Confucianism*. Analects 17.2

Whose deeds lower him, his pedigree cannot elevate.

*Islam*. Nahjul Balagha, Saying 21

By deeds, not by birth, is one a brahmin. By deeds one is a kshatriya, by deeds is one a vaishya, and by deeds is one a sudra.

*Jainism*. Uttaradhyayana Sutra 25.3

Four are the castes—brahmin, khatri, sudra,
and vaishya;
Four the stages of life—
Out of these, whoever on the Lord meditates,
is superior.

*Sikhism*. Adi Granth,
Gaund, M.4, p. 861

Not by matted hair, nor by family, nor by birth does one become a brahmin. But in whom there exist both truth and righteousness, pure is he, a brahmin is he.

I do not call him a brahmin merely because he is born of a brahmin womb or sprung from a brahmin mother. Being with impediments, he should address others as "sir." But he who is free from impediments, free from clinging—him I call a brahmin.

*Buddhism*. Dhammapada 393, 396

Confucius said, "In education there are no class distinctions."

*Confucianism*. Analects 15.38

**Galatians 3.28:** See comparable passages on unity, pp. 188-89.

**Qur'an 49.13:** Cf. Hadith of Baihaqi, p. 94.

**Ofudesaki 13.43-45:** All mankind—the wealthy (on high mountains) and the poor (in the valleys)—emanated from one point, 'this origin': their common ancestor was formed by God the Parent at the shrine at Tenri, navel of the world—compare the Shinto cosmogony in the Kojiki 4-6, p. 118. There they will finally return to their common root. On God's regret, see Ofudesaki 17.64-70, p. 326.

**Dhammapada 393, 396:** The Buddha gave new, spiritual definitions to Hindu racial and caste terms like aryian and brahmin. An aryian is not a member of a light-skinned race, but one who follows the aryian Eightfold Path. A brahmin is not a member of a privileged caste, but one who attains the stage of arahant. Cf. Dhammapada 402-22, p. 157.

So what of all these titles, names, and races?
They are mere worldly conventions.

*Buddhism*. Sutta Nipata 648

Lord God of glory is He to whom both the ariyans and the outcastes (*dasa*) belong.

*Hinduism*. Rig Veda 8.51.9

If the brahmin, kshatriya, etc. initiated into my holy order of equality still subscribe to castes and exult therein, they behave like unregenerate beings.

*Jainism*. Sutrakritanga 1.13.10-11

Know all human beings to be repositories of
Divine Light;
Stop not to inquire about their caste;
In the hereafter there are no castes.

*Sikhism*. Adi Granth, Asa, M.1, p. 349

Caste and dynastic pride are condemnable
notions;
The One Master shelters all existence.
Anyone arrogating superiority to himself shall
be disillusioned;
Says Nanak, Superiority shall be determined by
God,
Crediting such a one with honor.

*Sikhism*. Adi Granth,
Sri Raga Mahalla, M.1, p. 83

Unless the mother has a flow of blood
There is no place for the embryo to lodge;
The function of the seed is the same for
everyone.
Greed, lust, anger, joy: such passions are
common to all.
What is the use of your learning and erudition?
Where is the proof for your claim to be high
born?
You are a blacksmith if you heat,
You are a washerman if you beat,
A weaver if you lay the warp,
A brahmin if you read the scriptures.
Is anyone in this world born through the ear?
Therefore, whoever realizes the divine nature is
high born.

*Hinduism*. Basavanna, Vacana 589

To an earthly king, if a poor man greets him, or one who has a burn on his hand, it is a disgrace, and the king does not reply, but God is not so, everybody is acceptable to Him.

*Judaism*. Midrash Psalms 147.1

All those who take refuge in me, whatever their birth, race, sex, or caste, will attain the supreme goal; this realization can be attained even by those whom society scorns. Kings and sages, too seek this goal with devotion.

*Hinduism*. Bhagavad Gita 9.32-33

The Merciful demands that your servant be your equal. You should not eat white bread, and he black bread; you should not drink old wine, and he new wine; you should not sleep on a feather-bed and he on straw. Hence it was said, Whoever acquires a Hebrew slave acquires a master.

*Judaism*. Talmud, Kiddushin 20a

I appeal to you for my child, Onesimus... no longer as a slave but more than a slave, as a beloved brother, especially to me but how much more to you, both in the flesh and in the Lord. So if you consider me your partner, receive him as you would receive me.

*Christianity*. Philemon 10-17

**Asa, M.1** and **Sri Raga Mahalla, M.1:** At the Sikh communal meal or *Pangat*, all eat together while sitting in a single line, without distinction of caste, rank, or wealth. Kings and beggars, brahmins and garbagemen sit together as equals, thus destroying caste consciousness; see Kanara, M.5, p. 195. For among caste-conscious Hindus, it is taboo for a brahmin to eat at the same table with an untouchable.

**Vacana 589:** See Vacana 716, p. 574. The discussion of conception and birth is to mock the vedic tradition in Rig Veda 10.90.11-12, p. 189, that brahmins were set apart at the Creation by being born through the mouth of the cosmic Person. Cf. Itivuttaka 101, p. 406.

**Philemon 10-17:** Paul, while in prison, had converted Onesimus, a runaway slave, to Christianity. Paul finally sends him back to his master, Philemon, with a letter appealing that he treat Onesimus not as a runaway slave but as a brother in Christ. According to Roman law the master had absolute authority

"Are you not like the Ethiopians to me,
O people of Israel?" says the Lord.
"Did I not bring up Israel from the land of
Egypt,
and the Philistines from Caphtor and the
Syrians from Kir?"

*Judaism* and *Christianity*. Amos 9.7

When a stranger sojourns with you in your land, you shall not do him wrong. The stranger who sojourns with you shall be to you as the native among you, and you shall love him as yourself; for you were strangers in the land of Egypt.

*Judaism* and *Christianity*. Leviticus 19.33-34

Even a Gentile, if he practices the Torah, is equal to the High Priest.

*Judaism*. Sifra 86b

"You are a native of Kwangtung, a barbarian. How can you expect to be a Buddha?" asked the Patriarch.

Hui Neng replied, "Although there are northern men and southern men, north and south make no difference to their Buddha-nature. A barbarian is different from Your Holiness physically, but there is no difference in our Buddha-nature."

*Buddhism*. Sutra of Hui Neng 1

Have you not seen how that God sends down water from the sky, and therewith We bring forth with it fruits of diverse hues? And in the mountains are streaks white and red, of diverse hues, and pitch black.

Men too, and beasts and cattle are of diverse colors. Even so only those of His servants who have understanding fear God.

*Islam*. Qur'an 35.27-28

For the white to lord it over the black, the Arab over the non-Arab, the rich over the poor, the strong over the weak or men over women is out of place and wrong.

*Islam*. Hadith of Ibn Majah

What is the true color of love? White? Black? True love has no color. Anyone who is color-conscious cannot have true love at all. You have got to be color-blind.

*Unification Church*. Sun Myung Moon, 1-1-87

God created the human being in his own image, in the image of God he created him; male and female he created them.

*Judaism* and *Christianity*. Genesis 1.27

Thou art woman, Thou art man; Thou art youth and maiden... it is Thou alone who, when born, assumes diverse forms.

*Hinduism*. Svetasvatara Upanishad 4.3

And their Lord answers them, "I waste not the labor of any that labors among you, be you male or female—the one of you is as the other."

*Islam*. Qur'an 3.195

Shariputra: "Goddess, what prevents you from transforming yourself out of your female state, by nature filthy and an unfit vessel?"

Goddess: "Although I have sought my 'female state' for these twelve years, I have not yet found it. Reverend Shariputra, if a magician were to incarnate a woman by magic, would you ask her, 'What prevents you from transforming yourself out of your female state?'"

Shariputra: "No! Such a woman would not really exist, so what would there be to transform?"

"Just so, Reverend Shariputra, all things do not really exist. Now, would you think, 'What

over his slaves, but Paul is appealing to a higher law. Although Paul writes quite tactfully in this letter, eventually the principle set up in this passage would operate to abolish slavery altogether. Cf. 1 Corinthians 7.20-24, p. 508.

**Amos 9.7:** The prophet Amos warns Israel not to be overly proud of its position as God's chosen people. God has been working to save even Israel's worst enemies, the Philistines and the Syrians; cf. Matthew 5.45, p. 90; Megilla 10b, p. 367.

prevents one whose nature is that of a magical incarnation from transforming herself out of her female state?' " Thereupon, the goddess employed her magical power to cause the elder Shariputra to appear in her form and to cause herself to appear in his form. Then the goddess, transformed into Shariputra, said to Shariputra, transformed into a goddess, "Reverend Shariputra, what prevents you from transforming yourself out of your female state?"

And Shariputra, transformed into a goddess, replied, "I no longer appear in the form of a male! My body has changed into the body of a woman! I do not know what to transform!"

The goddess continued, "If the elder could again change out of the female state, then all women could also change out of their female states. All women appear in the form of women in just the same way as the elder appears in the form of a woman. While they are not women in reality, they appear in the form of women. With this in mind, the Buddha said, 'In all things, there is neither male nor female.'"

*Buddhism.*
Holy Teaching of Vimalakirti 7

The sister Soma... when she was returning from her alms-round, after her meal, entered Dark Wood for noonday rest, and plunging into its depths sat down under a certain tree. Then Mara the evil one, desirous of arousing fear, wavering and dread in her, desirous of making her desist from concentrated thought, went up to her and addressed her in verse,

That opportunity [for arahantship] the sages may attain
is hard to win. But with her two-finger wit
that may no woman ever hope to achieve.

Then Soma thought, "Who now is this, human or non-human, that speaks verse? Surely it is Mara the Evil One who speaks verse, desirous of arousing in me fear, wavering and dread...." The sister replied in verses:

What should the woman's nature signify
when consciousness is tense and firmly set,
when knowledge rolls ever on, when she
by insight rightly comprehends the Dhamma?

To one for whom the question arises:
Am I a woman [in these matters], or
am I a man, or what not am I then?
To such a one is Mara fit to talk.

Then Mara the Evil One thought, "Sister Soma recognizes me!" and sad and sorrowful he vanished.

*Buddhism.* Samyutta Nikaya i.128,
Suttas of Sisters

❖

**Holy Teaching of Vimalakirti 7:** The point of this story is not that in this world there should be equality among the sexes. Rather, Buddhism teaches that sexual differentiation belongs only to the phenomenal sphere, which is transient and illusory. In Reality, beyond all appearances, sexuality is transcended. Compare Matthew 22.30, p. 248.

A similar story can be found in chapter 12 of the Lotus Sutra, where the daughter of a dragon king transforms herself into the form of a man to attain Buddhahood, thereby showing Shariputra that he should not regard a woman to be a "filthy vessel" incapable of receiving the Law. And in the Surangama Sutra, the bodhisattva Dridamati asks Gopaka-deva what kind of merit enables a woman to transform her female body into a male body, and the god replies that the problem is not important for the aspirant of the Mahayana as the discrimination does not exist in the mind of an enlightened being.

**Samyutta Nikaya i.128:** For an exemplary female disciple of Jesus, see Mark 14.3-9, p. 547.

## *The People of God*

ANY GOOD SOCIETY, whether a church or a polity, is united with the Absolute and guided by the truth. Many religions, therefore, regard themselves as the unique people of God, bound corporately in a special, covenanted relationship with the Lord. Indeed, not one but several religions-Judaism, Islam, Christianity, Shinto, and Sikhism, among them—have understood themselves to be "chosen" by God and uniquely qualified to establish a godly society. Likewise, in Buddhism the Sangha is a special community, distinguished by its discipline and devotion to the Dhamma and blessed by people who have attained the highest goal. A people that recognizes itself to be the focus of God's special concern, or that devotes itself to the exemplary life called for by the truth, also recognizes that it is responsible to manifest the highest standards of faith and behavior. If it does so, it will be the recipient of great blessings.

Happy is the unity of the Sangha.
Happy is the discipline of the united ones.

*Buddhism*. Dhammapada 194

All jealousies have vanished in the society of the Saints.
All are my friends now, there being no enemy or stranger.

*Sikhism*. Adi Granth, Kanara, M.5, p. 1299

You are the best community that has been raised up for mankind. You enjoin right conduct and forbid indecency; and you believe in God.

*Islam*. Qur'an 3.110

If you will obey my voice and keep my covenant, you shall be my own possession among all peoples; for all the earth is mine, and you shall be to me a kingdom of priests and a holy nation.

*Judaism* and *Christianity*. Exodus 19.5-6

"Many waters cannot quench love" [Song of Solomon 8.7]. If the idolatrous nations of the world were to unite to destroy the love between God and Israel, they would be unable to do so.

*Judaism*. Midrash, Exodus Rabbah 49.1

The land of great Japan is the divine land. Through the divine protection of the gods, the country is at peace. And through the reverence of the nation, the divine dignity is increased.

*Shinto*. Records of Princess Yamatohime

**Kanara, M.5:** On the *Pangat*, the Sikh communal meal, see note to Asa, M.1 and Sri Raga Mahalla, M.1, p. 192.

**Qur'an 3.110:** The *Ummah*, the community of all Muslims, is the foundation of the Islamic state and the ideal of a pan-Islamic world state. Cf. Qur'an 3.103-5, pp. 187.

**Exodus 19.5-6:** Cf. Deuteronomy 6.20-8.20, pp. 764-65; Sanhedrin 11.1, p. 411; Sifra 93d, p. 681.

**Exodus Rabbah 49.1:** See Song of Solomon 8.6-7, p. 176. Cf. Canticles Rabbah 2.5, p. 546; compare Ephesians 5.32-33, pp. 180-81.

**Records of Princess Yamatohime:** This stresses the interdependence of the kami and humanity.

"And you are My witnesses, says the Lord, and I am God" [Isaiah 43.12]. Rabbi Simeon ben Yohai taught, "If you are 'my witnesses,' I am the Lord, and if you are not my witnesses, I am not, as it were, the Lord."

*Judaism*. Pesikta Kahana 102b

You are fellow citizens with the saints and members of the household of God, built upon the foundation of the apostles and prophets, Christ Jesus himself being the cornerstone, in whom the whole structure is joined together and grows into a holy temple in the Lord; in whom you also are built into it for a dwelling place of God in the Spirit.

*Christianity*. Ephesians 2.19-22

Jesus... said to them, "Who do you say that I am?" Simon Peter replied, "You are the Christ, the Son of the living God." And Jesus answered him, "Blessed are you, Simon Bar-Jona! For flesh and blood has not revealed this to you, but my Father who is in heaven. And I tell you, you are Peter, and on this rock I will build my church, and the powers of death shall not prevail against it. I will give you the keys of the kingdom of heaven, and whatever you bind on earth shall be bound in heaven, and whatever you loose on earth shall be loosed in heaven."

*Christianity*. Matthew 16.15-19

And the Lord called his people Zion, because they were of one heart and one mind, and dwelt in righteousness; and there was no poor among them.

*Church of Jesus Christ of Latter-day Saints*.
Pearl of Great Price, Moses 7.18

Immutable is the city of the Divine Master,
Wherein those contemplating the Name attain joy.
In this city founded by the Creator Himself
Are fulfilled desires of the heart:
The Lord Himself has founded it; all joys are obtained herein.
To our progeny, brothers and disciples has come the bloom of joy.
As they sing praise of the Lord, perfection incarnate,
Their objectives are fulfilled.

*Sikhism*. Adi Granth,
Suhi Chhant, M.5, p. 783

Whoever associates with pure love, and those whose love resembles God's, are received joyfully into the Kingdom of Heaven.

*Unification Church*.
Sun Myung Moon, 8-26-86

**Peskita Kahana 102b:** The people of God have the vocation to witness to the divine Reality. The honor and purposes of God Himself depends upon them. Compare John 17.20-21, p. 186.

**Matthew 16.15-19:** This passage founds the Christian church on the apostleship of Peter, the first disciple. Thus all Christians are first of all, like Peter, disciples of Christ. For Roman Catholics, the authority of Peter is the basis for the primacy of the Pope, who as the Bishop of Rome stands as a successor to Peter who founded the Roman church. The authority of Peter is symbolized by the 'keys'; it is the power to 'bind' and 'loose,' meaning the authority to decide on questions of religious law.

**Pearl of Great Price, Moses 7.18:** Cf. Book of Mormon, 3 Nephi 21, pp. 795-96; Isaiah 51.11, pp. 385-86.

**Suhi Chhant, M.5:** Guru Arjan Dev, the fifth Sikh Guru who composed this passage, built the Golden Temple at Amritsar in the Punjab which has become the central Sikh shrine and place of pilgrimage. It is regarded here as the substantiation of the ideal of the City of God—cf. Gauri, Ravidas, p. 794. The Sikhs regard themselves as a holy people, the *Khalsa*, the Pure.

**Sun Myung Moon, 8-26-86:** This speaks of the coming Kingdom of Heaven on earth, which will embrace people of all races and nations.

## The Ideal Society

THE IDEAL SOCIETY IS ONE where there is liberty, justice, kindness, and peace. Some of the verses of scripture which teach these human rights and social values have stirred people of every age to the struggle for freedom and justice. Additional material on this topic, particularly where it concerns the government's obligation to insure these rights, will be found throughout Chapter 20.

The scriptures give descriptions of an ideal society which is far removed from the decadent societies in the existing world. Some texts enunciate general principles. Others describe the ideal society as it was purportedly realized long ago in a golden age; thus the Chinese religions idealized the legendary days of the ancient sage-kings. In Judaism and Christianity, conversely, the ideal society is to be realized in the future, at the consummation of history, with the establishment of *The Kingdom of Heaven*, pp. 789-96.

Proclaim liberty throughout the land to all its inhabitants.

*Judaism* and *Christianity*. Leviticus 25.10

Take away from me the noise of your songs;
To the melody of your harps I will not listen.
But let justice roll down like waters,
and righteousness like an ever-flowing stream.

*Judaism* and *Christianity*. Amos 5.23-24

Lo! God enjoins justice and kindness, and giving to kinsfolk, and forbids lewdness and abomination and wickedness. He exhorts you in order that you may take heed!

*Islam*. Qur'an 16.90

The world stands upon three things: upon the Law, upon worship, and upon showing kindness.

*Judaism*. Mishnah, Abot 1.2

God said, "O My servants, I have forbidden wickedness for Myself and have made it forbidden among you, so do not do injustice to one another."

*Islam*. Forty Hadith of an-Nawawi 24

Two hundred cattle are under one stick, but two hundred human beings are under two hundred sticks.

*African Traditional Religions*. Nupe Proverb (Nigeria)

Thus says the Lord: Do justice and righteousness, and deliver from the hand of the oppressor him who has been robbed. And do no wrong or violence to the alien, the fatherless, and the widow, nor shed innocent blood.

*Judaism* and *Christianity*. Jeremiah 22.3

**Leviticus 25.10:** This well-known passage, which is carved on America's Liberty Bell, was originally a proclamation of the Jubilee Year, once every fifty years, in ancient Israel. At the jubilee, all debts were forgiven, all Hebrew slaves freed, all leases expired, and all property returned to its original owners. This practice was based upon the premise that the land belongs to God, to be granted to the clans and families of Israel in perpetuity; it is not private property to be bought and sold. It prevented the impoverishment of poor farmers by wealthy creditors.

**Amos 5.23-24:** Cf. Micah 6.6-8, pp. 615; Psalm 24.3-6, p. 155.

**Nupe Proverb:** People are by nature independent and can be expected to drive themselves. Cf. Qur'an 2.256, p. 486; Tao Te Ching 60, p. 752; Baba Batra 60b, p. 752.

Now is the gracious Lord's ordinance promulgated,
No one shall cause another pain or injury;
All mankind shall live in peace together,
Under a shield of administrative benevolence.

*Sikhism*. Adi Granth,
Sri Raga, M.5, p. 74

In this world may obedience triumph over disobedience,
May peace triumph over discord,
May generosity triumph over niggardliness,
May love triumph over contempt,
May the true-spoken word triumph over the false-spoken word,
May truth triumph over falsehood.

*Zoroastrianism*. Yasna 60.5

When the right principles of man operate, the growth of good government is rapid, and when the right principles of soil operate, the growth of vegetables is rapid. Indeed, government is comparable to a fast-growing plant. Therefore the conduct of government depends upon the men. The right men are obtained by the ruler's personal character. The cultivation of the person is to be done through the Way, and the cultivation of the Way is to be done through benevolence (*jen*).

*Confucianism*.
Doctrine of the Mean 20

I exist for my family, my family exists for our society, our society exists for our nation, our nation exists for the world, all the world exists for God, and God exists for you and me, for all mankind. In this great circle of give and take there is harmony, there is unity, and there is an eternal process of increasing prosperity. Furthermore, since in this circuit all existence will fulfill its purpose of creation, there is abundant and profound joy. This is the Kingdom of Heaven, in which feelings of happiness overflow.

*Unification Church*.
Sun Myung Moon, 10-20-73

If love and agreement are manifest in a single family, that family will advance, become illumined and spiritual; but if enmity and hatred exist within it, destruction and dispersion are inevitable. This is likewise true of a city. If those who dwell within it manifest a spirit of accord and fellowship, it will progress steadily and human conditions become brighter, whereas through enmity and strife it will be degraded and its inhabitants scattered. In the same way the people of a nation develop and advance toward civilization and enlightenment through love and accord, and are disintegrated by war and strife. Finally, this is true of humanity itself in the aggregate. When love is realized and the ideal spiritual bonds unite the hearts of men, the whole human race will be uplifted, the world will continually grow more spiritual and radiant, and the happiness and tranquillity of mankind be immeasurably increased. Warfare and strife will be uprooted, disagreement and dissension pass away, and Universal Peace unite the nations and peoples of the world. All mankind will dwell together as one family, blend as the waves of one sea, shine as stars of one firmament, and appear as fruits of the same tree. This is the happiness and felicity of humankind. This is the illumination of man, the glory eternal and life everlasting; this is the divine bestowal.

*Baha'i Faith*. 'Abdu'l-Baha,
The Promulgation of Universal Peace

Let there be a small country with a few inhabitants. Though there be labor-saving contrivances, the people would not use them. Let the people mind death and not migrate far. Though there be boats and carriages, there would be no occasion to ride in them. Though there be armor and weapons, there would be no occasion to display them.

Let people revert to the practice of knotting ropes [instead of writing], and be contented with their food, pleased with their clothing, satisfied with their houses, and happy with their customs. Though there be a neighboring

**Sri Raga, M.5:** Cf. Gauri, Ravidas, p. 794.
**Doctrine of the Mean 20:** See Great Learning, p. 491; Mencius II.A.6, p. 145; and Great Learning 8, p. 162.

country in sight, and the people hear each other's cocks crowing and dogs barking, they would grow old and die without having anything to do with each other.

*Taoism.* Tao Te Ching 80

When the eighty-four thousand kings of the eighty-four thousand cities of India are contented with their own territories and with their own kingly state and their own hoards of treasure, they will not attack one another or raise mutual strife. They will gain their thrones by the due accumulation of the merit of their former deeds; they will be satisfied with their own royal state, and will not destroy one another nor show their mettle by laying waste whole provinces. When all the eighty-four thousand kings of the eighty-four thousand capital cities of India think of their mutual welfare and feel mutual affection and joy... contented in their own domains... India will be prosperous, well-fed, pleasant, and populous.

*Buddhism.* Golden Light Sutra

And Judah and Israel dwelt in safety, from Dan even to Beer-sheba, every man under his vine and under his fig tree, all the days of Solomon.

*Judaism* and *Christianity.* 1 Kings 4.25

Rama, whose arms reached to his knees, the powerful elder brother of Lakshmana, ruled the earth in glory and performed many sacrifices with his sons, brothers, and kinsfolk. No widow was ever found in distress nor was there any danger from snakes or disease during his reign; there were no malefactors in his kingdom nor did any suffer harm; no aged person ever attended the funeral of a younger relative; happiness was universal; each attended to his duty and they had only to look to Rama to give up enmity. Men lived for a thousand years, each having a thousand sons who were free from infirmity and anxiety; trees bore fruit and flowers perpetually; Parjanya sent down rain when it was needed and Maruta blew auspiciously; all works undertaken bore happy results and all engaged in their respective duties and eschewed evil. All were endowed with good qualities; all were devoted to pious observances, and Rama ruled over the kingdom for ten thousand years.

*Hinduism.* Ramayana, Yuddha Kanda 130

Long, long ago, brethren, there was a sovereign overlord named Strongtyre, a righteous king ruling in righteousness, lord of the four quarters of the earth, conqueror, the protector of his people, possessor of the seven precious things. His were these seven precious things: the Wheel, the Elephant, the Horse, the Gem, the Woman, the House-father, the Counselor. More than a thousand sons also were his, heroes, vigorous of frame, crushers of the hosts of the enemy. He lived in supremacy over this earth to its ocean bounds, having conquered it, not by the scourge, not by the sword, but by righteousness....

King Strongtyre, having in due form established his eldest son on the throne, shaved hair and beard, donned yellow robes and went forth from home into the homeless state. But on the seventh day after the royal hermit had gone forth, the Celestial Wheel disappeared.

When the new king was informed that the Celestial Wheel had disappeared, he was grieved and afflicted with sorrow. He went to the royal hermit and told him, saying, "Know, sire, verily the Celestial Wheel has disappeared." The royal hermit replied, "Grieve not, dear son, that the Celestial Wheel has disappeared, nor be afflicted. The Celestial Wheel is no paternal heritage of yours. You yourself do good, as I did, and earn the Wheel. Act up to the noble ideal of the duty which is set before true world sovereigns. Then it well may be that if you carry out the noble duty of a Wheel-turning monarch, on the feast of the full moon when you go with bathed head to observe the feast on the chief upper terrace, the Celestial

**Tao Te Ching 80:** This is the ideal of simple village life rooted in tradition and interwoven with loving ties of family and friends. It is quite the opposite of life of the modern jet-setter who travels everywhere but has no roots. For a similar Buddhist image, see Digha Nikaya iii.74-75, pp. 792-93. Cf. Tao Te Ching 32, p. 750; Chuang Tzu 9, pp. 223-24.

Wheel will manifest itself with its thousand spokes, its tire, hub, and all its parts complete."

"But what, sire, is this noble duty of a Wheel-turning monarch?"

"This, dear son, that you, leaning on the Law, honoring, respecting, and revering it, doing homage to it, hallowing it, being yourself a banner of the Law, a signal of the Law, having the Law as your master, should provide the right watch, ward, and protection for your own people, for the army, for the nobles, for vassals, for brahmins, and householders, for town and country dwellers, for the religious world, and for beasts and birds. Throughout your kingdom let no wrongdoing prevail. And whosoever in your kingdom is poor, to him let wealth be given.

"And when, dear son, in your kingdom men of religious life, renouncing the carelessness arising from the intoxication of the senses and devoted to forbearance and compassion, each mastering self, each calming self, each perfecting self, shall come to you from time to time and question you concerning what is good and what is bad, what is criminal and what is not, what is to be done and what left undone, what line of action will in the long run work for weal or for woe, you should hear what they have to say.... This, dear son, is the noble duty of a sovereign of the world."

"Even so, sire," answered the anointed king, and obeying, carried out the noble duty of a sovereign lord. To him, thus behaving, when on the feast of the full moon he had gone in due observance with bathed head to the chief upper terrace, the Celestial Wheel revealed itself, with its thousand spokes, its tire, its hub, and all its parts complete. And seeing this it occurred to the king, "It has been told me that a king to whom on such an occasion the Celestial Wheel reveals itself completely becomes a Wheel-turning monarch. May I, even I, also become a sovereign of the world!"

Then, brethren, the king arose from his seat, and uncovering his robe from one shoulder, took in his left hand a pitcher, and with his right hand sprinkled up over the Celestial Wheel, saying, "Roll onward, O lord Wheel! Go forth and overcome, O lord Wheel!" Then the Celestial Wheel rolled onward toward the region of the East, and after it went the Wheel-turning king, and with him his army, horses and chariots and elephants and men. And in whatever place the Wheel stopped, there the king, the victorious war-lord, took up his abode, and with him his four-fold army. Then all the rival kings came to the sovereign king and said, "Come, O mighty king! Welcome, O mighty king! All is thine, O mighty king! Teach us, O mighty king!"

The king, the sovereign war-lord spoke thus, "You shall slay no living thing. You shall not take what has not been given. You shall not act wrongly, touching bodily desires. You shall speak no lie. You shall drink no maddening drink. Enjoy your possessions as you have been wont to do. Then, brethren, all that were enemy kings became vassals to the king, the Wheel-turner.

*Buddhism.* Digha Nikaya iii.59-62, Cakkavatti-Sihanada Suttanta

Confucius said, "The practice of the Great Tao and the eminent men of the Three Dynasties—this I have never seen in person, and yet I have a mind to follow them. When the Great Tao prevailed, the world was a commonwealth; men of talent and virtue were selected, mutual confidence was emphasized, and brotherhood was cultivated. Therefore, men did not regard as parents only their own parents, nor did they treat as sons only their own sons. Old people were able to enjoy their old age; young men were able to employ their talents; juniors respected their elders; helpless widows, orphans, and cripples were well cared for. Men

**Digha Nikaya iii.59-62:** The Wheel is the symbol of the Dhamma, which the Buddha turned on preaching his opening sermon at Deer Park near Varanasi. The ideal king rules according to right, not might, and all submit to him willingly; without warfare or bloodshed he conquers the world. This sutta describes the suffering and social degradation which follows when the Dhamma is not practiced, and predicts that the world will one day return to the practice of the truth and realize the social ideal once again at the coming of the Maitreya Buddha. See other excerpts of this sutta on pp. 751, 776, 786-87, and 792-93.

had their respective occupations, and women their homes. They hated to see wealth lying about in waste, and they did not hoard it for their own use. They hated not to use their energies, and they used their energies not for their own benefit. Thus evil schemings were repressed, and robbers, thieves, and traitors no longer appeared, so that the front door remained open. This was called the *Ta-tung* (Grand Unity).

"Now the Great Tao has fallen into obscurity, and the world is in the possession of families. Each regards as parents only his own parents and treats as sons only his own sons; wealth and labor are employed for selfish purpose. The sovereigns take it as the proper behavior (*li*) that their states should be hereditary; they endeavor to make their cities and suburbs strong, their ditches and moats secure. Propriety (*li*) and justice (*i*) are used as the norms to regulate the relationship between ruler and subject, to ensure affection between father and son, harmony between brothers, and concord between husband and wife; to set up institutions, organize farms and hamlets, honor the brave and the wise, and bring merit to the individual. Hence schemes and plottings come about and men take up arms."

*Confucianism.* Book of Ritual 7.1.2

It was when the Great Tao declined,
That there appeared the doctrines of humanity (*jen*) and righteousness (*i*).
It was when knowledge and wisdom arose,
That there appeared much hypocrisy.
It was when the six family relationships lost their harmony,
That there was talk of filial piety and paternal affection.
It was when the country fell into chaos and confusion,
That there was talk of loyalty and trustworthiness.

Banish sageliness, discard wisdom,
And the people will be benefited a hundredfold.
Banish humanity, discard righteousness,
And the people will return to filial piety and paternal affection.
Banish skill, discard profit,
And thieves and robbers will disappear.
These three are the ill-provided adornments of life,
And must be subordinated to something higher:
See the simple, embrace primitivity;
Reduce the self, lessen the desires.

*Taoism.* Tao Te Ching 18-19

**Book of Ritual 7.1.2:** More of this passage, p. 474, refers to the illustrious ideal rulers Yü, T'ang, Wen, Wu, and the Duke of Chou. Cf. Mencius I.A.1, pp. 758-59; I.A.7, p. 686. On the degradation of humanity, cf. Laws of Manu 1.81-86, pp. 307-8.

**Tao Te Ching 18-19:** Cf. Tao Te Ching 32, p. 750; 37, p. 393; 38, p. 308; 51, p. 205; I Ching 42, p. 752.

CHAPTER 5

# THE PURPOSE OF LIFE IN THE NATURAL WORLD

THIS CHAPTER TREATS THE PURPOSE FOR HUMAN LIFE in relation to the natural world. The religions give a two-fold teaching, for the human being is both a part of nature and yet qualitatively distinct as the highest and central entity in nature. One the one hand, since every creature has its value and purpose in the cosmos, scriptures teach an ethic of reverence for all life and stewardship of the environment. On the other hand, the scriptures teach, in various ways, that the human being is the crown of creation. The human is the microcosm of the cosmos, encompassing all things. He or she is uniquely in God's image and able to realize divinity. Hence humans are given the commission to take dominion over the things of creation. This right of dominion should not be misunderstood as sanctioning domination, but rather it means to contribute to and enhance the harmony and beauty of the natural world. When human beings are firmly at one with Absolute Reality, they emit a luster and a spiritual fragrance that perfects their environment.

We begin with a collection of teachings on the value of every creature, on the sanctity of the natural world, and on the earth as the great source of life. The second section brings together passages on the ethic of reverence for life and stewardship for the environment. The third section contains passages which describe the human being as the microcosm, encompassing in his or her being the totality of the earth and its creatures. In the fourth section are texts commissioning humans to take dominion over the earth and to rule the earth as God's "vicegerent." This right to rule is founded upon the unique position and qualification of human beings as manifestations of Ultimate Reality, endowed with divine creativity. In the fifth section are teachings on the lordship of human beings extending over the spiritual realms as well. The final group of passages describes the highest union of nature's inherent beauty and power with human creativity and love, when the creation is sanctified by ideal humanity and will "obtain the glorious liberty of the children of God."

# *The Sanctity of Nature*

REVERENCE FOR LIFE begins with the recognition that human beings are but one species of living beings. All living beings are God's sacred creations, endowed with spirit, consciousness, and intelligence. Our reverence is heightened by the recognition that the interdependent web of life is wonderfully self-sustaining and productive. We see the results of human depredation of the environment, which have damaged the original balance of nature. This section concludes with texts praising Mother Earth as the Source of life and its great Sustainer and Supporter.

The earth is the Lord's and the fulness thereof,
the world and those who dwell therein.

*Judaism* and *Christianity*. Psalm 24.1

This earth is a garden,
The Lord its gardener,
Cherishing all, none neglected.

*Sikhism*. Adi Granth,
Majh Ashtpadi 1, M.3, p. 118

Even in a single leaf of a tree, or a tender blade of grass, the awe-inspiring Deity manifests itself.

*Shinto*. Urabe-no-Kanekuni

The stream crosses the path, the path crosses
the stream:
Which of them is the elder?
Did we not cut the path to go and meet this
stream?
The stream had its origin long, long ago.
It had its origin in the Creator.
He created things pure, pure, *tano*.

*African Traditional Religions*.
Ashanti Verse (Ghana and Ivory Coast)

Have you considered the soil you till?
Do you yourselves sow it, or are We the
Sowers?
Did We will, We would make it broken orts,
and you will remain bitterly jesting—
"We are debt-loaded;
nay, we have been robbed."
Have you considered the water you drink?
Did you send it down from the clouds, or did
We send it?
Did We will, We would make it bitter; so why
are you not thankful?
Have you considered the fire you kindle?
Did you make its timber to grow, or did We
make it?
We Ourselves made it for a reminder,
and a boon to the desert-dwellers.

*Islam*. Qur'an 56.63-73

All you under the heaven! Regard heaven as your father, earth as your mother, and all things as your brothers and sisters.

*Shinto*. Oracle of Atsuta

No creature is there crawling on the earth,
no bird flying with its wings,
but they are nations like yourselves.
We have neglected nothing in the Book;
then to their Lord they shall be mustered.

*Islam*. Qur'an 6.38

**Urabe-no-Kanekuni:** Shinto is pantheistic and teaches the omnipresence of the kami. It speaks of the *yaoyorozu-no-kami*, Eight Million Kami, to stress this point. Cf. Nihon Shoki 22, p. 260.
**Oracle of Atsuta:** See p. 188n.

God's hand has touched even every small blade of grass which grows in the field.... All creatures we see contain God's deep heart and tell the story of God's deep love.

*Unification Church.* Sun Myung Moon, 6-28-59

I say, "Just as the consciousness of a man born without any sense organs [i.e., one who is blind, deaf, dumb, crippled, etc. from birth] is not manifest, likewise the consciousness of beings of earth-body [e.g., atoms, minerals] is also not manifest. Nevertheless such a man experiences pain when struck or cut by a weapon, and so also do the beings of earth-body. Likewise for water-beings... fire-beings... plants... animals... air beings: their consciousness and experiences of pain are [actual though] not manifest."

*Jainism.* Acarangasutra 1.28-161

Tao gave them birth;
The power of Tao reared them,
Shaped them according to their kinds,
Perfected them, giving to each its strength.

Therefore of the ten thousand things there is not one that does not worship Tao and do homage to its power. Yet no mandate ever went forth that accorded to Tao the right to be worshipped, nor to its power the right to receive homage. It was always and of itself so.

Therefore as Tao bore them and the power of Tao reared them, made them grow, fostered them, harbored them, brewed for them, so you must
Rear them, but do not lay claim to them;
Control them, but never lean upon them,
Be their steward, but do not manage them.
This is called the Mysterious Power.

*Taoism.* Tao Te Ching 51

Come back, O Tigers!, to the woods again,
and let it not be leveled with the plain.
For without you, the axe will lay it low.
You, without it, forever homeless go.

*Buddhism.* Khuddaka Patha

A horse or a cow has four feet. That is Nature. Put a halter around the horse's head and put a string through the cow's nose, that is man. Therefore it is said, "Do not let man destroy Nature. Do not let cleverness destroy destiny [the natural order]."

*Taoism.* Chuang Tzu 17

They gave the sacrifice to the East,
the East said, "Give it to the West,"
the West said, "Give it to God,"
God said, "Give it to Earth, for Earth is senior."

*African Traditional Religions.* Idoma Prayer

The solid sky,
the cloudy sky,
the good sky,
the straight sky.

The earth produces herbs.
The herbs cause us to live.
They cause long life.
They cause us to be happy.

The good life,
may it prevail with the air.
May it increase.
May it be straight to the end.

Sweet Medicine's earth is good.
Sweet Medicine's earth is completed.
Sweet Medicine's earth follows the eternal ways.
Sweet Medicine's earth is washed and flows.

*Native American Religions.* Cheyenne Song

**Tao Te Ching 51:** The Chinese word *te*, here translated 'power,' may also be translated 'virtue' in the sense of efficacy. This passage can also be taken in a political sense as prescribing the stewardship of good government.

**Chuang Tzu 17:** Cf. Chuang Tzu 10, pp. 571-72.

**Cheyenne Song:** cf. Cree Round Dance Song, p. 31.

In the land of Yamato there are many mountains;
Ascending to the heaven of Mount Kagu,
I gaze down on the country, and see
Smoke rising here and there over the land,
Sea gulls floating here and there over the sea.
A fine country is this,
The island of dragonflies, this
Province of Yamato.

*Shinto.* Man'yoshu 1

On the eastern side of this Himalaya, the king of mountains, are green-flowing streams, having their source in slight and gentle mountain slopes; blue, white, and the hundred-leafed, the white lily and the tree of paradise, in a region overrun and beautified with all manner of trees and flowing shrubs and creepers, resounding with the cries of swans, ducks, and geese, inhabited by troops of monks and ascetics....

*Buddhism.* Jataka

Perhaps if we are lucky,
Our earth mother
Will wrap herself in a fourfold robe of white meal,
Full of frost flowers;
A floor of ice will spread over the world,
The forests because of the cold will lean to one side,
Their arms will break beneath the weight of snow.
When the days are thus,
The flesh of our earth mother will crack with cold.
Then in the spring when she is replete with living waters,
Our mothers,
All different kinds of corn,
In their earth mother we shall lay to rest.
With their earth mother's living waters
They will be made into new beings;
Into their sun father's daylight
They will come out standing;
Yonder to all directions
They will stretch out their hands calling for rain.
Then with their fresh waters
The rain makers will pass us on our roads.
Clasping their young ones [the ears of corn] in their arms,
They will rear their children.
Gathering them into our houses,
Following these toward whom our thoughts bend,
With our thoughts following them,
Thus we shall always live.

*Native American Religions.* Zuni Song

Truth, Eternal Order that is great and stern,
Consecration, Austerity, Prayer, and Ritual—these uphold the Earth.
May she, Queen of what has been and will be,
make a wide world for us.

Earth, which has many heights and slopes and
the unconfined plain that bind men together,
Earth that bears plants of various healing powers,
may she spread wide for us and thrive.

Earth, in which lie the sea, the river, and other waters,
in which food and cornfields have come to be,
in which live all that breathes and that moves,
may she confer on us the finest of her yield....

Set me, O Earth, amidst what is thy center and thy navel,
and vitalizing forces that emanate from thy body.
Purify us from all sides. Earth is my Mother; her son am I;
and Heaven my Father: may he fill us with plenty....

There lies the fire within the Earth,
and in plants,

**Man'yoshu 1:** 'Smoke' and 'sea gulls' suggest the plentitude and harmony among man and nature. Cf. Kagura-uta, p. 90; Kojiki 110, p. 752.

**Jataka:** The mountains, pristine and full of natural beauty, have always been the preferred environment for ascetics, where they may most readily strive to penetrate the Absolute. In Asia, Buddhist monasteries and temples are often associated with nature preserves.

**Zuni Song:** Cf. Cree Round Dance Song, p. 31; Sioux Tradition, pp. 258-59; Winnebago Invocation, pp. 260-61.

and waters carry it;
the fire is in stone.
There is a fire deep within men,
a fire in the kine,
and a fire in horses:
The same fire that burns in the heavens;
the mid-air belongs to this divine Fire.
Men kindle this fire that bears the oblation
and loves the melted butter.

May Earth, clad in her fiery mantle,
dark-kneed,
make me aflame;
may she sharpen me bright....

Whatever I dig from thee, Earth,
may that have quick growth again.
O purifier, may we not injure thy vitals or thy heart....

As a horse scatters dust, so did Earth, since she was born,
scatter the people who dwelt on the land,
and she joyously sped on, the world's protectress,
supporter of forest trees and plants.

What I [Earth] speak, I speak with sweetness;
what I look at endears itself to me;
and I am fiery and impetuous: others who fly at me with wrath
I smite down.

Peaceful, sweet-smelling, gracious, filled with milk,
and bearing nectar in her breast,
may Earth give with the milk her blessings to me.

Thou art the vessel, the Mother of the people,
the fulfiller of wishes, far-extending.
Whatever is wanting in thee is filled
by Prajapati, first-born of Eternal Order.

May those born of thee, O Earth,
be, for our welfare, free from sickness and waste.
Wakeful through a long life, we shall become
bearers of tribute for thee.

Earth, my Mother! set me securely with bliss
in full accord with Heaven. Wise One,
uphold me in grace and splendor.

*Hinduism.* Atharva Veda 12.1

The earth was once a human being; Old One made her out of a woman. "You will be the Mother of all people," he said.

Earth is alive yet, but she has changed. The soil is her flesh, the rocks are her bones, the wind is her breath, trees and grass her hair. She lives spread out, and we live on her. When she moves we have an earthquake.

After taking the woman and changing her to earth, Old One gathered some of her flesh and rolled it into balls, as people do with mud or clay. He made the first group of these balls into the ancients, the beings of the early world. The ancients were people, yet also animals. In form some looked human while others walked on all fours like animals. Some could fly like birds; others could swim like fishes. All had the gift of speech, as well as greater powers and cunning than either animals or people.

Besides the ancients, real people and real animals lived on the earth at that time. Old One made the people out of the last balls of mud he took from the earth. He rolled them over and over, shaped them like Indians, and blew on them to bring them alive. They were so ignorant that they were the most helpless of all the creatures Old One had made. Old One made people and animals into males and females so that they might breed and multiply.

Thus all living beings came from the earth. When we look around, we see part of our Mother everywhere.

*Native American Religions.*
Okanogan Creation

**Atharva Veda 12.1:** Vv. 1-3, 12, 19-21, 35, 57-63. Cf. Rig Veda 1.164.49, p. 94; Candi Mahatmya 10, p. 401.

**Okanogan Creation:** Cf. Aitareya Upanishad 1-3, p. 213. Rig Veda 10.90.6-16, pp. 621-22; Bhagavad Gita 14.4, p. 95.

## *Reverence for Life*

PASSAGES IN THIS SECTION prescribe the ethic proper to reverence for life. There is, first of all, the ethic of *ahimsa*, nonviolence toward all living beings. Vegetarianism is often motivated by this ethic. Then we have passages on the ethic of proper stewardship, recognizing that the natural world is given to humans as a trust, to be tended, maintained, and made fruitful. These deal with doing kindness to animals in distress, the proper management of natural resources, agriculture, animal husbandry, hunting, and forestry.

As a mother with her own life guards the life of her own child, let all-embracing thoughts for all that lives be thine.

*Buddhism.* Khuddaka Patha, Metta Sutta

Have benevolence toward all living beings.

*Jainism.* Tattvarthasutra 7.11

The mode of living which is founded upon a total harmlessness toward all creatures or [in case of actual necessity] upon a minimum of such harm, is the highest morality.

*Hinduism.* Mahabharata, Shanti Parva 262.5-6

One should not injure, subjugate, enslave, torture, or kill any animal, living being, organism, or sentient being. This doctrine of nonviolence is immaculate, immutable, and eternal. Just as suffering is painful to you, in the same way it is painful, disquieting, and terrifying to all animals, living beings, organisms, and sentient beings.

*Jainism.* Acarangasutra 4.25-26

One going to take a pointed stick to pinch a baby bird should first try it on himself to feel how it hurts.

*African Traditional Religions.* Yoruba Proverb (Nigeria)

The Exalted One was entering Savatthi when he saw some youths ill-treating a snake with a stick. Then he uttered these verses of uplift:

Whoso wreaks injury with a rod
On creatures fain for happiness,
When for the self hereafter he seeks happiness,
Not his, it may be, happiness to win.

*Buddhism.* Udana 11-12

This is the quintessence of wisdom: not to kill anything. Know this to be the legitimate conclusion from the principle of reciprocity with regard to non-killing. He should cease to injure living beings whether they move or not, on high, below, and on earth. For this has been called the Nirvana, which consists in peace....

A true monk should not accept such food and drink as has been especially prepared for him involving the slaughter of living beings. He should not partake of a meal which contains but a particle of forbidden food: this is the Law of him who is rich in control. Whatever he suspects, he may not eat. A man who guards his soul and subdues his senses, should never assent to anybody killing living beings.

*Jainism.* Sutrakritanga 1.11.10-16

**Metta Sutta:** Cf. Lion's Roar of Queen Srimala 4, p. 221; Milarepa, p. 221; Holy Teaching of Vimalakirti 1, p. 731.

**Udana 11-12:** Cf. Anguttara Nikaya iv.41-45, p. 617, condemning the slaughter of animals for ritual sacrifice.

Without doing injury to living beings, meat cannot be had anywhere; and the killing of living beings is not conducive to heaven; hence eating of meat should be avoided.

*Hinduism*. Laws of Manu 5.48

If one is trying to practice meditation and is still eating meat, he would be like a man closing his ears and shouting loudly and then asserting that he heard nothing.... Pure and earnest bhikshus, when walking a narrow path, will never so much as tread on the growing grass beside the path. How can a bhikshu, who hopes to become a deliverer of others, himself be living on the flesh of other sentient beings? Pure and earnest bhikshus will never wear clothing made of silk, nor wear boots made of leather for it involves the taking of life. Neither will they indulge in eating milk or cheese because thereby they are depriving the young animals of that which is rightfully belongs to them.

*Buddhism*. Surangama Sutra

Buy captive animals and give them freedom.
How commendable is abstinence that dispenses with the butcher!
While walking be mindful of worms and ants.
Be cautious with fire and do not set mountain woods or forests ablaze.
Do not go into the mountain to catch birds in nets, nor to the water to poison fishes and minnows.
Do not butcher the ox that plows your field.

*Taoism*. Tract of the Quiet Way

At the openings of ant hills
Please have trustworthy men
Always put food and water,
Sugar and piles of grain.

Before and after taking food
Offer appropriate fare
To hungry ghosts, dogs,
Ants, birds, and so forth.

*Buddhism*. Nagarjuna, Precious Garland 249-50

"He that is wise, wins souls" [Proverbs 11.30]. The rabbis said, "This refers to Noah, for in the Ark he fed and sustained the animals with much care. He gave to each animal its special food, and fed each at its proper period, some in the daytime and some at night. Thus he gave chopped straw to the camel, barley to the ass, vine tendrils to the elephant, and glass to the ostrich. So for twelve months he did not sleep by night or day, because all the time he was busy feeding the animals."

*Judaism*. Tanhuma, Noah 15a

According to Abu Hurairah, the Messenger of God said, "A man travelling along a road felt extremely thirsty and went down a well and drank. When he came up he saw a dog panting with thirst and licking the moist earth. 'This animal,' the man said, 'is suffering from thirst just as much as I was.' So he went down the well again, filled his shoe with water, and taking it in his teeth climbed out of the well and gave the water to the dog. God was pleased with his act and granted him pardon for his sins."

Someone said, "O Messenger of God, will we then have a reward for the good done to our animals?" "There will be a reward," he replied, "for anyone who gives water to a being that has a tender heart."

*Islam*. Hadith of Bukhari

The Lord God took the man and put him in the garden of Eden to till it and keep it.

*Judaism* and *Christianity*. Genesis 2.15

Never does a Muslim plant trees or cultivate land, and birds or men or beasts eat out of them, but that is a charity on his behalf.

*Islam*. Hadith of Muslim

**Precious Garland 249-50:** Cf. Digha Nikaya ii.88, Nihon Shoki 22, p. 260.
**Hadith of Muslim:** And likewise if he should cause a stream to flow: see Hadith of Ibn Majah, p. 715.

For six years you shall sow your land and gather in its yield; but in the seventh year you shall let it rest and lie fallow, that the poor of your people may eat; and what they leave the wild beasts may eat. You shall do likewise with your vineyard, and with your olive orchard.

*Judaism* and *Christianity*. Exodus 23.10-11

A certain priest had been killed by the bite of a snake, and when they announced the matter to the Blessed One, he said, "Surely now, O priests, that priest never suffused the four royal families of snakes with his friendliness. For if that priest had suffused the four royal families of the snakes with his friendliness, that priest would not have been killed by the bite of a snake....

Creatures without feet have my love,
And likewise those that have two feet,
And those that have four feet I love,
And those, too, that have many feet.

May those without feet harm me not,
And those with two feet cause no hurt;
May those with four feet harm me not,
Nor those who many feet possess.

Let creatures all, all things that live,
All beings of whatever kind,
See nothing that will bode them ill!
May naught of evil come to them!"

*Buddhism*. Vinaya Pitaka, Cullavagga v.6

Behold this buffalo, O Grandfather, which you have given us.
He is the chief of all four-leggeds upon our Sacred Mother.
From him the people live and with him they walk the sacred path.

*Native American Religions*. Sioux Prayer

The cows have come and brought us good fortune,
may they stay in the stall and be pleased with us;
may they live here, mothers of calves, many-colored,
and yield milk for Indra on many dawns....

They are not lost, nor do robbers injure them, nor
the unfriendly frighten, nor wish to assail them;
the master of cattle lives together long
with these, and worships the gods and offers gifts.

The charger, whirling up dust, does not reach them,
they never take their way to the slaughtering stool,
the cows of the worshipping man roam about
over the widespread pastures, free from all danger.

To me the cows are Bhaga, they are Indra,
they [their milk] are a portion of the first-poured Soma.
These that are cows are Indra, O people!
the Indra I long for with heart and spirit.

Ye cows, you fatten the emaciated,
and you make the unlovely look beautiful,
make our house happy, you with pleasant lowings,
your power is glorified in our assemblies.

*Hinduism*. Rig Veda 6.28

**Exodus 23.10-11:** The Sabbath for the land signifies that God is the true landowner, and he gives the land to us as its stewards. Land, like man and beast, deserves periodic rest; it should not be overexploited. In addition, the fallow land provided food to the poor who had no property. Cf. Leviticus 25.1-7.

**Cullavagga v.6:** Buddha gives in these verses a song for protection against harm from wild animals.

**Sioux Prayer:** The buffalo, as the source of food, clothing, and all life's necessities for the Sioux, represents Mother Earth herself.

**Rig Veda 6.28:** Vv.1, 3-6. This special regard for cows as sacred animals has persisted in India from vedic times till today.

A man should not breed a savage dog, nor place a shaking ladder in his house.

*Judaism*. Talmud, Ketubot 41b

Confucius fished with a line but not with a net. While fowling he would not aim at a roosting bird.

*Confucianism*. Analects 7.26

If you do not allow nets with too fine a mesh to be used in large ponds, then there will be more fish and turtles than they can eat; if hatchets and axes are permitted in the forests on the hills only in the proper seasons, then there will be more timber than they can use... This is the first step along the kingly way.

*Confucianism*. Mencius I.A.3

When you besiege a city for a long time, making war against it in order to take it, you shall not destroy its trees by wielding an axe against them; for you may eat of them, but you shall not cut them down. Are the trees in the field men that they should be besieged by you?

*Judaism* and *Christianity*.
Deuteronomy 20.19

The destruction of vegetable growth is an offense requiring expiation.

*Buddhism*. Pacittiya 11

There is a type of man whose... aim everywhere is to spread mischief through the earth and destroy crops and cattle. But God loves not mischief.

*Islam*. Qur'an 2.205

Rabbi Yohanan ben Zakkai used to say, "If there be a plant in your hand when they say to you, 'Behold the Messiah!' go and plant the plant, and afterwards go out and greet him."

*Judaism*. Talmud,
Abot de Rabbi Nathan, Ver. B, 31

Rajah Koranya had a king banyan tree called Steadfast, and the shade of its widespread branches was cool and lovely. Its shelter broadened to twelve leagues.... None guarded its fruit, and none hurt another for its fruit. Now there came a man who ate his fill of fruit, broke down a branch, and went his way. Thought the spirit dwelling in that tree, "How amazing, how astonishing it is, that a man should be so evil as to break off a branch of the tree, after eating his fill. Suppose the tree were to bear no more fruit." And the tree bore no more fruit.

*Buddhism*. Anguttara Nikaya iii.368

❖

**Ketubot 41b:** Stewardship includes creating a safe environment. Cf. Deuteronomy 22.8, a biblical ordinance requiring flat-roofed houses to have parapets.

**Deuteronomy 20.19:** See also Deuteronomy 22.6-7, 25.4. But contrast Qur'an 59.5.

**Pacittiya 11:** This monastic rule refers to monks living in forest dwellings. It is interpreted to mean that monks should never cut down large trees to clear the land; they may only clear underbrush.

**Abot de Rabbi Nathan, Ver. B, 31:** Cf. Luke 14.16-24, p. 485.

**Anguttara Nikaya iii.368:** Cf. Nihon Shoki 22, p. 260.

## *The Microcosm*

THE HUMAN BEING IS A MICROCOSM of the universe, having the essences of all things in him- or herself. As the microcosm, human beings have the foundation to know, use, and enjoy all things. Of all creatures, humans have the widest scope of thought and action, encompassing all things, knowing and appreciating all things, guiding and prospering all things, and transcending all things.

All that the Holy One created in the world He created in man.

*Judaism*. Talmud, Abot de Rabbi Nathan 31

We shall show them Our signs in the horizons and in themselves, till it is clear to them that it is the truth.

*Islam*. Qur'an 41.53

One who knows the inner self knows the external world as well. One who knows the external world knows the inner self as well.

*Jainism*. Acarangasutra 1.147

The whole of existence arises in me,
In me arises the threefold world,
By me pervaded is this all,
Of naught else does this world consist.

*Buddhism*. Hevajra Tantra 8.41

The illimitable Void of the universe is capable of holding myriads of things of various shape and form, such as the sun, the moon, stars, mountains, rivers, worlds, springs, rivulets, bushes, woods, good men, bad men, dharmas pertaining to goodness or badness, deva planes, hells, great oceans, and all the mountains of the Mahameru. Space takes in all these, and so does the voidness of our nature. We say that the Essence of Mind is great because it embraces all things, since all things are within our nature.

*Buddhism*. Sutra of Hui Neng 2

Man is the product of the attributes of Heaven and Earth, by the interaction of the dual forces of nature, the union of the animal and intelligent souls, and the finest subtle matter of the five elements.

Heaven exercises the control of the strong and light force, and hangs out the sun and stars. Earth exercises the control of the dark and weaker force, and gives vent to it in the hills and streams. The five elements are distributed through the four seasons, and it is by their harmonious action that the moon is produced, which therefore keeps waxing for fifteen days and waning for fifteen. The five elements in their movements alternately displace and exhaust one another. Each one of them, in the revolving course of the twelve months of the four seasons, comes to be in its turn the fundamental one for the time.

The five notes of harmony, with their six upper musical accords, and the twelve pitch-tubes, come each, in their revolutions among themselves, to be the first note of the scale.

The five flavors, with the six condiments, and the twelve articles of diet, come each one, in their revolutions in the course of the year, to give its character to the food.

The five colors, with the six elegant figures, which they form on the two robes, come each one, in their revolutions among themselves, to give the character of the dress that is worn.

Therefore Man is the heart and mind of Heaven and Earth, and the visible embodiment of the five elements. He lives in the enjoyment

**Abot de Rabbi Nathan 31:** Cf. Berakot 10a, p. 141.
**Hevajra Tantra 8.41:** Cf. Samyutta Nikaya i.62, p. 488.

of all flavors, the discriminating of all notes of harmony, and the enrobing of all colors.

*Confucianism*. Book of Ritual 7.3.1-7

In the beginning the Self alone was here—no other thing that blinks the eye at all. He thought, "What if I were to emanate worlds?" He emanated these worlds, water, rays of light, death, the waters. Water is up there beyond the sky; the sky supports it. The rays of light are the atmosphere; death the earth; what is underneath, the waters.

He thought again, "Here now are these worlds. What if I were to emanate guardians?" He raised a Man (*Purusha*) up from the water and gave him a form.

He brooded over him; when he had finished brooding over him, a mouth broke open on him the likeness of an egg. From the mouth came speech and from speech Fire.

Nostrils broke open, from the nostrils came breath, from breath the Wind.

Eyes broke open, from the eyes came sight, from sight the Sun.

Ears broke open, from the ears came hearing, from hearing the Points of the Compass.

Skin broke out, from skin grew hairs, from the hairs plants and trees.

A heart broke out, from the heart came mind, from the mind the Moon.

A navel broke open, from the navel came the out-breath, from the out-breath Death.

A phallus broke forth, from the phallus came semen, from semen Water....

Those deities [the macrocosmic beings], Fire and the rest, after they had been sent forth, fell into the great ocean. Then he [the Self] besieged him [the Purusha] with hunger and thirst. The deities then spoke to him, "Allow us a place in which we may rest and take food."

He led a cow towards them. They said, "This is not enough." He led a horse towards them. They said, "This is not enough." He led man toward them. Then they said, "Well done, indeed." Therefore man is well done. He said to them, "Enter the man, each according to his place."

Then fire, having become speech, entered the mouth; the wind, having become breath, entered the nostrils; the sun, having become sight, entered the eyes; the regions, having become hearing, entered the ears; the plants and trees, having become hairs, entered the skin; the moon, having become mind, entered the heart; death, having become out-breathing, entered the navel; water, having become semen, entered the phallus....

The Self considered, "How could these guardians exist without me?"

Again he thought, "By what way shall I enter them?

"If, without me, speech is uttered, breath is drawn, eye sees, ear hears, skin feels, mind thinks, sex organs procreate, then what am I?"

He thought, "Let me enter the guardians." Whereupon, opening the center of their skulls, he entered. The door by which he entered is called the door of bliss.

*Hinduism*.
Aitareya Upanishad 1.1-3.12

Each man is a microcosm of the universe. Your body is made of all the elements of the world. Nature supplied all the ingredients that make your body, which means that the universe made you by donating itself. If nature demanded that you refund everything that nature loaned you, would there be anything left of you? You can feel that the universe gave you birth and made you, so nature is your first parent. Do you feel good that you are a microcosm

**Book of Ritual 7.3.1-7:** Cf. Gleanings from the Writings of Baha'u'llah 27, pp. 215-16.

**Aitareya Upanishad 1.1-3.12:** Vv. 1.1-4, 2.1-4, 3.11-12. The *Purusha* formed at the beginning of creation is the macrocosmic Person; his parts are then invested in man, the microcosm. Likewise, Hindu temples are built on the pattern of the human body: see Vacana 820, p. 142. For other accounts of creation out of the macrocosmic Person, cf. Rig Veda 10.90.6-16, pp. 621-22. Mundaka Upanishad 1.1.7-9, p. 85; Okanogan Creation, p. 207.

of the universe? All the universal formulas can be found in you. You could accurately say that you are a small walking universe that can move, whereas the cosmic universe is stationary. Because you can move and act, you can govern the universe. The universe would want you to exercise dominion over it, so your first duty would be to love nature. Then, wherever you are, you can love the creation and appreciate it.

*Unification Church.* Sun Myung Moon, 9-30-79

## *Dominion*

ALTHOUGH WE HUMANS are part of the natural world, we have a unique position in it that makes us superior to all other beings. This is not a matter of physical size or strength, for on that scale of things we are only infinitesimal specks on a planet that is itself but a speck in the infinite reaches of the universe. Rather, the reason humans are regarded as the crown of creation is due entirely to our unique spiritual endowment. Humans have the ability, unparalleled in the natural world, to know God and to attain the transcendent purpose. In the special intimacy which we share with God, humans are potentially of more value than the entire world of creation. In this light, the bounty of creation has been regarded as a gift of divine love.

In the Abrahamic religions, humans are said to have been created as God's "vicegerents" and granted the blessing of dominion over all things. All things exist for our benefit, by which we can develop ourselves to become co-creators with God. Furthermore, humans are uniquely able to have dominion because we can understand the nature of all other creatures—symbolized by our giving them names. The blessing of dominion was not originally sanction for developing technology to extract wealth and a comfortable artificial environment at the expense of nature; in the agricultural societies for which this mandate was first given, human creativity was seen as essentially in harmony with natural processes. Today it may be interpreted as a call for artistic and creative projects to enhance the beauty and productivity of nature and the quality of human life.

I will create a vicegerent on earth.

*Islam.* Qur'an 2.30

Do you not see that God has subjected to your use all things in the heavens and on earth, and has made His bounties flow to you in exceeding measure, both seen and unseen?

*Islam.* Qur'an 31.20

And God blessed them, and God said to them, "Be fruitful and multiply, and fill the earth and subdue it; and have dominion over the fish of the sea and over the birds of the air and over every living thing that moves upon the earth."

*Judaism* and *Christianity.* Genesis 1.28

**Sun Myung Moon, 9-30-79:** Cf. Gleanings from the Writings of Baha'u'llah 27, pp. 215-16.

**Qur'an 2.30:** See the complete passage, Qur'an 2.30-33, p. 218; see also Sun Myung Moon, 10-13-70, pp. 218-19.

**Genesis 1.28:** Cf. Shabbat 33b, p. 715.

When I look at thy heavens, the work of thy fingers,
the moon and the stars which thou hast established;
what is man that thou art mindful of him,
and the son of man that thou dost care for him?
Yet thou hast made him little less than God,
and dost crown him with glory and honor.
Thou hast given him dominion over the works of thy hands;
thou hast put all things under his feet.

*Judaism* and *Christianity*. Psalm 8.3-6

God is He who created the heavens and the earth, and sends down rain from the skies, and with it brings forth fruits to feed you; it is He who made the ships subject to you, that they may sail through the sea by His command; and the rivers He has made subject to you. And He made subject to you the sun and the moon, both diligently pursuing their courses; and the night and the day He has made subject to you. And He gives you of all that you ask for. But if you count the favors of God, never will you be able to number them. Verily, man is given up to injustice and ingratitude.

*Islam*. Qur'an 14.32-34

The whole world was created only for the sake of the righteous man. He weighs as much as the whole world. The whole world was created only to be united to him.

*Judaism*. Talmud, Shabbat 30b

Truly do I exist in all beings, but I am most manifest in man. The human heart is my favorite dwelling place.

*Hinduism*. Srimad Bhagavatam 11.2

We did indeed offer the Trust to the heavens and the earth and the mountains; but they refused to undertake it, being afraid of it. But man undertook it; he was indeed unjust and foolish.

*Islam*. Qur'an 33.72

His movement is of Heaven, his stillness of Earth. With his single mind in repose, he is king of the world; the spirits do not afflict him; his soul knows no weariness. His single mind reposed, the ten thousand things submit—which is to say that his emptiness and stillness reach throughout Heaven and Earth and penetrate the ten thousand things. This is what is called Heavenly joy. Heavenly joy is the mind of the sage by which he shepherds the world.

*Taoism*. Chuang Tzu 13

Man, as the manifestation of God, is the leader of all things, and no creature is more honorable than man. All things upon the earth, following their own individual names, fashioning their true way, will know that Thou hast brought them to sight for man's sake. All things whatsoever, forgetting not their source, deviating not from their determined pattern, are made to work as well as to understand their part; humbling themselves and honoring man, without anger, without haste, without anxiety, without grief, neither linked nor parted, they are made to work out their true personality.

*Perfect Liberty Kyodan*. The Ritual Prayer

Having created the world and all that lives and moves therein, He, through the direct operation of His unconstrained and sovereign Will, chose to confer upon man the unique distinction and capacity to know Him and to love Him—a capacity that must needs be regarded as the generating impulse and the primary purpose underlying the whole of creation.... Upon the inmost reality of each and every created thing He has shed the light of one of His

**Qur'an 33.72:** The 'Trust' means the responsibility to choose good and reject evil, to live by God's purposes. Among all created beings, only humans have free will and the responsibility it confers. Yet we have abused it. Cf. Shabbat 88b-89a, p. 219.

names, and made it a recipient of the glory of one of His attributes. Upon the reality of man, however, He has focused the radiance of all of His names and attributes, and made it a mirror of His own Self. Alone of all created things man has been singled out for so great a favor, so enduring a bounty.

*Baha'i Faith.* Gleanings from the Writings of Baha'u'llah 27

Rangi and Papa, or Heaven and Earth, were the source from which, in the beginning, all things originated. Darkness then rested upon the heaven and upon the earth, and they still both cleave together, and the children they had begotten were ever thinking amongst themselves what might be the difference between darkness and light. Hence the ancient saying, "There was darkness from the first division of time, unto the tenth, to the hundredth, to the thousandth."

At last the beings who had been begotten by Heaven and Earth, worn out by the continued darkness, consulted amongst themselves, saying, "Let us now determine what we should do with Rangi and Papa, whether it would be better to slay them or to rend them apart." Then spoke Tumatauenga, the fiercest of the children of Heaven and Earth, "Let us slay them." But Tane-mahuta, the father of forests and all things that inhabit them, said, "Nay, not so. It is better to rend them apart, and to let heaven stand far above us, and the earth lie beneath our feet. Let the sky become a stranger to us, but the earth remain close to us as a nursing mother." Five of the brothers consented to this proposal, but not Tawhiri-ma-tea, the father of winds and storms. He, fearing that his kingdom was about to be overthrown, grieved greatly at the thought of his parents being torn apart.

Then Rongo-ma-tane, the god and father of cultivated food, rises up to rend apart the heavens and the earth; he struggles, but is unable to rend them apart. Next Tangaroa, the god and father of fish and reptiles rises up; he struggles, but he is unable to rend them apart. Next Haumia-tikitiki, the god and father of the food which springs up without cultivation, rises up and struggles, but he, too, fails. At last, slowly rises Tane-mahuta, the god and father of forests, birds, and insects, and he struggles with his parents. With his head firmly planted on mother earth and his feet upraised and resting against the skies, he strains his back and limbs with mighty effort and rends apart Rangi and Papa, all the while insensible to their shrieks and cries. Thus it is said, "It was the fierce thrusting of Tane which tore the heaven from the earth, so that they were rent apart, and darkness was made manifest, and so was the light."

Then there arose in the breast of Tawhiri-ma-tea, the god and father of winds and storms, a fierce desire to wage war with his brothers, because they had rent apart their common parents without his consent. So he rises, follows his father to the realms above, and hurries to the sheltered hollows in the boundless skies; there he consults long with his father, and as the vast Heaven listens to the suggestions of Tawhiri-ma-tea, thoughts and plans are formed in his breast, and Tawhiri-ma-tea also understands what he should do. Then by himself and vast Heaven were begotten his numerous brood: the mighty winds, squalls, whirlwinds, dense clouds, massy clouds, gloomy thick clouds, fiery clouds, clouds reflecting glowing red light, and the wildly bursting clouds of thunderstorms. In the midst of these, Tawhiri-ma-tea sweeps wildly on. Alas! Alas! Then rages the fierce hurricane; and while Tane-mahuta and his gigantic forests stand unconscious and unsuspecting, the blast of the breath of the mouth of Tawhiri-ma-tea smites them, the gigantic trees are snapt off right in the middle. Alas! They are rent to atoms, dashed to the earth, with boughs and branches torn and scattered, lying on the earth, left for the insect, for the grub, and for loathsome rottenness.

Tawhiri-ma-tea next swoops down upon the seas, and lashes in his wrath the ocean. Ah! Ah! Waves steep as cliffs rise, with tops so lofty as to make one giddy; these soon eddy into whirlpools, and Tangaroa, the god of the ocean

**Gleanings from the Writings of Baha'u'llah 27:** Cf. Aitareya Upanishad 1.1-3.12, p. 213; Sun Myung Moon, 9-30-79, pp. 213-14; 10-13-70, pp. 218-19.

and father of all that dwell therein, flies affrighted through the seas....

Tawhiri-ma-tea next rushed on to attack his brothers Rongo-ma-tane and Haumia-tikitiki, the gods and progenitors of cultivated and uncultivated food, but Papa, to save these for her other children, caught them up and hid them in a place of safety; and so well were they concealed by their mother Earth that he sought for them in vain.

Tawhiri-ma-tea, having thus vanquished all his other brothers, next rushed against Tumatauenga, to try his strength against his; he exerted all his force against him, but he could neither shake him nor prevail against him. What did Tumatauenga care for his brother's wrath? He was the only one of the whole party of brothers who had proposed to kill their parents. Now, against the storm winds, he shows himself brave and fierce in war. His other brothers had been broken or fled or had been hidden, but Tumatauenga, or man, still stood erect and unshaken upon the breast of his mother Earth.

Tumatauenga reflected upon the cowardly manner in which his brothers had acted, in leaving him to show his courage alone, and he determined to turn against them. To injure Tane-mahuta, he collected leaves and made snares—ha! ha! The children of Tane fell before him, none could any longer fly in safety. To take revenge on his brother Tangaroa, he sought for his offspring leaping and swimming in the water. He netted nets with flax, dragged with them, and hauled the children of Tangaroa ashore. To be revenged upon his brothers Rongo-ma-tane and Haumia-tikitiki, he soon found them by their distinctive leaves, and scraping into shape a wooden hoe and plaiting a basket, he dug in the earth and pulled up all kinds of plants with edible roots.

Thus Tumatauenga deposed four of his brothers, and they became his food. But one of them, Tawhiri-ma-tea, he could not vanquish by eating him for food, so this last-born child of Heaven and Earth was left as an enemy for man, and still this brother ever attacks him in storms and hurricanes, to destroy him alike on sea and land.

*Maori Religion*. On the Origin of the Human Race (New Zealand)

❖

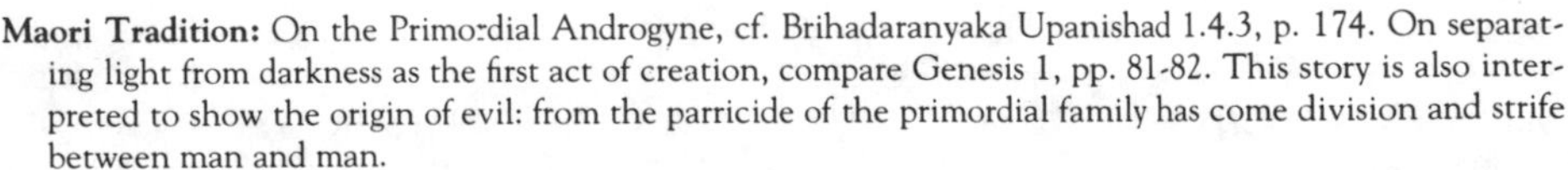

**Maori Tradition:** On the Primordial Androgyne, cf. Brihadaranyaka Upanishad 1.4.3, p. 174. On separating light from darkness as the first act of creation, compare Genesis 1, pp. 81-82. This story is also interpreted to show the origin of evil: from the parricide of the primordial family has come division and strife between man and man.

## *The Lord of Spirits*

THE NATURAL WORLD also includes the spiritual realm. Often enough, benevolent spiritual beings, angels, and devas are the objects of worship and supplication; see *Spiritual Benefactors*, pp. 256-62. Yet with deeper religious insight, it has been revealed that the human being is, in reality, Lord of spirits. Human beings who have received salvation, who are enlightened, or who have achieved the highest goal of life, easily outshine the angels in glory and surpass them in wisdom. Saints and sages, and even ordinary believers who have strong faith, can command the heavenly hosts to assist them in a righteous cause. They can also rebuke and cast out evil spirits in the name of God.

Furthermore, according to the doctrine of reincarnation, even unreconstructed human beings have more opportunity for spiritual advancement than do spirits. Only when incarnated as human beings may souls have an opportunity to progress to the point of their final liberation.

Do you not know that we are to judge angels? How much more, matters pertaining to this life!

*Christianity*. 1 Corinthians 6.3

When a man walks on the highway, a company of angels goes before him, proclaiming, "Make way for the Image of the Holy One!"

*Judaism*. Midrash Psalms 17.8

By converging to unity, all things may be accomplished. By the virtue which is without self-interest, even the supernatural may be subdued.

*Taoism*. Chuang Tzu 12

The wise ones who are intent on meditation, who delight in the peace of renunciation, such mindful, perfect Buddhas even the gods hold most dear.

*Buddhism*. Dhammapada 181

Behold, your Lord said to the angels, "I will create a vicegerent on earth." They said, "Wilt Thou place therein one who will make mischief therein and shed blood?—while we do celebrate Thy praises and glorify Thy holy name?" He said, "I know what you know not."

And He taught Adam the names of all things; then He placed them before the angels, and said, "Tell Me the nature of these, if you are right."

They said, "Glory to Thee! Of knowledge we have none, save what Thou hast taught us: in truth it is Thou who art perfect in knowledge and wisdom."

He said, "O Adam, tell them their natures." When he had told them, God said, "Did I not tell you that I know the secrets of heaven and earth, and I know what you reveal, and what you conceal?"

*Islam*. Qur'an 2.30-33

God created all things with forms, but the invisible God does not have any form.... However, without form, God could not have dominion over the world of form. Therefore, in

**1 Corinthians 6.3:** This refers not to humans generally, but only to saved Christians. Cf. Hebrews 1.14, p. 257; Qur'an 14.22, p. 315.

**Chuang Tzu 12:** Cf. Chuang Tzu 13, p. 215.

**Dhammapada 181:** Cf. Anguttara Nikaya i.279, p. 249; Digha Nikaya xi.67-83, pp. 264-65. For a Jain expression of this idea, see Upadesamala 448-49, p. 454.

**Qur'an 2.30-33:** Cf. Qur'an 17.61-64, pp. 312-13; Genesis 2.15-3.24, pp. 301-2; Brihadaranyaka Upanishad 1.4.10, p. 287.

the created world of material things, God created man, who [was to be given divine] personality and spirit, to be the master. God must have dominion not only over all earthly things, but also over the infinite spiritual world. Archangels and all other spiritual beings are invisible substantial beings [having form]. A certain central form is also necessary in order to have dominion over the invisible substantial world. Then where was that form available? It was only through Adam that God could have such a form. Accordingly, through Adam's form, God planned to have dominion over both the spiritual world and the physical world, with Adam as the center. That was the purpose of creation. God had to have a substantial relationship with the substantial being, Adam, in order to have dominion over all things.

*Unification Church.* Sun Myung Moon, 10-13-70

When Moses ascended on high, the ministering angels spoke before the Holy One, blessed be He, "Sovereign of the Universe! What business has one born of woman among us?" "He has come to receive the Torah," He answered them. They replied, "That secret treasure, which has been hidden by You for nine hundred and seventy-four generations before the world was created, You desire to give to flesh and blood! 'What is man, that Thou art mindful of him, And the son of man, that thou visitest him? O Lord our God, How excellent is thy name in all the earth! Who hast set thy glory [the Torah] upon the heavens!'" [Psalm 8.5, 2].

"Reply to them," said the Holy One to Moses....

Moses then spoke before Him, "Sovereign of the Universe! The Torah which You give me, what is written in it?" "I am the Lord your God, which brought you out of the Land of Egypt" [Exodus 20.2]. He said to the angels, "Did you go down to Egypt; were you enslaved to Pharaoh; why then should the Torah be yours? Again, what is written in it? 'You shall have no other gods' [Exodus 20.3]; do you dwell among peoples that engage in idol worship? Again, what is written in it? 'Remember the Sabbath day, to keep it holy' [Exodus 20.8]; do you perform work, that you need to rest?... Again, what is written in it? 'You shall not murder. You shall not commit adultery. You shall not steal' [Exodus 20.13-15]; is there any jealousy among you; is the evil Tempter among you?" Straightaway the angels conceded to the Holy One, blessed be He, for it is said, "O Lord our Lord, How excellent is Thy name in all the earth," whereas "Who hast set Thy glory upon the heavens" is not written [Psalm 8.10].

*Judaism.* Talmud, Shabbat 88b-89a

Thus I have heard: On a certain occasion the Exalted One was staying near Uruvela, on the bank of the river Neranjara, at the root of the mucalinda tree, having just won the highest wisdom. Now on that occasion the Exalted One was seated for seven days in one posture and experienced the bliss of release. Then arose a great storm of rain out of due season, and for seven days there was rainy weather, cold winds, and overcast skies. So Mucalinda, king of the snakes, coming forth from his haunt, encircled the body of the Exalted One seven times with his coils and stood rearing his great hood above the Exalted One's head, thinking, "Let not heat or cold or the touch of flies, mosquitoes, wind, or creeping things annoy the Exalted One."

Now after the lapse of those seven days the

**Sun Myung Moon, 10-13-70:** Cf. Sun Myung Moon, 9-30-79, pp. 213-14. This original blessing of dominion, and God's purpose in creating men to dwell on earth, was spoiled by the Fall. Fallen mankind has come under the false dominion of the archangel Satan. And God does not dwell in the personality of fallen man. Cf. 10-20-73, p. 332; Divine Principle I.1.2.3.4, p. 175.

**Shabbat 88b-89a:** This argument between God and the angels, with Moses acting as God's spokesman, is a midrash on Psalm 8 (p. 215), which proclaims the dominion of humankind. The angels quote verse 2 of the psalm to argue that God's Torah belongs in the heavens, but after Moses' arguments, they concede that the psalm concludes in verse 10 with God's name found only in the earth. The point seems to be responsibility, which humans alone possess. Cf. Qur'an 33.72, p. 215.

Exalted One roused himself from that concentration of mind. Then Mucalinda, king of the snakes, seeing that the sky was clear and free of clouds, unwrapped his folds from the Exalted One's body, and, withdrawing his own form and creating the form of a youth, stood before the Exalted One, holding up his clasped hands and doing reverence to him.

*Buddhism.* Udana 10, Mucalinda

Behold, I have given you authority to tread upon serpents and scorpions, and over all the power of the enemy; and nothing shall hurt you. Nevertheless, do not rejoice in this, that the spirits are subject to you; but rejoice that your names are written in heaven.

*Christianity.* Luke 10.19-20

The *Kesin* (long-haired sage) bears fire, he bears water,
the Kesin upholds earth and heaven,
the Kesin sees all visions of luster,
the Kesin is called the Light.

Munis with the wind for their girdle
wear the soiled yellow robe;
they go along the course of the wind
where the gods have gone before.

"In the ecstasy of Munihood
we have ascended on the wind,
and only these bodies of ours
are what you mortals ever see."

The Muni flies through mid-air
while he looks at varied forms,
and he is of every deva
a comrade in doing good.

*Hinduism.* Rig Veda 10.136.1-4

Blessed is human birth; even the dwellers in heaven desire this birth: for true wisdom and pure love may be attained only by man.

*Hinduism.* Srimad Bhagavatam 11.13

The universe is peopled by manifold creatures who are, in this round of rebirth, born in different families and castes for having done various actions.

Sometimes they go to the world of the gods, sometimes to the hells, sometimes they become demons in accordance with their actions. Sometimes they become soldiers, or outcastes and untouchables, or worms or moths....

Thus, living beings of sinful actions, who are born again and again in ever-recurring births, are not disgusted with the round of rebirth, but they are like warriors, never tired of the battle of life. Bewildered through the influence of their actions, distressed and suffering pains, they undergo misery in non-human births.

But by the cessation of karma, perchance, living beings will reach in due time a pure state and be born as men.

*Jainism.* Uttaradhyayana Sutra 3.1-7

**Udana 10:** Mucalinda is not a demon, but a heavenly serpent who represents good spiritual forces. His homage to the Buddha expresses the Buddha's lordship over the angelic world. The scene is well-known in Buddhist iconography. Compare Srimad Bhagavatam 10.16, p. 449.

**Luke 10.19-20:** Cf. Psalm 91.11-13, pp. 398-99.

## *Creation Rejoices*

THE NATURAL WORLD is not an object of our manipulation. It is a community of living, sentient beings that suffers or rejoices according to how it is treated by human beings. The scriptures teach that, for those who have eyes to see, nature is exquisitely sensitive to the spirit and attitude of people. The creation "groans in travail" when it is misused and defiled, and rejoices when it can serve God through serving the children of God. Indeed, the virtuous person brings redemption to nature.

Confucius said, "It is Goodness that gives to a neighborhood its beauty."

*Confucianism.* Analects 4.1

Whether in village or in forest, in vale or on hill, wherever arahants dwell—delightful, indeed, is that spot.

*Buddhism.* Dhammapada 98

The perfume of flowers blows not against the wind, nor does the fragrance of sandalwood, tagara and jasmine, but the fragrance of the virtuous blows against the wind; the virtuous man pervades every direction.

*Buddhism.* Dhammapada 54

The earth's condition is receptive devotion.
Thus the superior man who has breadth of character
Carries the outer world.

*Confucianism.* I Ching 2: The Receptive

May no living creatures, not even insects,
Be bound unto samsaric life; nay, not one of them;
But may I be empowered to save them all.

*Buddhism.* Milarepa

Good sons and daughters who accept the true Law, build the great earth, and carry the four responsibilities, become friends without being asked, for the sake of all living beings. In their great compassion, they comfort and sympathize with living beings, becoming the Dharma-mother of the world.

*Buddhism.* Lion's Roar of Queen Srimala 4

Only those who are absolutely sincere can fully develop their nature. If they can fully develop their nature, they can then fully develop the nature of others. If they can fully develop the nature of others, they can then fully develop the nature of things. If they can fully develop the nature of things, they can then assist in the transforming and nourishing process of Heaven and Earth. If they can assist in the transforming and nourishing process of Heaven and Earth, they can thus form with Heaven and Earth a trinity.

*Confucianism.* Doctrine of the Mean 22

There is a holy man living on faraway Ku-she Mountain, with skin like ice or snow, and gentle and shy like a young girl. He doesn't eat the five grains, but sucks the wind, drinks the dew, climbs up on the clouds and mist, rides a flying dragon, and wanders beyond the four seas. By concentrating his spirit, he can protect creatures from sickness and plague and make the

**Dhammapada 98:** Cf. Titus 1.15, p. 518.
**I Ching 2:** Cf. Chuang Tzu 12, p. 218.
**Lion's Roar of Queen Srimala 4:** Cf. Holy Teaching of Vimalakirti 1, p. 731.
**Doctrine of the Mean 22:** Cf. Doctrine of the Mean 1.4-5, p. 155. Srimad Bhagavatam 11.8, pp. 544-45; Nihon Shoki 22, p. 260.

harvest plentiful.... This man, with this virtue of his, is about to embrace the ten thousand things and roll them into one.

*Taoism*. Chuang Tzu 1

Mencius went to see King Hui of Liang. The king was standing over a pond. "Are such things enjoyed even by a good and wise man?" said he, looking round at his wild geese and deer.

"Only if a man is good and wise," answered Mencius, "is he able to enjoy them. Otherwise he would not, even if he had them.

"The Book of Songs says,

He surveyed and began the Sacred Terrace,
He surveyed it and measured it;
The people worked at it;
In less than no time they finished it.
He surveyed and began without haste;
The people came in ever-increasing numbers.
The king was in the Sacred Park.
The doe lay down;
The does were sleek;
The white birds glistened.
The king was at the Sacred Pond.
Oh! How full it was of leaping fish!

It was with the labor of the people that King Wen built his terrace and pond, yet so pleased and delighted were they that they named his terrace the Sacred Terrace and his pond the Sacred Pond, and rejoiced at his possession of deer, fish, and turtles. It was by sharing their enjoyments with the people that men of antiquity were able to enjoy themselves.

"The T'ang Shih says,

O Sun [the tyrant Chieh], when wilt thou perish?
We care not if we have to die with thee.

When the people were prepared 'to die with' him, even if the tyrant had a terrace and pond, birds and beasts, could he have enjoyed them all by himself?"

*Confucianism*. Mencius I.A.2

For the creation waits with eager longing for the revealing of the sons of God; for the creation was subjected to futility, not of its own will but by the will of him who subjected it in hope; because the creation itself will be set free from its bondage to decay and obtain the glorious liberty of the children of God. We know that the whole creation has been groaning in travail together until now; and not only the creation, but we ourselves, who have the first fruits of the Spirit, groan inwardly as we wait for adoption as sons, the redemption of our bodies.

*Christianity*. Romans 8.19-23

Since folk are ablaze with unlawful lusts, overwhelmed by depraved longings, depressed by wrong doctrines, on such as these the sky rains down not steadily. It is hard to get a meal. The crops are bad, afflicted with mildew and grown to mere stubs. Accordingly, many come to their end.

*Buddhism*. Anguttara Nikaya i.50

Hear the word of the Lord, O people of Israel;
for the Lord has a controversy with the inhabitants of the land.
There is no faithfulness or kindness,
and no knowledge of God in the land;
there is swearing, lying, killing, stealing, and committing adultery;
they break all bounds and murder follows murder.
Therefore the land mourns,
and all who dwell in it languish,
and also the beasts of the field,
and the birds of the air,
and even the fish of the sea are taken away.

*Judaism* and *Christianity*. Hosea 4.1-3

**Chuang Tzu 1:** Cf. Chuang Tzu 13, p. 215; Rig Veda 10.136.1-4, p. 220.

**Anguttara Nikaya i.50:** Cf. Golden Light Sutra 12, p. 770; Book of Songs, Ode 254, pp. 769-70; Chuang Tzu 10, pp. 571-72. Even the attitude of the spirits reflects the heart of people: cf. Vamana Purana 19.31-35, p. 315.

**Hosea 4.1-3:** Cf. Jeremiah 7.1-15, p. 768-69; Exodus 20.1-17, p. 110.

Enoch looked upon the earth; and he heard a voice from the bowels thereof, saying, "Woe, woe is me, the mother of men; I am pained, I am weary, because of the wickedness of my children. When shall I rest, and be cleansed from the filthiness which is gone forth out of me? When will my Creator sanctify me, that I may rest, and righteousness for a season abide upon my face?" And when Enoch heard the earth mourn, he wept, and cried unto the Lord, saying, "O Lord, wilt thou not have compassion upon the earth?"

*Church of Jesus Christ of Latter-day Saints.* Pearl of Great Price, Moses 7.48-49

To you did the soul of the ox complain:
"For whom did you create me? Who made me?
Fury and violence oppress me, and cruelty and tyranny.
I have no shepherd other than you: then obtain good pastures for me."

Then the creator of the ox asked the Right, "Hast thou a judge for the ox,
That you may give him, with the pasture, the care for the raising of the cattle?
Whom did you appoint his master who shall put to flight Fury together with the wicked?"

As Righteousness, reply was made: "No companion is there for the ox
That is free from hatred. Men do not understand
How the great deal with the lowly.
Of all beings he is the strongest
To whose aid I come at his call"....

"With hands outstreched we pray to the Lord,
We two, my soul and the soul of the mother-cow,
Urging the Wise One to command that no harm shall come to the honest man,
To the herdsman, in the midst of the wicked who surround him."

Then spoke the Wise Lord himself, he who understands the prayers in his soul:
"No master has been found, no judge according to Righteousness,
For the breeder and the herdsman has the creator fashioned you.

The ordinance of sprinkling the water of the cattle, for the welfare of the ox,
And the milk for the welfare of men desiring food,
This has the Wise Lord, the Holy One,
Fashioned by his decree, in accord with Righteousness."

The ox-soul:
"Whom hast thou, as Good Mind, who may take care of us two for men?"

"I know but this one, Zarathustra Spitama, the only one who has heard our teaching;
He will make known our purpose, O Wise One, and that of Righteousness.
Sweetness of speech shall be given to him."

And then moaned the ox-soul: "That I should have to be content
With the powerless word of a man without strength for a guardian,
I who wish for a strong master!
Will he ever be, he who shall help him with his hands?"

*Zoroastrianism.* Avesta, Yasna 29.1-9

In the days when natural instincts prevailed, men moved quietly and gazed steadily. At that time, there were no roads over mountains, nor boats, nor bridges over water. All things were produced, each for its own proper sphere. Birds and beasts multiplied; trees and shrubs grew up.

**Pearl of Great Price, Moses 7.48-49:** Cf. Pearl of Great Price, Moses 7.27-37, p. 324.

**Yasna 29.1-9:** In this dialogue in heaven, the soul of the ox complains that he is oppressed by the wicked. He asks for justice from his Lord, but the reply comes that there is no one. The soul of the ox and his mate pray again to God, who replies that the ox has been put in the power of man. But he also decrees laws of reciprocal service by which the oxen and mankind can live in harmony. The ox, not satisfied, asks for a righteous protector who will practice these laws. He is told he must make do with Zarathustra, who however lacks the power to actualize the teaching. When, the ox asks, will that teaching prevail, that he may be saved? Zoroastrianism in fact abolished the ritual slaughter of oxen which was practiced among the vedic Aryans.

The former might be led by the hand; you could climb up and peep into a raven's nest. For then man dwelt with the birds and beasts, and all creation was one. There were no distinctions of good and bad men; being all equally without knowledge, their virtue could not go astray. Being all equally without evil desires, they were in a state of natural integrity, the perfection of human existence.

*Taoism*. Chuang Tzu 9

The wolf shall dwell with the lamb,
and the leopard shall lie down with the kid,
and the calf and the lion and the fatling together,
and a little child shall lead them.
The cow and the bear shall feed;
their young shall lie down together;
and the lion shall eat straw like the ox.
The sucking child shall play over the hole of the asp,
and the weaned child shall put his hand on the adder's den.
They shall not hurt or destroy
in all my holy mountain;
for the earth shall be full of the knowledge of the Lord
as the waters cover the sea.

*Judaism* and *Christianity*. Isaiah 11.6-9

❖

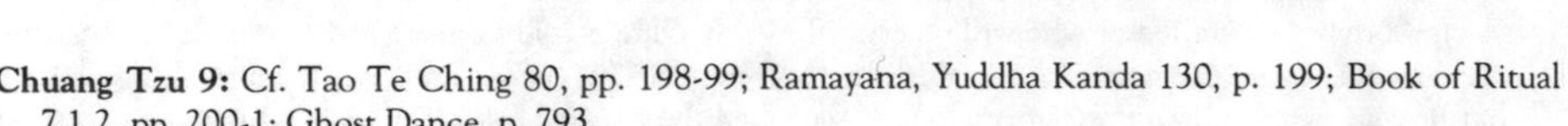

**Chuang Tzu 9:** Cf. Tao Te Ching 80, pp. 198-99; Ramayana, Yuddha Kanda 130, p. 199; Book of Ritual 7.1.2, pp. 200-1; Ghost Dance, p. 793.

**Isaiah 11.6-9:** Cf. Divine Principle I.1.3.1, p. 137.

CHAPTER 6

# LIFE BEYOND DEATH AND THE SPIRITUAL WORLD

NO TREATMENT OF ULTIMATE REALITY AND THE PURPOSES of human life would be complete without a discussion of death and the individual's destiny after death. All religions affirm that there is an aspect of the human person that lives on after the physical life has ended. The immortality of the spirit or soul or psychophysical individual (Buddhism does not admit an eternal metaphysical Soul) is the subject of many passages of scripture. Its destiny after the death of the body is to go into another existence—perhaps in heaven or hell, or as another sentient being on the earth, or in a resurrection body, or merged in eternal unity with the Absolute. Conceptions of the hereafter vary considerably from one religion to another, but there are ample common points which we can explore in making the comparisons in this chapter.

We open with selected passages which affirm the reality of the spiritual world, which corresponds to this material universe and exists "alongside" it. In the next section are passages about the immortal soul, the core of a person's individuality, which survives the death of the physical body: It may ascend to Heaven, descend into hell, or transmigrate into another body. Then, since human life is eternal, it is important to know how to prepare for life in the hereafter. This is the topic of the third section, which gathers passages urging us to use our lives in this world as preparation for life in the next world. In the fourth section we have texts dealing with the actual passage, at the time of physical death, into the next existence. This is usually depicted as fraught with some form of judgment or trial. The fifth section contains passages describing the beauties of heaven and the terrors of hell, using imagery which is sometimes fantastic, sometimes psychological.

The concluding sections contain texts on the assorted spiritual beings, angels, gods, and demons which populate the spiritual world. With power to influence events on earth, these spirits may be looked to for guidance and inspiration or propitiated by offerings. On the other hand, many religions recognize that the spirits are often in error. They have deep suspicions of spiritualism and spirit worship as liable to lead to idolatry and even demonic possession.

## *The Spiritual World: Mystery, Multiplicity, Analogy, Harmony*

THE GENERAL APPEARANCE of the spiritual world is the topic of this short section. Being invisible, it is not something that is easily fathomed, nor are its traces easily observed. However, three definite notions about the spiritual world are represented here: It is composed of a multiplicity of realms, it corresponds by analogy to the phenomenal world, and it operates in mystic harmony.

They will ask you concerning the Spirit. Say, "The Spirit is by command of my Lord, and of knowledge you have been vouchsafed but little."

*Islam*. Qur'an 17.85

No one in heaven or on the earth knows the Unseen save God; and they know not when they will be raised. Does [human] knowledge extend to the Hereafter? No, for they are in doubt concerning it. No, for they cannot see it.

*Islam*. Qur'an 27.65-66

For now we see through a glass, darkly; but then face to face: now I know in part; but then shall I know even as also I am known.

*Christianity*. 1 Corinthians 13.12

I [Paul] know a man in Christ who fourteen years ago was caught up to the third heaven—whether in the body or out of the body I do not know, God knows. And I know that this man was caught up into Paradise—whether in the body or out of the body I do not know, God knows—and he heard things that cannot be told, which man may not utter.

*Christianity*. 2 Corinthians 12.2-4

In my Father's house are many rooms.

*Christianity*. John 14.2

Of the nether worlds and heavens has He
created millions;
Men exhaust themselves trying to explore
them.

*Sikhism*. Adi Granth, Japuji 22, M.1, p. 5

There are celestial bodies and there are terrestrial bodies; but the glory of the celestial is one, and the glory of the terrestrial is another. There is one glory of the sun, and another glory of the moon, and another glory of the stars; for star differs from star in glory.

*Christianity*. 1 Corinthians 15.40-41

The church of the Firstborn... are they into whose hands the Father has given all things—they are they who are priests and kings, who have received of his fulness, and of his glory; and are priests of the Most High, after the order of Melchizedek, which was after the order of the Only Begotten Son. Wherefore, as it is written, they are gods, even the sons of God.... These are they whose bodies are celestial, whose glory is that of the sun, even the glory of

**Qur'an 17.85:** Cf. Rig Veda 3.54.5, p. 47.

**1 Corinthians 13.12:** This passage points to the future, the last days, the *eschaton*. It may be interpreted either as the time after death (personal eschatology), as we do here, or to the final consummation of history: cf. 1 John 3.2, p. 791.

**2 Corinthians 12.2-4:** Many interpreters think this man was Paul himself. On these manifestations of spiritual forces, cf. Doctrine of the Mean 16, p. 48.

**Japuji 22, M.1:** Cf. Taitiriya Upanishad 2.7-9, pp. 133-34.

**1 Corinthians 15.40-41:** Celestial bodies are those spirits who soar in divine love and grace; terrestrial bodies are earth-bound spirits who remain attached to worldly desires, but who may be lifted up through the ministrations of angels and higher beings.

God, the highest of all, whose glory the sun of the firmament is written of as being typical.

And again, we saw the terrestrial world, and behold and lo, these are they who are of the terrestrial, whose glory differs from that of the church of the Firstborn who have received the fulness of the Father, even as that of the moon differs from the sun in the firmament. Behold, these are they who died without law;... who received not the testimony of Jesus in the flesh, but afterwards received it. These are they who are honorable men of the earth, who were blinded by the craftiness of men.

These are they who receive of his glory, but not of his fulness. These are they who receive of the presence of the Son, but not of the fulness of the Father. Wherefore, they are bodies terrestrial, and not bodies celestial, and differ in glory as the moon differs from the sun. These are they who are not valiant in the testimony of Jesus; wherefore, they obtain not the crown over the kingdom of our God....

And again, we saw the glory of the telestial, which glory is that of the lesser, even as the glory of the stars differs from that of the glory of the moon in the firmament. These are they who received not the gospel of Christ, neither the testimony of Jesus. These are they who deny not the Holy Spirit. These are they who are thrust down to hell. These are they who shall not be redeemed from the devil until the last resurrection, until the Lord, even Christ the Lamb, shall have finished his work.

These are they who receive not of his fulness in the eternal world, but of the Holy Spirit through the ministration of the terrestrial; and the terrestrial through the ministration of the celestial. And also the telestial receive it of the administering of angels who are appointed to minister for them, or who are appointed to be ministering spirits for them; for they shall be heirs of salvation.

And thus we saw, in the heavenly vision, the glory of the telestial, which surpasses all understanding; and no man knows it except him to whom God has revealed it. And thus we saw the glory of the terrestrial which excels in all things the glory of the telestial, even in glory, and in power, and in might, and in dominion. And thus we saw the glory of the celestial, which excels in all things—where God, even the Father, reigns upon his throne forever and ever; before whose throne all things bow in humble reverence, and give him glory forever and ever.

*Church of Jesus Christ of Latter-day Saints.*
Doctrine and Covenants 76.54-93

All kingdoms have a law given;

And there are many kingdoms; for there is no space in which there is no kingdom; and there is no kingdom in which there is no space, either a greater or a lesser kingdom.

And unto every kingdom is given a law; and unto every law there are certain bounds also and conditions.

All beings who abide not in those conditions are not justified.

For intelligence cleaves unto intelligence; wisdom receives wisdom; truth embraces truth; virtue loves virtue; light cleaves unto light; mercy has compassion on mercy and claims her own; justice continues its course and claims its own; judgment goes before the face of him who sits upon the throne and governs and executes all things.

*Church of Jesus Christ of Latter-day Saints.*
Doctrine and Covenants 88.36-40

The spiritual world is connected with the physical world. The common factor connecting all things is true love.

*Unification Church.*
Sun Myung Moon, 12-18-85

**Doctrine and Covenants 76.54-93:** This is a visionary interpretation of the preceding passage which describes three spiritual realms. Latter-day Saints and their families who are members of the priesthood and who make active witness to the gospel may become celestial spirits. Honorable and conscientious Christians may become terrestrial spirits, and non-Christians, providing they do not blaspheme the Holy Spirit or commit gross crimes, may become telestial spirits. Cf. Doctrine and Covenants 131.1-3, p. 176.

**Doctrine and Covenants 88.36-40:** This teaches that people ascend to a 'kingdom' that suits their level of intelligence, virtue, light, mercy, and justice.

**Sun Myung Moon, 12-18-85:** Cf. Sun Myung Moon, 4-18-77, p. 248.

What is here [the phenomenal world], the same is there [in Brahman]; and what is there, the same is here.

*Hinduism*. Katha Upanishad 2.1.10

Thou who exists beyond the wide firmament,
mighty in thine own splendor and strong of
mind, hast made,
for our help, the earth a replica of thy glory,
and encompassed water and light up to the
heavens.

*Hinduism*. Rig Veda 1.52.12

We have such a high priest, one who is seated at the right hand of the throne of the Majesty in heaven, a minister in the sanctuary and the true tabernacle which is set up not by man but by the Lord.... There are priests who offer gifts according to the law. They serve a copy and shadow of the heavenly sanctuary; for when Moses was about to erect the tabernacle, he was instructed by God, saying, "See that you make everything according to the pattern which was shown to you on the mountain." But as it is, Christ has obtained a ministry which is much more excellent.

*Christianity*. Hebrews 8.1-6

The system of Change is tantamount to Heaven and Earth, and therefore can always handle and adjust the way of Heaven and Earth. Looking up, we observe the pattern of the heavens; looking down, we examine the order of the earth. Thus we know the causes of what is hidden and what is manifest. If we investigate the cycle of things, we shall understand the concepts of life and death.

Essence and material force are combined to become things. The wandering away of Spirit becomes change. From this we know that the characteristics and conditions of spiritual beings are similar to those of Heaven and Earth and therefore there is no disagreement between them. The knowledge [of Spirit] embraces all things and its way helps all under heaven, and therefore there is no mistake. It operates freely and does not go off course. It rejoices in Nature and understands destiny. Therefore there is no worry. As [things] are contented in their stations and earnest in practicing kindness, there can be love. It molds and encompasses all transformations of Heaven and Earth without mistake, and it stoops to bring things into completion without missing any. It penetrates to a knowledge of the course of day and night. Therefore Spirit has no spatial restriction and Change has no physical form.

*Confucianism*. I Ching,
Great Commentary 1.4.1-4

When King Solomon "penetrated into the depths of the nut garden" [Song of Solomon 6.11], he took up a nut shell and studying it, he saw an analogy in its layers with the spirits which motivate the sensual desires of humans....

God saw that it was necessary to put into the world so as to make sure of permanence all things having, so to speak, a brain surrounded by numerous membranes. The whole world,

**Katha Upanishad 2.1.10:** Cf. Rig Veda 6.47.18, p. 50; Basavanna, Vacana 239, p. 249; Cree Round Dance Song, p. 31; Pearl of Great Price, Moses 6.63, p. 50; Anguttara Nikaya i.279, p. 249; Dhammapada 15-18, pp. 238-39; Chun Boo Kyung, p. 62. This passage may also be interpreted as describing the mystical union of 'this' with Brahman—cf. Katha Upanishad 2.1.10-11, pp. 415-16.

**Hebrews 8.1-6:** The sacrifice which Jesus the High Priest offers for the forgiveness of sins in the heavenly tabernacle is said to be in every way superior to sacrifices at the Jerusalem temple which were offered to atone for sins according to the Jewish Law—cf. Hebrews 9.11-14, p. 371. This is based upon neo-Platonic philosophy, which regards the spiritual realm, the realm of forms, as Reality, while the earthly realm is but its copy, shadow, and reflection. Hebrews quotes Exodus 25.40 as supporting this view: God instructed Moses to construct the tabernacle according to the pattern of the heavenly tabernacle which he saw on Mount Sinai.

**I Ching, Great Commentary 1.4.1-4:** On the lawfulness common to heaven and earth as grounding their resemblance one to the other, cf. Atharva Veda 4.1.3, Rig Veda 10.85.1, p. 99; Proverbs 8.22-31, p. 100; Chuang Tzu 6, p. 101; Doctrine of the Mean 12, p. 101; etc.

upper and lower, is organized on this principle, from the primary mystic center to the very outermost of all the layers. All are coverings, the one to the other, brain within brain, spirit inside of spirit, shell within shell.

The primal center is the innermost light, of a translucence, subtlety, and purity beyond comprehension. That inner point extends to become a "palace" which acts as an enclosure for the center, and is also of a radiance translucent beyond the power to know it. The "palace" vestment for the incognizable inner point, while it is an unknowable radiance in itself, is nevertheless of a lesser subtlety and translucency than the primal point. The palace extends into a vestment for itself, the primal light. From then outward, there is extension upon extension, each constituting a vesture to the one before, as a membrane to the brain. Though membrane first, each extension becomes brain to the next extension.

Likewise does the process go on below; and after this design, man in the world combines brain and membrane, spirit and body, all to the more perfect ordering of the world.

*Judaism*. Zohar, Genesis 19b

God created the seven heavens in harmony.

*Islam*. Qur'an 71.15

Music expresses the harmony of the universe, while rituals express the order of the universe. Through harmony all things are influenced, and through order all things have a proper place. Music rises to heaven, while rituals are patterned on the earth... Therefore the Sage creates music to correlate with Heaven and creates rituals to correlate with the Earth. When rituals and music are well established, we have the Heaven and Earth functioning in perfect order.

*Confucianism*. Book of Ritual 19

❖

**Zohar, Genesis 19b:** The idea that the world is filled with a hierarchy of Being, with the Supreme as its uttermost point, is also expressed in Katha Upanishad 2.3.7-8, p. 60, 3.13, p. 601; Kena Upanishad 1.1-2, p. 75; Qur'an 24.35, p. 74; and the hadith describing seventy thousand curtains of light which veil the Presence, p. 56.

**Qur'an 71.15:** Cf. Gauri Sukhmani, M.5, p. 57; Ramkali Anandu, M.3, p. 134.

**Book of Ritual 19:** Cf. Ramkali Anandu, M.3, p. 134; Sun Myung Moon, 9-11-79, p. 116.

# *The Immortal Soul*

THE SOUL OR SPIRIT OF THE HUMAN individual may be characterized variously: by Hinduism as the divine Self, by Buddhism as the product of conditions and causes, and in Judaism, Christianity, and Islam as the core of the individual person, partaking of his or her choices and deeds. From the perspective of ontology, we note that Buddhism does not conceive of the soul as ultimately real; it parts company with the Hindu and Jain concept of the soul as identical with the divine Self (*Atman*). The Abrahamic religions understand the personal soul to be real, and yet at the same time distinct from God, who is fundamentally other and distinct from his creatures. But ontology is not at issue here; one may refer to passages under *Formless, Emptiness, Mystery*, pp. 55-60, and *Original Mind*, pp. 146-51. In this chapter we are only concerned with the soul as a phenomenological entity which carries the destiny of the individual person.

First of all, the soul, in any of these varied conceptions, is more essential to a person's identity than his body, which is made from clay and is but a vestment, a possession, something one *has* rather than what one *is*. Next, we examine notions of eternal life: how the soul survives the death of the physical body. Although the manner of its survival varies among the religions—it may remain close to earth, ascend to Heaven, descend into hell, participate in a general resurrection, merge into the Godhead, or transmigrate into another body—the fact of its survival is a common thread that unites them all. These texts include descriptions of a new "spiritual body" which will clothe the soul in the next life. Finally, we have several passages which liken the transition to the next life to waking up from a dream.

The body is the sheath of the soul.

*Judaism*. Talmud, Sanhedrin 108a

The dust returns to the earth as it was, and the spirit returns to God who gave it.

*Judaism* and *Christianity*. Ecclesiastes 12.7

Then the Lord God formed man out of the dust of the ground, and breathed into his nostrils the breath of life; and man became a living being.

*Judaism* and *Christianity*. Genesis 2.7

And He originated the creation of man out of clay,
then He fashioned his progeny of an extraction of mean water,
then He shaped him, and breathed His spirit in him.

*Islam*. Qur'an 32.8-9

The union of seed and power produces all things; the escape of the soul brings about change. Through this we come to know the conditions of outgoing and returning spirits.

*Confucianism*. I Ching, Great Commentary 1.4.2

**I Ching, Great Commentary 1.4.2:** Birth and death form one recurring cycle, like the alternation of the seasons. Spirit comes from the invisible realms to the visible, then returns to the invisible realms again.

Now my breath and spirit goes to the Immortal,
and this body ends in ashes;
OM. O Mind! remember. Remember the deeds.
Remember the actions.

*Hinduism*. Isha Upanishad 17

The outward form, brethren, of him who has won the truth stands before you, but that which binds it to rebirth is cut in twain.

*Buddhism*. Digha Nikaya: Brahmajala Sutta

The soul is characterized by knowledge and vision, is formless, an agent, has the same extent as its own body, is the enjoyer of the fruits of karmas, and exists in samsara. It is also enlightened and has a characteristic upward motion.

*Jainism*. Nemichandra, Dravyasangraha 2

Matter has no life, hence it has no real existence. Mind is immortal.

*Christian Science*. Science and Health, 584

A man *is* his own immortal soul.

*Scientology*. L. Ron Hubbard, A New Slant on Life

Knowing that this body is like foam, and comprehending that it is as unsubstantial as a mirage, one should destroy the flower-tipped shafts of sensual passions [Mara], and pass beyond the sight of the King of death.

*Buddhism*. Dhammapada 46

Know that the present life is but a sport and a diversion, an adornment and a cause of boasting among you, and a rivalry in wealth and children. It is as a rain whose vegetation pleases the unbelievers; then it withers, and you see it turning yellow, then it becomes straw. And in the Hereafter there is grievous punishment, and forgiveness from God and good pleasure; whereas the present life is but the joy of delusion.

*Islam*. Qur'an 57.20

Behold this beautiful body, a mass of sores, a heaped up lump, diseased, much thought of, in which nothing lasts, nothing persists.

Thoroughly worn out is this body, a nest of diseases, perishable. This putrid mass breaks up. Truly, life ends in death. Like gourds cast away in autumn are these dove-hued bones. What pleasure is there in looking at them?

Of bones is this house made, plastered with flesh and blood. Herein are stored decay, death, conceit, and hypocrisy.

Even ornamented royal chariots wear out. So too the body reaches old age. But the Dhamma of the Good grows not old. Thus do the Good reveal it among the Good.

*Buddhism*. Dhammapada 147-51

Man's real nature is primarily spiritual life,
which weaves its threads of mind to build a cocoon of flesh, encloses its own soul in the cocoon,
And, for the first time, the spirit becomes flesh.
Understand this clearly: The cocoon is not the silkworm;
In the same way, the physical body is not man but merely man's cocoon.
Just as the silkworm will break out of its cocoon and fly free,
So, too, will man break out of his body-cocoon and ascend to the spiritual world when his time is come.

**Isha Upanishad 17:** Also found in Yajur Veda 40.15.

**Brahmajala Sutta:** With liberation, the existential state of the soul may change without any alteration of a person's external bodily appearance.

**Dravyasangraha 2:** This speaks of the *jiva*, the individual soul.

**Science and Health, 584:** Cf. the Buddhist doctrine of Mind-only in Lankavatara Sutra 61-64, pp. 102-3.

**Dhammapada 46:** Cf. Sutra of Hui Neng 10, p. 310.

**Qur'an 57.20:** Cf. Qur'an 17.18-19, p. 237; 102, p. 239.

Never think that the death of the physical
body is the death of man.
Since man is life, he will never know death.

*Seicho-no-Ie.* Nectarean Shower of Holy Doctrines.

Ts'ai-wu said, "I have heard the names *kuei* and *shen*, but I do not know what they mean." The Master said, "The [intelligent] spirit is of the shen nature, and shows that in fullest measure; the animal soul is of the kuei nature, and shows that in fullest measure. It is the union of kuei and shen that forms the highest exhibition of doctrine.

"All the living must die, and dying, return to the ground; this is what is called kuei. The bones and flesh molder below, and, hidden away, become the earth of the fields. But the spirit issues forth, and is displayed on high in a condition of glorious brightness. The vapors and odors which produce a feeling of sadness, [and arise from the decay of their substance], are the subtle essences of all things, and also a manifestation of the shen nature."

*Confucianism.* Book of Ritual 21.2.1

Though our outer nature is wasting away, our inner nature is being renewed every day. For this slight momentary affliction is preparing us for an eternal weight of glory beyond all comparison, because we look not to the things that are seen but to the things that are unseen; for the things that are seen are transient, but the things that are unseen are eternal.

For we know that if the earthly tent we live in is destroyed, we have a building from God, a house not made with hands, eternal in the heavens. Here indeed we groan, and long to put on our heavenly dwelling, so that by putting it on we may not be found naked. For while we are still in this tent, we sigh with anxiety; not that we would be unclothed, but that we would be further clothed, so that what is mortal may be swallowed up by life. He who has prepared us for this very thing is God, who has given us the Spirit as a guarantee.

So we are always of good courage; we know that while we are at home in the body we are away from the Lord, for we walk by faith, not by sight. We are of good courage, and we would rather be away from the body and at home with the Lord. For we must all appear before the judgment seat of Christ, so that each one may receive good or evil, according to what he has done in the body.

*Christianity.* 2 Corinthians 4.16-5.10

Look upon life as a swelling tumor, a protruding goiter, and upon death as the draining of a sore or the bursting of a boil.

*Taoism.* Chuang Tzu 6

You prefer this life, although the life to come is better and more enduring. All this is written in earlier scriptures; the scriptures of Abraham and Moses.

*Islam.* Qur'an 87.16-19

Onyame does not die, I will therefore not die.

*African Traditional Religions.* Akan Proverb (Ghana)

Do not say, "They are dead!" about anyone who is killed for God's sake. Rather they are living, even though you do not notice it.

*Islam.* Qur'an 2.154

Those who are dead are never gone:
they are there in the thickening shadow.
The dead are not under the earth:
they are there in the tree that rustles,
they are in the wood that groans,
they are in the water that runs,
they are in the water that sleeps,
they are in the hut, they are in the crowd,
the dead are not dead.

**Nectarean Shower of Holy Doctrines:** As in popular Japanese Buddhism, the scripture of this new religion contrasts the realm of appearances and sense impressions with the realm of Reality. The body belongs to the realm of appearances, but the spiritual life belongs to the order of Reality.

**Akan Proverb:** 'Onyame' is the most common Akan name for the Supreme Being. It means, roughly, The One Who Gives Fulness.

**Qur'an 2.154:** This refers specifically to the martyrs, those killed in the struggle for God. Cf. Qur'an 3.169-74, p. 629; Hadith of Muslim, p. 627.

Those who are dead are never gone:
they are in the breast of the woman,
they are in the child who is wailing,
and in the firebrand that flames.
The dead are not under the earth:
they are in the fire that is dying,
they are in the grasses that weep,
they are in the whimpering rocks,
they are in the forest, they are in the house,
the dead are not dead.

*African Traditional Religions.* Birago Diop, Mali Poem

Who is whose mother? Who the father?
All relationships are nominal, false.
Ignorant man! Why do you babble as in a dream?
Know, by conjunction made by God, by His Ordinance,
You have come into the world.
All from one clay are made; in all one Light shines.
One breath pervades all, what point is any weeping over another?
Man wails over the loss of what he calls his:
Know, the Self is not perishable.

*Sikhism.* Adi Granth, Gauri, M.5, p. 188

One man believes he is the slayer, another believes he is the slain. Both are ignorant; there is neither slayer nor slain. You were never born; you will never die. You have never changed; you can never change. Unborn, eternal, immutable, immemorial, you do not die when the body dies. Realizing that which is indestructible, eternal, unborn, and unchanging, how can you slay or cause another to be slain?

As a man abandons his worn-out clothes and acquires new ones, so when the body is worn out a new one is acquired by the Self, who lives within.

The Self cannot be pierced with weapons or burned with fire; water cannot wet it, nor can the wind dry it. The Self cannot be pierced or burned, made wet or dry. It is everlasting and infinite, standing on the motionless foundation of eternity. The Self is unmanifested, beyond all thought, beyond all change. Knowing this, you should not grieve.

*Hinduism.* Bhagavad Gita 2.19-25

One who identifies himself with his soul regards bodily transmigration of his soul at death fearlessly, like changing one cloth for another.

*Jainism.* Pujyapada, Samadhishataka 77

Why is it thought incredible by any of you that God raises the dead?

*Christianity.* Acts 26.8

Just as the womb takes in and gives forth again, so the grave takes in and will give forth again.

*Judaism.* Talmud, Berakot 15b

It is We who give life, and make to die, and to Us is the homecoming.

*Islam.* Qur'an 50.43

And among His signs is this: you see the earth barren and desolate, but when We send down rain to it, it is stirred to life and yields increase. Truly, He who gives life to the dead earth can surely give life to men who are dead. For He has power over all things.

*Islam.* Qur'an 41.39

Some day the Great Chief Above will overturn the mountains and the rocks. Then the spirits that once lived in the bones buried there will

**Gauri, M.5:** Cf. Acarangasutra 4.32, p. 676; Brihadaranyaka Upanishad 2.4.4-5, p. 677.

**Bhagavad Gita 2.19-25:** The Self—which is all-pervasive Spirit—pre-exists its incarnation in the physical body, and will continue to exist through eternity, clothed in body after body. A different notion of pre-existence, whereby what pre-exists is the individual soul, is found in the Latter-day Saints; cf. Pearl of Great Price, Abraham 3.22-4.1, p. 258.

**Acts 26.8:** Cf. 1 Corinthians 15.52-57, pp. 411-12.

**Berakot 15b:** Cf. Ezekiel 37.1-14, p. 413.

**Qur'an 41.39:** Cf. Qur'an 3.27, p. 412; Ezekiel 37.1-14, p. 413.

go back into them. At present those spirits live in the tops of the mountains, watching their children on earth and waiting for the great change which is to come. The voices of these spirits can be heard in the mountains at all times. Mourners who wail for their dead hear spirit voices reply, and thus they know that their lost ones are always near.

*Native American Religions*. Yakima Tradition

The world beyond is as different from this world as this world is different from that of the child while still in the womb of its mother. When the soul attains the Presence of God, it will assume the form that best befits its immortality and is worthy of its celestial habitation. Such an existence is a contingent and not an absolute existence, inasmuch as the former is preceded by a cause, whilst the latter is independent thereof. Absolute existence is strictly confined to God, exalted be His glory.

*Baha'i Faith*. Gleanings from the Writings of Baha'u'llah 81

Birth is not a beginning; death is not an end. There is existence without limitation; there is continuity without a starting point. Existence without limitation is space. Continuity without a starting point is time. There is birth, there is death, there is issuing forth, there is entering in. That through which one passes in and out without seeing its form, that is the Portal of God.

*Taoism*. Chuang Tzu 23

Yama was the first to find us our abode,
a place that can never be taken away,
where our ancient Fathers have departed; all who are born go there by that path, treading their own.
Meet the Fathers, meet Yama, meet with the fulfillment of wishes in the highest heaven;
casting off imperfections, find anew your dwelling,
and be united with a lustrous body.

*Hinduism*. Rig Veda 10.14.2,8

But some one will ask, "How are the dead raised? With what kind of body do they come?" You foolish man! What you sow does not come to life unless it dies. And what you sow is not the body which is to be, but a bare kernel, perhaps of wheat or some other grain. But God gives it a body as He has chosen, and to each kind of seed its own body. For not all flesh is alike, but there is one kind for men, another for animals, another for birds, and another for fish. There are celestial bodies and there are terrestrial bodies; but the glory of the celestial is one, and the glory of the terrestrial is another. There is one glory of the sun, and another glory of the moon, and another glory of the stars; for star differs from star in glory.

So it is with the resurrection from the dead. What is sown is perishable, what is raised is imperishable. It is sown in dishonor, it is raised in glory. It is sown in weakness, it is raised in power. It is sown in a physical body, it is raised in a spiritual body. If there is a physical body, there is also a spiritual body.

*Christianity*. 1 Corinthians 15.35-44

It comes from the origin,
It returns to the original land
In the Plain of High Heaven—
That spirit is one and the same,
Not two.

The Way of death
Is found in one's own mind
And no other;
Inquire of it in your own heart,
In your own mind.

**Yakima Tradition:** Cf. Ghost Dance, p. 793; Ezekiel 37.1-14, p. 413.

**Gleanings from the Writings of Baha'u'llah 81:** Personal immortality is strictly distinguished from the Absolute in itself, in contrast to the Hindu conception of the eternal Atman which *is* Brahman.

**Chuang Tzu 23:** Cf. Chuang Tzu 6, p. 413.

**Rig Veda 10.14.2, 8:** On Yama, King of the dead, see p. 246.

Leave to the kami
The path ahead;
The road of the returning soul
Is not dark
To the land of Yomi,
To the world beyond.

In all things
Maintaining godly uprightness:
Such a one at last will see
All dark clouds cleared away.

All humanity born into
The land of sun-origin, this
Land of Japan,
Come from the kami,
And to the kami will return.

*Shinto.* Naokata Nakanishi, One Hundred Poems on The Way of Death

God takes the souls of men at death; and those that die not He takes during their sleep. Those on whom He has passed the decree of death He keeps back, but the rest he returns to their bodies for a term appointed. Verily in this are signs for those who reflect.

*Islam.* Qur'an 39.42

While one is in the state of dream, the golden, self-luminous being, the Self within, makes the body to sleep, though he himself remains forever awake and watches by his own light the impressions of deeds that have been left upon the mind. Thereafter, associating himself again with the consciousness of the organs of sense, the Self causes the body to awake.

While one is in the state of dream, the golden, self-luminous being, the Self within, the Immortal One, keeps alive the house of flesh with the help of the vital force, but at the same time walks out of this house. The Eternal goes wherever He desires.

The self-luminous being assumes manifold forms, high and low, in the world of dreams. He seems to be enjoying the pleasure of love, or to be laughing with friends, or to be looking at terrifying spectacles.

Everyone is aware of the experiences; no one sees the Experiencer.

Some say that dreaming is but another form of waking, for what a man experiences while awake he experiences again in his dreams. Be that as it may, the Self, in dreams, shines by Its own light....

As a man passes from dream to wakefulness, so does he pass at death from this life to the next.

*Hinduism.* Brihadaranyaka Upanishad 4.3.11-14, 35

How do I know that the love of life is not a delusion? How do I know that he who is afraid of death is not like a man who left his home as a youth and forgot to return? Lady Li was the daughter of the border warden of Ai. When she was first taken captive and brought to the state of Chin, she wept until the bosom of her robe was drenched with tears. But later, when she went to live in the royal palace, shared with the king his luxurious couch and sumptuous food, she regretted that she had wept. How do I know that the dead do not repent of their former craving for life? Those who dream of a merry drinking party may the next morning wail and weep. Those who dream of wailing and weeping may in the morning go off gaily to hunt. While they dream they do not know that they are dreaming. In their dream, they may even try to interpret their dream. Only when they have awakened do they begin to know that they have dreamed. By and by comes the great awakening, and then we shall know that it has all been a great dream.

Once upon a time, Chuang Tzu dreamed that he was a butterfly, a butterfly fluttering about, enjoying itself. It did not know that it was Chuang Tzu. Suddenly he awoke with a

**One Hundred Poems on The Way of Death:** All people, not only the Emperor, are children of the kami, find their roots within the kami, and are destined to become kami.

**Brihadaranyaka Upanishad 4.3.11-14, 35:** The thought comparing the passing over to the next existence at death to a sleeper waking from a dream continues in verses 4.3.34-4.4.4, pp. 240-41. Cf. Bhagavad Gita 5.15-16, p. 381.

start and he was Chuang Tzu again. But he did not know whether he was Chuang Tzu who had dreamed that he was a butterfly, or whether he was a butterfly dreaming that he was Chuang Tzu. Between Chuang Tzu and the butterfly there must be some distinction. This is what is called the transformation of things.

*Taoism.* Chuang Tzu 2

## *Prepare Now for Eternity*

GENERALLY, RELIGIONS DO NOT EXPOUND on the reality of a future life merely as a comfort to the bereaved or as an opiate for those oppressed in this life. Rather, the fact of a future life enhances the purpose and meaning of earthly existence. How a person lives in the world will do much to determine his or her ultimate destiny. Indeed, it is often taught that life in the world is the only chance to prepare for life in eternity. The link between deed and retribution is not severed by death; often it is only in the next life that what has been sown through actions while on earth is completely reaped. Likewise, a person's qualities of character survive death: As a person was good or evil in this life, so he will continue to enjoy goodness or be pained by evil in the next. Therefore, the wise person lives with an eye to eternity by accumulating merit, repenting for misdeeds, and seeking to clear up all accounts before the day of his death. Generally, the proper preparation for the life in the hereafter is seen as extending throughout life, even from one's youth. For one who prepares for death, death is not something to be feared. But to those who are heedless of this principle death comes suddenly, leaving them eternally full of regret. See also *Repentance*, pp. 641-46.

Prepare to meet your God, O Israel!

*Judaism* and *Christianity*. Amos 4.12

Every breath you take is a step towards death.

*Islam.* Nahjul Balagha, Saying 72

This world is like a vestibule before the World to Come; prepare yourself in the vestibule that you may enter the hall.

*Judaism.* Mishnah, Abot 4.21

As the fallow leaf of the tree falls to the ground, when its days are gone, even so is the life of men; Gautama, be careful all the while!

As the dew-drop dangling on the top of a blade of grass lasts but a short time, even so the life of men; Gautama, be careful all the while!

A life so fleet, and existence so precarious, wipe off the sins you ever committed; Gautama, be careful all the while!

A rare chance, in the long course of time, is human birth for a living being; hard are the consequences of actions; Gautama, be careful all the while!

*Jainism.* Uttaradhyayana Sutra 10.1-4

And we see that death comes upon mankind... nevertheless there was a space granted unto

**Amos 4.12:** Cf. Bhagavad Gita 8.5-7, p. 241.

man in which he might repent; therefore this life became a probationary state; a time to prepare to meet God; a time to prepare for that endless state which has been spoken of by us, which is after the resurrection of the dead.

*Church of Jesus Christ of Latter-day Saints.* Book of Mormon, Alma 12.24

Better is one hour of repentance and good works in this world than all the life of the World to Come, and better is one hour of calmness of spirit in the World to Come than all the life of this world.

*Judaism.* Mishnah, Abot 4.22

If any do wish for the transitory things of life, We readily grant them—such things as We will, to such persons as We will. But in the end We have provided hell for them; they will burn therein, disgraced and rejected. But those who wish for the things of the Hereafter, and strive for them with all due striving, and have faith—they are the ones whose striving is acceptable to God.

*Islam.* Qur'an 17.18-19

To prepare for heaven, we should live our daily lives with sacrifice and service.

*Unification Church.* Sun Myung Moon, 2-6-77

Tzu-lu asked how one should serve ghosts and spirits. The Master said, "Till you have learnt to serve men, how can you serve ghosts?" Tzu-lu then ventured upon a question about the dead. The Master said, "Till you know about the living, how are you to know about the dead?"

*Confucianism.* Analects 11.11

When the Master was very ill, Tzu-lu asked leave to perform the Rite of Expiation. The Master said, "Is there such a thing?" Tzu-lu answered saying, "There is. In one of the Dirges it says, 'We performed rites of expiation for you, calling upon the sky-spirits above and the earth-spirits below.'" The Master said, "My expiation began long ago!"

*Confucianism.* Analects 7.34

Do not lay up for yourselves treasures on earth, where moth and rust consume and where thieves break in and steal, but lay up for yourselves treasure in heaven, where neither moth nor rust consumes and where thieves do not break in and steal. For where your treasure is, there will your heart be also.

*Christianity.* Matthew 6.19-21

Men who have not led a religious life and have not laid up treasure in their youth, perish like old herons in a lake without fish.

Men who have not lived a religious life and have not laid up treasure in their youth lie like worn-out bows, sighing after the past.

*Buddhism.* Dhammapada 155-56

Wealth and sons are the adornment of the present world; but the abiding things, the deeds of righteousness, are better with God in reward, and better in hope.

*Islam.* Qur'an 18.46

O shrewd businessman, do only profitable
business:
Deal only in that commodity which shall
accompany you after death.

*Sikhism.* Adi Granth, Sri Raga, M.1, p. 22

**Book of Mormon, Alma 12.24:** Cf. Alma 34.33-35, p. 645.

**Qur'an 17.18-19:** Cf. Qur'an 39.53-58, p. 644.

**Matthew 6.19-21:** Cf. Luke 12.16-21, p. 666; also Matthew 25.14-30, pp. 715-16, and Uttaradhyayana Sutra 7.14-21, p. 716; Parable of the Talents in Christian and Jain versions.

**Dhammapada 155-56:** Cf. Majjhima Nikaya ii.72-73, p. 666; also Khuddaka Patha 8.

**Sri Raga, M.1:** See Uttaradhyayana Sutra 7.14-21, p. 716.

We are on a market trip on earth:
Whether we fill our baskets or not,
Once the time is up, we go home.

*African Traditional Religions*. Igbo Song (Nigeria)

[The soul] cannot be taken from its place of deposit; it does not perish anywhere by fire; if kings of surpassing grandeur are angry they cannot take it away; and therefore what any man should provide for his children as a legacy is learning. Other things are not real wealth.

*Jainism*. Naladiyar 134

Relatives and friends and well-wishers rejoice at the arrival of a man who had been long absent and has returned home safely from afar. Likewise, meritorious deeds will receive the good person upon his arrival in the next world, as relatives welcome a dear one on his return.

*Buddhism*. Dhammapada 219-20

Giving no pain to any creature, a person should slowly accumulate spiritual merit for the sake of acquiring a companion in the next world....

For in the next world neither father, nor mother, nor wife, nor sons, nor relations stay to be his companions; spiritual merit alone remains with him.

*Hinduism*. Laws of Manu 4.238-39

Rabbi Eliezer ben Jacob says, "He who carries out one good deed acquires one advocate in his own behalf, and he who commits one transgression acquires one accuser against himself. Repentance and good works are like a shield against calamity."

*Judaism*. Mishnah, Abot 4.13

O people! Fear God, and whatever you do, do it anticipating death. Try to attain everlasting blessing in return for transitory and perishable wealth, power and pleasures of this world.

Be prepared for a fast passage because here you are destined for a short stay. Always be ready for death, for you are living under its shadow. Be wise like people who have heard the message of God and have taken a warning from it.

Beware that this world is not made for you to live forever, you will have to change it for hereafter. God, glory be to Him, has not created you without a purpose and has not left you without duties, obligations, and responsibilities....

You must remember to gather from this life such harvest as will be of use and help to you hereafter.

*Islam*. Nahjul Balagha, Sermon 67

Now man is made of determination *(kratu)*; according to what his determination is in this world so will he be when he has departed this life.

*Hinduism*. Shankara, Vedanta Sutra 1.2.1

Both life and death of such as are firm in their penance and rules are good. When alive they earn merit and when dead they attain beatitude.

Both life and death of such as indulge in sins are bad. When alive they add to malice and when dead they are hurled into darkness.

*Jainism*. Dharmadasaganin, Upadesamala 443-44

Here he grieves, hereafter he grieves. In both states the evil-doer grieves. He grieves, he is afflicted, perceiving the impurity of his own deeds.

**Laws of Manu 4.238-39:** The thought continues in verses 4.241-243, p. 242. Cf. Srimad Bhagavatam 6.1, p. 646.

**Abot 4.13:** Cf. Tanhuma Numbers 19, p. 257; Tract of the Quiet Way, p. 711.

**Nahjul Balagha, Sermon 67:** Cf. Qur'an 39.53-58, p. 644.

**Vedanta Sutra 1.2.1:** Cf. Brihadaranyaka Upanishad 4.4.5-6, pp. 124-25; 4.4.6-7, p. 658; Svetasvatara Upanishad 5.11-12, p. 499; Laws of Manu 12.3-9, p. 125; Bhagavad Gita 4.31, p. 621.

**Upadesamala 443-44:** see following note.

Here he rejoices, hereafter he rejoices. In both states the well-doer rejoices. He rejoices, exceedingly rejoices, perceiving the purity of his own deeds.

Here he suffers, hereafter he suffers. In both states the evil-doer suffers. "Evil have I done"—thinking thus, he suffers. Having gone to a woeful state, he suffers even more.

Here he is happy, hereafter he is happy. In both states the well-doer is happy. "Good have I done"—thinking thus, he is happy. Upon going to a blissful state, he rejoices even more.

*Buddhism*. Dhammapada 15-18

Jesus said, "Truly, truly, I say to you, whatever you bind on earth shall be bound in heaven, and whatever you loose on earth shall be loosed in heaven."

*Christianity*. Matthew 18.18

As for that abode of the Hereafter, We assign it to those who seek not oppression in the earth, nor corruption. The sequel is for those who ward off evil. Whoever brings a good deed, he will have better than the same; while as for him who brings an ill deed, those who do ill deeds will be requited only what they did.

*Islam*. Qur'an 28.83-84

You can climb up the mountain and down again; you can stroll around the valley and return; but you cannot go to God and return.

*African Traditional Religions*. Nupe Proverb (Nigeria)

Sooner, do I declare, would a one-eyed turtle, if he were to pop up to the surface of the sea only once at the end of every hundred years, chance to push his neck through a yoke with one hole than would a fool, who has once gone to the Downfall, be reborn as a man.

*Buddhism*. Samyutta Nikaya v.455

Death carries away the man who gathers flowers, whose mind is attached to sensuality, even as a great flood sweeps away a slumbering village.

*Buddhism*. Dhammapada 47

Rivalry in worldly increase distracts you
Until you come to the graves.
Nay, but you will come to know!
Again, you will come to know!
Would that you knew now with certainty of
 mind!
For you will behold hell-fire;
Indeed, you will behold it with sure vision.
Then, on that day, you will be asked
 concerning pleasure.

*Islam*. Qur'an 102

The untrustworthy lord of death
Waits not for things to be done or undone;
Whether I am sick or healthy,
This fleeting life span is unstable.

Leaving all I must depart alone.
But through not having understood this
I committed various kinds of evil
For the sake of my friends and foes.

Yet my foes will become nothing.
My friends will become nothing.
I too will become nothing.
Likewise all will become nothing.

**Dhammapada 15-18:** Cf. Anguttara Nikaya i.279, p. 249; Basavanna, Vacana 239, p. 249; Sun Myung Moon, 4-18-77, p. 249.

**Matthew 18.18:** Jesus gives the authority to bind and loose to his disciples, and hence to the church; compare Matthew 16.19, p. 196, where that authority is given only to Peter. For Catholics, this passage refers mainly to the discipline and grace dispensed by the church, which, when determined on earth, endures in heaven. But for Protestants, who reject the mediation of a priesthood, the blessings of Christ are freely available to every believer as he avails himself of them through faith, prayer, and good deeds. Hence ultimately it is the individual's own binding or loosing, while on earth, that will bind or liberate in heaven.

**Qur'an 28.83-84:** Cf. Majjhima Nikaya i.389-90, p. 242.

**Samyutta Nikaya v.455:** The Buddha cautions those who rely on the doctrine of reincarnation against mistakenly thinking that they will soon get a second chance at this life.

Just like a dream experience,
Whatever things I enjoy
Will become a memory.
Whatever has passed will not be seen again.

Even within this brief life
Many friends and foes have passed,
But whatever unbearable evil I committed for them
Remains ahead of me....

While I am lying in bed,
Although surrounded by my friends and relatives,
The feeling of life being severed
Will be experienced by me alone.

When seized by the messengers of death,
What benefit will friends and relatives afford?
My merit alone shall protect me then,
But upon that I have never relied.

*Buddhism.* Shantideva, Guide to the Bodhisattva's Way of Life 2.33-41

❖

## *The Passage Beyond*

THE PASSAGE INTO THE NEXT LIFE at the moment of death is a nearly impenetrable mystery for us who have not yet experienced it. There are published accounts of near-death experiences by people who have been resuscitated from clinical death; they report a passing into another world, meeting a being of light, and feeling great warmth and accepting love. Perhaps they have experienced the first stages of the passage. But the religions of the world are nearly unanimous in describing another, less comfortable event: The individual undergoes a judgment where he must review his life with unsparing honesty. Yet even at that crucial moment the dying person may, by focusing his mind on God and accepting the Light that seems to embrace him, leap to a higher realm. Thus texts like the Tibetan Book of the Dead and the Bhagavad Gita give counsel on the way to assure a safe passage. Jainism, above all, emphasizes the importance of control in the transition from this life to the next by the ideal of *Sallekhana*, the holy death, which is attained by the aspirant as he exerts himself in fasting and meditation.

The Self, having in dreams enjoyed the pleasures of sense, gone hither and thither, experienced good and evil, hastens back to the state of waking from which he started.

As a man passes from dream to wakefulness, so does he pass from this life to the next.

When a man is about to die, the subtle body, mounted by the intelligent self, groans—as a heavily laden cart groans under its burden.

When his body becomes thin through old age or disease, the dying man separates himself from his limbs, even as a mango or a fig or a banyan fruit separates itself from its stalk, and by the same way that he came he hastens to his new abode, and there assumes another body, in which to begin a new life.

When his body grows weak and he becomes apparently unconscious, the dying man gathers his senses about him and, completely withdrawing their powers, descends into his heart. No more does he see form or color without.

He neither sees, nor smells, nor tastes. He does not speak, he does not hear. He does not think, he does not know. For all the organs, detaching themselves from his physical body, unite with his subtle body. Then the point of his heart, where the nerves join, is lighted by the light of the Self, and by that light he departs either through the eye, or through the gate of the skull, or through some other aperture of the body. When he thus departs, life departs; and when life departs, all the functions of the vital principle depart. The Self remains conscious, and, conscious, the dying man goes to his abode. The deeds of this life, and the impressions they leave behind, follow him.

As a caterpillar, having reached the end of a blade of grass, takes hold of another blade and draws itself to it, so the Self, having left behind it [a body] unconscious, takes hold of another body and draws himself to it.

As a goldsmith, taking an old gold ornament, molds it into another, newer and more beautiful, so the Self, having given up the body and left it unconscious, takes on a new and better form, either that of the Fathers, or that of the Celestial Singers, or that of the gods, or that of other beings, heavenly or earthly.

*Hinduism*. Brihadaranyaka Upanishad 4.3.34-4.4.4

Pre-recorded is the year and hour of nuptials:
Gather ye all to anoint the door-step.
Friend! Utter blessing that with the Lord,
the departed be united.
In each home arrives this courier-packet,
Calls continually keep arriving.
Says Nanak, Contemplate Him who sends the call.
May the day of union for each arrive!

*Sikhism*. Adi Granth, Kirtan Sohila, M.1, p. 12

O nobly-born... the body which you have now is called the thought-body of propensities. Since you do not have a material body of flesh and blood, whatever may come—sounds, lights, or rays—are, all three, unable to harm you; you are incapable of dying. It is quite sufficient for you to know that these apparitions are your own thought-forms. Recognize this to be the *Bardo* (the intermediate state after death).

*Buddhism*. Tibetan Book of the Dead

Those who remember me at the time of death will come to me. Do not doubt this. Whatever occupies the mind at the time of death determines the destiny of the dying; always they will tend toward that state of being. Therefore, remember me at all times....

Remembering me at the time of death, close down the doors of the senses and place the mind in the heart. Then, while absorbed in meditation, focus all energy upwards towards the head. Repeating in this state the divine Name, the syllable OM that represents the changeless Brahman, you will go forth from the body and attain the supreme goal.

*Hinduism*. Bhagavad Gita 8.5-7, 12-13

If this thought occurs to a monk, "I am sick and not able, at this time, to regularly mortify the flesh," that monk should regularly reduce his food; regularly reducing his food and diminishing his sins, he should take proper care of his body, being immovable like a beam; exerting himself he dissolves his body....

**Brihadaranyaka Upanishad 4.3.34-4.4.4:** Cf. Brihadaranyaka Upanishad 4.3.11-14, p. 235. These verses deal with rebirth for those who have not attained the highest. The Upanishad (4.4.6-7, p. 247) describes the passage of those who will pass beyond the realm of samsara to unity with Brahman.

**Kirtan Sohila, M.1:** The passage to death is welcomed with this Peal of Laudation, recited at the finale of the funeral service as well as daily as an evening prayer. Union with Creator is likened to marriage. Through absorption in praising God, the soul on departing the body will find union with God and escape the wheel of transmigration.

**Bhagavad Gita 8.5-13:** This teaches that one's prayer and attitude at the time of death is all-important for the soul's subsequent journey. Regardless of the quality of one's life, just remembering God at the time of death can lead to liberation. Yet since death may come suddenly, and may be accompanied by much pain and distraction, the habit of remembering God should be nurtured throughout life. Some Hindus name their children with divine names in order that, at the time of death, the natural human desire to think of one's children will cause them to meditate on the divine name and thus win beatitude. For instance, the story of Ajamil in Srimad Bhagavatam 6.1 describes a dishonest man who on his deathbed lay thinking of his youngest son called Narayana (a name of Krishna), and hence inadvertently he found liberation. In contrast to this view, see Qur'an 4.17-18, p. 645.

This is the truth: speaking truth, free from passion, crossing the samsara, abating irresoluteness, knowing all truth and not being known, leaving this frail body. Overcoming all sorts of pains and troubles through trust in this, he accomplishes this fearful religious death. Even thus he will in due time put an end to existence. This has been adopted by many who were free from delusion; it is good, wholesome, proper, beatifying, meritorious. Thus I say.

*Jainism.* Acarangasutra 7

At the moment of death the sum of all the experiences of life on earth comes to the surface of the mind—for in the mind are stored all impressions of past deeds—and the dying man then becomes absorbed in these experiences. Then comes complete loss of memory. Next there arises before man's mind the vision of his life to come, a vision regulated by his impressions of his past deeds; and he no longer recollects his life on earth. This complete forgetfulness of his past identity is death.

His complete acceptance of another state and identification with a new body is said to be his birth. He no longer remembers his past life, and, though he has existed before, he considers himself newly born.

His next birth is regulated by the deeds of the present life—the deeds which make up his character. If his character is dominated by light, he achieves a higher birth, that of a deva or of a sage; if by passion, he is returned to earth as a demon or as a man; and if by darkness he is born from the lower wombs.

*Hinduism.* Srimad Bhagavatam 11.15

Leaving the dead body on the ground like a log of wood or a clod of earth, the relatives depart with averted faces; but spiritual merit follows the soul.

Let him therefore always slowly accumulate spiritual merit, in order that it may be his companion after death; for without merit as his companion he will traverse a gloom difficult to traverse.

That companion speedily conducts the man who is devoted to duty and effaces his sins by austerities, to the next world, radiant and clothed with an ethereal body.

*Hinduism.* Laws of Manu 4.241-43

He, having effected an activity of body that is harmful, effected an activity of speech that is harmful, effected an activity of mind that is harmful, arises in a world that is harmful. Because he has uprisen in a world that is harmful, harmful sensory impingements assail him. He, being assailed by harmful sensory impingements, experiences a harmful feeling, without exception painful, even as do creatures in Niraya hell. In this way, there is the uprising of a being from what he has come to be; he uprises according to what he does; when he has uprisen sensory impingements assail him. So I speak thus: Creatures are heir to deeds.

*Buddhism.* Majjhima Nikaya i.389-90, Kukkuravatika Sutta

And every man's augury have we fastened to his own neck, and We shall bring forth for him on the Day of Resurrection a book which he

**Acarangasutra 7:** *Sallekhana* means to fast oneself to death while in the complete control of the passions through meditation and in full mindfulness. Such a holy death leads to Nirvana or to rebirth in the celestial realms. Lay people and monks alike may aspire to the holy death when the body has begun to deteriorate in old age or from a terminal illness. Then, under proper supervision and according to established ritual, they make an end that is at the same time a moment of purity, free of passion or delusion. Cf. Uttaradhyayana Sutra 4.7, pp. 527-28; Gittin 57b, p. 633.

**Srimad Bhagavatam 11.15:** 'Light' *(sattva)*, 'passion' *(rajas)*, and 'darkness' *(tamas)* are the three *gunas*, qualities of embodied existence; see Bhagavad Gita 18.40, p. 272. This passage speaks of a new embodied birth, and is not the way of the highest soul who is no longer entangled in the fetters of the gunas. Cf. Svetasvatara Upanishad 5.11-12, p. 499.

**Laws of Manu 4.241-43:** Cf. Laws of Manu 4.238-39, p. 238; Dhammapada 219-20, p. 238.

**Majjhima Nikaya i.389-90:** Cf. Qur'an 28.83-84, p. 239; Majjhima Nikaya iii.202-6, pp. 499-500; Garland Sutra 10, p. 125.

will find wide open. "Read your book! Your soul suffices as a reckoner against you this day."

*Islam.* Qur'an 17.13-14

Toward the wicked man and the righteous one
And him in whom right and wrong meet
Shall the Judge act in upright manner,
According to the laws of the present existence.

*Zoroastrianism.* Avesta, Yasna 33.1

Then I saw a great white throne and Him who sat upon it; from His presence earth and sky fled away, and no place was found for them. And I saw the dead, great and small, standing before the throne, and books were opened. Also another book was opened, which is the book of life. And the dead were judged by what was written in the books, by what they had done.

*Christianity.* Revelation 20.11-12

After you depart this life, God shall demand a reckoning of your deeds
That in His ledger are recorded.
Those that are rebellious, shall be summoned.
Azrael, the angel of death, will hover over them,
And trapped in a blind alley they will know not any escape.
Says Nanak, Falsehood must be destroyed;
Truth in the end shall prevail.

*Sikhism.* Adi Granth, Ramkali-ki-Var, M.1, p. 953

At the gates of the land of the dead
You will pass before a searching Judge.
His justice is true and he will examine your feet,
He will know how to find every stain,
Whether visible or hidden under the skin;
If you have fallen on the way he will know.
If the Judge finds no stains on your feet
Open your belly to joy, for you have overcome
And your belly is clean.

*African Traditional Religion.* Fon Song (Benin)

They that are born are destined to die; and the dead to be brought to life again; and the living to be judged, to know, to make known, and to be made conscious that He is God, He the Maker, He the Creator, He the Discerner, He the Judge, He the Witness, He the Complainant; He it is that will in future judge, blessed be He, with whom there is no unrighteousness, nor forgetfulness, nor respect of persons, nor taking of bribes. Know also that everything is according to reckoning; and let not your imagination give you hope that the grave will be a place of refuge for you. For perforce you were formed, and perforce you were born, and perforce you live, and perforce you will die, and perforce you will in the future have to give account and reckoning before the King of kings, the Holy One, blessed be He.

*Judaism.* Mishnah, Abot 4.29

Behold, two guardian angels appointed to learn [man's doings] learn and note them, one sitting on the right and one on the left. Not a word does he utter but there is a sentinel by him, ready to note it. And the stupor of death will bring truth before his eyes, "This was the thing which you were trying to escape!"

*Islam.* Qur'an 50.17-19

Anything evil refrain from doing; all good deeds do! So will you be released forever from the influence of evil stars, and always be encompassed by good guardian angels.

*Taoism.* Tract of the Quiet Way

The Good Spirit, who was born simultaneously with you, will come now and count out your

**Qur'an 17.13-14:** Cf. Qur'an 39.47-48, p. 126.
**Yasna 33.1:** Cf. Yasna 48.4, p. 290; Book of Mormon, Alma 41:3-4, p. 126.
**Revelation 20.11-12:** Cf. Matthew 25.31-45, p. 699; Abot 3.20, p. 124; Qur'an 99.6-8, p. 126.
**Abot 4.29:** Cf. Abot 3.20, p. 124.
**Qur'an 50.17-19:** Cf. Qur'an 13.10-11, p. 126; 41.30-31, p. 257.
**Tract of the Quiet Way:** Cf. Abot 4.13, p. 238.

good deeds with white pebbles, and the Evil Spirit, who was born simultaneously with you, will come and count out your evil deeds with black pebbles. Thereupon you will be greatly frightened, awed, and terrified, and will tremble; and you will attempt to tell lies, saying, "I have not committed any evil deed."

Then the Lord of Death will say, "I will consult the Mirror of karma." He will look in the Mirror, wherein every good and evil act is vividly reflected. Lying will be of no avail.

Then one of the executive furies of the Lord of Death will place a rope around your neck and drag you along; he will cut off your head, extract your heart, pull out your intestines, lick up your brain, drink your blood, eat your flesh, and gnaw your bones; but you will be incapable of dying. Although your body be hacked to pieces, it will revive again. The repeated hacking [symbolizing the pangs of the deceased's conscience] will cause intense pain and torture.

Even at the time that the pebbles are being counted out, be not frightened; tell no lies; and fear not the Lord of Death.

Your body being a mental body is incapable of dying even though beheaded and quartered. In reality, your body is of the nature of voidness; you need not be afraid. The Lords of Death are your own hallucinations. Your desire-body is a body of propensities, and void. Voidness cannot injure voidness; the qualityless cannot injure the qualityless. Apart from one's own hallucinations, in reality there are no such things existing outside oneself as Lord of Death, or god, or demon. Act so as to recognize this.

*Buddhism.* Tibetan Book of the Dead

The self is the maker and non-maker, and itself makes happiness and misery, is its own friend and its own foe, decides its own condition good or evil, and is its own river Veyarana [the river in which hell-beings are tormented].

*Jainism.* Magadhishloka

When we subject ourselves to the least discrimination or particularization, transformation takes place; otherwise, all things remain as void as space, as they inherently are. By dwelling our mind on evil things, hell arises. By dwelling our mind on good acts, paradise appears. Dragons and snakes are the transformations of venomous hatred, while heavenly Bodhisattvas are mercy personified. The upper regions are Wisdom crystallized, while the underworld is only another form of ignorance and infatuation.

*Buddhism.* Sutra of Hui Neng 6

Naturally every Hopi wants to join the spirits of his loved ones who have passed beyond. To that end he keeps his heart pure and is kind and generous to other people.

When a bad person, one who is known as "not-Hopi," dies, his fate is very different. Witches called the "Two Hearts" take him by the hand as soon as the breath is out of his body, and they lead him away to their own country. The country of the Two Hearts is as bad as they are themselves.

*Native American Religions.*
Hopi tradition

The Trumpet will be sounded, and whoever is in heaven and whoever is on earth will be stunned, except for someone God may wish. Then another [blast] will be blown and behold, they will stand there watching! The earth will shine through its Lord's light and the Book will be laid open. Prophets and witnesses will be brought in, and judgment will be pronounced among them formally, and they will not be harmed. Every soul will be repaid for whatever it has done; He is quite aware of what they are doing.

The ones who disbelieve will be driven along to hell in throngs until, just as they come up to it, its gates will swing open and its keepers will say to them, "Did not messengers come to you from among yourselves reciting your Lord's verses to you and warning you about meeting [Him] on this day of yours?" They will say, "Of course!" But the Sentence about torment has still come due for disbelievers.

**Tibetan Book of the Dead:** Cf. Milarepa, p. 266.
**Magadhishloka:** Cf. Guide to the Bodhisattva's Way of Life 4.28-35, p. 279.

Someone else will say, "Enter hell's gates to remain there. What an awful lodging will it be for the overbearing!"

The ones who have heeded their Lord will be driven along to the Garden in throngs until just as they come up to it, its gates will swing open and its keepers will tell them, "Peace be upon you! You have been good, so enter it to remain there." They will say, "Praise be to God who has held true to His promise for us and let us inherit the earth! We shall settle down anywhere we wish to in the Garden. How favored are such workers' wages!"

You will see the angels clustering around the Throne hymning their Lord's praise. Judgment will be pronounced on them formally, and they will say, "Praise be to God, Lord of the universe!"

*Islam.* Qur'an 39.68-75

Whoever, man or woman, O Wise Lord,
Shall give me what thou knowest is the best of this existence,
To wit—reward for righteousness and the dominion with the Good Mind—
And all those whom I shall induce to worship such as you,
With all those will I cross the Bridge of the Separator!
The sacrificers and the sorcerer princes
Have subdued mankind to the yoke of their dominion,
To destroy existence through evil deeds:
They shall be tortured by their own soul and their own conscience,
When they come to the Bridge of the Separator,
Forever to be inmates of the House of Evil.

*Zoroastrianism.* Avesta, Yasna 46.10-11

God will then set up a bridge over Gehenna and intercession will be allowed, and they will say, "O God, keep safe, keep safe." The believers will then pass over like the twinkling of an eye, like lightning, like wind, like a bird, like the finest horses and camels. Some will escape and be kept safe, some will be lacerated [by flesh-hooks and thorns which will rise up from Gehenna] and let go, and some will be pushed into the fire of Gehenna.

*Islam.* Hadith of Bukhari and Muslim

❖

**Qur'an 39.68-75:** Cf. Qur'an 69.13-37, p. 781.

**Yasna 46.10-11:** Zarathustra promises blessings for those who support him and help the teaching achieve dominion in the world, and woe for the evil-doers who practice false religion. The 'Bridge of the Separator,' where the righteous and the wicked will be sorted out, is an image also found in popular Islam, as in the following tradition. Compare also the Hindu theme of crossing the waters: see Atharva Veda 12.2.26-27, p. 386.

**Hadith of Bukhari and Muslim:** This bridge is called *Sirat.*

# *Heaven*

SOME CONCEPTION OF HEAVEN AND HELL is found universally among the religions of the world. Descriptions of these abodes are often full of graphic and fanciful imagery, conveying in metaphor a reality that can hardly be part of the ordinary experience of mortals. Are these realms objectively real? The scriptures are unanimous in affirming they are. Yet they do not have any physical location: "up" or "down" is a matter of spiritual geography, not of astronomy or geology. The view found in some texts, that Heaven or hell is derived from one's state of mind,[1] does not make it any less real. For the attitudes and desires of people's hearts, which may be hidden by the external features of mortal life, are the equivalent of material reality in the realms of spirit.

A number of the Hindu, Buddhist, and Taoist passages speak of Yama, the Indic god of the dead. Yama is not comparable to the devil or Satan who, in Christian belief, is the author of evil. In the Vedas, he presides over the bright realms and is the object of offerings and supplications for the benefit of the departed. As the lord of hell in Buddhism, his acts are strictly in accordance with divine law, meting out punishments according to people's karma, and in one Taoist text reprinted here he even gives an object lesson to turn people away from evil.

Some ambiguity plagues the descriptions of Heaven and hell in the scriptures of Judaism, Christianity, and Islam, which can be interpreted either to describe the state of the soul upon death or what will be after the future Resurrection. The qur'anic passages collected here which describe the opening of Paradise and hell are a few of many which refer to the Last Judgment. Most Muslims, therefore, regard the dead to be sleeping in the grave awaiting that momentous event. Yet other passages, such as the hadith describing Muhammad's Night Journey,[2] point to the present reality of Heaven as the dwelling place for the souls of the righteous. The biblical vision of Heaven from the Revelation and the passage from the same book about the lake of fire are visions of a future recompense after the tribulations of the Last Judgment. Those Christians who hold to a literal interpretation of these verses concur with their Muslim brothers and sisters that the souls of the dead are asleep in the grave, awaiting the future opening of Heaven and hell. But another strand of the Christian tradition, supported by biblical descriptions of the Sheol in Job 3.17-19, the heavenly Jerusalem in Hebrews 12.22-24, and the story of Lazarus and the rich man in Luke 16.19-31, teaches that upon death each person immediately enters his appointed place in Heaven or hell. The visions in Revelation are often interpreted in this way, and have spawned such classic descriptions as Dante's *Divine Comedy*. The concept of the World to Come in Jewish writings is similarly ambiguous: the World to Come may be a present heaven or describe a future redemption on earth.[3]

---

[1] E.g., Tibetan Book of the Dead, p. 241, Magadhishloka, p. 244, Sutra of Hui Neng 6, p. 244.

[2] See Qur'an 2.154, p. 232, and 39.42, p. 235.

[3] The resolution of these two doctrines comes at the eschatological time of redemption, when the realization of the Kingdom of God on earth brings with it a transformation of heaven, "a new heaven and a new earth"—cf. Revelation 21.1-22.5, pp. 794-95; Isaiah 24.18-23, p. 781; Qur'an 21.104-05, p. 789; 69.13-17, p. 781. The destruction of evil and the triumph of good, when God becomes all in all, effects liberation for the earthly realms and the spiritual realms alike. See also passages which teach that the words "life" and "death" often refer to a state of grace rather than physical life or death: Luke 9.60, p. 412; Qur'an 6.122, p. 412; Berakot 18ab, p. 412. In that light we can also understand resurrection to mean the enlivening and salvation of those in the spiritual realms as well as on earth.

The world's scriptures describe Heaven as a place of rest, or as an exalted spiritual state, full of divine splendor and communion with the Absolute. There are also descriptions using more graphic and materialistic imagery: gardens of delights, with riches and pleasures abounding. A number of texts describe it as a place of fellowship with the spirits of the departed or a fellowship of saints. We conclude with visions or tours of Heaven: the Buddhist description of the Pure Land, the vision of throngs surrounding the divine throne in the Book of Revelation, and Muhammad's Night Journey.

There the wicked cease from troubling,
and there the weary are at rest.
There the prisoners are at ease together;
they hear not the voice of the taskmaster.
The small and the great are there,
and the slave is free from his master.

*Judaism* and *Christianity*. Job 3.17-19

Chuang Tzu said, "Were I to prevail upon God to allow your body to be born again, and your bones and flesh to be renewed, so that you could return to your parents, to your wife, and to the friends of your youth, would you be willing?"

At this, the skull opened its eyes wide and knitted its brows and said, "How should I cast aside happiness greater than that of a king, and mingle once again in the toils and troubles of mortality?"

*Taoism*. Chuang Tzu 18

He in whom desire has been stilled suffers no rebirth. After death, having attained to the highest, desiring only the Self, he goes to no other world. Realizing Brahman, he becomes Brahman.

Freed from the body, he becomes one with the immortal spirit, Brahman, the Light eternal.

*Hinduism*. Brihadaranyaka Upanishad 4.4.6-7

When a son of the Buddha fulfils his course,
In the world to come he becomes Buddha.

*Buddhism*. Lotus Sutra 2

To the highest regions, in due order, to those regions where there is no delusion, and to those regions which are full of light where the glorious gods dwell—who have long life, great power, great luster, can change their shape at will, are beautiful as on their first day, and have the brilliance of many suns—to such places go those who are trained in self-control and penance, both monks and householders who have obtained liberation by absence of passion.

*Jainism*. Uttaradhyayana Sutra 5.26-28

Not like this world is the World to Come. In the World to Come there is neither eating nor drinking; no procreation of children or business transactions; no envy or hatred or rivalry; but the righteous sit enthroned, their crowns on their heads, and enjoy the luster of the Divine Splendor (*Shechinah*).

*Judaism*. Talmud, Berakot 17a

In the resurrection they neither marry nor are given in marriage, but are like angels in heaven.

*Christianity*. Matthew 22.30

**Lotus Sutra 2:** The teaching of the Lotus Sutra at this point is paralleled in Hindu Vedanta, e.g., Mundaka Upanishad 3.2.8-9, p. 414; Chandogya Upanishad 6.8.7, p. 414, and related passages. To realize one's Buddhahood is comparable to discerning Brahman—the Absolute and Ultimate. No longer immersed in temporal phenomena, one becomes joined to eternal Reality.

**Berakot 17a:** Cf. Hadith, p. 791.

And those Foremost [in faith] will be Foremost
[in the Hereafter].
These will be those nearest to God;
In Gardens of Bliss;
A number of people from those of old,
And a few from those of later times.
They will be on thrones encrusted, reclining
on them, facing each other.
Round about them will serve youths of perpetual freshness,
With goblets, shining beakers, and cups filled
out of clear-flowing fountains;
No after-ache will they receive therefrom, nor
will they suffer intoxication;
And with fruits, any that they may select,
And the flesh of fowls, any that they may
desire.
And there will be companions with beautiful,
big and lustrous eyes,
Like unto pearls well-guarded:
A reward for the deeds of their past life.
No frivolity will they hear therein, nor any
taint of ill,
Only the saying "Peace! Peace!"

*Islam.* Qur'an 56.10-27

Higher than all stands the Realm of Grace—
None can have access there except heroes of
supreme might,
Inspired by God-consciousness.
In that sphere abide numberless heroines like
Sita of surpassing praise
And beauty indescribable.
Those to God united suffer not mortality nor
delusion.
In that sphere abide devotees assembled from
the various universes,
Cherishing the holy Eternal ever in their
hearts.
In everlasting bliss.
The formless Supreme Being abides in the
Realm of Eternity.
Over His creation He casts His glance of grace.
In that realm are contained all the continents
and universes,
Exceeding in number all count.
Of creation, worlds upon worlds abide
therein—
All obedient to His Will;
He watches over them in bliss,
And has each constantly in mind.
Says Nanak, Such is that realm's [glory] that to
try to describe it is to attempt the impossible.

*Sikhism.* Adi Granth,
Japuji 37 M.1, p. 8

Make me immortal in the realm
where the son of Vivasvat [Yama] reigns,
where lies heaven's secret shrine, where
are those waters that are ever young.
For Indra, flow thou on, Indu!

Make me immortal in that realm
where movement is accordant to wish,
in the third region, the third heaven of heavens,
where the worlds are resplendent.
For Indra, flow thou on, Indu!

Make me immortal in that realm
where all wishes and longings go,
where spreads the Radiant One's region,
where holy bliss is, and happiness.
For Indra, flow thou on, Indu!

Make me immortal in that realm
where beatitude and joy and cheer
and transports of delight abound,
where the highest desires have been filled.
For Indra, flow thou on, Indu!

*Hinduism.* Rig Veda 9.113.8-11

What is heaven? Heaven is created by those people who love here on earth with unselfishness and an absolute, God-centered love. This is the most basic principle, and all other principles you learn are the expansion of this basic truth.

*Unification Church.*
Sun Myung Moon, 4-18-77

**Qur'an 56.10-27:** Cf. Qur'an 9.72, p. 133; 69.20-24, p. 781; 98.7-8, p. 411.
**Rig Veda 9.113.8-11:** Cf. Rig Veda 10.14.2,8, p. 234.
**Sun Myung Moon, 4-18-77:** Cf. Sun Myung Moon, 12-18-85, p. 227. 1 Corinthians 13, p. 160.

Behold! between the worlds
of mortals and of gods
There is no difference!
To speak the truth is the world of gods;
To speak untruth, the mortal world.
Good works is heaven,
Bad works is hell;
You are the witness, O Lord.

*Hinduism.* Basavanna, Vacana 239

Rabbi Joseph, son of Rabbi Joshua ben Levi, was ill and fell into a coma. When he recovered, his father asked him, "What did you see?" He replied, "I beheld a world the reverse of this one; those who are on top here were below there, and vice versa." He said to him, "My son, you have seen a corrected world. But what is the position of us students of Torah there?" He answered, "We are the same as here. I heard it stated, 'Happy is he who comes here possessed of learning'; and I further heard it said that martyrs occupy an eminence which nobody else can attain."

*Judaism.* Talmud, Pesahim 50a

Once Hatthaka, son of a deva [one reborn in heaven after death], when night was waning, lit up the whole of Jeta Grove with exceeding splendor and approached the Exalted One.... Then said the Exalted One, "Well, Hatthaka, do things go on now just the same as before, when you were in human shape?"

"Yes, Lord, they do. But there are also some things now going on which I did not experience when I was in human shape. Just as, Lord, the Exalted One now dwells surrounded by brethren and sisters, by lay-brothers and lay-sisters, by royalties and ministers, by sectarians and their followers—just so do I dwell surrounded by sons of devas. Even from a distance, Lord, do sons of the devas come saying, 'We'll hear the Norm from the lips of Hatthaka, son of a deva.'

"Of three things, Lord, I never got enough. I died regretful of three things. What were they? I never had enough of beholding the Exalted One. I died regretting it. I never had enough of hearing the good Norm. I died regretting it. I never had enough of serving the Order of Brethren. I died regretting it."

*Buddhism.* Anguttara Nikaya i.279

Where men of goodwill and good deeds rejoice,
Their bodies now made free from all disease,
Their limbs made whole from lameness or
defect—
In that heaven may we behold our parents and
our sons!

*Hinduism.* Atharva Veda 6.120.3

All who obey God and the Apostle are in the company of those on whom is the grace of God—of the Prophets who teach, the sincere lovers of Truth, the witnesses [martyrs] who testify, and the righteous who do good: Ah! What a beautiful fellowship!

*Islam.* Qur'an 4.69

You have come to Mount Zion and to the city of the living God, the heavenly Jerusalem, and to innumerable angels in festal gathering, and to the assembly of the first-born who are enrolled in heaven, and to a judge who is God of all, and to the spirits of just men made perfect, and to Jesus, the mediator of a new covenant.

*Christianity.* Hebrews 12.22-24

Komashtam'ho instructed the people in the nature of death: "When you die, you will be again with those you love who have gone before you. Again you will be young and

**Vacana 239:** Cf. Katha Upanishad 2.1.10, p. 228.

**Pesahim 50a:** Cf. 1 Samuel 2.4-9, p. 388; Hadith of Bukhari, p. 647.

**Anguttara Nikaya i.279:** Regret is a powerful emotion in the world beyond; it can create hell or spur one to self-betterment.

**Atharva Veda 6.120.3:** Cf. Atharva Veda 12.2.26-27, p. 386.

**Qur'an 4.69:** Cf. Gleanings from the Writings of Baha'u'llah 81, pp. 259-60.

**Hebrews 12.22-24:** Cf. Revelation 21.1-2, pp. 794-95; Isaiah 51.11, p. 794.

strong, though you might have been old and feeble on the day you died. In the spirit land the corn will grow and all will be happy, whether they were good or bad when they were alive. So death is not something to be afraid of."

*Native American Religions*. Yuma Tradition

For [the ancestors] Soma is purified,
some accept the molten butter;
to the company of those, for
whom the honey flows, let him go!

To the company of those who
are invincible by spiritual discipline (*tapas*),
and through spiritual discipline have gone to heaven,
to men of great spiritual fire, let him go!

To the company of those who
fight contested battles, heroes
who cast away their lives, to those who
made a thousand gifts, let him go!

To those ancient followers
of the Law, steadfast in the Law,
who furthered the Law, to the Fathers, Yama,
great in their spiritual fire, let him go!

To the sage-poets, the leaders
of thousands, those who protect the sun,
to the Rishis of great spiritual discipline,
born of spiritual discipline, Yama! Let him go!

*Hinduism*. Rig Veda 10.154.1-5

O Ananda, the world called Sukhavati, which is the world system of the Lord Amitabha, is rich and prosperous, comfortable, fertile, delightful, and crowded with many gods and men. And in this world, Ananda, there are no hells, no animals, no ghosts, no devils, and no inauspicious places of rebirth. And there do not appear in this world such gems as are known in the world Sukhavati.

And that world Sukhavati, Ananda, is fragrant with many sweet-smelling odors, rich in manifold flowers and fruits, adorned with jewel trees, and frequented by flocks of various birds with sweet voices, which have been produced by the miraculous power of the Tathagata. The jewel trees have various colors, many colors, many hundreds of thousands of colors. They are composed of varying combinations of the seven precious things: gold, silver, beryl, crystal, coral, red pearls, and emerald.... Their roots, trunks, branches, leaves, flowers, and fruits are pleasant to touch, and fragrant. And when these trees are moved by the wind, a sweet and delightful sound proceeds from them, which one never tires of hearing. Such jewel trees, and clusters of banana trees and rows of palm trees, all made of precious gems, grow everywhere in this Buddha-land. On all sides it is surrounded with golden nets, and all round covered with lotus flowers made of all the precious things. Some of the lotus flowers are half a mile in circumference, others up to ten miles. And from each jewel lotus issue thirty-six hundred thousand billions of rays of light. And at the end of each ray issue thirty-six hundred thousand billions of Buddhas, with golden-colored bodies, who bear the thirty-two marks of the great man, and who, in all the ten directions, go into the countless [lower] realms and there teach the Law.

And many kinds of rivers flow along in this Pure Land. There are great rivers there, one mile broad, and up to fifty miles broad and twelve miles deep. All these rivers flow along calmly; their water is fragrant with manifold agreeable odors, and in them are bunches of flowers to which various jewels adhere, and they resound with various sweet sounds. And the sound which issues from these great rivers is as pleasant as that of a musical instrument consisting of hundreds of thousands of billions of parts, and which, skillfully played, emits a heavenly music. It is deep, commanding, distinct, clear, pleasant to the ear, touching the heart, delightful, and one never tires of hearing it, as if it always said, "Impermanent, peaceful, calm, and not-self." Such is the sound that reaches the ears of those beings.

**Yuma Tradition:** Cf. Zuni Prayer, p. 170; Hopi Tradition, p. 244, Ghost Dance, p. 793.

**Rig Veda 10.154.1-5:** This is a prayer to Yama, the judge of the dead, to allow the deceased to enter the higher realms. Cf. Tibetan Book of the Dead, pp. 243-44.

And, Ananda, both banks of those great rivers are lined with variously scented jewel trees, and from them bunches of flowers, leaves, and branches of all kinds hang down. And if those beings wish to indulge in sports full of heavenly delights on those river-banks, then, after they have stepped into the water, the water in each case rises as high as they wish it to—up to the ankles, or to the knees, or to the hips, or to their sides, or to their ears. And heavenly delights arise. Again, if beings wish the water to be cold, for them it becomes cold; if they wish it to be hot, for them it becomes hot; if they wish it to be hot and cold, for them it becomes hot and cold, to suit their pleasure. And those rivers flow along, full of water scented with the best perfumes, covered with lilies, lotus, and all manner of beautiful flowers, resounding with the sounds of peacocks, sparrows, parrots, ducks, geese, herons, cranes, swans, and others, with small islands inhabited by flocks of birds, easy to ford, free from mud, and with golden sand on the bottom. And all the wishes those beings may think of, they will be fulfilled, as long as they are rightful.

*Buddhism.*
Larger Sukhavativyuha Sutra 15-18

After this I looked, and lo, in heaven an open door! And the first voice, which I had heard speaking to me like a trumpet, said, "Come up hither, and I will show you what must take place after this." At once I was in the Spirit, and lo, a throne stood in heaven, with one seated on the throne! And he who sat there appeared like jasper and carnelian, and round the throne was a rainbow that looked like an emerald. Round the throne were twenty-four thrones, and seated on the thrones were twenty-four elders, clad in white garments, with golden crowns upon their heads. From the throne issue flashes of lightning, and voices and peals of thunder, and before the throne burn seven torches of fire, which are the seven spirits of God; and before the throne there is as it were a sea of glass, like crystal.

And round the throne, on each side of the throne, are four living creatures, full of eyes in front and behind: the first living creature like a lion, the second living creature like an ox, the third living creature with the face of a man, and the fourth living creature like a flying eagle. And the four living creatures, each of them with six wings, are full of eyes round about and within, and day and night they never cease to sing,

Holy, holy, holy, is the Lord God Almighty,
who was and is and is to come!

After this I looked, and behold, a great multitude which no man could number, from every nation, from all tribes and peoples and tongues, standing before the throne and before the Lamb [Christ], clothed in white robes, with palm branches in their hands, and crying out with a loud voice, "Salvation belongs to our God who sits upon the throne, and to the Lamb!"...

Then one of the elders addressed me, saying, "Who are these, clothed in white robes, and whence have they come?" I said to him, "Sir, you know." And he said to me, "These are they who have come out of the great tribulation; they have washed their robes and made them white in the blood of the Lamb.

Therefore they are before the throne of God,
and serve him day and night within his temple;
and he who sits upon the throne will shelter
them with his presence.
They shall hunger no more, neither thirst any
more;
the sun shall not strike them, nor any
scorching heat.
For the Lamb in the midst of the throne will be
their shepherd,
and he will guide them to springs of living
water;
and God will wipe away every tear from their
eyes."

*Christianity.*
Revelation 4.1-8 and 7.9-17

**Revelation 4.1-8** and **7.9-17:** Cf. Revelation 21-22, pp. 794-95; Ezekiel 1.3-28, pp. 65-66; Doctrine and Covenants 76.54-93, p. 227.

Glory be to Him, who carried His servant by night from the Holy Mosque to the Further Mosque, the precincts of which We have blessed, that We might show him some of Our signs.

*Islam.* Qur'an 17.1

Anas ibn Malik said, "Abu Dharr recounted that the Messenger of God said, 'While I was at Mecca, the roof of my house opened and Gabriel entered. He opened my chest, washed me with the water of Zamzam, brought a golden basin full of faith and wisdom and emptied all of it into my chest. After that he closed it, took me by the hand and raised me towards the lowest heaven. When I arrived at the lowest heaven, Gabriel said to the door-keeper, "Open." "Who is there?" he asked. "Gabriel," the angel replied. "Is there anyone with you?" responded the door-keeper. "Yes," replied Gabriel, "Muhammad is with me." "Has he been commanded?" added the door-keeper. "Yes," said the angel. When the door-keeper had opened to us, we rose up within the lowest heaven, and suddenly we saw a man sitting, having some spirits on his right and others on his left. Every time he looked to the right he smiled, but as soon as he looked to the left he wept. He said, "Welcome virtuous prophet and virtuous son." "Who is this?" I asked Gabriel. "This man," he replied, "is Adam, and those spirits on the right are destined to Paradise, while the spirits on his left are destined to hell. That is why, when he looks to the right, he smiles, and when he looks to the left, he weeps."

"'Then Gabriel raised me up to the second heaven and said to the door-keeper, "Open." He asked the same questions as the first, and then opened to us.'" Anas recounted that Abu Dharr said that the Prophet found in the various heavens Adam, Idris, Moses, Jesus, and Abraham, but he was not certain which were the positions they occupied. What he does say is that Muhammad found Adam in the lowest heaven and Abraham in the sixth heaven.

Anas adds, "When Gabriel came with the Prophet into the presence of Idris, the latter said, 'Welcome virtuous prophet.'" "When I asked 'Who is this?'" the Prophet went on, "Gabriel answered me, 'It is Idris.' Then I went into the presence of Moses, who said, 'Welcome virtuous prophet and virtuous brother.' 'Who is this?' I asked. 'Moses' replied the angel. I then went into the presence of Jesus, who exclaimed, 'Welcome virtuous prophet and virtuous brother.' 'Who is it?' I said. 'Jesus,' replied Gabriel. I went after that into the presence of Abraham, who said, 'Welcome virtuous prophet and virtuous brother.' 'Who is it?' I asked. 'It is Abraham,' the angel said to me." Ibn Hazm records that Ibn 'Abbas and Abu Habba al-Ansari said that the Prophet used the following words, "Then the angel raised me until he brought me to a height where I heard the beating of wings.... Then Gabriel led me away and brought me to the lote-tree of the Boundary, which is covered with unspeakably beautiful colors. Next I entered Paradise. There are domes of pearls, and the sun there is made of musk."

*Islam.* Hadith of Bukhari

**Qur'an 17.1:** This is the Night Journey (*Mi'raj*) of Muhammad, where he was transported from the 'Holy Mosque' at Mecca to the 'Further Mosque' in Jerusalem, and then taken on a tour of the seven heavens, even to the throne of God. The following hadith gives details of the latter part of the journey.

**Hadith of Bukhari:** An episode from this description of the Mi'raj where God prescribes for Muslims fifty prayers a day and Muhammad, on Moses' advice, bargains with God to reduce their number to five, omitted here, may be found on p. 561.

## *Hell*

THE LOWER REALMS OF HELL are the subject of the following passages. Some say that hell is but a state of mind, yet as anyone knows who has experienced the pangs of intense loneliness, remorse, shame, guilt, or loss, such states of mind can be excruciatingly vivid. Furthermore, it is said that in the spiritual world it will not be possible to avoid such feelings, as is usually done while in the body, through such devices as forgetting, rationalization, or losing oneself in sense-pleasures or drink. There is no respite from unpleasant feelings, which remain to torture the unfortunate soul continually. To describe such pain, which is beyond comprehension, scriptures use concrete images: burning fire, boiling water, bitter cold, being crushed, hacked and dismembered, trampled, burned, and eaten alive.

As for the cowardly, the faithless, the polluted, as for murderers, fornicators, sorcerers, idolators, and all liars, their lot shall be in the lake that burns with fire and sulphur, which is the second death.

*Christianity*. Revelation 21.8

There is a stream of fire from which emerge
poisonous flames.
There is none else there except the self.
The waves of the ocean of fire are aflame
And the sinners are burning in them.

*Sikhism*. Adi Granth,
Maru Solahe, M.1, p. 1026

Hell is before him, and he is made to drink a festering water, which he sips but can hardly swallow. Death comes to him from every side, yet he cannot die—before him is a harsh doom.

*Islam*. Qur'an 14.15-16

Hell will lurk in ambush
to receive home the arrogant,
who will linger there for ages.
They will taste nothing cool in it nor any drink
except hot bathwater and slops,
a fitting compensation
since they have never expected any reckoning
and have wittingly rejected Our signs.
Everything We have calculated in writing.
"So taste! Yet We shall only increase torment
for you!"

*Islam*. Qur'an 78.21-30

After their lifetime's end
They will enter the Avici hell,
For a complete kalpa;
Reborn at each kalpa's end,
They thus go on revolving
Unto innumerable kalpas;
When they come out of hell,
They will degrade into animals,
Such as dogs or jackals,
With lean-cheeked forms,
Blue-black with scabs and sores,
The sport of men;
Moreover by men
Hated and scorned,

**Maru Solahe, M.1:** Cf. Magadhishloka, p. 244.
**Qur'an 14.15-16:** Cf. Qur'an 11.106-07, p. 368; 14.42-52, p. 782; 39.68-75, pp. 244-45; 69.13-17, p. 781.
**Qur'an 78.21-30:** See previous note.

Ever suffering hunger and thirst,
Bones and flesh withered up.
Alive, beaten with thorns,
Dead, with shards and stones;
By cutting themselves off from the Buddha seed,
They receive such recompense.

*Buddhism.* Lotus Sutra 3

He went from there to the east. There men were dismembering one another, cutting off each of their limbs, saying, "This to you, this to me!" He said: "O horrible! Men are here dismembering one another, cutting off each of their limbs!" They replied, "In this way they have treated us in the other world, and in the same way we now treat them in return." He asked, "Is there no expiation for this?" "Yes, there is." "What is it?" "Your father knows it."

*Hinduism.* Satapatha Brahmana 11.6.3

Some of the sinful are cut with saws, like firewood, and others, thrown flat on the ground, are chopped into pieces with axes. Some, their bodies half buried in a pit, are pierced in the head with arrows. Others, fixed in the middle of a press, are squeezed like sugarcane. Some are surrounded closely with blazing charcoal, enwrapped with torches, and smelted like a lump of ore. Some are plunged into heated butter, and others into heated oil, and like a cake thrown into the frying pan they are turned about. Some are thrown in the path of huge maddened elephants, and some with hands and feet bound are placed head downwards. Some are thrown into wells; some are hurled from heights; others, plunged into pits full of worms, are eaten away by them....

Having experienced in due order the torments below, he comes here again, purified.

*Hinduism.* Garuda Purana 3.49-71

Then the man of unwholesome deeds boils in water infested with worms. He cannot stay still—the boiling pots, round and smooth like bowls, have no surfaces which he can get hold of. Then he is in the jungle of sword blades, limbs mangled and hacked, the tongue hauled by hooks, the body beaten and slashed. Then he is in Vetarani, a watery state difficult to get through, with its two streams that cut like razors. The poor beings fall into it, living out their unwholesome deeds of the past. Gnawed by hungry jackals, ravens and black dogs, and speckled vultures and crows, the sufferers groan. Such a state is experienced by the man of unwholesome deeds. It is a state of absolute suffering. So a sensible person in this world is as energetic and mindful as he can be.

*Buddhism.* Sutta Nipata 672-76

There was a rich man, who was clothed in purple and fine linen and who feasted sumptuously every day. And at his gate lay a poor man named Lazarus, full of sores, who desired to be fed with what fell from the rich man's table; moreover the dogs came and licked his sores. The poor man died and was carried by the angels to Abraham's bosom. The rich man also died and was buried; and in Hades, being in torment, he lifted up his eyes, and saw Abraham far off and Lazarus in his bosom. And he called out, "Father Abraham, have mercy upon me, and send Lazarus to dip the end of his finger in water and cool my tongue; for I am in anguish in this flame." But Abraham said,

**Lotus Sutra 3:** Avici hell is the most severe of the Buddhist hells. In this passage, 'such people' means those who treat the Lotus Sutra with disrespect or who maltreat its followers. They will suffer the inevitable effect caused by accumulating such bad karma.

**Satapatha Brahmana 11.6.3:** In this passage the sage Bhrigu is given a tour of hell. Later, his father Varuna explains the expiation for these sins through offering the fire sacrifice, the *agnihotra*.

**Garuda Purana 3.49-71:** Vv. 49-54, 71. Regarding the last verse: The Eastern conception of hell in Hinduism, Buddhism, and Jainism is analagous to the Christian concept of Purgatory. There is no eternal damnation; hell is a place to expiate evil karma with the end that the purified soul can again advance to a higher plane of existence. Cf. Markandeya Purana 13-15, p. 693.

**Sutta Nipata 672-76:** Cf. Tibetan Book of the Dead, pp. 243-44; Guide to the Bodhisattva's Way of Life 4.28-35, p. 279.

"Son, remember that you in your lifetime received your good things, and Lazarus in like manner evil things; but now he is comforted here, and you are in anguish. And besides all this, between us and you a great chasm has been fixed, in order that those who would pass from here to you may not be able, and none may cross from there to us."

And he said, "Then I beg you, father, to send him to my father's house, for I have five brothers, so that he may warn them, lest they also come into this place of torment." But Abraham said, "They have Moses and the prophets; let them hear them." And he said, "No, father Abraham; but if some one goes to them from the dead, they will repent." He said to him, "If they do not hear Moses and the prophets, neither will they be convinced if someone should rise from the dead."

*Christianity*. Luke 16.19-31

In the garden of the city of Sieu-Shui-Siuen, there once lived a man by the name of Fan Ki, who led a wicked life. He induced men to stir up quarrels and lawsuits with each other, to seize by violence what did not belong to them, and to dishonor other men's wives and daughters. When he could not succeed easily in carrying out his evil purposes, he made use of the most odious stratagems.

One day he died suddenly, but came back to life twenty-four hours afterward and bade his wife gather together their relatives and neighbors. When all were assembled he told them that he had seen the king of the dark realm who said to him, "Here the dead receive punishment for their deeds of evil. The living know not the lot that is reserved for them. They must be thrown into a bed of coals whose heat is in proportion to the extent of their crimes and to the harm they have done their fellows."

The assembled company listened to this report as to the words of a feverish patient; they were incredulous and refused to believe the story. But Fan Ki had filled the measure of crime, and Yama, the king of hell, had decided to make an example of him so as to frighten men from their evil ways. At Yama's command Fan Ki took a knife and mutilated himself, saying, "This is my punishment for inciting men to dissolute lives." He put out both his eyes, saying, "This is my punishment for having looked with anger at my parents, and at the wives and daughters of other men with lust in my heart." He cut off his right hand, saying, "This is my punishment for having killed a great number of animals." He cut open his body and plucked out his heart, saying, "This is my punishment for causing others to die under tortures." And last of all he cut out his tongue to punish himself for lying and slandering.

The rumor of these occurrences spread afar, and people came from every direction to see the mangled body of the unhappy man. His wife and children were overcome with grief and shame, and closed the door to keep out the curious crowd. But Fan Ki, still living by the ordeal of Yama, said in inarticulate sounds, "I have but executed the commands of the king of hell, who wants my punishment to serve as a warning to others. What right have you to prevent them from seeing me?"

For six days the wicked man rolled upon the ground in the most horrible agonies, and at the end of that time he died.

*Taoism*. Treatise on Response and Retribution, Appended Tales

❖

# *Spiritual Benefactors*

THE WORLD'S RELIGIONS TESTIFY to the existence of a host of spiritual beings, occupying the various realms in the spiritual world. The good and beneficent spiritual beings are for Christians the angels and departed saints, for Mahayana Buddhists the great bodhisattvas, and for Shintoists the kami.

Indian religions speak of devas and devis, the Thirty-three, *gandharvas* or celestial musicians, and diverse other classes of spiritual beings. Chinese religion has among its ranks of gods the Yellow Emperor, the Jade Emperor, and countless personal spirits such as the Spirit of the Hearth. In Native American religions the spiritual benefactors are forces active in the natural world: viz., the Thunders, Mother Corn, sacred Stones, the Winds, Eagle, Sun, and Moon.

In the monotheistic religions, and in religions with an impersonal and utterly transcendent conception of Absolute Reality, these spiritual benefactors, no matter how exalted, are regarded as subordinate to Ultimate Reality. Yet since the Ultimate Reality is often inaccessible to humans, the higher spiritual beings are frequently revered as intermediaries. Gabriel, an angel, is the intermediary of divine revelation in Islam and the Latter-day Saints. For Buddhists, Bodhisattvas personify aspects of Ultimate Reality in ways that can be more easily apprehended by human beings who are too dull to grasp the perfect wisdom of Emptiness. In African traditional and Native American religions, in Shinto, and in Taoism the spirits of nature, the heavenly beings, and the most prominent ancestors constitute the fellowship of spiritual beings that together cause the movements of heaven and earth.

These spiritual beings have power. In many traditions the gods, goddesses, and benevolent spirits of nature dispense blessings to the human world and keep their devotees from harm. Therefore, it is requisite that they be worshipped and supplied with offerings. We also include traditions about making offerings for ancestors and relatives who have passed on. These offerings ease their way into the next world and give them additional spiritual merit.

O gods! All your names are to be revered, saluted and adored; all of you who have sprung from heaven and earth, listen here to my invocation.

*Hinduism.* Rig Veda 10.63.2

I [the Bodhisattva Samantabhadra] relieve the distress of the beings of all evil realms, and equally bestow happiness on them. I continue to do so through the lapse of boundless kalpas, and in the extent of the ten quarters of the universe. The benefits of all are eternal, and omnipresent.

*Buddhism.* Gandavyuha Sutra

The Lord Scripture Glory says, "For seventeen generations I have been incarnated as a high mandarin, and I have never oppressed my people nor maltreated my subordinates. I have helped them in misfortune; I have rescued

**Rig Veda 10.63.2:** Cf. Rig Veda 1.164.46, p. 34, Brihadaranyaka Upanishad 3.9.1, pp. 52-53.

**Gandavyuha Sutra:** The great bodhisattvas, who are worshipped in popular Buddhism, embody and symbolize different aspects of the Buddha. Samantabhadra, which means Universally Good, is the embodiment of the Buddha's vows and practices. Manjusri embodies the Buddha's wisdom. Avalokitesvara (Chinese *Kuan Yin*) embodies the Buddha's compassion for beings in distress. See also the hymn to Kuan Yin in Lotus Sutra 25, p. 402.

them from poverty; I have taken compassion on their orphans; I have forgiven their transgressions; I have extensively practiced secret virtue which is attuned to Heaven above. If you are able to keep your hearts as I have kept mine, Heaven will surely bestow upon you blessings."

*Taoism*. Tract of the Quiet Way

Parvati, on seeing her son Ganesha resuscitated, embraced him joyously and clothed him with new garments and ornaments. After kissing his face, she said, "O Ganesha, you have had great distress since your very birth. You are blessed and contented now. You will receive worship before all the gods. You will be free from distress. Vermillion is on your face now. Hence you will be worshipped with vermillion by all men always.

"All achievements certainly accrue to him who performs your worship with flowers, sandal paste, scents, auspicious food offerings, waving of lights, betel leaves, charitable gifts, circumambulations, and obeisance. All kinds of obstacles will certainly perish."

Shiva, Brahma, and Vishnu declared in unison, "O great gods, just as we three are worshipped in all the three worlds, so also Ganesha shall be worshipped by all of you. He is the remover of all obstacles and the bestower of the fruits of all rites."

*Hinduism*. Shiva Purana, Rudrasamhita 18

Are they [the angels] not all ministering spirits sent forth to serve, for the sake of those who are to obtain salvation?

*Christianity*. Hebrews 1.14

The work of the Holy Spirit is the phenomena which have been working to harmonize the spiritual world and the human world through love.

*Unification Church*. Sun Myung Moon, 5-1-81

Those who have said, "Our Lord is God," then have gone straight, upon them the angels descend, saying, "Fear not, neither sorrow; rejoice in Paradise that you were promised. We are your friends in the present life and in the world to come; therein you shall have all that your souls desire..."

*Islam*. Qur'an 41.30-31

If a man perform a religious precept, one angel is assigned to him; if he perform two precepts, two angels are assigned to him; if he perform all the precepts, many angels are assigned to him; as it is said, "For He shall give His angels charge over you, to keep you in all thy ways" [Psalm 91.11]. Who are these angels? They are his guardians from the harmful spirits; as it is said, "A thousand shall fall at your side and ten thousand at your right hand" [Psalm 91.7].

*Judaism*. Tanhuma Numbers 19

**Tract of the Quiet Way:** In popular Taoism the great officials and emperors of old have ascended to heaven and become blessed spirits. Lord Scripture Glory (Wen Chang) is one of the chief Taoist deities.

**Shiva Purana, Rudrasamhita 18:** Ganesha is depicted with an elephant head and a human body. His worship is popular among contemporary Hindus. In this, his foundation legend, Ganesha had been decapitated in battle, and to restore him to life the head of an elephant was affixed to his body. He is given blessings and is offered to humanity to be worshipped as 'the remover of all obstacles'—a role suitable to the symbolism of an elephant.

**Hebrews 1.14:** Cf. Qur'an 21.19-22, p. 54; Michi-no-Shiori, p. 53; Hebrews 13.2, p. 700. Many Christians revere the saints: chief among them Mary, the mother of Jesus—cf. The Rosary, p. 597—from whom emanate grace for the people of the world.

**Sun Myung Moon, 5-1-81:** Cf. Acts 2.1-18, pp. 408-9; Romans 8.26-27, p. 464.

**Qur'an 41.30-31:** Cf. Qur'an 13.10-11, p. 126; 50.17-19, p. 243.

**Tanhuma Numbers 19:** Cf. Midrash Psalms 17.8, p. 218; Abot 4.13, p. 238; Psalm 91.1-13, pp. 398-99; Tract of the Quiet Way, p. 711.

Now the Lord had shown to me, Abraham, the intelligences that were organized before the world was; and among all these there were many of the noble and great ones;

And God saw these souls that they were good, and he stood in the midst of them, and he said, "These I will make my rulers"; for he stood among those that were spirits, and he saw that they were good; and he said to me, "Abraham, you are one of them; you were chosen before you were born."

And there stood one among them who was like unto God [Jesus Christ], and he said to those who were with him, "We will go down, for there is space there, and we will take of these materials, and we will make an earth on which these may dwell;

"And we will prove them herewith, to see if they will do all things that the Lord their God shall command them...."

And the Lord said, "Let us go down." And they went down at the beginning, and they, that is the gods, formed the heavens and the earth.

*Church of Jesus Christ of Latter-day Saints.*
Pearl of Great Price, Abraham 3.22-4.1

*Sansang suira!*
There are eight peaks within the inner mountain,
And thirteen famous places in the outer mountain.
Within these famous mountains and the great heavens of all Buddhas,
The great altar of the nation is protected by the great generals.
Was not the general Chae Yong one of them?
The famous general of Korea,
Who was favored by his people....
Oh, I am the great mountain god.
If I sit down, I cover three thousand li [the entire land of Korea].
If I stand up, I stretch over ninety thousand li [the whole world].
If I look down with my clear mirror, I can observe ten thousand li.
Oh, I am the great mountain god.
What can you offer to satisfy me?
Is the whole pig covered with a red cloth enough?
Is the bundle of three different colored silks enough?
Offer many rich silks to me.
Oh, you, the husband and wife of this home.
Do you remember who gives you the food that sustains you?
Who gave you a home?
Who gave you wealth?
Who gave you long life?
I, the Sansang, gave you blessings and aid in times of need.

*Korean Shamanism.*
Invocation of the Mountain Spirit

I looked at the moss-covered stones. Some of them seemed to have the features of a man, but they could not answer me. Then I had a dream, and in my dream one of these small, round stones appeared to me and told me that the maker of all was Wakan Tanka, and that in order to honor him I must honor his works in nature. The stone said that by my search I had shown myself worthy of supernatural help. It said that if I were curing a sick person I might ask its assistance, and that all the forces of nature would help me work a cure.... Some believe that these stones descend with the lightning, but I believe they are on the ground

**Pearl of Great Price, Abraham 3.22-4.1:** In the teaching of the Latter-day Saints, all people pre-existed as spirits and as gods, and they participated with God in the creation of the world. The text goes on to review the contents of Genesis 1, pp. 81-82, but with 'the gods' acting at each stage of creation.

**Invocation of the Mountain Spirit:** Sansang is the Mountain God. As the mountain is a symbol of strength and power, Sansang is also the god of great generals, and is personified by the famous general Chae Yong of the Silla dynasty. The Mountan Spirit is also often symbolized by a tiger, who in legend inhabits the mountain recesses. The shamaness (*mudang*) who invokes Sansang by singing this song wears a general's costume and a hat with tiger's fur, and holds flags and a sword. Sansang is one of twelve spirits which are invoked in turn during the shamanist ritual, which is called a *kut*.

and are projected downwards by the bolt. In all my life I have been faithful to the sacred stones. I have lived according to their requirements, and they have helped me in all my troubles. I have tried to qualify myself as well as possible to handle these sacred stones. I know that I am not worthy to speak [directly] to Wakan Tanka, so I make my requests of these stones and they are my intermediaries.

*Native American Religions.* Sioux Tradition

"The path of the *hekura* is visible, luminous; there arises from it something like a fiery breath that makes the air heavy and almost unbreathable. One does not see the hekura, one feels the wind they raise when they move. During the hunt from which I just returned, I scattered the hekura who were in me."

"Ordinary men are unable to recognize them. Yet the wind tells us that they are there."

"I see them only at night, when I close my eyes."

"One can see them only then."

"Their paths become luminous for me. I am sleeping; they approach and summon me to answer them. They suddenly wake me by shaking my arm or pulling on my ankle."

"Those who are not truly shamans do not hear them. He who is really a shaman hears a kind of buzzing, 'bouu...' during his sleep, and this song echoes, rebounding off the celestial vault. He opens his eyes and says to himself, 'I am going to see them now!' The parrotlets sing, 'bre, bre, bre...,' he knows that it is they. A cool breeze then glides along his legs...."

"I saw the hekura walk on a rotten branch; I was passing right underneath."

"Indeed, it was they; but they were not friendly toward you. The strong odors of the smoking grill, the smell of singed hair, of scorched meat near the fire, all this drives them off. Yet they did seem inclined to approach you."

"They give off a heady perfume; it comes from the dyes and the magic plants they carry with them. Suddenly, I stopped smelling these aromas, my nostrils no longer perceived them."

"Therefore when one is at the end of the initiation, it is advisable not to hunt. If a flock of toucans takes flight and one of them lands near you, then all the others immediately follow suit. Be sure not to frighten them: stare at them fixedly and continue on your way; you be sure that they are hekura. Of course, there are those you drove away during the hunt; but don't be overly concerned, I foresee that those were not the good ones. The others remain, who came into your breast while you were lying in your hammock. Those are truly yours, they are in you."

*Native American Religions.* Yanomami Shaman's Instruction (Brazil)

"Ah, the spirits of my ancestors have looked down from heaven, watching over and helping me. The hosts of evil have now been subdued one and all, and we are without enemy or misfortune. Let us now therefore give worship to the heavenly deities, vowing to abide by the teachings of our imperial ancestors." With that, Emperor Jimmu prepared places of worship in the mountains of Tomi... and thus performed worship to the imperial ancestors and to the heavenly deities.

*Shinto.* Nihon Shoki 3

The light which these souls [of departed saints] radiate is responsible for the progress of the world and the advancement of its peoples. They are like leaven which leavens the world of being, and constitute the animating force

**Sioux Tradition:** Cf. Sioux Tradition, pp. 53-54; Cree Round Dance Song, p. 31; Cheyenne Song, p. 205; Zuni Song, p. 206; Gros Ventres Tradition of the Pipe Child, pp. 170-71.

**Yanomami Shaman's Instruction:** This is a conversation between an experienced shaman and his apprentice. Note how the shaman is trained to become sensitive to faint odors, sounds, and touch which indicate the presence of spirits. More of this instruction is given on p. 376.

**Nihon Shoki 3:** In Shinto, there is little difference between the kami and the spirits of ancestors, deceased emperors, great saints, and heroes. All are worthy of worship; all merge into the common spirit of divinity which guides Japan; see One Hundred Poems on the Jewelled Spear, p. 558. Cf. Book of Ritual 1.2.3.4.6-9, pp. 612-13, describing how ancestors are revered and worshipped in China.

through which the arts and wonders of the world are made manifest.... These souls and symbols of detachment have provided, and will continue to provide, the supreme moving impulse in the world of being.

*Baha'i Faith*. Gleanings from the Writings of Baha'u'llah 81

The spirit that eats a man's offering, pays him back with life.

*African Traditional Religions*. Proverb

The man who ignores Ogun will clear his farm with his bare hands.

*African Traditional Religions*. Yoruba Proverb (Nigeria)

Our ancestors the emperors of old governed the realm by first paying worship to the kami with reverence and awe. Widely worshipping the kami of mountain and river, they thereby had natural concourse with heaven and earth. For this reason, summer and winter also turned in their season, and the works of creation were in harmony.

*Shinto*. Nihon Shoki 22

In whatsoever place the prudent man shall
make his home,
Let him support the virtuous ones who live the
holy life.
To all the devas dwelling there let him make
offerings.
Thus honored, they will honor him; revered,
they'll him revere.
As a mother gives compassion to the child she
has borne,
Whom the devas compassion give ever see
good luck.

*Buddhism*. Digha Nikaya ii.88

Ala, come and drink and eat the kola nut.

Chukwu, come and drink and eat the kola nut.

Ancestors, come and drink and eat kola nut.

I was told by a man of Ngbwidi, one named Ehirim, that a man of Agunese had stolen his yams; and so I summoned the priests of Ala and Aro holders and elders in order that we might inquire into the matter. I called them, even as my father, who was priest of Njoku before me, used to do.

If any of these men, who have come to try the case, deal falsely in the matter, or if the accuser or accused or any person called to give evidence tells falsehood, then do you, Ala, Chukwu, Njoku, Ancestors, and Ofo, deal with that man.

*African Traditional Religions*. Igbo Invocation at a Trial (Nigeria)

"War-bundle owners, I greet you. Ye elders, I am about to pour tobacco for the spirits.

"Hearken Earthmaker, our father, I am about to offer you a handful of tobacco. My ancestor so-and-so concentrated his mind upon you. The fireplaces with which you blessed him, the small amount of life you granted to him, all, four times the blessings that you bestowed upon my ancestor, I ask of you directly. May I have no troubles in life.

**Gleanings from the Writings of Baha'u'llah 81:** Cf. Qur'an 4.69, p. 249. In Hebrews 11.1-12.2, pp. 539-40, the saints are described as a cloud of witnesses urging on the faithful.

**Yoruba Proverb:** Ogun is the god of iron, and hence of all tools, weapons, and machines. His worship is popular in Yoruba religion today, and in its offshoot, Santeria.

**Nihon Shoki 22:** The kami indwell the whole of life, and the divine can be seen within all the manifestations of nature—the mountains, the streams, the forests, etc. Hence respect for nature and respect for the gods are one in the same; see Urabe-no-Kanekuni, p. 204. Cf. Book of Ritual 1.2.3.4.6-9, pp. 612-13.

**Digha Nikaya ii.88:** Cf. Anguttara Nikaya iii.368, p. 211; Precious Garland 249-50, p. 209; Hebrews 13.2, p. 700.

**Igbo Invocation at a Trial:** Ala is the earth goddess, Chukwu is the Igbo name for God, the Creator; and Njoku is the yam deity. The Ofo and Aro are ritual sticks of wood or iron, specially consecrated, that create a channel for the spirits to operate in this world. Through their mediation, the gods can ferret out an evil-doer or a person who gives false testimony and punish him with misfortune. Cf. Igbo Consecration of the Ofo, p. 550.

"Chief of the Thunderbirds, who lives in the west, you strengthened my grandfather. I am about to offer you a handful of tobacco. The food, the pair of deer you gave him for his fireplaces, that I ask of you directly. May you accept this tobacco from me and may I not meet with troubles.

"Great Black Hawk, you also blessed my grandfather. I am about to offer you tobacco. Whatever food you blessed him with that I ask you directly. May I not meet with troubles.

"You [night spirits] on the other side, who live in the east, who walk in darkness, I am about to offer you tobacco to smoke. Whatever you blessed my ancestor with, I ask of you. If you smoke this tobacco I will never be a weakling.

"Disease-giver, you who live in the south; you who look like a man; who art invulnerable; who on one side of your body present death and on the other life, you blessed my ancestor in the daytime, in broad daylight. You blessed him with food and told him that he would never fail in anything. You promised to avoid his home. You placed animals before him that he might easily obtain food. I offer you tobacco that you may smoke it, and that I may not be troubled by anything.

"To you, Sun, Light-wanderer, I make an offering of tobacco....

"To you, Grandmother Moon, who blessed my grandfather with food, I am about to make an offering of tobacco....

"To you, too, South Wind, I offer a handful of tobacco....

"For you, Grandmother Earth, I will also pour tobacco....

"To you, Pair of Eagles, to whom my ancestor prayed, I offer tobacco....

"Hearken, all ye spirits to whom my ancestor prayed; to all of you I offer tobacco. My ancestor gave a feast to all those who had blessed him. Bestow upon us once again all the blessings you gave our ancestor, that we may not become weaklings. I greet you all."

*Native American Religion*. Winnebago Invocation at the Sweat Lodge

Outside the walls they stand, at the crossways and outside doors, to their own home returning. But when a plenteous meal is spread, of food and drink, no man remembers them [the dead]. Such is the way of things.

Wherefore do those who have pity on their kin make offerings due, of choice food and drink at seasonable times, saying, "Be this a gift to kinsmen, may our kinsmen be well pleased with it!" Then do those earth-bound [ghosts], kinsmen, gather there where a plenteous meal is spread of food and drink, and fail not to render thanks, saying, "Long live our kinsmen, thanks to whom we have this gift! To us this offering is made; not without fruit are they who give!"

For [in ghostland] no cattle-keeping, no ploughing of fields is seen. There is no trading there, as on earth, no trafficking with gold. We ghosts that have departed there exist on what is given here. Even as water gathered on high ground flows down into the marsh, so are offerings given here on earth of service to the ghosts....

Of a truth, wailing and grief and all manner of lamentation avail not anything. It helps not the ghosts that kinsmen stand lamenting thus.

Moreover, [if] this gift of charity is bestowed on the Order, it is bound to be of service [to the ghosts] for a long, long time.

Thus this duty done to kinsmen has been declared: unto the ghosts it is no mean offering of worship; unto the Brethren of the Order it is strength conferred; unto yourselves no small merit has been won.

*Buddhism*. Khuddaka Patha, Tirokudda Sutta

**Winnebago Invocation:** Cf. Sioux Tradition, pp. 53-54; Zuni Song, p. 206; Sioux Vision Quest, pp. 606-7; A Winnebago Father's Precepts, p. 671. On the origin of tobacco as a sacred mediator to the beneficent spirits, see Sioux Tradition of the Sacred Pipe, p. 610.

**Tirokudda Sutta:** Cf. Doctrine and Covenants 128.18, pp. 368-69.

There was a shrine to the water goddess in the village of Ch'ing Ch'i, and her image that was placed there was so nicely carved that it looked like a real goddess of splendid beauty. The villagers made her the guardian of the district and paid her great respect.

It was the second month of the year when the pear blossoms on the grounds were very pretty, that a party of young students was passing by and admired the flowers. One of them lifted the curtain that was hung before the image of the goddess and exclaimed, "How lovely she is! If she were alive I would make her my mistress!"

His friends were shocked, but he laughed at their scruples, saying that spirits and gods have no reality; that it is well enough for the people to believe in and fear them, because such superstition made them more amenable. He then composed a libelous poem and wrote it on the wall, but his friends did not say anything more, knowing the uselessness of their advice.

After this they all went to the examination hall, and stayed in the Wen Chang Dormitory. One evening the Lord Scripture Glory (Wen Chang) appeared to them in a dream, and they were greatly afraid to be in the presence of his august majesty. He had a roll on his table and declared to them, "As you know well, any student who is guilty of trifling with women is excluded from the list. Even a plain, ordinary woman should be respected by you; how much more this is true of a holy goddess, you all must know. According to a report I have received it seems there is one of your number who has insulted the goddess of Ch'ing Ch'i." Having ascertained the name of the offender, the Lord cancelled it from the list, adding that this was done because the man was guilty of wronging a woman.

When the students met the following morning, they learned that each had the same dream during the night. Yet the offender himself was obdurate and said, "What has the Lord of Literature to do with such trifles? What harm can an image of clay do to me?"

He entered the examination cell, and having written down his seven essays with unusual vigor and brilliancy, felt assured of his final success. But when the night was far advanced, there appeared before him the goddess of water with her attendants. She censured him for both his grave offence and impertinence, and then ordered her maids to strike him with their sticks until the student lost his mind and destroyed all of his papers. When he was carried out of the cell in the morning, he was unconscious, and soon died.

*Taoism*. Treatise on Response and Retribution, Appended Tales

❖

## *Spiritual Error and the Occult*

THERE IS A CURRENT OF DEEP DISTRUST for spirits and their communications within the major religions. Since they are not comparable to Ultimate Reality, spirits are not privy to the highest truth. Christianity, Judaism, and Islam have a tradition that groups of the angels have fallen into error and misunderstood the will of God. Buddhism even regards the Creator god (the Hindu god Brahma) as one of these subordinate deities, subordinate to the Dhamma revealed by the Buddha.

Spirits are often viewed as fallible, motivated by selfish ends, and liable to mislead those who rely on them for guidance. Furthermore, the spiritual world is also populated by evil spirits, demons, fallen angels, and Satan—see *Demonic Powers*, pp. 309-15—as well as intermediate spiritual beings including the jinn, spirits of the dead, and various classes of ghosts. Therefore, a person should "test the spirits to see whether they are of God," based on the higher authority of revealed truth. Occult practices, such as seeking information from mediums, witches, astrologers, and otherwise penetrating the world of spirits, is condemned in many scriptures because it can lead people astray through communication with spirits from the lower realms. Attachment to revelations from spirits can sometimes rival genuine faith in God. Belief in miracles can also lead astray. Faith, purity, adherence to revealed truth, and performance of good deeds are superior ways to insure fellowship with spiritual beings of the highest levels.

Even in his servants he puts no trust,
and his angels he charges with error.

*Judaism* and *Christianity*. Job 4.18

O Lord, how can a god or a demon know all the extent of your glory? You alone know what you are, by the light of your innermost nature.

*Hinduism*. Bhagavad Gita 10.14

They say, "The All-merciful has taken to Him a son." Glory be to Him! Nay, but they [whom they call 'sons'] are honored servants, that do not outstrip Him in speech; they perform as He commands. He knows what is before them and behind them, and they do not intercede except for the man with whom He is well-pleased. They tremble in awe of Him. If any of them says, "I am a god apart from Him," such a one We recompense with hell, even as We recompense those who do evil.

*Islam*. Qur'an 21.26-29

God has taken his place in the divine council;
in the midst of the gods he holds judgment:
"How long will you judge unjustly
and show partiality to the wicked?
Give justice to the weak and the fatherless;
maintain the right of the afflicted and the
destitute.
Rescue the weak and the needy;
deliver them from the hand of the wicked."
They have neither knowledge nor
understanding,
they walk about in darkness,
all the foundations of the earth are shaken.
I say, "You are gods,

**Qur'an 21.26-29:** This is directed against both polytheism and certain popular forms of Christianity which take Jesus to be a separate god, the offspring of God the Father. Orthodox Christianity denies this: God the Son, second Person of the Trinity, is not begotten, nor is he "a God apart from" the Father. Jesus as the incarnation of the Son was always obedient to the Father's will. The Trinity is One God; it should never be misunderstood as tri-theism. Cf. Qur'an 5.75, p. 469; also Qur'an 4.116-17, p. 287, and 21.19-20, p. 54.

sons of the Most High, all of you;
nevertheless you shall die like men,
and fall like any prince."
Arise, O God, judge the earth;
for to thee belong all the nations!

*Judaism* and *Christianity*. Psalm 82

Say, It has been revealed to me that a company of the jinn gave ear. Then they said, "We have indeed heard a Qur'an wonderful, guiding to rectitude. We believe in it, and we will not associate with our Lord anyone. He—exalted by our Lord's majesty!—has not taken to Himself either consort or a son.

"The fool among us spoke against God outrage, and we had thought that men and jinn would never speak against God a lie. But there were certain men of mankind who would take refuge with certain men of the jinn, and they increased them in vileness, and they thought, even as you also thought, that God would never raise up anyone.

"And we stretched toward heaven, but we found it filled with terrible guards and meteors. We would sit there on seats to hear; but any listening now finds a meteor in wait for him. And so we know not whether evil is intended for those in the earth, or whether their Lord intends for them rectitude.

"And some of us are righteous, and some of us are otherwise; we are sects differing. Indeed, we thought that we should never be able to frustrate God in the earth, neither be able to frustrate Him by flight. When we heard the guidance, we believed in it; and whosoever believes in his Lord, he shall fear never paltriness nor vileness.

"And some of us have surrendered, and some of us have deviated. Those who have surrendered sought rectitude; but as for those who have deviated, they have become firewood for hell."

*Islam*. Qur'an 72.1-15

Once upon a time, Kevaddha, there occurred to a certain monk in this very company of monks, a doubt on the following point: "Where now do these four basic elements—extension, cohesion, heat, and motion—pass away, leaving no trace behind?" Then that monk worked himself up into such a state of ecstasy that the way leading to the heaven of the gods became clear to his ecstatic vision.

Then that monk went up to the realm of the Four Great Kings and asked the gods there, "Where, my friends, do the four basic elements—extension, cohesion, heat, and motion—pass away, leaving no trace behind?" The gods of the heaven of the Four Great Kings replied, "We do not know that. But there are the Four Great Kings, more powerful and glorious than we. They will know."

Then that monk went up to the Four Great Kings and asked, "Where, my friends..." The Four Great Kings replied, "We do not know that. But there are the gods of the heaven of the Thirty-three... They will know."

Then that monk, putting the same question and getting the same reply, went to Sakka, king of the heaven of the Thirty-three... up to the Yama gods... to the Tusita gods... to the Nimmana-rati gods... to the Vasavatti gods... to the retinue of the gods of the Heaven of God Almighty....

Finally the monk drew near to God Almighty [Brahma] and asked, "Where, my friend, do the four basic elements—extension, cohesion, heat, and motion—pass away, leaving no trace behind?"

And the greatest god replied, "I am the Great God, Almighty, the Supreme One, the one who cannot be conquered by others, All-seeing, All-powerful, the Ruler, the Creator, the Excellent, the Almighty, the One who has already practiced Calm, the Father of all that are and all that are to be!"

The monk said, "I did not ask you as to whether you were indeed all that you now say you are; but I ask you where do the four basic elements cease, leaving no trace behind?" Then the god gave the same reply. And yet a third time the monk put the same question to god as before.

Then, Kevaddha, that greatest god took that monk by the arm and led him aside and said, "These gods, the retinue of God Almighty, think me, friend, to be such that there is nothing I cannot see, nothing I have not understood, nothing I have not realized. Therefore, I gave no answer to your question in their presence. I do not know the answer to your question. Therefore, you have done wrong, acted unskillfully, in that, going past the Buddha, you have undertaken this long search for an answer to this question. Go back now to the Exalted One and accept his answer."

*Buddhism*. Digha Nikaya xi.67-83, Kevaddha Sutta

Men of ignorance worship spirits and ghosts.

*Hinduism*. Bhagavad Gita 17.4

Do not turn to mediums or wizards; do not seek them out, to be defiled by them: I am the Lord your God.

*Judaism* and *Christianity*. Leviticus 19.31

My follower does not study the practice of magic and spells. He does not analyze dreams and signs in sleep and movements in the Zodiac.

*Buddhism*. Sutta Nipata 927

Cursed be occult and miracle-making powers.

*Sikhism*. Var Sorath M.3, p. 650

Confucius never discussed abnormal phenomena, physical exploits, disorderly conduct, or spiritual beings.

*Confucianism*. Analects 7.20

Because I see danger in the practice of miracles, I loathe and abhor and repudiate them.

*Buddhism*. Digha Nikaya xi.66, Kevaddha Sutta

Then a blind and dumb demoniac was brought to [Jesus], and he healed him, so that the dumb man spoke and saw. And all the people were amazed, and said, "Can this be the Son of David?" But when the Pharisees heard it they said, "It is only by Beelzebul, the prince of demons, that this man casts out demons."

*Christianity*. Matthew 12.22-24

Jesus answered them, "Truly, I say to you, you seek me, not because you saw signs [that I am the Christ] but because you ate your fill of the loaves. Do not labor for the food which perishes, but for the food which endures to eternal life, which the Son of Man will give to you."

*Christianity*. John 6.26-27

Beloved, do not believe every spirit, but test the spirits to see whether they are of God; for many false prophets have gone out into the world.

*Christianity*. 1 John 4.1

Now concerning spiritual gifts, brethren, I do not want you to be uninformed. You know that when you were heathen, you were led astray to dumb idols, however you may have been moved. Therefore I want you to understand that no one speaking by the Spirit of God ever says "Jesus be cursed!" and no one can say "Jesus is Lord!" except by the Holy Spirit.

*Christianity*. 1 Corinthians 12.1-3

Indeed, even the devas are jealous of a yogin, striving as he does to surpass them by attaining Brahman. They therefore try to lead him astray, in various ways, if they find him off his guard.

*Hinduism*. Srimad Bhagavatam 11.20

**Bhagavad Gita 17.4:** Cf. Brihadaranyaka Upanishad 1.4.10, p. 287.

**Matthew 12.22-24:** Jesus performed many miracles for the people. Yet to the skeptical leaders they proved nothing; the devil can also do miracles.

**John 6.26-27:** The common people also were more impressed by the miracle of multiplying the loaves and fishes (see Mark 6.30-44, pp. 456-57) than by Jesus himself and his message, and followed him to see the show rather than to receive his wisdom. Miracles are not conducive to lasting faith.

**1 John 4.1:** Cf. 1 Timothy 4.1-2, p. 317; 2 Corinthians 11.14, p. 313; Qur'an 6.112, p. 317; Lotus Sutra 3, pp. 313-14.

**1 Corinthians 12.1-3:** Cf. John 14.13-14, p. 598; Srimad Bhagavatam 6.1, p. 596; John 14.15-21, p. 462; Romans 8.26-27, p. 464.

**Srimad Bhagavatam 11.20:** Cf. Brihadaranyaka Upanishad 1.4.10, p. 287; Mahabharata, Anusasana Parva 40.5-12, p. 307; Vishnu Purana 3.17-18, p. 318; Qur'an 17.61-64, pp. 312-13.

God is the protecting friend of those who believe. He brings them out of darkness into light. As for those who disbelieve, their patrons are false deities. They bring them out of light into darkness.

*Islam.* Qur'an 2.257

Those who worship other gods with faith and devotion also worship Me, Arjuna, even if they do not observe the usual forms. I am the object of all worship, its enjoyer and Lord. But they know not My pure being, and because of this they must be reborn.

Those who worship the gods will go to the realm of the gods; those who worship their ancestors will be united with them after death. Those who worship phantoms will become phantoms; but My devotees will come to me.

*Hinduism.* Bhagavad Gita 9.23-25

To maintain the existence of a ghost,
Only brings about mischief;
To understand the non-existence of a ghost
Is the way of Buddha;
To know that ghost and Reality are one
Is the way to Liberation.
Knowing that the ghosts are all one's parents
Is the right understanding;
Realizing that the ghost itself is Self-mind
Is glory supreme.

*Buddhism.* Milarepa

❖

**Qur'an 2.257:** Cf. Qur'an 4.116-17, p. 287.
**Bhagavad Gita 9.23-25:** Cf. Vacana 616, p. 286.

Part Two

# *Evil, Sin, and the Human Fall*

# CHAPTER 7

# THE HUMAN CONDITION

DESPITE THE PURPOSES FOR HUMAN LIFE which are proclaimed by religion and, for the most part, nurtured as ideals in the breasts of men and women, the human condition is in reality characterized by suffering, war, oppression, poverty, vain striving, and disappointment. The starting point of Buddhism, the first of the Four Noble Truths, is that all life is Ill—full of trouble and suffering. All religions recognize the correctness of this assertion in its broadest sense, that the human condition contradicts and defeats a person's true purpose as ordained by God or established by divine principles. The Christian understanding of man's inveterate tendency to do evil and turn away from God is found in the doctrine of Original Sin. The texts describing these and other comparable notions are brought together in the first section.

A second way to understand the human condition is to recognize human nature as the arena where the desires to do good and evil are in protracted conflict. This may be understood as reflecting a fundamental dualism within nature itself, or more commonly as a defect within the human heart. Due to this war within, it is hardly possible to fulfill the highest aspirations to goodness and holiness.

A third way of describing the human condition is by the theme of ignorance. Specifically, most people pass their lives in ignorance of God, his laws, and his purposes. Blinded by illusion or caught up in false values of materialism and egoism, their striving is in the wrong direction, one that leads away from God and toward their own destruction. A related concept in the monotheistic faiths is idolatry, which can mean allegiance to such false gods as money, power, race, nation, or any partisan political cause when it is made an absolute end in itself. Then there is pride and egoism, a most insidious form of ignorance, by which a person falsely places himself over others.

In the last section we turn to the root of suffering in selfish desire and craving—the second of the Four Noble Truths of Buddhism. The self-destructive character of selfish desire is widely recognized in the scriptures of the world's religions. It is manifested in specific forms, including lust, anger, and greed.

The human condition is also understood as the result of a fall from a potential or primordial state of grace or as a deviation from humanity's original purpose. These themes and the scriptures which pertain to them will be treated in the next chapter.

## *Ill*

THE FIRST OF THE BUDDHA'S FOUR NOBLE TRUTHS is that human existence is suffering, or Ill (Pali *dukkha*), which connotes the idea of an illness generated by the self through its false attachments. Often this condition is described by the metaphor of a universal fire engulfing the world. In Hinduism, the human lot of samsara is to go through an endless cycle of death and rebirth, conditioned by nature (the *gunas*) and rooted in the results of past actions. This is likened to a universal tree, turned upside-down, whose roots and branches trace the sequences of actions (*karma*) back to the beginning of time: The whole of it is suffering. In Christianity, the doctrine of Original Sin conveys a similar idea: Humans are, by their fallen condition, cut off from God and hence unable to fulfill the true purpose of life. We may try to be good, but in spite of our best efforts, we miss the mark. Original Sin, like the Hindu notion of samsara, is understood to be a condition perpetuated throughout the generations of humankind. (The doctrine of Original Sin also includes an explanation of its cause in the primordial Fall of Man, but that topic is deferred to the next chapter.)

Analogous statements recognizing that the human condition is inveterately ill, deficient, or sinful can be found in the scriptures of many religions. No one is untainted by sin and evil. Few are they who truly seek truth, beauty, and goodness. Even when people begin with the best of intentions, their behavior usually degenerates and ends in acrimony, betrayal, or violence.

The Noble Truth of Suffering (*Dukkha*) is this: Birth is suffering; aging is suffering; sickness is suffering; death is suffering; sorrow and lamentation, pain, grief, and despair are suffering; association with the unpleasant is suffering; dissociation from the pleasant is suffering; not to get what one wants is suffering—in brief, the five aggregates of attachment are suffering.

*Buddhism*. Samyutta Nikaya lvi.11: Setting in Motion the Wheel of Truth

I look at what ordinary people find happiness in, what they all make a mad dash for, racing around as though they couldn't stop—they all say they're happy with it. I'm not happy with it and I'm not unhappy with it. In the end, is there really happiness or isn't there?

*Taoism*. Chuang Tzu 18

**Samyutta Nikaya lvi.11:** This is the first of the Four NobleTruths, taken from the Buddha's first sermon. The 'five aggregates,' or *skandhas*, are the elements of the personality to which we cling in our vain craving for existence. There are: body-form, feeling, perception, activities which make karma, and consciousness.

Affliction does not come from the dust,
nor does trouble sprout from the ground;
but man is born to trouble
as the sparks fly upward.

*Judaism* and *Christianity*. Job 5.6-7

This world, become ablaze,
by touch of sense afflicted,
utters its own lament.
Whatever conceit one has,
therein is instability.
Becoming other,
bound to becoming,
yet in becoming it rejoices.
Delight therein is fear,
and what it fears is ill.

*Buddhism*. Udana 32

Brothers, all is burning. And what is the all that is burning? Brothers, the eye is burning, visible forms are burning, visual consciousness is burning, visual impression is burning, also whatever sensation, pleasant or painful or neither-painful-nor-pleasant, arises on account of the visual impression, that too is burning. Burning with what? Burning with the fire of lust, with the fire of hate, with the fire of delusion; I say it is burning with birth, aging, and death, with sorrows, with lamentations, with pains, with griefs, with despairs.

The ear is burning, sounds are burning, auditory consciousness is burning, auditory impression is burning, also whatever sensation, pleasant or painful or neither-painful-nor-pleasant, arises on account of the auditory impression, that too is burning. Burning with what? Burning with the fire of lust, with the fire of hate, with the fire of delusion; I say it is burning with birth, aging, and death, with sorrows, with lamentations, with pains, with griefs, with despairs.

The nose is burning, odors are burning, olfactory consciousness is burning, olfactory impression is burning....

The tongue is burning, flavors are burning, consciousness of flavor is burning, taste impression is burning....

The body is burning, tangible things are burning, tactile consciousness is burning, tactile sensation is burning....

The mind is burning, thoughts are burning, consciousness of thought is burning.... Burning with what? Burning with the fire of lust, with the fire of hate, with the fire of delusion; I say it is burning with birth, aging, and death, with sorrows, with lamentations, with pains, with griefs, with despairs.

*Buddhism*. Samyutta Nikaya xxxv.28: The Fire Sermon

Farid, I thought I alone had sorrow;
Sorrow is spread all over the whole world.
From my roof-top I saw
Every home engulfed in sorrow's flames.

*Sikhism*. Adi Granth, Shalok, Farid, p. 1382

Kisa Gotami had an only son, and he died. In her grief she carried the dead child to all her neighbors, asking them for medicine, and the people said, "She has lost her senses. The boy is dead."

At length Kisa Gotami met a man who replied to her request, "I cannot give you medicine for your child, but I know a physician who can. Go to Sakyamuni, the Buddha."

Kisa Gotami repaired to the Buddha and cried, "Lord and Master, give me the medicine that will cure my boy."

The Buddha answered, "I want a handful of mustard seed." And when the girl in her joy promised to procure it, the Buddha added, "The mustard seed must be taken from a house where no one has lost a child, husband, parent, or friend."

Poor Kisa Gotami now went from house to house, and the people pitied her and said, "Here is the mustard seed, take it!" But when she asked, "Did a son or daughter, a father or

**Udana 32:** Cf. Lankavatara Sutra 24, p. 282; Svetasvatara Upanishad 1.6-8, p. 282.

**Samyutta Nikaya xxxv.28:** The theme of a world on fire is elaborated in the Lotus Sutra's Parable of the Burning House; see p. 93n. Cf. Genesis Rabbah 39.1, p. 421; Brihadaranyaka Upanishad 1.3.1-7, pp. 276-77.

mother, die in your family?" they answered her, "Alas! The living are few, but the dead are many. Do not remind us of our deepest grief." And there was no house but some beloved one had died in it.

Kisa Gotami became weary and hopeless, and sat down at the way-side, watching the lights of the city as they flickered up and were extinguished again. At last the darkness of night reigned everywhere. And she considered the fate of men, that their lives flicker up and are extinguished. And she thought to herself, "How selfish am I in my grief! Death is common to all; yet in this valley of desolation there is a path that leads him to immortality who has surrendered all selfishness."

Putting away the selfishness of her affection for her child, Kisa Gotami had the dead body buried in the forest. Returning to the Buddha, she took refuge in him and found comfort in the Dharma.

*Buddhism*. Buddhaghosa,
Parable of the Mustard Seed

For everything there is a season, and a time for every matter under heaven:
a time to be born, and a time to die;
a time to plant, and a time to pluck up what is planted;
a time to kill, and a time to heal;
a time to break down, and a time to build up;
a time to weep, and a time to laugh;
a time to mourn, and a time to dance;
a time to cast away stones, and a time to gather stones together;
a time to embrace, and a time to refrain from embracing;
a time to seek, and a time to lose;
a time to keep, and a time to cast away;
a time to rend, and a time to sew;
a time to keep silence, and a time to speak;
a time to love, and a time to hate;
a time for war, and a time for peace.

*Judaism* and *Christianity*.
Ecclesiastes 3.1-8

There is an eternal pipal tree, with roots on high and branches downward. The verses of Scripture are its leaves. Who understands this tree understands the Scriptures.

It stretches its branches upward and downward. The states of all things nurture the young shoots. The young shoots are the nourishment of our senses. And below, the roots go far into the world of men; they are the sequences of actions.

This understanding of the tree's shape—its end and its beginning, and its ground—is not open to the ordinary world. The roots of that pipal tree have spread far. With the strong axe of detachment a man should cut that tree.

*Hinduism*. Bhagavad Gita 15.1-3

No creature, whether born on earth or among the gods in heaven, is free from the conditioning of the three states of matter (*gunas*).

*Hinduism*. Bhagavad Gita 18.40

The question as to when the union of soul with karma occurred for the first time cannot arise, since this is a beginningless relation like gold and stone.

*Jainism*. Pancadhyayi 2.35-36

**Parable of the Mustard Seed:** This parable appears in various sources in the Buddhist tradition. It illustrates the principle of the impermanence of phenomena, the attachment to which is the basis of all suffering. Cf. Diamond Sutra 32, p. 79; Lankavatara Sutra 24, p. 282.

**Ecclesiastes 3.1-8:** This meditation on the impermanence of life is often recited at funerals. Cf. Isaiah 40:6-8, p. 78.

**Bhagavad Gita 15.1-3:** Cf. Suhi, M.5, pp. 282-83, Svetasvatara Upanishad 1.6-8, p. 282; Uttaradhyayana Sutra 3.1-7, p. 220; Udana 77, p. 379. On the 'states of all things' (*gunas*) see the following note.

**Bhagavad Gita 18.40:** The three *gunas* or qualities of matter are goodness or purity (*sattva*), energy or passion (*rajas*), and darkness or inertia (*tamas*). Every person contains all three qualities in different proportions, as all light is a mixture of the three primary colors. As forces operating within the world of matter (*prakriti*), the gunas condition human existence and obscure the way to the Self. Cf. Bhagavad Gita 13.19-22, p. 118.

If we say we have no sin, we deceive ourselves, and the truth is not in us.

*Christianity*. 1 John 1.8

Nor do I absolve my own self of blame; the human soul is certainly prone to evil, unless my Lord do bestow His mercy.

*Islam*. Qur'an 12.53

All men, both Jews and Greeks, are under the power of sin, as it is written,

> None is righteous, no, not one;
> no one understands, no one seeks for God.
> All have turned aside, together they have
> gone wrong;
> no one does good, not even one.

*Christianity*. Romans 3.9-12

Surely man was created fretful,
when evil visits him, impatient,
when good visits him, grudging,
save those that pray.

*Islam*. Qur'an 70.19-22

Behold, I was brought forth in iniquity,
and in sin did my mother conceive me.

*Judaism* and *Christianity*. Psalm 51.5

Each of us is destined at birth to bear the legacy of man's first and continuing rebellion against God. That legacy is the tendency to sin. A person sins when he succumbs to the inclination to contravene the divine will by pursuing inordinate desires. It is an inclination that lurks in the hearts of all people whether they believe in God or not, but many are not even aware of it.

*Sekai Kyusei Kyo*.
Mokichi Okada, Johrei

Confucius said, "I for my part have never yet seen one who really cared for Goodness, nor one who really abhorred wickedness. One who really cared for Goodness would never let any other consideration come first. One who abhorred wickedness would be so constantly doing Good that wickedness would never have a chance to get at him. Has anyone ever managed to do Good with his whole might even as long as the space of a single day? I think not. Yet I for my part have never seen anyone give up such an attempt because he had not the strength to go on."

*Confucianism*. Analects 4.6

Confucius remarked, "There is in the world now really no moral social order at all."

*Confucianism*. Doctrine of the Mean 5

There is a male monkey in every forest.

*African Traditional Religions*.
Tiv Proverb (Nigeria)

**1 John 1.8:** Cf. Mark 10.17-18, p. 468; Jeremiah 17.9, p. 323; also Shinran, p. 649.

**Qur'an 12.53:** Cf. Quran 4.28, p. 362. Not even Muhammad, the best of men, regarded himself blameless; cf. Qur'an 17.11, p. 277; Hadith of Muslim, p. 362. On the original uprightness of human nature, see Qur'an 30.30, p. 144.

**Romans 3.9-12:** Paul is quoting from Psalm 14, p. 281. Yet every person still has a measure of conscience and moral sense; see Romans 2.14-16, p. 215. Cf. Book of Mormon, Mosiah 3.19, p. 648.

**Qur'an 70.19-22:** Cf. Qur'an 95.4-6, p. 321.

**Psalm 51.5:** In the tradition of St. Augustine's explanation of original sin, Protestants and Catholics have generally regarded the act of procreation as instrumental in transmitting original sin from one generation to the next. But this does not make the act itself sinful. According to Vatican II, *Guadium et Spes*, conjugal love is a means of grace in Christian marriage.

**Johrei:** This idea reflects the influence of Christianity on the new religions of Japan. Compare also the Jewish concept of the evil inclination in Kiddushin 30b, p. 277, and Book of Mormon, Mosiah 3.19, p. 648.

**Analects 4.6:** The last sentence means that it is the will, not the way, that is wanting. Cf. Analects 14.2, p. 154.

**Tiv Proverb:** Every community has its troublemaker, bully, or thief.

The slanderers of the true dharma in the latter age of decay are as numerous as the soil of all the worlds in the universe is immeasurable. Those who keep the true dharma are as few in number as a bit of soil on a fingernail.

*Buddhism.* Mahaparinirvana Sutra

Since beginningless past, all sentient beings and I have been parents and children, brothers and sisters to each other. Being full of greed, hatred, and ignorance, pride, conceit, dishonesty, deception, and all other afflictions, we have therefore harmed each other, plundering, raping, and killing, doing all manner of evil. All sentient beings are like this—because of passions and afflictions they do not respect or honor each other, they do not agree with or obey each other, they do not defer to each other, they do not edify or guide each other, they do not care for each other—they go on killing and injuring each other, being enemies and malefactors to each other. Reflecting on myself as well as other sentient beings, we act shamelessly in the past, future, and present, while the Buddhas of past, future, and present see and know it all.

*Buddhism.* Garland Sutra 22

How vast is God,
The ruler of men below!
How arrayed in terrors is God,
With many things irregular in his ordinations.
Heaven gave birth to the multitudes of the people,
But the nature it confers is not to be depended upon.
All are good at first,
But few prove themselves to be so at the last.

*Confucianism.* Book of Songs, Ode 255

When men get together to pit their strength in games of skill, they start off in a light and friendly mood, but usually end up in a dark and angry one, and if they go on too long they start resorting to various underhanded tricks. When men meet at some ceremony to drink, they start off in an orderly manner, but usually end up in disorder, and if they go on too long they start indulging in various irregular amusements. It is the same with all things. What starts out being sincere usually ends up being deceitful. What was simple in the beginning acquires monstrous proportions in the end.

*Taoism.* Chuang Tzu 4

❖

**Mahaparinirvana Sutra:** Nichiren Buddhists regard the present age as the *Mappo*, the Age of the Degeneration of the Law, and for this reason the followers of the true Law are persecuted; cf. Lotus Sutra 13, p. 775.

**Book of Songs, Ode 255:** On being 'good at first,' cf. Mencius IV.B.12, p. 144, and Book of Ritual 38.18, p. 144; cf. Ecclesiastes 7.29, p. 321; Qur'an 95.4-6, p. 321.

# *The War Within*

RELIGIONS HAVE CONCEPTUALIZED the infirmity of the human condition as an interior war between two opposing natures, one good and the other evil. As long as people experience this state of contradiction, they can neither realize their divine self nor achieve a state of unity and wholeness. Paradoxically, while people immersed in worldly affairs may not always recognize the war within themselves, it is precisely in leading a conscientious life, when striving to do good and be good, that this conflict comes to the fore.

The world's religions conceptualize this conflict in various ways. The first group of passages locates the two natures in the fabric of creation itself: thus Zoroastrianism and Hinduism teach that the earth is a battlefield between two opposing good and evil powers, and Hinduism and Jainism distinguish between the divine Self and the material existence in which it is bound.

The monotheistic religions, however, cannot allow a dualism that locates the conflict in the fabric of creation itself, for that would raise insuperable problems for the doctrine of the unity of God. They delimit these warring powers to spiritual influences—see *Demonic Powers*, pp. 309-15—or to the carnal desires within the individual soul.[1] The next group of scripture passages hold this view: for example, Paul's observation of the war between spirit and flesh and the Jewish doctrine of the Good and Evil Inclinations. Buddhism, which regards material reality as resultant of mind and deals entirely on the level of psychology, likewise emphasizes the war within the person, between its innate emptiness and the fetters caused by craving for selfhood. We conclude with passages expressing the more general idea that the human self is often its own worst enemy.

This body is mortal, always gripped by death, but within it dwells the immortal Self. This Self, when associated in our consciousness with the body, is subject to pleasure and pain; and so long as this association continues, freedom from pleasure and pain can no man find.

*Hinduism.* Chandogya Upanishad 8.12.1

Just as knowledge, in spite of it being intangible, gets obliterated under the influence of wine, so the self, though originally intangible, gets its qualities obstructed under the influence of tangible karma particles. In its state of bondage, the soul, though intangible, conceives itself to be tangible [identical with the body].

*Jainism.* Pancadhyayi 2.57

Two birds, united always and known by the same name, closely cling to the same tree. One of them eats the sweet fruit; the other looks on without eating.

Seated on the same tree, the jiva moans, bewildered by his impotence. But when he beholds the other, the Lord worshipped by all, and His glory, he becomes free from grief.

When the seer beholds the self-luminous Creator, the Lord, the Purusha, the progenitor

**Pancadhyayi 2.57:** Cf. Pancadhyayi 2.35-36, p. 272.

[1] Thus, Satan only incites evil by resonating with man's evil desires.

of Brahma, then he, the wise seer, shakes off good and evil, becomes stainless, and reaches the supreme unity.

*Hinduism.* Mundaka Upanishad 3.1.1-3

The First Fundamental Principle is the primary cause of the succession of deaths and rebirths from beginningless time. It is the Principle of Ignorance, the outgoing principle of individuation, manifestation, transformation, succession and discrimination. From the working out of this Principle there has resulted the various differentiation of minds of all sentient beings, and all the time they have been taking these limited and perturbed and contaminated minds to be their true and natural Essence of Mind.

The Second Fundamental Principle is the primary cause of the pure unity of Enlightenment and Nirvana that has existed from beginningless time. It is the principle of integrating compassion, the indrawing, unifying principle of purity, harmony, likeness, rhythm, permanency, and peace. By the indrawing of this Principle within the brightness of your own nature, its unifying spirit can be discovered and developed and realized under all varieties of conditions.

*Buddhism.* Surangama Sutra

There are two orders of creation: one divine, the other demonic.

*Hinduism.* Bhagavad Gita 16.6

Yes, there are two fundamental spirits, twins which are renowned to be in conflict. In thought and in word, in action, they are two: the good and the bad. And between these two, the beneficent have correctly chosen, not the maleficent.

Furthermore, when these two spirits first came together, they created life and death, and now, in the end the worst existence shall be for the deceitful but the best thinking [Heaven] for the truthful person.

Of these two spirits, the deceitful one chose to bring to realization the worst things. But the very virtuous spirit, who is clothed in the hardest stones, chose the truth, and so shall mortals who shall satisfy the Wise Lord continuously with true actions.

*Zoroastrianism.* Avesta, Yasna 30.3-5

The offspring of Prajapati were of two kinds: gods and demons. Of these the gods were younger and the demons the older. They were disputing the possession of these worlds. The gods said, "Well, let us overpower the demons at the sacrifice with the *Udgitha* chant [chanting the Sama Veda]."

They said to speech, "Chant for us!" "Very well," she said. So speech chanted for them the Udgitha. Whatever delight is in speech, that she chanted for the Gods; whatever she speaks well, that is for herself. The demons knew: "By this singer they will overpower us." They attacked her and pierced her with evil. The evil that makes one speak what is improper, that is that evil.

Then they said to the breath, "Chant for us!"... Whatever delight is in breath, that he chanted for the gods; whatever fragrance he smells well, that is for himself. The demons... pierced him with evil. The evil that makes one smell what is improper, that is that evil.

Then they said to the eye, "Chant for us!"... Whatever delight is in the eye, that he chanted for the gods; whatever beautiful he sees, that is for himself. The demons... pierced him with evil. The evil that makes one see what is improper, that is that evil.

Then they said to the ear, "Chant for us!"... Whatever delight is in the ear, that he chanted for the gods; whatever he hears well, that is for

**Mundaka Upanishad 3.1.1-3:** The tree represents the body. The two birds are the *jiva* or individual soul and the *Atman* or Self. Cf. Bhagavad Gita 13.19-22, p. 118; Atharva Veda 19.51.1, p. 154.

**Surangama Sutra:** Cf. Dhammapada 1-2, p. 515.

**Bhagavad Gita 16.6:** Cf. Satapatha Brahmana 5.1.1.1-2, p. 313.

**Yasna 30.3-5:** Zoroastrianism demands a decision, to choose either the good or the evil spirit which rage in conflict within the self. Cf. Yasna 30.2, p. 486; Videvdad 1.3-11, p. 311.

himself. The demons... pierced him with evil. The evil that makes one hear what is improper, that is that evil.

Then they said to the mind, "Chant for us!"... Whatever delight there is in the mind, that he chanted for the gods; whatever he thinks well, that is for himself. The demons... pierced him with evil. The evil that makes one think what is improper, that is that evil. Thus they afflicted the senses with evil; they pierced them with evil.

Then they said to the Life Breath, "Chant for us!" "Very well," he said. So the Breath chanted for them. The demons knew, "By this singer they will overpower us." They attacked him and wanted to pierce him with evil. But just as a lump of earth is scattered when it strikes on a stone, in the same way they were scattered in all directions and perished. Therefore the gods increased and the demons diminished. He who knows this increases in himself and his enemies diminish.

*Hinduism.*
Brihadaranyaka Upanishad 1.3.1-7

The spirit is indeed willing, but the flesh is weak.

*Christianity.* Matthew 26.41

Man prays for evil as he prays for good; man is ever hasty.

*Islam.* Qur'an 17.11

Every person has both a bad heart and a good heart. No matter how good a man seems, he has some evil. No matter how bad a man seems, there is some good about him. No man is perfect.

*Native American Religions.*
Mohawk Tradition

The mind is said to be twofold:
The pure and also the impure;
Impure—by union with desire;
Pure—from desire completely free.

*Hinduism.* Maitri Upanishad 6.34

By the fetters of envy and selfishness are all bound—gods, men, demons, nagas, gandhabbas and every other great class of beings—so that although they wish, "Would that we might live in friendship, without hatred, injury, emnity or malignity," they still live in emnity, hating, injuring, hostile, malign.

*Buddhism.* Digha Nikaya ii.276,
Sakkapanha Suttanta

Rabbi Isaac said, "Man's evil inclination renews itself daily against him, as it is said, 'Every imagination of the thoughts of his heart was only evil every day.' [Genesis 6.5]." And Rabbi Simeon ben Levi said, "Man's evil inclination gathers strength against him daily and seeks to slay him... and were not the Holy One, blessed be He, to help him, he could not prevail against it."

*Judaism.* Talmud, Kiddushin 30b

**Brihadaranyaka Upanishad 1.3.1-7:** The senses, though created good, are hopelessly invaded by evil—cf. Samyutta Nikaya xxxv.28, p. 271; only the Life Breath (*prana*) remains inviolate. The prana is channeled through yoga; hence it is through yoga and meditative disciplines that one can establish an inviolate foundation of goodness within oneself.

**Qur'an 17.11:** Prayer is an expression of one's desire and intention; hence it is possible to pray for evil either out of ignorance or insincerity. Yet God does not necessarily treat all prayers alike, for he looks for true piety; cf. Qur'an 2.177, p. 615.

**Mohawk Tradition:** This is the conclusion to a creation account given in full on pp. 311-12.

**Maitri Upanishad 6.34:** Cf. Mueller's translation, p. 515. Cf. Dhammapada 1-2, p. 515; Bhagavad Gita 3.36-41, p. 294.

**Digha Nikaya ii.276:** Cf. Maitri Upanishad 3.2, p. 292.

**Kiddushin 30b:** This is the Jewish doctrine of the Evil Inclination. See Kiddushin 30b, p. 374; Berakot 5a, pp. 657-58; Shabbat 105b, p. 288; cf. James 4.1-3, p. 294; 1 Peter 2.11, p. 657.

# *Ignorance*

MANY RELIGIONS REGARD the evils of the human condition as a result of ignorance. Being ignorant of the truth about Ultimate Reality and the purpose of life, people's values become confused, and consequently they act wrongly. In Hinduism and Jainism, this blindness (*avidya*) is what binds people to the wheel of birth-and-death (*samsara*). In Buddhism, ignorance leads to grasping after self and begets delusion (*moha*). In the Christian Bible, the apostle Paul taught that ignorance of God lay at the root of all forms of license and immorality. In Islam it is the condition of forgetting God; as a result, people ever since Adam have deviated from the path and lost their souls. Taoist sages condemn knowledge of worldly things as a source of confusion about true values, and similarly we find in many scriptures warnings against the illusory goals and vanities that infect worldly life.

This selection of passages is arranged in roughly the following order: We begin with the practical observation that ignorance of Ultimate Reality spurs evil and demonic behavior. Next, it is due to ignorance, according to the religions of India, that humans are bound to suffer on the wheel of samsara, going through continual deaths and rebirths. Humanity's spiritual blindness is the subject of the third group of passages, beginning with passages which describe the veil of illusion (*maya*) that obscures the faculty of insight. Other passages describe humanity's blindness by such metaphors as frogs in a well and moths drawn to perish in a lamp. In our blindness, we are attracted to the vanities of this world which are ephemeral and deceiving, according to the next group of passages. We conclude with passages which reason that even evil itself is an illusion or a bad dream.

My people go into exile for want of knowledge.

*Judaism* and *Christianity*. Isaiah 5.13

Be not like those who forgot God, therefore He made them forget their own souls!

*Islam*. Qur'an 59.19

Only when men shall roll up space as if it were a simple skin,
Only then will there be an end of sorrow without acknowledging God.

*Hinduism*. Svetasvatara Upanishad 6.20

Whoever wants to do some evil against another does not remember God.

*African Traditional Religions*. Proverb

In sleep our nights wasted,
In filling our belly the days:
This life, precious as a jewel,
Is forfeited for a cowrie shell.
Ignorant fool!
You who have never realized God's Name,
In the end into regrets shall fall.

*Sikhism*. Adi Granth, Gauri Bairagani, M.1, p. 156

Although they knew God they did not honor him as God or give thanks to him, but they became futile in their thinking, and their senseless minds were darkened. Claiming to be wise, they became fools, and exchanged the glory of the immortal God for images resembling mortal man or birds or animals or reptiles. Therefore God gave them up in the lusts of their hearts to impurity, to the dishonoring of their bodies among themselves, because they exchanged the truth about God for a lie and worshipped and served the creature rather than the Creator, who is blessed for ever! Amen.

*Christianity*. Romans 1.21-25

The fool says in his heart,
"There is no God."
They are all corrupt, they do abominable
  deeds,
there is none that does good.
The Lord looks down from heaven
upon the children of men,
to see if there are any that act wisely,
that seek after God.
They have all gone astray,
they are all alike corrupt;
there is none that does good,
no, not one.
Have they no knowledge,
all the evildoers
who eat up my people as they eat bread,
and do not call upon the Lord?

*Judaism* and *Christianity*. Psalm 14.1-4

Rabbi Hananiah ben Hakinai said, "No man lies to his neighbor until he has denied the Root. It happened once that Rabbi Reuben was in Tiberias on the Sabbath, and a philosopher asked him, 'Who is the most hateful man in the world?' He replied, 'The man who denies his Creator.' 'How so?' said the philosopher. Rabbi Reuben answered, '"Honor thy father and thy mother, thou shalt do no murder, thou shalt not commit adultery, thou shalt not steal, thou shalt not bear false witness against thy neighbor, thou shalt not covet." No man denies the derivative [the Ten Commandments] until he has previously denied the Root [God], and no man sins unless he has denied Him who commanded him not to commit that sin.'"

*Judaism*. Tosefta Shebuot 3.6

The demonic do things they should avoid and avoid the things they should do. They have no sense of uprightness, purity, or truth.

"There is no God," they say, "no truth, no spiritual law, no moral order. The basis of life is sex; what else can it be?" Holding such distorted views, possessing scant discrimination, they become enemies of the world, causing suffering and destruction.

Hypocritical, proud, and arrogant, living in delusion and clinging to deluded ideas, insatiable in their desires, they pursue their unclean ends. Although burdened with fears that end only with death, they still maintain with complete assurance, "Gratification of lust is the highest that life can offer."

Bound on all sides by scheming and anxiety, driven by anger and greed, they amass by any means they can a hoard of money for the satisfaction of their cravings.

"I got this today," they say; "tomorrow I shall get that. This wealth is mine, and that will be mine too. I have destroyed my enemies. I shall destroy others too! Am I not like God? I enjoy what I want. I am successful. I am powerful. I am happy. I am rich and well-born. Who is equal to me? I will perform sacrifices and give gifts, and rejoice in my own generosity." This is how they go on, deluded by ignorance. Bound by their greed and entangled in a web of delusion, whirled about by a fragmented mind, they fall into a dark hell.

*Hinduism*. Bhagavad Gita 16.7-16

He who does not clearly understand Heaven will not be pure in virtue. He who has not mastered the Way will find himself without any acceptable path of approach. He who does not understand the Way is pitiable indeed!

*Taoism*. Chuang Tzu 11

**Romans 1.21-25:** Cf. Philippians 3.18-19, p. 288; Qur'an 45.23, p. 293.

**Psalm 14.1-4:** Cf. Isaiah 1.2-3, p. 323.

**Tosefta Shebuot 3.6:** Cf. Pesikta Rabbati, p. 111; Mekilta Exodus 12.6, p. 287.

**Bhagavad Gita 16.7-16:** Cf. Isaiah 5.21, p. 289; Bhagavad Gita 3.41, p. 294; Acarangasutra 2.1-3, pp. 296-97.

**Chuang Tzu 11:** Cf. Chuang Tzu 10, pp. 571-72, on ignorance that comes to pervade even the world of nature.

This vast universe is a wheel, the wheel of Brahman. Upon it are all creatures that are subject to birth, death, and rebirth. Round and round it turns, and never stops. As long as the individual self thinks it is separate from the Lord, it revolves upon the wheel in bondage to the laws of birth, death, and rebirth....

The Lord supports this universe, which is made up of the perishable and the imperishable, the manifest and the unmanifest. The individual soul, forgetful of the Lord, attaches itself to pleasure and thus is bound.

*Hinduism.* Svetasvatara Upanishad 1.6-8

By reason of the habit-energy stored up by false imagination since beginningless time, this world is subject to change and destruction from moment to moment; it is like a river, a seed, a lamp, wind, a cloud; like a monkey who is always restless, like a fly who is ever in search of unclean things and defiled places, like a fire which is never satisfied. Again, [thought] is like a water-wheel or a machine: it goes on rolling the wheel of transmigration, carrying varieties of bodies and forms... causing the wooden figures to move as a magician moves them. Mahamati, a thorough understanding concerning these phenomena is called comprehending the egolessness of persons.

*Buddhism.* Lankavatara Sutra 24

Intoxicated by the wine of illusion, like one intoxicated by wine; rushing about, like one possessed of an evil spirit; bitten by the world, like one bitten by a great serpent; darkened by passion, like the night; illusory, like magic; false, like a dream; pithless, like the inside of a banana-tree; changing its dress in a moment, like an actor; fair in appearance, like a painted wall—thus they call him.

*Hinduism.* Maitri Upanishad 4.2

Owing to delusion, one again passes through cycles of birth and death. In this unbroken chain of births and deaths, delusion keeps cropping up again and again.

*Jainism.* Acarangasutra 5.7-8

Few see through the veil of maya.

*Hinduism.* Bhagavad Gita 7.25

Long is the night to the wakeful; long is the league to the weary; long is samsara to the foolish who know not the sublime Truth.

*Buddhism.* Dhammapada 60

This world is as a juggler's show,
Wherein various disguises he assumes.
As he puts off his makeup, ended is His
  expanse [of creation].
Then is left the Sole Supreme Being.
How many various guises has He assumed and
  cast off?
To where have they gone? From where did they
  come?
From water arise innumerable waves;
From gold are shaped ornaments of various
  forms;
Many are the kinds of seeds sown:
As ripens the fruit, again is left the Sole
  Supreme Being.
Into thousands of pitchers falls reflection of the
  one sky;
As the pitcher is broken, the sole Light
  remains.

**Svetasvatara Upanishad 1.6-8:** Cf. Bhagavad Gita 15.1-3, p. 272; Mundaka Upanishad 1.2.7-10, p. 615. This wheel is similarly a Buddhist symbol of bondage to samsara, due to grasping.

**Lankavatara Sutra 24:** The impermanence of the world is essentially the impermanence of thought, out of which it is made. Cf. Dhammapada 171, p. 678; Holy Teaching of Vimalakirti 3, p. 148; Bhagavad Gita 15.1-3, p. 272.

**Maitri Upanishad 4.2:** See Bhagavad Gita 5.15-16, p. 381; cf. Nahjul Balagha, Sermon 86, p. 679.

**Acarangasutra 5.7-8:** Cf. Uttaradhyayana Sutra 3.1-7, p. 220; Acarangasutra 2.55-56, p. 292; Pancadhyayi 2.57, p. 275.

**Bhagavad Gita 7.25:** Maya is the magic show of creation's multiplicity, which blinds people to the truth of Brahman; see the following passage. Cf. Chandogya Upanishad 8.3.2, p. 147.

While thoughts of maya last, doubt, avarice,
  and attachment are found;
When illusion is lifted, only the Sole Supreme
  Being is left.

*Sikhism*. Adi Granth, Suhi, M.5, p. 736

The unbelievers...
Are like the depths of darkness
In a vast deep ocean,
Overwhelmed with billow,
Topped by billow,
Topped by dark clouds:
Depths of darkness,
One above another:
If a man stretches out his hand, he can hardly
  see it!
For any to whom God gives not light,
There is no light!

*Islam*. Qur'an 24.40

Within the Essence of Mind all things are intrinsically pure, like the azure of the sky and the radiance of the sun and the moon which, when obscured by passing clouds, may appear as if their brightness had been dimmed; but as soon as the clouds are blown away, brightness reappears and all objects are fully illuminated. Learned audience, our evil habits may be likened unto the clouds; while Sagacity and Wisdom are like the sun and the moon respectively. When we attach ourselves to outer objects, our Essence of Mind is clouded by wanton thoughts which prevent our Sagacity and Wisdom from sending forth their light.

*Buddhism*. Sutra of Hui Neng 6

It is not the eyes that are blind, but blind are the hearts within the breasts.

*Islam*. Qur'an 22.46

Fools dwelling in darkness, but thinking themselves wise and erudite, go round and round, by various tortuous paths, like the blind led by the blind.

*Hinduism*. Katha Upanishad 1.2.5

The god of this world has blinded the minds of the unbelievers, to keep them from seeing the light of the gospel of the glory of Christ, who is the likeness of God.

*Christianity*. 2 Corinthians 4.4

Confucius said, "In vain I have looked for a single man capable of seeing his own faults and bringing the charge home against himself."

*Confucianism*. Analects 5.26

They have hearts, but understand not with them; they have eyes, but perceive not with them; they have ears, but they hear not with them. They are like cattle; nay, rather they are further astray. Those—they are the heedless.

*Islam*. Qur'an 7.179

You shall indeed hear but never understand,
and you shall indeed see but never perceive.
For this people's heart has grown dull,
and their ears are heavy of hearing,
and their eyes they have closed,
lest they should perceive with their eyes,
and hear with their ears,
and understand with their heart,
and turn for me to heal them.

*Christianity*. Matthew 13.14-15

Blind is this world. Few are those who clearly see. As birds escape from a net, few go to a blissful state.

*Buddhism*. Dhammapada 174

**Qur'an 24.40:** Cf. Qur'an 24.35, p. 381; Nahjul Balagha, Sermon 86, p. 679.

**Sutra of Hui Neng 6:** Cf. Holy Teaching of Vimalakirti 3, p. 148; Anguttara Nikaya i.10, p. 322; Chandogya Upanishad 8.3.2, p. 147; Bhagavad Gita 5.15-16, p. 381.

**Qur'an 22.46:** Cf. Forty Hadith of an-Nawawi 6, p. 147; Luke 11.34-36, p. 147.

**Katha Upanishad 1.2.5:** Cf. Udana 68-69, p. 41.

**2 Corinthians 4.4:** Cf. John 8.43-45, pp. 309-10; Yasna 32.9, p. 309; Qur'an 35.5-6, p. 313.

**Matthew 13.14-15:** Cf. Mark 4.10-12, p. 574n.

**Dhammapada 174:** Cf. Udana 75-76, p. 294.

As is a well full of frogs
Ignorant of the wide world,
So is my mind deluded by evil passions
Keeping out all thought of the Beyond.
Lord of all universes! Show me for one instant
a sight of Thee.
Lord! My senses have been fouled;
Thy state I cannot encompass.
Shower on me Thy grace;
Remove my delusions;
Confer on me true wisdom.
Great yogis for all their praxis
Comprehend not thy Reality inexpressible.
Through love and devotion mayst Thou be
known—
Thus says Ravidas the cobbler.

*Sikhism*. Adi Granth,
Gauri Purabi, Ravidas, p. 346

On a certain occasion the Exalted One was seated in the open air, on a night of inky darkness, and oil lamps were burning. Swarms of winged insects kept falling into these oil lamps and thereby met their end, came to destruction and utter ruin. Seeing those swarms of winged insects so doing, the Exalted One saw the meaning in it and uttered this verse of uplift,

They hasten up and past, but miss the real;
a bondage ever new they cause to grow.
Just as the flutterers fall into the lamp,
so some are bent on what they see and hear.

*Buddhism*. Udana 72

The life of this world is but comfort of illusion.

*Islam*. Qur'an 3.185

Vanity of vanities! All is vanity. What does man gain by all the toil at which he toils under the sun?

I have seen everything that is done under the sun; and behold, all is vanity and a striving after wind.

*Judaism* and *Christianity*.
Ecclesiastes 1.2-3 and 1.14

Parable of those who reject their Lord: their works are as ashes on which the wind blows furiously on a stormy day. No power have they over aught that they have earned. That is straying far, far from the goal.

*Islam*. Qur'an 14.18

How do I know that loving life is not a delusion? How do I know that in hating death I am not like a man who, having left home in his youth, has forgotten the way back?

*Taoism*. Chuang Tzu 2

God, or good, never made man capable of sin. It is the opposite of good—that is, evil—which seems to make men capable of wrongdoing. Hence evil is but an illusion, and it has no real basis.

*Christian Science*.
Science and Health, 480

The Tathagata knows the polluted minds of beings for what they are. For he knows that the minds of ordinary people are not actually polluted by the polluting forces of perverted views, which, being nothing but wrong ideas, do not really find a place in them.

*Buddhism*. Perfection of Wisdom
in Eight Thousand Lines 12.3

**Gauri Purabi, Ravidas:** Cf. Jaitsari, M.5, p. 290.
**Udana 72:** Cf. Udana 75-76, p. 294.
**Qur'an 3.185:** Cf. Qur'an 57.20, p. 231.
**Perfection of Wisdom in Eight Thousand Lines 12.3:** Cf. Surangama Sutra, p. 322; Holy Teaching of Vimalakirti 6, p. 314; Pancastikaya 38, p. 322.

The power that is not good—that is, the power
that causes misfortune—is, after all, only a
bad dream.
The life that is not good—that is, disease—is,
after all, only a bad dream.
All discords and imperfections are, after all,
only bad dreams.
It is our bad dreams that give power to disease,
misfortune, discord, and imperfection.
It is like being tortured by some demon in our
dreams;
But when we awaken, we find that there is
actually no such power,
And that we had suffered at the hands of our
own mind.

*Seicho-no-Ie.*
Nectarean Shower of Holy Doctrines

❖

# Idolatry

FOR THE MONOTHEISTIC RELIGIONS, the chief manifestation of ignorance is idolatry. Literally the worship of images, idolatry in the broader sense means allegiance to false values that substitute for God. In the Qur'an idols are regarded as evil spirits and Satan; those who worship them are therefore enemies to God. The idol-gods, being spiritual beings, have the nature of creatures, rather than of God, and hence cannot profit their adherents—cf. *Spiritual Error and the Occult*, pp. 263-66. The Bible views idols as human artifacts, not as representations of deity. Hence idol worship is regarded as a form of materialism, and, conversely, any false reliance on human power or wealth is a form of idolatry. A more spiritual conception of idolatry is to identify it with egoism and human craving, since attachment to these false realities separates us from our true nature. In our century, the idols of nationalism, racism, and secular ideologies have captivated millions, with horrible results.

Verily We have raised in every nation a messenger, proclaiming, "Serve God and shun false gods."

*Islam.* Qur'an 16.36

The parable of those who take protectors other than God is that of the spider who builds for itself a house; but truly the flimsiest of houses is the spider's house—if they only knew!

*Islam.* Qur'an 29.41

Set forth your case, says the Lord;
bring your proofs, says the King of Jacob....
Declare to us the things to come,
tell us what is to come hereafter,
that we may know that you are gods.

Do good, or do harm,
that we may be dismayed and terrified.
Behold, you are nothing,
and your work is nought;
an abomination is he who chooses you.

*Judaism* and *Christianity.*
Isaiah 41.21-24

How can you call that flirt a chaste lady
Who kisses and embraces every man she meets
And shamelessly says, "O Honey, my dear!"...
Behold! A faithful wife has but one husband!
Behold! A true believer has but one God!
Look! The fellowship of other gods is
debauchery!
Look! To believe in different gods is harlotry!

*Hinduism.* Basavanna, Vacana 615-16

The Lord said to Hosea, "Go, take to yourself a wife of harlotry and have children of harlotry, for the land commits great harlotry by forsaking the Lord." So he went and took Gomer the daughter of Diblaim, and she conceived and bore him a son.

And the Lord said to him, "Call his name Jezreel, for yet a little while, and I will punish the house of Jehu for the blood of Jezreel, and I will put an end to the kingdom of the house of Israel. On that day, I will break the bow of Israel in the valley of Jezreel."

She conceived again and bore a daughter. And the Lord said to him, "Call her name Not Pitied, for I will no more have pity on the house of Israel, to forgive them at all."...

**Qur'an 29:41:** Cf. Qur'an 21.19-21, p. 54; 23.91-92, p. 54.

**Isaiah 41.21-24:** God is calling the idol gods to account before the heavenly court. Cf. 1 Corinthians 8.4-6, p. 54.

When she had weaned Not Pitied, she conceived and bore a son. And the Lord said, "Call his name Not My People, for you are not my people and I am not your God."

*Judaism* and *Christianity*. Hosea 1.2-8

The law against idolatry outweighs all other commandments.

*Judaism*. Mekilta Exodus 12.6

God forgives not joining other gods with Him; other sins than this He forgives whom He pleases. One who joins other gods with God has strayed far, far away. The pagans, leaving Him, call but upon female deities: they actually call upon Satan, the persistent rebel!

*Islam*. Qur'an 4.116-17

Whoever knows the self as "I am Brahman," becomes all this [universe]. Even the gods cannot prevent his becoming this, for he has become their Self.

Now, if a man worships another deity, thinking, "He is one and I am another," he does not know. He is like an animal to the gods. As many animals serve a man, so does each man serve the gods [with offerings]. Even if one animal is taken away, it causes anguish to the owner; how much more so when many are taken away! Therefore it is not pleasing to the gods that men should know the truth.

*Hinduism*. Brihadaranyaka Upanishad 1.4.10

Who sees Me by form,
Who seeks Me in sound,
Perverted are his footsteps upon the Way;
For he cannot perceive the Tathagata.

*Buddhism*. Diamond Sutra 26

Since you saw no form on the day that the Lord spoke to you at Horeb out of the midst of the fire, beware lest you act corruptly by making a graven image for yourselves, in the form of any figure, the likeness of male or female, the likeness of any beast that is on the earth, the likeness of any winged bird that flies in the air, the likeness of anything that creeps on the ground, the likeness of any fish that is in the water under the earth.

*Judaism* and *Christianity*. Deuteronomy 4.15-18

Our God is in the heavens;
he does whatever he pleases.
Their idols are silver and gold,
the work of men's hands.
They have mouths, but do not speak;
eyes, but do not see.
They have ears, but do not hear;
noses, but do not smell.
They have hands, but do not feel;
feet, but do not walk;
and they do not make a sound in their throat.
Those who make them are like them;
so are all who trust in them.

*Judaism* and *Christianity*. Psalm 115.3-8

**Hosea 1.2-8:** God instructed the prophet Hosea to marry a prostitute in order to dramatize through his own marriage Israel's religious apostasy. As Gomer was unfaithful to the prophet, so Israel was unfaithful to God. Gomer's children were given symbolic names as prophecies of coming judgment. On idolatry as harlotry, cf. Jeremiah 2-3.

**Mekilta Exodus 12.6:** Cf. Exodus 20.3-5, p. 110; Tosefta Shebuot 3.6, p. 281.

**Qur'an 4.116-17:** Cf. Qur'an 21.26-29, p. 263.

**Brihadaranyaka Upanishad 1.4.10:** Cf. Srimad Bhagavatam 11.20, p. 265; Qur'an 17.61-64, pp. 312-13.

**Diamond Sutra 26:** A similar stanza can be found in the Theravada scriptures, at Theragatha 469.

**Deuteronomy 4.15-18:** Cf. Romans 1.21-25, pp. 280-81.

**Psalm 115.3-8:** The Bible has a number of satires on idols as human creations, mere objects unable to do anything—for example Isaiah 44.9-20 and Jeremiah 10.1-10. Passages such as these have fostered a general disdain for visual representations of the divine in Judaism, Christianity, and Islam. Such satires are perhaps uncomprehending of genuine image-worship, in which the image is understood only as a representation of transcendent Reality and a means to focus the mind on God, who is beyond form. Yet veneration of images may become idolatry when the images are themselves regarded as having magical powers.

It is people who make the gods important.

If a spirit [idol] becomes too troublesome, it will be shown the tree from which it was carved.

*African Traditional Religions*. Kalabari Proverbs (Namibia)

Fools misjudge me when I take
a human form,
because they do not know my supreme
state as Lord of Beings.
Unconscious, they fall prey to beguiling nature
such as belongs to ogres and demons,
for their hopes [ascribing to God human
motives] are vain, and so
are their rituals and their search for wisdom.

*Hinduism*. Bhagavad Gita 9.11-12

Their land is filled with silver and gold,
and there is no end to their treasures;
their land is filled with horses,
and there is no end to their chariots.
Their land is filled with idols;
they bow down to the work of their hands,
to what their own fingers have made.
So man is humbled, and men are brought
low—
forgive them not!

*Judaism* and *Christianity*. Isaiah 2.7-9

When the people saw that Moses delayed to come down from the mountain, the people gathered themselves together to Aaron, and said to him, "Up, make us gods, who shall go before us; as for this Moses, the man who brought us up out of the land of Egypt, we do not know what has become of him." And Aaron said to them, "Take off the rings of gold which are in the ears of your wives, your sons, and your daughters, and bring them to me." So all the people took off the rings of gold which were in their ears, and brought them to Aaron. And he received the gold at their hand, and fashioned it with a graving tool, and made a molten calf; and they said, "These are your gods, O Israel, who brought you up out of the land of Egypt!" When Aaron saw this, he built an altar before it; and Aaron made proclamation and said, "Tomorrow shall be a feast to the Lord." And they rose up early on the morrow, and offered burnt offerings and brought peace offerings; and the people sat down to eat and drink, and rose up to play.

*Judaism* and *Christianity*. Exodus 32.1-6

Covetousness, which is idolatry.

*Christianity*. Colossians 3.5

"There shall be *in* you no strange god and you shall not worship a foreign god" [Psalm 81.10]. What is the "foreign god" within a man's body? It is the evil impulse.

*Judaism*. Talmud, Shabbat 105b

For many... live as enemies of the cross of Christ. Their end is destruction, their god is the belly, and they glory in their shame, with minds set on earthly things.

*Christianity*. Philippians 3.18-19

Have you seen him who makes his desire his god, and God sends him astray purposely, and seals up his hearing and his heart, and sets on his sight a covering? Who, then, will lead him after God [has condemned him]? Will you not then heed?

*Islam*. Qur'an 45.23

**Bhagavad Gita 9.11-12:** Cf. Bhagavad Gita 9.23-25, p. 266.
**Isaiah 2.7-9:** Cf. Matthew 6.24, p. 665.
**Shabbat 105b:** On the Evil Inclination, cf. Kiddushin 30b, p. 277.
**Philippians 3.18-19:** Cf. Romans 1.21-25, pp. 280-81.

Resolve to gain the victory over your own selves, that haply the whole earth may be freed and sanctified from its servitude to the gods of its idle fancies—gods that have inflicted such loss upon, and are responsible for the misery of, their wretched worshipers. These idols form the obstacle that impedes man in his efforts to advance in the path of perfection.

*Baha'i Faith*. Gleanings from the Writings of Baha'u'llah 43

## *Pride and Egoism*

THE CORRELATE OF IGNORANCE about Absolute Reality is pride and the inordinate preoccupation with one's own self. Pride and egoism blind one to recognizing transcendent Reality, or even to taking an accurate measure of oneself. Because of pride, a person thinks he is independent and cannot recognize that his very existence is dependent upon Ultimate Reality. He is blind to his relationships to other people, and neither can he conceive that there is a Deity who cares for him. In Christianity, pride is often regarded as the first step to the fall and rebellion against God. In Buddhism, grasping after the self and the sense of ego is the chief of all cravings and the deepest root of ignorance. In the Indic religions pride, like ignorance, is a fetter that binds humans to the wheel of rebirth. The passages collected below discuss pride as the cause of rebellion against God, as a hindrance to knowledge of Ultimate Reality, and as leading to improper estimation of oneself.

Pride goes before destruction,
and a haughty spirit before a fall.

*Judaism* and *Christianity*. Proverbs 16.18

The mightily proud ultimately rot in their own arrogance.

*Sikhism*. Adi Granth, Gauri Sukhmani, M.5, p. 278

Nay, but verily man is rebellious
For he thinks himself independent.
Lo! Unto thy Lord is the return.

*Islam*. Qur'an 96.6-8

Woe to those who are wise in their own eyes,
and shrewd in their own sight!

*Judaism* and *Christianity*. Isaiah 5.21

Selfishness may be sweet only for oneself, but no harmony of the whole can come from it.

*Tenrikyo*. Osashizu

We say that "Good" and "Harmony," and "Evil" and "Disharmony," are synonymous. Further we maintain that all pain and suffering are results of want of Harmony, and that the one terrible and only cause of the disturbance

**Proverbs 16.18:** Cf. Matthew 23.12, p. 387; Erubin 13b, p. 387.

**Gauri Sukhmani, M.5:** For more of this passage, see pp. 388 and 672-73. Cf. Bhagavad Gita 16.7-16, p. 281; 18.58, p. 492.

**Isaiah 5.21:** See Proverbs 3.5-6, p. 537; Luke 18.10-14, p. 642; cf. Bhagavad Gita 16.7-16, p. 281.

of Harmony is selfishness in some form or another.

*Theosophy*. Helena Blavatsky, The Key to Theosophy

He who makes his thought better and worse, O Wise One,
Better and worse his conscience, by deed and by word,
He follows his leanings, his wishes, his likings.
In thy mind's force, at the end of times, he shall be set apart.

*Zoroastrianism*. Avesta, Yasna 48.4

Turn not your cheek in scorn toward folk, nor walk with pertness in the land. Lo! God loves not each braggart boaster. Be modest in your bearing and subdue your voice. Lo! The harshest of all voices is the voice of the ass.

*Islam*. Qur'an 31.18-19

But Jeshurun waxed fat, and kicked;
you waxed fat, you grew thick, you became sleek;
then he forsook God who made him,
and scoffed at the Rock of his salvation.

*Judaism* and *Christianity*. Deuteronomy 32.15

I know that Western culture is characterized by individualism. However, selfish individualism is doomed. Sacrificial individualism will blossom. Individuality in itself is good. God gave each of us a unique way to serve. But individualism without God can only build castles on the sands of decay.

*Unification Church*. Sun Myung Moon, 10-20-73

Nzame (God) is on high, man is on the earth.
*Yeye O, Yalele*, God is God, man is man.
Everyone in his house, everyone for himself.

*African Traditional Religions*. Fang Tradition (Gabon)

Like a traveller on earth, overstuffed with pride,
Committing innumerable sins, in maya-hues dyed,
Sunk in avarice, attachment, and pride;
Forgetful of death, involved with progeny, companions, worldly transactions, wife,
Is their life passed.

*Sikhism*. Adi Granth, Jaitsari Chhant, M.5, p. 705

The pride of your heart has deceived you,
you who live in the clefts of the rock,
whose dwelling is high,
who say in your heart,
"Who will bring me down to the ground?"
Though you soar aloft like the eagle,
though your nest is set among the stars,
thence I will bring you down, says the Lord.

*Judaism* and *Christianity*. Obadiah 3-4

For the Lord of hosts has a day
against all that is proud and lofty,
against all that is lifted up and high;
against all the cedars of Lebanon
lofty and lifted up;
and against all the oaks of Bashan;
against all the high mountains
and against all the lofty hills;
against every high tower,
and against every fortified wall;
against all the ships of Tarshish,
and against all the beautiful craft.

**Key to Theosophy:** Cf. Sun Myung Moon, 10-20-73, p. 333.

**Qur'an 31.18-19:** Cf. Samanasuttam 135-36, p. 648; Doctrine of the Mean 33, p. 648.

**Deuteronomy 32.15:** Cf. 1 Timothy 6.10, p. 296; James 4.13-16, p. 649.

**Sun Myung Moon, 10-20-73:** Cf. Philippians 2.3-4, p. 650.

**Fang Tradition:** This selection is taken from a creation story, and describes the rebellion of primal man as springing from a false sense of of God's remoteness and man's independence.

**Jaitsari Chhant M.5:** Cf. Shalok, M.9, p. 278.

**Obadiah 3-4:** This passage is an indictment of the Edomites, who thought their fortresses in the high cliffs were impenetrable. Cf. 1 Samuel 2.4-9, p. 388; Qur'an 89.6-14, p. 767.

And the haughtiness of man shall be humbled,
and the pride of men shall be brought low;
and the Lord alone will be exalted in that day.

*Judaism* and *Christianity*. Isaiah 2.12-17

All our righteousnesses are as filthy rags.

*Judaism* and *Christianity*. Isaiah 64.6

If you desire to obtain help, put away pride. Even a hair of pride shuts you off, as if by a great cloud.

*Shinto*. Oracle of Kasuga

The Buddha restrained Shariputra, "If I preach this matter [the Lotus Sutra], all the gods, men, and asuras in all the worlds shall be alarmed, and the arrogant monks shall fall into a great trap. Indeed...

> My dharma is subtle and hard to imagine.
> Those of overweening pride,
> If they hear it, shall surely neither revere it
> nor believe in it."

Yet Shariputra again addressed the Buddha, "I beseech you to preach, I beseech you to preach!..." [The Buddha, prevailed upon by Shariputra, began to teach, but as he began,] in the assembly monks, nuns, lay brothers, and lay sisters to the number of five thousand straightway rose from their seats and, doing obeisance to the Buddha, withdrew. For what reason? This group had deep and grave roots of sin and overweening pride, imagining themselves to have attained and to have borne witness to what in fact they had not. Having such faults as these, therefore they did not stay. The World-honored One, silent, did not restrain them.

The Buddha declared to Shariputra, "My assembly has no more branches and leaves, it has only firm fruit. It is just as well that such arrogant ones as these have withdrawn. Now listen well, for I will preach to you."

*Buddhism*. Lotus Sutra 2

"Subhuti, what do you think? Does a holy one say within himself, 'I have obtained Perfective Enlightenment?'" Subhuti replied, "No, World-honored One... If a holy one of Perfective Enlightenment said to himself, 'Such am I,' he would necessarily partake of the idea of an ego-identity, a personality, a being, or a separated individuality."

*Buddhism*. Diamond Sutra 9

Shun all pride and jealousy. Give up all idea of "me" and "mine".... As long as there is consciousness of diversity and not of unity in the Self, a man ignorantly thinks of himself as a separate being, as the "doer" of actions and the "experiencer" of effects. He remains subject to birth and death, knows happiness and misery, is bound by his own deeds, good or bad.

*Hinduism*. Srimad Bhagavatam 11.4

He who has in his heart faith equal to a single grain of mustard seed will not enter hell, and he who has in his heart as much pride as a grain of mustard seed will not enter paradise.

*Islam*. Hadith of Muslim

**Isaiah 2.12-17:** Cf. 1 Samuel 2.4-9, p. 388; Matthew 23.12, p. 387; Erubin 13b, p. 387; Isaiah 24.18-23, p. 781.

**Isaiah 64.6:** This passage was originally a complaint by certain Israelites that they were being shunned by society despite their faithfulness to God. But in the Christian tradition, it is understood as an exclamation of the worthlessness of worldly fame or knowledge as mere pretense in the presence of the divine majesty.

**Oracle of Kasuga:** Cf. Sutta Nipata 798, p. 39; Sutra of Hui Neng 6, p. 283. The grand shrine of Kasuga, in Nara prefecture, is one of Japan's oldest Shinto shrines.

**Lotus Sutra 2:** The Buddha seeks to weed out the prideful and retain only sincere disciples before he begins to preach the wonderful Dharma of the Lotus Sutra. Cf. Sutta Nipata 798, p. 39.

**Diamond Sutra 9:** Cf. Dhammapada 63, p. 650; Tao Te Ching 71, p. 650; Shinran, p. 649.

**Hadith of Muslim:** Cf. Hadith of Bukhari, p. 647; Bhagavad Gita 18.58, p. 492.

Where egoism exists, Thou are not experienced,
Where Thou art, is not egoism.
You who are learned, expound in your mind
This inexpressible proposition.

*Sikhism*. Adi Granth,
Maru-ki-Var, M.1, p. 1092

In thinking, "This is I" and "That is mine," he binds himself with his self, as does a bird with a snare.

*Hinduism*. Maitri Upanishad 3.2

Travelling powerless, like a bucket travelling in a well:
First with the thought "I," misconceiving the self,
Then, arising attachment to things with the thought "mine."

*Buddhism*. Candrakirti,
Madhyamakavatara 3

Not knowing the consequence of good and evil karmas, he is afflicted and hurt. Nevertheless, he, due to his egotism, piles up karmas and undergoes births and deaths again and again.

*Jainism*. Acarangasutra 2.55-56

The fool who thinks he is wise is called a fool indeed.

*Buddhism*. Dhammapada 63

If I justify myself, my own mouth shall condemn me:
If I say, I am perfect, it shall also prove me perverse.

*Judaism* and *Christianity*. Job 9.20

Whoever proclaims himself good,
know, goodness approaches him not.

*Sikhism*. Adi Granth,
Gauri Sukhmani, M.5, p. 278

Confucius said, A faultless man I cannot hope ever to meet; the most I can hope for is to meet a man of fixed principles. Yet where all around I see Nothing pretending to be Something, Emptiness pretending to be Fullness, Penury pretending to be Affluence, even a man of fixed principles will be none too easy to find.

*Confucianism*. Analects 7.25

He who tiptoes cannot stand;
He who strides cannot walk.
He who shows himself is not conspicuous;
He who considers himself right is not illustrious;
He who brags will have no merit;
He who boasts will not endure.
From the point of view of the Way, these are like excessive food and useless excrescences
Which all creatures detest.
He who has the Way does not abide in them.

*Taoism*. Tao Te Ching 24

Pride has seven forms:

Boasting that one is lower than the lowly,
Or equal with the equal, or greater than
Or equal to the lowly
Is called the pride of selfhood.

Boasting that one is equal to those
Who by some quality are better than oneself
Is the pride of being superior. Thinking
That one is higher than the extremely high,

Who fancy themselves to be superior,
Is pride greater than pride;
Like an abscess in a tumor
It is very vicious.

Conceiving an "I" through ignorance
In the five empty [aggregates]
Which are called the appropriation
Is said to be the pride of thinking "I."

**Maitri Upanishad 3.2:** Cf. Digha Nikaya ii.276, p. 277; Bhagavad Gita 2.71, p. 638.

**Madhyamakavatara 3:** Candrakirti (ca. 560-640) wrote the Madhyamakavatara to explain Nagarjuna's view of sunyata. It consists of twelve chapters. Following the Dashabhumi Sutra, the first ten chapters explain the ten stages of perfections leading to the Buddha-wisdom, and the final two chapters explain the stages of Bodhisattva and of Buddha. Cf. Sutta Nipata 205-6, p. 650.

**Gauri Sukhmani, M.5:** See Gauri Sukhmani, M.5, pp. 672-73.

**Analects 7.25:** Cf. Chuang Tzu 1, pp. 650-51.

**Tao Te Ching 24:** Cf. Tao Te Ching 71, p. 650.

Thinking one has won fruits not yet
Attained is pride of conceit.
Praising oneself for faulty deeds
Is known by the wise as wrongful pride.

Deriding oneself, thinking
"I am senseless," is called
The pride of lowliness.
Such briefly are the seven prides.

*Buddhism.* Nagarjuna,
Precious Garland 406-12

❖

## *Selfish Desire, Lust, and Greed*

PASSION, GREED, COVETOUSNESS, hatred, lust: these emotions dominate the soul, causing blindness and leading to destruction. Every major religion recognizes that suffering and evil are caused by excessive desires or desires directed toward a selfish purpose. Buddhism has summed up this principle in the second of the Four Noble Truths and denotes these desires by the term "craving." Craving is a fetter: poisoning the heart, deluding the mind, and binding people to evil courses of action.

While all religions view selfish desire as baneful and the cause of much suffering, they differ in explaining these selfish desires in relation to human psychology. Buddhism, and similarly Jainism, reject desire of all kinds, even the grasping for existence itself, as harmful and a source of bondage. In the monotheistic religions: Christianity, Judaism, Islam, and in some texts from Sikhism and Hinduism, the passions of the flesh—which are evil—are distinguished from the healthy ambition for goodness and the passion for God. Chinese religion condemns only excessive desire and selfish desire: Desires themselves may be good if they are in harmony with the Tao. Similarly, Hinduism honors desire when it takes its rightful place within the dharma of family and society; this ambivalence is illustrated from a passage which identifies Kama, the god of desire, with the generative forces of nature.

To these condemnations of selfish desires, the reader may add many additional passages concerned with their renunciation, which may be found in Chapter 18.

The Noble Truth of the Origin of suffering is this: It is craving that leads back to birth, bound up with passionate greed. It finds fresh delight now here and now there, namely, craving for sense pleasures, craving for existence and becoming, and craving for non-existence.

*Buddhism.* Samyutta Nikaya lvi.11:
Setting in Motion the Wheel of Truth

Have you seen him who makes his desire his god, and God sends him astray purposely, and seals up his hearing and his heart, and sets on his sight a covering? Who, then, will lead him after God [has condemned him]? Will you not then heed?

*Islam.* Qur'an 45.23

**Samyutta Nikaya lvi.11:** Cf. Dhammapada 212-16, p. 658.

What causes wars, and what causes fighting among you? Is it not your passions that are at war in your members? You desire and do not have; so you kill. And you covet and cannot obtain; so you fight and wage war. You do not have, because you do not ask. You ask and do not receive, because you ask wrongly, to spend it on your passions.

*Christianity*. James 4.1-3

The man who gathers flowers [of sensual pleasure], whose mind is distracted and who is insatiate in desires, the Destroyer brings under his sway.

*Buddhism*. Dhammapada 48

Let no one say when he is tempted, "I am tempted by God"; for God cannot be tempted with evil and he himself tempts no one; but each person is tempted when he is lured and enticed by his own desire. Then desire when it has conceived gives birth to sin; and sin when it is full-grown brings forth death.

*Christianity*. James 1.13-15

In desire is man born;
From desire he consumes objects of various tastes;
By desire is he led away bound,
Buffeted across the face.
Bound by evil qualities is he chastised—

*Sikhism*. Adi Granth, Sri Raga Ashtpadi, M.1, p. 61

Envy and desire and ambition drive a man out of the world.

*Judaism*. Mishnah, Abot 4.28

There are three gates to self-destructive hell: lust, anger, and greed.

*Hinduism*. Bhagavad Gita 16.21

If a man fails to overcome illicit lustful desires, and pursues them, he will bring ruin upon himself. In the end, he will bring destruction to this world and universe.

*Unification Church*. Sun Myung Moon, 1-3-86

Arjuna:
What is the force that binds us to selfish deeds, O Krishna? What power moves us, even against our will, as if forcing us?

Krishna:
It is selfish desire and anger, arising from the state of being known as passion; these are the appetites and evils which threaten a person in this life.

Just as a fire is covered by smoke and a mirror is obscured by dust, just as an embryo is enveloped deep within the womb, knowledge is hidden by selfish desire—hidden, Arjuna, by this unquenchable fire for self-satisfaction, the inveterate enemy of the wise.

Selfish desire is found in the senses, mind, and intellect, misleading them and burying wisdom in delusion. Fight with all your strength, Arjuna! Controlling your senses, conquer your enemy, the destroyer of knowledge and realization.

*Hinduism*. Bhagavad Gita 3.36-41

Clinging, in bondage to desires, not seeing
in bondage any fault, thus bound and fettered,
never can they cross the flood so wide and mighty.

Blinded are beings by their sense desires
spread over them like a net; covered are they
by cloak of craving; by their heedless ways
caught as a fish in the mouth of a funnel-net.
Decrepitude and death they journey to,
just as a sucking calf goes to its mother.

*Buddhism*. Udana 75-76

**James 4.1-3:** Cf. 1 Peter 2.11, p. 657; also Great Learning 7, pp. 658-59; Maitri Upanishad 6.28, p. 744.
**Abot 4.28:** Cf. Itivuttaka 45, p. 278; Uttaradhyayana Sutra 23.38, p. 278; Sorath, M.3, p. 278.
**Bhagavad Gita 3.36-41:** Cf. Maitri Upanishad 6.34, p. 277.
**Udana 75-76:** Cf. Udana 72, p. 284.

The fish that is excessively attached to water,
without water dies.
For love of the lotus is the humming-bee
destroyed,
Finding not the way of escape...
Subdued by lust is the elephant caught,
Helpless under others' power.
For the love of sound the deer bows his head,
Thereby torn to pieces.
Beholding his family, by greed is man attracted,
With wealth involved:
Deeply in wealth involved, regarding it as his
own,
Which inevitably he must leave behind.
Whoever with other than the Lord forms love,
Know him to be eternally the sufferer.

*Sikhism*. Adi Granth, Dhanasari, M.5, pp. 670-71

Just as a tree with roots unharmed and firm, though hewn down, sprouts again, even so while latent craving is not rooted out, this sorrow springs up again and again.

If in anyone the thirty-six streams of craving that rush toward pleasureable thoughts are strong, such a deluded person torrential thoughts of lust carry off.

The streams of craving flow everywhere. The creeper sprouts and stands. Seeing the creeper that has sprung up, with wisdom cut off the root.

In beings there arise pleasures that rush toward sense-objects, and such beings are steeped in craving. Bent on happiness, they seek happiness. Verily, such men come to birth and decay.

Folk enwrapt in craving are terrified like a captive hare. Held fast by fetters and bonds, for long they come to sorrow again and again....

That which is made of iron, wood, or hemp, is not a strong bond, say the wise; the longing for jewels, ornaments, children, and wives is a far greater attachment. That bond is strong, say the wise. It hurls down, is supple, and is hard to loosen. This too the wise cut off, and leave the world, with no longing, renouncing sensual pleasures.

Those who are infatuated with lust fall back into the stream, as does a spider into the web spun by itself. This too the wise cut off, and wander, with no longing, released from all sorrow.

*Buddhism*. Dhammapada 338-47

Confucius said, "I have never seen anyone whose desire to build up his moral power was as strong as sexual desire."

*Confucianism*. Analects 9.17

There is no crime greater than having too
many desires;
There is no disaster greater than not being
content;
There is no misfortune greater than being
covetous.

*Taoism*. Tao Te Ching 46

They say that woman is an enticement.
No, No, she is not so.
They say that money is an enticement.
No, No, it is not so.
They say that landed property is an entice-
ment.
No, No, it is not so.
The real enticement is the insatiable appetite
of the mind,
O Lord Guheswara!

*Hinduism*. Allama Prabhu, Vacana 91

All things are full of weariness; a man cannot
utter it;
the eye is not satisfied with seeing, nor the ear
filled with hearing.

*Judaism* and *Christianity*. Ecclesiastes 1.8

**Dhanasari, M.5:** Cf. Gauri Purabi, Ravidas, p. 284.

**Dhammapada 338-47:** Vv. 338-42, 345-47. Cf. Dhammapada 334-37, p. 658; Itivuttaka 114-15, p. 385.

**Analects 9.17:** Repeated at Analects 15.12.

**Allama Prabhu, Vacana 91:** Allama Prabhu was a Shaivite contemporary of Basavanna. This passage opposes the tendency to despise women as responsible for men's downfall. Rather, men are at fault for their self-begotten lusts. Guheswara is a name of Shiva.

Desire never rests by enjoyment of lusts, as fire surely increases the more butter is offered to it.

*Hinduism*. Laws of Manu 2.94

Not by a shower of gold coins does contentment arise in sensual pleasures.

*Buddhism*. Dhammapada 186

Passion makes the bones rot.

*Judaism* and *Christianity*. Proverbs 14.30

The ignorant one craves for a life of luxury and repeatedly hankers after pleasures. Haunted by his own desires he gets benumbed and is rewarded only with suffering.

The benighted one is incompetent to assuage sufferings, because he is attached to desires and is lecherous. Oppressed by physical and mental pain, he keeps rotating in a whirlpool of agony. I say so.

*Jainism*. Acarangasutra 2.60, 74

The love of money is the root of all evils.

*Christianity*. 1 Timothy 6.10

Wealth is the fountainhead of inordinate craving.

*Islam*.
Nahjul Balagha, Saying 56

What is that love which is based on greed?
When there is greed, the love is false.

*Sikhism*. Adi Granth,
Shalok, Farid, p. 1378

He who loves money will not be satisfied with money; nor he who loves wealth, with gain: this also is vanity.

*Judaism* and *Christianity*.
Ecclesiastes 5.10

Even were the wealth of the entire world bestowed lavishly on a man, he would not be happy: contentment is difficult to attain.

*Jainism*. Uttaradhyayana Sutra 8.16

O my wealth-coveting and foolish soul, when will you succeed in emancipating yourself from the desire for wealth? Shame on my foolishness! I have been your toy! It is thus that one becomes a slave of others. No one born on earth did ever attain to the end of desire.... Without doubt, O Desire, your heart is as hard as adamant, since though affected by a hundred distresses, you do not break into pieces! I know you, O Desire, and all those things that are dear to you! The desire for wealth can never bring happiness.

*Hinduism*. Mahabharata,
Shanti Parva 177

He who considers wealth a good thing can never bear to give up his income; he who considers eminence a good thing can never bear to give up his fame. He who has a taste for power can never bear to hand over authority to others. Holding tight to these things, such men shiver with fear; should they let them go, they would pine in sorrow. They never stop for a moment of reflection, never cease to gaze with greedy eyes—they are men punished by Heaven.

*Taoism*. Chuang Tzu 14

Carnality is nothing but mundane existence, and mundane existence is nothing but carnality. Stupefied by the acute torments caused by tempting passions, a sensual person dwells in mundane existence, uttering, "My mother, my father, my brother, my sister, my wife, my son, my daughter, my daughter-in-law, my friend, my kith and kin, my vast property and means,

**1 Timothy 6.10:** This is frequently misquoted. It states that it is *the love of* money, not money itself, which is the root of all evils. Cf. Matthew 4.4, p. 664; 6.24, p. 665; 19.21-24, p. 666; Deuteronomy 32.15, p. 290.

**Shalok, Farid:** Cf. Asa-ki-Var, M.2, p. 706.

my food and clothes." Infatuated by deep attachments to these, he dwells with them. He lives constantly tormented by avidity; he endeavors to amass wealth in season and out of season; being desirous of sensual pleasures, he is avid for money, so much so that he becomes an out and out rogue committing theft or injury.... Such a man repeatedly becomes a killer of living beings.

*Jainism.* Acarangasutra 2.1-3

Do men delight in what they see?—they are corrupted by colors. Do they delight in what they hear?—they are corrupted by sounds. Do they delight in benevolence?—they bring confusion to virtue. Do they delight in righteousness?—they turn their backs on reason. Do they delight in rites?—they are aiding artificiality. Do they delight in music?—they are aiding dissolution. Do they delight in sageliness?—they are assisting artifice. Do they delight in knowledge?—they are assisting the fault-finders. As long as the world rests in the true form of its inborn nature and fate, it makes no difference whether these eight delights exist or not. But if the world does not rest in the true form of its nature and fate, then these eight delights will begin to grow warped and crooked, jumbled and deranged, and will bring confusion to the world. And if on top of that the world begins to honor them and cherish them, then the delusion of the world is great indeed!

*Taoism.* Chuang Tzu 11

The gods asked Shiva to revive Kama [Desire], and they said, "Without Desire the whole universe will be destroyed. How can you exist without Desire?" But Shiva replied in anger, "The universe must continue without Desire, for it was he who caused all the gods, including Indra, to fall from their places and become humble, and it is Desire who leads all creatures to hell. Without Desire a man can do no evil.... I burnt Desire in order to give peace to all creatures, and I will not revive him, since he is the evil at the root of all misery. Now all of you should set your minds on asceticism." The gods and sages said, "What you have said, Shiva, is no doubt the very best thing for us, but nevertheless, all of this universe was created by means of Desire, and all of it is the form of Desire, and that Desire cannot be killed. How can you have burnt Kama? You yourself made him and gave him the ability he has just used." But Shiva merely scowled and vanished.

*Hinduism.* Skanda Purana 1.1.21

❖

**Acarangasutra 2.1-3:** Cf. Bhagavad Gita 16.7-16, p. 281.

**Chuang Tzu 11:** Cf. Tao Te Ching 12, p. 662; Great Learning 7, pp. 658-59.

**Skanda Purana 1.1.21:** *Kama*, here personified, is the principle of desire. Later, Shiva accedes to the gods' request and revives Kama. The tension between asceticism and desire is a theme which continues throughout the cycle of Shiva myths. Pure asceticism, by whose ardor (*tapas*) the gods and sages sustain their divinity, and desire, whose energy engenders all life, are apparently irreconcilable, yet both are necessary. Kama (love) is praised as the divine source of all creation in Atharva Veda 9.2.19-20, p. 89.

CHAPTER 8

# FALL AND DEVIATION

THIS CHAPTER DEALS WITH TOPICS AROUND the theme of fall and deviation. This can refer to a primordial human fall such as posited by Christianity, or to a continual falling away from the purpose of existence in the life of each individual person, or both. In Adam's sin we all have sinned: this can mean we are genetically damaged by an Original Sin or that Adam was the archetypal sinner whose fall we repeat continually. Regardless of how the fall is understood, once having deviated, fallen humans do not manifest their purpose of existence. In particular, we no longer experience the immediate presence of God, nor are we truly ourselves. Hence we require salvation in order to be restored to our original purpose.

The theme of deviation includes the topic of demonic powers. These have no place in a world that fulfills its true purpose, yet they manifestly exist and wreak damage in our world. A related topic is heresy, where error masquerades as true teaching and leads people astray.

A fourth section describes how the original human nature has become defiled, occluded, or damaged. Animal instinct rather than wisdom has come to dominate behavior, and people's value as temples of the divine Spirit has been lost. The chapter closes with passages depicting the sadness, grief, and pity which this human deviation elicits from the heart of God.

❖

# The Human Fall

BELIEF THAT HUMANITY FELL from a primordial state of unity with God is a doctrine of the Abrahamic faiths, and similar beliefs are also found in the traditions of many African religions and in the doctrines of new religions influenced by Christianity. Among the Abrahamic faiths understandings of the Fall take varying forms. In Christianity, the sin of the original man and woman is imputed to all humanity, and created an enduring separation between humans and God which could only be remedied by Christ.[1] In Islam, on the other hand, Adam's sin was his alone, and he, like all human beings, could return to a position of acceptance by submission (*islam*) to God. He fell victim to the promptings of Satan, a trial which every person must face and which only some are able to endure. In Judaism we find a mixture of beliefs: Rabbinic passages gathered in this section which accept the biblical doctrine that the sin of Adam and Eve brought a curse into the world are counterbalanced by other passages emphasizing individual responsibility[2] and denying that we are culpable for the sin of our ancestor Adam. The Evil Inclination which directs the soul to do evil may have been induced by a fall, but then again, it may have been created by God.[3]

The human fall is a significant teaching only in certain religions. It is logically necessary only for religions in which (1) God is the only Creator, (2) the creation was purposed to be good, and (3) evil is regarded as real and contrary to the purpose of creation. But these three premises are found together only in the Abrahamic faiths and in some other theistic religions. In Zoroastrianism, where there are two creators—God and the devil—the origin of evil does not involve a fall. Neither is there a doctrine of a fall in Buddhism, which lacks a doctrine of creation. Hinduism, which (in *Sankhya* philosophy) regards matter as partaking of base elements, or in which creation is an act of play (*lila*) without moral purpose, also does not require a doctrine of the fall. Nevertheless, Buddhism and Hinduism have scriptures which speculate on a primordial fall from grace in order to explain the discrepancy between the cosmos' pure origin and its present state of suffering.

The first group of passages are derived from or related to the account of the Fall in Genesis. This story is full of symbolism and open to varied interpretations. The Tempter—variously called Satan, Lucifer, or Iblis—instigates Adam and Eve to disobey God's command, often with the hint that the act of the Fall involved sexual misconduct. While the Bible attributes the Fall mainly to the mistake of the woman, the Qur'an regards Adam and Eve as equally culpable. The next group of passages are independent traditions from the African religions, Hinduism, Buddhism, and Shinto which give some account of the cause for the present deviation of humanity from its pure origin. These traditions resemble the accounts of the fall in the Abrahamic faiths in one or more respects: disobedience, eating a forbidden food, sexual misconduct, and the culpability of the woman. The last group of passages, from the Eastern religions, describes a belief that this world has declined from an original golden age of purity and godliness. God's creation was originally pure, but with the progression of the ages the Law has gradually fallen into disuse and human nature has degenerated.

---

[1] 1 Corinthians 15.21-22, p. 388.

[2] Ezekiel 18, p. 490.

[3] Kiddushin 30b, p. 374.

The Lord God took the man [Adam] and put him in the Garden of Eden to till it and keep it. And the Lord God commanded the man, saying, "You may freely eat of every tree of the garden; but of the tree of the knowledge of good and evil you shall not eat, for in the day that you eat of it you shall die."

Then the Lord God said, "It is not good that the man should be alone; I will make him a helper fit for him." So out of the ground the Lord God formed every beast of the field and every bird of the air, and brought them to the man to see what he would call them; and whatever the man called every living creature, that was its name. The man gave names to all cattle, and to the birds of the air, and to every beast of the field; but for the man there was not found a helper fit for him. So the Lord God caused a deep sleep to fall upon the man, and while he slept took one of his ribs and closed up its place with flesh; and the rib which the Lord God had taken from the man he made into a woman and brought her to the man. Then the man said, "This at last is bone of my bones and flesh of my flesh; she shall be called Woman, because she was taken out of Man." Therefore a man leaves his father and his mother and cleaves to his wife, and they become one flesh. And the man and his wife were both naked, and were not ashamed.

Now the serpent was more subtle than any other wild creature that the Lord God had made. He said to the woman, "Did God say, 'You shall not eat of any tree of the garden'?" And the woman said to the serpent, "We may eat of the fruit of the trees of the garden; but God said, 'You shall not eat of the fruit of the tree which is in the midst of the garden, neither shall you touch it, lest you die.'" But the serpent said to the woman, "You will not die. For God knows that when you eat of it your eyes will be opened, and you will be like God, knowing good and evil." So when the woman saw that the tree was good for food, and that it was a delight to the eyes, and that the tree was to be desired to make one wise, she took of its fruit and ate; and she also gave some to her husband, and he ate. Then the eyes of both were opened, and they knew that they were naked; and they sewed fig leaves together and made themselves aprons.

And they heard the sound of the Lord God walking in the garden in the cool of the day, and the man and his wife hid themselves from the presence of the Lord God among the trees of the garden. But the Lord God called to the man, and said to him, "Where are you?" And he said, "I heard the sound of thee in the garden, and I was afraid, because I was naked; and I hid myself." He said, "Who told you that you were naked? Have you eaten of the tree of which I commanded you not to eat?" The man said, "The woman whom thou gavest to be with me, she gave me fruit of the tree, and I ate." Then the Lord God said to the woman, "What is this that you have done?" The woman said, "The serpent beguiled me, and I ate." The Lord God said to the serpent, "Because you have done this,

Cursed are you above all cattle,
and above all wild animals;
Upon your belly you shall go,
and dust you shall eat all the days of your life.
I will put enmity between you and the woman,
and between your seed and her seed;
He shall bruise your head,
and you shall bruise his heel."

To the woman he said,

"I will greatly multiply your pain in childbearing,
in pain you shall bring forth children,
Yet your desire shall be for your husband,
and he shall rule over you."

And to Adam he said, "Because you have listened to the voice of your wife, and have eaten of the tree of which I commanded you, 'You shall not eat of it,'

cursed is the ground because of you;
in toil you shall eat of it all the days of your life;
Thorns and thistles it shall bring forth to you;
and you shall eat the plants of the field.
In the sweat of your face you shall eat bread

till you return to the ground,
for out of it you were taken;
you are dust,
and to dust you shall return."

The man called his wife's name Eve, because she was the mother of all living. And the Lord God made for Adam and for his wife garments of skins, and clothed them.

Then the Lord God said, "Behold, the man has become like one of us, knowing good and evil; and now, lest he put forth his hand and take also of the tree of life, and eat, and live forever"—therefore the Lord God sent him forth from the Garden of Eden, to till the ground from which he was taken. He drove out the man; and at the east of the Garden of Eden he placed the cherubim, and a flaming sword which turned every way, to guard the way to the tree of life.

*Judaism* and *Christianity*.
Genesis 2.15-3.24

It is We who created you and gave you shape; then We bade the angels, "Bow down to Adam," and they bowed down; not so Iblis, he refused to be of those who bow down. [God] said, "What prevented you from bowing down when I commanded you?" He said, "I am better than he; You created me from fire, and him from clay." God said, "Get down from this place; it is not for you to be arrogant here; get out, for you are of the meanest of creatures." He said, "Give me respite till the day when they are raised up." God said, "Be among those who are to have respite."

He said, "Because you have thrown me out of the Way, lo! I will lie in wait for them on Your Straight Way: Then will I assault them from before them and behind them, from their right and their left: nor will You find, in most of them, gratitude." God said, "Get out from this, disgraced and expelled. If any of them follow you, I will fill hell with all of you.

"And Adam, dwell, you and your wife, in the Garden, and enjoy its good things as you wish, but approach not this tree, or you will run into harm and transgression."

Then Satan began to whisper suggestions to them, bringing openly before their minds all their shame that was previously unnoticed by them. He said, "Your Lord only forbade you this tree, lest you should become angels or such beings as live forever." And he swore to them both, that he was their sincere advisor. So by deceit he brought about their fall: when they tasted of the tree, their shame became apparent to them, and they began to sew together the leaves of the Garden over their bodies.

And their Lord called unto them, "Did I not forbid you that tree, and tell you that Satan was an avowed enemy unto you both?" They said, "Our Lord! we have wronged our own souls. If You do not forgive us and do not grant us Your mercy, we shall certainly be lost." God said, "Get you down, with enmity between yourselves. On earth will be your dwelling place and your means of livelihood—for a time. Therein shall you live, and therein you shall die; but from it shall you be brought forth at last."

O Children of Adam! We have bestowed raiment upon you to cover your shame, as well as to be an adornment to you. But the raiment of righteousness—that is the best. Such are among the signs of God, that they may receive admonition.

O Children of Adam! Let not Satan seduce you in the same manner as he got your parents out of the Garden, stripping them of their clothing in order to expose their private parts. He and his tribe watch you from where you cannot see them! We have made the devils friends only to those without faith.

*Islam*. Qur'an 7.11-27

**Genesis 2.15-3.24:** Cf. Luke 10.19-20, p. 220; Qur'an 2.30-33, p. 218. On the primitive harmony of paradise, cf. Chuang Tzu 9, p. 224.

**Qur'an 7.11-27:** Cf. Qur'an 17.61-64, pp. 312-13. In the last verses, the Qur'an relates Satan's deed in the Garden to the pagan orgies of Muhammad's day. It also compares this primordial purpose of clothing with the better way to protect one's purity, by modesty born of submission to God.

God created man incorruptible, and made him in the image of his own nature, but through the devil's envy, death came into the world.

*Christianity*.
Wisdom of Solomon 2.23-24

Rabbi Aha said, "God deliberated how to create man. He said to himself, 'If I create him like the angels, he will be immortal. If I create him like the beasts, he will be mortal.' God decided to leave man's conduct to his own free choice, and if he had not sinned, he would have been immortal."

*Judaism*. Midrash, Genesis Rabbah 8.11

Rabbi Abba said, "If Adam had not sinned, he would not have begotten children from the side of the evil inclination, but he would have borne offspring from the side of the holy spirit. But now, since all the children of men are born from the side of the evil inclination, they have no permanence and are but short-lived, because there is in them an element of the 'other side.' But if Adam had not sinned and had not been driven from the Garden of Eden, he would have begotten progeny from the side of the holy spirit—a progeny holy as the celestial angels, who would have endured for eternity, after the supernal pattern."

*Judaism*. Zohar, Genesis 61a

What was the wicked serpent contemplating at that time? He thought, "I shall go and kill Adam and wed his wife, and I shall be king over the whole world."

*Judaism*. Talmud,
Abot de Rabbi Nathan 1

Rabbi Joshua ben Qarhah said, "Why does the scripture not place the verse 'And the Lord God made for Adam and his wife garments of skin' [Genesis 3.21] immediately after 'And they were both naked, and were not ashamed' [Genesis 2.25]? It teaches you through what sin that wicked creature inveighed them: Because [the serpent] saw them engaged in their natural relations, he conceived a lust for her."

*Judaism*. Midrash,
Genesis Rabbah 18.6

After Adam and Eve had partaken of the forbidden fruit they were driven out of the Garden of Eden, to till the earth.

And they have brought forth children; yea, even the family of all the earth.

And the days of the children of men were prolonged, according to the will of God, that they might repent while in the flesh; wherefore, their state became a state of probation, and their time was lengthened, according to the commandments which the Lord God gave unto the children of men. For He gave commandment that all men must repent; for He showed unto all men that they were lost, because of the transgression of their parents.

**Wisdom of Solomon 2.23-24:** The Fall brought death into the world, meaning spiritual death and loss of our original relationship to God; cf. 1 Corinthians 15.21-22, p. 388; Romans 6.23, p. 410; cf. Berakot 18ab, p. 412; Genesis Rabbah 10.4, p. 791.

**Genesis Rabbah 8.11:** The prevailing Jewish conception of the Fall regards Adam as typical of all human beings. Like Adam, we all sin; we all fall. We are not condemned for an original sin; we all have the choice of death or eternal life placed before us—cf. Ezekiel 18, p. 490. If this passage is interpreted as referring specifically to Adam, it is affirming that God treated Adam as responsible and free to choose, contrary to certain views which regard the fall as an ascent from innocence to responsibility, to "knowledge of good and evil"—compare Book of Mormon, 2 Nephi 2.19-26, below.

**Zohar, Genesis 61a:** This passage speaks of an original sin, as Adam's sin is regarded as the source of the Evil Inclination which is inherited by all humankind; see also Shabbat 145b-146a, p. 389. On the other hand, in Kiddushin 30b, p. 374, there is the opinion that the Evil Inclination was created by God.

**Genesis Rabbah 18.6:** In the dominant Jewish tradition Adam and Eve enjoyed married life prior to the Fall. In the Christian tradition, on the other hand, they are usually depicted as living chaste while in the Garden. Illustrating the latter point of view we give the following passages from the Book of Mormon and Divine Principle. On the devil's lust, cf. Shabbat 145b-146, p. 389. For another Jewish interpretation of the forbidden fruit, see Sanhedrin 70ab, p. 354.

And now, behold, if Adam had not transgressed he would not have fallen, but he would have remained in the Garden of Eden. And all things which were created must have remained in the same state in which they were after they were created; and they must have remained forever, and had no end.

And they would have had no children; wherefore they would have remained in a state of innocence, having no joy, for they knew no misery; doing no good, for they knew no sin.

But behold, all things have been done in the wisdom of Him who knows all things.

Adam fell that men might be; and men are, that they might have joy.

And the Messiah comes in the fulness of time, that he may redeem the children of men from the fall. And because that they are redeemed from the fall they have become free forever, knowing good from evil; to act for themselves and not to be acted upon.

*Church of Jesus Christ of Latter-day Saints.*
Book of Mormon, 2 Nephi 2.19-26

All things were created to receive God's dominion through love. Love is the source of life and the essence of happiness; love is the ideal of all creation. Accordingly, the more one receives God's love, the more beautiful he or she becomes. So it was very natural that Eve looked most beautiful in Lucifer's eyes. Moreover, when [immature] Eve was susceptible to his temptation, Lucifer was strongly stimulated by an impulse of love toward Eve. At this point, Lucifer dared to seduce Eve at the risk of his life. Lucifer, who left his position due to excessive desire, and Eve, who desired to have her eyes opened like God's through a sexual relationship before she was ready for it, thus formed a reciprocal base, and had sexual intercourse with each other. The power of love derived from their give and take action was not based on the principle, and they fell into an illicit relationship of spiritual love.

Eve received certain elements from Lucifer when she joined in one body with him through love. First, she received from Lucifer the sense of fear, which came from his guilty conscience because of their violation of the purpose of creation. Second, she received wisdom enabling her to perceive that her intended spouse in the original nature of creation was not Lucifer but Adam.... Eve then seduced Adam in the hope that she might rid herself of the fear derived from the fall and stand before God by becoming, even then, one body with Adam, who was meant to be her spouse.

Adam and Eve were meant to have become husband and wife, eternally centered on God, after their perfection. However, at that time Eve was still in the period of immaturity. Eve joined with Adam after she had the illicit relationship with the archangel and while Adam, too, was in his period of immaturity. The premature conjugal relationship thus established between Adam and Eve was centered on Satan and caused the physical fall.

Eve, having become one body with the archangel through their illicit sexual relationship, was in the position of the archangel to Adam. Therefore Adam, whom God loved, looked very beautiful to her. Adam was Eve's only hope of returning to God. Feeling this, Eve tempted Adam, just as the archangel had tempted her. Adam and Eve formed a reciprocal base, and through their give and take action, the power of love drew them closer. This powerful love made Adam leave his original position and finally caused Eve and him to have an illicit sexual relationship.

Adam, by becoming one body with Eve, inherited all the elements Eve had received from Lucifer, in the same manner she did. These elements were then transmitted to their

**Book of Mormon, 2 Nephi 2.19-26:** The scriptures of the Latter-day Saints give positive value to the Human Fall, agreeing with a minority tradition in Christianity that views the Fall as a "happy fault" (*felix culpa*). The Fall was necessary both for procreation and for the exercise of moral agency—to know the joy of ethical living. In addition, without the Fall humankind could not know the grace of redemption in Christ. For these reasons, the Fall is considered to have been within the plan of God; compare Hadith of Muslim, p. 373. The contrary Jewish position—that unfallen humans were created endowed with moral agency, is given above in Genesis Rabbah 8.11. Cf. Pearl of Great Price, Moses 4.1-4, p. 313.

descendants... and mankind has multiplied sin to the present day, thus perpetuating the lineage of Satan.

*Unification Church.* Divine Principle I.2.2.2

You must know, monks, that after the floods [that put out the conflagration that ended the last cosmic cycle] receded and the earth came back into being, there was upon the face of the earth a film more sweet-smelling than ambrosia. Do you want to know what was the taste of that film? It was like the taste of grape wine in the mouth. And at this time the gods of the Abhasvara Heaven said to one another, "Let us go and see what it looks like in Jambudvipa now that there is earth again." So the young gods of that heaven came down into the world and saw that over the earth was spread this film. They put their fingers into the earth and sucked them. Some put their fingers into the earth many times and ate a great deal of this film, and these at once lost all their majesty and brightness. Their bodies grew heavy and their substance became flesh and bone. They lost their magic and could no longer fly. But there were others who ate only a little, and these could still fly about in the air. And those that had lost their magic cried out to one another in dismay, "Now we are in a very sad case. We have lost our magic. There is nothing for it but to stay here on earth; for we cannot possibly get back to heaven." They stayed and fed upon the film that covered the earth, and gazed at one another's beauty. Then those among them that were most passionate became women, and these gods and goddesses fulfilled their desires and pleasure in one another. And this was how it was, monks, that when the world began, love-making first spread throughout the world; it is an old and constant thing. And that woman should appear in the world, this too is an old thing, and not only a matter of today.

And the gods who had returned to heaven looked down and saw the young gods that had fallen, and they came down and reproached them, saying, "Why are you behaving in this unclean way?" Then the gods on earth thought to themselves, "We must find some way to be together without being seen by others." So they made houses that would cover and hide them. Monks, that was how houses first began.

[Now the people] seeing this thing of husbands and wives had begun, hated and despised such couples and seized them with the left hand, pushed them with the right hand and drove them away. But always after two months or maybe three they would come back again. Then the people hit them or pelted them with sticks, clods of earth, tiles or stones. "Go and hide yourselves! Go and hide yourselves properly!" That is why today when a girl is married she is pelted with flowers or gold or silver or pieces of clothing or rice, and the people as they pelt her say, "May peace and happiness, new bride, be yours!" Monks, in former times ill was meant by these things that were done, but nowadays good is meant.

*Buddhism.* Ekottara Agama 34 and Ch'i-shih Ching

**Divine Principle I.2.2.2:** The Fall is here regarded as a corruption of human love. Love is meant to be the most glorious and fulfilling emotion, expressing at the same time intimacy with God, but love was misused and degraded. The Fall was consummated when Adam and Eve had their first sexual relationship, at the instigation of Satan, and expressing an evil motivation. Since then, human love has been infected with self-centered elements. On the premise that an ideal world would have been perfected through the God-centered love of perfected Adam and Eve, married under God's blessing, see Divine Principle I.1.2.3.4, p. 175; cf. Sun Myung Moon, 10-20-73, p. 332; 3-30-90, p. 776; 8-20-89, p. 408.

**Ekottara Agama 34 and Ch'i-shih Ching:** These are both texts from the Chinese Tripitaka. The Ekkotara Agama is the Chinese translation of portions of the Anguttara Nikaya of the Pali scriptures. In the case of this text, however, the parallel Pali version is found not in the Anguttara Nikaya, but in Digha Nikaya iii.27, the Aggana Suttanta.

The deities Izanagi and Izanami descended from Heaven to the island Ono-goro and erected a heavenly pillar and a spacious palace.

At this time Izanagi asked his wife Izanami, "How is your body formed?" She replied, "My body, though it be formed, has one place which is formed insufficiently." Then Izanagi said, "My body, though it be formed, has one place which is formed to excess. Therefore, I would like to take that place in my body which is formed to excess and insert it into that place in your body which is formed insufficiently, and thus give birth to the land. How would this be?" "That will be good," said Izanami. "Then let us, you and me, walk in a circle around this heavenly pillar and meet and have conjugal intercourse," said Izanagi. "You walk around from the right, and I will walk around from the left and meet you."

After having agreed to this, they circled around; then Izanami said first, "How delightful! I have met a lovely lad!" Afterwards, Izanagi said, "How delightful! I have met a lovely maiden!" After each had spoken, Izanagi said to his wife, "It was not proper that the woman should speak first." Nevertheless, they commenced procreation and gave birth to a leech-child. They placed this child into a boat made of reeds and floated it away.

Then the two deities consulted together, "The child which we have just borne is not good. It is best to report this before the heavenly gods." So they ascended together and sought the will of the heavenly gods. The gods thereupon performed a grand divination, and said, "Because the woman spoke first, the child was not good. Descend once more and say it again."

Then they descended again and walked once more in a circle around the heavenly pillar as before. "How delightful! I have met a lovely maiden!" "How delightful! I have met a lovely lad!" Thus they united and gave birth to children, [the eight islands of Japan].

*Shinto.* Kojiki 4.1-6.1

The Creator, Fidi Mukullu, made all things including man. He also planted banana trees. When the bananas were ripe he sent the sun to harvest them. The sun brought back a full basket to Fidi Mukullu, who asked him if he had eaten any. The sun answered "no," and the Creator decided to put him to a test. He made the sun go down into a hole dug in the earth, then asked him when he wanted to get out. "Tomorrow morning, early," answered the sun. "If you did not lie," the Creator told him, "you will get out early tomorrow morning." The next day the sun appeared at the desired moment, confirming his honesty. Next the moon was ordered to gather God's bananas and was put to the same test. She also got out successfully. Then came man's turn to perform the same task. However, on his way to the Creator he ate a portion of the bananas, but denied doing so. Put to the same test as the sun and the moon, man said that he wanted to leave the hole at the end of five days. But he never got out. Fidi Mukullu said, "Man lied. That is why man will die and will never reappear."

*African Traditional Religions.*
Basonge Tradition (Zaire)

**Kojiki 4-6:** The deities Izanagi and Izanami represent the union of opposites, yang and yin, which is the source of all life divine and human—cf. I Ching, Great Commentary 1.1.i-iv, pp. 117-18. However, these deities at first erred in the ritual of conjugal intercourse by which they were to create the land and all things. Their mistake was in allowing the woman to take initiative—a parallel to Eve's haste to eat the fruit in the Genesis story. The 'leech-child' (*piru-go*) was a monstrosity who was allowed to die of exposure. Izanami, too, would eventually die in childbirth (Kojiki 7.22); compare the curses in Genesis 3.3 and 3.16.

The Japanese philosopher Nishida regards this myth as the Shinto version of Original Sin. According to Nishida, as Izanagi and Izanami were brother and sister, everything in the universe originated from an incestuous marriage. The procession around the heavenly pillar was a ritual designed to overcome the incest taboo, but the error in carrying out this ritual nullified its effect. Hence all humanity is the result of incest. The death of Izanami, the symbolic death of their daughter Amaterasu-omi-kami (Kojiki 15) and the expulsion of their son Susanoo (Kojiki 17.25) were punishments endured by the Shinto gods to atone for this original mistake.

In the beginning God was very close to man, for the sky then lay just above the earth. There was no death, sickness, sorrow, or hunger, and men were content with one grain of millet a day granted them by God. One day, a greedy woman, who wanted to pound more than the one grain permitted, used a long-handled pestle and struck the sky. This angered God, who withdrew with the sky to its present position far above the earth. Since then the country has become spoiled, and men are now subject to death, sickness, hunger, and disease.

*African Traditional Religions.* Dinka Tradition (Sudan)

In the olden days, when Imana (God) still lived among men, Death did not live among men. Whenever he happened to stray onto the earth, God would chase it away with his hunting dogs. One day during such a chase, Death was forced into a narrow space and would have been caught and destroyed. But in his straits he found a woman, and promised her that if she hid him he would spare her and her family. The woman opened her mouth and Death jumped inside. When God came to her and asked her if she had seen Death, she denied ever seeing him. But God, the All-seeing One, knew what happened, and told the woman that since she had hidden Death, in the future Death would destroy her and all her children. From that moment death spread all over the world.

*African Traditional Religions.* Hutu Tradition (Rwanda and Burundi)

Formerly, all creatures were virtuous, and by themselves they obtained divinity. Therefore the gods became worried, so Brahma created women in order to delude men. Then women, who had been virtuous, became wicked witches, and Brahma filled them with wanton desires, which they in turn inspired in men. He created anger, and henceforth all creatures were born in the power of desire and anger.

*Hinduism.* Mahabharata, Anusasana Parva 40.5-12

Formerly Prajapati brought forth pure creatures, who were truthful and virtuous. These creatures joined the gods in the sky whenever they wished, and they lived and died by their own wish. In another time, those who dwelt on earth were overcome by desire and anger, and they were abandoned by the gods. Then by their foul deeds these evil ones were trapped in the chain of rebirth, and they became atheists.

*Hinduism.* Mahabharata, Aranyaka Parva 181.11-20

In the Krita [golden age], Dharma is four-footed and entire, and so is Truth; nor does any gain accrue to men by unrighteousness.

In the other three ages, by reason of unjust gains, Dharma is deprived successively of one foot, and through the prevalence of theft, falsehood, and fraud the merit gained by men is diminished by one-fourth in each.

Men are free from disease, accomplish all their aims, and live four hundred years in the Krita age, but in the Treta [silver age] and in each of the succeeding ages their life is lessened by one quarter.

The life-[span] of mortals... the desired results of sacrificial rites and the supernatural power of embodied spirits are fruits apportioned among men according to the character of the age.

One set of duties is prescribed for men in the Krita age, different ones in the Treta and in the Dvapara, and again another set in the Kali, in

**Dinka Tradition:** Many African myths explain how in primordial times God withdrew far from the human realm. Variations on this particular version of the myth of God's withdrawal are found in the traditions of many African peoples. Cf. Dinka Song, p. 325; Fang Tradition, p. 290.

**Mahabharata, Anusasana Parva 40.5-12:** In this and similar Hindu traditions, the motive for the human fall lies with the gods, who grew jealous of people and desired to keep them out of heaven. This compares with the jealousy of the angels in the qur'anic and biblical accounts of the Fall. Cf. Srimad Bhagavatam 11.20, p. 265; Brihadaranyaka Upanishad 1.4.10, p. 287.

**Mahabharata, Aranyaka Parva 181.11-20:** Philosophical Hinduism explains evil by the doctrines of karma and reincarnation, but logically, karma itself must have an origin. This passage allows how, though the Creator be good, the chain of evil karma could begin.

proportion as those ages decrease in length.

In the Krita age the chief virtue is declared to be the performance of austerities, in the Treta divine knowledge, in the Dvapara the performance of sacrifices, and in the Kali liberality alone.

*Hinduism.* Laws of Manu 1.81-86

When the Tao was lost, there was virtue;
When virtue was lost, there was benevolence;
When benevolence was lost, there was rectitude;
When rectitude was lost, there were rules of propriety.
Propriety is a wearing thin of loyalty and good faith,
And the beginning of disorder.

*Taoism.* Tao Te Ching 38

❖

**Laws of Manu 1.81-86:** This is the Hindu doctrine of the four ages (*Yugas*), which together make up a complete world-cycle. We now live in the Kali Age, which is said to have begun with the death of Krishna shortly after the Mahabharata War (c. 1500-1000 B.C.). Cf. Vishnu Purana 4.24, pp. 777, 786; Linga Purana 1.40.72-83, p. 792; Bhagavad Gita 8.17-21, p. 78.

**Tao Te Ching 38:** On the harmony of the ancient golden age of the Great Tao, or Grand Unity, cf. Book of Ritual 7.1.2, pp. 200-1; Tao Te Ching 18-19, p. 201; Chuang Tzu 9, p. 224.

# Demonic Powers

THE SCRIPTURES OF ALL RELIGIONS testify to demonic beings and powers. Some regard them as real and rival powers to God (dualism); others consider them to be a manifestation of ignorance and ultimately unreal (monism). They testify that at their head is a chief, known by various names: Satan, Beelzebul, Lucifer, Iblis, Mara, and Angra Mainyu, among others. We have already met some of them in the various accounts of the human fall and the origin of evil. But the demonic powers are continually active, drawing people's hearts to do wickedness. While rationalists have difficulty accepting the reality of the devil, merely looking at the horrors of the twentieth century causes one to realize that the capability of human beings to inflict evil on one another transcends the realm of reason. Scriptures teach that when a person has the desire to do a small evil, the devil has a claim and may influence him to do something far worse. Conversely, many people on the religious path experience the temptations of the devil precisely at the point when they are about to make great progress in the path.

We begin with descriptions of the Evil One from the texts of many religions. Some emphasize the devil's power, some his enmity to God, and some his wrong teachings. Some identify him with death and disease, others with lusts and selfish desires. We then include two passages, one from Zoroastrianism and one from Native American religions, which describe a dualism in which the Evil One creates all evil in the world to counter God's good creation. However, for the monotheistic faiths that emphasize the goodness of God's creation, the demons themselves are resultant beings who must have fallen from being good creations of God. Thus, the following group of passages in this section portray the fall of the angels. A fourth selection of passages treats the theme of the devil's disguise as a being of light, including texts on the devil's positive role to test and prove the faith of human beings. Finally, we give texts on the devil's temptations and the manner in which people make themselves vulnerable to his influence.

The Evil Ruler spoils the Word,
The plan of life, by his teachings.
He, indeed, deprives me
Of the exalted goal of Good Thought.
With the word of my spirit,
I pray to You, O Wise One, and to truth!

*Zoroastrianism*. Avesta, Yasna 32.9

O believers, follow not the steps of Satan; for whoever follows the steps of Satan will assuredly be bid to indecency and dishonor. But for God's bounty to you and His mercy not one of you would have been pure ever; but God purifies whom He will; and God is All-hearing, All-knowing.

*Islam*. Qur'an 24.21

Jesus said to them... "Why do you not understand what I say? It is because you cannot bear to hear my word. You are of your father the devil, and your will is to do your father's desires. He was a murderer from the beginning, and has nothing to do with the truth, because there is no truth in him. When he lies, it is

**Yasna 32.9:** See Videvdad 19.1-7, pp. 445-46; cf. 2 Corinthians 4.4, p. 283.
**Qur'an 24.21:** Cf. Qur'an 4.116-17, p. 287; 4.118-20, p. 322.

according to his own nature, for he is a liar and the father of lies. But, because I tell the truth, you do not believe me."

*Christianity*. John 8.43-45

For we are not contending against flesh and blood, but against the principalities, against the powers, against the world rulers of this present darkness, against the spiritual hosts of wickedness in the heavenly places.

*Christianity*. Ephesians 6.12

The foremost of your armies is that of Desire, the second is called Dislike. The third is Hunger-thirst and the fourth is Craving. The fifth is the army of Lethargy-laziness and the sixth is Fear. The seventh is Doubt and the eighth is Obstinacy-restlessness. Then there are Material Gain, Praise, Honor, and Fame... These, O Mara, are your forces, the attackers of the Evil One. One less than a hero will not be victorious over them and attain happiness.

*Buddhism*. Sutta Nipata 436-39

The Essence of Mind or Suchness is the real
Buddha,
While heretical views and the three poisonous
elements [greed, anger, delusion] are Mara.
Enlightened by right views, we call forth the
Buddha within us.
When our nature is dominated by the three
poisonous elements
We are said to be possessed by the devil;
But when right views eliminate from our mind
these poisonous elements
The devil will be transformed into a real
Buddha.

*Buddhism*. Sutra of Hui Neng 10

You, trees, hear my words, and you, grass, hear my words, and you, Divinity, hear my words, and you, earth, hear my words. Repeat, ee! O Divinity, because of sickness, you help out my tongue. For we have dedicated the ox and invoked over it. And if a man has hated Akol [and his sickness is the result of malice] then that man will find what he deserves.... And you, ox, we have given you to the Power [the illness]. And you fetish-bundles, they say that you kill people. Leave off, you are shamed. You fetish, I have separated you, cease! And you, Macardit, they say that you kill people, I have separated you, cease! Thus!

*African Traditional Religions*. Dinka Invocation at an Ox Sacrifice (Sudan)

Seated on his golden throne, blazing like flame, Ravana resembled a great fire kindled on an altar kept alive by sacrificial offerings. Unconquered by gods, gandharvas, rishis or other creatures, that warrior, who resembled death itself with wide-open jaws, bore on his person the wounds inflicted by the thunderbolts in the war between gods and titans... He, the scourge of the gods, who transgressed every moral law, the ravisher of others' wives, the wielder of celestial weapons, the destroyer of sacrifices, who descended into the city of Bhogavati and subdued the serpent Vasuki, from whom, on his defeat, he stole the gentle consort; he who scaled Mount Kailasha and overcame Kuvera depriving him of his aerial chariot Pushpaka, which transported him wherever he desired; he who in his anger destroyed the garden of Chaitraratha, the lotus pool and the Nandana Grove and all the pleasurable retreats of the gods... proud of his strength, he stole the Soma juice, sanctified by mantras, before its pressing by the twice-born

**John 8.43-45:** Cf. Matthew 12.22-24, p. 265.

**Sutta Nipata 436-39:** Cf. Buddhacarita 13, pp. 446-47.

**Sutra of Hui Neng 10:** Buddhism traditionally identifies Mara with cravings and delusions, the nature of our own (evil) mind, just as Buddha is within us, the nature of our own true mind. Cf. Dhammapada 46, p. 231.

**Dinka Invocation:** An ox is being sacrificed in order to propitiate the evil powers that are causing illness in a man named Akol. These evil powers include Macardit, the malign divinity who is for the Dinka the final cause of suffering and death. A *fetish* is a bundle of medicine imbued with black magic. It is used to gain influence over another person or cause him harm. But if the owner of a fetish neglects it, its magic will come back upon his head.

in the sacrifice; this perverse wretch, Ravana of evil deeds, slayer of the brahmins, ruthless, pitiless, delighting in causing harm to others, was verily a source of terror to all beings.

*Hinduism.*
Ramayana, Aranya Kanda 32

The first of the good lands and countries which I, Ahura Mazda, created, was Paradise, by the good river Araxes. Thereupon came Angra Mainyu, who is all death, and he counter-created by his witchcraft the serpent in the river and winter, a work of the devils.

The second of the good lands and countries which I, Ahura Mazda, created, was the plains in Samarkand. Thereupon came Angra Mainyu, who is all death, and he counter-created by his witchcraft the fly Skaitya, which brings death to the cattle.

The third of the good lands and countries which I, Ahura Mazda, created, was the strong, holy Merv. Thereupon came Angra Mainyu, who is all death, and he counter-created by his witchcraft sinful lusts....

The eighth of the good lands and countries which I, Ahura Mazda, created, was Urva of the rich pastures. Thereupon came Angra Mainyu, who is all death, and he counter-created by his witchcraft the sin of pride.

*Zoroastrianism.* Videvdad 1.3-11

Many winters in the past, the Earth was entirely covered by a great blanket of water. There was no sun, moon, or stars and so there was no light. All was darkness. At that time, the only living creatures of the earth were water animals such as the beaver, muskrat, duck, and loon. Far above the earth was the Land of Happy Spirits where lived Rawennio, the Great Ruler. In the center of this upper world was a giant apple tree whose roots sank deep into the ground.

One day, Rawennio pulled this giant tree up by its roots. The Great Spirit called his daughter, who lived in the Upper World, and commanded her to look into the pit caused by the uprooted tree. This woman, who was to be the mother of the Good and Evil Spirits, came and looked into the hole by the uprooted tree. She saw far below her the Lower World covered with water and surrounded by heavy clouds. "You are to go to this world of darkness," said the Great Spirit. Gently lifting her, he dropped her into the hole. She floated downward....

[The water animals then dive beneath the water to find some dry land for her to land upon; they erect the land on the back of a giant turtle.]

After a time, the Sky Woman gave birth to twins. One, who became the Good Spirit, was born first. The other, the Evil Spirit, while being born, caused her mother so much pain that she died during his birth.

The Good Spirit immediately took his mother's head and hung it in the sky. It became the sun. From his mother's body he fashioned the moon and stars and placed them in the sky. The rest of his mother's body he buried under the earth. That is why living things find nourishment in the soil. They spring from Mother Earth.

The Evil Spirit put darkness in the western sky to drive the sun before it.

The Good Spirit created many things which he placed upon the earth. The Evil Spirit tried to undo the work of his brother by creating evil. The Good Spirit made tall and beautiful trees such as the pine and hemlock. The Evil Spirit stunted some trees. In others he put knots and gnarls. He covered some with thorns, and placed poison fruit on them. The Good Spirit made animals such as the deer and the bear. The Evil Spirit made poisonous animals, lizards and serpents to destroy the animals of the Good Spirit's creation. The Good Spirit made springs and streams of good, pure water. The Evil Spirit breathed poison into many of the springs. He put snakes into others. The Good Spirit made beautiful rivers protected by high hills. The Evil Spirit pushed rocks

**Ramayana, Aranya Kanda 32:** Ravana is the chief of the demons, who terrorizes the worlds of gods and humans. Rama, the avatar of Vishnu, appears on earth to defeat him. Cf. Ramayana, Bala Kanda 15, pp. 447-48.

**Videvdad 1.3-11:** Cf. Yasna 30.3-5, p. 276.

and dirt into the rivers causing the current to become swift and dangerous. Everything that the Good Spirit made, his wicked brother tried to destroy.

Finally, when the earth was completed, the Good Spirit fashioned man out of some red clay. He placed man upon the earth, and told him how he should live. The Evil Spirit, not to be outdone, fashioned a creature out of the white foam of the sea. What he made was the monkey.

After mankind and the other creatures of the world were created, the Good Spirit bestowed a protecting spirit upon each of his creations. He then called the Evil Spirit, and told him that he must cease making trouble upon the earth. This the Evil Spirit refused to do. The Good Spirit became very angry with his wicked brother and challenged him to combat, the victor to become ruler of the earth. They fought for many days; finally the Evil Spirit was overcome. The Good Spirit now became ruler over the earth. He banished his wicked brother to a dark cave under the earth. There he must always remain.

But the Evil Spirit has wicked servants who roam the earth. These wicked spirits can take the shape of any creature that the Evil Spirit desires them to take. They are constantly influencing the minds of men, thus causing men to do evil things. The Good Spirit continues to create and protect mankind. He controls the spirits of good men after death. The Evil Spirit takes charge of the souls of wicked men after death.

That is why every person has both a bad heart and a good heart. No matter how good a man seems, he has some evil. No matter how bad a man seems, there is some good about him. No man is perfect.

*Native American Religions.*
Mohawk Tradition

How you are fallen from heaven,
O Lucifer, son of the morning!
How you are cut down to the ground,
you who weakened the nations!
For you said in your heart,
"I will ascend into heaven,
I will exalt my throne above the stars of God;
I will sit also upon the mount of the
congregation,
in the recesses of the north;
I will ascend above the heights of the clouds;
I will be like the Most High."
Yet you shall be brought down to hell,
to the depths of the pit.

*Judaism* and *Christianity.*
Isaiah 14.12-15

And when We said to the angels, "Bow yourselves to Adam," they bowed themselves, save Iblis; he said, "Shall I bow myself to one whom You have created of clay?" He said, "What do you think? This [creature] whom You have honored above me, if You defer me until the Day of Resurrection I shall assuredly master his seed, save a few."

Said He, "Depart! Those of them that follow you—surely hell shall be your recompense, an

**Isaiah 14.12-15:** In the Christian tradition these verses are taken to describe the primeval fall of Lucifer and the beginning of sin. Lucifer was the angel of the intellect who was puffed up with willful pride. His ambition was to exceed God. But he was cast down from heaven and became Satan, who would then work his malignant will on humankind. This story of the primeval rebellion of the angels is greatly elaborated in the Book of Enoch. The word 'Lucifer,' which is Latin for Light-bearer, was first used in the Vulgate; and this name for the devil passed into English-speaking Christianity through the King James version. However most modern Bibles return to the Hebrew and translate Morning Star or Day Star. This passage lies within a taunt by the prophet Isaiah against the king of Babylon. He made use of a Canaanite variant of the myth of the rebellious angel, one which identified the angel with the atmospheric phenomenon of the morning star which shines brightly in the sky until it is quenched by the brightness of the rising sun. Cf. Psalm 82, pp. 263-64.

ample recompense! And startle any of them whom you can with your voice; and rally against them your horsemen and your foot [soldiers], and share with them in their wealth and their children, and promise them!"

But Satan promises them naught, except delusion.

*Islam.* Qur'an 17.61-64

The Lord God spoke to Moses, saying, "That Satan... is the same who was from the beginning, and he came before me, saying, 'Behold, here am I; send me, I will be thy son, and I will redeem all mankind, that not one soul shall be lost. Surely I will do it; therefore give me my honor.'

"But my Beloved Son, who was my Beloved and Chosen from the beginning, said to me, 'Father, thy will be done, and the glory be thine forever.'

"Therefore, because that Satan rebelled against me, and sought to destroy the agency of man, which I, the Lord God, had given him, and also, that I should give to him my own power; by the power of my Only Begotten [Christ], I caused that he should be cast down;

"And he became Satan, yea, even the devil, the father of all lies, to deceive and to blind men, and to lead them captive at his will, even as many as would not hearken unto my voice."

*Church of Jesus Christ of Latter-day Saints.*
Pearl of Great Price, Moses 4.1-4

The gods and the demons, both having the Creator as their origin, were rivals of each other. So the demons, swollen with pride, said, "In what, pray, should we place the oblation?" And they proceeded to place the oblation in their own mouths. The gods then proceeded to place their oblations each in the mouth of one of his fellows. And the Creator gave himself over to them. In this way they became owners of sacrifice, for sacrifice is really the food of the gods.

*Hinduism.*
Satapatha Brahmana 5.1.1.1-2

Even Satan disguises himself as an angel of light.

*Christianity.* 2 Corinthians 11.14

Mara the Evil One will expound to the bodhisattva a counterfeit of the Path.

*Buddhism.*
Large Sutra on Perfect Wisdom 382

O men, God's promise is true; so let not the present life delude you, and let not the Deluder delude you concerning God. Surely Satan is an enemy to you; so take him for an enemy. He calls his party only that they may be among the inhabitants of the Fire.

*Islam.* Qur'an 35.5-6

When I first heard Buddha preaching the
Greater Vehicle,
In my heart I was greatly alarmed:
"Surely Mara is playing Buddha,
Confusing my thoughts!"
The Buddha by resort to various means,

**Qur'an 17.61-64:** Cf. Qur'an 2.30-33, p. 218; Qur'an 7.11-27, p. 302; Srimad Bhagavatam 11.20, p. 265; Brihadaranyaka Upanishad 1.4.10, p. 287.

**Pearl of Great Price, Moses 4.1-4:** Satan's request to God contained two errors: he wanted to claim all the glory and credit for man's salvation when credit is due only to God, and he would save humanity by compulsion—'not one soul shall be lost,' without regard for man's free agency. Christ, the Beloved Son, correctly offers to God the credit for salvation. God then ordered Christ to cast Satan down to the earth, where he continues to seek to enslave humankind. Cf. Book of Mormon, 2 Nephi 2.19-26, pp. 303-4.

**Satapatha Brahmana 5.1.1.1-2:** There are two orders of spiritual beings: gods and demons; cf. Bhagavad Gita 16.6, p. 276; Vishnu Purana 3.17-18, p. 318. The chief difference between demons and gods is that the demons are self-centered while the gods are generous and share with others.

**2 Corinthians 11.14:** Cf. 1 John 4.1, p. 265; Srimad Bhagavatam 11.20, p. 265; Sun Myung Moon, 1-1-68, p. 595.

**Large Sutra on Perfect Wisdom 382:** Cf. Perfection of Wisdom in Eight Thousand Lines 17.2, p. 317.

**Qur'an 35.5-6:** Cf. Qur'an 22.52-53, pp. 444-45.

Parables, and cunning phrases preaches,
But his thought is as calm as the sea;
When I hear him, my net of doubt is severed....

The World-honored One preaches the Real Path,
While Mara has none of this.
By this token I know for a certainty
That this is no Mara playing Buddha,
But that I, through having fallen into a net of doubt,
Thought this was the work of Mara.
When I hear the Buddha's gentle voice,
Profound, far removed from the ordinary understanding, and extremely subtle,
Setting forth the pure Dharma,
My heart is overjoyed,
My doubts and second thoughts are cleared away forever.

*Buddhism.* Lotus Sutra 3

The Maras who play the devil in the innumerable universes of the ten directions are all bodhisattvas dwelling in the Inconceivable Liberation, who are playing the devil in order to develop living beings through their skill in liberative technique. Those miserable beggars who come to the bodhisattvas to ask for a hand, a foot, an ear, a nose... a kingdom, a wife, a son, gold, silver, jewels... these demanding beggars are usually bodhisattvas living in the Inconceivable Liberation who, through their skill in liberative technique, wish to test and thus demonstrate the firmness of the high resolve of the bodhisattvas. Why? Bodhisattvas must demonstrate that firmness by means of terrible austerities.

*Buddhism.* Holy Teaching of Vimalakirti 6

Now there was a day when the sons of God came to present themselves before the Lord, and Satan also came among them. The Lord said to Satan, "Whence have you come?" Satan answered the Lord, "From going to and fro on the earth, and from walking up and down on it." And the Lord said to Satan, "Have you considered my servant Job, that there is none like him on the earth, a blameless and upright man, who fears God and turns away from evil?" Then Satan answered the Lord, "Does Job fear God for naught? Hast thou not put a hedge about him and his house and all that he has, on every side? Thou hast blessed the work of his hands, and his possessions have increased in the land. But put forth thy hand now, and touch all that he has, and he will curse thee to thy face." And the Lord said to Satan, "Behold, all that he has is in your power."

*Judaism* and *Christianity*. Job 1.6-12

Be sober, be watchful. Your adversary the devil prowls around like a roaring lion, seeking some one to devour.

*Christianity*. 1 Peter 5.8

**Lotus Sutra 3:** The 'Greater Vehicle' is the teaching of the Lotus Sutra, the doctrine of the One Vehicle. Shariputra's initial doubts were due to the novelty of the Sutra's teaching. For a story where Mara in fact comes in disguise to give a false teaching, see Samyutta Nikaya i.128, p. 194. On discerning the spirit, cf. 1 John 4.1, p. 265.

**Holy Teaching of Vimalakirti 6:** This passage explains that the Maras and other temptations are not to be seen as fundamentally evil, but should rather be appreciated as offering trials and lessons to humans on the path to enlightenment. They may even be liberated bodhisattvas disguised as Maras as an expedient device (*upaya*) for the purpose of guiding and educating living beings. According to Udana 21-24, p. 720, even the Buddha once tempted his disciple Nanda with visions of heavenly damsels in order to spur him to enlightenment. For another instance of a bodhisattva's deception, see Mahaparinirvana Sutra 424-33, pp. 538-39. On the unreality of evil, cf. Nectarean Shower of Holy Doctrines, p. 285; Science and Health, 480, p. 284.

**Job 1.6-12:** In Job, as in the previous Buddhist passage, the devil is not fundamentally evil and opposed to God, but is rather the one whom God allows to test Job's integrity. In proving Job, Satan is serving a divine purpose. For more of this story, and Job's legendary patience, see Job 1.13-22, p. 532; 2.7-10, p. 506. God often tries people through confronting them with evils; cf. 2 Corinthians 12.7-10, p. 405, on Paul's thorn; Genesis Rabbah 56, p. 445, on the temptation of Abraham; and Qur'an 21.35, p. 404.

**1 Peter 5.8:** Cf. Sun Myung Moon, 1-1-68, p. 595.

One of the nights [when I "lamented"] the bad spirits came and started tearing the offerings off the poles; and I heard their voices under the ground, and one of them said, "Go and see if he is crying." And I heard rattles, but all the time they were outside the sacred place and could not get in, for I had resolved not to be afraid, and did not stop sending my voice to Wakan-Tanka for aid.

*Native American Religions.* Black Elk, Sioux Tradition

When a man grasps at things, Mara stands beside him.

*Buddhism.* Sutta Nipata 1103

The Lord said to Cain, "Why are you angry, and why has your countenance fallen? If you do well, will you not be accepted? And if you do not do well, sin is couching at the door; its desire is for you, but you must master it."

*Judaism* and *Christianity.* Genesis 4.6-7

The Messenger of God said, "There is none among you with whom is not an attache from among the jinn." The Companions said, "With you, too?" He said, "Yes, but God helps me against him and so I am safe from his hand."

*Islam.* Hadith of Muslim

And Satan says, when the issue is decided, "God surely promised you a true promise; I also promised you, then I failed you, for I had no authority over you, but that I called you, and you answered me. So do not blame me, blame yourselves."

*Islam.* Qur'an 14.22

"We do not do all the evil that we do because of our own desire," said the rakshasa. "It is because of your evil karma, and your disfavor toward us. Our faction increases because of the brahmins who behave like rakshasas and the evil actions of the other three classes. Those who dishonor brahmins become rakshasas, and their ranks are swelled by the sexual sins of evil women."

*Hinduism.* Vamana Purana 19.31-35

Whoever lives contemplating pleasant things, with senses unrestrained, in food immoderate, indolent, inactive, him verily Mara overthrows, as the wind blows down a weak tree.

Whoever lives contemplating the impurities of the body, with senses restrained, in food moderate, full of faith, full of sustained energy, him Mara overthrows not, as the wind cannot shake a rocky mountain.

*Buddhism.* Dhammapada 7-8

Shall I inform you on whom it is that the devils descend? They descend on every lying, wicked person, into whose ears they pour hearsay vanities, and most of them are liars. And the poets—it is those straying in Evil, who follow them: do you not see them wandering distracted in every valley? They preach what they never practice.

*Islam.* Qur'an 26.221-26

Endowed with two dharmas does the bodhisattva become one hard to assail by the evil Maras: He surveys all phenomena from Emptiness, and does not abandon any being. Endowed with two other dharmas does the bodhisattva become one hard to assail by the evil Maras: as he speaks so he acts, and he is brought to mind by the Buddhas, the Lords.

*Buddhism.* Large Sutra on Perfect Wisdom 431

**Genesis 4.6-7:** Cf. Mahabharata, p. 278.
**Hadith of Muslim:** Cf. Qur'an 114, p. 32.
**Qur'an 14.22:** Cf. Qur'an 5.105, p. 488.

## *Heresy*

AMONG THE MOST INSIDIOUS CAUSES of deviation from the religious path is the lure of false teaching, or heresy. The scriptures of every major religion warn against it. "Heresy" means opinion, and the wisdom of orthodox tradition is not something to be denied or perverted on the basis of mere opinion. The orthodox tradition carries with it the deposit of wisdom inherited from the founders, prophets, saints, and sages who have had the surest and deepest insight into truth. It is rare that a novel teaching can hope to attain the same level of insight.

Yet every genuine religion, when it was first born, was branded a heresy by the leaders of the orthodox establishment. The founders of religion gave their teachings based on profound religious insights or new revelation, not mere opinion. But how could members of the establishment orthodoxy know that? How, beyond the criterion of orthodoxy, do we distinguish a false teaching from a true one? This requires careful discernment.

The fundamental error of heresy is that it deceives innocent people by leading them to deny the truth. A number of the passages gathered below also attack false prophets and heretics for having base motives: They are hypocrites using religion for worldly gain (although orthodox teachers could have the same flaw). Others point to their rotten fruits: licentious living, greed, and the sowing of dissension. Still others attribute these false teachings to the work of demons and evil spirits. But some heresies deceive through advocating a standard of conduct even more austere or a faith even more extreme than what is called for in the correct path. These selections conclude with two examples: First is the schism of the Buddhist order led by Devadatta, who advocated extreme austerities beyond those of the Middle Path. The second is the conflict between Jeremiah and the false prophet Hananiah; while Jeremiah expected God to judge Israel for its sins, Hananiah had such extreme "faith" that he believed God would defend Jerusalem at all costs.

Beware of false prophets, who come to you in sheep's clothing but inwardly are ravenous wolves. You will know them by their fruits.

*Christianity*. Matthew 7.15-16

God's Messenger is reported as saying, "In the last times men will come forth who will fraudulently use religion for worldly ends and wear sheepskins in public to display meekness. Their tongues will be sweeter than sugar, but their hearts will be the hearts of wolves. God will say, 'Are they trying to deceive Me, or are they acting presumptuously towards Me? I swear by Myself that I shall send trial upon those people which will leave the intelligent men among them confounded.'"

*Islam*. Hadith of Tirmidhi

The prophets who lead my people astray,
who cry "Peace" when they have something to eat,
but declare war against him who puts nothing into their mouths.

*Judaism* and *Christianity*. Micah 3.5

There will be false teachers among you, who will secretly bring in destructive heresies, even denying the Master who brought them, bring-

**Matthew 7.15-16:** Cf. Matthew 7.16-20, p. 330; 1 John 4.1, p. 265.

ing upon themselves swift destruction. And many will follow their licentiousness, and because of them the way of truth will be reviled. And in their greed they will exploit you with false words; from of old their condemnation has not been idle, and their destruction has not been asleep.

*Christianity.* 2 Peter 2.1-3

Some shameless men, becoming monks, propagate a doctrine of their own. And others believe in it, put their faith in it, adopt it, saying, "Well, you speak the truth, O brahmin or O shramana! We shall present you with food, drink, spices, and sweetmeats, with a robe, a bowl, or a broom." Some have induced others to honor them, and some have made their proselytes to honor them. Before, they were determined to become [genuine] shramanas, poor monks who would have neither sons nor cattle, to eat only what should be given them by others, and to commit no sins. But after having entered the religious life they do not cease from committing sins, they cause others to commit sins, and they assent to another's committing sins. Thus they are given to pleasures, amusements, and sensual lust; they are greedy, fettered, passionate, covetous, the slaves of love and hate; therefore they cannot free themselves nor free anyone else.

*Jainism.* Sutrakritanga 2.1.18-19

Thus have We appointed unto every Prophet an adversary—devils of humankind and jinn—who inspire in one another plausible discourse through guile.

*Islam.* Qur'an 6.112

Now the Spirit expressly says that in later times some will depart from the faith by giving heed to deceitful spirits and doctrines of demons, through the pretensions of liars whose consciences are seared.

*Christianity.* 1 Timothy 4.1-2

Brahma and Vishnu were arguing, each shouting that he was supreme. In anger, Brahma cursed Vishnu, "You will be deluded and your devotees will have the appearance of brahmins, but they will be against the Vedas and the true path of release."

*Hinduism.* Paraśara Purana 3

Mara, the Evil One, may come along in the guise of a teacher, and say, "Give up what you have heard up to now!... What you have heard just now, that is not the word of the Buddha. It is poetry, the work of poets. But what I here teach to you, that is the teaching of the Buddha, that is the word of the Buddha." If, on hearing that, a bodhisattva wavers and is put out, then one should know that he has not been predicted by the Tathagata, that he is not fixed on full enlightenment. But... an arhat, a monk whose outflows are dried up, does not go by someone else whom he puts his trust in, for he has placed the nature of Dharma directly before his own eyes.

*Buddhism.* Perfection of Wisdom in Eight Thousand Lines 17.2

Indeed, the causes of discord and rebellion against religion are that in opposition to the laid-down orders of the Book of God, people follow dictates of their mind and introduce innovations and schism. Consequently, in spite of the commands of God, such persons are considered heads of religion who know nothing about religion.

The fact is, had falsehood been allowed to show separately from truth, seekers of truth would have easily discerned it, and would have kept away from falsehood. And had truth been

**Sutrakritanga 2.1.18-19:** Cf. Mark 7.6-7, p. 348.

**1 Timothy 4.1-2:** Cf. 1 John 4.1, p. 265.

**Parasara Purana 3:** In this passage the sectarian feuds in Hinduism—here the devotees of the Vaishnavite bhakti sects are labelled heretics—have their origins in quarrels among the gods. The very human quarrels and jealousies of the gods in Hindu popular traditions should be counterpoised with the philosophical vedic and upanishadic doctrine that all the gods are transcendentally One.

**Perfection of Wisdom in Eight Thousand Lines 17.2:** Cf. Large Sutra on Perfect Wisdom 382, p. 313.

allowed to appear distinct from falsehood, people would not have found [it] easy to criticize religion. But unfortunately men started mixing parts of truth with falsehood, and Satan exploited this situation, and got complete control over the minds of its followers. Only such persons can escape its trap, who have advanced with the help of God towards sober and rational ways of meditation.

*Islam.* Nahjul Balagha, Sermon 55

Be not those who ascribe partners unto God—those who split up their religion and become schismatics, each sect exulting in its tenets.

*Islam.* Qur'an 30.31-32

The demons, led by Prahlada, had stolen the sacrificial portions of the gods, but they were so full of svadharma, Vedic worship, and asceticism that they could not be conquered. Vishnu created a man of delusion to lead the demons from the path of the Vedas; the man was naked, bald, carrying a peacock feather fan; he went where the demons were practicing asceticism at the banks of the Narmada and made them all into arhats, discouraging them from their asceticism and teaching them contradictory tenets about dharma.... Then the man put on red garments and taught the rest of the demons that the sacrifice of animals was an evil act. He taught, "If the animal slaughtered in the sacrifice is assured of arrival in heaven, why does the sacrificer not kill his own father?" Then the demons became Buddhists, and they caused others to become heretics, abandoning the Vedas and reviling the gods and brahmins, discarding their armor of svadharma. The gods attacked them and killed them.

*Hinduism.* Vishnu Purana 3.17-18

As Devadatta was meditating in private, a reasoning arose in his mind thus, "Whom could I now please so that, because he is pleased with me, much gain and honor would accrue to me?" And he thought of Prince Ajatasattu. Throwing off his own form and assuming that of a young boy clad in a girdle of snakes, he became manifest in the prince's lap. Terrified, he asked who he was.

"I am Devadatta."

"If that is really so, please become manifest in your own form." And Devadatta, throwing off the young boy's form stood, wearing his outer cloak and his robes and carrying his bowl, before Prince Ajatasattu. Greatly pleased with this wonder of psychic power, morning and evening he went to wait on him with five hundred chariots, bringing five hundred offerings of rice cooked in milk as a gift of food. And in Devadatta, overcome by the gains, honors, and fame, his mind obsessed by them, there arose the longing to be the one to lead the Order of monks. But at its very occurrence Devadatta declined in his psychic power.

Moggallana then warned the Lord of Devadatta's longing. He replied, "Moggallana, this foolish man of himself will now betray himself. The teacher who is not pure in moral habit, or in mode of livelihood, or in teaching Dhamma, or in the exposition, or in the vision of knowledge... pretends that he is pure, and that his moral habit, etc., are pure, clean, untarnished. Although disciples know this about him, they think, 'If we should tell this to householders, he would not like it, and how could we speak about what he would would not like? Moreover [by his reputation] we receive the requisite of robes, alms food, lodgings, and medicines...' Disciples protect such a teacher

**Qur'an 30.31-32:** The schismatic, by exalting in human opinions, is in effect joining other gods with God.

**Vishnu Purana 3.17-18:** In Vaishnavite Hinduism, the Buddha is regarded as an avatar of Vishnu who teaches heresy in order to delude the demons. Thus, begrudgingly, Buddha is honored as a savior against the demons while his teaching is condemned. In this passage the Buddha avatar is a composite figure: he walks naked like a Jain, and he also teaches a second heresy recognizable as Materialism by its satire on the traditional rationalization for animal sacrifices. In this case, as in Mahabharata, Anusasana Parva 40, p. 307, and Srimad Bhagavatam 11.20, p. 265, spiritual beings of high status are jealous of other beings with superior virtue; compare Brihadaranyaka Upanishad 1.4.10, p. 287; Isaiah 14.12-15, p. 312; Qur'an 17.61-64, pp. 312-13. In Hinduism, traditions about demons aspiring for divinity are often metaphors for people of inferior caste aspiring to a destiny beyond their station; sometimes they are successful—cf. Matsya Purana 180.5, p. 508, and Vishnu Purana 1.17-20, pp. 635-36—but in this case their aspirations are foiled.

and such a teacher expects protection from them. But I, Moggallana, am pure in moral habit, in mode of livelihood... Disciples do not protect me and I do not expect protection from them.

"Do not, monks, envy Devadatta's gains, honors, and fame. For as long as Prince Ajatasattu goes to him morning and evening, Devadatta's wholesome mental states may be expected to decline, not to grow, just as a fierce dog would become much fiercer if a bladder were thrown at his nose. Devadatta's gains, honors and fame bring about his own hurt and destruction."

Now at that time the Lord was sitting down teaching Dhamma surrounded by a large company which included a king. And Devadatta got up, saluted the Lord and spoke thus, "Lord, the Lord is now old, stricken in years and at the close of his life. Let him be content to abide in ease here and now, and hand over the Order of monks to me. It is I who will lead the Order of monks."

"Enough, Devadatta, please do not lead the Order of monks. I would not hand over the Order even to Sariputta and Moggallana. How then to you, a wretched one to be vomited up like spittle?"

And Devadatta, angry and displeased at having been disparaged, went away. The Lord addressed the Order of monks, saying, "Let the Order carry out a formal act of information against Devadatta, to the effect that whereas Devadatta's nature was formerly of one kind, now it is of another; and that whatever he should do by gesture or by voice, in that neither the Buddha nor the Dhamma nor the Order is to be seen, but only Devadatta."

On hearing the news Devadatta sought to deprive the recluse Gotama of life. He saw the Lord pacing up and down in the shade of Mount Vulture Peak, and having climbed it he hurled down a great stone. But two mountain peaks, meeting, crushed it and only a fragment fell down; but it drew blood on the Lord's foot. Looking upward he said to Devadatta, "You have produced much demerit, foolish man, in that you, with your mind malignant and set on murder, drew the Tathagata's blood."

Then Devadatta appealed to some friends of his, saying, "Come, we will approach the Lord and ask for five policies, saying, 'Lord, the Lord in many a figure speaks in praise of desiring little, of being contented, of expunging evil, of being punctilious, etc. Lord, the following five policies are conducive thereto: Monks must be forest dwellers for as long as they live; whoever should abide in a village, sin would besmirch him. They must be beggars for alms; whoever should accept an invitation to a meal would commit sin. They should wear rags; whoever accepts a robe given by a householder, commits sin. They should dwell at the root of a tree; whoever should go under cover commits sin. They should never eat fish and flesh; whoever eats fish or flesh commits sin.' The recluse Gotama will not allow these five policies, but we will win the people over to them."

Devadatta's friends replied, "It is possible, with these five policies, to make a schism in the recluse Gotama's Order, a breaking of the concord. For, your reverence, people esteem austerity."

So Devadatta and his friends approached the Lord, and put the matter of these five policies before him.

"Enough, Devadatta," he said. "Whoever wishes, let him be a forest dweller, whoever wishes, let him stay near a village; whoever wishes, let him be a beggar for alms; whoever wishes, let him accept an invitation; whoever wishes, let him wear rags; whoever wishes, let him accept robes given by a householder..."

Devadatta was joyful and elated that the Lord did not accept these five policies. He entered Rajagaha and taught them to the people, and such people as were of little faith thought that Devadatta and his friends were punctilious while Gotama was permissive of profligacy. But the people who had faith and were believing complained to the monks that Devadatta was creating a schism, and the monks told the Lord. He said to Devadatta, who acknowledged the truth of the complaint,

"Do not let there be a schism in the Order, for a schism in the Order is a serious matter, Devadatta. He who splits an Order that is united sets up demerit that endures for an eon and he is boiled in hell for an eon. But he who unites an Order that is split sets up sublime merit and rejoices in heaven for an eon."

*Buddhism*. Vinaya Pitaka ii.184-98

In the beginning of the reign of Zedekiah the son of Josiah, king of Judah, this word came to Jeremiah from the Lord. Thus the Lord said to me, "Make yourself thongs and yoke-bars, and put them on your neck. Send word to... Zedekiah king of Judah, 'Bring your necks under the yoke of the king of Babylon, and serve him and his people, and live. Why will you and your people die by the sword, by famine, and by pestilence, as the Lord has spoken concerning any nation which will not serve the king of Babylon? Do not listen to the words of the prophets who are saying to you, "You shall not serve the king of Babylon, for it is a lie which they are prophesying to you. 'I have not sent them, says the Lord, but they are prophesying falsely in my name, with the result that I will drive you out and you will perish, you and the prophets who are prophesying to you.'"

In that same year... Hananiah the son of Azzur, the prophet from Gibeon, spoke to me in the House of the Lord, in the presence of the priests and all the people, saying, "Thus says the Lord of Hosts, the God of Israel, I have broken the yoke of the king of Babylon. Within two years I will bring back to this place all the vessels of the Lord's House, which Nebuchadnezzar king of Babylon took away from this place and carried to Babylon. I will also bring back to this place Jeconiah the son of Jehoiakim, king of Judah, and all the exiles from Judah who went to Babylon, says the Lord, for I will break the yoke of the king of Babylon."

Then Jeremiah the prophet spoke to Hananiah the prophet in the presence of the priests and all the people who were standing in the House of the Lord; and the prophet Jeremiah said, "Amen! May the Lord do so; may the Lord make the words which you have prophesied come true, and bring back to this place from Babylon the vessels of the House of the Lord, and all the exiles. Yet hear now this word which I speak in your hearing and the hearing of all the people: The prophets who preceded you and me from ancient times prophesied war, famine, and pestilence against many countries and great kingdoms. As for the prophet who prophesies peace, when the word of that prophet comes to pass, then it will be known that the Lord has truly sent the prophet."

Then the prophet Hananiah took the yoke-bars from the neck of Jeremiah the prophet, and broke them. And Hananiah spoke in the presence of all the people, saying, "Thus says the Lord, 'Even so will I break the yoke of Nebuchadnezzar king of Babylon from the neck of all the nations within two years.'" But Jeremiah the prophet went his way.

Sometime after... Jeremiah the prophet said to the prophet Hananiah, "Listen, Hananiah, the Lord has not sent you, and you have made this people trust in a lie. Therefore thus says the Lord, 'Behold, I will remove you from the face of the earth. This very year you shall die, because you have uttered rebellion against the Lord.'" In that same year, in the seventh month, the prophet Hananiah died.

*Judaism* and *Christianity*.
Jeremiah 27-28

❖

**Vinaya Pitaka ii.184-98:** Cf. Itivuttaka 11, p. 188; Digha Nikaya i.167, p. 672. King Ajatasattu (Skt. Ajatasatru) is later healed by the Buddha; see Mahaparinirvana Sutra 575-76, p. 375.

# Degraded Human Nature

HUMAN NATURE HAS FALLEN far from the ideal of love and holiness which is exalted by the world's religions. In previous chapters, we have gathered passages which testify to humanity's true status as the highest sentient being; the purity and goodness of the original human nature; and the perfection of human existence, filled with divine love and compassion. Yet in fact, most people exhibit a character that is more animal-like than divine.

The Darwinian theory of evolution regards the animal within human beings as an integral part of human nature, an inheritance from our ape-like progenitors. And it is undeniable that the human being, by virtue of having a body, possesses instinctive and animal-like appetites and desires. But the position of most religions is that the essence of the human being is to be found in his spirit, which should dominate and control the body. Perhaps the meaning of evolution is the emergence of human beings as spiritual and ethical beings who transcend the animal stage. If so, this evolutionary birthright is barely manifest in most people, who allow their spiritual essence to be dominated by lower instinctual impulses.

Thus, while human behavior often may be instinctual and low, it is not the expression of the human essence. It is rather a corruption of human nature and a regression from realizing the true purpose of life. In theistic religions, such behavior is viewed as the result of humankind's separation from God. A degraded human being may be regarded as even lower than an animal, for at least an animal strives to realize its limited purpose, while benighted humans stray far from theirs.

The scripture passages gathered here approach this theme in three ways. Most people have deviated from their original nature, their hearts having become defiled and alienated from communion with God. The accumulation of sinful deeds, deluded thoughts, and base passions creates fetters that enslave those who indulge in them. Being thus degraded, they have sunk to the level of beasts and even lower.

God made man upright, but they have sought out many devices.

*Judaism* and *Christianity*. Ecclesiastes 7.29

Surely We created man of the best stature;
Then We reduced him to the lowest of the low,
Save those who believe and do good works,
and theirs is a reward unfailing.

*Islam*. Qur'an 95.4-6

A little confusion can alter the sense of direction; a great confusion can alter the inborn nature.

*Taoism*. Chuang Tzu 8

Be not like those who forget God, and therefore He made them forget their own souls!

*Islam*. Qur'an 59.19

The effect of wrong belief is so dominant that the self does not evince its inborn inclination

**Ecclesiastes 7.29:** Cf. Romans 1.21-25, pp. 280-81; Book of Songs, Ode 255, p. 274.
**Qur'an 95.4-6:** Cf. Qur'an 70.19-22, p. 273.
**Chuang Tzu 8:** Cf. Chuang Tzu 11, p. 297; Book of Songs, Ode 255, p. 274.

to the real path, just as the invasion of a bile-infected fever brings an aversion to sweet juice.

*Jainism*. Nemichandra, Gomattasara

This consciousness is luminous, but it is defiled by adventitious defilements.

*Buddhism*. Anguttara Nikaya i.10

Delusion is a sort of demonic force. People's original mind is pure but it becomes perverted due to delusion and other karmas.

*Jainism*. Kundakunda, Pancastikaya 38

Satan said, "I will take of Thy servants a portion marked off; I will mislead them, and I will create in them false desires; I will order them... to deface the fair nature created by God." Whoever, forsaking God, takes Satan for a friend, has of a surety suffered a loss that is manifest. Satan makes them promises, and creates in them false desires; but Satan's promises are nothing but deception.

*Islam*. Qur'an 4.118-20

Your mind, having become diseased and bewildered because of the false sense-conceptions accumulated since beginningless time, has developed many desires, attachments, and habits. From these there have arisen, incident to the ever-changing processes of life, arbitrary conceptions concerning self and not-self and as to what is true and what is not true. These arbitrary conceptions have not developed in a normal way from your pure Mind Essence, but in an abnormal way because of the prior false conceptions that had their origin in the sense organs, like the sight of blossoms in the air that come to diseased minds. They falsely appear to have had their origin in the enlightening and Essential Mind but, in truth, they have arisen because of diseased conditions.

*Buddhism*. Surangama Sutra

Behold, the Lord's hand is not shortened, that
it cannot save,
or his ear dull, that it cannot hear;
but your iniquities have made a separation
between you and your God,
and your sins have hid his face from you so that
he does not hear.

*Judaism* and *Christianity*. Isaiah 59.1-2

All vices are like chains thrown around the neck.

*Sikhism*. Ádi Granth, Sorath, M.1 p. 595

Jesus answered them, "Truly, truly, I say to you, everyone who commits sin is a slave to sin."

*Christianity*. John 8.34

Through wrong belief, indulgence, negligence, passions, and activities the individual self attracts particles of matter which are fit to turn into karma, as the self is actuated by passions. This influx of karma results in bondage.

*Jainism*. Tattvarthasutra 8.1-2

Denizens of hell are bound by hate,
Hungry ghosts by misery,
And beasts by blindness.
Men by lust are bound,
By jealousy, asuras,
And the devas in heaven by pride.
These Six Fetters are the obstacles to liberation.

*Buddhism*. Milarepa

**Anguttara Nikaya i.10:** 'Luminous consciousness' is *citta*. Cf. Sutra of Hui Neng 6, p. 283; Perfection of Wisdom in Eight Thousand Lines 12.3, p. 284; Holy Teaching of Vimalakirti 3, p. 148; Mahaparinirvana Sutra 214-15, p. 147.

**Surangama Sutra:** Cf. Chuang Tzu 11, p. 297; Sutra of Hui Neng 6, p. 283.

**Sorath, M.1:** Cf. Gauri Ashtpadi, M.1, p. 378.

**Tattvarthasutra 8.1-2:** Cf. Pancadhyayi 2.57, p. 275.

**Milarepa:** Cf. Dhammapada 345-46, p. 295; Digha Nikaya ii.276, p. 277; Udana 75-76, p. 294; Sutta Nipata 948, p. 378.

Bound by the fetters of the fruits of good and evil, like a cripple; without freedom, like a man in prison... thus they call him.

*Hinduism*. Maitri Upanishad 4.2

The heart is deceitful above all things, and desperately corrupt; who can understand it?

*Judaism* and *Christianity*, Jeremiah 17.9

Mencius said, "Slight is the difference between man and the brutes. The common man loses this distinguishing feature, while the gentleman retains it."

*Confucianism*. Mencius IV.B.19

By doing evil the self becomes a rogue, an animal, or inhabitant of hell; and always beset by thousands of pains, it strays incessantly.

*Jainism*. Kundakunda, Pravacanasara 1.12

Having attained human birth, which is an open gateway to Brahman, one who... remains attached to the ties of the world is not fit to be called human. Pleasures of sense may be had in all lives: leave them, then, to the brutes!

*Hinduism*. Srimad Bhagavatam 11.3

That man in whom there never kindles
One spark of the love of God,
Know, Nanak, that his earthly vesture
Is no better than that of a swine or dog!

*Sikhism*. Adi Granth, Shalok, M.9, p. 1428

Hear, O heavens, and give ear, O earth,
for the Lord has spoken:
"Sons I have reared and brought up,
but they have rebelled against me.
The ox knows its owner,
and the ass its master's crib;
but Israel does not know,
my people does not understand."

*Judaism* and *Christianity*. Isaiah 1.2-3

And recite to them the tiding of him to whom We gave Our signs, but he cast them off, and Satan followed after him, and he became one of the perverts. And had We willed, We would have raised him up, but he inclined toward the earth and followed his lust. So the likeness of him is as the likeness of a dog; if you attack it it lolls its tongue out, or if you leave it it lolls its tongue out. That is that people's likeness who cried lies to Our signs. So relate the story; haply they will reflect....

We have created for hell many jinn and men; they have hearts, but understand not with them; they have eyes, but perceive not with them; they have ears, but they hear not with them. They are like cattle; nay, rather they are further astray. Those—they are the heedless.

*Islam*. Qur'an 7.175-79

If man does worthily, they say to him, "You were created before the angels of the service"; if he does not, they say to him, "The fly, the gnat, and the worm were created before you."

*Judaism*. Midrash, Genesis Rabbah 8.1

Greed and evil are king and minister, falsehood
their officer;
Lust the counsellor who is called for advice—
all three hold conclave to chalk out plans.
The subjects, bereft of understanding, are
carcasses full of straw.

*Sikhism*. Adi Granth, Asa-ki-Var, M.1, pp. 468-69

**Maitri Upanishad 4.2:** Cf. Maitri Upanishad 3.2, p. 292; Bhagavad Gita 3.36-37, p. 294; Mundaka Upanishad 2.2.8, p. 377.

**Pravacanasara 1.12:** Cf. Brihadaranyaka Upanishad 1.4.10, p. 287.

**Isaiah 1.2-3:** Cf. Exodus Rabbah 31.15, p. 117.

**Asa-ki-Var, M.1:** Cf. Sorath, M.3, p. 278; Luke 9.60, p. 412; Berakot 18ab, p. 412; Maitri Upanishad 6.28, p. 744.

# *God's Grief*

IN RELIGIOUS TRADITIONS which revere a personal God, the fall and degradation of human beings is often recognized to cause God sorrow. Particularly where God is known as the divine Parent and human beings as his children, the heart of God must feel great sadness over the children's bondage, degradation, and rebellion. In Judaism, and in Islam where God is called the Compassionate One, the suffering of God is an integral part of the tradition. In Christianity, the passion of Jesus Christ has regularly represented the divine grief, but the biblical witness to God's sadness is often eclipsed by the Aristotelian conception that God's perfection requires that God be impassible. Recently, however, Christian theologians have begun to reaffirm that God the Father and Creator also suffers. In Mahayana Buddhism, the compassion of Shakyamuni Buddha is regarded as a specific instance of the compassionate heart of the cosmic Buddha who is the Father of all humanity. The suffering heart of God is a central affirmation in several of the new religions.

The Lord saw that the wickedness of man was great in the earth, and that every imagination of the thoughts of his heart was only evil continually. And the Lord was sorry that he had made man on the earth, and it grieved him to his heart.

*Judaism* and *Christianity*. Genesis 6.5-6

Before he brought on the flood, God himself kept seven days of mourning, for he was grieved at heart.

*Judaism*. Tanhuma, Shemini 11a

And it came to pass that the God of heaven looked upon the residue of the people, and he wept; and Enoch bore record of it, saying, "How is it that the heavens weep, and shed forth their tears as the rain upon the mountains?" And Enoch said unto the Lord, "How is it that you can weep, seeing you are holy, and from all eternity to all eternity?..."

The Lord said unto Enoch, "Behold these your brethren; they are the workmanship of my own hands, and I gave to them their knowledge... and commandment, that they should love one another, and that they should choose me, their Father; but behold, they are without affection, and they hate their own blood; and the fire of my indignation is kindled against them; and in my hot displeasure will I send in the floods upon them... misery shall be their doom; and the whole heavens shall weep over them, even all the workmanship of my hands; wherefore should not the heavens weep, seeing these shall suffer?"

*Church of Jesus Christ of Latter-day Saints*. Pearl of Great Price, Moses 7.28-37

Abu Dharr reported God's Messenger as saying, "I see what you do not see and I hear what you do not hear; heaven has groaned, and it has a right to groan."

*Islam*. Hadith of Ahmad, Tirmidhi, and Ibn Majah

**Genesis 6.5-6:** This passage introduces the story of the Deluge. It has given rise to numerous reflections on God's sorrow, illustrated by the next two selections.

**Pearl of Great Price, Moses 7.28-37:** This is a conversation between Enoch and God shortly before God sent the Flood upon the earth. Like the previous rabbinic passage, it is a meditation on Genesis 6.5-6. Cf. Moses 7.48-49, p. 223.

God's heart was torn asunder and broke with indescribable grief and tears the moment Adam and Eve fell.

*Unification Church.* Sun Myung Moon, 10-11-59

No one is more patient over injury which he hears than God. Men attribute a son to Him, yet He preserves them and provides for them.

*Islam.* Hadith of Bukhari and Muslim

O Jerusalem, Jerusalem, killing the prophets and stoning those who are sent to you! How often would I have gathered your children together as a hen gathers her brood under her wings, and you would not!

*Christianity.* Matthew 23.37

Rabbi Me'ir said, "When man is sore troubled, the Shechinah says, 'How heavy is my head, how heavy is my arm.' If God suffers so much for the blood of the wicked, how much more for the blood of the righteous."

*Judaism.* Mishnah, Sanhedrin 6.5

"In all their afflictions he was afflicted" [Isaiah 53.9]. So God said to Moses, "Do you not notice that I dwell in distress when the Israelites dwell in distress? Know from the place whence I speak with you, from the midst of thorns [the burning bush], it is as if I stand in their distresses."

*Judaism.* Midrash, Exodus Rabbah 2.5

Abuk, mother of Deng,
Leave your home in the sky and come to work in our homes,
Make our country to become clean like the original home of Deng,
Come make our country as one:
The country of Akwol
Is not as one, either by night or by day,
The child called Deng, his face has become sad,
The children of Akwol have bewildered their Chief's mind.

*African Traditional Religions.* Dinka Song (Sudan)

My sickness comes from ignorance and the thirst for existence, and it will last as long as do the sicknesses of all living beings. Were all living beings to be free from sickness, I also would not be sick. . . . As the parents will suffer as long as their only son does not recover from his sickness, just so, the bodhisattva loves all living beings as if each were his only child. He becomes sick when they are sick and is cured when they are cured.

*Buddhism.* Holy Teaching of Vimalakirti 5

My grief is beyond healing,
my heart is sick within me.
Hark, the cry of the daughter of my people
from the length and breadth of the land:
"Is the Lord not in Zion?
Is her King not in her?"

**Sun Myung Moon, 10-11-59:** Cf. Sun Myung Moon, 5-1-77, pp. 434-35.

**Hadith of Bukhari and Muslim:** This brings to mind Genesis 3.21, p. 302, when after Adam and Eve fell, God still made garments of skins for them.

**Matthew 23.37:** In these words Jesus lamented over the people who rejected him and refused the great salvation which he offered. On God's longing in general, cf. Yebamot 64a, p. 137.

**Sanhedrin 6.5:** Cf. Hagiga 5b, p. 752. For a Sikh passage intimating the divine burden, see Japuji 16, M.1, p. 89.

**Dinka Song:** Deng is the ancestor of the Dinka people and the chief deity, identified with Divinity as a whole and manifest in the fertilizing rain. Abuk is the first woman, earth, and the female principle. This song may refer to the tradition of the separation of heaven and earth at the origin of humanity; cf. Dinka Tradition, p. 307.

**Holy Teaching of Vimalakirti 5:** Vimalakirti, apparently sick in bed, utters words which signify the true spirit of a bodhisattva who commiserates with the suffering of all living beings. Cf. Mahaparinirvana Sutra 470-71, pp. 162-63.

Why have they provoked me to anger with
their graven images,
and with their foreign idols?
"The harvest is past,
the summer is ended,
and we are not saved."
For the wound of the daughter of my people is
my heart wounded,
I mourn, and dismay has taken hold on me.
Is there no balm in Gilead?
Is there no physician there?
Why then has the health of the daughter of my
people not been restored?
O that my head were waters,
and my eyes a fountain of tears,
that I might weep day and night
for the slain of the daughter of my people!

*Judaism* and *Christianity*. Jeremiah 8.18-9.1

In the perilous round of mortality,
In continuous, unending misery,
Firmly tied to the passions
As a yak is to its tail;
Smothered by greed and infatuation,
Blinded and seeing nothing;
Seeking not the Buddha, the Mighty,
And the Truth that ends suffering,
But deeply sunk in heresy,
By suffering seeking riddance of suffering;
For the sake of all these creatures,
My heart is stirred with great pity.

*Buddhism*. Lotus Sutra 2

Whatever kind of regret I, God, may have borne, until now I have overlooked it and kept still patiently....

Never think of this regret as slight! It is the result of the regret which has been accumulated and piled up.

For Me, Tsukihi, all people of the whole world are My children. Although I single-heartedly love them, unaware of this, each and every one of them equally is thinking only of dust.

Think of the regret of God over these dusty minds! It is far beyond expression of My words.

*Tenrikyo*. Ofudesaki 17.64-70

When Israel was a child, I loved him,
and out of Egypt I called my son.
The more I called them,
the more they went from me;
they kept sacrificing to the Baals,
and burning incense to idols.

Yet it was I that taught Ephraim to walk,
I took him up in my arms;
but they did not know that I healed them.
I led them with cords of compassion,
with the bands of love,
and I became to them as one
who eases the yoke on their jaws,
and I bent down to them and fed them.

They shall return to the land of Egypt,
and Assyria shall be their king,
because they have refused to return to me.
The sword shall rage against their cities,
consume the bars of their gates,
and devour them in their fortresses.
My people are bent on turning away from me;
so they are appointed to the yoke,
and none shall remove it.

How can I give you up, O Ephraim!
How can I hand you over, O Israel!
How can I make you like Admah!
How can I treat you like Zeboiim!
My heart recoils within me,
my compassion grows warm and tender.
I will not execute my fierce anger,
I will not again destroy Ephraim;

**Jeremiah 8.18-9.1:** The prophet Jeremiah, like the bodhisattva in the previous passage, laments heartsick over his people's suffering, ignorance, and unbelief. At the same time, the prophet is speaking the words of God and expressing the divine pathos.

**Ofudesaki 17.64-70:** In Tenrikyo sin is not endemic in human beings; it is the dust which collects on intrinsically pure minds and which needs to be swept away. See also Ofudesaki 7.109-11, p. 137; 13.43-44, p. 191.

for I am God and not man,
the Holy One in your midst,
and I will not come to destroy.

*Judaism* and *Christianity*. Hosea 11.1-9

My children,

The Enlightened One, because He saw mankind drowning in the great sea of birth, death, and sorrow, and longed to save them, for this was moved to pity.

Because He saw the men of the world straying in false paths, and none to guide them, for this He was moved to pity.

Because He saw that they lay wallowing in the mire of the Five Lusts, in dissolute abandonment, for this He was moved to pity.

Because He saw them still fettered to their wealth, their wives and their children, knowing not how to cast them aside, for this He was moved to pity.

Because He saw them doing evil with hand, heart, and tongue, and many times receiving the bitter fruits of sin, yet ever yielding to their desires, for this He was moved to pity.

Because He saw that they slaked the thirst of the Five Lusts as it were with brackish water, for this He was moved to pity.

Because He saw that though they longed for happiness, they made for themselves no karma of happiness; and though they hated pain, yet willingly made for themselves a karma of pain; and though they coveted the joys of heaven, would not follow His commandments on earth, for this He was moved to pity.

Because He saw them afraid of birth, old age, and death, yet still pursuing the works that lead to birth, old age, and death, for this He was moved to pity.

Because He saw them consumed by the fires of pain and sorrow, yet knowing not where to seek the still waters of samadhi, for this He was moved to pity.

Because He saw them living in an evil time, subjected to tyrannous kings and suffering many ills, yet heedlessly following after pleasure, for this He was moved to pity.

Because He saw them living in a time of wars, killing and wounding one another; and knew that for the riotous hatred that had flourished in their hearts they were doomed to pay an endless retribution, for this He was moved to pity.

Because many born at the time of His incarnation had heard Him preach the Holy Law, yet could not receive it, for this He was moved to pity.

Because some had great riches that they could not bear to give away, for this He was moved to pity.

Because He saw the men of the world ploughing their fields, sowing the seed, trafficking, huckstering, buying, and selling; and at the end winning nothing but bitterness, for this He was moved to pity.

*Buddhism*. Upasaka Sila Sutra

**Hosea 11.1-9:** The prophet Hosea uttered these words of divine pathos while prophesying against the corruption of Ephraim, the northern kingdom of Israel. He recalls God's motherly love for Israel as a child, when God brought Israel forth from the land of Egypt and raised her as an infant; compare Deuteronomy 32.10-12, p. 93; Isaiah 1.2-3, p. 323. Admah and Zeboiim were cities destroyed long ago along with Sodom and Gomorrah.

**Upasaka Sila Sutra:** The Enlightened One is the all-pervading cosmic Buddha (*Dharmakaya*), as well as the historical Shakyamuni. See Lion's Roar of Queen Srimala 5, p. 466. This sutra is found in the Chinese Tripitaka.

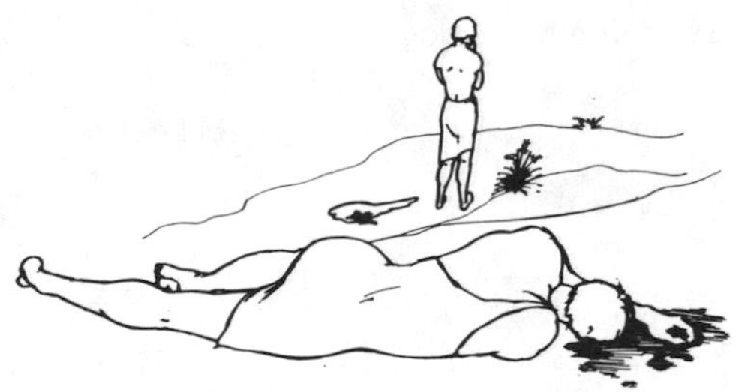

CHAPTER 9

# THE MAJOR SINS

IN THIS CHAPTER WE TURN FROM THE CAUSES and motivations of evil to its specific manifestations in daily life. In the opening section, we have selected passages on the difference between good and evil. The remaining sections treat each of the major sins individually.

There are various ways of classifying evil deeds: sins of the mind, of the mouth, and of the body, for example. Most commonly, however, the variety of evil deeds can be classified according to four major sins: (1) sexual immorality, (2) murder, (3) stealing, and (4) lying. Crimes of the tongue may be further subdivided: lying and deliberate deception, hypocrisy—especially in matters of religion, slander and bearing false witness, and foul speech. The final section deals with addictions to liquor, drugs, and gambling, the so-called "victimless crimes" which are really crimes against oneself.

The world's religions are quite unanimous in their condemnation of these sins and group them together in listing the most serious evils. We refer to injunctions in various expressions of the *Decalogue*, pp. 110-13, and to the following typical passages:

> Whoso in this world destroys life, tells lies, takes what is not given, goes to others' wives, and is addicted to intoxicating drinks, such a one digs up his own root in this world.
>
> *Buddhism*. Dhammapada 246-47

> Do you not know that the unrighteous will not inherit the kingdom of God? Do not be deceived; neither the immoral, nor idolators, nor adulterers, nor sexual perverts, nor thieves, nor the greedy, nor drunkards, nor revilers, nor robbers will inherit the kingdom of God.
>
> *Christianity*. 1 Corinthians 6.9-10

The plunderer of gold, the liquor-drinker,
the invader of a teacher's bed, the brahmin-killer:
These four sink downward in the scale—
And, fifth, he who consorts with them.

*Hinduism.* Chandogya Upanishad 5.10.9

## *Good and Evil*

HOW CAN WE DEFINE what is good and what is evil? Are there universal indicators behind, within, or consequent upon an action by which one can determine whether it was a good or an evil act? How can one tell whether a person is good or evil? The scriptures of the world's religions provide a variety of answers to these questions.

The first group of passages define good and evil by their fruits. A good person or a good deed bears good fruits; and an evil person or an evil deed produces evil fruits. From the fruits, the person's heart and sincerity can be known. Among the good fruits, of special importance for their traditions are the Confucian Five Happinesses and the Christian Fruits of the Spirit.

Second are passages which define good and evil by purpose and intention. Purpose may mean to follow an objective standard: the Dhamma or the will of God or Way of Heaven. Or, intention may be known inwardly and intuitively. Defining good and evil by purpose or intention permits one to know good or evil even when the result is not visible. But since intention is often hidden, it may have to be brought to light by testing, as in the final selections.

You will know them by their fruits. Are grapes gathered from thorns, or figs from thistles? So, every sound tree bears good fruit, but the bad tree bears evil fruit. A sound tree cannot bear evil fruit, nor can a bad tree bear good fruit. Every tree that does not bear good fruit is cut down and thrown into the fire. Thus you will know them by their fruits.

*Christianity.* Matthew 7.16-20

If you, Rahula, are desirous of doing a deed with the body, you should reflect on that deed of your body, thus: "That deed that I am desirous of doing with the body is a deed of my body that might conduce to the harm of self and that might conduce to the harm of others and that might conduce to the harm of both; this deed of body is unskilled, its yield is anguish, its result is anguish." If you, Rahula, reflecting thus, should find it so, a deed of body like this, Rahula, is certainly not to be done by you.

*Buddhism.* Majjhima Nikaya i.415, Ambalatthika-Rahulovada Sutta

**Majjhima Nikaya i.415:** Similar reflection is recommended with respect to deeds of speech and deeds of thought. It should be done before, during, and subsequent to one's action so that the moral quality of the deed can be experientially tested in light of these criteria. The Pali term *akusala,* translated 'unskill,' is the principal ethical term used in the sense of immoral in the Theravada scriptures. Cf. Dhammapada 361, p. 651; Srimad Bhagavatam 11.7, p. 652.

The five sources of happiness: the first is long life; the second, riches; the third, soundness of body and serenity of mind; the fourth, love of virtue; the fifth is an end crowning the life. Of the six extreme evils, the first is misfortune shortening the life; the second, sickness; the third, distress of mind; the fourth, poverty; the fifth, wickedness; the sixth, weakness.

*Confucianism*. Book of History 5.4.9

Now the works of the flesh are plain: fornication, impurity, licentiousness, idolatry, sorcery, enmity, strife, jealousy, anger, selfishness, dissension, party spirit, envy, drunkenness, carousing, and the like. I warn you, as I warned you before, that those who do such things shall not inherit the kingdom of God. But the fruit of the Spirit is love, joy, peace, patience, kindness, goodness, faithfulness, gentleness, self-control; against such there is no law.

*Christianity*. Galatians 5.19-23

God's messenger said, "Do you know the thing which most commonly brings people into Paradise? It is fear to God and good character. Do you know what most commonly brings people into hell? It is the two hollow things: the mouth and the private parts."

*Islam*.
Hadith of Tirmidhi and Ibn Majah

Hear and understand: not what goes into the mouth defiles a man, but what comes out of the mouth, this defiles a man.... Do you not see that whatever goes into the mouth passes into the stomach, and so passes on? But what comes out of the mouth proceeds from the heart, and this defiles a man. For out of the heart come evil thoughts, murder, adultery, fornication, theft, false witness, slander. These are what defile a man.

*Christianity*. Matthew 15.11-20

How can activity be good or wicked? That which is performed with good intention is good; and that which is performed with evil intention is wicked.... That which purifies the soul or by which the soul is purified, is merit—producing a happy feeling. That which keeps the soul away from good is demerit—producing an unhappy feeling.

*Jainism*. Pujyapada, Sarvarthasiddhi 6.3

Is there a "righteous man" who is good and a righteous man who is not good? He who is good to Heaven and good to man, he is a righteous man who is good; good to Heaven but not good to man, that is a righteous man who is evil... But a wicked man who is evil to Heaven and evil to man, he is a wicked man who is evil; he who is evil to Heaven but not evil to man, that is a wicked man who is not evil.

*Judaism*. Talmud, Kiddushin 40a

"All who commit crimes, robbing, stealing, practicing villainy and treachery, and who kill men or violently assault them to take their property, being reckless and fearless of death—these are abhorred by all."

The king says, "O Feng, such great criminals are greatly abhorred, and how much more detestable are the unfilial and unbrotherly—as the son who does not reverently discharge his duty to his father, but greatly wounds his father's heart, and the father who can no longer love his son, but hates him; as the younger brother who does not think of the manifest will of Heaven, and refuses to respect his elder brother, and the elder brother who does not think of the toil of their parents in bringing up their children, and is very unfriendly to his junior. If we who are charged with government do not treat parties who proceed to such wickedness as offenders, the laws of our nature given by Heaven to our people

**Galatians 5.19-23:** Cf. James 3.13-18, p. 571.
**Matthew 15.11-20:** Cf. Dhammapada 1-2, p. 515.
**Kiddushin 40a:** Cf. Shabbat 31a, p. 718.

will be thrown into great disorder and destroyed. You must resolve to deal speedily with such according to the penal laws of King Wen, punishing them severely and not pardoning."

*Confucianism.* Book of History 5.9

Whosoever seeks, by whatever means, merely the happiness of cyclic existence for personal ends, he is to be understood as a mean person.

Whosoever reverses deeds done from base motives and turns back the happiness of worldly pleasures for the sake of his own liberation, that person is called middling.

Whosoever wishes to eliminate completely the sufferings of others through his own sufferings, that is the excellent person.

*Buddhism.* Bodhipathapradipa

God's definition of goodness is total giving, total service, and absolute unselfishness. We are to live for others. You live for others and others live for you. God lives for man and man lives for God. The husband lives for his wife and the wife lives for her husband. This is goodness. And here unity, harmony, and prosperity abound.

Evil is the emergence of selfishness into this world. God's principle of unselfish giving was twisted into an ungodly principle of selfish taking. The ungodly position of desiring to be served rather than to serve was thereby established. The origin of evil is Satan. He was in the position to serve God, but instead he posed as another god and subjugated man for his own benefit.... His motivation was selfishness. Out of his selfishness comes the origin of evil and sin.

*Unification Church.*
Sun Myung Moon, 10-20-73

Evil and good are not equal, even though the abundance of evil may amaze you; so heed God, you men of wits, so that you may prosper!

*Islam.* Qur'an 5.100

Easily known is the progressive one; easily known the one who declines. He who loves Dhamma progresses, he who hates it declines.

*Buddhism.* Sutta Nipata 92

The things which men greatly desire are comprehended in meat and drink and sexual pleasure; those which they greatly dislike are comprehended in death, exile, poverty, and suffering. Thus liking and disliking are the great elements in men's minds. But men keep them hidden in their minds, where they cannot be fathomed or measured. The good and the bad of them being in their minds, and no outward manifestation of them being visible, if it be wished to determine these qualities in one uniform way, how can it be done without the use of the rules of propriety?

*Confucianism.* Book of Ritual 7.2.20

The Master said, "The true gentleman is easy to serve, yet difficult to please. For if you try to please him in any manner inconsistent with the Way, he refuses to be pleased; but in using the services of others he only expects of them what they are capable of performing. Common people are difficult to serve, but easy to please. Even though you try to please them in a manner inconsistent with the Way, they will still be pleased; but in using the services of others they expect them [irrespective of their capacities] to do any work that comes along."

*Confucianism.* Analects 13.25

**Book of History 5.9:** On relations towards parents and brothers as 'the trunk of Goodness,' see Analects 1.2, p. 171; also Classic on Filial Piety 1, pp. 171-72.

**Bodhipathapradipa:** This short work (Tib. *Byan-chub lam-gyi sgron-ma*) by Atisha consits of 68 stanzas that discuss the proper path leading to the attainment of enlightenment. Cf. Hadith of Bukhari, p. 688.

**Sun Myung Moon, 10-20-73:** Cf. Key to Theosophy, pp. 289-90; Sun Myung Moon, 10-20-73, p. 290.

**Book of Ritual 7.2.20:** One purpose of religious rites and social laws and norms is to help to reveal a person's character and inward intentions; good people will adhere to them, evil people will violate them. Cf. Romans 13.1-7, p. 748; Tanhuma Shemini 15b, p. 612.

**Analects 13.25:** Cf. Analects 1.16, p. 703; 12.16, p. 703; 15.20, p. 489.

That again which is virtue may, according to time and place, be sin. Thus appropriation of what belongs to others, untruth, and injury and killing, may, under special circumstances, become virtue.

Acts that are apparently evil, when undertaken from considerations connected with the gods, the scriptures, life itself, and the means by which life is sustained, produce consequences that are good.

*Hinduism*. Mahabharata, Shanti Parva 37.11, 14

No creature shall be harmed for one's own sake, one's own enjoyment. All depends upon the purpose; not even a blade of grass shall be cut without a worthy purpose. What is called sin becomes a merit if it is done for a higher purpose, even as what is considered uplifting becomes a force for binding if done in disregard of the higher Truth. Rightly used, rightly directed, the very means of fall become the means for rise....

[In Tantric ritual] wine is not to be taken as wine nor flesh as flesh; nor is it permissible to partake in the ceremonies as a mere human animal ridden with greed and desire. The wine is the Shakti, the Divine Energy; flesh is the Shiva, the Divine Substance, and he who partakes is none other than Bhairava himself, the Divine Enjoyer. The bliss that arises when all these three are fused in the consciousness of the worshipper is real Release. Bliss is the intimate form of Brahman and it is there installed in each individual body; wine brings out, releases into manifestation this indwelling Bliss... and awakens the sense of godhood which unties the knots of life. To be otherwise, to do otherwise, is simply to be drunk.

*Hinduism*. Kularnava Tantra 5

And verily We shall try you until We know those of you who really strive and are steadfast, and until We test your record.

*Islam*. Qur'an 47.31

Once there lived a housewife named Vedehika who had a reputation for gentleness, modesty, and courtesy. She had a housemaid named Kali who was efficient and industrious and who managed her work well. Then it occurred to Kali the housemaid, "My mistress has a very good reputation; I wonder whether she is good by nature, or is good because my work, being well-managed, makes her surroundings pleasant. What if I were to test my mistress?"

The following morning Kali got up late. Then Vedehika shouted at her maid, "Hey, Kali!" "Yes, madam?" "Hey, what makes you get up late?" "Nothing in particular, madam." "Nothing in particular, eh, naughty maid, and you get up late?" And being angry and offended, she frowned.

Then it occurred to Kali, "Apparently, my mistress does have a temper inwardly, though she does not show it because my work is well-managed. What if I were to test her further?" Then she got up later. Thereupon Vedehika shouted at her maid, "Hey, Kali, why do you get up late?" "No particular reason, madam." "No particular reason, eh, and you are up late?" she angrily hurled at her words of indignation.

Then it occurred to Kali, "Apparently, my mistress does have a temper inwardly, though she does not show it because my work is well-managed. What if I were to test her still further?" She got up still later. Thereupon Vedehika shouted at her, "Hey, Kali, why do you get up late?" and she angrily took up the bolt of the door-bar and hit her on the head, cutting it. Thereupon Kali, with cut head and

**Mahabharata, Shanti Parva 37.11,14:** See Mahabharata, Shanti Parva 329.13, p. 719; cf. Yogacarya Bhumi Shastra, p. 341.

**Kularnava Tantra 5:** In Tantric practice, purification of inner intention allows the adept to employ the objects of ordinary desire in the service of self-transcendence. Yet such entirely subjective standards can easily be corrupted.

**Qur'an 47.31:** Cf. Qur'an 29.2-3, p. 405; Sirach 6.7-17, p. 184; Udana 65-66, p. 184.

blood trickling down, denounced her mistress before the neighbors, saying, "Madam, look at the work of the gentle lady, madam, look at the action of the modest lady, madam, look at the action of the quiet lady. Why must she get angry and offended because I got up late and hit me, her only maid, cutting me on the head?" Thus the housewife lost her good reputation.

Analogously, brethren, a person here happens to be very gentle, very humble, and very quiet as long as unpleasant things do not touch him. It is only when unpleasant things happen to a person that it is known whether he is truly gentle, humble, and quiet.

*Buddhism.* Majjhima Nikaya i.123-24, Kakacupama Sutta

❖

**Majjhima Nikaya i.123-24:** Cf. Udana 65-66, p. 184; Sirach 6.7-17, p. 184; 2 Corinthians 12.7-10, p. 405.

# *Adultery*

THE FOREMOST OF SINFUL ACTIONS is adultery or fornication. No other sin has such a baneful effect on the spiritual life. Because it is committed in secret, by mutual consent, and often without fear of the law, adultery is especially a sin against God and against the goal of life. Modern secular societies can do little to inhibit adultery and sexual promiscuity. Only the norms of morality which are founded on religion can effectively curb this sin.

Most of the passages collected here condemn adultery, fornication, and sexual promiscuity in general. A number of passages seek to demarcate limits of behavior that verge on fornication. At the conclusion are passages on related behaviors: divorce and homosexuality.

Approach not adultery: for it is a shameful deed and an evil, opening the road to other evils.

*Islam.* Qur'an 17.32

Let marriage be held in honor among all, and let the marriage bed be undefiled; for God will judge the immoral and the adulterous.

*Christianity.* Hebrews 13.4

We find that to every sin God is long-suffering, except to the sin of unchastity. Rabbi Azariah said, "All things can God overlook save lewdness."

*Judaism.* Midrash, Leviticus Rabbah 23.9

Be sure of this, that no fornicator or impure man... has any inheritance in the kingdom of Christ and of God.

*Christianity.* Ephesians 5.5

Neither fornicate, for whosoever does that shall meet the price of sin—doubled shall be the chastisement for him on the Resurrection Day.

*Islam.* Qur'an 25.68-69

Violating and misusing love is the gravest of all crimes. Abusing love is a greater crime than cutting the universal root of life [murder].

*Unification Church.* Sun Myung Moon, 3-20-77

Both learning and the practice of the Teaching are lost to him who is given to sexual intercourse. He employs himself wrongly. That is what is ignoble in him.

*Buddhism.* Sutta Nipata 815

A wise man has nothing to do with lust. Lust is nothing but death, and lack of it is serenity. How can one who perceives this indulge in wanton behavior?

*Jainism.* Acarangasutra 2.61

Four misfortunes befall a careless man who commits adultery: acquisition of demerit, disturbed sleep, third, blame; and fourth, a state of woe. There is acquisition of demerit as well as evil destiny. Brief is the joy of the frightened man and woman. The king imposes a heavy punishment. Hence no man should frequent another man's wife.

*Buddhism.* Dhammapada 309-10

**Sutta Nipata 815:** Cf. Sutra of Forty-two Sections 25, p. 660.

When a family declines, ancient traditions are destroyed. With them are lost the spiritual foundations for life, and the family loses its sense of unity. Where there is no sense of unity, the women of the family become corrupt; and with the corruption of its women, society is plunged into chaos. Social chaos is hell for the family and for those who have destroyed the family as well.

*Hinduism.* Bhagavad Gita 1.40-42

Immorality in the house is like a worm in the vegetables.

*Judaism.* Talmud, Sota 3b

Do not approach thy neighbor's wife or maids.

*Taoism.* Tract of the Quiet Way

Let those who cannot find a match keep chaste till God give them independence by His grace.

*Islam.* Qur'an 24.33

Whoever has illicit affairs with the wives of his relatives or friends, either by force or through mutual consent, he is to be known as an outcast.

*Buddhism.* Sutta Nipata 123

The philanderer lusting after numerous women
does not give up seeking in others' homes.
What he does daily only brings regrets—
in sorrow and greed he is shrivelled up.

*Sikhism.* Adi Granth, Dhanasari, M.5, p. 672

A man should not think incontinently of another's wife, much less address her to that end; for such a man will be reborn in a future life as a creeping insect. He who commits adultery is punished both here and hereafter; for his days in this world are cut short, and when dead he falls into hell.

*Hinduism.* Vishnu Purana 3.11

The lips of a loose woman drip honey,
and her speech is smoother than oil;
but in the end she is bitter as wormwood,
sharp as a two-edged sword.
Her feet go down to death;
her steps follow the path to Sheol;
she does not take heed to the path of life;
her ways wander, and she does not know it....

Drink water from your own cistern,
flowing water from your own well.
Should your springs be scattered abroad,
streams of water in the streets?
Let them be for yourself alone,
and not for strangers with you.
Let your fountain be blessed,
and rejoice in the wife of your youth,
a lovely hind, a graceful doe.
Let her affection fill you at all times with delight,
be infatuated always by her love.
Why should you be infatuated, my son, with a loose woman
and embrace the bosom of an adventuress?
For a man's ways are before the eyes of the Lord,
and he watches all his paths.
The iniquities of the wicked ensnare him,
and he is caught in the toils of his sin.
He dies for lack of discipline,
and because of his great folly he is lost.

*Judaism* and *Christianity.* Proverbs 5.3-23

If you are handsome, do not go astray after lewdness, but honor your Creator, and fear Him, and praise Him with the beauty which He has given you.

*Judaism.* Pesikta Rabbati 127a

The body is not meant for immorality, but for the Lord... Do you not know that your bodies are members of Christ? Shall I therefore take the members of Christ and make them members of a prostitute? Never! Do you not know that he who joins himself to a prostitute becomes one body with her? For, as it is written, "The two shall become one flesh." But he who is united to the Lord becomes one spirit with him. Shun immorality. Every other sin which a man commits is outside the body; but the immoral man sins against his own body. Do you not know that your body is a temple of the

Holy Spirit within you, which you have from God?

*Christianity*. 1 Corinthians 6.13-19

Offering presents to a woman, romping with her, touching her ornaments and dress, sitting with her on a bed, all these are considered adulterous acts.

*Hinduism*. Laws of Manu 8.357

A monk who, with sexual desire and a perverse intention, contacts a woman, holding her hand or holding a braid of her hair or rubbing against any part of her body, commits an offense, requiring formal meetings of the Order for its exoneration.

*Buddhism*. Vinaya Pitaka

Because the daughters of Zion are haughty
and walk with outstretched necks,
glancing wantonly with their eyes,
mincing along as they go,
tinkling with their feet;
the Lord will smite with a scab
the heads of the daughters of Zion,
and the Lord will lay bare their secret parts.

*Judaism* and *Christianity*. Isaiah 3.16-17

Tell the believing men to lower their gaze and be modest. That is purer for them. Lo! God is Aware of what they do.

And tell the believing women to lower their gaze and be modest, and to display of their adornment only that which is apparent, and to draw their veils over their bosoms, and not to reveal their adornment save to their own husbands or fathers... or children who know naught of women's nakedness. And let them not stamp their feet so as to reveal what they hide of their adornment. And turn unto God together, O believers, in order that ye may succeed.

*Islam*. Qur'an 24.30-32

A master has said, "He who beholds a beautiful woman should say, 'Blessed be He who hath created such in His universe.'" But is even mere looking permitted? The following can surely be raised as an objection: "Thou shalt keep from every evil thing" [Deuteronomy 23.10] implies that one should not look intently at a beautiful woman, even if she be unmarried, nor at a married woman, even if she be ugly, nor at a woman's gaudy garments, nor at male and female asses or at a pig and a sow or at fowls when they are mating.

*Judaism*. Talmud, Aboda Zara 20ab

The lawful thing which God hates most is divorce.

*Islam*. Hadith of Abu Dawud

The Lord was witness to the covenant between you and the wife of your youth, to whom you have been faithless, though she is your companion and your wife by covenant.... "For I hate divorce," says the Lord.

*Judaism* and *Christianity*. Malachi 2.14-16

The husband receives his wife from the gods; he does not wed her according to his own will; doing what is agreeable to the gods, he must always support her while she is faithful.

**1 Corinthians 6.13-19:** Cf. 1 Corinthians 3.16-17, p. 141, on the sacredness of the human body as God's temple. Paul is quoting Genesis 2.24, p. 175.

**Vinaya Pitaka:** The Vinaya Pitaka is the standard text of monastic discipline for Theravada monks.

**Qur'an 24.30-32:** Wearing the veil by Muslim women was instituted in the Qur'an as a practical protection against the temptation to adultery.

**Aboda Zara 20ab:** Cf. Treatise on Response and Retribution, p. 661.

**Hadith of Abu Dawud:** The Islamic law on divorce is found in Qur'an 2.226-32. There a waiting period of four months is prescribed, to allow the decision to be reconsidered.

**Malachi 2.14-16:** Christian and Jewish marriage is not like a secular contract which can be anulled at will; it is a covenant to which God is witness and third partner.

"Let mutual fidelity continue until death;" this may be considered as a summary of the highest law for husband and wife.

*Hinduism*. Laws of Manu 9.95, 101

And Pharisees came up and in order to test him [Jesus] asked, "Is it lawful for a man to divorce his wife?" He answered them, "What did Moses command you?" They said, "Moses allowed a man to write a certificate of divorce, and to put her away." But Jesus said to them, "For your hardness of heart he wrote you this commandment. But from the beginning of creation, 'God made them male and female.' 'For this reason a man shall leave his father and mother and be joined to his wife, and the two shall become one flesh.' So they are no longer two but one flesh. What therefore God has joined together, let not man put asunder."

And in the house the disciples asked him about this matter. And he said to them, "Whoever divorces his wife and marries another, commits adultery against her; and if she divorces her husband and marries another, she commits adultery."

*Christianity*. Mark 10.2-12

You shall not lie with a male as with a woman; it is an abomination.

*Judaism* and *Christianity*. Leviticus 18.22

The bodhisattva does not approach the five kinds of unmanly men in order to be friendly with or close to them.

*Buddhism*. Lotus Sutra 14

And Lot said to his people, "You commit lewdness, such as no people in creation ever committed before you. Do you indeed come in unto males?"

*Islam*. Qur'an 29.28-29

God gave them up to dishonorable passions. Their women exchanged natural relations for unnatural, and the men likewise gave up natural relations with women and were consumed with passion for one another, men committing shameless acts with men and receiving in their own persons the due penalty for their error.

*Christianity*. Romans 1.26-27

**Laws of Manu 9.95, 101:** Divorce is permitted, but it is not done by virtuous people. According to Narada Dharma Sutra 12.92-100 and Laws of Manu 9.76-81, a man may divorce his wife on the grounds of adultery, profligacy, procuring an abortion, drunkenness, malicious speech, or failure to produce a male heir. A woman may divorce her husband if he becomes a religious ascetic, is impotent, is expelled from his caste, or is long absent. A waiting period of one to eight years is normally required.

**Mark 10.2-12:** In the parallel attestation in Matthew 19.3-9, there is an exception for 'unchastity.' Current biblical scholarship does not see this exception as sanctioning divorce on the grounds of marital infidelity. 'Unchastity' is not the same word as adultery; it is thought to refer to the incestuous relations practiced by some pagans before their conversion to Christianity. Jesus is quoting Genesis 1.27, p. 193, and Genesis 2.24, p. 175.

**Lotus Sutra 14:** The 'five kinds of unmanly men' includes homosexuals, hermaphrodites, eunuchs, and those suffering from various kinds of impotence. The Sangha did not want anyone to join the order as an escape; it likewise barred from membership debtors who wanted to renege on their debts and young novices who did not have their parents' permission.

**Qur'an 29.28-29:** This passage refers to the story of Sodom and Gomorrah. According to the Bible (Genesis 19.4-11), when two angels came to Lot's home to warn him of the city's impending destruction, the mob demanded that Lot give the men over to them, that they might rape and sodomize them. Lot defended them and offered his daughters instead; at which point the mob sought to lay hands on Lot, but the angels rescued him.

**Romans 1.26-27:** The 'due penalty' may refer to venereal disease, but there is in addition the spiritual damage to the personality of one who engages in such behavior.

# Murder

MURDER IS CONDEMNED by all faiths, as by reason itself. Nevertheless, there is often a line between murder and sanctioned violence, and this line is drawn in various ways. In Jainism, and among some Buddhists, Hindus, and Taoists, the concept of absolute nonviolence (*ahimsa*) encompasses all animals and living beings. In Judaism, Christianity, and Islam, on the other hand, the scriptural prohibitions against murder are restricted to the killing of human beings.

Some passages in the Christian, Buddhist, Taoist, and Jewish scriptures may be interpreted as teaching that killing a human being is a sin under any and all circumstances. Hence, some in these traditions regard it as wrong to use violent means to defend against harm—cf. *Turn the Other Cheek*, pp. 708-10. Pacifism and objections to capital punishment likewise derive from this scriptural foundation. Other passages, a selection of which are given here, may be interpreted as restricting the definition of murder to an individual killing for selfish purposes. They permit killing in self-defense, permit killing to prevent greater crimes, sanction state enforcement of the death penalty, and support the waging of war for just cause. Nevertheless, killing in such circumstances should still be viewed as evil, albeit the lesser evil. The inferior morality of killing in self-defense or in retaliation is highlighted in the two versions of the story of Cain and Abel from the Bible and the Qur'an. In the biblical story God grants Cain a mark to protect him from retaliation, and in the qur'anic version Abel shows his righteousness by refusing to defend himself from Cain's aggression.

Related crimes which are treated in the latter part of this section include infanticide, abortion, and suicide. Abortion is a topic of much current controversy in the West—many religious people regard it as a crime analogous to infanticide—yet there is no mention in the Bible. Abortion is often condemned in the scriptures of Eastern religions. We have also selected a few representative scriptural condemnations of suicide. However, Jainism approves of religious suicide as an extremely effective means of penance;[1] and in the Orient suicide may be a virtuous act where honor is at stake.

You shall not kill.

*Judaism* and *Christianity*. Exodus 20.13

The essence of right conduct is not to injure anyone; one should know only this, that non-injury is religion.

*Jainism*. Naladiyar 14-15

He who commits murder must be considered as the worst offender, more wicked than a defamer, than a thief, and than he who injures with a staff.

*Hinduism*. Laws of Manu 8.345

Anyone who kills a believer intentionally will have his reward in hell, to remain there. God will be angry with him and curse him, and prepare awful torment for him.

*Islam*. Qur'an 4.92

**Naladiyar 14-15:** 'Non-injury,' that is, *ahimsa*. Cf. Acarangasutra 5.101-2, p. 114.

[1] Cf. Acarangasutra 7, pp. 241-42.

Only one single man [Adam] was created in the world, to teach that, if any man has caused a single soul to perish, Scripture imputes it to him as though he had caused the whole world to perish, and if any man saves alive a single soul, Scripture imputes it to him as though he had saved the whole world.

*Judaism.* Mishnah, Sanhedrin 4.5

All tremble at the rod. All fear death. Comparing others with oneself, one should neither strike nor cause to strike.

All tremble at the rod. Life is dear to all. Comparing others with oneself, one should neither strike nor cause to strike.

Whoever, seeking his own happiness, harms with the rod other pleasure-loving beings, experiences no happiness hereafter.

Whoever, seeking his own happiness, harms not with the rod other pleasure-loving beings, experiences happiness hereafter.

*Buddhism.* Dhammapada 129-32

In wars to gain land, the dead fill the plains; in wars to gain cities, the dead fill the cities. This is known as showing the land the way to devour human flesh. Death is too light a punishment for such men [who wage war]. Hence those skilled in war should suffer the most severe punishments.

*Confucianism.* Mencius IV.A.14

Victory breeds hatred, for the defeated live in pain. Happily live the peaceful, giving up victory and defeat.

*Buddhism.* Dhammapada 201

A man once came before Raba and said to him, "The ruler of my city has ordered me to kill a certain person, and if I refuse he will kill me." Raba told him, "Be killed and do not kill; do you think that your blood is redder than his? Perhaps his is redder than yours."

*Judaism.* Talmud, Pesahim 25b

We could surmise that murdering an enemy whom all people, as well as yourself, dislike cannot be a crime. But even the hated man has the same cosmic value as you. Murdering is a crime, because by murdering a person you infringe upon a cosmic law.

*Unification Church.* Sun Myung Moon, 9-30-79

Then they came up and laid hands upon Jesus and seized him. And behold, one of those who were with Jesus stretched out his hand, and drew his sword, and struck the slave of the high priest, and cut off his ear. Then Jesus said to him, "Put your sword back into its place; for all who take the sword will perish by the sword."

*Christianity.* Matthew 26.51-52

Fine weapons are instruments of evil.
They are hated by men.
Therefore those who possess Tao turn away from them....
Weapons are instruments of evil, not the instruments of a good ruler.
When he uses them unavoidably, he regards calm restraint as the best principle.

Even when he is victorious, he does not regard it as praiseworthy,
For to praise victory is to delight in the slaughter of men.
He who delights in the slaughter of men will not succeed in the empire....
For the slaughter of the multitude, let us weep with sorrow and grief.
For a victory, let us observe the occasion with funeral ceremonies.

*Taoism.* Tao Te Ching 31

If a man comes to kill you, forestall it by killing him.

*Judaism.* Talmud, Sanhedrin 72a

**Sanhedrin 4.5:** This scripture is quoted in Qur'an 5.32, below.

**Dhammapada 129-32:** Cf. Dhammapada 201, p. 708; Sutta Nipata 705, p. 114; Acarangasutra 5.101-2, p. 114; Samyutta Nikaya v.353, pp. 114-15.

**Matthew 26.51-52:** Cf. Treatise on Response and Retribution 5, p. 123.

Do not take life—which God has made sacred—except for just cause. And if anyone is slain wrongfully, we have given his heir authority to demand retribution; but let him not exceed bounds in the matter of taking life, for he is helped by the law.

*Islam*. Qur'an 17.33

O sons of 'Abdul Muttalib, let there be no retaliation for the act of murder. Do not roam about with a drawn sword... and do not start a massacre of my opponents and enemies. See that only one man, that is my murderer, is killed in punishment for the crime of murder, and that nobody else is molested or harmed or harassed. The punishment to the man who attempted the murder shall take place only when I die of the wound delivered by him, and this punishment shall be only one stroke of the sword to end [his] life. He should not be tortured before his death; his hands and feet should not be cut off, because I have heard the Holy Prophet saying, "Do not cut off the hands and feet of anybody, be it a biting dog."

*Islam*.
Nahjul Balagha, Letter 47

Suppose a bodhisattva sees that a vicious robber intends to kill many people for the sake of wealth; or intends to harm virtuous shravakas, pratyekabuddhas, or bodhisattvas; or intends to do other things that will cause him to fall into the Uninterrupted hell. When seeing this, the bodhisattva will think, "If I kill that person, I will fall into the hells; if I do not kill him, he will commit crimes which will lead him to the Uninterrupted hell, where he will suffer greatly. I would rather kill him and fall to the hells myself than let him undergo great suffering in the Uninterrupted hell."

Then, deeply regretting the necessity for this action, and with a heart full of compassion, he will kill that person. In doing this, he does not violate the bodhisattva precepts; instead, he generates many merits.

*Buddhism*. Yogacarya Bhumi Shastra

Now Adam knew Eve his wife, and she conceived and bore Cain... and again, she bore his brother Abel. Now Abel was a keeper of sheep, and Cain a tiller of the ground. In the course of time Cain brought to the Lord an offering of the fruit of the ground, and Abel brought of the firstlings of the flock and of their fat portions. And the Lord had regard for Abel and his offering, but for Cain and his offering He had no regard. So Cain was very angry, and his countenance fell. The Lord said to Cain, "Why are you angry, and why has your countenance fallen? If you do well, will you not be accepted? And if you do not do well, sin is couching at the door; its desire is for you, but you must master it."

Cain said to Abel his brother, "Let us go out into the field." And when they were in the field, Cain rose up against his brother Abel, and killed him. Then the Lord said to Cain, "Where is Abel your brother?" He replied, "I do not know; am I my brother's keeper?" And the Lord said, "What have you done? The voice of your brother's blood is crying to me from the ground. And now you are cursed from the ground, which has opened its mouth to receive your brother's blood from your hand. When you till the ground, it shall no longer yield to you its strength; you shall be a fugitive and a wanderer on the earth." Cain said to the Lord, "My punishment is greater than I can bear. Behold, you have driven me this day away from the ground; and from your face I shall be hidden; and I shall be a fugitive and a wanderer on the earth, and whoever finds me will slay me." Then the Lord said to him, "Not so! If any one slays Cain, vengeance shall be taken on him sevenfold." And the Lord put a mark on Cain, lest any who came upon him should kill him. Then Cain went away from the presence of the Lord, and dwelt in the land of Nod, east of Eden.

*Judaism* and *Christianity*.
Genesis 4.1-16

**Nahjul Balagha:** 'Ali spoke these words as he lay dying of a wound delivered by an assassin. He urged that there be no acts of vengeance outside of the rule of law.

**Yogacarya Bhumi Shastra:** 'Uninterrupted' (*Avici*) hell is the lowest Buddhist hell.

And recite for them the story of the two sons of Adam truthfully, when they offered a sacrifice, and it was accepted of one of them, and not accepted of the other. "I will surely slay you," said one. "God accepts only of the godfearing," said the other.

"Yet if you stretch out your hand against me, to slay me, I will not stretch out my hand against you, to slay you; I fear God, the Lord of all Beings. I desire that you should be laden with my sin and your sin, and so become an inhabitant of the Fire; that is the recompense of the evildoers."

Then his soul prompted him to slay his brother, and he slew him, and became one of the losers.

Then God sent forth a raven, scratching into the earth, to show him how he might conceal the vile body of his brother. He said, "Woe is me! Am I unable to be as this raven, and so conceal my brother's vile body?" And he became one of the remorseful.

Therefore We prescribed for the Children of Israel that whoever kills a human being, except to retaliate for manslaughter or for corruption done in the land, it shall be as if he had killed all of humankind; and whoso saves the life of one, it shall be as if he had saved the lives of all humankind.

*Islam*. Qur'an 5.27-32

[Evil-doers] kill the baby and cause abortion of the unborn.

*Taoism*. Treatise on Response and Retribution

Slay not your children, fearing a fall to poverty. We shall provide for them and for you. Lo! the slaying of them is great sin.

*Islam*. Qur'an 17.31

It is a capital crime to destroy an embryo in the womb.

*Judaism*. Talmud, Sanhedrin 57b

If a woman is in hard travail, one cuts up the child in her womb and brings it forth member by member, because her life comes before the child.

*Judaism*. Mishnah, Ohalot 7.6

A bhikkhu who intentionally kills a human being, down to procuring abortion, is no ascetic and no follower of the Fraternity of the Buddha.

*Buddhism*. Vinaya, Mahavagga i.78.4

Those versed in the sacred law state that there are three acts only which make women outcastes: the murder of the husband, slaying a learned brahmin, and the destruction of the fruit of their womb.

*Hinduism*. Vasishtha Dharma Sutra 28.7

He who takes his own or another's life becomes an outcaste.

*Hinduism*. Apastamba Dharma Sutra 1.10.28.17

Let him [the ascetic] not desire to die... let him wait for his appointed time, as a servant waits for the payment of his wages.

*Hinduism*. Laws of Manu 6.45

"Surely your blood of your lives will I require." [Genesis 9.5]. This includes suicide, except in a case like that of Saul.

*Judaism*. Midrash, Genesis Rabbah 34.13

**Qur'an 5.27-32:** The Qur'an cites the Mishnah, Sanhedrin 4.5, above.

**Qur'an 17.31:** The motives for female infanticide in pre-Islamic Arabia, where the practice was common, were mainly economic. They are little different from some of the more questionable contemporary rationales for abortion.

**Laws of Manu 6.45:** In contrast to Jainism, see Acarangasutra 7, pp. 241-42.

**Genesis Rabbah 34.13:** King Saul killed himself on the battlefield rather than allow himself to be captured by the enemy and become a taunt to Israel; see 1 Samuel 31.1-6. For another noble suicide, see Gittin 57b, p. 633; Shih Chi 47, p. 433.

He who killed himself with steel would be the eternal denizen of the Fire of hell, and he would have that weapon in his hand and would be thrusting that into his stomach for ever and ever; he who killed himself by drinking poison would sip that in the Fire of hell where he is doomed for ever and ever; and he who killed himself by falling from a mountain would constantly be falling in the Fire of hell.

*Islam.* Hadith of Muslim

A monk who intentionally deprives a human being of his life, or provides the means for suicide, or praises death, or incites one to commit suicide, saying, "Of what use to you is this evil, difficult life? Death is better for you than life," thus having his mind set on the other's death and with the idea that he should die, praises death in various ways or incites him to commit suicide, commits an offense entailing loss of monkhood.

*Buddhism.* Vinaya Pitaka

# *Theft*

THEFT MEANS to take property that belongs to another or to the public. It encompasses fraud, usury, extortion, and dishonest trading.

You shall not steal.

*Judaism* and *Christianity*. Exodus 20.15

Where you did not sow, do not reap.

*African Traditional Religions*. Igala Proverb (Nigeria)

Because what is yours is not yours, how then can you regard what is not yours as yours?

*Judaism*. Talmud, Derek Eretz Zuta 2.5

To take to oneself unrighteous wealth is like satisfying one's hunger with putrid food, or one's thirst with poison wine. It gives a temporary relief, indeed, but death also follows it.

*Taoism*. Treatise on Response and Retribution 5

The wickedness of evil-minded thieves, who secretly prowl over this earth, cannot be restrained except by punishment.

*Hinduism*. Laws of Manu 9.263

As for the thief, both male and female, cut off their hands. It is the reward of their own deeds, an exemplary punishment from God.

*Islam*. Qur'an 5.38

Lo! those who devour the wealth of orphans wrongfully, they do but swallow fire into their bellies, and they will be exposed to burning flame.

*Islam*. Qur'an 4.10

Says Nanak, "To grasp what is another's is as evil
As pig's flesh to the Muslim and cow's flesh to the Hindu.
The Teacher shall intercede for his follower
Only when he has not eaten carrion."

*Sikhism*. Adi Granth, Var Majh, M.1, p. 141

These acts are included in stealing: prompting another to steal, receiving stolen goods, creating confusion to overcharge or underpay, using false weights and measures, and deceiving others with artificial or imitation goods.

*Jainism*. Akalanka, Tattvartharajavartika 7.27

Woe unto the defrauders,
Those who when they take the measure from mankind demand it full,
But if they measure unto them or weigh for them, they cause them loss.

*Islam*. Qur'an 83.1-3

Whoever steals what is considered to belong to others, whether it be situated in villages or the forest, he is to be known as an outcast.

Whoever having contracted debts defaults when asked to pay, retorts, "I am not indebted to you," he is to be known as an outcast.

Whoever is desirous of stealing even a trifle and kills a person going along the road in order to take it, he is to be known as an outcast.

*Buddhism*. Sutta Nipata 119-21

**Derek Eretz Zuta 2.5:** Even one's own possessions are 'not yours' because they belong to God; we have been given them as a trust.

**Var Majh, M.1:** 'Carrion' refers to ill-gotten gains.

Hear this, you who trample upon the needy,
and bring the poor of the land to an end,
saying, "When will the new moon be over,
that we may sell grain?
And the sabbath,
that we may offer wheat for sale,
that we may make the ephah small and the shekel great,
and deal deceitfully with false balances,
that we may buy the poor for silver
and the needy for a pair of sandals,
and sell the refuse of the wheat?"
The Lord has sworn by the pride of Jacob,
"Surely I will never forget any of their deeds.
Shall not the land tremble on this account,
and every one mourn who dwells in it?"

*Judaism* and *Christianity*. Amos 8.4-8

[Evil-doers] impoverish others for their own gain.
For private ends they neglect public duties.
They break into others' houses to take their property and valuables.
They misdirect the water and light fires to destroy the people's homes.
They upset others' plans so as to prevent their success.
They spoil a worker's utensils to hamper his efficiency.
With violence they seize, with violence they demand.
They delight in fraud, they delight in robbery, they make raids and commit depradations to get rich.
They shorten the foot, they narrow the measure, they lighten the scales, they reduce the peck.
They adulterate the genuine, and they seek profit in illegitimate business.

*Taoism*. Treatise on Response and Retribution

O ye who believe! Devour not usury, doubling and quadrupling [the sum lent].

*Islam*. Qur'an 3.130

If you lend money to any of my people with you who is poor, you shall not be to him as a creditor, and you shall not exact interest from him.

*Judaism* and *Christianity*. Exodus 22.25

Do not men despise a thief if he steals
to satisfy his appetite when he is hungry?

*Judaism* and *Christianity*. Proverbs 6.30-31

**Qur'an 3.130:** All modern societies agree that usury, when it is understood to mean charging exhorbitant interest, 'doubling and quadrupling,' is an evil whose prohibition is consistent with sound economics. But the absolute proscription of usury, when it is understood as prohibiting loaning money for any amount of interest whatsoever, has always proved difficult to practice in a mercantile economy. In the Islamic tradition, the wealthy will often make personal loans at no interest to those in need as a form of charity, but this does not apply to loans for business. Where there is a need to raise capital, either by entrepreneurs or by the state, loans are required, and people with capital will lend it only at a price. Therefore, both Christian and Muslim societies that have tried to enforce this prohibition have often winked at loopholes. One typical loophole is to permit loans from nonbelievers. Thus in Medieval Europe Jewish bankers were the accepted creditors for Christians, and today Western banks are often permitted to lend money in Islamic nations. Today, Islamic banks are developing new policies consistent with the Qur'an. Most notable of these is investment as profit sharing. Banks will lend to entrepreneurs in return for a percentage of the profits rather than for a fixed rate of interest. The bank then prospers as the business succeeds, but makes nothing should it fall into the red.

**Exodus 22.25:** Lending at interest is prohibited specifically in the case where the borrower is poor. Cf. Exodus Rabbah 31.15, p. 117.

**Proverbs 6.30-31:** In traditional Roman Catholic moral teaching, when a person is in dire need he may be justified in stealing food to keep from starving. In that case, food is regarded as 'common property.' Cf. Chuang Tzu 25, p. 755.

## *Lying and Deceit*

IT IS SAID THAT THE PEN is mightier than the sword. Similarly, a lie may do more damage than a gun fired in anger. Lying is the doorway to any number of evils. But we may distinguish between lying in the sense of teaching a falsehood about Reality—e.g., propagating atheism or a false doctrine—and lying in the sense of deliberately misleading and deceiving another about a matter of which he has certain knowledge. The first type of lie may in fact be based on honest conviction; the second type of lie is deliberate deception. In this section, we have gathered passages on lying and falsehood only in the latter sense of deliberate deception; untruth in the former sense may be classed as *Ignorance*, pp. 280-85. Even so, often there is only a short distance between ignorance about truth and lying to one's neighbor, as several passages in this section affirm.

Lying lips are an abomination to the Lord.

*Judaism* and *Christianity*. Proverbs 12.22

Do not assert with your mouth what your heart denies.

*Taoism*. Tract of the Quiet Way

No man should talk one way with his lips and think another way in his heart.

*Judaism*. Talmud, Baba Metzia 49

Dishonesty in business or the uttering of lies causes inner sorrow.

*Sikhism*. Adi Granth, Maru Solahe, M.3, p. 1062

O you who believe, wherefore do you say what you do not?
Very hateful is it to God, that you say what you do not.

*Islam*. Qur'an 61.2-3

No man who practices deceit shall dwell in my house;
no man who utters lies shall continue in my presence.

*Judaism* and *Christianity*. Psalm 101.7

A speaker of falsehood reaches purgatory; and again so does one who, having done a misdeed, says, "I did not." Both of them, men of base deeds, become equal in the other world.

*Buddhism*. Dhammapada 306

Lying does not mean that one could not be rich;
Treachery does not mean you may not live to old age;
But it is the day of death [judgment] about which one should be baffled.

*African Traditional Religions*. Yoruba Proverb (Nigeria)

Falsehood implies the making of a wrong statement by one who is overwhelmed by intense passions.

*Jainism*. Upasakadasanga Sutra

**Qur'an 61.2-3:** Cf. Matthew 23.2-3, p. 579; Analects 2.13, p. 579; Dhammapada 51-52, p. 579; James 1.22-24, pp. 579-80.

**Psalm 101.7:** Cf. Psalm 24.3-6, p. 155; Shabbat 31a, p. 718.

**Yoruba Proverb:** Don't think that just because you have used lying to advantage in this world, that lying will similarly avail you in the hereafter. Cf. Yoruba Proverbs, p. 718.

You brood of vipers! how can you speak good, when you are evil? For out of the abundance of the heart the mouth speaks. The good man out of his good treasure brings forth good, and the evil man out of his evil treasure brings forth evil. I tell you, on the day of judgment men will render account for every careless word they utter; for by your words you will be justified, and by your words you will be condemned.

*Christianity*. Matthew 12.34-37

There is no evil that cannot be done by the liar, who has transgressed the one law of truthfulness and who is indifferent to the world beyond.

*Buddhism*. Dhammapada 176

All things are determined by speech; speech is their root, and from speech they proceed. Therefore he who is dishonest with respect to speech is dishonest in everything.

*Hinduism*. Laws of Manu 4.256

There are three characteristics of a hypocrite: when he speaks, he lies; when he makes a promise, he acts treacherously; and when he is trusted, he betrays.

*Islam*. Hadith of Muslim

Confucius said, "I do not see what use a man can be put to, whose word cannot be trusted. How can a wagon be made to go if it has no yoke-bar, or a carriage if it has no collar-bar?"

*Confucianism*. Analects 2.22

The Venerable Rahula saw the Lord coming in the distance; seeing him he made ready a seat and water for washing the feet. The Lord sat down on the seat made ready; as he was sitting down he bathed his feet. And Rahula, having greeted the Lord, sat down at a respectful distance.

Then the Lord put a little quantity of water that was left over into the water vessel and addressed Rahula, saying, "Do you, Rahula, see this little quantity of water that is left over and that is put into the water vessel?"

"Yes, revered sir."

"Even so, Rahula, little is the recluseship of those who have no shame at intentional lying."

Then the Lord, having thrown away that little quantity of water, addressed Rahula, saying, "Do you, Rahula, see this little quantity of water that has been thrown away?"

"Yes, revered sir."

"Even so, Rahula, thrown away is the recluseship of those who have no shame at intentional lying."

*Buddhism*. Majjhima Nikaya i.414, Ambalatthika-Rahulovada Sutta

A liar lies to himself as well as to the gods. Lying is the origin of all evils; it leads to rebirth in the miserable planes of existence, to breach of the pure precepts, and to corruption of the body.

*Buddhism*. Maharatnakuta Sutra 27, Bodhisattva Surata's Discourse

Woe to those who call evil good and good evil,
who put darkness for light and light for darkness,
who put bitter for sweet and sweet for bitter!

*Judaism* and *Christianity*. Isaiah 5.20

Beings who are ashamed of what is not shameful, and are not ashamed of what is shameful, embrace wrong views and go to a woeful state.

Beings who see fear in what is not to be feared, and see no fear in the fearsome, embrace false views and go to a woeful state.

Beings who imagine faults in the faultless and perceive no wrong in what is wrong, embrace false views and go to a woeful state.

*Buddhism*. Dhammapada 316-18

**Matthew 12.34-37:** Cf. Matthew 15.11-20, p. 614.

**Dhammapada 176:** Cf. Tosefta Shebuot 3.6, p. 281.

**Laws of Manu 4.256:** Cf. Markandeya Purana, p. 351; Matthew 15.11-20, p. 614; James 3.6-9, p. 352.

**Analects 2.22:** Cf. Analects 15.5, p. 718.

**Maharatnakuta Sutra 27:** The Maharatnakuta Sutra is is a collection of Mahayana sutras in the Chinese Tripitaka.

# *Hypocrisy*

WHEREVER PEOPLE SUBSCRIBE to a religion or any doctrine of moral excellence, there may arise the sin of hypocrisy. The hypocrite wishes to enjoy the approval of his peers and even the perquisites of a religious office by appearing outwardly moral or religious, while inwardly he is not. Or, where religion makes serious demands upon people's lives, such as Islam's call to *jihad* or Buddhism's strict precepts of monastic discipline, the hypocrite tries to circumvent these demands while appearing outwardly righteous. The hypocrite does not pay the price of commitment to the religious life and hence does not reap its spiritual benefits; he remains at a low state. Furthermore, when hypocrites rise to high position, they set a bad example for ordinary believers and bring religion itself into disrepute.

Woe to you, scribes and Pharisees, hypocrites! for you are like whitewashed tombs, which outwardly appear beautiful, but within they are full of dead men's bones and all uncleanness. So you also outwardly appear righteous to men, but within you are full of hypocrisy and iniquity.

*Christianity.* Matthew 23.27-28

King Alexander Jannaeus said to his wife, "Fear not the [true] Pharisees nor the non-Pharisees, but those hypocrites who ape the Pharisees."

*Judaism.* Talmud, Sota 22b

And Jesus said to them, "Well did Isaiah prophesy of you hypocrites, as it is written,

This people honors me with their lips,
but their heart is far from me;
in vain do they worship me,
teaching as doctrines the precepts of men."

*Christianity.* Mark 7.6-7

The man of superior "righteousness" takes action, and has an ulterior motive to do so.
The man of superior "propriety" takes action,
And when people do not respond to it, he will stretch his arms and force it on them.

*Taoism.* Tao Te Ching 38

What is the use of your matted hair, O witless man? What is the use of your antelope skin garment? Within, you are full of passions; without, you embellish yourself [with the paraphernalia of an ascetic].

*Buddhism.* Dhammapada 394

Some go to bathe at holy places—
With hearts impure and faculties false.
As one part of impurity they wash, twice more freshly stick to them.
They washed themselves outside; inside they are full of deadly poison.
The pure in soul are pure even without ritual bathing;

**Matthew 23.27-28:** Cf. Matthew 7.15-16, p. 316; 12.34-37, p. 347; 23.2-3, p. 579; Hadith of Tirmidhi, p. 316. A good example of hypocrisy is the attitude of the priest and Levite to the mugging victim on the road in the Parable of the Good Samaritan, Luke 10.25-37, p. 686-87.

**Sota 22b:** Although among Christians the term 'Pharisee' has come to mean people with a rigid, formalistic religion, the historical Pharisees were a party of sincere Jewish believers. The New Testament's condemnation of the Pharisees should be taken to refer to the hypocrites among them.

**Mark 7.6-7:** Jesus is quoting Isaiah 29.13. Cf. Matthew 7.21, p. 580; James 3.13-18, p. 571; Pearl of Great Price, Joseph Smith 2, p. 426.

**Tao Te Ching 38:** Lao Tzu is criticizing action according to conventional ethical and social norms as leading to self-righteousness and legalism.

**Dhammapada 394:** Cf. Tevijja Sutta, Digha Nikaya xiii.33-34, pp. 140-41.

The wicked will be wicked in all ritual performances.

*Sikhism.* Adi Granth, Var Suhi, M.1, p. 789

The brahmin's sacred thread binds not his
passions and lust for woman.
Each morning his face is covered with shame.
By the thread his feet and hands are not
restrained;
Nor his slanderous tongue and lustful eyes...
Listen, O world! to this marvel:
This man, blind in soul, is called wise.

*Sikhism.* Adi Granth, Asa-ki-Var, M.1, p. 471

He who has the character of a sinner, though he lays great stress on the outward signs of his religious calling as a means of living, he who does not control himself though he pretends to do so, will come to grief for a long time.

As hemlock kills him who drinks it, as a weapon cuts him who awkwardly handles it, as a demon harms him who does not incant it, so the Law harms him who mixes it up with sensuality.

*Jainism.* Uttaradhyayana Sutra 20.43-44

Many with a yellow robe on their necks are of evil disposition and uncontrolled. Evil-doers on account of their evil deeds are born in a woeful state.

Better to swallow a red-hot iron ball [which would consume one] like a flame of fire than to be an immoral and uncontrolled person feeding on the alms offered by the devout....

Any loose act, any corrupt practice, a life of dubious holiness—none of these is of much fruit.

*Buddhism.* Dhammapada 307-12

Whoever derives a profit for himself from the words of the Torah is helping on his own destruction.

*Judaism.* Mishnah, Abot 4.7

Not every one who says to me, "Lord, Lord," shall enter the kingdom of heaven, but he who does the will of my Father who is in heaven.

*Christianity.* Matthew 7.21

God's Messenger is reported as saying, "When one commits fornication he is not a believer, when one steals he is not a believer, when one drinks wine he is not a believer, when one takes plunder on account of which men raise their eyes at him he is not a believer, and when one of you defrauds he is not a believer; so beware, beware!"

*Islam.* Hadith of Bukhari and Muslim

The opulent man who is liberal towards strangers, while his family lives in distress, has counterfeit virtue which will first make him taste the sweets [of fame], but afterwards make him swallow the poison [of punishment in hell].

*Hinduism.* Laws of Manu 11.9

Woe to those who pray
and are heedless of their prayers,
to those who make display
and refuse charity.

*Islam.* Qur'an 107.4-7

Beware of practicing your piety before men in order to be seen by them; for then you have no reward from your Father who is in heaven.

Thus, when you give alms, sound no trumpet before you, as the hypocrites do in the synagogues and in the streets, that they may be praised by men. Truly, I say to you, they have their reward. But when you give alms, do not

**Var Suhi, M.1:** Cf. Var Majh, M.1, p. 344, Udana 6, p. 614.
**Uttaradhyayana Sutra 20.43-44:** Cf. Sutrakritanga 2.1.18-19, p. 317.
**Dhammapada 308:** Cf. Lotus Sutra 2, p. 291; Var Sarang, M.1, p. 714; Oracle of Hachiman, p. 520.
**Abot 4.7:** Cf. 2 Thessalonians 3.8-12, p. 714; James 3.13-18, p. 571; Var Sarang, M.1, p. 714.
**Matthew 7.21:** Cf. Abot 1.17, p. 580.
**Hadith of Bukhari and Muslim:** Cf. Qur'an 6.151-53, p. 111; 25.63-76, pp. 157-58; Jeremiah 7.1-15, pp. 768-69.
**Qur'an 107.4-7:** Cf. Qur'an 2.177, p. 615; Shinto Uden Futsujosho, p. 595.

let your left hand know what your right hand is doing, so that your alms may be in secret; and your Father who sees in secret will reward you.

*Christianity*. Matthew 6.1-4

O believers, void not your freewill offerings with reproach and injury, as one who expends of his substance to show off to men and believes not in God and the Last Day. The likeness of him is as the likeness of a smooth rock on which is soil, and a torrent smites it, and leaves it barren. They have no power over anything that they have earned. God guides not the people of the unbelievers.

*Islam*. Qur'an 2.264

When We show favor to a man, he withdraws and turns aside, but when ill touches him then he abounds in prayer.

*Islam*. Qur'an 41.51

I know your works: you are neither cold nor hot. Would that you were cold or hot! So, because you are lukewarm, I will spew you out of my mouth.

*Christianity*. Revelation 3.15-16

And of mankind are some who say, "We believe in God and the Last Day," when they believe not. They think to beguile God and those who believe, and they beguile none save themselves; but they perceive not. In their hearts is a disease, and God increases their disease. A painful doom is theirs because they lie. And when it is said to them, "Make not mischief on the earth," they say, "We are only peacemakers." Behold they are indeed the mischief-makers but they perceive not.

*Islam*. Qur'an 2.8-12

As for you, son of man, your people who talk together about you by the walls and at the doors of the houses, say to one another, each to his brother, "Come, and hear what the word is that comes forth from the Lord." And they come to you as people come, and they sit before you as my people, and they hear what you say but they will not do it; for with their lips they show much love, but their heart is set on their gain.

*Judaism* and *Christianity*. Ezekiel 33.30-31

The evildoers who pursue Devotion held
sacred by thine initiate,
Because they have no part in the Good Mind,
O Lord,
From them she shrinks back, with
Righteousness,
As far as the wild beasts of prey shrink back
from us!

*Zoroastrianism*. Avesta, Yasna 34.9

Many are the gurus who are proficient to the utmost in Vedas and Shastras; but rare is the guru who has attained to the supreme Truth.

Many are the gurus on earth who give what is other than the Self; but rare is the guru who brings to light the Atman.

Many are the gurus who rob the disciple of his wealth; but rare is the guru who removes the disciple's afflictions.

Many are they who are given to the discipline and conduct according to caste, stage, and family; but he who is devoid of all volition is a guru rare to find.

He is the guru by whose very contact there flows the supreme bliss; the intelligent man shall choose such a one as the guru and no other.

*Hinduism*. Kularnava Tantra 13

**Matthew 6.1-4:** Cf. Matthew 6.5-8, p. 594; Mencius VII.B.11, p. 696.

**Qur'an 2.264:** Cf. Qur'an 2.271, p. 624; Matthew 5.23-24, p. 701.

**Revelation 3.15-16:** This was said to the wealthy church of Laodicea, whose comfortable and lukewarm Christianity was nauseating.

**Qur'an 2.8-12:** 'We are only peacemakers': these were the lukewarm Muslims of Medinah who wanted to maintain their peaceful lives and a comfortable coexistence with the unbelievers, when Muhammad was calling the people to total commitment to the cause of Islam.

**Ezekiel 33.30-31:** Cf. Micah 3.5, p. 316.

## *Slander, Gossip, and Foul Speech*

A MALICIOUS OR LOOSE TONGUE is the cause of much evil in the world. Since talk can cause damage to others and to oneself, one's words should be weighed carefully.

The crime of bearing false witness in a court of law is singled out in the Ten Commandments as a specially grievous sin, since its consequences for the unjustly accused are so dire. In the ancient Mesopotamian law code of Hammurabi, a witness who falsely accused another of a crime was liable, if his perjury were uncovered, to a punishment identical to that for the crime which he laid upon the innocent party. Beyond the court of law, there are many other situations where a person is asked about some event or about the behavior of others. These are opportunities either to be truthful, or to bear false witness and cause others injury by damaging their reputations, sowing discord and mistrust between husband and wife or between friends, or even falsely implicating them in crimes.

Furthermore, much damage can come from words said without careful deliberation and from tales repeated to others without first ascertaining whether they are true. One should be aware of the character and mind of the person to whom the words are said. Also, harsh and foul speech, cursing and reviling others, can lead to fighting and violence.

You shall not bear false witness against your neighbor.

*Judaism* and *Christianity*. Exodus 20.16

One giving false evidence or uttering falsehood goes to Raurava hell.

*Hinduism*. Markandeya Purana 10

Whoever commits a delinquency or crime, then throws the blame upon the innocent, has burdened himself with falsehood and a flagrant crime.

*Islam*. Qur'an 4.112

When he is cited and questioned as a witness before a council or a company or amid his relations or amid a guild or a royal family, and is told, "Now, my good man, say what you know," although he does not know, he says, "I know," and although he knows, he says, "I do not know"; although he has not seen, he says, "I saw," and although he has seen, he says, "I did not see." Thus his speech becomes intentional lying either for his own sake or for that of another or for the sake of some material gain or other. And he is a slanderer; having heard something at one place, he makes it known elsewhere for causing variance among those people... In this way he sows discord among those who were in harmony or foments those who were at variance. Discord is his pleasure, his delight, his joy, the motive of his speech.... If this kind of vocal conduct is followed, unskilled states of mind grow much, skilled states of mind decrease.

*Buddhism*. Majjhima Nikaya iii.47-48, Sevitabbaasevitabba Sutta

You who believe, if some perverse man should come up to you with some piece of news, clear up the facts lest you afflict some folk out of ignorance and some morning feel regretful for what you may have done....

**Qur'an 4.112:** Cf. Qur'an 4.135, p. 718.

You who believe, do not let one folk ridicule another folk. Perhaps they are better than they are. Nor let women mistreat other women; perhaps they are better than themselves. Nor should you find fault with one another nor shout at one another using nicknames; it is bad to use a dirty name instead of one you can believe in. Those who do not turn away from it are wrongdoers.

You who believe, refrain from being overly suspicious: even a little suspicion is a vice. Do not spy on one another, nor yet any of you slander others. Would one of you like to eat his dead brother's flesh? You would loathe it! Heed God, for God is Relenting, Merciful.

*Islam*. Qur'an 49.6-12

There are eight faults that men may possess... you must not fail to examine these carefully. To do what is not your business to do is called officiousness. To rush forward when no one has nodded in your direction is called obsequiousness. To echo a man's opinions and try to draw him out in speech is called sycophancy. To speak without regard for what is right and wrong is called flattery. To delight in talking about other men's failings is called calumny. To break up friendships and set kinfolk at odds is called maliciousness. To praise falsely and hypocritically so as to cause injury and evil to others is called wickedness. Without thought for right and wrong, to try to face in two directions at once so as to steal a glimpse of the other party's wishes is called treachery. These eight faults inflict chaos on others and injury on the possessor. A gentleman will not befriend the man who possesses them, an enlightened ruler will not have him for a minister.

*Taoism*. Chuang Tzu 31

You shall not go up and down as a talebearer among your people.

*Judaism* and *Christianity*. Leviticus 19.16

If the ear does not hear malicious gossip, the heart is not grieved.

*African Traditional Religions*. Yoruba Proverb (Nigeria)

They [young widows] learn to be idlers, gadding about from house to house, and not only idlers but gossips and busybodies, saying what they should not.

*Christianity*. 1 Timothy 5.13

The tongue is an unrighteous world among our members, staining the whole body, setting on fire the cycle of nature, and set on fire by hell. For every kind of beast and bird, of reptile and sea creature, can be tamed and has been tamed by humankind, but no human being can tame the tongue—a restless evil, full of deadly poison. With it we bless the Lord and Father, and with it we curse men, who are made in the likeness of God.

*Christianity*. James 3.6-9

A person is born with an axe in his mouth. He whose speech is unwholesome cuts himself with his axe.

When a person praises someone who should be blamed, or attacks someone worthy of praise, then this man is accumulating evil with his mouth and this evil will not lead to happiness.

It is little harm if one loses money in gambling with dice, even losing everything, including oneself; but if one bears ill-will toward well-conducted ones it is greater harm indeed. Insulting men of real worth, bearing ill-will in thought and speech, leads to eons upon eons in the states of misery.

*Buddhism*. Sutta Nipata 657-60

A noisy bird builds a bad nest.

*African Traditional Religions*. Kanufi Proverb (Nigeria)

**Qur'an 49.6-12:** Vv. 6, 11-12.
**Leviticus 19.16:** Cf. Abot 3.17, p. 653.

The origin of all trouble
Within this world
Is a single word
Spoken in haste.

*Shinto.* Moritake Arakida, One Hundred Poems About The World

Speak not harshly to anyone. Those thus addressed will retort. Painful, indeed, is vindictive speech. Blows in exchange may bruise you.

*Buddhism.* Dhammapada 133

The Master said, "Where disorder develops, words are the first steps. If the prince is not discreet, he loses his servant. If the servant is not discreet, he loses his life. If germinating things are not handled with discretion, the perfecting of them is impeded."

*Confucianism.* I Ching, Great Commentary 1.8.10

To be always talking is against nature. For the same reason a hurricane never lasts a whole morning, nor a rain storm all day. Who is it that makes the wind and rain? It is Heaven and earth. And if even Heaven and earth cannot blow or pour for long, how much less in his utterances should man?

*Taoism.* Tao Te Ching 23

The Messenger of God... took hold of his tongue and said, "Restrain this." I said, "O Prophet of God, will what we say be held against us?" He said, "May your mother be bereaved of you, Mu'adh! Is there anything that topples people on their faces into hell-fire other than the harvests of their tongues?"

*Islam.* Forty Hadith of an-Nawawi 29

❖

**I Ching, Great Commentary 1.8.10:** Cf. Micah 7.5-7, p. 674; Yoruba Song, p. 675.
**Forty Hadith of an-Nawawi 29:** Cf. Hadith of Tirmidhi and Ibn Majah, p. 331.

## *Addiction*

ADDICTION TO LIQUOR, drugs, or gambling is a cause of people's downfall in every society. These so-called victimless crimes render man's spirit blind to the light of God and deaf to the promptings of his conscience. Addictions typically lead to antisocial behavior, destroy families, and promote criminal acts. Despite contemporary medical models of addiction which regard it as a disease, the world's religions generally affirm that people are responsible for their own actions and should be taught to steer clear of addictions.

You who believe! Intoxicants and gambling... are an abomination—of Satan's handiwork: eschew such that you may prosper. Satan's plan is to stir up enmity and hatred among you by means of liquor and gambling, and to hinder you from the rememberance of God and from prayer. Will you not then abstain?

*Islam*. Qur'an 5.90-91

Men who are grave and wise,
Though they drink, are mild and masters of themselves;
But those who are benighted and ignorant
Are devoted to drink, and more so daily.
Be careful, each of you, of your deportment—
What heaven confers, when once lost, is not regained.

*Confucianism*. Book of Songs, Ode 196

Do not get drunk with wine, for that is debauchery; but be filled with the Spirit.

*Christianity*. Ephesians 5.18

Woe to those who rise early in the morning,
that they may run after strong drink,
who tarry late into the evening
till wine inflames them!
They have lyre and harp,
timbrel and flute and wine at their feasts,
but they do not regard the deeds of the Lord,
or see the work of his hands.

*Judaism* and *Christianity*. Isaiah 5.11-12

Who has woe? Who has sorrow?
Who has strife? Who has complaining?
Who has wounds without cause?
Who has redness of eyes?
Those who tarry long after wine,
those who go to try mixed wine.
Do not look at wine when it is red,
when it sparkles in the cup
and goes down smoothly.
At the last it bites like a serpent,
and stings like an adder.
Your eyes will see strange things,
and your mind utter perverse things.
You will be one who lies down in the midst of the [rolling] sea,
like one who totters to and fro like the top of a mast.
"They struck me," you will say, "but I was not hurt;
they beat me, but I did not feel it.
When shall I awake?
I will seek another drink."

*Judaism* and *Christianity*. Proverbs 23.29-35

Rabbi Isaac said, quoting Proverbs 23.31, "Wine makes the faces of the wicked red in this world, but pale in the world to come." Rabbi Me'ir said, "The tree of which Adam ate was a vine, for it is wine that brings lamentation to man."

*Judaism*. Talmud, Sanhedrin 70ab

**Ephesians 5.18:** Cf. Wadhans, M.1, p. 161; Acts 2.1-18, pp. 408-9.

What are the six channels for dissipating wealth? Taking intoxicants; loitering in the streets at unseemly hours; constantly visiting shows and fairs; addiction to gambling; association with evil companions; the habit of idleness....

Gambling and women, drink and dance and song,
Sleeping by day and prowling around by night,
Friendship with wicked men, hardness of heart,
These causes six bring ruin to a man.

Gambling and drinking, chasing after those
Women as dear as life to other men,
Following the fools, not the enlightened ones,
He wanes as the darker half of the moon.

The drunkard always poor and destitute;
Even while drinking, thirsty; haunting bars;
Sinks into debt as into water stone,
Soon robs his family of their good name.

One who habitually sleeps by day
And looks upon the night as time to rise
Licentious and a drunkard all the time,
He does not merit the rank of householder.

*Buddhism.* Digha Nikaya iii.182-85, Sigalovada Sutta

Excessive eating is prejudicial to health, to fame, and to bliss in Heaven; it prevents the aquisition of spiritual merit and is odious among men; one ought, for these reasons, to avoid it carefully.

*Hinduism.* Laws of Manu 2.57

The Gambler:
These nuts that once tossed on tall trees in the wind
but now smartly roll over the board, how I love them!
As alluring as a draught of Soma on the mountain,
the lively dice have captured my heart.

My faithful wife never quarreled with me
or got angry; to me and my companions
she was always kind, yet I've driven her away
for the sake of the ill-fated throw of a die.

Chorus:
His wife's mother loathes him, his wife rejects him,
he implores people's aid but nowhere finds pity.
A luckless gambler is no more good
than an aged hack to be sold on the market.

Other men make free with the wife of a man
whose money and goods the eager dice have stolen.
His father and mother and brothers all say,
"He is nothing to us. Bind him, put him in jail!"

The Gambler:
I make a resolve that I will not go gaming.
So my friends depart and leave me behind.
But as soon as the brown nuts are rattled and thrown,
to meet them I run, like an amorous girl.

Chorus:
To the meeting place the gambler hastens.
Shall I win? he asks himself, hoping and trembling,
But the throws of the dice ruin his hopes,
giving the highest scores to his opponent.

Dice, believe me, are barbed: they prick and they trip,
they hurt and torment and cause grievous harm.
To the gambler they are like children's gifts, sweet as honey,
but they turn on the winner in rage and destroy him.

Fifty-three strong, this band jumps playfully,
like Savitri, the god whose statutes are true.
They pay no heed to the anger of the powerful;
the king himself bows down before them.

Downward they roll, then jump in the air!
Though handless, they master those who have hands!
Unearthly coals thrown down on the board,
though cold they burn the player's heart to ashes.

Abandoned, the wife of the gambler grieves.
Grieved too, is his mother as he wanders to nowhere.
Afraid and in debt, ever greedy for money,
he steals in the night to the home of another.

He is seized by remorse when he sees his wife's lot,
beside that of another with well-ordered home.
In the morning, however, he yokes the brown steeds

and at the evening falls stupid before the cold embers.

The Gambler to the dice:
To the mighty chieftain of your whole band,
the one who has become the king of your troop,
to him I show my ten fingers extended.
No wealth do I withhold! I speak truly!

Chorus:
Steer clear of dice. Till well your own field.
Rejoice in your portion and value it highly.
See there, O Gambler, your cattle, your wife.
This is the counsel of the noble Savitri.

The Gambler to the dice:
Grant us your friendship, have mercy upon us!
Do not overwhelm us with your fierce attack!
May your anger and evil intention be assuaged!
Let the brown dice proceed to ensnare another!

*Hinduism*. Rig Veda 10.34

❖

Part Three

# Salvation and the Savior

CHAPTER 10

# SALVATION–LIBERATION–ENLIGHTENMENT

DUE TO HUMANKIND'S CONDITION OF DEPRAVITY, ignorance, and bondage to desire, the task of reaching the goal and purpose of life is no simple matter. Chains must be broken, sins forgiven, and ignorance dispelled. Causes of spiritual and physical oppression and bondage must be removed. Once that is done, people may come into intimate communion with God, become clear about the truth of reality, have their innate energies liberated, recover their original selves, and find peace. This process, and its goal, is called variously salvation, liberation, and enlightenment. It is the prerequisite for proper fulfillment of the purposes of life described in Part One.

We begin with a discussion of grace, the divine mercy that wills our salvation. We are in desperate need of grace, for—according to religious teachings with a severe view of human fallenness—we are hopelessly lost, corrupted, and afflicted by evil. The second section extends the theme to the question of universal salvation: Is God's grace so all-encompassing and irresistible that all humankind will ultimately be saved? In the remainder of this chapter we gather passages which describe salvation, liberation, and enlightenment under twelve heads which cover a broad range of meanings: (1) atonement, forgiveness, and cleansing of sins; (2) healing of the ills of both body and soul; (3) liberation from the bondage of sin or the fetters of craving; (4) enlightenment, by which primordial ignorance is overcome through wisdom; (5) a journey, crossing the waters of life's suffering to find the shore and solid ground; (6) reversal of an upside-down world or restoration of a broken reality to its original trueness; (7) peace and a calm spirit; (8) help and deliverance in times of distress or oppression; (9) the refining fire to smelt away impurities of the heart; (10) the experience of being born anew as a new person and a child of God; (11) eternal life, the state where death has no sway; and (12) the unitive state of mystic oneness with all Reality.

# Grace

MOST RELIGIONS RECOGNIZE that, due to humanity's fallen and degraded condition, it is difficult if not impossible for an individual to attain the goal and purpose of life unaided. In fact, help is available; God's grace is sufficient support for people on the journey of faith. The scriptures often emphasize the priority of divine grace; it is present even before a person responds, eliciting faith in those who otherwise would have no clue of how to escape their mean lot.

First we have selected passages which describe God as the savior of benighted and sinful people. Grace is entirely God's initiative, given to people regardless of their attitude or merit. Furthermore, God's grace far overshadows the merit gained by good works; indeed, nothing can come of a person's good works or austerities endured for the purpose of salvation, in the absence of divine grace. God's grace is also described as sufficient, regardless of the person's burden or strength to bear it.

The section ends with the two Parables of the Prodigal Son, one from the New Testament and one from the Lotus Sutra. The teachings of these two stories differ in important respects: The Christian version cautions against self-righteousness on the part of the faithful believer as represented by the prodigal's brother, while the Buddhist version teaches the Buddha's skill in means through the devices of the rich father. Yet the theme of divine compassion for errant humanity shines through both.

Through Thy power, O Lord,
Make life renovated, real at Thy will.

*Zoroastrianism*. Avesta, Yasna 34.15

God is the best to take care of man, and He is the Most Merciful of those who show mercy!

*Islam*. Qur'an 12.64

Lord! You are the uninvoked savior, motiveless compassionate being, a well-wisher even when unprayed, a friend even when unrelated.

*Jainism*. Vitaragastava 13.1

For God so loved the world that he gave his only Son, that whoever believes in him should not perish but have eternal life.

*Christianity*. John 3.16

Since all have sinned and fall short of the glory of God, they are justified by his grace as a gift, through the redemption which is in Christ Jesus, whom God put forward as an expiation by his blood, to be received by faith.

*Christianity*. Romans 3.23-25

God the Rescuer,
God the Savior,
Almighty, whom we joyfully adore,
Powerful God,
Invoked by all men,
May he, the bounteous, grant us his blessings!

*Hinduism*. Rig Veda 7.100.4

Always created beings He cherishes;
The Creator looks to the weal of all.

**Qur'an 12.64:** Cf. Qur'an 39.53, p. 369.

**Vitaragastava 13.1:** Cf. Tao Te Ching 62, p. 90.

**Romans 3.23-25:** See Ephesians 2.8-9, p. 540.

**Rig Veda 7.100.4:** Cf. Black Yajur Veda 6.6, p. 90, invoking the grace of God as Shiva; also Bhagavad Gita 18.58, p. 396.

Lord! Invaluable are Thy blessings;
Without extent is His bounty.

*Sikhism.* Adi Granth, Kirtan Sohila, M.1, p. 12

And the Almighty said to Moses, "I am One and Eternal, so you, too, shall be united as one and you will be an eternal people." He further said, "Thus shall you say to the Children of Israel, 'The Eternal, Who is determined to remove cruelty from all human existence, has sent me to you.'"

*Judaism.* Torah Yesharah, Exodus 3.14

I am the Tathagata,
The Most Honored among men;
I appear in the world
Like unto this great cloud,
To pour enrichment on all
Parched living beings,
To free them from their misery
To attain the joy of peace,
Joy of the present world,
And joy of Nirvana.

*Buddhism.* Lotus Sutra 5

The Lord is my shepherd, I shall not want;
he makes me lie down in green pastures.
He leads me beside still waters;
he restores my soul.
He leads me in paths of righteousness
for his name's sake.
Even though I walk through the valley of
the shadow of death,
I fear no evil;
for thou art with me;
thy rod and thy staff,
they comfort me.
Thou preparest a table before me
in the presence of my enemies;
thou anointest my head with oil,
my cup overflows.
Surely goodness and mercy shall follow me
all the days of my life;
and I shall dwell in the house of the Lord
for ever.

*Judaism* and *Christianity.* Psalm 23

If we are faithless, he remains faithful—for he cannot deny himself.

*Christianity.* 2 Timothy 2.13

God is always impartial and compassionate. At least three times he tries to lead even the most wicked men [to salvation] by way of their minds.

*Unification Church.* Sun Myung Moon

We who live in the world, still attached to karmas, can overcome the world by thy grace alone.

*Hinduism.* Srimad Bhagavatam 11.2

All need grace, for even Abraham, for whose sake grace came plenteously into the world, himself needed grace.

*Judaism.* Midrash, Genesis Rabbah 60.2

God promises you His forgiveness and bounties; and God cares for all and He knows all things. He grants wisdom to whom He pleases, and he to whom wisdom is granted receives indeed a benefit overflowing; but none will grasp the Message but men of understanding.

*Islam.* Qur'an 2.268-69

**Torah Yesharah:** This is a traditional interpretive translation of Torah by Obadiah Sforno (1475-1550). It renders the way many Jews have traditionally understood the meaning of the Tetragrammaton. Compare the modern translation of Exodus 3.13-15, p. 76. Cf. 1 Timothy 2.3-4, p. 366.

**Lotus Sutra 5:** Buddhism is basically a religion of salvation or liberation, as derived from the Four Noble Truths, which both diagnose mankind's ills and explain the process of liberation from them. This passage is from the Parable of the Rain Cloud, pp. 91-92; cf. Lotus Sutra 7, pp. 455-56; Larger Sukhavativyuha Sutra 8.18, p. 457; Tannisho of Shinran, p. 542.

**Psalm 23:** Cf. Psalm 145.8-9, p. 88; John 10.11-16, p. 457, on Jesus the Good Shepherd.

**2 Timothy 2.13:** Cf. Canticles Rabbah 2.5, p. 546.

**Genesis Rabbah 60.2:** Cf. Kiddushin 30b, p. 277. Mention of Abraham recalls Paul's argument for faith as superior to works in Galatians 3.1-9, p. 540-41.

**Qur'an 2.268-69:** Cf. Qur'an 18.23-24, p. 649; 42:19, p. 87; 49.7, p. 538.

The Self is not to be obtained by instruction,
Nor by intellect, nor by much learning.
He is to be obtained only by the one whom He chooses.
To such a one the Self reveals His own person.

*Hinduism*. Mundaka Upanishad 3.2.3

Abu Huraira reported God's Messenger as saying, "There is none whose deeds alone would entitle him to get into Paradise." Someone said, "God's Messenger, not even you?" He replied, "Not even I, but that my Lord wraps me in mercy."

*Islam*. Hadith of Muslim

By assuming numerous garbs [of ascetics], learning, induced meditation, or stubborn practices,
Has none attained Him.
Says Nanak, By His grace alone does one attain to sainthood and enlightenment.

*Sikhism*. Adi Granth, Gauri Bawan Akkhari, M.5, p. 251

Now, if it had not been been for the plan of redemption, which was laid from the foundation of the world, there could have been no resurrection of the dead; but there was a plan of redemption laid, which shall bring to pass the resurrection of the dead.

*Church of Jesus Christ of Latter-day Saints*. Book of Mormon, Alma 12.25

God desires to lighten things for you, for man was created a weakling.

*Islam*. Qur'an 4.28

God is faithful, and he will not let you be tempted beyond your strength, but with the temptation will also provide the way of escape, that you may be able to endure it.

*Christianity*. 1 Corinthians 10.13

God charges no soul save to its capacity;
standing to its account is what it has earned,
and against its account what it has deserved.
Our Lord! Take us not to task if we forget, or make mistake.
Our Lord! Charge us not with a load as that which You laid upon those before us.
Our Lord! Burden us not beyond what we have the strength to bear.
Pardon us, forgive us, and have mercy on us.

*Islam*. Qur'an 2.286

And Jesus said, "There was a man who had two sons; and the younger of them said to his father, 'Father, give me the share of property that falls to me.' And he divided his living between them. Not many days later, the younger son gathered all he had and took his journey into a far country, and there he squandered his property in loose living. And when he had spent everything, a great famine arose in that country, and he began to be in want. So he went and joined himself to one of the citizens of that country, who sent him into his fields to feed swine. And he would gladly have fed on the pods that the swine ate; and no one gave him anything. But when he came to himself he said, 'How many of my father's hired servants have bread enough and to spare, but I perish here with hunger! I will arise and go to my father, and I will say to him, 'Father, I have sinned against heaven and before you; I am no longer worthy to be called your son; treat me as one of your hired servants.' And he arose and came to his father. But while he was yet at a

**Mundaka Upanishad 3.2.3:** For a different interpretation of this ambiguous text, see p. 492.

**Hadith of Muslim:** Cf. Qur'an 12.53, p. 273; Hadith of Muslim, p. 315; Nahjul Balagha, Sermon 57, p. 557.

**Gauri Bawan Akkhari, M.5:** Cf. Shalok, M.9, p. 278; Gauri Purabi, Ravidas, p. 284; Isaiah 64.6, p. 291.

**Book of Mormon, Alma 12.25:** The 'plan of redemption' refers to the inevitable Last Judgment and eschatological redemption of the righteous. The ultimate justice of God is founded upon his Word, which was declared before the creation of the world. Cf. 2 Peter 3.3-10, pp. 781-82; Proverbs 8.22-31, p. 100; John 1.1-4, pp. 99-100.

**1 Corinthians 10.13** and **Qur'an 2.286:** Cf. Qur'an 65.7, p. 492; Jeremiah 10.23-24, p. 404; Matthew 11.28-30, p. 461; Romans 8.26-27, p. 464; Guide to the Bodhisattva's Way of Life 7.22-24, p. 404-5.

distance, his father saw him and had compassion, and ran and embraced him and kissed him. And the son said to him, 'Father, I have sinned against heaven and before you; I am no longer worthy to be called your son.' But the father said to his servants, 'Bring quickly the best robe, and put it on him; and put a ring on his hand, and shoes on his feet; and bring the fatted calf and kill it, and let us eat and make merry; for this my son was dead, and is alive again; he was lost, and is found.' And they began to make merry.

"Now his elder son was in the field; and as he came and drew near to the house, he heard music and dancing. And he called one of his servants and asked what this meant. And he said to him, 'Your brother has come, and your father has killed the fatted calf, because he has received him safe and sound.' But he was angry and refused to go in. His father came out and entreated him, but he answered his father, 'Lo, these many years I have served you, and I never disobeyed your command; yet you never gave me a kid, that I might make merry with my friends. But when this son of yours came, who has devoured your living with harlots, you killed for him the fatted calf!' And he said to him, 'Son, you are always with me, and all that is mine is yours. It was fitting to make merry and be glad, for this your brother was dead, and is alive; he was lost, and is found.'"

*Christianity*. Luke 15.11-32: Parable of the Prodigal Son

It is like a youth who, on attaining manhood, leaves his father and runs away. For long he dwells in some other country, ten, or twenty, or fifty years. The older he grows, the more needy he becomes. Roaming about in all directions to seek clothing and food, he gradually wanders along till he unexpectedly approaches his native country. From the first the father searched for his son but in vain, and meanwhile has settled in a certain city. His home becomes very rich; his goods and treasures are incalculable....

At this time, the poor son, wandering through village after village, and passing through countries and cities, at last reaches the city where his father has settled. Always has the father been thinking of his son, yet, though he has been parted from him over fifty years, he has never spoken of the matter to any one, only pondering over it within himself and cherishing regret in his heart, as he reflects, "Old and worn, I own much wealth—gold, silver, and jewels, granaries and treasuries overflowing; but I have no son. Some day my end will come and my wealth will be scattered and lost, for there is no one to whom I can leave it... If I could only get back my son and commit my wealth to him, how contented and happy should I be, with never a further anxiety!"

Meanwhile the poor son, hired for wages here and there, unexpectedly arrives at his father's house. Standing by the gate, he sees from afar his father seated on a lion-couch, his feet on a jeweled footstool, revered and surrounded by Brahmans, warriors, and citizens, and with strings of pearls, worth thousands and myriads, adorning his body; attendants and young slaves with white chowries wait upon him right and left... The poor son, seeing his father possessed of such great power, was seized with fear, regretting that he had come to this place, and secretly reflects thus, "This must be a king, or someone of royal rank; it is no place for me to obtain anything for hire of my labor. I had better go to some poor hamlet, where there is a place for letting out my labor, and food and clothing are easier to get. If I tarry here long, I may suffer oppression and forced service." Reflecting thus, he hastens away.

Meanwhile the rich elder on his lion-seat has recognized his son at first sight, and with great joy in his heart has also reflected, "Now I

**Luke 15.11-32:** Jesus' Parable of the Prodigal Son speaks not only of God's grace and forgiveness (represented by the father), but also of the ethic that righteousness (represented by the elder brother) be accompanied by forgiveness and compassion for sinners (the younger brother). On the elder brother's attitude, compare Jonah 3.3-10, p. 643n.

have some one to whom I may bequeath my treasuries of wealth. Always I have been thinking of this my son, with no means of seeing him; but suddenly he himself has come and my longing is satisfied. Though worn with years, I yearn for him as of old."

Instantly he dispatches his attendants to pursue him quickly and fetch him back. Thereupon the messengers hasten forth to seize him. The poor son, surprised and scared, loudly cries his complaint, "I have committed no offense against you; why should I be arrested?" The messengers all the more hasten to lay hold of him and compel him to go back. Thereupon the poor son, thinking within himself that though he is innocent yet he will be imprisoned, and that now he will surely die, is all the more terrified, faints away and falls prostrate on the ground. The father, seeing this from afar, sends word to the messengers, "I have no need for this man. Do not bring him by force. Sprinkle cold water on his face to restore him to consciousness and do not speak to him any further." Wherefore? The father, knowing that his son's disposition is inferior, knowing that his own lordly position has caused distress to his son, yet convinced that he is his son, tactfully does not say to others, "This is my son."

A messenger says to the son, "I now set you free; go wherever you will." The poor son is delighted, thus obtaining the unexpected. He rises from the ground and goes to a poor hamlet in search of food and clothing. Then the elder, desiring to attract his son, sets up a device. Secretly he sends two men, doleful and shabby in appearance, saying, 'You go and visit that place and gently say to the poor man, "There is a place for you to work here… we will hire you for scavenging, and we both also will work along with you.'" Then the two messengers go in search of the poor son and, having found him, place before him the above proposal. Thereupon the poor son, having received his wages beforehand, joins with them in removing a refuse heap.

His father, beholding the son, is struck with compassion for, and wonder at, him. Another day he sees at a distance, through a window, his son's figure, gaunt, lean, and doleful, filthy and unclean with dirt and dust; thereupon he takes off his strings of jewels, his soft attire, and puts on a coarse, torn and dirty garment, smears his body with dust, takes a basket in his right hand, and with an appearance fear-inspiring says to the laborers, "Get on with your work, don't be lazy." By such a device he gets near to his son, to whom he afterwards says, "Ay, my man, you stay and work here, do not go again elsewhere; I will increase your wages; give whatever you need, bowls, utensils, rice, wheat-flour, salt, vinegar, and so on; have no hesitation; besides there is an old and worn-out servant whom you shall be given if you need him. Be at ease in your mind; I am, as it were, your father; do not be worried again. Wherefore? I am old and advanced in years, but you are young and vigorous; all the time you have been working, you have never been deceitful, lazy, angry or grumbling; I have never seen you, like the other laborers, with such vices as these. From this time forth you shall be as my own begotten son."

Thereupon the elder gives him a new name and calls him a son. Then the poor son, though he rejoices at this happening, still thinks of himself as a humble hireling. For this reason, during twenty years he continues to be employed in scavenging. After this period, there grows mutual confidence between them, and he goes in and out and at his ease, though his abode is still in a small hut.

Then the elder becomes ill and, knowing that he will die before long, says to the poor son, "Now I possess abundance of gold, silver, and precious things, and my granaries and treasuries are full to overflowing. The quantities of these things, and the amounts which should be received and given, I want you to understand in detail. Such is my mind, and you must agree to this my wish. Wherefore? Because now I and you are of the same mind. Be increasingly careful so that there be no waste."

The poor man accepts his instruction and commands, and becomes acquainted with all the goods… but has no idea of expecting to inherit as much as a meal, while his abode is still the original place and he is yet unable to abandon his sense of inferiority.

After a short time has again passed, the father notices that his son's ideas have gradually been enlarged, his aspirations developed, and that he despises his previous state of mind. On seeing that his own end is approaching, he commands his son to come, and gathers together his relatives, and the kings, ministers, warriors, and citizens. When they are all assembled, he addresses them saying, "Now, gentlemen, this is my son, begotten by me. It is over fifty years since, from a certain city, he left me and ran away to endure loneliness and misery. His former name was so-and-so and my name was so-and-so. At that time in that city I sought him sorrowfully. Suddenly in this place I met and regained him. This is really my son and I am really his father. Now all the wealth which I possess belongs entirely to my son, and all my previous disbursements and receipts are known by this son."

When the poor son heard these words of his father, great was his joy at such unexpected news, and thus he thought, "Without any mind for, or effort on my part, these treasures now come of themselves to me."

World-honored One! The very rich elder is the Tathagata, and we are all as the Buddha's sons. The Buddha has always declared that we are his sons. But because of the three sufferings, in the midst of births-and-deaths we have borne all kinds of torments, being deluded and ignorant and enjoying our attachment to trifles. Today the World-honored One has caused us to ponder over and remove the dirt of all diverting discussions of inferior things. In these we have hitherto been diligent to make progress and have got, as it were, a day's pay for our effort to reach Nirvana. Obtaining this, we greatly rejoiced and were contented, saying to ourselves, "For our diligence and progress in the Buddha-law what we have received is ample"... The Buddha, knowing that our minds delighted in inferior things, by his tactfulness taught according to our capacity, but still we did not perceive that we are really Buddha's sons... Therefore we say that though we had no mind to hope or expect it, yet now the Great Treasure of the King of the Law has of itself come to us, and such things that Buddha-sons should obtain, we have all obtained.

*Buddhism*. Lotus Sutra 4:
Parable of the Prodigal Son

**Lotus Sutra 4:** In the Buddhist Parable of the Prodigal Son, the rich elder represents the Buddha and the son is the ordinary person. The Buddha cannot show his grace directly, so in compassion he resorts to an expedient in order to reach his low-minded son. Cf. the Parable of the Good Physician, Lotus Sutra 16, p. 721; also 1 Corinthians 9.19-22, p. 719.

## *Universal Salvation*

THE COMPASSION AND GRACE OF GOD know no bounds. In some passages from scripture, the extent of God's saving work is predicted eventually to embrace all humankind. Thus does the Divine Parent's heart yearn for all his children. In Buddhist terms, the essential purpose of absolute Truth is to liberate all sentient beings, and Mahayana Buddhist scriptures express the universality of grace in the Vow of the Buddha Amitabha. His Vow is a bodhisattva vow to save all beings, and in popular Buddhism the great Bodhisattvas who attend the Buddha are revered as manifesting the gracious aspects of Ultimate Reality.

Universal salvation is compatible with the belief that there is only one valid and true religion. Salvation may come to all people through one central point: thus in Abraham "shall all the families of the earth be blessed" (Genesis 12.3). For those who believe in one religion as the only way, the divine mandate to save all humankind is a powerful impetus to missionary activity.

We conclude with several passages which offer salvation to souls in hell. If salvation is to be available universally, to every soul who has ever lived regardless of his or her earthly life, the doctrine may appear at odds with beliefs about hell and the Last Judgment. If God is most essentially just, how can the wicked receive salvation? On the other hand, if God is most essentially gracious and compassionate, how can he permit any creature to suffer in hell eternally? Compassion and justice must go together. Buddhism, Hinduism, and Jainism reconcile these aspects of Ultimate Reality by regarding all states of hell as purgatories, designed to mete out punishments for a limited period of time, that evil karma might be burned up and the soul have a future opportunity to find the Path. Christian and Islamic theologians dispute this question among themselves—some upholding an eternal hell, others looking to universal salvation. The Latter-day Saints practice baptism for the dead, thereby emptying hell of its dead through the efforts of the living.

God our Savior, who desires all men to be saved and to come to the knowledge of the truth.

*Christianity*. 1 Timothy 2.3-4

The daily concern of the Parent is single-heartedly how best I can advance arrangements to save all of you.

*Tenrikyo*. Ofudesaki 14.35

We will make offering unto thee with worship,
O Lord, and to the Right,
That you may achieve through Good Mind the
destiny of all creatures in the Dominion.
For the salvation of the man of insight among
such as you,
O Wise One, will hold good for everyone.

*Zoroastrianism*. Avesta, Yasna 34.3

**1 Timothy 2.3-4:** Cf. 2 Timothy 2.13, p. 361; Torah Yesharah, p. 361.

**Yasna 34.3:** The passage asks that these prayers to God cause all creatures, not just the wise man, to achieve their destiny in God's Kingdom.

The Dharma of the Buddhas
by the constant use of a single flavor
Causes the several worlds
universally to attain perfection,
By gradual practice
all obtain the Fruit of the Way.

*Buddhism.* Lotus Sutra 5

As I live, says the Lord God, I have no pleasure in the death of the wicked.

*Judaism* and *Christianity*. Ezekiel 33.11

When Israel crossed the Red Sea, the angels were about to break forth in song, but the Holy One rebuked them, "My children are drowning, and you would sing?"

*Judaism.* Talmud, Megilla 10b

God it is who has sent His Messenger with the guidance and the Religion of Truth, that He may cause it to prevail over all religion, however much the idolators may be averse.

*Islam.* Qur'an 9.33

Turn to me and be saved,
all the ends of the earth!
for I am God, and there is no other.
By myself I have sworn,
from my mouth has gone forth in righteousness
an irrevocable decree:
"To me every knee shall bow,
every tongue shall swear."

*Judaism* and *Christianity*.
Isaiah 45.22-23

Miqdad reported that he heard God's messenger say, "There will not remain on the face of the earth a mud-brick house or a camel's hair tent which God will not cause the confession of Islam to enter, bringing both mighty honor and abject abasement. God will either honor the occupants and put them among its adherents, or will humiliate them and they will be subject to it." Miqdad said, "God will then receive complete obedience."

*Islam.* Hadith of Ahmad

God is on the watch for the nations of the world to repent, so that He may bring them under His wings.

*Judaism.* Midrash,
Numbers Rabbah 10.1

I testify that Thou art the Lord of all creation, and the Educator of all beings, visible and invisible. I bear witness that Thy power hath encompassed the entire universe, and that the hosts of the earth can never dismay Thee, nor can the dominion of all peoples and nations deter Thee from executing Thy purpose. I confess that Thou hast no desire except the regeneration of the whole world, and the establishment of the unity of its peoples, and the salvation of all them that dwell therein.

*Baha'i Faith.* Gleanings from the
Writings of Baha'u'llah 115

Behold my servant, whom I uphold,
my chosen, in whom my soul delights;
I have put my Spirit upon him,
he will bring forth justice to the nations.
He will not cry or lift up his voice,
or make it heard in the street;
a bruised reed he will not break,
and a dimly burning wick he will not quench;
he will faithfully bring forth justice.

**Lotus Sutra 5:** This is the conclusion to the long Parable of the Rain Cloud, pp. 91-92.

**Megilla 10b:** 'My children' are the Egyptians who drowned in the waters while the Israelites escaped—Exodus 15.1-11, p. 400-1. On God's love for Israel's enemies, cf. Amos 9.7, p. 193.

**Qur'an 9.33:** Cf. Qur'an 22.56, p. 789.

**Isaiah 45.22-23:** Cf. Isaiah 2.2-4, p. 790; 56.7, p. 188; Zechariah 14.9, p. 789.

**Hadith of Ahmad:** Cf. Qur'an 21.104-05, p. 789.

**Gleanings from the Writings of Baha'u'llah 115:** Cf. Gleanings from the Writings of Baha'u'llah 111, p. 188; 'Abdu'l-Baha, Promulgation of Universal Peace, pp. 198, 795.

He will not fail or be discouraged
till he has established justice in the earth;
and the coastlands wait for his law.

*Judaism* and *Christianity*. Isaiah 42.1-4

The Tathagatas do not enter ultimate liberation until all living beings have entered ultimate liberation.

*Buddhism*. Holy Teaching of Vimalakirti 4

God did not call me for myself. He called me expecting that I would develop the universal personality [that can relate well with all people and things].

*Unification Church*. Sun Myung Moon, 4-14-57

I establish the Vows unexcelled,
And reach the highest path, Bodhi.
Were these Vows unfulfilled,
I would never attain Enlightenment.

I will be the great provider
Throughout innumerable ages.
Should I fail to save all in need,
I would never attain Enlightenment.

Upon my attaining Enlightenment,
If my Name were not heard anywhere
In the ten quarters of the universe,
I would never attain Enlightenment.

Practicing the Holy Way—selflessness,
Depth in right reflection and pure wisdom,
Aspiring toward the highest path,
I will be the teacher of devas and men.

My wondrous power by its great light
Brightens countless lands throughout,
Removes the darkness of the three defilements
And delivers all from suffering and pain.

*Buddhism*. Larger Sukhavativyuha Sutra 9.1-5: Juseige

Those who are wretched shall be in the Fire... they will dwell therein for all the time that the heavens and the earth endure, except as your Lord wills; for your Lord is the sure Accomplisher of what He plans.

*Islam*. Qur'an 11.106-7

For Christ also died for sins once for all, the righteous for the unrighteous, that he might bring us to God, being put to death in the flesh but made alive in the spirit; in which he went and preached to the spirits in prison, who formerly did not obey, when God's patience waited in the days of Noah, during the building of the ark.

*Christianity*. 1 Peter 3.18-20

It is sufficient to know, in this case, that the earth will be smitten with a curse unless there is a welding link of some kind or other between the fathers and the children, upon some subject or other—and behold what is that subject? It is the baptism for the dead. For we without them cannot be made perfect; neither can they without us be made perfect. Neither can they nor we be made perfect without those who have died in the gospel also; for it is necessary in the ushering in of the dispensation of the

**Isaiah 42.1-4:** This Servant Song is understood differently by Jews and Christians. Jews interpret the servant to be Israel, and view the passage as a statement of Israel's vocation to be a light to the world. Christians understand the fuller meaning of the servant as realized in Christ.

**Larger Sukhavativyuha Sutra 9.1-5:** This is one of the chief hymns of the Pure Land school. One should not interpret this passage as speaking of God's love in the western sense of the divine Being's love for his creatures. Rather, the ideal of the bodhisattva illustrates the Mahayana Buddhist principle that Ultimate Reality is itself all-embracing, inclusive of every living being and of the nature of compassion. One who truly understands this principle cannot help but feel suffering as long as there is even one individual who suffers, for that unfortunate individual is one's very self. This is the essence of the Bodhisattva Vow; see Sikshasamuccaya 280-81, p. 692; Garland Sutra 23, p. 692; see also the Eighteenth Vow of Buddha Amitabha, Larger Sukhavativyuha Sutra 8.18, p. 457.

**Qur'an 11.106-7:** Based on this verse, some Muslim theologians have deduced that the penalties in hell are not eternal, for 'the time that the heavens and the earth endure' has a limit; in the end they are to be dissolved and renewed.

**1 Peter 3.18-20:** This passage is usually interpreted to mean that Jesus preached to the spirits in hell. Or, if the doctrine of eternal hell is to be upheld, then the 'prison' may be interpreted as an intermediate state of purgatory. Compare Markandeya Purana 13-15, p. 693.

fullness of times, which dispensation is now beginning to usher in, that a whole and complete and perfect union, and welding together of dispensations, and keys, and powers, and glories should take place.

*Church of Jesus Christ of Latter-day Saints.* Doctrine and Covenants 128.18

## *Atonement and Forgiveness*

FOR PEOPLE SOILED BY SIN and hence unworthy to enter the presence of God, or corrupted by evil deeds and hence unable to realize their true inner nature, an essential prerequisite for salvation is the forgiveness of sins. The experience of divine forgiveness and pardon is universal, reaching to supplicants in all the world's religions.

The opening passages express God's forgiving nature; it is ever God's desire to forgive. The next few passages treat the idea of atonement; some expiation must be made for sin, either by a Savior, or by a priest, or by the supplicant's own acts of penance and devotion. Several texts discuss the cleansing of sin. We conclude with passages which emphasize the magnitude of divine forgiveness, which can encompass even the most gargantuan evils. Some passages suggest that God even desired sin or favors sinners in order that he may demonstrate his gracious and forgiving nature.

I, I am he who blots out your transgressions for my own sake, and I will not remember your sins.

*Judaism* and *Christianity*. Isaiah 43.25

All evil effects of deeds are destroyed, when He who is both personal and impersonal is realized.

*Hinduism*. Mundaka Upanishad 2.2.9

Say, If you love God, follow me, and God will love you, and forgive you all your sins; God is All-forgiving, All-compassionate.

*Islam*. Qur'an 3.31

In him we have redemption through his blood, the forgiveness of our trespasses, according to the riches of his grace which he lavished upon us.

*Christianity*. Ephesians 1.7-8

Say, O my Servants who have transgressed against their souls! Despair not of the mercy of God: for God forgives all sins: for He is Oft-forgiving, Most Merciful.

*Islam*. Qur'an 39.53

**Doctrine and Covenants 128.18:** The baptism for the dead is an important rite of the Latter-day Saints, bringing salvation to those who have passed away in ignorance—'those who have died in the gospel' are Christians ignorant of the new dispensation—and bringing wholeness and complete salvation to the cosmos. Notice the Bible references to Malachi 4.6 and Hebrews 11.39-40. Cf. Doctrine and Covenants 76.54-93, pp. 226-27.

**Isaiah 43.25:** Cf. Isaiah 1.16-20, p. 520.

**Ephesians 1.7-8:** This passage speaks of the blood of Christ, shed on the cross for the forgiveness of sins. Cf. Romans 3.23-25, p. 360; Hebrews 9.11-14, below; John 1.29, p. 455; 1 Corinthians 11.23-25, p. 609.

**Qur'an 39.53:** Cf. Qur'an 26.77-82, p. 88; 40.55, p. 529.

Let every person ask pardon of the Great Light Asis,
The Molder of us all.

*African Traditional Religions*. Kipsigis Tradition (Kenya)

If we have sinned against the man who loves us,
have wronged a brother, a dear friend, or a comrade,
the neighbor of long standing or a stranger,
remove from us this stain, O King Varuna.

*Hinduism*. Rig Veda 5.85.7

Though a man be soiled with the sins of a lifetime, let him but love me, rightly resolved, in utter devotion. I see no sinner, that man is holy. Holiness soon shall refashion his nature to peace eternal. O son of Kunti, of this be certain: The man who loves me shall not perish.

*Hinduism*. Bhagavad Gita 9.30-31

Anyone that is fallen into the grip of lust, wrath, or attachment,
Attached to stingy greed,
Guilty of the four cardinal sins and evils,
And demonic sins like murder;
Who never has attended to scriptures, holy music, or sacred verse—
By contemplation of the Supreme Being,
With a moment's remembrance of God shall he be saved.

*Sikhism*. Adi Granth, Sri Raga, M.5, p. 70

Hide thy face from my sins,
and blot out all my iniquities.
Create in me a clean heart, O God,
and put a new and right spirit within me.

*Judaism* and *Christianity*. Psalm 51.9-10

Shining brightly, Agni, drive away
our sin, and shine wealth on us.
Shining bright, drive away our sin.

For good fields, for good homes, for wealth,
we made our offerings to thee.
Shining bright, drive away our sin....

So that Agni's conquering beams
may spread out on every side,
Shining bright, drive away our sin.

Thy face is turned on every side,
thou pervadest everywhere.
Shining bright, drive away our sin.

*Hinduism*. Rig Veda 1.97.1-6

Of the sin against the gods thou art atonement;
Of the sin against men thou art atonement;
Of the sin against myself thou art atonement;
Of every kind of sin thou art atonement.
The sin that I have committed knowingly,
and that I have committed unawares,
Of all sins thou art atonement.

*Hinduism*. Yajur Veda 8.13

Let him utter the name, Buddha Amitayus. Let him do so serenely with his voice uninterrupted; let him be continually thinking of Buddha until he has completed ten times the thought, repeating, "Adoration to Buddha Amitayus." On the strength of [his merit of] uttering the Buddha's name he will, during every repetition, expiate the sins which involve him in births and deaths during eighty million kalpas.

*Buddhism*. Meditation on Buddha Amitayus 3.30

**Kipsigis Tradition:** Cf. p. 642.

**Rig Veda 5.85.7:** Cf. Rig Veda 7.86.2-5, p. 643 and note.

**Bhagavad Gita 9.30-31:** Cf. Bhagavad Gita 18.66, p. 551; Srimad Bhagavatam 6.1, p. 646.

**Sri Raga, M.5:** On the four cardinal sins, cf. Chandogya Upanishad 5.10.9, p. 330. Cf. Shalok Vadhik, M.3, p. 642-43.

**Rig Veda 1.97.1-6:** This is a litany for the fire ritual. Agni, deity embodied in fire, symbolically burns away sin and mental pollution through the ritual fire. Cf. Rig Veda 10.9.8-9, p. 611.

**Meditation on Buddha Amitayus:** In Pure Land Buddhism, compassion reaches to the nethermost hells! The grace of Buddha Amitayus, the Buddha of Infinite Life, or Buddha Amitabha (Jap. Amida), the

Aaron shall offer the bull as a sin offering for himself, and shall make atonement for himself and for his house. Then he shall take the two goats, and set them before the Lord at the door of the tent of meeting; and Aaron shall cast lots upon the two goats, one lot for the Lord and the other lot for Azazel. And Aaron shall present the goat on which the lot fell for the Lord, and offer it as a sin offering; but the goat on which the lot fell for Azazel shall be presented alive before the Lord to make atonement over it.... He shall kill the goat of the sin offering which is for the people, and bring its blood within the veil, and sprinkle it upon the mercy seat and before the mercy seat; thus he shall make atonement for the holy place, because of the uncleannesses of the people of Israel.... And Aaron shall lay both his hands upon the head of the live goat, and confess over him all the iniquities of the people of Israel, and all their transgressions, all their sins; and he shall put them upon the head of the goat, and send him away into the wilderness by the hand of a man who is in readiness. The goat shall bear all their iniquities upon him to a solitary land.... And it shall be a statute to you for ever that in the seventh month, on the tenth day of the month... on this day shall atonement be made for you, to cleanse you; from all your sins you shall be clean before the Lord.

*Judaism.* Leviticus 16.6-30

But when Christ appeared as the high priest of the good things that have come, then through the greater and more perfect tent (not made with hands, that is, not of this creation) he entered once and for all into the Holy Place, taking not the blood of goats and calves but his own blood, thus securing an eternal redemption. For if the sprinkling of defiled persons with the blood of goats and bulls and with the ashes of a heifer sanctifies for the purification of the flesh, how much more shall the blood of Christ, who through the eternal Spirit offered himself without blemish to God, purify your conscience from dead works to serve the living God.

*Christianity.* Hebrews 9.11-14

[The Bodhisattva] Vajrasattva is white, with one face and two hands, holding a scepter in his right hand and a bell in his left. He is sitting in the adamantine posture embracing his consort, Dor-je Nyem-ma, who is white, with one face and two hands, holding a curved knife in her right hand and a skull-cap in her left.... Above a moon in Vajrasattva's heart is a HUM and on the edge of the moon revolves the hundred-syllable mantra.

[I pray], "O Endowed Transcendent Destroyer Vajrasattva, I myself and others request that you cleanse wrongs and hindrances from all sentient beings and purify every weakened and broken sacred word of

Buddha of Infinite Light (who are one in the same), is sufficient to save even the most reprobate sinner. In the Amida Buddha's original vow, he pledged to save all sentient beings who would repeat his name ten times; see Larger Sukhavativyuha Sutra 8.18, p. 457.

**Leviticus 16.6-30:** This is the ancient ritual for the Day of Atonement. The Bible prescribes that the high priest (Aaron) purify the altar and holy place with blood from the bull and goat which are sacrificed, and that the sins of the congregation be placed upon the head of a remaining goat (the 'scapegoat') who is led into the wilderness. In modern Judaism the Day of Atonement is observed with solemn fasting and the "sacrifice of prayer" which replace this archaic ritual. Cf. Menahot 110a, p. 618.

**Hebrews 9.11-14:** This passage compares the sacrifice of Christ, who shed his blood on the cross for the forgiveness of sins, with the above ritual of the Day of Atonement. It emphasizes that Christ's sacrifice was 'once and for all,' 'securing an eternal redemption,' while the atoning rites of the Old Testament were only temporary and had to be repeated every year. Since Hebrews was written after the Temple had been destroyed (in 70 A.D.) and its rites had ceased, the implication is that Christ's sacrifice is the only effective means of atonement. Other rituals of purification from the Old Testament, such as the rite of the red heifer (Numbers 19.1-10) are also mentioned in the comparison. Cf. Romans 3.23-25, p. 360; John 1.29, p. 455; Hebrews 2.14-18, p. 469; 1 Corinthians 11.23-25, p. 609.

honor." Having requested like this, from the HUM and the mantra-rosary in his heart shine out radiant lights, cleansing the wrongs and hindrances from all sentient beings, who come presenting offerings that delight the Awakened Beings and their spiritual sons. Every excellence of their body, speech and mind collects in the form of light and dissolves into the mantra-rosary and the HUM. From there a white stream of nectar flows, pouring from the place of union of the Lord and consort. It enters through the pour aperture at the crown of my head, filling my whole body with a stream of nectar of pristine awareness. I become purified by the cleansing of all evils and hindrances from my three doors.

"Through my ignorance and delusions I have transgressed and weakened my pledges. O my spiritual master, protect me and be my refuge. Lord who holds the adamantine scepter, the embodiment of great compassion, the chief of beings, I go to you for refuge."

In answer Vajrasattva replies, "O child of my family, your wrongs and hindrances and every broken and weakened commitment are cleansed and purified." Having spoken thus, he dissolves into me and my three doors become inseparable from the perfect body, speech, and mind of Vajrasattva.

*Buddhism*. Cakrasamvara Tantra

Thus hearing the litany, and that there be
No blot of sin in the court or the country,
May the deities bestow their purification that
No offense remain, and
As the wind blows from its origin
To carry away the clouds of heaven,
Even as the wind of morning and the wind of evening
Clears away the morning and evening mists,
As the ship in harbor casts off its moorings stem and stern
To be borne out onto the great plain of the sea, and
As the rank grasses beyond the river
Are swept away with the clean stroke of the scythe—
Even so, may the deity Seoritsuhime-no-kami,
Dwelling in the swift-flowing stream that
Falls from the high mountains and low hills,
Carry away these sins and pollutions
Without remain, to the wide sea plain.
Our sins thus swept away,
May the goddess Hayaakitsuhimi-no-kami,
Who lives in the stream of the sea plain,
Open wide her great mouth
To engulf those sins and impurities, and
When they are thus imbibed,
May the god Ibukidonushi-no-kami,
Dwelling in the place where breath is breathed,
Blow them out with a great rushing breath.
And when he has thus banished them to the underworld,
May the goddess Hayasasurahime-no-kami disperse them one and all.
Even in this way, may the sins of
All in the realm, from officials of the court
On down, every transgression within the land,
Be washed away.

*Shinto*. Engishiki 8

Allah the Almighty has said, "O son of Adam, so long as you call upon Me and ask of Me, I shall forgive you for what you have done, and I shall not mind. O son of Adam, were your sins to reach the clouds of the sky and were you to then ask forgiveness of Me, I would forgive you. O son of Adam, were you to come to Me with sins nearly as great as the earth and were you to then face Me, ascribing no partner to Me, I would bring you forgiveness nearly as great as the earth."

*Islam*. Forty Hadith of an-Nawawi 42

**Engishiki 8:** This is a traditional litany for purification, recited at Shinto shrines. Cf. Kojiki 11, pp. 520-21.
**Forty Hadith of an-Nawawi 42:** Cf. Pesikta Rabbati 32b-33a, p. 561; Canticles Rabbah 2.5, p. 546.

Flowers like the lotus... do not grow on the dry ground in the wilderness, but do grow in the swamps and mud banks. Just so, the Buddha-qualities do not grow in living beings certainly destined for the uncreated but do grow in those living beings who are like swamps and mud banks of passion.

*Buddhism.* Holy Teaching of Vimalakirti 8

If you were not to commit sins, God would have swept you out of existence and would have replaced you with another people who have committed sin, and then asked God's forgiveness, that He might grant them pardon.

*Islam.* Hadith of Muslim

## *Healing*

THE CONDITION OF FALLEN HUMANITY has been likened to an infirmity and a disease of the soul. Our ignorance of Reality renders us blind to the truth and deaf to God's voice. Our hearts are heavy with pain and suffering. Hence, salvation may be regarded as healing the soul of its infirmity and restoring it to health where it can realize its true potential. Religious teaching may be regarded as a sovereign remedy, and the founder who bears the truth may be likened to a master physician.

But there is also a causal, psychosomatic relationship between healing of the soul and health of the body. Physical health is thus a welcome by-product of spiritual health. Jesus performed miraculous healings and exorcisms; today healings are performed in every part of the world by spiritual healers of all religions.

O Mankind! There has come to you an exhortation from your Lord, a balm for that which is in the breasts, a guidance and mercy for believers.

*Islam.* Qur'an 10.57

Whatever defect I have of eye, of heart, of mind,
or whatever excess there is,
may Brihaspati remedy it.
Gracious to us be the Lord of the world.

*Hinduism.* Yajur Veda 36.2

The Buddha, the Truly Enlightened One, the unexcelled master physician... having developed and perfected the medicines of the Teaching over countless eons, having cultivated and learned all skills in application of means, and fully consummated the power of illuminating spells, is able to quell all sentient beings' afflictions.

*Buddhism.* Garland Sutra 37

Then the eyes of the blind shall be opened,
and the ears of the deaf unstopped;

**Hadith of Muslim:** Cf. Book of Mormon, 2 Nephi 2.19-26, pp. 303-4n.

**Qur'an 10.57:** Cf. Qur'an 26.77-80, p. 88.

**Garland Sutra 37:** Cf. the Parable of the Good Physician, Lotus Sutra 16, p. 721; Guide to the Bodhisattva's Way of Life 7.22-24, pp. 404-5.

then shall the lame man leap like a hart,
and the tongue of the dumb sing for joy.
For waters shall break forth in the wilderness,
and streams in the desert.

*Judaism* and *Christianity*. Isaiah 35.5-6

The Way is like an empty vessel
That yet may be drawn from
Without ever needing to be filled.
It is bottomless; the very progenitor of all things in the world.
In it all sharpness is blunted,
All tangles untied,
All glare tempered,
All dust smoothed.
It is like a deep pool that never dries.

*Taoism*. Tao Te Ching 4

Under shelter of the Supreme Being, not a whiff of hot air touches us—
All around us is drawn the mystic circle of divine protection,
Keeping away suffering.
We have met the holy Preceptor, perfection incarnate,
Who has established this state.
He has administered medicine of the divine Name,
And attached our devotion to the Sole Lord.
The divine Preserver has preserved us, and all maladies removed.
Says Nanak, In His grace has the Lord come to succor us.

*Sikhism*. Adi Granth, Bilaval, M.5, p. 819

Come, let us return to the Lord;
for he has torn, that he may heal us;
he has stricken, and he will bind us up.
After two days he will revive us;
on the third day he will raise us up,
that we may live before him.

*Judaism* and *Christianity*. Hosea 6.1-2

The antidote, assuredly, for the elemental soul [bound to samsara] is this: study of the knowledge of the Veda and pursuit of one's own duty.

*Hinduism*. Maitri Upanishad 4.3

The words of the Torah are like a perfect remedy. This may be compared to a man who inflicted a big wound upon his son, and then put a plaster on his wound, saying, "My son! As long as this plaster is on your wound you can eat and drink what you like, and bathe in cold or warm water, and you will suffer no harm. But if you remove it, it will break out into sores." Even so did God say to the Israelites, "My children! I created within you the Evil Inclination, but I created the Law as its antidote. As long as you occupy yourselves with the Torah, the Evil Inclination will not rule over you. But if you do not occupy yourselves with the Torah, then you will be delivered into its power, and all its activity will be against you."

*Judaism*. Talmud, Kiddushin 30b

The physical healing of Christian Science results now, as in Jesus' time, from the operation of divine Principle, before which sin and disease lose their reality in human consciousness and disappear as naturally and as necessarily as darkness gives place to light and sin to reformation. Now, as then, these mighty works are not supernatural, but supremely natural. They are the sign of Immanuel, or "God with us,"—a divine influence ever present in human consciousness.

*Christian Science*. Science and Health, xi

A great crowd followed [Jesus] and thronged about him. And there was a woman who had had a flow of blood for twelve years, and who had suffered much under many physicians, and had spent all that she had, and was no better but rather grew worse. She had heard the reports about Jesus, and came up behind him in

**Isaiah 35.5-6:** Cf. Luke 4.16-21, p. 378.
**Tao Te Ching 4:** Cf. Dhammapada 82, p. 393; Elegant Sayings 173, p. 396.
**Bilaval, M.5:** Cf. Sri Raga, M.5, p. 393.
**Hosea 6.1-2:** Cf. Qur'an 26.77-80, p. 88; 2 Chronicles 7.14, p. 642.
**Kiddushin 30b:** Cf. Kiddushin 30b, p. 277; Genesis Rabbah 10.4, p. 791; Numbers Rabbah 17.6, pp. 791-92.

the crowd and touched his garment. For she said, "If I touch even his garments, I shall be made well." And immediately the hemorrhage ceased; and she felt in her body that she was healed of her disease. And Jesus, perceiving in himself that power had gone forth from him, immediately turned about in the crowd, and said, "Who touched my garments?" And his disciples said to him, "You see the crowd pressing around you, and yet you say, 'Who touched me?'" And he looked around to see who had done it. But the woman, knowing what had been done to her, came in fear and trembling and fell down before him, and told him the whole truth. And he said to her, "Daughter, your faith has made you well; go in peace, and be healed of your disease."

*Christianity*. Mark 5.24-34

Now Peter and John were going up to the temple at the hour of prayer, the ninth hour. And a man lame from birth was being carried, whom they laid daily at the gate of the temple which is called Beautiful to ask alms of those who entered the temple. Seeing Peter and John about to go into the temple, he asked for alms. And Peter directed his gaze at him, with John, and said, "Look at us." And he fixed his attention upon them, expecting to receive something from them. But Peter said, "I have no silver and gold, but I give you what I have; in the name of Jesus Christ of Nazareth, walk." And he took him by the right hand and raised him up; and immediately his feet and ankles were made strong. And leaping up he stood and walked and entered the temple with them, walking, and leaping, and praising God.

*Christianity*. Acts 3.1-8

The World-honored One, the All-compassion and Guide, for the sake of King Ajatasatru, entered into the moonlight-samadhi. Having entered the samadhi, a great light issued. The light was pure and cool, and it went to the king and shone in the king's body. The boils on his body got cured and the choking pains died out. Relieved of the pains of the boils and feeling cool in body, the king said to the Buddha, "Where does this light come from? It shines on me and touches me; it cures all boils, and the body feels peace." The Buddha answered, "O great king! This is the light of the heaven of heavens. This light has no root; it is boundless.... It is seen only where there is a desire to save.... O King, you said before that there was no good doctor in the world who could cure the body and mind. Because of this, this light is first sent out. It first cures your body, and then, your mind."

*Buddhism*.
Mahaparinirvana Sutra 575-76

Sickness arises from total involvement in the process of misunderstanding from beginningless time. It arises from the passions that result from unreal mental constructions, and hence ultimately nothing is perceived which can be said to be sick.

What is the elimination of this sickness? It is the elimination of egoism and possessiveness. What is the elimination of egoism and possessiveness? It is the freedom from dualism. What is freedom from dualism? It is the absence of involvement with either the external or the internal. What is absence of involvement with either external or internal? It is nondeviation, nonfluctuation, and nondistraction from equa-

**Mark 5.24-34:** Cf. Mark 9.17-24, p. 543; Matthew 12.22-24, p. 265; John 9.1-7, p. 503; Isaiah 53.4, pp. 457-58.

**Mahaparinirvana Sutra 575-76:** Healing King Ajatasatru shows the Buddha's great benevolence to even the most undeserving of grace. For King Ajatasatru (Pali Ajatasattu) was no friend of the Buddha, being a patron of the heretic Devadatta (cf. Vinaya Pitaka ii.184-98, pp. 318-20.), and having killed his father the pious King Bimbisara and imprisoned his mother Queen Vaidehi (according to Meditation on Buddha Amitayus). It is said that the king at last repented and learned the Teaching.

nimity. What is equanimity? It is the equality of everything from self to liberation. Why? Because both self and liberation are void.

*Buddhism.* Holy Teaching of Vimalakirti 5

I [God] feel extreme pity for the present world which indulges in excessive use of medicine.... Medicine should be used only in unavoidable instances and with full understanding of its true character. I reveal to you that the true nature of what modern science calls medicine is poison. Although you have been enjoying this poison, even naming it "medicine," you should know that its true nature... has the function of hardening and contaminating your spiritual and physical body. This results in your suffering and in shortening your life span. Nevertheless, humans have made light of this... and moreover have rejected the divine art of deep spiritual cleansing. In addition, you have utilized medicine as a means for making money and have been polluting the earth and atmosphere. You have thus committed a heavy sin toward the Creator of heaven and earth and humans. As a result of the sin and negative karma, you humans are bringing God's judgment upon yourselves. It is truly a pitiful condition.

Therefore, God is finally going to intensely cleanse the poison of your triple self—the spiritual, astral, and physical bodies collectively—and develop your positive spiritual power. Otherwise, the true children of God would lose their original vitality, which would make fruitless the purpose for which God created His children, the earth, and food prepared for them. For this reason, God must finally carry out deep spiritual cleansing....

Those who become obedient to God, come to a realization, come closer to God, and repent, shall receive the Baptism for deep spiritual cleansing by the holy spiritual essence of fire. They shall spiritually receive directly, the True Positive Light through your triple body, which is the way to lessen their compensation. This world shall be saved from the immense number of disturbances working against people's souls by Mahikari-no-Waza.

*Mahikari.* Goseigen

The *hekura*... help you bring back stolen souls; thanks to them you don't lose your way. You can repel the demons of disease; they enable you to recognize them by their smell. Each one has its particular odor, and their hammocks are impregnated with it; it comes from the *watota*, which they all possess. A high-quality hallucinogen enables you to see and name the demon who has just stolen a soul. You think, "It is so-and-so who is guilty!" And it is your turn to hurl your familiar hekura after him.

*Native American Religions.* Yanomami Shaman's Instruction (Brazil)

**Holy Teaching of Vimalakirti 5:** Vimalakirti rises from his sick bed and teaches that his sickness was ultimately unreal (*sunya*); by not being attached to or involved with an illusory reality he is no longer sick. From that demonstration Vimalakirti gives a deeper lesson. Both 'self' and 'liberation' are void because these are mere names, and because such opposing concepts do not possess reality. Even attachment to the idea of void is nothing but void. Compare Christian Science healing, above, which is realized only with faith—a faith that overcomes attachment to self and to the self's perception of illness, and places complete trust in the power of God.

**Goseigen:** Mahikari-no-Waza, also called *okiyome*, is a form of spiritual healing by divine Light. Its purpose is not only to heal individual illnesses, but further to purify the earth of pollution, greed, violence, and all spiritual evils. In this revelation, Yoshikazu Okada (1901-1974) is promised that he himself will be the channel for this 'True Positive Light.' This addresses a problem faced by all spiritual healers, which is the inevitable weakening of the healer's power as he or she begins to absorb into his or her own person 'compensation' for the patient's illness. In Mahikari, each practitioner is given a pendant called the *omitama* through which the Light can be connected to the founder's channel, and thus each can transmit the healing power without absorbing any ill effects. We note that Oriental medicine has, since the time of the *Classic of the Yellow Emperor*, regarded drugs as heavy poisons to be used only in certain types of illnesses or in conjunction with other forms of treatment such as acupuncture, herbs, and changes in diet or environment.

**Yanomami Shaman's Instruction:** Disease of the body is understood to be the symptom of a stolen soul. Evil spirits steal the soul, which robs the person of his vitality; hence he falls ill. By recovering the soul

# Liberation

THE SPIRITUAL FREEDOM experienced by those who are released from the fetters of desires and attachments to worldly things is called Liberation (Skt. *moksha*). It is an inner experience of freedom that can be present regardless of the person's external circumstances. The saint is free even in prison, while people with all worldly opportunities and unlimited wealth may be caught in dire bondage. The Christian scriptures speak of a comparable experience of Christian liberty that gives the believer an unlimited sense of freedom to live according to the spirit of Christ independent of external custom or constraint. Naturally, people should have the opportunity to realize the fruits of their spiritual liberation in a free society; inner freedom engenders and is completed through external freedom. Salvation as liberation from external oppression will be discussed under *Help and Deliverance*, pp. 396-402.

Passages in this section first assert that liberation is found only in the presence of God. Next come passages which describe the nature of liberation: release from bondage to desire, peace of mind, freedom to travel throughout the universe of spirit, freedom from the fetters of karma. Several concluding passages assert that truth, natural law, or divine law is necessary and conducive to liberation. Law is the way to freedom—just as, in driving an automobile, rules of the road are required in order to have the freedom to travel to any destination in safety. Thus freedom should not be interpreted as freedom to disregard spiritual law; to do so would return one to a state of bondage.

Proclaim liberty throughout the land to all its inhabitants.

*Judaism* and *Christianity*. Leviticus 25.10

Liberation is the best thing, as the moon is best among the stars.

*Jainism*. Sutrakritanga 1.11.22

Now the Lord is the Spirit, and where the Spirit of the Lord is, there is freedom.

*Christianity*. 2 Corinthians 3.17

The fetters of the heart are broken, all doubts are resolved, and all works cease to bear fruit, when He is beheld who is both high and low.

*Hinduism*. Mundaka Upanishad 2.2.8

The Self, indeed, is below. It is above. It is behind. It is before. It is to the south. It is to the north. The Self, indeed, is all this. Verily, he who sees this, reflects on this, and understands this delights in the Self, sports with the Self, rejoices in the Self, revels in the Self. Even while living in the body he becomes a

and restoring it to the body, the shaman effects a cure. For help in this recovery, the shaman calls upon his familiar spirits, called *hekura*. For more concerning the hekura, see p. 259.

Other texts on healing in traditional religions are found scattered throughout this anthology. A comparable passage on the Iglulik Eskimo Shaman Initiation, p. 382, describes how one can recover stolen souls and souls that have been taken to the Land of the Dead. In a Sioux Tradition, pp. 258-59, sacred stones are used to call forth the natural powers of healing. The Dinka might sacrifice an ox (p. 310) to appease the malevolent spiritual powers which are understood to be causing disease. African prayers contain supplications to God to heal disease, for example the Anuak Prayer, p. 54. A Yoruba Hymn, p. 483, ascribes to Ifa the power to heal the earth.

**Mundaka Upanishad 2.2.8:** Cf. Maitri Upanishad 3.2, p. 292; Svetasvatara Upanishad 2.15, pp. 602-3.

self-ruler. He wields unlimited freedom in all the worlds. But those who think differently from this have others for their rulers; they live in perishable worlds. They have no freedom at all in the worlds.

*Hinduism.* Chandogya Upanishad 7.25.2

And [Jesus] came to Nazareth, where he had been brought up; and he went to the synagogue, as his custom was, on the sabbath day. And he stood up to read; and there was given to him the book of the prophet Isaiah. He opened the book and found the place where it was written,

The Spirit of the Lord is upon me,
because he has anointed me to preach good news to the poor.
He has sent me to proclaim release to the captives
and recovering of sight to the blind.
to set at liberty those who are oppressed,
to proclaim the acceptable year of the Lord.

And he closed the book, and gave it back to the attendant, and sat down; and the eyes of all in the synagogue were fixed on him. And he began to say to them, "Today this scripture has been fulfilled in your hearing."

*Christianity.* Luke 4.16-21

Desire is a chain, shackled to the world, and it is a difficult one to break. But once that is done, there is no more grief and no more longing; the stream has been cut off and there are no more chains.

*Buddhism.* Sutta Nipata 948

The quest of pleasure brings nothing but torment abounding;
Man thus makes of his evil desires only a shackle about the neck.
You seeker of false delights, liberation comes only through the love of God.

*Sikhism.* Adi Granth, Gauri Ashtpadi, M.1, p. 222

If there is a man who can dominate Satan, the liberation of the spiritual and physical worlds will take place.

*Unification Church.* Sun Myung Moon, 2-22-87

Yea, happily he lives, the brahmin set free,
Whom lusts defile not, who is cooled and loosed from bonds,
Who has all barriers burst, restraining his heart's pain.
Happy the calm one lives who wins peace of mind.

*Buddhism.* Anguttara Nikaya i.137

As the path of the birds in the air or of fishes in the water is invisible, even so is the path of the possessors of wisdom.

*Hinduism.* Mahabharata, Shanti Parva 67.63

He whose corruptions are destroyed, he who is not attached to food, he who has Deliverance, which is void and signless, as his object—his path, like that of birds in the air, cannot be traced.

*Buddhism.* Dhammapada 93

**Chandogya Upanishad 7.25.2:** Cf. Acarangasutra 2.173, p. 47.

**Luke 4.16-21:** Jesus is reading from the Old Testament, Isaiah 61.1-2. Historically, Isaiah was proclaiming to a community of impoverished exiles liberation from oppression, captivity, and indebtedness, and the dawn of a new time when God will once again favor Israel with abundance. But for Jesus, it is a proclamation of all-encompassing liberation: release to those captive to sin and enlightenment to the spiritually blind as well as liberty to those suffering external oppression. With liberation comes the fulfillment of all creation, the 'acceptable year of the Lord.'

**Sutta Nipata 948:** Cf. Digha Nikaya ii.276, p. 277; Dhammapada 345-46, p. 295; Milarepa, p. 322.

**Gauri Ashtpadi, M.1:** Cf. Sorath, M.1, p. 322.

**Anguttara Nikaya i.137:** Buddha uses the term 'brahmin' not in the sense of a member of the brahmin caste, but as a title for one who is truly liberated. See Dhammapada 393, 396, p. 191.

**Mahabharata, Shanti Parva 67.63** and **Dhammapada 93:** The invisible path refers to the fact that the liberated do not leave a trail of karma. This is because whatever he does is done with detachment, without a sense of "I," without any desire for reward. Cf. Bhagavad Gita 4.19-21, p. 555.

The wind blows where it wills, and you hear the sound of it, but you do not know whence it comes or whither it goes; so it is with every one who is born of the Spirit.

*Christianity*. John 3.8

Open yourself, create free space;
release the bound one from his bonds!
Like a newborn child, freed from the womb,
be free to move on every path!

*Hinduism*. Atharva Veda 6.121.4

Immediately after attaining release from all karmas, the soul goes up to the end of the universe. Previously driven [by karmas], the soul is free from the bonds of attachment, the chains have been snapped, and it is its nature to dart upwards. The liberated self, in the absence of the karmas which had led it to wander in different directions in different states of existence, darts upwards as its nature is to go up.

*Jainism*. Samantabhadra, Ratnakarandasravakacara 10

He has no branches, how then leaves? Whose
root is not in the ground.
Who is worthy to praise that man inspired,
from bondage free?

*Buddhism*. Udana 77

When a man is free from all sense pleasures and depends on nothingness he is free in the supreme freedom from perception. He will stay there and not return again.

It is like a flame struck by a sudden gust of wind. In a flash it has gone out and nothing more can be known about it. It is the same with a wise man freed from mental existence: In a flash he has gone out and nothing more can be known about him.

When a person has gone out, then there is nothing by which you can measure him. That by which he can be talked about is no longer there for him; you cannot say that he does not exist. When all ways of being, all phenomena are removed, then all ways of description have also been removed.

*Buddhism*. Sutta Nipata 1072-76

You will know the truth, and the truth will make you free.

*Christianity*. John 8.32

No man is free, but he who labors in the Torah.

*Judaism*. Mishnah, Abot 6.2

That disciplined man
with joy and light within,
becomes one with God
and reaches the freedom that is God's.

*Hinduism*. Bhagavad Gita 5.24

Subhuti, if you should conceive the idea that anyone in whom dawns the Consummation of Incomparable Enlightenment declares that all manifest standards are ended and extinguished, do not countenance such thoughts.

*Buddhism*. Diamond Sutra 27

**John 3.8:** Cf. Romans 8.26-27, p. 464.

**Atharva Veda 6.121.4:** Cf. Tao Te Ching 55, p. 156.

**Ratnakarandasravakacara 10:** This is the state of Nirvana; cf. Ratnakarandasravakacara 131, p. 88. Liberation is also enlightenment; cf. Tattvarthasutra 10.1-2, p. 383.

**Udana 77:** This is the tree of karma of Indian thought, discussed in Bhagavad Gita 15.1-3, p. 272. Cf. Svetasvatara Upanishad 3.9, p. 412; Anguttara Nikaya ii.37-39, p. 468.

**Sutta Nipata 1072-76:** This is a good expression of the freedom that comes from absence of self. Cf. Mumonkan 8, p. 414; Samyutta Nikaya iii.68, p. 640; Anguttara Nikaya ii.37-39, p. 468; Seng Ts'an, pp. 150-51; Bhagavad Gita 4.19-21, p. 555.

**John 8.32:** Cf. James 1.25, p. 105.

**Abot 6.2:** Cf. Abot 3.6, p. 551; Baba Metzia 10a, p. 551.

**Bhagavad Gita 5.24:** Cf. Bhagavad Gita 3.31-32, p. 107; Katha Upanishad 2.6.11, p. 600.

For freedom Christ has set us free; stand fast therefore, and do not submit again to a yoke of slavery... For you were called to freedom, brethren; only do not use your freedom as an opportunity for the flesh, but through love be servants of one another.

*Christianity*. Galatians 5.1 and 5.13

## *Enlightenment*

ENLIGHTENMENT MEANS DISPELLING the darkness of ignorance. Enlightenment is the primary term used to describe the experience of salvation in Hinduism and Buddhism, yet the experience of enlightenment is common to most religions. According to the manner in which Reality is perceived in the different traditions, enlightenment may be either the intuitive grasping of inner wisdom, illumination by the truth of the Word, or direct apprehension of transcendent Reality. The true self, formerly obscured by false habits of thinking and vain desires, is suddenly revealed. The inner eye, which was blinded by defilements of worldly living, opens to a vision of the true Reality. From that moment life can never be the same, as the enlightened person begins to live by the knowledge he has acquired.

The first group of passages compare God or God's word to a light that shines into the soul. Second are passages which describe enlightenment as inner knowledge, opening the inner eye or the "eye of the heart." It is recognizing one's *Original Mind*, pp. 146-51. Third, we have passages on enlightenment as knowing God, the eternal source of truth. The concluding passage describes one experience of enlightenment: a sudden apprehension of a new gestalt, a quantum leap in thinking, a powerful conversion.

Your word is a lamp to my feet and a light to my path.

*Judaism* and *Christianity*. Psalm 119.105

The truth has come, and falsehood has vanished away. Surely falsehood is ever certain to vanish.

*Islam*. Qur'an 17.85

Jesus spoke to them, saying, "I am the light of the world; he who follows me will not walk in darkness, but will have the light of life."

*Christianity*. John 8.12

Those who believe will stand alongside [the Prophet], their light streaming on ahead of them and to their right. They will say, "Our Lord, perfect our light for us, and forgive us!"

*Islam*. Qur'an 66.8

**Galatians 5.1 and 5.13:** Christian freedom means that the believer is not justified according to how well he or she obeys religious laws. One is justified by faith. Yet in faith, the believer lives by the divine laws because they are helpful in maintaining his or her relationship with Christ. A Christian can still fall into the slavery of passions.

**Qur'an 17.85:** Cf. Mundaka Upanishad 3.1.6, p. 451; Qur'an 39.23, p. 105.

**Qur'an 66.8:** Cf. Qur'an 33.45-46, p. 454; Hadith of Muslim, p. 56.

Him the sun does not illumine, nor the moon, nor the stars, nor the lightning—nor, verily, fires kindled upon the earth. He is the one light that gives light to all. He shines; everything shines.

*Hinduism.* Katha Upanishad 5.15

It is wonderful, Lord! It is wonderful, Lord! It is as if, Lord, one might set upright that which had been upturned, or might reveal what was hidden, or might point out the path to one who had gone astray, or might bring an oil lamp into the darkness so that those with eyes might see material shapes.

*Buddhism.* Udana 49

The holy Preceptor by the Word lighted a
lamp;
Thereby was shattered darkness of the temple
of the self,
And the unique chamber of jewels thrown
open.
Wonderstruck were we in extreme on
beholding it—
Its greatness beyond expression.

*Sikhism.* Adi Granth,
Bilaval, M.5, p. 821

Your eye is the lamp of your body; when your eye is sound, your whole body is full of light; but when it is not sound, your body is full of darkness. Therefore be careful lest the light in you be darkness. If then your whole body is full of light, having no part dark, it will be wholly bright, as when a lamp with its rays gives you light.

*Christianity.* Luke 11.34-36

The Atman is the light:
The light is covered by darkness:
This darkness is delusion:
That is why we dream.
When the light of Atman
Drives out our darkness
That light shines forth from us,
A sun in splendor,
The revealed Brahman.

*Hinduism.* Bhagavad Gita 5.15-16

God is the Light of the heavens and the earth.
The parable of His Light
is as if there were a Niche,
and within it a Lamp;
the Lamp enclosed in Glass:
The Glass as it were a brilliant star:
Lit from a blessed Tree,
an olive neither of the East nor of the West,
whose oil is well-nigh luminous,
though fire scarce touched it.
Light upon Light!
God guides whom He will to His Light:
God sets forth parables for men, and God
knows all things.

*Islam.* Qur'an 24.35

Since all Dharmas are immanent in our mind there is no reason why we should not realize intuitively the real nature of Suchness. The Bodhisattva Sila Sutra says, "Our Essence of Mind is intrinsically pure, and if we knew our mind and realized what our nature is, all of us would attain Buddhahood."

*Buddhism.* Sutra of Hui Neng 2

I am blind and do not see the things of this world; but when the light comes from above, it

**Udana 49:** For a vivid pictorial representation of the Buddha's enlightening wisdom, see Garland Sutra 2, pp. 64-65.

**Luke 11.34-36:** Cf. Forty Hadith of an-Nawawi 6, p. 147; Qur'an 22.46, p. 283; Bhagavad Gita 15.9-11, p. 148.

**Bhagavad Gita 5.15-16:** Cf. Svetasvatara Upanishad 2.14, pp. 602-3.

**Qur'an 24.35:** See p. 74n.

**Sutra of Hui Neng 2:** Cf. Sutra of Hui Neng 3, p. 147; Seng Ts'an, pp. 150-51. Meditation on Buddha Amitayus 17, p. 462.

enlightens my heart and I can see, for the Eye of my heart sees everything; and through this vision I can help my people. The heart is a sanctuary at the center of which there is a little space, wherein the Great Spirit dwells, and this is the Eye. This is the Eye of the Great Spirit by which He sees all things, and through which we see Him. If the heart is not pure, the Great Spirit cannot be seen.

*Native American Religions.*
Black Elk, Sioux Tradition

The Self within the heart is like a boundary which divides the world from That. Day and night cross not that boundary, nor old age, nor death; neither grief nor pleasure, neither good nor evil deeds. All evil shuns That. For That is free from impurity: by impurity can it never be touched.

Wherefore he who has crossed that boundary, and has realized the Self, if he is blind, ceases to be blind; if he is wounded, ceases to be wounded; if he is afflicted, ceases to be afflicted. When that boundary is crossed, night becomes day; for the world of Brahman is light itself.

*Hinduism.*
Chandogya Upanishad 4.1-2

It is as if some man goes into an intimate friend's house, gets drunk, and falls asleep. Meanwhile his friend, having to go forth on official duty, ties a priceless jewel within the man's garment as a present, and then departs. The man, being asleep, knows nothing of this. On arising he travels onwards till he reaches some other country where, striving for food and clothing, he labors diligently, undergoes exceeding great hardship, and is content even if he can obtain but a little. Later, his friend happens to meet him and speaks thus—"Tut! Sir! How is it you have come down to this, merely for the sake of food and clothing? Wishing you to be in comfort and able to satisfy your five senses, I, formerly in such a year and month and on such a day, tied a priceless jewel within your garment. Now as of old it is present there, yet you in ignorance are slaving and worrying to keep yourself alive. How very stupid! Go you now and exchange that jewel for what you need, and for ever hereafter live as you will, free from poverty and shortage."

*Buddhism.* Lotus Sutra 8

The enlightenment consists of a mysterious light which the shaman suddenly feels in his body, inside his head, within the brain, an inexplicable searchlight, a luminous fire... for he can now, even with closed eyes, see through darkness and perceive things and coming events which are hidden from others: thus they look into the future and into the secrets of others.

The candidate obtains this mystical light after long hours of waiting, sitting on a bench in his hut and invoking the spirits. When he experiences it for the first time, it is as if the house in which he is suddenly rises, he sees far ahead of him, through mountains, exactly as if the earth were one great plain, and his eyes could reach to the end of the earth. Nothing is hidden from him any longer; not only can he see things far, far away, but he can also discover souls, stolen souls, which are either kept concealed in far, strange lands or have been taken up or down to the Land of the Dead.

*Native American Religions.*
Iglulik Eskimo Shaman Initiation

Brahman is all in all. He is action, knowledge, goodness supreme. To know him, hidden in the lotus of the heart, is to untie the knot of ignorance.

*Hinduism.* Mundaka Upanishad 2.1.10

**Black Elk:** Cf. Forty Hadith of an-Nawawi 6, p. 147; Bhagavad Gita 15.9-11, p. 148.

**Lotus Sutra 8:** The jewel is the man's own original mind; to find it is enlightenment. For variations of this parable, see Mahaparinirvana Sutra 214-15, p. 147; Chandogya Upanishad 8.3.2, p. 147.

**Iglulik Eskimo Shaman Initiation:** Cf. Yanomami Shaman's Instruction, p. 376.

**Mundaka Upanishad 2.1.10:** Cf. Bhagavad Gita 15.9-11, p. 148; Kena Upanishad 1.1-2, p. 75; Svetasvatara Upanishad 1.11-12, p. 414; Isha Upanishad 6-7, p. 416.

Perfect knowledge is attained on the destruction of deluding karmas, of karmas which obscure knowledge and perception, and of karmas which obstruct [faith]. With the absence of the cause of bondage, the annihilation of all karmas is liberation.

*Jainism*. Tattvarthasutra 10.1-2

To know the eternal is called enlightenment.
Not to know the eternal is to act blindly to result in disaster.
He who knows the eternal is all-embracing.
Being all-embracing, he is impartial.
Being impartial, he is kingly [universal].
Being kingly, he is one with Nature.
Being one with nature, he is in accord with Tao.
Being in accord with Tao, he is everlasting,
And is free from danger throughout his lifetime.

*Taoism*. Tao Te Ching 16

For support, O Far-sighted One,
Reveal unto me that which is unique:
That of Thy Kingdom, O Lord,
Which are blessings of Good Thought,
Forth, O Beneficent Right-mindedness,
Dost Thou reveal Religious commands!

*Zoroastrianism*. Avesta, Yasna 33.13

Yet among the mature we do impart wisdom, although it is not a wisdom of this age or of the rulers of this age, who are doomed to pass away. But we impart a secret and hidden wisdom of God, which God decreed before the ages for our glorification. None of the rulers of this age understood this; for if they had, they would not have crucified the Lord of glory. But, as it is written,

What no eye has seen, nor ear heard,
nor the heart of man conceived,
what God has prepared for those who love him,

God has revealed to us through the Spirit. For the Spirit searches everything, even the depths of God.

*Christianity*. 1 Corinthians 2.6-10

The Sixth Patriarch was pursued by the monk Myo as far as Taiyu Mountain. The patriarch, seeing Myo coming, laid the Robe and Bowl [of office] on a rock and said, "This robe represents the faith; it should not be fought over. If you want to take it away, take it now." Myo tried to move it, but it was as heavy as a mountain and would not budge. Faltering and trembling, he cried out, "I came for the Dharma, not for the robe. I beg you, please give me your instruction."

The patriarch said, "Think neither good nor evil. At this very moment, what is the original self of the monk Myo?" At these words, Myo was directly illuminated. His whole body was covered with sweat. He wept and bowed, saying, "Besides the secret words and secret meaning you have just now revealed to me, is there anything else, deeper still?" The patriarch said,

"What I have told you is no secret at all. When you look into your own true self, whatever is deeper is found right there."

*Buddhism*. Mumonkan 23

**Tao Te Ching 16:** The phrase 'to know the eternal is enlightenment' is repeated in several passages of the Tao Te Ching; see Tao Te Ching 16, p. 601; 55, p. 156.

**1 Corinthians 2.6-10:** Cf. 1 Corinthians 1.20-25, p. 570; 2.12-16, p. 575.

**Mumonkan 23:** This incident, when Hui Neng the Sixth Patriarch was fleeing from the followers of his rival Shen Hsiu, is also recounted in the Sutra of Hui Neng. In Zen, enlightenment frequently occurs in such a manner: A sudden realization grows from an experience of crisis and extreme desperation. When it comes, one no longer depends on cognition or knowledge or secret lore. The authentic self shines forth; cf. Mumonkan 1, pp. 601-2; Seng Ts'an, pp. 150-51.

## Crossing the Waters

THE RELIGIONS BORN IN INDIA share a common symbol of salvation as crossing the waters. The waters represent the painful existence in the world, plagued by ills, a continual passing from life to death in samsara. Tossed about on the turbulent sea, the wayfarer finds rest only on the other shore, the firm ground of Nirvana. In the Judeo-Christian scriptures, crossing the waters is also a symbol of salvation, drawn from the historical tradition of the Israelites crossing the Red Sea under divine protection and later crossing the Jordan River to reach the promised land.

Carry us across, as by a boat
across the sea, for our good.
Shining bright, drive away our sin.

*Hinduism.* Rig Veda 1.97.8

The body, they say, is a boat and the soul is the sailor. Samsara is the ocean which is crossed by the great sages.

*Jainism.* Uttaradhyayana Sutra 23.73

Even if you were the most sinful of sinners, Arjuna, you could cross beyond all sin by the raft of spiritual wisdom.

*Hinduism.* Bhagavad Gita 4.36

Strive and cleave the stream. Discard, O brahmin, sense-desires. Knowing the destruction of conditioned things, be a knower of the Unmade.

*Buddhism.* Dhammapada 383

As they call the great ocean a boundless flood of water, difficult to traverse with the arms alone, so should the learned one know and renounce it [samsara]: that sage is called "Maker of the End."

*Jainism.* Acarangasutra 25.10

Few are there among men who go across to the further shore; the rest of mankind only run about on the bank. But those who act rightly according to the teaching, as has been well taught, will cross over to the other shore, for the realm of passions is so difficult to cross.

*Buddhism.* Dhammapada 85-86

Save me, O God! For the waters have come up
to my neck.
I sink in deep mire, where there is no foothold;
I have come into deep waters, and the flood
sweeps over me.

*Judaism* and *Christianity*. Psalm 69.1-2

The Lord reigns, he is robed in majesty;
the Lord is robed, he is girded with strength.
Yea, the world is established;
it shall never be moved.
Thy throne is established from of old,
thou art from everlasting.

The floods have lifted up, O Lord,
the floods have lifted up their voice,
the floods lift up their roaring.
Mightier than the thunders of many waters,
mightier than the waves of the sea,
the Lord on high is mighty!

**Rig Veda 1.97.8:** Cf. Satapatha Brahmana 4.2.5.10, p. 620.

**Uttaradhyayana Sutra 23.73:** See Uttaradhyayana Sutra 10.34, p. 531.

**Bhagavad Gita 4.36:** Cf. Bhagavad Gita 12.5-7, p. 544; Mundaka Upanishad 2.2.6, p. 600; Narada Dharma Sutra 1.210, p. 105; Svetasvatara Upanishad 2.8, pp. 602-3.

**Dhammapada 383:** Cf. Sutta Nipata 948, p. 378; Dhammapada 414, p. 157.

**Dhammapada 85-86:** On desires as the stream, see Dhammapada 338-47, p. 295. On the metaphor of the Teaching as a raft for crossing to the other shore, see Majjhima Nikaya i.134-135, p. 573.

Thy decrees are very sure;
holiness befits thy house,
O Lord, for evermore.

*Judaism* and *Christianity*. Psalm 93

Once Rabbi Phinehas was going to the house of study, and the river Ginai which he had to pass was so swollen that he could not cross it. He said, "O river, why do you prevent me from getting to the house of study?" Then it divided its waters, and he passed over. And his disciples said, "Can we too pass over?" He said, "He who knows that he has never insulted an Israelite can pass over unharmed."

*Judaism*.
Jerusalem Talmud, Demai 22a

Suppose, monks, a man is carried along a river by a current which looks delightful and charming. Then a sharp-sighted man standing on the bank sees him and calls out, "My friend! Though you are being carried along in the river by a current which seems delightful and charming, yet further down here is a pool with waves and whirlpools, with monsters and demons. My friend, when you get there you will come by your death or mortal pain!" Hearing the other's call, that man struggles against the stream with hands and feet.

This parable, monks, I use to explain my meaning. The river current is craving; "looking delightful and charming" refers to one's own sphere of perception. The pool lower down is the five fetters belonging to this lower world; its waves are the five pleasures of sense; monsters and demons refer to women. His going against the stream refers to renunciation; struggle with hands and feet means to put forth energy. The sharp-sighted man standing on the bank is the Wayfarer, Arahant, a Rightly-awakened One.

*Buddhism*. Itivuttaka 114-15

Man's life is a poison-laden ship, tossed into the ocean;
The shore is not visible as it floats in the midst of the waters.
Neither is there oar in hand, nor is there a pilot in this terrible vast sea.
Friend! The world is caught in a mighty snare,
Only by Divine grace and meditating on the holy Name
May man remain afloat.
God is the ship; the holy Word the pilot.
Where there is God's Word, neither wind nor fire, nor waves,
Nor any frightful forms have power:
There the holy eternal Name alone abides,
Which carries man across the ocean of worldliness.
Those going over it, by divine grace reach the other shore.
Engrossed in devotion to the Eternal;
Their transmigration is ended;
Their light is merged into the light of the infinite.

*Sikhism*. Adi Granth,
Maru Ashtpadi, M.1, p. 1009

Awake, awake, put on strength,
O arm of the Lord;
awake, as in days of old,
the generations of long ago.
Was it not you that cut Rahab in pieces,
that pierced the dragon?
Was it not you that dried up the sea,
the waters of the great deep;

**Demai 22a:** Stories of sages crossing a physical body of water are common to many traditions. There are stories of the Buddha crossing a river to his disciples; Jesus walking on water in Matthew 14.24-31, p. 543; a Taoist sage walking through a cataract in Chuang Tzu 19; and Moses crossing the Red Sea in Exodus 14, pp. 439-40.

**Itivuttaka 114-15:** Cf. Dhammapada 338-47, p. 295. 'Wayfarer,' etc. are titles of the Buddha.

**Maru Ashtpadi, M.1:** Cf. Suhi Chhant, M.5, p. 639.

that made the depths of the sea a way
for the redeemed to pass over?
And the ransomed of the Lord shall return,
and come to Zion with singing;
everlasting joy shall be upon their heads;
they shall obtain joy and gladness,
and sorrow and sighing shall flee away.

*Judaism* and *Christianity*. Isaiah 51.9-11

When you go over the Jordan, and live in the land which the Lord your God gives you to inherit, and when he gives you rest from all your enemies round about... you shall rejoice before the Lord your God.

*Judaism* and *Christianity*. Deuteronomy 12.10-12

The rocky stream flows on: Hold you all together,
quit you like heroes, and cross over, my friends!
Leave here all those that are evil-minded,
let us cross to powers who are undiseased.

Stand erect, and cross you over, my comrades!
This rocky river flows on before us.
Abandon here all those that are malicious,
let us cross to powers, benign and pleasant.

*Hinduism*. Atharva Veda 12.2.26-27

❖

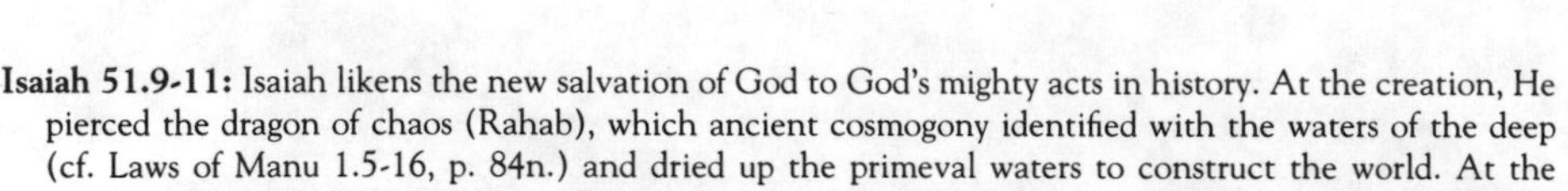

**Isaiah 51.9-11:** Isaiah likens the new salvation of God to God's mighty acts in history. At the creation, He pierced the dragon of chaos (Rahab), which ancient cosmogony identified with the waters of the deep (cf. Laws of Manu 1.5-16, p. 84n.) and dried up the primeval waters to construct the world. At the Exodus God divided the Red Sea and opened a way for the Israelites to cross dry-shod; cf. Exodus 14, pp. 439-40.

**Deuteronomy 12.10-12:** In the faith of Black Americans, crossing the Jordan River is a metaphor for crossing from the troubles of this world to the peaceful abode of Heaven.

**Atharva Veda 12.2.26-27:** These verses are sung at funeral ceremonies. On a bridge to cross over the waters of hell, cf. Yasna 46.10-11, p. 245; Hadith of Bukhari and Muslim, p. 245.

## *Reversal and Restoration*

SALVATION AS RESTORATION refers to the undoing of bad habits, modes of thinking, ways of behaving, social relations, and political systems which have grown corrupt and deviated from the proper way. It is a return to the origin, in order to restore the original way of life according to the true principles and purposes of God. Salvation is pictured as a great reversal. God will act to turn the existing social and political order upside down; no longer will the wealthy and powerful lord it over the honest and god-fearing. Internally, salvation brings with it the insight that the way to God is the reverse of the way of the world. Enlightenment brings, as it were, a one-hundred-and-eighty degree change in orientation.

Some passages describe the great reversal as a political image. Others describe an inner reversal: dying to self in order to live, seeking darkness in order to find the light, and abasing the self in order to become prominent. Further passages speak of returning to an original harmony or blessedness which was lost: reversal of the Original Sin that occurred at the human fall or a recovery of the original mind which is by nature enlightened. An important expression of this theme of reversion to the origin is found in the Buddhist doctrine of Dependent Origination (*Paticcasamuppada*), which is not just a law of causality but more properly the insight that all causes leading to downfall must be reversed.

The last will be first, and the first last.

*Christianity*. Matthew 20.16

Whoever exalts himself will be humbled, and whoever humbles himself will be exalted.

*Christianity*. Matthew 23.12

Him who humbles himself, God exalts; him who exalts himself, God humbles; from him who searches for greatness, greatness flies; him who flies from greatness, greatness searches out: with him who is importunate with circumstances, circumstance is importunate; by him who gives way to circumstance, circumstance stands.

*Judaism*. Talmud, Erubin 13b

The way of Heaven,
Is it not like stretching a bow?
What is high up is pressed down,
What is low down is lifted up;
What has surplus is reduced,
What is deficient is supplemented.

The way of Heaven,
It reduces those who have surpluses,
To supplement those who are deficient.
The way of man is just not so:
It reduces those who are deficient,
To offer to those who have surpluses.
Who can offer his surpluses to the world?
Only a person of Tao.

*Taoism*. Tao Te Ching 77

**Matthew 23.12:** Cf. Luke 18.10-14, p. 642; Isaiah 2.12-17, pp. 290-91; Proverbs 16.18, p. 289; Matthew 5.5, p. 647; Philippians 2.6-11, p. 440.

**Erubin 13b:** Cf. Isaiah 2.12-17, pp. 290-91; Hosea 6.1-2, p. 374.

**Tao Te Ching 77:** Cf. Tao Te Ching 56, p. 601.

The bows of the mighty are broken,
but the feeble gird on strength.
Those who were full have hired themselves out for bread,
but those who were hungry have ceased to hunger.
The barren has borne seven,
but she who has many children is forlorn.
The Lord kills and brings to life;
he brings down to Sheol and raises up.
The Lord makes poor and makes rich;
he brings low, he also exalts.
He raises up the poor from the dust;
he lifts the needy from the ash heap,
to make them sit with princes
and inherit a seat of honor.
For the pillars of the earth are the Lord's,
and on them he has set the world.
He will guard the feet of his faithful ones;
but the wicked shall be cut off in darkness;
for not by might shall a man prevail.

*Judaism* and *Christianity*. 1 Samuel 2.4-9

Whoever is proud of his royal authority
falls into hell, becomes a dog.
Whoever fancies himself for his beauty
takes birth as a filthy worm.
Whoever proclaims his meritorious deeds
whirls in transmigration, fallen into numerous births.
Whoever is proud of wealth and estates
is thoughtless, blind, senseless.
But whoever in whose heart He, in His grace, lodges humility
finds, says Nanak, liberation in this life,
bliss in the hereafter.

Whoever is proud of his wealth,
know not even a blade of grass shall accompany him.
Whoever pins his confidence on large hoardes and servants
is destroyed in an instant.
Whoever reckons himself powerful over all
is reduced in an instant to ashes.
Whoever in his pride reckons none as his equal
in the end is treated with ignominy by the Master of Law.
Whoever by the Master's grace has his pride anulled,
says Nanak, finds acceptance at the Divine Portal.

*Sikhism*. Adi Granth, Gauri Sukhmani, M.5, p. 278

Sentient beings wish to return to their origin where their nature will be in perfect unity.

*Buddhism*. Surangama Sutra

Always to know the standard is called profound and secret virtue.
Virtue becomes deep and far reaching,
And with it all things return to their original natural state.
Then complete harmony will be reached.

*Taoism*. Tao Te Ching 65

Confucius said, "To subdue one's self and return to propriety, is perfect virtue. If a man can for one day subdue himself and return to propriety, all under heaven will ascribe perfect virtue to him."

*Confucianism*. Analects 12.1.1

For as by a man came death, by a man has come also the resurrection of the dead. For as in Adam all die, so also in Christ shall all be made alive.

*Christianity*. 1 Corinthians 15.21-22

**1 Samuel 2.4-9:** This is the Song of Hannah. A similar song is sung by Mary—the Magnificat—in Luke 1.47-55. Cf. Pesahim 50a, p. 249; Isaiah 2.12-17, pp. 290-91.

**Tao Te Ching 65:** Cf. Tao Te Ching 16, p. 601; Chuang Tzu 12, p. 416.

**Analects 12.1.1:** On the human being's original state as one of propriety, see Book of Ritual 38.18, p. 144; Doctrine of the Mean 1.4-5, p. 155; Mencius II.A.6, p. 145.

**1 Corinthians 15.21-22:** Cf. Revelation 1.18, p. 463; also Romans 5.12-19. This and the following two passages describe salvation as a reversal of the primordial human Fall. Paul is arguing from the Jewish doctrine that the Fall brought death into the world; cf. Genesis Rabbah 8.11, p. 303; 10.4, p. 791; Wisdom of Solomon 2.23-24, p. 303.

Why are idolators lustful? Because they did not stand at Mount Sinai. For when the serpent came upon Eve he injected lust into her; as for the Israelites who stood at Mount Sinai, their lustfulness departed; but as for the idolators who did not stand at Mount Sinai, their lustfulness did not depart.

*Judaism.* Talmud, Shabbat 145b-46a

To save a sick man is to restore him to the status he had before the sickness occurred. To save a drowning man is to restore him to the state he was in before he began to drown. Likewise, to save a man fallen into sin means to restore him to the original sinless position which he enjoyed in the beginning. Therefore, God's providence of salvation is the providence of restoration.

*Unification Church.* Divine Principle I.3.2.1

Just as if, brethren, a man faring through the forest, through the great wood, should see an ancient path, and ancient road traversed by men of former days... And that man, brethren, should bring word to the prince, "Pardon, lord, know this. I have seen as I fared through the forest, through the great wood, an ancient path, an ancient road traversed by men of former days. I have been along it, and going along it I have seen an ancient city, an ancient prince's domain, wherein dwelt men of former days, having gardens, groves, pools, foundations of walls, a goodly spot. Lord, restore that city." And, brethren, the prince or his minister should restore that city. That city should thereafter become prosperous and flourishing, populous, teeming with folk, grown and thriving. Even so have I, brethren, seen an ancient Path, an ancient road traversed by the Rightly Enlightened Ones of former times.

*Buddhism.* Samyutta Nikaya ii.106

If you wish to untie a knot, you must first understand how it was tied.

*Buddhism.* Surangama Sutra

I will teach you Dhamma: If this is, that comes to be; from the arising of this, that arises; if this is not, that does not come to be; from the stopping of this, that is stopped.

*Buddhism.* Majjhima Nikaya ii.32

The world, O Kaccana, is for the most part bound up in a seeking, attachment, and proclivity, but a monk does not sympathize with this seeking and attachment, nor with the mental affirmation, proclivity, and prejudice which affirms an Ego. He does not doubt or question that it is only evil that springs into existence, and only evil that ceases from existence, and his conviction of this fact is dependent on no one besides himself. This, O Kaccana, is what constitutes Right Belief.

That things have being, O Kaccana, constitutes one extreme of doctrine; that things have no being is the other extreme. These extremes have been avoided by the Tathagata, and it is a Middle doctrine he teaches:

On ignorance depends karma;
On karma depends consciousness;
On consciousness depend name and form;
On name and form depend the six organs of sense;
On the six organs of sense depends contact;
On contact depends sensation;
On sensation depends desire;
On desire depends attachment;

**Shabbat 145b-146a:** The Israelites who stood at Mount Sinai are understood to include all Jews whenever and wherever they live. On lust as the infirmity of soul brought on through the Fall, see Genesis Rabbah 18.6, p. 303; 10.4, p. 791.

**Divine Principle I.3.2.1:** Restoration is through "indemnity," which means to lay conditions of faith, obedience, and sacrifice, thereby reversing Adam's unbelief, rebellion, and selfish heart at the time of the Fall; see Sun Myung Moon, 9-11-72, p. 552. Restoration also means to make reparations for the sins of the individual, family, nation, and so on, that have accrued through the course of history.

**Samyutta Nikaya ii.106:** Cf. Lankavatara Sutra 61, pp. 102-3.

**Majjhima Nikaya ii.32:** This is a short formula for the doctrine of Dependent Origination (Pali *Paticcasamuppada*). A more complete formulation follows.

On attachment depends existence;
On existence depends birth;
On birth depend old age and death, sorrow, lamentation, misery, grief, and despair. Thus does this entire aggregation of misery arise.

But on the complete fading out and cessation of ignorance ceases karma;
On the cessation of karma ceases consciousness;
On the cessation of consciousness ceases name and form;
On the cessation of name and form cease the six organs of sense;
On the cessation of the six organs of sense ceases contact;
On the cessation of contact ceases sensation;
On the cessation of sensation ceases desire;
On the cessation of desire ceases attachment;
On the cessation of attachment ceases existence;
On the cessation of existence ceases birth;
On the cessation of birth cease old age and death, sorrow, lamentation, misery, grief, and despair. Thus does this entire aggregation of misery cease.

*Buddhism*. Samyutta Nikaya xxii.90

For whoever would save his life will lose it, and whoever loses his life for my sake will find it.

*Christianity*. Matthew 16.25

The sage awakes to light in the night of all creatures. That which the world calls day is the night of ignorance to the wise.

*Hinduism*. Bhagavad Gita 2.69

The Way out into the light often looks dark,
The way that goes ahead often looks as if it went back.
The way that is least hilly often looks as if it went up and down,
The virtue that is really loftiest looks like an abyss,
What is sheerest white looks sullied.

*Taoism*. Tao Te Ching 41

Sights, sounds, tastes, odors, things touched and objects of mind are, without exception, pleasing, delightful, and charming—so long as one can say "They are";

These are considered a source of happiness by the world with its gods—and when they cease, this is by them considered suffering.

The cessation of phenomenal existence is seen as a source of happiness by us ariyans—this insight of those who can see is the reverse of that of the whole world:

What others say is a source of happiness, that, we say, is suffering; what others say is suffering, that, we know, as a source of happiness. Behold this doctrine, hard to understand, wherein the ignorant are bewildered.

*Buddhism*. Samyutta Nikaya iv.127-28

To yield is to to be preserved whole.
To be bent is to become straight
To be empty is to be full.
To be worn out is to be renewed.
To have little is to possess.
To have plenty is to be perplexed.
Therefore the sage embraces the One
And becomes the model of the world.
He does not show himself; therefore he is luminous.
He does not justify himself; therefore he becomes prominent.

**Samyutta Nikaya xxii.90:** This enumerates all twelve links in the chain of Dependent Origination, first forwards to show the origin of ill, then backwards to show its cessation. 'Right Belief' is the first step in the Noble Eightfold Path (see p. 113), namely to understand the Four Noble Truths, of which Dependent Origination is a more detailed explanation. Cf. Buddhacarita 14, p. 437.

**Matthew 16.25:** Cf. Mark 8.34-36, p. 638; John 12.24-25, p. 638; Hadith of Muslim, p. 627; Philippians 2.6-11, p. 440; Hidden Words of Baha'u'llah, Arabic 7, p. 639.

**Tao Te Ching 41:** Note the pun on the way out, which is the Way (*Tao*).

**Bhagavad Gita 2.69:** Cf. Samanasuttam 135-36, p. 648.

He does not boast of himself; therefore he is given credit.
He does not brag; therefore he can endure for long.
It is precisely because he does not compete that the world cannot compete with him.
Is the ancient saying, "To yield is to be preserved whole" empty words?
Truly he will be preserved, and all will come to him.

*Taoism.* Tao Te Ching 22

"Blessed One, what is meant by this term Nirvana?" Replied the Buddha, "When the self-nature and the habit-energy of all the sense-discriminations, including ego (*alaya*), intellect (*manas*), and the faculty of judgment (*manovijnana*), from which issue the habit-energy of wrong speculations—when all these go through a revulsion, I and all the Buddhas declare that there is Nirvana. The way and the self-nature of this Nirvana is emptiness, which is the state of reality."

*Buddhism.* Lankavatara Sutra 38

❖

**Tao Te Ching 22:** Cf. Tao Te Ching 28, p. 648; 48, p. 639; I Ching, Great Commentary 2.5.2-3, p. 117; Hidden Words of Baha'u'llah, Arabic 7, p. 639.

**Lankavatara Sutra 38:** This 'revulsion,' turning all previous ways of thinking upside-down, is the sudden enlightenment of the Zen school. For comparable Theravada passages, see Udana 49, p. 381; Anguttara Nikaya v.322, p. 392.

# *Peace*

PEACE IS ONE OF THE MOST DESIRABLE fruits of salvation in all the world's religions. We begin with passages describing the fruit of inner peace. The peace that comes with reaching Ultimate Reality brings tranquillity to the heart and clarity to the mind. It is the absence of passions, desires, anxieties, and wandering thoughts; the heart becomes cool and content. Nirvana is often translated 'Peace.' The scriptures praise the peace and tranquillity that come to the soul that is firm in faith. The soul of the saint is likened to a deep pond whose surface remains undisturbed by waves despite the many currents or streams that flow into it.

A second group of passages describe the peace of God that brings harmony among people and nations. Outward peace is emphasized in the Abrahamic faiths, for whom the work of God has a social and historical dimension. The love of God breaks down the walls of hostility between people, and thus becomes the foundation for their lasting peace. Yet peace in this social and political sense is not only given by God, it must also be built by the efforts of human beings. Those who are blessed with inner peace have the responsibility to become peacemakers, reconciling conflict.

Peace I leave with you; my peace I give to you; not as the world gives do I give to you.

*Christianity*. John 14.27

In the remembrance of God do hearts find satisfaction.

*Islam*. Qur'an 13.28

The Master said, "In the morning, hear the Way; in the evening, die content!"

*Confucianism*. Analects 4.8

This is peace, this is the excellent, namely the calm of all the impulses, the casting out of all "basis," the extinction of craving, dispassion, stopping, Nirvana.

*Buddhism*. Anguttara Nikaya v.322

O tranquil soul,
return to your Lord
so pleasant and well-pleased!
Enter among My servants
and enter My garden!

*Islam*. Qur'an 89.27-30

May the Lord lift up his countenance upon you, and give you peace.

*Judaism* and *Christianity*. Numbers 6.26

And the peace of God, which passes all understanding, will keep your hearts and your minds in Christ Jesus.

*Christianity*. Philippians 4.7

He it is who sent down peace of reassurance into the hearts of the believers, that they might add faith to their faith.

*Islam*. Qur'an 48.4

Thou dost keep him in perfect peace,
whose mind is stayed on thee,
because he trusts in thee.

*Judaism* and *Christianity*. Isaiah 26.3

**Anguttara Nikaya v.322:** Nirvana is the Ultimate Good because it is the complete end of all the impulses and passions that produce evil. Cf. Dhammapada 96, p. 156.

**Qur'an 89.27-30:** Cf. Qur'an 56.27, p. 248.

**Numbers 6.26:** Part of the Aaronic benediction, Numbers 6.24-26, p. 31.

If a man sings of God and hears of Him,
And lets love of God sprout within him,
All his sorrows shall vanish,
And in his mind, God will bestow abiding
peace.

*Sikhism.* Adi Granth,
Japuji 5, M.1, p. 2

Just as a deep lake is clear and still, even so, on hearing the teachings and realizing them, the wise become exceedingly peaceful.

*Buddhism.* Dhammapada 82

As rivers flow into the ocean but cannot make the vast ocean overflow, so flow the streams of the sense-world into the sea of peace that is the sage.

*Hinduism.* Bhagavad Gita 2.70

Men do not mirror themselves in running water—they mirror themselves in still water. Only what is still can still the stillness of other things.

*Taoism.* Chuang Tzu 5

The monk looks for peace within himself, and not in any other place. For when a person is inwardly quiet, there is nowhere a self can be found; where, then, could a non-self be found?

There are no waves in the depths of the sea; it is still, unbroken. It is the same with the monk. He is still, without any quiver of desire, without a remnant on which to build pride and desire.

*Buddhism.* Sutta Nipata 919-20

The Lord lives in the heart of every creature. He turns them round and round upon the wheel of his Maya. Take refuge utterly in Him. By His grace you will find supreme peace, and the state which is beyond all change.

*Hinduism.* Bhagavad Gita 18.61-62

Should anyone be victim of great anxiety, his
body racked with maladies,
Beset with problems of home and family,
With pleasure and pain alternating,
Wandering in all four directions without peace
or rest—
Should he then contemplate the Supreme
Being,
Peaceful shall his mind and body become.

*Sikhism.* Adi Granth,
Sri Raga, M.5, p. 70

Victory breeds hatred, for the defeated live in pain. Happily live the peaceful, giving up victory and defeat.

*Buddhism.* Dhammapada 201

Tao invariably takes no action, and yet there is
nothing left undone.
If kings and barons can keep it, all things will
transform spontaneously.
If, after transformation, they should desire to
be active,
I would restrain them with simplicity, which
has no name.
Simplicity, which has no name, is free of
desires.
Being free of desires, it is tranquil.
And the world will be at peace of its own
accord.

*Taoism.* Tao Te Ching 37

Some children were playing beside a river. They made castles of sand, and each child defended his castle and said, "This one is

**Dhammapada 82:** Cf. Anguttara Nikaya i.137, p. 378; Dhammapada 413, p. 157.

**Bhagavad Gita 2.70:** Cf. Bhagavad Gita 6.7-9, p. 153.

**Chuang Tzu 5:** Only a person at peace with himself can calm others. Cf. Tao Te Ching 4, p. 374; Great Learning, p. 602; Tao Te Ching 56, p. 601.

**Sutta Nipata 919-20:** Cf. Dhammapada 279, p. 640. The peace which comes from finding union in the midst of the world's bewildering diversity is also expressed in the Peace Chant of the Isha Upanishad, p. 31. Cf. Katha Upanishad 3.13, p. 601, Bhagavad Gita 5.10-12, p. 554. On the wheel of Maya, see Svetasvatara Upanishad 1.6.8, p. 282.

**Dhammapada 201:** Cf. Nitivakyamrita 344, p. 743.

**Tao Te Ching 37:** Cf. Chuang Tzu 7, p. 416; Tao Te Ching 80, pp. 198-99.

mine." They kept their castles separate and would not allow any mistakes about which was whose. When the castles were all finished, one child kicked over someone else's castle and completely destroyed it. The owner of the castle flew into a rage, pulled the other child's hair, struck him with his fist and bawled out, "He has spoiled my castle! Come along all of you and help me to punish him as he deserves." The others all came to his help. They beat the child with a stick and then stamped on him as he lay on the ground.... Then they went on playing in their sand castles, each saying, "This is mine; no one else may have it. Keep away! Don't touch my castle!" But evening came, it was getting dark and they all thought they ought to be going home. No one now cared what became of his castle. One child stamped on his, another pushed his over with both hands. Then they turned away and went back, each to his home.

*Buddhism*. Yogacara Bhumi Sutra 4

Glory to God in the highest, and on earth peace, good will toward men!

*Christianity*. Luke 2.14

The whole of the Torah is for the purpose of promoting peace.

*Judaism*. Talmud, Gittin 59b

All things exist for world peace.

*Perfect Liberty Kyodan*. Precept 14

God is peace, His name is peace, and all is bound together in peace.

*Judaism*. Zohar, Leviticus 10b

For Christ Jesus is our peace, who has made us both one, and has broken down the dividing wall of hostility.

*Christianity*. Ephesians 2.14

Our Father, it is thy universe, it is thy will:
Let us be at peace, let the souls of the people be cool.
Thou art our Father, remove all evil from our path.

*African Traditional Religions*. Nuer Prayer (Sudan)

They shall beat their swords into plowshares,
and their spears into pruning hooks;
nation shall not lift up sword against nation,
neither shall they learn war any more.

*Judaism* and *Christianity*. Isaiah 2.4

Now is the gracious Lord's ordinance promulgated,
No one shall cause another pain or injury;
All mankind shall live in peace together,
Under a shield of administrative benevolence.

*Sikhism*. Adi Granth, Sri Raga, M.5, p. 74

Blessed are the peacemakers, for they shall be called sons of God.

*Christianity*. Matthew 5.9

He brings together those who are divided, he encourages those who are friendly; he is a peacemaker, a lover of peace, impassioned for peace, a speaker of words that make for peace.

*Buddhism*. Digha Nikaya xiii.75, Tevijja Sutta

**Yogacara Bhumi Sutra 4:** In this parable Nirvana is likened to the diminution of jealousy and passion for existence with the cool of evening. In the Pali version (Samyutta Nikaya iii.188) the sand castles are likened to the body, which had been the object of grasping; with Release it becomes a thing to be disregarded and broken up.

**Luke 2.14:** The proclamation of the angelic hosts at the birth of Jesus, the Prince of Peace; see the larger passage Luke 1.26-2.14, p. 424. Cf. Yasna 60.5, p. 198.

**Precept 14:** A sentiment common to most of the new religions of Japan.

**Zohar, Leviticus 10b:** In Hebrew, *shalom* includes the concepts peace, wellness, and wholeness. Cf. Numbers 6.24-26, p. 31; the Kaddish prayer, p. 30.

**Ephesians 2.14:** Cf. John 17.20-21, p. 186; Atharva Veda 7.52.1-2, p. 187.

**Matthew 5.9:** Cf. Abot 1.12, p. 161.

If two parties of believers fall to fighting, then make peace between them. And if one party of them does wrong to the other, fight that wrong-doer until it returns to the ordinance of God; then, if it returns, make peace between them justly, and act equitably. Lo! God loves the equitable.

*Islam.* Qur'an 49.9

During the short eons of swords,
They meditate on love,
Introducing to nonviolence
Hundreds of millions of living beings.

In the midst of great battles
They remain impartial to both sides;
For bodhisattvas of great strength
Delight in reconciliation of conflict.

*Buddhism.*
Holy Teaching of Vimalakirti 8

Peace be to earth and to airy spaces!
Peace be to heaven, peace to the waters,
peace to the plants and peace to the trees!
May all the gods grant me peace!
By this invocation of peace may peace be diffused!
By this invocation of peace may peace bring peace!
With this peace the dreadful I appease,
with this peace the cruel I appease,
with this peace all evil I appease,
so that peace may prevail, happiness prevail!
May everything for us be peaceful!

*Hinduism.* Atharva Veda 19.9.14

❖

# *Help and Deliverance*

IN TIMES OF DISTRESS, danger, and oppression, believers in every tradition look to God for support and help. In times of crisis, in combat, and when confronting death, even non-believers will turn to God for help. And time and again, they find deliverance in ample measure. Conversely, the scriptures warn against reliance on one's own power, allies, or wealth to prevail in the fight when the true source of power is available through faith.

The passages include expressions of confidence in divine deliverance, supplications for help, and texts which describe God's grace as an unassailable refuge. There are several accounts of God's saving deeds in history: from the Bible, Moses at the Red Sea; from the Qur'an, the battle of Badr; and from the Mahabharata, a counsel on the inevitable victory of Krishna in the battle between the Kurus and the Pandavas. The section closes with two hymns: one to the Hindu Goddess Durga, to whom is attributed a great victory in the primeval war between the gods and the demons, and the other praising Kuan Yin, in Chinese Buddhism the bodhisattva of divine compassion who is said to be ready and able to save anyone in distress. Related passages, exhorting people to do battle in the name of faith or justice with the confidence that God or Right is on their side, may be found under *War Against Evil*, pp. 740-47.

If God is for us, who can be against us?

*Christianity*. Romans 8.31

United with me, you shall overcome all difficulties by my grace.

*Hinduism*. Bhagavad Gita 18.58

Not by might, nor by power, but by my Spirit, says the Lord of hosts.

*Judaism* and *Christianity*. Zechariah 4.6

O you who believe! If you help God's cause, He will help you and will make your foothold firm.

*Islam*. Qur'an 47.7

God, the Lord, is my strength;
he makes my feet like hind's feet,
he makes me tread upon high places.

*Judaism* and *Christianity*. Habakkuk 3.19

To those who have conformed themselves to the Way, the Way readily lends its power. To those who have conformed themselves to the power, the power readily lends more power.

*Taoism*. Tao Te Ching 23

Men of little ability, too,
By depending upon the great, may prosper;
A drop of water is a little thing,
But when will it dry away if united to a lake?

*Buddhism*. Elegant Sayings 173

Up dost Thou raise me, O Lord,
Through devotion dost Thou grant me endurance,
Through the Most Holy Spirit,
O Wise One, good award of prayer,
Through Right powerful vigor,
And through Good Thought leadership!

*Zoroastrianism*. Avesta, Yasna 33.12

**Tao Te Ching 23:** 'Power' (*te*) means the latent power or virtue inherent in nature and in Ultimate Reality.

**Elegant Sayings 173:** Cf. Tao Te Ching 4, p. 374.

Should the lord bestow His might on the tiny
ant,
Hordes million-strong it may destroy.
Whomsoever He Himself sends not to death,
He guards by the strength of His arm.
Despite all his efforts,
All man's endeavors turn fruitless.
None other is savior or destroyer:
He Himself is guardian of all beings.
O man! Why all this anxiety?
Says Nanak, Contemplate Him who is beyond
your understanding,
Who is so wonderful.

*Sikhism.* Adi Granth
Gauri Sukhmani, M.5, pp. 285-86

Have you not known?
Have you not heard?
The Lord is the everlasting God
the Creator of the ends of the earth
He does not grow weary, he does not tire,
his understanding is unsearchable.
He gives strength to the weary,
and to him who has no might he increases
strength.
Youths may faint and be weary,
and young men may fall, exhausted;
but they who hope in the Lord shall renew
their strength.
They shall mount up with wings like eagles,
they shall run and not be weary,
they shall walk and not grow faint.

*Judaism* and *Christianity*.
Isaiah 40.28-31

God does not leave his child tied up overnight.

*African Traditional Religions*.
Tiv Proverb (Nigeria)

Whosoever keeps his duty to God, God will appoint a way out for him, and will provide for him in a way that he cannot foresee. And whosoever puts his trust in God, He will suffice him. Lo! God brings His command to pass. God has set a measure for all things.

*Islam*. Qur'an 65.2-3

Leave your fight to Olodumare and look on, for he is defender of the defenseless.

*African Traditional Religions*.
Yoruba Proverb (Nigeria)

God is our refuge and strength,
a very present help in trouble.
Therefore we will not fear though the earth
should change,
though the mountains shake in the heart of the
sea;
though its waters roar and foam,
though the mountains tremble with its tumult.

*Judaism* and *Christianity*. Psalm 46.1-3

A king is not saved by his great army,
a warrior is not delivered by his great strength.
The war horse is a vain hope for victory,
and by its great might it cannot save.
Behold, the eye of the Lord is on those who
fear him,
on those who hope in his steadfast love,
that he may deliver their soul from death,
and keep them alive in famine.
Our soul waits for the Lord;
he is our help and our shield.

*Judaism* and *Christianity*.
Psalm 33.16-20

Altar Mountain of the Sacred Forest,
Where, since the divine age,
It has been said the myriad gods descended
To make offerings for safe passage
In the land of abundant rice on the
Plain of reeds.
Spring, and your spring mists rise,
Come the fall, and aflush with rouge,

**Gauri Sukhmani, M.5:** Cf. Devgandhari, M.4, p. 542; Gaund Kabir, pp. 629-30.

**Isaiah 40.28-31:** Cf. 1 Samuel 2.4-9, p. 388; 17.4-51, pp. 746-47.

**Tiv Proverb:** This is said when help arrives unexpectedly. Cf. Dinka Prayer, p. 94.

**Yoruba Proverb:** 'Olodumare' is a Yoruba name for the Supreme Being. Cf. Psalm 55.22, p. 592.

**Psalm 46.1-3:** The imagery is one of cosmic destruction in the latter days. This psalm was the inspiration for Martin Luther's famous hymn, "A Mighty Fortress is Our God." Cf. Psalm 23, p. 361; Psalm 93, pp. 384-85; Rig Veda 8.69.8, p. 548.

You, mountain god of the forest altar,
Take for belt the stream of the River Asuka,
Whose current so swift,
No easy birth her stony pillows give to the
moss,
Yet still moss on them abounds.
I shall beseech you each new night,
Show me in divined dreams
The way I should pass in peace!
Oh, god with sword-like awe enshrined.

*Shinto*. Man'yoshu 13

Free us, Indra, from the fear of all that we are
afraid of.
May thou, with thy saving power,
turn away the hater and the enemy.

We call on Indra, bounteous Giver,
we will be prosperous in men and cattle.
Let not the demon hosts approach us;
turn the hostiles away on all sides.

Adorable Indra, our Savior,
Vritra-slayer and Furtherer of our highest aims,
may he be our Protector from the end,
from the middle, from behind, and from in
front.

Lead us to a free world, Wise One,
where lie divine luster, sunlight, and security.
Valiant are the arms of thee, the Powerful;
we will take to their vast shelter.

*Hinduism*. Atharva Veda 19.15.1-4

Good God of this earth, my Lord!
You are above me, I am below you.
When misfortune comes to me,
As trees keep off the sun from me,
May you keep off misfortune;
My Lord, be my shadow!

Calling upon you, I pass the day.
Calling upon you, I pass the night.
When this moon rises, do not forsake me;
When I rise, I do not forsake you;
Let the danger pass by me.
God, my Lord, you Sun with thirty rays,
When the enemy comes, let not your worm be
killed upon the earth;
Keep him off, as we seeing a worm upon the
earth,
Crush him if we like, spare him if we like.
As we tread upon and kill a worm upon the
earth,
Thus, if you please, you crush us upon the
earth.
God, you go, holding the bad and the good in
your hand;
My Lord, let us not be killed,
We your worms, we are praying to you.

*African Traditional Religions*.
Boran Prayer (Kenya)

If God gives you a cup of wine and an evil-minded person kicks it over, He fills it up for you again.

*African Traditional Religions*.
Akan Proverb (Ghana)

He who dwells in the shelter of the Most High,
who abides in the shadow of the Almighty,
will say to the Lord, "My refuge and my
fortress;
my God, in whom I trust."
For he will deliver you from the snare of the
fowler,
and from the deadly pestilence;
he will cover you with his pinions,
and under his wings you will find refuge;
his faithfulness is a shield and buckler.

You will not fear the terror of the night,
nor the arrow that flies by day,
nor the pestilence that stalks in darkness,
nor the destruction that wastes at noonday.
A thousand may fall at your side,
ten thousand at your right hand;
but it will not come near you.
You will only look with your eyes
and see the recompense of the wicked.

**Atharva Veda 19.15.1-4:** Indra is the chief vedic god, who established justice throughout the cosmos by slaying the serpent-demon Vritra, the personification of all evil, lawlessness, darkness, and drought; see Rig Veda 1.80. Cf. Rig Veda 10.103, p. 743; Bhagavad Gita 11.26-34, pp. 738-39.

**Akan Proverb:** Cf. Banyarawanda Proverb, p. 69.

Because you have made the Lord your refuge,
the Most High your habitation,
no evil shall befall you,
no scourge come near your tent.
For he will give his angels charge of you
to guard you in all your ways.
On their hands they will bear you up,
lest you dash your foot against a stone.
You will tread on the lion and the adder,
the young lion and the serpent you will trample
under foot.

*Judaism* and *Christianity*.
Psalm 91.1-13

Knowing It one is not touched by evil action. Therefore he who knows It as such becomes self-controlled, calm, withdrawn into himself, patient, and collected; he sees the Self in his own self; he sees all as the Self. Evil does not overcome him, but he overcomes all evil. Evil does not afflict him, but he consumes all evil.

*Hinduism*.
Brihadaranyaka Upanishad 4.4.23

One who has a true hold on life, when he walks on land does not meet tigers or wild buffaloes; in battle he is not touched by weapons of war. Indeed, a buffalo that attacked him would find nothing for his horns to butt, a tiger would find nothing for its claws to tear, a weapon would find no place for its blade to lodge. And why? Because such men have no "death-spot" in them.

*Taoism*. Tao Te Ching 50

Those who are devoted to the perfection of wisdom should expect therefrom many advantages here and now. They will not die an untimely death, nor from poison, or sword, or fire, or water, or staff, or violence. When they bring to mind and repeat this perfection of wisdom, the calamities which threaten them from kings and princes, from king's counsellors and king's ministers, will not take place. If kings, etc., would try to do harm to those who again and again bring to mind and repeat the perfection of wisdom, they will not succeed; because the perfection of wisdom upholds them. Although kings, etc., may approach them with harmful intent, they will instead decide to greet them, to converse with them, to be polite and friendly to them. For this perfection of wisdom entails an attitude of friendliness and compassion toward all beings. Therefore, even though the devotees of the perfection of wisdom may be in the middle of a wilderness infested with venomous vipers, neither men nor ghosts can harm them, except as a punishment for past deeds.

*Buddhism*. Perfection of Wisdom
in Eight Thousand Lines 75-76

Master Lieh Tzu said to Barrier Keeper Yin, "The Perfect Man can walk under water without choking, can tread on fire without being burned, and can travel above the ten thousand things without being frightened. May I ask how he manages this?"

The Barrier Keeper Yin replied, "This is because he guards the pure breath—it has nothing to do with wisdom, skill, determination, or courage. Sit down and I will tell you about it. All that have faces, forms, voices, colors—these are all mere things. How could one thing and another thing be far removed from each other? And how could any of them be capable of leading you to what preceded them? They are forms, colors—nothing more. But that which creates things has no form, and it rests where there is no change. If a man can get hold of *this* and exhaust it fully, then how can things stand in his way? He may rest within the bounds that know no excess, hide within the borders that know no source, wander where the ten thousand things have their end and beginning, unify his nature, nourish his breath, unite his virtue, and thereby communicate with that which creates all things. A man like this guards what belongs to Heaven and keeps it whole. His spirit has no flaw, so how can things enter in and get at him?

**Psalm 91.1-13:** Cf. Luke 10.19-20, p. 220; Matthew 4.1-11, p. 444; Joshua 1.1-9, p. 745; Daniel 3.1-28, pp. 630-31; Acts 16.19-30, p. 635.

**Tao Te Ching 50:** Cf. Tao Te Ching 16, p. 383.

"When a drunken man falls from a carriage, though the carriage may be going very fast, he won't be killed. He has bones and joints the same as other men, and yet he is not injured as they would be, because his spirit is whole. He didn't know he was riding, and he doesn't know he has fallen out. Life and death, alarm and terror do not enter his breast, and so he can bang against things without fear of injury. If he can keep himself whole like this by means of wine, how much more can a man keep himself whole by means of Heaven! The sage hides himself in Heaven—hence there is nothing that can do him harm."

*Taoism*. Chuang Tzu 19

O Apostle! Sufficient for you is God—for you and for those who follow you among the believers.

O Apostle! Rouse the believers to the fight. If there are twenty among you, patient and persevering, they will vanquish two hundred; if a hundred, they will vanquish a thousand of the unbelievers, for these are a people without understanding.

For the present, God has lightened your task, for He knows that there is a weak spot in you; but even so, if there are a hundred of you, patient and persevering, they will vanquish two hundred, and if a thousand, they will vanquish two thousand, with the leave of God; for God is with those who patiently persevere.

*Islam*. Qur'an 8.64-66

O you who believe! Remember the grace of God on you, when there came down on you hosts; but We sent against them a hurricane and forces you could not see: but God sees clearly all that you do. Behold! They came on you from above you and from below you, and behold, the eyes became dim and the hearts gaped up to the throats, and you imagined various vain thoughts about God! In that situation were the believers tried; they were shaken as by a tremendous shaking....

And God turned back the unbelievers, for all their fury; no advantage did they gain; and enough is God for the believers in their fight. And God is full of Strength, Able to enforce His will.

*Islam*. Qur'an 33.9-25

O king, I say to you that Krishna is Eternal and Unfading... the Supreme Lord of all creatures, the great Master. He is warrior, He is Victory, He is Victor, and He is the Lord of all nature. O king, He is full of goodness and divested of all the qualities of darkness and passion. There, where Krishna is, there righteousness is; and where righteousness is, there is victory. It is by the Yoga of his Supreme Excellence, and the Yoga of his Self, that the sons of Pandu, O king, are supported. Victory, therefore, will surely be theirs. He it is that always imparts to the Pandavas understanding endued with righteousness and strength in battle; and He it is who always protects them from danger.

*Hinduism*. Mahabharata, Bhishma Parva 66

Then Moses and the people of Israel sang this
song to the Lord:
"I will sing to the Lord,
for he has triumphed gloriously;
the horse and his rider
he has thrown into the sea.

**Chuang Tzu 19:** Based on this tradition, the drunken man or the fool who is so pliant that he can stagger about and always escape harm is a stock character in Chinese drama. Cf. Tao Te Ching 55, p. 156; Chuang Tzu 6, p. 413.

**Qur'an 8.64-66:** This revelation was given on the eve of the battle of Badr, where the Companions of Muhammad, ill-equipped (the 'weak spot'), defeated a force that outnumbered them by more than three to one.

**Qur'an 33.9-25:** Vv. 9-11, 25. This sura describes the Battle of the Trench (A.H. 5), when a confederacy of opponents, with a force of ten thousand men, beseiged the Muslims in Medina for more than two weeks. Cf. Qur'an 2.214, p. 628.

**Mahabharata, Bhishma Parva 66:** These words of advice and warning were spoken to King Duryodhana, the arrogant and vain chief of the Kurus, on the eve of the great battle with the Pandavas. Krishna, avatar of Vishnu the Supreme Godhead, was on the side of the Pandavas as Arjuna's charioteer. Duryodhana took no notice of this sage advice. Cf. Bhagavad Gita 11.26-34, pp. 738-39.

The Lord is my strength and my song,
and he has become my salvation;
this is my God, and I will praise him,
my father's God, and I will exalt him.
The Lord is a man of war;
the Lord is his name.

"Pharaoh's chariots and his host
he cast into the sea;
and his picked officers
are sunk in the Red Sea.
The floods cover them;
they went down into the depths like a stone.

Your right hand, O Lord, glorious in power,
your right hand, O Lord, shatters the enemy.

In the greatness of your majesty
you overthrow your adversaries;
you send forth your fury,
it consumes them like stubble.
At the blast of your nostrils
the waters piled up,
the floods stood up in a heap;
the deeps congealed in the heart of the sea.

The enemy said, 'I will pursue,
I will overtake,
I will divide the spoil,
my desire shall have its fill of them.
I will draw my sword,
my hand shall destroy them.'
You blew them away with your wind,
the sea covered them;
they sank as lead
in the mighty waters.

"Who is like thee, O Lord, among the gods?
Who is like thee, majestic in holiness,
terrible in glorious deeds, doing wonders?"

*Judaism* and *Christianity*. Exodus 15.1-11

O Goddess, who removest the suffering of thy suppliants, be gracious!
Be gracious, O Mother of the whole world!
Be gracious, O Queen of the universe; safeguard the universe!
Thou, O Goddess, art Queen of all that is movable and immovable!
Thou alone hast become the support of the world,
Because thou dost subsist in the form of the earth!
By thee, who existest in the form of water, all
This universe is filled, O thou inviolable in thy valor!
Thou art Vishnu's energy, boundless in thy valor;
Thou art the Germ of the universe, thou art Illusion sublime!
All this world has been bewitched, O Goddess;
Thou indeed when attained art the cause of the final emancipation from existence on earth!...
O Goddess, be gracious! Protect us wholly from fear of our foes
Perpetually, as thou hast at this very time saved us promptly by the slaughter of the demons!
And bring thou quickly to rest the sins of all the worlds
And the great calamities which have sprung from the maturing of portents!
To us who are prostrate be thou gracious,
O goddess, who takest away affliction from the universe!
O thou worthy of praise from the dwellers in the three worlds,
Bestow thou boons on the worlds!

*Hinduism*. Markandeya Purana, Candi Mahatmya 10

**Exodus 15.1-11:** These verses are taken from the victory song which Moses and the Israelites sung at the Red Sea, at the great manifestation of God's power on which the biblical nation of Israel was founded. For other accounts of God's miraculous defeat of the Egyptians at the Red Sea, see Exodus 14, pp. 439-40 and Qur'an 10.75-92, pp. 438-39; cf. Megilla 10b, p. 367.

**Candi Mahatmya 10:** Worship of the Mother Goddess or feminine principle is prominent in contemporary Hinduism. She is identified with the earth—Atharva Veda 12.1, p. 207; with prakriti/matter, and maya/illusion—cf. Shiva Purana, p. 118. Often she is depicted in her terrible aspect as a dread warrior and destroyer of evil. The Goddess is known by various names: Durga, Kali, Shakti, Devi; in this text she is called by the name Candika.

World-honored Lord and Perfect One,
I pray thee now declare
Wherefore this holy Bodhisat
Is known as Kuan Shih Yin [Hearer of the
Cries of the World]?
To this the Perfect One replied
By uttering this song:

The echoes of her holy deeds
Resound throughout the world.
So vast and deep the vows she made
When, after countless eons
Of serving hosts of Perfect Ones,
She voiced her pure desire
[To liberate afflicted beings].

Now hearken to what came of it—
To hear her name or see her form,
Or fervently recite her name
Delivers beings from every woe.

Were you with murderous intent
Thrust within a fiery furnace,
One thought of Kuan Yin's saving power
Would turn those flames to water!

Were you adrift upon the sea
With dragon-fish and fiends around you,
One thought of Kuan Yin's saving power
Would spare you from the hungry waves.

Suppose from Mount Sumeru's peak
Some enemy should cast you down,
One thought of Kuan Yin's saving power
And sun-like you would stand in space.

Were you pursued by evil men
And crushed against the Iron Mountain,
One thought of Kuan Yin's saving power
And not a hair would come to harm.

Were you amidst a band of thieves,
Their cruel knives now raised to slay,
One thought of Kuan Yin's saving power
And pity must restrain their blows.

Suppose the king now wroth with you,
The headsman's sword upraised to strike,
One thought of Kuan Yin's saving power
Would dash the sword to pieces.

Were you close pent by prison walls,
Your wrists and ankles bound by chains,
One thought of Kuan Yin's saving power
Would instantly procure release.

Had you imbibed some fatal draught
And lay now at the point of death,
One thought of Kuan Yin's saving power
Would nullify its poison....

Imbued with supernatural power
And wise in using skilful means,
In every corner of the world
She manifests her countless forms.

No matter what black evils gather—
What hell-spawned demons, savage beasts,
What ills of birth, age, sickness, death,
Kuan Yin will one by one destroy them.

True Kuan Yin! Pure Kuan Yin!
Immeasurably wise Kuan Yin!
Merciful and filled with pity,
Ever longed-for and revered!

O Radiance spotless and effulgent!
O night-dispelling Sun of Wisdom!
O Vanquisher of storm and flame!
Your glory fills the world!

*Buddhism*. Lotus Sutra 25

❖

**Lotus Sutra 25:** Kuan Yin (Jap. Kannon) is the Bodhisattva Avalokitesvara, The One who Hears Cries, and thus represents the divine attribute of grace and help to people in distress. In Chinese Buddhism Kuan Yin is a female—the Goddess of compasssion—and this passage is often recited to invoke her aid and offer her worship. Hence we have used a translation of the Lotus Sutra which describes her as a female bodhisattva, even though in the Sanskrit original Avalokitesvara is depicted as a male. Other bodhisattavas are also invoked for protection, notably Samantabhadra, whose worship flourished in Japan during the Heian period; cf. Lotus Sutra 28.

## *The Refining Fire*

THE PRESENCE OF SUFFERING and hardship in life cannot always be explained on the basis of divine justice. Why, if God is just and gracious, and the true teaching brings forth love and peace, do the righteous seem to suffer about as much as the wicked? The problem of theodicy, particularly when it concerns the problem of the righteous sufferer, has occupied the minds of some of the greatest religious thinkers. Passages relevant to the problem of theodicy are found scattered throughout this anthology according to the various solutions which are posited in scripture: E.g., the human condition is inevitably *Ill*, pp. 270-74; people are deluded by *Ignorance*, pp. 280-85; infected by Original Sin from a primordial *Human Fall*, pp. 300-308; fated to work out accumulated *Karma* and *Inherited Sin*, pp. 498-503; or influenced by *Demonic Powers*, pp. 309-15. One may have an *Argument with God*, pp. 559-62, that such suffering is unjust; or empathize with *God's* own *Grief*, pp. 324-27.

Another way in which the suffering of the righteous is frequently understood is as a means to spiritual advancement and hence a manifestation of God's grace. Suffering tries and tests people, purifies their faith, corrects their flaws, and refines their character. This suffering is an expression of grace and love because once people have come out of the refining fire and accepted correction, they will shine with a tested and confirmed faith and a splendid character. Especially those whom God wishes to entrust with a special responsibility, or who are desirous of reaching the highest goal, will be most severely tested and most thoroughly refined. The passages gathered below treat this gracious side of suffering: the refining fire.

Welcome to thy wrath and to thy glow!
Our welcome be to thy flame!
Let thy missles burn our enemies,
Be our purifier, be gracious to us!

*Hinduism.* Yajur Veda 36.20

Just as a great conflagration
Can burn up all things,
So does Buddha's field of blessings
Burn up all fabrication.

*Buddhism.* Garland Sutra 10

As the heat of a fire reduces wood to ashes, the fire of knowledge burns to ashes all karma. Nothing in this world purifies like spiritual wisdom.

*Hinduism.* Bhagavad Gita 4.37

Just as a fire quickly reduces decayed wood to ashes, so does an aspirant who is totally absorbed in the inner self and completely unattached to all external objects shake to the roots, attenuate, and wither away his karma-body.

*Jainism.* Samantabhadra, Aptamimamsa 24-27

"From His right hand went forth a fiery law for them" [Deuteronomy 33.2]. The words of Torah are compared to fire, for both were given from heaven, and both are eternal. If a man draws near the fire, he derives benefit; if he keeps afar, he is frozen, so with the words of the Torah: if a man toils in them, they are life to him; if he separates from him, they kill him.

*Judaism.* Sifre Deuteronomy 143a

**Garland Sutra 10:** Cf. Dhammapada 239, p. 510; Ramayana, Yuddha Kanda 118-20, p. 560.

I will put this third into the fire,
and refine them as one refines silver,
and test them as gold is tested.

*Judaism* and *Christianity*. Zechariah 13.9

Ambrosia can be extracted even from poison; elegant speech even from a child; good conduct even from an enemy, gold even from impurity.

*Hinduism*. Laws of Manu 2.239

Make chastity your furnace, patience your smithy,
The Master's word your anvil, and true knowledge your hammer.
Make awe of God your bellows, and with it kindle the fire of austerity.
And in the crucible of love, melt the nectar Divine.
Only in such a mint, can man be cast into the Word.

*Sikhism*. Adi Granth, Japuji 38, M.1, p. 8

Devotion to God's Name is my lamp;
In this lamp is poured the oil of suffering.
The light of realization burns away this oil,
Lifted is the encounter with Death.
Let not the world ridicule this as an idle boast:
Vast loads of firewood are reduced to ashes by a tiny spark of fire.

*Sikhism*. Adi Granth, Asa, M.1, p. 358

Every soul must taste of death, and We try you with evil and with good, for ordeal. And unto Us you will be returned.

*Islam*. Qur'an 21.35

Rabbi Yohanan said, "The Israelites are compared to an olive tree, because as the olive yields its oil only by hard pressure, so the Israelites do not return to righteousness except through suffering."

*Judaism*. Talmud, Menahot 53b

We rejoice in our sufferings, knowing that suffering produces endurance, and endurance produces character, and character produces hope, and hope does not disappoint us, because God's love has been poured into our hearts.

*Christianity*. Romans 5.3-5

In the whole world it is said that some part of the body is afflicted and painful. It is truly a signpost or guidance from God, though you are ignorant of it.

*Tenrikyo*. Ofudesaki 2.22

My son, do not despise the Lord's discipline
or be weary of his reproof,
for the Lord reproves him whom he loves,
as a father the son in whom he delights.

*Judaism* and *Christianity*. Proverbs 3.11-12

I know, O Lord, that the way of man is not in himself,
that it is not in man who walks to direct his steps.
Correct me, O Lord, but in just measure;
not in thy anger, lest thou bring me to nothing.

*Judaism* and *Christianity*. Jeremiah 10.23-24

Yet the suffering
Involved in my awakening will have a limit;
It is like the suffering of having an incision made
In order to remove and destroy greater pain.

Even doctors eliminate illness
With unpleasant medical treatments,
So in order to overcome manifold sufferings
I should be able to put up with some discomfort.

**Zechariah 13.9:** Cf. Hidden Words of Baha'u'llah, Arabic 54, p. 664.
**Japuji 38, M.1:** Cf. Book of Certitude, 68-69, p. 575.
**Menahot 53b:** Cf. Canticles Rabbah 2.5, p. 546.
**Proverbs 3.11-12:** Quoted in Hebrews 12.5-11. Cf. Job 1.6-12, p. 314; Deuteronomy 6.20-8.20, p. 764-65; Book of Mormon, Mosiah 3.19, p. 648.

But the Supreme Physician does not employ
Common medical treatments such as these,
With an extremely gentle technique
He remedies all the greatest sins.

*Buddhism*. Shantideva, Guide to the Bodhisattva's Way of Life 7.22-24

Do men imagine that they will be left [at ease] because they say, "We believe," and will not be tested with affliction? Lo! We tested those who were before you. Thus God knows those who are sincere, and knows those who feign.

*Islam*. Qur'an 29.2-3

Mencius said, "Shun rose from the fields; Fu Yüeh was raised to office from among the builders; Chiao Ke from amid the fish and salt; Kuan Chung from the hands of the prison officer; Sun Shu-ao from the sea and Po-li Hsi from the market. That is why Heaven, when it is about to place a great burden on a man, always first tests his resolution, exhausts his frame and makes him suffer starvation and hardship, frustrates his efforts so as to shake him from his mental lassitude, toughen his nature, and make good his deficiencies."

*Confucianism*. Mencius VI.B.15

If the Holy One is pleased with a man, he crushes him with painful sufferings. For it is said, "And the Lord was pleased with him, hence he crushed him by disease" [Isaiah 53.10]. Now, you might think that this is so even if he did not accept them with love. Therefore it is said, "To see if his soul would offer itself in restitution." Even as the trespass-offering must be brought by consent, so also the sufferings must be endured with consent. And if he did accept them, what is his reward? "He will see his seed, prolong his days." And more than that, his knowledge [of Torah] will endure with him. For it is said, "The purpose of the Lord will prosper in his hand."

*Judaism*. Talmud, Berakot 5a

And to keep me from being too elated by the abundance of revelations, a thorn was given me in the flesh, a messenger of Satan, to harass me, to keep me from being too elated. Three times I [Paul] besought the Lord about this, that it should leave me; but he said to me, "My grace is sufficient for you, for my power is made perfect in weakness." I will all the more gladly boast of my weaknesses, that the power of Christ may rest upon me. For the sake of Christ, then, I am content with weaknesses, insults, hardships, persecutions, and calamities; for when I am weak, then I am strong.

*Christianity*. 2 Corinthians 12.7-10

**Qur'an 29.2-3:** Cf. Qur'an 2.153-57, p. 530; 6.165, p. 506; 47.31, p. 333; Majjhima Nikaya i.123-24, pp. 333-34; Job 1.6-12, p. 314; Sirach 6.7-17, p. 184; Fon Song, p. 530.

**Mencius VI.B.15:** Cf. Luke 12.48, p. 506.

**Berakot 5a:** The Talmud is explicating on Isaiah 53.10, pp. 457-58, a verse from Isaiah's portrayal of God's suffering servant. Cf. Job 23.3-10, p. 560.

**2 Corinthians 12.7-10:** Paul never specifies the nature of his 'thorn'; it was most likely a physical ailment. When he petitioned God for relief, instead he received the response 'My grace is enough for you...' which he takes to be a manifestation in his person of the message of the cross.

## Born Anew

TO LEAVE THE CONDITION OF WORLDLY EXISTENCE and enter the realm of God's grace is often understood as a second, spiritual birth. Jesus said, "You must be born anew." The Christian who is born again in Christ becomes a child of God, experiences an intimacy with God, and has the spirit of Christ dwelling in him. The old self dies away, with its worldly desires and false views. To be born again, the Christian must undergo the rite of Baptism, by which he becomes open to receive Christ and the Holy Spirit. Among the passages from the Christian scriptures, we offer the account of the first Pentecost. The gifts of the Spirit, especially the gift of speaking in tongues, are essential signs confirming the veracity of a person's rebirth in Pentecostal Christian churches.

In Hinduism and Buddhism, the twice-born are those who have received religious instruction and have realized its truths. Their life is now grounded in Dharma, and they have rejected a life of sense gratification. The Hindu's second birth is the student's initiation into the mysteries of vedic knowledge; it must be mediated by an able teacher. In Buddhism rebirth means to become a "son of the Buddha" after education and training, through which the old ways of looking at life are replaced by the new eyes of the Dharma. Buddha's sons and daughters make vows to follow the path that will lead them to eventual Arahantship or Buddhahood. Initiations in the primal religions may similarly bring about a new birth.[1] The mystic transformation of rebirth is integral to salvation as offered through several new religions, most notably the Change of Blood Lineage in the Unification Church.

Today I indeed know that I am really a son of Buddha, born from the mouth of Buddha, evolved from the Law, and have obtained a place in the Buddha-law.

*Buddhism*. Lotus Sutra 3

To all who received him [Jesus], who believed in his name, he gave power to become children of God; who were born, not of blood nor of the will of the flesh nor the will of man, but of God.

*Christianity*. John 1.12-13

Monks, I am a brahmin, one to ask a favor of, ever clean-handed, wearing my last body, incomparable physician and surgeon. You are my own true sons, born of my mouth, born into the doctrine, created in the doctrine, my spiritual heirs, not carnal heirs.

*Buddhism*. Itivuttaka 101

Jesus answered him, "Truly, truly, I say to you, unless one is born anew, he cannot see the kingdom of God." Nicodemus said to him, "How can a man be born when he is old? Can

**Lotus Sutra 3:** The Mahayana goal is that each person himself become a Buddha. Cf. Parable of the Prodigal Son, Lotus Sutra 4, pp. 363-65.

**John 1.12-13:** Cf. Book of Mormon, Mosiah 3.19, p. 648.

**Itivuttaka 101:** In traditional Hinduism, the term 'twice-born' applies only to those who undertake instruction from a brahmin. Shakyamuni Buddha was not a brahmin in the conventional meaning; his caste was kshatriya. But as the Enlightened One, he declared himself to be a brahmin in the true sense

[1] See Sioux Vision Quest, pp. 606-7.

he enter a second time into his mother's womb and be born?" Jesus answered, "Truly, truly, I say to you, unless one is born of water and the Spirit, he cannot enter the kingdom of God. That which is born of the flesh is flesh, and that which is born of the Spirit is spirit. Do not marvel that I say to you, 'You must be born anew.'"

*Christianity*. John 3.3-7

Repentance makes man a new creature; hitherto dead through sin, he is fashioned afresh.

*Judaism*. Midrash Psalms 18

He from whom the pupil gathers the knowledge of his religious duties is called the teacher. Him he should never offend. For he causes the pupil to be born a second time by imparting to him sacred learning. The second birth is the best; the father and the mother produce the body only.

*Hinduism*.
Apastamba Dharma Sutra 1.1

In the eighth year after conception, one should perform the initiation (*upanayana*) of a brahmin, in the eleventh year after conception of a kshatriya, and in the twelfth that of a vaishya.

Thus has been described the rule for the initiation of the twice-born, which indicates a new birth, and sanctified.

Of him who gives natural birth and him who gives the knowledge of the Veda, the giver of the Veda is the more venerable father; for the birth for the sake of the Veda ensures eternal rewards both in this life and after death.

*Hinduism*.
Laws of Manu 2.36, 68 and 146

But you are not in the flesh, you are in the Spirit, if in fact the Spirit of God dwells in you. Any one who does not have the Spirit of Christ does not belong to him. But if Christ is in you, although your bodies are dead because of sin, your spirits are alive because of righteousness. If the Spirit of him who raised Jesus from the dead dwells in you, he who raised Christ Jesus from the dead will give life to your mortal bodies also through his Spirit which dwells in you.

So then, brethren, we are debtors, not to the flesh, to live according to the flesh—for if you live according to the flesh you will die, but if by the Spirit you put to death the deeds of the body you will live. For all who are led by the Spirit of God are sons of God. For you did not receive the spirit of slavery to fall back into fear, but you have received the spirit of sonship. When we cry, "Abba! Father!" it is the Spirit himself bearing witness with our spirit that we are children of God, and if children, then heirs, heirs of God and fellow heirs with Christ, provided we suffer with him in order that we may also be glorified with him.

*Christianity*. Romans 8.9-17

These same people, though wrapt in all these veils of limitation, and despite the restraint of such observances, as soon as they drank the immortal draught of faith, from the cup of certitude, at the hand of the Manifestation of the All-glorious, were so transformed that they would renounce for his sake their kindred, their substance, their lives, their beliefs, yea, all else save God! So overpowering was their yearning for God, so uplifting their transports of ecstatic delight, that the world and all that

of one who has attained Brahman. Thus he was qualified to initiate his followers into the Buddha doctrine and give them a second birth. The words 'born of my mouth' is an allusion to the Vedic myth of the creation of the castes—see Rig Veda 10.90.11-12, p. 189, in which the brahmins were born out of the mouth of the Supreme Being. Buddha is abolishing the caste system by declaring that all his followers are, as it were, brahmins, born out of the mouth of the Buddha by virtue of receiving his instruction. Compare Vacana 589, p. 192.

**John 3.3-7:** To be 'born of water and the Spirit' refers to baptism with water, through which one receives the gift of the Holy Spirit: cf. Acts 2.38, p. 611; Romans 6.3-11, pp. 611-12.

**Apastamba Dharma Sutra 1.1:** Cf. Atharva Veda 6.121.4, p. 379.

**Romans 8.9-17:** Cf. Mark 8.34-36, p. 638; Galatians 2.20, p. 639.

is therein faded before their eyes into nothingness. Have not this people exemplified the mysteries of "rebirth"... ?

... Nothing short of this mystic transformation could cause such spirit and behavior, so utterly unlike their previous habits and manners, to be manifest in the world of being. For their agitation was turned into peace, their doubt into certitude, their timidity into courage. Such is the potency of the Divine Elixir, which, swift as the twinkling of an eye, transmutes the souls of men!

*Baha'i Faith.* Book of Certitude, 155, 157

Do you have true love? True Parents have absolute and eternal love. But we inherited the wrong root of love through the fall. Here in the Western world, many deny that the fall occurred: "Who has fallen? What has anyone in my lineage done wrong?" But love, in the beginning of mankind, started in the wrong direction. Without recognizing this, then salvation and a religious life become meaningless. What is the final purpose of salvation? Mankind, represented by a tree, has multiplied fallen nature throughout the world. Restoration of love, life, and blood lineage must occur.... For the original "me" to emerge, I must originate in God's love, God's life, and God's lineage. It did not happen [at the time of Adam and Eve], therefore we are still trying to connect to these three things....

In restoring all of these three elements it is necessary to have the parent/child relationship. Fallen man exists only as a shell. Inside he is nothing; it's just like a scarecrow with a form but nothing else. He must receive love and become one with the parents. Before finding new life, there has to be love. In our case, we have life, but since there was no true love, our originating point was not God....

Most Christianity emphasizes Jesus' blood. Why is the blood so meaningful? Jesus' blood means the parents' blood before the fall: true blood.

Can [True] Father alone, by himself, bequeath these three things? Not without [True] Mother! That is why the goal in the Old Testament was to have the Marriage of the Lamb.

Where do fallen people belong? They are born and become mature physically, but in essence they have not been truly born. It is written in the Bible, "Unless you are born again, you cannot be saved," which means exactly that. They have to go back into the mother's womb and even before that—back into the father's bone marrow. That means his blood lineage is mine, his love is mine, his life is my life.... Basically all that we have to know is that True Parents embody the new love, life, and blood lineage. Unless you connect with all three, you cannot connect with God.

*Unification Church.* Sun Myung Moon, 8-20-89

When the day of Pentecost had come, they were all together in one place. And suddenly a sound came from heaven like the rush of a mighty wind, and it filled all the house where they were sitting. And there appeared to them tongues as of fire, distributed and resting on each one of them. And they were all filled with the Holy Spirit and began to speak in other tongues, as the Spirit gave them utterance.

Now there were dwelling in Jerusalem Jews, devout men from every nation under heaven. And at this sound the multitude came together, and they were bewildered, because each one heard them speaking in his own language. And they were amazed and wondered, saying, "Are not all these who are speaking Galileans? And how is it that we hear, each of us in his own

**Sun Myung Moon, 8-20-89:** Rebirth means to leave the lineage of Adam and Eve—fallen humanity stained by the original sin (cf. Divine Principle I.2.2.2, pp. 304-5)—and be engrafted into the lineage of the True Parents, who embody God's true love—as God purposed for Adam and Eve had they not fallen (cf. Divine Principle I.1.2.3.4, p. 175). This Change of Blood Lineage occurs spiritually at the holy wedding; it is substantiated through a God-centered way of life which embodies the True Parents' standard of godly love.

native language? Parthians and Medes and Elamites and residents of Mesopotamia, Judea and Cappadocia, Pontus and Asia, Phrygia and Pamphylia, Egypt and the parts of Lybia belonging to Cyrene, and visitors from Rome, both Jews and proselytes, Cretans and Arabians, we hear them telling in our own tongues the mighty works of God." But others mocking said, "They are filled with new wine."

But Peter, standing with the eleven, lifted up his voice and addressed them, "Men of Judea and all who dwell in Jerusalem, let this be known to you, and give ear to my words. For these men are not drunk, as you suppose, since it is only the third hour of the day; but this is what was spoken by the prophet Joel:

And in the last days it shall be, God
declares,
that I will pour out my Spirit upon all flesh,
and your sons and your daughters shall
prophesy,
and your young men shall see visions,
and your old men shall dream dreams;
yea, and on my menservants and my maidservants in those days
I will pour out my Spirit; and they shall
prophesy.

*Christianity.* Acts 2.1-18

❖

**Book of Certitude, 155, 157:** See Hidden Words of Baha'u'llah, Arabic 7, p. 639.

**Acts 2.1-18:** This is the Bible's account of the first Christian Pentecost. In Judaism, the Pentecost is the day commemorating the giving of the Law to Moses on Mount Sinai. The gift of tongues to the disciples, on the very day commemorating the giving of the Law ages before, marks the beginning of a new dispensation of God's grace, a 'dispensation of the Spirit'—see 2 Corinthians 3.7-16, p. 454. By quoting the prophet Joel, Peter declared that these phenomena of tongues and prophesy are signs of the Last Days and testimony to the messiahship of Jesus Christ, who had been crucified. Jews and Christians alike, who even today look to a future new age, often describe it as an age of the Spirit, when the Spirit of God will become manifest in the hearts of all people; see Jeremiah 31.31-34, p. 792, and Numbers Rabbah 17.6, pp. 791-92. Note also that testimony to the Lord in every tongue is a characteristic of the Last Days according to the Jewish prayer Alenu, p. 790, and in the Great Commission to preach the gospel to all nations—see Matthew 28.18-20, p. 723. Hence the Christian Pentecost is regarded both as the beginning of a new dispensation of the Spirit and as the momentary sign of an even greater outpouring of the Spirit which is yet to come. The gift of tongues is a living reality for Pentecostal Christians, manifesting the power of the Spirit to transform their lives and make them new creatures in Christ. Cf. John 3.8, p. 379; Ephesians 5.18, p. 354.

## *Eternal Life*

THE GOAL OF THE RELIGIOUS QUEST is often described as immortality or eternal life. Humanity has always chafed under the limitations of mortality, and people have found in religion the means to transcend the death which seems to proscribe the possibilities of human existence. Yet we have already gathered under *Immortal Soul*, pp. 230-36, passages from scripture which recognize that every person has an eternal spirit as his or her birthright. Everyone will continue eternally in some form of existence after the end of this physical life. The question of eternal life, therefore, does not mean eternal existence *per se*, but rather what form it will take, and whether death will remain a barrier to human fulfillment.

We find that the scriptures of many religions give two meanings to the terms "life" and "death." There is the physical meaning of life: existence in this physical realm, and there is the spiritual meaning of life: the state of blessedness which is enduring from life to life and hence transcends death. There is the physical death: the dropping of the body which is an event in the voyage of every soul, and the spiritual death: the condition of distance from God, ignorance, and a hellish existence in the hereafter.

Hence when the question of salvation is at issue, the outcomes called "eternal life" and "immortality" are often ciphers to describe the condition of blessedness. This condition is present already in the physical life of the person who realizes Truth or lives in God's grace, and it will continue, unabated, in the hereafter. The person who gains eternal life has accomplished the goal of life, and hence death is not to be feared as a limitation, as it is for a worldly person who has tied all hopes to his possessions and pleasures in the world.

Some Taoist scriptures, on the other hand, promote the ideal of physical immorality. The eternal youth of the Taoist Immortals is a consequence of their life being totally at one with the Tao of nature. Likewise, the doctrine of the resurrection is interpreted by some Christians, Jews, and Muslims as requiring the reconstitution of the dead in their physical bodies, to dwell forever on this earth. Yet these physical interpretations are also based on a spiritual concept of life and death: Only the spiritually alive are qualified to enjoy immortality or the fruits of the resurrection.

We note that Buddhist scriptures generally avoid speaking of the state of blessedness as eternal life. Buddhist teaching views the desire for life as a kind of grasping, and hence a fetter to liberation.

For the wages of sin is death, but the free gift of God is eternal life in Christ Jesus our Lord.

*Christianity.* Romans 6.23

Jesus said to her, "I am the resurrection and the life; he who believes in me, though he die, yet shall he live, and whoever lives and believes in me shall never die."

*Christianity.* John 11.25

**Romans 6.23:** Cf. John 3.16, p. 360; 12.50, p. 454; Midrash Psalms 18, p. 407.
**John 11.25:** Cf. John 12.24-25, p. 638; Mark 8.34-36, p. 638; Romans 8.9-17. p. 407; Job 19.25-26, p. 415.

From the unreal lead me to the Real!
From darkness lead me to light!
From death lead me to immortality!

*Hinduism.* Brihadaranyaka Upanishad 1.3.28

All Israel have part in the world to come, as it is said, "and thy people shall be all righteous; they shall inherit the land forever, the branch of my planting, the work of my hands that I may be glorified" [Isaiah 60.21].

*Judaism.* Mishnah, Sanhedrin 11.1

Those who have faith and do righteous deeds, they are the best of creatures. Their reward is with God: Gardens of Eternity, beneath which rivers flow; they will dwell therein for ever; God well pleased with them, and they with Him; all this for such as fear their Lord and Cherisher.

*Islam.* Qur'an 98.7-8

Having realized the Self, which is soundless, intangible, formless, undecaying, and likewise tasteless, eternal, and odorless; having realized That which is without beginning and end, beyond the Great, and unchanging—one is freed from the jaws of death.

*Hinduism.* Katha Upanishad 1.3.15

Being in accord with Tao, he is everlasting.

*Taoism.* Tao Te Ching 16

Eternity does not exist apart from true love.

*Unification Church.* Sun Myung Moon, 8-18-88

Where one sees nothing but the One, hears nothing but the One, knows nothing but the One—there is the Infinite. Where one sees another, hears another, knows another—there is the finite. The Infinite is immortal, the finite is mortal.

It is written, He who has realized eternal Truth does not see death, nor illness, nor pain; he sees everything as the Self, and obtains all.

*Hinduism.* Chandogya Upanishad 7.23 and 7.27

Then do I proclaim what the Most Beneficent spoke to me,
The Words to be heeded, which are best for mortals:
Those who shall give hearing and reverence
Shall attain unto perfection and immortality
By the deeds of good spirit of the Lord of Wisdom!

*Zoroastrianism.* Avesta, Yasna 45.5

The supreme stage of the Soul is free from birth, old age and death; he is supreme, pure, and devoid of eight karmas; he possesses infinite knowledge, intuition, bliss, and potency; he is indivisible, indestructible, and inexhaustible. Besides, he is supersensuous and unparalleled, is free from obstructions, merit, demerit, and rebirth, and is eternal, steady, and independent.

*Jainism.* Kundakunda, Niyamasara 176-77

There is the nine-portalled lotus
covered under three bands, in which
lives the spirit with the Atman within,
that the Veda-knowers know.

Desireless, serene, immortal, Self-existent,
contented with the essence, lacking nothing, is he.

**Brihadaranyaka Upanishad 1.3.28:** Cf. Rig Veda 9.113.8-11, p. 248.

**Sanhedrin 11.1:** All Jews are entitled to an eternal kingdom by virtue of membership in the Jewish people and God's heritage and promise which they have received.

**Qur'an 98.7-8:** Cf. Qur'an 25.75-76, p. 158; 56.10-27, p. 248.

**Katha Upanishad 1.3.15:** Cf. Brihadaranyaka Upanishad 4.4.25, p. 76; Bhagavad Gita 8.20-21, p. 78; 9.30-31, p. 370. Cf. Lotus Sutra 16, p. 791.

**Chandogya Upanishad 7.23 and 27:** Cf. Brihadaranyaka Upanishad 4.4.6-7, p. 658.

**Niyamasara 176-77:** In Jainism there is no pre-existent Supreme Being, but rather the state of Godhood (*Paramatman*) which is humanity's goal and highest good.

One has no fear of death who has known him,
the Atman—serene, ageless, youthful.

*Hinduism.* Atharva Veda 10.8.43-44

Death is but another phase of the dream that existence can be material. Nothing can interfere with the harmony of being nor end the existence of man in Science. Man is the same after as before a bone is broken or the body guillotined. If man is never to overcome death, why do the Scriptures say, "The last enemy that shall be destroyed is death"? The tenor of the Word shows that we shall obtain the victory over death in proportion as we overcome sin. The great difficulty lies in ignorance of what God is. God, Life, Truth, and Love make man undying. Immortal Mind, governing all, must be acknowledged as supreme in the physical realm, so-called, as well as in the spiritual.

*Christian Science.* Science and Health, 427

Higher than this is Brahman, the Supreme, the Great.
Hidden in all things, body by body,
The One embracer of the universe—
By knowing him as Lord men become immortal.

I know this mighty Person
Of the color of the sun, beyond darkness.
Only by knowing him does one pass over death.
There is no other path for going there.

Than whom there is naught else higher,
Than whom there is naught else smaller, naught greater,
The One stands like a tree established in heaven.
By him, the Person, this whole world is filled.

That which is beyond this world
Is without form and without ill.
They who know That, become immortal;
But others go only to sorrow.

*Hinduism.* Svetasvatara Upanishad 3.7-10

Leave the dead to bury their own dead; but as for you, go and proclaim the kingdom of God.

*Christianity.* Luke 9.60

Can he who was dead, to whom We gave life, and a Light whereby he can walk among men, be like him who is in the depths of darkness from which he can never come out?

*Islam.* Qur'an 6.122

"For the living know that they shall die" [Ecclesiastes 9.5]: These are the righteous who in their death are called living... "but the dead know nothing": These are the wicked who in their lifetime are called dead.

*Judaism.* Talmud, Berakot 18ab

Thou bringest forth the living from the dead, and thou bringest forth the dead from the living.

*Islam.* Qur'an 3.27

For the trumpet will sound, and the dead will be raised imperishable, and we shall be changed. For this perishable nature must put on the imperishable, and this mortal nature must put on immortality. When the perishable puts on the imperishable, and the mortal puts on immortality, then shall come to pass the saying that is written,

**Atharva Veda 10.8.43-44:** The 'nine-portalled lotus' is the "city of nine gates" (Bhagavad Gita 5.13), that is, the body. Cf. Kena Upanishad 1.1-2, p. 75, Svetasvatara Upanishad 2.12, p. 603. On immortality in the Sikh scriptures, see Ramkali Dakhni Onkar, M. 1, p. 555.

**Svetasvatara Upanishad 3.7-10:** Cf. Rig Veda 10.90.1-4, p. 63. Note the image of the tree—compare Bhagavad Gita 15.1-3, p. 272, and of the Supreme Being likened to the Sun—see Isha Upanishad 15-16, p. 47. Cf. Lotus Sutra 16, p. 791.

**Luke 9.60:** Jesus uses two different meanings for the word 'dead' in this proverb. The first 'dead' are those that are physically alive but spiritually dead, in contrast to the true follower of Jesus who shares in eternal life.

**Qur'an 6.122:** Cf. Hidden Words of Baha'u'llah, Arabic 7, p. 639.

**Berakot 18ab:** Cf. Asa-ki-Var, M.1, p. 323.

Death is swallowed up in victory.
O Death, where is thy victory?
O Death, where is thy sting?

The sting of death is sin, and the power of sin is the law. But thanks be to God, who gives us the victory through our Lord Jesus Christ.

*Christianity*. 1 Corinthians 15.52-57

The hand of the Lord was upon me, and he brought me out by the Spirit of the Lord, and set me down in the midst of the valley; it was full of bones... and lo, they were very dry. And he said to me, "Son of man, can these bones live?" And I answered, "O Lord God, thou knowest."

Again he said to me, "Prophesy to these bones, and say to them, O dry bones, hear the word of the Lord. Thus says the Lord God to these bones, Behold, I will cause breath to enter you, and you shall live. And I will lay sinews upon you, and will cause flesh to come upon you, and cover you with skin, and put breath in you, and you shall live. And you shall know that I am the Lord."

So I prophesied as I was commanded; and as I prophesied, there was a noise, and behold, a rattling; and the bones came together, bone to its bone. And as I looked, there were sinews on them, and flesh came upon them, and skin covered them.... and breath came into them, and they lived, and stood upon their feet, an exceedingly great host.

Then he said to me, "Son of man, these bones are the whole house of Israel. Behold, they say, 'Our bones are dried up, and our hope is lost; we are clean cut off.' Therefore prophesy, and say to them, Thus says the Lord God, Behold, I will open your graves, and raise you from your graves, O my people, and I will bring you home into the land of Israel.... And I will put my Spirit within you, and you shall live, and I will place you in your own land; then you shall know that I, the Lord, have spoken, and I have done it, says the Lord."

*Judaism* and *Christianity*.
Ezekiel 37.4-14

Nan-po Tzu-k'uei said to the woman Nü Yü, "You are old, and yet your complexion is like that of a child. How is this?"

Nü Yü replied, "I have learned Tao."

"Could I get Tao by studying it?" asked the other.

"I fear not," said Nü Yü. "You are not the sort of person. There was Pu-liang Yi. He had the qualifications of a sage... so I began teaching him. In three days, all distinctions of high and low, good and bad, had ceased to exist. Seven days more, and the external world had ceased to be. In nine more days, he became unconscious of his own existence. He first became ethereal, next possessed of perfect wisdom, then without past and present, and finally was able to enter where life and death are no more—where killing does not take away life, nor does giving birth add to it. In that state, there is nothing he does not welcome, nothing he does not send off, nothing he does not destroy, nothing he does not construct. This is to be at Peace in Strife. He who can be at peace in strife is on the way to perfection."

*Taoism*. Chuang Tzu 6

❖

**1 Corinthians 15.52-57:** The resurrection brings immortality and victory over death only by virtue of Jesus' victory over death. It is through faith in Jesus that Christians have confidence in their immortality. Otherwise, they will be stung by death, as 'the sting of death is sin.' Cf. 1 Corinthians 15.21-22, p. 388; 15.24-26, p. 793; 2 Corinthians 4.16-5.10, p. 232; Romans 6.3-11, pp. 611-12; 8.9-17, p. 407.

**Ezekiel 37.4-14:** This passage is traditionally understood to be a prophesy of the resurrection of the dead. In its literal, historical sense it speaks figuratively of the reconstitution of the nation of Israel after years of exile in Babylon. Cf. Berakot 15b, Qur'an 41.39, p. 233; Yakima Tradition, pp. 233-34.

**Chuang Tzu 6:** On the little child, cf. Tao Te Ching 10, p. 601; 20, p. 434; 55, p. 156.

## *The Unitive State*

THE UNITIVE STATE IS THE FINAL GOAL of salvation in the great religions of the East. The experience of this unity is profound and can be hinted at only vaguely by the words of scripture. It encompasses both union with God or Absolute Reality and union with all existence, the dissolution of subject and object, knower and known. Mystical union is less common in the Abrahamic faiths, which in their uncompromising monotheism have always insisted upon an absolute distinction between the infinite God and even the most saintly of his creatures. Yet the scriptures of Judaism and Christianity speak of a Beatific Vision, an encounter with God's presence that transforms the viewer. In Islam, traditions attributed to Muhammad himself undergird the unitive experiences of Sufi mystics.

Brahman is the end of the journey. Brahman is the supreme goal.

*Hinduism.* Katha Upanishad 1.3.11

Rooted in Nibbana, the holy life is lived. Nibbana is its goal, Nibbana is its end.

*Buddhism.* Samyutta Nikaya iii.188

Meditate upon him and transcend physical consciousness. Thus will you reach union with the Lord of the universe. Thus will you become identified with him who is One without a second. In him all your desires will find fulfillment.

The truth is that you are always united with the Lord. But you must *know* this.

*Hinduism.*
Svetasvatara Upanishad 1.11-12

As rivers flow into the sea and in so doing lose name and form, so even the wise man, freed from name and form, attains the Supreme Being, the Self-luminous, the Infinite. He who knows Brahman becomes Brahman.

*Hinduism.*
Mundaka Upanishad 3.2.8-9

Gettan Osho said, "Keichu, the first wheelmaker, made a cart whose wheels had a hundred spokes. Now, suppose you took a cart and removed both the wheels and the axle. What would you have?"

Mumon's Comment: "If anyone can directly master this topic, his eye will be like a shooting star, his spirit like a flash of lightning."

When the spiritual wheels turn,
Even the master fails to follow them.
They travel in all directions above and below,
North, south, east, and west.

*Buddhism.* Mumonkan 8

That which is the finest essence—this whole world has that as its Self. That is Reality. That is the Self. That art thou.

*Hinduism.*
Chandogya Upanishad 6.8.7

When I love him, I am his hearing by which he hears; and his sight by which he sees; his hand by which he strikes; and his foot by which he walks.

*Islam.* Forty Hadith of an-Nawawi 38

**Katha Upanishad 1.3.11:** Cf. Brihadaranyaka Upanishad 4.4.6-7, p. 247.

**Svetasvatara Upanishad 1.11-12:** Cf. Bhagavad Gita 5.24, p. 379; Isha Upanishad 15-16, p. 47.

**Mundaka Upanishad 3.2.8-9:** Cf. Chandogya Upanishad 7.23, 27, p. 411; Katha Upanishad 3.13, p. 601; Maru Ashtpadi, M.1, p. 385.

**Mumonkan 8:** 'The wheels and the axle' means the body and mind. Cf. Sutta Nipata 1072-76, p. 379.

**Forty Hadith of an-Nawawi 38:** This is a sacred hadith, with God himself the speaker.

Heaven and earth contain me not, but the heart of my faithful servant contains me.

*Islam*. Hadith of Suhrawardi

If the heart of God is not moving within your heart... once the invisible but powerful axis of the heart of God is moved out of you, everything becomes empty. Once the heart of God dwells within you, no matter how lonely you may be you will be filled and the universe will be filled. A person who is completely filled is a joyful person because he lacks nothing.

*Unification Church*. Sun Myung Moon, 9-11-77

Now are for us no entanglements or snares,
Nor a bit of egoism left.
Now is all distance annulled, nor are curtains drawn between us.
Thou art mine, I Thine.

*Sikhism*. Adi Granth, Bilaval, M.5, p. 821

I know that my Redeemer lives,
and at last he will stand upon the earth;
and after my skin has been thus destroyed,
then from my flesh I shall see God.

*Judaism* and *Christianity*. Job 19.25-26

Beloved, we are God's children now; it does not yet appear what we shall be, but we know that when he appears we shall be like him.

*Christianity*. 1 John 3.2

And we all, with unveiled face, beholding the glory of the Lord, are being changed into his likeness from one degree of glory to another; for this comes from the Lord who is the Spirit.

*Christianity*. 2 Corinthians 3.18

Some persons asked the Prophet, "Shall we see God on the day of resurrection?" He answered, "Do you feel any trouble in seeing the moon on the night when it is full? Do you feel any trouble in seeing the sun on a cloudless day?" They answered, "No." He said, "In the same way you will see your Lord."

*Islam*. Hadith of Muslim

Veiled by ignorance,
The minds of man and Buddha
Appear to be different;
Yet in the realm of Mind Essence
They are both of one taste. Some-
Time they will meet each other
In the great Dharmadhatu.

*Buddhism*. Milarepa

Buddha said, "Through the Consummation of Incomparable Enlightenment I acquired not even the least thing. *This* is altogether everywhere, without differentiation or degree."

*Buddhism*. Diamond Sutra 22-23

Whatever is here, that is there.
What is there, that again is here.
He obtains death after death
Who seems to see a difference here.

By the mind, indeed, is this realization to be attained:
There is no difference here at all!
He goes from death to death

**Sun Myung Moon, 9-11-77:** Cf. Sun Myung Moon, 10-20-73, p. 132.

**Bilaval, M.5:** Cf. Majh, M.5, p. 132; Maru Ashtpadi, M.1, p. 385.

**Job 19.25-26:** Cf. Isha Upanishad 15-16, p. 47.

**1 John 3.2:** That is, we shall all become perfect and Christ-like. Thomas Aquinas described this Beatific Vision as "the ultimate goal for the redeemed." Cf. 1 Corinthians 13.12, p. 226.

**2 Corinthians 3.18:** Cf. 2 Corinthians 3.7-16, p. 454.

**Hadith of Muslim:** Cf. Hadith, p. 56; Isha Upanishad 15-16, p. 47.

**Milarepa:** The '*Dharmadhatu*' is the world of Reality, unclouded by temporal phenomena or grasping for existence, as perceived by those who have attained enlightenment. Cf. Sutra of Hui Neng 3, p. 147; 2, p. 381; Seng Ts'an, pp. 150-51; Surangama Sutra, p. 388; Isha Upanishad 15-16, p. 47.

**Diamond Sutra 22-23:** Cf. Mulamadhyamaka Karika 25, pp. 59-60. Lankavatara Sutra 78, p. 121.

Who seems to see a difference here.

*Hinduism*. Katha Upanishad 2.1.10-11

Those who see all creatures within themselves
And themselves in all creatures know no fear.
Those who see all creatures in themselves
And themselves in all creatures know no grief.
How can the multiplicity of life
Delude the one who sees its unity?

*Hinduism*. Isha Upanishad 6-7

T'ien Ken was travelling to the south of Yin Mountain. He had reached the river Liao when he met a nameless sage, to whom he said, "I beg to ask about governing the world."

"Go away," said the nameless man, "you are a low fellow. How unpleasant is your question! I would be in companionship with the Maker of things. When wearied, I would mount on the bird of ease and emptiness, proceed beyond the world, wander in the land of nowhere, and live in the domain of nothingness. Why do you come to worry me with the problem of setting the world in order?"

T'ien Ken again asked his question, and the nameless man replied, "Make excursion in simplicity. Identify yourself with nondistinction. Follow the nature of things and admit no personal bias, then the world will be at peace."

*Taoism*. Chuang Tzu 7

In the Great Beginning, there was non-being. It had neither being nor name. The One originates from it; it has oneness but not yet physical form. When things obtain it and come into existence, that is called virtue [power which gives them their individual character]. That which is formless is divided [into yang and yin], and from the very beginning going on without interruption is called destiny. Through movement and rest it produces all things. When things are produced in accordance with the principle of life, there is physical form. When the physical form embodies and preserves the spirit so that all activities follow their own specific principles, that is nature.

By cultivating one's nature one will return to virtue. When virtue is perfect, one will be one with the Beginning. Being one with the Beginning, one becomes vacuous, and being vacuous, one becomes great. One will then be united with the sound and breath of things. When one is united with the sound and breath of things, one is then united with the universe. This unity is intimate and seems to be stupid and foolish. This is called profound and secret virtue, this is complete harmony.

*Taoism*. Chuang Tzu 12

Homage to the Perfection of Wisdom, the lovely, the holy!

Avalokita, the holy Lord and Bodhisattva, was moving in the deep course of the wisdom which has gone beyond. He looked down from on high, he beheld but five heaps, and he saw that in their own-being they were empty.

Here, O Shariputra, form is emptiness, and the very emptiness is form; emptiness does not differ from form, form does not differ from emptiness; whatever is form, that is emptiness, whatever is emptiness, that is form. The same is true of feelings, perceptions, impulses, consciousness.

Here, O Shariputra, all dharmas are marked with emptiness; they are not produced or stopped, not defiled or immaculate, not deficient or complete.

Therefore, O Shariputra, in emptiness there is no form, nor feeling, nor perception, nor impulse, nor consciousness; No eye, ear, nose, tongue, body, mind; no forms, sounds, smells, tastes, touchables or objects of mind; No sight-organ element [and so on to] no mind-consciousness element; There is no ignorance, no

**Katha Upanishad 2.1.10-11:** Cf. Chandogya Upanishad 7.23, p. 411; Lankavatara Sutra 78, p. 121; Mulamadhyamaka Karika 25, pp. 59-60; Chuang Tzu 2, p. 120.

**Isha Upanishad 6-7:** Cf. Chandogya Upanishad 7.23, p. 411; 7.25.2, pp. 377-78; Chuang Tzu 22, p. 64.

**Chuang Tzu 7:** 'Identify yourself with nondistinction': see Seng Ts'an, pp. 150-51; Chuang Tzu 2, p. 120.

**Chuang Tzu 12:** This account of creation of all things from non-being leads to the principle that when a person becomes vacuuous he can be united with all things. See Tao Te Ching 40, p. 58; 65, p. 388; Chuang Tzu 15, p. 602; 19, pp. 399-400; Doctrine of the Mean 1.4-5, p. 155.

extinction of ignorance [and so on through the twelve links of the chain of dependent origination to] there is no decay and death, no extinction of decay and death. There is no suffering, no origination, no stopping, no path. There is no cognition, no attainment, and no non-attainment.

Therefore, O Shariputra, it is because of his indifference to any kind of personal attainment that a bodhisattva, through having relied on the perfection of wisdom, dwells without thought-coverings. In the absence of thought coverings he has not been made to tremble, he has overcome what can upset, and in the end he attains to Nirvana.

All those who appear as Buddhas in the three periods of time [are] fully awake to the utmost, right and perfect enlightenment because they have relied on the perfection of wisdom.

Therefore one should know the perfection of wisdom as the great spell, the spell of great knowledge, the utmost spell, the unequalled spell, allayer of all suffering, in truth—for what could go wrong? By the Perfection of Wisdom has this spell been delivered. It runs like this, "Gone, Gone, Gone beyond, gone altogether beyond, O what an awakening, all hail!"

This completes the Heart of perfect wisdom.

*Buddhism*. Heart Sutra

A monk asked Tozan, "What is Buddha?" Tozan replied, "Three pounds of flax!"

*Buddhism*. Mumonkan 18

❖

**Heart Sutra:** It is said that this short sutra gives the essence of the pefection of wisdom. 'Heaps' in the first paragraph are the *skandhas*: form, feelings, perceptions, impulses, consciousness. These, the five constituents of human personality, are declared to be in reality empty. Their emptiness is described in the paradoxical dialectic, 'form is emptiness... emptiness is form,' which also describes the transcendental unity of subject and object, self and world, samsara and nirvana that is realized by the bodhisattva coursing in perfect wisdom. The 'dharmas' in the third paragraph refer not to 'things' or 'laws' but to a group of 75 mental and experiental factors enumerated in Buddhst Abhidharma philosophy; many are listed in the following paragraph: the five skandhas, six sense-organs, six sense-objects, six corresponding forms of consciousness, twelve links of the chain of causation, Four Noble Truths, gnosis, and attainment of the fruits of meditation. They are likewise declared to be empty. The final 'spell' or mantra, delivered by Wisdom personified, describes the experience of awakening to the realization of this wisdom. Cf. Lankavatara Sutra 61-64, pp. 102-3.

**Mumonkan 18:** This Zen koan stresses the folly of definition. You do not define the truth; you enter into it. If you think you can simply understand this koan to mean that the Buddha nature enters into everything, what do you make of Mumonkan 1, p. 572? Cf. Chuang Tzu 22, p. 64, and Mumonkan 21, p. 64n.

# CHAPTER 11
# THE FOUNDER

THIS CHAPTER CONTAINS PASSAGES ON THE LIFE and work of the founders of religion, who first discovered the truth that leads to salvation, offered their whole lives to enlighten and save others, provided for subsequent generations models of the ideal person, and continue to shed grace and light into the hearts of people everywhere. Among these great souls are Jesus, Muhammad, the Buddha, Confucius, Abraham, Moses, Zarathustra, Lao Tzu, Mahavira, Nanak, and the ancient Hindu rishis. Hindu scriptures also chronicle the exploits of Krishna and Rama, avatars of the Lord Vishnu. Confucian scriptures eulogize the lives of the ancient sage-kings Wen, Yao, Shun, and the Duke of Chou. We also include passages on the founders of some of the newer religions, such as Joseph Smith, Baha'u'llah, and Sun Myung Moon.

This consideration of the founders of religion as a genus should not be construed as leveling them to figures of equal significance. Each one is unique, and each stands in a unique position in relation to the religion which he spawned. For the Christian, it is the saving work of Christ alone that saves, notwithstanding the accomplishments of other founders, no matter how great they may be. Similarly, the Muslim's faith is defined uniquely by the message of Muhammad, and the Buddhist's by the enlightenment and teachings of Siddhartha. The committed believer is confronted with one individual as the standard of truth and love who defines the true way. The declaration, "I am the Way, the Truth, and the Life; no one comes to the Father but by me" (John 14.6) is echoed by similar statements in many religions: "Outside the Buddha's dispensation there is no saint" (Dhammapada 254); "Muhammad is the Seal of the Prophets" (Qur'an 33.40); "Glory be to Lord Mahavira, the teacher of the world" (Nandi Sutra 2). The reader should be faithful to the founder of his own tradition, who sets before him the truth and offers him the gracious help that guides his life. That being his faith, he cannot but cleave to it. Then, on that foundation, he may observe the comparisons made in this chapter. He may find that the founders of other faiths have also been given insight into divine truth and have lived out that truth in an exemplary manner. He may regard them worthy of respect, if he finds that their faith is comparable to the standard of faith set by his own tradition.

Another difficulty which besets any treatment of the founders of religions is that in certain traditions they are regarded as gods or as possessed of divine attributes—a topic which in itself is worthy of consideration in this chapter. Thus Jesus of Nazareth is the incarnation of the Second Person of the blessed Trinity; Siddhartha is a manifestation of the eternal Buddha or *Dharmakaya*, Krishna and Rama are incarnations of Vishnu, who in his cosmic form pervades the entire universe, and the Shinto culture heroes are gods who have come down from heaven. Yet to the extent that the founders are regarded as divine, their very human accomplishments—suffering persecution and rejection, struggling with temptation, and extending themselves in the service of others—may be mitigated. What, after all, is persecution or temptation to a god? What is so praiseworthy about a person helping others if he is omnipotent and endowed with all treasures? Hence, in this chapter we have tried to avoid particularly Docetic passages in favor of passages where the founders are regarded as subject to the ordinary limitations of being human.

Similarly, any distinction between the salvation wrought of God and the saving work of a human founder becomes blurred when the founder is at the same time the very deity who is continually offering salvation. We have treated the theme of salvation as divine activity in Chapter 10. There we have placed many passages on the saving work of Jesus, Buddha, and Krishna as it is a function of their representing divinity, while reserving passages which describe their more particularly human existence for this chapter.

These founders, saviors, and pathfinders are compared in various aspects of their life, faith, work, and character by bringing together comparable passages. We will consider first the founders' call and their initial embarkation on the path, second their difficult course of persecution and rejection by the world, and third their victory, triumphing over all difficulties and fully realizing the divine purpose. One section gathers passages describing their struggle with and victory over evil and demonic powers. Another contains descriptions of their roles as revealers and teachers, bringing new truth and light for the people of their age and subsequent ages. Other texts show the founders to be supreme examples of self-sacrifice and service to others as they gave of themselves to the mission of saving and enlightening this dark world. Their accomplishments not being limited to their own lifetimes, a seventh grouping of texts describe these founders as forever alive in peoples' hearts, as the continuing light and inspiration for every age, and forever making intercession on people's behalf. An eighth section treats various conceptions of the founder's person—e.g., his humanity and divinity. We have gathered texts foundational to Christian reflections on Christ's divinity, Buddhist reflections on the three bodies of the Buddha, and similar ideas in other religions, as well as passages which express the ordinary humanity of Muhammad, Moses, Confucius, and other founders from traditions which deny that their founders are divine. The final section relates each founder of religion to a long line of prophets, Buddhas, Tirthankaras, Avatars, teachers, or sages who preceded him and who may follow him in the future.

## *Call and Awakening*

EARLY IN THE LIFE OF EACH FOUNDER comes the moment when he is awakened to his special vocation. In the Abrahamic traditions, the founder was called from the ordinary pursuits of life through a special appearance of divinity. This call was both a revelation of God and a challenge to take up a mission. Often, as was true for Moses and Muhammad, the founder first tried to resist the divine call before he finally accepted it.

We do not know when Jesus first recognized his special vocation. The Bible depicts him as predestined from birth, yet one particular moment of realization may have come at his baptism at the Jordan River with the descent of the Spirit.

In India, where countless ascetics strenuously exert themselves on the path to enlightenment, the founders of Buddhism and Jainism began as two of the thousands of similar seekers for God. Instead of God coming down and calling them, as in the West, they strove toward truth and finally attained it. Nevertheless, in the biographies of the Buddha and Mahavira we have accounts of their first awakenings. When the young Buddha, living a sheltered life as a prince, saw suffering in others, he was distressed and his sensitive mind was awakened to the quest for truth.

Now the Lord said to Abram, "Go from your country and your kindred and your father's house to the land that I will show you. And I will make of you a great nation, and I will bless you, and make your name great, so that you will be a blessing. I will bless those who bless you, and him who curses you I will curse; and by you all the families of the earth shall bless themselves."

*Judaism* and *Christianity*. Genesis 12.1-3

A man... was travelling from place to place when he saw a building in flames. "Is it possible that the building lacks a person to look after it?" he wondered. The owner of the building looked out and said, "I am the owner of the building." Similarly, when Abraham our father said, "Is it conceivable that the world is without a guide?" the Holy One, blessed be He, looked out and said to him, "I am the Guide, the Sovereign of the Universe."

*Judaism*. Genesis Rabbah 39.1

Now Moses was keeping the flock of his father-in-law, Jethro, the priest of Midian; and he led his flock to the west side of the wilderness, and came to Horeb, the mountain of God. And the angel of the Lord appeared to him in a flame of fire out of the midst of a bush; and he looked, and lo, the bush was burning, yet it was not consumed. And Moses said, "I will turn aside and see this great sight, why the bush is not burnt." When the Lord saw that he turned aside to see, God called to him out of the bush, "Moses, Moses!" And he said, "Here am I." Then he said, "Do not come near; put off your shoes from your feet, for the place on which

**Genesis 12.1-3:** This is the call of Abraham. In return for following God into an unknown land, he is promised a three-fold blessing: receiving a land, becoming a nation, and mediating God's blessing to the world. Cf. Hebrews 11.8-10, p. 539; Abot 5.4, p. 438n.; Qur'an 21.71, p. 428. For the call of Jacob, his vision of the ladder reaching to heaven, see Genesis 28.10-17, p. 65.

**Genesis Rabbah 39.1:** For more traditions on Abraham's call, see Zohar, Genesis 68a and Qur'an 6.75-79, p. 50. On the world in flames, see the Buddha's Fire Sermon, Samyutta Nikaya xxxv.28, p. 271, and the Parable of the Burning House in Lotus Sutra 3, p. 93n.

you are standing is holy ground." And he said, "I am the God of your father, the God of Abraham, the God of Isaac, and the God of Jacob." And Moses hid his face, for he was afraid to look at God.

Then the Lord said, "I have seen the affliction of my people who are in Egypt, and have heard their cry because of their taskmasters; I know their sufferings, and I have come down to deliver them out of the hand of the Egyptians, and to bring them up out of that land to a good and broad land, a land flowing with milk and honey, to the place of the Canaanites, the Hittites, the Amorites, the Perizzites, the Hivites, and the Jebusites. And now, behold, the cry of the people of Israel has come to me, and I have seen the oppression with which the Egyptians oppress them. Come, I will send you to Pharaoh, that you may bring forth my people, the sons of Israel, out of Egypt." But Moses said to God, "Who am I that I should go to Pharaoh, and bring the sons of Israel out of Egypt?" He said, "But I will be with you; and this shall be the sign for you, that I have sent you: when you have brought forth the people out of Egypt, you shall serve God upon this mountain."

Then Moses said to God, "If I come to the people of Israel and say to them, 'The God of your fathers has sent me to you,' and they ask me, 'What is his name,' what shall I say to them?" God said to Moses, "I Am Who I Am." He said, "Say this to the people of Israel, 'I Am has sent me to you.'"...

But Moses said to the Lord, "Oh, my Lord, I am not eloquent, either heretofore or since you have spoken to your servant; but I am slow of speech and of tongue." Then the Lord said to him, "Who has made man's mouth? Who makes him dumb, or deaf, or seeing, or blind? Is it not I, the Lord? Now therefore go, and I will be with your mouth and teach you what you shall speak." But he said, "Oh, my Lord, send, I pray, some other person." Then the anger of the Lord was kindled against Moses and he said, "Is there not Aaron, your brother, the Levite? I know that he can speak well; and behold, he is coming out to meet you, and when he sees you he will be glad in his heart. And you shall speak to him and put the words in his mouth; and I will be with your mouth and with his mouth, and will teach you what you shall do. He shall speak for you to the people; and he shall be a mouth for you."

*Judaism* and *Christianity*.
Exodus 3.1-4.16

I, an idle bard, by Thee a task am assigned:
In primal time was I commanded night and day
  to laud Thee.
The bard was summoned by the Master to the
  Eternal Mansion,
And was honored with the robe of divine
  laudation and praise.
On the holy Name ambrosial was he feasted.
As by the Master's guidance on this he has
  feasted, has felt blessed.
The bard has spread and proclaimed divine
  laudation by the holy Word.
Says Nanak, By laudation of the holy Eternal
Is the Supreme Being, all-perfection, attained.

*Sikhism*. Adi Granth,
Var Majh, M.1, p. 150

Lo! We revealed it on the Night of Power.
Ah, what will convey unto you what the Night
  of Power is!
The Night of Power is better than a thousand
  months.
The angels and the Spirit descend therein, by
  the permission of their Lord, with all
  decrees.
It means peace until the rising of the dawn.

*Islam*. Qur'an 97.1-5

**Exodus 3.1-4.16:** Typically when God calls someone to a great mission, he may first offer excuses and try to refuse his request. Moses finally agreed to lead the Israelites when God gave him Aaron as a helper and spokesman. For more on the Name of God, see note to Exodus 3.13-15, p. 76n., and Torah Yesharah, p. 361.

By the Star when it sets,
your comrade errs not, nor is deceived,
nor does he speak of his own desire.
It is naught but an inspiration that is inspired,
which one of mighty powers has taught him,
one vigorous; and he grew clear to view
when he was on the uppermost horizon.
Then he drew near and came down
till he was two bows' length away or even nearer,
and He revealed unto His slave that which He revealed.
The heart lied not in what he saw;
will you then dispute with him what he has seen?

*Islam.* Qur'an 53.1-12

In the month of Ramadan in which God willed concerning him what He willed of His grace, the Apostle set forth to Hira as was his wont, and his family with him. When it was the night on which God honored him with his mission and showed mercy on His servants thereby, Gabriel brought him the command of God. "He came to me," said the Apostle of God, "while I was asleep, with a coverlet of brocade whereupon was some writing, and said, 'Read!' I said, 'I cannot read.' He pressed me with it so tightly that I thought it was death; then he let me go and said, 'Read!' I said, 'I cannot read.' He pressed me with it again so that I thought it was death; then he let me go and said, 'Read!' I said, 'I cannot read.' He pressed me with it the third time so that I thought it was death and said, 'Read!' I said, 'What then shall I read?'—and this I said only to deliver myself from him, lest he should do the same to me again. He said,

> Read! In the name of thy Lord who created,
> Who created man of blood coagulated.
> Read! Thy Lord is the most beneficent,
> Who taught by the pen,
> Taught that which they knew not unto men.

"So I read it, and he departed from me. And I awoke from my sleep, and it was as though these words were written on my heart. Now none of God's creatures was more hateful to me than an ecstatic poet or a man possessed: I could not even look at them. I thought, Woe is me, a poet or possessed—never shall the Quraysh say this of me! I will go to the top of the mountain and throw myself down that I may kill myself and gain rest. So I went forth to do so, and then, when I was midway on the mountain, I heard a voice from heaven saying, 'O Muhammad! thou art the Apostle of God and I am Gabriel.' I raised my head toward heaven to see who was speaking, and lo, Gabriel in the form of a man with feet astride the horizon, saying, 'O Muhammad! thou art the Apostle of God and I am Gabriel.' I stood gazing at him, moving neither forward nor backward; then I began to turn my face away from him, but toward whatever region of the sky I looked, I saw him as before. And I continued standing there, neither advancing nor turning back, until Khadija sent her messengers in search of me and they gained the high ground above Mecca and returned to her while I was standing in the same place; then he parted from me and I from him, returning to my family.

"And I came to Khadija and sat by her thigh and drew close to her. She said, 'O Abu'l-Qasim, where have you been? By God, I sent my messengers in search of you, and they reached the high ground above Mecca and returned to me.' I said to her, 'Woe is me, a poet or one possessed.' She said, 'I take refuge in God from that, O Abu'l-Qasim. God would not treat you thus, since He knows your truthfulness, your great trustworthiness, your fine character, and your kindness. This cannot be, my dear. Perhaps you did see something.' 'Yes, I did,' I said. Then I told her of what I had seen; and she said, 'Rejoice, O son of my uncle, and be of good heart. Verily, by Him in whose hand is Khadija's soul, I have hope that you will be the Prophet of this people.' Then she arose and gathered her garments and set forth to her cousin Waraqa, who had become a Christian and read the scriptures and learned from those that follow the Torah and the Gospel. And when she related to him what the Apostle of God told her he had seen and heard, Waraqa

**Qur'an 53.1-12:** This passage describes Muhammad's vision of the Angel Gabriel on Mount Hira.

cried, 'Holy! Holy! Verily by Him in whose hand is Waraqa's soul, if you have spoken to me the truth, Khadija, there came to him the greatest *Namus* (Gabriel) who came to Moses aforetime, and lo, he is the Prophet of this people.'"

*Islam.* Sirat Rasul Allah

The angel Gabriel was sent from God to a city of Galilee named Nazareth, to a virgin betrothed of a man whose name was Joseph, of the house of David; and the virgin's name was Mary. And he came to her and said, "Hail, O favored one, the Lord is with you!" But she was greatly troubled at the saying, and considered in her mind what sort of greeting this might be. And the angel said to her, "Do not be afraid, Mary, for you have found favor with God. And behold, you will conceive in your womb and bear a son, and you shall call his name Jesus.

He will be great, and will be called the Son of the Most High;
and the Lord God will give to him the throne of his father David,
and he will reign over the house of Jacob for ever;
and of his kingdom there will be no end."

And Mary said to the angel, "How shall this be, since I have no husband?" And the angel said to her,

"The Holy Spirit will come upon you,
and the power of the Most High will overshadow you;
therefore the child to be born will be called holy,
the Son of God...

For with God, nothing will be impossible." And Mary said, "Behold, I am the handmaid of the Lord; let it be to me according to your word." And the angel departed from her.

In those days a decree went out from Caesar Augustus that all the world should be enrolled. This was the first enrollment, when Quirinius was governor of Syria. And all went to be enrolled, each to his own city. And Joseph also went up from Galilee, from the city of Nazareth, to Judea, to the city of David, which is called Bethlehem, because he was of the house and lineage of David, to be enrolled with Mary, his betrothed, who was with child. And while they were there, the time came for her to be delivered. And she gave birth to her first-born son and wrapped him in swaddling cloths, and laid him in a manger, because there was no place for them in the inn.

And in that region there were shepherds out in the field, keeping watch over their flock by night. And an angel of the Lord appeared to them, and the glory of the Lord shone around them, and they were filled with fear. And the angel said to them, "Be not afraid; for behold, I bring you good news of a great joy which will come to all the people; for to you is born this day in the city of David a Savior, who is Christ the Lord. And this will be a sign for you: you will find a babe wrapped in swaddling cloths and lying in a manger." And suddenly there was with the angel a multitude of the heavenly host praising God and saying,

Glory to God in the highest,
and on earth peace, good will among men!

*Christianity.* Luke 1.26-2.14

In those days Jesus came from Nazareth of Galilee and was baptized by John in the Jordan. And when he came up out of the water, immediately he saw the heavens opened and the Spirit descending upon him like a dove; and a voice came from heaven, "Thou art my beloved Son; with thee I am well pleased."

*Christianity.* Mark 1.9-11

**Sirat Rasul Allah:** The quotation, from Qur'an 96.1-5, is the content of the angel Gabriel's first revelation to Muhammad. Khadija was Muhammad's first wife and a firm support for her husband in the difficult days of his early ministry in Mecca.

**Mark 1.9-11:** The baptism of Jesus marks the beginning of his ministry. In Mark's account, Jesus is the recipient of revelation and empowerment; God speaks to him, the dove descends upon him, and the Spirit enters into him. In similar accounts in Matthew 3.17 and John 1.32-34, the baptism is regarded rather as a sign to John the Baptist of Jesus' messiahship and divinity.

Although his parents were unwilling and tears poured down their cheeks, the recluse Gotama, having cut off hair and beard and donned saffron robes, went forth from home into homelessness.

*Buddhism*. Digha Nikaya i.115

The king of the Shakya, having heard from the sage Asita that the goal of the prince was to attain supreme bliss, sought to engage the prince in sensual pleasures, lest he should wish to go off to the forest.

On one occasion, however, the prince heard about woods filled with songs, abounding in fresh grass, with trees in which the cuckoos sounded, adorned with many lotus ponds. The king, learning of the desire of his dear son, arranged an excursion befitting his affection, majesty, and his son's age. Yet he ordered that all commoners suffering any affliction should be kept off the royal road lest the tender-hearted prince be distressed at the sight of them....

The prince saw the man overcome with old age, different in form from other people, and his curiosity was aroused. "Oh, charioteer! Who is this man with gray hair, supported by a staff in his hand, his eyes sunken under his eyebrows, his limbs feeble and bent? Is this transformation a natural state or an accident?" The charioteer, when he was thus asked, his intelligence being confused by the gods, saw no harm in telling the prince its significance, which should have been discreetly withheld from him, "Old age, it is called, the destroyer of beauty and vigor, the source of sorrow, the depriver of pleasures, the slayer of memories, the enemy of sense organs. That man has been ruined by old age. He, too, in his infancy had taken milk and, in due time, had crawled on the ground; he then became a handsome youth, and now he has reached old age.... People in the world are aware of old age, the destroyer of beauty; yet, they seek pleasures."... For a long while, the prince kept his gaze on the decrepit man, sighing and shaking his head. "Turn back the horses, charioteer; go home quickly. How can I enjoy myself in the garden when the fear of death is revolving in my mind?"

[On a second excursion, the prince is similarly distressed at the sight of a man afflicted by disease. On a third excursion, he sees a corpse carried by mourners.]

The charioteer then said to him, "This is the last state of all men. Death is certain for all, whether they be of low, middle, or high degree." Though he was a steadfast man, the prince felt faint as soon as he heard about death. Leaning his shoulders against the railing, he said in a sad tone, "This is the inescapable end for all men; yet, people in the world harbor no fear and seem unconcerned. Men must be hardened indeed to be so at ease as they walk down the road leading to the next life. Charioteer, turn back, for this is not the time for the pleasure-ground. How can a man of intelligence, aware of death, enjoy himself in this fateful hour?"...

Longing for solitude, the prince kept his followers back and approached a lonely spot at the foot of a Jambu tree, covered all over with beautiful leaves. There he sat on the clean ground where the soft grass glittered like beryl. Contemplating the birth and death of beings, he undertook to steady his mind in meditation. In no time his mind became firm; he was released from mental distractions such as the desire for objects of sense, and attained the first trance of calmness. Having acquired the concentration of mind which springs from solitude, the prince was filled with extreme joy and bliss; then meditating on the course of the world, he thought that this state was indeed supreme. "Alas, wretched is he who, out of ignorance and the blindness of pride, ignores others who are distressed by old age, sickness, or death, though he himself, being likewise subject to disease, old age, and death, is helpless!" As he thus perceived clearly the evils of disease, old age, and death in the world, the false pride in self, arising from a belief in one's strength, youth, and life, left him instantly....

While this passionless, pure insight of that great-souled one grew, a man in mendicant's clothes approached him without being seen by others. The prince asked, "Tell me, who are you?" The man replied, "Oh best of men, I am a mendicant who, in fear of birth and death, has renounced the world for the sake of deliverance. In this world which is characterized by destruction, I eagerly search for the blessed and indestructible state. I regard both kinsmen and strangers as equals, and I am free from the evils of passion arising from objects of sense. Living wherever I happen to be—at the foot of a tree, in a deserted house, in the mountains, or in the woods—I wander about, living on the alms I receive, without ties to person or place and with no expectation save for the attainment of the ultimate goal."... The prince now knew what he should do, and began thinking of a way to leave his home.

*Buddhism.* Ashvaghosha,
Buddhacarita 3-5

While I was laboring under the extreme difficulties caused by the contests of these parties of religionists, I was one day reading the Epistle of James, first chapter and fifth verse, which reads: "If any of you lack wisdom, let him ask of God, that giveth to all men liberally, and upbraideth not; and it shall be given him."

Never did any passage of scripture come with more power to the heart of man than this did at this time to mine. It seemed to enter with great force into every feeling of my heart. I reflected on it again and again, knowing that if any person needed wisdom from God, I did; for how to act I did not know, and unless I could get more wisdom than I had then had, I would never know; for the teachers of religion of the different sects understood the same passages of scripture so differently as to destroy all confidence in settling the question by an appeal to the Bible.

Finding myself alone, I kneeled down and began to offer up the desire of my heart to God. I had scarcely done so, when immediately I was seized upon by some power which entirely overcame me, and had such an astonishing influence over me as to bind my tongue so that I could not speak. Thick darkness gathered around me, and it seemed to me for a time as if I were doomed to sudden destruction.

But, exerting all my powers to call upon God to deliver me out of the power of this enemy which had seized me, and at the very moment when I was ready to sink into despair and abandon myself to destruction... I saw a pillar of light exactly over my head, above the brightness of the sun, which descended gradually until it fell upon me.

It no sooner appeared than I found myself delivered from the enemy which held me bound. When the light rested upon me I saw two Personages, whose brightness and glory defy all description, standing above me in the air. One of them spoke to me, calling me by name and said, "This is My Beloved Son. Hear Him!"

My object in going to inquire of the Lord was to know which of all the sects was right, that I might know which to join. No sooner, therefore, did I get possession of myself, so as to be able to speak, than I asked the Personages who stood above me in the light, which of all the sects was right—and which I should join.

I was answered that I must join none of them, for they were all wrong; and the Personage who addressed me said that all their creeds were an abomination in his sight; that those professors were all corrupt; that "they draw near me with their lips, but their hearts are far from me, they teach for doctrines the commandments of men, having the form of godliness, but they deny the power thereof."

He again forbade me to join with any of them; and many other things did he say to me, which I cannot write at this time. When I came to myself again, I found myself lying on my back, looking up into heaven. When the light had departed, I had no strength; but soon recovering in some degree, I went home.

*Church of Jesus Christ of Latter-day Saints.*
Pearl of Great Price, Joseph Smith 2.11-20

**Pearl of Great Price, Joseph Smith 2.11-20:** This was the first revelation to Joseph Smith, years before he received the golden plates on which were written the Book of Mormon. Here he was first oppressed by a satanic force—compare Genesis 32.24-30, p. 447—but with desperate prayers he was delivered. He saw two beings, whom he identified as God and Jesus. Based in part on this revelation, Latter-day Saints theology understands God to have a physical body; cf. Pearl of Great Price, Abraham 3.22-4.1, p. 258.

## *Rejected by the World*

THE FOUNDERS OF RELIGION inevitably met resistance, disbelief, and persecution when they attempted to spread their message. Thus Moses endured the murmurings of his people, Muhammad was branded a charlatan and pursued by his fellow tribesmen of the Quraysh, and Jesus was rejected and slandered by many of the Jews of his day and eventually was executed as an insurrectionist. Confucius was unsuccessful in his efforts to get his teachings accepted by the leaders of his day, and Lao Tzu describes his plight as that of a social outcast. Mahavira and even Buddha, whose ministry is glorified by later traditions, were abused and ridiculed as they wandered from town to town. Yet even more profound than the pains and travails which they suffered in the body was the inner agony of loneliness as these founders wandered about, with no one to understand them or sympathize with their minds. Their only solace was their single-minded devotion to God or their conviction about the truth which they, alone in the world, could understand.

Moses and Aaron went to Pharaoh and said, "Thus says the Lord, the God of Israel, 'Let my people go, that they may hold a feast to me in the wilderness.'" But Pharaoh said, "Who is the Lord, that I should heed his voice and let Israel go? I do not know the Lord, and moreover I will not let Israel go." Then they said, "The God of the Hebrews has met with us; let us go, we pray, a three days' journey into the wilderness, and sacrifice to the Lord our God, lest he fall upon us with pestilence or with the sword." But the king of Egypt said to them, "Moses and Aaron, why do you take the people away from their work? Get to your burdens."... The same day Pharaoh commanded the taskmasters of the people and their foremen, "You shall no longer give the people straw to make bricks, as heretofore; let them go and gather straw for themselves. But the number of bricks which they made heretofore you shall lay upon them, you shall by no means lessen it; for they are idle; therefore they cry, 'Let us go and offer sacrifice to our God.' Let heavier work be laid upon the men that they may labor at it and pay no regard to lying words."...

The foremen of the people of Israel saw that they were in evil plight, when they said, "You shall by no means lessen your daily number of bricks." They met Moses and Aaron, who were waiting for them, as they came forth from Pharaoh; and they said to them, "The Lord look upon you and judge, because you have made us offensive in the sight of Pharaoh and his servants, and have put a sword in their hand to kill us."

Then Moses turned again to the Lord and said, "O Lord, why have you done evil to this people? Why did you ever send me? For since I came to Pharaoh to speak in your name, he has done evil to this people, and you have not delivered your people at all." But the Lord said to Moses... "I will harden Pharaoh's heart, and though I multiply my signs and wonders in the land of Egypt, Pharaoh will not listen to you; then I will lay my hand upon Egypt and bring forth my hosts, my people the sons of Israel, out of the land of Egypt by great acts of judgment. And the Egyptians shall know that I am the Lord, when I stretch forth my hand upon Egypt and bring out the people of Israel from among them."

*Judaism* and *Christianity*.
Exodus 5.1-7.5

The whole congregation of the people of Israel murmured against Moses and Aaron in the wilderness, and said to them, "Would that we had died by the hand of the Lord in the land of

Egypt, when we sat by the fleshpots and ate bread to the full; for you have brought us out into this wilderness to kill this whole assembly with hunger."

*Judaism* and *Christianity*. Exodus 16.2-3

We gave Abraham of old his proper course, for We were aware of him, when he said to his father and his people, "What are these images to which you pay devotion?" They said, "We found our fathers worshippers of them." He said, "Truly you and your fathers were in plain error." They said, "Do you bring us the truth, or are you some jester?" He said, "No, but your Lord is the Lord of the heavens and the earth, who created them; and I am of those who testify to that. And, by God, I shall circumvent your idols after you have gone away and turned your backs." Then he reduced them to fragments, all save the chief of them, that perhaps they might have recourse to it.

They said, "Who has done this to our gods? Surely it must be some evildoer." [Others] said, "We heard a youth make mention of them, one called Abraham." They said, "Bring him here before the people's eyes that they may testify." They said, "Are you the one who has done this to our gods, Abraham?" He said, "No, their chief has done it. So question them, if they can speak." Then they gathered apart and said, "You yourselves are the wrongdoers," and they were utterly confounded. Then they said [to Abraham], "You know well that they do not speak." He said, "Do you worship instead of God that which cannot profit you at all, nor harm you? Fie on you and all that you worship instead of God! Have you then no sense?"

They said, "Burn him and stand by your gods, if you will!" We said, "O fire, be coolness and peace for Abraham!" They wished to set a snare for him, but We made them the greater losers. And we rescued him and Lot, and brought them to the land that We have blessed for all peoples.

*Islam*. Qur'an 21.51-71

The true light that enlightens every man was coming into the world. He was in the world, and the world was made through him, yet the world knew him not. He came to his own home, and his own people received him not.

*Christianity*. John 1.9-11

A scribe came up and said to him, "Teacher, I will follow you wherever you go." And Jesus said to him, "Foxes have holes, and birds of the air have nests, but the Son of man has nowhere to lay his head."

*Christianity*. Matthew 8.19-20

He went away from there and came to his own country; and his disciples followed him. And on the sabbath he began to teach in the synagogue; and many who heard him were astonished, saying, "Where did this man get all this? What is the wisdom given to him? What mighty works are wrought by his hands! Is not this the carpenter, the son of Mary and brother of James and Joses and Judas and Simon, and are not his sisters here with us?" And they took offense at him. And Jesus said to them, "A prophet is not without honor, except in his own country, and among his own kin, and in his own house."

*Christianity*. Mark 6.1-4

And [Jesus] came out, and went, as was his custom, to the Mount of Olives; and the disciples followed him. And when he came to the place

**Exodus 16.2-3:** Moses struggled with a rebellious people even after they had escaped from Egypt. Having been raised with a slave mentality, it was not easy for the Hebrews to have the courage to go forward into the Promised Land.

**Qur'an 21.51-71:** Though this episode is not found in the Bible, some confrontation with his parents and the idolators is well attested in Jewish and Christian traditions. See Qur'an 19.41-58, pp. 475-76. On trial by fire, see Daniel 3.1-28, pp. 630-31; Ramayana, Yuddha Kanda 118-20, p. 560.

**John 1.9-11:** Cf. Matthew 23.37, p. 325.

**Matthew 8.19-20:** Cf. Forty Hadith of an-Nawawi 40, p. 679.

**Mark 6.1-4:** On the persecution which Jesus endured during his lifetime, see also Mark 3.31-35, p. 677n.; Matthew 5.11-12, p. 628; 10.24-25, pp. 586-87; 12.9-14, p. 616; 12.22-24, p. 265; Acts 7.51-53, pp. 634-35; Isaiah 53.1-12, pp. 458.

he said to them, "Pray that you may not enter into temptation." And he withdrew from them about a stone's throw, and knelt down and prayed, "Father, if thou art willing, remove this cup from me; nevertheless not my will, but thine, be done." And there appeared to him an angel from heaven, strengthening him. And being in an agony he prayed more earnestly; and his sweat became like great drops of blood falling down upon the ground. And when he rose from prayer, he came to the disciples and found them sleeping for sorrow, and he said to them, "Why do you sleep? Rise and pray that you may not enter into temptation."

While he was still speaking, there came a crowd, and the man called Judas, one of the twelve, was leading them. He drew near to Jesus to kiss him; but Jesus said to him, "Judas, would you betray the Son of man with a kiss?" And when those who were about him saw what would follow, they said, "Lord, shall we strike with the sword?" And one of them struck the slave of the high priest and cut off his right ear. But Jesus said, "No more of this!" And he touched his ear and healed him. Then Jesus said to the chief priests and officers of the temple and the elders, who had come out against him, "Have you come out as against a robber, with swords and clubs? When I was with you day after day in the temple, you did not lay hands on me. But this is your hour, and the power of darkness." Then they seized him and led him away, bringing him into the high priest's house....

Now the men who were holding Jesus mocked him and beat him; they also blindfolded him and asked him, "Prophesy! Who is it that struck you?" And they spoke many other words against him, reviling him.

When day came, the assembly of the elders of the people gathered together, both chief priests and scribes; and they led him away to their council, and they said, "If you are the Christ, tell us." But he said to them, "If I tell you, you will not believe; and if I ask you, you will not answer. But from now on the Son of man shall be seated at the right hand of the power of God." And they all said, "Are you the Son of God, then?" And he said to them, "You say that I am." And they said, "What further testimony do we need? We have heard it ourselves from his own lips."

Then the whole company of them arose, and brought him before Pilate. And they began to accuse him, saying, "We found this man perverting our nation, and forbidding us to give tribute to Caesar, saying that he himself is Christ a king. And Pilate asked him, "Are you the King of the Jews?" And he answered him, "You have said so." And Pilate said to the chief priests and the multitudes, "I find no crime in this man.... Behold, nothing deserving of death has been done by him. I will therefore chastise him and release him."

But they all cried out together, "Away with this man, and release to us Barabbas"—a man who had been thrown into prison for an insurrection started in the city, and for murder. Pilate addressed them once more, desiring to release Jesus; but they shouted out, "Crucify, crucify him!" A third time he said to them, "Why, what evil has he done? I have found in him no crime deserving death; I will therefore chastise him and release him." But they were urgent, demanding with loud cries that he should be crucified. And their voices prevailed. So Pilate gave sentence that their demand should be granted. He released the man who had been thrown into prison for insurrection and murder, but Jesus he delivered up to their will.

And as they led him away, they seized one Simon of Cyrene, who was coming in from the country, and laid on him the cross, to carry it behind Jesus....

Two others also, who were criminals, were led away to be put to death with him. And when they came to the place which is called The Skull [Calvary], there they crucified him, and the criminals, one on the right and one on the left. And Jesus said, "Father, forgive them; for they know not what they do." And they cast lots to divide his garments. And the people stood by, watching; but the rulers scoffed at him, saying, "He has saved others; let him save himself, if he is the Christ of God, his Chosen One!" The soldiers also mocked him, coming up and offering him vinegar, and saying, "If you are the King of the Jews, save yourself!" There was also an inscription over him, "This is the King of the Jews."

One of the criminals who were hanged railed at him, saying, "Are you not the Christ? Save yourself and us!" But the other rebuked him, saying, "Do you not fear God, since you are under the same sentence of condemnation? And we indeed justly; for we are receiving the due reward of our deeds; but this man has done nothing wrong." And he said, "Jesus, remember me when you come into your kingdom." And he said to him, "Truly I say to you, today you will be with me in Paradise."

It was now about the sixth hour, and there was darkness over the whole land until the ninth hour, while the sun's light failed; and the curtain of the temple was torn in two. Then Jesus, crying with a loud voice, said, "Father, into Thy hands I commit my spirit!" And having said this he breathed his last.

*Christianity*. Luke 22.39-23.46

The Messenger says, "O my Lord, behold, my people have taken this Qur'an as a thing to be shunned." Even so We have appointed to every Prophet an enemy from among the sinners; but your Lord suffices as a guide and as a helper.

*Islam*. Qur'an 25.30-31

When you recite the Qur'an We place between you and those who believe not in the hereafter a hidden barrier; and We place upon their hearts veils lest they should understand it, and in their ears a deafness; and when you make mention of your Lord alone in the Qur'an, they turn their backs in aversion.

*Islam*. Qur'an 17.45-46

By the Pen and by the record which men write, you are not, by the grace of your Lord, mad or possessed. Nay, verily for you is a reward unfailing, and you stand on an exalted standard of character. Soon you will see, and they will see, which of you is afflicted with madness. Verily it is your Lord who knows best, who among men has strayed from His path: and He knows best those who receive guidance.

*Islam*. Qur'an 68.1-7

When the Apostle openly displayed Islam as God ordered him his people did not withdraw or turn against him, so far as I have heard, until he spoke disparagingly of their gods. When he did that they took great offense and resolved unanimously to treat him as an enemy, except those whom God had protected by Islam from such evil, but they were a despised minority. Abu Talib, his uncle, treated the Apostle kindly and protected him, the latter continuing to obey God's commands, nothing turning him back. When the Quraysh saw that he would not yield to them and withdrew from them and insulted their gods and that his uncle treated him kindly and stood up in his defense and would not give him up to them, some of their leading men went to Abu Talib... and said, "O Abu Talib, your nephew has cursed our gods, insulted our religion, mocked our way of life and accused our forefathers of error; either you must stop him or you must let us get at him, for you yourself are in the same position as we are in opposition to him and we will rid you of him." He gave them a conciliatory reply and a soft answer and they went away.

The Apostle continued on his way, publishing God's religion and calling men thereto. In consequence his relations with Quraysh deteriorated and men withdrew from him in enmity. They were always talking about him and inciting one another against him. Then they went to Abu Talib a second time and said, "You have a high and lofty position among us, and we have asked you to put a stop to your nephew's activities but you have not done so. By God, we cannot endure that our fathers should be reviled, our customs mocked and our gods insulted. Until you rid us of him we will fight

**Luke 22-23:** This is a narrative of Jesus' passion. Cf. Isaiah 53.1-12, p. 458, which this passion fulfills in many of its details.

**Qur'an 25.30-31:** Cf. Qur'an 6.112, p. 317; 43.22-25, p. 484.

**Qur'an 17.45-46:** Cf. Qur'an 62.11, p. 665.

the pair of you until one side perishes," or words to that effect. Thus saying, they went off. Abu Talib was deeply distressed at the breach with his people and their enmity but he could not desert the Apostle and give him up to them.

After hearing these words from the Quraysh, Abu Talib sent for his nephew and told him what his people had said. "Spare me and yourself," he said. "Do not put on me a burden greater than I can bear." The Apostle thought that his uncle had the idea of abandoning and betraying him, and that he was going to lose his help and support. He answered, "O my uncle, by God, if they put the sun in my right hand and the moon in my left on condition that I abandoned this course, until God has made it victorious or I perish therein, I would not abandon it." Then the Apostle broke into tears, and got up. As he turned away his uncle called him and said, "Come back, my nephew," and when he came back, he said, "Go and say what you please, for by God I will never give you up on any account."

*Islam.* Sirat Rasul Allah

The Thaqif... stirred up their louts and slaves to insult him and cry after him until a crowd came together, and compelled him to take refuge in an orchard belonging to 'Utba ibn Rabi'a and his brother Shayba who were in it at the time. The louts who had followed him went back, and he made for the shade of a vine and sat there while the two men watched him, observing what he had to endure from the local louts....

When the Apostle reached safety he said, so I am told, "O God, to Thee I complain of my weakness, little resource, and lowliness before men. O Most Merciful, Thou art the Lord of the weak, and Thou art my Lord. To whom wilt Thou confide me? To one afar who will misuse me? Or to an enemy to whom Thou hast given power over me? If Thou art not angry with me I care not. Thy favor is more wide for me. I take refuge in the light of Thy countenance by which the darkness is illumined, and the things of this world and the next are rightly ordered, lest Thy anger descend upon me or Thy wrath light upon me. It is for Thee to be satisfied until Thou art well pleased. There is no power and no might save in Thee."

*Islam.* Sirat Rasul Allah

As an elephant in the battlefield withstands the arrows shot from a bow, even so will I endure abuse.

*Buddhism.* Dhammapada 320

Now at that time very distinguished young men belonging to the respectable families in Magadha were living the holy life under the Lord. People looked down upon, criticized, spread it about, saying, "The recluse Gotama gets along by making [us] childless, the recluse Gotama gets along by making [us] widows, the recluse Gotama gets along by breaking up families... Who now will be led away by him?"

*Buddhism.* Vinaya Pitaka, Mahavagga i.43

Bhaddiya, it seems that some recluses and brahmins are vain and empty liars and misrepresent me contrary to facts as being one who holds such a view, in saying, "The recluse Gotama is a conjurer and he knows a conjuring technique by means of which he lures away the followers of other sects."

*Buddhism.* Anguttara Nikaya ii.193

At one time Sakyamuni Buddha was staying in the town of Kosambi. In this town there was one who resented him and who bribed wicked men to circulate false stories about him. Under these circumstances it was difficult for his disciples to get sufficient food from their begging, and there was much abuse.

Ananda said to Sakyamuni, "We had better not stay in a town like this. There are other and better towns to go to. We had better leave this town."

The Blessed One replied, "Suppose the next town is like this, what shall we do then?"

"Then we move to another."

The Blessed One said, "No, Ananda, there will be no end in that way. We had better remain here and bear the abuse patiently until it ceases, and then we move to another place.

There are profit and loss, slander and honor, praise and abuse, suffering and pleasure in this world; the Enlightened One is not controlled by these external things; they will cease as quickly as they come."

*Buddhism.* Dhammapada Commentary

In the province called Laat, local dogs often attacked the Lord. While some people warded them off or shooed them away, and other monks traversing that region carried sticks to frighten the dogs... the Lord had no stick nor any other safety device. He ambulated across the region by virtue of his rugged will.

In Laat province certain people would injure the Lord with sticks, fists, lances, blades, stones, and broken utensils. Others would lacerate the Lord's body. A few would spit on him. Others would throw dust at him. Some people jeered him and pulled him to the ground.... When the Lord sat in a meditative posture, it seemed strange to the onlookers and they would forcibly change his posture. The Lord suffered all this maltreatment as if he had nothing to do with his body....

The Lord never craved anybody's protection. Frequently, human beings or the organic world tortured him. Some people volunteered to save him from such discomforts but the Lord invariably declined such offers. It was his conviction that one cannot realize oneself while seeking another's refuge.

*Jainism.* Acarangasutra 9

To what land shall I flee? Where bend my steps?
I am thrust out from family and tribe;
I have no favor from the village to which I would belong,
Nor from the wicked rulers of the country:
How then, O Lord, shall I obtain thy favor?
I know, O Wise One, why I am powerless:
My cattle are few, and I have few men.
To thee I address my lament: attend unto it, O Lord,
And grant me the support which friend would give to friend.
As Righteousness, teach the possession of the Good Mind.

When, O Wise One, shall the wills of the future saviors come forth,
The dawns of the days when, through powerful judgment,
The world shall uphold Righteousness?
To whom will help come through the Good Mind?
To me, for I am chosen for the revelation by thee, O Lord.

*Zoroastrianism.* Avesta, Yasna 46.1-3

Confucius went on to Cheng, and the Master and disciples lost track of each other. While Confucius stood alone at the east gate of the outer city the natives reported to Tsekung, "There is a man at the east gate whose forehead is like that of Emperor Yao, whose neck resembles that of an ancient minister, Kaoyao.... He looks crestfallen like a homeless, wandering dog." Tsekung told Confucius this story, and Confucius smiled and said, "I don't know about the descriptions of my figure, but as for resembling a homeless, wandering dog, he is quite right, he is quite right!"

*Confucianism.*
Ssu-ma Ch'ien, Shih Chi 47

In the spring of the fourteenth year of Duke Ai of Lu (481 B.C.) there was a hunt in the country and Baron Shusun's driver, by the name of Chusang, caught a strange animal which was regarded as bad luck. Confucius looked at it and declared it was a unicorn, and then the people brought the animal home.

**Dhammapada Commentary:** Once the order was falsly accused by religions rivals of murdering a female ascetic. The Buddha remarked, "This noise, monks, will not last long. It will last just seven days. After seven days it will vanish away." (Udana 45)

**Yasna 46.1-3:** Zarathustra, like Confucius, fled his enemies and wandered about preaching the doctrine while looking for a prince to support him. But he had more success in life than did Confucius, for he found a prince, Vishtaspa, who accepted his teaching and put it into practice. Cf. Yasna 53.1-2, p. 441.

**Shih Chi 47:** Cf. Analects 3.24, pp. 441-42.

Confucius then said, "Alas, no tortoise bearing magic anagrams has appeared in the Yellow River, and no sacred writings have come out of the River Lo. I have given up."... And he heaved a sigh, saying, "There is no one in the world who understands me." And Tsekung said, "Why do you say that there is no one in the world who understands you?" And Confucius said, "I don't blame Heaven, and I don't blame mankind. All I try to do is my best to acquire knowledge, and to aim at a higher ideal. Perhaps Heaven is the only one who understands me!"

*Confucianism.*
Ssu-ma Ch'ien, Shih Chi 47

When under siege in K'uang, the Master said, "With King Wen dead, is not culture (*wen*) invested here in me? If Heaven intends culture to be destroyed, those who come after me will not be able to have any part of it. If Heaven does not intend this culture to be destroyed, then what can the men of K'uang do to me?"

*Confucianism.* Analects 9.5

[Being surrounded and short of food], Confucius knew that his disciples were angry and disappointed at heart, so he asked Tselu to come in and questioned him. "It is said in the Book of Songs, 'Neither buffaloes, nor tigers, they wander in the desert' [A comparison to themselves]. Do you think that my teachings are wrong? How is it that I find myself now in this situation?" Tselu replied, "Perhaps we are not great enough and have not been able to win people's confidence in us. Perhaps we are not wise enough and people are not willing to follow our teachings." "Is that so?" said Confucius. "Ah Yu, if the great could always gain the confidence of the people, why did Po I and Shu Ch'i have to go and die of starvation in the mountains? If the wise men could always have their teachings followed by others, why did Prince Pikan have to commit suicide?"

Tselu came out and Tsekung went in, and Confucius said, "Ah Sze, it is said in the Book of Songs, 'Neither buffaloes, nor tigers, they wander in the desert.' Are my teachings wrong? How is it that I find myself now in this situation?" Tsekung replied, "The Master's teachings are too great for the people, and that is why the world cannot accept them. Why don't you come down a little from your heights?" Confucius replied, "Ah Sze, a good farmer plants the field but cannot guarantee the harvest, and a good artisan can do a skillful job, but he cannot guarantee to please his customers. Now you are not interested in cultivating yourselves, but are only interested in being accepted by the people. I am afraid you are not setting the highest standard for yourself."

Tsekung came out and Yen Hui went in, and Confucius said, "Ah Hui, it is said in the Book of Songs, 'Neither buffaloes, nor tigers, they wander in the desert.' Are my teachings wrong? How is it that I find myself now in this situation?" Yen Hui replied, "The Master's teachings are so great. That is why the world cannot accept them. However, you should just do your best to spread the ideas. What do you care if they are not accepted? The very fact that your teachings are not accepted shows that you are a true gentleman. If the truth is not cultivated, the shame is ours; but if we have already strenuously cultivated the teachings of a moral order and they are not accepted by the people, it is the shame of those in power. What do you care if you are not accepted? The very fact that you are not accepted shows that you are a true gentleman." And Confucius was pleased and said smilingly, "Is that so? Oh, son of Yen, if you were a rich man, I would be your butler!"

*Confucianism.*
Ssu-ma Ch'ien, Shih Chi 47

**Shih Chi 47:** Confucius was continually frustrated during his lifetime, for no prince in authority recognized his mission to bring true ethical government and peace to China. In this passage he complains that none of the traditional omens signalling the appearance of a true philosopher-king had appeared, and even a possible omen of the appearance of a sage—the unicorn—was not believed to be so by the people.

All men, indeed, are wreathed in smiles,
As though feasting after the Great Sacrifice,
As though going up to the Spring Carnival.
I alone am inert, like a child that has not yet given sign,
Like an infant that has not yet smiled.
I droop and drift, as though I belonged nowhere.
All men have enough to spare;
I alone seem to have lost everything.
Mine is indeed the mind of a very idiot,
So dull am I.
The world is full of people that shine;
I alone am dark.
They look lively and self-assured;
I alone, depressed.
I seem unsettled as the ocean;
Blown adrift, never brought to a stop.
All men can be put to some use;
I alone am intractable and boorish.
But wherein I most am different from men
Is that I prize no sustenance that comes not from the Mother's breast.

*Taoism.* Tao Te Ching 20

Some brand me a ghost, some a goblin,
Some call me mad; Nanak is a simple, humble man.
Nanak is mad after the divine King, after Him crazy.
Other than the Lord I recognize none.
To be really crazy is to be fear-crazed of God,
And other than the Lord, none other to recognize.
A man would be mad, if he were to engage in this one sole task:
He should realize the Lord's command and discard other kinds of understanding.
Truly mad would he be, should he love the Lord,
Should he look upon himself as foul,
And the rest of the world as good.

*Sikhism.* Adi Granth, Maru, M.1, p. 991

I have tasted prison life, not only under the communist regime but also in free Korea. I can never forget one former member who came up to me when I was being taken to the West Gate prison in Seoul. He looked at me and laughed scornfully, "You fool! Are you still doing this stupid thing?" I can never forget that man. At that moment I did not say anything to him, but in my heart I prayed, "God, give me a chance to testify to how righteous You are, and how I was obedient to You." This is just one instance of personal betrayal; there are too many to count. When I close my eyes and start to pray, tears always come forth. I have experienced so much agony and pain and heartbreak that I know God, and I am in a position to comfort Him.

No one understands me. My parents never understood, even my wife and children can never really understand. My understanding of God is a lonely understanding. You also can be a companion to that lonely God. I always feel how vulnerable and weak I am, but I know that God trusts and is depending on me to fulfill. When I see God's expectation I just have no way to sit still. I feel, "God, You are Almighty. You can do anything You want, but because of Your own precious children's failure You put Yourself in a position of such suffering. You don't need to suffer, but You have been helpless, waiting so long for some man You could depend on. God, I really sympathize with You. I understand You."

If anyone truly knew me internally then he just could not help but be crushed by sorrow. When spiritually enlightened people pray about me, God's response is always the same; He responds to their prayer in tears because when God thinks about His lonely champion here on earth, God just weeps. The vast entanglement of human history seems utterly impossible to ever reorganize, and even God hardly knew where to begin the dispensation. But one lonely man found the secret and lived through

**Tao Te Ching 20:** The Taoist sages also wandered about seeking a reception for their message of righteousness and peace; cf. Chuang Tzu 33, p. 725.

**Maru, M.1:** Guru Nanak was branded a madman by some people shortly after the revelation came to him at Sultanpur Lodhi. This verse is his response to that charge.

everything to bring the dispensation this far. Even for God, that was something to behold.

Day after day I continuously wept. My eyes became swollen and painful because the tears poured out in gallons. I could not even open my eyes to the sunlight. So many tears were shed in laying the foundation of this church. I will not explain this to you completely; if I were to tell you, then you would be responsible to also go that way, and I do not want that. I would rather leave an easier way for you.

*Unification Church.*
Sun Myung Moon, 5-1-77

To seal the testimony of this book and the Book of Mormon, we announce the martyrdom of Joseph Smith the Prophet, and Hyrum Smith the Patriarch. They were shot in Carthage jail, on the 27th of June, 1844, about five o'clock p.m., by an armed mob—painted black—of from 150 to 200 persons. Hyrum was shot first and fell calmly, exclaiming: "I am a dead man!" Joseph leaped from the window, and was shot dead in the attempt, exclaiming, "O Lord my God!" They were both shot after they were dead, and both received four balls.

*Church of Jesus Christ of Latter-day Saints.*
Doctrine and Covenants 135.1

❖

**Sun Myung Moon, 5-1-77:** Sun Myung Moon's ministry encountered such hostility that he was imprisoned six times: once in Japan, twice in North Korea, twice in South Korea, and once in the United States. Cf. Divine Principle I.3.5.2, pp. 779-80. On the imprisonment of Baha'u'llah, see Tablets of Baha'u'llah Revealed After the Kitab-i-Aqdas, p. 459.

## *The Victor*

THE FOUNDER IS STEADFAST through his trials, and finally emerges the victor. In the case of Buddha and Mahavira, these trials were largely internal struggles to realize the truth through sustained meditation and austerities. Upon the conquest of his passions and the attainment of the highest liberation, Gotama became the Buddha, the Wayfarer who had reached the Goal, the "trackless one" who had transcended the cycle of birth and death. Jain sutras describe Mahavira's victory, by which he becomes a Tirthankara, in similar terms.

In the Abrahamic faiths the founders maintained an attitude of faith despite rejection and persecution, and are finally vindicated. Abraham was the first great victor of faith, who was tested ten times according to Jewish tradition. His ultimate test came when God asked him to sacrifice his son Isaac. Moses demonstrated unshakable faith in confronting Pharaoh with God's demand that he free the Israelites. Risking imprisonment and ridicule even from his own people, he persevered and led the people out of Egyptian slavery under the divine protection that he alone knew was available to them. Jesus' victory transcends death itself: Obedient to death on the cross, he was resurrected and exalted to the right hand of God. St. Paul describes how Jesus, though essentially divine, offered himself to be humiliated and killed, according to the will of God, and thereby received divine approval and exaltation. His willingness to empty himself and suffer is itself part of his victorious standard of faith. Then we include the account of Jesus' resurrection appearances from the Gospel of Luke. Muhammad's vindication came during his lifetime. He returned victorious to Mecca after years of exile, brought an end to paganism in Arabia, and established the new nation of Islam. Zarathustra, also, was vindicated in his lifetime through gaining as a patron Prince Vishtaspa, whom he convinced to put his doctrines into practice. Confucius, on the other hand, never lived to see his teachings adopted in China. His victory was total, nevertheless, as China would eventually come entirely under the tutelage of Confucian teachings.

All these great founders of religion had courage, steadfastness of purpose, and fidelity to the goal which they sought, the cause which they championed, the reality which they realized, and the revelation with which they had been entrusted. With these qualities they could be victorious.

All have I overcome. All do I know. From all am I detached. All have I renounced. Wholly absorbed am I in the destruction of craving. Having comprehended all by myself, whom shall I call my teacher?

*Buddhism.* Dhammapada 353

Through many a birth I wandered in samsara, seeking but not finding the builder of this house. Sorrowful is it to be born again and again.

O house-builder! You are seen. You shall build no house again. All your rafters are broken. Your ridgepole is shattered. My mind has attained the unconditioned. Achieved is the end of craving.

*Buddhism.* Dhammapada 153-54

**Dhammapada 153-54:** The 'house-builder' is the chain of causation that binds humanity to existence and suffering; see the following passage. It is not God the Creator.

Having mastered perfectly all the methods of trance, the prince recalled, in the first watch of the night, the sequence of his former births.

Next the Rightly-illumined One perceived [the chain of causation], and thus was decisively awakened: When birth is destroyed, old age, and death ceases; when becoming is destroyed, then birth ceases; when attachment is destroyed, becoming ceases; when craving is destroyed, attachment ceases; when sensations are destroyed, craving ceases; when contact is destroyed, sensation ceases; when the six sense organs are destroyed, contact ceases; when the psycho-physical organism is destroyed, the six sense organs cease; when consciousness is destroyed, the psycho-physical organism ceases; when psychic constructions are destroyed, consciousness ceases; when ignorance is destroyed, psychic constructions cease.

Reflecting his right understanding, the great hermit arose before the world as Buddha, the Enlightened One. He found self nowhere, as the fire whose fuel has been exhausted. Then he conceived the Eightfold Path, the straightest and safest path for the attainment of this end.

For seven days, the Buddha with serene mind contemplated the Truth that he had attained and gazed at the Bodhi tree without blinking: "Here on this spot I have fufilled my cherished goal; I now rest at ease in the Dharma of selflessness."

*Buddhism*. Ashvaghosha, Buddhacarita 14

The Venerable One lived... indifferent alike to the smell of ordure and of sandal [wood], to straw and jewels, dirt and gold, pleasure and pain, attached neither to this world nor to that beyond, desiring neither life nor death; he arrived at the shore of samsara, and he exerted himself for the suppression of the defilement of karma.

With supreme knowledge, with supreme intuition, with supreme conduct, in blameless lodgings, in blameless wandering, with supreme valor, with supreme uprightness, with supreme mildness, with supreme dexterity, with supreme patience, with supreme freedom from passions, with supreme control, with supreme contentment, with supreme understanding, on the supreme path to final liberation, which is the fruit of veracity, control, penance, and good conduct, the Venerable One meditated on himself for twelve years.

During the thirteenth year, in the second month of summer, in the fourth fortnight, the light of the month Vaisakha, on its tenth day, when the shadow had turned towards the east .... after fasting two-and-a-half days without drinking water, being engaged in deep meditation, he reached the highest knowledge and intuition, called wholeness (*kevala*), which is infinite, supreme, unobstructed, unimpeded, complete, and full!

When the venerable ascetic Mahavira had become a Jina and Saint, he was a Liberated One, omniscient and comprehending all objects; he knew and saw all conditions of the world, of gods, men, and demons: whence they come, whither they go, whether they are born as men or animals or become gods or beings in purgatory, the ideas, the thoughts of their minds, the food, doings, desires, the open and secret deeds of all the living beings in the whole world; he the Saint, for whom there is no secret, knew and saw all conditions of all living beings in the world, what they thought, spoke, or did at any moment.

*Jainism*. Kalpa Sutra 120-21

**Buddhacarita 14:** This describes the Buddha's enlightenment. Its fundamental doctrinal expression is the chain of Dependent Origination, given here and in Samyutta Nikaya xxii.90, p. 390.

**Kalpa Sutra 120-21:** This describes Mahavira's enlightenment to become the supreme soul, called a Jina, a saint, a *Kevalin*, and a Tirthankara.

With ten trials Abraham our father was tried, and he bore them all, to make known how great was the love of Abraham our father.

*Judaism*. Mishnah, Abot 5.4

After these things God tested Abraham, and said to him, "Abraham!" And he said, "Here am I." He said, "Take your son, your only son Isaac, whom you love, and go to the land of Moriah, and offer him there as a burnt offering upon one of the mountains of which I shall tell you."

So Abraham rose early in the morning, saddled his ass, and took two of his young men with him, and his son Isaac; and he cut the wood for the burnt offering, and arose and went to the place of which God had told him. On the third day Abraham lifted up his eyes and saw the place afar off. Then Abraham said to his young men, "Stay here with the ass; I and the lad will go yonder and worship, and come again to you." And Abraham took the wood of the burnt offering, and laid it on Isaac his son; and he took in his hand the fire and the knife. So they went both of them together.

And Isaac said to his father Abraham, "My father!" And he said, "Here am I, my son." He said, "Behold, the fire and the wood; but where is the lamb for a burnt offering?" Abraham said, "God will provide himself the lamb for a burnt offering, my son." So they went both of them together.

When they came to the place of which God had told him, Abraham built an altar there, and laid the wood in order, and bound Isaac his son, and laid him on the altar, upon the wood. Then Abraham put forth his hand, and took the knife to slay his son. But the angel of the Lord called to him from heaven, and said, "Abraham, Abraham!" And he said, "Here am I." He said, "Do not lay your hand on the lad or do anything to him; for now I know that you fear God, seeing you have not withheld your son, your only son, from me." And Abraham lifted up his eyes and looked, and behold, behind him was a ram, caught in a thicket by his horns; and Abraham went and took the ram, and offered it up as a burnt offering instead of his son.

So Abraham called the name of that place The Lord will provide; as it is said to this day, "On the mount of the Lord it shall be provided."

And the angel of the Lord called to Abraham a second time from heaven, and said, "By myself I have sworn, says the Lord, because you have done this, and have not withheld your son, your only son, I will indeed bless you, and I will multiply your descendants as the stars of heaven and as the sand which is on the seashore. And your descendants shall possess the gate of their enemies, and by your descendants shall all the nations of the earth bless themselves, because you have obeyed my voice."

*Judaism* and *Christianity*.
Genesis 22.1-18

Then We sent forth, after them, Moses and Aaron to Pharaoh and his council with Our signs, but they waxed proud, and were a sinful people. So when the truth came to them from

**Abot 5.4:** The ten trials: in Babylon when he confronted the idolators (Qur'an 21.51-71, p. 428), his call to depart for an unknown land (Genesis 12.1, p. 675), and thence to Egypt (Genesis 12.10), the test involving his wife in Egypt (Genesis 12.11-20) and again in Gerar (Genesis 20.1-18), the war with the kings (Genesis 14), the covenant between the pieces (Genesis 15), the covenant of circumcision (Genesis 17), the casting out of Hagar and Ishmael (Genesis 21.10-13), and the sacrifice of Isaac (Genesis 22, below). Ten is the traditional number, corresponding to the Ten Words by which God created the world; the exact enumeration of the trials may vary. Cf. Hebrews 11.8-19, pp. 539-40.

**Genesis 22.1-18:** The binding of Isaac, the *Akkedah*, was Abraham's ultimate test of faith. Isaac was his only son by his wife Sarah, born miraculously by God's hand after she was long past child-bearing age; furthermore, he was the one by whom God's promise of numerous descendants was to be fulfilled. Such was the love and attachment that Abraham had for his son. Yet at God's command, he willingly offered him up, though it was more difficult than to sacrifice his own life. In interfaith discussions among Jews and Christians, Isaac's self-sacrifice is sometimes compared to Jesus' crucifixion. For three of the many Jewish reflections on the binding of Isaac, see Genesis Rabbah 56, p. 445; 56.11, p. 626; Rosh Hashanah 16a, pp. 463-64. A Christian reflection is found in Hebrews 11.17-19, pp. 539-40.

Us, they said, "Surely this is a manifest sorcery."... So none believed in Moses, save a seed of his people, for fear of Pharaoh and their council, that they would persecute them; and Pharaoh was high in the land, and he was one of the prodigals. Moses said, "O my people, if you believe in God, in Him put your trust, if you have surrendered." They said, "In God we have put our trust. Our Lord, make us not a temptation to the people of the evildoers, and deliver us by Thy mercy from the people of the unbelievers."...

Moses said, "Our Lord, You have given to Pharaoh and his council adornment and possessions in this present life. Our Lord, let them go astray from Your way; our Lord, obliterate their possessions, and harden their hearts so that they do not believe, till they see the painful chastisement." He said, "Your prayer is answered; so go you straight, and follow not the way of those that know not."

And We brought the children of Israel over the sea; and Pharaoh and his hosts followed them insolently and impetuously till, when the drowning overtook them, he said, "I believe that there is no god but He in whom the children of Israel believe; I am of those that surrender." "Now? And before you were a rebel, one of those who did corruption. So today We shall deliver you with your body, that you might be a sign to those after you. Surely many men are heedless of Our signs."

*Islam*. Qur'an 10.75-92

When the king of Egypt was told that the people had fled, the mind of Pharaoh and his servants was changed toward the people, and they said, "What is this we have done, that we have let Israel go from serving us?" So he made ready his chariot and took his army with him, and took six hundred picked chariots and all the other chariots of Egypt with officers over all of them.... The Egyptians pursued them, all Pharaoh's horses and chariots and his horsemen and his army, and overtook them encamped by the sea, by Pi-ha-hiroth, in front of Baal-zephon.

When Pharaoh drew near, the people of Israel lifted up their eyes, and behold, the Egyptians were marching after them; and they were in great fear. And the people of Israel cried out to the Lord; and they said to Moses, "Is it because there are no graves in Egypt that you have taken us away to die in the wilderness? What have you done to us, in bringing us out of Egypt? Is not this what we said to you in Egypt, 'Let us alone and let us serve the Egyptians'? For it would have been better for us to serve the Egyptians than to die in the wilderness."

And Moses said to the people, "Fear not, stand firm, and see the salvation of the Lord, which he will work for you today; for the Egyptians whom you see today you shall never see again. The Lord will fight for you, and you have only to be still."...

Then Moses stretched out his hand over the sea; and the Lord drove the sea back by a strong east wind all night, and made the sea dry land, and the waters were divided. And the people of Israel went into the midst of the sea on dry ground, the waters being a wall to them on their right hand and on their left. The Egyptians pursued, and went in after them into the midst of the sea, all Pharaoh's horses, his chariots, and his horsemen. And in the morning watch the Lord in a pillar of fire and of cloud looked down upon the host of the Egyptians, and discomfited the host of the Egyptians, clogging their chariot wheels so that they drove heavily; and the Egyptians said, "Let us flee from before Israel; for the Lord fights for them against the Egyptians."

Then the Lord said to Moses, "Stretch out your hand over the sea, that the water may come back upon the Egyptians, upon their chariots, and upon their horsemen." So Moses stretched forth his hand over the sea, and the sea returned to its wonted flow when the morning appeared; and the Egyptians fled into it, and the Lord routed the Egyptians in the midst of the sea. The waters returned and covered the chariots and the horsemen and all the host of Pharaoh that had followed them into the sea; not so much as one of them remained. But the people of Israel walked on dry ground through the sea, the waters being a wall to them on their right hand and on their left.

Thus the Lord saved Israel from the hand of the Egyptians; and Israel saw the Egyptians dead upon the seashore. And Israel saw the great work which the Lord did against the Egyptians, and the people feared the Lord; and they believed in the Lord and in his servant Moses.

*Judaism* and *Christianity*. Exodus 14.5-31

Christ Jesus, who,
though he was in the form of God,
did not count equality with God a thing to be grasped,
but emptied himself,
taking the form of a servant,
being born in the likeness of men.
And being found in human form he humbled himself
and became obedient unto death,
even death on a cross.
Therefore God has highly exalted him
and bestowed on him the name which is above every name,
that at the name of Jesus every knee should bow,
in heaven and on earth and under the earth,
and every tongue confess that Jesus Christ is Lord,
to the glory of God the Father.

*Christianity*. Philippians 2.6-11

But on the first day of the week, at early dawn, they went to the tomb, taking the spices which they had prepared. And they found the stone rolled away from the tomb, but when they went in they did not find the body. While they were perplexed about this, behold, two men stood by them in dazzling apparel; and as they were frightened and bowed their faces to the ground, the men said to them, "Why do you seek the living among the dead? Remember how he told you, while he was still in Galilee, that the Son of man must be delivered into the hands of sinful men, and be crucified, and on the third day rise." And they remembered his words, and returning from the tomb they told all this to the eleven and to all the rest. Now it was Mary Magdalene and Joanna and Mary the mother of James and the other women with them who told this to the apostles; but these words seemed to them an idle tale, and they did not believe them.

That very day two of them were going to a village called Emmaus, about seven miles from Jerusalem, and talking with each other about all these things that had happened. While they were talking and discussing together, Jesus himself drew near and went with them. But their eyes were kept from recognizing him. And he said to them, "What is this conversation which you are holding with each other as you walk?" And they stood still, looking sad. Then one of them, named Cleopas, answered him, "Are you the only visitor to Jerusalem who does not know the things that have happened there in these days?" And he said to them, "What things?" And they said to him, "Concerning Jesus of Nazareth, who was a prophet mighty in deed and word before God and all the people, and how our chief priests and rulers delivered him up to be condemned to death, and crucified him. But we had hoped that he was the one to redeem Israel. Yes, and besides all this, it is now the third day since this happened. Moreover, some women of our company amazed us. They were at the tomb early in the morning and did not find his body; and they came back saying that they had even seen a vision of angels, who said that he was alive. Some of those who were with us went to the tomb, and found it just as the women had said; but him they did not see." And he said to them, "O foolish men, and slow of heart to believe all that the prophets have spoken! Was it not necessary that the Christ should suffer these things and enter into his glory?" And beginning at Moses and all the prophets, he interpreted to them in all the scriptures the things concerning himself.

**Exodus 14.5-31:** Cf. Exodus 15.1-11, pp. 400-1.

**Philippians 2.6-11:** This is the well-known hymn of Christ's *kenosis*, or self-emptying. By grasping at nothing and denying himself totally, Jesus laid the condition to be totally vindicated and exalted by God. Cf. Mark 8.34-36, p. 638.

So they drew near to the village to which they were going. He appeared to be going further, but they constrained him, saying, "Stay with us, for it is toward evening, and the day is now far spent." So he went in to stay with them. When he was at table with them, he took the bread and blessed, and broke it, and gave to them. And their eyes were opened and they recognized him; and he vanished out of their sight. They said to each other, "Did not our hearts burn within us while he talked to us on the road, while he opened to us the scriptures?" And they rose that same hour and returned to Jerusalem; and they found the eleven gathered together and those who were with them, who said, "The Lord has risen indeed, and has appeared to Simon!" Then they told what had happened on the road, and how he was known to them in the breaking of bread.

As they were saying this, Jesus himself stood among them and said to them, "Peace to you!" But they were startled and frightened, and supposed that they had seen a spirit. And he said to them, "Why are you troubled, and why do questionings rise in your hearts? See my hands and my feet, that it is I myself; handle me, and see; for a spirit has not flesh and bones, as you see that I have." And while they still disbelieved for joy, and wondered, he said to them, "Have you anything here to eat?" They gave him a piece of broiled fish, and he took it and ate before them.

Then he said to them, "These are my words which I spoke to you, while I was still with you, that everything written about me in the law of Moses and the prophets and the psalms must be fulfilled." Then he opened their minds to understand the scriptures, and said to them, "Thus it is written, that the Christ should suffer and on the third day rise from the dead, and that repentance and forgiveness of sins should be preached in his name to all nations, beginning from Jerusalem. You are witnesses of these things. And behold, I send the promise of my Father upon you; but stay in the city, until you are clothed with power from on high."

Then he led them out as far as to Bethany, and lifting up his hands he blessed them. While he blessed them, he parted from them, and was carried up into heaven. And they returned to Jerusalem with great joy, and were continually in the temple blessing God.

*Christianity*. Luke 24.1-53

The best possession of Zarathustra Spitama has been revealed:
It is that the Wise Lord has granted, through the Right, eternal bliss
To him and to all those who have observed and practiced
The words and deeds of his good religion.

By the thought of him, by words and deeds,
Shall Prince Vishtaspa and Spitama, Zarathustra's son,
And Frashaostra strive willingly
To please the Wise One and to pray in His praise,
Making even the paths to the religion of the savior,
Which the Lord has ordained.

*Zoroastrianism*. Yasna 53.1-2

The border warden requested to be introduced to Confucius, saying, "When men of superior virtue have come to this [exile], I have never been denied the privilege of seeing them." The followers introduced him, and when he came out from the interview, he said, "My friends, why are you distressed by your master's loss of office? The kingdom has long been without the

**Luke 24.1-53:** Immediately after the tragic events leading to Christ's crucifixion as recounted in Luke 22.39-23.46, pp. 428-30, comes the glorious victory over death and evil that is Christ's resurrection. This description of the resurrection begins with the discovery of the empty tomb, thence his appearance among the disciples on the road to Emmaus and his partaking of a meal with them, and concludes with his ascension into heaven. Another resurrection appearance, to Thomas, is given in John 20.24-29, p. 467.

**Yasna 53.1-2:** Cf. Yasna 28.7, p. 733.

principles of truth and right; Heaven is going to use your master as a bell with its wooden tongue."

*Confucianism.* Analects 3.24

Did We not expand your breast for you
and lift from you your burden,
the burden that weighed down on your back?
Did We not exalt your fame?
So truly with hardship comes ease,
truly with hardship comes ease.
So when you are empty, labor,
and let your Lord be your Quest.

*Islam.* Qur'an 94

A declaration of immunity from God and His Apostle, to those of the pagans with whom you have contracted mutual alliances... and an announcement from God and His Apostle, to the people assembled on the day of the Great Pilgrimage, that God and His Apostle dissolve treaty obligations with the pagans. If then, you repent, it will be best for you; but if you turn away, know that you cannot frustrate God. And proclaim a grievous penalty to those who reject Faith. But the treaties are not dissolved with those pagans with whom you have entered into alliance and who have not subsequently failed you in aught, nor aided any one against you. So fulfill your engagements with them to the end of their term: God loves the righteous.

But when the forbidden months are past, then fight and slay the pagans wherever you find them, and seize them, beleaguer them, and lie in wait for them in every strategem of war; but if they repent, and establish regular prayers and practice regular charity, then open the way for them: for God is Oft-forgiving, Most Merciful. If one among the pagans asks you for asylum, grant it to him, so that he may hear the Word of God; and then escort him to where he can be secure....

O you who believe! Truly the pagans are unclean; so let them not, after this year of theirs, approach the Sacred Mosque. And if you fear poverty [from loss of their trade], soon God will enrich you, if He wills, out of His bounty, for God is All-knowing, All-wise.

*Islam.* Qur'an 9.1-6, 28

The Apostle continued his pilgrimage and showed the men the rites and taught them the customs of their hajj. He made a speech in which he made things clear. He praised and glorified God, then he said, "O men, listen to my words. I do not know whether I shall ever meet you in this place again after this year. Your blood and your property are sacrosanct until you meet your Lord, as this day and this month are holy. You will surely meet your Lord and He will ask you of your works. I have told you. He who has a pledge let him return it to him who entrusted him with it; all usury is abolished, but you have your capital. Wrong not and you shall not be wronged.... All blood shed in the pagan period is to be left unavenged. The first claim on blood I abolish is that of ibn Rabi'a ibn al-Harith ibn 'Abdu'l-Muttalib. It is the first blood shed in the pagan period which I deal with. Satan despairs of ever being worshipped in your land, but if he can be obeyed in anything short of worship, he will be pleased in matters you may be disposed to think of little account, so beware of him in your religion.... Time has completed its cycle and is as it was on the day that God created the heavens and the earth."

*Islam.* Sirat Rasul Allah

**Qur'an 94:** This early Meccan sura, called "Solace," describes the Prophet's inward assurance at a time of difficulty and persecution. The revelation foretells future victory as though it is already accomplished; coming as it does from a plane beyond time.

**Qur'an 9.1-6, 28:** These are among the verses given at the time of the Muslims' final victory over the pagans, as they began to organize a new nation, and in anticipation of the victorious pilgrimage to Mecca in A.H. 9 (October, 630 A.D. ). They were read there to the assembled pilgrims by Ali as a statement of state policy. This declaration of immunity granted the pagans relief from any blood debts due to having previously violated their agreements with the Muslims (see below). At the same time, the pagans were welcomed to sincerely embrace Islam or face extinction.

The United States of America declared war against me. The battle has been fought, and the United States was defeated. Throughout the world, the established religions joined the opposition: Christianity, Buddhism, Confucianism—every religion on earth united against me. But when I counterattacked, they all utterly fell down. Who protected me? God! No matter how strongly they came against me, they could not move my position away from the vertical standing point, from the center of God's love.

From this center position... I was steadfast and stirred up this world to make a victorious foundation by fighting all of Satan's power. You must never forget how I gained this foundation. I was named the victor. Only one man in history has ever defeated all of Satan's world. Now I am leading world humanity into unity.

Everything I had was poured into America so that with love, we could restore the original way. I made oneness with everyone, western and eastern people, centering only on true love. Everyone who has come against me, even Satan, cannot deny that I have made that kind of foundation a reality on the earth. Of course God is enjoying my victory and He is raising His hand, "My son! My victor! Welcome to My place of Heart!"

Now wherever I go, there will be no opposition because I have brought unity between East and West, North and South on the individual level, family, tribal, national, world, and cosmic levels. At the time of Jesus, even though he came as the Messiah, he was whipped from day one until the end. There was opposition and crucifixion, just the opposite of what should have been. I received similar persecution, but from this day on we can go forward without any opposition because the world is looking for hope which cannot be found anywhere except with me!

*Unification Church.*
Sun Myung Moon, 9-3-89

❖

**Sun Myung Moon, 9-3-89:** Sun Myung Moon triumphed through receiving persecution without complaint, and doing his best to give God's love in return. In the United States, where he suffered intense persecution, including imprisonment, he nevertheless continuously sought to serve and guide the American people, pouring resources into numerous educational and social projects. Thus his integrity and godliness became manifest to people in the very organizations which had persecuted him. By such a victorious love, he 'made oneness with everyone.' On the True Parents as the cosmic center of God's love, cf. Divine Principle I.1.2.3.4, p. 175.

## He who Subjugates Satan

SATAN, MARA, ANGRA MAINYU, or the devil by whatever name, who holds sway over the world and over the inner desires of human beings, is the final obstacle which must be overcome if the founder is to realize the ultimate victory. The devil is only a spiritual creature who improperly dominates human beings, and hence he inevitably comes into conflict with those exceptional souls who dare to take their rightful place as true human beings, the Lords of creation: see *Lord of Spirits*, pp. 218-20. Every religious founder must gain the qualification to reveal the truth through winning a contest with the devil. In more mythological texts, the founder may be represented as battling a many-headed serpent or dragon—surely an appropriate symbol for the irrational power of evil. In psychological terms, the founder engages in an internal struggle to overcome the selfish elements that cling to the heart. Thus in various forms, the scriptures of many faiths depict their founder as vanquishing a spiritual foe and showing the way for ordinary people to do the same.

In all the texts here, with the possible exception of the episode from the boyhood of Krishna, the founder's struggle with the devil is a purely human one. Although there are traditions, especially in Hinduism, where the battle between the gods and the demons can be decided by the power of deity alone, it is a recognized spiritual principle that human beings have responsibility to subjugate Satan. God's grace does not obviate man's responsibility to deal with the temptations of his environment and the struggle within his own soul. In this struggle, the founders lead the way.

Then Jesus was led up by the Spirit into the wilderness to be tempted by the devil. He fasted forty days and forty nights, and afterward he was hungry. And the tempter came and said to him, "If you are the Son of God, command these stones to become loaves of bread." But he answered, "It is written,

'Man shall not live by bread alone,
but by every word that proceeds from the
mouth of God.'"

Then the devil took him to the holy city, and set him on the pinnacle of the temple, and said to him, "If you are the Son of God, throw yourself down; for it is written,

'He will give his angels charge of you,'

and

'On their hands they will bear you up,
lest you strike your foot against a stone.'"

Jesus said to him, "Again it is written,

'You shall not tempt the Lord your God.'"

Again, the devil took him to a very high mountain, and showed him all the kingdoms of the world and the glory of them, and he said to him, "All these I will give you, if you will fall down and worship me." Then Jesus said to him, "Begone Satan! for it is written,

'You shall worship the Lord your God
and Him only shall you serve.'"

Then the devil left him, and behold, angels came and ministered to him.

*Christianity*. Matthew 4.1-11

Never did We send an apostle or a prophet before you, but, when he framed a desire, Satan threw some vanity into his desire. But God will cancel anything vain that Satan throws in, and God will confirm His signs—for God is full of knowledge and wisdom: that He may make the

**Matthew 4.1-11:** Cf. Luke 10.19-20, p. 220; Psalm 91.11-13, pp. 398-99; Matthew 12.22-24, p. 265; Deuteronomy 8.3, pp. 764-65.

suggestions thrown in by Satan but a trial for those in whose hearts is a disease and who are hardened of heart.

*Islam.* Qur'an 22.52-53

On their way to Mount Moriah, Abraham and Isaac met Satan disguised as an old man. "Where are you going, Abraham?" asked Satan.

"I'm on my way to pray," answered Abraham.

"Why then the wood and the fire and the sacrificial knife?"

"We shall be on top of Mount Moriah several days and will use them to prepare our food."

"You are an old man and you have only one son with your wife Sarah, yet you are willing to sacrifice him," mocked Satan.

"As God told me to do, so shall it be," answered Abraham.

Satan then addressed Isaac, "Where are you going, Isaac?"

"To study God's wisdom," said Isaac.

"Do you intend to study after you are dead? For your father intends to sacrifice you."

"If God wishes to accept me as a sacrifice, I am glad to do His will."

Satan ran ahead to the foot of Mount Moriah and caused the stream to rise and overflow. Abraham and Isaac tried to wade across but the water reached over their heads.

"You have asked me to sacrifice my son," Abraham prayed, "but I shall not be able to fulfill Your will if I drown."

The waters at once receded and father and son proceeded to the top of the mountain.

*Judaism.* Midrash, Genesis Rabbah 56

From the region of the north, from the regions of hell, forth rushed Angra Mainyu, the deadly, the arch-devil. And thus spoke the guileful one, the evil-doer Angra Mainyu, the deadly, "Demon, rush down upon him! destroy the holy Zarathustra!" The demon came rushing along, the demon Buiti, the unseen death, the hell-born.

Zarathustra chanted aloud the [prayer] Ahuna-Vaira, "The will of the Lord is the Law of holiness; the riches of good thought shall be given to him who works in this world for Mazda, and wields according to the will of the Lord the power He gave him to relieve the poor... profess the Law of the worshippers of Mazda!" The demon, dismayed, rushed away, the demon Buiti, the unseen death, the hell-born.

And the demon, the guileful one, said unto Angra Mainyu, "O baneful Angra Mainyu! I see no way to kill him, so great is the glory of the holy Zarathustra."

Zarathustra saw all this from within his soul, "The evil-doing devils and fiends take counsel together for my death."

Up started Zarathustra, forward went Zarathustra, unshaken by the evil spirit, by the hardness of his malignant riddles, swinging stones in his hand, stones as big as a house, which he obtained from the Maker, Lord Mazda, he the holy Zarathustra.

[Said Angra Mainyu,] "At what on this wide, round earth, whose ends lie afar, at what do you swing those stones, you who stand by the river Dareja, upon the mountains, in the mansion of Pourushaspa?"

Thus Zarathustra answered Angra Mainyu, "O evil-doer, Angra Mainyu! I will smite the creation of the devil!"...

Again to him said the guileful one, the maker of the evil world, Angra Mainyu, "Do not destroy my creatures, O holy Zarathustra! You are the son of Pourushaspa [whom I know], born of your mother [who invoked me]. Renounce the good Law of the worshippers of

**Qur'an 22.52-53:** This passage may refer to the so-called "satanic verses" which were allegedly uttered as Muhammad struggled with the temptation to compromise with the polytheists of Mecca. Muhammad overcame this temptation; hence the revelation in the Qur'an is a pure expression of truth.

**Genesis Rabbah 56:** See the story of the sacrifice of Isaac in Genesis 22, p. 438. Isaac is quite aware that he is about to be sacrificed, and his faith is tested as much as is Abraham's. Similar stories of demons testing a person's faith are common in Buddhism: see Samyutta Nikaya i.128, p. 194; Mahaparinirvana Sutra 424-33, pp. 538-39; Lotus Sutra 3, pp. 313-14.

Mazda, and you will gain such a boon as the murderer [King Zohak] gained, the ruler of the nations."

Thus in answer to him said Zarathustra Spitama, "No! Never will I renounce the good law of the worshippers of Mazda, though my body, my life, my soul should burst!"

*Zoroastrianism.*
Videvdad 19.1-7

When the future Buddha sat down at the foot of the Bodhi tree with his soul fully resolved to obtain the highest knowledge, the whole world rejoiced; but Mara, the enemy of good law, was afraid. He whom they call the God of Pleasure, the owner of various weapons, the flower-arrowed, the lord of the course of desire—it is he whom they also style Mara, the enemy of liberation. His three sons, Confusion, Gaiety, and Pride, and his three daughters, Lust, Delight, and Craving, asked him the reason for his despondency, and thus he answered them,

"This sage, wearing the armor of resolution, and having drawn the arrow of wisdom with the barb of truth, sits yonder intending to conquer my realms—hence my mind is despondent. If he succeeds in overcoming me and proclaims to the world the path of final bliss, all this my realm will today become empty... While, therefore, he stands within my reach and while his spiritual eyesight is not yet attained, I will assail him to break his vow as the might of a swollen river assails a dam."

Then, seizing his flower-made bow and his five arrows of infatuation, the Great Disturber of the minds of living beings, together with his children, approached the root of the Bodhi tree. Placing his left hand on the end of the barb and playing with the arrow, Mara addressed the calm seer as he sat on his seat preparing to cross to the further side of the ocean of existence,

"Up, up, O Kshatriya, afraid of death! Follow your own duty [as member of the warrior caste] and abandon this path of liberation. Conquer the lower worlds by force of arms, and gain the higher worlds as well! That is a glorious path to travel, which has been followed by leaders of men for generations. This mendicant life is ill-suited for one born of royalty to follow. But if you will stubbornly refuse to rise, then be firm, if you will... When pierced by this weapon, even the son of Ida, the grandson of the moon, became mad; and Santanu also lost his self-control. How much more then will one of feebler powers succumb, now that the age has become degenerate? Therefore quickly rise and come to your senses, for this arrow is ready, darting out its tongue."

But even when thus addressed, the Shakya saint, unheeding, did not change his posture. Mara then discharged his arrow of love at him and set in front of him his daughters Lust, Delight, and Craving, and his sons Confusion, Gaiety, and Pride. Still he gave no heed and swerved not from his firmness. Mara, beholding him thus, sank down, and slowly pondered,

"He does not even notice the arrow, the very one by which the god Shambhu was pierced with love for the daughter of the mountain and shaken from his vow. Can he be devoid of all feeling? He is not worthy of my flower-shaft, nor my arrow Excitation, nor even my sending my daughter Sexual Delight to tempt him. He deserves the terrors, attacks, and blows from all the gathered hosts of the demons."

Then Mara called to mind his own army, mustering them for the overthrow of the Shakya saint. His followers swarmed around, wearing different forms and carrying arrows, trees, darts, clubs, and swords in their hands; with faces of boars, fishes, horses, asses, and camels, of tigers, bears, lions, and elephants—one-eyed, many-faced, three-headed, with protuberant bellies and speckled bellies; blended with goats, with knees swollen like pots, armed with tusks and claws, carrying headless trunks in their hands, assuming many forms, with half-mutilated faces and monstrous mouths.... Before these dreadful monsters, the great sage remained untroubled, sporting with them as if they were only rude children. Then one of them, his eyes rolling wildly, lifted a club against him; but his arm was instantly para-

**Videvdad 19.1-7:** Cf. Yasna 32.9, p. 309.

lyzed, like Indra's of old with its thunderbolt. Some, having lifted up stones and trees, found themselves unable to throw them against the sage.... Another hurled upon him a mass of blazing straw as big as a mountain peak.... Despite all these various scorching assaults on his body and his mind, and all these missiles showered down upon him, the Shakya saint did not in the least degree move from his posture nor deviate from his firm resolution....

Then some being of invisible shape, but of preeminent glory, standing in the heavens and beholding Mara thus malevolent against the seer, addressed him in a loud voice unruffled by enmity, "Take not on yourself, O Mara, this vain labor; throw aside your malevolence and retire to your home; this sage cannot be shaken by you any more than the mighty mountain Meru by the wind.... Let not your greatness, O Mara, be mixed with pride. It is not well to be confident—fortune is unstable. Why do you accept a position whose base is tottering?"

Having listened to his words, and having seen the unshaken firmness of the great saint, Mara departed dispirited and broken in purpose with those very arrows of desire by which, O world, you are smitten in your heart. With their strength at an end, their labor all fruitless, and all their stones, straw, and trees thrown away, that host fled in all directions, like some hostile army when its camp has been destroyed by the enemy.

When the flower-armed god thus fled away vanquished with his hostile forces, and the passionless sage remained victorious, having conquered all the power of darkness, the heavens shone out with the moon like a maiden with a smile, and a sweet-smelling shower of flowers fell down wet with dew. With the wicked one thus vanquished, the different regions of the sky grew clear, the moon shone forth, showers of flowers fell down from the sky upon the earth, and the night gleamed out like a spotless maiden.

*Buddhism.* Ashvaghosha, Buddhacarita 13

And Jacob was left alone; and a man wrestled with him until the breaking of the day. When the man saw that he did not prevail against Jacob, he touched the hollow of his thigh; and Jacob's thigh was put out of joint as he wrestled with him. Then he said, "Let me go, for the day is breaking." But Jacob said, "I will not let you go, unless you bless me." And he said to him, "What is your name?" "Jacob." "Your name shall no more be called Jacob, but Israel, for you have striven with God and with men, and have prevailed." Then Jacob asked him, "Tell me, I pray, your name." But he said, "Why is it that you ask my name?" And there he blessed him. So Jacob called the name of the place Peniel, saying, "For I have seen God face to face, and yet my life is preserved."

*Judaism* and *Christianity.* Genesis 32.24-30

[The hosts of celestial beings address Brahma,] "O Blessed Lord, having been favored by thee, the rakshasa Ravana perpetually troubles us since thou hast granted a boon to him, and we are helpless and forced to endure his fearful oppression! The Lord of the demons has inspired terror in the Three Worlds. Provoking the sages, brahmins, and other beings, he tramples them underfoot, he who has become insufferable through pride, being under thy protection. In his presence, the sun ceases to

**Buddhacarita 13:** In this account Mara is depicted as a Cupid-like figure similar to Kama, the Hindu god of desire. But while in the Hindu myths of the battle between Kama and Shiva, Shiva revives Kama because he is a necessary part of creation (see Skanda Purana 1.1.21.82-99, p. 297), in Buddhism Mara is entirely evil. For another version of this encounter, cf. Sutta Nipata 436-39, p. 310. On Mara's argument that Buddha should abandon his asceticism and follow his duty (*svadharma*) as a member of the kshatriya caste, see Bhagavad Gita 18.44-48, p. 505; Matsya Purana 180.5-7, p. 508.

**Genesis 32.24-30:** The struggle of Jacob is usually interpreted as not against a demon, but against an angel whom God was using to test Jacob. The result is nevertheless the same—Jacob is victorious in the spiritual struggle. Cf. Pearl of Great Price, Joseph Smith 2.11-20, p. 426; Mahaparinirvana Sutra 424-33, pp. 538-39.

shine, the wind fails to blow, and, before him, the ocean, garlanded with waves, is still. O Blessed One, be pleased to devise some means for his destruction!"

Brahma reflected awhile and answered, "Here is a way of bringing about the end of that perverse being! 'May I not be destroyed by gandharvas, yakshas, gods or demons,' was Ravana's request, but thinking man to be of no account, he did not ask to be made invulnerable in regard to him; therefore, none but man can destroy him."

At that time, the immortal Vishnu, Lord of the World, attired in yellow, bearing the conch, discus, and mace in his hands, appeared mounted on Garuda, like unto the sun above the clouds. All the celestial beings prostrated themselves before him and said, "O Lord, for the good of all creatures, we address this prayer to thee! The monarch Dasharatha who reigns in Ayodhya, a virtuous and liberal prince, has three consorts, distinguished by chastity and good qualities. O Vishnu, do thou incarnate in them by dividing thyself into four parts! Become a mortal and the vanquisher in combat of Ravana, the powerful tormentor of the worlds, who cannot be slain by the gods."

Vishnu replied, "Have no fear, from now on be happy; Ravana, that cruel and insufferable monster, the terror of the gods and rishis, with his sons and grandsons, his ministers, relations, and allies, for the good of all, will be slain by me, and during eleven thousand years, I shall dwell in the world of men and protect the earth."

*Hinduism.* Ramayana, Bala Kanda 15

Susano-o... descended to the upper reaches of the Pi river in the land of Idumo. There he found an old man and an old woman, with a maiden between them, crying.... "Why are you crying?" he asked. The old man replied, "We originally had eight daughters. But the eight-tailed dragon of Kosi has come every year and eaten them one by one. We are crying because it is now time for him to come again." He asked, "What is its appearance?" He replied, "His eyes are like red ground-cherries; his one body has eight heads and eight tails. On his body grow moss and cypress and cryptomeria trees. His length is such that he spans eight valleys and eight mountain peaks. If you look at his belly, you see that blood is oozing out all over it." Then Susano-o said to the old man, "Will you give me your daughter?" He answered, "Awed as I am, I do not know your name." Then he replied, "I am the brother of the Sun Goddess and have just descended from heaven." Then the old parents said, "If that is so, then we will with fearful reverence present her to you." Then Susano-o transformed the maiden into a hair-comb, which he inserted into his hair-bunch and said to them, "Distill thick *sake* of eight-fold brewings; build a fence, and make eight doors in the fence. At each door, tie together eight platforms, and on each of these platforms place a wine barrel. Fill each barrel with the thick wine, and wait." They made the preparations as he had instructed, and as they waited, the eight-tailed dragon came indeed, as predicted. Putting one head into each of the barrels, he drank the wine; then, becoming drunk, he lay down and slept. Then Susano-o unsheathed the sword ten hands long which he was wearing at his side, and hacked the dragon to pieces, so that the Pi river ran with blood. When he cut the dragon's middle tail, the blade of his sword broke. Thinking this strange, he thrust deeper with the stub of his sword, until a great sharp sword appeared. He took this sword out and, thinking it an extraordinary thing, presented the sword to Amaterasu. This is the sword *Kusa-nagi*.

*Shinto.* Kojiki 19

**Ramayana, Bala Kanda 15:** The demon Ravana can only be conquered by man; hence Vishnu agrees to incarnate himself as Rama, son of King Dasaratha, and then as a man to defeat Ravana in combat. On the doctrine of avatars, see Bhagavad Gita 4.7-8, p. 474n.

**Kojiki 19:** Susano-o is chiefly worshipped in the shrine at Izumo. Izumo was headquarters of an ancient Japanese clan and was the rival of the shrine at Ise, where the Sun Goddess Amaterasu-omi-kami is worshipped. The Kojiki sees the two kami as rivals, with Amaterasu winning out. Her victory symbolizes the all-conquering imperial family, which is seen as descending from Amaterasu. Thus Susano-o, as patron kami of a losing clan, is given an ambiguous role in the mythology, at once a primal culture hero of Japan and yet an impetuous character who offends the gods of heaven. This story represents his heroic

The serpent Kaliya, who was full of pride because of the virulence of his poison... entered a pool in the river Kalindi.... When Krishna, who had become incarnate to restrain the wicked, perceived that the river had been polluted by that serpent whose poison was so virulent and swiftly active, he climbed a very high Kadamba tree, clapped his hands, girded his loins tightly, and plunged into the poisoned water. The mass of water in that pool of serpents was swelled by the poison emitted by serpents who were shaken by the blast caused by the vigorous dive of the Man, and it overflowed for a hundred bow lengths on all sides with terrible waves tawny with poison, but this did nothing to him of infinite thought.

When Kaliya heard the noise of the whirling of the club-like arms of Krishna, who was playing in the pool like a rogue elephant, and saw his own residence overwhelmed, he was unable to bear the sight and sound, and he slithered out. He enveloped angrily with his coils and bit in his vital spots that Boy whose feet were like the inside of a lotus, beautiful to see in his youth, adorned with the Srivatsa, wearing yellow garments, with a beautiful smile on his face, playing fearlessly. When Krishna's dear friends the cattle-tenders saw him caught up in the coils of the serpent, apparently motionless, they were greatly distressed... the cows and bulls and calves lowed in their misery... and the cow-herds' wives... were burnt by great sorrow and saw the triple world as empty, for it was devoid of their Beloved.

Krishna, seeing that his own village, with its women and children, was so miserable because of him, and knowing that it had no refuge other than him, conformed to the way of mortals and, staying for a moment, rose up from the serpent's grip. The serpent's hoods were tortured by the expanding body of Krishna, and he released him; he raised his hoods angrily and stood spitting venom through his hissing nostrils; he stared at Hari with his unblinking eyes that were like frying pans, and he licked the two corners of his mouth with his forked tongue, and his very gaze was full of fire and virulent poison. Playfully, Krishna circled about him, like Garuda, the lord of birds, and Kaliya also moved about, watching for an opportunity. When the serpent's strength was exhausted by moving about in this way, the First bent down the snake's raised shoulder and mounted upon his broad heads. Then the Master of all musical arts danced, his lotus feet made bright red by their contact with the multitude of rubies on the serpent's head. When the wives of the gandharvas, siddhas, celestial players, and gods saw that he was preparing to dance, they approached him joyfully with offerings of drums and musical instruments and songs and flowers and praises.

He who bears a cruel rod of punishment trampled with his feet whatever head of the hundred-headed one was yet unbent, and the serpent, his life span spent but still writhing, vomited clotted blood from his mouth and fell, suffering horribly. The Ancient Man danced on the serpent, who still spewed poison from his eyes and hissed loudly in his anger, and he trampled down with his feet whatever head the serpent raised, subduing him calmly as if he were being worshipped with flowers. Kaliya, his umbrella of hoods shattered by the gay dance of death, his limbs broken, vomiting blood copiously from his mouths, remembered the Guru of all who move and are still, the Ancient Man, Narayana, and he surrendered to him in his heart.

*Hinduism.* Srimad Bhagavatam 10.16

aspect. It represents the myth of the hero defeating the demonic forces that is widespread among many cultures: e.g., St. George and the dragon, or Perseus and Andromeda. *Kusa-nagi* is one of the three symbols of Shinto in the possession of the emperor; cf. Kojiki 39.2-3, p. 609.

**Srimad Bhagavatam 10.16:** This passage is as much an expression of Krishna's compassion to his devotees and their utter dependence on him as it is an account of his vanquishing a demon. By surrendering to Krishna, even the serpent Kaliya, in death, attains liberation. In the Bible, the motif of divine punishment of the wicked being meted out in a festal dance is found in Isaiah 30.29-33 and 1 Chronicles 20.20-23. On the submission of the serpent to the Buddha, see Udana 10, pp. 219-20. On the Christian's power over serpents and evil powers, see Luke 10:19-20, p. 220.

## The Revealer of Truth

EVERY RELIGION REGARDS ITS FOUNDER as the revealer of the truth and the true source of the teaching for all to follow. In fact, one of the primary ways in which we encounter the founder is through his teaching. His teaching is based on his own attainments or on the revelation granted him; it is not dependent upon anyone else. It is always distinct from and superior to the beliefs which were prevalent before him; it becomes the standard upon which to measure all ideas that arise after him; and it remains as the continuing wellspring for all later expressions of doctrine.

In this section, we begin with passages which declare the founder's teaching to be the true and only way. As explained in the introduction to this chapter, the fact that several founders have made this claim is not meant to invalidate or relativize their claims; each in his own way stands at the summit of truth unrivaled by anyone else. Every reader must inevitably face this radical claim of authority and uniqueness, first by the founder of his own tradition. We should not think that we are able to arrive at truth merely by the power of our own intellects; rather we should be instructed by those guides who have seen much further than we are able.

Other passages describe the ways in which the founders have arrived at their incomparable teachings. These are mainly two: by receiving divine revelation from a transcendent source, and through extensive striving, study, and meditation. Yet even where the mode of realizing truth is through study and meditation, there is often a revelatory element. Thus the passage from the Vedas indicates that, despite their best efforts to strain and sift, only certain noted sages received the gift of divine speech.

Several passages describe the founders as teachers and bringers of light, even outshining all previous teachers. In the concluding passage, which describes the Buddha as not uttering any words at all, we recognize that these founders do not just preach a truth, but realize it, embody it, and convey it by their example. This brings us back full circle to the opening passages, where Jesus, Krishna, Buddha, and others are not only the revealers of an objective Word but the embodiments of Truth itself.

Jesus said to him, "I am the way, the truth, and the life; no one comes to the Father, but by me."

*Christianity*. John 14.6

I [Krishna] am the goal of the wise man, and I am the way. I am his prosperity. I am his heaven. There is nothing dearer to him than I.

*Hinduism*. Srimad Bhagavatam 11.12

In the sky there is no track. Outside [the Buddha's dispensation] there is no saint. Mankind delights in obstacles. The Tathagatas are free from obstacles.

*Buddhism*. Dhammapada 254

Muhammad is... the Messenger of God and the Seal of the Prophets.

*Islam*. Qur'an 33.40

**Qur'an 33.40:** When a document is sealed, it is complete and there can be no further addition. As 'the Seal of the Prophets' Muhammad is regarded as the last prophet, completing for all time the testimony of God's revelation. For Islam, God's teaching will continue in later ages through reformers, sages, and saints, but no more through a Prophet.

Glory be to Lord Mahavira, the source of the Scripture, supreme Tirthankara, the teacher of the world.

*Jainism*. Nandi Sutra 2

Oh, how great is the divine moral law of the Sage Confucius. Overflowing and illimitable, it gives birth and life to all created things and towers high up to the very heavens. How magnificent it is! How imposing the three hundred principles and three thousand rules of conduct! They await the man who can put the system into practice.

*Confucianism*. Doctrine of the Mean 27

The Eternal thought, "Shall I hide from Abraham what I am going to do, seeing that Abraham is to become a large and powerful nation, and that all nations of the world are to seek bliss like his? I have chosen him that he may charge his sons and his household after him to follow the directions of the Eternal by doing what is good and right."

*Judaism*. Genesis 18.17-19

The Truth has come, and falsehood has vanished away. Surely falsehood is ever certain to vanish.

*Islam*. Qur'an 17.85

Truth is victorious, never untruth.
Truth is the way; truth is the goal of life,
Reached by sages who are free from self-will.

*Hinduism*. Mundaka Upanishad 3.1.6

The best of paths is the Eightfold Path. The best of truths are the Four Noble Truths. Non-attachment is the best of mental states. The best of human beings is the Seeing One.

This is the only Way. There is no other that leads to the purity of insight. You should follow this path, for this is what bewilders Mara.

Embarking upon that path, you will make an end of pain. This path has been declared by me after having learned the way for the removal of thorns.

*Buddhism*. Dhammapada 273-75

The whole world seeks to attain the transcendent state—
Without the true Preceptor's aid it is not attained.
Exhausted with learning, pandits and astrologers
Fall into sects and are lost in delusion.
The transcendent state is attained only on meeting the Preceptor,
Should he of his will show grace.
Brother! Except through the Preceptor the transcendent state may not arise.

*Sikhism*. Adi Granth, Sri Raga, M.3, p. 68

No one has ever seen God; the only Son, who is in the bosom of the father, he has made him known.

*Christianity*. John 1.18

Through Vyasa's grace, I have heard the supreme secret of spiritual union directly from the Lord of Yoga, Krishna himself.

*Hinduism*. Bhagavad Gita 18.75

**Qur'an 17.85:** The truth was revealed to Muhammad.

**Mundaka Upanishad 3.1.6:** In Hinduism, the ancient sages who composed the Vedas while in a state of enlightenment are regarded as the sources of revealed scripture.

**Dhammapada 273-75:** Cf. Lotus Sutra 2, p. 102.

**Sri Raga, M.3:** Cf. Bilaval, M.5, p. 381.

**Bhagavad Gita 18.75:** The Vedas, which were handed down in a long line of oral transmission, are said to have been collected and compiled by the sage Vyasa. Traditionally, Vyasa is also responsible for compiling the Mahabharata, the Srimad Bhagavatam, and numerous other sacred works. Yet ultimately, the sage is transparent to the divine revelation he transmits.

To me, Zarathustra, the prophet and sworn
friend of righteousness,
Lifting my voice with veneration, O Wise One,
May the creator of the mind's force show, as
Good Mind,
His precepts, that they may be the path of my
tongue.

*Zoroastrianism*. Yasna 50.6

Stir not your tongue [O Muhammad] to hasten it [the Qur'an]. Lo! upon Us rests the putting together thereof and the reading thereof. And when We read it to you, follow the reading; then lo! upon Us rests its explanation.

*Islam*. Qur'an 75.16-19

It belongs not to any mortal that God should speak to him, except by revelation, or from behind a veil, or that He should send a messenger and he reveal whatsoever He will, by His leave; surely He is All-high, All-wise. Even so We have revealed to thee [O Muhammad] a Spirit of Our bidding. You knew not what the Book was, nor belief; but We made it a light, whereby We guide whom We will of Our servants. And you, surely you shall guide unto a straight path—the path of God.

*Islam*. Qur'an 42.51-53

Looking all over the world and through all ages, I find no one who has understood My heart. No wonder that you know nothing, for so far I have taught nothing to you. This time I, God, revealing Myself to the fore, teach you all the truth in detail.

*Tenrikyo*. Ofudesaki 1.1-3

When, Lord of our prayer! The first of Speech,
and the foremost,
the sages uttered, giving the unnamed a name,
which was their best, and their most stainless,
then they
with love revealed the divine secret in their
souls.

Where the sages formed the Speech with their
mind,
straining it as they strain flour with the sieve,
therein have friends discovered bonds of
friendship,
whose holy beauty lies hidden in that Speech.

With worship they followed the steps of the
Speech
and found it installed in the hearts of sages.
They acquired it and gave it at many places,
and seven singers intone it together.

There is the man who sees but has not seen
Speech;
there is the man who hears but has not heard
her,
but to another she reveals her lovely form
like a loving wife, finely robed, to her husband.

*Hinduism*. Rig Veda 10.71.1-4

The Lord said to Moses, "Come up to me on the mountain, and wait there, and I will give you the tables of stone, with the law and the commandment, which I have written for their instruction." So Moses rose with his servant Joshua, and Moses went up into the mountain of God.... Now the appearance of the glory of the Lord was like a devouring fire on the top of the mountain in the sight of the people of Israel. And Moses entered the cloud, and went up on the mountain. And Moses was on the mountain forty days and forty nights.

*Judaism*. Exodus 14.12-18

Moses said to Israel, "Know you not with what travail I gained the Torah! What toil, what labor, I endured for its sake. Forty days and forty nights I was with God. I entered among the angels, the Living Creatures, the Seraphim, of whom any one could blast the whole universe in flame. My soul, my blood, I gave for the Torah. As I learnt it in travail, so do you learn it in travail, and as you learn it in travail, so do you teach it in travail."

*Judaism*. Sifre Deuteronomy 131b

Know then, that from time to time a Tathagata is born into the world, a fully Enlightened One, blessed and worthy, abounding in wisdom

**Yasna 50.6:** Cf. Yasna 33.13, p. 383; 45.5, p. 105.
**Rig Veda 10.71.1-4:** *Vac*, divine 'Speech,' is the divine revelation in the Vedas.

and goodness, happy with the knowledge of the worlds, unsurpassed as a guide to erring mortals, a teacher of gods and men, a blessed Buddha. He thoroughly understands this universe, as though he saw it face to face.... The Truth does he proclaim both in its letter and in its spirit, lovely in its origin, lovely in its progress, lovely in its consummation. A higher life does he make known in all its purity and in all its perfection.

*Buddhism.*
Digha Nikaya xiii, Tevijja Sutta

The holy sages were able to survey all the movements under heaven. They contemplated the way in which these movements met and became interrelated, to take their course according to eternal laws. Then they appended judgments, to distinguish between the good fortune and the misfortune indicated.... They speak of the most confused diversities without arousing aversion. They speak of what is most mobile without causing confusion. This comes from the fact that they observed before they spoke and discussed before they moved. Through observation and discussion they perfected the changes and transformations.

*Confucianism.* I Ching,
Great Commentary 1.8.2-4

Above, he [Chuang Tzu] wandered with the Creator, below he made friends with those who have gotten outside of life and death, who know nothing of beginning or end. As for the Source, his grasp of it was broad, expansive, and penetrating; profound, liberal, and unimpeded. As for the Ancestor, he may have said to have turned and accommodated himself to it and to have risen on it to the greatest heights. Nevertheless, in responding to change and expounding on the world of things, he set forth principles that will never cease to be valid, an approach that can never be shuffled off. Veiled and arcane, he is one who has never been completely comprehended.

*Taoism.* Chuang Tzu 33

Behold, there shall be a record kept among you; and in it you [Joseph Smith] shall be called a seer, a translator, a prophet, an apostle of Jesus Christ, an elder of the church through the will of God the Father, and the grace of your Lord Jesus Christ, being inspired of the Holy Ghost to lay its foundation, and to build it up into the most holy faith. Which church was organized and established in the year of your Lord eighteen hundred and thirty, in the fourth month, and on the sixth day of the month which is called April.

Wherefore, meaning the church, you shall give heed unto all his words and commandments which he shall give to you as he receives them, walking in all holiness before me; for his word you shall receive, as if from my own mouth, in all patience and faith. For by doing these things the gates of hell shall not prevail against you; yea, and the Lord God will disperse the powers of darkness from before you, and cause the heavens to shake for your good, and His name's glory.

For thus says the Lord God, "Him have I inspired to move the cause of Zion in mighty power for good, and his diligence I know, and his prayers I have heard."

*Church of Jesus Christ of Latter-day Saints.*
Doctrine and Covenants 21.1-7

Say, "Obey God, and obey the Messenger; then, if you turn away, only upon him rests what is laid on him, and upon you rests what is laid on you. If you obey him, you will be guided. It is only for the Messenger to deliver the manifest Message."

*Islam.* Qur'an 24.54

**I Ching, Great Commentary 1.8.2-4:** This describes the way in which the oracles in the I Ching were discovered, by empirical observation.

**Doctrine and Covenants 21.1-7:** Joseph Smith was a 'translator' of ancient documents—the golden plates of the Book of Mormon and the papyri of Abraham and Moses in the Pearl of Great Price—but not in the modern sense of one who is an expert in languages and strives for literal accuracy. His translation was by the gift of spiritual inspiration, using certain special stones called interpreters and focusing on his mind's inner eye to divine the meaning. Cf. Book of Mormon, Ether 3.21-28, 4.5; Mosiah 8.9-19.

**Qur'an 24.54:** Cf. Qur'an 4.79-80, p. 489.

The Tirthankaras do not forcibly guide one to the good or take one away from the evil. They only preach and open the eyes of the people to the consequences of treading a forbidden path. He who listens to such preaching becomes the Lord not only of men but also of the gods.

*Jainism.* Dharmadasaganin, Upadesamala 448-49

O Prophet, we have sent you as a witness, and good tidings to bear and warning, calling unto God by His leave, and as a light-giving lamp.

*Islam.* Qur'an 33.45-46

I have come as a light into the world, that whoever believes in me may not remain in darkness. If anyone hears my sayings and does not keep them, I do not judge him; for I did not come to judge the world but to save the world. He who rejects me and does not receive my sayings has a judge; the word that I have spoken will be his judge on the last day. For I have not spoken on my own authority; the Father who sent me has himself given me commandment what to say and what to speak. And I know that his commandment is eternal life.

*Christianity.* John 12.46-50

The glowworm shines so long as the light-bringer has not arisen. But when the shining one has come up, its light is quenched, it glows no longer. Such is the shining of the sectarians. So long as the rightly awakened ones arise not in the world, the sophists get no light, nor do their followers, and those of wrong views cannot be released from Ill.

*Buddhism.* Udana 73

Now if the dispensation of death, carved in letters on stone, came with such splendor that the Israelites could not look on Moses' face because of its brightness, fading as this was, will not the dispensation of the Spirit be attended with greater splendor? For if there was splendor in the dispensation of condemnation, the dispensation of righteousness must far exceed it in splendor. Indeed, in this case, what once had splendor has come to have no splendor at all, because of the splendor that surpasses it.... Yes, to this day, whenever Moses is read, a veil lies over their minds; but when a man turns to the Lord, the veil is removed.

*Christianity.* 2 Corinthians 3.7-16

Mahamati said, "It is said by the Blessed One that from the night of the Enlightenment till the night of the Parinirvana [at his death], the Tathagata has not uttered even a word, nor will he ever utter a word. According to what deeper sense is that not-speaking the Buddha's speaking?"

The Blessed One replied, "By reason of two things of the deeper sense, Mahamati, this statement is made: the truth of self-realization and an eternally-abiding reality.... Of what deeper sense is the truth of self-realization? What has been realized by the Tathagatas, that is my own realization, in which there is neither decreasing nor increasing; for the realm of self-realization is free from words and discriminations, having nothing to do with dualistic ways of speaking.

"What is meant by an eternally-abiding reality? The ancient road of reality has been there all the time, like gold, silver, or pearl preserved

**Upadesamala 448-49:** See Ratnakarandasravakacara 7-10, p. 456. On the hearer attaining lordship, cf. Dhammapada 181, p. 218. On individual responsibility to receive the message, compare Sutta Nipata 1063-64, p. 489.

**Qur'an 33.45-46:** Cf. Bilaval, M.5, p. 381.

**John 12.46-60:** Cf. Matthew 7.24-27, p. 106.

**2 Corinthians 3.7-16:** Cf. Galatians 3.10-13, 21-26, p. 108. Yet there is also continuity between the new revelation and the old; see Matthew 5.17-18, p. 474. Cf. Book of Certitude, 33-41, p. 779.

in the mine; the substance of truth abides forever, whether the Tathagata appears in the world or not.... What has been realized by myself and other Tathagatas is this reality, the eternally-abiding reality, the self-regulating reality; the suchness of things, the realness of things, the truth itself. For this reason it is stated by me that from the night of the Tathagata's Enlightenment till the night of his entrance into Nirvana, he has not in the meantime uttered, nor ever will utter, one word."

*Buddhism.* Lankavatara Sutra 61

❖

## *The Man for Others*

THE FOUNDER IS THE MAN FOR OTHERS, who gives his life and substance to save them. He manifests the quality of divine compassion and becomes the savior of humanity. The diverse passages in this section describe how each of the founders showed selfless love for others. Some texts recount his compassionate deeds of serving the people and giving of his means; some describe his self-sacrifice and bearing others' burdens; some describe his earnest efforts to preach and impart wisdom to lead the ignorant to enlightenment; and some describe how the founder put himself at risk in order to overcome ignorance and enmity.

We sent you [O Muhammad] not save as a mercy for the peoples.

*Islam.* Qur'an 21.107

Behold the Lamb of God, who takes away the sin of the world!

*Christianity.* John 1.29

This man, the holy one through righteousness,
Holds in his spirit the force which heals existence,
Beneficent unto all, as a sworn friend,
O Wise One.

*Zoroastrianism.* Yasna 44.2

The Tathagata with unimpeded compassion pities the three worlds. The reason the Tathagata appeared in this world is to propagate the Buddha's teachings, to save all sentient beings, and to bestow true benefit upon them.

*Buddhism.* Larger Sukhavativyuha Sutra 2

The World-honored One is very rare;
Only with difficulty can he be encountered.
Fully endowed with incalculable merits,
He can rescue and preserve all.
The great teacher of gods and men,

**Lankavatara Sutra 61:** The worldless nature of the Buddha's words is well captured by the Zen story of how the Elder Kashyapa inherited the Dharma, Mumonkan 6, p. 585. Cf. Lankavatara Sutra 76, p. 573; Diamond Sutra 21, p. 572; Mulamadhyamaka Karika 24.8-12, pp. 719-20.

**Qur'an 21.107:** See Hadith of Ibn Sa'd, p. 464.

**John 1.29:** Cf. Galatians 2.20, p. 639; Romans 3.23-25, p. 360; John 3.16, p. 360.

**Yasna 44.2:** 'This man' is Zarathustra.

**Larger Sukhavativyuha Sutra 2:** Cf. Mahaparinirvana Sutra 575-76, p. 375n.

He takes pity on the world,
And living beings in the ten directions
All everywhere receive his favors.

*Buddhism*. Lotus Sutra 7

When evil prevailed upon earth, when truth had been forgotten and life had become a sinful burden to mankind, there went out a prayer to God entreating him to come down upon the earth as a Savior of humanity. The omniscient, omnipresent Lord knew the sufferings of mankind, and out of his great and all-consuming love for his children wished to lift the veil of ignorance which covered their sight—to be born as man, Krishna, in order to show them once more how to ascend toward himself.

*Hinduism*. Srimad Bhagavatam 10

The Tirthankara or Supreme Lord is adorable, endowed with omniscience, uncontaminated by human infirmities, immaculate and pure, devoid of any desire whatsoever, without beginning, middle, or end, and uniquely benevolent—all these are the characteristics of the Supreme Lord. Besides, without any selfish design, he preaches for the benefit of the unemancipated and suffering beings. True scripture, which flows spontaneously out of the Supreme Lord, is irrefutable, is salutary for the well-being of all kinds of beings, is capable of undermining the perverse path, and reveals the objective nature of things.

*Jainism*. Samantabhadra, Ratnakarandasravakacara 7-10

Confucius said, "From the very poorest upwards—beginning even with the man who could bring no better present than a bundle of dried flesh—none has ever come to me without receiving instruction."

*Confucianism*. Analects 7.7

And as he sat at table in the house, behold, many tax collectors and sinners came and sat down with Jesus and his disciples. And when the Pharisees saw this, they said to his disciples, "Why does your teacher eat with tax collectors and sinners?" But when he heard it, he said, "Those who are well have no need of a physician, but those who are sick. Go and learn what this means, 'I desire mercy, and not sacrifice.' For I came not to call the righteous, but sinners."

*Christianity*. Matthew 9.10-13

Seated under a palm tree the Holy One pondered, "The profound wisdom so hard to be understood is now known by me. These sin-defiled worlds understand not this most excellent Law, and the unenlightened shamelessly censure both me and my wisdom. Shall I proclaim this Law? It is only produced by knowledge; having attained it thus in my lonely pondering, do I feel strong enough to deliver the world?" Having remembered all that he had heard before, he again pondered; and resolved, "I will explain it for the sake of delivering the world."

*Buddhism*. Ashvaghosha, Buddhacarita 15.79-82

The apostles returned to Jesus... and he said to them, "Come away by yourselves to a lonely place, and rest a while." For many were coming

**Lotus Sutra 7:** The Lotus Sutra is full of parables depicting the Buddha's compassion. See the Parable of the Prodigal Son, Lotus Sutra 4, pp. 363-65.; the Parable of the Good Physician, Lotus Sutra 16, p. 721; and the Parable of the Burning House, Lotus Sutra 3, p. 93n.; cf. Lotus Sutra 4, p. 557.

**Srimad Bhagavatam 10:** The avatar is a manifestation of divine grace. Cf. Bhagavad Gita 4.7-8, p. 474; Ramayana, Bala Kanda 15, p. 448.

**Matthew 9.10-13:** This expresses Jesus' preference for sinners and outcasts. He was critical of a society which sharply distinguished the "good" and upright people from sinners and those, like tax-collectors, whom society scorned. He taught that God's mercy embraces even the meanest and most sinful of His creatures; compare Tannisho, p. 542.

**Buddhacarita 15.79-82:** This episode comes shortly after Buddha won enlightenment but prior to his first sermon at Varanasi.

and going, and they had no leisure even to eat. And they went away in the boat to a lonely place by themselves. Now many saw them going, and knew them, and they ran there on foot from all the towns, and got there ahead of them. As he landed he saw a great throng, and he had compassion on them, because they were like sheep without a shepherd; and he began to teach them many things. And when it grew late, his disciples came to him and said, "This is a lonely place, and the hour is now late; send them away, to go into the country and villages round about and buy themselves something to eat." But he answered them, "You give them something to eat." And the disciples said to him, "Shall we go and buy two hundred denarii worth of bread, and give it to them to eat?" And he said to them, "How many loaves have you? Go and see." And when they had found out, they said, "Five, and two fish." Then he commanded them all to sit down by companies upon the green grass. So they sat down in groups, by hundreds and by fifties. And taking the five loaves and two fish he looked up to heaven, and blessed, and broke the loaves, and gave them to the disciples to set before the people; and he divided the two fish among them all. And they all ate and were satisfied. And they took up twelve baskets full of broken pieces and of the fish. And those who ate the loaves were five thousand men.

*Christianity*. Mark 6.30-44:
Miracle of the Loaves and the Fishes

If, after my obtaining Buddhahood, all the beings in the ten quarters who, with sincerity of heart hold faith and wish to be reborn in my country, repeating my name perhaps ten times, are not so born, may I not achieve the highest enlightenment. Excluded only are those who have committed the five deadly sins and those who have abused the true Dharma.

*Buddhism*.
Larger Sukhavativyuha Sutra 8.18

I am the good shepherd. The good shepherd lays down his life for his sheep. He who is a hireling and not a shepherd, whose own the sheep are not, sees the wolf coming and leaves the sheep and flees; and the wolf snatches them and scatters them. He flees because he is a hireling and cares nothing for the sheep. I am the good shepherd; I know my own and my own know me, as the Father knows me and I know the Father; and I lay down my life for the sheep. And I have other sheep, that are not of this fold; I must bring them also, and they will heed my voice. So there shall be one flock, one shepherd.

*Christianity*. John 10.11-16

Who has believed what we have heard?
And to whom has the arm of the Lord been
 revealed?
For he grew up like a pale shoot,
like a root out of dry ground;
he had no form or comeliness that we should
 look at him,

**Mark 6.30-44:** While tradition regards the feeding of the five thousand as a supernatural miracle, some scholars explain it by saying that when Jesus brought out the five loaves and two fish to share with the multitudes, his generosity led many others in the audience to bring out the food which they had carried with them for the journey and share it with their fellows. As the spirit of generosity multiplied, the people found that they had more than enough food. This episode from Jesus' life is reflected in the fellowship of the Christian common meal. Other manifestations of Jesus' mercy can be found in his healings; see Mark 5.24-34, p. 374-75.

**Larger Sukhavativyuha Sutra 8.18:** The Eighteenth Vow of the Amitabha Buddha—to effect universal salvation before he sets foot in Nirvana—is at the heart of Pure Land Buddhism. It represents the highest degree of the Buddha's compassion. At the same time, one who relies on this vow and its power can avoid the traps of self-dependence and striving, which only bind one to samsara. Striving on the path is useless; rather it is through faith in the power of this vow, called by Shinran the Power of Another, that one can have confidence in salvation; see Tannisho, p. 542. See Larger Sukhavativyuha Sutra 9.1-5, p. 368; compare Galatians 3.21-22, p. 108. On the 'five deadly sins,' see p. 123n.

and no beauty that we should desire him.
He was despised and rejected by men;
a man of sorrows, and acquainted with grief;
and as one who from whom men hide their faces
he was despised, and we esteemed him not.

Surely he has borne our griefs
and carried our sorrows;
yet we esteemed him stricken,
smitten by God, and afflicted.
But he was wounded for our transgressions,
he was bruised for our iniquities;
upon him was the chastisement that made us whole,
and with his stripes we are healed.
All we like sheep have gone astray;
we have turned every one to his own way;
and the Lord has laid upon him
the iniquity of us all.

He was oppressed, and he was afflicted,
yet he opened not his mouth;
like a lamb that is led to the slaughter,
and like a sheep that is before its shearers is dumb,
so he opened not his mouth.
Arrested and convicted, he was taken away;
and as for his generation, who considered
that he was cut off out of the land of the living,
stricken for the transgression of my people?
And they made his grave with the wicked,
and his tomb with demons,
although he had done no violence,
and there was no deceit in his mouth.

Yet it was the will of the Lord to bruise him;
he has put him to grief;
when he makes himself an offering for sin,
he shall see his offspring, he shall prolong his days;
the will of the Lord shall prosper in his hand;
he shall see the fruit of the travail of his soul and be satisfied;
by his knowledge shall the righteous one, my servant,
make many to be accounted righteous;
and he shall bear their iniquities.
Therefore I will divide him a portion with the great,
and he shall divide the spoil with the strong;
because he poured out his soul to death,
and was be numbered with the transgressors;
yet he bore the sin of many,
and made intercession for the transgressors.

*Judaism* and *Christianity*. Isaiah 53.1-12

A man should share in the distress of the community, for so we find that Moses, our teacher, shared in the distress of the community.

*Judaism*. Talmud, Taanit 11a

At the end of forty days and forty nights the Lord gave me [Moses] the two tables of stone, the tables of the covenant. Then the Lord said to me, "Arise, go down quickly from here; for your people whom you have brought from Egypt have acted corruptly; they have turned aside quickly out of the way which I commanded them; they have made themselves a molten image.... Let me alone, that I may destroy them and blot out their name from under heaven; and I will make of you a nation mightier and greater than they."

So I turned and came down from the mountain, and the mountain was burning with fire; and the two tables of the covenant were in my two hands. And I looked, and behold, you had sinned against the Lord your God; you had

**Isaiah 53.1-12:** This is the famous prophecy of the Suffering Servant. It contains imagery of a man who is stricken with illness, a leper, and an innocent man who is convicted and executed. Yet in this man of sorrows is revealed the power and mercy of God. Though he makes himself an offering, suffering to atone for the sins of others, in the end he is vindicated by God. For Christianity, this passage is regarded as a prophecy which is fulfilled in the suffering life of Jesus Christ; see Luke 22-23, pp. 428-30. Rabbinic Judaism similarly applies these verses to the suffering of the Messiah to come; see Pesikta Rabbati 162b-63a, pp. 784-85. More commonly, Jews interpret the servant to be Israel itself, or the faithful in Israel. In either interpretation, the Servant's suffering brings redemption for all humanity. In fact, some Jews and Christians have come to understand their relatedness as peoples of God through their vocations to fulfill the role of suffering servant. Cf. Isaiah 42.1-4, p. 368, on the Servant as a light to the nations, where the same range of interpretations applies.

made yourselves a molten calf; you had turned aside quickly from the way which the Lord had commanded you. So I took hold of the two tables, and cast them out of my two hands, and broke them before your eyes. Then I lay prostrate before the Lord as before, forty days and forty nights; I neither ate bread nor drank water, because of all the sin which you have committed… because the Lord had said that he would destroy you. And I prayed to the Lord, "O Lord God, destroy not your people and your heritage, whom you have redeemed through your greatness, whom you have brought out of Egypt with a mighty hand. Remember your servants, Abraham, Isaac, and Jacob; do not regard the stubbornness of this people, or their wickedness, or their sin, lest the land from which you brought us say, 'Because the Lord was not able to bring them into the land which he promised them, and because he hated them, he has brought them out to slay them in the wilderness.' For they are your people and your heritage, whom you brought out by your great power and by your outstretched arm."

*Judaism.* Deuteronomy 9.11-29

T'ang said, "I, Lu, the little one, dare to offer a black bull and to make this declaration before the great God. I dare not pardon those who have transgressed. I shall present thy servants as they are so that the choice rests with thee alone. If I transgress, let not the ten thousand states suffer because of me; but if the ten thousand states transgress, the guilt is mine alone."

*Confucianism.* Analects 20.1.3

My Lord! Others have fallen back in showing compassion to their benefactors as you have shown compassion even to your malefactors. All this is unparalleled.

*Jainism.* Vitaragastava 14.5

We, truly, have come for your sakes, and have borne the misfortunes of the world for your salvation. Do you flee the one [Baha'u'llah] who has sacrificed his life that you may be quickened?… Do you imagine that he seeks his own interests, when he has, at all times, been threatened by the swords of the enemies; or that he seeks the vanities of the world, after he has been imprisoned in the most desolate of cities?…

Verily, he has consented to be sorely abased that you may attain glory, and yet, you are disporting yourselves in the vale of heedlessness. He, in truth, lives in the most desolate of abodes for your sakes, while you dwell in your palaces.

*Baha'i Faith.* Tablets of Baha'u'llah Revealed after the Kitab-i-Aqdas

Now Esau hated Jacob because of the blessing with which his father had blessed him, and Esau said to himself, "The days of mourning for my father are approaching; then I will kill my brother Jacob." But the words of Esau her older son were told to Rebekah; so she sent and called Jacob her younger son, and said to him, "Behold, your brother Esau comforts himself by planning to kill you. Now therefore, my son, obey my voice; arise, flee to Laban my brother in Haran, and stay with him a while, until your brother's fury turns away."…

[After twenty years with Laban, Jacob arose, and] sent messengers before him to Esau his brother in the land of Seir, the country of Edom, instructing them, "Thus you shall say to my lord Esau, 'Thus says your servant Jacob, "I have sojourned with Laban, and stayed until now; and I have oxen, asses, flocks, menservants, and maidservants; and I have sent to tell my lord, in order that I may find favor in your sight."'"

And the messengers returned to Jacob, saying, "We came to your brother Esau, and he is coming to meet you, and four hundred men with him." Then Jacob was greatly afraid and distressed; and he divided the people that were

**Deuteronomy 9.11-29:** Cf. Pesikta Rabbati 32b-33a, p. 561. For an example of Muhammad's intercession on behalf of the people, see the Hadith of Bukhari, p. 561, describing his Night Journey, where he bargains with God to reduce the number of statutory prayers. Cf. Hadith of Bukhari, p. 464.

**Vitaragastava 14.5:** On the Buddha's compassion for his enemies, see Mahaparinirvana Sutra 575-76, p. 375n.

with him, and the flocks and herds and camels, into two companies, thinking, "If Esau comes to the one company and destroys it, then the company which is left will escape."

And Jacob said, "O God of my father Abraham and God of my father Isaac, O Lord who said to me, 'Return to your own country and to your kindred, and I will do you good,' I am not worthy of the least of all the steadfast love and all the faithfulness which you have shown to your servant, for with only my staff I crossed this Jordan; and now I have become two companies. Deliver me, I pray, from the hand of my brother, from the hand of Esau, for I fear him, lest he come and slay us all, the mothers with the children. But you said, 'I will do you good, and make your descendants as the sand of the sea, which cannot be numbered for multitude.'"

So he lodged there that night, and took from what he had with him a present for his brother Esau, two hundred she-goats and twenty he-goats, two hundred ewes and twenty rams, thirty milch camels and their colts, forty cows and ten bulls, twenty she-asses and ten he-asses. These he delivered into the hand of his servants, every drove by itself, and said to his servants, "Pass on before me, and put a space between drove and drove." He instructed the foremost, "When Esau my brother meets you, and asks you, 'To whom do you belong? Where are you going? And whose are these before you?' then you shall say, 'They belong to your servant Jacob; they are a present sent to my lord Esau; and moreover he is behind us.'" He likewise instructed the second and the third and all who followed the droves, "You shall say the same thing to Esau when you meet him, and you shall say, 'Moreover your servant Jacob is behind us.'" For he thought, "I may appease him with the present that goes before me, and afterwards I shall see his face; perhaps he will accept me."...

And Jacob lifted up his eyes and looked, and behold, Esau was coming, and four hundred men with him. So he divided his children among Leah and Rachel and the two maids. He put the maids with their children in front, then Leah with her children, and Rachel and Joseph last of all. He himself went on before them, bowing himself to the ground seven times, until he came near to his brother.

But Esau ran to meet him, and embraced him, and fell on his neck and kissed him, and they wept. And when Esau raised his eyes and saw the women and children, he said, "Who are these with you?" Jacob said, "The children whom God has graciously given your servant." Then the maids drew near, they and their children, and bowed down; Leah likewise and her children drew near and bowed down; and last Joseph and Rachel drew near, and they bowed down. Esau said, "What do you mean by all this company which I met?" Jacob answered, "To find favor in the sight of my lord." But Esau said, "I have enough, my brother, keep what you have for yourself." Jacob said, "No, I pray you, if I have found favor in your sight, then accept my present from my hand; for truly to see your face is like seeing the face of God, with such favor have you received me."

*Judaism* and *Christianity*.
Genesis 27.41-44; 32.3-20; 33.1-10

❖

**Genesis 27-33:** Cf. Matthew 5.44, p. 705; Tosefta, Baba Metzia 2.26, p. 706, and related passages.

## *The Living Presence*

BESIDES THE INCOMPARABLE ACTS OF CHARITY which the founders, during their lifetime, did to save and enlighten humanity, in every age the founder abides as a living presence. Thus, according to the Christian Gospels, Jesus abides in the hearts of all believers and has sent the Holy Spirit to enliven and instill God's love within them. The Lotus Sutra declares that the Buddha is eternally manifest and is forever saving living beings. In the traditions of the Sunnah, Muhammad is ever beside the believers; he also intercedes on their behalf before the throne of God. The living presence of the founder in the hearts of believers is an experience of personal mystical union—"I am in my Father, and you in me, and I in you"—that is comparable to the impersonal mystical experience of *The Unitive State*, pp. 414-17.

Lo, I am with you always, even to the close of the age.

*Christianity*. Matthew 28.20

The Prophet is closer to the believers than their own selves, and his wives are their mothers.

*Islam*. Qur'an 33.6

Verily I am beside you, as a father is beside his children.

*Islam*. Hadith of Abu Dawud

Be aware of me always, adore me, make every act an offering to me, and you shall come to me; this I [Krishna] promise, for you are dear to me. Abandon all supports and look to me for protection. I shall purify you from the sins of the past; do not grieve.

*Hinduism*. Bhagavad Gita 18.65-66

[Jesus declared,] "Come to me, all who labor and are heavy laden, and I will give you rest. Take my yoke upon you, and learn from me; for I am gentle and lowly in heart, and you will find rest for your souls. For my yoke is easy, and my burden is light."

*Christianity*. Matthew 11.28-30

I am the Tathagata, the Worshipful, the All-wise, the Perfectly Enlightened in Conduct, the Well-departed, the Understander of the World, the Peerless Leader, the Controller, the Teacher of Gods and Men, the Buddha, the World-honored One. Those who have not yet been saved, I cause to be saved; those who have not yet been set free, to be set free; those who have not yet been comforted, to be comforted; those who have not yet obtained Nirvana, to obtain Nirvana. I know the present world and the world to come as they really are. I am the All-knowing, the All-seeing, the Knower of the Way, the Opener of the Way, the Preacher of the Way. Come to me, all you gods, men, and demons, to hear the Law.

*Buddhism*. Lotus Sutra 5

**Matthew 28.20:** This is spoken by the resurrected Jesus as he commissions his disciples to go out and teach all nations.

**Qur'an 33.6:** Though this passage was uttered of the historical Muhammad, it is often taken to signify a living spiritual relationship which believers of any age may have with the Prophet and his family; thus the following hadith.

**Matthew 11.28-30:** Cf. Revelation 3.20, p. 493.

If you love me, you will keep my commandments. And I will pray to the Father, and he will give you another Counselor, to be with you forever, even the Spirit of Truth, whom the world cannot receive, because it neither sees him nor knows him; you know him, for he dwells with you, and will be in you.

I will not leave you desolate; I will come to you. Yet a little while, and the world will see me no more, but you will see me; because I live, you will live also. In that day you will know that I am in my Father, and you in me, and I in you. He who has my commandments and keeps them, he it is who loves me; and he who loves me will be loved by my Father, and I will love him and manifest myself to him.

*Christianity*. John 14.15-21

He it is who sent down peace of reassurance into the hearts of the believers, that they might add faith to their faith.

*Islam*. Qur'an 48.4

Says Nanak, The Master is a tree of contentment and forbearance;
Righteousness its flower, enlightenment the fruit.
This tree by joy in God keeps ever fresh and green;
By practice of meditation is it ripened.
With joy in the Lord is it consumed,
By such as dispense the supreme charity of selfless action.

*Sikhism*. Adi Granth, Var Majh, M.1, p. 147

Abide in me, and I in you. As the branch cannot bear fruit by itself, unless it abides in the vine, neither can you, unless you abide in me. I am the vine, you are the branches. He who abides in me, and I in him, he it is that bears much fruit, for apart from me you can do nothing. If a man does not abide in me, he is cast forth as a branch and withers; and the branches are gathered, thrown into the fire and burned. If you abide in me, and my words abide in you, ask whatever you will, and it shall be done for you. By this my Father is glorified, that you bear much fruit, and so prove to be my disciples. As the Father has loved me, so have I loved you; abide in my love. If you keep my commandments, you will abide in my love, just as I have kept my Father's commandments and abide in his love. These things I have spoken to you, that my joy may be in you, and that your joy may be full.

*Christianity*. John 15.4-11

Every Buddha Tathagata is one whose [spiritual] body is the Principle of Nature (*Dharmadhatukaya*), so that he may enter into the mind of any being. Consequently, when you have perceived Buddha, it is indeed that mind of yours that possesses those thirty-two signs of perfection and eighty minor marks of excellence [which you see in Buddha]. In fine, it is your mind that becomes Buddha, nay, it is your mind that is indeed Buddha. The ocean of true and universal knowledge of all the Buddhas derives its source from one's own mind and thought. Therefore you should apply your thought with an undivided attention to a careful meditation on that Buddha Tathagata, Arhat, the Holy and Fully Enlightened One.

*Buddhism*. Meditation on Buddha Amitayus 17

**John 14.15-21:** 'Counselor,' and 'Spirit of Truth' are names for the Holy Spirit, which descended upon the disciples at Pentecost and which continues to infuse the hearts of sincere Christians. At the same time, the Counselor is identified with Jesus Christ, who comes to dwell with the faithful. Jesus is also one with the Father. Thus, according to the doctrine of the Trinity, the Father, the Son, and the Holy Spirit are one. On the Spirit abiding in us, cf. Romans 8.9-17, p. 407.

**Var Majh, M.1:** This and the following passage express the image of the founder as a Tree of Life. For more on this image, see Psalm 1:1-3, p. 106; Qur'an 14.24-27, p. 106, and Revelation 22.1-5, pp. 794-95.

**John 15.4-11:** Cf. Romans 6.3-11, pp. 611-12.

**Meditation on Buddha Amitayus 17:** Cf. Lion's Roar of Queen Srimala 5, p. 466; Garland Sutra 37, p. 62; Sutra of Hui Neng 2, p. 381.

May the Lord of Lords [Mahavira], whom all the hosts of saints keep in mind, all the rulers of men and angels praise, and all the scriptures—Vedas, Puranas, and Shastras—extol, make my heart his abode.

May the Lord of Lords, who is of the nature of perception, cognition, and bliss, is free from all mundane imperfections, is comprehensible through concentrated contemplation, and is known as the Highest Self, be enshrined in my heart.

May the Lord of Lords, who cuts asunder the net of worldly afflictions and sorrows, perceives the innermost secrets of the universe, and is the pure introvert Self capable of being visualized by the yogins, reside in my heart.

May the Lord of Lords, who is the expounder of the path of liberation, is beyond the reach of the miseries like those of birth and death, is the seer of the three worlds, and is bodiless and faultless, make my heart his abode.

May the Lord of Lords, who is free from all blemishes like attachment and aversion which hold in tight bondage all embodied beings, who has no need of sense organs, is knowledge itself and eternally independent, be enshrined in my heart.

May the Lord of Lords, whose cognition pervades all the objects in the cosmos, who has attained liberation and perfection, is fully enlightened and absolutely free from the bondage of karma, and whose contemplation destroys all spiritual aberrations, reside in my heart.

*Jainism.* Samayika Patha

In order to save all creatures,
I expediently speak of Nirvana,
Yet truly I am not extinct,
But ever here preaching the Law.
I ever remain in this world,
In supernatural power,
So that all perverted creatures
Fail to see me, though near,
Looking on me as extinct,
Everywhere worshipping my relics,
Cherishing desire for goodness
And thirsting with aspiration.
When all creatures have submitted,
Are upright, and gentle in mind,
Wholeheartedly looking for Buddha,
Not caring for their own lives,
Then I with all the Sangha
On the Spirit Vulture Peak appear,
And then I tell all creatures
That I exist here, forever undying,
By means of expedients revealing
Myself as dead, yet not dead.
If in other regions there are beings,
Reverent and joyful in faith,
Again I am in their midst
To preach the supreme Law.
You, not hearing of this,
Only say I am extinct.
I, beholding all living creatures
Sunk in the sea of suffering,
At first do not show myself,
But set them expectant and thirsting,
Then, when their hearts are longing,
I appear to preach the Law.
In supernatural power,
Through kalpas numberless,
On the Spirit Vulture Peak am I,
And in other dwelling places.

*Buddhism.* Lotus Sutra 16

I am the first and the last, and the living one; I died, and behold I am alive for evermore, and I have the keys to Death and Hades.

*Christianity.* Revelation 1.18

Who shall bring any charge against God's elect? It is God who justifies; who is to condemn? Is it Christ Jesus, who died, yes, who was raised from the dead, who is at the right hand of God, who indeed intercedes for us?

*Christianity.* Romans 8.33-34

Why [on Rosh Hashanah] do we blow on a ram's horn? The Holy One said, "Sound before

**Samayika Patha:** On these recitations, see p. 604n.
**Lotus Sutra 16:** Cf. Lotus Sutra 16, the prose version, p. 77.
**Revelation 1.18:** Cf. 1 Corinthians 15.21-22, p. 388.

me a ram's horn so that I may remember on your behalf the binding of Isaac the son of Abraham, and account it to you as if you had bound yourselves before me.

*Judaism.* Talmud, Rosh Hashanah 16a

My life is a mercy and a blessing for you: in my presence you speak, and an answer is given you. When I die my death will be a mercy and a blessing for you: After death, your deeds will be sent to me and I will look at them: If you worked righteousness, I will praise God for this. If you worked evil, I will ask God that you be forgiven.

*Islam.* Hadith of Ibn Sa'd

Likewise the Spirit helps us in our weakness; for we do not know how to pray as we ought, but the Spirit himself intercedes for us with sighs too deep for words. And he who searches the hearts of men knows what is the mind of the Spirit, because the Spirit intercedes for the saints according to the will of God.

*Christianity.* Romans 8.26-27

According to Anas, the Prophet said, "At the Judgment Day the believers will assemble and will say, 'Let us ask someone to intercede for us.' They will go and find Adam and say to him, 'You are the father of mankind; God has created you with His hand, He has taught the angels to kneel before you, and He has taught you the names of all things. Intercede to the Lord on our behalf in order that He may deliver us from our present predicament.' He will reply, 'I am not the one you are needing. Go and find Noah; he is the first messenger whom God sent to mankind.' They will find Noah, and he will say, 'I am not the one you need.' He will remind them that he asked the Lord about things of which he could have no knowledge, and he would be ashamed to intercede for them. 'Go,' he will say to them, 'and find the Friend of the Merciful [Abraham].' They will do as they are bid, and the latter will say, 'Go and ask Moses, this worshipper to whom God has addressed a word and to whom He has given the Torah.' They will go and find Moses, and he will say to them, 'I am not he whom you need.' He will tell them that he killed a man who was not guilty, and that he is ashamed before his Lord. Then he arranges for them to approach Jesus, the worshipper of God and His messenger, the Word of God and the Spirit of God. But Jesus will say to them, 'I am not the one whom you need; go and find Muhammad (God bless and preserve him!); he is the servant for whom God has pardoned all faults, past and future.'

"Then they will come to me; I shall go to the Lord and ask Him if He will listen to me. He will grant me my request, and when I see Him, I shall fall down on my knees and remain there as long as it pleases Him. Then He will say to me, 'Look up; ask and you shall receive; speak and you will be heard; intercede and your intercession will be granted.' Then I shall raise my head; I shall praise the Lord, following the formula which He will teach me; then I shall intercede. The Eternal One will show me a group of people, for whom I shall gain access into Paradise. This done, I shall return to the Lord, and when I have seen Him, under the same condition as before, I shall intercede afresh. He will show me a second group, for whom I shall gain access to Paradise. Then I shall do the same a third and a fourth time, and shall say, 'There are no more for hell except those whom the Qur'an has condemned to it, and who must live in it forever.'"

*Islam.* Hadith of Bukhari

**Rosh Hashanah 16a:** Rosh Hashanah is the Jewish New Year; it is invoked by sounding the ram's horn. On the binding of Isaac, see Genesis 22, p. 438.

**Romans 8.26-27:** The Holy Spirit enters the hearts of believers and helps them in their weakness, sanctifying them by transforming their minds into the image of the Son, the mind of Christ. The Spirit leads people to testify to Jesus Christ: see 1 Corinthians 12.1-3, p. 265; Matthew 10.19-20, pp. 586-87. The Spirit is liberating: see John 3.8, p. 379. For another conception of the Holy Spirit as all God-centered, loving spiritual influences, see Sun Myung Moon, 5-1-81, p. 257.

# The Person and Character of the Founder

THIS SECTION CONTAINS PASSAGES which describe either the divinity of the founder as a manifestation of God, or the humanity of the founder as a person with a unique and striking personality. In some religions the founder, as the human being who is completely one with Absolute Reality, is described as divine. The concurrence of humanity and divinity in a single person is a mystery which is described in various ways: Christology is the theological and doctrinal reflection by which Jesus is characterized as fully God and fully man. Jainism holds that the Tirthankara has realized the state of *paramatman*, or perfected soul, who alone is divine and absolute. Hinduism understands the concurrence of divinity and humanity through the doctrines of the *Avatar* and the indwelling of divinity in the soul of the Sage.

Jesus Christ is also recognized as the incarnation of the Second Person of the Trinity: Three persons—Father, Son, and Holy Spirit—united and manifesting the creative, redemptive, and sanctifying activity of God in the world. The comparable Mahayana Buddhist doctrine of the *Trikaya*, the Buddha's three bodies, holds at one the *Dharmakaya*, Eternal Buddha, which is the substance of Enlightenment and Truth itself; the *Sambhogakaya*, the compassion and wisdom of the Buddha by which people are led to salvation; and the *Nirmanakaya*, the bodily manifestations of the Buddha, the latest being the historical Siddhartha Gautama. The Hindu Trinity of Brahma, Vishnu, and Shiva, the Creator, Preserver, and Destroyer, is not strictly comparable; it deals with a three-fold manifestation of the Godhead quite apart from any incarnation.[1]

In the orthodox traditions of Islam, Judaism, Theravada Buddhism, and Confucianism, on the other hand, the founder is a human being and emphatically distinct from deity. The majority of traditions about the founder in these religions describe his character in very human terms, in order to avoid any attempt to make him into a god. And yet, mystical and popular strands in many of these religions cherish traditions about the founder's person that recognize in him qualities like unto Ultimate Reality.

## The Divine Person

Whoever sees me [Muhammad] has seen God.
*Islam.* Hadith of Bukhari and Muslim

He who sees the Norm, he sees me; he who sees me, he sees the Norm.
*Buddhism.* Samyutta Nikaya iii.120

Do you not know me, Philip? He who has seen me has seen the Father; how can you say, "Show us the Father?" Do you not believe that I am in the Father and the Father in me?
*Christianity.* John 14.9-10

Says Nanak, "The Master is the Lord's image;
The Lord in the Master pervasive—
Brother! between these lies no difference."
*Sikhism.* Adi Granth, Asa Chhant, M.4, p. 442

**Samyutta Nikaya iii.120:** 'Norm,' that is, the Dhamma.

[1] See Vishnu Purana 1, p. 53.

Glory be to Lord Mahavira, in whose mirror of enlightenment are reflected vividly the terrestrial and the extra-terrestrial, and whose complexion resembles the interior of a blooming lotus and burnished gold.

*Jainism*. Virasena, Jayadhavala 3

In the beginning was the Word, and the Word was with God, and the Word was God. He was in the beginning with God; all things were made through him, and without him was not anything made that was made. In him was life, and the life was the light of men.... And the Word became flesh and dwelt among us, full of grace and truth; we have beheld his glory, glory as of the only Son of the Father.

*Christianity*. John 1.1-4, 14

The grace of the Lord Jesus Christ and the love of God and the fellowship of the Holy Spirit be with you all.

*Christianity*. 2 Corinthians 13.14

The supreme, complete enlightenment is the realm of Nirvana. The realm of Nirvana is the Dharma-body of the Tathagata [the Eternal Buddha]. Attaining the absolute Dharma-body is [attaining] the absolute One Vehicle. The Tathagata is not different from the Dharma-body. The Tathagata is identical with the Dharma-body.... The Absolute is unlimited and unceasing.

O Lord, the Tathagata, who is not limited by time... is without limitation. His great compassion also is unlimited, bringing peace and comfort to the world. His unlimited great compassion brings unlimited peace and comfort to the world. This explanation is a good explanation concerning the Tathagata. If one again speaks of the inexhaustible Dharma, the eternally abiding Dharma which is the refuge of all worlds—this is also a good explanation concerning the Tathagata. Therefore, in a world that has not been saved, a world without a refuge, there is an inexhaustible, eternally abiding refuge equal to the utmost limit: the Tathagata, Arhat, Completely Enlightened One.

*Buddhism*. Lion's Roar of Queen Srimala 5

Jesus said to them, "Truly, truly, I say to you, before Abraham was, I am."

*Christianity*. John 8.58

Outwardly, we are last of all, but inwardly we preceded everyone.

*Islam*. Hadith of Bukhari

I have been Manu and also Surya,
I am the wise rishi Kakshivat,
I have befriended Kutsa, Arjuni's son,
and I am the poet Ushanas; behold Me!

*Hinduism*. Rig Veda 4.26.1

**Jayadhavala 3:** Cf. Ratnakarandasravakacara 7-10, p. 456.

**John 1.1-4:** See pp. 99-100n.

**2 Corinthians 13.14:** This Trinitarian benediction suggests the distinctive activities of the persons of the Trinity: the grace of Christ, who died as atonement for our sins, leads us to the love of God, and the Holy Spirit manifests God's love through producing fellowship with God and among people.

**Lion's Roar of Queen Srimala 5:** A statement of the Trikaya doctrine: the Tathagata is at once the realm of Nirvana and of Absolute Suchness, or the *Dharmakaya*, the Dharma of compassion that fills the world, or *Sambhogakaya*, and the person of the human Tathagata, the Arhat. For texts on the Dharmakaya, cf. Garland Sutra 37, p. 62; Holy Teaching of Vimalakirti 12, pp. 62-63; for a visual depiction of the Sambhogakaya, see Garland Sutra 2, pp. 64-65.

**John 8.58:** As the pre-existent Word, Jesus preceded Abraham, even all human beings.

**Hadith of Bukhari:** This refers to Muhammad, who is outwardly the last of the prophets but inwardly preceded them.

**Rig Veda 4.26.1:** As the 'Poet of poets' God (Indra) infuses the vedic sages and gives them their holy utterance. This is the vedic foundation for the later Hindu doctrine of Avatars.

Whenever truth is forgotten in the world, and wickedness prevails, the Lord of Love becomes flesh to show the way, the truth, and the life to humanity. Such an incarnation is an avatar, an embodiment of God on earth.

*Hinduism*. Srimad Bhagavatam 1.1

Jesus took with him Peter and James and John his brother, and led them up a high mountain apart. And he was transfigured before them, and his face shown like the sun, and his garments became white as light. And behold, there appeared to them Moses and Elijah, talking with him. And Peter said to Jesus, "Lord, it is well that we are here; if you wish, I will make three booths here, one for you and one for Moses and one for Elijah." He was still speaking, when lo, a bright cloud overshadowed them, and a voice from the cloud said, "This is my beloved Son, with whom I am well pleased; listen to him." When the disciples heard this, they fell on their faces, and were filled with awe. But Jesus came and touched them, saying, "Rise, and have no fear." And when they lifted up their eyes, they saw no one but Jesus only.

*Christianity*. Matthew 17.1-8

O Krishna, it is right that the world delights and rejoices in your praise, that all the saints and sages bow down to you and all evil flees before you to the far corners of the universe. How could they not worship you, O Lord? You are the eternal Spirit, who existed before Brahma the Creator and who will never cease to be. Lord of the gods, you are the abode of the universe. Changeless, you are what is and what is not, and beyond the duality of existence and nonexistence....

Sometimes, because we were friends, I rashly said, "Oh, Krishna!" "Say, friend!"—casual, careless remarks. Whatever I may have said lightly, whether we were playing or resting, alone or in company, sitting together or eating, if it was disrespectful, forgive me for it, O Krishna. I did not know the greatness of your nature, unchanging and imperishable.

*Hinduism*. Bhagavad Gita 11.36-42

Now Thomas, one of the twelve, called the Twin, was not with them when Jesus came. So the other disciples told him, "We have seen the Lord." But he said to them, "Unless I see in his hands the print of the nails, and place my finger in the mark of the nails, and place my hand in his side, I will not believe." Eight days later, his disciples were again in the house, and Thomas was with them. The doors were shut, but Jesus came and stood among them, and said, "Peace be with you." Then he said to Thomas, "Put your finger here, and see my hands; and put out your hand, and place it in my side; do not be faithless, but believing." Thomas answered him, "My Lord and my God!" Jesus said to him, "Have you believed because you have seen me? Blessed are those who have not seen and yet believed."

*Christianity*. John 20.24-29

When Confucius returned from his visit with Lao Tzu, he did not speak for three days. His disciples said, "Master, you've seen Lao Tzu—what estimation would you make of him?" Confucius said, "At last I may say that I have seen a Dragon—a Dragon that coils to show his body at its best, that sprawls out to display his patterns at their best, riding on the breath

**Srimad Bhagavatam 1.1:** See Bhagavad Gita 4.7-8, p. 474, the classic statement on avatars. Cf. Srimad Bhagavatam 10, p. 456; Ramayana, Bala Kanda 15, p. 448; Kularnava Tantra 13, pp. 583-84; Swaiyya Guru, Kala, pp. 474-75.

**Matthew 17.1-8:** This is the Transfiguration, when Jesus' disciples first become aware of his divinity. Cf. John's vision of the resurrected Jesus in Revelation 1.9-19, p. 65.

**Bhagavad Gita 11.36-42:** Arjuna spoke these words just after being awe-struck by a vision of Krishna's transcendental form in Bhagavad Gita 11.3-34, pp. 66-68, 738-39. For other of Krishna's transcendental manifestations, see Srimad Bhagavatam 10.5, p. 547, and Srimad Bhagavatam 10.16, pp. 448-49.

**John 20.24-29:** This is the account of doubting Thomas. The resurrection of Jesus in a tangible body is one proof of his divinity; cf. Luke 24, pp. 440-41. Others prove Jesus' divinity by citing his miracles, such as walking on water, see Matthew 14.24-31, p. 543.

of the clouds, feeding on the yin and yang. My mouth fell open and I couldn't close it; my tongue flew up and I couldn't even stammer. How could I possibly make any estimation of Lao Tzu?"

*Taoism*. Chuang Tzu 14

At one time the Lord was journeying along the highroad between Ukkattha and Setabbya; so also was the brahmin Dona. He saw on the Lord's footprints the wheels with their thousand spokes, their rims and hubs and all their attributes complete, and he thought, "Indeed, how wonderful and marvelous—it cannot be that these are the footprints of a human being."

Then Dona, following the Lord's footprints, saw that he was sitting under a tree, comely, faith-inspiring, his sense-faculties and his mind peaceful.... Dona approached the Lord and said, "Is your reverence a god?"

"No indeed, brahmin, I am not a god."

"Then an angel?"

"No indeed, brahmin."

"A fairy, then?"

"No indeed, brahmin, I am not a fairy."

"Then is your reverence a human being?"

"No indeed, brahmin, I am not a human being."

"You answer No to all my questions. Who then is your reverence?"

"Brahmin, those outflows whereby, if they had not been extinguished, I might have been a god, angel, fairy, or a human being—those outflows are extinguished in me, cut off at the root, made like a palm-tree stump that can come to no further existence in the future. Just as a blue, red, or white lotus, although born in the water, grown up in the water, when it reaches the surface stands there unsoiled by the water—just so, brahmin, although born in the world, grown up in the world, having overcome the world, I abide unsoiled by the world. Take it that I am Buddha."

*Buddhism*. Anguttara Nikaya ii.37-39

## *The Human Person*

Say, I do not say to you, "I possess the treasuries of God"; I know not the Unseen. And I say not to you, "I am an angel"; I only follow what is revealed to me.

*Islam*. Qur'an 6.50

Say, I am only a mortal the like of you; it is revealed to me that your God is one God. So let him who hopes for the encounter with his Lord work righteousness, and not associate with his Lord's service anyone.

*Islam*. Qur'an 18.110

Monks, an inquiring monk, learning the range of another's mind, should make a study of the Tathagata, so as to distinguish whether he is a fully self-awakened one or not.

*Buddhism*. Majjhima Nikaya i.318

A man ran up and knelt before him, and asked him, "Good Teacher, what must I do to inherit eternal life?" And Jesus said to him, "Why do you call me good? No one is good but God alone."

*Christianity*. Mark 10.17-18

The Master said, "As to being a Divine Sage or even a Good Man, far be it from me to make any such claim. As for unwearying effort to

**Chuang Tzu 14:** Chuang Tzu often casts Confucius in the role of a poor and benighted sage whose wisdom cannot compare with that of the Taoist masters. Such was then the rivalry between the two schools.

**Anguttara Nikaya ii.37-39:** The Buddha's transcendental nature cannot be comprehended by conventional notions of divinity, for the Hindu gods are merely another class of creatures, as are *gandharvas* (angels) and *yakkhas* (fairies). These beings still live in samsara, with passions untamed, producing karmic 'outflows.' Only in Nirvana as attained by the Buddha is desire and its outflows entirely extinguished and the world of phenomena thus overcome. He is beyond any form or phenomena of existence. Cf. Dhammapada 93, p. 378; Sutta Nipata 1072-76, p. 379.

**Majjhima Nikaya i.318:** The Buddha lays himself open to inquiry by inviting others to observe his behavior and judge his mental purity. He invites them to judge him as a man.

**Mark 10.17-18:** Cf. 1 John 1.8, p. 273; also Qur'an 12.53, p. 273; Hadith of Muslim, p. 362.

learn and unflagging patience in teaching others, those are merits that I do not hesitate to claim."

*Confucianism.* Analects 7.33

They do blaspheme who say, "God is Christ, the son of Mary." But said Christ, "O Children of Israel! Worship God, my Lord and your Lord." Whoever joins other gods with God—God will forbid him the Garden, and the Fire will be his abode.

*Islam.* Qur'an 5.75

Since the children share in flesh and blood, he [Jesus] himself likewise partook of the same nature, that through death he might destroy him who has the power of death, that is, the devil, and deliver all those who through fear of death were subject to lifelong bondage.... Therefore he had to be made like his brethren in every respect, so that he might become a merciful and faithful high priest in the service of God, to make expiation for the sins of the people. For because he himself has suffered and been tempted, he is able to help those who are tempted.

*Christianity.* Hebrews 2.14-18

Lo! God and His angels shower blessings on the Prophet. O you who believe! Ask blessings on him and salute him with a worthy salutation.

*Islam.* Qur'an 33.56

Miriam and Aaron spoke against Moses because of the Cushite woman whom he had married, for he had married a Cushite woman; and they said, "Has the Lord indeed spoken only through Moses? Has he not spoken through us also?" And the Lord heard it. Now the man Moses was very meek, more than all men that were on the face of the earth. And suddenly the Lord said to Moses and to Aaron and Miriam, "Come out, you three, to the tent of meeting." And the three of them came out. And the Lord came down in a pillar of cloud, and stood at the door of the tent, and called Aaron and Miriam; and they both came forward. And he said, "Hear my words: If there is a prophet among you, I the Lord make myself known to him in a vision, I speak with him in a dream. Not so with my servant Moses; he is entrusted with all my house. With him I speak mouth to mouth, clearly, and not in dark speech; and he beholds the form of the Lord. Why then were you not afraid to speak against my servant Moses?"

*Judaism.* Numbers 12.1-8

What are the eighteen special dharmas of a Buddha? From the night when the Tathagata knows full enlightenment, to the day when he becomes extinct in Nirvana, during all this time the Tathagata 1) does not stumble, 2) is not rash or noisy in his speech, 3) is never robbed of his mindfulness. 4) He has no perception of difference. 5) His thought is never unconcentrated. 6) His evenmindedness is not due to lack of consideration. 7) His zeal, 8) vigor, 9) mindfulness, 10) concentration, 11) wisdom, and 12) deliverance never fail. 13) All the deeds of his body, 14) voice, and 15) mind are preceded by cognition and continue to conform to cognition. 16) His cognition and vision regarding the past, 17) future, and 18) present period of time proceeds unobstructed and freely. And all that is without taking anything as a basis.

*Buddhism.* Large Sutra on Perfect Wisdom 211-12

**Qur'an 5.75:** Muslims consider the belief that Jesus is God, or the son of God—'son' understood in the sense of procreation or partaking of divinity—as one of the chief errors of Christian theology. In Islam there is an absolute distinction between God and human beings. Cf. Qur'an 21.26-29, p. 263n.

**Hebrews 2.14-18:** This conveys the necessity for Jesus to be a human being; by his having shared in the lot of humanity, he is able to save humanity.

**Qur'an 33.56:** By this command all Muslims, when they mention the name of the Prophet, will recite a blessing.

**Large Sutra on Perfect Wisdom 211-12:** This is one of several lists of the Buddha's qualities: his 18 dharmas, which describe qualities of mind, word, and deed; his 32 marks, which are the physical signs of a superman, and his 80 secondary marks.

The Master said, "The thought that,
I have left my moral power untended,
My learning unperfected;
I have heard of righteous men, but have been unable to go to them,
I have heard of evil men, but have been unable to reform them.
—it is these thoughts that disquiet me."

The Master said, "Give me a few more years, so that I may have spent a whole fifty years in study, and I believe that after all I should be fairly free from error."

The Duke of She asked Tzu-lu about Confucius. Tzu-lu did not reply. The Master said, "Why did you not say 'This is the character of the man: so intent upon enlightening the eager that he forgets his hunger, and so happy in doing so, that he forgets the bitterness of his lot and does not realize that old age is at hand. That is what he is.'"

The Master said, "Even when walking in a party of no more than three I can always be certain of learning from those I am with. There will be good qualities that I can select for imitation and bad ones that will teach me what requires correction in myself."

*Confucianism.* Analects 7

The Lord abstained from frequent speech. He uttered a few words, if and when necessary. If somebody asked, "Who is there inside?" he would respond, "It is I, a monk."

The Lord slept sparingly. He frequently meditated standing and even then retained full consciousness. During his spiritual pursuit he had very little sleep. During twelve and a half years he slept for less than a *muhurta* (48 minutes).... When sleep would be too irresistible, he would wander a little to conquer it and thus ceaselessly stay awake.

The Lord was conversant with the precise quantity of food and water required for a human body and consumed these accordingly.... The Lord was not biased towards savory dishes. He experimented variously in matters of diet. Once he took dry food. He subsisted on fatless rice and cereals... three kinds of food only for a full eight months.

The Lord abandoned water also during his fasts. Once, he dispensed with water for a fortnight. He extended that to live without water for fasts of one, two, and six months.

The Lord never rubbed his eyes nor scratched the itching part.... The Lord ever kept his arms spread out even during the winter, instead of clasping his arms across his chest.... While the people shivered in winter and many monks sought warm places to nestle into, protected from the chilly blasts, warming themselves with hearths indoors, the Lord meditated in the open with no clothes and no shelter.... He suffered stoically.

*Jainism.* Acarangasutra 9

One gopi said, "Do you know that when Krishna lies on the ground he rests on his left elbow, and his head rests on his left hand. He moves his attractive eyebrows while playing his flute with his delicate fingers, and the sound he produces creates such a nice atmosphere that the denizens of the heavenly planets, who travel in space with their wives and beloved, stop their airplanes, for they are stunned by the vibration of the flute. The wives of the demigods who are seated in the planes then become very much ashamed of their singing and the quality of their musicianship. Not only that, but they become afflicted with conjugal love, and their hair and tightened dresses immediately loosen."

One of the gopis told mother Yashoda, "My dear mother, your son is very expert among the cowherd boys. He knows all the different arts, how to tend the cows and how to play the flute. He composes his own songs, and to sing them he puts his flute to his mouth. When he plays, either in the morning or in the evening, all the demigods, like Lord Shiva, Brahma, Indra, and Candra, bow their heads and listen

**Analects 7:** Vv. 3,16,18,21. Confucius' character is also illuminated by Analects 2.4, p. 510; 7.7, p. 456; 7.20, p. 265; 7.26, p. 210; 9.10, p. 585; and 9.16, p. 529.

with great attention. Although they are very learned and expert, they cannot understand the musical arrangements of Krishna's flute. They simply listen attentively and try to understand, but become bewildered and nothing more."

*Hinduism.* Srimad Bhagavatam 10.34

Anas said, "I served the Prophet for ten years and he never said to me, 'Shame!' or 'Why did you do such and such?' or 'Why did you not do such and such?'"

He said, "When I was walking with God's Messenger, who was wearing a Najrani cloak with a coarse fringe, a nomadic Arab caught up on him, and gave his cloak a violent tug, pulling God's Prophet back against his chest, and I saw that the side of God's Messenger's shoulder was marked by the fringe of the cloak because of the violence of the man's tug. He said, 'Command that I be given some of God's property which you have, Muhammad,' and God's Messenger turned around to him and laughed, then ordered that he be given something."

He said, "God's Messenger was the best of men, the most generous of men, the bravest of men. One night the people of Medina were startled; when they went in the direction of the sound they were met by the Prophet, who had gone out toward the sound ahead of them, and he was saying, 'You have nothing to fear.' He was on a barebacked horse with no saddle belonging to Abu Talha and had a sword slung on his neck. He said, 'I found it could run like a great river.'"

Abu Huraira told that when God's Messenger was asked to invoke a curse on the polytheists he replied, "I was not sent as one given to cursing; I was sent only as a mercy."

'Aisha said, "God's Messenger was never given his choice between two things without taking the lesser of them, provided it involved no sin, for if it did, no one kept further away from it than he. And God's Messenger never took revenge on his own behalf for anything unless something God had forbidden had been transgressed, in which event he took revenge for it for God's sake."

Anas said, "I served God's Messenger for ten years from the time I was eight years old and he never blamed me for anything which was destroyed at my hand. If any member of his family blamed me he said, 'Leave him alone, for if anything were decreed it would happen.'"

'Aisha said, "God's Messenger was not unseemly or lewd in his language, nor was he loud-voiced in the streets, nor did he return evil for evil, but he would forgive and pardon."

She said, "God's Messenger used to patch his sandals, sew his garment and conduct himself at home as anyone of you does in his house. He was a human being, searching his garment for lice, milking his sheep, and doing his own chores."

She reported God's Messenger as saying, "If I wished, 'Aisha, mountains of gold would go with me. An angel whose waist was as high as the Kaaba came to me and told me that my Lord sent me a greeting and said that if I wished I could be a prophet and a servant, or if I wished I could be a prophet and a king. I looked at Gabriel and he gave me a sign to humble myself. I then said that I would be a prophet and a servant." After that God's Messenger did not eat reclining, saying he would eat like a slave and sit like a slave.

*Islam.* Hadith

**Srimad Bhagavatam 10.34:** Krishna as a youth was beloved of the *gopis*, the cowherd girls of Vrindavan. They were irresistibly attracted to him and joined in his pastimes, for he is the center radiating divine love. Yet Krishna also manifested his transcendental powers in delighting the gopis; cf. Srimad Bhagavatam 10.5, p. 547.

**Hadith:** These traditions are from a collection of hadith from many sources. Other passages on the character of Muhammad include Qur'an 12.53, p. 273; Hadith of Muslim, p. 315; and Hadith of Muslim, p. 362. On his frequent prayer vigils, see Qur'an 73.1-8, p. 593.

I have become a legend in the Gloucester [Mass.] area.... When the New Hope put out to sea and dropped anchor, often many other boats would follow and anchor in the vicinity. When we had a tuna strike, other fishermen would bring out their binoculars and watch what I was doing. At first the negative people would want the tuna to break loose and escape, but after a few days of successful catches they began to change their thinking, and the rumor began that I have something good working for me.

I was always the first one out to sea. Some of the seasoned professional fishermen would go out early to outdo me, but no matter how early they got out, the New Hope was already there. The fishermen were not only inspired by this, but when they tried to compete with me they had to work so hard that they had no time for their usual drinking or laziness. By the end of the summer a rumor was going around that declining town that I am the only one who can save Gloucester.

Without exception I got up every day at three a.m. The New Hope went out in the moonlight and in many cases returned home with the stars and moon shining. Do you like to get up early in the morning? The staff members working on the boat were never told what time to get up, but since I arose at three they followed me, no matter how sleepy they were.

This has been my tradition for four years in America. It is not easy to follow me, because no one can outwork me. My crew knows what I would do, and if I tell them to be out by 1:30 on the Atlantic they get up and go out with no grumbling. I have even set the tradition of staying out and working all night.

This summer I did not earn much in terms of money, but in terms of tradition, I earned billions of dollars worth.... Even though fishing is hard work, I wanted to give myself without any reservation to set the tradition for the posterity of the Unification Church.

*Unification Church.*
Sun Myung Moon, 9-11-77

❖

## *The Succession of Founders and Messengers*

RELIGIONS DO NOT SPRING UP without a root in this world. Each great founder of religion has acknowledged his debt to his spiritual forebears, whose teachings and traditions he cherishes and passes on anew. Thus Muhammad comes after a long line of holy prophets; Shakyamuni is only the most recent of countless past Buddhas; Mahavira passes on the tradition of twenty-two previous Tirthankaras; and Jesus comes on the foundation of Moses and the Old Testament prophets. Confucius and Lao Tzu looked back to the sages and exemplary rulers of ancient China. Traditions of sages and elders handing on a tradition are found in the Vedas and in the scriptures of rabbinic Judaism. The lineage of the Latter-day Saints' priesthood extends back to Adam.

In some religions, the succession of sages also extends into the future; thus the nine historical avatars of Vishnu will be followed by a future avatar, the Kalkin; and the Shakyamuni Buddha who comes on the foundation of a succession of countless former Buddhas will in turn be followed by a future Buddha, the Maitreya. We will consider this theme under the topic *Messiah*, pp. 783-88.

Naught is said unto you [Muhammad] save what was said unto the messengers before you.

*Islam*. Qur'an 41.43

I have seen an ancient Path, an ancient road traversed by the rightly enlightened ones of former times.

*Buddhism*. Samyutta Nikaya ii.106

The Master said, "I have transmitted what was taught to me without making up anything of my own. I have been faithful to and loved the Ancients."

*Confucianism*. Analects 7.1

On the whole twenty-three Tirthankaras have appeared, the venerable Mahavira being the last of the Tirthankaras.

*Jainism*. Kalpa Sutra 2

The Lord your God will raise up for you a prophet like me [Moses] from among you, from your brethren—him you shall heed.

*Judaism* and *Christianity*. Deuteronomy 18.15

In many and various ways God spoke of old to our fathers by the prophets; but in these last days he has spoken to us by a Son, whom he appointed the heir of all things.

*Christianity*. Hebrews 1.1-2

**Samyutta Nikaya ii.106:** See more of this passage on p. 389; cf. Lankavatara Sutra 61, p. 103.

**Deuteronomy 18.15:** Many of the prophets, most notably Elijah, understood themselves to be successors to the mission of Moses, and called the people to return to the covenant with God which Moses first established. Moses is also a forerunner of Jesus, and these words are often taken as announcing his future advent; cf. Acts 3.22, 7.37.

**Hebrews 1.1-2:** Cf. 2 Corinthians 3.7-16, p. 454.

Whenever the Law declines and the purpose of life is forgotten, I manifest myself on earth. I am born in every age to protect the good, to destroy evil, and to re-establish the Law.

*Hinduism*. Bhagavad Gita 4.7-8

Think not that I have come to abolish the law and the prophets; I have not come to abolish them but to fulfil them. For truly, I say to you, till heaven and earth pass away, not an iota, not a dot, will pass from the law until all is accomplished.

*Christianity*. Matthew 5.17-18

Of yore I followed countless Buddhas,
And perfectly trod the Ways
Of the profound and mystic Law,
Hard to perceive and perform.
During infinite kotis of kalpas,
Having followed all these Ways,
Attaining fruition on the Wisdom-throne,
I could perfectly understand.

*Buddhism*. Lotus Sutra 2

Lo! We inspired you [O Muhammad] as We inspired Noah and the prophets after him, as We inspired Abraham and Ishmael and Isaac and Jacob and the tribes, and Jesus and Job and Jonah and Aaron and Solomon, and as we imparted unto David the Psalms; and messengers We have mentioned to you before and messengers We have not mentioned to you... messengers of good cheer and of warning, in order that mankind might have no argument against God after the messengers. God was ever Mighty, Wise.

*Islam*. Qur'an 4.163-65

It was in this way that Emperor Yü, Kings T'ang, Wen, Wu, Ch'eng, and the Duke of Chou achieved eminence: all these six noble men paid attention to propriety, made manifest their justice, and acted in good faith. They exposed their errors, made humaneness their law and prudence their practice, thus showing the people wherein they should constantly abide. If there were any who did not follow these principles, he would lose power and position and be regarded by the multitude as dangerous.

*Confucianism*. Book of Ritual 7.1.2

In Sati Yuga you practiced supreme yoga, and
assuming the Dwarf's form, defeated haughty Bali;
In Treta again you practiced supreme yoga and
were called Rama, the Lord of the Raghu race;
In Dwapar you appeared as Krishna, slayer of
Mura, and slew Kamsa;
And conferring kingship on Ugrasen, rendered
your devotees fear-free;

**Bhagavad Gita 4.7-8:** This is the classic verse on the doctrine of Vishnu's incarnations, or *avatars*. Each avatar came for a specific mission to save the world and establish righteousness (*dharma*), according to the scriptures. There are ten classical avatars of Vishnu: the fish, the tortoise, the boar, the man-lion, the dwarf, Rama, Rama-with-the-Axe, Krishna, the Buddha, and the future Kalkin. Cf. Srimad Bhagavatam 1.1, p. 467; Kularnava Tantra 13, pp. 583-84n.; Bhagavad Gita 4.7-8, p. 786n., on future avatars.

**Matthew 5.17-18:** Matthew understands the Gospel to be the fulfillment of the Jewish Torah and Jesus to be its preeminent interpreter. In truth, many statements of Jesus find parallels in the sayings of the rabbis. On the other hand, compare the view of Paul in Galatians 3.10-13, 21-26, p. 108, and 2 Corinthians 3.7-16, p. 454.

**Lotus Sutra 2:** Shakyamuni is speaking of his own gradual progress to perfect enlightenment over countless past lives following countless Buddhas. Cf. Anagatavamsa, p. 786.

**Book of Ritual 7.1-2:** On the primary virtues of 'propriety' *(li)*, 'justice' *(i)*, and 'humaneness' *(jen)*, see Mencius II. A. 6, p. 145.

In Kali Yuga you were verily Nanak, and
assumed the names Angad and Amar Das;
Declared the Supreme Being, "The reign of the
holy Guru shall be immutable, eternal."

*Sikhism.* Adi Granth,
Swaiyya Guru, Kala, p. 1390

I [Krishna] told this eternal secret to Vivasvat. Vivasvat taught Manu, and Manu taught Ikshvaku. Thus, Arjuna, eminent sages received knowledge of yoga in a continuous tradition. But through time the practice of yoga was lost in the world. The secret of these teachings is profound. I have explained them to you today because you are my friend and devotee.

*Hinduism.* Bhagavad Gita 4.1-3

Moses received the Torah on Sinai and delivered it to Joshua, and Joshua [delivered it] to the elders, and the elders to the prophets, and the prophets delivered it to the men of the Great Synagogue.

*Judaism.* Mishnah, Abot 1.1

When Moses reached heaven, he beheld the Law written in black fire upon skins of white fire, and he also beheld the Lord seated upon the Throne of Glory and occupied in adding and ornamenting the letters of the Torah with crowns. He asked, "Why art thou now adding these crown-like ornamentations to the letters?"

Whereto the Lord replied, "In days to come there will be born a man named Rabbi Akiba, a scholar in Israel, full of knowledge and wisdom, to whom the secret of these dots and ornamentations will be revealed. He will interpret them, basing upon their interpretations numerous laws and injunctions."

"If it is thy will," said Moses, "may I be permitted to behold this wise man?"

"Look behind you," said the Lord.

Moses did as he was bidden, and lo, he saw a house full of students, sitting at the feet of a master who was explaining to them the secrets and mysteries of the Torah. Moses heard their discussions, but could not follow them and was greatly grieved. Thereupon he heard the disciples asking their master, "Whence do you know this?" and Rabbi Akiba replied, "What I have told you has already been explained to Moses the son of Amram, on Mount Sinai." When Moses heard these words, he was content.

In his modesty, however, the prophet turned to God, saying, "Lord of the Universe! Thou wilt one day create a man like Rabbi Akiba who will excel me in knowledge and wisdom; why dost thou not give the Torah to Israel through him instead of me?"

But the Lord replied, "Such is my decree."

*Judaism.* Talmud, Menahot 29b

Mention Abraham in the Book. He was a truthful prophet when he told his father, "My father, why do you worship something that neither hears nor perceives, and does not benefit you in any way? My father, I have been given some knowledge which has not come to you, so follow me: I'll guide you along a Level Road. My father, do not serve Satan! Satan was defiant towards the Mercy-giving. My father, I fear lest some torment from the Mercy-giving should afflict you, and you become a partisan of Satan."

He said, "Peace be upon you! I'll seek forgiveness for you from my Lord; He has been so gracious towards me. I'll move away from you and from anything you appeal to instead of

**Swaiyya Guru, Kala:** The founders of Sikhism, Guru Nanak, Angad, and Amar Das, are ascribed as avatars of Vishnu, successors of Rama and Krishna. Similarly, many modern Hindu spiritual leaders have been regarded as avatars; see Bhagavad Gita 4.7-8, p. 786n. This passage is one of a number of laudatory stanzas written by bards called Bhatts, who were attached to the Gurus' houshold.

**Abot 1.1:** 'Torah' means not only the words written in the first five books of the Bible. This passage speaks of an 'oral Torah' which was transmitted through the chain of succession to the rabbis. Its practical clarifications and inner teachings define the way of life which is true to the written commandments. The rabbis wrote the Mishnah and the Talmud as codifications of this oral Torah. See the following passage from the Talmud.

God. I shall appeal to my Lord; perhaps I'll not feel quite so miserable with my Lord's appeal."

When he moved away from them and what they worshipped instead of God, We bestowed Isaac and Jacob on him. Each We made a prophet. We bestowed some of Our mercy on them and granted them a sublime tongue for telling truth.

Mention Moses in the Book. He was sincere, and was a messenger, a prophet. We called out to him from the right side of the mountain, and brought him close to confide in. We bestowed his brother Aaron on him as a prophet through Our mercy.

Mention Ishmael in the Book. He kept true to the Promise, and was a messenger, a prophet. He used to order his people to pray and pay the welfare tax; he was approved by his Lord.

Mention Idris in the Book. He was a truthful prophet; We raised him to a lofty place.

Those are some of the prophets from Adam's offspring whom God has favored, and some of those We transported along with Noah, and some of Abraham's and Ishmael's offspring, as well as some others We have guided and chosen. Whenever the Mercy-giving's signs are recited to them, they drop down on their knees and weep!

*Islam.* Qur'an 19.41-58

Inasmuch as these Birds of the Celestial Throne are all sent down from the heaven of the Will of God, and as they all arise to proclaim His irresistible Faith, they therefore are regarded as one soul and the same person. For they all drink from the one Cup of the love of God, and all partake of the fruit of the same Tree of Oneness. These Manifestations of God have each a twofold station. One is the station of pure abstraction and essential unity. In this respect, if you call them all by one name, and ascribe to them the same attribute, you have not erred from the truth. Even as He has revealed, "No distinction do We make between any of His Messengers!" For they one and all summon the people of the earth to acknowledge the Unity of God....

The other is the station of distinction, and pertains to the world of creation and to its limitations. In this respect, each Manifestation of God has a distinct individuality, a definitely prescribed mission, a predestined Revelation, and specially designated limitations. Each one of them is known by a different name, is characterized by a special attribute, fulfills a definite Mission, and is entrusted with a particular Revelation.

*Baha'i Faith.*
Book of Certitude, 152, 176

And the sons of Moses, according to the Holy Priesthood which he received under the hand of his father-in-law Jethro; and Jethro received it under the hand of Caleb; and Caleb received it under the hand of Elihu; and Elihu under the hand of Jeremy; and Jeremy under the hand of Gad; and Gad under the hand of Esaias; and Esaias received it under the hand of God.

Esaias also lived in the days of Abraham, and was blessed of him—which Abraham received the priesthood from Melchizedek, who received it through the lineage of his fathers, even till Noah; and from Noah till Enoch, through the lineage of their fathers; and from Enoch to Abel, who was slain by the conspiracy of his brother, who received the priesthood by the commandment of God, by the hand of his father Adam, who was the first man—which priesthood continues in the church of God in all generations, and is without beginning of days or end of years.

And the Lord confirmed a priesthood also upon Aaron and his seed, throughout all their

**Qur'an 19.41-58:** On the superiority of Muhammad to the other prophets, see Qur'an 33:40, p. 450, and Hadith of Bukhari, p. 464. The Qur'an gives a lofty position to Ishmael, the ancestor of the Arab peoples, who according to the Bible was the less-favored son of Abraham.

**Book of Certitude, 152, 176:** Cf. Book of Certitude, 33-41, p. 779.

generations, which priesthood also continues and abides forever with the priesthood which is after the holiest order of God. And this greater priesthood administers the gospel and holds the key of the mysteries of the kingdom, even the key of the knowledge of God.

*Church of Jesus Christ of Latter-day Saints.*
Doctrine and Covenants 84.6-19

**Doctrine and Covenants 84.6-19:** The restored priesthood includes the Aaronic priesthood and the Melchizedek priesthood; these are open to all qualified males among the Latter-day Saints. The various ranks of the priesthood have obligations for missionary and church work.

PART FOUR

# THE RELIGIOUS LIFE

CHAPTER 12

# RESPONSIBILITY AND PREDESTINATION

RESPONSIBILITY AND PREDESTINATION ARE INTERRELATED TOPICS. On the one hand, the scriptures affirm that every individual is responsible before God. We are given freedom in the context of the responsibility to fulfill the purpose of life. Individual responsibility begins with a decision to follow a righteous path—the topic of the first section. The second section has passages on the unalienable responsibility which every individual has for his own self, which cannot be passed off to another or excused by circumstance or surrendered to the grace of a savior. Human responsibility also cannot be coerced; it requires freedom of thought and freedom of action, freedom to believe and freedom to disbelieve. The third section has texts on the synergistic cooperation of responsibility and grace. Our responsibility is seen as undergirded and prompted by God's grace, and as we do our portion we find that God has been helping us all along.

At the same time, a person's scope of action is ordinarily limited by conditions which are beyond his or her control. Some people are blessed with an easy life; others have a hard lot. For some faith comes easily, and they advance on the path with seemingly effortless ease, while for others the burdens of life are heavy, and despite strenuous efforts they continually fall into temptation and despair. These variations in ability, circumstance, and fortune are explained in various ways. Doctrines of predestination, expressed by texts gathered in the fourth section, attribute differences in endowment and fate to the hand of God, who is omnipotent and controls all. God's grace is the only efficacious power, beside which human effort counts for very little.

In the fifth section, variations in individual endowment and fate are explained as caused by prior actions. The doctrine of karma explains personal existence as continuous with countless prior lives. Deeds committed in past lives bear fruit in the present life, causing variations in circumstance and endowment. This doctrine is founded upon a belief in reincarnation. For religions which regard the passage through life as a singular event, a persons's life is conditioned by the sins inherited through family and lineage. The sins of the fathers are passed on to their descendants in the form of difficult burdens and tragic circumstances, while the merits of the fathers appear as blessings. Individuals are also subject to conditions by virtue of belonging to a group or nation; its collective history has created debts or benefits which are shared by its members.

To regard human beings as totally free and responsible for their lives, and to regard life as totally predetermined by external factors, are two extremes of a spectrum within which lies the actual human situation. This leads to the topic of duty. Texts gathered in the concluding section teach that we should accept our lot in life and then strive to do our best with what we have been given. They teach us to be confident of God's provision, whatever it may be, as an adequate starting point for accomplishing our individual responsibility.

## Decision

THE RELIGIOUS LIFE begins with a decision. It is not something that comes in the natural course of an unexamined life, but it must be consciously chosen and cleaved to. Neither can the decision be compelled by human authorities, nor by the power of Heaven. The call to faith must be entered into freely. Often the call to decision is an exhortation to awaken to the real dangers and fragility of human life: the inevitability of death, the awareness of the sinfulness of one's life, the looming threat of hell and punishment. In the light of these dangers, religion offers a sure refuge and way to salvation. This decision is commonly described as between two possibilities: life or death, the narrow gate or the wide gate, two roads. This decision also requires a commitment based upon knowledge sufficient that one will not later be swayed by doubts.

"Men, what must I do to be saved?" And they said, "Believe in the Lord Jesus, and you will be saved, you and your household."

*Christianity*. Acts 16.30-31

Say, O mankind, I am the Messenger of God to you all, of Him to whom belongs the sovereignty of the heavens and the earth. There is no God but He. He gives life, and He makes to die. So believe in God, and His messenger, the Prophet who can neither read nor write, who believes in God and in His words, and follow Him that haply you may be led aright.

*Islam*. Qur'an 7.158

Seek refuge with the Lord alone,
with your whole being, Bharata.
By His grace, you will reach
supreme peace, an everlasting estate.

*Hinduism*. Bhagavad Gita 18.62

To many a refuge fear-stricken men betake themselves—to hills, woods, groves, trees, and shrines. Nay, no such refuge is safe, no such refuge is supreme. Not by resorting to such a refuge is one freed from all ill.

He who has gone for refuge to the Buddha [the Teacher], the Dhamma [the Teaching], and the Sangha [the Taught], sees with right knowledge the Four Noble Truths: Sorrow, the Cause of Sorrow, the Transcending of Sorrow, and the Noble Eightfold Path which leads to the Cessation of Sorrow. This, indeed, is refuge secure. This, indeed, is refuge supreme. By seeking such refuge one is released from all sorrow.

*Buddhism*. Dhammapada 188-92

Young person, run to embrace Ifa.
Young person, run to embrace Ifa.
If people deceive you,
Do not accept.
If people deceive you,
Do not accept.
Truth is bitter.

The future of the world belongs to Ifa
It will certainly not be spoiled in our own time.
It will not be spoiled in our own time.
The world will not be spoiled in our own time.
Ifa will mend it.

*African Traditional Religions*.
Yoruba Hymn (Nigeria)

**Dhammapada 188-92:** Cf. Khuddaka Patha, p. 29.

**Yoruba Hymn:** Ifa is the name of one of the high Yoruba divinities, but it also means Yoruba religion as a whole. Both meanings are meant here.

Confucius said, "Set your heart upon the Way, support yourself by its power, lean upon goodness, seek distraction in the arts."

*Confucianism*. Analects 7.6

Arise! Awake! Approach the great and learn. Like the sharp edge of a razor is that path—so the wise say—hard to tread and difficult to cross.

*Hinduism*. Katha Upanishad 1.3.14

Enter by the narrow gate; for the gate is wide and the way is easy that leads to destruction, and those who enter by it are many. For the gate is narrow and the way is hard that leads to life, and those who find it are few.

*Christianity*. Matthew 7.13-14

Man always stands at the crossroads of good and evil.

*Perfect Liberty Kyodan*. Precept 18

Surely, the path that leads to worldly gain is one, and the path that leads to Nibbana is another; understanding this, the bhikkhu, the disciple of the Buddha, should not rejoice in worldly favors, but cultivate detachment.

*Buddhism*. Dhammapada 75

Have We not granted him two eyes,
and a tongue, and two lips,
and guided him on the two high roads?
Yet he has not assaulted the Steep!
What will make you realize what is the Steep?
To free a slave,
or to give food at a time of hunger,
to an orphan near of kin
or a needy man in misery;
then to become one who believes, and to
counsel each other to be steadfast, and to
counsel each other to be merciful.

*Islam*. Qur'an 90.8-17

Thus says the Lord:
Stand by the roads, and look,
and ask for the ancient paths,
where the good way is; and walk in it,
and find rest for your souls.

*Judaism* and *Christianity*. Jeremiah 6.16

They say only, "Lo! We found our fathers following a religion, and we are guided by their footprints." And even so We sent not a warner before you [Muhammad] into any township, but its luxurious ones said, "Lo! We found our fathers following a religion, and we are following their footprints." And the warner said, "What! Even though I bring you better guidance than that you found your fathers following?" They answered, "Lo! In what you bring we are disbelievers." We have requited them; see what was the consequence for the deniers.

*Islam*. Qur'an 43.22-25

Jesus said to them, "No one puts new wine into old wineskins; if he does, the new wine will burst the skins and will be spilled, and the skins will be destroyed. But new wine must be put into fresh wineskins."

*Christianity*. Luke 5.37-38

Were I possessed of the least knowledge, I would, when walking on the great Way, fear only paths that lead astray. The great Way is easy, yet people prefer bypaths.

**Katha Upanishad 1.3.14**: Cf. Bhagavad Gita 4.34-35, p. 582; Uttaradhyayana Sutra 10.28-33, p. 680.

**Dhammapada 75**: See previous note.

**Qur'an 90.8-17**: The two highways are the steep and difficult path of virtue—called the Steep—and the easy path of vice and self-centered living. On the Straight Path, see Qur'an 1, pp. 29-30.

**Qur'an 43.22-25**: In contrasting this and the preceding passage, recall that Muhammad was a prophet who brought a new teaching that differed from the traditions of the polytheists, while Jeremiah was a prophet who called his people back to the fundamentals of the Covenant of Moses.

**Luke 5.37-38**: Jesus brought a new message, 'new wine'; it could not abide with those who were attached to the conventional wisdom, the 'old wineskins.' Cf. Luke 9.60, p. 412.

The court is corrupt,
The fields are overgrown with weeds,
The granaries are empty;
Yet there are those dressed in fineries,
With swords at their sides,
Filled with food and drink,
And possessed of too much wealth.
This is known as taking the lead in robbery.
Far indeed is this from the Way.

*Taoism.* Tao Te Ching 53

A man once gave a great banquet, and invited many; and at the time for the banquet he sent his servant to say to those who had been invited, "Come; for all is now ready." But they all alike began to make excuses. The first said to him, "I have bought a field, and I must go out and see it; I pray you, have me excused." And another said, "I have bought five yoke of oxen, and I go to examine them; I pray you, have me excused." And another said, "I have married a wife, and therefore I cannot come." So the servant came and reported this to his master. Then the householder in anger said to his servant, "Go out quickly to the streets and lanes of the city, and bring in the poor and maimed and blind and lame." And the servant said, "Sir, what you commanded has been done, and still there is room." And the master said to his servant, "Go out to the highways and hedges, and compel people to come in, that my house may be filled. For I tell you, none of those men who were invited shall taste my banquet."

*Christianity.* Luke 14.16-24: Parable of the Banquet

He who is not with me is against me.

*Christianity.* Matthew 12.30

God puts forth a parable: A man belonging to many partners at variance with each other, and a man belonging entirely to one master: are those two equal in comparison?

*Islam.* Qur'an 39.29

No one can serve two masters; for either he will hate the one and love the other, or he will be devoted to one and despise the other. You cannot serve God and mammon.

*Christianity.* Matthew 6.24

If by giving up a lesser happiness one may behold a greater one, let the wise man give up the lesser happiness in consideration of the greater happiness.

*Buddhism.* Dhammapada 290

Both the good and the pleasant present themselves to a man. The calm soul examines them well and discriminates. Yea, he prefers the good to the pleasant; but the fool chooses the pleasant out of greed and avarice.

*Hinduism.* Katha Upanishad 1.2.2

The Self-existent pierced sense openings outward;
therefore a man looks out, not in.
But a certain wise man, in search of immortality,
turned his gaze inward and saw the Self within.

The foolish go after outward pleasures
and walk into the snare of all-embracing death.

**Tao Te Ching 53**: The 'bypaths' mean ways of avoiding or rationalizing away one's obligations for the sake of personal gain. Cf. Tao Te Ching 12, p. 662.

**Luke 14.16-24**: In this parable, Jesus laments that the most qualified people make excuses that worldly occupations keep them from participating in God's kingdom. So God must call the poor and impoverished, who have nothing to lose. Cf. Matthew 16.26, p. 681; Luke 9.60, p. 412; 9.62, p. 528; Abot 2.8, p. 679; Digha Nikaya iii.185, p. 714. On the other hand, compare Abot de Rabbi Nathan Ver. B, 31, p. 211.

**Matthew 12.30**: Compare Bhagavad Gita 6.5-6, p. 278.

**Matthew 6.24**: Cf. Matthew 16.26, p. 681.

**Dhammapada 290**: Cf. Holy Teaching of Vimalakirti 4, p. 132.

**Katha Upanishad 1.2.2**: Cf. Chandogya Upanishad 7.23, p. 133; Dhammapada 7-8, p. 315.

The wise, however, discerning immortality,
do not seek the permanent among things
impermanent.

*Hinduism.* Katha Upanishad 4.1-2

The kingdom of Heaven is like treasure hidden in a field, which a man found and covered up; then in his joy he goes and sells all he has and buys that field.

The kingdom of Heaven is like a merchant in search of fine pearls, who, on finding one pearl of great price, went and sold all he had and bought it.

*Christianity.* Matthew 13.44-46

Hear with your ears that which is the sovereign good;
With a clear mind look upon the two sides
Between which each man must choose for himself,
Watchful beforehand that the great test may be accomplished in our favor.

Now at the beginning the twin spirits have declared their nature,
The better and the evil,
In thought and word and deed. And between the two
The wise ones choose well, not so the foolish.

*Zoroastrianism.* Avesta, Yasna 30.2-3

Behold, I [Moses] set before you this day a blessing and a curse: the blessing, if you obey the commandments of the Lord your God, which I command you this day, and the curse, if you do not obey the commandments of the Lord your God, but turn aside from the way which I command you this day, to go after other gods.

*Judaism* and *Christianity.* Deuteronomy 11.26-28

And now remember, remember my brethren, that whosoever perishes, perishes unto himself; and whosoever does iniquity, does it to himself; for behold, you are free; you are permitted to act for yourselves; for behold, God has given you a knowledge and has made you free.

He has given to you that you might know good from evil; and he has given to you that you might choose life or death; and you can do good and be restored to that which is good, or have that which is good restored to you; or you can do evil, and have that which is evil restored to you.

*Church of Jesus Christ of Latter-day Saints.* Book of Mormon, Helaman 14.30-31

No compulsion is there in religion; rectitude has been distinguished from error.

*Islam.* Qur'an 2.256

I [Krishna] give you these precious words of wisdom; reflect on them and then do as you choose.

*Hinduism.* Bhagavad Gita 18.63

I am not biased in favor of Mahavira, nor averse to Kapila or other teachers. I am committed to the preaching that is truly rational.

*Jainism.* Haribhadra, Loktattvanirnaya 38

**Katha Upanishad 4.1-2**: Truth is found through meditation and fixing attention on the Self within, not by dealing with the deceptive and transient phenomena of the world. This is the most fundamental statement of Upanishadic philosophy. Cf. Mahabharata, Shanti Parva 177, p. 133; Udana 11, p. 133; Sifre Deuteronomy 143a, p. 403.

**Yasna 30.2-3**: Cf. Yasna 30.3-5, p. 276, 49.3, p. 681.

**Deuteronomy 11.26-28**: Cf. Deuteronomy 6.20-8.20, pp. 764-65.

**Qur'an 2.256**: Cf. Qur'an 10.94-95, p. 543; 10.99-100, p. 39; Analects 12.19, p. 756.

**Loktattvanirnaya 38:** Haribhadra was an 8th century Shvetambara sage who sought to compare the various philosophies and yogic systems in India at that time. Kapila was an exponent of dualistic Sankhya philosophy.

Do not be misled by reports, or tradition, or hearsay. Be not misled by the authority of religious texts, nor by mere logic or inference, nor by considering appearances, nor by the delight in speculative opinions, nor by seeming possibilities, nor by the idea: "This is our teacher." But when you know for yourselves that certain things are unwholesome and wrong, and bad, then give them up.... And when you know for yourselves that certain things are wholesome and good, then accept them and follow them.

*Buddhism.*
Anguttara Nikaya i.190-91

## *Individual Responsibility*

RESPONSIBILITY IS CENTRAL to what it means to be human. Other creatures have life, consciousness, intelligence, and even some limited linguistic ability; but only human beings are responsible to choose their manner of life and hence their destiny. All the religions of the world emphasize, in one way or another, individual responsibility in matters of faith and practice.

However, the definition and limits of individual responsibility are discerned differently by the various religions. Theravada Buddhism, Jainism, and nontheistic Hinduism regard the journey on the path to liberation as entirely the responsibility of the individual. Each person is "a lamp unto himself"; each works out his own salvation alone and by himself. In several of the passages from Buddhism and Islam given here, there is explicit rejection of reliance upon a savior from without, and both Buddha and Muhammad reject characterization of themselves as saviors.

On the other hand, in Christianity, Judaism, and Islam, individual responsibility is given in the context of prevenient grace; as a person works out his own salvation, at the same time God is at work within. Salvation is offered as a gift, and it is our responsibility to receive it and not reject it. These viewpoints, by which God and human beings are jointly responsible for salvation, are covered in the following section on *Synergy.*

A person's destiny is arguably bound by God's predestination, past karma, or the burden of inherited sin. But several texts in this section reject the notion that such conditions impinge in any way on one's individual responsibility. They argue against a fatalistic attitude born of the belief that one's life is predestined. They also repudiate any illusion that the results of an individual's evil behavior can be mitigated by rank or family connections. Regardless of the conditions by which one person may be afflicted and another favored, every person is a responsible agent who will be called to account for his own deeds.

Individual responsibility means an attitude of self-criticism. We should not blame others for our own difficulties, but rather look for the cause within ourselves. This is an especially prominent theme in Chinese religion, which makes self-rectification the basis for all ethical and political life.

**Anguttara Nikaya i.190-91**: Cf. Majjhima Nikaya i.318, p. 468; i.101, p. 543; Vinaya ii.10, pp. 37-38.

"And now, brethren, I take my leave of you. All the constituents of being are transitory. Work out your salvation with diligence." This was the last word of the Tathagata.

*Buddhism.* Digha Nikaya ii.155-56,
Mahaparinibbana Suttanta

Work out your own salvation with fear and trembling.

*Christianity.* Philippians 2.12

In fear and trembling,
With caution and care,
As though on the brink of a chasm,
As though treading thin ice.

*Confucianism.* Analects 8.3

O ye who believe! You have charge over your own souls.

*Islam.* Qur'an 5.105

I have heard and realized that bondage and salvation are both within yourself.

*Jainism.* Acarangasutra 5.36

If I am not for myself who is for me? And when I am for myself what am I? And if not now, when?

*Judaism.* Mishnah, Abot 1.14

Not by travelling to the end of the world can one accomplish the end of ill. It is in this fathom-long carcass, friend, with its impressions and its ideas that, I declare, lies the world, and the cause of the world, and the cessation of the world, and the course of action that leads to the cessation of the world.

*Buddhism.* Samyutta Nikaya i.62

Single is each being born; single it dies; single it enjoys the reward of its virtue; single it suffers the punishment of its sin.

*Hinduism.* Laws of Manu 4.240

The soul indulges in actions, bears fruits, takes birth, dies and transmigrates, all in utter solitariness. I have always been solitary; I belong to no one else; I behold no one to whom I can say I belong; I behold no one whom I can designate as mine.

*Jainism.* Acarangasutra 4.32

By self do you censure yourself. By self do you examine yourself. Self-guarded and mindful, O bhikkhu, you will live happily.

Self, indeed, is the protector of self. Self, indeed, is one's refuge. Control, therefore, your own self as a merchant controls a noble steed.

*Buddhism.* Dhammapada 379-80

So, Ananda, you must be lamps unto yourselves. Rely on yourselves, and do not rely on external help. Hold firm to the truth as a lamp and a refuge, and do not look for refuge to anything besides yourselves. A brother becomes his own lamp and refuge by continually looking on his body, feelings, perceptions, moods, and ideas in such a manner that he conquers the cravings and depressions of ordinary men and is always strenuous, self-possessed, and collected in mind. Whoever among my disciples does this, either now or when I am dead, if he is anxious to learn, will reach the summit....

*Buddhism.* Digha Nikaya ii.99-100,
Mahaparinibbana Suttanta

**Philippians 2.12**: But see the following verse, Philippians 2.13, p. 493, which acknowledges the accompanying divine grace. Individual responsibility is emphasized strongly by the Latter-day Saints; see Pearl of Great Price, Moses 4.1-4, p. 313.

**Analects 8.3**: This is a quotation from Book of Songs, Ode 195.

**Qur'an 5.105**: Cf. Qur'an 14.22, p. 315; 33.72, p. 215.

**Samyutta Nikaya i.62**: Cf. Sutta Nipata 919-20, p. 393.

**Acarangasutra 4.32**: For more of this passage, see p. 676. Cf. Samayika Patha, p.604.

**Dhammapada 379-80**: Cf. Dhammapada 25, p. 511.

Man should discover his own reality
and not thwart himself.
For he has his self as his only friend,
or as his only enemy.

A person has the self as friend
when he has conquered himself,
but if he rejects his own reality,
the self will war against him.

*Hinduism.* Bhagavad Gita 6.5-6

Everything is in the hand of Heaven except the fear of Heaven.

*Judaism.* Talmud, Berakot 33b

Human responsibility is the absolute law of God, and unless you fulfill it you have no way to get into heaven.

*Unification Church.*
Sun Myung Moon, 12-21-86

Whoever works righteousness benefits his own soul; whoever works evil, it is against his own soul: Your Lord is never unjust to His servants.

*Islam.* Qur'an 41.46

Oneself, indeed, is one's savior, for what other savior could there be? With oneself well controlled one obtains a savior difficult to find.

*Buddhism.* Dhammapada 160

Hoen of Tozan said, "Even Shakya[muni] and Maitreya are servants of another. I want to ask you, who is he?"

*Buddhism.* Mumonkan 45

And We have sent you to men a Messenger; God suffices for a witness. Whosoever obeys the Messenger, thereby obeys God; and whosoever turns his back—We have not sent you to be a watcher over them.

*Islam.* Qur'an 4.79-80

"Please, Man of Shakya," said Dhotaka, "free me from confusion!" "It is not in my practice to free anyone from confusion," said the Buddha. "When you have understood the most valuable teachings, then you yourself will cross this ocean."

*Buddhism.* Sutta Nipata 1063-64

The Master said, "What the superior man seeks is in himself; what the mean man seeks is in others."

*Confucianism.* Analects 15.20

Confucius remarked, "In the practice of archery we have something resembling the principle in a moral man's life. When the archer misses the center of the target, he turns round and seeks for the cause of his failure within himself."

*Confucianism.*
Doctrine of the Mean 14

An individual natively desires to be cause. He tries not to become a bad effect.

You try to help people and people try to help you because you and they want to be cause. When something bad happens, neither one wishes to be cause.

You want to be an effect. Then you find the effect bad. You try not to be an effect. And then you blame something or somebody.

*Scientology.* L. Ron Hubbard,
Handbook for Preclears

**Berakot 33b**: Cf. Sanhedrin 105a, p. 530. The rabbis have high regard for freedom of the human will, and believe that it is beyond the control even of God Almighty.

**Qur'an 4.79-80**: Cf. Qur'an 24.54, p. 453.

**Sutta Nipata 1063-64**: The truth is not to be defined or handed out on a platter; it is to be entered through the enlightenment experience. To grasp the truth intuitively is to *arrive*. For a Jain version of this idea, see Upadesamala 448-49, p. 454.

**Analects 15.20**: Cf. Analects 12.21, p. 523.

**Doctrine of the Mean 14**: Cf. Matthew 7.1-5, p. 703; Analects 12.16, p. 703; Romans 14.10-12, pp. 703-4.

**Handbook for Preclears**: To 'be cause' means to take responsibility for one's actions and for all events that impinge on oneself. To reach the state of Clear means to fully be a cause, never blaming others when things go poorly but always taking responsibility oneself. The way to be a cause is the way of giving.

Or has he not been told of what is in the scrolls
of Moses,
and of Abraham, he who paid his debt in full?
That no soul laden bears the load of another,
and that a man shall have to his account only
as he has labored,
and that his laboring shall surely be seen,
then he shall be recompensed for it with the
fullest recompense,
and that the final end is unto your Lord.

*Islam*. Qur'an 53.36-42

The word of the Lord came to me again: "What do you mean by repeating this proverb concerning the land of Israel, 'The fathers have eaten sour grapes, and the children's teeth are set on edge'? As I live, says the Lord God, this proverb shall no more be used by you in Israel. Behold, all souls are mine; the soul of the father as well as the soul of the son is mine, the soul that sins shall die...."

Yet you say, "Why should not the son suffer for the iniquity of the father?" When the son has done what is lawful and right, and has been careful to observe all my statutes, he shall surely live. The soul that sins shall die. The son shall not suffer for the iniquity of the father, nor the father suffer for the iniquity of the son; the righteousness of the righteous shall be upon himself, and the wickedness of the wicked shall be upon himself.... Therefore I will judge you, O house of Israel, every one according to his ways, says the Lord God.

*Judaism* and *Christianity*. Ezekiel 18

There are certain recluses and brahmins who teach thus: Whatsoever weal or woe or neutral feeling is experienced, all is due to some previous action.... Then I say to them, "So then, owing to a previous action, men will become murderers, thieves, unchaste, liars, slanderers, abusive, babblers, covetous, malicious, and perverse in view. Thus for those who fall back on a former deed as the essential reason [for their behavior] there is neither desire to do, nor effort to do, nor necessity to do this deed or abstain from that deed. So then, the necessity for action or inaction not being found to exist in truth and verity, the term 'recluse' cannot reasonably be applied to yourselves, since you live in a state of bewilderment with faculties unguarded."

Others teach thus: Whatsoever weal or woe or neutral feeling is experienced, all that is due to the creation [predestination] of a Supreme Deity.... Then I say to them, "So then, owing to the creation of a Supreme Deity, men will become murderers, thieves, unchaste... perverse in view. Thus for those who fall back on the creation of a Supreme Deity as the essential reason [for their behavior] there is neither desire to do, nor effort to do, nor necessity to do this deed or abstain from that deed. So then, the necessity for action or inaction not being found to exist in truth and verity, the term 'recluse' cannot reasonably be applied to yourselves, since you live in a state of bewilderment with faculties unguarded."

*Buddhism*.
Anguttara Nikaya i.173-74

**Ezekiel 18**: Vv. 1-3,19-20,30. This important passage was uttered by the prophet Ezekiel to counter the fatalism which was prevalent among the Jews who had been exiled to Babylon and who blamed their lot on the sins of previous generations. In denying a determining role for inherited sin and stressing individual responsibility, he restored a measure of their faith and self-respect. In the Christian era, this passage has been a basis for Jewish arguments against the Christian doctrines of Original Sin and the vicarious Atonement of Christ. Many Jews argue that those doctrines compromise strict individual accountability for sin.

**Anguttara Nikaya i.173-74**: Here Buddha argues against fatalism based on belief in karma or predestination. One's accumulated karma or the predestination of God are minor factors, conditioning but not determining one's life. There is always room to apply oneself, gain merit, and advance on the path towards the ultimate goal. Cf. the Simile of the One-eyed Turtle, Samyutta Nikaya v.455, p. 239, in which the Buddha argues against the easy belief that through reincarnation we will have many and frequent chances at life in this world.

The ancients who wished to manifest their clear character to the world would first bring order to their states. Those who wished to bring order to their states would first regulate their families. Those who wished to regulate their families would first cultivate their personal lives. Those who wished to cultivate their personal lives would first rectify their minds. Those who wished to rectify their minds would first make their wills sincere. Those who wished to make their wills sincere would first extend their knowledge. The extension of knowledge consists in the investigation of things. When things are investigated, knowledge is extended; when knowledge is extended, the will becomes sincere; when the will is sincere, the mind is rectified; when the mind is rectified, the personal life is cultivated; when the personal life is cultivated, the family will be regulated; when the family is regulated, the state will be in order; when the state is in order, there will be peace throughout the world. From the Son of Heaven down to the common people, all must regard cultivation of the personal life as the root or foundation. There is never a case when the root is in disorder and yet the branches are in order.

*Confucianism.* Great Learning

## *Synergy*

IN THE THEISTIC RELIGIONS human efforts are undertaken in the context of God's grace. The relationship between effort and grace is what Thomas Aquinas called synergy: Effort calls forth grace, and grace prompts effort. A number of texts stress human initiative as calling forth grace—"God helps those who help themselves"; conversely, others describe grace as preceding and overshadowing human effort. The concluding texts describe the conjoint action of human effort and divine providence, including the paradoxical nature of their relationship. For texts that regard salvation as by grace alone, see *Grace*, pp. 360-65.

Be mindful of me, and I will be mindful of you.

*Islam.* Qur'an 2.152

If you say yes, your God will say yes.

*African Traditional Religions.* Igbo Proverb (Nigeria)

Resist the devil and he will flee from you.
Draw near to God and he will draw near to you.

*Christianity.* James 4.7-8

God changes not what is in a people, until they change what is in themselves.

*Islam.* Qur'an 13.11

Those who honor me I will honor, and those who despise me shall be lightly esteemed.

*Judaism* and *Christianity.* 1 Samuel 2.30

**Great Learning**: Cf. Chuang Tzu 5, p. 393; Gleanings from the Writings of Baha'u'llah 43, p. 289.
**Qur'an 13.11**: Cf. Abot 2.4, p. 551.
**1 Samuel 2.30**: Cf. Sukka 53a, p. 73; Berakot 55a, p. 513; Matthew 13.12, p. 513.

Realization of the holy Word is granted to those who place themselves under God's shelter.

*Sikhism*. Adi Granth, Wadhans Chhant, M.5, p. 571

He who longs for the Self—by him alone is the Self attained. To him does the Self reveal His true being.

*Hinduism*. Mundaka Upanishad 3.2.3

Remembering me, you shall overcome all difficulties through my grace. But if you will not heed me in your self-will, nothing will avail you.

*Hinduism*. Bhagavad Gita 18.58

He who conforms to the Way is gladly accepted by the Way; he who conforms to virtue is gladly accepted by virtue; he who conforms to loss is gladly accepted by loss.

*Taoism*. Tao Te Ching 23

If a man sanctify himself a little, he becomes much sanctified; if he sanctify himself below, he becomes sanctified from above; if he sanctify himself in this world, he becomes sanctified in the world to come.

*Judaism*. Talmud, Yoma 39a

If you wish to find the true way,
Right action will lead you to it directly;
But if you do not strive for Buddhahood
You will grope in the dark and never find it.

*Buddhism*. Sutra of Hui Neng 2

In the Book of Changes it is said, "He is blessed by Heaven. Good fortune. Nothing that does not further."

The Master said, "To bless means to help. Heaven helps the man who is devoted; men help the man who is true. He who walks in truth and is devoted in his thinking, and furthermore reveres the worthy, is blessed by Heaven. 'He has good fortune, and there is nothing that would not further' [Hexagram 42: Increase]."

*Confucianism*. I Ching, Great Commentary 1.12.1

Ask, and it will be given to you; seek, and you will find; knock, and it will be opened to you. For every one who asks receives, and he who seeks finds, and to him who knocks it will be opened. Or what man of you, if his son asks him for bread, will give him a stone? Or if he asks for fish, will give him a serpent? If you, then, who are evil, know how to give good gifts to your children, how much more will your Father who is in heaven give good things to those who ask him!

*Christianity*. Matthew 7.7-11

God has declared: I am close to the thought that My servant has of Me, and I am with him whenever He recollects Me. If he remembers Me in himself, I remember him in Myself, and if he remembers Me in a gathering I remember him better than those in the gathering do, and if he approaches Me by as much as one hand's length, I approach him by a cubit.... If he takes a step towards Me, I run towards him.

*Islam*. Hadith

God asks nothing of any soul save that which He has given it.

*Islam*. Qur'an 65.7

**Mundaka Upanishad 3.2.3**: Cf. Bhagavad Gita 7.21-23, p. 518. For a different and more grace-centered interpretation of this same text, in which it is the Self who chooses whom he will, see p. 362.

**Bhagavad Gita 18.58**: Cf. Hadith of Muslim, p. 543.

**Tao Te Ching 23**: Cf. Analects 7.6, p. 484; 7.29, p. 72. On 'conforming to loss,' see Bhagavad Gita 7.21-23, Holy Teaching of Vimalakirti 6, p. 518; Makkot 10b, p. 517; Abot 4.12, p. 512.

**Yoma 39a**: Cf. Abot 2.4, p. 551; Berakot 55a, p. 513; Jerusalem Talmud, Kiddushin 1.9, p. 513.

**Matthew 7.7-11**: Cf. Luke 6.38, p. 694; Book of Mormon, 3 Nephi 18.19-21, p. 593.

**Hadith**: A sacred hadith transmitted by Ibn Hanbal, the great Muslim jurist. Cf. Sukka 53a, p. 73; Romans 8:26-27, p. 464.

**Qur'an 65.7**: Cf. Qur'an 2.286, p. 362; 48.4, p. 462; 1 Corinthians 10.13, p. 362.

God gives each person a hook with which to pluck his fruit.

*African Traditional Religions.* Igbo Proverb (Nigeria)

Behold, I stand at the door and knock; if any one hears my voice and opens the door, I will come in to him and eat with him, and he with me.

*Christianity.* Revelation 3.20

For by grace you have been saved through faith; and this is not your own doing, it is the gift of God—not because of works, lest any man should boast. For we are his workmanship, created in Christ Jesus for good works, which God prepared beforehand, that we should walk in them.

*Christianity.* Ephesians 2.8-10

Lo! This is an admonishment, that whosoever will may choose a way unto his Lord; yet you will not, unless God wills. Lo! God is Knower, Wise. He makes whom He will to enter His mercy, and for evildoers has prepared a painful doom.

*Islam.* Qur'an 76.29-31

Rabbi Akiba says, "Everything is foreseen, yet freedom of choice is given; the world is judged by grace, yet all is according to the preponderance of works."

*Judaism.* Mishnah, Abot 3.19

By man's actions is acquired the vesture of
human incarnation;
By God's grace is attained the Door of
Liberation.
Nanak! Know the All-holy to be Almighty,
Absolute.

*Sikhism.* Adi Granth, Japuji 4, M.1, p. 2

Work out your own salvation with fear and trembling; for God is at work in you, both to will and to work for his good pleasure.

*Christianity.* Philippians 2.12-13

No affliction befalls, except it be by the leave of God. Whosoever believes in God, He will guide his heart. And God has knowledge of everything.

*Islam.* Qur'an 64.11

Should you do anything that is beautiful, God
has caused it to be beautiful.
Should you do anything evil, God has caused it
to be evil.

*African Traditional Religions.* Nupe Proverb (Nigeria)

O My servants, everyone of you is in error, except the one I have guided, so ask guidance from Me and I will guide you. O My servants, everyone of you is hungry, except him whom I have fed, so ask food of Me and I will feed you. O My servants, everyone of you is naked except him whom I have clothed, so ask clothing of Me and I will clothe you. O My servants, you sin day and night, and I pardon your sins; so ask pardon of Me and I will pardon you.

*Islam.* Forty Hadith of an-Nawawi 24

All undertakings in this world depend both on the ordering of fate and on human exertion; but among these two the ways of fate are unfathomable; in the case of man's work action is possible.

*Hinduism.* Laws of Manu 7.205

All by Thee is accomplished, Thine is the
might,
Thou watcheth Thy handiwork,
With chess pieces raw and ripe.

**Revelation 3.20**: Cf. John 15.4-11, p. 462.

**Ephesians 2.8-10**: The two halves of this passage balance the grace of God with the obligation for good works. Priority is given to grace, by which we are transformed and enabled to do the good works.

**Qur'an 76.29-31**: Cf. Qur'an 49.7, p. 538.

**Abot 3.19**: This passage juxtaposes two pairs of contraries: divine foreknowledge and human freedom, and the divine attributes of mercy and justice. Cf. Exodus 33.19, p. 494; Berakot 33b, p. 489.

**Philippians 2.12-13**: Individual responsibility and the indwelling grace of God are juxtaposed in this passage. Cf. Romans 8.26-27, p. 464.

All that into the world have come, must depart
hence—
All shall by turns go.
Why put out of mind the Lord, master of life
and death?
By one's own hands is one's affairs set straight.

*Sikhism*. Adi Granth, Asa-ki-Var,
M.1, pp. 473-74

Lord Mahavira! Your word sometimes supports the view of providence, at other times calls events spontaneously occurring or ascribes destiny to external factors. At times you hold the deeds of individuals to be the mold of their desert, at other times find that another's deeds project their moral reflection on the individual. The miracle is that none blames you for these paradoxical utterances!

*Jainism*. Siddhasena,
Dvatrimshika 3.8

## *Predestination*

DOCTRINES OF PREDESTINATION provide one explanation for the fact that individuals are subject to variations in endowment, fortune, and circumstances that are beyond their control. According to this explanation, all such differences are attributed to the hand of God, who is omnipotent and controls all. There are degrees of predestination. Absolute predestination means that the individual's eternal destiny—heaven or hell—is predetermined before his birth. Milder forms of predetermination describe God as apportioning blessings and hardship as he wills, then permitting human beings limited freedom to make the best of their lot. Predestination is given particular emphasis in Islam, Christianity, Sikhism, and African traditional religions.

This section opens with passages on God's unconstrained freedom to grant mercy or impose hardship as he wills. Next we offer passages which describe human free action as constrained by God's irresistible decrees. Further passages describe how God's predestination is realized through easing and guiding people to perform the deeds which will lead them to their predetermined good or evil destiny. The concluding passages describe one event in human life which certain scriptures say is predestined: the time of one's death.

The order that God has arranged, mortal man
cannot upset.

*African Traditional Religions*.
Akan Proverb (Ghana)

I will be gracious to whom I will be gracious,
and I will show mercy on whom I will show
mercy.

*Judaism* and *Christianity*.
Exodus 33.19

**Asa-ki-Var, M.1**: The image of God in heaven moving chess pieces which determine man's destiny on earth is evocative of absolute predestination. Yet that is all the more reason to be mindful of God, Master of the game; for who knows on what basis he decides his moves, or whether he will not choose to move the pieces again?

**Akan Proverb**: Cf. Nupe Proverb, p. 493.

God makes the provision wide for whomever of His servants He will, and straitens it for whomever He will. Lo! God is Aware of all things.

*Islam*. Qur'an 29.62

The Lord is the Doer, cause of all:
What avail man's designs?
As is the Lord's will, so it happens.
The Lord is Almighty, without impediment to
His will.
All that is done is by His pleasure:
From each He is far, to each close.
All He considers, watches over,
discriminates—
Himself He is sole and all.

*Sikhism*. Adi Granth,
Gauri Sukhmani, M.5, p. 279

We know that in everything God works for good with those who love him, who are called according to his purpose. For those whom he foreknew he also predestined to be conformed to the image of his Son, in order that he might be the first-born among many brethren. And those whom he predestined he also called; and those whom he called he also justified; and those whom he justified he also glorified.

*Christianity*. Romans 8.28-30

Neither utterance nor silence lies within man's
power;
Neither to ask nor to give.
Neither life nor death depends on man's effort.
Authority, wealth, or command—none of
these come by man's own endeavor;
Nor meditation, enlightenment, or cogitation.
Neither by his effort nor praxis may man
escape free of worldliness.
God alone who has the power, exercises it.
Says Nanak, All before Him are alike—none
high or low.

*Sikhism*. Adi Granth,
Japuji 33, M.1, p. 7

Nothing will happen to us except what God has decreed for us: He is our Protector.

*Islam*. Qur'an 9.51

No man bruises his finger here on earth unless it was so decreed against him in Heaven.

*Judaism*. Talmud, Hullin 7b

Where you fall, there your God pushed you down.

*African Traditional Religions*.
Igbo Proverb (Nigeria)

God has both the yam and the knife;
only those whom he gives a slice can eat!

*African Traditional Religions*.
Igbo Proverb (Nigeria)

The Lord's favors cannot be forced out of His
hand:
Some even while awake attain them not;
On others he confers these, shaking them
awake.

*Sikhism*. Adi Granth,
Sri Raga Mahalla, M.1, p. 83

Whatever you do not wish to do
because of your delusions,
you will do even against your will,

**Exodus 33.19**: Cf. James 4.13-16, p. 649; Abot 3.19, p. 493.

**Qur'an 29.62**: Cf. Qur'an 49.7, p. 538; 76.29-31, p. 493.

**Gauri Sukhmani, M.5**: Cf. Asa-ki-Var, M.1, pp. 493-94.

**Romans 8.28-30**: Some interpret this passage to allow room for human free will; since it may be that not all among 'those whom he called' will be justified, should they not believe; and not all among 'those whom he justified' will be glorified, should they not continue to live a sanctifying life. Cf. 2 Peter 1.5-11.

**Qur'an 9.51**: Cf. Qur'an 18.23-24, p. 649; Psalm 127.1-2, p. 553.

bound by your natural duty [karma].
The Lord, Arjuna, is present
inside all beings,
moving them like puppets
by his magic power.

*Hinduism*. Bhagavad Gita 18.60-61

It may be that one of you will be performing the works of the people of Paradise, so that between him and Paradise there is the distance of only an arm's length, but then what is written for him overtakes him, and he begins to perform the works of the people of hell, into which he will go. Or maybe one of you will be performing the works of the people of hell, so that between him and hell there is the distance of only an arm's length, but then what is written for him will overtake him, and he will begin to perform the works of the people of Paradise, into which he will go.

*Islam*. Forty Hadith of an-Nawawi 4

I will harden Pharaoh's heart, and though I multiply my signs and wonders in the land of Egypt, Pharaoh will not listen to you.

*Judaism* and *Christianity*. Exodus 7.3-4

The Word has been realized against most of them, yet they do not believe. Surely We have put on their necks fetters up to the chin, so their heads are raised; and We have put up before them a barrier and behind them a barrier; and We have covered them, so they do not see. Alike it is to them whether you have warned them or you have not warned them: they do not believe.

*Islam*. Qur'an 36.7-10

Yüeh-cheng Tzu saw Mencius. "I mentioned you to the prince," said he, "and he was to have come to see you. Amongst his favorites is one Tsang Ts'ang who dissuaded him. That is why he failed to come."

"When a man goes forward," said Mencius, "there is something which urges him on; when he halts, there is something which holds him back. It is not in his power either to go forward or to halt. It is due to Heaven that I failed to meet the Marquis of Lu. How can this fellow Tsang be responsible for my failure?"

*Confucianism*. Mencius I.B.16

Is there injustice on God's part? By no means! For he said to Moses, "I will have mercy on whom I have mercy, and I will have compassion on whom I have compassion." So it depends not upon man's will or exertion, but upon God's mercy. For the scripture says to Pharaoh, "I have raised you up [in hardness of heart] for the very purpose of showing my power in [against] you, that my name may be proclaimed in all the earth." So then he has mercy upon whomever he wills, and he hardens the heart of whomever he wills.

You will say to me then, "Why does he still find fault? For who can resist his will?" But who are you, a man, to answer back to God? Will what is molded say to its molder, "Why have you made me thus?" Has the potter no right over the clay, to make out of the same lump one vessel for beauty and another for menial use? What if God, desiring to show his wrath and to make known his power, has endured with much patience the vessels of wrath made for destruction, in order to make known the riches of his glory for the vessels of mercy, which he has prepared beforehand for glory, even us whom he has called?

*Christianity*. Romans 9.14-24

'Ali said, "We were one day at a funeral in the Baqi' al-Gharqad, when the Prophet—upon whom be Allah's blessing and peace—came and sat, and we sat around him." He had with him a staff and he bowed his head and began to make marks with his staff on the ground. Then he said, "There is no one of you, no soul that

**Bhagavad Gita 18.60-61**: This passage appears to bridge the topics of predestination and karma. The bondage to God's will is realized through karma, which is itself a manifestation of God's material aspect (*prakriti*).

**Romans 9.14-24**: The figure of the potter and clay is a frequent one in the Bible. In Jeremiah 18.3-11, p. 764, it is used to illustrate the different lesson that God is responsive to human action.

has been born, but has his place in Paradise or in hell already decreed for him, or, to put it otherwise, his unhappy or his happy fate has been decreed for him." A man spoke up, "O Apostle of Allah, shall we not then just entrust ourselves to what is written for us, and renounce works, since he amongst us who belongs to the Blessed will inevitably be led to the works of the Blessed, and he amongst us who belongs to the Damned will inevitably be led to the works of the Damned?" He answered, "As for those who are to be among the Blessed, the works of the Blessed will be made easy for them, and as for those [who will be among the] Damned, the works of the Damned will be made easy for them." Then he recited,

> So as for him who gives and shows piety,
> And gives credence to what is best,
> We shall ease the way for him to that which is easy,
> But as for him who is miserly
> And takes pride in wealth,
> And treats what is best as false,
> For him We shall ease the way to that which is hard,
> Nor will his wealth avail him when he is perishing.
> It is Ours to give guidance,
> And to Us belong both the last and the first.

*Islam.* Hadith of Bukhari

No man, though he had a hundred souls, can outlive the statute of the gods.

*Hinduism.* Rig Veda 10.33.9

For not of your will were you formed, and not of your own will were you born, and not of your will do you live, and not of your own will will you die, and not of your will are you to give account and reckoning before the Supreme King of kings, the Holy One, Blessed be He.

*Judaism.* Mishnah, Abot 4.29

Like the waves in large rivers, that which has been done before cannot be turned back, and, like the tide of the sea, the approach of death is hard to stem. Bound by the fetters of the fruits of good and evil, like a cripple; without freedom, like a man in prison; beset by many fears, like one standing before the Judge of the dead; intoxicated by the wine of illusion, like one intoxicated by wine; rushing about, like one possessed of an evil spirit; bitten by the world, like one bitten by a great serpent; darkened by passion, like the night; illusory, like magic; false, like a dream; pithless, like the inside of a banana tree; changing its dress in a moment, like an actor, fair in appearance, like a painted wall—thus they call him.

*Hinduism.* Maitri Upanishad 4.2

Time is no one's friend and no one's enemy; when the effect of his acts in a former existence, by which his present existence is caused, has expired, he snatches a man away forcibly. A man will not die before his time has come, even though he has been pierced by a thousand shafts; he will not live after his time is out, even though he has only been touched by the point of a blade of grass. Neither drugs, nor magical formulas, nor burnt offerings, nor prayers will save a man who is in the bonds of death or old age. An impending evil cannot be averted even by a hundred precautions; what reason then for you to complain?

*Hinduism.* Institutes of Vishnu 20.43-46

**Hadith of Bukhari**: The recitation is from the Qur'an 92.5-13.
**Abot 4.29**: For more of this passage, see p. 243.
**Maitri Upanishad 4.2**: Cf. Lankavatara Sutra 24, p. 282; Svetasvatara Upanishad 1.6-8, p. 282.

## *Karma and Inherited Sin*

MANY RELIGIONS EXPLAIN differences in people's fortunes and native endowments as a consequence of inheritance from the past. This inheritance is conceived in two ways, either as karma from past lives or as the inherited sins of the fathers. These doctrines encourage us to accept our lot in life and to suffer it patiently, in order to expiate past deeds and earn merit. Furthermore, they teach that the individual is not an island unto himself or herself. Rather, we each stand in solidarity with the larger community of the human race and necessarily partake of its good and evil within ourselves.

*Karma* means action, and all actions have consequences for good or ill. In accordance with the theory of reincarnation, which is common to the religions born in India, differences in fortune, social position, and endowment are the inherited consequences of actions done in previous lifetimes. In Hinduism this doctrine affirms the absolute justice of the universe with its many inequalities; for who is man to try to change what has been fated by his own past deeds?

The doctrine of karma has been criticized for fostering fatalistic and complacent acceptance of the caste system, poverty, and social injustice. But with careful understanding, we may regard karma as explaining the inequalities in human life without justifying them. After all, if a person escapes from his caste, or a caste is given preferential favors by government decree, or the caste system is dissolved altogether, may not such also be seen as the fruit of previous good deeds?

On the other hand, Buddhism cautions against interpreting karma as a deterministic principle.[1] In Theravada Buddhism, karma is but one among twenty-four factors (*paccaya*) that condition a person's life, and a particular tendency due to past karma may be actualized only when other circumstances, some under the volitional control of the individual, are conducive to its expression. Some Hindu scriptures teach that divine grace can annul and supersede the effects of past deeds.[2]

In religions which do not accept the doctrine of reincarnation, the individual's connectedness to the larger humanity through time may be understood through lineage and family rather than through the continuity of a single soul inhabiting many past lives. The sins of the fathers, when they have not been properly expiated, are passed on and lead to evil consequences for subsequent generations. Likewise, an ancestor's merits and good works, when they are not reaped as blessings in his own life, will accrue as blessings for his descendants. Inherited sin, like karma, is passed on from birth, but its transmission is analogous to the transmission of the parents' biological endowment rather than through the entry into the womb of a previously incarnate soul.

Individuals are also connected to the larger humanity through space; they are a part of the collectives of nation, race, tribe, religion, and suffer or prosper with the fortunes of those collectives. When a community or a nation sins and faces punishment—war, famine, disease, or an epidemic of drugs and crime, each of its members suffers as a consequence of belonging to that community

---

[1] See, for example, Anguttara Nikaya i.173-74, p. 490.

[2] See Mundaka Upanishad 2.2.9, p. 369; Bhagavad Gita 9.30, p. 370; and Srimad Bhagavatam 11.2, p. 361.

even though their personal lives may be blameless. We may call this collective sin, and it also helps to explain people's unequal fortunes. Inherited sin, karma, and collective sin each give a partial explanation for the inequalities of the world within which the individual must find his way.

Like the waves in great rivers, there is no turning back of that which has previously been done.... [The soul is] like a lame man—bound with the fetters made of the fruit of good and evil.

*Hinduism.* Maitri Upanishad 4.2

By the delusions of imagination, touch, and sight,
And by eating, drinking, and impregnation there is a birth and development of the self.
According to his deeds (*karma*) the embodied one successively
Assumes forms in various conditions.
Coarse and fine, many in number,
The embodied one chooses forms according to his own qualities.
Each subsequent cause of his union with them is seen to be
Because of the quality of his acts and of himself.

*Hinduism.* Svetasvatara Upanishad 5.11-12

If it be that good men and good women, who receive and retain this discourse, are downtrodden, their evil destiny is the inevitable retributive result of sins committed in their past mortal lives. By virtue of their present misfortunes the reacting effects of their past will be thereby worked out, and they will be in a position to attain the Consummation of Incomparable Enlightenment.

*Buddhism.* Diamond Sutra 16

The wise priest knows he now must reap
The fruits of deeds of former births.
For be they many or but few,
Deeds done in covetousness or hate,
Or through infatuation's power,
Must bear their needful consequence.
Hence not to covetousness, nor hate,
Nor to infatuation's power
The wise priest yields, but knowledge seeks
And leaves the way to punishment.

*Buddhism.* Anguttara Nikaya iii.33

"Frequently I have been born in a high family, frequently in a low one; I am not mean, nor noble, nor do I desire social preferment." Thus reflecting, who would brag about his family or about his glory, or for what should he long? Therefore a wise man should neither be glad nor angry about his lot: he should know and consider about the happiness of all living creatures. Carefully conducting himself, he should mind this: "I will always experience blindness, deafness, dumbness, be one-eyed, hunchbacked, black, white, and every color; because of my carelessness I am born in many births, experience many feelings."

*Jainism.* Acarangasutra 2.50-55

Subha, the son of Toddeya, asked the Exalted One, "What is the cause and what is the reason, O Gotama, for which among men and the beings who have been born as men there is found to be lowness and excellence? For some people are of short life span and some of long life span; some suffer from many illnesses and some are free from illness; some are ugly and some beautiful; some are of little account and some have great power; some are poor and some are wealthy; some are born into lowly

**Maitri Upanishad 4.2**: Cf. Sutta Nipata 654, p. 102; Dhammapada 127, p. 124.
**Svetasvatara Upanishad 5.11-12**: Cf. Brihadaranyaka Upanishad 4.4.5-6, pp. 124-25.
**Anguttara Nikaya iii.33**: Cf. Garland Sutra 10, p. 125.

families and others into high families; some are devoid of intelligence and some possess great wisdom. What is the cause, what the reason for which among men and the beings who have been born as men there is to be found lowness and excellence?"

"Men have, O young man, deeds as their very own, they are inheritors of deeds, deeds are their matrix, deeds are their kith and kin, and deeds are their support. It is deeds that classify men into high or low status.

"Here, O young man, some woman or man is a taker of life, fierce, with hands stained by blood, engaged in killing and beating, without mercy for living creatures. As a result of deeds thus accomplished, thus undertaken, he is reborn on the breakup of the body, after death, into a state of woe, of ill plight, of purgatory or hell, or if he comes to be born as a man, wherever he may be reborn he is of a short life span. This course—that he is a taker of life, fierce, with hands stained by blood, engaged in killing and beating, without mercy for living creatures, leads to shortness of life.

"Here, on the other hand, O young man, some woman or man gives up killing, totally refraining from taking life and abides laying down the rod, laying down the weapon, conscientious, endowed with mercy and sensitive to the weal of all living beings. As a result of the deeds thus accomplished, thus undertaken, he is reborn on the breakup of the body, after death, into a happy state, into a heavenly world, or if he comes to be born as a man, wherever he is reborn he has a long life span. This course—that one gives up taking life and abides laying down the rod, laying down the weapon, conscientious, endowed with mercy for living creatures, leads to longevity.

"Here some woman or man is by nature a tormentor of living creatures.... As a result of the deeds thus accomplished... wherever he is reborn he suffers much from sickness.... But here some woman or man is not by nature a tormentor of living beings... he is free from sickness.

"Here some woman or man is wrathful... wherever he is reborn he is ugly.... But here some woman or man is not wrathful... he is handsome.

"Here some woman or man is jealous-minded... wherever he is born he is of little account.... But here some woman or man is not jealous-minded... he has great power.

"Here some woman or man is not a giver to ascetic or brahmin... wherever he is born he is poor.... Here some woman or man is a giver... he is wealthy.

"Thus men have, O young man, deeds as their very own, they are inheritors of their deeds, their deeds are their kith and kin, and their deeds their support. It is their deeds that classify men into this low or high status."

*Buddhism.*
Majjhima Nikaya iii.202-206,
Culakammavibhanga Sutta

The murderer of a brahmin becomes consumptive, the killer of a cow becomes hump-backed and imbecile, the murderer of a virgin becomes leprous—all three born as outcastes. The slayer of a woman and the destroyer of embryos becomes a savage full of diseases; who commits illicit intercourse, a eunuch; who goes with his teacher's wife, disease-skinned. The eater of flesh becomes very red; the drinker of intoxicants, one with discolored teeth.... Who steals food becomes a rat; who steals grain becomes a locust... perfumes, a muskrat; honey, a gadfly; flesh, a vulture; and salt, an ant.... Who commits unnatural vice becomes a village pig; who consorts with a sudra woman becomes a bull; who is passionate becomes a lustful horse.... These and other signs and births are seen to be the karma of the embodied, made by themselves in this world. Thus the makers of bad karma, having experienced the tortures of hell, are reborn with the residues of their sins, in these stated forms.

*Hinduism.* Garuda Purana 5

**Majjhima Nikaya iii.202-206**: Cf. Majjhima Nikaya i.389-90, p. 242.

In the flower-named city, Pataliputta, in the best part of the earth, were two bhikkhunis, members of the Shakya clan, possessed of good qualities, one of them called Isidasi, the second called Bodhi, both possessed of virtue, delighting in meditation and study, having great learning, with defilements shaken off. Seated happily in a lonely place, Bodhi asked, "You are lovely, noble Isidasi, your youth has not yet faded. Having seen what fault [in household life] are you then intent on renunciation?"...

"Hear, Bodhi, how I went forth. My father was a merchant in Ujjeni, and I was his only daughter, dear, charming, and beloved. Then a wealthy merchant from Saketa sent men to woo me; to him my father gave me as a daughter-in-law....

"I myself adorned my lord, like a servant-girl. I myself prepared the rice gruel; I myself washed the bowl; as a mother to her only son, so I looked after my husband. Yet my husband took offense at me, who in this way had shown him devotion, an affectionate servant, with humbled pride, an early riser, not lazy, virtuous. He said to his parents, 'I shall not be able to live together with Isidasi in one house.... She does me no harm, but to me she is odious. I have had enough; I am leaving her.' Hearing this utterance my father-in-law and mother-in-law asked me, 'What offense has been committed by you? Speak confidently how it really was.' 'I have not offended at all; I have not harmed; I have not said any evil utterance; what can be done when my husband hates me?' I said. Downcast, overcome by pain, they led me back to my father's house, saying, 'While keeping our son safe, we have lost the goddess of beauty incarnate.'

"Then my father gave me to the household of a second rich man for half the bride price for which the merchant had taken me. In his house too I lived a month, then he too rejected me, although I served him like a slave girl, virtuously. Then my father spoke to one wandering for alms, a tamer of others and self-tamed, 'Be my son-in-law; throw down your cloth and pot.' He too, having lived with me for a fortnight, returned me to my father, saying, 'Give me my cloth and pot and cup; I shall beg for alms again.'...

"When he departed, I thought, 'I shall ask leave and go to die, or else I shall go forth.' Then the noble lady Jinadatta, expert in the discipline, having great learning, possessed of virtue, on her begging round came to my father's house. Seeing her in our house, rising up from my seat, I offered it to her; having paid homage to her feet when she had sat down, I gave her food. Having completely satisfied her with food and drink, I said, 'Noble lady, I wish to go forth.' My father implored me, 'Stay home and practice the doctrine, child; and with food and drink satisfy ascetics and brahmins who come here.' But lamenting, I begged my father, 'Evil indeed was the action done by me [the karma leading to my misfortune]; I shall destroy it.' Then my father said, 'Attain enlightenment and the foremost doctrine and obtain quenching, which the best of men have realized.' Saluting my parents and relatives, I went forth. In seven days I attained the three knowledges.

"I know now my own last seven births; I shall relate to you the actions of which this misfortune is the fruit and result; listen to it attentively. In the city of Erakaccha I was a wealthy goldsmith. Intoxicated by pride in my youth, I had sexual intercourse with another's wife. Having fallen from there, I was cooked in hell; I cooked for a long time; and rising up from there I entered the womb of a female monkey. A great monkey, leader of the herd, castrated me when I was seven days old; this was the fruit of the action of having seduced another's wife. I died in the Sindhava forest and entered the womb of a one-eyed, lame she-goat. As a goat I was castrated, worm-eaten, tail-less, unfit, because of having seduced another's wife. Next I was born of a cow belonging to a cattle-dealer; a lac-red calf. I was castrated after twelve months and drew the plough, pulled the cart, and became blind, tail-less, unfit, because of having seduced another's wife. Then I was born of a household slave in the street, neither as a woman or a man, because of having seduced another's wife. In my thirtieth year I died; I was born as a girl in a carter's family which was poor and much in debt. To satisfy the creditors, I was sold to a caravan leader and dragged off, wailing, from my home. Then in my sixteenth year, when I had arrived at marriageable age, his son, Giridasa by name, took me as a wife. But he had another wife, virtuous and possessed of good qualities, who was affectionate towards her husband; with her I stirred up enmity. This [my misfortunes] were fruit of that last action, that men rejected me though I served like a slave girl. Even of that I have now made an end."

*Buddhism.* Therigatha 400-447, Isidasi Sutta

If the punishment does not fall on the offender himself, it falls on his sons; if not on the sons, on his grandsons.

*Hinduism.* Laws of Manu 4.173

For I the Lord your God am a jealous God, visiting the iniquity of the fathers upon the children to the third and the fourth generation of those who hate me, but showing steadfast love to the thousands of those who love me and keep my commandments.

*Judaism* and *Christianity.* Exodus 20.5-6

Loose us from the yoke of the sins of our fathers
and also of those which we ourselves have committed.

*Hinduism.* Rig Veda 7.86.5

In this world the fate of every posterity is similar to that of its ancestors. Neither death leaves off the work of destruction, nor the survivors give up their sinful activities. Human beings follow in each others' footsteps; groups after groups and nations after nations end their days without mending their ways.

*Islam.* Nahjul Balagha, Sermon 86

If at death there remains guilt unpunished, judgment extends to his posterity.... When parties by wrong and violence take the money of others, an account is taken, and set against its amount, of their wives and children and all the members of their families, when these gradually die. If they do not die, there are disasters from water, fire, thieves, and robbers, from losses of property, illnesses, and evil tongues to balance the value of their wicked appropriations.

*Taoism.* Treatise on Response and Retribution 4-5

You who are so powerful as to enter inside the small medicine gourd to shelter yourself from danger,
Have you forgotten your children?
Have you forgotten your wife?
The evil seeds a man sows
Shall be reaped by his offspring.
Cruelty, like a troublesome chicken, is inevitably punished.
However late it is,
The punishment will come when it will.

*African Traditional Religions.* Yoruba Song (Nigeria)

Happy are the righteous! Not only do they acquire merit, but they bestow merit upon their children and children's children to the end of all generations, for Aaron had several sons who deserved to be burned like Nadab and Abihu, but the merit of their father helped them. Woe unto the wicked! Not alone that they render themselves guilty, but they bestow guilt upon their children and children's children unto the end of all generations. Many sons did Canaan have, who were worthy to be ordained like Tabi, the slave of Rabbi Gamaliel, but the guilt of their ancestor caused them [to lose their chance].

*Judaism.* Talmud, Yoma 87a

Rabbi Phinehas the Priest said in reference to Proverbs 11.21, "If you have fulfilled a command, do not seek its reward from God straightaway, lest you not be acquitted of sin, but be regarded as wicked because you have not sought to cause your children to inherit

**Exodus 20.5-6:** But compare Ezekiel 18, p. 490.

**Yoruba Song:** The image of a troublesome chicken at the mercy of the farmer well illustrates the powerlessness of a wicked man in the hands of God.

anything. For if Abraham, Isaac, and Jacob had sought the reward of the good deeds which they performed, how could the seed of these righteous men [e.g., Israel] have been delivered?"

*Judaism*. Midrash, Exodus Rabbah 44.3

As he passed by, he saw a man blind from his birth. And his disciples asked him, "Rabbi, who sinned, this man or his parents, that he was born blind?" Jesus answered, "It was not that this man sinned, or his parents, but that the works of God might be made manifest in him."... As he said this, he spat on the ground and made clay of the spittle and anointed the man's eyes with the clay, saying to him, "Go, wash in the pool of Siloam." So he went and washed and came back seeing.

*Christianity*. John 9.1 7

Even those who are pious and innocent suffer for the misdeeds of others through their contact, as fish in a snake-infested lake.

*Hinduism*. Ramayana, Aranya Kanda 38

All of you are pledges one for the other: all of you, aye the world, exist through the merit of a single righteous man among you, and if but one man sin, the whole generation suffers.

*Judaism*. Tanhuma ed. Buber 25a

Justice is turned back,
and righteousness stands afar off;
for truth has fallen in the public squares,
and uprightness cannot enter.
Truth is lacking,
and he who departs from evil makes himself a prey.

*Judaism* and *Christianity*. Isaiah 59.14-15

Ibn 'Umar reported God's Messenger as saying, "When God causes punishment to descend on a people, those righteous ones among them will be smitten by the punishment, but afterwards they will be resurrected according to their deeds."

*Islam*. Hadith of Bukhari and Muslim

❖

**John 9.1-7**: Jesus rejects his disciples' speculation about inherited sin, for it does not serve any positive purpose. Our burdens of sin are only the contexts in which we may establish faith in order that God's grace may shine forth.

**Tanhuma ed. Buber 25a**: See Genesis 18.20-33, p. 561, where God destroys the people of Sodom and Gomorrah for want of ten righteous men. Cf. Hullin 92a, p. 730.

**Isaiah 59.14-15**: Cf. Asa, M.1, p. 768.

# *Duty*

IN THE MIDST OF LIFE'S uncontrollable circumstances, scripture advocates an attitude that is responsible and dutiful. Just as *Synergy*, pp. 491-94, describes the conjunction of responsibility and grace, Duty describes the conjunction of responsibility and destiny.

Admonitions to be responsible for one's own duty and station may refer to the obligations of one's role in society, what in Hinduism is called *svadharma*. By fulfilling the obligations incumbent upon one's position, the entire social order is supported and the community as a whole benefits. This is the case whether one's duty is that of a prince or a janitor; every role is valuable in building the whole. One's obligations are often proportionate to one's gifts and abilities, "to whom much is given, will much be required." Similarly, on the path of spiritual ascent, a person should not neglect his own welfare to compare himself to others and envy those who progress faster. Even to be preoccupied with helping others is flawed if done without regard to one's own spiritual growth, for how can a person properly guide others to enlightenment when his own soul is deep in ignorance? Our duty is to fulfill our individual covenant with God. Duty to God should transcend the varying fortunes of life; we should never seek to escape or avoid it. The example of Job reminds us that even in difficulty we should willingly "drink from the cup" which God has provided.

We then move to the ethics of fulfilling one's duty. To do one's duty is a challenge, particularly when to shirk responsibility appears as an inviting temptation. The ethical imperative of duty is a reliable beacon for directing one's steps in the face of adversity or temptations of worldly ease. In the Confucian doctrine of Rectification of Names, the call to conform to one's station is a challenge in the sense that most people stray far from the duties which their positions would properly entail. In particular, people in high positions are duty-bound to serve the public and show compassion to those below them, but they rarely fulfil this, being rulers in name but not in fact. Thus, the ethic of fulfilling one's duty is seen as the root of what is most honorable and noble in man.

The concluding passages reject fatalism and see in duty an opportunity for action. Implicit is a distinction between the fetters of conventional social duties and the higher duty to fulfil one's potential as a child of God.

There is not one of us but has his appointed position, and we are verily ranged in ranks [for service].

*Islam*. Qur'an 37.164-65

Through your sojourn in the world,
Know your station in life.
Know it well, you in the world,
Know it well.

*Shinto*. Moritake Arakida, One Hundred Poems about the World

**One Hundred Poems about the World:** This passage reflects the fusion of Confucian and Shinto ideas in Japanese religion. The notion of 'station in life' comes largely from the Confucian hierarchic system.

For the sake of others' welfare, however great, let not one neglect one's own welfare. Clearly perceiving one's own welfare, let one be intent on one's own goal.

*Buddhism*. Dhammapada 166

By devotion to one's own particular duty, everyone can attain perfection. Let me tell you how. By performing his own work, one worships the Creator who dwells in every creature. Such worship brings that person to fulfillment.

It is better to perform one's own duties imperfectly than to master the duties of another. By fulfilling the obligations he is born with, a person never comes to grief. No one should abandon duties because he sees defects in them.

Every action, every activity, is surrounded by defects as a fire is surrounded by smoke.

*Hinduism*. Bhagavad Gita 18.44-48

Leaving alone things which do not concern him is one of the good things in a man's Islam.

*Islam*. Forty Hadith of an-Nawawi 12

If one does not perform duty to one whom the duty is due, one becomes a thief of the duty.

*Zoroastrianism*. Avesta, Videvdad 4.1

Borrowed trousers and garments
Never fit a man well;
They are usually either too tight
Or too loose.
Proper fitting is achieved
When one wears one's own dress.

*African Traditional Relgions*.
Yoruba Proverb (Nigeria)

Let him not despise what he has received, nor should he live envying the gains of others. The disciple who envies the gains of others does not attain concentration.

Though receiving but little, if a disciple does not despise his own gains, even the gods praise such a one who is pure in livelihood and is not slothful.

*Buddhism*. Dhammapada 365-66

The little that one produces [oneself] with a broken hoe is better than the plenty that another gives you.

*African Traditional Religions*.
Buji Proverb (Nigeria)

You cannot use your hand to force the sun to set.

*African Traditional Religions*.
Bette Proverb (Nigeria)

All appointments are from Heaven, even that of a janitor.

*Judaism*. Talmud, Baba Batra 91b

A favorite saying of the rabbis of Jabneh was, I am God's creature and my peasant neighbor is God's creature. My work is in the town and his work is in the country. I rise early for my work and he rises early for his work. Just as he does not presume to do my work, so I do not presume to do his work. Will you say, I do much and he does little? We have learned, One may do much or one may do little; it is all the same, provided he directs his heart to Heaven.

*Judaism*. Talmud, Berakot 17a

**Bhagavad Gita 18.44-48**: By 'defects' the Bhagavad Gita is defending the imperfections of the caste system against Buddhist and Jain critiques. At the same time, this is practical advice that can be applied to many of life's situations.

**Dhammapada 365-66**: On complaint and envy, see Bhagavad Gita 3.31-32, p. 107.

**Bette Proverb**: This means that you cannot succeed in overstepping your position or seeking to do that for which you have no ability.

Every one to whom much is given, of him will much be required.

*Christianity*. Luke 12.48

He has raised you in ranks, some above others, that He may try you in the gifts He has given you.

*Islam*. Qur'an 6.165

Shall I not drink the cup which the Father has given me?

*Christianity*. John 18.11

In the day of prosperity be joyful, and in the day of adversity consider; God made the one as well as the other, so that man may not find out anything that will be after him.

*Judaism* and *Christianity*. Ecclesiastes 7.14

Nanak, for man it is idle to ask for pleasure
when suffering comes;
Pleasure and suffering are like robes which man
must wear as they come.
Where arguing is of no avail, it is best to be
contented.

*Sikhism*. Adi Granth,
Var Majh, M.1, p. 149

I go out at the north gate,
With my heart full of sorrow.
Straitened am I and poor,
And no one takes knowledge of my distress.
So it is! Heaven has done it;—
What then shall I say?

*Confucianism*. Book of Songs, Ode 40

Satan went forth from the presence of the Lord, and afflicted Job with loathsome sores from the sole of his foot to the crown of his head. And he took a potsherd with which to scrape himself, and sat among the ashes. Then his wife said to him, "Do you still hold fast to your integrity? Curse God, and die." But he said to her, "You speak as one of the foolish women would speak. Shall we receive good at the hand of God, and shall we not receive evil?"

*Judaism* and *Christianity*. Job 2.7-10

All a gentleman can do in starting an enterprise is to leave behind a tradition which can be carried on. Heaven alone can grant success.

*Confucianism*. Mencius I.B.14

When one follows unswervingly the path of virtue it is not to win advancement. When one invariably keeps one's word it is not to establish the rectitude of one's actions. A gentleman merely follows the norm and awaits his destiny.

*Confucianism*. Mencius VII.B.33

It is not your duty to complete the work, but neither are you free to desist from it; if you have studied much Torah, much reward will be given you; for faithful is your Employer to pay you the wages for your labor. Know that the grant of reward to the righteous will be in the time to come.

*Judaism*. Abot 2.21

Duke Ching of Ch'i asked Confucius about government. Confucius replied saying, "Let the prince be a prince, the minister a minister, the father a father, and the son a son." The Duke said, "How true! For indeed, when the prince is not a prince, the minister not a minister, the father not a father, the son not a son, one may have a dish of millet in front of one and yet not know if one will live to eat it."

*Confucianism*. Analects 12.11

**John 18.11**: Compare Jesus' prayer in the Garden of Gethsemane, where he reluctantly accepted the cup of dying on the cross; see Luke 22.42, p. 429.

**Book of Songs, Ode 40**: The officer's silence under his burden and distress shows his submission to Heaven.

**Job 2.7-10**: In this story, Satan is acting only on God's permission, so Job's plight is ultimately due to the hand of God. See Job 1.6-12, p. 314n.

**Analects 12.11**: This passage gives the Confucian doctrine of Rectification of Names. Cf. Mencius I.B.8, p. 741; II.B.4, p. 736.

He who does not fulfil his duty is not respected by honest men. It is how he acts that reveals the nobility or baseness of a man and distinguishes the honest or the dishonest person; otherwise the ignoble would resemble the noble, and he who is devoid of honor would resemble a man of integrity; he who is unworthy would be deemed worthy and he who is depraved would be considered to be a man of virtue. If, under the pretext of duty, I adopt this unrighteous course, calculated to produce the confusion of social roles, and do acts not recognized by the scriptures, I should, renouncing good, have to reap evil only! What sensible man, able to discern what is just and unjust, would respect me in this world, if I behaved viciously and dishonorably?...

Duty, the essence of which is truth, is said to be the root of all in this world; it is truth that is the support of duty; everything has truth as its basis; there is nothing greater than the truth. Offerings, sacrifices, libations, mortifications, asceticism, and the Vedas all have truth as their foundation; therefore truth is before all. Alone it supports the world, alone it supports the family; its non-observance sends one to hell; it alone is exalted in heaven. Why should I not fulfil the command of my father, who was a devotee of truth? Neither ambition, forgetfulness, nor pride would cause me to destroy the bridge of morality!

*Hinduism.* Ramayana, Ayodhya Kanda 109

The moral man conforms himself to his life circumstances; he does not desire anything outside his position. Finding himself in a position of wealth and honor, he lives as becomes one living in a position of wealth and honor. Finding himself in a position of poverty and humble circumstances, he lives as becomes one living in a position of poverty and humble circumstances. Finding himself in uncivilized countries, he lives as becomes one living in uncivilized countries. Finding himself in circumstances of danger and difficulty, he acts according to what is required of a man under such circumstances. In one word, the moral man can find himself in no situation in life in which he is not master of himself.

In high position he does not domineer over his subordinates. In a subordinate position he does not court the favors of his superiors. He puts in order his own personal conduct and seeks nothing from others; hence he has no complaint to make. He complains not against God, nor rails against men.

Thus it is that the moral man lives out the even tenor of his life, calmly waiting for the appointment of God, whereas the vulgar person takes to dangerous courses, expecting the uncertain chances of luck.

*Confucianism.* Doctrine of the Mean 14

Tzu-kao, Duke of She, who was being sent on a mission to Ch'i, consulted Confucius. "The king is sending me on a very important mission. Ch'i will probably treat me with great honor but will be in no hurry to do anything more. Even a commoner cannot be forced to act, much less one of the feudal lords. I am very worried about it...."

Confucius said, "In the world, there are two great decrees: one is fate and the other is duty. That a son should love his parent is fate—you cannot erase this from his heart. That a subject should serve his ruler is duty—there is no place he can go and be without his ruler, no place he can escape to between heaven and earth. These are called the great decrees. Therefore, to serve your parents and be content to follow them anywhere—this is the perfection of filial piety. To serve your ruler and be content to do anything for him—this is the peak of loyalty. And to serve your own mind so that sadness or joy do not sway or move it; to understand what you can do nothing about and be content with

**Ramayana, Ayodhya Kanda 109**: Rama rejects his friends' arguments that he should seize the throne and abrogate the command of his father that he retire to the forest. He regards the duty of a filial son to obey his father's wishes to be more precious than a kingdom.

**Doctrine of the Mean 14**: Compare 1 Corinthians 9.19-22, p. 719.

it as with fate—this is the perfection of virtue. As a subject and a son, you are bound to find things you cannot avoid. If you act in accordance with the state of affairs and forget about yourself, then what leisure will you have to love life and hate death?...

"Just go along with things and let your mind move freely. Resign yourself to what cannot be avoided and nourish what is within you—this is best. What more do you have to do to fulfill your mission? Nothing is as good as following orders—that is how difficult it is!"

*Taoism*. Chuang Tzu 4

Every one should remain in the state in which he was called. Were you a slave when called? Never mind. But if you can gain your freedom, avail yourself of the opportunity. For he who was called in the Lord as a slave is a freedman of the Lord. Likewise he who was free when called is a slave of Christ. You were bought with a price; do not become slaves of men. So, brethren, in whatever state each was called, there let him abide with God.

*Christianity*. 1 Corinthians 7.20-24

Mencius said, "Though nothing happens that is not due to destiny, one accepts willingly only what is one's proper destiny. That is why he who understands destiny does not stand under a wall on the verge of collapse. He who dies after having done his best in following the Way dies according to his proper destiny. It is never anyone's proper destiny to die in fetters."

*Confucianism*. Mencius VII.A.2

There was a demon named Harikesha, devoted to the brahmins and to dharma. From his very birth he was a devotee of Shiva. His father said, "I think you cannot be my son, or else you are indeed ill-begotten. For this is not the behavior (*svadharma*) for families of demons. You are by your inborn nature cruel-minded, flesh-eating, destructive. Do not behave in this evil way [that is, worshipping brahmins and Shiva]; the behavior ordained by the Creator for demons should not be abandoned; just as householders should not perform actions appropriate to the hermitage. Abandon this human nature with its complicated scale of rites; you must have been born from a mortal man, to be set on this wrong path. Among mortals, the appropriate ritual duty arises according to caste; and I too have ordained your duty in the proper way." But Harikesha went to Benares and performed asceticism until Shiva accepted him as a great yogi, one of his own hosts.

*Hinduism*. Matsya Purana 180.5-7

❖

**1 Corinthians 7.20-24**: Christianity does not sanction slavery. However, in the Roman Empire, when Paul wrote this letter, many slaves became Christians. Paul counseled them to fulfill their social duties, internally living in the spiritual freedom of Christ, and all the while looking for an opportunity to gain lawfully their external freedom as well. Cf. Philemon 10-17, p. 192.

**Matsya Purana 180.5-7**: This and similar stories of the good demon who aspires to a destiny beyond that ordained for his race are understood as metaphors for any person who aspires to a destiny beyond his caste. However, it is not always the case that, as in this example, will triumphs over blood. See Vishnu Purana 3.17-18, p. 318; cf. Sanhedrin 105a, p.530.

CHAPTER 13

# SELF-CULTIVATION AND SPIRITUAL GROWTH

A RESPONSIBLE LIFE IS NOT REALIZED IN A MOMENT. Throughout a lifetime, effort must be invested continually for spiritual growth and self-development. A growing and fragile self, like any growing thing, requires cultivation. Good character is realized through constant cultivation of goodness. In particular, a mature person will have cultivated an attitude of sincerity, a pure heart, and a measure of self-control. Virtues which are required on the way include: a proper start, heedfulness and vigilance during the journey, and perseverance to reach the goal.

## *Spiritual Growth*

LIFE AS A PROCESS OF GROWTH is spiritual as well as physical, from one stage to the next. These stages may be described in many ways, but fundamentally they include: a foundation stage when the knowledge of truth or the gift of salvation is first acquired; a growth stage where the person practices that truth and develops virtue, self-control, insight, and self-confidence; and finally the stage of maturity where the person realizes the fulness of perfection: the stage of arahant, bodhisattva, or oneness with Christ. The process of growth is sometimes expressed by the metaphor of sprouting grain.

O man! Verily you are ever toiling on toward your Lord—painfully toiling—but you shall meet Him.... You shall surely travel from stage to stage.

*Islam*. Qur'an 84.6, 19

We must begin... with the more simple demonstrations of control, and the sooner we begin the better. The final demonstration takes time for its accomplishment. When walking, we are guided by the eye. We look before our feet, and if we are wise, we look beyond a single step in the line of spiritual advancement.

*Christian Science*.
Science and Health, 428-29

To the pupil training, in the straight way walking,
By ending [his sins] first comes knowledge;
Straight follows insight; by that insight freed
He knows in very truth: Sure is my freedom
By wearing out the fetter of becoming.

*Buddhism*. Itivuttaka 53

Practicing step by step,
One gradually fulfills all Buddha teachings.
It is like first setting up a foundation
Then building the room:
Generosity and self-control, like this,
Are bases of enlightening beings' practices.

*Buddhism*. Garland Sutra 10

The Master said, "At fifteen I set my heart upon learning. At thirty, I had planted my feet upon firm ground. At forty, I no longer suffered from perplexities. At fifty, I knew what were the biddings of Heaven. At sixty, I heard them with a docile ear. At seventy, I could follow the dictates of my own heart; for what I desired no longer overstepped the boundaries of right."

*Confucianism*. Analects 2.4

Through constant effort over many lifetimes, a person becomes purified of all selfish desires and attains the supreme goal of life.

*Hinduism*. Bhagavad Gita 6.45

By degrees, little by little, from time to time, a wise person should remove his own impurities as a smith removes the dross from silver.

*Buddhism*. Dhammapada 239

We rejoice in our sufferings, knowing that suffering produces endurance, and endurance produces character, and character produces hope, and hope does not disappoint us, because God's love has been poured into our hearts.

*Christianity*. Romans 5.3-5

Study of Torah leads to precision, precision to zeal, zeal to cleanliness, cleanliness to restraint, restraint to purity, purity to holiness, holiness to meekness, meekness to fear of sin, fear of sin to saintliness, saintliness to the holy spirit, and the holy spirit to life eternal.

*Judaism*. Talmud, Aboda Zara 20b

The kingdom of God is as if a man should scatter seed upon the ground, and should sleep and rise night and day, and the seed should sprout and grow, he knows not how. The earth produces of itself, first the blade, then the ear, then the full grain in the ear. But when the grain is ripe, at once he puts in the sickle, because the harvest has come.

*Christianity*. Mark 4.26-29:
Parable of the Sprouting Seed

Muhammad is the Apostle of God; and those who are with him are strong against unbelievers, but compassionate amongst each other.... And their similitude in the Gospel is: Like a

**Qur'an 84.6, 19**: Cf. Qur'an 91.7-10, p. 511; Chun Boo Kyung, p. 119.

**Bhagavad Gita 6.45**: What in some religious conceptions requires many lifetimes, other doctrines regard as attainable in one life, through God's grace. Yet the seeker who attains the supreme goal may look back to the efforts of his ancestors or his own incarnations in previous lives, grateful for the foundations of faith and good works which they sowed and which he could finally reap.

**Mark 4.26-29**: This parable represents the growth of the Kingdom of Heaven—interpreted either corporately or within the heart of the individual believer—as a natural process that occurs mysteriously and gradually, enlivened by God's fertilizing grace. It is likened to the growth of grain in three stages of formation—'the blade,' growth—'the ear,' and maturity—'the full grain,' followed by a fourth stage of returning to God—'the harvest.'

seed which sends forth its blade, then makes it strong; it then becomes thick, and it stands on its own stem, filling the sowers with wonder and delight.

*Islam.* Qur'an 48.29

Grace was given to each of us according to the measure of Christ's gift.... to equip the saints for the work of ministry, until we all attain to the unity of the faith and of the knowledge of the Son of God, to mature manhood, to the measure of the stature of the fulness of Christ; so that we may no longer be children, tossed to and fro on every wind of doctrine, by the cunning of men, by their craftiness in deceitful wiles. Rather, speaking the truth in love, we are to grow up in every way into him who is the head, into Christ—from whom the whole body, joined and knit together by every joint with which it is supplied, when each part is working properly, makes bodily growth and upbuilds itself in love.

*Christianity.* Ephesians 4.7-16

## Cultivate the Good

IF, CONTINUALLY AND OVER a long time, a person practices good deeds, he will form good habits. Good habits cultivated over a long time lead to the formation of good character. According to the Parable of the Sower, the human spirit is like a field that must be sowed, cultivated, and weeded if it is to bear a good crop. People can only develop good habits by constant practice; otherwise they will develop bad habits that become progressively more difficult to break. Thus good begets good, while evil begets evil. We also include several passages which suggest that even doing good for bad or base motives can be beneficial by encouraging good habits.

Not to do any evil, to cultivate good, to purify one's mind—this is the teaching of the Buddhas.

*Buddhism.* Dhammapada 183

Immaturity:
A watery hole at the foot of a mountain amidst uncultivated growth.
The superior man by determined good conduct nourishes his virtue.

*Confucianism.* I Ching 4: Immaturity

By the... soul, and Him who perfected it
and inspired it with conscience of what is wrong for it and right for it:
He is indeed successful who causes it to grow,
and he is indeed a failure who stunts it.

*Islam.* Qur'an 91.7-10

By sustained effort, earnestness, discipline, and self-control, let the wise man make for himself an island which no flood can overwhelm.

*Buddhism.* Dhammapada 25

**Qur'an 48.29**: The 'similitude in the Gospel' is Mark 4.26-29, preceding.

**Ephesians 4.7-16**: The gift of salvation is only the beginning of the saint's spiritual growth to 'mature manhood' which is oneness with Christ.

**Dhammapada 183**: This may well be the most famous aphorism of the Buddha.

Train yourself in godliness; for while bodily training is of some value, godliness is of value in every way, as it holds promise for the present life and also for the life to come.

*Christianity*. 1 Timothy 4.7-8

This Atman, resplendent and pure, whom the sinless disciples behold residing within the body, is attained by unceasing practice of truthfulness, austerity, right knowledge, and continence.

*Hinduism*. Mundaka Upanishad 3.1.5

Birth does not lead to greatness; but cultivation of numerous virtues by a man leads him to greatness. It is a pearl that possesses real greatness and not the pair of shells in which it is produced.

*Jainism*. Vajjalagam 687

Gain:
The superior man, seeing what is good, imitates it;
Seeing what is bad, he corrects it in himself.

*Confucianism*. I Ching 42: Gain

The domain of voidness, yet where one cultivates all types of virtues, such is the domain of the bodhisattva.

*Buddhism*. Holy Teaching of Vimalakirti 5

Make every effort to supplement your faith with virtue, and virtue with knowledge, and knowledge with self-control, and self-control with steadfastness, and steadfastness with godliness, and godliness with brotherly affection, and brotherly affection with love. For if these things are yours and abound, they keep you from being ineffective or unfruitful in the knowledge of our Lord Jesus Christ. For whoever lacks these things is blind and shortsighted and has forgotten that he was cleansed from his old sins. Therefore, brethren, be the more zealous to confirm your call and election, for if you do this you will never fall; so there will be richly provided for you an entrance into the eternal kingdom of our Lord and Savior Jesus Christ.

*Christianity*. 2 Peter 1.5-11

Run to do even a slight precept, and flee from transgression; for precept draws precept in its train, and transgression, transgression; for the recompense of a precept is a precept, and the recompense of a transgression is a transgression.

*Judaism*. Mishnah, Abot 4.2

Make haste in doing good; check your mind from evil; for the mind of him who is slow in doing meritorious actions delights in evil.

Should a person commit evil, he should not do it again and again; he should not find pleasure therein: painful is the accumulation of evil.

Should a person perform a meritorious action, he should do it again and again; he should find pleasure therein: blissful is the accumulation of merit.

*Buddhism*. Dhammapada 116-18

Do not disregard evil, saying, "It will not come nigh unto me": by the falling of drops even a water jar is filled; likewise the fool, gathering little by little, fills himself with evil.

Do not disregard merit, saying "It will not come nigh unto me": by the falling of drops of water even a water jar is filled; likewise the wise man, gathering little by little, fills himself with good.

*Buddhism*. Dhammapada 121-22

**1 Timothy 4.7-8**: Paul frequently compares inner training to the physical training of an athlete: see 1 Corinthians 9.24-27, p. 530. Cf. Dhammapada 80, p. 522; Chuang Tzu 19, p. 136.

**Mundaka Upanishad 3.1.5**: Cf. Bhagavad Gita 5.24, p. 379.

**I Ching 42**: Cf. Analects 7.3, 7.21, p. 470.

**Holy Teaching of Vimalakirti 5**: This and the following passage teach that attaining enlightenment or receiving salvation are not excuses for ceasing to cultivate the good. Mahayana Buddhism teaches that everything phenomenal is void *(sunya)*, yet that void is the womb of everything. Voidness correctly realized generates wisdom and compassion; these direct one to cultivate the good.

Black goats must be caught early, before it is dark.

*African Traditional Religions.* Igala Proverb (Nigeria)

If you neglect the Torah, many causes for neglecting it will present themselves to you.

*Judaism.* Mishnah, Abot 4.12

Mencius said to Kau Tzu, "A trail through the mountains, if used, becomes a path in a short time, but, if unused, becomes blocked by grass in an equally short time. Now your heart is blocked by grass."

*Confucianism.* Mencius VII.B.21

If one guards himself against sin three times, the Holy One guards him from then on.

*Judaism.* Jerusalem Talmud, Kiddushin 1.9

Engage in Torah and charity even with an ulterior motive, for the habit of right doing will lead also to right motivation.

*Judaism.* Talmud, Pesahim 50b

The Master said, "The inferior man is not ashamed of unkindness and does not shrink from injustice. If no advantage beckons he makes no effort. If he is not intimidated he does not improve himself, but if he is made to behave correctly in small matters he is careful in large ones. This is fortunate for the inferior man. This is what is meant when it is said in the I Ching, 'His feet are fastened in the stocks, so that he cannot walk. No blame' [Hexagram 21: Biting Through].

"If good does not accumulate, it is not enough to make a name for a man. If evil does not accumulate, it is not enough to destroy a man. Therefore the inferior man thinks to himself, Goodness in small things has no value, and so neglects it. He thinks, Small sins do no harm, and so does not give them up. Thus his sins accumulate until they can no longer be covered up, and his guilt becomes so great that it can no longer be wiped out. In the I Ching it is said, 'His neck is fastened in the wooden cangue, so that his ears are hidden. Misfortune' [Hexagram 21: Biting Through]."

*Confucianism.* I Ching, Great Commentary 2.5.7-8

The Holy One gives wisdom only to him who has wisdom.

*Judaism.* Talmud, Berakot 55a

For to him who has will more be given, and he will have abundance; but from him who has not, even what he has will be taken away.

*Christianity.* Matthew 13.12

If there is no host on the inside to receive it [the Tao], it will not stay; if there is no mark on the outside to guide it, it will not go. If what is brought forth from the inside is not received on the outside, then the sage will not bring it forth. If what is taken in from the outside is not received by a host on the inside, the sage will not entrust it.

*Taoism.* Chuang Tzu 14

Listen! A sower went out to sow. And as he sowed, some seed fell along the path, and the birds came and devoured it. Other seed fell on rocky ground, where it had not much soil, and immediately it sprang up, since it had no depth of soil; and when the sun rose it was scorched, and since it had no root it withered away. Other seed fell among thorns, and the thorns grew up and choked it. And other seeds fell into good soil and brought forth grain, growing up and increasing and yielding thirtyfold, and sixtyfold, and a hundredfold....

Do you not understand this parable?... The sower sows the word. And these are the ones along the path, where the word is sown; when they hear, Satan immediately comes and takes

**Igala Proverb**: This means nip problems in the bud before they escalate.

**Matthew 13.12**: Cf. the Parable of the Talents, Matthew 25.14-30, pp. 715-16.

**Chuang Tzu 14**: Cf. Tao Te Ching 41, p. 575.

away the word which is sown in them. And these in like manner are the ones sown upon rocky ground, who, when they hear the word, immediately receive it with joy; and they have no root in themselves, but endure for a while; then, when tribulation or persecution arises on account of the word, immediately they fall away. And others are the ones sown among thorns; they are those who hear the word, but the cares of the world, and the delight in riches, and the desire for other things, enter in and choke the word, and it proves unfruitful. But those that were sown upon good soil are the ones who hear the word and accept it and bear fruit, thirtyfold and sixtyfold and a hundredfold.

*Christianity*. Mark 4.3-20: Parable of the Sower

## *Sincerity*

SINCERITY OF HEART is the starting point of spiritual practice and ethical living. A person's inner intention goes far toward determining the extent to which a particular action is *Good and Evil*, pp. 330-34. In theistic traditions, God sees into the heart and requites a person according to his or her inmost reality. For Shinto, sincerity *(makoto)* means the inner, harmonious coherence of thought and action, of the individual's will and the will of the kami. Or in Buddhism, as the Dhammapada so forcefully states, action begins with the mind; it is created by the mind; it goes forth according to the inner state of the mind. In some of the passages gathered here, sincerity means the natural and spontaneous flow of the mind, devoid of all pretense and all egoistic grasping. Other passages view the matter differently, and call for self-examination and self-cultivation in order to manifest true sincerity.

Even when the outward form of an act is obedient and faithful, the person's inner intentions become manifest in the end. The concluding passages examine how differences in the progress made in the religious life are due to the different hearts with which people approach the same task.

Sincerity is the single virtue that binds divinity and man in one.

*Shinto*. Takatomi Senge

It matters not whether you do much or little, so long as your heart is directed to Heaven.

*Judaism*. Talmud, Berakot 17a

A man becomes pure through sincerity of intellect; thereupon, in meditation, he beholds Him who is without parts.

*Hinduism*. Mundaka Upanishad 3.1.8

**Mark 4.3-20**: The individual's capacity for truth determines the degree of its reception. Yet that capacity is itself something to be cultivated, by clearing away the thorns and pulling up the weeds so that the Word of God may bear fruit. Cf. Tao Te Ching 41, p. 575.

**Berakot 17a**: Berakot 5.1, p. 600; Baraita Kallah, p. 620; Psalm 145.18, p. 592.

**Mundaka Upanishad 3.1.8**: Cf. Rig Veda 10.151.4-5, p. 538.

Sincerity (*ihsan*): You should worship God as if you saw Him; for although you do not see Him, He sees you.

*Islam*. Forty Hadith of an-Nawawi 2

Sincerity (*makoto*) is the mind of the kami. Accordingly, when serving the kami in worship, if one has a mind of sincerity, the kami will surely respond.

*Shinto*. Ekken Kaibara, Divine Injunctions

"The one true God is Spirit"; therefore, when you pray to the Divine Spirit, you must be true in spirit.

*Omoto Kyo*. Michi-no-Shiori

Abu Huraira reported God's Messenger as saying, "God does not look at your forms and your possessions, but He looks at your hearts and your deeds."

*Islam*. Hadith of Muslim

Through the best righteousness,
Through the highest righteousness,
May we catch sight of Thee,
May we approach Thee,
May we be in perfect friendship with Thee.

*Zoroastrianism*. Yasna 60.21

A worship without love
And an unfeeling act,
Behold, my brothers, is
A pictured loveliness—
No joy in its embrace;
A painted sugarcane—
No relish in its taste.
O Lord, without sincerity
Is no piety.

*Hinduism*. Basavanna, Vacana 126

No matter how dark, the hand always knows the way to the mouth.

*African Traditional Religions*. Idoma Proverb (Nigeria)

Mind is the forerunner of all evil states. Mind is chief; mind-made are they. If one speaks or acts with wicked mind, because of that suffering follows one, even as the wheel [of the cart] follows the hoof of the draught ox.

Mind is the forerunner of all good states. Mind is chief; mind-made are they. If one speaks or acts with pure mind, because of that happiness follows one, even as one's shadow that never leaves.

*Buddhism*. Dhammapada 1-2

Thoughts alone cause the round of births (*samsara*); let a man strive to purify his thoughts. What a man thinks, that he is: this is an old secret.

By the serenity of his thoughts a man blots out all actions, whether good or bad. Dwelling within his Self with serene thoughts, he obtains imperishable happiness.

If the thoughts of a man were so fixed on Brahman as they are on the things of this world, who would not then be freed from bondage?

The mind, it is said, is of two kinds, pure and impure: impure from the contact with lust, pure when free from lust.

When a man, having freed his mind from sloth, distraction, and vacillation, becomes as it were delivered from his mind, that is the highest point.

*Hinduism*. Maitri Upanishad 6.34.3-7

**Forty Hadith of an-Nawawi 2**: Compare Analects 3.12, p. 620.

**Divine Injunctions**: Cf. Records of the Enshrinement of the Two Imperial Deities at Ise, p. 594; One Hundred Poems on the Jeweled Spear, p. 550.; also Boran Prayer, p. 594; Chuang Tzu 23, p. 524.

**Michi-no-Shiori**: Cf. Records of the Enshrinement of the Two Imperial Deities at Ise, p. 594; also Sifre Deuteronomy 80a, p. 594; Boran Prayer, p. 594; Psalm 145.18, p. 592.

**Idoma Proverb**: This means that regardless of the circumstances, you can always know yourself.

**Dhammapada 1-2**: These are the justly famous opening verses of the Dhammapada. Cf. Lankavatara Sutra 64, p. 103; 78, p. 121; Matthew 15.11-20, p. 331; Sarvarthasiddhi 6.3, p. 332.

By the Truth I mean purity and sincerity in their highest degree. He who lacks purity and sincerity cannot move others. Therefore he who forces himself to lament, though he may sound sad, will awaken no grief. He who forces himself to be angry, though he may sound fierce, will arouse no awe. And he who forces himself to be affectionate, though he may smile, will create no air of harmony. True sadness need make no sound to awaken grief; true anger need not show itself to arouse awe; true affection need not smile to create harmony. When a man has the Truth within himself, his spirit may move among external things. That is why the Truth is to be prized!

*Taoism*. Chuang Tzu 31

The truly upright is that which flows out of your genuine innermost self as a result of the sincerity shown by the kami; on all occasions, you must exert this sincerity to the utmost, even in the most minor of your activities. Courtesy and ritual without this sincerity and honesty are mistaken and insufficient. It is like drawing a bow and merely releasing the string blindly without firming your hand, or like trying to move in a boat without an oar.

*Shinto*. Mochimasa Hikita,
Records of the Divine Wind

You should speak with your mind—your inmost self. If it is sympathetic with others, you can become one with God and automatically know the truth of the universe.

*Unification Church*.
Sun Myung Moon, 11-19-78

Brother! Without guidance of the Preceptor
comes not illumination (*sahaj*).
From the holy Word arises equipoise (*sahaj*),
And is the holy Lord attained.
What in serenity (*sahaj*) is sung is properly
rewarded;
Without serenity all utterance is in vain.
From equipoise arises devotion;
From equipoise comes love and dispassion
toward the world.
From equipoise arise joy and peace;
Without equipoise is life a waste.

*Sikhism*. Adi Granth,
Sri Raga Ashtpadi, M.3, p. 68

You shall love the Lord your God with all your heart, with all your soul, and with all your might.

*Judaism* and *Christianity*.
Deuteronomy 6.5

Because you are lukewarm, and neither cold nor hot, I will spew you out of my mouth.

*Christianity*. Revelation 3.16

We should examine ourselves and learn what is the affection and purpose of the heart, for in this way only can we learn what we honestly are.

*Christian Science*.
Science and Health . 8

What is meant by "making the will sincere" is allowing no self-deception, as when we hate a bad smell or love a beautiful color. This is called satisfying oneself. Therefore the superior man will always be watchful over himself when alone.

**Chuang Tzu 31**: Cf. Chuang Tzu 13, p. 148; Doctrine of the Mean 20.18, p. 154.

**Records of the Divine Wind**: Cf. Chuang Tzu 13, p. 148; 23, p. 524.

**Sri Raga Ashtpadi, M.3**: The key term in this passage is *sahaj*, variously translated illumination, equipoise, serenity, sponaneous devotion. It is essentially an unforced, spontaneous dawning of the self, born from within. Sikhism is opposed to hatha yoga, a term which it uses to classify all yogic practices involving forced austerities, extreme effort, and asceticism. Instead it seeks to cultivate a spontaneous sense of harmony and poise: *sahaj*. Hence a comparison with Taoist and Shinto concepts of spontaneity and sincerity is useful. Cf. Chuang Tzu 23, p. 524.

**Deuteronomy 6.5**: This is taken from The Shema, Deuteronomy 6.4-9, p. 31.

**Revelation 3.16**: This letter, sent to the wealthy church of Laodicea, complains that their lukewarm Christianity is nauseating. It is the antithesis of the absolute sincerity called for in the previous passage.

When the inferior man is alone and leisurely, there is no limit to which he does not go in his evil deeds. Only when he sees a superior man does he then try to disguise himself, concealing his evil and showing off the good in him. But what is the use? For other people see him as if they see his very heart. This is what is meant by the saying that what is true in a man's heart will be shown in his outward appearance. Therefore the superior man will always be watchful over himself when alone.

Tseng Tzu said, "What ten eyes are beholding and what ten hands are pointing to—isn't it frightening?"

Wealth makes a house shining and virtue makes a person shining. When one's mind is broad and his heart generous, his body becomes big and is at ease. Therefore the superior man always makes his will sincere.

*Confucianism.* Great Learning 6.1-4

Truth [sincerity] means the fulfilment of our self; and moral law means following the law of our being. Truth is the beginning and end, the substance, of material existence. Without truth there is no material existence. It is for this reason that the moral man values truth.

Truth is not only the fulfilment of our own being; it is that by which things outside of us have an existence. The fulfilment of our being is moral sense. The fulfilment of the nature of things outside of us is intellect. These, moral sense and intellect, are the powers or faculties of our being. They combine the inner or subjective and the outer or objective use of the power of the mind. Therefore, with truth, everything done is right.

*Confucianism.* Doctrine of the Mean 25

If, brethren, a woman or man or a young lad fond of self-adornment, on examining the reflection of his own face in a bright clean mirror or bowl of clear water, should see therein a stain or speck, he will strive to remove that stain or speck; and when he no longer sees it there he is pleased and satisfied, thinking, "A gain it is to me that I am clean." Likewise a monk's introspection is most fruitful in good conditions, thus: "Do I or do I not generally live covetous? Do I or do I not generally live malevolent in heart? Do I or do I not generally live possessed by sloth and torpor? Do I or do I not generally live excited in mind? Do I generally live in doubt and wavering, or have I crossed beyond it? Do I generally live wrathful or not? Do I generally live with soiled thoughts or clean thoughts? Do I generally live with body passionate or not? Do I generally live sluggish or full of energy? Do I generally live uncontrolled or well controlled?"

If on self-examination a monk finds thus: "I generally live covetous, malevolent in heart, possessed by sloth and torpor, excited in mind, doubtful and wavering, wrathful, with body passionate, sluggish, uncontrolled"—then that monk must put forth extra desire, effort, endeavor, exertion, impulse, mindfulness, and attention for the abandoning of those wicked, unprofitable states.

*Buddhism.* Anguttara Nikaya v.66

A man is allowed to follow the road he wishes to pursue.

*Judaism.* Talmud, Makkot 10b

Like a clear mirror
Reflecting images according to the forms,
So from Buddha's field of blessings
Rewards are obtained according to one's heart.

*Buddhism.* Garland Sutra 10

**Great Learning 6.1-4**: These two Confucian passages and the following Buddhist text describe a more active and mindful type of sincerity, one requiring constant effort at practice and self-examination. It is quite a different concept from that of the Taoist and Sikh passages just given. See Doctrine of the Mean 33, p. 71; Mencius II.A.2, p. 527.

**Doctrine of the Mean 25**: 'Truth' means trueness, the state of the fullest expression of one's being. Hence it may also be translated 'sincerity.' The necessary complementarity of internal and external, of morality and material production, is characteristic of Chinese thought.

**Anguttara Nikaya v.66**: Cf. Majjhima Nikaya i.55-63, pp. 604-5.

**Garland Sutra 10**: Cf. Kularnava Tantra 13, pp. 583-84.

To the pure all things are pure, but to the corrupt and unbelieving nothing is pure; their very minds and consciences are corrupted.

*Christianity*. Titus 1.15

Actions are but by intention and every man shall have but that which he intended. Thus he whose migration was for Allah and His Messenger, his migration was for Allah and His Messenger, and he whose migration was to achieve some worldly benefit or to take some woman in marriage, his migration was for that for which he migrated.

*Islam*. Forty Hadith of an-Nawawi 1

When a person is devoted to something with complete faith, I unify his faith in that. Then, when his faith is completely unified, he gains the object of his devotion. In this way, every desire is fulfilled by me. Those whose understanding is small gain only transient satisfaction; those who worship the gods go to the gods. But my devotees come to me.

*Hinduism*. Bhagavad Gita 7.21-23

The Dharma is without taint and free of defilement. He who is attached to anything, even to liberation, is not interested in the Dharma but is interested in the taint of desire. The Dharma is not an object. He who pursues [the Dharma as an] object is not interested in the Dharma but is interested in objects... The Dharma is not a secure refuge. He who enjoys [it as] a secure refuge is not interested in the Dharma but is interested in a secure refuge... The Dharma is not a society. He who seeks to associate with the Dharma is not interested in the Dharma but is interested in association.

*Buddhism*.
Holy Teaching of Vimalakirti 6

If you pray to God (*Imana*) for blessing while sitting on a hearth he anoints you with ashes.

*African Traditional Religions*.
Hutu Proverb (Rwanda and Burundi)

When the monks assembled before the midday meal to listen to his lecture, the great Hogen of Seiryo pointed at the bamboo blinds. Two monks simultaneously went and rolled them up. Hogen said, "One gain, one loss."

Mumon's comment: "Tell me, who gained and who lost? If you have an eye to penetrate the secret, you will see where their teacher failed. However, I warn you strongly against discussing gain and loss."

*Buddhism*. Mumonkan 26

**Forty Hadith of an-Nawawi 1**: The migration was the exile of Muhammad and his Companions from Mecca to Yathrib (Medina). Yet the point of this tradition is universally applicable. Cf. Analects 7.29, p. 72.

**Bhagavad Gita 7.21-23**: Cf. Bhagavad Gita 7.3,17,28, p. 538; Tao Te Ching 23, p. 492; Analects 7.29, p. 72.

## *Purity*

PURITY IS THE COUNTERPART to sincerity. It is prized and sought after in every religion as the foundation for proper action. The religions of China and Japan emphasize that even before exerting effort, a person should purify his or her heart. Passages in this section use the motifs of the mirror and washing with water to set forth the idea of inward purity of mind. Such ideas of purity are found everywhere, but purity is particularly central to Shinto, as represented here by a central chapter from the Kojiki in which the very creation of the gods takes place through purification.

Blessed are the pure in heart, for they shall see God.

*Christianity*. Matthew 5.8

By purity of heart alone is the holy Eternal attained.

*Sikhism*. Adi Granth, Asa-ki-Var, M.1, p. 472

Filth on hands, feet, and body may be washed off with water;
Clothes fouled by dirt may be washed with soap;
The mind fouled by sin and evil
May only be cleansed by devotion to God.

*Sikhism*. Adi Granth, Japuji 20, M.1, p. 4

For everything there is an appropriate way of polishing; the heart's polishing is the remembrance of God.

*Islam*. Hadith of Tirmidhi

O my brother! A pure heart is as a mirror; cleanse it with the burnish of love and severance from all save God, that the true sun may shine within it and the eternal morning dawn.

*Baha'i Faith*. The Seven Valleys and the Four Valleys, 21

Even as a mirror stained by dust
Shines brilliantly when it has been cleansed,
So the embodied one, on seeing the nature of the Self,
Becomes unitary, his end attained, from sorrow freed.

*Hinduism*. Svetasvatara Upanishad 2.14

All you who come before me, hoping to attain the accomplishment of your desires, pray with hearts pure from falsehood, clean within and without, reflecting the truth like a mirror.

*Shinto*. Oracle of Temmangu

The mind of the perfect man is like a mirror. It does not lean forward or backward in its response to things. It responds to things but conceals nothing of its own. Therefore it is able to deal with things without injury to [its reality].

*Taoism*. Chuang Tzu 7

**Matthew 5.8**: Cf. Psalm 24.3-6, p. 155; Dhammapada 183, p. 511.

**Hadith of Tirmidhi**: Cf. Qur'an 2.222, p. 641.

**Svetasvatara Upanishad 2.14**: The mirror of the soul is cleansed through meditation, pp. 602-3.

**Oracle of Temmangu**: Here *makoto* is translated 'truth,' but it in fact connotes sincerity and inner coherence. See Divine Injunctions, p. 515. On Temmangu, see p. 169n.

**Chuang Tzu 7**: Cf. Dhammapada 95, p. 156; Garland Sutra 10. This verse also has to do with an attitude of detachment; see Diamond Sutra 10, p. 662.

Though I had nothing to eat but a red-hot ball of iron, I will never accept the most savory food offered by a person with an impure mind.

Though I were sitting upon a blazing fire hot enough to melt copper, I will never go to visit the place of a person with a polluted mind.

*Shinto*. Oracle of Hachiman

Should clothing be rendered impure if blood-stained,
How reckon pure the way of those who suck human blood?
Says Nanak, Utter God's Name with thy tongue in purity of heart—
That alone is true religion;
All else is worldly show and false deeds.

*Sikhism*. Adi Granth, Var Majh, M.1, p. 140

The body is cleansed by water, the internal organ is purified by truthfulness, the individual soul by sacred learning and austerities, the intellect by true knowledge.

*Hinduism*. Laws of Manu 5.109

If any one purifies himself from what is ignoble, then he will be a vessel consecrated and useful to the Master of the house, ready for any good work. So shun youthful passions and aim at righteousness, faith, love, and peace, along with those who call upon the Lord from a pure heart.

*Christianity*. 2 Timothy 2.21-22

Behold, thou desirest truth in the inward being;
therefore teach me wisdom in my secret heart.
Purge me with hyssop, and I shall be clean;
wash me, and I shall be whiter than snow.
Fill me with joy and gladness;
let the bones which thou hast broken rejoice.
Hide thy face from my sins,
and blot out all my iniquities.
Create in me a clean heart, O God,
and put a new and right spirit within me.

*Judaism* and *Christianity*. Psalm 51.6-10

"Wash yourselves, make yourselves clean;
remove the evil of your doings from before my eyes.
Cease to do evil, learn to do good.
Seek justice, correct oppression.
Defend the fatherless, plead for the widow.

"Come now, let us reason together," says the Lord.
"Though your sins are like scarlet,
they shall be as white as snow;
though they are red like crimson,
they shall become like wool.
If you are willing and obedient
you shall eat the good of the land;
but if you refuse and rebel,
you shall be devoured by the sword;
for the mouth of the Lord has spoken."

*Judaism* and *Christianity*. Isaiah 1.16-20

Izanagi said, "I have been to a most unpleasant, a horrible, unclean land [the underworld]. Therefore I shall purify myself." Arriving at the plain Ahakihara by the river-mouth of Tachibana in Himuka in Tsukushi, he purified and exorcised himself....

After taking off the articles worn on his body, he said, "The current of the upper stream is a current too swift; the current in the lower

**Oracle of Hachiman**: Hachiman, the patron deity of warriors, is one of the most popular Shinto dieties in Japan; nearly half the registered Shinto shrines are dedicated to him. He is also regarded as a Buddhist bodhisattva, Hachiman Daibosatsu. This is one of the Oracles of the Three Shrines, printed on hanging scrolls and found in homes throughout Japan.

**Var Majh, M.1**: Cf. Asa-ki-Var, M.1, p. 152.

**Laws of Manu 5.109**: Cf. Bhagavad Gita 4.37-38, p. 565; Udana 6, p. 614.

**2 Timothy 2.21-22**: Cf. Hebrews 9.11-14, p. 371; Titus 1.15, p. 518; Analects 2.2, p. 657.

stream is a current too weak." Then, when he went down and dived into the middle stream and bathed, there came into existence a deity named Yasomagatsuhi-no-kami [Numerous Forces of Misfortune]; next, Omagatsuhi-no-kami [Spirit of Great Calamity]. These two deities came into existence from the pollution which he took on when he went to that unclean land.

Next, in order to rectify these evils, there came into existence the deity Kannaobi-no-kami [Divine Renewal God]; next, Onaobi-no-kami [Great Renewal God]; next, Izunome-no-kami.

Next, when he bathed at the bottom of the water, there came into existence the deity named Sokotsuwatatsumi-no-kami [Bottom Sea-spirit Deity] and Sokotsutsunoo-no-kami [Bottom Spirit Male Lord]. Next, when he bathed in the middle, there came into existence the deity named Nakatsuwatatsumi-no-kami [Middle Sea-spirit Deity] and Nakatsutsunoo-no-kami [Middle Spirit Male Lord]. When he bathed at the surface of the water, there came into existence the deity named Uwatsuwatatsumi-no-kami [Upper Sea-spirit Deity] and Uwatsutsunoo-no-kami [Upper Spirit Male Lord]....

Then when he washed his left eye, there came into existence a deity named Amaterasu-omi-kami.

Next, when he washed his right eye, there came into existence a deity named Tsukiyomi-no-mikoto [the Moon god].

Next, when he washed his nose, there came into existence the deity named Susanoo-no-mikoto.

*Shinto.* Kojiki 11

**Kojiki 11**: Izanagi must purify himself after visiting the land of the dead. The first fruits of his purification are deities of misfortune, representing the pollutions which he is casting off; the next three deities are the great gods of purification who are entreated in the Shinto rite of *shubatsu* (purification) to this day. The following three pairs of kami are ancestral deities of various clans in Japan, and the final fruits of purification are the major deities: Amaterasu, the Sun Goddess and chief Shinto diety, and Susanoo, Amaterasu's rival and a storm god; see Kojiki 19, p. 448n. This passage is a scriptural root for the widespread concern for purification of both body and mind in Shinto. Cf. Engishiki 8, p. 372.

# Self-control

SELF-CONTROL IS NECESSARY for any spiritual progress. Unruly thoughts, attractions of the senses, lustful desires, anger, covetousness, and avarice constantly arise in the mind of the person who has no mental discipline; and these impel him to do evil deeds. If a person cannot direct his thoughts, desires, and actions according to his own will, how can he possibly direct his soul to God and keep his life on the path of truth? Unless the higher mind is strengthened and given the will power to master the impulses of the flesh mind, there will be little room for God to dwell with that mind. Thus, central to the religious life is self-control.

The passages in this section feature two nearly universal metaphors employed to describe self-control: military conquest and the horse and rider. More relevant passages are gathered under the topics *Restraint*, pp. 651-54, *Control Anger*, pp. 655-57, and *Subdue Desires*, pp. 657-61.

Irrigators lead the waters. Fletchers bend the shafts. Carpenters bend wood. The virtuous control themselves.

*Buddhism*. Dhammapada 80 and 145

With the conquest of my mind, I have conquered the whole world.

*Sikhism*. Adi Granth, Japuji 28, M.1, p. 6

Though one should conquer a million men on the battlefield, yet he, indeed, is the noblest victor who has conquered himself.

*Buddhism*. Dhammapada 103

Though a man should conquer thousands and thousands of valiant foes, greater will be his victory if he conquers nobody but himself.

Fight with yourself; why fight with external foes? He who conquers himself through himself will obtain happiness....

Difficult to conquer is oneself; but when that is conquered, everything is conquered.

*Jainism*. Uttaradhyayana Sutra 9.34-36

Before you desire to control the universe, you must first be able to completely control yourself.

*Unification Church*. Sun Myung Moon, 11-22-70

He who is slow to anger is better than the mighty,
and he who rules his spirit than he who takes a city.

*Judaism* and *Christianity*. Proverbs 16.32

**Dhammapada 80**: Self-control is as necessary to the inner life as skill in shaping wood, metal, or water is required for good industry. Spiritual training is the counterpart to learning a secular trade; cf. Guide to the Bodhisattva's Way of Life 4.40, p. 530. For the comparisons to the physical training of an athlete, see 1 Timothy 4.7-8, p. 512; 1 Corinthians 9.24-27, p. 530.

**Japuji 28, M.1**: Cf. Shalok Sehskriti, M.5, pp. 744-45; Bhagavad Gita 6.5-6, p. 489.

**Dhammapada 103**: Cf. Dhammapada 42, p. 279; Guide to the Bodhisattva's Way of Life 4.28-35, p. 279.

**Uttaradhyayana Sutra 9.34-36**: Cf. Acarangasutra 2.78, p. 657; Gleanings from the Writings of Baha'u'llah 43, p. 289.

**Sun Myung Moon, 11-22-70**: 'To control the universe,' that is, to have any good influence over the affairs of the world, first one's self-control should be perfect.

**Proverbs 16.32**: Cf. 1 Peter 2.11, p. 657.

Who is strong? He who controls his passions.
*Judaism.* Mishnah, Abot 4.1

Abu Huraira reported God's Messenger as saying, "The strong man is not the good wrestler; the strong man is only he who controls himself when he is angry."
*Islam.* Hadith of Bukhari and Muslim

That man is disciplined and happy
who can prevail over the turmoil
that springs from desire and anger,
here on earth, before he leaves his body.
*Hinduism.* Bhagavad Gita 5.23

The Prophet declared, "We have returned from the lesser holy war (*al jihad al-asghar*) to the greater holy war (*al jihad al-akbar*)." They asked, "O Prophet of God, which is the greater war?" He replied, "Struggle against the lower self."
*Islam.* Hadith

Attack the evil that is within yourself; do not attack the evil that is in others.
*Confucianism.* Analects 12.21

He who knows others is wise;
He who knows himself is enlightened.
He who conquers others has physical strength;
He who conquers himself is strong.
*Taoism.* Tao Te Ching 33

It is true that the mind is restless and difficult to control. But it can be conquered, Arjuna, through regular practice and detachment. Those who lack self-control will find it difficult to progress in meditation; but those who are self-controlled, striving earnestly through the right means, will attain the goal.
*Hinduism.* Bhagavad Gita 6.35-36

The flickering, fickle mind, difficult to guard, difficult to control—the wise person straightens it as a fletcher straightens an arrow.

Like a fish that is drawn from its watery abode and thrown upon land, even so does this mind flutter. Hence should the realm of the passions be shunned.

The mind is hard to check, swift, flits wherever it lists: to control it is good. A controlled mind is conducive to happiness.

The mind is very hard to perceive, extremely subtle, flits wherever it lists. Let the wise person guard it; a guarded mind is conducive to happiness.

Faring far, wandering alone, bodiless, lying in a cave, is the mind. Those who subdue it are freed from the bonds of Mara.
*Buddhism.* Dhammapada 33-37

Man makes a harness for his beast; all the more should he make one for the beast within himself, his evil desire.
*Judaism.* Jerusalem Talmud, Sanhedrin 10.1

Be not like a horse or a mule, without understanding,
which must be curbed with bit and bridle,
else it will not keep with you.
*Judaism* and *Christianity*. Psalm 32.9

Excellent are trained mules, so are thoroughbred horses of Sindh and noble tusked elephants; but far better is he who has trained himself.

Formerly this mind went wandering where it liked, as it wished and as it listed. Today with attentiveness I shall completely hold it in

**Abot 4.1**: The verse goes on to quote Proverbs 16.32, above. Cf. Berakot 5a, pp. 657-58.
**Bhagavad Gita 5.23**: Cf. Bhagavad Gita 3.41, p. 294; 6.5-6, p. 489.
**Hadith**: This tradition is prized in Sufism. The 'lesser jihad' is jihad in the ordinary sense: the war against external foes. The 'greater jihad' is the spiritual war, whose battleground is the soul.
**Analects 12.21**: Cf. Analects 12.1, p. 388; 2.2, p. 657; 5.21-23, p. 635; 16.7, p. 659.
**Bhagavad Gita 6.35-36**: Cf. Bhagavad Gita 6.10-27, p. 603.
**Dhammapada 33-37**: Cf. Dhammapada 25, p. 511; Guide to the Bodhisattva's Way of Life 4.28-35, p. 279.

check, as a mahout controls an elephant in must.

*Buddhism.* Dhammapada 322 and 326

Know that the Self is the rider, and the body the chariot; that the intellect is the charioteer, and the mind the reins.

The senses, say the wise, are the horses; the roads they travel are the mazes of desire....

When a man lacks discrimination and his mind is uncontrolled, his senses are unmanageable, like the restive horses of a charioteer. But when a man has discrimination and his mind is controlled, his senses, like the well-broken horses of a charioteer, lightly obey the rein.

*Hinduism.* Katha Upanishad 1.3.3-6

## *Preparing the Start*

IF ANY VENTURE IS TO SUCCEED, it must begin well. The Oriental proverb, "Well begun is half done," describes the theme of the passages in this section. A good beginning means, first of all, internal preparation. A person should purify his heart prior to starting any venture; furthermore, he must steel himself with firm resolution and gather sufficient means to bear any and all burdens on the way to the goal. This is practical advice, but it applies especially to activity in the spiritual quest: It should not be embarked upon lightly or frivolously, lest the aspirant fall into straits worse than where he was when he started.

The superior man does not embark upon any affair until he has carefully planned the start.

*Confucianism.* I Ching 6: Conflict

Success is the result of foresight and resolution; foresight depends upon deep thinking and planning to keep your secrets to yourself.

*Islam.* Nahjul Balagha, Saying 46

He who wants to expand the field of happiness, let him lay the foundation of it on the bottom of his heart.

*Taoism.* Tract of the Quiet Way

If you do not perceive the sincerity within yourself and yet try to move forth, each movement will miss the mark.

*Taoism.* Chuang Tzu 23

One must not stand up and say the Tefillah except in a serious frame of mind. The pious men of old used to wait an hour, and then say the prayer, in order to direct their hearts to their Father in Heaven.

*Judaism.* Mishnah, Berakot 5.1

**Dhammapada 322, 326**: Cf. Dhammapada 94, p. 156; 380, p. 488.

**Katha Upanishad 1.3.3-6**: Cf. Svetasvatara Upanishad 2.9, pp.602-3.

**I Ching 6**: Cf. Great Learning, p. 602.

**Chuang Tzu 23**: Cf. Records of the Divine Wind, p. 516; Chandogya Upanishad 7.22, p. 134; Sutta Nipata 506, p. 620.

**Berakot 5.1**: The 'Tefillah' refers to the Amidah, or Eighteen Benedictions, one of the central daily prayers of Judaism. Cf. Berakot 30b, p. 594.

Before you climb a tree you must start at the bottom.

*African Traditional Religions.* Buji Proverb (Nigeria)

Check the edge of the axe before splitting wood.

*African Traditional Religions.* Njak Proverb (Nigeria)

The superior man gathers together his weapons in order to provide against the unforeseen.

*Confucianism.* I Ching 45: Gathering Together

For which of you, desiring to build a tower, does not first sit down and count the cost, whether he has enough to complete it? Otherwise, when he has laid a foundation, and is not able to finish, all who see it begin to mock him, saying, "This man began to build, and was not able to finish." Or what king, going to encounter another king in war, will not sit down first and take counsel whether he is able with ten thousand to meet him who comes against him with twenty thousand?

*Christianity.* Luke 14.28-31

A ship, which is not well prepared, in the ocean
Goes to destruction, together with its goods and merchants.
But when a ship is well prepared, and well joined together,
Then it does not break up, and all the goods get to the other shore.
Just so a bodhisattva, exalted in faith,
But deficient in wisdom, swiftly comes to a failure in enlightenment.
But when he is well joined to wisdom, the foremost perfection,
He experiences, unharmed and uninjured, the enlightenment of the Jinas.

*Buddhism.* Verses on the Perfection of Wisdom which is the Storehouse of Precious Virtues 14.7-8

Woodworker Ch'ing carved a piece of wood and made a bell stand, and when it was finished, everyone who saw it marveled, for it seemed to be the work of gods or spirits. When the Marquis of Lu saw it, he asked, "What art is it you have?" Ch'ing replied, "I am only a craftsman—how would I have any art? There is one thing, however. When I am going to make a bell stand, I never let it wear out my energy. I always fast in order to still my mind. When I have fasted for three days, I no longer have any thought of congratulations or rewards, of titles or stipends. When I have fasted for five days, I no longer have any thought of praise or blame, of skill or clumsiness. And when I have fasted seven days, I am so still that I forget I have four limbs and a form and body. By that time, the ruler and his court no longer exist for me. My skill is concentrated and all outside distractions fade away. After that, I go into the mountain forest and examine the Heavenly nature of the trees. If I find one of superlative form, and I can see a bell stand there, I put my hand to the job of carving; if not, I let it go. This way I am simply matching up 'Heaven' with 'Heaven.' That's probably the reason that people wonder if the results were not made by spirits."

*Taoism.* Chuang Tzu 19

❖

# Vigilance

VIGILANCE, AND SIMILAR MENTAL ATTITUDES of heedfulness, wakefulness, and concentration, are necessary for progress on the spiritual path. Heedfulness is necessary because life is a continuous stream: Every moment is an occasion to think, will, and act either within the discipline of the spiritual path or to violate its teachings. Despite one's initial burst of enthusiasm for the Way, it is all too easy to slip back into fallen and worldly habits. Only continued vigilance can preserve our life.

In the religions of the East, vigilance often refers to watching over one's thoughts in *Meditation*, pp. 599-607. Intense concentration is required, minding the condition of one's thoughts and exercising restraint over one's actions. In Western religions vigilance often refers to being mindful of God, who is ever present. By such wakefulness, one is alert against any sin or diversion from a life lived in accordance with God's will. Islam calls us constantly to remember *(dhikr)* God, his commandments, and his mercies, and reminds us through the duty of daily *Prayer*, pp. 592-95. Christian scriptures warn us that the Lord comes "like a thief in the night" and encourage constant wakefulness through such passages as the Parable of the Wise and Foolish Maidens. At the conclusion we give several passages describing how a moment of weakness, of "looking back," can potentially ruin a lifetime of spiritual progress.

Keep your heart with all vigilance,
for from it flow the springs of life.

*Judaism* and *Christianity*. Proverbs 4.23

We verily have displayed Our warnings in this Qur'an that they may take heed.

*Islam*. Qur'an 17.41

Men of understanding [are] such as remember God, standing, sitting, and reclining.

*Islam*. Qur'an 3.190-91

One who walks, stands, sits, sleeps, eats, and speaks with vigilance, no sin accrues.

*Jainism*. Dashavaikalika Sutra 4.8

The firm control of the senses is what is called yoga. One must then be vigilant; for yoga can be both beneficial and injurious.

*Hinduism*. Katha Upanishad 2.3.11

Heedfulness is the path to the deathless; heedlessness is the path to death. The heedful do not die; the heedless are like unto the dead.

Distinctly understanding this difference, the wise, intent on heedfulness, rejoice in heedfulness, delighting in the realm of the noble ones.

The constantly meditative, the ever steadfast ones, realize the bond-free, supreme Nibbana.

The glory of him who is energetic, mindful, pure in deed, considerate, self-controlled, right-living, and heedful steadily increases....

**Proverbs 4.23**: Cf. 1 Thessalonians 5.17, p. 593.

**Qur'an 17.41**: Cf. Qur'an 33.45-46, p. 454; Hadith of Darimi, p. 593.

**Qur'an 3.190-91**: Cf. Qur'an 11.114, p. 592; 18.23-24, p. 649; 29.45, p. 592; Hadith of Darimi, p. 593.

**Dashavaikalika Sutra 4.8**: Cf. the example of Mahavira in Acarangasutra 9, p. 470.

**Katha Upanishad 2.3.11**: Yoga becomes injurious when its powers disorient and overwhelm the young aspirant who lacks sufficient control, or when it is used for personal gain.

The ignorant, foolish folk indulge in heedlessness; the wise man guards earnestness as the greatest treasure.

*Buddhism.* Dhammapada 21-26

I [Mahavira] say, "What is the conduct that distinguishes a monk from a secular man? A monk is he whose conduct is ingenuous, who has devoted himself to the path of achieving salvation, and who never indulges in hypocrisy. One should preserve, without the slightest diminution, the faith which one had at the time of renunciation. One should not be swept away by the eddies of a mercurial mind."

*Jainism.* Acarangasutra 1.35-37

If while going, standing, sitting or reclining when awake, a thought of sensuality, hatred or aggressiveness arises in a monk, and he tolerates it, does not reject, discard, and eliminate it, does not bring it to an end, that monk, who in such a manner is ever and again lacking in earnest endeavor and moral shame, is called indolent and void of energy.

If while going, standing, sitting, or reclining when awake, a thought of sensuality, hatred, or aggressiveness arises in a monk, and he does not tolerate it, but rejects, discards, and eliminates it, brings it to an end, that monk, who in such a manner ever and again shows earnest endeavor and moral shame, is called energetic and resolute.

*Buddhism.* Itivuttaka 110

Kung-sun Ch'ou asked Mencius, "May I ask what your strong points are?"

"I have an insight into words. I am good at cultivating my 'flood-like ch'i.'"

"May I ask what this 'flood-like ch'i' is?"

"It is difficult to explain. This is a ch'i which is, in the highest degree, vast and unyielding. Nourish it with integrity and place no obstacle in its path and it will fill the space between heaven and earth. It is a ch'i which unites righteousness and the Way. Deprive it of these and it will collapse. It is born of accumulated rightness and cannot be appropriated by anyone through a sporadic show of rightness. Whenever one acts in a way that falls below the standard set in one's heart, it will collapse.... You must work at it and never let it out of your mind. At the same time, while you must never let it out of your mind, you must not forcibly help it grow either."

*Confucianism.* Mencius II.A.2

And watch! Lo! I am a watcher with you.

*Islam.* Qur'an 11.93

I slept, but my heart was awake.
Hark! My Beloved is knocking.

*Judaism* and *Christianity.* Song of Solomon 5.2

Be mindful when you are alone, in the shadow of your coverlet.

*Taoism.* Tract of the Quiet Way

If one holds oneself dear, one should protect oneself well. During every one of the three watches the wise man should keep vigil.

*Buddhism.* Dhammapada 157

Though others sleep, be thou awake! Like a wise man, trust nobody, but be always on the alert; for dangerous is the time and weak the

**Acarangasutra 1.35-37**: The same principles apply to householders; see Tattvarthasutra 6.18-24, p. 166.

**Itivuttaka 110**: Cf. Anguttara Nikaya v.66, p. 517; Digha Nikaya ii.99-100, p. 488.

**Mencius II.A.2**: In Chinese thought, *ch'i (qi)* is life breath or life energy. It is essential to health and can be focused and enhanced by disciplines such as T'ai-chi, Chi Gong, and Kung Fu. Ch'i has both physical and spiritual aspects, uniting mind and body. For Mencius, the power of ch'i is founded on truth and righteousness. See Chuang Tzu 15, p. 602n.; cf. Great Learning 6.1-4, p. 516-17; Analects 6.5, p. 600.

**Qur'an 11.93**: Muhammad often kept prayer vigils into the early morning hours, Qur'an 73.1-8, p. 593. Cf. Hadith, p. 545.

**Song of Solomon 5.2**: Cf. Revelation 3.20, p. 493, Psalm 42.1-3, p. 545.

**Tract of the Quiet Way**: Cf. Great Learning 6.1-4, p. 516-17; Doctrine of the Mean 33, p. 71.

**Dhammapada 157**: The 'three watches' may be interpreted as the three periods in a person's life.

body. Be as watchful as the two-headed bharunda bird!

A monk should step carefully in his walk, supposing everything to be a snare for him. First, he must bestow care on his life till he wins the Stake, and afterwards he should despise it, annihilating its sins.

*Jainism.* Uttaradhyayana Sutra 4.6-7

You yourselves know well that the day of the Lord will come like a thief in the night. When people say, "There is peace and security," then sudden destruction will come upon them as travail comes upon a woman with child, and there will be no escape. But you are not in darkness, brethren, for that day to surprise you like a thief. For you are all sons of light and sons of the day; we are not of the night or of darkness. So then let us not sleep, as others do, but let us keep awake and be sober.

*Christianity.* 1 Thessalonians 5.2-6

The kingdom of Heaven shall be compared to ten maidens who took their lamps and went to meet the bridegroom. Five of them were foolish, and five were wise. For when the foolish took their lamps, they took no oil with them; but the wise took flasks of oil with their lamps. As the bridegroom was delayed, they all slumbered and slept. But at midnight there was a cry, "Behold, the bridegroom! Come out to meet him." Then all those maidens rose and trimmed their lamps. And the foolish said to the wise, "Give us some of your oil, for our lamps are going out." But the wise replied, "Perhaps there will not be enough for us and for you; go rather to the dealers and buy for yourselves." And while they went to buy, the bridegroom came, and those who were ready went in with him to the marriage feast; and the door was shut. Afterward the other maidens came also, saying, "Lord, lord, open to us." But he replied, "Truly, I say to you, I do not know you." Watch therefore, for you know neither the day nor the hour.

*Christianity.* Matthew 25.1-13

No one who puts his hand to the plow and looks back is fit for the kingdom of God.

*Christianity.* Luke 9.62

Those journeying to heaven do not look back; they ascend the heaven, the two worlds.

*Hinduism.* Satapatha Brahmana 9.2.3.27

But Lot's wife behind him looked back, and she became a pillar of salt.

*Judaism* and *Christianity.* Genesis 19.26

Even those who have much learning,
Faith, and willing perseverance
Will become defiled by a [moral] fall
Due to the mistake of lacking alertness.

The thieves of unalertness,
In following upon the decline of mindfulness,
Will steal even the merits I have firmly gathered.
I shall then descend to the lower realms.

*Buddhism.* Shantideva, Guide to the Bodhisattva's Way of Life 5.26-27

**Uttaradhyayana Sutra 4.6-7**: The first verse calls for vigilance against temptations of the world. The second verse describes care for the body: one should guard one's life well until one wins Enlightenment, 'the Stake.' Then one despises the body to the point of the Holy Death (*Sallekhana*)—cf. Acarangasutra 7, pp. 241-42.

**1 Thessalonians 5.2-6**: This is often taken to refer to the wait for the Second Advent of Christ; see 2 Peter 3.3-10, pp. 781-82; also Luke 21.34-36.

**Luke 9.62**: Cf. Luke 9.60, p. 412; 14.16-24, p. 485.

**Genesis 19.26**: When Lot and his family were fleeing Sodom and Gomorrah, they were instructed not to look back at the destruction which was consuming the cities.

The Master said, "Danger arises when a man feels secure in his position. Destruction threatens when a man seeks to preserve his worldly estate. Confusion develops when a man has put everything in order. Therefore the superior man does not forget danger in his security, nor ruin when he is well established, nor confusion when his affairs are in order. In this way he gains personal safety and is able to protect the empire. In the I Ching it is said: 'What if it should fail? What if it should fail?' In this way he ties it to a cluster of mulberry shoots [makes success certain]."

*Confucianism.* I Ching, Great Commentary 2.5.9

## *Perseverance and Patience*

SPIRITUAL GROWTH IS A LONG PROCESS that requires perseverance and patience. Once the resolution is made and the journey is begun, it should not be abandoned, for the result is often not decided until the very end. Patience is not merely to wait for fate to intervene; rather it means to persevere in the practices of the discipline until the goal is achieved. The scriptures express the virtue of perseverance through various metaphors: running a race, climbing a tree, digging a well, and boring to the pith of a tree.

To conclude this section, we have singled out two passages which tell stories of great patience. One, from the story of Job in the Bible, describes his patience and faith in the midst of suffering. The other, from the Qur'an, tells the story of Moses' mystic journey, where the mark of a patient man is that he can accept the vicissitudes of life, as unlikely as they might be, without doubting the ever-present but unseen hand of God.

Be patient; surely God's promise is true. And ask forgiveness for your sin, and proclaim the praise of your Lord at evening and dawn.

*Islam.* Qur'an 40.55

Though he be ever so tired by repeated failure, let him begin his operations again and again; for fortune greatly favors the man who perseveres in his undertakings.

*Hinduism.* Laws of Manu 9.300

And let us not grow weary in well-doing, for in due season we shall reap, if we do not lose heart.

*Christianity.* Galatians 6.9

How long can you continue to sacrifice with a heart of love? This is what determines whether you have victory or defeat.

*Unification Church.* Sun Myung Moon, 9-11-72

Once when the Master was standing by a stream, he said, "Could one but go on and on like this, never ceasing day or night!"

*Confucianism.* Analects 9.16

The snail has no hands,
The snail has no feet,
Gently the snail climbs the tree.

*African Traditional Religions.* Yoruba Proverb (Nigeria)

**I Ching, Great Commentary 2.5.9**: Cf. I Ching, Great Commentary 1.8.7, p. 653; Micah 7.5-7, p. 674.

If fishermen, hunters, and farmers,
Thinking merely of their own livelihood,
Endure the sufferings of heat and cold,
Why am I not patient for the sake of the
world's joy?

*Buddhism*. Shantideva, Guide to the Bodhisattva's Way of Life 4.40

He who endures to the end will be saved.

*Christianity*. Mark 13.13

The day that the sun sets and does not rise again is indeed an evil day.

*African Traditional Religions*. Igala Proverb (Nigeria)

Perseverance prevails even against Heaven.

*Judaism*. Talmud, Sanhedrin 105a

Prosperity forsakes those who always dream of fate and favors those who persevere. One should therefore always be active and alert.

*Hinduism*. Matsya Purana 221.2

Master Tseng said, "The true Knight of the Way must perforce be both broad-shouldered and stout of heart; his burden is heavy and he has far to go. For Goodness is the burden he has taken upon himself; and must we not grant that it is a heavy one to bear? Only with death does his journey end; then must we not grant that he has far to go?"

*Confucianism*. Analects 8.7

Life is like a hill.
Mawu the Creator made it steep and slippery,
To right and left deep waters surround it,
You cannot turn back once you start to climb.
You must climb with a load on your head.
A man's arms will not help him, for it's a trial,
The world is a place of trial.

*African Traditional Religions*. Fon Song (Benin)

You who believe, seek help through patience and prayer; God stands alongside the patient!... We will test you with a bit of fear and hunger, and a shortage of wealth and souls and produce. Proclaim such to patient people who say, whenever disaster strikes them, "We are God's, and are returning to Him!" Such will be granted their prayers by their Lord as well as mercy. Those are guided!

*Islam*. Qur'an 2.153-57

Race with one another for forgiveness from your Lord and a Garden.

*Islam*. Qur'an 57.21

Heedful among the heedless, wide awake amongst the slumbering, the wise man advances as does a swift horse, leaving a weak jade behind.

*Buddhism*. Dhammapada 29

Do you not know that in a race all the runners compete, but only one receives the prize? So run that you may obtain it. Every athlete exercises self-control in all things. They do it to receive a perishable wreath, but we an imperishable. Well, I do not run aimlessly, I do not box as one beating the air; but I pommel my body and subdue it, lest after preaching to others I myself should be disqualified.

*Christianity*. 1 Corinthians 9.24-27

**Guide to the Bodhisattva's Way of Life 4.40**: Cf. Dhammapada 80, p. 522, another comparison of the spiritual task to worldly labors.

**Igala Proverb**: Even the worst problems have solutions if one only perseveres.

**Sanhedrin 105a**: 'Heaven' here may mean one's God-ordained destiny. Cf. Matsya Purana 180.5-7, p. 508.

**Matsya Purana 221.2**: Cf. Acarangasutra 1.35-37. p. 527.

**Analacts 8.7**: Cf. I Ching 58, p. 134; Lotus Sutra 13, p. 630.

**Qur'an 2.153-57**: Cf. Qur'an 2.177, p. 615; 3.186, p. 628.

**1 Corinthians 9.24-27**: Cf. 1 Timothy 4.7-8, p. 512; Hebrews 12.1-2, p. 540.

You will be running to the four corners of the universe:
To where the land meets the big water;
To where the sky meets the land;
To where the home of winter is;
To the home of rain.
Run this! Run!
Be strong!
For you are the mother of a people.

*Native American Religions.* Apache Song

Scripture credits with performance not him who begins a task, but him who completes it.

*Judaism.* Talmud, Sota 13b

You have crossed the great ocean; why do you halt so near the shore? Make haste to get on the other side, Gautama; be careful all the while!

*Jainism.* Uttaradhyayana Sutra 10.34

Mencius said, "To try to achieve anything is like digging a well. You can dig a hole nine fathoms deep, but if you fail to reach the source of water, it is just an abandoned well."

*Confucianism.* Mencius VII.A.29

Rabbi Akiba, illiterate at forty, saw one day a stone's perforation where water fell from a spring, and having heard people say, "Waters wear stones," he thought, "If soft water can bore through a rock, surely iron-clad Torah should, by sheer persistence, penetrate a tender mind"; and he turned to study.

*Judaism.* Talmud, Abot de Rabbi Nathan 6

Suppose a man goes to the forest to get some of the pith that grows in the center of a tree and returns with a burden of branches and leaves, thinking that he has secured what he went after; would he not be foolish?

A person seeks a path that will lead him away from misery; and yet, he follows that path a little way, notices some little advance, and immediately becomes proud and conceited. He is like the man who sought pith and came back satisfied with a burden of branches and leaves.

Another man goes into the forest seeking pith and comes back with a load of branches. He is like the person on the path who becomes satisfied with the progress he has made by a little effort, and relaxes his effort and becomes proud and conceited.

Another man comes back carrying a load of bark instead of the pith he was looking for. He is like the person who finds that his mind is becoming calmer and his thoughts clearer, and then relaxes his effort and becomes proud and conceited.

Then another man brings back a load of the woody fiber of the tree instead of the pith. Like him is one who has gained a measure of intuitive insight, and then relaxes his effort. All of these seekers, who become easily satisfied after insufficient effort and become proud and overbearing, relax their efforts and easily fall into idleness. All these people will inevitably face suffering again.

*Buddhism.* Majjhima Nikaya i.192-95: Simile of the Pith

It matters not what you learn; but when you once learn a thing, you must never give it up until you have mastered it. It matters not what you inquire into, but when you inquire into a thing, you must never give it up until you have thoroughly understood it. It matters not what you try to think out, but when you once try to think out a thing you must never give it up until you have got what you want. It matters not what you try to sift out, but when you once try to sift out a thing, you must never give it up until you have sifted it out clearly and distinctly. It matters not what you try to carry out, but when you once try to carry out a thing you must never give it up until you have done it thoroughly and well. If another man succeed by one effort, you will use a hundred efforts. If

**Apache Song**: This is a song for the girls' initiation to adulthood, which takes place at puberty.
**Mencius VII.A.29**: Cf. Luke 14.28-31, p. 525.
**Majjhima Nikaya i.192-95**: Cf. Parable of the Sower, Mark 4.3-20, pp. 513-14.

another man succeed by ten efforts, you will use a thousand efforts. Let a man really proceed in this manner, and though dull, he will surely become intelligent; though weak, he will surely become strong.

*Confucianism.*
Doctrine of the Mean 20

Now there was a day when [Job's] sons and daughters were eating and drinking wine in their eldest brother's house; and there came a messenger to Job, and said, "The oxen were plowing and the asses feeding beside them; and the Sabeans fell upon them and took them, and slew the servants with the edge of the sword; and I alone have escaped to tell you." While he was yet speaking, there came another, and said, "The fire of God fell from heaven and burned up the sheep and the servants, and consumed them; and I alone have escaped to tell you." While he was yet speaking, there came another, and said, "The Chaldeans formed three companies, and made a raid upon the camels and took them, and slew the servants with the edge of the sword; and I alone have escaped to tell you." While he was yet speaking, there came another, and said, "Your sons and daughters were eating and drinking wine in their eldest brother's house; and behold, a great wind came across the wilderness, and struck the four corners of the house, and it fell upon the young people, and they are dead; and I alone have escaped to tell you."

Then Job arose, and rent his robe, and shaved his head, and fell upon the ground, and worshipped. And he said, "Naked I came from my mother's womb, and naked shall I return; the Lord gave, and the Lord has taken away; blessed be the name of the Lord."

In all this, Job did not sin or charge God with wrong.

*Judaism* and *Christianity*.
Job 1.13-22

Moses... found one of Our servants to whom We had given mercy from Ourself and taught him knowledge from Our very presence. Moses said to him, "May I follow you so you may teach me some of the common sense you have been taught?" He said, "You will never have any patience with me! How can you show any patience with something that is beyond your experience?"

He said, "You will find me patient, if God so wishes. I will not disobey you in any matter." He said, "If you follow me, do not ask me about anything until I tell you something to remember it by."

So they both started out until, as they boarded a ship, he bored a hole in her. [Moses] said, "Have you scuttled her to drown her crew? You have done such a weird thing!" He said, "Didn't I say that you would not manage to show any patience with me?" He said, "Do not take me to task for what I have forgotten, nor weigh me down by making my case too difficult for me."

They journeyed on and when they met a youth, he killed him. Moses said, "Have you killed an innocent soul, who himself had not murdered another? You have committed such a horrible deed!" He said, "Did I not tell you that you would never manage to have any patience with me?" He said, "If I ever ask you about anything after this, do not let me accompany you. You have found an excuse so far as I am concerned."

They both proceeded further till when they came to the people of a town, they asked its inhabitants for some food, and they refused to treat either of them hospitably. They found a wall there which was about to tumble down, so he set it straight. Moses said, "If you had wished, you might have accepted some payment for it." He said, "This means a parting between you and me. Yet I shall inform you about the interpretation of what you had no patience for.

**Job 1.13-22**: Cf. Job 2.7-10, p. 506; Anguttara Nikaya iii.33, p. 499.

"As for the ship, it belonged to some poor men who worked at sea. I wanted to damage it because there was a king behind them seizing every ship by force. The young man's parents were believers, and we dreaded lest he would burden them with arrogation and disbelief. We wanted the Lord to replace him for them with someone better than him in purity and nearer to tenderness. The wall belonged to two orphan boys in the city, and a treasure of theirs lay underneath it. Their father had been honorable, so your Lord wanted them to come of age and claim their treasure as a mercy from your Lord. That is the interpretation of what you showed no patience for."

*Islam*. Qur'an 18.65-82

**Qur'an 18.65-82**: The biblical Moses had the weaknesses of anger and impatience; once he killed an Egyptian and as a consequence had to flee Egypt and live in exile in Midian; cf. Numbers 20.2-13, p. 656. This parable about Moses has no parallel in the Bible. Moses seeks a teacher, which shows that despite his great faith and wisdom, he was always humble to truth and eager to learn more. The unnamed teacher whom he meets is one who is deeply acquainted with the secrets of life; tradition assigns him the name Khidr. He has such spiritual insight that he can see the reality behind appearances. For Moses, and all of us who lack such unusual powers of insight, the truth is hidden, and we make mistakes if we rely on quick judgments. The truth can only be found out through patience and trust in God. Cf. Proverbs 3.5-6, p. 537.

# CHAPTER 14
# FAITH

THIS WORLD IS AFFLICTED BY MANY ACCUMULATED LAYERS of sin and delusion, and most people are not in touch with their original, true selves. God cannot easily be felt or experienced; the truth cannot easily be understood or practiced. Without God and the guidance of truth, the mind is rudderless, drifting aimlessly in a sea of vain desires and false conceptions. In such a condition, even the best efforts at spiritual growth may fail. Yet time and again God reveals himself to those who seek him in faith. This chapter gathers passages on faith and other attitudes of mind with which one seeks Ultimate Reality: faith itself; devotion and longing for God; fear of God, submission to God, and obedience to Heaven's commandments; confidence in God's provision that dispenses with worldly cares; gratitude for God's favors; and even the honesty of daring to argue with God. Through these attitudes a person lives in faith, lifts up his heart to God, and finds a relationship with his Lord.

## *Faith*

FAITH HAS MANY DIMENSIONS and aspects. There is faith which is belief, faith which is knowledge, faith which is vision, faith which is trust, and faith which is the heart's intention. Some people are willing to die for faith, others experience genuine faith as mixed with doubt. In several scriptures the value of faith is set above the efficacy of works, for faith means acceptance of God's all-sufficient grace while works signify self-reliance and a kind of unbelief. Other texts consider faith to be the starting point for knowledge and the basis for proper effort in the religious path.

This section opens with passages in which faith is assent to a particular belief. The content of faith is sometimes stated as a creed, giving in a few words the basic tenets of religion. Based upon this belief, a person is rightly guided to a true relationship with God and progress in the religious life.

The next passages describe faith as an attitude of receptive devotion to God and trust in God's providence. It is faith in the sense of faithfulness. Such faith has the attributes of vision and hope, giving people the will to persevere in the path despite persecution and seeming lack of results.

Third, we have brought together some key passages on the faith of Abraham. Abraham is depicted as the exemplar of faith in Judaism, Christianity, and Islam. In the Qur'an, Abraham is called the first Muslim, literally "One who Submits" his will to God. Submission, *islam*, is regarded as the fundamental attitude of all Muslims; see *Fear, Submission, Obedience*, pp. 549-52. In the Christian Bible, Paul makes the faith of Abraham the basis for his distinction between faith and works. Faith is the acceptance of God's grace through Jesus Christ which alone is sufficient to bring salvation, while the works of the law are human efforts which can only confirm man's powerlessness to save himself; see *Grace*, pp. 360-65.

On this topic of faith and works we include other passages as well: from the Lotus Sutra, the scriptures of Pure Land Buddhism, the Talmud, and the Adi Granth. The Buddhist saint Shinran emphasizes the power of faith and the insufficiency of works to a degree comparable to the Lutheran Christian doctrine of *sola fide*, Faith Alone. The passage from the Talmud shows that Judaism does not accept Paul's characterization of the law as human striving antithetical to faith, but rather places faith at the peak of the law.

The last group of passages illustrates the extremes of absolute faith and doubt: the faith that can move mountains and the doubt that withers any benefits of faith. Absolute faith in these passages means trust in God, even when it appears unrealistic and even hazardous to do so. Yet it is precisely in such circumstances that doubt most often appears.

Right belief, right knowledge, right conduct, these together constitute the path to liberation.

*Jainism*. Tattvarthasutra 1.1

He who does not understand the will of Heaven cannot be regarded as a gentleman.

*Confucianism*. Analects 20.3.1

Unless you have believed, you will not understand.

*Judaism* and *Christianity*. Isaiah 7.9

Without faith there is no knowledge, without knowledge there is no virtuous conduct, without virtues there is no deliverance, and without deliverance there is no perfection [Nirvana].

*Jainism*. Uttaradhyayana Sutra 28.30

They said to him, "What must we do, to be doing the works of God?" Jesus answered them, "This is the work of God, that you believe in him whom he has sent."

*Christianity*. John 6.28-29

**Isaiah 7.9**: This is a translation from the Septuagint; the Hebrew text, which is accepted for all modern Bibles, reads: "Unless you are faithful, you will not be established." Yet since the time of St. Augustine, this reading has been immensely influential as a foundation for the Christian theological tradition of "faith seeking understanding."

O you who believe, believe in God and His Apostle and the scripture which He has sent to His Apostle and the scriptures which He sent down to those before. Whoever denies God, His angels, His books, His apostles, and the Day of Judgment, has gone far, far astray.

*Islam*. Qur'an 4.136

*Iman* (faith)... is to believe in Allah, His angels, His books, His messengers, and the Last Day, and to believe in divine destiny, both the good and the evil thereof.

*Islam*. Forty Hadith of an-Nawawi 2

There are four kinds of faith. The first is the faith in the Ultimate Source. Because of this faith a man comes to meditate with joy on the principle of Suchness. The second is the faith in the numberless excellent qualities of the Buddhas. Because of this faith a man comes to meditate on them always, to draw near to them in fellowship, to honor them, and to respect them, developing his capacity for goodness and seeking after the all-embracing knowledge. The third is the faith in the great benefits of the Dharma. Because of this faith a man comes constantly to remember and practice the various disciplines leading to enlightenment. The fourth is faith in the Sangha, whose members are able to devote themselves to the practice of benefitting both themselves and others. Because of this faith a man comes to approach the assembly of bodhisattvas constantly and with joy to seek instruction from them in the correct practice.

*Buddhism*.
Awakening of Faith in Mahayana

The righteous shall live by being faithful.

*Judaism* and *Christianity*.
Habakkuk 2.4

By faith you shall be free and go beyond the world of death.

*Buddhism*. Sutta Nipata 1146

When the Israelites saw the Egyptians lying dead on the seashore, and saw the great power which the Lord had put forth against Egypt, the people were in awe of the Lord and put their faith in him and in Moses his servant.

*Judaism*. Exodus 14.30-31

The true believers are those whose hearts are filled with awe at the mention of God, and whose faith grows stronger as they listen to His revelations. They put their trust in their Lord, pray steadfastly, and give in alms of that which We have given them. Such are the true believers. They shall be exalted and forgiven by their Lord, and a generous provision shall be made for them.

*Islam*. Qur'an 8.2-4

Put your trust on the Exalted in Might, the Merciful—Who sees you standing forth in prayer, and your movements among those who prostrate themselves. For it is He who hears and sees all things.

*Islam*. Qur'an 26.218-20

Trust in the Lord with all your heart,
and do not rely on your own insight.
In all your ways acknowledge him
and he will make straight your paths.

*Judaism* and *Christianity*.
Proverbs 3.5-6

**Qur'an 4.136**: In this passage and the following tradition, faith means to believe the central tenets of Islam. They recite the Muslim creed in five clauses. Cf. Qur'an 2.177, p. 615.

**Forty Hadith of an-Nawawi 2**: See the previous note.

**Awakening of Faith in Mahayana**: This description of the four faiths includes faith in the traditional Three Jewels—the Buddha, the Dharma, and the Sangha—preceded by faith in the particularly Mahayanist teaching about the Absolute, or Suchness, which is all-inclusive, unconditional, transcendent, and immanent. This work, whose Sanskrit title is Mahayana Shraddahotpada Shastra, is attributed to Ashvaghosha. In China it is among the most highly regarded of Buddhist scriptures and is used by most of its major schools.

**Proverbs 3.5-6**: Cf. Qur'an 18.65-82, pp. 532-33; Gleanings from the Writings of Baha'u'llah 127, p. 136.

God has endeared the Faith to you, and has made it beautiful in your hearts, and He has made hateful to you unbelief, wickedness, and rebellion: such indeed are those who walk in righteousness—a grace and favor from God.

*Islam.* Qur'an 49.7

Faith is composed of the heart's intention.
Light comes through faith.
Through faith men come to prayer,
Faith in the morning, faith at noon and at the setting of the sun.
O Faith, give us faith!

*Hinduism.* Rig Veda 10.151.4-5

The faith of every man, O Arjuna, accords with his nature. Man is made up of faith; as is his faith, so is he.

The threefold austerity [of body, speech, and mind] practiced with faith by men of balanced mind, without any expectation of reward, is said to be pure.

Without faith, whatever offering or gift is made or work done or penance performed, it is reckoned "not-being" both now and hereafter.

*Hinduism.* Bhagavad Gita 17.3,17, and 28

Inexpressible is the state of faith;
Whoever attempts to describe it shall in the end regret his rashness.
This state pen and paper cannot record,
Nor cogitation penetrate its secret.
The great, immaculate Name of God
May only be realized by one
Whose mind is firmly fixed in faith.

Through faith the mind and intellect find concentration;
And to the seeker are revealed all the stages of enlightenment.
Through faith one will not receive blows in the hereafter,
Nor be subjected to death's terror.
The great, immaculate Name of God
May only be realized by one
Whose mind is firmly fixed in faith.

Through faith man meets no obstacle on the Path,
And shall proceed to his abode with God with his honor universally proclaimed.
One with faith shall not stray into sects and byways,
But be fixed in true religion.
The great, immaculate Name of God
May only be realized by one
Whose mind is firmly fixed in faith.

Through faith man finds the Door of Liberation:
Even his relatives are liberated through him.
Through faith are both Preceptor and disciple liberated.
Says Nanak, One with faith
Need not wander about begging for divine grace.
The great, immaculate Name of God
May only be realized by one
Whose mind is firmly fixed in faith.

*Sikhism.* Adi Granth, Japuji 12-15, M.1, p. 3

Where there is no vision, the people perish.

*Judaism* and *Christianity.* Proverbs 29.18

Once there was a person who sought the True Path in the Himalayas. He cared nothing for all the treasures of the earth or even for all the delights of heaven, but he sought the teaching that would remove all mental delusions. The gods were impressed by the man's earnestness and sincerity and decided to test his mind. So one of the gods disguised himself as a demon and appeared in the Himalayas, singing,

> Everything changes,
> Everything appears and disappears.

**Qur'an 49.7**: Cf. Qur'an 48.4, p. 392; Yasna 60.21, p. 515.

**Rig Veda 10.151.4-5**: Cf. Mundaka Upanishad 3.1.8, p. 514.

**Bhagavad Gita 7.3,17,28**: This meaning of faith is somewhat akin to sincerity: see Bhagavad Gita 7.21-23, p. 518; Taittiriya Upanishad 1.11.3, p. 620.

The seeker heard this song which pleased him so, as if he had found a spring of cool water for his thirst or as if he were a slave unexpectedly set free. He thought, "At last I have found the true teaching that I have sought for so long." He followed the voice and at last came upon the frightful demon. With an uneasy mind he approached the demon and said, "Was it you who sang the holy song that I have just heard? If it was you, please sing more of it." The demon replied, "Yes, it was my song, but I can not sing more of it until I have had something to eat; I am starving." The man begged him in earnest, saying, "It has a sacred meaning to me and I have sought its teaching for a long time. I have only heard a part of it; please let me hear more." The demon said again, "I am starving, but if I can taste the warm flesh and blood of a man, I will finish the song." The man, in his eagerness to hear the teaching, promised the demon that he could have his body after he had heard the teaching. Then the demon sang the complete song,

Everything changes,
Everything appears and disappears,
There is perfect tranquillity
When one transcends both life and extinction.

Hearing this, the man, after he wrote the poem on rocks and trees around, quietly climbed a tree and hurled himself to the feet of the demon, but the demon had disappeared and, instead, a radiant god received the body of the man unharmed.

*Buddhism.*
Mahaparinirvana Sutra 424-33

Now faith is the assurance of things hoped for, the conviction of things not seen. For by it the men of old received divine approval. By faith we understand that the world was created by the word of God, so that what is seen was made out of things which do not appear.

By faith Abel offered to God a more acceptable sacrifice than Cain, through which he received approval as righteous, God bearing witness by accepting his gifts; he died, but through his faith he is still speaking. By faith Enoch was taken up so that he should not see death; and he was not found, because God had taken him. Now before he was taken he was attested as having pleased God. And without faith it is impossible to please him. For whoever would draw near to God must believe that he exists and that he rewards those who seek him.

By faith Noah, being warned by God concerning events as yet unseen, took heed and constructed an ark for the saving of his household; by this he condemned the world and became an heir of the righteousness which comes by faith.

By faith Abraham obeyed when he was called to go out to a place which he was to receive as an inheritance; and he went out, not knowing where he was to go. By faith he sojourned in the land of promise, as in a foreign land, living in tents with Isaac and Jacob, heirs with him of the same promise. For he looked forward to the city which has foundations, whose builder and maker is God. By faith Sarah herself received power to conceive, even when she was past the age, since she considered him faithful who had promised. Therefore from one man, and him as good as dead, were born descendants as many as the stars of heaven and as the innumerable grains of sand by the seashore.

These all died in faith, not having received what was promised, but having seen it and greeted it from afar, and having acknowledged that they were strangers and exiles on the earth. For people who speak thus make it clear that they are seeking a homeland. If they had been thinking of that land from which they had gone out, they would have had opportunity to return. But as it is, they desire a better country, that is, a heavenly one. Therefore God is not ashamed to be called their God, for he has prepared for them a city.

By faith Abraham, when he was tested, offered up Isaac, and he who had received the promises was ready to offer up his only son, of

**Mahaparinirvana Sutra 424-33**: Cf. Holy Teaching of Vimalakirti 6, p. 314; Qur'an 18.65-82, pp. 532-33; Daniel 3.1-28, pp. 630-31; Gittin 57b, p. 633.

whom it was said, "Through Isaac shall your descendants be named." He considered that God was able to raise men even from the dead; hence, figuratively speaking, he did receive him back...

By faith Moses, when he was born, was hid for three months by his parents, because they saw that the child was beautiful; and they were not afraid of the king's edict. By faith Moses, when he was grown up, refused to be called the son of Pharaoh's daughter, choosing rather to share ill-treatment with the people of God than to enjoy the fleeting pleasures of sin. He considered abuse suffered for the Christ greater wealth than the treasures of Egypt, for he looked to the reward. By faith he left Egypt, not being afraid of the anger of the king; for he endured as seeing him who is invisible. By faith he kept the Passover and sprinkled the blood, so that the Destroyer of the first-born might not touch them.

By faith the people crossed the Red Sea as if on dry land; but the Egyptians, when they attempted to do the same, were drowned. By faith the walls of Jericho fell down after they had been encircled for seven days. By faith Rahab the harlot did not perish with those who were disobedient, because she had given friendly welcome to the spies.

And what more shall I say? For time would fail me to tell of Gideon, Barak, Samson, Jephthah, of David and Samuel and the prophets—who through faith conquered kingdoms, enforced justice, received promises, stopped the mouths of lions, quenched raging fire, escaped the edge of the sword, won strength out of weakness, became mighty in war, put foreign armies to flight. Women received their dead by resurrection. Some were tortured, refusing to accept release, that they might rise again to a better life. Others suffered mocking and scourging, and even chains and imprisonment. They were stoned, they were sawn in two, they were killed with the sword, they went about in skins of sheep and goats, destitute, afflicted, ill-treated—of whom the world was not worthy—wandering over deserts and mountains, and in dens and caves of the earth.

And all these, though well attested by their faith, did not receive what was promised, since God had foreseen something better for us, that apart from us they should not be made perfect.

Therefore, since we are surrounded by so great a cloud of witnesses, let us also lay aside every weight, and sin which clings so closely, and let us run with perseverance the race that is set before us, looking to Jesus the pioneer and perfecter of our faith, who for the joy that was set before him endured the cross, despising the shame, and is seated at the right hand of the throne of God.

*Christianity*. Hebrews 11.1-12.2

He [Abraham] believed the Lord, and he reckoned it to him as righteousness.

*Judaism* and *Christianity*. Genesis 15.6

For by grace you have been saved through faith; and this is not your own doing, it is the gift of God—not because of works, lest any man should boast.

*Christianity*. Ephesians 2.8-9

O foolish Galatians! Who has bewitched you, before whose eyes Jesus Christ was publicly portrayed as crucified? Let me [Paul] ask you only this, Did you receive the Spirit by works of the law, or by hearing with faith? Are you so foolish? Having begun with the Spirit, are you now ending with the flesh? Did you experience

**Hebrews 11.1-12.2**: The 'promise' which the saints whose stories are recounted here had not received was the salvation wrought through Jesus Christ, the 'perfecter of our faith'—and of theirs as well. They live still as witnesses, encouraging us. Cf. Acts 7.1-60, pp. 634-35; Daniel 3, pp. 630-31; Gittin 57b, p. 633; Gleanings from the Writings of Baha'u'llah 81, pp. 259-60. On the metaphor of the foot race, cf. 1 Corinthians 9.24-27, p. 530.

**Ephesians 2.8-9**: Cf. Galatians 2.20, p. 639.

so many things in vain?—if it really is in vain. Does he who supplies the Spirit to you and works miracles among you do so by works of the law, or by hearing with faith? Thus Abraham "believed God, and it was reckoned to him as righteousness." So you see that it is men of faith who are sons of Abraham....

Now it is evident that no man is justified before God by the law; for "He who through faith is righteous shall live"; but the law does not rest on faith, for "He who does them shall live by them."

*Christianity*. Galatians 3.1-7, 11-12

Rabbi Simlai said, "Six hundred and thirteen commandments were given to Moses, 365 negative commandments, answering to the number of the days of the year, and 248 positive commandments, answering to the number of a man's members. Then David came and reduced them to eleven [Psalm 15]. Then came Isaiah, and reduced them to six [Isaiah 33.15]. Then came Micah, and reduced them to three [Micah 6.8]. Then Isaiah came again, and reduced them to two, as it is said, 'Keep judgment and do righteousness.' Then came Amos, and reduced them to one, as it is said, 'Seek me and live.' Or one may say, then came Habakkuk [2.4], and reduced them to one, as it is said, 'The righteous shall live by his faith.'"

*Judaism*. Talmud, Makkot 23b-24a

Who therefore shrinks from the religion of Abraham, except he be foolish-minded? Indeed, We chose him in the present world, and in the world to come he shall be among the righteous. When his Lord said to him, "Surrender," he said, "I have surrendered myself to the Lord of all Being." And Abraham charged his sons with this and Jacob likewise, "My sons, God has chosen for you the religion; see that you die not save in surrender." Why, were you witnesses when death came to Jacob? When he said to his sons, "What will you serve after me?" They said, "We will serve your God and the God of your fathers Abraham, Ishmael and Isaac, One God; to Him we surrender." That is a nation that has passed away; there awaits them that they have earned, and there awaits you what you have earned; you shall not be questioned concerning the things they did.

And they say, "Be Jews or Christians and you shall be guided." Say, "Nay, rather the creed of Abraham, a man of pure faith; he was no idolator." Say you, "We believe in God, and in that which has been sent down on us and sent down on Abraham, Ishmael, Isaac and Jacob, and the Tribes, and that which was given to Moses and Jesus and the Prophets; of their Lord; we make no division between any of them, and to Him we surrender."

*Islam*. Qur'an 2.130-36

**Galatians 3.1-7**: Paul is quoting from Genesis 15.6 on the faith of Abraham to contrast the value of faith with the worthlessness of relying on human efforts to observe the many ordinances on ritual, diet, and worship found in the Law of Moses. More of this passage, dealing with the incompleteness of works of the Law, is given at pp. 107-8. Cf. Mundaka Upanishad 1.2.7-11, p. 108; Sutra of Hui Neng 6, pp. 108-9.

**Galatians 3.11-12**: Paul quotes Habakkuk 2.4 to support the priority of faith over the obligations of the Law. The second quotation, from Leviticus 18.5, states that a man shall live by doing the commandments of the Torah. By quoting this, Paul is arguing that faith and the Law are two independent and opposing principles; one can live either by faith or by the Law. Yet, he argues, justification through the Law is impossible—cf. Romans 3.19-20, pp. 107-8. This is contrary to the Jewish view that faith is the core of the Law, as in the following passage from the Talmud. Also compare James 2.14-26, p. 712, on the necessity of good works which demonstrate true faith.

**Makkot 23b-24a**: Judaism does not accept Paul's characterization, above, that faith is opposed to the Law. the rabbis teach that faith is the core and concrescence of the Law. This passage also quotes Habakkuk 2.4, but here it is interpreted to mean that 'the righteous shall *live* by his faith' and not merely profess it. Cf. Genesis Rabbah 60.2, p. 361.

**Qur'an 2.130-36**: The word *islam* means Submission or 'the Surrender.' Abraham's faith is exemplary for the Muslim, just as for the Jew and the Christian. Therefore Judaism, Christianity, and Islam are called the Abrahamic religions.

All the shravakas,
And pratyekabuddhas,
Cannot by their powers
Attain unto this sutra.
Shariputra!
Even you, into this sutra
Enter only by faith.

*Buddhism*. Lotus Sutra 3

As far as I, Shinran, am concerned, it is only because the worthy Honen taught me so that I believe salvation comes from Amida by saying the Nembutsu. Whether the Nembutsu brings rebirth in the Pure Land or leads one to hell, I myself have no way of knowing. But even if I had been misled by Honen and went to hell for saying the Nembutsu, I would have no regrets. If I were capable of attaining Buddhahood on my own through the practice of some other discipline, and yet went down to hell for saying the Nembutsu, then I might regret having been misled. But since I am incapable of practicing such disciplines, there can be no doubt that I would be doomed to hell anyway....

"If even a good man can be reborn in the Pure Land, how much more so a wicked man!" People generally think, however, that if even a wicked man can be reborn in the Pure Land, how much more so a good man! This latter view may at first sight seem reasonable, but it is not in accord with the purpose of the Original Vow [of Amida Buddha], with faith in the Power of Another. The reason for this is that he who, relying on his own power, undertakes to perform meritorious deeds, has no intention of relying on the Power of Another and is not the object of the Original Vow of Amida. Should he, however, abandon his reliance on his own power and put his trust in the Power of Another, he can be born in the True Land of Recompense. We who are caught in the net of our own passions cannot free ourselves from bondage to birth and death, no matter what kind of austerities or good deeds we try to perform. Seeing this and pitying our condition, Amida made his Vow with the intention of bringing wicked men to Buddhahood. Therefore the wicked man who depends on the Power of Another is the prime object of salvation.

*Buddhism*. Shinran, Tannisho

Exhausted after all effort, to the Lord's shelter I go,
Now that to His shelter I have come, say I,
"Lord, preserve me or ruin me as may please Thee!"

*Sikhism*. Adi Granth, Devgandhari, M.4, p. 527

For truly, I say to you, if you have faith as a grain of mustard seed, you will move this mountain, "Move from here to there," and it will move; and nothing will be impossible to you.

*Christianity*. Matthew 17.20

**Lotus Sutra 3**: Faith is the key to acquiring the teaching of the Lotus Sutra. The shravakas and pratyekabuddhas, for whom Buddhism is a matter of training and efforts at Nirvana, cannot attain it by their works or acquired wisdom. In the Buddhist tradition, Shariputra is often described as the wisest of the disciples of Shakyamuni Buddha. Yet even he can acquire the teaching of the Lotus Sutra 'only by faith,' not by his own powers of understanding. Cf. Lotus Sutra 2, p. 291.

**Tannisho**: Shinran is the founder of the Jodo Shinshu school of Pure Land Buddhism in Japan; his teacher Honen founded the Jodo Shu school. The Original Vow of Amida Buddha is found in the Larger Sukhavativyuha Sutra 8.18, p. 457. The teaching that sinners have an easier time being reborn in the Pure Land than do the righteous is linked to the Buddha's teaching of No-self (*anatta*). By throwing oneself entirely on the grace of the Buddha and accounting one's own accomplishments as nothing, there is no question of any attachment to self. A wicked person who repents completely accounts his self as nothing, but good people are more likely to have residual pride in their own virtues or attainments and hence are blocked from the goal. Cf. Shinran, p. 649. Compare Lotus Sutra 2, p. 291; Isaiah 64.6, p. 291; Matthew 9.10-13, p. 456; Luke 18.10-14, p. 642.

**Devgandhari, M.4**: Cf. Shalok, M.9, p. 278; Gauri Bawan Akkhari, M.5, p. 362.

Ibn Mas'ud reported God's Messenger as saying, "He who has in his heart faith equal to a single grain of mustard seed will not enter hell, and he who has in his heart as much pride as a grain of mustard seed will not enter paradise."

*Islam*. Hadith of Muslim

If you are in any doubt concerning what We have sent down to you, then question those who have read the Book before you; Truth has come to you from your Lord, so do not be a waverer; do not be someone who rejects God's signs, so you be a loser.

*Islam*. Qur'an 10.94-95

A man of faith, absorbed in faith, his senses controlled, attains knowledge, and, knowledge attained, quickly finds supreme peace. But the ignorant man, who is without faith, goes doubting to destruction. For the doubting self there is neither this world, nor the next, nor joy.

*Hinduism*. Bhagavad Gita 4.39-40

One of the crowd said [to Jesus], "Teacher, I brought my son to you, for he has a dumb spirit; and whenever it seizes him, it dashes him down; and he foams and grinds his teeth and becomes rigid... have pity on us and help us." And Jesus said to him, "If you can! All things are possible to him who believes." Immediately the father of the child cried out and said, "I believe; help my unbelief!"

*Christianity*. Mark 9.17-24

Whatever monk has doubts about the Teacher, is perplexed, is not convinced, is not sure, his mind does not incline to ardor, to continual application, to perseverance, to striving. This is the first mental barrenness that thus comes not to be got rid of by him whose mind does not incline to ardor, to continual application, to perseverance, to striving.

And again, this monk has doubts about the Dhamma... has doubts about the Order... has doubts about the training, is perplexed, is not convinced, is not sure... his mind does not incline to ardor... to striving. If these mental barrennesses are not rooted out, that he should come to growth, expansion, and maturity in this dhamma and discipline—such a situation does not occur.

*Buddhism*. Majjhima Nikaya i.101, Cetokhila Sutta

The boat was many furlongs distant from the land, beaten by the waves... And in the fourth watch of the night he [Jesus] came to them, walking on the sea. But when the disciples saw him walking on the sea, they were terrified, saying, "It is a ghost!" And they cried out in fear. But immediately he spoke to them, saying, "Take heart, it is I; have no fear."

And Peter answered him, "Lord, if it is you, bid me come to you on the water." He said, "Come." So Peter got out of the boat and walked on the water and came to Jesus; but when he saw the wind, he was afraid, and beginning to sink he cried out, "Lord, save me." Jesus reached out his hand and caught him, saying to him, "O man of little faith, why did you doubt?"

*Christianity*. Matthew 14.24-31

❖

**Hadith of Muslim**: Cf. Bhagavad Gita 18.58, p. 492.

**Mark 9.17-24**: Throughout the synoptic Gospels, Jesus heals only those who have faith. See Mark 5.24-34, pp. 374-75.

**Majjhima Nikaya i.101**: Cf. Sutta Nipata 249, p. 614; Anguttara Nikaya i.190-91, p. 487.

**Matthew 14.24-31**: Cf. the episode of Doubting Thomas, John 20.24-29, p. 467.

# Devotion and Praise

DEVOTION TO GOD is the love for God that expresses itself in joyful and emotional outpourings of praise and worship and a constant longing for God's sweet presence. This powerful mode of religious consciousness is particularly manifest in the bhakti tradition of Hinduism and Sikhism, in the dancing and songs of Sufi Muslims and Hassidic Jews, and in pietistic and devotional movements throughout the history of Christianity. Many of these passages describe this mystical emotion as a transformed and sublime love of a bride for her beloved, as in the Song of Solomon in the Bible, in the love poetry of the Adi Granth, and in the amorous episodes of Krishna and the cowherd girls in the Srimad Bhagavatam. Other passages express devotion to God in songs and psalms of praise.

Whatever you do, do all to the glory of God.

*Christianity*. 1 Corinthians 10.31

The supreme Lord who pervades all existence, the true Self of all creatures, may be realized through undivided love.

*Hinduism*. Bhagavad Gita 8.22

Heaven and earth contain me not, but the heart of my faithful servant contains me.

*Islam*. Hadith of Suhrawardi

He is the Living One; there is no god but He: call upon Him, giving Him sincere devotion. Praise be to God, Lord of the Worlds!

*Islam*. Qur'an 40.65

"And you shall love the Lord"—namely, you shall make the Lord beloved.

*Judaism*. Talmud, Yoma 86

Those who remember the Lord with every
  breath, each morsel,
And in whose mind ever abides the spell of the
  Lord's Name—
Says Nanak, are blessed, perfect devotees.

*Sikhism*. Adi Granth, Gauri Var, M.5, p. 319

Lord! In praying to you I violate the restraint of tongue, in remembering you I violate the restraint of mind, and in prostrating to you I violate the restraint of body. Be it as it may, I vow to ever pray to you, remember you, and prostrate myself before you.

*Jainism*. Jinasena, Adipurana 76.2

Greater is he who acts from love than he who acts from fear.

*Judaism*. Talmud, Sota 31a

The path to the Unmanifest is very difficult for embodied souls to realize [by effort at meditation]. But quickly I come to those who offer me every action, who worship me only, their dearest delight, with undaunted devotion. Because they love me, these are my bondsmen, and I shall save them from mortal sorrow and all the waves of life's deathly ocean.

*Hinduism*. Bhagavad Gita 12.5-7

He who loves me is made pure; his heart melts in joy. He rises to transcendental consciousness by the rousing of his higher emotional nature. Tears of joy flow from his eyes, his hair stands on end, his heart melts in love. The bliss in that state is so intense that, forgetful of himself

**Yoma 86**: Quoting Deuteronomy 6.5, p. 516.

**Sota 31a**: Compare 1 John 4.18, pp. 159-60.

**Bhagavad Gita 12.5-7**: Cf. Bhagavad Gita 18.65-66, p. 461; Srimad Bhagavatam 6.1, p. 646; Japuji 20, M.1, p. 519; Gauri Purabi, Ravidas, p. 284.

and his surroundings, he sometimes weeps profusely, or laughs, or sings, or dances; such a devotee is a purifying influence upon the whole universe.

*Hinduism*. Srimad Bhagavatam 11.8

Holy is the man of devotion;
Through thoughts and words and deed
And through his conscience he increases
Righteousness;
The Wise Lord as Good Mind gives the
dominion.
For this good reward I pray.

I know that my greatest good is to worship
The Wise Lord and those that have been and
are.
By their names will I worship them
And come before them with praise.

*Zoroastrianism*. Avesta,
Yasna 51.21-22

Be wakeful, for the longing of the righteous to see Me has increased, and verily My longing toward them has increased more.

*Islam*. Hadith

As a hart longs for flowing streams,
so longs my soul for thee, O God.
My soul thirsts for God,
for the living God.
When shall I come and behold
the face of God?
My tears have been my food
day and night.

*Judaism* and *Christianity*.
Psalm 42.1-3

The chakora bird longs for the moonlight,
The lotus longs for sunrise,
The bee longs to drink the flower's nectar,
Even so my heart anxiously longs for thee, O
Lord.

*Hinduism*. Basavanna, Vacana 364

My beloved speaks and says to me,
"Arise, my love, my fair one, and come away;
for lo, the winter is past,
the rain is over and gone.
The flowers appear on the earth;
the time of singing has come,
and the voice of the turtledove is heard in our
land.
The fig tree puts forth its figs,
and the vines are in blossom;
they give forth fragrance.
Arise, my love, my fair one, and come away."

*Judaism* and *Christianity*.
Song of Solomon 2.10-13

How may I live, Mother, without the Lord?
Glory to Thee, Lord of the Universe!
To praise Thee I seek;
Never without the Lord may I live.
The Bride is athirst for the Lord;
All night is she awake lying in wait for Him.
The Lord has captured my heart;
He alone knows my agony:
Without the Lord the soul is in travail and
pain—
Seeking His Word and the touch of His feet.
Show Thy grace, Lord; immerse me in Thyself.

*Sikhism*. Adi Granth,
Sarang, M.1, p. 1232

**Srimad Bhagavatam 11.8**: Cf. Chandogya Upanishad 7.23, p. 134; Sun Myung Moon, 10-20-73, p. 132.

**Yasna 51.21-22**: The translation of this Gatha portrays an historical conception of the religion of Zarathustra which may differ from the monotheism of modern Parsees: it appears to have been a henotheism in which the Wise Lord Ahura Mazda is served by subordinate divine entities.

**Hadith**: Cf. Qur'an 11.93, p. 527; Song of Solomon 5.2 , p. 527.

**Song of Solomon 2.10-13**: This book is also called Canticles or Song of Songs. Scholars regard it as originally a collection of some twenty-five songs of love and courtship such as might be sung at weddings. Despite its secular origins, this book has been prized by mystics as lyrically portraying the intimate experience of divine love for the individual soul. Christians have taken it as an allegory of Christ's love for the church, his Bride: see Ephesians 5.21-33, pp. 180-81; Revelation 21.2, pp. 794-95. In the Jewish tradition it describes God's love for Israel: see Canticles Rabbah 2.5, below; Canticles Rabbah 4.4.3, p. 652; Exodus Rabbah 49.1, p. 195.

**Sarang, M.1**: Cf. Rig Veda 1.164.49, p. 94.

My heart is joy-filled, blossoming with love;
Ravished am I by His love—
Love of my eternal Lord.
He is the immortal Lord Supreme,
Whose will nothing restrains;
Gracious, compassionate,
In each one's life involved.
He is my sole knowledge, object of meditation, adoration,
His name in my soul lodged:
Neither ritual garb nor wandering nor austere yoga
Know I to win Him over:
Nanak, true devotion alone conquers His love.

Agreeable is the cool night, followed by happy day;
Thou who art asleep in thy own ego, the Beloved calls thee.
Awakened is the youthful bride to the Lover's call,
In aspect pleasing to Him.
Thou youthful bride! discard falsehood, deceit,
Maya-absorption, concern with the world.
Round my neck I wear the pearl-string of His Name,
The jewel string of His holy Word.
With hands folded Nanak makes supplication:
Show Thy grace, take me into Thy favor!

*Sikhism.* Adi Granth,
Bilaval Chhant, M.1, p. 843-44

Upon my bed by night
I sought him whom my soul loves;
I sought him, but found him not;
I called him, but he gave no answer.
"I will rise now and go about the city,
in the streets and in the squares;
I will seek him whom my soul loves."
I sought him, but found him not.
The watchmen found me,
as they went about the city.
"Have you seen him whom my soul loves?"
Scarcely had I passed them,
when I found him whom my soul loves.
I held him, and would not let him go
until I had brought him into my mother's house,
and into the chamber of her that conceived me.
I adjure you, O daughters of Jerusalem,
by the gazelles or the hinds of the field,
that you not stir up or awaken love
until it please.

*Judaism* and *Christianity*.
Song of Solomon 3.1-5

"For I am love-sick" [Song of Solomon 2.5]. Said the community of Israel before the Holy One, "Sovereign of the Universe, all the maladies which Thou bringest upon me are to make me more beloved of Thee."

Another explanation: The community of Israel said before the Holy One, "Sovereign of the Universe, the reason for all the sufferings which the nations inflict upon me is because I love Thee."

Another explanation: "Although I am sick [i.e., sinful], I am beloved of Him."

*Judaism.* Midrash,
Canticles Rabbah 2.5

To the shepherd girls, Krishna was their beloved friend, lover, and companion. When Sri Krishna played on his flute, the shepherd girls forgot everything; unconscious even of their own bodies, they ran to him, drawn by his great love. Once Krishna, to test their devotion to him, said to them, "O you pure ones, your duties must be first to your husbands and children. Go back to your homes and live in their service. You need not come to me. For if you only meditate on me, you will gain salvation." But the shepherd girls replied, "O thou cruel lover, we desire to serve only thee! Thou knowest the scriptural truths, and dost advise

**Song of Solomon 3.1-5**: Cf. Book of Songs, Ode 1, pp. 176-77; note to Song of Solomon 2.10-13, above.

**Canticles Rabbah 2.5**: The first interpretation speaks of how suffering is for the purpose of love, bringing Israel nearer to God; see Menahot 53b, p. 404. The second interpretation refers to the fact that those who love God naturally attract persecution from the fallen world; cf. Matthew 15:11-12, p. 628; Berakot 61b, p. 629; Gittin 57b, p. 633; Hebrews 11, pp. 539-40. On the third interpretation, cf. Forty Hadith of an-Nawawi 42, p. 372; 2 Timothy 2.13, p. 361.

us to serve our husbands and children. Very well; we shall abide by thy teaching. Since thou art all in all, and art all, by serving thee we shall be serving them also."

Krishna, who gives delight to all and who is blissful in his own being, divided himself into as many Krishnas as there were shepherd girls, and danced and played with them. Each girl felt the divine presence and divine love of Sri Krishna. Each felt herself the most blessed. Each one's love for Krishna was so absorbing that she felt herself one with Krishna—nay, knew herself to be Krishna.

Truly has it been said that those who meditate on the divine love of Sri Krishna, and upon the sweet relationship between him and the shepherd girls, become free from lust and sensuality.

*Hinduism.* Srimad Bhagavatam 10.5

O Rama... I wish to be with thee! I shall experience no fatigue in following thee, even if I may no longer rest near thee on a luxurious couch. The kusha grass, the reeds, the rushes and thorny briars on the way, in thy company, will seem as soft as lawns or antelope skins! The dust raised by the tempest that covers me will resemble rare sandalwood paste, O my dear Lord. When, in the dense forest, I sleep beside thee on a grassy couch, soft as a woollen coverlet, what could be more pleasant to me? Leaves, roots, fruits, whatever it may be, little or much, that thou hast gathered with thine own hand to give to me, will taste of amrita!... To be with thee is heaven, to be without thee is hell, this is the truth!

*Hinduism.* Ramayana, Ayodhya Kanda 30

Now when Jesus was at Bethany in the house of Simon the leper, as he sat at table, a woman came with an alabaster flask of ointment of pure nard, very costly, and she broke the flask and poured it over his head. But there were some who said to themselves indignantly, "Why was the ointment thus wasted? For this ointment might have been sold for more than three hundred denarii, and given to the poor." And they reproached her. But Jesus said, "Let her alone; why do you trouble her? She has done a beautiful thing to me. For you always have the poor with you, and whenever you will, you can do good to them; but you will not always have me. She has done what she could; she has anointed my body beforehand for burying. And truly, I say to you, wherever the gospel is preached in the whole world, what she has done will be told in memory of her."

*Christianity.* Mark 14.3-9

Once, while Yashoda was holding the baby Krishna on her lap, she set him down suddenly to attend to some milk that was boiling over on the oven. At this the child was much vexed. In his anger he broke a pot containing curdled milk, went to a dark corner of the room taking some cheese with him, smeared it over his face, and began feeding a monkey with the crumbs. When his mother returned and saw him, she scolded him. As a punishment, she decided to tie him with a rope to a wooden mortar. But to her surprise the rope, although long enough, seemed too short. She took more rope, but still it was too short. Then she used all the ropes she could find, but still Krishna could not be tied. This greatly mystified Yashoda. Krishna smiled within himself, but now, seeing that his mother was completely tired out and perplexed, he gently allowed himself to be bound.

He who has neither beginning, nor middle, nor end, who is all-pervading, infinite, and omnipotent, allowed himself to be bound by Yashoda only because of her great love. He is the Lord omnipotent, the Lord of all beings, the controller of all; yet he permits himself to be controlled by those who love him.

*Hinduism.* Srimad Bhagavatam 10.3

**Srimad Bhagavatam 10.5**: Cf. Srimad Bhagavatam 10.34, pp. 470-71; 10.16, pp. 448-49.

**Ramayana**: Sita expresses her undying love for Rama. Since Rama is God incarnate, Sita's devotion is representative of every true devotee of the Lord. See Ramayana, Sundara Kanda 19-22, p. 632.

**Srimad Bhagavatam 10.3**: The last line from this account of an episode from the life of Krishna expresses an important truth: love is the one power which can control even the Almighty God.

Sing you all, and sing aloud!
Devotees, sing your songs.
Let children, too, sing. Sing to him
who is like a mighty fortress.
Let the viol send down its strains,
the lute raise its voice around,
the bow string strike its echoing sound:
to Indra is our hymn upraised.

*Hinduism*. Rig Veda 8.69.8-9

Praise the Lord!
Praise God in his sanctuary;
praise him in his mighty firmament!
Praise him for his mighty deeds;
praise him according to his exceeding greatness!
Praise him with trumpet sound;
praise him with lute and harp!
Praise him with timbrel and dance;
praise him with strings and pipe!
Praise him with sounding cymbals;
praise him with loud clashing cymbals!
Let everything that breathes praise the Lord!
Praise the Lord!

*Judaism* and *Christianity*. Psalm 150

Come together, you all, with the power of spirit,
to the Lord of heaven, who is One, the Guest of the people.
He, the ancient, desires to come to the new,
to him all pathways turn; verily he is One.

We all here are thine, O Indra, praised by many,
We who go about, attached to thee, Lord of wealth!
O Lover of song, none but thee receives our songs.
Love these our words as the earth loves her creatures.

Loud songs have sounded to the bounteous Indra,
One worthy of praise, the Supporter of mankind,
to the much invoked, waxing strong with lovely hymns,
and the immortal One who is sung day by day.

Toward Indra have all our loving songs, joined
to the heavenly light, proceeded in unison;
as a wife embraces her husband, comely bride-groom,
so they encompass the bounteous One for his grace.

*Hinduism*. Sama Veda 372-75

❖

**Rig Veda 8.69.8-9**: Cf. Ramkali Anandu, M.3, p. 134.
**Psalm 150**: Cf. Psalm 100, p. 135.

## *Fear, Submission, and Obedience*

IN THIS SECTION ARE GATHERED representative passages on the fear of God, submission to God, and obedience to God's will. The fear of God sometimes means to serve God out of fear of punishment, as in the texts from the Upanishad on the fearsomeness of Shiva and from the African traditional ritual of Ofo. But usually the fear of God is a more exalted emotion, an awe and respect for Ultimate Reality who has graciously provided for our lives. Fear includes the notions of duty and loyalty to God, who is worthy of all service because of his continual blessings and help. It includes the idea of awe and respect, since God is awesome, mighty, and wonderful. It also includes the notions of shame and the fear of the consequences of sin, which guard people from unseemly behavior and sins which would cause injury to themselves.

Submission or surrender to God is a theme especially prominent in Islam, whose name means Submission; but it is also an important theme of Vaishnavite Hinduism, wherein surrender to Krishna is regarded as the core teaching of the Bhagavad Gita. The virtue of obedience to God is particularly significant in the Abrahamic religions, which envision God as a Person who acts in history and in the lives of individuals. In Eastern religions we also find passages calling us to conform to the will of Heaven and to conform our will to the nature of Ultimate Reality.

O you who believe! Fear God as He should be feared, and die not except in a state of *islam*.

*Islam*. Qur'an 3.102

And now, Israel, what does the Lord your God require of you, but to fear the Lord your God with all your heart and with all your soul, and to keep the commandments and statutes of the Lord, which I [Moses] command you this day for your good?

*Judaism*. Deuteronomy 10.12-13

The friendship of the Lord is for those who fear him,
and he makes known to them his covenant.

*Judaism* and *Christianity*. Psalm 25.14

Call on Him with fear and longing in your hearts: for the Mercy of God is near to those who do good.

*Islam*. Qur'an 7.56

To fear God and commune with Him is the whole secret of faith for those who serve the cause of the true God.

*Omoto Kyo*. Michi-no-Shiori

The Lord is in his holy temple;
let all the earth keep silence before him.

*Judaism* and *Christianity*. Habakkuk 2.20

**Qur'an 3.102**: Cf. Qur'an 2.130-36, p. 541; Hadith of Tirmidhi and Ibn Majah, p. 332.

**Deuteronomy 10.12-13**: Cf. Exodus 14.30-31, p. 537; Deuteronomy 6.20-8.20, pp. 764-65.

**Psalm 25.14**: The Covenant is the agreement defining the relationship between God and Israel, and by extension to all people, with its specific obligations and promised blessings for obedience, curses for disobedience.

**Qur'an 7.56**: Cf. Qur'an 8.2-4, p. 537; Hadith of Darimi, p. 593; Nahjul Balagha, Sermon 67, p. 238.

**Habakkuk 2.20**: This expresses the awesome sense of the numinous.

Divine things,
Proceeding from the mind
Of the unseen kami—
How awesome, and
Not to be taken lightly!

*Shinto*. Norinaga Motoori, One Hundred Poems on the Jewelled Spear

O my Father, Great Elder,
I have no words to thank you,
But with your deep wisdom
I am sure that you can see
How I value your glorious gifts.
O my Father, when I look upon your greatness,
I am confounded with awe.
O Great Elder,
Ruler of all things earthly and heavenly,
I am your warrior,
Ready to act in accordance with your will.

*African Traditional Religions*. Kikuyu Prayer (Kenya)

Shiva, the sovereign of the gods, He in whom all the worlds rest, He who rules over all two-footed and four-footed beings, to that god let us sacrifice an oblation.

"Thou art unborn," with these words some come near to Thee, trembling. O Rudra, let Thy gracious face protect me for ever! O Rudra! hurt us not in our offspring and descendants, hurt us not in our own lives, nor in our cows, nor in our horses! Do not slay our men in Thy wrath, for, holding oblations, we call on Thee always.

*Hinduism*. Svetasvatara Upanishad 4.13, 21-22

This Ofo we have come today to consecrate you. You will start today to be effective. Anybody that has poison that can kill, any man or woman or anybody who steals and denies it, if he is brought and if this Ofo is brought and he or she swears on it, may you kill him or her. Anybody that commits an incest or any other kind of abomination against the earth deity, may this Ofo kill him.

You the holder of this Ofo, if you commit any of these crimes, may this Ofo kill you. Earth goddess, you have heard. Thunder, you have heard. Ebirike, our ancestors have you heard? Yam goddess listen, water spirit and the spirit of the latrine, you have all heard. Be our witness today that anybody who commits abomination should die! I think I am correct? Yes!

*African Traditional Religion*. Igbo Consecration (Nigeria)

May your fear of Heaven be as strong as your fear of man!

*Judaism*. Talmud, Berakot 28b

The fear of God is mighty and of great weight.
Egoism is worthless and just vociferous.
Walk under the weight of such great fear;
And through Divine grace obtain knowledge of God.
None crosses the ocean of existence unless he bear fear;
Through fear the fear-directed life is beautified with divine love.
Through fear of God, the fire of fear blazes in the human frame.
Through fear of God and love is molded spiritual beauty.
Without fear of God all that is uttered is misshapen and worthless—
The mold and the shaping strokes both blind....
Through fear of God vanish worldly fears.
The fear of God which eliminates all other fear—

**Svetasvatara Upanishad 4.13, 21-22**: Shiva has many aspects, one of which is the God of destruction. In this fearful aspect he is worshipped in this passage from the Upanishads. Rudra is an epithet of Shiva.

**Igbo Consecration**: The Ofo stick is a central religious symbol of the Igbo. It represents the connection between the human world and the spiritual world, and is used to connect with spiritual power, give blessings, empower curses, solemnize oaths, enforce justice, and bring the collective wisdom and power of the ancestors to bear on social and political decisions. Cf. Igbo Trial, p. 260.

**Berakot 28b**: For a Chinese story about someone who had no fear of heaven, see Treatise on Response and Retribution, p. 262. Cf. Analects 3.13, p. 593.

How may it be called fear?
No other resting place is except Thee;
All that happens is Thy will.
One might be afraid of it if anything other than God held any fear—
To be shaken with such fears is sheer perturbation of mind.

*Sikhism.* Adi Granth, Gauri, M.1. p. 151

The fear of the Lord is the beginning of wisdom.

*Judaism* and *Christianity.* Proverbs 9.10

He in whom the fear of sin comes before wisdom, his wisdom will endure; but he in whom wisdom comes before the fear of sin, his wisdom will not endure.

*Judaism.* Mishnah, Abot 3.11

Monks, two bright things guard the world: shame and fear of blame. If these two bright things did not guard the world... the world would fall into promiscuity, as is the case with goats, sheep, poultry, pigs, dogs, and jackals.

*Buddhism.* Itivuttaka 36

Whosoever submits his will to God, while doing good, his wage is with his Lord, and no fear shall be upon them, neither shall they sorrow.

*Islam.* Qur'an 2.112

Abandon all supports and look to me for protection. I shall purify you from the sins of the past; do not grieve.

*Hinduism.* Bhagavad Gita 18.66

He who submits to the yoke of the Torah liberates himself from the yoke of circumstance. He rises above the pressures of the state and above the fluctuations of worldly fortune.

*Judaism.* Mishnah, Abot 3.6

"They are My servants" [Leviticus 25.55]—not servants' servants.

*Judaism.* Talmud, Baba Metzia 10a

I have come down from heaven, not to do my own will, but the will of him who sent me.

*Christianity.* John 6.38

O you who believe! Be mindful of your duty to God, and seek the way to approach unto Him, and strive in His way in order that you may succeed.

*Islam.* Qur'an 5.35

A sacrificial vessel:
The superior man, taking his stance as righteousness requires, adheres firmly to Heaven's decrees.

*Confucianism.* I Ching 50: Sacrificial Vessel

The most excellent action is love for God's sake and hatred for God's sake.

*Islam.* Hadith of Abu Dawud

Make [God's] will as your will,
so that He may make your will as His will;
make naught your will before His will,
so that He may make naught the will of others before your will.

*Judaism.* Mishnah, Abot 2.4

**Itivuttaka 36**: This fear is only a beginning stage of faith, a guard at the gate of hell rather than the way to heaven. Cf. I Ching, Great Commentary 1.3.4, p. 642.

**Qur'an 2.112**: On Muhammad's absolute obedience to God, see Qur'an 6.50, p. 468.

**Bhagavad Gita 18.66**: This passage gives the essence of surrendering to God in the Hindu bhakti tradition.

**Baba Metzia 10a**: Cf. Bhagavad Gita 12.5-7, p. 544; Abot 1.3, p. 667.

**John 6.38**: Cf. Matthew 7.21, p. 580; Patet 6, p. 642.

**I Ching 50**: Cf. Analects 20.3.1, p. 536.

**Hadith of Abu Dawud**: By 'hatred for God's sake' is meant hatred of sin and evil, not the self-centered hatred of a person who has done us wrong.

**Abot 2.4**: Cf. Dharmasangiti Sutra, p. 107; Proverbs 3.5-6, p. 537; Patet 6, p. 642.

Do not yield your members to sin as instruments of wickedness,
but yield yourselves to God as men who have been brought from death to life,
and your members to God as instruments of righteousness.

*Christianity*. Romans 6.13

Abiding by your commandment is preferable to worshipping you. Obeying your commandment conduces to deliverance and contravenes from bondage.

*Jainism*. Vitaragastava 19.4

Has the Lord as great delight in burnt offerings and sacrifices
as in obeying the voice of the Lord?
Behold, to obey is better than sacrifice,
and to hearken than the fat of rams.

*Judaism* and *Christianity*. 1 Samuel 15.22

What is thy command? What is thy wish?
Is it for praise? Is it for worship?
Proclaim, O Wise One, that we may hear
for which of the decrees rewards shall be assigned—
instruct us through Right,
paths good to tread, of Good Mind!

*Zoroastrianism*. Avesta, Yasna 34.12

Why does God require of us obedience?... Man must push away and overcome the factors of the Fall [of man]. Because the Fall originated from disobedience, God must order us to have absolute obedience as a necessary condition to restore this. Therefore in our religious way of life we cannot complain. We have no excuse; we must have absolute obedience.

*Unification Church*. Sun Myung Moon, 9-11-72

Ritual purification, though million-fold, may not purify the mind.
Nor may absorption in trance still it, however long and continuous.
Possessing worlds multiple quenches not the rage of avarice and desire.
A thousand million feats of intellect bring not emancipation.
How then to become true to the Creator?
How to demolish the wall of illusion?
Through obedience to His Ordinance and Will.
Says Nanak, This blessing too is pre-ordained.

*Sikhism*. Adi Granth, Japuji 1, M.1, p. 1

❖

**1 Samuel 15.22**: Cf. Micah 6.6-8, p. 615.

**Yasna 34.12**: Cf. Yasna 33.14, p. 626; Patet 6, p. 642.

**Sun Myung Moon, 9-11-72**: On not complaining, see Bhagavad Gita 3.31-32, p. 107; Book of Songs, Ode 40, p. 506; Var Majh, M.1, p. 506.

**Japuji 1, M.1**: Cf. Micah 6.6-8, p. 615.

## *Anxiety*

A PERSON WHO HAS FAITH and confidence in God's provision need not worry about worldly cares. For one who has deep insight into Reality, concerns about possessions and acquisitions seem ephemeral and meaningless. Hence the scriptures counsel the traveller in the spirit to avoid meaningless attachments to possessions, position, or fame. The faithless person, being attached to these things, becomes anxious when they are lacking, and he is constantly driven to grasp after them. But in the life of faith there is a simplicity and detachment that produces neither anxiety nor care. To live like the birds of the air or the animals of the forest, for whom God provides the necessities of life; to trust in God and the spiritual principle that God will protect and provide for those who put Heaven first; to be selfless, and hence unconcerned about such mundane matters as life or death: this is the attitude of the wise man.

Any who believes in his Lord has no fear, either of loss or of any injustice.

*Islam*. Qur'an 72.13

All are afraid of death; nowhere is there fearlessness. But the virtuous saints never fear death and the state after death.

*Hinduism*. Matsya Purana 212.25

My Lord, boundless as
The sun and moon
Lighting heaven and earth;
How then can I have concerns
About what is to be?

*Shinto*. Man'yoshu 20

One who has mastered Dhamma, one much learned,
Has no such thought as, Ah! 'tis well with me!
Look you! how tortured is he that has possessions!
One to another human folk are bound.

*Buddhism*. Udana 13

Day in, day out, I am with Amida;
Let the sun set whenever it pleases.
How grateful indeed I am!
Namu-Amida-Butsu!

*Buddhism*. Myokonin

Unless the Lord builds the house,
those who build it labor in vain.
Unless the Lord watches over the city,
the watchman stays awake in vain.
It is in vain that you rise up early and go late to rest,
eating the bread of anxious toil;
for he gives his beloved sleep.

*Judaism* and *Christianity*. Psalm 127.1-2

Do not strain your eyes in longing for the things We have given for enjoyment to parties of them, the splendor of the life of this world, through which We test them: but the provision of your Lord is better and more enduring.... We do not ask you to provide sustenance; We

**Qur'an 72.13**: Cf. Qur'an 2.112, p. 551.

**Udana 13**: Cf. Suhi, M.5, p. 665.

**Myokonin**: The Myokonin is a collection of poems by Japanese Pure Land saints. Pure Land Buddhists keep the mind fixed on Ultimate Reality by constantly chanting *Namu-Amida-Butsu*, All Hail to Amitabha Buddha; see Meditation on Buddha Amitayus 3.30, p. 597.

provide it for you. The fruit of the Hereafter is for righteousness.

*Islam*. Qur'an 20.131-32

Those who surrender to God all selfish attachments are like the leaf of a lotus floating clean and dry in water. Sin cannot touch them. Renouncing their selfish attachments, those who follow the path of service work with body, senses, and mind for the sake of self-purification. Those whose consciousness is unified abandon all attachment to the results of action and attain supreme peace.

*Hinduism*. Bhagavad Gita 5.10-12

How many animals do not carry their own provision! God provides for them and for you. He is Alert, Aware.

*Islam*. Qur'an 29.60

In the Changes it is said, "If a man is agitated in mind, and his thoughts go hither and thither, only those friends on whom he fixes his conscious thoughts will follow" [Hexagram 31: Influence].

The Master said, "What need has nature of thought and care? In nature all things return to their common source and are distributed along different paths; through one action, the fruits of a hundred thoughts are realized. What need has nature of thought, of care?"

*Confucianism*. I Ching,
Great Commentary 2.5.1

Therefore I tell you, do not be anxious about your life, what you shall eat or what you shall drink, nor about your body, what you shall put on. Is not life more than food, and the body more than clothing? Look at the birds of the air: they neither sow nor reap nor gather into barns, and yet your heavenly Father feeds them. Are you not of more value than they? And which of you by being anxious can add one cubit to his span of life? And why are you anxious about clothing? Consider the lilies of the field, how they grow; they neither toil nor spin; yet I tell you, even Solomon in all his glory was not arrayed like one of these. But if God so clothes the grass of the field, which today is alive and tomorrow is thrown into the oven, will he not much more clothe you, O men of little faith? Therefore do not be anxious, saying, "What shall we eat?" or "What shall we wear?" For the Gentiles seek all these things; and your heavenly Father knows that you need them all. But seek first his kingdom and his righteousness, and all these things shall be yours as well.

*Christianity*. Matthew 6.25-33

Whoever has bread in his basket and says, "What am I going to eat tomorrow?" only belongs to those who are little in faith.

*Judaism*. Talmud, Sota 48b

"My clothes are torn, I shall soon go naked," or "I shall get a new suit": such thoughts should not be entertained by a monk. At one time he will have no clothes, at another time he will have some. Knowing this to be a salutary rule, a wise monk should not complain about it.

*Jainism*. Uttaradhyayana Sutra 2.12-13

Though the fig tree does not blossom,
nor fruit be on the vines,
the produce of the olive fail
and the fields yield no food,
the flock be cut off from the fold
and there be no herd in the stalls,
yet I will rejoice in the Lord,
I will exult in the God of my salvation.

*Judaism* and *Christianity*.
Habakkuk 3.17-18

**Qur'an 20.131-32**: An important element in the attitude of trust in God's provision is to avoid comparing oneself with others.

**Bhagavad Gita 5.10-12**: Cf. Bhagavad Gita 2.47-50, p. 667; Srimad Bhagavatam 9, p. 700.

**Matthew 6.25-33**: Cf. Srimad Bhagavatam 9, p. 700.

**Habakkuk 3.17-18**: Cf. Sri Raga, M.1, p. 625.

The Exalted One said to Bhaddiya, "Bhaddiya, what motive have you, who are wont to resort to forest-dwelling, to the roots of trees, to lonely spots, in exclaiming, 'Ah! 'tis bliss! Ah! 'tis bliss!'?"

"Formerly, sir, when I enjoyed the bliss of royalty as a householder, within my palace guards were set and outside my palace guards were set. So also in the district and outside. Thus, sir, though guarded and protected, I dwelt fearful, anxious, trembling, and afraid. But now, sir, as I resort to forest-dwelling, to the roots of trees, to lonely spots, though alone, I am fearless, assured, confident, and unafraid. I live at ease, unstartled, lightsome, with heart like that of some wild creature. This, sir, was the motive I have for exclaiming, 'Ah! 'tis bliss! Ah! 'tis bliss!'"

*Buddhism.* Udana 19-20

The restless mind is not fixed at one spot;
Like a deer it nibbles at tender shoots.
Should man lodge in mind the divine lotus feet,
His life span is lengthened, his mind awakened, immortal he becomes.
All beings are in the grip of anxiety;
But by contemplation of God comes joy.

*Sikhism.* Adi Granth, Ramkali Dakhni Onkar, M.1, p. 932

The awakened sages call a person wise when all his undertakings are free from anxiety about results; all his selfish desires have been consumed in the fire of knowledge. The wise, ever satisfied, have abandoned all external supports. Their security is unaffected by the results of their action; even while acting, they really do nothing at all [i.e., nothing producing karma]. Free from expectations and from all sense of possession, with mind and body firmly controlled by the Self, they do not incur sin by the performance of physical action.

*Hinduism.* Bhagavad Gita 4.19-21

The man who has had his feet cut off in punishment discards his fancy clothes—because praise and blame no longer touch him. The chained convict climbs the highest peak without fear—because he has abandoned all thought of life and death. These two are submissive and unashamed because they have forgotten other men, and by forgetting other men they have become men of Heaven. You may treat such men with respect and they will not be pleased; you may treat them with contumely and they will not be angry. Only because they are one with the Heavenly Harmony can they be like this.

*Taoism.* Chuang Tzu 23

❖

**Ramkali Dakhni Onkar, M.1**: Cf. Sri Raga, M.1, p. 625; Atharva Veda 10.8.43-44, pp. 411-12.

**Bhagavad Gita 4.19-21**: Cf. Bhagavad Gita 2.47-50. p. 667; Tao Te Ching 2, p. 667; Sutta Nipata 1072-76, p. 379.

**Chuang Tzu 23**: It is a well-known phenomenon that people who have faced death, imprisonment, or absolute disgrace can rise above ordinary notions of good and evil and become people of profound wisdom. Cf. Chuang Tzu 6, pp. 158-59; 31, p. 680.

## Gratitude

A SENSE OF GRATITUDE AND INDEBTEDNESS to others is an important wellspring of a generous and virtuous life. All people can recognize that they are indebted to their parents, who gave them birth and raised them at considerable sacrifice. But our indebtedness extends much further than that. Fundamentally, we are indebted to God our Creator and the powers of nature that nourish and sustain our life. Then, since the food we eat travels from the soil to our dining table by passing through many hands—that cultivate, harvest, clean, package, transport, sell, and prepare it—we should recognize that we rely on the labors of many people in order to survive. A sense of gratitude to others is thus acknowledging our interdependent existence; it is an antidote to the illusion of egoism. Such gratitude is recalled and expressed in the prayer of grace or thanks offered before meals.

Another dimension of gratitude is directed toward those who are responsible for our education and enlightenment in the way of truth and salvation. Gratitude toward one's teachers, and especially toward the sages and founders of religions who offered their lives to find the truth, is a proper attitude of faith. Most of all, we should be grateful to God, who quietly has been guiding and nurturing each person toward salvation, and without whose grace the world would be plunged in darkness.

And whatever you do, in word or deed, do everything in the name of the Lord Jesus, giving thanks to God the Father through him.

*Christianity*. Colossians 3.17

O you who believe! Eat of the good things that We have provided for you, and be grateful to God, if it is Him that you worship.

*Islam*. Qur'an 2.172

God created foods to be received with thanksgiving by those who believe and know the truth. For everything created by God is good, and nothing is to be rejected if it is received with thanksgiving; for then it is consecrated by the word of God and prayer.

*Christianity*. 1 Timothy 4.3-5

Abraham caused God's name to be mentioned by all the travellers whom he entertained. For after they had eaten and drunk, and when they arose to bless Abraham, he said to them, "Is it of mine that you have eaten? Surely it is of what belongs to God that you have eaten. So praise and bless Him by whose word the world was created."

*Judaism*. Talmud, Sota 10b

The unworthy man is ungrateful, forgetful of benefits [done to him]. This ingratitude, this forgetfulness is congenial to mean people... But the worthy person is grateful and mindful of benefits done to him. This gratitude, this mindfulness, is congenial to the best people.

*Buddhism*. Anguttara Nikaya i.61

One upon whom We bestow kindness
But will not express gratitude,
Is worse than a robber
Who carries away our belongings.

*African Traditional Religions*.
Yoruba Proverb (Nigeria)

**Colossians 3.17**: Cf. Psalm 100, p. 135.

Be not like those who honor their gods in prosperity and curse them in adversity. In pleasure or pain, give thanks!

*Judaism.* Mekilta Exodus 20.20

Even if you cry your heart out, hurt your eyes by constant weeping, and even if you lead the life of an ascetic till the end of the world, all these untiring efforts of yours will not be able to make compensation for a tithe of His good will and kindness, for His bounties and munificence and for His mercy and charity in directing you toward the path of truth and religion.

*Islam.* Nahjul Balagha, Sermon 57

It is God who has made the night for you, that you may rest therein, and the day, as that which helps you to see. Verily God is full of grace and bounty to men, yet most men give no thanks.

It is God who has made for you the earth as a resting place, and the sky as a canopy, and has given you shape—and made your shapes beautiful—and has provided for you sustenance of things pure and good; such is God, your Lord. So glory to God, the Lord of the Worlds!

*Islam.* Qur'an 40.61, 64

You, the World Honored One, are a great
  benefactor.
By doing this rare thing,
You taught and benefited us
Out of your compassion toward us.

No one will be able to repay your favors
Even if he tries to do it
For many hundreds of millions of kalpas.
No one will be able to repay your favors
Even if he bows to you respectfully,
And offers you his hands or feet or anything
  else.
No one will be able to repay your favors
Even if he carries you on his head or shoulders
And respects you from the bottom of his heart
For as many kalpas
As there are sands in the River Ganges.

*Buddhism.* Lotus Sutra 4

All human bodies are things lent by God. With what thought are you using them?

*Tenrikyo.* Ofudesaki 3.41

When a man is born, whoever he may be, there is born simultaneously a debt to the gods, to the sages, to the ancestors, and to men.

When he performs sacrifice it is the debt to the gods which is concerned. It is on their behalf, therefore, that he is taking action when he sacrifices or makes an oblation.

And when he recites the Vedas it is the debt to the sages which is concerned. It is on their behalf, therefore, that he is taking action, for it is said of one who has recited the Vedas that he is the guardian of the treasure store of the sages.

And when he desires offspring, it is the debt to the ancestors which is concerned. It is on their behalf, therefore, that he is taking action, so that their offspring may continue, without interruption.

And when he entertains guests, it is the debt to man which is concerned. It is on their behalf, therefore, that he is taking action if he entertains guests and gives them food and drink. The man who does all these things has performed a true work; he has obtained all, conquered all.

*Hinduism.* Satapatha Brahmana 1.7.2.1-5

**Qur'an 40.61, 64**: Cf. Qur'an 14.32-34, p. 215; 16.10-18, p. 91; 32.4-9, pp. 80-81; Wadhans, M.5, p. 649; Kikuyu Prayer, p. 550. On gratitude to parents, see Qur'an 46.15-16, p. 172.

**Lotus Sutra 4**: The value of the Buddha's teaching is immeasurable. It touches eternity, which all temporal phenomena rolled up together cannot hope to attain. Hence no temporal acts of gratitude can possibly be worthy of it. Cf. Myokonin, p. 553.

**Ofudesaki 3.41**: Cf. Sun Myung Moon, 9-30-79, pp. 213-14.

**Satapatha Brahmana 1.7.2.4**: On gratitude to one's parents, cf. Anguttara Nikaya i.61, p. 172; Classic on Filial Piety 1, pp. 171-72.

Ah, children—
Be not arrogant, but
Assist the deities of
Marvelous spirit power
In their work.

Even the grains, and the
Teeming grass and trees—
Even these are favored with
Blessings from Amaterasu,
Great Goddess of the Sun.

Morning and evening,
At each meal you take,
Consider the blessings of
Toyouke-no-kami,
You people of the world.

The blessings of the
Gods of heaven and earth—
Without these,
How could we exist,
Even for a day, even for a night?

Forget not the grace
Of generations of ancestors;
From age to age, the ancestors
Are our own *ujigami*,
Gods of our families.

Father and mother
Are gods of the family;
Even so, honor them as gods with
Heartfelt service,
All you of human birth.

*Shinto.* Norinaga Motoori,
One Hundred Poems
on the Jewelled Spear

❖

**One Hundred Poems on the Jewelled Spear**: The *ujigami* are eponymous ancestors of the clan; one's ancestors should be reverenced. Toyouke-no-kami is the Food Goddess worshipped at the Outer Shrine of the Temple at Ise, and Amaterasu is the Sun Goddess; they represent all the productive forces of nature and humanity which provide our food.

## *Argument with God*

WHERE GOD IS KNOWN AND EXPERIENCED as a real Person, one who loves and cares for human beings as his children, the seeker after God may not be satisfied with love expressed only as devotion, obedience, or blind trust. He may desire an encounter that is more dramatic and definite: a stand, a confrontation, an argument. The fact that Almighty God will countenance such arguments is an indication of his profound love for humanity. This is not the argument of the doubter or the atheist, nor the complaint of one with little faith,[1] but an encounter motivated by a burning desire for deeper insight into God's truth and experience of his compassionate Presence.

Job argued with God because conventional wisdom said that his suffering must be the just punishment for his sins. Yet he knew himself to be innocent of any crimes, and he wanted to meet God face to face rather than accept platitudes which he knew to be untrue. Although God did not quite grant his innocence as he had conceived it, Job was more than transformed by the encounter itself. In the Ramayana, Sita went through an ordeal by fire to prove her innocence to her husband, the divine Rama, who had spurned her without cause. She submitted to the fire to prove her faithfulness; thus she proved herself and was reconciled to her Lord. The great bhakti saints such as Basavanna had such pure and ardent devotion that they could argue for the integrity of their relationship with God. The Hebrew prophets often interceded with God in attempting to change his mind and win pardon for their people; thus Abraham interceded for the cities of Sodom and Gomorrah, challenging God to show his mercy rather than his wrath. In a similar manner Muhammad, on his heavenly tour during the Night Journey (*Mi'raj*), argued with God and won a reduction of the number of obligatory prayers incumbent on all Muslims. A well-known passage from the Talmud depicts the sages arguing with God to illustrate how much God values human free choice.

Let me have silence, and I will speak,
and let come on me what may.
I will take my flesh in my teeth,
and put my life in my hand.
Behold, he will slay me; I have no hope;
yet I will defend my ways to his face.
This will be my salvation,
that a godless man shall not come before him.
Listen carefully to my words,
and let my declaration be in your ears.
Behold, I have prepared my case;
I know that I shall be vindicated.
Who is there that will contend with me?
For then I would be silent and die.
Only grant two things to me,
then I will not hide myself from thy face:
withdraw thy hand far from me,
and let not dread of thee terrify me.
Then call, and I will answer;
or let me speak, and do thou reply to me.
How many are my iniquities, and my sins?
Make me know my transgression and my sin.
Why dost thou hide thy face,
and count me as thy enemy?

*Judaism* and *Christianity*.
Job 13.13-24

---

[1] On not complaining, see Bhagavad Gita 3.31-32, p. 107; Sun Myung Moon, 9-11-72, p. 552; Job 2.7-10, p. 506; Var Majh, M.1, p. 506; John 18.11, p. 506; Book of Songs, Ode 40, p. 506.

Oh that I knew where I might find him,
that I might come even to his seat!
I would lay my case before him
and fill my mouth with arguments.
I would learn what he would answer me,
and understand what he would say to me.
Would he contend with me in the greatness of
his power?
No; he would give heed to me.
There an upright man could reason with him,
and I should be acquitted forever by my judge.
Behold, I go forward, but he is not there;
and backward, but I cannot perceive him;
on the left hand I seek him, but I cannot
behold him;
I turn to the right hand, but I cannot see him.
But he knows the way that I take;
when he has tried me, I shall come forth as
gold.

*Judaism* and *Christianity*. Job 23.3-10

After the death of Ravana, Rama sent for Sita.... When Sita eagerly arrived, after her months of loneliness and suffering, she was received by her husband in full view of a vast public. But she could not understand why her lord seemed preoccupied and moody and cold. Rama suddenly said, "My task is done. I have now freed you. I have fulfilled my mission. All this effort has been not to attain personal satisfaction for you or me. It was to vindicate the honor of the Ikshvaku race and to honor our ancestors' codes and values. After all this, I must tell you that it is not customary to admit back to the normal married fold a woman who has resided all alone in a stranger's house. There can be no question of our living together again. I leave you free to go where you please and to choose any place to live in. I do not restrict you in any manner."

On hearing this, Sita broke down. "My trials are not ended yet," she cried. "I thought with your victory our troubles were at an end...! So be it." She beckoned to Lakshmana and ordered, "Light a fire at once, on this very spot."

Lakshmana hesitated and looked at his brother, wondering whether he would countermand the order. But Rama seemed passive and acquiescent. Lakshmana gathered faggots and got ready a roaring pyre within a short time. The entire crowd watched, stunned, while the flames rose higher and higher. Still Rama made no comment. He watched. Sita approached the fire, prostrated herself before it, and said, "O Agni, great god of fire, be my witness." She jumped into the fire.

From the heart of the flame rose the god of fire, bearing Sita, and presented her to Rama with words of blessing. Rama, now satisfied that he had established his wife's integrity in the presence of the world, welcomed Sita back to his arms.

Ramayana, Yuddha Kanda 118-20

I do act as I talk
And live up to my words in deed;
Take a balance and weights in your hands
Oh my Lord!
If my words and deeds
Should differ slightly
By even a barley grain,
You kick me and go,
Oh Lord Kudala Sangama!

*Hinduism*. Basavanna, Vacana 440

I am the cattle; you are the herdsman.
Before I am caught and thrashed as the beast,
O Lord Kudala Sangama!
Please see to it that you are not blamed:
"Who the heck is grazing this one here!"

*Hinduism*. Basavanna, Vacana 53

**Ramayana, Yuddha Kanda 118-20**: Although Sita had remained chaste while in Ravana's captivity (see Ramayana, Sundara Kanda 19-22, p. 632), Rama still was unwilling to take her back. Rama is God incarnate; why would he not know of her chastity and fidelity and accept her? The text says that he was swayed by the suspicions and scruples of the crowd, and that he momentarily doubted his true identity as Vishnu. Thus it is up to Sita herself to prove her innocence through an ordeal by fire.

**Vacana 440**: The sage is so full of self-confidence that he can challenge the divine Judge. Kudala Sangama is Basavanna's personal name for Lord Shiva; it is the name of a temple where he studied in his youth.

**Vacana 53**: Just as the herdsman should be vigilant enough not to let his cattle go astray and graze in another's field, so God should save his ardent devotee for the sake of his own good name.

The Lord said, "Because the outcry against Sodom and Gomorrah is great and their sin is very grave, I will go down to see whether they have done altogether according to the outcry which has come to me; and if not, I will know."

So the men turned from there, and went toward Sodom; but Abraham still stood before the Lord. Then Abraham drew near, and said, "Will you indeed destroy the righteous with the wicked? Suppose there are fifty righteous within the city; will you still destroy the place and not spare it for the fifty righteous who are in it? Far be it from you to do such a thing, to slay the righteous with the wicked, so that the righteous fare as the wicked! Far be that from you! Shall not the Judge of all the earth do right?"

And the Lord said, "If I find at Sodom fifty righteous in the city, I will spare the whole place for their sake."

Abraham answered, "Behold, I have taken upon myself to speak to the Lord, I who am but dust and ashes. Suppose five of the fifty righteous are lacking? Will you destroy the whole city for lack of five?"

And he said, "I will not destroy it if I find forty-five there."

"Suppose forty are found there."

"For the sake of forty I will not do it."

"Oh let not the Lord be angry, and I will speak. Suppose thirty are found there."

"I will not do it, if I find thirty there."

"Behold, I have taken upon myself to speak to the Lord. Suppose twenty are found there."

"For the sake of twenty I will not destroy it."

"Oh let not the Lord be angry, and I will speak again but this once. Suppose ten are found there."

"For the sake of ten I will not destroy it." And the Lord went his way when he had finished speaking to Abraham; and Abraham returned to his place.

*Judaism* and *Christianity*. Genesis 18.20-33

God said, "When I conquer, I lose. When I am conquered, I gain. I conquered the generation of the flood. But did I not lose, for I destroyed my world? So, too, with the generation of the Tower of Babel. So, too, with the men of Sodom. But at the sin of the golden calf I was conquered; Moses prevailed over me [to forgive their sin], and I gained, in that I did not destroy Israel."

*Judaism*. Pesikta Rabbati 32b-33a

"When the angel raised me [through the heavens]," said the Prophet, "then God prescribed for my people fifty prayers [a day]. As I came back with this regulation, I passed near Moses. 'What has God prescribed for your people?' he asked. 'He has prescribed fifty prayers,' I replied. 'Go back to the Lord,' said Moses, 'for your people will not be strong enough to endure that.' So I went back into the presence of God, who reduced the number by half. Then when I came near Moses, I said to him, 'They have been reduced by half.' 'Go back to the Lord,' he said, 'for your people will not be strong enough to endure that.' I went back into the presence of God, who reduced the number again by half. Coming back to Moses, I told him of this new reduction. 'Go back to the Lord,' he replied, 'for your people will not have the strength to endure that.' I went back into the presence of God and He said to me, 'There will be five prayers then, but they will be worth fifty in my eyes, for nothing can be changed of what has been spoken in my presence.' I went back to Moses, who said to me again, 'Go back to the Lord.' 'I am ashamed before the Lord,' I replied."

*Islam*. Hadith of Bukhari

On that day Rabbi Eliezer brought forward all of the arguments in the world [in favor of his position on a certain matter of ritual cleanliness], but they [his colleagues] did not accept them from him.

**Pesikta Rabbati 32b-33a**: On Moses' intercession for Israel, see Deuteronomy 9.11-29, pp. 458-59.

**Hadith of Bukhari**: This is a portion of the hadith of the *Mi'raj*, Muhammad's Night Journey. For more of this hadith, where Muhammad flies through the seven heavens, see p. 252.

He said to them, "If the law agrees with me, let this carob tree prove it." The carob tree leaped a hundred cubits from its place in the garden. The sages replied, "No proof can be brought from a carob tree."

He said to them, "If the law agrees with me, let this stream of water prove it." The stream of water began to flow backwards. The sages replied, "No proof can be brought from a stream of water."

Again he said to them, "If the law agrees with me, let the walls of this schoolhouse prove it." The walls began to shake and incline to fall. Rabbi Joshua leaped up and rebuked the walls saying, "When disciples of sages engage in legal dispute what is your relevance?" In honor of Rabbi Joshua the walls did not tumble. In honor of Rabbi Eliezer they did not right themselves, and are still inclined even to this day.

Again Rabbi Eliezer said to the sages, "If the law agrees with me, let it be proved from Heaven." A divine voice came forth and said, "Why do you dispute with Rabbi Eliezer, for in all matters the law agrees with him!"

But Rabbi Joshua rose to his feet again and exclaimed, '"It is not in heaven.'"

Some time later, Rabbi Nathan met the prophet Elijah and asked him, "What did the Holy One, blessed be He, do when rebuked by Rabbi Joshua?" Elijah replied, "He laughed with joy, saying, 'My children have defeated me, my children have defeated me.'"

*Judaism*. Talmud, Baba Metzia 59ab

❖

**Baba Metzia 59ab:** Rabbi Joshua's rebuke of the divine voice is a quotation of Deuteronomy 30.12. It implies that God has left the divine law in human hands and open to human interpretation regardless of God's position. The report of Elijah is based upon the tradition that, having been taken up to heaven in a whirlwind (2 Kings 2.11), he lives with God and enjoys his confidence; see Sanhedrin 98a, p. 784.

CHAPTER 15

# WISDOM

TO RECOGNIZE ULTIMATE REALITY REQUIRES KNOWLEDGE—not conceptual knowledge, but knowledge to be practiced in life, to be understood by the heart, and to be realized in spirit. It is divine knowledge, as revealed in scripture or imparted through the teachings of people who have realized truth. This chapter deals with this intellectual aspect of the life of faith.

We begin with passages on the search for knowledge in general. Passages in the second section affirm that scripture and tradition are the most reliable repositories of truth, whose study and practice is efficacious for gaining knowledge. The third section deals with the limitations of conceptual learning and the accumulation of facts, which fill libraries but may be of little value for spiritual advancement. Indeed, the most essential knowledge is not confined to words, but must be apprehended directly by experience and realization. Furthermore, there are limitations to scripture itself: Cast in parables and limited by words, it is often clouded by interpretation; and as a finite vessel, it cannot encompass the infinity of Ultimate Reality. The fifth section deals with the requirement that knowledge, if it is to be of any value, must be practiced. Another section has texts on the way of gaining wisdom through the discipline of discipleship. Some traditions advise the seeker to become the student of a living teacher; others call one to follow the example of founders and spiritual giants of the past. The chapter concludes with a section entitled *New Wine and Old Wineskins*, on the wisdom of the aged and the need to devote oneself to learning in one's youth.

❖

# The Search for Knowledge

THE SEARCH FOR KNOWLEDGE is incumbent upon every human being. Education and diligent study elevates and ennobles the human person. The most important knowledge is spiritual wisdom—the Way or the Dhamma—which not only enlightens the intellect but also elevates the spirit and fosters a good will. When a person finds a deep truth, it awakens an emotion of inner joy, because that truth corresponds with what is already within his or her original mind.

The search for knowledge is an obligation laid on every Muslim.

*Islam.* Hadith of Ibn Majah and Baihaqi

A good, all-round education, appreciation of the arts, a highly trained discipline and pleasant speech; this is the highest blessing.

*Buddhism.* Sutta Nipata 261

Confucius said, "Broaden your knowledge of the Classics, restrain it with ritual, and you are unlikely to deviate from the Way."

*Confucianism.* Analects 12.15

There is no greater wealth than wisdom; no greater poverty than ignorance; no greater heritage than culture.

*Islam.* Nahjul Balagha, Saying 52

When Confucius was going to Wei, Jan Ch'iu drove him. The Master said, "What a dense population!" Jan Ch'iu said, "When the people have multiplied, what next should be done for them?" The Master said, "Enrich them." Jan Ch'iu said, "When one has enriched them, what next should be done for them?" The Master said, "Instruct them."

*Confucianism.* Analects 13.9

A disciple in training will comprehend this earth, the realm of death and the realm of the gods. A disciple in training will investigate the well-taught Path of Virtue, even as an expert garland-maker picks flowers.

*Buddhism.* Dhammapada 45

The Master said, "A gentleman can see a question from all sides without bias. The small man is biased and can see a question only from one side."

*Confucianism.* Analects 2.14

There are three things that occasion sorrow to a superior man [who is devoted to learning]: If there be any subject of which he has not heard, and he cannot get to hear of it; if he hear of it, and cannot get to learn it; if he have learned it, and cannot get to carry it out in practice.

*Confucianism.* Book of Ritual 18.2.2.20

The parents of a child are but his enemies when they fail to educate him properly in his boyhood. An illiterate boy, like a heron amidst swans, cannot shine in the assembly of the learned. Learning imparts a heightened charm to a homely face. Knowledge is the best treasure that a man can secretly hoard up in life. Learning is the revered of the revered.

**Nahjul Balagha, Saying 52:** Cf. Lamentations Rabbah, Proem 2, pp. 731-32.

**Dhammapada 45:** Cf. Verses on the Perfection of Wisdom which is the Storehouse of Precious Virtues 14.7-8, p. 525.

Knowledge makes a man honest, virtuous, and endearing to society. It is learning alone that enables a man to better the condition of his friends and relations. Knowledge is the holiest of holies, the god of the gods, and commands respect of crowned heads; shorn of it a man is but an animal. The fixtures and furniture of one's house may be stolen by thieves; but knowledge, the highest treasure, is above all stealing.

*Hinduism*. Garuda Purana 115

Does not wisdom call,
does not understanding raise her voice?
On the heights beside the way,
in the paths she takes her stand;
beside the gates in front of the town,
at the entrance of the portals she cries aloud;
"To you, O men, I call,
and my cry is to the sons of men.
O simple ones, learn prudence;
O foolish men, pay attention.
Hear, for I will speak noble things,
and from my lips will come what is right;
for my mouth will utter truth;
wickedness is an abomination to my lips.
All the words of my mouth are righteous;
there is nothing twisted or crooked in them.
They are all straight to him who understands
and right to those who find knowledge.
Take my instruction instead of silver,
and knowledge rather than choice gold;
for wisdom is better than jewels,
and all that you may desire cannot compare
with her.

*Judaism* and *Christianity*. Proverbs 8.1-11

If any of you lacks wisdom, let him ask God who gives to all men generously and without reproaching, and it will be given him.

*Christianity*. James 1.5

[God] gives wisdom to whom He will, and he to whom wisdom is given has truly received abundant good. But none remember except men of understanding.

*Islam*. Qur'an 2.269

What thing I am I do not know.
I wander secluded, burdened by my mind.
When the Firstborn of Truth has come to me
I receive a share in that selfsame Word.

*Hinduism*. Rig Veda 1.164.37

Mencius said, "A gentleman steeps himself in the Way because he wishes to find it in himself."

*Confucianism*. Mencius IV.B.14

He who imbibes the Dhamma abides in happiness with mind pacified; the wise man ever delights in the Dhamma revealed by the Noble Ones.

*Buddhism*. Dhammapada 79

When they listen to that which has been revealed unto the Messenger, you see their eyes overflow with tears because of their recognition of the Truth. They say, "Our Lord, we believe. Inscribe us as among the witnesses."

*Islam*. Qur'an 5.83

As the heat of a fire reduces wood to ashes, the fire of knowledge burns to ashes all karma. Nothing in this world purifies like spiritual wisdom. It is the perfection achieved in time through the path of yoga, the path which leads to the Self within.

*Hinduism*. Bhagavad Gita 4.37-38

**Proverbs 8.1-11:** Wisdom is personified here, and in Proverbs 8.22-23, p. 100; Perfection of Wisdom in Eight Thousand Lines 7.1, pp. 100-1; and Sirach 24.28-29, p. 576. Cf. 1 Corinthians 2.6-10, p. 383.

**James 1.5:** God is the ultimate source of wisdom, and he who doubts is invited to bring the matter before God in prayer. Cf. Pearl of Great Price, Joseph Smith 2, p. 426.

**Qur'an 2.269:** Cf. Proverbs 9.10, p. 569.

**Rig Veda 1.164.37:** This is the cosmic law as imparted by a teacher.

**Bhagavad Gita 4.37-38:** Cf. Laws of Manu 5.109, p. 520; Narada Dharma Sutra 1.210, p. 105; Sifre Deuteronomy 143a, p. 403.

Those who see Truth and speak Truth,
Their bodies and minds become truthful.
Truth is their evidence, Truth is their instruction,
True is the praise of the truthful.
Those who have forgotten Truth cry in agony and weep while departing.

*Sikhism.* Adi Granth, Sri Raga, M.3, p. 69

The end and aim of wisdom is repentance and good deeds.

*Judaism.* Talmud, Berakot 17

True learning induces in the mind service of mankind.

*Sikhism.* Adi Granth, Asa, M.1, p. 356

## *Scripture and Tradition*

EVERY RELIGION has its store of received truth. This truth is recorded in scriptures and in the accumulated wisdom and tradition of the generations. The passages in this section recommend the study of scripture and received tradition as the way to reliable knowledge of truth, wisdom for living, and understanding of the way to approach God.

Neglect not study of the Vedas.

*Hinduism.* Taittiriya Upanishad 1.11.1

O how I love thy law! It is my meditation all the day.

*Judaism* and *Christianity*. Psalm 119.97

Lo! It is an unassailable Scripture. Falsehood cannot come at it from before it or behind it. It is a revelation from the Wise, the Owner of Praise.

*Islam.* Qur'an 41.41-42

Absorbed in the Scriptures and their purport, he transcends the cycle of birth and death.

*Jainism.* Acarangasutra 5.122

Hillel said, "He who has acquired words of Torah has acquired for himself the life of the world to come."

*Judaism.* Mishnah, Abot 2.8

I am leaving you a trust. So long as you cling to it you can't go wrong. That is the rope God has extended from heaven to earth. That is the Qur'an.

*Islam.* Hadith of Darimi 1

Know that he who reads and recites the Law-flower Sutra—that man has adorned himself with the adornment of the Buddha, and so is carried by the Tathagata on his shoulder.

*Buddhism.* Lotus Sutra 10

**Berakot 17** and **Asa, M.1:** Cf. James 3.13-18, p. 571; Book of Certitude, 69, p. 571; Precepts of Divine Learning, p. 571.

**Taittiriya Upanishad 1.11.1:** On study of the Vedas as an offering, see Satapatha Brahmana 11.5.6.1-3, p. 617.

**Psalm 119.87:** Cf. Menahot 110a, p. 618.

**Hadith of Darimi 1:** Cf. Qur'an 3.103, p. 187.

**Lotus Sutra 10:** Cf. Dhammapada 79, p. 565.

The work which the sages saw in the sacred sayings
Are manifestly spread forth in the triad of the Vedas.
Follow them constantly, you lovers of truth!
This is your path to the world of good deeds.

*Hinduism.* Mundaka Upanishad 1.2.1

This age stands in need of the holy Preceptor's teaching.
The holy Word is the Preceptor; by devoted meditation on it am I its disciple.
By absorbing the discourse of the Inexpressible I remain free from the taint of illusion.

*Sikhism.* Adi Granth, Ramkali Siddha Goshti, M.1, p. 943

And you shall love the Lord your God with all your heart, and with all your soul, and with all your might. And these words which I [Moses] teach you shall be upon your heart; and you shall teach them diligently to your children, and shall talk of them when you sit in your house, and when you walk by the way, and when you lie down, and when you rise. And you shall bind them for a sign upon your hand, and they shall be as frontlets between your eyes. And you shall write them upon the doorposts of your house and on your gates.

*Judaism.* Deuteronomy 6.5-9

We have sent down the Qur'an in Truth, and in Truth has it descended: and We sent you [Muhammad] but to give glad tidings and to warn sinners. It is a Qur'an which We have divided into parts from time to time, in order that you might recite it to men at intervals; We have revealed it by stages. Say: Whether you believe in it or not, it is true that those who were given prior insight, when it is recited to them, fall down on their faces in humble prostration, and say: "Glory to our Lord! Truly has the promise of our Lord been fulfilled!" They fall down on their faces in tears, and it increases their earnest humility.

*Islam.* Qur'an 17.105-9

Tradition endures.

*African Traditional Religions.* Akan Proverb (Ghana)

Without proverbs [traditional wisdom], the language would be but a skeleton without flesh, a body without a soul.

*African Traditional Religions.* Zulu Proverb (South Africa)

The superior man acquaints himself with many sayings of antiquity
And many deeds of the past,
In order to strengthen his character thereby.

*Confucianism.* I Ching 26: Taming Power of the Great

On Thee alone we ever meditate,
And ponder over the teachings of the loving mind,
As well as the acts of the holy men,
Whose souls accord most perfectly with truth.

*Zoroastrianism.* Avesta, Yasna 34.2

But as for you, continue in what you have learned and have firmly believed, knowing from whom you learned it and how from childhood you have been acquainted with the sacred writings which are able to instruct you for salvation through faith in Christ Jesus. All scripture is inspired by God and profitable for teaching, for reproof, for correction, and for training in righteousness, that the man of God

**Ramkali Siddha Goshti, M.1:** From the decree of Gobind Singh, the tenth Guru, Sikhism has relied on Scripture as the embodiment of the Guru's wisdom. Hence the Adi Granth is called the Guru Granth Sahib and is the central object of veneration.

**Deuteronomy 6.5-9:** For Jews, this central text of the Torah commands teaching and study. In addition, it is the basis for the ritual use of passages of the Torah wrapped inside the phylacteries worn on the forehead and the arm at times of prayer, and inside the mezuzzah affixed to the doorframes of every home. Cf. Psalm 19.7-10, pp. 105-6.

**Qur'an 17.105-09:** Cf. Qur'an 75.16-19, 42.51-53, p. 452.

**Yasna 34.2:** Cf. Yasna 45.5, p. 105.

may be complete, equipped for every good work.

*Christianity.* 2 Timothy 3.14-17

O leaders of religion! Weigh not the Book of God with such standards and sciences as are current among you, for the Book itself is the unerring Balance established among men. In this most perfect Balance whatever the peoples and kindreds possess must be weighed, while the measure of its weight should be tested according to its own standard, did you but know it.

*Baha'i Faith.*
Epistle to the Son of the Wolf, 128

The Book of Changes contains the fourfold Tao of the holy sages. In speaking, we should be guided by its judgments; in action, we should be guided by its changes; in making objects, we should be guided by its images; in seeking an oracle, we should be guided by its pronouncements.

Therefore the superior man, whenever he has to make or do something, consults the Changes, and he does so in words. It takes up his communications like an echo; neither far nor near, neither dark nor deep exist for it, and thus he learns of the things of the future. If this book were not the most spiritual thing on earth, how could it do this?

*Confucianism.* I Ching,
Great Commentary 1.10.1-2

The Taoist priest... looked around the middle hall and said, "You have a rare gem in your house; for when I entered I saw the radiance of a holy light. Where do you keep your treasure?"

Wan Teh-hsü answered, "In this poor dwelling there is nothing worthy of the name of a treasure."

The priest then took him by the hand and led him to the place where the Treatise on Response and Retribution lay, saying, "This holy book is the treasure. All the holy men of the three religions selected and compiled it to point out the way of virtue on which every one should walk. If a man disciplines himself according to its instructions, the truth will shine forth in all its glory, and every letter in the sacred writing will emit rays of divine light. But if you recite the sacred text with a secret desire for profit or reward, selfishness will darken its native glory, and the writing will show no illumination."

*Taoism.* Treatise on Response
and Retribution, Appended Tales

❖

**2 Timothy 3.14-17:** On scripture, see Matthew 7.24-27, p. 106. On tradition, cf. Jeremiah 6.16, p. 484.

**Treatise on Response and Retribution:** The 'three religions' are Taoism, Buddhism, and Confucianism, which, by the time of the Sung dynasty, came to coexist in China. They each have contributed aspects to the formation of Chinese culture. None insists on exclusive allegiance, and it is quite natural for people to believe in the truth of all three simultaneously. On the spiritual illumination of holy scriptures, cf. Forty Hadith of an-Nawawi 36, p. 186; Abot 3.2, p.186; Perfection of Wisdom in Eight Thousand Lines 7.1, pp. 100-1; Menahot 29b, p. 475.

# *Poverty of Conceptual Learning*

ALL RELIGIONS DISTINGUISH between intellectual study and the apprehension of spiritual knowledge that is conducive to salvation. Intellectual and conceptual knowledge, for all its utility in the world, does not profit the spiritual seeker, and may even impede the realization of Truth. The gulf between Athens and Jerusalem—between the conceptual systems of secular philosophy and the scriptural truth of Western religions—is the subject of the first group of passages. Against the apparent knowledge gained through philosophy and scientific reason is placed the seeming folly of the cross, the minutiae of sacrificial lore in the Torah, and the absolute claim of the Word of God. We include several passages on the evils of knowledge that is not restrained or directed by spiritual wisdom: it leads to arrogance, and excessive domination by which people are oppressed and the environment damaged.

Turning to Eastern religions, especially Buddhism and Taoism, we find that the truth which is realized in the experience of enlightenment is too profound to be stated in words. Words themselves become impediments to enlightenment when they lead to discriminative thought, attachment to one thing, and aversion to another thing. Thus the Zen koan, "Has a dog the Buddha nature?" only leads the questioner into a welter of mental confusion until he realizes that the way out is beyond any "nothingness" understood as a concept. Words can be at best a vehicle to the meaning that lies beyond, as a finger points to an object beyond itself, or as a raft that carries a man across the stream is discarded once he reaches the other shore.

The poverty of conceptual learning extends to the concepts in scripture. Knowledge of scripture according to the letter is, like any other intellection, defective by itself. Direct intuitive knowledge or inner realization of God is far superior.

Of making many books there is no end, and much study is a weariness of the flesh.

*Judaism* and *Christianity*.
Ecclesiastes 12.12

A thousand and hundred thousand feats of intellect shall not accompany man in the hereafter.

*Sikhism*. Adi Granth,
Japuji 1, M.1, p. 1

Whoever goes after unreasonable and unnecessary rationalization will never be able to reach truth.

*Islam*.
Nahjul Balagha, Saying 30

The fear of the Lord is the beginning of wisdom.

*Judaism* and *Christianity*.
Proverbs 9.10

This is true knowledge: to seek the Self as the true end of wisdom always. To seek anything else is ignorance.

*Hinduism*. Bhagavad Gita 13.11

**Ecclesiastes 12.12:** Cf. Isaiah 64.6, p. 291.
**Japuji 1, M.1:** Cf. Ramkali, M.5, p. 36.
**Proverbs 9.10:** Cf. Isaiah 7.9, p. 536; Abot 3.11, p. 551.

Knowledge puffs up, but love builds up. If any one imagines that he knows something, he does not yet know as he ought to know. But if one loves God, one is known by him.

*Christianity.* 1 Corinthians 8.1-3

Rabba ben Huna said, "Whoever possesses knowledge of the Torah without having fear of the Lord is likened to a treasurer who has been entrusted with the inner keys of the treasury but from whom the outer keys were witheld."

*Judaism.* Talmud, Shabbat 31a

Rabbi Eleazar Hisma said, "Offerings of birds and purifications of women, these, yea these, are the essential precepts. Astronomy and geometry are but fringes to wisdom."

*Judaism.* Mishnah, Abot 3.23

My now-deceased mother really scolded me. She said, "Go away somewhere into the wilderness; since all you seem to do is look at books. For all the days to come you will be pitiful because the book blocks your path. Never will anything be revealed to you in a vision, for you live like a white man."

*Native American Religions.* Delaware Testimony

Perfected is the Word of your Lord in truth and justice. There is naught that can change His words. He is the Hearer, the Knower. If you obeyed most of those on earth they would mislead you far from God's way; they follow naught but an opinion, and they do but guess.

*Islam.* Qur'an 6.115-16

True words are not fine-sounding;
Fine-sounding words are not true.
The good man does not prove by argument;
And he who proves by argument is not good.
True wisdom is different from much learning;
Much learning means little wisdom.

*Taoism.* Tao Te Ching 81

Human philosophy has made God manlike. Christian Science makes man Godlike. The first is error; the latter is truth. Metaphysics is above physics, and matter does not enter into metaphysical premises or conclusions. The categories of metaphysics rest on one basis, the divine Mind.

*Christian Science.* Science and Health, 269

The Unification Church is a school far greater than Harvard or Yale or Princeton, and is a place where only the elite of the universe can enroll. Harvard University can graduate a Ph.D., but that person can only turn around and teach theories on a blackboard. Even a thousand Harvards cannot create one son of God, but our school turns out sons of God every day.

*Unification Church.* Sun Myung Moon, 5-1-77

Where is the wise man? Where is the scribe? Where is the debater of this age? Has not God made foolish the wisdom of the world? For since, in the wisdom of God, the world did not know God through wisdom, it pleased God through the folly of what we preach to save those who believe. For the Jews demand signs and the Greeks seek wisdom, but we preach Christ crucified, a stumbling block to Jews and folly to Gentiles, but to those who are called, both Jews and Greeks, Christ the power of God and the wisdom of God. For the foolishness of God is wiser than men, and the weakness of God is stronger than men.

*Christianity.* 1 Corinthians 1.20-25

**1 Corinthians 8.1-3:** Cf. Mark 7.6-7, p. 348; 2 Corinthians 3.6, p. 574; Sutta Nipata 798, p. 39; Tao Te Ching 71, p. 650; Kena Upanishad 2.1-3, p. 56.

**Abot 3.23:** Offerings and purity laws are God's commandments in scripture, while the sciences are knowledge of human devising.

**Qur'an 6.115-16:** Cf. Nahjul Balagha, Sermon 1, p. 56.

**Tao Te Ching 81:** Cf. Tao Te Ching 71, p. 650; Chuang Tzu 2, p. 120; 13, p. 148; Gauri Sukhmani, M.5, p. 650.

**1 Corinthians 1.20-25:** Cf. 1 Corinthians 2.6-10, p. 383; Dhammapada 63, p. 650.

Know verily that knowledge is of two kinds: divine and satanic. The one wells out from the fountain of divine inspiration; the other is but a reflection of vain and obscure thoughts. The source of the former is God Himself; the motive force of the latter the whisperings of selfish desire. The one is guided by the principle: "Fear God; God will teach you"; the other is but a confirmation of the truth: "Knowledge is the most grievous veil between man and his Creator." The former brings forth the fruit of patience, of longing desire, of true understanding, and love; while the latter can yield naught but arrogance, vainglory, and conceit.

*Baha'i Faith.* Book of Certitude, 69

Who is wise and understanding among you? By his good life let him show his works in the meekness of wisdom. But if you have bitter jealousy and selfish ambition in your hearts, do not boast and be false to the truth. This wisdom is not such as comes down from above, but is earthly, unspiritual, devilish. For where jealousy and selfish ambition exist, there will be disorder and every vile practice. But wisdom from above is first pure, then peaceable, gentle, open to reason, full of mercy and good fruits, without uncertainty or insincerity. And the harvest of righteousness is sown in peace by those who make peace.

*Christianity.* James 3.13-18

"Some say that broad learning is an impediment in the study of Shinto; is that really so?"

"It is not extensive learning itself which is an impediment. It all depends on the mind of the scholar with such erudition, whether it becomes a benefit or a hindrance. Learning has as its original function knowledge of the way of mankind, becoming familiar with all the things within the realm, and producing human virtue. In spite of this fact, current scholarship concerns itelf with matters of absolutely no value to the way of man, aiming merely for the approbation of fellow scholars, becoming merely a tenacious attachment to books, and thus dark and confused, without any illumination at all. Such is an evil to Shinto."

*Shinto.* Ieyuki Asai,
Precepts of Divine Learning

Of all things seen in the world
Only mind is the host;
By grasping forms according to interpretation
It becomes deluded, not true to reality.

All philosophies in the world
Are mental fabrications;
There has never been a single doctrine
By which one could enter the true essence of things.

By the power of perceiver and perceived
All kinds of things are born;
They soon pass away, not staying,
Dying out instant to instant.

*Buddhism.* Garland Sutra 10

As long as men in high places covet knowledge and are without the Way, the world will be in great confusion. How do I know this is so? Knowledge enables men to fashion bows, crossbows, nets, stringed arrows, and like contraptions, but when this happens the birds flee in confusion to the sky. Knowledge enables men to fashion fishhooks, lures, seines, dragnets, trawls, and weirs, but when this happens the fish flee in confusion to the depths of the water. Knowledge enables men to fashion pitfalls, snares, cages, traps, and gins, but when this happens the beasts flee in confusion to the swamps. And the flood of rhetoric that enables men to invent wily schemes and poisonous slanders, the glib gabble of "hard" and "white," the foul fustian of "same" and "different," bewilder the understanding of common men. So the world is dulled and darkened by great confusion. The blame lies in the coveting of knowledge.

In the world everyone knows enough to pursue what he does not know, but no one knows enough to pursue what he already knows.

**Book of Certitude, 69:** Cf. Epistle to the Son of the Wolf, 128, p. 568; Book of Certitude, 68-69, p. 575.
**James 3.13-18:** Cf. Galatians 5.19-23, p. 331; Mark 7.6-7, p. 348.
**Garland Sutra 10:** Cf. Lankavatara Sutra 63, pp. 102-3.

Everyone knows enough to condemn what he takes to be no good, but no one knows enough to condemn what he has already taken to be good. This is how the great confusion comes about, blotting out the brightness of sun and moon above, searing the vigor of hills and streams below, overturning the round of the four seasons in between. There is no insect that creeps and crawls, no creature that flutters and flies, that has not lost its inborn nature. So great is the confusion of the world that comes from coveting knowledge!

*Taoism.* Chuang Tzu 10

Lord Mahavira said to Gautama, "When Dharma is not seen by the seer directly it is seen through the wire mesh of words. Conjecture is the wire mesh that covers that window. Multiple sects and systems result from such an indirect observation. The path suggested to you, Gautama, is the direct path of the seer. Be vigilant and a seer of Dharma."

*Jainism.* Uttaradhyayana Sutra 10.31

Knowledge is of five kinds, namely: sensory knowledge, scriptural knowledge, clairvoyance, telepathy, and omniscience. These five kinds of knowledge are of two types: the first two kinds are indirect knowledge and the remaining three constitute direct knowledge. In sensory knowledge... there is only the apprehension of indistinct things.... But clairvoyance, telepathy, and omniscience is direct knowledge; it is perceived by the soul in a vivid manner without the intermediary of the senses or the scriptures.

*Jainism.* Tattvarthasutra 1.19-29

The kami-faith is caught, not taught.

*Shinto.* Proverb

A monk asked Joshu, "Has a dog the Buddha nature?" Joshu answered, "Mu."

Mumon's comment: To attain this subtle realization, you must completely cut off the way of thinking.

*Buddhism.* Mumonkan 1

Subhuti, do not say that the Tathagata conceives the idea: I must set forth a Teaching. For if anyone says that the Tathagata sets forth a Teaching he really slanders Buddha and is unable to explain what I teach. As to any Truth-declaring system, Truth is undeclarable; so "an enunciation of Truth" is just a name given to it.

*Buddhism.* Diamond Sutra 21

It is because every one under heaven recognizes beauty as beauty that the idea of ugliness exists.
And if every one recognized virtue as virtue, this would merely create fresh conceptions of wickedness.
For truly,
"Being and Not-being grow out of one another:
Difficult and easy complete one another.
Long and short test one another;
High and low determine one another.
Pitch and mode give harmony to one another,
Front and back give sequence to one another."
Therefore the sage relies on actionless activity,
And carries on wordless teaching.

*Taoism.* Tao Te Ching 2

**Chuang Tzu 10:** Cf. Tao Te Ching 18-19, p. 201; Chuang Tzu 13, p. 148.

**Tattvarthasutra 1.19-29:** Omniscience, the highest form of knowledge, is attained only by a perfected soul. Cf. 2 Corinthians 3.6, p. 574.

**Mumonkan 1:** 'Mu' means emptiness, but emptiness cannot be realized conceptually. Proper meditation requires complete denial of the intellect. Cf. the commentary to this koan, pp. 601-2; Lankavatara Sutra 63, pp. 102-3; Holy Teaching of Vimalakirti 5, p. 58.

**Diamond Sutra 21:** This and all the Perfection of Wisdom sutras are written for the student who is aspiring for truth; there is nothing nihilistic about them. But since truth is based in Sunyata, this text advises that 'an enunciation of truth' is also empty and not to be made an object of grasping. Cf. Lankavatara Sutra 61, pp. 454-55; Mumonkan 6, p. 585; Holy Teaching of Vimalakirti 5, p. 58; Kena Upanishad 2.1-3, p. 56; Seng Ts'an, pp. 150-51; Mulamadhyamaka Karika 24.8-12, pp. 719-20.

**Tao Te Ching 2:** Cf. Tao Te Ching 18-19, p. 201; 48, p. 639; Chuang Tzu 2, pp. 40-41; 2, p. 120; Katha Upanishad 2.1.10-11, pp. 415-16.

Mahamati, the Tathagatas do not teach a doctrine that is dependent upon letters. As to letters, their being or non-being is not attainable; it is otherwise with thought that is never dependent upon letters. Again, Mahamati, anyone that discourses on a truth that is dependent upon letters is a mere prattler because truth is beyond letters. For this reason, it is declared in the canonical text by myself and other Buddhas and bodhisattvas that not a letter is uttered or answered by the Tathagatas. For what reason? Because truths are not dependent on letters....

Therefore, Mahamati, let the son or daughter of a good family take good heed not to get attached to words as being in perfect conformity with meaning, because truth is not of the letter. Be not like the one who looks at the fingertip. When a man with his fingertip points out something to somebody, the fingertip may be taken wrongly for the thing pointed at. In like manner, simple and ignorant people are unable even unto their death to abandon the idea that in the fingertip of words there is the meaning itself, and will not grasp ultimate reality because of their intent clinging to words, which are no more than the fingertip.... Be not like one who, grasping his own fingertip, sees the meaning there. You should rather energetically discipline yourself to get at the meaning itself.

*Buddhism.* Lankavatara Sutra 76

"O monks, a man is on a journey. He comes to a vast stretch of water. On this side the shore is dangerous, but on the other it is safe and without danger. No boat goes to the other shore which is safe and without danger, nor is there any bridge for crossing over. He says to himself, 'This sea of water is vast, and the shore on this side is full of danger; but on the other shore it is safe and without danger. No boat goes to the other side, nor is there a bridge for crossing over. It would be good therefore if I would gather grass, wood, branches, and leaves to make a raft, and with the help of the raft cross over safely to the other side, exerting myself with my hands and feet.' Then that man gathers grass, wood, branches, and leaves and makes a raft, and with the help of that raft crosses over safely to the other side, exerting himself with his hands and feet. Having crossed over and gotten to the other side, he thinks, 'This raft was of great help to me. With its aid I have crossed safely over to this side, exerting myself with my hands and feet. It would be good if I carry this raft on my head or on my back wherever I go.'

"What do you think, O monks, if he acted in this way would that man be acting properly with regard to the raft?"

"No, sir."

"In which way, then, would he be acting properly with regard to the raft? Having crossed and gone over to the other side, suppose that man should think, 'This raft was a great help to me. With its aid I have crossed safely over to this side, exerting myself with my hands and feet. It would be good if I beached this raft on the shore, or moored it and left it afloat, and then went on my way wherever it may be.' Acting in this way would that man act properly with regard to the raft.

"In the same manner, O monks, I have taught a doctrine similar to a raft—it is for crossing over, and not for carrying. You who understand that the teaching is similar to a raft, should give up attachment to even the good Dhamma; how much more then should you give up evil things."

*Buddhism.* Majjhima Nikaya i.134-35:
Parable of the Raft

The fish trap exists because of the fish; once you've gotten the fish, you can forget the trap. The rabbit snare exists because of the rabbit; once you've gotten the rabbit, you can forget the snare. Words exist because of meaning; once you've gotten the meaning, you can forget the words. Where can I find a man who has forgotten words so I can have a word with him?

*Taoism.* Chuang Tzu 26

❖

**Lankavatara Sutra 76:** Cf. Lankavatara Sutra 61, pp. 454-55; Mumonkan 6, p. 585; Zohar, Numbers 152a, p. 574.

**Majjhima Nikaya i.134-35:** Cf. Dhammapada 85-86, p. 384; Bhagavad Gita 2.42-46, p. 576; Mulamadhyamaka Karika 24.8-12, pp. 719-20.

# Scripture Teaches in Parables

THE SCRIPTURES CONTAIN PASSAGES which qualify the truth of their own doctrines. Recognizing that scripture may be expressed in parables and symbolic language, they teach that spiritual discernment is required for its proper interpretation. Scripture also cautions us from believing that any system of doctrine contains the entirety of truth, for in reality, God's truth is infinite. Rather, as the Buddhist texts tell us, the teachings of religion are limited to what is needful and useful for humankind's salvation.

We have put forth for men in this Qur'an every kind of parable, in order that they may receive admonition.

*Islam.* Qur'an 39.27

Knowing that all the living have many and various desires deep-rooted in their minds, I have, according to their capacity, expounded the various laws by which these [desires] could be overcome with various reasonings, parabolic expressions, and expedients.

*Buddhism.* Lotus Sutra 2

And when he was alone, those who were about him with the twelve [disciples] asked [Jesus] concerning the parables. And he said to them, "To you has been given the secret of the kingdom of God, but for those outside everything is in parables; so they may indeed see but not perceive, and may indeed hear but not understand; lest they should turn again, and be forgiven."

*Christianity.* Mark 4.10-12

It is He who sent down upon you the Book, wherein are verses clear that are the Essence of the Book, and others ambiguous. As for those in whose hearts is swerving, they follow the ambiguous part, desiring dissension, and desiring its interpretation; and none knows its interpretation, save only God. And those firmly rooted in knowledge say, "We believe in it; all is from our Lord"; yet none remembers, but men possessed of minds.

*Islam.* Qur'an 3.7

The written code kills, but the Spirit gives life.

*Christianity.* 2 Corinthians 3.6

Look, I will draw my sword to fight the Vedas,
I will put shackles on the Shastras,
I will whip the back of the books of Logic,
And I will chop off the nose of the Agamas.
[I don't give a damn about my high birth;
I have no hesitation to say,]
I am the son of the cobbler Chennyye.
O most bountiful Lord, Kudala Sangama.

*Hinduism.* Basavanna, Vacana 716

**Mark 4.10-12:** Jesus gives the reason he teaches in parables by quoting from Isaiah 6.9-10. The prophet Isaiah's words are a bitter commentary on the people's rejection of his ministry; though he preached God's words, the people's minds were darkened and they could not respond. Jesus was similarly misunderstood. Yet he still endeavored to give a gentle and gradual message, one that could be received even by babes, through teaching in simple parables. These could be understood by those who had ears to hear. Cf. Matthew 13.14-15, p. 283.

**Qur'an 3.7:** Cf. Qur'an 2.269, p. 565; Pearl of Great Price, Joseph Smith 2, p. 426.

**Vacana 716:** Basavanna, a brahmin by birth, regarded the cobblers and untouchables as his brothers and sisters, fathers and mothers. For this breach of caste taboos he was constantly rebuked by brahmins quoting scripture. Cf. Vacana 589, p. 192.

The biblical tales are only the Torah's outer garments, and woe to him who regards these as being the Torah itself!

*Judaism.* Zohar, Numbers 152a

He who does not know that indestructible Being of the Rig Veda, that highest ether-like Self wherein all the gods reside, of what use is the Rig Veda to him? Those only who know It rest contented.

*Hinduism.* Svetasvatara Upanishad 4.8

First take up the words,
Ponder their meaning,
Then the fixed rules reveal themselves.
But if you are not the right man,
The meaning will not manifest itself to you.

*Confucianism.* I Ching, Great Commentary 2.8.4

When the man of highest capacities hears the Tao
He does his best to put it into practice.
When the man of middling capacity hears the Tao
He is in two minds about it.
When the man of low capacity hears Tao
He laughs loudly at it.
If he did not laugh, it would not be worth the name of Tao.

*Taoism.* Tao Te Ching 41

Jesus answered them, "My teaching is not mine, but his who sent me; if any man's will is to do his will, he shall know whether this teaching is from God or whether I am speaking from my own authority."

*Christianity.* John 7.16-17

In the unessential they imagine the essential, in the essential they see the unessential—they who entertain such wrong thoughts never realize the essence.

What is essential they regard as essential, what is unessential they regard as unessential—they who entertain such right thoughts realize the essence.

*Buddhism.* Dhammapada 11-12

Were you to cleanse the mirror of your heart from the dust of malice, you would apprehend the meaning of the symbolic terms revealed by the all-embracing Word of God made manifest in every dispensation, and would discover the mysteries of divine knowledge. Not, however, until you consume with the flame of utter detachment those veils of idle learning, that are current among men, can you behold the resplendent morn of true knowledge.

*Baha'i Faith.* Book of Certitude, 68-69

Now we have received not the spirit of the world, but the Spirit which is from God, that we might understand the gifts bestowed on us by God. And we impart this in words not taught by human wisdom but taught by the Spirit, interpreting spiritual truths to those who possess the Spirit. The unspiritual man does not receive the gifts of the Spirit of God, for they are folly to him, and he is not able to understand them because they are spiritually discerned. The spiritual man judges all things, but is himself to be judged by no one. "For who has known the mind of the Lord so as to instruct him?" But we have the mind of Christ.

*Christianity.* 1 Corinthians 2.12-16

**Svetasvatara Upanishad 4.8:** Cf. Pancastikaya 170, p. 146; Ramkali, M.5, p. 36.

**Tao Te Ching 41:** See Chuang Tzu 14, p. 513, and the Parable of the Sower, Mark 4.3-20, pp. 513-14.

**Book of Certitude, 68-69:** For an example of Baha'i interpretation of symbols from the Bible, see Book of Certitude, 33-41, p. 779.

**1 Corinthians 2.12-16:** Interpretation of scripture should be by the inspiration of the Spirit. It is said that even the devil can quote scripture. Only with the discernment born of the Spirit of God is the Word of God understood in all its depth and power. The quotation is from Isaiah 40.13. Cf. 1 Corinthians 2.6-10, p. 383.

Undiscerning men, theologians
preoccupied with scriptural lore,
who claim there is nothing else,
utter words with ephemeral results.
Their words promise better births through cultic acts,
dwell at length on various rites,
and aim at pleasure and power.
These men are full of desire, zealous for heaven.
They cling to pleasures and power
and are fooled by their own discourses.
They have no knowledge consisting in commitment,
fixed in concentration.

The Scriptures speak to the world's weave of integrity
passion, and sloth. Transcend it, Arjuna,
free from opposites, forever in integrity,
detached from things, in command of yourself.
All the Scriptures mean as much—no more, no less—
to the discerning spiritual man
as a water tank
in a universal flood.

*Hinduism*. Bhagavad Gita 2.42-46

And if all the trees in the earth were pens, and the sea, with seven more seas to help it [were ink], the words of God could not be spent. Lo! God is Mighty, Wise.

*Islam*. Qur'an 31.27

The water from the ocean contained in a pot can neither be called an ocean nor non-ocean, but it can be called only part of the ocean. Similarly, a doctrine, though arising from the Absolute Truth, is neither the Truth nor not the Truth.

*Jainism*. Vidyanandi, Tattvarthaslokavartika 116

The Word is measured in four quarters.
The wise who possess insight know these four divisions.
Three quarters, concealed in secret, cause no movement.
The fourth is the quarter that is spoken by men.

*Hinduism*. Rig Veda 1.164.45

Just as the first man did not know her [Wisdom] perfectly,
the last one has not fathomed her;
for her thought is more abundant than the sea,
and her counsel deeper than the great abyss.

*Christianity*. Sirach 24.28-29

Behold, you are my son; wherefore look, and I will show you the workmanship of my hands; but not all, for my works are without end, and also my words, for they never cease.

*Church of Jesus Christ of Latter-day Saints*. Pearl of Great Price, Moses 1.4

I have yet many things to say to you, but you cannot bear them now. When the Spirit of truth comes, he will guide you into all the truth.

*Christianity*. John 16.12-13

For our knowledge is imperfect and our prophecy is imperfect; but when the perfect comes, the imperfect will pass away. When I was a child, I spoke like a child, I thought like a child, I reasoned like a child; when I became a man, I gave up childish ways. For now we see in a mirror dimly, but then face to face. Now I know in part; then I shall understand fully.

*Christianity*. 1 Corinthians 13.9-12

**Bhagavad Gita 2.42-46:** Cf. the Parable of the Raft, Majjhima Nikaya i.134-35, p. 573; Mulamadhyamaka Karika 24.8-12, pp. 719-20.

**Tattvarthaslokavartika 116:** Cf. Sanmatitarka 1.28, pp. 39-40; Parable of the Blind Men and the Elephant, Udana 68-69, p. 41.

**Rig Veda 1.164.45:** Cf. Rig Veda 10.90.1-4, p. 63; Kena Upanishad 2.1-3, p. 56.

**John 16.12-13:** Jesus only had three years to teach his disciples, and many truths of heaven were left unrevealed. The Spirit continues to inspire us with new and deeper insights into truth.

And We sent Messengers before you, and We assigned to them wives and seed; and it was not for any Messengers to bring a sign, but by God's leave. Every term has a Book.

God blots out, and He establishes whatsoever He will; and with Him is the Essence of the Book.

Whether We show you a part of that We promise them, or We call you unto Us, it is yours only to deliver the message, and Ours is the reckoning.

*Islam*. Qur'an 13.38-40

Thus I have heard.

On a certain occasion the Blessed One was dwelling at Savatthi in Jetavana monastery in Anathapindika's Park. Now it happened to the venerable Malunkyaputta, being in seclusion and plunged in meditation, that a consideration presented itself to his mind, as follows:

"These theories which the Blessed One has left unelucidated, has set aside and rejected—that the world is eternal, that the world is not eternal, that the world is finite, that the world is infinite, that the soul and the body are identical, that the soul is one thing and the body another, that the saint exists after death, that the saint does not exist after death, that the saint both exists and does not exist after death, that the saint neither exists nor does not exist after death—these the Blessed One does not elucidate to me. And the fact that the Blessed One does not elucidate them to me does not please me nor suit me. Therefore I will draw near to the Blessed One and inquire of him concerning these matters. If the Blessed One will elucidate to me, either that the world is eternal or that the world is not eternal..., in that case I will lead the religious life under the Blessed One. If the Blessed One will not elucidate [these matters] to me..., in that case I will abandon religious training and return to the lower life of a layman."

Then the venerable Malunkyaputta arose at eventide from his seclusion, drew near to where the Blessed One was; and having drawn near and greeted the Blessed One, he sat down respectfully at one side. And seated respectfully at one side, Malunkyaputta asked his question....

[The Buddha replied], "Pray, Malunkyaputta, did I ever say to you, 'Come, Malunkyaputta, lead the religious life under me, and I will elucidate to you either that the world is eternal, or that the world is not eternal, etc.'?"

"Nay, verily, reverend sir."

"Or did you ever say to me, 'Reverend sir, I will lead the religious life under the Blessed One, on condition that the Blessed One elucidate to me these things'?"

"Nay, verily, reverend sir."

"That being the case, vain man, whom are you so angrily denouncing? Malunkyaputta, any one who should say, 'I will not lead the religious life under the Blessed One until the Blessed One shall elucidate to me either that the world is eternal or that the world is not eternal...'—that person would die before the Tathagata had ever elucidated this to him.

"It is as if, Malunkyaputta, a man had been wounded by an arrow thickly smeared with poison, and his friends and companions, relatives and kinsfolk, were to procure for him a physician or surgeon; and the sick man were to say, 'I will not have this arrow taken out until I have learned whether the man who wounded me belonged to the warrior caste, or to the brahmin caste, or to the farmers' caste, or to the menial caste.'

"Or again he were to say, 'I will not have this arrow taken out until I have learned the name of the man who wounded me, and to what clan he belongs.'

"Or again he were to say, 'I will not have this arrow taken out until I have learned whether the man who wounded me was tall, or short, or of middle height.'

"Or again he were to say, 'I will not have this arrow taken out until I have learned whether the man who wounded me was black, or dusky, or of a yellow skin.'

**Qur'an 13.38-40:** The 'Essence of the Book' is the fulness of truth known only to God; what is revealed in the Qur'an and in the previous scriptures may only be a part of this fulness of truth. How is Muhammad or any of the prophets, who are but mortals, to know?

"Or again he were to say, 'I will not have this arrow taken out until I have learned whether the man who wounded me was from this or that village, town, or city.'

"Or again he were to say, 'I will not have this arrow taken out until I have learned whether the bow which wounded me was a capa, or a kodanda.'

"Or again he were to say, 'I will not have this arrow taken out until I have learned whether the bowstring which wounded me was made from swallow-wort, or bamboo, or sinew, or maruva, or from milkweed.'

"Or again he were to say, 'I will not have this arrow taken out until I have learned whether the shaft which wounded me was a kaccha or a ropima.'

"Or again he were to say, 'I will not have this arrow taken out until I have learned whether the shaft which wounded me was feathered from the wings of a vulture, or of a heron, or of a falcon, or of a peacock, or of a sithilahanu.'

"Or again he were to say, 'I will not have this arrow taken out until I have learned whether the shaft which wounded me was wound round with the sinews of an ox, or of a buffalo, or of a deer, or of a monkey.'

"Or again he were to say, 'I will not have this arrow taken out until I have learned whether the arrow which wounded me was an ordinary arrow, or a claw-headed arrow, or a vekanda, or an iron arrow, or a calf-tooth arrow, or a karavirapatta.' That man would die, Malunkyaputta, without ever having learnt this.

"In exactly the same way, Malunkyaputta, any one who should say, 'I will not lead the religious life under the Blessed One until the Blessed One shall elucidate to me either that the world is eternal or that the world is not eternal, etc.'—that person would die before the Tathagata had ever elucidated this to him.

"The religious life does not depend on the dogma that the world is eternal; nor does the religious life depend on the dogma that the world is not eternal. Whether the dogma obtain, that the world is eternal, or that the world is not eternal, there still remain birth, old age, death, sorrow, lamentation, misery, grief, despair, for the extinction of which in the present life I am prescribing.... This profits not, nor has to do with the fundamentals of religion, nor tends to aversion, absence of passion, cessation, quiescence, the supernatural faculties, supreme wisdom, and Nirvana; therefore have I not elucidated it.

"And what, Malunkyaputta, have I elucidated? Misery I have elucidated; the cessation of misery I have elucidated; and the path leading to the cessation of misery I have elucidated. And why, Malunkyaputta, have I elucidated this? Because this does profit, has to do with the fundamentals of religion, and tends to aversion, absence of passion, cessation, quiescence, knowledge, supreme wisdom, and Nirvana; therefore I have elucidated it. Accordingly, Malunkyaputta, bear always in mind what it is that I have not elucidated, and what it is that I have elucidated."

Thus spoke the Blessed One; and, delighted, the venerable Malunkyaputta applauded the speech of the Blessed One.

*Buddhism.* Majjhima Nikaya i.426-31:
Cula-Malunkya Sutta

❖

**Majjhima Nikaya i.426-31:** Cf. Parable of the Raft, Majjhima Nikaya i.134-35, p. 573.

## *Learning and Practice*

WHEN A TRUTH IS LEARNED, it must be practiced. Indeed, knowledge that is not put into practice is not truly learned; it soon fades away like a mirage. The person who claims to be wise and devout, but who never acts on his wisdom, is engaging in *Hypocrisy*, pp. 348-51. Conversely, as the concluding story of Mary and Martha shows, action without learning is also foolish. In the East, people are taught the virtue of being reserved and taciturn in order that they might not display knowledge that they have not yet mastered in practice. It is far better first to act on an idea in private and see its result than to announce it to others while it is yet untested and unmastered. This reserve is especially apt in the case of religious and moral teaching, whose practice is not easy. Only a teacher who has first mastered and embodied his teaching is worthy of respect.

I do act as I talk
And live up to my words in deed.

*Hinduism.* Basavanna, Vacana 440

Tzu-kung asked about the true gentleman. The Master said, "He does not preach what he practices until he has practiced what he preaches."

*Confucianism.* Analects 2.13

The scribes and the Pharisees sit on Moses' seat; so practice and observe whatever they tell you, but not what they do; for they preach, but do not practice.

*Christianity.* Matthew 23.2-3

O you who believe, wherefore do you say what you do not?
Very hateful is it to God, that you say what you do not.

*Islam.* Qur'an 61.2-3

Realization of Truth is higher than all else;
Higher still is truthful living.

*Sikhism.* Adi Granth, Sri Raga Ashtpadi, M.1, p. 62

Just as a man or a woman has known what is truth, so he or she should practice that truth with zeal, and should teach it those persons who should practice it so, as it is!

*Zoroastrianism.* Avesta, Yasna 35.6

As a flower that is lovely and beautiful, but is scentless, even so fruitless is the well-spoken word of one who does not practice it.

As a flower that is lovely, beautiful and scent-laden, even so fruitful is the well-spoken word of one who practices it.

*Buddhism.* Dhammapada 51-52

That knowledge is very superficial which remains only on your tongue: the intrinsic merit and value of knowledge is that you act up to it.

*Islam.* Nahjul Balaga, Saying 90

Be doers of the word, and not hearers only, deceiving yourselves. For if any one is a hearer of the word and not a doer, he is like a man who observes his natural face in a mirror; for

**Analects 2.13:** This is close to the Confucian meaning of sincerity; see Doctrine of the Mean 25, p. 517.
**Matthew 23.2-3:** Cf. Qur'an 26.221-26, p. 315.
**Dhammapada 51-52:** Cf. Large Sutra on Perfect Wisdom 431, p. 315.

he observes himself and goes away and at once forgets what he was like.

*Christianity*. James 1.22-24

The Master said, "A gentleman is ashamed to let his words outrun his deeds."

*Confucianism*. Analects 14.29

Not study is the chief thing, but action; and whoso multiplies words, multiplies sin.

*Judaism*. Mishnah, Abot 1.17

Not every one who says to me, "Lord, Lord," shall enter the kingdom of Heaven, but he who does the will of my Father who is in heaven.

*Christianity*. Matthew 7.21

The Master said, "Do not be too ready to speak of it, lest the doing of it should prove to be beyond your powers."

*Confucianism*. Analects 14.21

The one who would have the worst position in God's sight on the Day of Resurrection would be a learned man who did not profit from his learning.

*Islam*. Hadith of Darimi

Though he recites many a scriptural text, but does not act accordingly, that heedless man is like a cowherd who counts others' cattle. He has no share in the fruits of the religious life.

Though he can recite few scriptural texts, but acts in accordance with the teaching, forsaking lust, hatred, and ignorance, with right awareness and mind well emancipated, not clinging to anything here or in the next life, he shares the fruits of the religious life.

*Buddhism*. Dhammapada 19-20

Now as they went on their way, he entered a village; and a woman named Martha received him into her house. And she had a sister called Mary, who sat at the Lord's feet and listened to his teaching. But Martha was distracted with much serving; and she went to him and said, "Lord, do you not care that my sister has left me to serve alone? Tell her then to help me." But the Lord answered her, "Martha, Martha, you are anxious and troubled about many things; one thing is needful. Mary has chosen the good portion, which shall not be taken away from her."

*Christianity*. Luke 10.38-42

❖

**James 1.22-24:** If a teaching is not put into practice, it may readily be forgotten. This frequently happens to sensitive people who receive spiritual revelations; if not acted upon they rapidly slip away. Cf. James 2.14-26, p. 712.

**Matthew 7.21:** Cf. John 9.31, p. 594; James 2.14-26, p. 712.

**Luke 10.38-42:** Martha's constant serving, though an effort to please the Lord, was out of place. Receiving a new teaching is of special value, during which time life's ordinary duties, even what is regarded as obligatory good practice, should be put aside.

# Teacher and Disciple

KNOWLEDGE OF SPIRITUAL AND RELIGIOUS TRUTH is often best imparted by a teacher. The personal relationship between a worthy teacher and his disciple allows a level of guidance and intimate communication of truth beyond what may be attained by the private study of scripture or through personal prayer and meditation. The teacher should have a mature faith, rich experience, and accomplishment by which he can set an example for his students and convey to them the insights born of his experience and mastery. The students, for their part, should be obedient to the teacher and willing to receive discipline.

In some Eastern religions, where the teacher is the embodiment of truth through his own self-realization, he is regarded as the ultimate authority. In Christianity, Judaism, and Islam, on the other hand, the teacher is not to be trusted by virtue of his own personal spiritual or intellectual prowess. He is but a servant of God, and he must be true to the traditions and doctrinal foundations established by the founder, passed on by the elders, and laid down in scripture.

Discipleship in many religions can also refer to following directly the example of the founder, who is the supreme teacher. The disciple not only heeds the words of the founder, who is the *Revealer of Truth*, pp. 450-55; he also follows in the founder's footsteps by imitating his example, life-style, and attitude of heart. Furthermore, in many religions the succession of disciples extending from the living teacher back to the founder establishes the Apostolic Succession, the proper chain of authority for teaching and administration.

Finally, discipleship is a call to help and support the founder in his mission. The disciples of Jesus and the Companions of Muhammad were willing to die for their lord in service of the cause of God. The disciple proclaims the founder's message to the world; he shares in his persecution and sufferings; for "a servant is not above his master." This discipleship has its cost, but it also brings with it the honor of being a co-worker with God.

One not knowing a land asks of one who
knows it,
he goes forward instructed by the knowing one.
Such, indeed, is the blessing of instruction,
one finds a path that leads him straight
onward.

*Hinduism*. Rig Veda 10.32.7

Let your house be a place of meeting for the wise, and dust yourself with the dust of their feet, and drink their words with thirst.

*Judaism*. Mishnah, Abot 1.4

Just as cold disappears by sitting near the fire,
So are sins destroyed in the congregation of
saints.

*Sikhism*. Adi Granth,
Ramkali Ashtpadi, M.5, p. 914

One *faqih* (scholar in religion) is more annoying to Satan than a thousand of the faithful who perform only their ceremonial duties.

*Islam*. Hadith of Tirmidhi

**Rig Veda 10.32.7:** Cf. Katha Upanishad 1.3.14, p. 484. In Jainism, respect for teachers who have attained liberation is expressed in the Namokar Mantra, pp. 30-31.

Approach someone who has realized the purpose of life and question him with reverence and devotion; he will instruct you in this wisdom. Once you attain it, you will never be deluded. You will see all creatures in the Self, and all in Me.

*Hinduism*. Bhagavad Gita 4.34-35

Should one see a wise man, who, like a revealer of treasure, points out faults and reproves; let one associate with such a wise person; it will be better, not worse, for him who associates with such a one.

Let him advise, instruct, and dissuade one from evil; truly pleasing is he to the good, displeasing is he to the bad.

*Buddhism*. Dhammapada 76-77

Stand in the assembly of the elders.
Who is wise? Cleave to him.
Be ready to listen to every narrative,
and do not let wise proverbs escape you.
If you see an intelligent man, visit him early;
let your foot wear out his doorstep.

*Christianity*. Sirach 6.34-36

He who sees through the eye tells proverbs.

*African Traditional Religions*. Igala Proverb (Nigeria)

To many it is not given to hear of the Self. Many, though they hear of it, do not understand it. Wonderful is he who speaks of it. Intelligent is he who learns of it. Blessed is he who, taught by a good teacher, is able to understand it.

The truth of the Self cannot be fully understood when taught by an ignorant man, for opinions regarding it, not founded in knowledge, vary one from another. Subtler than the subtlest is this Self, and beyond all logic. Taught by a teacher who knows the Self and Brahman as one, a man leaves vain theory behind and attains to truth.

The awakening which you have known does not come through the intellect, but rather, in fullest measure, from the lips of the wise....

Words cannot reveal him. Mind cannot reach him. Eyes do not see him. How then can he be comprehended, save when taught by those seers who indeed have known him?

*Hinduism*. Katha Upanishad 1.2.7-9 and 2.6.12

Whoever does not have a guide, Satan is his guide.

*Islam*. Hadith

It is very important for a person who wishes to "lament" to receive aid and advice from a *wichasha wakan* (holy man), so that everything is done correctly, for if things are not done in the right way, something very bad can happen, and even a serpent could come and wrap itself around the lamenter.

*Native American Religions*. Black Elk, Sioux Tradition

The teacher, brethren, should regard the pupil as his son. The pupil should regard the teacher as his father. Thus these two, by mutual reverence and deference joined, dwelling in community of life, will win increase, growth, progress in this Norm-discipline.

*Buddhism*. Vinaya Pitaka, Mahavagga iii.1

As in the sky flies the white-clothed crane,
Keeping its mind behind,
In its heart continually remembering its young ones;
So the true Guru keeps the disciple absorbed in the love of God,
And also keeps him in his heart.

*Sikhism*. Adi Granth, Gauri, M.4

**Igala Proverb:** Only one with much life experience, who sees with the eye of wisdom, is qualified to instruct others.

**Hadith:** This tradition is from Sufi circles. The role of the teacher is particularly important in the Sufi orders, for it is the teacher who preserves and conveys the esoteric wisdom essential to spiritual advancement on the Path.

**Black Elk:** To 'lament' means to enter a place of total isolation and cry for a vision; see Sioux Vision Quest, pp. 606-7.

Set the believers an example in speech and conduct, in love, in faith, in purity. Till I come, attend to the public reading of scripture, to preaching, to teaching. Do not neglect the gift you have, which was given you by prophetic utterance when the council of elders laid their hands upon you. Practice these duties, devote yourself to them, so that all may see your progress. Take heed to yourself and to your teaching; hold to that, for by so doing you will save both yourself and your hearers.

*Christianity*. 1 Timothy 4.12-16

The sage always excels in saving people, and so abandons no one;
Always excels in saving things, and so abandons nothing.
This is called following one's discernment.
Hence the good man is the teacher the bad learns from;
And the bad man is the material the good works on.
Not to value the teacher
Nor to love the material
Though it seems clever, betrays great bewilderment.

*Taoism*. Tao Te Ching 27

Much Torah have I learned from my teachers, more from my colleagues, but from my students most of all.

*Judaism*. Talmud, Taanit 7a

The Master said, "Even when walking in a party of no more than three I can always be certain of learning from those I am with. There will be good qualities that I can select for imitation and bad ones that will teach me what requires correction in myself."

*Confucianism*. Analects 7.21

The Master said, "Only one who bursts with eagerness do I instruct; only one who bubbles with excitement do I enlighten. If I hold up one corner and a man cannot come back to me with the other three, I do not continue the lesson."

*Confucianism*. Analects 7.8

What then is Apollos? What is Paul? Servants through whom you believed, as the Lord assigned to each. I planted, Apollos watered, but God gave the growth. So neither he who plants nor he who waters is anything, but only God who gives the growth. He who plants and he who waters are equal, and each shall receive his wages according to his labor. For we are God's fellow workers; you are God's field, God's building.

According to the grace of God given to me, like a skilled master builder I laid a foundation, and another man is building upon it. Let each man take care how he builds upon it. For no other foundation can any one lay than that which is laid, which is Jesus Christ.

*Christianity*. 1 Corinthians 3.5-11

The guru, it is declared, is the very Lord himself. To approach the guru, to worship the guru, is to approach the Lord, worship the Lord. Why should the Lord choose to manifest through the guru, why should he not act directly?

**1 Timothy 4.12-16:** The teaching positions in the church: bishop, priest, and deacon, are endowed in a ceremony of the laying of hands. Thus the gift of apostolic authority, first given to Peter (see Matthew 16.15-19, p. 196), is passed on.

**Tao Te Ching 27:** Cf. Chuang Tzu 14, p. 513.

**Analects 7.8:** Confucius used the Socratic method in his instruction, often putting questions before his students and drawing out their own opinions; for example, see Shih Chi 47, p. 433. He expected his students to learn by thinking through the matter on their own and coming up with well-reasoned arguments, thus holding up 'the other three.' He also encouraged his students to ask him questions about his philosophy. Yet traditional Confucian education long ago abandoned this method for a more strictly didactic approach in which the students are only to memorize the maxims, as the silent, passive recipients of knowledge.

**1 Corinthians 3.5-11:** Paul is writing to a community in which disputes have arisen over the doctrines of different teachers. Paul reminds them that a teacher is no more than a servant of God and Christ, and that all true teaching is built on Christ's foundation, not the constructions of human reason.

Shiva is really all-pervading, above the mind, without features, imperishable... infinite; how can such a one be worshipped? That is why, out of compassion for his creatures, He takes the form of the guru and, when so worshipped in devotion, grants liberation and fulfillment. Shiva has no binding form, Shiva is not perceivable by the human eye; therefore He protects the disciple conforming to Dharma in the form of the guru. The guru is none other than the supreme Shiva enclosed in human skin; he walks the earth, concealed, for bestowing grace on the good disciples.... To him who is loaded with sinful karma, the guru appears to be human; but to him whose karma is auspicious, meritful, the guru appears as Shiva.

*Hinduism*. Kularnava Tantra 13

The disciple that takes abode in the Master's home to receive guidance
Should with his heart the Master's guidance accept.
He should nowise show off his ego;
He should ever in his heart meditate on the Name Divine.
The disciple that has abandoned himself to the Master—
All his objectives shall be fulfilled.
One that serves and seeks no recompense,
Finds union with the Lord.

*Sikhism*. Adi Granth, Gauri Sukhmani, M.5, p. 286

After having taught the Veda, a teacher instructs the pupil, "Say what is true! Do your duty! Do not neglect the study of the Veda! After having brought to your teacher his proper reward, do not cut off the line of children! Do not swerve from the truth! Do not swerve from duty! Do not neglect what is useful! Do not neglect greatness! Do not neglect the learning and teaching of the Veda!

"Do not neglect the [sacrificial] works due to the gods and the fathers! Let your mother be to you like unto a god! Let your father be to you like unto a god! Let your teacher be to you like unto a god! Let your guest be to you like unto a god! Whatever good works have been performed by us, those should be observed by you."

*Hinduism*. Taittiriya Upanishad 1.11.1-2

During many kalpas I was long a king and vowed to seek the Supreme Wisdom, my mind never relenting.... For the sake of the Law, I gave up the throne of my domain, deputed my government to the prince-royal, and with beating drum and open proclamation, sought everywhere for the truth, promising, "Whoever is able to tell me of a Great Vehicle, him I will all my life provide for, and be his footman." At that time a certain hermit came to me, the king, and said, "I have a Great Vehicle, named Wonderful Law-flower Sutra. If you will not disobey me, I will explain it to you." I, the king, hearing what the hermit said, became ecstatic with joy and instantly followed, providing for his needs, gathering fruit, drawing water, collecting fuel, laying his food, even of my body making his seat and bed, yet never feeling fatigue of body or mind. While I thus served, a millennium passed, and for the sake of the Law, I zealously waited on him that he should lack nothing.

*Buddhism*. Lotus Sutra 12

**Kularnava Tantra 13:** On the teacher as avatar or infused by God, see Bhagavad Gita 4.7-8, p. 786n.; Rig Veda 4.26.1, p. 466; Asa Chhant, M.4, p. 465; Swaiyya Guru, Kala, pp. 474-75. Only the student with a sincere mind sees God in his teacher; cf. Bhagavad Gita 11.41-42, p. 467; Garland Sutra 10, p. 517. This tantra also addresses the problem of hypocritical teachers; see pp. 350-51.

**Taittiriya Upanishad 1.11.1-2:** Cf. Bhagavad Gita 13.7, p. 648; Qur'an 31.17, p. 169; Oracle of Temmangu, p. 169.

**Lotus Sutra 12:** The Buddha recounts a story of one of his previous lives, where as a bodhisattva in training he served his teacher to obtain the teaching of the Lotus Sutra. This episode inspired Gyoki (668-749 A.D.) who was famed for his devotion to social welfare work.

Verily in the Messenger of God you have a good example for him who looks unto God and the Last Day, and remembers God much.

*Islam*. Qur'an 33.21

Look to the rock from which you were hewn,
and to the quarry from which you were digged.
Look to Abraham your father
and to Sarah who bore you;
for when he was but one I called him,
and I blessed him and made him many.

*Judaism* and *Christianity*. Isaiah 51.1-2

I will follow the examples of the Buddhas from thought to thought. Even though the void of space has end, and the worlds of beings, the karmas of beings, the sorrows of beings all have end, yet my practice and following the examples of the Buddhas will not be ended. Thought succeeds thought without interruption, and in deeds of body, speech, and mind, without weariness.

*Buddhism*. Gandavyuha Sutra, Vows of Samantabhadra

Yen Hui said with a deep sigh, "The more I strain my gaze up towards it, the higher it soars. The deeper I bore down into it, the harder it becomes. I see it in front; but suddenly it is behind. Step by step the Master skillfully lures one on. He has broadened me with culture, restrained me with ritual. Even if I wanted to stop, I could not. Just when I feel that I have exhausted every resource, something seems to rise up, standing out sharp and clear. Yet though I long to pursue it, I can find no way of getting to it at all."

*Confucianism*. Analects 9.10

When [Jesus] had washed their feet, and taken his garments, and resumed his place, he said to them, "Do you know what I have done to you? You call me Teacher and Lord; and you are right, for so I am. If I then, your Lord and Teacher, have washed your feet, you also ought to wash one another's feet. For I have given you an example, that you also should do as I have done to you. Truly, truly, I say to you, a servant is not greater than his master; nor is he who is sent greater than he who sent him. If you know these things, blessed are you if you do them."

*Christianity*. John 13.12-17

When Shakyamuni Buddha was at Vulture Peak, he held out a flower to his listeners. Everyone was silent. Only Kashyapa the Great broke into a broad smile. The Buddha said, "I have the True Dharma Eye, the Marvelous Mind of Nirvana, the True Form of the Formless, and the Subtle Dharma Gate, independent of words and transmitted beyond doctrine. This I have entrusted to Kashyapa the Great."

*Buddhism*. Mumonkan 6

Moses received the Torah on Sinai, and delivered it to Joshua, and Joshua to the elders, and the elders to the prophets, and the prophets

**Qur'an 33.21:** Cf. Sun Myung Moon, 9-11-77, p. 472.

**Isaiah 51.1-2:** The patriarchs Abraham and Sarah are models of faith and obedience, who established a tradition for later generations of Jews, Christians, and Muslims. Cf. Galatians 3.1-7, pp. 540-41; Qur'an 2.130-36, p. 541; 1 Peter 3.1-6, p. 180; Hebrews 11.8-13, pp. 539-40.

**Analects 9.10:** Yen Hui was Confucius' favorite disciple, and he excelled all the others. Yet he, above all, was aware of how far away he was from the standard of his master. Other passages on Hui are Analects 6.9, p. 665, and Shih Chi 47, p. 433.

**John 13.12-17:** The essence of discipleship to Jesus is to love and serve others, and to witness for the Gospel; see Matthew 28.18-20, p. 723.

**Mumonkan 6:** Successful discipleship in Zen requires the wordless communication of enlightenment; cf. Lankavatara Sutra 61, pp. 454-55; Diamond Sutra 21, p. 572. The lineage of Zen masters runs from Shakyamuni Buddha to his disciple Kashyapa, then through Bodhidharma, the First Patriarch of Chinese Buddhism, and Hui Neng (Jap. Eno), the Sixth Patriarch. Thence the teaching proliferated into many schools of Zen in Japan and China. Cf. Sutra of Hui Neng 1, p. 149.

delivered it to the men of the Great Synagogue. These said three things: Be deliberate in judging, and raise up many disciples, and make a hedge for the Torah.

*Judaism*. Mishnah, Abot 1.1

Truly, truly, I say to you, he who believes in me will also do the works that I do; and greater works than these will he do, because I go to the Father.

*Christianity*. John 14.12

When your view is the same as your teacher's, you destroy half your teacher's merit; when your view surpasses your teacher's, you are worthy to succeed him.

*Buddhism*. Zen Proverb

And with how many a prophet have there been a number of devoted men who fought [beside him]. They quailed not for whatever befell them in the way of God, nor did they weaken, nor were they brought low. God loves the steadfast.

Their cry was only, "Our Lord! Forgive us for our sins and wasted efforts, make our foothold sure, and give us victory over the disbelieving folk."

*Islam*. Qur'an 3.145-147

Then the Exalted One said to the brethren, "I am released, brethren, from all bonds, those that are divine and those that are human. You also, brethren, are released from all bonds, those that are divine and those that are human. Go forth, brethren, on your journey, for the profit of the many, for the bliss of the many, out of compassion for the world, for the welfare, the profit, the bliss of devas and mankind!

Go not any two together. Proclaim, brethren, the Norm, goodly in its beginning, goodly in its middle, goodly in its ending. Both in the spirit and in the letter make known the all-perfected, utterly pure righteous life. There are beings with but little dust of passion on their eyes. They are perishing through not hearing the Norm. There will be some who will understand.

*Buddhism*. Vinaya Pitaka i.21

And [Jesus] called to him his twelve disciples and gave them authority over unclean spirits, to cast them out, and to heal every disease and every infirmity. The names of the twelve apostles are these: first, Simon, who is called Peter, and Andrew his brother; James the son of Zebedee, and John his brother; Philip and Bartholomew; Thomas and Matthew the tax collector; James the son of Alphaeus, and Thaddaeus; Simon the Cananaean, and Judas Iscariot, who betrayed him.

These twelve Jesus sent out, charging them, "Go nowhere among the Gentiles, and enter no town of the Samaritans, but go rather to the lost sheep of the house of Israel. And preach as you go, saying, 'The kingdom of Heaven is at hand.' Heal the sick, raise the dead, cleanse lepers, cast out demons. You received without paying, give without pay. Take no gold, nor silver, nor copper in your belts, no bag for your journey, nor two tunics, nor sandals, nor a staff; for the laborer deserves his food. And whatever town or village you enter, find out who is wor-

**Abot 1.1:** The essence of discipleship to Moses is to study Torah, according to Sifre Deuteronomy 131b, p. 452. Rabbinic Judaism, which emphasizes the study of Torah above all else, began with Great Synagogue, a council of elders which existed from the time of Ezra (c. 428 B.C.). The three maxims set down by these early rabbis were meant for the guidance of teachers, and they are the basis of the casuistry of the Talmud and the method of rabbinic instruction. To be deliberate in judging means to look at a question from every angle and take account of every possible contingency. To make disciples has always been an aim of rabbinic Judaism: Until the age of Constantine, Jews actively evangelized among Gentile peoples, and after repression by the Christian state the rabbis renounced evangelism but continued to make disciples of Jewish youth. But students did not disciple so much to a particular teacher as to the accumulated wisdom of the tradition. To make a hedge around the Torah means to take every precaution to keep the revelation from the harmful encroachments of the world; see Abot 3.17, p. 653.

**Zen Proverb:** The place of the teacher is very important in Zen Buddhism, but straight imitation is not!

thy in it, and stay with him until you depart. As you enter the house, salute it. And if the house is worthy, let your peace come upon it; but if it is not worthy, let your peace return to you. And if any one will not receive you or listen to your words, shake off the dust from your feet as you leave that house or town. Truly, I say to you, it shall be more tolerable on the day of judgment for the land of Sodom and Gomorrah than for that town.

"Behold, I send you out as sheep in the midst of wolves; so be wise as serpents and innocent as doves. Beware of men; for they will deliver you up to councils, and flog you in their synagogues, and you will be dragged before governors and kings for my sake, to bear testimony before them and the Gentiles. When they deliver you up, do not be anxious how you are to speak or what you are to say; for what you are to say will be given to you in that hour; for it is not you who speak, but the Spirit of your Father speaking through you....

"A disciple is not above his teacher, nor a servant above his master; it is enough for a disciple to be like his teacher, and the servant like his master. If they have called the master of the house Beelzebul, how much more will they malign those of his household."

*Christianity*. Matthew 10.1-25

❖

**Matthew 10.1-25:** Cf. Matthew 16.24-25, p. 625; 28.18-20, p. 723; Mark 6.7-9, p. 665; Romans 8.35-39, p. 628; 2 Corinthians 5.20-6.13, p. 724.

# *New Wine and Old Wineskins*

THE WISDOM OF OLD AGE is the fruit of a lifetime of living a moral life and practicing the discipline of a religious path. However, the effort which it takes to realize the fulness of spiritual wisdom should be undertaken from one's youth. Strength and adaptability are required, and once old age has drawn nigh it becomes too difficult to practice and too late to change. Old age is a time to manifest either the wisdom gained as the fruits of that effort or the decrepitude of a wasted life.

Jesus said to them, "No one puts new wine into old wineskins; if he does, the new wine will burst the skins and will be spilled, and the skins will be destroyed. But new wine must be put into fresh wineskins.

"And no one after drinking old wine desires new; for he says, 'The old is good.'"

*Christianity*. Luke 5.37-39

Elisha ben Abuya said, "If one learns as a child, what is it like? Like ink written on clean paper. If one learns as an old man, what is it like? Like ink written on blotted paper."

Rabbi Jose ben Judah said, "He who learns from the young, to what is he like? To one who eats unripe grapes, or drinks wine from the vat. And one who learns from the old, to what is he like? To one who eats ripe grapes, or drinks old wine."

Rabbi Meir said, "Look not at the flask, but at what it contains: there may be a new flask full of old wine, and an old flask that has not even new wine in it."

*Judaism*. Mishnah, Abot 4.25-27

You can only coil a fish when it is fresh.

*African Traditional Religions*.
Nupe Proverb (Nigeria)

The Master said, "Respect the young. How do you know that they will not one day be all that you are now? But if a man has reached forty or fifty and nothing has been heard of him, then I grant there is no need to respect him."

*Confucianism*. Analects 9.22

At fifteen I set my heart upon learning. At thirty, I had planted my feet upon firm ground. At forty, I no longer suffered from perplexities. At fifty, I knew what were the biddings of Heaven. At sixty, I heard them with a docile ear. At seventy, I could follow the dictates of my own heart, for what I desired no longer overstepped the boundaries of right.

*Confucianism*. Analects 2.4

**Luke 5.37-39:** The first saying speaks to the fact that a new teaching is more readily learned by the young, whose minds are still open and impressionable. The old person, being full of concepts and long-established habits of mind, cannot easily learn new things. Furthermore, since Jesus' words were challenging to the conventional wisdom, they could hardly be received by people bound to the traditions of the past: see Luke 9.60, p. 412; 9.62, p. 528; 14.16-24, p. 485; Qur'an 43.33-35, p. 484. The second saying, conversely, praises the wisdom of the elder who is well-versed in faith, wisdom, and life experience.

**Abot 4.25-27:** The first two sayings have meanings which correspond to the New Testament passage above: that the young are better learners and the old are better teachers. The third saying, that one cannot judge a book by its cover, may be a retort by a young teacher to Rabbi Jose's saying.

**Nupe Proverb:** A person can only be educated when he is young and flexible.

**Analects 2.4:** Confucius' own growth in wisdom, described in this passage, could be a model for all wise people who apply themselves to learning and spiritual discipline throughout life. Cf. Analects 16.7, p. 659.

If the hair has become white, a man does not on that account become old; though a man may be young, if he is learned the gods look upon him as old.

*Hinduism*. Laws of Manu 2.136

You cannot prolong your life, therefore be not careless; you are past help when old age approaches.

*Jainism*. Uttaradhyayana Sutra 4.1

You have gathered nothing in your youth; how can you find anything in your old age?

*Christianity*. Sirach 25.3

The man of little learning grows old like the ox. His muscles grow but his wisdom grows not.

*Buddhism*. Dhammapada 152

He is not thereby an elder merely because his head is gray. Ripe is he in age; "old in vain" is he called. In whom are truth, virtue, harmlessness, restraint, and self-control, that wise man who is purged of impurities is, indeed, called an elder.

*Buddhism*. Dhammapada 260-61

Yuan Jang sat waiting for the Master in a sprawling position. The Master said, "Those who when young show no respect to their elders achieve nothing worth mentioning when they grow up. And merely to live on, getting older and older, is to be a useless pest."

*Confucianism*. Analects 14.46

Before the gray descends on your cheek,
the wrinkles plow your chin,
and the body becomes a cage of bones;
Before the teeth fall off from your mouth,
the back bends to the earth,
and you become a burden to others;
Before you hold a stick in one hand
and lean heavily with the other on your knee;
Before age corrodes your bodily beauty
and you feel the pangs of death;
Adore our Lord Kudala Sangama!

*Hinduism*. Basavanna, Vacana 161

Remember also your Creator in the days of your youth, before the evil days come, and the years draw nigh, when you will say, "I have no pleasure in them"; before the sun and the light and the moon and the stars are darkened and the clouds return after the rain; in the day when the keepers of the house tremble, and the strong men are bent, and the grinders cease because they are few, and those that look through the windows are dimmed, and the doors on the street are shut; when the sound of the grinding is low, and one rises up at the voice of a bird, and all the daughters of song are brought low; they are afraid also of what is high, and terrors are in the way; the almond tree blossoms, the grasshopper drags itself along and desire fails; because man goes to his eternal home, and the mourners go about the streets; before the silver cord is snapped, or the golden bowl is broken, or the pitcher is broken at the fountain, or the wheel broken at the cistern, and the dust returns to the earth as it was, and the spirit returns to God who gave it.

*Judaism* and *Christianity*.
Ecclesiastes 12.1-7

❖

**Dhammapada 152:** Cf. Qur'an 91.7-10, p. 511.
**Ecclesiastes 12.1-7:** This passage describes in metaphorical language the body's deterioration in old age.

CHAPTER 16

# WORSHIP

THIS CHAPTER IS DEVOTED TO PRAYER, MEDITATION, chanting, and various rituals through which people worship God, seek God's presence, and find their connection with Ultimate Reality. Through prayer, chanting the name of God, worship, and ritual, a person lifts up his or her heart to God and opens to receive God's guidance, succor, and inspiration. Through meditation, a person may contact and realize the Ultimate Reality that resides within, or make the heart properly receptive to the transcendent God who is also "nearer to him than the jugular vein." We conclude with a section on the limitations of ritual, when it is not accompanied by a sincere and loving heart or when it becomes an end in itself.

Worship is not a matter of practices alone. True worship should be accompanied by a proper attitude of faith by which the soul opens itself to the divine Presence. It should also be complemented by humility and acts of sacrifice and self-denial by which selfishness and egoism, the chief impediments to self-transcendence, are destroyed.

# Prayer

PRAYER LIES AT THE CORE of worship in most religions. We have already given some representative prayers in the *Invocation*, pp. 29-32, which opens this anthology. The passages here discuss the efficacy of prayer and give guidance on how to pray. There are general exhortations to prayer, with the promises that God indeed hears and heeds prayers and that prayer restrains one from evil. Other texts give instruction on how to pray. Prayer should be done constantly, sometimes with vigils far into the night. Prayer should be honest; it is quiet and sincere conversation in one's own words and from the heart. Prayer should be accompanied by deeds; the prayer of the hypocrite is without effect. Among the best prayers are those for the welfare of others ahead of oneself.

Your Lord says, "Call on Me; I will answer your prayer."

*Islam*. Qur'an 40.60

The Lord is near to all who call upon him,
to all who call upon him in truth.

*Judaism* and *Christianity*. Psalm 145.18

When My servants ask you concerning Me, I am indeed Close to them. I listen to the prayer of every suppliant when he calls on Me.

*Islam*. Qur'an 2.186

Cast your burden on the Lord, and he will sustain you.

*Judaism* and *Christianity*. Psalm 55.22

If the poorest of mankind come here once for worship, I will surely grant their heart's desire.

*Shinto*. Oracle of Itsukushima

Prayer restrains one from shameful and unjust deeds; and remembrance of God is the greatest thing in life, without doubt.

*Islam*. Qur'an 29.45

Beings possessed by carnal passions, anger, or infatuation have but to revere and remember the Bodhisattva Kuan Shih Yin and they will be set free from their passions.

*Buddhism*. Lotus Sutra 25

Establish regular prayers at the two ends of the day and at the approaches of the night: for those things that are good remove those that are evil. This is a word of remembrance to those who remember.

*Islam*. Qur'an 11.114

O Shariputra, having perceived this cause and effect, I with reverence say thus, "Every son and every daughter of a family ought with their whole mind to make fervent prayer for [rebirth in] the Pure Land of Buddha Amitayus."

*Buddhism*. Smaller Sukhavativyuha Sutra 10

**Psalm 145.18:** Cf. Psalm 57.15, p. 73.

**Qur'an 2.186:** God is the one who is 'Close' to man. Close is one of the Ninety-nine Most Beautiful Names of Allah; see Qur'an 59.22-24, p. 598n. Cf. Qur'an 50.16, p. 72.

**Qur'an 29.45:** Cf. Qur'an 70.19-22, p. 273; Berakot 5a, pp. 657-58.

**Lotus Sutra 25:** On the merits of worshipping the Bodhisattva Kuan Yin (Skt. Avalokitesvara), see Lotus Sutra 25, p. 402, and Gandavyuha Sutra 39, p. 256n.

**Qur'an 11.114:** For more on the *salat*, the five obligatory prayers, see Hadith of Muslim, p. 598n. Cf. Qur'an 26.218-20, p. 537; 40.55, p. 529; 70.19-22, p. 273.

Lord of creation! no one other than thee
pervades all these that have come into being.
May that be ours for which our prayers rise,
may we be masters of many treasures!

*Hinduism.* Rig Veda 10.121.10

Wang-sun Chia asked about the saying,

Better pay court to the stove
Than pay court to the shrine.

Confucius said, "It is not true. He who has put himself in the wrong with Heaven has no means of expiation left."

*Confucianism.* Analects 3.13

You must always pray unto the Father in my name; and whatsoever you shall ask the Father in my name, which is right, believing that you shall receive, behold it shall be given unto you. Pray in your families unto the Father, always in my name, that your wives and your children may be blessed.

*Church of Jesus Christ of Latter-day Saints.* Book of Mormon, 3 Nephi 18.19-21

O believers, when you stand up to pray wash your faces, and your hands up to the elbows, and wipe your heads, and your feet up to the ankles. If you are defiled, purify yourselves; but if you are sick or on a journey, or if any of you comes from the privy, or have touched women, and you can find no water, then have recourse to wholesome dust and wipe your faces and hands with it. God does not desire to make any impediment for you; but He desires to purify you, and that He may complete His blessing upon you; haply you will be thankful.

*Islam.* Qur'an 5.6

Is any one among you suffering? Let him pray. Is any cheerful? Let him sing praise. Is any among you sick? Let him call for the elders of the church, and let them pray over him, anointing him with oil in the name of the Lord; and the prayer of faith will save the sick man, and the Lord will raise him up; and if he has committed sins, he will be forgiven. Therefore confess your sins to one another, and pray for one another, that you may be healed. The prayer of a righteous man has great power in its effects. Elijah was a man of like nature with ourselves and he prayed fervently that it might not rain, and for three years and six months it did not rain on the earth. Then he prayed again and heaven gave rain, and the earth brought forth its fruit.

*Christianity.* James 5.13-18

Pray constantly.

*Christianity.* 1 Thessalonians 5.17

Rabbi Yohanan said, "Would that man could pray all day, for a prayer never loses its value."

*Judaism.* Jerusalem Talmud, Berakot 1.1

The fire of hell has been forbidden to these two eyes: the eye that remained sleepless through watching in the ways of God, and the eye that wept with spirit trembling at the fear of God.

*Islam.* Hadith of Darimi

O you wrapped up in your raiment!
Keep vigil the night long, save a little—
A half thereof, or abate a little thereof
Or add [a little] thereto and chant the Qur'an
in measure,
For We shall charge you with a word of weight.
Lo! The vigil of the night is when impression is
more keen and speech more certain.
Lo! You have by day a chain of business.
So remember the name of your Lord and
devote yourself with complete devotion.

*Islam.* Qur'an 73.1-8

Call on your Lord with humility and in private.

*Islam.* Qur'an 7.55

**Book of Mormon, 3 Nephi 18.19-21:** Cf. John 14.13-14, p. 598, Matthew 7.7-11, p. 492.
**Qur'an 73.1-8:** Cf. Qur'an 11.93, p. 527. Muhammad kept frequent prayer vigils through the night.
**Qur'an 7.55:** Cf. Qur'an 23.1-5, p. 647.

When we pray alone to God, shedding tears, we will not feel lonely; God is surely with us.

*Unification Church.* Sun Myung Moon, 2-15-67

Worship me through meditation in the sanctuary of the heart.

*Hinduism.* Srimad Bhagavatam 11.5

There is a polish for everything that becomes rusty, and the polish for the heart is the remembrance of God.

*Islam.* Hadith of Tirmidhi

"To serve the Lord your God with all your heart" [Deuteronomy 11.13]. What is a service with the heart? It is prayer.

*Judaism.* Sifre Deuteronomy 80a

Of all prayers of the heart, the best prayer is the prayer to the Master to be given the grace of properly praising the Lord.

*Sikhism.* Adi Granth, Maru Ashtpadi, M.5, p. 1018

Set me free, I entreat thee from my heart;
If I do not pray to thee with my heart,
Thou hearest me not.
If I pray to thee with my heart,
Thou knowest it and art gracious unto me.

*African Traditional Religions.* Boran Prayer (Kenya)

People are granted birth into this world by the kami. Accordingly, the mind of a person is something which communes with the will of the kami, and one must thus avoid doing anything which would impair that mind. To be visited with the blessings of the kami, one must first direct one's mind wholeheartedly to prayer; to be granted the protection of the kami, one must make a foundation of honesty. In this way, the person's pristine, undefiled mind will be awakened to the original, profound way.

*Shinto.* Records of the Enshrinement of the Two Imperial Deities at Ise

Always let a man test himself: if he can direct his heart, let him pray; if he cannot, let him not pray.

*Judaism.* Talmud, Berakot 30b

Prayer should not be recited as if a man were reading a document.

*Judaism.* Jerusalem Talmud, Berakot 4.3

For the Great Spirit is everywhere; he hears whatever is in our minds and hearts, and it is not necessary to speak to him in a loud voice.

*Native American Religion.* Black Elk, Sioux Tradition

And when you pray, you must not be like the hypocrites; for they love to stand and pray in the synagogues and at the street corners, that they may be seen by men. Truly, I say to you, they have received their reward. But when you pray, go into your room and shut the door and pray to your Father who is in secret; and your Father who sees in secret will reward you.

And in praying do not heap up empty phrases as the Gentiles do; for they think that they will be heard for their many words. Do not be like them, for your Father knows what you need before you ask him.

*Christianity.* Matthew 6.5-8

We know that God does not listen to sinners, but if anyone is a worshipper of God and does his will, God listens to him.

*Christianity.* John 9.31

**Srimad Bhagavatam 11.5:** Here we begin several passages on prayers of the heart. When meditation is directed towards God conceived as a Person—here the Lord Krishna—it is in fact indistinguishable from prayer.

**Sifre Deuteronomy 80a:** Cf. Deuteronomy 6.5, p. 516; Berakot 17a, p. 514.

**Records of the Enshrinement of the Two Imperial Deities at Ise:** cf. Oracle of Temmangu, p. 519; Divine Injunctions, p. 515; Michi-no-Shiori, p. 515.

**Berakot 30b:** Cf. Berakot 5.1, p. 600.

**John 9.31:** Cf. Matthew 7.21, p. 580.

Prayers to the Deity accompanied by monetary gifts secured by injustice are sure not to be granted. Pray in all righteousness and the Deity will be pleased to listen to your supplication. Foolish is he who, in impatient eagerness and without following the path of righteousness, hopes to obtain divine protection.

*Shinto*. Shinto Uden Futsujosho

He who prays for his fellowman, while he himself has the same need, will be answered first.

*Judaism*. Talmud, Baba Kamma 92a

The pure whom you have found worthy for their righteousness and their good mind,
Fulfil their desire, O Wise Lord, let them attain it!
I know that words of prayer which serve a good end
Are successful before you.

*Zoroastrianism*. Avesta, Yasna 28.10

What is the most important and necessary thing for us in our daily life? It is the life of prayer. Through prayer we should know the invisible enemy and distinguish the invisible enemy from ourselves. Don't pray for yourself. This is my teaching.

*Unification Church*.
Sun Myung Moon, 1-1-68

Sitting cross-legged,
They should wish that all beings
Have firm and strong roots of goodness
And attain the state of immovability.

Cultivating concentration,
They should wish that all beings
Conquer their minds by concentration
Ultimately, with no remainder.

When practicing contemplation,
They should wish that all beings
See truth as it is
And be forever free of opposition and contention.

*Buddhism*. Garland Sutra 11

❖

**Sun Myung Moon, 1-1-68:** The 'invisible enemy' is Satan, who is constantly seeking to influence our thoughts, confusing us to the point where we think that his ideas are our own. Cf. Qur'an 114, p. 32; 1 Peter 5.8, p. 314.

# The Name of God

PRAISING OR CHANTING THE NAME OF GOD is a special form of prayer. In many religions, the excellence of chanting the name(s) of God lies in the mystic syllables which invoke God's purity and sovereign power. The various mantras in Hinduism and Buddhism, such as OM, *Hari Krishna*, *Namu Myo Ho Renge Kyo*, *Om Mani Padme Hum*, and the Roman Catholic practice of chanting the Rosary, all focus the mind on Ultimate Reality and call forth its mystical elevating influence. In Christianity, prayers are offered in the name of Jesus Christ, who promises to do whatever is asked in faith.

On the other hand, in the Jewish tradition the explicit name of God is too holy to be uttered by the human tongue. In particular, the Tetragrammaton, which is translated "the Lord" in modern Bibles, is never to be spoken. To show respect, God is often referred to paraphrastically by such terms as the Lord, Heaven, the King, the Almighty, the Name, and G-d. Thus, to praise and bless the name of God, as in the psalm quoted here, means to extol God's greatness and mighty works without mentioning his sacred name.

Of special mention are traditions of the many names of God which enumerate his many attributes. The Qur'an contains the Ninety-nine Most Beautiful Names of Allah, and in an excerpt from the Mahabharata we give a few of Vishnu's Thousand Names. To recite these names is to give a magnificent description of the height, depth, and breadth of divinity.

Verily nothing is more purifying than the holy name of God.

*Hinduism*. Srimad Bhagavatam 6.1

Wonderful is the teacher, Sri Krishna;
Wonderful are his deeds.
Even the utterance of his holy name
Sanctifies him who speaks and him who hears.

*Hinduism*. Srimad Bhagavatam 10

Contemplate solely the Name of God—
Fruitless are all other rituals.

*Sikhism*. Adi Granth, Suhi, M.1, p. 728

Contemplate the Name yourself; inspire it to others;
By attending to it, discoursing of it, living by it, obtain liberation.
The true essence, eternal is the Lord's Name:
By spontaneous devotion, says Nanak, chant the Lord's praise.

*Sikhism*. Adi Granth, Gauri Sukhmani, M.5, p. 289

**Srimad Bhagavatam 6.1:** In Vaishnavite Hinduism, the names of God are Krishna, Rama, Hari, Narayana, and other titles of Vishnu.

**Suhi, M.1:** In Sikhism God is formless; worship of idols, which in Hinduism is the practice of puja, is not permitted. *Nam*, the Name of God, imageless sound, is the only substantial form of God that can be apprehended by humans; it signifies the presence of Divine Reality. Hence the Name is the medium of communication between God and man. The supreme name of God is *Ek Oankar*, and repeating or contemplating this or any of God's other names or titles is the chief form of prayer and devotion. The word Nam also signifies this devotion. Cf. Var Majh, M.1, p. 520; Asa Chhant, M.5, p. 600.

All Buddhas in the universe throughout past, present, and future invariably attain Buddhahood with the seed of the five characters of *Namu Myo Ho Renge Kyo.*

*Buddhism.* Nichiren

If there be anyone who commits evil deeds... let him utter the name Buddha Amitayus serenely and with voice uninterrupted; let him be continually thinking of Buddha until he has completed ten times the thought, repeating, *Namu Amida Butsu.* On the strength of uttering Buddha's name he will, during every repetition, expiate the sins.

*Buddhism.*
Meditation on Buddha Amitayus 3.30

Hail Mary, full of grace! Blessed art thou among women, and blessed is the fruit of thy womb, Jesus.

Holy Mary, Mother of God, pray for us sinners, now and at the hour of our death.

*Christianity.* The Rosary

The goal which all the Vedas declare, which all austerities aim at, and which men desire when they lead a life of continence, I will tell you briefly: it is OM.

This syllable OM is indeed Brahman. This syllable is the Highest. Whosoever knows this syllable obtains all that he desires.

*Hinduism.* Katha Upanishad 1.2.15-16

OM! This syllable is this whole world. Its further explanation is: the past, the present, the future—everything is just the word OM. And whatever else that transcends threefold time—that, too, is just the word OM.

For truly everything here is Brahman; this Self *(Atman)* is Brahman. This same Self has four fourths: the waking state, outwardly cognitive... the dreaming state, inwardly cognitive... the deep sleep state, unified, a cognition-mass... and the state of being one with the Self, the cessation of phenomena, tranquil....

This is the Self with regard to the word OM, with regard to its elements. The elements are the fourths, the elements: the letter A, the letter U, the letter M.

The waking state, the common-to-all-men, is the letter A... the sleeping state, the Brilliant, is the letter U... the deep-sleep state, the Cognitional, is the letter M... The fourth is without an element, with which there can be no dealing, the cessation of phenomena, benign, without a second. This AUM is the Self indeed.

*Hinduism.* Mandukya Upanishad

**Nichiren:** Nichiren (b. 1222), the great Buddhist reformer in Japan, set up these five words as the Daimoku; the words mean Homage to the Lotus Sutra. The Lotus Sutra, which is seen as the epitome of the truth, may only be received through faith (see Lotus Sutra 3, p. 542). Hence to chant its praises is to align oneself with the teaching of the sutra and so receive its benefits. Chanting the Daimoku is the prevalent practice in the various religious organizations which descend from Nichiren and revere the Lotus Sutra, such as Nichiren Shu, Soka Gakkai, and Rissho Kosei Kai.

**Meditation on Buddha Amitayus 3.30:** Pure Land Buddhists in Japan keep the mind fixed on Ultimate Reality by constantly chanting *Namu Amida Butsu,* All Hail to Amitabha Buddha. Cf. Myokonin, p. 553.

**The Rosary:** For Roman Catholics, frequent repetition of this chant is a devotion and a penance that expiates sin. Mary is 'Mother of God' in that she is the mother of Jesus, yet she is by no means God herself, but a human being, 'blessed among women.' As first among the saints in heaven, she serves God alongside the angels as a mediator of divine grace (compare Gleanings from the Writings of Baha'u'llah 81, p. 260n.). The first half of the Rosary is a quotation of Luke 1.42.

**Katha Upanishad 1.2.15-16:** A number of passages in the Upanishads praise the mystic syllable OM, which is chanted at the beginning of all sacred discourse. See the Mandukya Upanishad (below), Mundaka Upanishad 2.2.6, p. 600; Bhagavad Gita 8.13, p. 241; also Taittiriya Upanishad 1.8 and Prasna Upanishad 5.1-7.

**Mandukya Upanishad:** Although, in fact, OM is not pronounced 'AUM,' in Sanskrit the vowel O is a dipthong contracted from AU. Hence the Upanishad can analyze OM as three letters A-U-M. These

Minds arising dependent
On a sense and an object
Are said to be *man*;
*Tra* means protection.

Protection by means of all the vajras,
Of the pledges and vows explained,
Free from the ways of the world,
Is called "the practice of *mantra*."

*Buddhism.* Guhyasamaja Tantra 18.69c-71b

Whatever you ask in my name, I will do it, that the Father may be glorified in the Son; if you ask anything in my name, I will do it.

*Christianity.* John 14.13-14

God's Messenger is reported as saying, "The words dearest to God are four: Glory be to God, Praise be to God, there is no god but God, and God is most great."

*Islam.* Hadith of Muslim

I will extol thee, my God and King,
and bless thy name for ever and ever.
Every day I will bless thee,
and praise thy name for ever and ever.
Great is the Lord, and greatly to be praised,
and his greatness is unsearchable.

*Judaism* and *Christianity.* Psalm 145.1-3

He is God, there is no god but He.
He is the Knower of the unseen and the visible;
He is the all-Merciful, the all-Compassionate.

He is God, there is no God but He.
He is the King, the Holy, the Peaceable,
The Faithful, the Preserver,
The Mighty, the Compeller, the Sublime.
Glory be to God, above that they associate!

He is God, the Creator, the Maker, the Shaper.
To Him belong the Names Most Beautiful.
All that is in the heavens and the earth
magnifies Him;
He is the Mighty, the Wise.

*Islam.* Qur'an 59.22-24

The Thousand Names of the great Lord which are based on his qualities, and which the sages have sung, I shall proclaim for the weal of the world:

"He who is in the form of the Universe and is All-pervasive, who is of the form of Sacrifice, who is the Lord of the past, future, and present, the Creator of all living beings, their Sustainer and their Existence, their Indweller and Well-wisher; the Pure and Supreme Being, the highest Goal of the liberated, the imperishable Spirit that is the Onlooker and the eternal Knower of the body; who is the Path and the Leader among those who know the path, himself Matter, Spirit, and God, the Supreme

are invested with mystical significance. The last non-element is the end of the sound, unutterable, fading away, merging with silence. Uttering the mystic syllable OM corresponds with the movement of the soul from the external senses through successively deeper levels of being towards ultimate merging with the Unattributed. See Katha Upanishad 3.13, p. 601.

**John 14.13-14:** Christians pray in the name of Jesus Christ, calling upon him who assures the efficacy of their prayers; cf. Colossians 3.17, p. 556. Latter-day Saints do likewise; see 3 Nephi 18.19-21, p. 593.

**Hadith of Muslim:** These words are spoken in the five obligatory daily prayers, called *salat*, and in phrases which the Muslim continually repeats throughout the day. Each repetition (*rak'a*) of the salat begins with the words "God is most great," and ends with the words "Glory be to my Lord, the Most High." It includes a recitation of the opening sura of the Qur'an, pp. 29-30, which includes the words "Praise be to God, Lord of the Worlds." The *Kalima*, or Declaration of Faith, reads, "There is no god but God, and Muhammad is His prophet."

**Psalm 145.1-3:** This is the beginning of an acrostic psalm, for which each verse begins with the next letter in order of the Hebrew alphabet. In Jewish tradition, God is too holy to be spoken of directly by his proper name, the Tetragrammaton. Hence, to praise the name of God means to praise God's attributes and mighty works.

**Qur'an 59.22-24:** Islamic tradition lists Allah's Ninety-nine Most Beautiful Names, each one drawn from the Qur'an.

Being who took the form of the Man-lion, who has rays of light as hair, and possesses the Goddess of Fortune; the All, the Destroyer, the Beneficent, the Steadfast, the Prime Source of beings, the Inexhaustible Repository, who manifests himself as he pleases, the Benefactor, the Protector, One whose birth is unique, the Capable, the Master; the Self-born, the Giver of happiness, the Solar Deity, the Lotus-eyed, the Speaker of the sublime sound named Veda... the King, the Destroyer of sins; he who holds the Conch, the Sword, the Discus, the Bow, and the Mace, the Discus-armed, the Unperturbed, he who can use anything as a weapon for striking."

Thus these Thousand from among the divine Names of the Great Kesava, fit to be sung, have been fully told. He who listens to this or recites it daily shall encounter nothing untoward here or in the hereafter.

*Hinduism.* Mahabharata, Anusasana Parva 254

## *Meditation*

MEDITATION CLEANSES THE HEART of all obstructions and opens to the Ultimate Reality that lies within. Meditation takes several forms, and the scriptures teach several meditative techniques.

Hindu, Jain, Taoist, and Buddhist scriptures describe meditation as sitting in a quiet spot, restricting all sense stimuli, controlling the mind's wandering thoughts and feelings, and finally attaining a stillness that reveals the true self-nature within. This self-nature may be the original Nothingness, or a union with the creative Spirit that flows through all things. In Confucian meditation this tranquillity makes the mind clear and receptive to the impartial evaluation of knowledge.

Meditative spiritual practices are also widespread in Christianity, Judaism, and Islam. Most of these practices were developed by mystics and monastics long after the scriptures had been compiled, and regrettably they are underrepresented in an anthology which is limited to scripture. Some are meditations *on* scripture: For example, in Roman Catholicism the *Spiritual Exercises* of St. Ignatius Loyola and *The Dark Night of the Soul* by St. John of the Cross instruct one to meditate on events in Jesus' life and passion and identify one's own spiritual journey with them. Muslim Sufis often base their meditations on one or several of the Qur'an's Ninety-nine Most Beautiful Names of God.[1] Jewish mystics may meditate on a verse of Torah to uncover its hidden meaning. Many Jews and Christians employ silent meditation as a valuable preparation for prayer; it is a time of quiet when the mind is calmed and clarified before communing with God.

The distinctive Theravada Buddhist discipline of the Four Arousings of Mindfulness aims at achieving awareness of all movements, sensations, feelings, thoughts, and ideas as they come and go in the body and mind. The Buddha taught in the Satipatthana Sutta that one should become mindful at every moment on the ever-changing phenomena of body, senses, and thought.

**Mahabharata, Anusasana Parva 254:** Reciting this list of God's Thousand Names, which are actually God's attributes, is a major form of Hindu devotion.

[1] See Qur'an 59.22-24, p. 598.

Through this meditation, a person realizes that everything in his body and all the phenomena of his mind are transitory and unreal, and he thus realizes the truth of Dependent Origination. A Mahayana Buddhist meditation is to construct a mental image: for example an image of Buddha, a Bodhisattva, or the Pure Land.

Finally, there is shamanistic meditation, where the goal is to receive a vision from the spiritual plane. After a communal initiation, assisted by songs, fasting, and invoking the spirits, the person on a vision quest goes to a lonely spot free from distraction. There he remains, meditating, until the moment when he breaks through beyond ordinary consciousness to receive a supernatural vision that gives purpose to his life and endows him with spiritual powers.

Verily, from meditation arises wisdom. Without meditation wisdom wanes.

*Buddhism.* Dhammapada 282

Concentration is unafflicted one-pointedness.

*Buddhism.* Nagarjuna, Precious Garland 437

The Master said, "Hui is capable of occupying his whole mind for three months on end with no thought but that of Goodness. The others can do so, some for a day, some even for a month, but that is all."

*Confucianism.* Analects 6.5

Within the lotus of the heart he dwells, where the nerves meet like the spokes of a wheel at its hub. Meditate on him as OM. Easily may you cross the sea of darkness.

*Hinduism.* Mundaka Upanishad 2.2.6

In the cool, dew-drenched night are shining
the stars:
At this hour are awake the devotees, lovers of
God,
Meditating each day on the Name—
Their hearts meditating on the lotus feet of
God,
Whom they forsake not for an instant.

*Sikhism.* Adi Granth, Asa Chhant, M.5, p. 459

Let the words of my mouth
and the meditation of my heart
be acceptable in thy sight, O Lord,
my rock and my redeemer.

*Judaism* and *Christianity.* Psalm 19.14

One must not stand up and say the Tefillah except in a serious frame of mind. The pious men of old used to wait an hour, and then say the prayer, in order to direct their hearts to their Father in heaven.

*Judaism.* Mishnah, Berakot 5.1

Commune with your own heart upon your bed, and be silent.

*Judaism* and *Christianity.* Psalm 4.4

Calm is his mind, calm is his speech, calm is his action, who, rightly knowing, is wholly freed, perfectly peaceful and equipoised.

*Buddhism.* Dhammapada 96

When all the senses are stilled, when the mind is at rest, when the intellect wavers not—then, say the wise, is reached the highest state.

This calm of the senses and the mind has been defined as yoga. He who attains it is freed from delusion.

*Hinduism.* Katha Upanishad 2.6.10-11

**Precious Garland 437:** The same definition is given in Bhagavad Gita 6.12, pp. 603-4.

**Analects 6.5:** Cf. Mencius II.A.2, p. 527.

**Mundaka Upanishad 2.2.6:** Cf. Mandukya Upanishad, p. 597; Bhagavad Gita 8.12-13, p. 241.

**Berakot 5.1:** The 'Tefillah' refers to the Amidah, the Eighteen Benedictions, one of the chief Jewish prayers. Cf. Berakot 30b, p. 594; Chuang Tzu 23, p. 524.

**Katha Upanishad 2.6.10-11:** Cf. Bhagavad Gita 5.24, p. 379; Katha Upanishad 4.1-2, pp. 485-86.

Block the passages,
Shut the doors,
Let all sharpness be blunted,
All tangles untied,
All glare tempered,
All dust smoothed.
This is called mysterious levelling.

*Taoism.* Tao Te Ching 56

Attain utmost vacuity;
Hold fast to quietude.
While the myriad things are stirring together,
I see only their return.
For luxuriantly as they grow,
Each of them will return to its root.
To return to the root is called quietude,
Which is also said to be reversion to one's destiny.
This reversion belongs with the eternal:
To know the eternal is enlightenment.

*Taoism.* Tao Te Ching 16

Can you keep the unquiet physical soul from straying, hold fast to the Unity, and never quit it?
Can you, when concentrating your breath, make it soft like that of a little child?
Can you wipe and cleanse your vision of the Mystery till all is without blur?

*Taoism.* Tao Te Ching 10

The wise man should surrender his words to his mind;
and this he should surrender to the Knowing Self;
and the Knowing Self he should surrender to the Great Self;
and that he should surrender to the Peaceful Self.

*Hinduism.* Katha Upanishad 3.13

Bodhisattvas should leave behind all phenomenal distinctions and awaken the thought of the Consummation of Incomparable Enlightenment by not allowing the mind to depend upon notions evoked by the sensible world—by not allowing the mind to depend upon notions evoked by sounds, odors, flavors, touch-contacts, or any qualities. The mind should be kept independent of any thoughts which arise within it. If the mind depends upon anything it has no sure haven.

*Buddhism.* Diamond Sutra 14

Arouse your entire body with its three hundred and sixty bones and joints and its eighty-four thousand pores of skin; summon up a spirit of great doubt and concentrate on the word "mu" (nothingness). Carry it continually day and night. Do not form a nihilistic conception of vacancy, or a relative conception of "has" or "has not." It will be just as if you swallowed a red-hot iron ball, which you cannot spit out even if you try. All the illusory ideas and delusive thoughts accumulated up to the present will be exterminated, and when the time comes, internal and external will be spontaneously united. You will know this, but for yourself only, like a dumb man who has had a dream. Then all of a sudden an explosive con-

**Tao Te Ching 56:** Cf. Chuang Tzu 5, p. 393; 23, p. 659.

**Tao Te Ching 16:** Cf. Chuang Tzu 12, p. 416.

**Tao Te Ching 10:** Cf. Chuang Tzu 6, p. 413; on the figure of the little child, see Tao Te Ching 55, p. 156; 20, p. 434; Atharva Veda 6.121.4, p. 379.

**Katha Upanishad 3.13:** Yoga is a process of absorption into Brahman. Sense activities and outward expression (words) should be stopped and attention drawn into the mind. Then the mind should be concentrated on the *buddhi*, or the highest spiritual faculty of the soul, the individualized Atman. This too should be submerged into the Great Self or Cosmic Mind, thereby losing all notions of separate individuality. Finally, this Great Self, which still knows itself, is to dissolve into the Absolute, the Peaceful Self which is devoid of any distinction or difference whatsoever. Compare the four states of the soul in Mandukya Upanishad, p. 597, the four or five levels of being in Katha Upanishad 2.3.7-8, p. 60, the four nets in Maitri Upanishad 6.28, p. 744, and the four meditations in the Buddha's Noble Eightfold Path, p. 113.

**Diamond Sutra 14:** Cf. Sutta Nipata 1072-76, p. 379; Sutra of Hui Neng 6, p. 283; Perfection of Wisdom in Eight Thousand Lines 12.3, p. 284; Seng Ts'an, pp. 150-51.

version will occur, and you will astonish the heavens and shake the earth.

*Buddhism.* Mumonkan 1

Pure spirit reaches in the four directions, flows now this way, now that—there is no place it does not extend to. Above, it brushes heaven; below, it coils on the earth. It transforms and nurses the ten thousand things, but no one can make out its form. Its name is called One-with-Heaven. The way to purity and whiteness is to guard the spirit, this alone; guard it and never lose it, and you will become one with spirit, one with its pure essence, which communicates and mingles with the Heavenly Order.

*Taoism.* Chuang Tzu 15

The Way of learning to be great consists in manifesting the clear character, loving the people, and abiding in the highest good.

Only after knowing what to abide in can one be calm. Only after having been calm can one be tranquil. Only after having achieved tranquillity can one have peaceful repose. Only after having peaceful repose can one begin to deliberate. Only after deliberation can the end be attained. Things have their roots and their branches. Affairs have their beginnings and their ends. To know what is first and what is last will lead one near the Way.

*Confucianism.* Great Learning

On one occasion a certain monk was seated not far from the Buddha in cross-legged posture, holding his body upright, enduring pain that was the fruit born of former action, pain racking, sharp, and bitter; but he was mindful, composed, and uncomplaining. Seeing the monk so seated and so employed, the Buddha gave this utterance:

For the monk who has left behind all karma,
And shaken off the dust aforetime gathered,
Who stands fast without thought of "I" or "mine"—
For such there is no need to talk to people.

*Buddhism.* Udana 20

Holding the body steady, with the three upper parts erect,
And causing the senses with the mind to enter into the heart,
A wise man with the Brahma-boat should cross over
All the fear-bringing streams.

Having repressed his breathings here in the body, and having his movements checked,
One should breathe through his nostrils with diminished breath.
Like that chariot yoked with vicious horses,
His mind the wise man should restrain undistractedly.

In a clean, level spot, free from pebbles, fire, and gravel,
By the sound of water and other propinquities
Favorable to thought, not offensive to the eye,
In a hidden retreat protected from the wind, one should practice yoga.

Fog, smoke, sun, fire, wind,
Fireflies, lightning, a crystal, a moon—
These are the preliminary appearances,
Which produce the manifestation of Brahman in yoga.

**Mumonkan 1:** Zen (Ch'an) stresses the immediacy of the experience of enlightenment, which is not dependent upon logical progression or reflection. It can only be realized through intense meditation. This passage describes what must be done to understand the koan, "Has a dog the Buddha Nature?"; see p. 572.

**Chuang Tzu 15:** *Ch'i* (*qi*) is the spiritual energy pervading all things. Taoist meditation called Chi Gong and martial arts such as T'ai-chi employ physical exercises in order to cultivate the ch'i, unite with its flow, and harness its power, resulting in inner tranquillity and spiritual vigor. Cf. Mencius II.A.2, p. 527; also Chuang Tzu 6, p. 413; 12, p. 416.

**Great Learning:** Confucian meditation, called Quiet Sitting, has as its aim neither to find the Self nor to empty the mind, but rather to make the mind level and receptive to knowledge. According to the school of Wang-yang Ming, investigation of outward reality should begin with the investigation of one's own mind. Cf. Doctrine of the Mean 1.4-5, p. 155; Great Learning 7, pp. 658-59; Chuang Tzu 5, p. 393; 23, p. 659.

When the fivefold quality of yoga has been
produced,
Arising from earth, water, fire, air, and space,
No sickness, old age, no death has he
Who has obtained a body made out of the fire
of yoga.

Lightness, healthiness, steadiness,
Clearness of countenance and pleasantness of
voice,
Sweetness of odor, and scanty excretions—
These, they say, are the first stage in the
progress of yoga.

Even as a mirror stained by dust
Shines brilliantly when it has been cleansed,
So the embodied one, on seeing the nature of
the Soul,
Becomes unitary, his end attained, from sorrow
freed.

When with the nature of the self, as with a
lamp,
A practicer of yoga beholds here the nature of
Brahman,
Unborn, steadfast, from every nature free—
By knowing God, one is released from all
fetters!

*Hinduism.* Svetasvatara Upanishad 2.8-15

Those who aspire to the state of self-discipline should seek the Self in inner solitude through meditation, controlling body and mind, free from expectations and attachment to material possessions.

Select a clean spot, neither too high nor too low, and seat yourself firmly on a cloth, a deerskin, and kusha grass. Then, once seated, strive to still your thoughts. Make your mind one-pointed in meditation, and your heart will be purified. Hold your body, head, and neck firmly in a straight line, and keep your eyes from wandering. With all fears dissolved in the peace of the Self and all desires dedicated to God, controlling the mind and fixing it on Me, sit in meditation with Me as your only goal. With senses and mind constantly controlled through meditation, united with the Self within, an aspirant attains Nirvana, the state of abiding joy and peace in Me.

Arjuna, those who eat too much or eat too little, who sleep too much or sleep too little, will not succeed in meditation. But those who are temperate in eating and sleeping, work and recreation, will come to the end of sorrow through meditation. Through constant effort they learn to withdraw the mind from selfish cravings and absorb it in the Self. Thus they attain the state of union.

When meditation is mastered, the mind is unwavering like the flame of a lamp in a windless place. In the still mind, in the depths of meditation, the eternal Self reveals itself. Beholding the Self by means of the Self, an aspirant knows the joy and peace of complete fulfilment. Having attained that abiding joy beyond the senses, revealed in the stilled mind, he never swerves from the central truth. He desires nothing else, and cannot be shaken by the heaviest burden of sorrow.

The practice of meditation frees one from all affliction. This is the path of yoga. Follow it with determination and sustained enthusiasm. Renouncing wholeheartedly all selfish desires and expectations, use your will to control the senses. Little by little, through patience and repeated effort, the mind will become stilled in the Self.

Wherever the mind wanders, restless and diffuse in its search for satisfaction without, lead it within; train it to rest in the Self. Abiding joy comes to those who still the mind. Freeing themselves from the taint of self-will, with their consciousness unified, they become one with God.

*Hinduism.* Bhagavad Gita 6.10-27

**Svetasvatara Upanishad 2.8-15:** The unity realized by the adept in meditation is described in Atharva Veda 19.51.1, p. 154. On the self-control required in meditation, see Bhagavad Gita 5.21-23, p. 133; 6.35-36, p. 523; Dhammapada 33-37, p. 523.

**Bhagavad Gita 6.10-27:** See the previous note.

As long as I am seated in this meditation, I shall patiently suffer all calamities that might befall me, be they caused by an animal, a human being or a god.

I renounce, for the duration [of this meditation], my body, all food, and all passions. Attachment, aversion, fear, sorrow, joy, anxiety, self-pity... all these I abandon with body, mind, and speech. I further renounce all delight and all repulsion of a sexual nature.

Whether it is life or death, whether gain or loss, whether defeat or victory, whether meeting or separation, whether friend or enemy, whether pleasure or pain, I have equanimity towards all.

In [attaining] knowledge, insight, and proper conduct, [the cause] is invariably nothing but my own soul. Similarly, my soul [is cause] for both the influx of karmas and the stopping of that influx.

One and eternal is my soul, characterized by intuition and knowledge; all other states that I undergo are external to me, for they are formed by associations. Because of these associations my soul has suffered the chains of misery; therefore I renounce with body, mind, and speech, all relationships based on such associations.

Thus have I attained to equanimity and to my own self-nature.
May this state of equanimity be with me until I attain salvation.

*Jainism.* Samayika Patha

There is this one way, monks, for the purification of beings, for the overcoming of sorrow and misery, for the destruction of pain and grief, for winning the right path, for the attainment of Nibbana, namely the Four Arousings of Mindfulness. What are these four?

Here a monk lives contemplating the body in the body, ardent, clearly conscious and mindful, having overcome, in this world, covetousness and dejection; he lives contemplating feelings in feelings, ardent, clearly conscious and mindful, having overcome, in this world, covetousness and dejection; he lives contemplating consciousness in consciousness, ardent, clearly conscious and mindful, having overcome, in this world, covetousness and dejection; he lives contemplating mental objects in mental objects, ardent, clearly conscious and mindful, having overcome in this world, covetousness and dejection.

And how, monks, does a monk live contemplating body in the body? Here a monk, having gone to the forest, sits down cross-legged keeping his body erect and setting up mindfulness in front of him. Mindful he breathes in, mindful he breathes out. Breathing in long, he knows, "I breathe in long." Breathing out long, he knows, "I breathe out long." Breathing in short, he knows, "I breathe in short." Breathing out short, he knows, "I breathe out short." "Experiencing the whole body I shall breathe out," thus he trains himself....

And further, a monk knows when he is going, "I am going"; he knows when he is standing, "I am standing"; he knows when he is sitting, "I am sitting"; he knows when he is lying down, "I am lying down"; or just as the body is disposed so he knows it....

And further, a monk reflects on this very body enveloped by the skin and full of manifold impurity from the soles up and from the crown of the head down, thinking, "There are in this body: hair of the head, hair of the body, nails, teeth, skin, flesh, sinews, bones, marrow, kidney, heart, liver, membranes, spleen, lungs, bowels, intestines, mesentery, feces, bile, phlegm, pus, blood, sweat, fat, saliva, mucus, synovic fluid, urine."...

And further, if a monk sees a body dead for one day, or two or three, swollen, discolored, decomposing, thrown aside in the cemetery, he applies this perception to his own body, "Truly, this body of mine, too, is of the same nature, it will become like that and will not escape it."...

And how, monks, does a monk live contemplating feelings in feelings?

**Samayika Patha:** This is one of many recitations, *samayika patha*, inwardly repeated during the layperson's meditation, the *samayika*. Usually performed at dusk, when the day's activities have come to an end, the layperson sits in a yoga posture, asks forgiveness of all beings, puts his mind in a state of calm, and begins his meditation. This Jain practice allows laypeople a taste of the ascetic life.

Here a monk when experiencing a pleasant feeling knows, "I experience a pleasant feeling"; when experiencing a painful feeling knows, "I experience a painful feeling"; when experiencing a feeling that is neither pleasant nor painful knows, "I experience a neither pleasant nor painful feeling."...

And how does a monk live contemplating consciousness in consciousness?

Here, monks, a monk knows the consciousness with craving as with craving; the consciousness without craving as without craving; the consciousness with anger as with anger; the consciousness without anger as without anger; the consciousness with ignorance as with ignorance; the consciousness without ignorance as without ignorance... the freed state of consciousness as the freed state; the unfreed state of consciousness as the unfreed....

And how does a monk live contemplating mental objects in mental objects?

Here, monks, a monk lives contemplating mental objects in the mental objects of the five hindrances. When sense desire is present, a monk knows, "There is sense desire in me," or when sense desire is not present he knows, "There is no sense desire in me." He knows how the arising of the non-arisen sense desire comes to be; he knows how the abandoning of the arisen sense desire comes to be; he knows how the non-arising in the future of the abandoned sense desire comes to be. When anger is present, he knows... when sloth and torpor is present, he knows... when restlessness and worry are present, he knows... when doubt is present, he knows....

Truly, monks, whoever practices these Four Settings up of Mindfulness for seven years, then one of two results may be expected by him: highest knowledge here and now or, if some remainder of clinging is yet present, the state of non-returning.

*Buddhism*. Majjhima Nikaya i.55-63, Satipatthana Sutta

Buddha then replied to Vaidehi, "You and all other beings besides ought to make it their only aim, with concentrated thought, to get a perception of the Western Quarter. You will ask how that perception is to be formed. I will explain it now. All beings, if not blind from birth, are uniformly possessed of sight, and they all see the setting sun. You should sit down properly, looking in the western direction, and prepare your thought for a close meditation on the sun; cause your mind to be firmly fixed on it so as to have an unwavering perception by the exclusive application of your thought, and gaze upon it when it is about to set and looks like a suspended drum.

"After you have thus seen the sun, let that image remain clear and fixed, whether your eyes be shut or open—such is the perception of the sun, which is the First Meditation.

"Next you should form the perception of water; gaze on the water clear and pure, and let [this image] also remain clear and fixed; never allow your thought to be scattered or lost.

"When you have thus seen the water you should form the perception of ice. As you see the ice shining and transparent, you should imagine the appearance of lapis lazuli.

"After that has been done, you will see the ground consisting of lapis lazuli, transparent and shining both within and without. Beneath this ground of lapis lazuli there will be seen a golden banner with the seven jewels, diamonds and the rest, supporting the ground. It extends to the eight points of the compass, and thus the eight corners [of the ground] are perfectly filled up. Every side of the eight quarters consists of a hundred jewels, every jewel has a thousand rays, and every ray has eighty-four thousand colors which, when reflected in the ground of lapis lazuli, look like one hundred thousand million suns, and it is difficult to see them all one by one. Over the surface of that ground of lapis lazuli there are stretched golden ropes intertwined crosswise; divisions are made by means of [strings of] seven jewels with every part clear and distinct.

**Majjhima Nikaya i.55-63:** This sutta teaches the distinctively Buddhist technique of meditation called the Four Arousings of Mindfulness. Cf. Digha Nikaya ii.99-100, p. 488, Anguttara Nikaya v.66, p. 517.

"Each jewel has rays of five hundred colors which look like flowers or like the moon and stars. Lodged high up in the open sky these rays form a tower of rays, whose stories and galleries are ten millions in number and built of a hundred jewels. Both sides of the tower have each ten thousand million flowery banners furnished and decked with innumerable musical instruments. Eight kinds of cool breezes proceed from the brilliant rays. When those musical instruments are played, they emit the sounds 'suffering,' 'non-existence,' 'impermenance,' and 'non-self'—such is the perception of the water, which is the Second Meditation.

"When this perception has been formed, you should meditate on its constituents one by one and make the images as clear as possible, so that they may never be scattered or lost, whether your eyes be shut or open. Except only during the time of your sleep, you should always keep this in your mind. One who has reached this stage of perception is said to have dimly seen the Land of Highest Happiness (*Sukhavati*).

"One who has obtained samadhi is able to see the Land clearly and distinctly: this state is too much to be explained fully—such is the perception of the Land, and it is the Third Meditation."

*Buddhism*. Meditation on Buddha Amitayus 9-11

Before I could go on my vision quest, I had to purify myself in the *oinikaga* tipi, the *inipi*, the sweat lodge.... With the buffalo-horn ladle, Good Lance poured ice-cold water over the red-glowing stones. There was a tremendous hiss as we were instantly enveloped in a cloud of searing white steam. It was so hot, it came like a shock wave upon me... I dared not breathe; I thought that if I did I would burn my lungs into charcoal. But I did not cry out. I just stuck my head between my knees. Good Lance prayed. He used ancient words, "This steam is the holy breath of the universe. Hokshila, boy, you are in your mother's womb again. You are going to be reborn." They all sang two songs, very ancient songs, going way back to the days when we Sioux roamed the prairie. Suddenly I felt wise with the wisdom of generations. These men, my relatives, sang loud and vigorously.... The little hut was shaken as if in the grip of a giant hand. It was trembling as a leaf trembles in the wind. Beneath us the earth seemed to move. "Grandfather is here," said Good Lance. "The spirits are here; the Eagle's wisdom is here." We believed it; we knew it. The pipe was passed.... Four times we smoked. After the last time, Good Lance told me, "Hokshila, you have been purified; you are no longer a child; you are ready now and made strong to go up there and cry for a dream."...

Our vision pit was an L-shaped hole dug into the ground, first straight down and then a short horizontal passage deep under the roots of the trees. You sit at the end of that passage and do your fasting. A grown-up man fasts anywhere from one to four days... in my case, it was decided that I should stay up there alone without food or water for two days and two nights.

[After some preparations] it was time for me to strip and go down into the hole. My father and uncle wrapped me in a star quilt and tied me up in it with a deer hide thong.... They patted me on the back, mumbled some encouragements, and left me there.

**Meditation on Buddha Amitayus 9-11:** Meditating upon the Pure Land of Amitabha in the Western direction through contemplating the setting sun was a popular practice in ancient Japan. The Western gate of Shi-tenno-ji in Osaka was believed to be the gate to the Pure Land, and it is said that many followers gathered there at the spring and autumn equinoxes when the sun set directly through the gate. The meditation itself continues through sixteen stages, dwelling in turn upon the exquisite beauty of the Pure Land, the glory of the Buddha and the great Bodhisattvas, and the destinies of beings of various grades of character. In this passage we have mention of the Four Noble Truths. Meditation on Buddha Amitayus 17, p. 462, is a meditation on the Tathagata himself. Cf. the description of the Pure Land in Larger Sukhavativyuha Sutra 15-18, pp. 250-51.

The first hours were the hardest. It was pitch dark and deathly still. I sat there without moving. My arms and legs went asleep. I could neither hear nor see nor feel. I became almost disembodied, a thing with a heart and wild thoughts but no flesh or bones. Would I ever be able to see and hear again?… I don't know how long I sat there. All sense of time had left me long ago. I didn't know whether it was day or night, had not even a way to find out. I prayed and prayed, tears streaming down my cheeks. I wanted water but kept praying. Toward evening of the second day—and this time is only a wild guess—I saw wheels before my eyes forming up into one fiery hoop and then separating again into bright, many-colored circles, dancing before my eyes and again contracting into one big circle, a circle with a mouth and two eyes.

Suddenly, I heard a voice. It seemed to come from within the bundle that was me, a voice from the dark. It was hard to tell exactly where it came from. It was not a human voice; it sounded like a bird speaking like a man. My hackles rose… "Remember the hoop" said the voice, "this night we will teach you." And I heard many feet walking around in my small vision pit. Suddenly I was out of my hole, in another world, standing in front of a sweat bath on a prairie covered with wildflowers, covered with herds of elk and buffalo.

I saw a man coming toward me; he seemed to have no feet; he just floated toward me out of a mist, holding two rattles in his hand. He said, "Boy, whatever you tell your people, do not exaggerate; always do what your vision tells you. Never pretend." The man was wearing an old-fashioned buckskin outfit decorated with quillwork. I stretched out my hands to touch him, when suddenly I was back inside my star quilt, clutching my medicine bundle of stones and tobacco ties. I still heard the voice, "Remember the hoop; remember the pipe; be its spokesman." I was no longer afraid; whoever was talking to me meant no harm.

Suddenly before me stretched a coal-black cloud with lightning coming out of it. The cloud spread and spread; it grew wings; it became an eagle. The eagle talked to me: "I give you a power, not to use for yourself, but for your people. It does not belong to you; it belongs to the common folks." I saw a rider on a gray horse coming toward me, he held in his one hand a hoop made of sage. He held it high… and again everything dissolved into blackness. Again out of the mist came a strange creature floating up, covered with hair, pale, formless. He wanted to take my medicine away from me, but I wrestled with him, defended it. He did not get my medicine. He, too, disappeared.

Suddenly somebody shook me by the shoulder. "Wake up, boy." My father and my uncle had come for me. The two days and two nights were over.

*Native American Religions.*
Leonard Crow Dog, Sioux Vision Quest

❖

**Sioux Vision Quest:** The vision quest began with an invocation to the spirits in the sweat lodge; cf. the Winnebago Invocation at the Sweat Lodge, pp. 260-61.

# Ritual

SPACE DOES NOT PERMIT *World Scripture* to do justice to the wide variety of rituals and rites by which people of the world worship God. The rituals ordained in the scriptures of the world's religions fall into several broad classes. Some texts mandate the worship and remembrance of the transcendent God through symbols and images. The Christian Eucharist represents in the bread and wine the body and blood of Christ; the Hindu *puja* is a rite in which images of the gods are worshipped with bathing, flowers, food offerings, obeisance, and mantras; fire represents God's righteousness in Zoroastrian fire worship; veneration of relics is common to many religions, particularly Buddhism; the three great symbols of Shinto represent the Sun Goddess Amaterasu; and the peace pipe in Native American religion brings forth the blessings of the Great Spirit.

Other rituals center on sacred space and time. Pilgrimage, the journey to the sacred place, is a religious duty in many religious traditions. In Islam the *hajj*, the pilgimage to Mecca, is a central rite. Muhammad observed the hajj on his victorious return to Mecca, but according to the Qur'an this rite was first ordained by Abraham. Rituals to set apart sacred time can include the many actions and symbols to mark the beginning or ending of festival days; thus the Jewish law of the Sabbath sets it apart from the rest of the week as a day of rest.

Many rituals are concerned with purity and purification. Ritual bathing, baptism, hand-washing, and other forms of cleansing are symbolic of purification of the soul. The Vedas teach the merit of bathing in the Ganges, and the Bible prescribes the Christian rite of baptism. Dietary laws, prohibiting one from eating certain unclean foods or requiring foods to be prepared in a prescribed manner, such as the Jewish laws of *kashrut* and Hindu teachings on vegetarianism, are helpful for purifying body and spirit.

The concluding passages deal with worship through offering animal sacrifices. Since only the rituals of living religions are relevant for modern man, we must distinguish these from the ritual practice of the ancients as preserved in scripture. Offerings of animals are still made in contemporary Chinese religion, in Islam as one rite of the hajj, in some primal religions, and rarely in Hinduism. But for most Hindus the vedic sacrifices have been spiritualized and supplanted by puja, and Judaism regards study and prayer as fulfilling the biblical commandments to sacrifice animals.[1]

Let us do it
The way it is usually done
So that we may have the usual result.

*African Traditional Religions*. Yoruba Proverb (Nigeria)

Those who, knowing my true nature, worship me steadfastly are my true devotees. Worship me in the symbols and images which remind you of me, and also in the hearts of my devotees, where I am most manifest.... Observe the forms and rituals set forth in the scriptures, without losing sight of their inner spirit.

*Hinduism*. Srimad Bhagavatam 11.5

**Srimad Bhagavatam 11.5:** Cf. Kularnava Tantra 5, p. 333, on the mystical meaning of several of the objects used in Tantric ritual.

[1] See the relevant passages: Satapatha Brahmana 11.5.6.1-3, p. 617, and Menahot 110a, p. 618.

Ascribe to the Lord, O families of the peoples,
ascribe to the Lord glory and strength!
Ascribe to the Lord the glory due his name;
bring an offering, and come into his courts!
Worship the Lord in holy array;
tremble before him, all the earth!

*Judaism* and *Christianity*. Psalm 96.7-9

Thy fire, O Lord, mighty through
Righteousness, swift and powerful—
We would that it may be a resplendent support
For him who exalts it; but for the enemy, O
Wise One,
According to the powers of thy hand, the clear
showing of his trespasses!

*Zoroastrianism*. Avesta, Yasna 34.4

The Lord Jesus on the night when he was betrayed took bread, and when he had given thanks, he broke it, and said, "This is my body which is [broken] for you. Do this in remembrance of me." In the same way also the cup, after supper, saying, "This cup is the new covenant in my blood. Do this, as often as you drink it, in remembrance of me."

*Christianity*. 1 Corinthians 11.23-25

Then the Sun Goddess Amaterasu imparted unto the first emperor the myriad Maga-tama beads and the mirror which had been used to lure her out of the cave as well as the sword Kusa-nagi... and said, "This mirror—have it with you as my spirit, and worship it just as you would worship in my very presence."

*Shinto*. Kojiki 39.2-3

In due time they purified the bones of the deceased Saint with the finest water, and, placing them in golden pitchers in the city of Mallas, they chanted hymns of praise, "The jars hold great relics, full of virtue, like the jewelled ore of a great mountain, and the relics are unharmed by fire, just as the sphere of Brahma in heaven is unharmed [though the whole earth be burned up]. These bones, pervaded with universal benevolence, and not liable to burning by the fire of passion, are preserved under the influence of devotion; though they are cold, they still warm our hearts."

The wise know the virtues of the Buddha to be such that, given equal purity of mind, the same fruit will be won either by reverencing the Seer during his worldly existence or by doing obeisance to his relics after the Parinirvana.

*Buddhism*. Ashvaghosha, Buddhacarita 27.76-78, 28.69

With a love for the happiness of different beings Shiva Puja shall be performed—so say the wise men. The pedestal represents Shiva's consort Parvati and his phallic emblem represents the sentient being. Just as lord Shiva remains ever in close embrace of the Goddess Parvati, so also the phallic emblem holds on to the pedestal forever.... The devotee shall install the phallic emblem and worship it with the sixteen prescribed types of homage and services: invocation, offering the seat, water offering, washing the feet, water for rinsing the mouth as a mystical rite, oil bath, offering of cloth, scents, flowers, incense, lamps, and food, waving of lights, betel leaves, obeisance, and

**Yasna 34.4:** Fire is the central symbol of Zoroastrian worship. It represents both God's righteousness and the ordeal at the judgment by which the wicked are separated from the righteous.

**1 Corinthians 11.23-25:** These words are spoken at the Eucharistic service in Christian churches.

**Kojiki 39.2-3:** These three sacred symbols of Shinto are in the possession of the emperor of Japan. But the mirror, which is placed at the center of Shinto altars, is especially significant. Besides being a symbol of the sun, it represents the kami within. The reflection of the self is the reflection of kami. On the origin of the sword, see Kojiki 19, p. 448.

mystical discharge and conclusion.... Everywhere Shiva accords benefit as befitting the endeavor put in.

*Hinduism*. Shiva Purana, Vidyeshvarasamhita 11.22-35

You are as wide as the world and sky
And wider still!
Your feet go deeper than the abyss
And deeper still!
Your crown stands high above the universe
And higher still!
You are imperceptible, past understanding,
Unlimited and incomparable.
But coming to the palm of my hand
You have taken the form of Linga,
So small and effulgent:
O Lord Kudala Sangama!

*Hinduism*. Basavanna, Vacana 743

The woman entered the circle... a very beautiful woman, dressed in the softest deerskin which was ornamented with fringes and colors more beautiful than any woman of the Lakota had ever worked. Then she served the men with food, and when they had feasted she told them that she wished to serve them always. She said that they had first seen her as smoke, and they should always see her as smoke.

Then she took from her pouch a pipe and willow bark and tobacco and filled the pipe with bark and tobacco and lit it with a burning coal. She smoked a few whiffs and handed the pipe to the chief and told him to smoke and hand it to another. Thus the pipe was passed until all had smoked. She then instructed the council how to gather the bark and the tobacco and prepare it, and gave the pipe into their keeping, telling them that as long as they preserved this pipe she would serve them. But she would serve them in this way. When the smoke came from the pipe she would be present and hear their prayers and take them to the Wakan Tanka and plead for them that their prayers should be answered.

After she remained in the camp for many days... she called all the people together and had them sit in a circle about the fire. She stood in the midst of the circle, and when the fire had burned to coals, she directed the shaman to place sweetgrass on it, making a cloud of smoke. The woman entered the smoke and disappeared. Then the shamans knew that it was Wohpe who had given the pipe. They appointed a custodian for it; it was to be kept sacred and used only on the most solemn and important occasions.

*Native American Religions*. Sioux Tradition of the Sacred Pipe

And when We settled for Abraham the place of the House, "You shall not associate with Me anything. And do purify My House for those that shall go about it and those that stand, for those that bow and prostrate themselves;

"And proclaim among men the Pilgrimage, and they shall come unto you on foot and upon every lean beast, they shall come from every deep ravine, that they may witness things profitable to them and mention God's name on

**Shiva Purana:** *Puja* is the rite of image worship with its many ceremonies. It is the chief style of worship in popular Hinduism. This passage is an extract from a lengthy discussion of the worship of Shiva as represented by the linga. Note that the linga is devoid of any connotation of sexual license; it is a spiritual symbol of the cosmic unity of male and female principles. It has taken on an abstract and aniconic character, in contrast to the images of gods and goddesses which adorn most Hindu worship. Cf. Shiva Purana, Rudrasamhita 18.3-22, p. 257.

**Vacana 743:** The Lingayats of South India worship Shiva in the form of the *Ishta-linga*, a personal linga carried in a small container suspended on the neck. It is a tiny stone, oval in shape and black in color, which symbolizes the transcendent Deity. Meditating on the Ishta-linga, surrounded by all the articles of puja (as mentioned in the previous passage from the Puranas)—flowers, rosary beads, sacred ash, incense, candles—the devotee gazes on the linga held in the open left palm raised to the level of one's nose while reciting the Shiva mantra and singing devotional songs. Use of the Ishta-linga as a symbol for deity emancipated worship from the temple and priesthood, as each individual became his own temple of God; see Vacana 820, p. 142.

**Sioux Tradition of the Sacred Pipe:** Cf. Gros Ventres Tradition of the Pipe Child, p. 171; Winnebago Invocation at the Sweat Lodge, pp. 260-61.

days well-known over such beasts of the flocks as He has provided them, 'So eat thereof, and feed the wretched poor.' Let them then finish with their self-neglect and let them fulfill their vows, and go about the Ancient House."...

And the beasts of sacrifice—We have appointed them for you as among God's way-marks; therein is good for you. So mention God's name over them, standing in ranks; then, when their flanks collapse, eat of them and feed the beggar and the suppliant. So We have subjected them to you; haply you will be thankful.

The flesh of them shall not reach God, neither their blood, but godliness from you shall reach Him. So He has subjected them to you, that you may magnify God for that He has guided you.

*Islam*. Qur'an 22.26-37

And the Lord said to Moses, "Say to the people of Israel, You shall keep my Sabbaths, for this is a sign between me and you throughout your generations, that you may know that I, the Lord, sanctify you. You shall keep the Sabbath, because it is holy for you; everyone who profanes it shall be put to death; whoever does any work on it, that soul shall be cut off from among his people. Six days shall work be done, but the seventh day is a Sabbath of solemn rest, holy to the Lord; whoever does any work on the Sabbath day shall be put to death. Therefore the people of Israel shall keep the Sabbath, observing the Sabbath throughout their generations, as a perpetual covenant. It is a sign for ever between me and the people of Israel that in six days the Lord made heaven and earth, and on the seventh day he rested, and was refreshed."

*Judaism* and *Christianity*. Exodus 31.12-17

Wash away, Waters, whatever
sin is in me, what wrong I have done,
what imprecation I have uttered,
and what untruth I have spoken.

Today I have sought the Waters,
we have mingled with their essence;
approach me, Agni, with thy power,
and fill me, as such, with brilliance.

*Hinduism*. Rig Veda 10.9.8-9

Repent, and be baptized every one of you in the name of Jesus Christ for the forgiveness of your sins; and you shall receive the gift of the Holy Spirit.

*Christianity*. Acts 2.38

Do you not know that all of us who have been baptized into Christ Jesus were baptized into his death? We were buried therefore with him by baptism into death, so that as Christ was raised from the dead by the glory of the Father, we too might walk in newness of life. For if we have been united with him in a death like his, we shall certainly be united with him in a resurrection like his. We know that our old self was crucified with him so that the sinful body

**Qur'an 22.26-37:** These verses sanction the *hajj*, the pilgrimage to Mecca, and describe some of its rites. The origin of the pilgrimage to Mecca, and the Kaaba that houses the sacred black stone, goes back to Abraham. The rites had been corrupted by the pagan Arabs, who installed their idols at the Kaaba, and only with Muhammad was the rite restored to its original purpose: to magnify the One God. The first hajj was the crowning achievement of Muhammad's own life, when he could successfully subjugate the idolators and return from exile to the city of his birth (see Qur'an 9.1-28 and Sirat Rasul Allah, p. 442). Ever since, the pilgrimage to Mecca once in a lifetime has been a religious aspiration for all Muslims. Note the inner purpose of the ritual and its sacrifice: not to satisfy God's hunger for worship, but that the people may express holiness and magnify God.

**Exodus 31.12-17:** See Exodus 20.1-17, p. 110. Jews observe the Sabbath day on Saturday as a solemn day of rest, study, and worship. Most Christians observe the Lord's Day, Sunday, as the day of Sabbath rest and worship; it was on a Sunday that Jesus rose from the dead, and on Sundays that Christians meet and break bread together to commemorate his resurrection.

**Rig Veda 10.9.8-9:** Bathing at the Ganges is efficacious in washing away sins and receiving divine grace.

**Acts 2.38:** Cf. John 3.3-7, pp. 406-7; Matthew 28.18-20, p. 723.

might be destroyed, and we might no longer be enslaved to sin. For he who has died is freed from sin. But if we have died with Christ, we believe that we shall also live with him. For we know that Christ being raised from the dead will never die again; death no longer has dominion over him. The death he died he died to sin, once for all, but the life he lives he lives to God. So you also must consider yourselves dead to sin and alive to God in Christ Jesus.

*Christianity*. Romans 6.3-11

You shall not eat any abominable thing. These are the animals you may eat: the ox, the sheep, the goat, the hart, the gazelle, the roebuck, the wild goat, the ibex, the antelope, and the mountain sheep. Every animal that parts the hoof and chews the cud, among the animals, you may eat. Yet of those that chew the cud or have the hoof cloven you shall not eat these: the camel, the hare, and the rock badger, because they chew the cud but do not part the hoof, are unclean to you. And the swine, because it parts the hoof but does not chew the cud, is unclean for you. Their flesh you shall not eat, and their carcasses you shall not touch. Of all that are in the waters you may eat these: whatever has fins and scales you may eat. And whatever does not have fins and scales you shall not eat; it is unclean for you.

You shall not eat anything that dies of itself; you may give it to the alien who is within your towns, that he may eat it, or you may sell it to a foreigner; for you are a people holy to the Lord your God....

You shall not boil a kid in its mother's milk.

*Judaism*. Deuteronomy 14.3-21

What does God care whether a man kills an animal in the proper way and eats it, or whether he strangles the animal and eats it? Or what does God care whether a man eats unclean animals or clean animals? "If you are wise, for yourself you are wise, but if you scorn, you alone shall bear it" [Proverbs 9.12]. So you learn that the Commandments were given only to purify God's creatures, as it says, "God's word is purified, it is a protection to those who trust in Him" [2 Samuel 22.31].

*Judaism*. Tanhuma, Shemini 15b

Revered Elder who lives on Mount Kenya, you who make mountains tremble and rivers flood, we offer to you this sacrifice that you may bring us rain. People and children are crying, sheep, goats, and cattle are crying. Nwene-ngai, we beseech you with the blood and fat of this lamb which we are going to sacrifice to you.

*African Traditional Religions*.
Kikuyu Prayer (Kenya)

The son of Heaven sacrifices to Heaven and Earth; to the spirits presiding over the four quarters; to the spirits of the hills and rivers; and offers the five sacrifices of the house—all in the course of the year. The feudal princes

**Deuteronomy 14.3-21:** The rabbis, following the principle to 'put a fence around the Torah' (see Abot 1.1, pp. 585-86), interpreted these commandments of Torah strictly in formulating the laws of *kashrut*, determining what foods are kosher. The injunction not to 'boil a kid in its mother's milk' became the basis for the law that milk and meat shall not be eaten at the same meal.

**Tanhuma, Shemini 15b:** The rabbis knew that the ritual commandments of scripture are often arbitrary; not only were they ridiculed by educated Gentiles, but many Jews themselves found them uncomfortable. This text gives a functional meaning to rituals such as the dietary laws. The commandments have no intrinsic value in themselves. Their purpose is to be a means whereby people can prove their sincerity towards God, to discipline and purify, and that people can make a condition of faith by which God can justify the worshipper. This could be a reply to Jesus' words in Matthew 15.11-20, p. 614. Cf. Sifra 93d, p. 681; also Book of Ritual 7.2.20, p. 332.

**Kikuyu Prayer:** For other passages on animal sacrifice, see Dinka Invocation, p. 310, over an ox sacrifice to propitiate a malevolent power, and the Korean Shaman's Invocation of the Mountain Spirit, p. 258.

present oblations, each to the spirits of its hills and rivers; and offer the five sacrifices of the house—all in the course of the year. Great officers present the oblations of the five sacrifices of the house—all in the course of the year. Other officers present oblations to their ancestors.... The son of Heaven uses an ox of one color, pure and unmixed; a feudal prince, a fatted ox; a great officer, an ox selected for the occasion; an ordinary officer, a sheep or a pig.

*Confucianism.*
Book of Ritual 1.2.3.4.6-9

## *Beyond Ritual*

RITUAL IS A POWERFUL WAY to evoke the mystery, awe and holiness of the divine Presence. However, ritual has sometimes been misused to cover hypocrisy. Overly relied upon, it may imbue an aura of sanctity which is not matched by wisdom or deeds. Ritual is no substitute for inward piety, love for one's neighbor, and personal realization of God. And whenever ritual is practiced, it should be done mindfully and with a proper attitude; indeed one purpose of ritual is to cultivate a heart that is sincere and devoted. Nearly every religion has its own internal critique of ritualism. Even when, as in some of these passages, the scripture of one religion is apparently criticizing the ritualism of another religion, the critique is essentially a teaching for its own people.

In Buddhism, Hinduism, and Jainism, the ultimate goal—unity with Brahman or the peace of Nirvana—cannot be gained through ritual or meritorious work. Offerings and ritual are fruitful only for gaining the temporary bliss of heaven; but life in heaven is temporary. Soon enough, the soul returns to a body and to suffering in the world. Rather, the Upanishads and Sutras teach that the path to the ultimate goal requires the inner discipline and realization that comes through meditation.

Then there is the question of what to do when a request for charity conflicts with ritual taboos. The question was put to Jesus, "Is it lawful to heal on the Sabbath?" Mencius was asked whether a man can stretch out his hand to save a drowning woman even though ritually men and women should not touch each other. A Shinto passage praises hospitality to strangers even when it means breaking ritual abstinence.

Finally, there is a general tendency in all religions to see in acts of devotion, study, and charity the essence of the formal rituals required by scripture. The Talmud describes how Judaism spiritualized ritual once ritual practice had become impossible, when the Temple in Jerusalem, the only proper place for offering sacrifices and burnt offerings, was in ruins. Thus an act of charity to one's neighbor is regarded as the equivalent of sacrificing a lamb as a sin offering. In a different context, the Buddha criticized animal sacrifice as creating evil karma by killing life, and instead taught a spiritual meaning of sacrifice as fulfilled in honoring parents, caring for family, and charity to the monks.

**Book of Ritual 1.2.3.4.6-9** On auspicious days, when seeking help, or when giving thanks for good fortune, Chinese customarily offer a cooked whole pig or chicken either at the hearth or the temple. They also offer them at the graves of their ancestors on the anniversaries of their deaths. On offering food to spirits and ancestors, see Precious Garland 249-50, p. 209; Digha Nikaya ii.88, p. 260; Khuddaka Patha, p. 261; Satapatha Brahmana 11.5.6.1-3, p. 617.

The Master said, "A man who is not humane, what can he have to do with ritual?"

*Confucianism*. Analects 3.3

Not by sacred water is one pure, although
many folk bathe in it.
In whom is truth and dhamma, he is pure; he is
a brahmin.

*Buddhism*. Udana 6

Look, you brothers, who bathe in the holy
waters,
Look, you monks, who bathe in the stream.
Give up, give up, your unholy thoughts;
Give up lustful thoughts for another man's
wife,
Give up coveting after another man's wealth.
If you bathe in the waters without giving up
these,
It is as if bathing in a stream that has run dry.

*Hinduism*. Basavanna, Vacana 642

What is Shinto? Not
In the shrines the worldly minded
Frequent for gifts
In vain, but in good deeds, pure
Of heart, lies real religion.

*Shinto*. Genchi Kato

Hear and understand, not what goes into the mouth defiles a man, but what comes out of the mouth, this defiles a man.... Do you not see that whatever goes into the mouth passes into the stomach, and so passes on? But what comes out of the mouth proceeds from the heart, and this defiles a man. For out of the heart come evil thoughts, murder, adultery, fornication, theft, false witness, slander. These are what defile a man.

*Christianity*. Matthew 15.11-20

Abstaining from fish or flesh, nakedness, shaving of the head, wearing the hair matted, smearing with ashes, wearing rough deerskins, attending the sacrificial fire, all the various penances performed for immortality, neither incantations, oblations, sacrifices, nor observing seasonal feasts will cleanse a man who has not overcome his doubt.

*Buddhism*. Sutta Nipata 249

Whoever, therefore, eats the bread or drinks the cup of the Lord in an unworthy manner will be guilty of profaning the body and blood of the Lord. Let a man examine himself, and so eat of the bread and drink of the cup. For any one who eats and drinks without discerning the body eats and drinks judgment upon himself.

*Christianity*. 1 Corinthians 11.27-29

Even three times a day to offer
Three hundred cooking pots of food
Does not match a portion of the merit
Acquired in one instant of love.

*Buddhism*. Nagarjuna,
Precious Garland 283

**Udana 6:** Cf. Var Suhi, M.1, pp. 348-49; Laws of Manu 5.109, p. 520. The original sanction for bathing in the Ganges is given by such texts as Rig Veda 10.9.8-9, p. 611.

**Vacana 642:** Cf. Vacana 126, p. 515.

**Genchi Kato:** See Oracle of Hachiman, p. 520.

**Matthew 15.11-20:** This saying was uttered in a dispute over the Jewish dietary laws (see Deuteronomy 14.3-21, p. 612), yet it applies generally to any ritualism that ascribes righteousness to certain material forms. The key to purity is the intention of the heart. Cf. Tanhuma, Shemini 15b, p. 612; Var Majh, M.1, p. 344.

**Sutta Nipata 249:** Cf. Digha Nikaya i.167, p. 672. The same verse is found in Dhammapada 141.

**1 Corinthians 11.27-29:** Cf. Kularnava Tantra 5, p. 334.

**Precious Garland 283:** Cf. Itivuttaka 19, p. 685; 1 Corinthians 13, p. 160; Oracle of Kasuga, p. 685.

With what shall I come before the Lord?
and bow myself before God on high?
Shall I come before him with burnt offerings,
with calves a year old?
Will the Lord be pleased with thousands of rams,
with ten thousands of rivers of oil?
Shall I give my first-born for my transgression,
the fruit of my body for the sin of my soul?
He has showed you, O man, what is good;
and what does the Lord require of you
but to do justice, and to love kindness,
and to walk humbly with your God?

*Judaism* and *Christianity*. Micah 6.6-8

It is not piety that you turn your faces [in prayer] to the East and to the West. True piety is this:

to believe in God, and the Last Day, the angels, the Book, and the Prophets,

to give of one's substance, however cherished, to kinsmen, and orphans, the needy, the traveller, beggars, and to ransom the slave, to perform the prayer, to pay the alms.

And they who fulfil their covenant, when they have engaged in a covenant, and endure with fortitude misfortune, hardship, and peril, these are they who are true in their faith, these are the truly God-fearing.

*Islam*. Qur'an 2.177

Make your mosque of compassion, your prayer mat of sincerity;
Your Qur'an of honest and legitimate earning.
Be modesty your circumcision, noble conduct your Ramadan fast—
Thus shall you be a true Muslim.
Make good deeds your Kaaba; truth your preceptor;
Good action your creed and daily prayers.
Make your rosary of what pleases God:
Thus will you be honored at the last reckoning.

*Sikhism*. Adi Granth, Var Majh, M.1, p. 140

Finite and transient are the fruits of sacrificial rites. The deluded, who regard them as the highest good, remain subject to birth and death.... Attached to works, they know not God. Works lead them only to heaven, whence, to their sorrow, their rewards quickly exhausted, they are flung back to earth. Considering religion to be observance of rituals and performance of acts of charity, the deluded remain ignorant of the highest good. Having enjoyed in heaven the reward of their good works, they enter again into the world of mortals. But the wise, self-controlled, and tranquil souls, who are contented in spirit, and who practice austerity and meditation in solitude and silence, are freed from all impurity, and attain by the path of liberation the immortal, the truly existing, the changeless Self.

*Hinduism*. Mundaka Upanishad 1.2.7-11

People under delusion accumulate tainted merits but do not tread the Path.
They are under the impression that to accumulate merits and to tread the Path are one and the same thing.
Though their merits for alms-giving and offerings are infinite
They do not realize that the ultimate source of sin lies in the three poisons within their own mind.
They expect to expiate their sins by accumulating merit

**Micah 6.6-8:** Cf. 1 Samuel 15.22, p. 552; Amos 5.23-24, p. 197; Shabbat 31a, p. 718; Japuji 1, M.1, p. 552; 1 Corinthians 13, p. 160; Oracle of Kasuga, p. 685.

**Qur'an 2.177:** Cf. Digha Nikaya iii.185, pp. 167-68; Qur'an 107.4-7, p. 349.

**Var Majh, M.1:** Cf. Gauri Sukhmani, M.5, pp. 672-73; Var Suhi, M.1, pp. 348-49; Var Majh, M.1, p. 344. It should be remembered that Guru Nanak lived prior to the consolidation of Sikhism as a separate religion; he lived as a Hindu among Hindus and a Muslim among Muslims. He was critical of superficial ritualism in both religions and taught devotion to the One God as the true path of both religions.

**Mundaka Upanishad 1.2.7-11:** See the following note; cf. Chandogya Upanishad 7.22, p. 134.

Without knowing that felicities obtained in future lives have nothing to do with the expiation of sins.
Why not get rid of the sin within our own mind,
For this is true repentance?

*Buddhism*. Sutra of Hui Neng 6

[Jesus] went on from there, and entered their synagogue. And behold, there was a man with a withered hand. And they asked him, "Is it lawful to heal on the sabbath?" so that they might accuse him. He said to them, "What man of you, if he has one sheep and it falls into a pit on the sabbath, will not lay hold of it and lift it out? Of how much more value is a man than a sheep! So it is lawful to do good on the sabbath." Then he said to the man, "Stretch out your hand." And the man stretched it out, and it was restored, whole like the other. But the Pharisees went out and took counsel against him, how to destroy him.

*Christianity*. Matthew 12.9-14

Ch'un-yü K'un said, "Is it prescribed by the rites that, in giving and receiving, man and woman should not touch each other?"

"It is," said Mencius.

"When one's sister-in-law is drowning, does one stretch out a hand to help her?"

"Not to help a sister-in-law who is drowning is to be a brute. It is prescribed by the rites that, in giving and receiving, man and woman do not touch each other, but in stretching out a helping hand to the drowning sister-in-law one uses one's discretion."

*Confucianism*. Mencius IV.A.17

Of old, one of the ancestral gods was roaming through the land of his descendant gods, and he came to Mount Fuji in the province of Suruga, just as it was becoming evening, so he went to the home of the god of Mount Fuji and begged to be provided with a place to stay for the night. The god of Mount Fuji, however, replied, "Unfortunately, today is the day that the first fruits are being offered to the gods, and all of my family are under taboos of purification and abstinence. As a result, it would not be fitting for us to put up an unknown stranger. On this day of all days, please excuse me from being more courteous to you."

With this, the other deity was filled with resentment, and said, "I am your ancestor! Even so, will you not put me up? For this I will make it snow both winter and summer on this very mountain in which you live, cover it with mist and cold the year long, so that no person may climb it to give you offerings!"

And with these words, he ascended instead Mount Tsukuba in the province of Hitachi, and begged there for a place to stay the night. The god of Tsukuba replied, "Tonight we are keeping the abstinence of the first fruits, but we cannot refuse your request." And so he respectfully provided the visiting deity with food and a place to stay.

Thereupon, the ancestor deity was filled with joy, and said, "How dear, my child, you are to me, and how majestic your shrine. Here, may you prosper forever with the heavens and earth, with the sun and moon, and may people gather here forever to present you with food offerings, so that your generations continue in ease without end."

As a result, Mount Fuji became covered with snow year-round so that it could not be climbed. Mount Tsukuba, on the other hand, is a gathering place for many people, who enjoy themselves with singing and dancing to this day.

*Shinto*. Hitachi Fudoki

**Sutra of Hui Neng 6:** Buddhist teaching, like that of the Upanishads (above), regards offerings and ritual as effective only for gaining the temporary bliss of heaven. Offerings made from a desire to earn a place in heaven are tainted by selfishness; hence they still produce karma and cannot bring about liberation from bondage. Liberation comes only through the internal gnosis of dependent origination and the reality of Nothingness.

**Hitachi Fudoki:** The Fudoki are gazeteers first prepared at the order of Empress Genmei (c. 715 A.D.) to record local traditions and legends regarding the origins of names of local districts and villages, features of the land, local products, etc. See Oracle of Kasuga, p. 685; compare Luke 10.25-37, p. 687n.

Once, when the Exalted One dwelt near Savatthi in Anathapindika's Park at Jeta Grove, a great sacrifice was being prepared for brahmin Uggatasarira: five hundred bulls, five hundred steers, and as many heifers, goats, and rams were brought to the post for sacrifice. Now brahmin Uggatasarira went and visited the Exalted One, greeted him, exchanged the usual polite talk and sat down at one side. He said, "I have heard that the laying of the fire and the setting up of the pillar are very fruitful, very advantageous.... I am indeed anxious, Master Gotama, to lay the fire, to set up the pillar; let Master Gotama counsel and instruct me for my happiness and welfare for many a day."

"Brahmin, even before the sacrifice, a man who lays the fire, who sets up the pillar, sets up three swords, evil, ill in yield, ill in fruit. Even before the sacrifice, a man laying a fire, setting up a pillar, causes to rise such thoughts as, 'Let there be slain for the sacrifice so many bulls, steers, heifers, goats, rams!' Thinking to make merit, he makes demerit; thinking to do good, he does evil; thinking he seeks the way of happy going, he seeks the way of ill going. He sets up firstly this thought-sword, which is evil, ill in yield, ill in fruit. Again, brahmin, even before the sacrifice... he speaks such words as, 'Let there be slain so many bulls, steers, heifers, goats, rams!'... he sets up secondly this word-sword.... Moreover, brahmin, even before the sacrifice, he himself first sets foot on the business, saying, 'Let them slay.'... he sets up thirdly this deed-sword....

"Brahmin, these three fires, when esteemed, revered, venerated, respected, must bring best happiness. What three? The fires of the venerable, the householder, the gift-worthy. And what is the fire of the venerable? Consider the man who honors his father and mother—this is called the fire of the venerable.... And what is the fire of the householder? Consider, brahmin, the man who honors his sons, womenfolk, slaves, messengers, workmen—this is called the fire of the householder.... And what is the fire of the gift-worthy? Consider, brahmin, those recluses and godly men who abstain from pride and indolence, who bear things patiently and meekly, each taming self, each calming self, each cooling self—this is called the fire of the gift-worthy.... These three fires, when esteemed, revered, venerated, respected, must bring the best happiness."

*Buddhism.*
Anguttara Nikaya iv.41-45

There are five great sacrifices, namely, the great ritual services: the sacrifice to all beings, sacrifice to men, sacrifice to the ancestors, sacrifice to the gods, sacrifice to Brahman. Day by day a man offers sustenance to creatures; that is the sacrifice to beings. Day by day a man gives hospitality to guests, including a glass of water; that is the sacrifice to men. Day by day a man makes funerary offerings, including a glass of water; that is the sacrifice to the ancestors. Day by day a man makes offerings to the gods, including wood for burning; that is the sacrifice to the Gods. And the sacrifice to Brahman? The sacrifice to Brahman consists of sacred study.

*Hinduism.*
Satapatha Brahmana 11.5.6.1-3

**Anguttara Nikaya iv.41-45:** Zoroastrianism and Jainism similarly opposed the ritual slaughter of animals as practiced by the vedic Aryans. See Yasna 29.1-9, p. 223.

**Satapatha Brahmana 11.5.6.1-3:** This text shows a spiritualization of sacrifice in Hinduism. Since Brahman is higher than the gods, the sacrifice to Brahman, namely study and realization of truth, is more essential to religion than offerings of fire and animals to the gods. Similarly, feeding animals and acts of charity which are done daily in ordinary life are regarded as holy sacrifices. See the following passage.

"And in every place offerings are burned and presented unto My name" [Malachi 1.11]. '"In every place!' Is this possible?" Rabbi Samuel ben Nahmai said in the name of Rabbi Jonathan, "This refers to the scholars who devote themselves to the study of the Torah in whatever place they are: [God says], 'I account it to them as though they burned and presented offerings to My name.'..."

"Bless the Lord, all you servants of the Lord, who stand in the house of the Lord in the night seasons" [Psalm 134.1]. "What is the meaning of 'in the night seasons'?" Rabbi Yohanan said, "This refers to the scholars who devote themselves to the study of the Torah at nights: Holy Writ accounts it to them as though they were occupied with the Temple service...."

Rabbi Isaac said, "What is the significance of the verses, 'This is the law of the sin offering' [Leviticus 6.18] and 'This is the law of the guilt offering' [Leviticus 7.1]? They teach that whosoever occupies himself with the study of the laws of the sin offering is as though he were offering the sin offering, and whosoever occupies himself with the study of the laws of the guilt offering is as though he were offering a guilt offering."

*Judaism.* Talmud, Menahot 110a

❖

**Menahot 110a:** Judaism regards the fruit of study of the Torah as a holiness equivalent to the fruit of sacrifice in the Temple, which had become impossible after its destruction in 70 A.D. Cf. Abot de Rabbi Nathan 6, p. 685.

CHAPTER 17

# OFFERING AND SACRIFICE

THE PRACTICE OF RELIGION MAY BE CHARACTERIZED as the way of offering and sacrifice. There are offerings from one's wealth and possessions, but these are only an outward manifestation of offering. For the essence of the offering is to give the self—with its desires, loves, talents, vocation, possessions, relations, and its very identity—to God and to the service of his will. Whatever is held most dear makes the best offering; in an affluent society those occasional tax-deductible donations to a church or charity may be paltry offerings indeed. The true seeker for God makes his whole life an offering in the sense that he lives for God, works for God, and continually directs all his thoughts and deeds to God. The requirements of the sacrifice may include enduring persecution, even to the point of martyrdom. The sections in this chapter explore these various kinds of sacrifice.

## *Offering*

THE WAY OF OFFERING begins from the heart, is manifest in deeds, and extends to the entire cosmos. All tasks should be done with an attitude of offering—in other words, doing them for God's sake, not for one's personal gain. People should offer up the thing that is dearest, with a willing and cheerful heart, for an offering expresses a person's very self. Several important Hindu texts describe sacrifice as central to the creation and maintenance of the cosmos.

Every sacrifice is a boat to heaven.

*Hinduism.* Satapatha Brahmana 4.2.5.10

Lo! We have given you abundance; so pray to your Lord, and sacrifice.

*Islam.* Qur'an 108.1-2

Let all your deeds be done for the sake of Heaven.

*Judaism.* Mishnah, Abot 2.17

Whatever you do, do all to the glory of God.

*Christianity.* 1 Corinthians 10.31

You will not attain piety until you expend of what you love; and whatever thing you expend, God knows of it.

*Islam.* Qur'an 3.92

Whatever is given should be given with faith, not without faith—with joy, with modesty, with fear, with kindness.

*Hinduism.* Taittiriya Upanishad 1.11.3

Each one must do as he has made up his mind, not reluctantly or under compulsion, for God loves a cheerful giver.

*Christianity.* 2 Corinthians 9.7

Whether we bring much or little, it matters not, if only we fix our heart upon our Father in heaven.

*Judaism.* Talmud, Berakot 17a

"Make your offering," said the Master. "As you make it be pleased in mind. Make your mind completely calm and contented. Focus and fill the offering-mind with the giving. From this secure position you can be free from ill will."

*Buddhism.* Sutta Nipata 506

Of the saying, The word "sacrifice" is like the word "present"; one should sacrifice to a spirit as though the spirit were present, Confucius said, "If I am not present at the sacrifice, it is as though there were no sacrifice."

*Confucianism.* Analects 3.12

Rabbi Meir was once asked, "Why do the scriptures tell us in some passages that sacrifice is very pleasant unto the Lord, while in others it is said that God dislikes sacrifices?" He answered, "It depends whether a man's heart is sacrificed at the time he brings the sacrifice."

*Judaism.* Baraita Kallah 8

Whatever I am offered in devotion with a pure heart—a leaf, a flower, fruit, or water—I partake of that love offering. Whatever you do, make it an offering to me—the food that you eat, the sacrifices that you make, the help you give, even your suffering. In this way you will be freed from the bondage of karma, and from its results both pleasant and painful. Then, firm in renunciation and yoga, with your heart free, you will come to me.

*Hinduism.* Bhagavad Gita 9.26-28

**Abot 2.17:** Cf. Abot 2.4, p. 551.

**1 Corinthians 10.31:** Cf. Matthew 7.21, p. 580.

**Qur'an 3.92:** Cf. Qur'an 47.38, p. 664.

**Taittiriya Upanishad 1.11.3:** Cf. Chandogya Upanishad 7.22, p. 134; Svetasvatara Upanishad 4.13,21-22, p. 550.

**Berakot 17a:** Cf. Berakot 30b, p. 594. But attention to one's personal state of mind may not be all that is required; see Matthew 5.23-24, p. 701.

**Sutta Nipata 506:** See previous note.

**Analects 3.12:** Cf. Forty Hadith of an-Nawawi 2, p. 515.

**Baraita Kallah 8:** Cf. Berakot 30b, p. 594.

**Bhagavad Gita 9.26-28:** Cf. Bhagavad Gita 7.3,17,28, p. 538.

The offering is not of myself, but rather of
The heavenly goddess Toyookahime—
It is the offering of her palace,
The offering of her palace.

Would that I were an offering,
Taken up in the kami's hand,
Drawn near to my god,
Drawn near to my god.

*Shinto.* Kagura-uta

The essence of the offering is that it be analogous to the sin, and that a man offer to God his desires and passions, for this is more acceptable than all. Blessed are the righteous, that they bring this offering every day.

*Judaism.* Zohar, Leviticus 9b

The dedication of the offering is God; that which is offered is God; God offers it on God's fire. God is attained by those who concentrate on God's work.

Some aspirants offer material sacrifices; others offer selfless service upon the altar of God. Some renounce all enjoyment of the senses, sacrificing them in the fire of asceticism. Others partake of sense objects but offer them in service through the fire of the senses. Some offer the workings of the senses and the vital forces through the fire of self-control, kindled in the path of knowledge.

Some offer wealth; others offer asceticism and suffering. Some take vows and offer knowledge and study of the scriptures; and some make the offering of meditation. Some offer the forces of vitality, regulating their inhalation and exhalation, offering their life-breath as they breathe in and breathe out. Others offer the forces of vitality by fasting. All these understand the meaning of sacrifice and will be cleansed of their impurities.

In the offering is true sustenance, and through it a man or woman reaches the eternal Reality. But those who do not seek to serve are without a home in this world. Arjuna, how can they be at home in any world to come?

Thus many kinds of offerings are made, and each guides mankind along a path to God. Know that they are born of action, and understanding this, you will attain liberation.

*Hinduism.* Bhagavad Gita 4.24-32

So great is the power of sacrifice that it is the Self of the gods. When, out of the essence of sacrifice, the gods had made their own Self, they took their seat in the world of heaven. Similarly, the one who sacrifices now, when out of the essence of sacrifice he has made his own Self, takes his seat in the world of heaven.

*Hinduism.* Satapatha Brahmana 6.1.10

When with the Supreme Being as the offering
the gods performed a sacrifice,
spring was the molten butter, summer
the fuel, and autumn the oblation.

On the grass they besprinkled him,
the Sacrificed Supreme Being, the first born.
With him the gods sacrificed,
and those Sadhyas and the sages.

From that sacrifice, fully offered,
was gathered mixed milk and butter.
And the birds of the air arose,
the forest animals and the domestic.

From that sacrifice, fully offered,
the Rig and the Saman [Vedas] were born,
the Chandas was born of that,
and from that were born the Sacrificial
formulae.

From that were born horses, and the
animals with two rows of teeth;
yea, kine were born of that, and
of that were born the goat and the sheep....

From his mind was born the moon, and
from his eye the sun. From his mouth
were Indra and Agni born,
and Vayu (wind) was born from his breath.

From his navel came the mid-air,
from his head the sky was fashioned,
from his feet the earth, and from his ear
the quarters. Thus they formed the worlds.

Seven were the sticks of the enclosure,
thrice seven the logs of wood prepared,
when the gods, performing the rite,
bound, as their victim, the Supreme Being.

With sacrifice the gods worshipped the
Supreme Sacrifice.
Those were the earliest holy ordinances.

*Hinduism.*
Rig Veda 10.90.6-10, 13-16

## *Donations*

FOR THOSE WHO DO NOT PURSUE A RELIGIOUS VOCATION, the offering is most often a donation of money and material possessions to honor God and support the community of the faithful. The liberal donor puts the wealth and honor of God and God's representatives ahead of his own needs; through his donation he offers what he holds most dear. As a standard for the faithful giver, the Bible recommends a tithe, or ten percent of one's earnings. Through such gifts the believer is promised a reward.

Contributions to the faith are not always distinguished from *Charity*, pp. 697-700, to the less fortunate. In the Qur'an, the duty to give alms covers both meanings interchangeably, though Islam sometimes distinguishes *zakat*, the obligatory tithing to the religious authorities, from *sadaqa*, meaning almsgiving to the less fortunate above the legal requirement. In Islamic and Christian societies, mosques and churches typically devote most of the funds contributed for the faith to charitable purposes: to feed, clothe, and tend to the needs of the poor, infirm, widows, orphans, and homeless.

On the other hand, religious offerings differ from charity given directly to the poor in that they are meant to show devotion to God or to those who represent Truth in the highest degree. Thus, some of the passages in the latter part of this section address the questions of how and to whom donations should be given. For an offering to have the highest spiritual merit, both the donor and the recipient should be worthy. The donor should give with a pure mind and without expecting any reward or benefit from his gift. As to the recipient, in Buddhist terms he should be a suitable "field of merit" where the donations that are sown may bear abundant fruit.

He who gives liberally goes straight to the gods;
on the high ridge of heaven he stands exalted.

*Hinduism.* Rig Veda 1.125.5

All the tithe of the land, whether of the seed of the land or of the fruit of the trees, is the Lord's; it is holy to the Lord.

*Judaism* and *Christianity.*
Leviticus 27.30

**Rig Veda 10.90.6-10,13-16:** The theme of this well-known hymn is sacrifice as the method of creation. The world comes into being through the sacrifice and dismemberment of the primordial Person. The first fruits of sacrifice were the scriptures: Rig Veda, Sama Veda, *Chandas* (Atharva Veda) and 'Sacrificial formulae' (Yajur Vedas). Following the Word came the physical world and humankind. Cf. Aitareya Upanishad 1-3, p. 213; Mundaka Upanishad 1.1.7-9, p. 85; also Okanogan Creation, p. 207. In the ellipsis go the well-known verses on the origin of the four castes, which are given in another context—see Rig Veda 10.90.11-12, p. 189.

**Leviticus 27.30:** The custom of giving a tithe, or ten percent of one's income, is derived from this verse.

As water surely will wash away blood, so the giving of food to homeless or virtuous saints will certainly destroy the sins incidental to a householder's life.

*Jainism*. Samantabadhra, Ratnakarandasravakacara 114

Verily, misers go not to the celestial realms. Fools do not indeed praise liberality. The wise man rejoices in giving and thereby becomes happy thereafter.

*Buddhism*. Dhammapada 177

We should resolve to offer not only one-tenth but three-tenths of our earnings for the building of the Kingdom of God. One-tenth is for your country, one-tenth is for the people of the world, and one-tenth is for the Kingdom of Heaven.

*Unification Church*. Sun Myung Moon, 4-15-61

And [Jesus] sat down opposite the treasury [of the Temple], and watched the multitude putting money into the treasury. Many rich people put in large sums. And a poor widow came, and put in two copper coins, which make a penny. And he called his disciples to him and said to them, "Truly, I say to you, this poor widow has put in more than all those who are contributing to the treasury. For they all contributed out of their abundance, but she out of her poverty has put in everything she had, her whole living."

*Christianity*. Mark 12.41-44

The word of the Lord came by Haggai the prophet, "Is it a time for you yourselves to dwell in your paneled houses, while this temple lies in ruins? Now therefore thus says the Lord of Hosts: Consider how you have fared. You have sown much, and harvested little; you eat, but you never have enough; you drink, but you never have your fill; you clothe yourselves, but no one is warm; and he who earns wages earns wages to put them in a bag with holes.... Go up to the hills, and bring wood and build the temple, that I may take pleasure in it and that I may appear in my glory, says the Lord."

*Judaism* and *Christianity*. Haggai 1.3-8

Weeds are the bane of fields, lust is the bane of mankind. Hence what is given to those without lust yields abundant fruit.

Weeds are the bane of fields, hatred is the bane of mankind. Hence what is given to those rid of hatred yields abundant fruit.

Weeds are the bane of fields, delusion is the bane of mankind. Hence what is given to those rid of delusion yields abundant fruit.

Weeds are the bane of fields, craving is the bane of mankind. Hence what is given to those rid of craving yields abundant fruit.

*Buddhism*. Dhammapada 356-59

The likeness of those who spend their wealth in God's way is as the likeness of a grain which grows seven ears, in every ear a hundred grains. God gives increase manifold to whom He will. God is All-embracing, All-knowing.

Those who spend their wealth for the cause of God and afterward make not reproach and injury to follow that which they have spent; their reward is with their Lord, and there shall no fear come upon them, neither shall they grieve.

*Islam*. Qur'an 2.261-62

**Mark 12.41-44:** Cf. 2 Corinthians 9.6-11, p. 695.

**Haggai 1.3-8:** This was the attitude of the Pilgrims, who when they arrived in America, first built the church and school before providing for their own homes.

**Dhammapada 356-59:** The notion that the saints are a field of merit is behind the metaphor in these verses. Cf. Digha Nikaya ii.88, p. 260.

When you give alms, do not let your left hand know what your right hand is doing, so that your alms may be in secret; and your Father who sees in secret will reward you.

*Christianity*. Matthew 6.3-4

O you who believe, spend of the good things which you have earned, and of that which We bring forth from the earth for you, and seek not the bad with intent to spend it in charity when you would not take it for yourselves save with disdain; and know that God is Absolute Owner of Praise....

Whatever alms you spend, or vow you vow, lo! God knows it. Wrongdoers have no helpers.

If you publish your almsgiving, it is well, but if you hide it and give it to the poor, it will be better for you, and will atone for some of your ill-deeds. God is Informed of what you do....

And whatever good thing you spend, it is for yourselves, when you spend it not save in search of God's countenance; and whatever good thing you spend, it will be repaid to you in full, and you will not be wronged.

[Alms are] for the poor who are straitened for the cause of God, who cannot travel in the land [for trade]. The unthinking man accounts them wealthy because of their restraint. You shall know them by their mark: They do not beg of men with importunity. And whatever good thing you spend, lo! God knows it.

Those who spend their wealth by night and day, by stealth and openly, verily their reward is with their Lord, and there shall no fear come upon them, neither shall they grieve.

*Islam*. Qur'an 2.267-74

A gift is a gift of integrity
when it is given at the right place and time to the proper person,
to one who cannot be expected to return the gift—
and given merely because it should be given.

But what is given to get a gift in return,
or for the sake of some result,
or unwillingly,
that is a gift in the sphere of passion.

A gift is called slothful when it is given
not at the right time and place,
nor to a worthy person,
nor with proper ceremony, but with contempt.

*Hinduism*. Bhagavad Gita 17.20-22

He who receives a prophet because he is a prophet shall receive a prophet's reward, and he who receives a righteous man because he is a righteous man will receive a righteous man's reward. And whoever gives to one of these little ones even a cup of cold water because he is a disciple, truly, I say to you, he shall not lose his reward.

*Christianity*. Matthew 10.41-42

Those who build shrines of stone,
Of sandalwood or aloes,
Of brick and tiles, or clay;
Or those who, in the wilds,
Built Buddha-shrines of earth;
Even children who, in play,
Gathered sand for a Buddha's stupa;
Such men and beings as these
Have all attained to Buddhahood.

*Buddhism*. Lotus Sutra 2

**Qur'an 2.267-74:** These and Qur'an 2.261-62 (above) are verses selected from a long discussion of donations (*zakat*). Verse 273 condemns indiscriminate acts of charity, and defines the proper beneficiaries as those doing volunteer service, religious teaching and ministry, those in exile, and those persecuted for their faith.

**Lotus Sutra 2:** Cf. Hadith of Ibn Majah, p. 715.

Just as much seed sown in a sterile field will not yield abundant fruit nor please the husbandman, even so, bountiful giving bestowed upon the wicked does not yield abundant fruit, nor delight the donor. And just as when scanty seed is sown in good ground the harvest gladdens the farmer when there is plenty of rain, even so when paid to the righteous, the virtuous, a deed, though it be slight, becomes merit fraught with great return.

*Buddhism.* Petavatthu ii.9.68-71

## *Self-sacrifice*

THE MOST NOBLE SACRIFICE is self-sacrifice: to dedicate one's body, mind, and spirit in the service of God and humanity. In time of persecution and oppression, self-sacrifice may mean to willingly give up one's life as a martyr—see the following section. In times of relative ease, self-sacrifice means to be a living sacrifice, dedicating everything to the divine purpose. Self-sacrifice is also the supreme expression of love for others: see *Sacrifical Love*, pp. 691-94.

Man, in truth, is himself a sacrifice.

*Hinduism.* Chandogya Upanishad 3.16.1

In accepting the true Dharma, may I abandon body, life, and property, and uphold the true Dharma.

*Buddhism.* Lion's Roar of Queen Srimala 3

Jesus told his disciples, "If any man would come after me, let him deny himself and take up his cross and follow me. For whoever would save his life will lose it, and whoever loses his life from my sake will find it."

*Christianity.* Matthew 16.24-25

I appeal to you therefore, brethren, by the mercies of God,
to present your bodies as a living sacrifice,
holy and acceptable to God,
which is your spiritual worship.

*Christianity.* Romans 12.1

With whatever Thou dost provide, am I content;
no other door is there for me to knock.
Nanak this supplication makes,
may my life and body ever to Thee be dedicated!

*Sikhism.* Adi Granth, Sri Raga, M.1, p. 25

**Petavatthu ii.9.68-71:** Many of the stories in this book deal with the spirits of the departed, "hungry ghosts" who fail to find satisfaction from the food offerings made by their kinfolk. They return to their kin and explain to them that they would be far more satisfied were they to make offerings to the Sangha in their name. Cf. Khuddaka Patha, Tirokudda Sutta, p. 261.

**Lion's Roar of Queen Srimala 3:** See Lotus Sutra 13, p. 630; Mahaparinirvana Sutra 424-33, p. 539; Lotus Sutra 12, p. 584; cf. Kularnava Tantra 2, p. 628.

**Matthew 16.24-25:** This saying, central to Jesus' message, describes the essence of Christian discipleship. Each person should 'take up his cross,' enduring suffering and all difficulties for the sake of others, just as Jesus offered himself on the cross for the salvation of all mankind. The saying is repeated in several different forms throughout the gospels; see Mark 8.34-35, p. 638; John 12.24-25, p. 638. Cf. Romans 8.35-39, p. 628; Isaiah 53.1-12, pp. 457-58; Hadith of Muslim, p. 627.

**Romans 12.1:** Cf. Romans 6.13, p. 552; Suhi Chhant, M.5, p. 639.

To Thee as a sacrifice Zarathustra offers
the very life and being of his self;
he dedicates the first fruits of his loving
thoughts to Ahura Mazda;
he offers the best of his words and deeds
and willing obedience to the Divine Law.

*Zoroastrianism.* Avesta, Yasna 33.14

Let us all carry in ourselves the heart of parents and the body of a servant, and let us shed sweat for the sake of earth, tears for the sake of mankind, and blood for the sake of heaven. Let us never forget that we carry on our shoulders the historical cross: the responsibility to remove the grief and heartache of our Parent, the Great Lord of all creation. Let us all move forward to the way of salvation of the world.

*Unification Church.* Sun Myung Moon, 3-30-90

The wind was churning by his side
and pounding what was hard to bend,
when Kesin from the poison cup
drank in Rudra's company.

*Hinduism.* Rig Veda 10.136.7

Isaac willingly and gladly went with his father to Mount Moriah, to offer up his young life to the God whom he adored. As they were wending their way to perform the will of God, Isaac said to his father, "O father, I am yet young, and I am fearful lest my body tremble at the sight of the knife, causing you grief; I am fearful lest the offering shall not be a perfect one, perfect as I should like it to be."

*Judaism.* Midrash, Genesis Rabbah 56.11

It is better to suffer for doing right, if that is God's will, than for doing wrong.

*Christianity.* 1 Peter 3.17

It is not only physical bravery that counts. One must have the courage to face life as it is, to go through sorrows, and always sacrifice oneself for the sake of others.

*African Traditional Religions.* Kipsigis Saying (Kenya)

A sacrificial vessel:
The superior man, taking his stance as righteousness requires, adheres firmly to Heaven's decrees.

*Confucianism.* I Ching 50: Sacrificial Vessel

The Master said, "The determined scholar and the man of virtue will not seek to live at the expense of injuring their virtue. They will even sacrifice their lives to preserve their virtue complete."

*Confucianism.* Analects 15.8

Mencius said, "Fish is what I want; bear's palm is also what I want. If I cannot have both, I would rather take the bear's palm than fish. Life is what I want; dutifulness is also what I want. If I cannot have both, I would rather take dutifulness than life. On the one hand, though life is what I want, there is something I want more than life. That is why I do not cling to life at all costs. On the other hand, though death is what I loathe, there is something I loathe more than death. That is why there are troubles I do not avoid. If there is nothing a

**Yasna 33.14:** Cf. Yasna 34.12, p. 552; Suhi Chhant, M.5, p. 639.

**Sun Myung Moon 3-30-90:** Cf. Sun Myung Moon, 9-11-72, p. 529; 9-11-72, p. 691.

**Rig Veda 10.136.7:** Here the sacrifices of the *Kesin*, the long-haired ascetic, are likened to the draught of poison first drunk by Shiva (Rudra) by which he saved the world from calamity. According to a frequently reported tradition, when the gods and demons first churned the primeval ocean in order to create the universe and the ambrosial Soma, they also churned up a virulent poison which covered the universe with smoke and fumes. Shiva, for the sake of protecting all beings, swallowed the poison, whence, it is said, his throat became blue. The sage, by his self-sacrifice, finds God Shiva standing beside him. Cf. Sioux Sun Dance, pp. 693-94.

**Genesis Rabbah 56.11:** See Genesis 22.1-13, p. 438; Genesis Rabbah 56, p. 445.

**1 Peter 3.17:** Suffering and hardships come to all people, hence one might as well suffer for a godly purpose.

**Kipsigis Saying:** On sacrifice for the sake of others, see John 15.13, p. 691; Garland Śutra 23, p.692.

**Analects 15.8:** Cf. Analects 5.22 and 16.12, p. 635; Gittin 57b, p. 633.

man wants more than life, then why should he have scruples about any means, so long as it will serve to keep him alive? If there is nothing a man loathes more than death, then why should he have scruples about any means, so long as it helps him to avoid trouble? Yet there are ways of remaining alive and ways of avoiding death to which a man will not resort. In other words, there are things a man wants more than life and there are also things he loathes more than death. This is an attitude not confined to the moral man but common to all men. The moral man simply never loses it."

*Confucianism*. Mencius VI.A.10

## *Persecution and Martyrdom*

THE SUMMIT OF SACRIFICE is often thrust upon a man or woman in the form of persecution and even martyrdom. Few desire to be persecuted, yet persecution can be a blessing, for it pushes people to the realm of total self-sacrifice and self-denial. Hence we have the paradoxical fact of history that religion thrives in times of persecution.

Persecution is of no value if the person is crushed by it. But those who persevere with faith—even unto death—and gain victory over persecution achieve the highest goal and fellowship with God. They can enter the realm of the miraculous; they can attain the highest heaven, reserved for the martyrs and saints. In view of the beatification which comes through sacrifice, it is not surprising that those who receive persecution in faith often lose any negative feelings of hate or vengefulness toward their persecutors and even develop compassion for them.

This chapter begins with general passages on persecution, followed by passages on martyrdom. It concludes with specific examples of faithful people who have endured persecution and triumphed over it.

The Messenger of God said, "Surely, the gates of Paradise are beneath the shadow of swords."

*Islam*. Hadith of Muslim

As the elephant in the battlefield withstands the arrows shot from a bow, even so will I endure abuse; verily most people are lacking in virtue.

*Buddhism*. Dhammapada 320

In Ch'en, supplies ran short and his followers became so weak that they could not drag themselves onto their feet. Tzu-lu came to the Master and said indignantly, "Is it right that even gentlemen should be reduced to such straits?" The Master said, "A gentleman can withstand hardships; it is only the small man who, when submitted to them, is swept off his feet."

*Confucianism*. Analects 15.1

**Mencius VI.A.10:** cf. Chuang Tzu 4, p. 507-8.

**Hadith of Muslim:** This hadith recommends *jihad*, struggle on the way to God. The meaning of such struggles for God lies not in the killing of others, but in offering one's own life to defend true religion. Cf. Matthew 16.24-25, p. 625.

**Analects 15.1:** Cf. Mencius VI.A.10, pp. 626-27.

Blessed are you when men revile you and persecute you and utter all kinds of evil against you falsely on my account. Rejoice and be glad, for your reward is great in heaven, for so men persecuted the prophets who were before you.

*Christianity*. Matthew 5.11-12

Assuredly you will be tried in your property and in your persons, and you will hear much wrong from those who were given the Scripture before you and from the idolators. But if you persevere and ward off [evil], then that is of the steadfast heart of things.

*Islam*. Qur'an 3.186

The right attitude for the seeker of truth on this lofty Path is, "Let my people look askance; let my wife and children forsake me; let men deride; let kings punish; but I shall be steadfast, O Supreme Deity; I shall serve and ever serve Thee with mind, speech, body, and act; I shall not leave Thy Law."

*Hinduism*. Kularnava Tantra 2

Or do you think that you shall enter the Garden without such trials as came to those who passed away before you? They encountered suffering and adversity, and were so shaken in spirit that even the Apostle and those of faith who were with him cried, "When will come the help of God?" Ah! Verily the help of God is always near!

*Islam*. Qur'an 2.214

Monks, this is the meanest of callings, this of an almsman. A term of abuse in the world is this, to say "You scrap-gatherer! With bowl in hand you roam about!" Yet this is the calling entered on by those clansmen who are bent on the good because of good, not led thereto by fear.

*Buddhism*. Itivuttaka 89

It is painful never to take but what is freely given, and begging is a hard task. Common people say that men become monks because they will not work and are wretched. Weak men who are unable to bear these insults in villages or towns become disheartened like cowards in the battle. Perhaps a snarling dog will bite a hungry monk; in that case the weak will become disheartened like animals burnt by fire. Some who hate monks, revile them, "Those who lead such a miserable life are but atoning for their sins." Some call them names, as "naked, lowest of beggars, baldhead, scabby, filthy, nasty."... Some fools in outlying countries take a pious monk for a spy or a thief, bind him, and insult him with angry words. A weak monk, being hurt with a stick or a fist or a fruit, remembers his kind relations, just as a woman who in a fit has left her husband. All these hardships are difficult to bear; the weak return to their house like elephants who break down when covered with arrows.

*Jainism*. Sutrakritanga 1.3.1.6-17

Who shall separate us from the love of Christ? Shall tribulation, or distress, or persecution, or famine, or nakedness, or peril, or sword? As it is written,

> For thy sake we are being killed all the day long;
> we are regarded as sheep to be slaughtered.

No, in all these things we are more than conquerors through him who loved us. For I am sure that neither death, nor life, nor angels, nor principalities, nor things present, nor things to come, nor powers, nor height, nor depth, nor anything else in all creation, will be able to separate us from the love of God in Christ Jesus our Lord.

*Christianity*. Romans 8.35-39

**Matthew 5.11-12:** Cf. Matthew 10.24-25, pp. 586-87; Hebrews 11.1-38, pp. 539-40; Canticles Rabbah 2.5, p. 546.

**Qur'an 2.214:** Cf. Qur'an 3.145-47, p. 586; 4.75-76, pp. 742-43.

**Romans 8.35-39:** Cf. Matthew 10.1-20, pp. 586-87; 16.24-25, p. 625; 2 Corinthians 5.20-6.13, p. 724.

Precious in the sight of the Lord is the death of his saints.

*Judaism* and *Christianity*. Psalm 116.15

If you win over absolute persecution, you can stand as the object of God and God can intervene on your behalf. The reason for the development of religions is that they have overcome a great deal of persecution.

*Unification Church*. Sun Myung Moon, 4-3-83

Count not those who were slain in God's way as dead, but rather living with their Lord, by Him provided, rejoicing in the bounty that God has given them, and joyful in those who remain behind and have not joined them, because no fear shall be upon them, neither shall they sorrow, joyful in the blessing and bounty from God, and that God leaves not to waste the wage of the believers. And those who answered God and the Messenger after the wound had smitten them—to all those of them who did good and feared God—shall be a mighty wage.

To those to whom men said, "The people have gathered against you, therefore fear them"; but it increased them in faith, and they said, "God is sufficient for us; an excellent Guardian is He." So they returned with blessing and bounty from God, untouched by evil; they followed the good pleasure of God; and God is of bounty abounding.

*Islam*. Qur'an 3.169-74

Holy is the death of heroic men,
Who lay down their lives in an approved cause.
Such alone may be called heroes, as at the
Divine Portal obtain true honor:
Obtaining honor at the Divine Portal, with
honor they depart,
And in the hereafter they suffer not.
Such reward they shall obtain if on the Sole
Lord they meditate,
Whose service drives away all fears.
They utter not aloud their suffering; they bear
all in their minds—
The Lord Himself knows all.
Holy is the death of heroic men,
Who lay down their lives in an approved cause.

*Sikhism*. Adi Granth, Wadhans, Alahaniyan Dirges, M.1, pp. 579f.

Miracles were performed for our ancestors... because they were ready to sacrifice their lives for the sanctification of God's Name.

*Judaism*. Talmud, Berakot 20a

When Rabbi Akiba was taken out for execution, it was the hour for the recital of the Shema, and while they combed his flesh with iron combs, he was accepting upon himself the kingship of heaven [by reciting the Shema]. His disciples said to him, "Our teacher, even to this point?" He said to them, "All my days I have been troubled over this verse, "with all your soul" [Deuteronomy 6.5], [which I interpret] "even if He takes your soul." When shall I have the opportunity of fulfilling this? Now that I have the opportunity shall I not fulfill it?" He prolonged the last word [of the prayer] until he expired while saying it.

*Judaism*. Talmud, Berakot 61b

Arms pinioned, was I thrown down in a heap.
The elephant violently was goaded in the
head.
The elephant ran away trumpeting,
Declaring, "To this prostrate figure am I a
sacrifice;
Lord, in You alone lies my strength."
The Kazi urged the mahout to goad on the
elephant,

**Psalm 116.15:** Cf. Doctrine and Covenants 135.1, p. 435, on the martyrdom of Joseph Smith.

**Qur'an 3.169-74:** Cf. Qur'an 4.74-76, pp. 742-43; A Winnebago Father's Precepts, p. 742.

**Berakot 20a:** The sanctification of God's Name is to suffer martyrdom with the Jewish confession of faith, the Shema (p. 31), on the lips. See the following passage.

**Berakot 61b:** See the previous note and Canticles Rabbah 2.5, p. 546.

Threatening, "Mahout! I shall cut you to
 pieces!
Goad and drive the elephant!"
But the elephant, meditating on God, would
 not move:
In his heart was lodged the Lord.
The people queried, "What offense has this
 holy man committed,
That in bonds he is thrown to be trampled by
 the elephant?"
The elephant bowed again and again to the
 heap before it.
The benighted Kazi did not realize this;
Three times he ordered this trial
But his hard heart still was not softened.
Says Kabir, The Lord is my guardian.
In absorption in Him lies His servant's life.

*Sikhism*. Adi Granth, Gaund, Kabir, p. 870

After the Buddha's extinction,
In the last dread evil age,
We will proclaim this sutra.
Though many ignorant men
Will with evil mouth abuse us,
And beat us with swords and staves,
We will endure it all.
Monks in that evil age,
Heretical, warped, suspicious,
Crying "attained" when they have not,
Will have minds full of arrogance....
Others, greedy for gain,
Will preach the Law to laymen
And be revered by the world as arhats
Of the six transcendent powers;
These men, cherishing evil minds,
Ever thinking of earthly things,
Assuming the name of "forest dwellers,"
Will love to calumniate us,
Saying words such as these—
"All these bhikshu-fellows,
Because of love of gain,
Preach an heretical doctrine;
Themselves have composed this sutra
To delude the people of the world;
For the sake of acquiring fame,
They specialize in this sutra."
Always in the assemblies,
In order that they may ruin us,
To kings and to their ministers,
To brahmins and to citizens,
To other groups of bhikshus,
Of us they will speak slanderously,
Saying, "These are men with false views,
Who proclaim heretical doctrines."
But, from reverence for Buddha
We will endure those evils.
Though contemptuously addressed as—
"All you Buddhas!"
Even such scorn and arrogance
We will patiently endure
In the corrupt kalpa's evil age.
Abounding in fear and dread,
Devils will take possession of them
To curse, abuse, and insult us.
But we, reverently believing Buddha,
Will wear the armor of long-suffering;
For the sake of preaching this sutra
Every hard thing we will endure.
We will not love body nor life,
But care only for the Supreme Way.

*Buddhism*. Lotus Sutra 13

King Nebuchadnezzar made an image of gold, whose height was sixty cubits and its breadth six cubits. He set it up on the plain of Dura, in the province of Babylon.... [At] the dedication of the image... the herald proclaimed aloud, "You are commanded, O peoples, nations, and languagues, that when you hear the sound of the horn, pipe, lyre, trigon, harp, bagpipe, and every kind of music, you are to fall down and worship the golden image that King Nebuchadnezzar has set up; and whoever does

**Gaund, Kabir:** The Adi Granth contains numerous compositions by Indian saints, both Hindu and Muslim, called *bhaktas*, who preceded Guru Nanak. Among them the poet Kabir (1380-1460 A.D.) has pride of place; over 500 of his hymns are recorded in the Adi Granth. This hymn describes one of his trials.

**Lotus Sutra 13:** This stanza, called the Kanji-hon, gave inspiration and fortitude to Nichiren, Japan's leading champion of the Lotus Sutra, when he was exiled and persecuted by the leaders of rival Buddhist schools for his dedication to spreading its message.

not fall down and worship shall immediately be cast into a burning fiery furnace." Therefore, as soon as all the peoples heard the sound of the horn, pipe, lyre, trigon, harp, bagpipe, and every kind of music, all the peoples, nations, and languages fell down and worshipped the golden image which King Nebuchadnezzar had set up.

At that time certain Chaldeans came forward and maliciously accused the Jews. They said to King Nebuchadnezzar, "O king, live for ever! You, O king, have made a decree, that every man who hears the sound of the horn, pipe, lyre, trigon, harp, bagpipe, and every kind of music, shall fall down and worship the golden image; and whoever does not fall down and worship shall be cast into a burning fiery furnace. There are certain Jews whom you have appointed over the affairs of the province of Babylon: Shadrach, Meshach, and Abednego. These men, O king, pay no heed to you; they do not serve your gods or worship the golden image which you have set up."

Then Nebuchadnezzar in furious rage commanded that Shadrach, Meshach, and Abednego be brought. Then they brought these men before the king. Nebuchadnezzar said to them, "Is it true, O Shadrach, Meshach, and Abednego, that you do not serve my gods or worship the golden image which I have set up? Now if you are ready when you hear the sound of the horn, pipe, lyre, trigon, harp, bagpipe, and every kind of music, to fall down and worship the image which I have made, well and good; but if you do not worship, you shall immediately be cast into a burning fiery furnace; and who is the god that will deliver you out of my hands?"

Shadrach, Meshach, and Abednego answered the king, "O Nebuchadnezzar, we have no need to answer you in this matter. If it be so, our God whom we serve is able to deliver us from the burning fiery furnace; and he will deliver us out of your hand, O king. But if not, be it known to you, O king, that we will not serve your gods or worship the golden image which you have set up."

Then Nebuchadnezzar was full of fury, and the expression of his face was changed against Shadrach, Meshach, and Abednego. He ordered the furnace heated seven times more than it was wont to be heated. And he ordered certain mighty men of his army to bind Shadrach, Meshach, and Abednego, and to cast them into the burning fiery furnace. These men bound them in their mantles, their tunics, their hats, and their other garments, and cast them into the burning fiery furnace. Because the king's order was strict and the furnace very hot, the flame of the fire slew those men who took up Shadrach, Meshach, and Abednego. And these three men, Shadrach, Meshach, and Abednego, fell bound into the burning fiery furnace.

Then King Nebuchadnezzar was astonished and rose up in haste. He said to his counselors, "Did we not cast three men bound into the fire?" They answered the king, "True, O king." He answered, "But I see four men loose, walking in the midst of the fire, and they are not hurt; and the appearance of the fourth is like a son of the gods."

Then Nebuchadnezzar came near to the door of the burning fiery furnace and said, "Shadrach, Meshach, and Abednego, servants of the Most High God, come forth, and come here!" Then Shadrach, Meshach, and Abednego came out from the fire. And the satraps, the prefects, the governors, and the king's counselors gathered together and saw that the fire had not had any power over the bodies of those men; the hair of their heads was not singed, their mantles were not harmed, and no smell of the fire had come upon them. Nebuchadnezzar said, "Blessed be the God of Shadrach, Meshach, and Abednego, who has sent his angel and delivered his servants, who trusted in him, and set at nought the king's command, and yielded up their bodies rather than serve and worship any god except their own God."

*Judaism* and *Christianity*.
Daniel 3.1-28

**Daniel 3.1-28:** Cf. Qur'an 21.51-71, p. 428; Ramayana, Yuddha Kanda 118-20, p. 560; Mahaparinirvana Sutra 424-33, pp. 538-39; Hebrews 11.32-34, pp. 539-40.

Seated on the naked ground, Sita, who was fixed in virtue, resembled a branch severed from a tree that had fallen to earth. Her limbs covered with a soiled cloth, she, who was worthy of ornaments, now no longer adorned, resembled a lotus stalk stained with mud and, though radiant, her beauty was dimmed. In imagination, she took refuge with that lion among men, Rama, her mind a chariot drawn by the steeds of resolution. Yet that charming princess, devoted to Rama, emaciated, weeping, separated from her kinfolk, was a prey to anxiety and grief and saw no end to her misfortune....

And beholding that blameless Maithili [Sita] with her beautiful dark eyes and graceful lashes, Ravana, to his own destruction, sought to seduce her: "O lady, whose thighs resemble the trunk of an elephant, who, beholding me seeks to conceal your breasts and your body as if you feared me, O lady of large eyes, I love you. Be gracious to me, O lady of charming looks, adored by all the world! There is no man present here nor any titan able to change his form at will; therefore banish the fear which I inspire in you, O Sita.

"It has ever been the unquestioned and special privilege of titans to unite themselves with the wives of others, either taking them of their own free will or bearing them away by force. In spite of this, O Maithili, I shall not lay hands on you since you have no affection for me but, for myself, I am completely under your sway. Therefore trust in me and respond to my love. O goddess, have no fear of me, take courage, O dear one, and do not let yourself be consumed with grief. To wear but a single plait, to lie on the earth in soiled attire and fast unnecessarily does not become you. In my company, O Maithili, enjoy garlands, perfumes, sandalwood, ornaments, wine, rich beds and seats, singing, dancing, and music. You are a pearl among women; do not remain in this condition; adorn yourself as heretofore. Having united yourself with me, O lady of lovely form, what will not be yours?..."

Hearing the words of that terrible titan, Sita, overwhelmed with grief, answered in a faint and feeble voice. The unfortunate Sita, afflicted and trembling, faithful to her lord and anxious to preserve her virtue, her heart fixed on Rama, placed a straw between Ravana and herself and with a sweet smile answered him, saying, "Take back your heart and set it on your own consorts. As a sinner may not aspire to heaven, so you should not expect to win me. That which should never be done and is condemned in a woman faithful to her lord, I shall never do. Born in a noble house, I have been joined to a pious family."

Then turning her back on him, she continued, "You are not able to tempt me with wealth and riches; as the light of the sun cannot be separated from the sun so do I belong to Raghava [Rama]. Having rested on the arm of that Lord of Men, how should I depend on any other? Like unto the spiritual truth known to a brahmin faithful to his vows, I belong to the Lord of the World alone and am lawfully wedded to him. It is to your own advantage to restore me to Rama, wretched as I am like a she-elephant anxiously awaiting her mate in the forest. It behoves you to seek Rama's friendship, that lion among men, if you desire to preserve Lanka and do not wish to bring about your own destruction...."

Ravana, lord of the titans, was filled with indignation, and said, "I shall grant you two months as the term assigned to you, after which you must share my bed. If you should refuse, my cooks shall mince your limbs for my morning repast."

*Hinduism.* Ramayana, Sundara Kanda 19-22

When Joseph attained his full manhood, We gave him power and knowledge; thus do We reward those who do right. But the woman in whose house he lived sought to seduce him from his true self: she bolted the doors and said, "Now come, dear!" He said, "God forbid! Truly

**Ramayana, Sundara Kanda 19-22:** In addition to remaining unmoved by Ravana's threats, Sita must further prove her fidelity to Rama, and she submits herself to an ordeal by fire; see Yuddha Kanda 118-20, p. 560.

your husband is my lord! He made my sojourn agreeable! Truly to no good come those who do wrong!" And with passion did she desire him, and he would have desired her, but that he saw the evidence of his Lord: thus did We order that We might turn away from him all evil and shameful deeds, for he was one of Our servants, sincere and purified. So they both raced each other to the door, and she tore his shirt from the back; and they met her husband near the door.

She said, "What is the penalty for one who formed an evil design against your wife but prison or a grievous chastisement?" He said, "It was she that sought to seduce me—from my true self." And one of her household saw and bore witness, "If it be that his shirt is rent from the front, then is her tale true, and he is a liar! But if it be that his shirt is torn from the back, then is she the liar, and he is telling the truth!" So when he saw his shirt, that it was torn at the back, her husband said, "Behold, it is a snare of you women! Truly, mighty is your snare! O Joseph, pass this over! O wife, ask forgiveness for your sin, for truly you have been at fault."

Ladies said in the city, "The wife of the 'Aziz is seeking to seduce her slave from his true self; truly he has inspired her with violent love; we see she is evidently going astray." When she heard of their malicious talk, she sent for them and prepared a banquet for them; she gave each of them a knife and said [to Joseph], "Come out before them." When they saw him, they did extol him and cut their hands; they said, "God preserve us! No mortal is this! This is none other than a noble angel!" She said, "There before you is the man about whom you blamed me! I did seek to seduce him from his true self, but he did firmly save himself guiltless.... And now, if he does not do my bidding, he shall certainly be cast into prison and be of the company of the vilest!"

*Islam*. Qur'an 12.22-32

On one occasion four hundred boys and girls were carried off for immoral purposes. They divined what they were wanted for and said to themselves, "If we drown in the sea we shall attain the life of the future world." The eldest among them expounded, " 'The Lord said, I will bring them back from Bashan, I will bring them back from the depths of the sea' [Psalm 68.23].... 'I will bring them back from the depths of the sea,' [refers to] those who drown in the sea." When the girls heard this they all leaped into the sea. The boys then drew the moral for themselves, saying, "If those for whom it is natural [to succumb] act so, shall not we, for whom it is unnatural?" They also leaped into the sea. Of them the text says, "Yea, for Thy sake we are killed all the day long, we are counted as sheep for the slaughter" [Psalm 44.23].

*Judaism*. Talmud, Gittin 57b

Jeremiah stood in the court of the temple of the Lord, and said to all the people, "Thus says the Lord of hosts, the God of Israel, Behold, I am bringing upon this city and upon all its towns all the evil that I have pronounced against it, because they have stiffened their neck, refusing to heed my words." Now Pashhur the priest, the son of Immer, who was chief officer in the temple of the Lord, heard Jeremiah prophesying these things. Then Pashhur beat Jeremiah the prophet and put him in the stocks that were in the upper Benjamin Gate of the temple....

**Qur'an 12.22-32:** For the Bible's version of this story, and subsequent events when Joseph is cast into prison on account of the charges made against him, see Genesis 39-40.

**Gittin 57b:** Another well-known instance where Jews preferred suicide to enslavement occurred at the defense of Masada. This desert fortress, defended by less than 1,000, including women and children, was besieged by a Roman army of 15,000 for almost two years after the fall of Jerusalem in 70 A.D. When the Romans finally breached the walls, they found that the defenders had taken their own lives. Today Masada has become a symbol of Israeli national heroism. Cf. Analects 15.8, p. 626; Hebrews 11.35-37, pp. 539-40; Acarangasutra 7, pp. 241-42; Canticles Rabbah 2.5, p. 546.

O Lord, thou hast deceived me,
and I was deceived;
Thou art stronger than I,
and thou hast prevailed.
I have become a laughingstock all the day;
every one mocks me.
For whenever I speak, I cry out,
I shout, "Violence and destruction!"
For the word of the Lord has become for me
a reproach and derision all day long.
If I say, "I will not mention him,
or speak any more in his name,"
there is in my heart as it were a burning fire
shut up in my bones;
and I am weary of holding it in,
and I cannot.
For I hear many whispering,
"Terror is on every side!"
"Denounce him! Let us denounce him!"
say all my familiar friends,
watching for my fall.
"Perhaps he will be deceived,
then we can overcome him,
and take our revenge on him."
But the Lord is with me as a dread warrior;
therefore my persecutors will stumble,
they will not overcome me.
They will be greatly shamed,
for they will not succeed.
Their eternal dishonor
will never be forgotten.
O Lord of hosts, who triest the righteous,
who seest the heart and the mind,
let me see thy vengeance upon them,
for to thee have I committed my cause.

*Judaism* and *Christianity*.
Jeremiah 19.14-20.2, 20.7-12

And Stephen, full of grace and power, did great wonders and signs among the people. Then some of those who belonged to the congregation of the Freedmen [as it was called], and some of the Cyrenians, the Alexandrians, and those from Cilicia and Asia, arose and disputed with Stephen. But they could not withstand the wisdom and the spirit with which he spoke. Then they secretly instigated men, who said, "We have heard him speak blasphemous words against Moses and God." And they stirred up the people and the elders and the scribes, and they came upon him and seized him and brought him before the council, and set up false witnesses who said, "This man never ceases to speak words against this holy place and the Law; for we have heard him say that this Jesus of Nazareth will destroy this place [the temple], and will change the customs which Moses delivered to us." And gazing at him, all who sat in the council saw that his face was like the face of an angel.

And the high priest said, "Is this so?" And Stephen said, "Brethren and fathers, hear me.... The Most High does not dwell in houses made with hands; as the prophet says,

Heaven is my throne,
and the earth is my footstool.
What house would you build for me, says
the Lord,
or what is the place of my rest?
Did not my hand make all these things?

You stiff-necked people, uncircumcised in heart and ears, you always resist the Holy Spirit. Which of the prophets did not your fathers persecute? And they killed those who announced beforehand the coming of the Righteous One, whom you have now betrayed and murdered, you who received the Law as delivered by angels and did not keep it."

Now when they heard these things they were enraged, and they ground their teeth against him. But he, full of the Holy Spirit, gazed into heaven and saw the glory of God, and Jesus standing at the right hand of God; and he said, "Behold, I see the heavens opened, and the Son of man standing at the right hand of God." But they cried out with a loud voice and stopped their ears and rushed together

**Jeremiah 20.7-12:** The people mock Jeremiah by his own words, 'Terror on every side.' Yet it was not long before Jeremiah's prophecies of terror and destruction came to pass and Jerusalem was laid waste. For other verses on the suffering of the prophets, see Micah 2.6-11, p. 734; Amos 7.10-17, pp. 735-36; Mark 6.4, p. 428; Qur'an 25.31, p. 430; Hebrews 11.32-38, pp. 539-40; Matthew 23.37, p. 325; Acts 7.51-52, below.

against him. Then they cast him out of the city and stoned him; and the witnesses laid down their garments at the feet of a young man named Saul. And as they were stoning Stephen, he prayed, "Lord Jesus, receive my spirit." And he knelt down and cried with a loud voice, "Lord, do not hold this sin against them." And when he had said this, he died.

*Christianity*. Acts 6.8-7.60

When the Rajah of Kalinga mutilated my body, I was at that time free from the idea of an ego-identity, a personality, a being, and a separated individuality. Wherefore? Because then when my limbs were cut away piece by piece, had I been bound by the distinctions aforesaid, feelings of anger and hatred would have been aroused within me.

*Buddhism*. Diamond Sutra 14

The Master said, "Po I and Shu Ch'i never bore old ills in mind and had but the faintest feelings of rancor.

"Po I and Shu Ch'i starved at the foot of Mount Shou-yang; yet the people sing their praises down to this day."

*Confucianism*. Analects 5.22, 16.12

They seized Paul and Silas and dragged them into the marketplace before the rulers; and when they had brought them to the magistrates they said, "These men are Jews and they are disturbing our city. They advocate customs which it is not lawful for us Romans to practice." The crowd joined in attacking them; and the magistrates tore their garments off them and gave orders to beat them with rods. And when they had inflicted many blows upon them, they threw them into prison, charging the jailer to keep them safely. Having received this charge, he put them into the inner prison and fastened their feet in the stocks.

But about midnight Paul and Silas were praying and singing hymns to God, and the prisoners were listening to them, and suddenly there was a great earthquake, so that the foundations of the prison were shaken; and immediately all the doors were opened and everyone's fetters were unfastened. When the jailer woke and saw that the prison doors were open, he drew his sword and was about to kill himself, supposing that the prisoners had escaped. But Paul cried with a loud voice, "Do not harm yourself, for we are all here." And he called for lights and rushed in, and trembling with fear he fell down before Paul and Silas, and brought them out and said, "Men, what must I do to be saved?"

*Christianity*. Acts 16.19-30

The demon-king Hiranyakashipu had formerly brought the three worlds under his authority, usurped the sovereignty of Indra, and exercised of himself the functions of the sun, of air, of water, of fire, of the moon. He himself was the god of riches, and he appropriated all to himself.

One day his son Prahlada came to the court and bowed before his father. Hiranyakashipu said to him, "Repeat, boy, what you have acquired in your studies." "Hear, sire," replied Prahlada, "the substance of what I have learned. I have learned to adore Him who is

**Acts 6.8-7.60:** Stephen's classmate Saul helped instigate his death. Later Saul would convert and, renamed Paul, become the greatest of the Apostles. Note Stephen's last words of utter forgiveness for those who killed him, following the example of Jesus on the cross; see Luke 23.34, pp. 428-30; Matthew 10.24-25, pp. 586-87; also Sun Myung Moon, 10-20-73, p. 702. Under the Roman persecutions of the first three centuries, tens of thousands of Christians would follow Stephen's example of faith when offered the choice: deny Christ or be thrown to the lions.

**Diamond Sutra 14:** Buddha is referring to one of his previous incarnations, the lives of whom are popularized in the Jataka tales.

**Analects 5.22 and 16.12:** Po I and Shu Ch'i were legendary brothers who, out of loyalty, refused to take up arms against their wicked overlord when the occasion arose, despite his having wronged them. Rather, without complaint, they resigned their rights of accession to their state and lived in poverty. Their example is a model of goodness, according to Confucius. Cf. Analects 15.8, p. 626; Shih Chi 47, p. 433.

without beginning, middle, or end, increase or diminution; the imperishable Lord of the world, the universal Cause." On hearing these words, the sovereign of the demons, his eyes red with wrath and lips swollen with indignation, turned to his son's preceptor and said, "Vile brahmin, what is this preposterous commendation of my foe that, in disrespect to me, you have taught this boy to utter?" "King of the demons," replied the guru, "do not give way to passion; that which your son has uttered, he has not been taught by me." "By whom, then, boy, has this lesson been taught you?" "Vishnu, father," answered Prahlada, "is the instructor of the whole world: what else should anyone teach or learn, save Him, the Supreme Spirit?" "Blockhead," exclaimed the king. "Who is this Vishnu, whose name you thus reiterate so impertinently before me, who am the sovereign of the three worlds? Are you desirous of death, fool, that you give the title of supreme lord to anyone whilst I live?" "Vishnu, who is God," said Prahlada, "is the Creator and Protector, not of me alone, but of all human beings, and even, father, of you: He is the Supreme Lord of all. Why should you, sire, be offended?"...

Prahlada returned to his studies. Later he again came before his father, who asked him to recite a poem. Prahlada began, "May He from whom matter and soul originate, He who is the cause of all this creation, Vishnu, be favorable to us." On hearing which, Hiranyakashipu exclaimed, "Kill the wretch; he is not fit to live, a traitor to his friends, a burning brand to his own race!" and his attendents obediently snatched up their weapons and rushed in crowds upon Prahlada to destroy him. The prince calmly looked upon them, and said, "Demons, as truly as Vishnu is present in your weapons and in my body, so truly shall these weapons fail to harm me," and accordingly, although struck heavily and repeatedly by hundreds of the demons, the prince felt not the least pain, and his strength was ever renewed.

[After suffering many tortures at the hands of his father for the sake of his devotion to Vishnu, Vishnu finally appeared to him.]

Prahlada said [to Vishnu], "I have been hated, for that I assiduously proclaimed Thy praise, do Thou, O Lord, pardon in my father this sin that he has committed. Weapons have been hurled against me; I have been thrown into the flames; I have been bitten by venomous snakes; and poison has been mixed with my food; I have been bound and cast into the sea; and heavy rocks have been heaped upon me, but all this, and whatever ill besides has been wrought against me; whatever wickedness has been done to me, because I put my faith in Thee; all, through Thy mercy, has been suffered by me unharmed. Do Thou therefore free my father from this iniquity."

*Hinduism.* Vishnu Purana 1.17-20

❖

**Vishnu Purana 1.17-20:** For variations on the theme of a righteous son to a demonic father, see Matsya Purana 180.5-7, p. 508; Vishnu Purana 3.17-88, p. 318.

CHAPTER 18

# SELF-DENIAL AND RENUNCIATION

BECAUSE SIN, IGNORANCE, AND THE EVIL PASSIONS cloud our original nature, it is exceedingly difficult to reach God or the goal of religion simply through faith, prayer, worship, offerings, and good works. Our turbid and inconstant self, strengthened by the passions and desires of the body, causes even our good motives and desires to become distorted and confused. The ego gets in the way of a true relationship to God. We are caught up in pride, bound to our possessions and relations, desirous of having ample food and drink and comforts of life. For these reasons, the religious life is not only a straight path towards God, but also a negative path to deny the self, the body, and all the bright and attractive things of the world.

The path of self-denial includes denial of self, mind, desires, body, wealth, family, the world, and life itself. Through self-denial and separation from everything tempting and attractive about the world, the soul is purified and becomes an absolute void. In Buddhist terms, it realizes the truth of Emptiness. From a theistic perspective, we can say that only when the soul becomes empty of ego does it become a vessel suitable to be filled by God.

❖

# *Self-denial and No-self*

SELF-DENIAL IS NECESSARY to overcome the hindrances of egoism, pride, and selfish desires which obscure the true nature within. The person who is always concerned with himself or herself, is trapped in the "ego-cage of 'I,' 'me,' and 'mine.' " Consequently, he can neither realize his own true self nor relate to Ultimate Reality. From a Hindu perspective, denying "I," "me," and "mine" is, in fact, a way to find the true "I" that is transcendent and one with Reality. In the Christian perspective it is a way to recover the true self, which is loving and compassionate, having been created in the image of God. Both perspectives affirm the paradox that "he who loves his life loses it, and he who hates his life will keep it." For more on this paradox, see *Reversal and Restoration*, pp. 387-91.

Buddhism also teaches that the path to the religious goal requires one to deny the self and all egoistic grasping. But it goes further, grounding the practice of self-denial on the ontological statement that any form of a self is illusory. Buddhism is most sensitive to the insight that self-denial, when done for the purpose of seeking unity with an Absolute Self or God, can become subtly perverted into a form of pride and self-affirmation. Total self-denial should therefore dispense even with the goal of a transcendent Self. There is no self, either on earth or in heaven; all forms are transient, subject to birth and death. A number of texts explaining this doctrine of No-self (*anatta*) are collected here: more may be found under *Formless, Emptiness, Mystery*, pp. 55-60, and *Original Mind, No-mind*, pp. 146-51.

He who has no thought of "I" and "mine" whatever toward his mind and body, he who grieves not for that which he has not, he is, indeed, called a bhikkhu.

*Buddhism*. Dhammapada 367

They are forever free who renounce all selfish desires and break away from the ego-cage of "I," "me," and "mine" to be united with the Lord. Attain to this, and pass from death to immortality.

*Hinduism*. Bhagavad Gita 2.71

If any man would come after me, let him deny himself and take up his cross and follow me. For whoever would save his life will lose it; and whoever loses his life for my sake and the gospel's will save it.

*Christianity*. Mark 8.34-36

Truly, truly, I say to you, unless a grain of wheat falls into the earth and dies, it remains alone; but if it dies, it bears much fruit. He who loves his life loses it, and he who hates his life in this world will keep it for eternal life.

*Christianity*. John 12.24-25

**Dhammapada 367:** Cf. Madhyamakavatara 3, p. 292; Diamond Sutra 14, p. 635.

**Bhagavad Gita 2.71:** Cf. Bhagavad Gita 5.10-12, p. 554; Maitri Upanishad 3.2, p. 292; Srimad Bhagavatam 11.4, p. 291; Katha Upanishad 3.13, p. 601.

**Mark 8.34-36:** To bear the cross and sacrifice oneself for others, one must first deny the self and its desires. Cf. Matthew 10.24-25, pp. 586-87; 23.12, p. 387; Luke 14.26, p. 676; Philippians 2.6-11, p. 440; Romans 8.9-17, p. 407; Acts 6.8-7.60, pp. 634-35.

**John 12.24-25:** Cf. Matthew 16.24-25, p. 625.

O Son of Man! If you love Me, turn away from yourself; and if you seek My pleasure, regard not your own; that you may die in Me and I may eternally live in you.

*Baha'i Faith.* Hidden Words of Baha'u'llah, Arabic 7

The Man of the Way wins no fame,
The highest virtue wins no gain,
The Great Man has no self.

*Taoism.* Chuang Tzu 17

Torah abides only with him who regards himself as nothing.

*Judaism.* Talmud, Sota 21b

Where egoism exists, Thou art not experienced,
Where Thou art, is not egoism.
You who are learned, expound in your mind
This inexpressible proposition.

*Sikhism.* Adi Granth, Maru-ki-Var, M.1, p. 1092

Yen Yüan asked about perfect virtue. The Master said, "To subdue one's self and return to propriety is perfect virtue. If a man can for one day subdue himself and return to propriety, all under heaven will ascribe perfect virtue to him."

*Confucianism.* Analects 12.1.1

The pursuit of learning is to increase day after day.
The pursuit of Tao is to decrease day after day.
It is to decrease and further decrease until one reaches the point of taking no action.
No action is undertaken, and yet nothing is left undone.

*Taoism.* Tao Te Ching 48

If you do not deny yourself completely, restoration through indemnity is impossible. Indemnity conditions can be realized only by completely denying yourself. The standard of absolute denial should be established toward the individual, the family, the race, the world, the cosmos, and God.

*Unification Church.* Sun Myung Moon, 4-3-83

Would one die while living, thus crossing the ocean of existence.

*Sikhism.* Adi Granth, Suhi Chhant, M.5, p. 777

In the evening do not expect [to live till] morning, and in the morning do not expect evening. Prepare as long as you are in good health for sickness, and so long as you are alive for death.

*Islam.* Forty Hadith of an-Nawawi 40

I have been crucified with Christ; it is no longer I who live, but Christ who lives in me; and the life I now live in the flesh I live by faith in the Son of God, who loved me and gave himself for me.

*Christianity.* Galatians 2.20

Remember, those who fear death shall not escape it, and those who aspire to immortality shall not achieve it.

*Islam.* Nahjul Balagha, Sermon 43

Seek not for life on earth or in heaven. Thirst for life is delusion. Knowing life to be transitory, wake up from this dream of ignorance and strive to attain knowledge and freedom.

*Hinduism.* Srimad Bhagavatam 11.13

**Sota 21b:** Cf. Abot 2.4, p. 551.

**Maru-ki-Var, M.1:** Cf. Diamond Sutra 9, p. 650.

**Tao Te Ching 48:** Cf. Tao Te Ching 16, p. 601; 19, p. 657; 22, pp. 390-91; Chuang Tzu 6, p. 413.

**Sun Myung Moon, 4-3-83:** Indemnity and self-denial are necessary because of the Fall; see Divine Principle I.3.2.1, p. 389n. Cf. Luke 14.26, p. 676.

**Galatians 2.20:** Cf. Romans 8.9-17, p. 407; 12.1, p. 625; Ephesians 2.8-10, p. 540.

You, who sit on the top of a hundred-foot pole, although you have entered the Way, you are not yet genuine. Proceed on from the top of the pole, and you will show your whole body in the ten directions.

Mumon's Comment: If you go on further and turn your body about, no place is left where you are not the master. But even so, tell me, how will you go on further from the top of a hundred-foot pole? Eh?

*Buddhism.* Mumonkan 46

A monk asked Baso, "What is the Buddha?" Baso answered, "No mind, no Buddha."

*Buddhism.* Mumonkan 33

"All states are without self." When one sees this in wisdom, then he becomes dispassionate toward the painful. This is the path to purity.

*Buddhism.* Dhammapada 279

"The body, brethren, is not the self. If body were the self, this body would not be subject to sickness, and one could say of body, 'Let my body be thus; let my body not be thus.' But inasmuch as body is not the self, that is why body is subject to sickness, and one cannot say of body, 'Let my body be thus; let my body not be thus.'

"Feeling is not the self. If feeling were the self, then feeling would not be subject to sickness, and one could say of feeling, 'Let my feeling be thus; let my feeling not be thus.'...

"Likewise perception... the [volitional] activities... and consciousness are not the self. If consciousness were the self, then consciousness would not be subject to sickness, and one could say of consciousness, 'Let my consciousness be thus; let my consciousness not be thus'; but inasmuch as consciousness is not the self, that is why consciousness is subject to sickness, and that is why one cannot say of consciousness, 'Let my consciousness be thus; let my consciousness not be thus.'

"Now what do you think, brethren, is body permanent or impermanent?"

"Impermanent, Lord."

"And is the impermanent painful or pleasant?"

"Painful, Lord."

"Then what is impermanent, painful, and unstable by nature, is it fitting to consider as, 'this is mine, this am I, this is my self'?"

"Surely not, Lord."

"So also is it with feeling, perception, the activities, and consciousness. Therefore, brethren, every body whatever, be it past, future, or present, be it inward or outward, gross or subtle, lowly or eminent, far or near—every body should be thus regarded, as it really is, by right insight—'this is not mine; this am not I; this is not my self.'

"Every feeling whatever, every perception whatever, all activities whatsoever, every consciousness whatever [must likewise be so regarded].

"Thus perceiving, brethren, the well-taught noble disciple feels disgust for body, feels disgust for feeling, for perception, for the activities, for consciousness. Feeling disgust he is repelled; being repelled, he is freed; knowledge arises that in the freed is emancipation; so he knows, 'destroyed is rebirth; lived is the religious life; done is my task; for life in these conditions there is no hereafter.'"

*Buddhism.* Samyutta Nikaya iii.68

**Mumonkan 46:** The issue is grasping and dependence upon the body and sense experience, and fear of going beyond its limits. See Seng Ts'an, pp. 150-51.

**Mumonkan 33:** Implicit in this koan is the instruction to deny not only the self but also any object of attainment—even the Buddha himself; see Sutta Nipata 1072-76, p. 379; 919-20, p. 393; Sutra of Hui Neng 2, p. 58. The third of the Four Noble Truths speaks of the eradication of desire or striving, even striving after enlightenment. Compare Mumonkan 30, p. 74, which asserts the seeming opposite.

**Dhammapada 279:** The self is rightly denied because it truly does not exist; this is the Buddhist teaching on no-self (*anatta*). See Sutta Nipata 1072-76, p. 379; 919-20, p. 393.

**Samyutta Nikaya iii.68:** Matter (the body), sensation (feelings), cognition (perception), volition (the activities), and the consciousness which depends upon them are called the five aggregates (*skandhas*). The Buddha taught that these aggregates, which are commonly thought to constitute the self, are not the self. They are impermanent and unreal, and so is the self which is thought to consist of them. Cf. Majjhima Nikaya i.142-45, p. 659; Diamond Sutra 14, p. 635; Sutta Nipata 1072-76, p. 379.

## *Repentance, Confession, and Restitution*

REPENTANCE IS A STEP on the road to recovery of a relationship with God or realization of the original nature. Sins, attachments, and mistaken views must be acknowledged as such; then it is possible to turn away from the old life and set out on the new path of faith. Since accumulated sins and delusions form a barrier obscuring the presence of God or the true self, repentance is a condition for God to forgive the sin and eradicate illusion, that the divine Presence may once again grace the penitent's life.

Repentance is sometimes misunderstood as being fulfilled by words of contrition uttered in prayer. Words of contrition are indeed significant when they reflect a fresh inner realization that a particular course of action was wrong, and when they are accompanied by a sincere vow not to repeat the sin. But that is only the first stage of repentance. The second stage, one far more efficacious, is to confess the sin to others, particularly a confession to the person who had been wronged. The humiliation and shame which accompanies confessing one's sin to another makes such repentance extremely serious, and laying one's sins out in the open is a powerful cathartic. The third stage of repentance is to make some substantial compensation for the past misdeed. This means to do penance or to make restitution to the person who had been wronged, or, if that is not possible, to someone else representing that person. Finally, repentance should result in an actual change of direction in the life of the penitent, as he endeavors to perform good deeds and eschew his former transgressions.

The passages in this section cover these dimensions of repentance. First are texts setting forth repentance as a remedy for sin. Next we have several typical prayers of repentance. Third are texts enjoining the penitent to confess his sins to others, holding nothing back. Several texts are critical of delaying such confessions till the time of death. Fourth are texts which recommend acts of penance and restitution. Finally, we have gathered texts evaluating the firmness of repentance, chiefly by whether or not the penitent slides back to repeating the behavior for which he had repented, and whether his mind and spirit are truly renewed.

Repent, for the kingdom of heaven is at hand.

*Christianity*. Matthew 3.2

Truly, God loves those who repent, and He loves those who cleanse themselves.

*Islam*. Qur'an 2.222

Great is repentance; it turns premeditated sins into incentives for right conduct.

*Judaism*. Talmud, Yoma 86b

The grace of the Lord of heaven and earth is infinite and boundless; He has endowed you with the Beautiful Gift, called the Spirit of Repentance, with which to light up and purify yourself from sin.

*Omoto Kyo*. Michi-no-Shiori

**Matthew 3.2:** Here the Kingdom of Heaven is 'at hand' not only in the eschatological sense that the time of the Messiah has drawn near—as was the case in Jesus' day. The Kingdom of Heaven is also at hand for each person as he prepares himself for it. Cf. Acts 2.38, p. 611; Abot 4.22, p. 237.

**Qur'an 2.222:** Cf. Forty Hadith of an-Nawawi 42, p. 372; Isaiah 57.15, p. 73.

Concern over remorse and humiliation depends on the borderline. The urge to blamelessness depends on remorse.

*Confucianism.* I Ching, Great Commentary 1.3.4

If one hides the evil, it adds and grows. If one bares it and repents, the sin dies out. Therefore all Buddhas say that the wise do not hide sin.

*Buddhism.* Mahaparinirvana Sutra 560

The sacrifice acceptable to God is a broken
spirit;
a broken and contrite heart, O God, thou wilt
not despise.

*Judaism* and *Christianity.* Psalm 51.17

If my people who are called by my name humble themselves, and pray and seek my face, and turn from their wicked ways, then I will hear from heaven, and will forgive their sin and heal their land.

*Judaism* and *Christianity.* 2 Chronicles 7.14

Let us rid ourselves of evil doings.
Let every person ask pardon of the Great Light
Asis,
The molder of us all,
Who has given us this land to inhabit, and to
multiply in.

*African Traditional Religions.* Kipsigis Poem (Kenya)

The sin which makes you sad and repentant is liked better by the Lord than the good deed which turns you vain and conceited.

*Islam.* Nahjul Balagha, Saying 44

Two men went up to the temple to pray, one a Pharisee and the other a tax collector. The Pharisee stood and prayed thus with himself, "God, I thank thee that I am not like other men, extortioners, unjust, adulterers, or even like this tax collector. I fast twice a week, I give tithes of all that I get." But the tax collector, standing far off, would not even lift up his eyes to heaven, but beat his breast, saying, "God, be merciful to me a sinner!" I tell you, this man went down to his house justified rather than the other; for every one who exalts himself will be humbled, but he who humbles himself will be exalted.

*Christianity.* Luke 18.10-14

As was the will of God, so I ought to have
thought;
As was the will of God, so I ought to have
spoken;
As was the will of God, so I ought to have
acted.
If I have not so thought, so spoken, so acted,
Then do I repent for the sin,
Do I repent by my thought, word, and deed.
Do I repent with all my heart and conscience.

*Zoroastrianism.* Patet 6

You should become the person who prays as follows: "All the sins of the past and present are my responsibility. Father! Forgive me!"

*Unification Church.* Sun Myung Moon, 2-21-60

Our transgressions are past counting,
There is no end to our sins,
Be merciful, forgive us, O Lord;
We are great sinners and wrongdoers.
There is no hope of our redemption.
O Lord, dear Lord, our deeds weighed in the
balance

**I Ching, Great Commentary 1.3.4:** The 'borderline' refers to one's scruples about what is good and what is evil. An educated conscience is a prerequisite to repentance. Cf. Itivuttaka 36, p. 551.

**Psalm 51.17:** Cf. Psalm 51.6-10, p. 370; Isaiah 57.15, p. 73; Jeremiah 10.23-24, p. 404; Hosea 6.1-2, p. 374.

**2 Chronicles 7.14:** Cf. Jeremiah 18.3-11, p. 764; Midrash Psalms 18, p. 407.

**Nahjul Balagha, Saying 44:** Cf. Hadith of Muslim, p. 325; Forty Hadith of an-Nawawi 42, p. 372; Tannisho, p. 542.

**Luke 18.10-14:** Cf. Matthew 9.10-13, p. 456; Tannisho, p. 542.

Would get us no place in Thy court!
Forgive us and make us one with Thyself
Through the grace of the Guru.
If the Lord God can be attained to,
Then all evil is destroyed.

*Sikhism*. Adi Granth,
Shalok Vadhik, M.3, p. 1416

I muse on my heart and I ponder this question:
When shall I again be at one with Varuna?
Will he accept without rancor my offering?
When, reassured, shall I taste of his mercy?

I question myself on my sin, O Varuna,
desirous to know it. I seek out the wise
to ask them; the sages all give me this answer,
"The God, great Varuna, is angry with you."

What, then, O God, is my greatest transgression
for which you would ruin your singer, your friend?
Tell me, O God who knows all and lacks nothing,
so that, quickly prostrating, I may sinless crave pardon.

Loose us from the yoke of the sins of our fathers
and also from those we ourselves have committed.
Release your servant, as a thief is set free
from his crime or as a calf is loosed from its cord.

*Hinduism*. Rig Veda 7.86.2-5

Jonah arose and went to Nineveh, according to the word of the Lord. Now Nineveh was an exceedingly great city, three days' journey in breadth. Jonah began to go into the city, going a day's journey. And he cried, "Yet forty days, and Nineveh shall be overthrown!" And the people of Nineveh proclaimed a fast, and put on sackcloth, from the greatest of them to the least of them. Then tidings reached the king of Nineveh, and he arose from his throne, removed his robe, and covered himself with sackcloth, and sat in ashes. And he made proclamation and published through Nineveh, "By the decree of the king and his nobles: Let neither man nor beast, herd nor flock, taste anything; let them not feed, or drink water, but let man and beast be covered with sackcloth, and let them cry mightily to God; yea, let every one turn from his evil way and from the violence which is in his hands. Who knows, God may yet repent and turn from his fierce anger, so that we perish not?" When God saw what they did, how they turned from their evil way, God repented of the evil which he had said he would do to them; and he did not do it.

*Judaism* and *Christianity*. Jonah 3.3-10

Confess your sins to one another, and pray for one another, that you may be healed.

*Christianity*. James 5.16

Whosoever looks upon his wrongdoing as wrongdoing, makes amends by confessing it as such, and abstains from it in the future, will progress according to the Law.

*Buddhism*. Digha Nikaya i.85,
Samannaphala Sutta

By public confession, repentance, penance, repetition of holy mantras, and by gifts, the sinner is released from guilt.

In proportion as a man who has done wrong, himself confesses it, even so is he freed from guilt, as a snake from its slough.

In proportion as his heart loathes his evil deed, even so far is his body freed from that guilt.

*Hinduism*. Laws of Manu 11.228-30

**Rig Veda 7.86.2-5:** Cf. Rig Veda 5.85.7, p. 370.

**Jonah 3.3-10:** This story contains an irony, for Jonah himself was unhappy that Nineveh, the capital city of Israel's most hated enemies, heeded his message and repented. He would rather that they had ignored him, that God might have destroyed it. Thus God sets up for Jonah a lesson on self-righteousness. As a lesson on repentance, the story of Jonah is recited by Jews on the Day of Atonement. Cf. Jeremiah 18.3-11, p. 764; Parable of the Prodigal Son, Luke 15.11-32, pp. 362-63; Berakot 10a, p. 743.

**Laws of Manu 11.228-30:** Cf. Laws of Manu 8.314-16, p. 762.

"I wish to reverence you, ascetic who suffers with equanimity, with intense concentration."

"So be it."

"You will have passed the day auspiciously with little disturbance."

"Yes."

"You make spiritual progress."

"And you also."

"I wish to ask pardon for transgressions."

"I ask for it too."

"I must confess, ascetic who suffers with equanimity, for lack of respect and day-to-day transgressions of the mind, speech, or body; through anger, pride, deceit, or greed; false behavior and neglect of the Teaching; and whatever offense I have committed I here confess, repudiate, and repent of it and set aside my past deeds."

*Jainism*. Vandana Formula

[Certain brethren, having wrongly expelled another from the Order, came to the Master to confess their fault.] They fell at the feet of the Exalted One, and said to him,

"Transgression, Lord, overcame us: such was our folly, such was our stupidity, such was our wrongdoing, in that we expelled a brother who was pure and faultless without ground and without reason. May the Exalted One, O Lord, accept this our confession of guilt as such, for our self-restraint in the future."

"Truly, brethren, transgression overcame you, such was your folly.... Nevertheless, brethren, as you have seen your transgression as transgression, and have made confession as is fit and proper, I do accept it from you. For this, brethren, is growth in the Noble Discipline when, having seen our transgression as such, we make confession as is fit and proper, for the future practice of self-restraint."

*Buddhism*. Vinaya Pitaka, Mahavagga ix.1

Sin disappears with repentance.

Does not darkness vanish simultaneously with exposure to light?

Those who do not repent, retain their sins.

Is it not true that unexposed darkness remains darkness?

Confession may be made in secret, or you may write a letter to a leader of the teachings. However, there is nothing to be gained by disclosing your sin in darkness or before people who will only ridicule you.

What is the use of exposing darkness to darkness?

When once man sincerely repents, from that very instant his original perfection as a child of God becomes manifested as if his whole being were cleansed and purified.

After sincerely repenting, you feel at peace within yourself because you are truly My children and I am one with all of you.

Divine Spirit flows abundantly through you, and your spirit will grow and finally attain Infinite Life.

*Seicho-no-Ie*. Holy Sutra for Spiritual Healing

Say, O My slaves who have been prodigal to their own hurt! Despair not of the mercy of God, who forgives all sins. Lo! He is the Forgiving, the Merciful. Turn to Him repentant, and surrender unto Him, before there can come upon you the doom, when you cannot be helped. And follow the better of that which has been revealed unto you from your Lord, before the doom comes on you suddenly when you know not. Lest any soul should say, "Alas, my grief that I was unmindful of God, and I was indeed among the scoffers!" Or should say, "If God had but guided me, I should have been among the dutiful!" Or should say, when it sees the doom, "Oh, that I had but a second chance, that I might be among the righteous!"

*Islam*. Qur'an 39.53-58

**Vandana Formula:** This is spoken by lay people to monks of the Jain order. Lay people are encouraged to apply the teachings insofar as they are able to learn from the monks, who practice them fully, as their examples and teachers.

**Vinaya Pitaka, Mahavagga ix.1:** Cf. Cakrasamvara Tantra, pp. 371-72.

**Qur'an 39.53-58:** Cf. Anguttara Nikaya i.279, p. 249; Abot 4.22, p. 237. But in contrast, see Bhagavad Gita 8.5-13, p. 241n., on the efficacy of last-minute repentance.

But God shall not turn toward those who do evil deeds until, when one of them is visited by death, he says, "Indeed now I repent," neither to those who die disbelieving; for them We have prepared a painful chastisement.

*Islam.* Qur'an 4.17-18

Do not procrastinate the day of your repentance until the end; for after this day of life, which is given us to prepare for eternity, behold, if we do not improve our time while in this life, then comes the night of darkness wherein there can be no labor performed. You cannot say, when you are brought to that awful crisis, that I will repent, that I will return to my God. Nay, you cannot say this; for that same spirit which possesses your bodies at the time that you go out of this life, that same spirit will have power to possess your body in that eternal world. For behold, if you have procrastinated the day of your repentance even until death, behold, you have become subjected to the spirit of the devil, and he has sealed you his.

*Church of Jesus Christ of Latter-day Saints.* Book of Mormon, Alma 34.33-35

O dweller in the body, make reparation for whatever you have done!

*Hinduism.* Garuda Purana 2.35

If anyone commits a sin and [by confessing] has inflicted on him the prescribed punishment for that sin, it is atonement for him.

*Islam.* Hadith in Sharh as-Sunna

There was a rich man named Zacchaeus; he was a chief tax collector, and rich.... And Zacchaeus stood and said to the Lord, "Behold, Lord, the half of my goods I give to the poor, and if I have defrauded anyone of anything, I restore it fourfold." And Jesus said to him, "Today salvation has come to this house."

*Christianity.* Luke 19.2,8-9

Again, though I say to the wicked, "You shall surely die," yet if he turns from his sin and does what is lawful and right, if the wicked restores the pledge, gives back what he has taken by robbery, and walks in the statutes of life, committing no iniquity; he shall surely live, he shall not die. None of the sins that he has committed shall be remembered against him; he has done what is lawful and right, he shall surely live.

*Judaism* and *Christianity.* Ezekiel 33.14-16

And whosoever repents and does good, he verily repents toward God with true repentance.

*Islam.* Qur'an 25.71

If a man finds that he has made a mistake, then he must not be afraid of admitting the fact and amending his ways.

*Confucianism.* Analects 1.8.4

If one has, indeed, done deeds of wickedness, but afterward alters his way and repents, resolved not to do anything wicked, but to practice reverently all that is good, he is sure in the long run to obtain good fortune—this is called changing calamity into blessing.

*Taoism.* Treatise on Response and Retribution 5

Whoever was heedless before and afterwards is not; such a one illumines this world like the moon freed from clouds.

Whoever, by a good deed, covers the evil done, such a one illumines this world like the moon freed from clouds.

*Buddhism.* Dhammapada 172-73

How is one proved a repentant sinner? Rab Judah said, "If the object which caused his original transgression comes before him on two occasions, and he keeps away from it."

**Qur'an 4.17-18:** See previous note.

**Book of Mormon, Alma 34.33-35:** Cf. Book of Mormon, Alma 12.24, pp. 236-37.

**Hadith in Sharh as-Sunna:** Cf. Hadith of Abu Dawud, p. 762.

**Ezekiel 33.14-16:** Cf. Isaiah 1.16-20, p. 520; Matthew 5.23-24, p. 701; 1 Peter 4.8, p. 711.

**Analects 1.8.4:** Cf. Analects 12.1.1, p. 639.

**Dhammapada 172-73:** Cf. Qur'an 11.114, p. 711.

Rabbi Jose ben Judah said, "If a man commits a transgression, the first, second, and third time he is forgiven; the fourth time he is not forgiven."

*Judaism*. Talmud, Yoma 86b

He who has committed a sin and has repented, is freed from that sin, but he is purified only by resolving to cease: "I will do so no more."...

He who, having either unintentionally or intentionally committed a reprehensible deed, desires to be freed from it, must not commit it a second time.

If his mind be uneasy with respect to any deed, let him repeat the penances prescribed for it until they fully satisfy his conscience.

*Hinduism*. Laws of Manu 11.231-34

If a man commits sinful acts which he does not expiate in this life, he must pay the penalty in the next life; and great will be his suffering. Therefore, with a self-controlled mind, a man should expiate his sins here on earth.

Expiation and repentance, to a man who continues to commit sinful acts, knowing them to be harmful, are of no avail. Futile is it to bathe an elephant if he is straightway to roll again in the mud. All sinful thoughts and evil deeds are caused by ignorance. True expiation comes from illumination. As fire consumes all things, so does the fire of knowledge consume all evil and ignorance. Complete transformation of the inner life is necessary; and this is accomplished by control of the mind and the senses, by the practice of concentration, and by following and living the Truth.

The great secret of this complete transformation is the development of love for God. As when the sun rises the dewdrops vanish away, so when love grows all sin and ignorance disappear.

*Hinduism*. Srimad Bhagavatam 6.1

❖

**Srimad Bhagavatam 6.1:** Cf. Bhagavad Gita 9.30-31, p. 370; Japuji 20, M.1. p 519.

# *Humility*

HUMILITY IS AN ESSENTIAL ATTITUDE FOR SUCCESS in the spiritual life. Any self-conceit, whether nurtured by superior intelligence, wealth, a high position, or the praise of others, is an obstacle on the path. Genuine humility is not posturing. It requires a constant willingness to deny oneself, to be critical of oneself, and to be open to Heaven's guidance even when it differs from one's own preconceived concepts.

We open with passages which set forth the value of humility, meekness, and modesty. Humility requires sincerity and honesty; thus some passages liken the humble person to a little child, whose natural spontaneity and acceptance of life is the antithesis of the often complicated personality of the adult with its many masks, hidden resentments, and prejudices. Here is also the wisdom of the paradox (see *Reversal*, pp. 397-91) that the person who is humble and self-effacing ultimately prospers and wins more respect from others than the person who is proud and powerful. Next come passages enjoining humility before God and the recognition that the success of all our endeavors ultimately depends on God's favor. This is the attitude expressed by the common Muslim saying *insha'llah*, "God willing." The humble person does not regard his possessions or accomplishments as his own, but as a gift of God, to whom is due all gratitude. A third group of passages meditate on the insignificance, transience, and lowness of the human being, who is nothing but a puff of wind, a bag of excrement, food for worms. We conclude with passages which warn against letting the praise of others or great learning or high position go to the head and cause self-conceit. Indeed, it is those who are most favored with talent, intelligence, and worldly success who most often succumb to pride and thus lose their way.

Blessed are the meek, for they shall inherit the earth.

*Christianity*. Matthew 5.5

It is humility that exalts one and favors him against his friends.

*African Traditional Religions*. Kipsigis Proverb (Kenya)

Successful indeed are the believers
Who are humble in their prayers,
and who shun vain conversation,
and who are payers of the poor-due,
and who guard their modesty.

*Islam*. Qur'an 23.1-5

The Lamenter [who is seeking a vision] cries, for he is humbling himself, remembering his nothingness in the presence of the Great Spirit.

*Native American Religions*. Black Elk, Sioux Tradition

Harithah ibn Wahb al-Khuza'i tells how he heard the Prophet say, "Have I not taught you how the inhabitants of Paradise will be all the humble and the weak, whose oaths God will accept when they swear to be faithful? Have I not taught you how the inhabitants of hell will be all the cruel beings, strong of body and arrogant?"

*Islam*. Hadith of Bukhari

**Matthew 5.5:** Cf. Matthew 23.12, p. 387; Philippians 2.6-11, p. 440.
**Qur'an 23.1-5:** Cf. Qur'an 31.18-19, p. 290; 7.55, p. 593. On the Prophet's humility, see Hadith, p. 471.

Within the world
the palace pillar is broad,
but the human heart
should be modest.

*Shinto*. Moritake Arakida,
One Hundred Poems about the World

Be humble, be harmless,
Have no pretension,
Be upright, forbearing;
Serve your teacher in true obedience,
Keeping the mind and body in cleanness,
Tranquil, steadfast, master of ego,
Standing apart from the things of the senses,
Free from self;
Aware of the weakness in mortal nature.

*Hinduism*. Bhagavad Gita 13.7-8

Subdue pride by modesty, overcome hypocrisy by simplicity, and dissolve greed by contentment.

*Jainism*. Samanasuttam 136

Let the children come to me, and do not hinder them, for to such belongs the kingdom of God. Truly, I say to you, whoever does not receive the kingdom of God like a child shall not enter it.

*Christianity*. Luke 18.16-17

For the natural man is an enemy to God, and has been from the fall of Adam, and will be, forever and ever, unless he yields to the enticings of the Holy Spirit, and puts off the natural man and becomes a saint through the atonement of Christ the Lord, and becomes as a child, submissive, meek, humble, patient, full of love, willing to submit to all things which the Lord sees fit to inflict upon him, even as a child submits to his father.

*Church of Jesus Christ of Latter-day Saints*.
Book of Mormon, Mosiah 3.19

In the Book of Songs it is said,

Over her brocaded robe
She wore a plain and simple dress,

in that way showing her dislike of the loudness of its color and magnificence. Thus the ways of the moral man are unobtrusive and yet they grow more and more in power and evidence; whereas the ways of the vulgar person are ostentatious, but lose more and more in influence until they perish and disappear.

The life of the moral man is plain, and yet not unattractive; it is simple, and yet full of grace; it is easy, and yet methodical. He knows that accomplishment of great things consists in doing little things well. He knows that great effects are produced by small causes. He knows the evidence and reality of what cannot be perceived by the senses. Thus he is enabled to enter into the world of ideas and morals.

*Confucianism*.
Doctrine of the Mean 33

He who knows the masculine but keeps to the feminine,
Becomes the ravine of the world.
Being the ravine of the world,
He dwells in constant virtue,
He returns to the state of the babe.

He who knows the white but keeps to the black,
Becomes the model of the world.
Being the model of the world,
He rests in constant virtue,
He returns to the infinite.

He who knows glory but keeps to disgrace,
Becomes the valley of the world.
Being the valley of the world,
He finds contentment in constant virtue,
He returns to the Uncarved Block.

*Taoism*. Tao Te Ching 28

**Bhagavad Gita 13.7-8:** Cf. Gauri Sukhmani, M.5, p. 584.

**Luke 18.16-17:** Cf. Matthew 18.1-3, p. 144.

**Book of Mormon, Mosiah 3.19:** Cf. Proverbs 3.11-12, p. 404; John 1.12-13, p. 406.

**Doctrine of the Mean:** Cf. Qur'an 31.18-19, p. 290.

**Tao Te Ching 28:** The 'Uncarved Block' is the state of primitive simplicity without any pretense or artificiality. It can also mean the purity of one's original nature. Cf. Tao Te Ching 22, pp. 390-91; 55, p. 156.

Do not say about anything, "I am going to do that tomorrow," without adding, "If God will." Remember your Lord whenever you forget, and say, "Perhaps my Lord will guide me even closer than this to proper conduct."

*Islam*. Qur'an 18.23-24

Come now, you who say, "Today or tomorrow we will go into such and such a town and spend a year there and trade and get gain"; whereas you do not know about tomorrow. What is your life? For you are a mist that appears for a little time and then vanishes. Instead you ought to say, "If the Lord wills, we shall live and we shall do this or that." As it is, you boast in your arrogance. All such boasting is evil.

*Christianity*. James 4.13-16

Without merit am I; all merit is Thine.
Thine, Lord, are all merits—by what tongue
have I power to praise Thee?

*Sikhism*. Adi Granth, Wadhans, M.5, p. 577

Though I seek my refuge in the true faith of
the Pure Land,
Yet my heart has not been truly sincere.
Deceit and untruth are in my flesh,
And in my soul is no clear shining.
In their outward seeming all men are diligent
and truth speaking,
But in their souls are greed and anger and
unjust deceitfulness,
And in their flesh do lying and cunning
triumph.
Too strong for me is the evil of my heart.
I cannot overcome it.
Therefore my soul is like unto the poison of
serpents;
Even my righteous deeds, being mingled with
this poison,
Must be named deeds of deceitfulness.
Shameless though I be and having no truth in
my soul,
Yet the virtue of the Holy Name, the gift of
Him that is enlightened,
Is spread throughout the world through my
words,
Although I am as I am.
There is no mercy in my soul.
The good of my fellow man is not dear in my
eyes.
If it were not for the Ark of Mercy,
The divine promise of the Infinite Wisdom,
How should I cross the Ocean of Misery?
I, whose mind is filled with cunning and deceit
as the poison of reptiles,
Am impotent to practice righteous deeds.
If I sought not refuge in the gift of our Father,
I should die the death of the shameless.

*Buddhism*. Shinran

All men are children of Adam, and Adam was created from soil.

*Islam*. Hadith of Tirmidhi

Be of an exceedingly humble spirit, for the end of man is the worm.

*Judaism*. Mishnah, Abot 4.4

O Lord, what is man, that thou dost regard him,
or the son of man, that thou dost think of him?
Man is like a breath,
his days are like a passing shadow.

*Judaism* and *Christianity*. Psalm 144.3-4

**James 4.13-16:** Cf. Isaiah 40.6-8, p. 78.

**Shinran:** Shinran (1173-1262) honestly looked into his own mind and recognized the power of evil within. He realized that even the most determined saint cannot attain salvation through dependence on his or her own mind; compare 1 John 1.8, p. 273; Romans 3.9-12, p. 273. For Shinran, salvation is possible only through the Power of Another—the Orignal Vow of Buddha Amitabha to save all sentient beings (Larger Sukhavativyuha Sutra 8.18, p. 457). See Tannisho, p. 542.

**Abot 4.4:** Cf. Erubin 13b, p. 387.

**Psalm 144.3-4:** Cf. Isaiah 40.6-8, p. 78.

The body is impure, bad-smelling, and replete with various kinds of stench which trickle here and there. If one, possessed of such a body, thinks highly of himself and despises others—that is due to nothing other than his lack of insight.

*Buddhism.* Sutta Nipata 205-6

A rabbit that a huntsman brings,
They pay for it the proper price;
But none will give a betel nut
For the corpse of a ruler of the land!
A man's body is less worth than a rabbit's.

*Hinduism.* Basavanna, Vacana 158

Reflect upon three things, and you will not come within the power of sin: Know from where you came, to where you are going, and before whom you will in future have to give account and reckoning. From where you came—from a fetid drop; to where are you going—to a place of dust, worms, and maggots; and before whom you will in future have to give account and reckoning—before the Supreme King of kings, the Holy One, blessed be He.

*Judaism.* Mishnah, Abot 3.1

Even if all the world tells you, "You are righteous," consider yourself wicked.

*Judaism.* Talmud, Nidda 30b

A brahmin should ever shrink from honor as from poison, and should always be desirous of disrespect as if of ambrosia.

*Hinduism.* Laws of Manu 2.162

Confucius said, "A gentleman does not grieve that people do not recognize his merits; he grieves at his own incapacities."

*Confucianism.* Analects 14.32

To know when one does not know is best. To think one knows when one does not know is a dire disease.

*Taoism.* Tao Te Ching 71

The fool who knows that he is a fool is for that very reason a wise man; the fool who thinks he is wise is called a fool indeed.

*Buddhism.* Dhammapada 63

Do nothing from selfishness or conceit, but in humility count others better than yourselves.

*Christianity.* Philippians 2.3

Whoever proclaims himself good,
Know, goodness approaches him not.
He whose heart becomes dust of the feet of all,
Says Nanak, pure shall his repute be.

*Sikhism.* Adi Granth,
Gauri Sukhmani, M.5, p. 278

Subhuti, what do you think? Does a holy one say within himself, "I have obtained Perfective Enlightenment"? Subhuti replied, "No, World-honored One... If a holy one of Perfective Enlightenment said to himself, Such am I, he would necessarily partake of the idea of an ego-identity, a personality, a being, a separated individuality."

*Buddhism.* Diamond Sutra 9

In the barren north, there is a sea, the Celestial Lake. In it there is a fish, several thousand li in width, and no one knows how many li in length. It is called the leviathan (*kun*). There is also a bird, called the roc (*p'eng*), with a back like Mount T'ai and wings like clouds across the sky. Upon a whirlwind it soars up to a height of ninety thousand li. Beyond the clouds and atmosphere, with only the blue sky above it, it then turns south to the southern ocean.

**Sutta Nipata 205-6:** The many Buddhist meditations on the body as filthy and worthless are mainly to cultivate an attitude of detachment from sense desires and bodily pleasures. Cf. Dhammapada 350, p. 660; Therigatha, p. 663; Precious Garland 149-57, p. 660; Akkamahadevi, Vacana 33, p. 660.

**Tao Te Ching 71:** Cf. Tao Te Ching 81, p. 570.

**Dhammapada 63:** Cf. 1 Corinthians 1.20-25, p. 570, where the word of the cross seems folly because it teaches the way of humility and self-sacrifice.

**Gauri Sukhmani, M.5:** Cf. Tao Te Ching 81, p. 570.

A quail laughs at it, saying, "Where is that bird trying to go? I spurt up with a bound, and I drop after rising a few yards. I just flutter about among the brushwood and the bushes. This is also the perfection of flying. Where is that bird trying to go?" This is the difference between the great and the small.

Similarly, there are some men whose knowledge is sufficient for the duties of some office. There are some men whose conduct will benefit some district. There are some men whose virtue befits him for a ruler. There are some men whose ability wins credit in the country. In their opinion of themselves, they are just like what is mentioned above.

*Taoism.* Chuang Tzu 1

## *Restraint and Moderation*

ADMONITIONS TO REFRAIN FROM EVIL, which are found in every religion, open this section. Notable is restraint in Jainism, where *ahimsa* (nonviolence) is practiced to the extent that one is careful as one walks, eats, drinks, and breathes not to kill even insects or microscopic animals. There are admonitions to refrain from acting wrongly, even when the mind is full of evil promptings, or when the crowd is urging. Silence and discretion are valuable allies in this regard. Some texts urge us to set up a fence and honor a clear boundary line, marked by prohibitions and moral principles, so that good and evil may be clearly distinguished. The ground must be swept clean of confusing debris, and areas of gray avoided, lest we fall unwittingly into a mistake.

The section concludes with passages which counsel moderation in all things. Excessive behavior of any kind—stinginess or profligacy, mortification of the flesh or drowning in sense pleasures, self-righteous action or action to please others—should be eschewed in favor of the Golden Mean or Middle Path.

Forsake the outward sin, and the inward; surely the earners of sin shall be recompensed for what they have earned.

*Islam.* Qur'an 6.120

Just as a wealthy merchant with only a small escort avoids a perilous route; just as one desiring to live avoids poison; even so should one shun evil things.

*Buddhism.* Dhammapada 123

Good is restraint in deed; good is restraint in speech; good is restraint in mind; good is restraint in everything. The bhikkhu, restrained at all points, is freed from sorrow.

*Buddhism.* Dhammapada 361

Realizing the retributive nature of karmas, a wise man refrains from accumulating them.

*Jainism.* Acarangasutra 4.51

**Chuang Tzu 1:** Cf. Analects 7.25, p. 292.

**Dhammapada 361:** Cf. Dhammapada 183, p. 511; Majjhima Nikaya i.415, p. 331. On restraint of speech, see Dhammapada 133, p. 353.

**Acarangasutra 4.51:** Karma is accumulated through evil deeds and desires, but most especially through crimes of violence against other creatures; see below.

The highest charity is refraining from violence.
*Hinduism.* Srimad Bhagavatam 11.12

Let him who believes in Allah and the last day either speak good or be silent.
*Islam.* Forty Hadith of an-Nawawi 15

The very first principle of religion laid down by Lord Mahavira is *ahimsa*—non-injury to living beings—which must be observed very scrupulously and thoroughly, and behaving toward all living beings with proper restraint and control.
*Jainism.* Dashavaikalika Sutra 6.9

He who acts, harms; he who grabs, lets slip.
Therefore the sage does not act, and so does not harm,
Does not grab, and so does not let slip.
*Taoism.* Tao Te Ching 64

Restrain yourself with those that call upon their Lord at morning and evening, desiring His countenance, and let not your eyes turn away from them, desiring the adornments of the present life; and obey not him whose heart We have made neglectful of Our remembrance so that he follows his own lust, and his affair has become all excess.
*Islam.* Qur'an 18.8

Why endeavor in the way of evil,
As therefrom is received evil retribution?
If you take a long view, you would not practice evil at all.
Throw your dice in a manner
That with the Lord you lose not the game.
Direct your endeavor to profit.
*Sikhism.* Adi Granth, Asa-ki-Var, M.1, p. 474

A single bangle does not make a sound.
*African Traditional Religions.* Igala Proverb (Nigeria)

Verily God forgives my people the evil promptings which arise within their hearts as long as they do not speak about them and did not act upon them.
*Islam.* Hadith of Muslim

Mencius said, "Only when a man will not do some things is he capable of doing great things."
*Confucianism.* Mencius IV.B.8

The emptiest of you are as well-packed with religious observances as a pomegranate with seeds. For everyone who has the opportunity of committing a sin and escapes it and refrains from doing it performs a highly religious act. How much more, then, is this true of those "behind your veil," the modest and self-restrained among you!
*Judaism.* Midrash, Canticles Rabbah 4.4.3

Under the sway of strong impulse, the man who is devoid of self-control willfully commits deeds that he knows to be fraught with future misery. But the man of discrimination, even though moved by desires, at once becomes conscious of the evil that is in them, and does not yield to their influence but remains unattached.
*Hinduism.* Srimad Bhagavatam 11.7

My son, if sinners entice you,
do not consent.
If they say, "Come with us, let us lie in wait for blood,

**Tao Te Ching 64:** Any form of acquisitiveness or activism is out of harmony with the Tao, and will lead to bad results.

**Igala Proverb:** It takes two to quarrel, so do not accuse another of being quarrelsome.

**Hadith of Muslim:** Cf. Forty Hadith of an-Nawawi 29, p. 353; Ephesians 4.26-27, p. 655.

**Canticles Rabbah 4.4.3:** This is a midrash on "Your cheeks are like halves of a pomegranate behind your veil" (Song of Solomon 4.3).

**Srimad Bhagavatam 11.7:** Cf. Majjhima Nikaya i.415, p. 330.

let us wantonly ambush the innocent;
like Sheol let us swallow them alive
and whole, like those who go down to the Pit;
we shall find all precious goods,
we shall fill our houses with spoil;
throw in your lot among us,
we will all have one purse"—
my son, do not walk in the way with them,
hold back your foot from their paths;
for their feet run to evil,
and they make haste to shed blood.

*Judaism* and *Christianity*. Proverbs 1.10-16

Whenever there is attachment in my mind
And whenever there is the desire to be angry,
I should not do anything nor say anything,
But remain like a piece of wood....

Whenever I am eager for praise
Or have the desire to blame others;
Whenever I have the wish to speak harshly and cause dispute;
At such times I should remain like a piece of wood.

Whenever I desire material gain, honor or fame;
Whenever I seek attendants or a circle of friends,
And when in my mind I wish to be served;
At [all] these times I should remain like a piece of wood.

Whenever I have the wish to decrease or to stop working for others
And the desire to pursue my welfare alone,
If [motivated by such thoughts] a wish to say something occurs,
At these times I should remain like a piece of wood.

*Buddhism*. Shantideva, Guide to the Bodhisattva's Way of Life 5.48-52

Do only such actions as are blameless.... If at any time there is doubt with regard to right conduct, follow the practice of great souls, who are guileless, of good judgment, and devoted to truth.

*Hinduism*. Taittiriya Upanishad 1.11.2, 4

Rabbi Akiba said, "Laughter and levity accustom a man to immorality. Tradition is a fence for Torah. Tithes are a fence for riches. Vows are a fence for saintliness. A fence for wisdom is silence."

*Judaism*. Mishnah, Abot 3.17

What is lawful is obvious, and what is unlawful is obvious; and between them are matters which are ambiguous and of which many people are ignorant. Hence, he who is careful in regard to the ambiguous has justified himself in regard to his religion and his honor; but he who stumbles in the ambiguous has stumbled in the forbidden, as the shepherd pasturing around a sanctuary is on the verge of pasturing in it. Is it not true that every king has a sanctuary, and is not the sanctuary of God that which He has forbidden?

*Islam*. Forty Hadith of an-Nawawi 6

"To spread white rushes underneath. No blame" [Hexagram 28: Preponderence of the Great].

The Master said, "It does well enough simply to place something on the floor. But if one puts white rushes underneath, how could that be a mistake? This is the extreme of caution. Rushes in themselves are worthless, but they can have a very important effect. If one is as cautious as this in all that one does, one remains free of mistakes."

*Confucianism*. I Ching, Great Commentary 1.8.7

**Abot 3.17:** Cf. Abot 1.1, pp. 585-86 and note; Abot 2.8, p. 679; Sifra 93d, p. 681; I Ching, Great Commentary 1.3.4, p. 642.

**Forty Hadith of an-Nawawi 6:** Muhammad himself was scrupulous in this regard; see Hadith, p. 471.

**I Ching, Great Commentary 1.8.7:** On discretion, see I Ching, Great Commentary 1.8.10, p. 353, 2.5.9, p. 529.

Be generous but not extravagant, be frugal but not miserly.

*Islam.*
Nahjul Balagha, Saying 32

However hungry you are, you do not eat with both hands.

*African Traditional Religions.*
Akan Proverb (Ghana)

The Master said, " 'The Ospreys!' Pleasure not carried to the point of debauch; grief not carried to the point of self-injury."

*Confucianism.* Analects 3.20

Be not righteous overmuch, and do not make yourself overwise; why should you destroy yourself? Be not wicked overmuch, neither be a fool; why should you die before your time?

*Judaism* and *Christianity.*
Ecclesiastes 7.16-17

In practicing the ordinary virtues and in the exercise of care in ordinary conversation, when there is deficiency, the superior man never fails to make further effort, and where there is excess, never dares to go to the limit.

*Confucianism.*
Doctrine of the Mean 13.4

That things have being, O Kaccana, constitutes one extreme of doctrine; that things have no being is the other extreme. These extremes have been avoided by the Tathagata, and it is a middle doctrine he teaches.

*Buddhism.* Samyutta Nikaya xxii.90

Your name or your person, which is dearer?
Your person or your goods, which is worth more?
Gain or loss, which is the greater bane?
That is why excessive meanness is sure to lead to great expense;
Too much store is sure to end in immense loss.
Know contentment, and you will suffer no disgrace;
Know when to stop, and you will meet with no danger.
You can then endure.

*Taoism.* Tao Te Ching 44

❖

**Nahjul Balagha, Saying 32:** cf. Qur'an 31.19, p. 290.

**Akan Proverb:** This proverb means that as you restrain yourself when eating to stay within the bounds of good manners, you should also in all things resist temptation and act within the bounds of propriety.

**Analects 3.20:** 'The Ospreys!' refers to Ode 1 of the Book of Songs, pp. 176-77. Confucius interprets this ode as describing a model of conduct according to the Golden Mean: faithfulness in both joy and affliction.

**Samyutta Nikaya xxii.90:** In practice, the 'middle doctrine' (*madhyamaka*) means avoiding both the extremes of worldliness ('things have being') and total renunciation ('things have no being'). On the extreme of renunciation, see the story of Devadatta, Vinaya Pitaka ii.184-98, pp. 318-20.

## Control Anger

ANGER IS ONE EXPRESSION of extreme, unrestrained emotion that must be brought under control if one is to make spiritual progress. Anger is a natural feeling that arises upon seeing unrighteousness, yet uncontrolled it can cause much damage. Of the great founders of religion, we see that Moses manifested anger as a weakness. He displayed it, to his own loss, at the incident of striking the rock at Meribah. For a related theme, see *Turn the Other Cheek*, pp. 708-10.

Conquer anger by love.

*Buddhism.* Dhammapada 223

Anger dissolves affection.... Therefore man should subvert anger by forgiveness.

*Jainism.* Samanasuttam 135-36

The fly cannot be driven away by getting angry at it.

*African Traditional Religions.* Idoma Proverb (Nigeria)

The anger of man does not work the righteousness of God.

*Christianity.* James 1.20

Anger deprives a sage of his wisdom, a prophet of his vision.

*Judaism.* Talmud, Pesahim 66b

He who is slow to anger is better than the mighty,
And he who rules his spirit than he who takes a city.

*Judaism and Christianity.* Proverbs 16.32

Abu Huraira reported God's Messenger as saying, "The strong man is not the good wrestler; the strong man is only he who controls himself when he is angry."

*Islam.* Hadith of Bukhari and Muslim

Be angry but do not sin; do not let the sun go down on your anger, and give no opportunity for the devil.

*Christianity.* Ephesians 4.26-27

When a man goes to sacrifice he must remain peaceful, without a hot heart. He must stay thus for at least a day. If he quarrels on that day or is hot in his heart he becomes sick and destroys the words of the lineage and of the sacrifice.

*African Traditional Religions.* Luhya Saying (Kenya)

If an evil man, on hearing of what is good, comes and creates a disturbance, you should hold your peace. You must not angrily upbraid him; then he who has come to curse you will merely harm himself.

*Buddhism.* Sutra of Forty-two Sections 7

Brethren, if outsiders should speak against me, or against the Doctrine, or against the Order, you should not on that account either bear

**Dhammapada 223:** Cf. Dhammapada 3-5, p. 705.
**James 1.19-20:** Cf. Analects 16.7, p. 659.
**Idoma Proverb:** Anger solves nothing.
**Ephesians 4.26-27:** To practice this teaching, by resolving each day's quarrels and meditating to digest each day's resentments before going to bed each night, is a valuable spiritual exercise. For when anger is stored up day after day, it becomes much harder to eradicate.
**Sutra of Forty-two Sections 7:** Cf. Romans 12.19-20, p. 710.

malice, or suffer resentment, or feel ill will. If you, on that account, should feel angry and hurt, that would stand in the way of your own self-conquest.

*Buddhism*. Digha Nikaya i.3, Brahmajala Sutta

You have heard that it was said to the men of old, "You shall not kill; and whoever kills shall be liable to judgment." But I say to you that everyone who is angry with his brother shall be liable to judgment; whoever insults his brother shall be liable to the council, and whoever says "You fool!" shall be liable to the hell of fire.

*Christianity*. Matthew 5.21-22

Why, sir, do you get angry at someone
Who is angry with you?
What are you going to gain by it?
How is he going to lose by it?
Your physical anger brings dishonor on yourself;
Your mental anger disturbs your thinking.
How can the fire in your house burn the neighbor's house
Without engulfing your own?

*Hinduism*. Basavanna, Vacana 248

Now there was no water for the congregation; and the people contended with Moses, and said... "Why have you made us come out of Egypt, to bring us to this evil place? It is no place for grain, or figs, or vines, or pomegranates; and there is no water to drink." Then the Lord said to Moses, "Take the rod, and assemble the congregation, you and Aaron your brother, and tell the rock before their eyes to yield its water; so you shall bring water out of the rock for them; so you shall give drink to the congregation and their cattle."

Then Moses and Aaron gathered the assembly together before the rock, and he said to them, "Hear now, you rebels; shall we bring forth water for you out of this rock?" And Moses lifted up his hand and struck the rock with his rod twice; and water came forth abundantly, and the congregation drank, and their cattle. And the Lord said to Moses and Aaron, "Because you did not believe in me, to sanctify me before the eyes of the people of Israel, therefore you shall not bring this assembly into the land which I have given them."

*Judaism* and *Christianity*. Numbers 20.2-13

**Digha Nikaya i.3:** Cf. Chuang Tzu 2, pp. 40-41; Lotus Sutra 20, pp. 709-10; Guide to the Bodhisattva's Way of Life 5.48, p. 653; Itivuttaka 110, p. 527; Anguttara Nikaya v.66, p. 517.

**Matthew 5.21-22:** Cf. Matthew 5.27-28, p. 661.

**Basavanna, Vacana 248:** Cf. Jerusalem Talmud, Nedarin 9.4, p. 701.

**Numbers 20.2-13:** As punishment for this mistake at the waters of Meribah, Moses would die in the wilderness and never set foot in the promised land (Deuteronomy 32.48-52). Instead of sanctifying God and showing forth God's blessings, Moses angrily rebuked the congregation; in his anger he struck the rock twice, when one strike, done with dignity, would have been appropriate (Exodus 17.6-7). Another example of Moses' anger was his act of killing the Egyptian (Exodus 2.11-14), for which he was forced to flee Egypt and live as an exile in Midian.

## *Subdue Desires and Passions*

ALL RELIGIONS AGREE that the seeker after Ultimate Reality must restrain his desires and subdue the passions of the flesh. But lest the religions be viewed as advocating one uniform position, we should distinguish between the view of Buddhism, Taoism, and Jainism, where any desire, including the desire to be righteous or the desire to annihilate desire, is a fetter to be overcome in the path to holiness, and the position of Judaism, Christianity, Islam, and Confucianism where *Selfish Desire, Lust, and Greed*, pp. 293-97, are to be subdued while good desires may be encouraged.

At the end of this chapter is the motif, found in the texts of many scriptures, that the thought is akin to the deed, for "everyone who looks at a woman lustfully has already committed adultery with her in his heart." Therefore extreme care should be taken to avoid tempting situations which would inflame the mind with passion. For even if a person has a strong will to restrain his actions, once the mind is inflamed with desire, how can his soul be tranquil and composed?

For related passages on the theme of self-conquest and the metaphor of the horse, bridle, and reins, in which the desires of the senses must be reined in by the mind—or better, be trained to obey the mind with only a light tap of the reins—see *Self-control*, pp. 522-24.

Through the abandonment of desire the Deathless is realized.

*Buddhism*. Samyutta Nikaya xlvii.37

Manifest plainness,
Embrace simplicity,
Reduce selfishness,
Have few desires.

*Taoism*. Tao Te Ching 19

Confucius said, "If out of the three hundred Songs I had to take one phrase to cover all my teachings, I would say, 'Let there be no evil in your thoughts.'"

*Confucianism*. Analects 2.2

Realizing that pleasure and pain are personal affairs, one should subjugate his mind and senses.

*Jainism*. Acarangasutra 2.78

Beloved, I beseech you... to abstain from the passions of the flesh that wage war against your soul.

*Christianity*. 1 Peter 2.11

Is he who relies on a clear proof from his Lord like those for whom the evil that they do seems pleasing while they follow their own lusts?

*Islam*. Qur'an 47.14

That man is disciplined and happy
who can prevail over the turmoil
that springs from desire and anger,
here on earth, before he leaves his body.

*Hinduism*. Bhagavad Gita 5.23

A man should always incite the good impulse in his soul to fight against the evil impulse. If he subdues it, well and good; if not, let him

**Acarangasutra 2.78:** Cf. Uttaradhyayana Sutra 9.34-36, p. 522.

**1 Peter 2.11:** Cf. Proverbs 16.32, p. 522; 2 Timothy 2.21-22, p. 520; Jerusalem Talmud, Sanhedrin 10.1, p. 523.

**Qur'an 47.14:** Cf. Qur'an 4.25, p. 179.

**Bhagavad Gita 5.23:** Cf. Bhagavad Gita 3.41, p. 294; 6.23-26, p. 603; 16.21, p. 294; Maitri Upanishad 6.34.7, p. 515; Mahabharata, Shanti Parva 177, p. 133.

study Torah.... If [by that] he subdues it, well and good; if not, let him pray upon his bed.

*Judaism.* Talmud, Berakot 5a

Whoever quenches the fire of desire through the holy Word,
Spontaneously is his illusion of duality banished.
Such is he in whose heart the Name dwells, by the Master's guidance.

*Sikhism.* Adi Granth, Gauri Ashtpadi, M.1, p. 222

To whatever extent the five senses, the four taints of emotions, and the four instinctive appetites are suppressed by a person who is well established in the path of righteousness, to such extent the doorway for the entrance of evil is closed for that person.

*Jainism.* Acarangasutra 4.15

Put to death what is earthly in you: fornication, impurity, passion, evil desire, and covetousness, which is idolatry. On account of these the wrath of God is coming. In these you once walked, when you lived in them. But now put them all away: anger, wrath, malice, slander, and foul talk from your mouth.

*Christianity.* Colossians 3.5-8

From endearment springs grief, from endearment springs fear; for him who is wholly free from endearment there is no grief, much less fear.

From affection springs grief, from affection springs fear; for him who is wholly free from affection there is no grief, much less fear.

From attachment springs grief, from attachment springs fear; for him who is wholly free from attachment there is no grief, much less fear.

From lust springs grief, from lust springs fear; for him who is wholly free from lust there is no grief, much less fear.

From craving springs grief, from craving springs fear; for him who is wholly free from craving there is no grief, much less fear.

*Buddhism.* Dhammapada 212-16

We live in accordance with our deep, driving desire. It is this desire at the time of death that determines what our next life is to be. We will come back to earth to work out the satisfaction of that desire.

But not for those who are free from desire; they are free because all their desires have found fulfillment in the Self. They do not die like the others; but realizing Brahman, they merge in Brahman. So it is said:

When all the desires that surge in the heart
Are renounced, the mortal becomes immortal.

When all the knots that strangle the heart
Are loosened, the mortal becomes immortal,
Here in this very life.

*Hinduism.* Brihadaranyaka Upanishad 4.4.6-7

The craving of a person addicted to careless living grows like a creeper. He jumps from life to life like a fruit-loving monkey in the forest. Whomsoever in this world this base clinging thirst overcomes, his sorrows flourish like well-watered birana grass.

Whoso in the world overcomes this base unruly craving, from him sorrows fall away like water drops from a lotus leaf. This I say to you: Dig up the root of craving like one in quest of the birana's sweet root. Let not Mara crush you again and again as a flood crushes a reed.

*Buddhism.* Dhammapada 334-37

What is meant by saying that cultivation of the personal life depends on the rectification of the mind is that when one is affected by wrath to any extent, his mind will not be correct. When one is affected by fear to any extent, his mind will not be correct. When he is affected by fondness to any extent, his mind will not be

**Berakot 5a:** Cf. Kiddushin 30b, p. 277; Qur'an 29.45, p. 592.

**Dhammapada 212-16:** Cf. Dhammapada 338-47, p. 295; Itivuttaka 47, p. 662.

**Dhammapada 334-37:** Cf. Dhammapada 338-47, p. 295; Guide to the Bodhisattva's Way of Life 4.28-35, p. 279.

correct. When he is affected by worries and anxieties, his mind will not be correct. When the mind is not present, we look but do not see, listen but do not hear, and eat but do not know the taste of food. This is what is meant by saying that the cultivation of the personal life depends on the rectification of the mind.

*Confucianism.* Great Learning 7

Wipe out the delusions of the will, undo the snares of the heart, rid yourself of the entanglements to virtue; open up the roadblocks in the Way. Eminence and wealth, recognition and authority, fame and profit—these six are the delusions of the will. Appearances and carriage, complexion and features, temperament and attitude—these six are the snares of the heart. Loathing and desire, joy and anger, grief and happiness—these six are the entanglements of virtue. Rejecting and accepting, taking and giving, knowledge and ability—these six are the roadblocks of the Way. When these four sixes no longer seethe within the breast, then you will achieve uprightness; being upright, you will be still; being still, you will be enlightened; being enlightened, you will be empty; and being empty, you will do nothing, and yet there will be nothing that is not done.

*Taoism.* Chuang Tzu 23

Confucius said, "There are three things against which a gentleman is on his guard. In his youth, before his blood and vital humors have settled down, he is on his guard against lust. Having reached his prime, when the blood and vital humors have finally hardened, he is on his guard against strife. Having reached old age, when the blood and vital humors are already decaying, he is on his guard against avarice."

*Confucianism.* Analects 16.7

Thus I have heard. At one time when the Lord was staying in the Jeta Grove, the venerable Kassapa the Boy was staying in Blind Men's Grove. One night, a certain being, having illuminated the grove, spoke thus to Kassapa the Boy, "Monk, this anthill smokes by night and blazes up by day. A wise brahmin says, 'Clever one, bring a spade and dig into it.' He digs into it and finds a bolt and tells the brahmin, who says, 'Take out the bolt, and dig on.' The clever one digs into it again and finds in turn a frog, a pitchfork, a basket, a tortoise, a butcher knife, and a piece of meat, and each time the brahmin instructs him to take it out. He digs into it again and finds a cobra, and the brahmin says, 'Let the cobra be, do not touch the cobra, do reverence to the cobra.'"

Then Kassapa the Boy approached the Lord and described the parable to him, asking for its interpretation. The Lord replied, "The anthill is a symbol for the body made of the four elements, originated from mother and father, nourished on gruel... Whatever one thinks upon and ponders upon during the night concerning the day's affairs, this is smoking by night. Whatever affairs one sets going by day, having reflected the previous night, this is blazing up by day. The wise brahmin is the Tathagata, and the clever one is a monk who is a learner. The spade symbolizes intuitive wisdom, and digging means putting out effort.

"Among the things which the man digs up and takes out, the bolt symbolizes ignorance, the frog is the turbulence of wrath, the pitchfork is perplexity, and the basket is the five hindrances—the holding on to desire for sense pleasures, hatred, laziness, restlessness, delusion. The tortoise is the five Aggregates, the butcher knife is five sense pleasures, and the piece of meat is the resulting desire that causes one to covet satisfaction. These are all to be taken out and thrown away.

"The cobra means the person whose cankers are destroyed. If one digs into himself with the spade of wisdom, he will finally come to his cobra. It is worthy of reverence."

*Buddhism.* Majjhima Nikaya i.142-45: Parable of the Anthill

**Great Learning 7:** Cf. James 4.1-3, p. 294; Chuang Tzu 11, p. 297.

**Chuang Tzu 23:** Cf. Tao Te Ching 56, p. 601.

**Majjhima Nikaya i.142-45:** The five 'Aggregates' are the skandhas; the 'five sense pleasures,' are the pleasures of sight, sound, smell, taste, and touch. Cf. Mahaparinirvana Sutra 214-15, p. 147; Matthew 5.29-30, p. 663; Samyutta Nikaya iii.68, p. 640.

The greatest problem of any man is woman.

*African Traditional Religions*. Igala Proverb (Nigeria)

Confucius said, "I have never seen anyone whose desire to build up his moral power was as strong as sexual desire."

*Confucianism*. Analects 9.17

The Buddha said, "Of all longings and desires, there is none stronger than sex. Sex as a desire has no equal. Rely on the Oneness. No one under heaven is able to become a follower of the Way if he accepts dualism [the attraction of opposites]."

*Buddhism*. Sutra of Forty-two Sections 25

Those who abstain from sex,
Except with those joined to them in the marriage bond....
But those whose desires exceed those limits are transgressors....
These will be the heirs
Who will inherit Paradise.

*Islam*. Qur'an 23.5-11

He who delights in subduing evil thoughts, who meditates on the loathsomeness of the body, who is ever mindful—it is he who will make an end of craving. He will sever Mara's bond.

*Buddhism*. Dhammapada 350

The mouth is a vessel filled with foul
Saliva and filth between the teeth,
The nose with fluids, snot, and mucus,
The eyes with their own filth and tears.

The body is a vessel filled
With excrement, urine, lungs, and liver;
He whose vision is obscured and does not see
A woman thus, lusts for her body.

This filthy city of a body,
With protruding holes for the elements
Is called by stupid beings
An object of pleasure.

Why should you lust desirously for this
While recognizing it as a filthy form
Produced by a seed whose essence is filth,
A mixture of blood and semen?

He who lies on the filthy mass
Covered by skin moistened with
Those fluids, merely lies
On top of a woman's bladder.

Nagarjuna, Precious Garland 149-57

Get back, I hate you!
Don't hold my sari, you fool!
A she-buffalo is worried of its life,
And the butcher, of its killing!
The pious think of virtues,
And the wicked, of vices;
I am worried of my soul,
And you, of lust....

Fie on this body!
Why do you damn yourself

**Igala Proverb:** This means that a wife or lover leads to unforeseen troubles, hence the desire for sex should be disciplined.

**Sutra of Forty-two Sections:** This may be a criticism of Tantric Buddhism, with its "secret yoga" of sexual union as the way to enlightenment. For an example of a dualistic Tantric conception of enlightenment, see Hevajra Tantra 8.26-29, p. 119

**Dhammapada 350:** On 'meditating on the loathsomeness of the body,' see the following passages; also Sutta Nipata 205-06, p. 650 and the story of Subha, Therigatha 366-99, p. 663. For the setting up of mindfulness, see Majjhima Nikaya i.55-63, Satipatthana Sutta, pp. 604-5.

**Precious Garland 149-57:** Vv. 149-50, 154, 156-57. Gautama Buddha himself came to such a realization about the body's loathsomeness one evening when his father tempted him with courtesans in an effort to keep him from leaving home and beginning his spiritual quest. This is an excerpt from a meditation about bodies in general, and is not intended to denigrate women. Cf. Sutta Nipata 205-6, p. 650; Therigatha 366-99, p. 663.

In love of it—this pot of excrement,
The vessel of urine, the frame of bones,
This stench of purulence!
Think of Lord Shiva,
You fool!

*Hinduism*. Akkamahadevi, Vacana 15 and 33

Continence is to regard the wife of another as one's own sister or daughter, and to realize that the bodies of women are full of impurity and that charm can only delude the mind.

*Jainism*. Kartikeya, Anupreksa 337-39

Treat younger men like brothers, older women like mothers, younger women like sisters, in all purity.

*Christianity*. 1 Timothy 5.1-2

The Buddha said, "Be careful not to look at women and do not talk with them. If you must speak with them, be properly mindful and think, 'I am a shramana living in a turbid world. I should be like the lotus flower and not be defiled by the mud.' Regard old women the way you regard your mother. Regard those who are older than you the way you regard your elder sisters; regard those who are younger than you as your younger sisters, and regard children as your own. Bring forth thoughts to rescue them, and put an end to bad thoughts."

*Buddhism*. Sutra of Forty-two Sections 29

You have heard that it was said, "You shall not commit adultery." But I say to you that every one who looks at a woman lustfully has already committed adultery with her in his heart.

*Christianity*. Matthew 5.27-28

He who excites himself by lustful thoughts will not be allowed to enter the division of the Holy One.

*Judaism*. Talmud, Nidda 13b

The adultery of the eye is the lustful look, and the adultery of the tongue is the licentious speech, and the heart desires and yearns, which the parts may or may not put into effect.

*Islam*. Hadith of Muslim

It is true that you commit no actual crimes; but when you meet a beautiful woman in another's home and cannot banish her from your thoughts, you have committed adultery with her in your heart. Consider a moment! Would you have sufficient control over yourself to imitate the sage Lu Nan-tze if you were placed in a similar position? When he once found himself obliged to pass the night in a house whose only other occupant was a woman, he lighted a lamp and read aloud until morning to avoid exposing her to unjust suspicions.

*Taoism*. Treatise on Response and Retribution, Appended Tales

❖

**Akkamahadevi, Vacana 33:** Akkamahadevi (12th century) was a Virashaiva woman saint. Once, when a certain king tried to molest her, she suddenly threw away all her clothes and stepped out into the streets nude. This act of purity so stunned the king that he repented of his foolish lust. Akkamahadevi wandered about as a naked ascetic, clad only in her long hair, enduring the taunts of men and teaching an example of purity and devotion to God Shiva.

**Anupreksa 337-39:** Cf. Skanda Purana 5.2.11, p. 672.

**Nidda 13b:** cf. Aboda Zara 20ab, p. 337.

## *Detachment from the Senses*

THE PASSIONS AND CRAVINGS OF THE FLESH often arise from the perceptions of the senses. Therefore, subduing desire begins by cultivating an attitude of detachment towards sense perceptions, by regarding them as impermanent, transient, and of no account. This teaching is stressed in the Bhagavad Gita and in Buddhist scriptures. Related is the injunction by Jesus that "if your right eye causes you to sin, pluck it out and throw it away," which is illustrated by the story of the Buddhist nun Subha.

Just as one does not touch a sensuous woman entering an empty house, so is he who does not touch the sense objects that have entered into him, a renouncer, an ascetic, a self-sacrificer.

*Hinduism.* Maitri Upanishad 6.10

All bodhisattvas, lesser and great, should develop a pure, lucid mind, not depending upon sound, flavor, touch, odor, or any quality. A bodhisattva should develop a mind which alights upon no thing whatsoever; and so should he establish it.

*Buddhism.* Diamond Sutra 10

When the senses contact sense objects, a person experiences cold or heat, pleasure or pain. These experiences are fleeting; they come and go. Bear them patiently, Arjuna. Those who are not affected by these changes, who are the same in pleasure and pain, are truly wise and fit for immortality. Assert your strength and realize this!...

The disunited mind is far from wise; how can it meditate? How can it be at peace? When you know no peace, how can you know joy? When you let your mind follow the call of the senses, they carry away your better judgment as storms drive a boat off its charted course on the sea. Use all of your power to free the senses from attachment and aversion alike, and live in the full wisdom of the Self.

*Hinduism.* Bhagavad Gita 2.14-15, 66-68

Monks, there are these three feelings. What three? Pleasant feeling, painful feeling, and feeling that is neither painful nor pleasant. Pleasant feeling, monks, should be looked upon as pain, painful feeling should be looked upon as a barb, feeling that is neither painful nor pleasant should be looked upon as impermanent. When these three feelings are looked upon in these ways by a monk, that monk is called "rightly seeing."

*Buddhism.* Itivuttaka 47

The five colors make man's eyes blind;
The five notes make his hears deaf;
The five flavors injure his palate;
Riding and hunting make his mind go mad.
Goods hard to come by serve to hinder his progress.
Hence the sage is for the belly and not the eye.
Therefore he discards the one and takes the other.

*Taoism.* Tao Te Ching 12

**Diamond Sutra 10:** Cf. Chuang Tzu 7, p. 519.

**Itivuttaka 47:** Cf. Dhammapada 212-14, p. 658.

**Tao Te Ching 12:** Some interpret this passage as a criticism of attachment to the senses: 'The belly' is man's inner power, or *ch'i*, which should be cultivated through meditation while ignoring distractions of the senses. Others interpret the passage in a political sense: The extravagances of the court, pleasing to the eye, ear, and palate, should be rejected in favor of providing ample food for the people, 'the belly.'

If your right eye causes you to sin, pluck it out and throw it away; it is better that you lose one of your members than that your whole body be thrown into hell. And if your right hand causes you to sin, cut it off and throw it away; it is better that you lose one of your members than that your whole body go into hell.

*Christianity*. Matthew 5.29-30

In Jivaka's pleasant wood walked Subha the bhikkhuni. A gallant met her there and barred the way. Subha said this to him,

"What have I done to offend you, that you stand obstructing me? For it is not fitting, sir, that a man should touch a sister in orders. This has my Master ordained in the precepts we honor and follow. So has the Well-come One taught in the training wherein they have trained me to be purified, disciplined, holy. Why do you stand blocking my pathway? I am pure; you impure of heart; I am passionless, you of vile passions; I am wholly freed in spirit and blameless. Why do you obnoxiously stand obstructing me?"

"You are young, maiden, and faultless—what do you seek in the holy life? Cast off that yellow robe and come! In the blossoming woodland let us seek our pleasure. Filled with the incense of blossoms, the trees waft sweetness. See, the spring is at the prime, the season of happiness. Come with me then to the flowering woodland, and let us seek our pleasure....

"Dearer and sweeter to me than are you is no creature on earth, you with languid and slow-moving eyes of an elf in the forest. If you will do my bidding, come where the joys of the sheltered life await you; dwell in a house of verandas and terraces, with handmaidens serving you. Robe yourself with delicate garments, don garlands, use unguents. I will give you many and varied ornaments, fashioned with precious stones, gold work, and pearls. You will mount on a couch fair and sumptuous, carved in sandalwood, fragrant with essences, spread with new pillows, coverlets fleecy and soft..."

"What so infatuates you about this carcass, filled with carrion, to fill a grave, so fragile, that it seems to warrant such words?"

"Eyes you have like a gazelle's, like an elf's in the heart of the mountains—'tis those eyes of yours, sight of which feeds the depth of my passion. Shrined in your dazzling, immaculate face as in the calyx of a lotus, 'tis those eye of yours, sight of which feeds the strength of my passion. Though you be far from me, how could I ever forget you, O maiden, you of long-drawn eyelashes, you of eyes so miraculous?..."

"O you are blind! You chase a sham, deluded by puppet shows seen in the midst of the crowd; you deem of value and genuine conjurer's trickwork.... What is this eye but a little ball lodged in the fork of a hollow tree, bubble of film, anointed with tear-brine, exuding slime-drops, compost wrought in the shape of an eye of manifold aspects?"

Forthwith the maiden so lovely tore out her eye and gave it to him. "Here, then! Take your eye!" Her heart unattached, she sinned not.

Straightaway the lust in him ceased and he begged her pardon. "O pure and holy maid, would that you might recover your sight! Never again will I do such a thing. You have sore smitten my sin; blazing flames have I clasped to my bosom; a poisonous snake I have handled—but O, be healed and forgive me!"

Freed from molesting, the bhikkhuni went on her way to the Buddha, chief of the Awakened. There in his presence, seeing those features born of utmost merit, her eye was restored.

*Buddhism*. Therigatha 366-99,
Subha Jivakambavanika Sutta

**Matthew 5.29-30:** Cf. Majjhima Nikaya i.142-45, p. 659.
**Therigatha 366-99:** Cf. Akkamahadevi, Vacana 15 and 33, pp. 660-61; Precious Garland 149-57, p. 660; Sutta Nipata 205-6, p. 650.

# *Renunciation of Wealth*

ALL SCRIPTURES REGARD ATTACHMENT TO WEALTH and possessions as a fetter to spiritual progress. Attachment promotes greed and avarice, which draw the mind downward into the mire of self-centered desire. Therefore the path to Transcendence requires renunciation of wealth and the desire for its benefits.

Renunciation of wealth is of two kinds. One is total renunciation, the vow of poverty incumbent upon the monk. The other is the more moderate rejection of acquisitiveness: Wealth should be regarded as a secondary end, never overshadowing the purposes of God or the goal of spiritual advancement. One's work may result in gain, but that gain should never be grasped at, nor even desired if it would conflict with the demands of righteousness and require the exploitation of others. For more texts on total renunciation, see the next section on asceticism; also *Anxiety*, pp. 553-55.

We may divide these passages into three groups. Those in the first group distinguish true religion from concern for wealth. A person must put God first; attachment to riches is an obstacle to realizing the spiritual goal. A second group of texts recommends an attitude of non-possessiveness. People should not work with the expectation of reward, nor grasp after possessions. The Bhagavad Gita describes work done without attachment or desire for reward as liberated and not productive of karma. Taoist texts describe Non-action (*wu-wei*), which is devoid of self-interest, as the way to manage everything. Texts in the last group describe a hierarchy of values: Rightness and duty come above personal gain. As long as the former is upheld, gain is permissible; but it is incorrect to seek gain at the expense of rightness.

What avail riches for the practice of religion?

*Jainism.* Uttaradhyayana Sutra 14.16

Man shall not live by bread alone, but by every word that proceeds from the mouth of God.

*Judaism* and *Christianity.*
Deuteronomy 8.3, Matthew 4.4

Do not race after riches, do not risk your life for success, or you will let slip the Heaven within you.

*Taoism.* Chuang Tzu 29

Busy not yourself with this world, for with fire We test the gold, and with gold We test Our servants.

*Baha'i Faith.* Hidden Words of Baha'u'llah, Arabic 54

Anyone who is stingy, is stingy only with his own soul. God is Wealthy while you are poor.

*Islam.* Qur'an 47.38

Woe is he... who has gathered riches and counted them over, thinking his riches have made him immortal!

*Islam.* Qur'an 104.1-3

**Chuang Tzu 29:** Cf. Tao Te Ching 12, p. 662; John 2.13-16, p. 745.
**Qur'an 47.38:** Cf. Qur'an 107.4-7, p. 349; Osashizu, p. 289.
**Qur'an 104.1-3:** Cf. Qur'an 107.4-7, p. 349.

No one can serve two masters; for either he will hate the one and love the other, or he will be devoted to the one and despise the other. You cannot serve God and mammon.

*Christianity*. Matthew 6.24

When they see merchandise or diversion they scatter off to it, and they leave you standing. Say, "What is with God is better than diversion and merchandise. God is the best of providers."

*Islam*. Qur'an 62.11

Riches ruin the foolish, but not those in quest of the Beyond. Through craving for riches the ignorant man ruins himself as he does others.

*Buddhism*. Dhammapada 355

And he [Jesus] called to him the twelve, and began to send them out two by two, and gave them authority over the unclean spirits. He charged them to take nothing for their journey except a staff; no bread, no bag, no money in their belts; but to wear sandals and not put on two tunics.

*Christianity*. Mark 6.7-9

This is the way of Torah: A morsel with salt shall you eat and water by measure shall you drink; and you shall lie upon the earth, and you shall live a life of hardship, and labor in the Torah. If you do thus, happy shall you be and it shall be well with you.

*Judaism*. Mishnah, Abot 6.4

The Master said, "Incomparable was Hui! A handful of rice to eat, a gourdful of water to drink, living in a mean street—others would have found it unendurably depressing, but to Hui's cheerfulness it made no difference at all. Incomparable indeed was Hui!"

*Confucianism*. Analects 6.9

Blessed is the straw hut where God's praises are chanted;
Worthless the white mansions where remembrance of God is not.
Poverty with the holy while contemplating God is bliss itself.
Burn that pride of high state that involves the self with maya.
Grinding grain with rough clothing brings to the mind joy and contentment.
What worth kingship without peace of soul?

*Sikhism*. Adi Granth, Suhi, M.5, p. 745

Yajnavalkya [addressing his wife]: "Maitreyi, I am resolved to renounce the world and begin the life of renunciation. I wish therefore to divide my property between you and my other wife, Katyayani."

Maitreyi: "My Lord, if this whole earth belonged to me, with all its wealth, should I through its possession attain immortality?"

"No. Your life would by like that of the rich. None can possibly hope to attain immortality through wealth."

"Then what need have I of wealth? Please, my lord, tell me what you know about the way to immortality."

*Hinduism*. Brihadaranyaka Upanishad 2.4.1-3

'Ali ibn Abu Talib said, "When we were sitting with God's Messenger in the mosque, Mus'ab ibn 'Umair came to us wearing only a cloak of his patched with fur, and when God's Messenger saw him he wept to think of his former affluence and his condition at that time. He then said, 'How will it be with you when one of you goes out in the morning wearing a mantle and goes out in the evening wearing another, when one dish is placed before him

**Matthew 6.24:** Cf. 1 Timothy 6.10, p. 296; Matthew 16.26, p. 681.

**Dhammapada 355:** A man may have wealth as long as he does not crave it but places it in service of the higher goal—cf. Holy Teaching of Vimalakirti 2, p. 682.

**Mark 6.7-9:** Cf. Matthew 10.9-10, pp. 586-87.

**Analects 6.9:** Yen Hui was Confucius' favorite disciple; see Analects 9.10, p. 585; Shih Chi 47, p. 433.

**Brihadaranyaka Upanishad 2.4.1-3:** Cf. Lotus Sutra 12, p. 584, the story of a king who renounces his wealth to follow a mendicant teacher and learn the truth. The Shakyamuni's own life is, of course, the best example of a rich man renouncing a kingdom and its riches for the sake of a higher goal; see Buddhacarita of Ashvaghosha 3-5, pp. 425-26.

and another removed, and you cover your houses as the Kaaba is covered?' On receiving the reply, 'Messenger of God, we shall then be better than we are today, having leisure for worship and possessing all we require,' he said, 'No, you are better today than you will be at that time.'"

*Islam.* Hadith of Tirmidhi

Running after that cur, money,
I have forgotten you, O Lord.
What a shame! I have time only for making
  money, not for you.
How can a dog who loves rotten meat, relish
  the nectar?

*Hinduism.* Basavanna, Vacana 313

Beautified for mankind is love of the joys [that come] from women and offspring, and stored-up heaps of gold and silver, and horses branded, and cattle and land. That is comfort of the life of the world. God! With Him is a more excellent abode. Say, Shall I inform you of something better than that? For those who keep from evil, with their Lord are Gardens underneath which rivers flow, and pure companions, and contentment from God.

*Islam.* Qur'an 3.14-15

Jesus said to [the rich young man], "If you would be perfect, go, sell what you possess and give to the poor, and you will have treasure in heaven; and come, follow me." When the young man heard this he went away sorrowful; for he had great possessions.

And Jesus said to his disciples, "Truly, I say to you, it will be hard for a rich man to enter the kingdom of Heaven. Again I tell you, it is easier for a camel to go through the eye of a needle than for a rich man to enter the kingdom of God."

*Christianity.* Matthew 19.21-24

And [Jesus] told them a parable, saying, "The land of a rich man brought forth plentifully; and he thought to himself, 'What shall I do, for I have nowhere to store my crops?' And he said, 'I will do this: I will pull down my barns, and build larger ones; and there I will store all my grain and my goods. And I will say to my soul, Soul, you have ample goods laid up for many years; take your ease, eat, drink, be merry.' But God will say to him, 'Fool! This night your soul is required of you; and the things you have prepared, whose will they be?' So is he who lays up treasure for himself, and is not rich toward God."

*Christianity.* Luke 12.16-21

I see men of wealth in the world—
acquiring property, from delusion they give not
  away;
out of greed a hoard of wealth they make,
and hanker sorely after more sense pleasures....

Heirs carry off his wealth;
but the being goes on according to kamma.
Wealth does not follow him who is dying,
nor child or wife, nor wealth or kingdom.

Long life is not gained from wealth,
nor is old age banished by property.
"For brief is this life," the wise say,
non-eternal, subject to change.

Rich and poor feel the touch [of death],
fool and wise are touched alike.
But the fool, as though struck down by folly,
  prostrate lies,
While the wise, touched by the touch, trembles
  not.

Wherefore better than wealth is wisdom
by which one here secures Accomplishment.

*Buddhism.*
Majjhima Nikaya ii.72-73,
Rattapala Sutta

**Matthew 19.21-24:** Cf. 1 Timothy 6.10, p. 296; Matthew 6.19-21, p. 237; 13.44-46, p. 486; John 2.13-16, p. 745.

**Luke 12.16-21:** Cf. Matthew 6.19-21, p. 237.

**Majjhima Nikaya ii.72-73:** Buddhism does not condemn the acquisition of wealth in the life of a layman. He may energetically acquire wealth as long as he does not exploit others. Attachment to wealth and miserliness are condemned. Furthermore, far better than wealth is to realize enlightenment, arahantship, 'Accomplishment.'

The great man—his face and form blend with the Great Unity, the Great Unity which is selfless. Being selfless, how can he look upon possession as possession?

*Taoism.* Chuang Tzu 11

The impulse "I want" and the impulse "I'll have"—lose them! That is where most people get stuck; without those, you can use your eyes to guide you through this suffering state.

*Buddhism.* Sutta Nipata 706

On gaining the desired object, one should not feel elated. On not receiving the desired object, one should not feel dejected. In case of obtaining anything in excess, one should not hoard it. One should abstain from acquisitiveness. One who sees Reality should consume things in a manner different from that of a layman.

*Jainism.* Acarangasutra 2.114-19

The sage manages affairs without action,
Carries out the teaching without speech.
Ten thousand things arise and he does not
 initiate them,
They come to be and he claims no possession
 of them,
He works without holding on to,
Accomplishes without claiming merit.
Because he does not claim merit,
His merit does not go away.

*Taoism.* Tao Te Ching 2

You have the right to work, but never to the fruit of work. You should never engage in action for the sake of reward, nor should you long for inaction. Perform work in this world, Arjuna, as a man established within himself—without selfish attachments, and alike in success and defeat. For discipline is perfect evenness of mind.

Seek refuge in the attitude of detachment and you will amass the wealth of spiritual awareness. Those who are motivated only by desire for the fruits of action are miserable, for they are constantly anxious about the results of what they do. When consciousness is unified, however, all vain anxiety is left behind. There is no cause for worry, whether things go well or ill.

*Hinduism.* Bhagavad Gita 2.47-50

The Master said, "A superior man takes as much trouble to discover what is right as lesser men take to discover what will pay."

*Confucianism.* Analects 4.16

Be not like servants who minister to their master upon the condition of receiving a reward; but be like servants who minister to their master without the condition of receiving a reward; and let the fear of Heaven be upon you.

*Judaism.* Mishnah, Abot 1.3

Virtue is the root; wealth is the result.

If he makes the root his secondary object, and the result his primary, he will only wrangle with his people, and teach them rapine.

Hence, the accumulation of wealth is the way to scatter the people; and the letting it be scattered among them is the way to collect the people.

*Confucianism.* Great Learning 10.7-9

Wealth and rank are what every man desires; but if they can only be retained to the detriment of the Way he professes, he must relinquish them. Poverty and obscurity are what every man detests; but if they can only be avoided to the detriment of the Way he professes, he must accept them. The gentleman who ever parts company with goodness does not fulfill that name. Never for a moment does a gentleman quit the way of goodness. He is never so harried but that he cleaves to this; never so tottering but that he cleaves to this.

*Confucianism.* Analects 4.5

**Tao Te Ching 2:** Cf. Tao Te Ching 64, p. 652; Chuang Tzu 6, pp. 158-59. 'Without action,' *wu-wei*, is the benevolent principle of Heaven; cf. Tao Te Ching 34, pp. 90-91; 37, p. 87; 52, p. 679.

**Bhagavad Gita 2.47-50:** Cf. Bhagavad Gita 4.19-21, p. 555.

**Abot 1.3:** Cf. Micah 3.5, p. 316; Shalok, Farid, p. 296.

**Analects 4.5:** Cf. Mencius VI.A.10, pp. 626-27; Chuang Tzu 4, pp. 507-8.

# *Asceticism and Monasticism*

MATERIAL COMFORTS WHICH CATER to the desires of the body have always been recognized as obstacles to finer sensitivity in matters of the spirit. Asceticism, austerities, and severe discipline of the body are therefore recommended in order to reduce the claims of the body on the concerns of the soul. Fasting, chastity, simple food, and control of sleep are salutary practices for enriching the spiritual life. One who wishes to devote himself purely to a religious goal might even wish to sever him or herself entirely from the competing claims of worldly affairs by adopting the secluded and sometimes solitary life of a monk or nun. The paths of asceticism and monasticism are the topics of this section.

The first group of passages deal with the ascetic life as practiced in the religions of South Asia. Hindu tradition—in the passage from the Laws of Manu quoted here—advocates that every brahmin spend the last quarter of his life, after his children are grown, as a solitary ascetic in the forest, devoting himself to meditation and the goal of liberation (*moksha*) as he formerly had devoted himself to success at worldly affairs. He would receive his sustenance by begging in the neighboring villages, and villagers earn religious merit by offering of their food to the wandering ascetics.

This ideal of renunciation in retirement is difficult enough; few Hindus actually practice it. But there have always been heroic souls who dedicate their entire lives to the solitary path. Rather than a stage of life, monkhood may be a religious vocation for anyone serious about reaching the goal of liberation and Nirvana. Lifelong renunciation is the practice of Buddhist and Jain monks, who follow the examples of their founders; Buddha and Mahavira began as leaders of monastic orders.

The next several passages enjoin fasting; it is salutary for all people, not only monastics. In Islam, fasting is a duty for every Muslim during the month of Ramadan. A text from Native American religion encourages fasting as a way to gain spiritual support and help in life's trials.

The Christian teaching on chastity was originally meant for anyone who could receive it; many of the early disciples sought to practice this ideal by having chaste marriages. Based on this scriptural foundation, Christian monasticism grew and took institutional form in order to provide a supportive setting for those who wished to take vows of poverty and chastity, who valued the love of Christ which surpasses the love of women. As a later development, Christian monasticism is not explicitly regulated by scripture. It has taken a wide variety of forms: solitary hermits, cloistered monasteries, and orders dedicated to nursing, teaching, scholarship, and other forms of service to the world.

The last group of passages is critical of asceticism and monasticism; such critiques of asceticism are found in nearly every tradition where it is practiced. They are of two kinds: The first critique is that the ascetic practice is fraught with striving for spiritual achievement that is itself egotistical and vain. The true spiritual path is self-emptying, but accomplishing severe austerities can cause one to be puffed up with pride. Without denying the value of asceticism, there are various correctives to its abuse: pure faith, devotion, charity, and the inner path of meditation. The second criticism is that monkhood is incompatible with the generative and productive life in the world which is ordained by God. Thus Hinduism counterposes to the efficacy of asceticism for spiritual success the requirement to have progeny and care for them as the measure of worldly responsibility; there is a proper dharma for each in its own time and place. Islam and Sikhism both condemn monasticism, or at least those varieties of monasticism which take people out of the economic and social life where they should be contributing and leavening the society by their godly example.

The blue-necked peacock which flies through the air never approaches the speed of the swan. Similarly, the householder can never resemble the monk who is endowed with the qualities of the sage, who meditates, aloof, in the jungle.

*Buddhism.* Sutta Nipata 221

They who practice austerity and faith in the forest,
The peaceful knowers who live on alms,
Depart passionless through the door of the sun,
To where is that immortal Person, even the imperishable Spirit.

*Hinduism.* Mundaka Upanishad 1.2.11

"Revile not, harm not, live by rule restrained;
Of food take little; sleep and sit alone;
Keep thy mind bent upon the higher thought."
Such is the message of awakened ones.

*Buddhism.* Udana 43

Go on the begging tour, stay in a forest, eat but a little, speak only measured words, put up with misery, conquer sleep, practice friendship with all and non-attachment in an excellent manner.

*Jainism.* Vattakera, Mulacara 981

In the first place the sage should relinquish attachments to objects, whether animate or inanimate; he should then subdue his mind and senses; and finally he should resort to mortification of the flesh in progressively increasing intensity.... Only on complete obliteration of sensuality can one forsake violence. This is the truth: realize it.

*Jainism.* Acarangasutra 4.40, 45

To fill life to the brim is to invite [evil] omens.
If the heart makes calls upon the life-breath, rigidity follows.
Whatever has a time of vigor also has a time of decay.
Such things are against the Tao,
And whatever is against the Tao is soon destroyed.

*Taoism.* Tao Te Ching 55

The gods themselves for a sight of Thee have done penance, fasted, and performed ablutions:
Yogis and celibates have practiced austerities and adopted ochre robes.
For Thee, Lord, are all seekers dyed in devotion.
Innumerable Thy names, countless Thy forms, inexpressible Thy attributes.
The devotees questing after Thee have renounced home,
Mansions luxurious, elephants and chargers,
And sojourned into strange lands.
Saints and prophets, seekers and devotees—
Such have renounced the world and met with Thy acceptance.
They renounced pleasures, comfort, joys of the palate;
Gave up clothing and wrapped themselves in hides.
Ever restless, making agonized search for Thy Portal,
They dyed themselves in Thy name, and trod the hermit's path.

*Sikhism.* Adi Granth, Asa, M.1, p. 358

**Mulacara 981:** On the Rule for Jain ascetics, see Acarangasutra 2.15, p. 112.

**Acarangasutra 4.40, 45:** Cf. the description of Mahavira's ascetic life in Acarangasutra 9, p. 470.

**Asa, M.1:** In Sikhism, devotion to God is the root of all true asceticism. Austerities are valueless as exercises in themselves; they have value only when done in devotion.

But having passed the third part of life in the forest, a man may live as an ascetic during the fourth part of his existence, after abandoning all attachment to worldly objects....

Worlds, radiant in brilliancy, become the portion of him who recites [the texts regarding] Brahman and departs from his house as an ascetic, after giving a promise of safety to all created beings.

For that twice-born man, by whom not the smallest danger even is caused to created beings, there will be no danger from any quarter, after he is freed from his body.

Departing from his house fully provided with the means of purification, let him wander about absolutely silent, and caring nothing for enjoyments that may be offered to him.

Let him always wander alone, without any companion, in order to attain [final liberation], fully understanding that the solitary man, who neither forsakes nor is forsaken, gains his end.

He shall neither possess a fire, nor a dwelling; he may go to a village for his food, indifferent to everything, firm in purpose, meditating and concentrating his mind on God.

A potsherd [for an alms-bowl], the roots of trees [for a dwelling], coarse worn-out garments, life in solitude, and indifference toward everything are the marks of one who has attained liberation.

Let him not desire to die, let him not desire to live; let him wait for [his appointed] time, as a servant for the payment of his wages.

Let him put down his foot purified by his sight [i.e., watching not to step on any creature], let him drink water purified by straining with a cloth [so as not to swallow any creature], let him utter speech purified by truth, let him keep his heart pure.

Let him patiently bear hard words, let him not insult anybody, and let him not become anybody's enemy for the sake of his body.

Against an angry man let him not in return show anger, let him bless when he is cursed, and let him not utter speech, devoid of truth, scattered at the seven gates.

Delighted in what refers to the Soul, sitting [in yoga postures], independent, entirely abstaining from sensual enjoyments, with himself for his only companion, he shall live in this world, desiring the bliss [of liberation]....

Let him go to beg once a day, let him not be eager to obtain a large quantity of alms; for an ascetic who eagerly seeks alms attaches himself also to sensual enjoyments.

When no smoke ascends from the kitchen, when the pestle lies motionless, when the embers have been extinguished, when the people have finished their meal, when the remnants in the dishes have been removed, let the ascetic always go to beg.

Let him not be sorry when he obtains nothing, nor rejoice when he obtains, let him accept only so much as will sustain life, let him not care about the utensils.

Let him disdain all obtained in consequence of humble salutations, for even an ascetic who has attained final liberation is fettered by accepting food given in consequence of humble salutations.

By eating little, and by standing and sitting in solitude, let him restrain his sense, if they are attracted to sensual objects.

By the restraint of his senses, by the destruction of love and hatred, and by the abstention from injuring the creatures, he becomes fit for immortality.

*Hinduism.* Laws of Manu 6.33-60

O believers, prescribed for you is the Fast, even as it was prescribed for those that were before you—haply you will be god-fearing—

for days numbered; and if any of you be sick, or if he be on a journey, then a number of other days; and for those who are able, a redemption by feeding a poor man. Yet better it is for him who volunteers good, and that you should fast is better for you, if you know;

the month of Ramadan, wherein the Qur'an was sent down to be a guidance to the people, and as clear signs of the Guidance and the Salvation. So let those of you, who are present

**Laws of Manu 6.33-60:** This is the fundamental rule of Hindu asceticism, adopted with only minor variations by Jains and Buddhists as well. Cf. Uttaradhyayana Sutra 2.12-13, p. 554; Matthew 10.1-25, pp. 586-87.

at the month, fast it; and if any of you be sick, or if he be on a journey, then a number of other days; God desires ease for you, and desires not hardship for you; and that you fulfill the number, and magnify God that He has guided you, and haply you will be thankful.

*Islam*. Qur'an 2.183-85

My son, you ought to be of some help to your fellow men, and for that reason I counsel you to fast. Our grandfather who stands in our midst sends forth all kinds of blessings. Try then and obtain one of these. Try to have one of our grandfathers, one of the War Chiefs, pity you. Then some day as you travel along the road [of life], you will know what to do and encounter no obstacles. Without any trouble you will then be able to seek the prize you desire. Then the honor will be yours to glory in, for without any exertion have you obtained it. All the war power that exists has been donated to our grandfathers who are in control of warfare, and, if, reverently, you thirst yourself to death, then they will bestow blessings upon you. Now if you do not wear out your feet, if you do not blacken your face with charcoal, it will be for naught that you inflict suffering upon yourself. These blessings are not obtainable without effort. Try to have one of all the spirits created by Earthmaker take pity upon you. Whatever he says will come about. If you do not possess a spirit to strengthen you, you will be of no consequence and the people will show you little respect.

*Native American Religions*.
A Winnebago Father's Precepts

[Jesus] said to them, "Not all men can receive this saying, but only those to whom it is given. For there are eunuchs who have been so from birth, and there are eunuchs who have been made eunuchs by men, and there are eunuchs who have made themselves eunuchs for the sake of the kingdom of Heaven. He who is able to receive this, let him receive it."

*Christianity*. Matthew 19.12

It is well for a man not to touch a woman, but because of the temptation to immorality, each man should have his own wife and each woman her own husband.... I say this by way of concession, not of command. I wish that all were as I myself am. But each has his own special gift from God, one of one kind and one of another....

I want you to be free from anxieties. The unmarried man is anxious about the Lord, how to please the Lord; but the married man is anxious about worldly affairs, how to please his wife, and his interests are divided. And the unmarried woman or virgin is anxious about the affairs of the Lord, how to be holy in body and spirit; but the married woman is anxious about worldly affairs, how to please her husband. I say this for your own benefit, not to lay any restraint upon you, but to promote good order and to secure your undivided devotion to the Lord.

*Christianity*. 1 Corinthians 7.1-35

Some invent harsh penances. Motivated by hypocrisy and egoism, they torture their innocent bodies and Me who dwells within. Blinded by their strength and passion, they act and think like demons.

*Hinduism*. Bhagavad Gita 17.5-6

**Winnebago Father's Precepts:** The grandfathers are spirits created by Earthmaker who are in control of the powers for victory on the journey of life, which is metaphorically represented by the warpath. The 'grandfather who stands in our midst' is the spirit of the fire around which this teaching was given. The expression 'wear out your feet' refers to frequent journeys to the fasting lodge, which is of some distance from the village. On the value of fasting, cf. Chuang Tzu 19, p. 525.

**1 Corinthians 7.1-35:** Vv.1-2, 6-7, 32-35. Paul himself lived a celibate life, wholly devoted to the Lord. He recognized that his ability to function as a celibate apostle was a 'special gift' which he valued highly, and he wished that all could live as he did. Celibacy is valuable, because the unmarried person is free to devote him or herself totally to God, while the person caught up in the affairs of home and family has divided attentions. Paul advises those who are able to follow his example, but he also recognizes that it is a difficult course that is not for everyone.

**Bhagavad Gita 17.5-6:** This and the following passages condemn ascetic striving which is motivated by egoism or infected by pride. Any austerities done for the purpose of attaining something are futile.

Engaged in much difficult fasting, over six years his body became steadily emaciated.... But tormenting his body through such austerities availed him nothing. "This is not the way to achieve passionlessness, enlightenment, liberation. How can it be reached by a man who is not calm and at ease, who is so exhausted by hunger and thirst that his mind is unbalanced?"

*Buddhism*. Ashvaghosha, Buddhacarita 12.95-101

O brother, wither away your sensuality, passions, and egotism. There is no benefit in emaciating this gross body [through penances]. We will never praise you merely because of your withered body.

*Jainism*. Nisithabhasya 3758

If with Christ you died to the elemental spirits of the universe, why do you live as if you still belonged to the world? Why do you submit to regulations, "Do not handle, Do not taste, Do not touch" (referring to things which all perish as they are used), according to human precepts and doctrines? These have indeed an appearance of wisdom in promoting rigor of devotion and self-abasement and severity to the body, but they are of no value, serving only to indulge the flesh. If then you have been raised with Christ, seek the things that are above, where Christ is, seated at the right hand of God. Set your minds on things that are above, not on things that are on earth.

*Christianity*. Colossians 2.20-3.2

Formerly in the Pine Forest there were brahmins doing austerities, vying with each other in various ways, but they did not achieve success. Then they thought, "The sages did not speak the truth when they said that success in everything is obtained by asceticism." Overcome by impatience, they put aside their asceticism and became atheists. But at this time a voice said to them, "Do not despise the scriptures, do not blame asceticism or dharma, but blame yourselves. You strive against each other, desiring success, and because of that your asceticism is fruitless, destroyed by desire, egoism, anger, and greed. A man achieves perfection in asceticism only when he looks upon another man's wife as if she were his mother. Propitiate the linga of Shiva and you will obtain success."

*Hinduism*. Skanda Purana 5.2.11

If a man should go naked... feed on potherbs, wild rice, or Nivara seeds... wear coarse hempen cloth, or carry out any other [ascetic] practices... yet the state of blissful attainment in conduct, in heart, in intellect, have not been practiced by him, realized by him, then he is far from shramanaship, far from brahminship. But from the time, O Kassapa, when a monk has cultivated the heart of love that knows no anger, that knows no ill will—from the time when, by the destruction of the deadly intoxications, he dwells in that emancipation of heart, that emancipation of mind, that is free from those intoxications, and that he, while yet in this visible world, has come to realize and know—from that time, O Kassapa, is it that the monk is called a shramana, is called a brahmin!

*Buddhism*. Digha Nikaya i.167, Kassapa-Sihanada Sutta

Should one perform a million ritual acts and of these be proud,
They leave him only fatigued, and are of little avail.

**Skanda Purana 5.2.11:** The context of this passage is the story of the sages' mistrust of their wives, whom they believed to have been seduced by Shiva. Devotion to Shiva permits the brahmins to transcend their jealousy as well as the egoistic motivation for their asceticism.

**Digha Nikaya i.167:** Asceticism does not help one who has not overcome his doubts, according to Sutta Nipata 249, p. 614. Devadatta taught an excessive rigorism in order to cause a schism in the order: see Vinaya Pitaka ii.184-98, pp. 318-20. The 'deadly intoxications' are: lusts of the flesh, craving after being (immortality), and the defilements of delusion and ignorance.

One who performs innumerable austerities and
for these bears pride,
Shall remain caught in transmigration, moving
between heaven and hell.
With all a man's effort, should his self not turn
compassionate,
How may he have access to the Divine Portal?

*Sikhism*. Adi Granth, Gauri Sukhmani, M.5, p. 278

There was a great seer of strict vows, foremost of those wise in the law, the learned ascetic Mandapala. He followed the path of the seers who held up their seed [in chastity], austere and master of his senses. After he had abandoned his body, he attained to the world of the ancestors. Yet he failed to find the fruit of his acts there. Finding his worlds without reward, although he had won them with his asceticism, he questioned the celestials: "Why are these worlds that I won with my austerities closed to me? Where did I fail that this should be the results of my acts?" They said, "Men are born indebted to rites, to the study of the Veda, and to offspring, doubt it not. You are an ascetic and a sacrificer, but you have no offspring; these worlds are closed to you because of this matter of offspring. A son saves his father from the hell called *Put*, Hermit. Therefore, O brahmin, strive for the continuity of children!"

*Hinduism*. Mahabharata, Adi Parva 220

We sent Jesus son of Mary, and gave him the Gospel, and placed compassion and mercy in the hearts of those who followed him. But monasticism they invented—We ordained it not for them—only seeking God's pleasure, and they observed it not with right observance. So We give those who believe their reward, but many of them are evil-livers.

*Islam*. Qur'an 57.27

❖

**Gauri Sukhmani:** Cf. Suhi, M.1, p. 682; Var Sarang, M.1, p. 714; Itivuttaka 19, p. 685; Precious Garland 406-12, pp. 292-93.

**Mahabharata, Adi Parva 220:** Asceticism and procreation are apparently incompatible, yet both are necessary goods. In the story, Mandapala is given another opportunity to bear offspring by mating with a Sharngaka bird and begetting four Sharngaka bird-sages as his sons. Generally, the offspring of a saintly ascetic are the spiritual children whom he or she leads to enlightenment and salvation. On the kinds of indebtedness, see Satapatha Brahmana 1.7.2.1-5, p. 557. Cf. Laws of Manu 11.10, p. 676.

**Qur'an 57.27:** Muslim commentators note that the Qur'an approves of the asceticism and humility enjoined by the gospels: see Qur'an 5.82-83, p. 40. But monasticism is rejected, inasmuch as in its cloistered forms it takes believers out of the world while they should be mingling with others and upholding the Truth through service and example. Sikhism has a similar critique of otherworldly asceticism; see Suhi, M.1, p. 682. Mahayana Buddhism also downplays the value of otherworldliness, as seen in the Holy Teaching of Vimalakirti 2, p. 682.

## *Separation from Family*

WHILE THE FAMILY WHICH IS IMBUED WITH GOD'S LOVE can realize one of the great purposes of life, and it is indeed a joy to be a member of such a family, oftentimes the person who is called to a spiritual quest finds attachment to family and relations a hindrance on the path. The members of his family may not understand his passion for the spiritual life. They may not respect his lack of concern for material wealth and worldly success—which they take as the all-important values—as he pursues what he regards as a higher purpose. Hence they may come to oppose him and seek to tempt him away from the religious life.

The passages given below describe this most painful struggle between the aspirant and the possessive and ignorant members of his or her family. He is commanded to love God and his religious teacher more than his father and mother and brothers and sisters. He is warned to beware of other family members who would betray his trust and tempt him into sin. Entry into the religious life may even require the aspirant to leave his family, divorce his wife, and abandon his children and property. Some scriptures describe family ties as attachments, which partake of illusion and which are to be overcome in order to achieve tranquillity, enlightenment, and the highest goal.

To reject one's family is an extreme position, and several more moderate courses are suggested in the last group of texts. Believers may constitute new families which are devoted to God. Or they may find a way to live within families yet maintain a detached perspective, "in the world yet not of the world." This latter position will be treated further in the next section.

Do not think that I have come to bring peace on earth; I have come not to bring peace, but a sword. For I have come to set a man against his father, and a daughter against her mother, and a daughter-in-law against her mother-in-law; and a man's foes will be those of his own household. He who loves father or mother more than me is not worthy of me; and he who loves son or daughter more than me is not worthy of me.

*Christianity*. Matthew 10.34-37

O believers, take not your fathers and brothers to be your friends, if they prefer unbelief to belief; whosoever of you takes them for friends, those—they are the evildoers.

Say, If your fathers, your sons, your brothers, your wives, your clan, your possessions that you have gained, commerce you fear may slacken, dwellings you love—if these are dearer to you than God and His Messenger, and to struggle in His way, then wait till God brings His command: God guides not the people of the ungodly.

*Islam*. Qur'an 9.23-24

You who believe! Among your wives and your children there are enemies for you; therefore beware of them.... Your wealth and your children are only a temptation, whereas God, with Him is an immense reward.

*Islam*. Qur'an 64.14-15

Put no trust in a neighbor,
have no confidence in a friend;
guard the doors of your mouth
from her who lies in your bosom;
for the son treats the father with contempt,
the daughter rises up against her mother,
the daughter-in-law against her mother-in-law;
a man's enemies are the men of his own house.
But as for me, I will look to the Lord,
I will wait for the God of my salvation;
my God will hear me.

*Judaism* and *Christianity*. Micah 7.5-7

The thin skin that covers the stomach
Does not allow us to see the interior of a
treacherous person.
Keep your secret to yourself; never share it with
any man.
There's no honest man nowadays,
All people are now deceitful.
The person we asked to help us rub our back
with a sponge,
Added thorns to the sponge in his hand.
The person we asked to help us blow dust from
our eyes,
First put some pepper in his mouth.
The man on whose generosity we rested
assured
To obtain and enjoy sweet oranges,
Gave us sour oranges to suck.
The man we wished to confide in,
Turned out to be a garrulous person.
When people make themselves your close
associates,
Be cautious; confide only in yourself.
Only in yourself.

*African Traditional Religions*. Yoruba Song (Nigeria)

Now the Lord said to Abram, "Go from your country and your kindred and your father's house to the land that I will show you..."

*Judaism* and *Christianity*. Genesis 12.1

Every one who has left houses or brothers or sisters or father or mother or children or lands, for my name's sake, will receive a hundredfold, and inherit eternal life.

*Christianity*. Matthew 19.29

He who forsakes his home in the cause of God, finds in the earth many a refuge, wide and spacious; should he die as a refugee from home for God and His Apostle, his reward becomes due and sure with God: and God is Oft-forgiving, Most Merciful.

*Islam*. Qur'an 4.100

In awe of my lord's command,
I skirt the coastal borders and
Traverse the plain of the sea,
—Leaving father and mother behind.

*Shinto*. Man'yoshu 20

One day she who was formerly the mate of the venerable Sangamaji came towards him, drew near and said, "Recluse, support me with our little child." At these words the venerable Sangamaji was silent. So a second time and yet a third time his former wife repeated her words, and still the venerable Sangamaji was silent. Thereupon she set down the child in front of him and went away, saying, "Here is your child, recluse! Support him!" But the venerable Sangamaji neither looked at the child nor spoke to him. When from a distance she saw this, she thought to herself, "This recluse needs not even his own child." So she turned back, took up the child and went away.

*Buddhism*. Udana 5-6

"How could I be diligent, good Sariputta, when there are my parents to support, my wife and children to support, my slaves, servants and work-people to support, when there are services to perform for friends and acquaintances, services to perform for kith and kin, services to perform for guests, rites to perform for the ancestors, rites to perform for the gods, duties to perform for the king—and this body too must be satisfied and looked after!"

"What do you think, Dhananjani? Suppose someone failed to live the holy life because of his parents [and so on]; because of this failure... the guardians of Niraya hell might drag him off to their hell. Would he gain anything by saying, 'I failed to live the holy life because of my parents [and so forth]'?"

*Buddhism*. Majjhima Nikaya ii.186-87

**Qur'an 4.100:** The Companions of Muhammad had to leave their homes and families in the face of persecution, particularly in the emigration (*hejrat*) from Mecca to Medina.
**Udana 5-6:** Cf. Vinaya Pitaka, Mahavagga i.43, p. 431.
**Majjhima Nikaya ii.186-87:** Cf. 1 Corinthians 7.32-35, p. 671.

We have instructed man to treat his parents kindly. Yet if they should strive to make you associate anything with Me which you have no knowledge of, do not obey them.

*Islam*. Qur'an 29.8

If any one comes to me and does not hate his own father and mother and wife and children and brothers and sisters, yes, and even his own life, he cannot be my disciple.

*Christianity*. Luke 14.26

From concern with family, all the concerns of life, arise attachment.
Discard attachment, from which arises doings that are totally evil.
Brother! discard your detachment and illusion—
Then will the holy Name in your heart and body disport.

*Sikhism*. Adi Granth, Asa M.1, p. 356

Free from selfish attachment, they do not get compulsively entangled even in home and family. They are even-minded through good fortune and bad. Their devotion to me is undivided. Enjoying solitude and not following the crowd, they seek only me. This is true knowledge, to seek the Self as the true end of wisdom always. To seek anything else is ignorance.

*Hinduism*. Bhagavad Gita 13.9-11

If a man does anything for the sake of his happiness in another world, to the detriment of those whom he is bound to maintain, that produces evil results for him, both while he lives and when he is dead.

*Hinduism*. Laws of Manu 11.10

I have always been solitary; I belong to none else; I behold no one whom I can say I belong to nor do I behold one whom I can designate as mine. The path of worldliness is nothing but disaster. Who, whose, and where are one's kith and kin? Who, whose, and where are strangers, all going round in cycles of birth and death? At times, the kith and kin become strangers, and vice versa. Ponder thus, "I am all alone. Nobody was mine in the past, nor will ever be in the future. It is because of my karmas that I delude myself and consider others as mine. The truth is that I was alone in the past and will ever be all alone."

*Jainism*. Acarangasutra 4.32

He who is kind toward much-beloved friends loses his own good from his mind, becoming partial; observing such danger in friendship, let one walk alone like a rhinoceros.

As a spreading bush of bamboo is entangled in various ways, so is the longing for children and wives: not clinging to these, even like a bamboo just sprouting forth, let one walk alone like a rhinoceros....

If one lives in the midst of company, love of amusement and desire arises; strong attachment for children arises; let therefore one who dislikes separation, which must happen sooner or later from these beloved, walk alone like a rhinoceros....

Having abandoned the different kinds of desire, founded on child, wife, father, mother, wealth, corn, relations, let one walk alone like a rhinoceros.

Let a wise man, having discovered that such is attachment, that there is in it but little happiness, that it is but insipid, that there is more

**Luke 14.26:** In this hard saying, the injunction to hate one's parents is understood in the same way as to hate one's own life: It is a matter of hating any ties and attachments which have become fetters to the disciple's devotion to God and Christ and his will. Cf. Sun Myung Moon, 4-3-83, p. 639.

**Bhagavad Gita 13.9-11:** Cf. Kularnava Tantra 2, p. 628.

**Laws of Manu 11.10:** The obligations to family are not to be taken lightly; discipleship and shramanaship going to the point of breaking these obligations is a serious step. Cf. Mahabharata, Adi Parva 220, p. 673.

**Acarangasutra 4.32:** This is the declaration of the Jain who leaves home for the life of a solitary monk. It is also an ontological statement about human existence which is held in some form by all the religions of India; cf. Laws of Manu 4.238-39, p. 238; Gauri, M.5, p. 233.

affliction in it than comfort, that it is a fishhook, walk alone like a rhinoceros.

Having cast off the bonds, like a fish which breaks the net in the water, like a fire that returns not to the spot already burned up, let one walk alone like a rhinoceros.

*Buddhism.* Sutta Nipata 37-62: Rhinoceros Discourse

[Jesus'] mother and his brothers came; and standing outside they sent to him and called him. And a crowd was sitting about him; and they said to him, "Your mother and your brothers are outside, asking for you." And he replied, "Who are my mother and my brothers?" And looking around on those who sat about him, he said, "Here are my mother and my brothers! Whoever does the will of God is my brother, and sister, and mother."

*Christianity.* Mark 3.31-35

It is not for the sake of the husband, my beloved, that the husband is dear, but for the sake of the Self.

It is not for the sake of the wife, my beloved, that the wife is dear, but for the sake of the Self.

It is not for the sake of the children, my beloved, that the children are dear, but for the sake of the Self.

*Hinduism.* Brihadaranyaka Upanishad 2.4.4-5

Enlightening beings at home
Should wish that all beings
Realize the nature of "home" is empty
And escape its pressures.

While serving their parents,
They should wish that all beings
Serve the Buddha,
Protecting and nourishing everyone.

While with their spouses and children,
They should wish that all beings
Be impartial toward everyone
And forever give up attachment.

When attaining desires,
They should wish that all beings
Pull out the arrow of lust
And realize ultimate peace.

*Buddhism.* Garland Sutra 11

❖

**Sutta Nipata 37-62:** Vv.37-38, 41, 60-62. The rhinoceros-like aloofness recommended by this discourse is meant for monks still in training, for whom the attachments of family and friends might be distractions and obstacles to Nibbana. For those firmly established in enlightenment, family and friends should be no obstacles at all—see the excerpt from the Garland Sutra, below, and Holy Teaching of Vimalakirti 2, p. 682. Cf. Parable of the Mustard Seed, pp. 271-72.

**Mark 3.31-35:** Jesus spent long hours teaching his disciples, to the dismay of his family. When they tried to call him out, Jesus rebuked them thus. The Gospels reveal that Jesus was misunderstood and alienated from his family. At the marriage at Cana (John 2.3-4), when Jesus' mother asked him to perform a miracle and provide wine for the wedding, he said to her, "Woman, what have you to do with me? My hour has not yet come," suggesting that she had but a shallow understanding of his mission. See also Mark 6.1-4, p. 428.

**Brihadaranyaka Upanishad 2.4.4-5:** The Self refers to Ultimate Reality immanent in the heart, and certainly not to the egoistic self.

**Garland Sutra 11:** Cf. Holy Teaching of Vimalakirti 2, p. 682.

# *Separation from the World*

A PERSON WITH A RELIGIOUS GOAL cannot brook the standards of worldly life. A worldly lifestyle, seeking pleasure, wealth, fame, and material comforts, will inevitably distract from pursuing any spiritual purpose. Hence the aspirant must separate himself from the world or maintain some detachment from it. Separation from the world can be achieved either by physical isolation in a monastic community or by living an outwardly ordinary life yet without attachment to its prevailing values.

The scriptures contain numerous admonitions to avoid conforming to the world and its values. The wise man regards the worldly achievement as an illusion; he keeps his mind free of worldly cares or *Anxiety*, pp. 553-55. He does not delight in worldly pleasures, but devotes himself to pursuing his spiritual goal. He lives detached from worldly thoughts and sense impressions. He measures achievement by spiritual progress, rather than by the standards of worldly success.

These are followed by passages which deal with the social dimension of separation. A passage from the Midrash ascribes the reason for Judaism's severe ritual and moral injunctions to the fact that God separated the Jews from all the other peoples of the earth. In Buddhism and Christianity, the imperative that the Sangha or Church be a purified and separated environment for the sake of members' spiritual progress requires that miscreants be disciplined and even excommunicated.

We conclude with texts on being in the world but not of the world. Such an understanding of separation from the world is the norm in Confucianism, Islam, and Christianity. But in Buddhism and Hinduism, which have had to contend with the opinion that salvation requires monkhood, this meaning of separation from the world has been the subject of much discussion. The Holy Teaching of Vimalakirti, in particular, praises the householder's life as a middle way between the total renunciation of monkhood and a life of dissolute pleasure. Throughout this scripture, the householder Vimalakirti is an enlightened bodhisattva who displays insight, powers, and attainments superior to those of the monks.

Do not be conformed to this world, but be transformed by the renewal of your mind, that you may prove what is the will of God, what is good and acceptable and perfect.

*Christianity*. Romans 12.2

Do not serve mean ends. Do not live in heedlessness. Do not embrace false views. Do not be one who upholds the world.

*Buddhism*. Dhammapada 167

Come, behold this world which is like unto an ornamented royal chariot, wherein fools flounder, but for the wise there is no attachment.

*Buddhism*. Dhammapada 171

Pleasure lies in gold, silver, women, and
delectable objects;
Pleasure lies in mounts, soft beds, mansions,
and attractions of the palate.
With all such pleasures, how may the Name
find place in the mind?

*Sikhism*. Adi Granth, Sri Raga, M.1, p. 15

**Dhammapada 167:** Cf. Dhammapada 75, p. 484.
**Sri Raga, M.1:** Cf. Katha Upanishad 1.2.2, p. 485.

Hillel used to say, "More flesh, more worms; more wealth more care; more women more witchcraft; more maidservants more lewdness; more menservants more thieving; more Torah more life; more assiduity more wisdom; more counsel more understanding; more charity more peace."

*Judaism.* Mishnah, Abot 2.8

The streams of this world are dirty and its springs are turbid. Its window dressing and its show is beautiful but destructive. It is a quickly ending deception, a speedily fading light, a hurrying shade, and a weak and unreliable protection. It is so deceptive that it waits till those who abhor it start taking interest in it, and those who do not know its deception are attracted by it, and are satisfied with it, then it shows scanty regard for them, it snares and captivates them, and tying the rope of death round their necks drags them to their graves.

*Islam.* Nahjul Balagha, Sermon 86

Be in the world as if you were a stranger or a traveler.

*Islam.* Forty Hadith of an-Nawawi 40

A man came to the Prophet and said, "O Messenger of Allah, direct me to an act which, if I do it, will cause Allah to love me and people to love me." He said, "Renounce the world and Allah will love you; renounce what people possess and people will love you."

*Islam.* Forty Hadith of an-Nawawi 31

A complete disregard for all worldly things, perfect contentment, abandonment of hope of every kind, and patience—these constitute the highest good of one who has subjugated his senses and acquired a knowledge of Self.

No need of attaching yourself to things of this world. Attachment to worldly objects is productive of evil.

*Hinduism.* Mahabharata, Shanti Parva 329

He who has found the Mother [Tao]
And thereby understands her sons [things of the world],
And having understood the sons,
Still keeps to its Mother,
Will be free from danger throughout his lifetime.
Close the mouth,
Shut the doors [of cunning and desire],
And to the end of life there will be peace without toil.
Open the mouth,
Meddle with affairs,
And to the end of life there will be no salvation.

*Taoism.* Tao Te Ching 52

The Self-existent pierced sense openings outward;
therefore a man looks out, not in.
But a certain wise man, in search of immortality,
turned his gaze inward and saw the Self within.

The foolish go after outward pleasures
and walk into the snare of all-embracing death.
The wise, however, discerning immortality,
do not seek the permanent among things impermanent.

*Hinduism.* Katha Upanishad 4.1-2

**Abot 2.8:** Cf. Abot 3.17, p. 653; Luke 14.16-24, p. 485.

**Forty Hadith of an-Nawawi 40:** Cf. Matthew 8.19-20, p. 428.

**Forty Hadith of an-Nawawi 31:** On sacrifice and being loved by people, see John 15.13, p. 691; Hadith of Bukhari, p. 700; Kojiki 110, p. 752.

**Mahabharata, Shanti Parva 329:** Cf. Katha Upanishad 1.2.2, p. 485.

**Tao Te Ching 52:** The nature of the world should be understood from the vantage point of knowledge of Ultimate Reality, the Tao. Then it will be seen that things of the world change naturally, in accordance with the Tao. This leads to the concept of *wu-wei*, Non-action, which is to let the Tao operate and not to meddle with things according to human ambitions. Cf. Tao Te Ching 2, p. 667.

**Katha Upanishad 4.1-2:** Truth is found through meditation and fixing attention on the Self within, not by dealing with the deceptive and transient phenomena of the world. This is a most fundamental statement of Upanishadic philosophy.

What is the path of the Word? It is that a person gives up his desire for the world and has a deep yearning for God's world. We should love God's world more than we love any person: parents, children, or spouse.

*Unification Church.*
Sun Myung Moon, 8-9-70

The sage patterns himself on Heaven, prizes the Truth, and does not allow himself to be cramped by the vulgar. The stupid man does the opposite of this. He is unable to pattern himself on Heaven and instead frets over human concerns. He does not know enough to prize the Truth but instead, plodding along with the crowd, he allows himself to be changed by vulgar ways, and so is never content.

*Taoism.* Chuang Tzu 31

Adepts in yoga speak in the manner of the uncivil, behave as if ignorant, appear like the lowly. They do so in order that men may ignore them and not flock to them; they talk nothing at all. Though realized in freedom, the yogi will sport like a child, may conduct himself like a dullard, talk like one intoxicated. Such a yogi lives in a way that this world of men may laugh, feel disgust, revile, and seeing, pass at a distance, leaving him alone. He would go about in different guises, at times like one worthy, at times like one fallen, at times like a ghost or demon. If the yogi accepts things of life it is for the good of the world and not out of desire. Out of compassion for all men, he will sport on the earth.

*Hinduism.* Kularnava Tantra 9

To conserve his stock of virtue, the superior man withdraws into himself and thus escapes from the evil influences around him. He declines all temptations of honor and riches.

*Confucianism.*
I Ching 12: Stagnation

As a sweet-smelling, lovely lotus may grow upon a heap of rubbish thrown by the highway, even so a disciple of the Fully Enlightened One outshines the ignorant worldly people in wisdom.

*Buddhism.* Dhammapada 58-59

Cast aside from you all attachments, as the leaves of a lotus let drop of the water of the autumn rains; exempt from every attachment, Gautama, be careful all the while!

Give up your wealth and your wife; you have entered the state of the houseless; do not, as it were, return to your vomit. Gautama, be careful all the while!

Leave your friends and relations, the large fortune you have amassed; do not desire them a second time; Gautama, be careful all the while!...

Now you have entered on the path from which the thorns have been cleared, the great path; walk in the right path, Gautama, be careful all the while!

Do not get into an uneven road like a weak burden-bearer; for you will repent of it afterward; Gautama, be careful all the while!

*Jainism.*
Uttaradhyayana Sutra 10.28-33

**Chuang Tzu 31:** Cf. Chuang Tzu 23, p. 555.

**Kularnava Tantra 9:** Yogis may appear as fools or madmen, be meek or act repulsively, all the while in a state of higher awareness. They may make ordinary people uncomfortable by their disregard of worldly manners and conventions. The biblical prophets were often thought to be crazy: compare 1 Samuel 19.23-24. Compare also the Taoist images of the convict from Chuang Tzu 23, p. 555, and of the drunkard from Chuang Tzu 19, pp. 399-400.

**I Ching 12:** 'Virtue' has the sense of inner force and power by which one can act decisively and with conviction. It should not be restricted to 'morality,' though virtue in the sense of morality is one source of inner power.

**Dhammapada 58-59:** The pure lotus flower, which grows in muddy swamps, is a Buddhist symbol of one who leaves worldly life to accept the Dharma, train according to its teaching, and flower as an enlightened being. In Hinduism, it symbolizes one who lives sinless, untouched by the dirt of the world; cf. Bhagavad Gita 5.10, p. 554.

**Uttaradhyayana Sutra 10.28-33:** Cf. Katha Upanishad 1.3.14, p. 484.

For what is a man profited, if he shall gain the whole world and lose his own soul? Or what shall a man give in exchange for his soul?

*Christianity.* Matthew 16.26

What worth kingship without peace of soul?

*Sikhism.* Adi Granth, Suhi, M.5, p. 745

Better than absolute sovereignty over the earth, better than going to heaven, better than even lordship over all the worlds is the fruit of a Stream-winner.

*Buddhism.* Dhammapada 178

Jesus answered, "My kingship is not of this world; if my kingship were of this world, my servants would fight, that I might not be handed over to the Jews; but my kingship is not from the world."

*Christianity.* John 18.36

Confucius said, "Of T'ai Po it may indeed be said that he attained to the very highest pitch of moral power. No less than three times he renounced the sovereignty of all things under heaven [the throne of the empire], without the people getting a chance to praise him for it."

*Confucianism.* Analects 8.1

Righteousness, O Wise One, was set up for our
choice, to be our blessing,
Evil for the godless, for his undoing!
Therefore I seek union with the Good Mind,
And I forbid all traffic with the wicked.

*Zoroastrianism.* Avesta, Yasna 49.3

"And ye shall be holy unto me, for I, the Lord, am holy" [Leviticus 20.26]. Even as I am holy, so be you holy. As I am separate, so be you separate. And "I have severed you from the other peoples that you should be mine" [idem.]. If you sever yourselves from the other peoples, then you belong to me; but if not, then you belong to Nebuchadnezzar and his fellows." Rabbi Eliezer said, "How can we know that a man must not say, 'I have no desire to eat pig, I have no desire to have intercourse with a woman whom I may not marry'; but he must say, 'Yes, I would like to do these acts, but what can I do? My Father who is in heaven has forbidden them.' Because it says, 'I have severed you from among the nations to be mine.' He who is separated from iniquity receives to himself the Kingdom of Heaven."

*Judaism.* Sifra 93d

I wrote to you in my letter not to associate with immoral men; not at all meaning the immoral of this world, or the greedy and robbers, or idolators, since then you would need to go out of the world. But rather I wrote to you not to associate with any one who bears the name of brother if he is guilty of immorality or greed, or is an idolator, reviler, drunkard, or robber—not even to eat with such a one. For what have I to do with judging outsiders? Is it not those inside the church whom you are to judge? God judges those outside. "Drive out the wicked person from among you."

*Christianity.* 1 Corinthians 5.9-13

Just as the mighty ocean consorts not with a dead body; for when a dead body is found in the mighty ocean it quickly wafts it ashore, throws it up on the shore; even so, monks, whatsoever person is immoral, of a wicked nature, impure, of suspicious behavior, of covert deeds, one who is no recluse though claiming to be such, one rotten within, full of lusts, a rubbish-heap of filth—with such the Order consorts not, but gathering together

**Matthew 16.26:** Cf. Matthew 13.44-46, p. 486; Luke 14.16-24, p. 485.

**Suhi, M.5:** Cf. Udana 13, p. 553.

**Dhammapada 178:** The stage of Stream-winner is only a low grade of attainment on the way to Nibbana. He sees a glimpse of the goal, and, if he perseveres, he comes to have assurance of attaining sainthood.

**Sifra 93d:** Cf. Abot 3.17, p. 653.

**1 Corinthians 5.9-13:** Cf. Garuda Purana 112, p. 185; Tract of the Quiet Way, p. 185; Itivuttaka 68-69, p. 185. On the other hand, out of loving-kindness, Jesus ate with sinners and sought to help those afflicted with moral weakness: see Matthew 9.10-13, p. 685; also Romans 15.1-3, p. 691; Mencius IV.B.7, pp. 691-92.

quickly throws him out. Though he be seated in the midst of the Order, yet he is far away from the Order; far away is the Order from him.

*Buddhism*. Udana 55

Krishna, thou Lord of the senses, though moving amongst the objects of sense, remain unaffected by them. Thou hast indeed shown us the ideal: to live in the world and yet not be of it.

*Hinduism*. Srimad Bhagavatam 11.1

They are not of the world, even as I am not of the world. Sanctify them in truth; thy word is truth. As thou didst send me into the world, so I have sent them into the world. And for their sake I consecrate myself, that they also may be consecrated in truth.

*Christianity*. John 17.16-19

The world of the kami does not transcend that of man, and man does not need to enter a divine, transcendental world to attain salvation. He seeks salvation by bringing the kami into the human world, into the daily life of the home, the marketplace....

*Shinto*. S. Ono

Yoga consists not in frequenting wild places,
tombs and cremation grounds,
Nor in falling into trances;
Nor lies it in wandering about the world,
Nor in ritual bathing.
To live immaculate amidst the impurities of the
world—
This is true yoga practice.

*Sikhism*. Adi Granth, Suhi, M.1, p. 730

Vimalakirti wore the white clothes of a layman, yet lived impeccably like a religious devotee. He lived at home, but remained aloof from the realm of desire, the realm of pure matter, and the immaterial realm. He had a son, a wife, and female attendants, yet always maintained continence. He appeared to be surrounded by servants, yet lived in solitude. He appeared to be adorned with ornaments, yet always was endowed with the auspicious signs and marks. He seemed to eat and drink, yet always took nourishment from the taste of meditation. He made his appearance at the fields of sports and in the casinos, but his aim was always to mature those people who were attached to games and gambling. He visited the fashionable heterodox teachers, yet always kept unswerving loyalty to the Buddha. He understood the mundane and transcendental sciences and esoteric practices, yet always took pleasure in the delights of the Dharma. He mixed in all crowds, yet was respected as foremost of all.... He engaged in all sorts of businesses, yet had no interest in profit or possessions. To train living beings, he would appear at crossroads and on street corners, and to protect them he participated in government.

*Buddhism*. Holy Teaching of Vimalakirti 2

**Udana 55:** Cf. Lotus Sutra 2, p. 291; Garuda Purana 112, p. 185; Itivuttaka 68-69, p. 185.

**Suhi, M.1:** Cf. Var Sarang, M.1, p. 714; Qur'an 57.27, p. 673.

**Holy Teaching of Vimalakirti 2:** Among Mahayana texts, this scripture most clearly denies the necessity for the aspirant to enlightenment to become a monk. The logical culmination of the doctrine of Sunyata is the thought that there is no difference between Samsara and Nirvana, for both are empty—see Mulamadhyamaka Karika 25, pp. 59-60; Lankavatara Sutra 80, p. 158. Hence a person may dwell in perfect enlightenment while outwardly pursuing an ordinary life, as long as all thoughts, words, and actions are based upon a mind of compassion, which is the manifestation of Emptiness. Lay Buddhism has been particularly popular in Japan ever since the time of Shinran, who, believing that salvation is by faith alone and any ascetic practice is in vain, abandoned his monastic vows and married. Many of the popular modern sects of Nichiren Buddhism are also lay movements. Cf. Garland Sutra 11, p. 677.

CHAPTER 19

# LIVE FOR OTHERS

THIS CHAPTER TREATS ACTS OF CHARITY, LOVING-kindness, and righteousness which are the outward manifestations of an interior faith. The spiritual life which begins with faith and devotion to Ultimate Reality finds its completion in deeds of compassion, loving-kindness, service, and witness which manifest the Heart of Ultimate Reality in the world: "We love, because He first loved us" (1 John 4.19). Indeed, religion has been convincing to many because it has produced people of love who could surpass the standards of worldly affections.

Living for others is ultimately not a burden or a sacrifice. For those who have reached the goal of life, who have become one with Ultimate Reality, the motivation to give, serve, and love others flows spontaneously from their inmost being. They wish to give and serve for the sake of the other, without seeking any benefit for themselves. Their love is full of forgiveness and tolerance for those who do them wrong, whether from ignorance or from malice. They never find satisfaction in exacting revenge on their enemies, but only in bringing them to salvation. This is the ideal manifested by men and women of *True Love*, pp. 159-63. But living for others is also an ethic and a discipline which must be cultivated and practiced, for the human heart is often selfish and mean, when compared with the lofty standard of divine love.

Here we gather texts on the various ways in which scripture instructs people of faith to treat others and to love them properly. These include: (1) an attitude of loving-kindness and compassion; (2) selfless service for the sake of others; (3) sacrificial and suffering love; (4) the principle of giving and receiving, that is, of giving first without seeking to receive a return; (5) charity to the poor and hospitality to strangers; (6) forgiveness of those who do us wrong and tolerance of others' failings; (7) cautions against judging others, for who is without fault?; (8) loving your enemy and requiting evil with good; (9) turning the other cheek; (10) good works; (11) honest labor and good industry which benefits the community as well as oneself; (12) honesty and truthfulness; and (13) witnessing to the Truth in order to share with others the blessings of salvation.

# *Loving-kindness*

TEXTS ON LOVING-KINDNESS, compassion, and heartfelt love for others include general admonitions to kindness, benevolence, and gentleness. Next come passages which recommend loving-kindness and mercy as superior to ritual observances. Other passages stress the impartiality and universality of the heart of mercy; it transcends considerations of family, race, nationality, or religion. Love that naturally develops between members of a family should be extended to embrace all beings. Among the texts gathered here is Jesus' Parable of the Good Samaritan; also a text from the Upanishads on the Voice of Thunder, who utters three "Das" to describe the three interrelated virtues of self-control, giving, and compassion.

Those who act kindly in this world will have kindness.

*Islam*. Qur'an 39.10

Those who do not abandon mercy will not be abandoned by me.

*Shinto*. Oracle of Itsukushima

Love covers a multitude of sins.

*Christianity*. 1 Peter 4.8

Mencius said, " 'Benevolence' means 'man.' When these two are conjoined, the result is 'the Way.' "

*Confucianism*. Mencius VII.B.16

Have benevolence toward all living beings, joy at the sight of the virtuous, compassion and sympathy for the afflicted, and tolerance towards the indolent and ill-behaved.

*Jainism*. Tattvarthasutra 7.11

God enjoins justice, kindness, and charity to one's kindred, and forbids indecency, abomination, and oppression. He admonishes you so that you may take heed.

*Islam*. Qur'an 16.90

The world stands upon three things: upon the Law, upon worship, and upon showing kindness.

*Judaism*. Mishnah, Abot 1.2

Gentle character it is which enables the rope of life to stay unbroken in one's hand.

*African Traditional Religions*. Yoruba Proverb (Nigeria)

He who can find no room for others lacks fellow feeling, and to him who lacks fellow feeling, all men are strangers.

*Taoism*. Chuang Tzu 23

Treat people in such a way and live amongst them in such a manner that if you die they will weep over you; alive they crave for your company.

*Islam*. Nahjul Balagha, Saying 9

What sort of religion can it be
without compassion?
You need to show compassion
to all living beings.
Compassion is the root
of all religious faiths.

*Hinduism*. Basavanna, Vacana 247

**Mencius VII.B.16:** In Chinese characters, 'benevolence' and 'man' are cognates.
**Nahjul Balagha:** See Hadith, p. 471, on the Prophet's mercy, which made such a strong impression.

The bhikkhu who abides in loving-kindness, who is pleased with the Buddha's teaching, attains to that state of peace and happiness, the stilling of conditioned things, Nibbana.

Let him be cordial in all his ways and refined in conduct; filled thereby with joy, he will make an end of ill.

*Buddhism.* Dhammapada 368, 376

Rabbi Yohanan ben Zakkai said, "Go forth and see which is the good way to which a man should cleave." Rabbi Eliezar said, "A good eye"; Rabbi Joshua said, "A good friend"; Rabbi Jose said, "A good neighbor"; Rabbi Simeon said, "One who foresees the fruit of an action"; Rabbi Elazar said, "A good heart." Thereupon he said to them, "I approve the words of Elazar ben Arach, rather than your words, for in his words yours are included."

*Judaism.* Mishnah, Abot 2.13

Monks, whatsoever grounds there be for good works undertaken with a view to [favorable] rebirth, all of them are not worth one-sixteenth part of that goodwill which is the heart's release; goodwill alone, which is the heart's release, shines and burns and flashes forth in surpassing them.

*Buddhism.* Itivuttaka 19

Even though it be the home of someone who has managed for long to avoid misfortune, we gods will not enter into the dwelling of a person with perverse disposition. Even though it be a dwelling where a man be in mourning for father and mother, if he be a man of compassion, we deities will enter in there.

*Shinto.* Oracle of Kasuga

And as he sat at table in the house, behold, many tax collectors and sinners came and sat down with Jesus and the disciples. And when the Pharisees saw this, they said to his disciples, "Why does your teacher eat with tax collectors and sinners?" But when he heard it, he said, "Those who are well have no need of a physician, but those who are sick. Go and learn what this means, 'I desire mercy, and not sacrifice.'"

*Christianity.* Matthew 9.10-13

Once, as Rabbi Yohanan ben Zakkai was coming forth from Jerusalem, Rabbi Joshua followed after him and beheld the Temple in ruins. "Woe unto us," Rabbi Joshua cried, "that this, the place where the iniquities of Israel were atoned for, is laid waste!"

"My son," Rabbi Yohanan said to him, "be not grieved. We have another atonement as effective as this. And what is it? It is acts of loving-kindness, as it is said, 'For I desire mercy and not sacrifice' [Hosea 6.6]."

*Judaism.* Talmud, Abot de Rabbi Nathan 6

As a mother with her own life guards the life of her own child, let all-embracing thoughts for all that lives be thine.

*Buddhism.* Khuddaka Patha, Metta Sutta

**Dhammapada 368, 376:** See Digha Nikaya xiii.76-77, pp. 161-62.

**Abot 2.13:** Cf. Kiddushin 40a, p. 332.

**Itivuttaka 19:** While Mahayana Buddhism often criticizes the Theravada discipline as a path of self-seeking, this Theravada text takes the position that such self advancement is inferior to goodwill. By loving others, the heart is released from egoism and stands on a truly selfless, universal foundation. Cf. Precious Garland 283, p. 614; Micah 6.6-8, p. 615; Gauri Sukhmani, M.5, pp. 672-673.

**Oracle of Kasuga:** Shinto regards a dwelling where such mourning is going on to be polluted by death, normally a state which the gods would strictly avoid. Cf. Precious Garland 283, p. 614; Micah 6.6-8, p. 615.

**Matthew 9.10-13:** Jesus is quoting Hosea 6.6; cf. Micah 6.6-8, p. 615. The term 'sacrifice' connotes the ritual laws, including prohibitions against consorting with sinners and the unclean. But sinners and the unfortunate ones are the objects of 'mercy.' See the Parable of the Good Samaritan, below.

**Abot de Rabbi Nathan 6:** This passage from the Talmud also quotes Hosea 6.6 to make a similar point.

**Metta Sutta:** Cf. Lion's Roar of Queen Srimala 4, p. 221; Leviticus 19.18, p. 114.

Anas and 'Abdullah reported God's Messenger as saying, "All [human] creatures are God's children, and those dearest to God are those who treat His children kindly."

*Islam*. Hadith of Baihaqi

Do not rebuke an older man but exhort him as you would a father; treat younger men like brothers, older women like mothers, younger women like sisters, in all purity.

*Christianity*. 1 Timothy 5.1-2

A man once asked the Prophet what was the best thing in Islam, and the latter replied, "It is to feed the hungry and to give the greeting of peace both to those one knows and to those one does not know."

*Islam*. Hadith of Bukhari

The bodhisattva should adopt the same attitude toward all beings, his mind should be even toward all beings, he should not handle others with an uneven mind, but with a mind which is friendly, well-disposed, helpful, free from aversions, avoiding harm and hurt; he should handle others as if they were his mother, father, son, or daughter. As a savior of all beings should a bodhisattva behave toward all beings. So should he train himself if he wants to know full enlightenment.

*Buddhism*. Perfection of Wisdom in Eight Thousand Lines 321-22

Treat the aged of your own family in a manner befitting their venerable age and extend this treatment to the aged of other families; treat your own young in a manner befitting their tender age and extend this to the young of other families, and you can roll the empire on your palm. The Book of Songs says,

> He set an example for his consort
> And also for his brothers,
> And so ruled over the family and the state.

In other words, all you have to do is take this very heart here and apply it to what is over there. Hence one who extends his bounty can bring peace to the Four Seas; one who does not cannot bring peace even to his own family. There is just one thing in which the Ancients greatly surpassed others, and that is the way they extended what they did.

*Confucianism*. Mencius I.A.7

A lawyer stood up to put Jesus to the test, saying, "Teacher, what shall I do to inherit eternal life?" He said to him, "What is written in the Law? How do you read?" And he answered, "You shall love the Lord your God with all your heart, and with all your soul, and with all your strength, and with all your mind; and your neighbor as yourself." And he said to him, "You have answered right; do this, and you will live."

But he, desiring to justify himself, said to Jesus, "And who is my neighbor?" Jesus replied, "A man was going down from Jerusalem to Jericho, and he fell among robbers, who stripped him and beat him, and departed, leaving him half-dead. Now by chance a priest was going down that road; and when he saw him he passed by on the other side. So likewise a Levite, when he came to the place and saw him, passed by on the other side. But a Samaritan, as he journeyed, came to where he was; and when he saw him, he had compassion, and went to him and bound up his wounds, pouring on oil and wine; then he set him on his own beast and brought him to an inn, and took care of him. And the next day he took out two denarii and gave them to the innkeeper, saying, 'Take care of him; and whatever more

**1 Timothy 5.1-2:** Cf. Anupreksa 337-39, p. 661; Sutra of Forty-two Sections 29, p. 661.

**Perfection of Wisdom in Eight Thousand Lines 321-22:** Cf. Perfection of Wisdom in Eight Thousand Lines 402-3, p. 724; Garland Sutra 11, p. 595.; Digha Nikaya xiii.76-77, pp. 161-62; and the Bodhisattva Vow: Sikshasamuccaya 280-81, p. 692, and Garland Sutra 23, p. 692. On treating others as members of one's own family, see Gandavyuha Sutra, p. 699; Mahaparinirvana Sutra 470-71, pp. 162-63; Digha Nikaya iii.185-90, pp. 167-68; also Sutra of 42 Sections 29, p. 661.

**Mencius I.A.7:** The principle of extending the heart of love within the family to others outside the family is the Confucian answer to the allegation that Confucian ethics leads to partiality. Cf. Book of Ritual 7.1.2, p. 474; Chuang Tzu 23, p. 162; Analects 4.3-4, p. 161.

you spend, I will repay you when I come back.' Which of these three, do you think, proved neighbor to the man who fell among the robbers?" He said, "The one who showed mercy on him." And Jesus said to him, "Go, and do likewise."

*Christianity*. Luke 10.25-37:
Parable of the Good Samaritan

The same thing does the divine voice here, thunder, repeat, *Da*! *Da*! *Da*! that is, restrain yourselves, give, be compassionate. One should practice this same triad, self-restraint, giving, compassion.

*Hinduism*.
Brihadaranyaka Upanishad 5.2.2:
The Voice of Thunder

The threefold offspring of Prajapati—gods, men, and demons—dwelt with their father Prajapati as students of sacred knowledge.

Having lived the life of a student of sacred knowledge, the gods said, "Speak to us, sir." To them then he spoke this syllable, "*Da*." "Did you understand?" "We did understand," said they. "You said to us, 'Restrain yourselves (*damyata*).'" "Yes (*Om*)!" said he. "You did understand."

So then the men said to him, "Speak to us, sir." To them he spoke this syllable, "*Da*." "Did you understand?" "We did understand," said they. "You said to us, 'Give (*datta*).'" "Yes (*Om*)!" said he. "You did understand."

So then the demons said to him, "Speak to us, sir." To them he spoke this syllable, "*Da*." "Did you understand?" "We did understand," said they. "You said to us, 'Be compassionate (*dayadhvam*).'" "Yes (*Om*)!" said he. "You did understand."

I have three treasures. Guard and keep them:
The first is deep love,
The second is frugality,
The third is not to dare to take the lead in the world.
Because of deep love, one is courageous.
Because of frugality, one is generous.
Because of not daring to take the lead in the world, one becomes the leader of the world.
Now, to be courageous by forsaking deep love,
To be generous by forsaking frugality,
And to take the lead in the world by forsaking following behind—
This is fatal.
For deep love helps one to win in case of attack,
And to be firm in the case of defense.
When Heaven is to save a person,
Heaven will protect him through deep love.

*Taoism*. Tao Te Ching 67

**Luke 10.25-37:** This parable is both a lesson on universal compassion and a warning against self-righteousness on the part of religious people. 'My neighbor' means the man half-dead on the road, whom the priest passed by on the other side because of the ritual prohibition against touching a dead body; this recalls the controversy over healing on the Sabbath, see Matthew 12.9-14, p. 616; also Hitachi Fudoki, p. 616. Such concern for ritual purity must yield before the demand for compassion. Then it is the Samaritan, long despised as a heretic by right-thinking Jews, who properly shows mercy and fulfills the Law, while the priest and Levite, who were respected religious leaders, did not.

**Brihadaranyaka Upanishad 5.2.2:** Cf. Matthew 22.36-40, p. 115.

# *Serving Others*

THE WAY OF SERVING OTHERS is the topic of passages in this section. The purest service is to help others and to seek the welfare of others without the expectation of reward. On the contrary, the way of selfishness brings only disharmony and failure; the selfish person eventually will find himself alone and without friends in his time of need. In the Bhagavad Gita, and paralleled by passages in the Tao Te Ching, the way of selfless service is described as the fundamental principle by which God creates and sustains the universe. Whenever a person acts selflessly in the service of others, that act is born of God. Another group of passages connects service with true lordship. While the conventional rulers abuse their powers by seeking to be served by their charges, the true leader is a servant to his people; as exemplified by Jesus, who came "not to be served, but to serve."

Bear one another's burdens, and so fulfill the law of Christ.

*Christianity*. Galatians 6.2

Rendering help to another is the function of all human beings.

*Jainism*. Tattvarthasutra 5.21

All men are responsible for one another.

*Judaism*. Talmud, Sanhedrin 27b

The best of men are those who are useful to others.

*Islam*. Hadith of Bukhari

Let no one seek his own good, but the good of his neighbor.

*Christianity*. 1 Corinthians 10.24

Without selfless service are no objectives fulfilled; in service lies the purest action.

*Sikhism*. Adi Granth, Maru, M.1, p. 992

He who prays for his fellowman, while he himself has the same need, will be answered first.

*Judaism*. Talmud, Baba Kamma 92a

The man of perfect virtue, wishing to be established himself, seeks also to establish others; wishing to be enlarged himself, he seeks also to enlarge others.

*Confucianism*. Analects 6.28.2

I tell you these things that you may learn wisdom; that you may learn that when you are in the service of your fellow beings you are only in the service of your God.

*Church of Jesus Christ of Latter-day Saints*. Book of Mormon, Mosiah 2.17

One who serves and seeks no recompense
Finds union with the Lord.
Such a servant alone takes the Master's guidance, says Nanak,
As on him is divine grace.

*Sikhism*. Adi Granth, Gauri Sukhmani, M.5, pp. 286f.

**Galatians 6.2:** Cf. John 15.13, p. 183. This fulfills not only a law of Christ, but also a dhamma of Buddhism; cf. Guide to the Bodhisattva's Way of Life 8.112-16, p. 120.

**Hadith of Bukhari:** Cf. Bodhipathapradipa, pp. 332-33.

**1 Corinthians 10.24:** Cf. Galatians 5.13, p. 380; Philippians 2.3, p. 650.

Do nothing from selfishness or conceit, but in humility count others better than yourselves. Let each of you look not only to his own interests, but also to the interests of others.

*Christianity*. Philippians 2.3-4

God's definition of goodness is total giving, total service, and absolute unselfishness. We are to live for others. You live for others and others live for you. God lives for man and man lives for God. The husband lives for his wife and the wife lives for her husband. This is goodness. And here unity, harmony, and prosperity abound.

*Unification Church*. Sun Myung Moon, 10-20-73

Until now each and everyone throughout the world has been concerned only with himself. How pitiful it is! You have no mind to help others, however hard you may think it over. Henceforth, replace your mind definitely! I, Tsukihi, request it from you all equally. If you ask what kind of mind it is, it is the mind to save single-heartedly all people of the world. Henceforth, if only all people of the world equally help each other on any and every matter, believe that I, Tsukihi, will accept your minds and will work any and every kind of salvation!

*Tenrikyo*. Ofudesaki 12.89-94

Do not seek to benefit only yourself, but think of other people also. If you yourself have an abundance, do not say, "The others do not concern me, I need not bother about them!" If you were lucky in hunting, let others share it. Moreover, show them the favorable spots where there are many sea lions which can be easily slain. Let others have their share occasionally. If you want to amass everything for yourself, other people will stay away from you and no one will want to be with you. If you should one day fall ill, no one will visit you because, for your part, you did not formerly concern yourself about others.

Grant other people something also. The Yamana do not like a person who acts selfishly.

*Native American Religions*. Yamana Eskimo Initiation

Heaven is eternal and Earth everlasting.
They can be eternal and everlasting because they do not exist for themselves,
And for this reason can exist forever.
Therefore the sage places himself in the background,
But finds himself in the foreground.
He puts himself away, and yet he always remains.
Is it not because he has no personal interests?
This is the reason why his personal interests are fulfilled.

*Taoism*. Tao Te Ching 7

At the beginning, mankind and the obligation of selfless service were created together. "Through selfless service, you will always be fruitful and find the fulfillment of your desires": this is the promise of the Creator....

Every selfless act, Arjuna, is born from the eternal, infinite Godhead. God is present in every act of service. All life turns on this law, O Arjuna. Whoever violates it, indulging his senses for his own pleasure and ignoring the needs of others, has wasted his life. But those who realize the God within are always satisfied. Having found the source of joy and fulfillment, they no longer seek happiness from the external world. They have nothing to gain or lose by any action; neither people nor things can affect their security.

Strive constantly to serve the welfare of the world; by devotion to selfless work one attains the supreme goal in life. Do your work with the welfare of others always in mind. It was by such work that Janaka attained perfection; others, too, have followed this path.

What the outstanding person does, others will try to do. The standards such people set will be followed by the whole world. There is nothing

**Sun Myung Moon, 10-20-73:** See Sun Myung Moon, 10-20-73, p. 290; Key to Theosophy, pp. 289-90.

in the three worlds for me to gain, Arjuna, nor is there anything I do not have; I continue to act, but I am not driven by any need of my own. If I ever refrained from continuous work, everyone would immediately follow my example. If I stopped working I would be the cause of cosmic chaos, and finally of the destruction of this world and these people.

The ignorant work for their own profit, Arjuna; the wise work for the welfare of the world, without thought to themselves. By abstaining from work you will confuse the ignorant, who are engrossed in their actions. Perform all work carefully, guided by compassion.

*Hinduism*. Bhagavad Gita 3.10-26

Guardianship is not to give an order but to give one's self.

*African Traditional Religions*.
Nyika Proverb (Kenya and Tanzania)

Jesus said, "You know that the rulers of the Gentiles lord it over them, and their great men exercise authority over them. It shall not be so among you; but whoever would be great among you must be your servant, and whoever would be first among you must be your slave; even as the Son of man came not to be served but to serve, and to give his life as a ransom for many."

*Christianity*. Matthew 20.25-28

The sage does not accumulate for himself.
The more he uses for others, the more he has himself.
The more he gives to others, the more he possesses of his own.
The Way of Heaven is to benefit others and not to injure.
The Way of the sage is to act but not to compete.

*Taoism*. Tao Te Ching 81

If, for my own sake, I cause harm to others,
I shall be tormented in hellish realms;
But if for the sake of others I cause harm to myself,
I shall acquire all that is magnificent.

By holding myself in high esteem
I shall find myself in unpleasant realms, ugly and stupid;
But should this [attitude] be shifted to others
I shall acquire honors in a joyful realm.

If I employ others for my own purposes
I myself shall experience servitude,
But if I use myself for the sake of others
I shall experience only lordliness.

*Buddhism*. Shantideva, Guide to the
Bodhisattva's Way of Life 8.126-28

❖

**Bhagavad Gita 3.10-26:** Vv. 10, 15-26. See Bhagavad Gita 3.4-9, pp. 714-15; 5.10-12, p. 554; Satapatha Brahmana 5.1.1.1-2, p. 313. On Gandhi's interpretation of selfless action as *satyagraha*, see Bhagavad Gita 2.31-38, p. 742n.

**Matthew 20.25-28:** Cf. Guide to the Bodhisattva's Way of Life 5.51-52, p. 653.

**Tao Te Ching 81:** Cf. Tao Te Ching 64, p. 652.

## *Sacrificial Love*

SACRIFICIAL LOVE IS SELF-SACRIFICE with the pure motivation to alleviate the suffering of others. This supreme love is suffering love, love that requires involvement in the knotty problems of the world, love that bears with the failings and weaknesses of others, love that is committed to helping others regardless of the cost. We have the example of Jesus Christ, who offered his life to redeem sinful humanity, and Moses, who risked his life before Pharaoh for the sake of his people. We have the example of the bodhisattva, who vows to devote himself to save all beings and to accept their sufferings as his own. He regards his own happiness as incidental to the happiness of others. He does not claim the merit of his spiritual progress for himself, but offers it for the liberation of others. A Hindu example of this sacrificial attitude and of the practice of "transfer of merit" is found in the story of King Vipascit, who would rather ease the suffering of the denizens of hell than enjoy by himself the bliss of heaven. We conclude with a description of the painful Native American ritual called the Sun Dance, which is performed in times of famine, disease, or other danger to the community. The dancer afflicts his flesh in a sacred rite in order to procure spiritual help for his people.

One who stays in the shade does not know the sun's heat.

*African Traditional Religions.* Igala Proverb (Nigeria)

Greater love has no man than this, that a man lay down his life for his friends.

*Christianity.* John 15.13

The position of love can be established when one sacrifices oneself and gives oneself for others. Thus sacrifice accompanies love.

*Unification Church.* Sun Myung Moon, 9-11-72

A man should share in the distress of the community, for so we find that Moses, our teacher, shared in the distress of the community.

*Judaism.* Talmud, Taanit 11a

The believer who participates in human life, exposing himself to its torments and suffering, is worth more than the one who distances himself from its suffering.

*Islam.* Hadith of Ibn Majah

It is not always physical bravery that counts. One must have the courage to face life as it is, to go through sorrows and always sacrifice oneself for the sake of others.

*African Traditional Religions.* Kipsigis Saying (Kenya)

We who are strong ought to bear with the failings of the weak, and not to please ourselves; let each of us please his neighbor for his good, to edify him. For Christ did not please himself; but, as it is written, "The reproaches of those who reproached thee fell on me."

*Christianity.* Romans 15.1-3

Mencius said, "Those who are morally well-adjusted look after those who are not; those who are talented look after those who are not.

**Igala Proverb:** A criticism of those who, enjoying luxuries, forget that others are suffering.
**John 15.13:** Cf. 2 Timothy 2.3-4, p. 741.
**Sun Myung Moon, 9-11-72:** Cf. Sun Myung Moon, 9-11-72, p. 529; 3-30-90, p. 626; 9-30-79, p. 99.
**Romans 15.1-3:** Cf. 2 Corinthians 5.20-6.13, p. 724.

That is why people are glad to have good fathers and elder brothers. If those who are morally well-adjusted and talented abandon those who are not, then scarcely an inch will separate the good from the depraved."

*Confucianism.* Mencius IV.B.7

A bodhisattva resolves, "I take upon myself the burden of all suffering; I am resolved to do so; I will endure it. I do not turn or run away, do not tremble, am not terrified, nor afraid, do not turn back or despond.

"And why? At all costs I must bear the burdens of all beings. In that, I do not follow my own inclinations. I have made the vow to save all beings. All beings I must set free. The whole world of living beings I must rescue from the terrors of birth, of old age, of sickness, of death and rebirth, of all kinds of moral offense, of all states of woe.... My endeavors do not merely aim at my own deliverance. For with the help of the boat of the thought of all-knowledge, I must rescue all these beings from the stream of Samsara, which is so difficult to cross.... I myself must grapple with the whole mass of suffering of all beings. To the limit of my endurance I will experience in all the states of woe, found in any world system, all the abodes of suffering. And I must not cheat all beings out of my store of merit. I am resolved to abide in each single state of woe for numberless eons; and so I will help all beings to freedom, in all states of woe that may be found in any world system whatsoever.

"And why? Because it is surely better that I alone should be in pain than that all these beings should fall into the states of woe. Therefore I must give myself away as a pawn through which the whole world is redeemed from the terrors of hells, of animal birth, of the world of Death, and with this my own body I must experience, for the sake of all beings, the whole mass of painful feelings. And on behalf of all beings I give surety for all beings, and in doing so I speak truthfully, am trustworthy, and do not go back on my word. I must not abandon all beings."

*Buddhism.* Sikshasamuccaya 280-81, Vajradhvaja Sutra

"I should be a hostel for all sentient beings, to let them escape from all painful things. I should be a protector for all sentient beings, to let them all be liberated from all afflictions. I should be a refuge for all sentient beings, to free them from all fears....

"I should accept all sufferings for the sake of sentient beings, and enable them to escape from the abyss of immeasurable woes of birth and death. I should accept all suffering for the sake of all sentient beings in all worlds, in all states of misery, for ever and ever, and still always cultivate foundations of goodness for the sake of all beings. Why? I would rather take all this suffering on myself than to allow sentient beings to fall into hell. I should be a hostage to those perilous places—hells, animal realms, the nether world—as a ransom to rescue all sentient beings in states of woe and enable them to gain liberation.

"I vow to protect all sentient beings and never abandon them. What I say is sincerely true, without falsehood. Why? Because I have set my mind on enlightenment in order to liberate all sentient beings; I do not seek the unexcelled Way for my own sake."

*Buddhism.* Garland Sutra 23

**Mencius IV.B.7:** See Chuang Tzu 33, p. 725; Njak Proverb, p. 189.

**Sikshasamuccaya 280-81:** This is a version of the Bodhisattva Vow. It includes the practice of dedicating one's merits, won through years of effort at spiritual discipline and selfless deeds, for the benefit of others. To regard one's own suffering in solidarity with the suffering of others empties one's suffering of selfhood. Hence the pride of suffering and pride in one's own spiritual accomplishment is overcome. See Mahaparinirvana Sutra 470-71, pp. 162-63; Larger Sukhavativyuha Sutra 9.1-5, p. 368; Perfection of Wisdom in Eight Thousand Lines 321-22, p. 686; 402-3, p. 724; Lankavatara Sutra 80, p. 158; Bodhipathapradipa, pp. 332-33.

**Garland Sutra 23:** See previous note.

"Ho! servant of Yama! Say, what sin have I committed, for which I have incurred this deepest hell, frightful for its torments? Known as King Vipascit, I protected the earth with uprightness; I let no fighting rage; no guest departed with averted countenance; nor did I offend the spirits of the ancestors, the gods, ascetics, or my servants; nor did I covet other men's wives, or wealth, or aught else belonging to them. How, then, have I incurred this very terrible hell?"

Yama's officer: "Come then, we go elsewhere. You have now seen everything, for you have seen hell. Come then, let us go elsewhere."

Thereupon the king prepared to follow him; but a cry went up from all the men that abode in torment: "Be gracious, O king! stay but a moment, for the air that clings to thy body gladdens our mind and entirely dispels the burning and the sufferings and pains from our bodies, O tiger-like man! Be gracious, O king!"

Vipascit: "Neither in heaven nor in Brahma's world do men experience such joy as arises from conferring bliss on suffering creatures. If, while I am present, torment does not hurt these men, here then will I remain, firm as a mountain."

Yama's officer: "Come, O king; we proceed. Enjoy the delights won by your own merit; leave here the evildoers to their torments."

Vipascit: "As long as these beings are in sore suffering, I will not go. From my presence the denizens of hell grow happy. Fie on the sickly protection-begging life of that man who shows no favor to one distressed, even though he be a resolute foe! Sacrifices, gifts, austerities do not work for the welfare of him who has no thought for the succor of the distressed.... To grant deliverance to these men excels, I consider, the joy of heaven. If many sufferers shall obtain happiness while only I undergo pain, shall I not in truth embrace it?"

Dharma [the Law]: "These evil-doers have come to hell in consequence of their own deeds; you also, O king, must go to heaven in consequence of your meritorious deeds. I lead you to heaven; mount this heavenly chariot and linger not; let us go."

Vipascit: "Men in thousands, O Dharma, suffer pain here in hell; and being in affliction they cry to me to save them; hence I will not depart."

Dharma: "O king! Your merit is truly beyond reckoning. In evincing now this compassion here in the hells, your merit has amounted even higher. Come, enjoy the abode of the immortals; let these unfortunates consume away in hell the sin arising from their own actions!"

Vipascit: "Whatever good deeds I possess, O Lord of the Thirty Gods, by means thereof let the sinners who are undergoing torment be delivered from hell!"

Indra: "So be it, O king! You have gained an even more exalted station: see too these sinners delivered from hell!"

*Hinduism.* Markandeya Purana 13-15

When all the preparations were finished, the dancers stood at the foot of the sacred tree, at the west, and, gazing up at the top of the tree, they raised their right hands and blew upon the eagle-bone whistles. As they did this, Kablaya prayed,

"O Grandfather, Wakan Tanka, bend down and look upon me as I raise my hand to You. You see here the faces of my people... You have beheld the sacred place and the sacred center which we have fixed, and where we shall suffer. I offer all my suffering to You on behalf of the people... Be merciful to me, O Great Spirit, that my people may live!"

Then all the singers chanted together, "O Wakan Tanka, be merciful to me! I am doing this that my people may live!"

The dancers all moved around to the east, looking toward the top of the sacred tree at the west, and, raising up their hands, they sang, "Our Grandfather, Wakan Tanka, has given to me a path which is sacred!"

The dancers moved now to the south... to the west... to the north, and again to the west, all the time blowing upon their shrill eagle-bone whistles. Then the dancers all began to

**Markandeya Purana 13-15:** Compare Christ's tour of hell in 1 Peter 3.18-20, p. 368. For another Hindu story of exemplary sacrificial love, see the account of Rantideva, Srimad Bhagavatam 9, p. 700.

cry, and Kablaya was given a long thong and two wooden pegs, and with these he went to the center, and grasping the sacred tree he cried, "O Wakan Tanka, be merciful to me. I do this that my people may live!"...

As the singers and drummers increased the speed of their chanting and drumming, the helpers rushed up and, grasping Kablaya roughly, threw him on the ground. The helper then pulled up the skin of Kablaya's left breast, and through this loose skin a sharp stick was thrust; and in the same manner the right breast was pierced. The long rawhide rope had been tied at its middle around the sacred tree, toward its top, and then the two ends of the rope were tied to the pegs in Kablaya's chest. The helpers stood Kablaya up roughly, and he blew upon his whistle, and, leaning back upon the thongs, he danced, and continued to dance in this manner until the thongs broke loose from his flesh.

*Native American Religions.* Sun Dance, Sioux Tradition

# *Giving and Receiving*

THE SPIRITUAL PRINCIPLE OF GIVING and receiving is the subject of this section. When we give to one another, freely and without conditions, sharing our blessings with others and bearing each other's burdens, the giving multiplies and we receive far more than what was given. Even when there is no immediate prospect of return, Heaven keeps accounts of giving, and in the end blessing will return to the giver, multiplied manyfold. We must give first; to expect to receive without having given is to violate the universal law. On the other hand, giving in order to receive—with strings attached, with the intention of currying favor, or in order to make a name for oneself—is condemned. See also *The Golden Rule*, pp. 114-15.

Give, and it will be given to you... for the measure you give will be the measure you get back.

*Christianity.* Luke 6.38

Those who do not abandon mercy will not be abandoned by me.

*Shinto.* Oracle of Itsukushima

He who gives liberally goes straight to the gods; on the high ridge of heaven he stands exalted.

*Hinduism.* Rig Veda 1.125.5

Who is honored? He who honors mankind.

*Judaism.* Mishnah, Abot 4.1

Those who act kindly in this world will have kindness.

*Islam.* Qur'an 39.10

**Sun Dance:** The dancer has his chest pierced with wooden pegs tied with ropes to the top of a sacred tree; as he dances the ropes become taut until the pegs rip off from his flesh. The dancer sacrifices his body on behalf of his people, that the people may live. Cf. Rig Veda 10.136.7, p. 626.

**Luke 6.38:** Cf. Matthew 7.7-11, p. 492.

**Abot 4.1:** Cf. Matthew 25.31-46, p. 699; Gandavyuha Sutra, p. 699.

**Qur'an 39.10:** Cf. Forty Hadith of an-Nawawi 36, p. 699; Hadith of Muslim, p. 699.

Understand that through saving others you shall also be saved.

*Tenrikyo*. Ofudesaki 3.47

It is only when one does not have enough faith in others that others will have no faith in him.

*Taoism*. Tao Te Ching 17

One must pour cold water on the ground before he can tread on soft soil.

*African Traditional Religions*. Yoruba Proverb (Nigeria)

You will not attain piety until you expend of what you love; and whatever thing you expend, God knows of it.

*Islam*. Qur'an 3.92

If beings knew, as I know, the fruit of sharing gifts, they would not enjoy their use without sharing them, nor would the taint of stinginess obsess the heart and stay there. Even if it were their last bit, their last morsel of food, they would not enjoy its use without sharing it, if there were anyone to receive it.

*Buddhism*. Itivuttaka 18

The Buddha said, "When you see someone practicing the Way of giving, aid him joyously, and you will obtain vast and great blessings." A shramana asked, "Is there an end to those blessings?" The Buddha said, "Consider the flame of a single lamp. Though a hundred thousand people come and light their own lamps from it so that they can cook their food and ward off the darkness, the first lamp remains the same as before. Blessings are like this, too."

*Buddhism*. Sutra of Forty-two Sections 10

The accumulation of wealth is the way to scatter the people, and the letting it be scattered among them is the way to collect the people.

*Confucianism*. Great Learning 10.9

He who sows sparingly will also reap sparingly, and he who sows bountifully will also reap bountifully. Each one must do as he has made up his mind, not reluctantly or under compulsion, for God loves a cheerful giver. And God is able to provide you with every blessing in abundance, so that you may always have enough of everything and may provide in abundance for every good work. As it is written,

> He scatters abroad, he gives to the poor;
> his righteousness endures forever.

He who supplies seed to the sower and bread for food will supply and multiply your resources and increase the harvest of your righteousness. You will be enriched in every way for great generosity.

*Christianity*. 2 Corinthians 9.6-11

It is more blessed to give than to receive.

*Christianity*. Acts 20.35

Give not with the thought to gain,
and be patient unto thy Lord.

*Islam*. Qur'an 74.6-7

When you give alms, do not let your left hand know what your right hand is doing.

*Christianity*. Matthew 6.3

Giving simply because it is right to give, without thought of return, at a proper time, in proper circumstances, and to a worthy person, is enlightened giving. Giving with regrets or in the expectation of receiving some favor or of getting something in return, is selfish giving.

*Hinduism*. Bhagavad Gita 17.20-21

He who gives his wealth to purify himself,
and confers no favor on any man for
recompense,
only seeking the Face of his Lord the Most
High;
he shall surely be satisfied.

*Islam*. Qur'an 92.18-21

**Ofudesaki 3.47:** This is the basis of Tenrikyo's *hinokishin*, voluntary service for the well-being of the community, when one seeks neither praise nor reward.

**Yoruba Proverb:** In other words, be kind and generous to others if you expect others to help you.

**Qur'an 92.18-21:** Cf. Qur'an 2.261-62, p. 623; 2.267-74, p. 624.

Enlightening beings are magnanimous givers, bestowing whatever they have with equanimity, without regret, without hoping for reward, without seeking honor, without coveting material benefits, but only to rescue and safeguard all living beings.

*Buddhism.* Garland Sutra 21

"If I give this, what shall I enjoy?"—
Such selfish thinking is the way of the ghosts;
"If I enjoy this, what shall I give?"—
Such selfless thinking is a quality of the gods.

*Buddhism.* Shantideva, Guide to the Bodhisattva's Way of Life 8.125

Mencius said, "A man who is out to make a name for himself will be able to give away a state of a thousand chariots, but reluctance would be written all over his face if he had to give away a basketful of rice and a bowlful of soup when no such purpose was served."

*Confucianism.* Mencius VII.B.11

When a greeting is offered you, meet it with a greeting still more courteous, or at least of equal courtesy. God takes careful account of all things.

*Islam.* Qur'an 4.86

There was presented to me a papaya,
And I returned for it a beautiful *keu* gem;
Not as a return for it,
But that our friendship might be lasting.

There was presented to me a peach,
And I returned for it a beautiful *yaou* gem;
Not as a return for it,
But that our friendship might be lasting.

There was presented to me a plum,
And I returned for it a beautiful *kew* stone;
Not as a return for it,
But that our friendship might be lasting.

*Confucianism.* Book of Songs, Ode 64

Love cannot return unless you give it. People who love each other can continue the give and take action of love with more power than they invest. We can conclude that the word "eternity" can only be formed through love.

*Unification Church.* Sun Myung Moon, 12-5-71

❖

**Guide to the Bodhisattva's Way of Life 8.125:** This distinction between gods and demons is made in Satapatha Brahmana 5.1.1.1-2, p. 313.

**Book of Songs, Ode 64:** It is commonplace for people to give gifts with the intention of securing a favor in return. In such calculations, the gift and its return would be of roughly equal value. To return a gift of immensely greater value might burden the recipient with a feeling of indebtedness. This passage, however, describes an exchange of gifts with a purer motive: friendship that goes beyond the calculations of obligation.

## *Charity and Hospitality*

GIVING ALMS TO THE POOR and hospitality to strangers are traditional virtues encouraged by all religions. A relationship to the Highest Good naturally builds a bond among all members of the community—for all people are as brothers and sisters with the absolute value of (potential) enlightened beings or God's children. Giving alms and charity is a concrete expression of this spiritual bond. Along with admonitions to practice charity, texts such as the Parable of the Sheep and the Goats from the New Testament liken helping a poor man to giving offerings to God or the highest saints. Charity is not excused even for the poorest giver, according to several texts. Finally, we have passages on hospitality, including two texts lauding exemplary acts of charity, by a Companion of the Prophet Muhammad and the Hindu householder Rantideva, who gave food and water to guests even though it meant that they would have to go without.

Blessed is he who considers the poor; the Lord delivers him in the day of trouble.

*Judaism* and *Christianity*. Psalm 41.1

They feed with food the needy wretch, the orphan, and the prisoner, for love of Him, saying, "We wish for no reward nor thanks from you."

*Islam*. Qur'an 76.8-9

Charity—to be moved at the sight of the thirsty, the hungry, and the miserable and to offer relief to them out of pity—is the spring of virtue.

*Jainism*.
Kundakunda, Pancastikaya 137

"Ye shall walk after the Lord your God" [Deuteronomy 13.4]. But how can a man walk after God who "is a devouring fire"? [Deuteronomy 4.24]. It means, walk after His attributes: clothe the naked, visit the sick, comfort the mourner, bury the dead.

*Judaism*. Talmud, Sota 14a

Relieve people in distress as speedily as you must release a fish from a dry rill [lest he die]. Deliver people from danger as quickly as you must free a sparrow from a tight noose. Be compassionate to orphans and relieve widows. Respect the old and help the poor.

*Taoism*. Tract of the Quiet Way

Each person's every joint must perform a charity every day the sun comes up: to act justly between two people is a charity; to help a man with his mount, lifting him onto it or hoisting up his belongings onto it is a charity; a good word is a charity; every step you take to prayers is a charity; and removing a harmful thing from the road is a charity.

*Islam*. Forty Hadith of an-Nawawi 26

Be kind to parents, and the near kinsman, and to orphans, and to the needy, and to the neighbor who is of kin, and to the neighbor who is a stranger, and to the companion at your side, and to the traveller, and to [slaves] that your right hands own. Surely God loves not the proud and boastful such as are niggardly, and

**Psalm 41.1:** Cf. Var Sarang, M.1, p. 714.
**Qur'an 76.8-9:** Cf. Qur'an 2.264, p. 350; 16.90, p. 684; 90.8-17, p. 484.
**Sota 14a:** Cf. Gittin 61a, p. 42.
**Tract of the Quiet Way:** Cf. Great Learning 10.7-9, p. 667.
**Forty Hadith of an-Nawawi 26:** Cf. Hadith of Ibn Majah, p. 715.

bid other men to be niggardly, and themselves conceal the bounty that God has given them.

*Islam*. Qur'an 4.36-37

If there is among you a poor man, one of your brethren, in any of your towns within your land which the Lord your God gives you, you shall not harden your heart or shut your hand against your poor brother, but you shall open your hand to him, and lend him sufficient for his need, whatever it may be.... You shall give to him freely, and your heart shall not be grudging when you give to him; because for this the Lord your God will bless you in all your work and in all that you undertake. For the poor will never cease out of the land; therefore I command you, You shall open wide your hand to your brother, to the needy and to the poor, in the land.

*Judaism* and *Christianity*. Deuteronomy 15.7-11

The gods have not ordained that humans die of
hunger;
even to the well-fed man death comes in many
shapes.
The wealth of the generous man never wastes
away,
but the niggard has none to console him.

He who, possessed of food, hardens his heart
against the weak man, hungry and suffering,
who comes to him for help, though of old he
helped him—
surely he finds none to console him.

He is liberal who gives to anyone who asks for
alms,
to the homeless, distressed man who seeks
food;
success comes to him in the challenge of battle,
and for future conflicts he makes an ally.

He is no friend who does not give to a friend,
to a comrade who comes imploring for food;
let him leave such a man—his is not a home—
and rather seek a stranger who brings him
comfort.

Let the rich man satisfy one who seeks help;
and let him look upon the long view:
For wealth revolves like the wheels of a chariot,
coming now to one, now to another.

In vain does the mean man acquire food;
it is—I speak the truth—verily his death;
he who does not cherish a comrade or a friend,
who eats all alone, is all sin.

*Hinduism*. Rig Veda 10.117.1-6

There are three kinds of persons existing in the world: one is like a drought, one who rains locally, and one who pours down everywhere.

How is a person like a drought? He gives nothing to all alike, not giving food and drink, clothing and vehicle, flowers, scents and unguents, bed, lodging and light, neither to recluses and brahmins nor to wretched and needy beggars. In this way, a person is like a drought.

How is a person like a local rainfall? He is a giver to some, but to others he gives not.... In this way, a person is like a local rainfall.

How does a person rain down everywhere? He gives to all, be they recluses and brahmins or wretched, needy beggars; he is a giver of food and drink, clothing... lodging and lights. In this way a person rains down everywhere.

*Buddhism*. Itivuttaka 65

When the Holy One loves a man, He sends him a present in the shape of a poor man, so that he should perform some good deed to him, through the merit of which he may draw to himself a cord of grace.

*Judaism*. Zohar, Genesis 104a

**Qur'an 4.36-37:** Cf. Qur'an 2.177, p. 615; 107.4-7, p. 349. On the Prophet's charity, see Hadith, p. 471.

**Deuteronomy 15.7-11:** Cf. Matthew 6.1-4, pp. 349-50.

**Itivuttaka 65:** This and the other Hindu and Buddhist passages in this section take a different point of view from the Hindu and Buddhist doctrine of the Field of Merit, in Dhammapada 356-59, p. 623; Petavatthu ii.69-71, p. 625; Bhagavad Gita 17.20-22, p. 624, which regards only people of spiritual attainment as the proper recipients of gifts. Cf. Great Learning 10.9, p. 695.

Whoever removes a worldly grief from a believer, Allah will remove from him one of the griefs on the Day of Judgment. Whosoever alleviates the lot of a needy person, Allah will alleviate his lot in this world and the next. Whosoever shields a Muslim, Allah will shield him in this world and the next. Allah will aid a servant of His so long as the servant aids his brother.

*Islam*. Forty Hadith of an-Nawawi 36

When the Son of man comes in his glory, and all the angels with him, then he will sit on his glorious throne. Before him will be gathered all the nations, and he will separate them one from another as a shepherd separates the sheep from the goats, and he will place the sheep at his right hand, but the goats at his left. Then the King will say to those at his right hand, "Come, O blessed of my Father, inherit the kingdom prepared for you from the foundation of the world; for I was hungry and you gave me food, I was thirsty and you gave me drink, I was a stranger and you welcomed me, I was naked and you clothed me, I was sick and you visited me, I was in prison and you came to me." Then the righteous will answer him, "Lord, when did we see you hungry and feed you, or thirsty and give you drink? And when did we see you a stranger and welcome you, or naked and clothe you? And when did we see you sick or in prison and visit you?" And the King will answer them, "Truly, I say to you, as you did it to one of the least of these my brethren, you did it to me." Then he will say to those at his left hand, "Depart from me, you cursed, into the eternal fire prepared for the devil and his angels; for I was hungry and you gave me no food, I was thirsty and you gave me no drink, I was a stranger and you did not welcome me, naked and you did not clothe me, sick and in prison and you did not visit me." Then they also will answer, "Lord, when did we see you hungry or thirsty or a stranger or naked or sick or in prison, and did not minister to you?" Then he will answer them, "Truly, I say to you, as you did it not to one of the least of these, you did it not to me." And they will go away into eternal punishment, but the righteous into eternal life.

*Christianity*. Matthew 25.31-46:
Parable of the Sheep and the Goats

On the day of judgment God Most High will say, "Son of Adam, I was sick and you did not visit Me." He will reply, "My Lord, how could I visit Thee when Thou art the Lord of the Universe!" He will say, "Did you not know that My servant so-and-so was ill and yet you did not visit him? Did you not know that if you had visited him you soon would have found Me with him?"

*Islam*. Hadith of Muslim

All beings should be accommodated and served by me as attentively as I would show filial respect to my parents, due respect to my teachers, to elders, and arhats, up to the Tathagatas, all in equality. I would be a good physician to the sick, a guide to those who have wandered from the path, setting their feet in the right way. I would be a light to those who wander in darkness. I would enable the people in poverty to discover vaults of treasure. A bodhisattva should thus benefit all beings in equal treatment, and bestow his loving care on all beings alike. And why? Because if a bodhisattva serves all beings, that is equal to serving Buddhas dutifully. To hold all beings in high esteem, and render them respectful services, that is equal to reverencing and serving the Tathagatas. To make all beings happy, is to please the Tathagatas.

*Buddhism*. Gandavyuha Sutra,
Vows of Samantabhadra

One should give even from a scanty store to him who asks.

*Buddhism*. Dhammapada 224

Even a poor man who himself subsists on charity should give charity.

*Judaism*. Talmud, Gittin 7b

**Matthew 25.31-46:** Cf. Matthew 19.21-24, p. 666; Luke 10.25-37, pp. 686-87.

Not having enough of anything can cause one to become a miser.

*African Traditional Religions*. Yoruba Proverb (Nigeria)

He who has two coats, let him share with him who has none; and he who has food, let him do likewise.

*Christianity*. Luke 3.11

See to it that whoever enters your house obtains something to eat, however little you may have. Such food will be a source of death to you if you withhold it.

*Native American Religions*. A Winnebago Father's Precepts

Do not neglect to show hospitality to strangers, for thereby some have entertained angels unawares.

*Christianity*. Hebrews 13.2

Let him who believes in Allah and the Last Day be generous to his neighbor, and let him who believes in Allah and the Last Day be generous to his guest.

*Islam*. Forty Hadith of an-Nawawi 15

The husband and wife of the house should not turn away any who comes at eating time and asks for food. If food is not available, a place to rest, water for refreshing one's self, a reed mat to lay one's self on, and pleasing words entertaining the guest—these at least never fail in the houses of the good.

*Hinduism*. Apastamba Dharma Sutra 8.2

According to Abu Hurairah, a man came to find the Prophet and the latter asked his wives for something to give him to eat. "We have absolutely nothing," they replied, "except water." "Who wants to share his meal with this man?" asked the Prophet. A man of the Companions then said, "I." Then he led this man to his wife and said to her, "Treat generously the guest of the Messenger of God." She replied, "We have nothing except our children's supper." "Oh, well," he replied, "get your meal ready, light your lamp, and when your children want supper, put them to bed." So the woman prepared the meal, lit the lamp, put the children to bed, then, getting up as if to trim the lamp, she extinguished it. The Companion and his wife then made as if to eat, but in fact they spent the night with empty stomachs. The next day when the Companion went to find the Messenger of God, the latter said to him, "This night God smiled." It was then that God revealed these words, "and they prefer the others before themselves, although there be indigence among them" [Qur'an 59.9].

*Islam*. Hadith of Bukhari

The fame of Rantideva is sung in this and the other world, Rantideva, who, though himself hungry, was in the habit of giving away his wealth as it came, while trusting in God to provide his needs. Even in time of famine, Rantideva continued his generosity though his family was reduced to poverty.

For forty-eight days he and his family were starving; a little liquid, and that enough for only one, was all that remained. As he was about to drink it, an outcaste came begging for water. Rantideva was moved at the sight and said, "I do not desire from God the great state attended by divine powers or even deliverance from rebirth. Establishing myself in the hearts of all beings, I take on myself their suffering so that they may be rid of their misery." So saying, the compassionate king gave that little liquid to the outcaste, though he himself was dying of thirst.

The gods of the three worlds came and desired to bestow upon him manifold blessings, but Rantideva, who had no attachment or desire, merely bowed to Lord Vasudeva [Krishna] in devotion.

*Hinduism*. Srimad Bhagavatam 9

**Yoruba Proverb:** Meaning that since it is bad to become a miser, you should give even though you yourself are in need.

**Hebrews 13.2:** Cf. Hitachi Fudoki, p. 616.

**Apastamba Dharma Sutra 8.2:** Cf. Hitachi Fudoki, p. 616.

## *Forgiveness and Reconciliation*

THE SCRIPTURES ADVOCATE a large-hearted attitude of forgiveness and tolerance of others' mistakes, even when they cause offense or injury. Forgiveness is far preferable to holding a grudge, which would only fester and poison the spirit. It is preferable to exacting revenge—see *Love Your Enemy*, pp. 705-7. Furthermore, we are advised to take responsibility for the grudges and injuries which others feel toward us. This is the first of several sections which deal with overcoming disputes, enmity, grudges, and prejudices in personal relationships.

Subvert anger by forgiveness.

*Jainism*. Samanasuttam 136

The best deed of a great man is to forgive and forget.

*Islam*. Nahjul Balagha, Saying 201

Where there is forgiveness, there is God Himself.

*Sikhism*. Adi Granth, Shalok, Kabir, p. 1372

If you efface and overlook and forgive, then lo! God is forgiving, merciful.

*Islam*. Qur'an 64.14

The superior man tends to forgive wrongs and deals leniently with crimes.

*Confucianism*. I Ching 40: Release

If you are offering your gift at the altar, and there remember that your brother has something against you, leave your gift there before the altar and go; first be reconciled to your brother, and then come and offer your gift.

*Christianity*. Matthew 5.23-24

The Day of Atonement atones for sins against God, not for sins against man, unless the injured person has been appeased.

*Judaism*. Mishnah, Yoma 8.9

Show endurance in humiliation and bear no grudge.

*Taoism*. Treatise on Response and Retribution

You shall not take vengeance or bear any grudge against the sons of your own people, but you shall love your neighbor as yourself: I am the Lord.

*Judaism* and *Christianity*. Leviticus 19.18

Who takes vengeance or bears a grudge acts like one who, having cut one hand while handling a knife, avenges himself by stabbing the other hand.

*Judaism*. Jerusalem Talmud, Nedarim 9.4

Moses son of 'Imran said, "My Lord, who is the greatest of Thy servants in Thy estimation?" and received the reply, "The one who forgives when he is in a position of power."

*Islam*. Hadith of Baihaqi

**Shalok, Kabir:** On tolerance of the ill-behaved, see Tattvarthasutra 7.11, p. 684.

**Matthew 5.23-24** and **Yoma 8.9:** Not only will God not accept the offering of a hypocrite whose piety is a mask for robbery and injury—see Qur'an 2.264, p. 350—he also will not accept our offering if another person has a grievance against us, though we might think our actions were justified. Therefore we should take responsibility for others' grievances against us, and avoid all temptations to self-righteousness.

**Treatise on Response and Retribution:** Cf. Analects 14.11, p. 709.

**Jerusalem Talmud, Nedarim 9.4:** Cf. Vacana 248, p. 656; Digha Nikaya i.3, pp. 655-56.

**Hadith of Baihaqi:** Muhammad attributes this teaching to Moses.

Better and more rewarding is God's reward to those who believe and put their trust in Him: who avoid gross sins and indecencies and, when angered, are willing to forgive... Let evil be rewarded by like evil, but he who forgives and seeks reconciliation shall be rewarded by God. He does not love the wrongdoers.... True constancy lies in forgiveness and patient forbearance.

*Islam*. Qur'an 42.36-43

In reconciling a great injury,
Some injury is sure to remain.
How can this be good?
Therefore the sage holds the left-hand tally
[obligation] of a contract;
He does not blame others.
The person of virtue attends to the obligation;
The person without virtue attends to the
exactions.

*Taoism*. Tao Te Ching 79

Then Peter came up and said to him, "Lord, how often shall my brother sin against me, and I forgive him? As many as seven times?" Jesus said to him, "I do not say to you seven times, but seventy times seven."

"Therefore the kingdom of Heaven may be compared to a king who wished to settle accounts with his servants. When he began the reckoning, one was brought to him who owed him ten thousand talents; and as he could not pay, his lord ordered him to be sold, and his wife and children and all that he had, and payment to be made. So the servant fell on his knees, imploring him, 'Lord, have patience with me, and I will pay you everything.' And out of pity for him the lord of that servant released him and forgave him the debt. But that same servant, as he went out, came upon one of his fellow servants who owed him a hundred denarii; and seizing him by the throat he said, 'Pay what you owe.' So his fellow servant fell down and besought him, 'Have patience with me, and I will pay you.' He refused and went and put him in prison till he should pay the debt. When his fellow servants saw what had taken place, they were greatly distressed, and they went and reported to their lord all that had taken place. Then his lord summoned him and said to him, 'You wicked servant! I forgave you all that debt because you besought me; and should not you have had mercy on your fellow servant, as I had mercy on you?' And in anger his lord delivered him to the jailers, till he should pay all his debt. So also my heavenly Father will do to every one of you, if you do not forgive your brother from your heart."

*Christianity*. Matthew 18.21-35:
Parable of the Wicked Servant

When Jesus was crucified, Roman soldiers pierced him. And Jesus prayed for his enemies: "Father, forgive them; for they know not what they do" [Luke 23.34]. Even at the moment of death on the cross, Jesus was so earnest in forgiving. His very last act was motivated by his love for his enemies. He was the supreme form of giving—a paragon of love. The example of Jesus Christ is the absolute standard for all mankind. Just imagine an entire nation composed of Jesus-like men. What would you call it? The Kingdom of Heaven on earth—it could be nothing less.

*Unification Church*.
Sun Myung Moon, 10-20-73

**Qur'an 42.36-43:** Vv. 36-37, 40, 43. The Qur'an exalts forgiveness as the way in which the best of people respond to being wronged, yet as a concession to human weakness, it allows that to take revenge is not a sin—see Qur'an 17.33, p. 340. Muhammad in the traditions consistently praises those who would forgive rather than take revenge. On Muhammad's own forgiving nature, see Hadith, p. 471. 'Ali likewise prohibited his followers from taking revenge for his murder; see Nahjul Balagha, Letter 47, p. 341. Cf. Forty Hadith of an-Nawawi 32, p. 708.

**Tao Te Ching 79:** Cf. Handbook for Preclears, p. 489; Matthew 7.1-5, p. 703; Dhammapada 252-53, p. 703, and related passages on not judging others before correcting oneself.

**Matthew 18.21-35:** Cf. The Parable of the Prodigal Son, Luke 15.11-32, pp. 362-63.

**Sun Myung Moon, 10-20-73:** On Jesus' and his disciples' attitude of forgiveness even at their deaths, see Luke 23.34, pp. 428-30; Acts 7.60, p. 635. Cf. Sun Myung Moon, 3-30-90, p. 707.

## Judge Not

SCRIPTURE CAUTIONS US not to be harsh and judgmental of others' faults, even where they are evident, because neither are we perfect and free from error. The admonition not to regard the speck in your neighbor's eye before removing the log from your own eye finds parallels in many scriptures. Rather than justify ourselves and blame others, we should look into ourselves for having such feelings of resentment. We should look into ourselves for where we may have been at fault, and from that starting point we can sincerely strive for reconciliation.

The vile are ever prone to detect the faults of others, though they be as small as mustard seeds, and persistently shut their eyes against their own, though they be as large as Vilva fruit.

*Hinduism*. Garuda Purana 112

Judge not, that you be not judged. For with the judgment that you pronounce you will be judged, and the measure you give will be the measure you get. Why do you see the speck that is in your brother's eye, but do not notice the log that is in your own eye? Or how can you say to your brother, "Let me take the speck out of your eye," when there is the log in your own eye? You hypocrite, first take the log out of your own eye, and then you will see clearly to take the speck out of your brother's eye.

*Christianity*. Matthew 7.1-5

A man holding a basket of eggs does not dance on stones.

*African Traditional Religions*. Buji Proverb (Nigeria)

Easily seen are others' faults, hard indeed to see are one's own. Like chaff one winnows others' faults, but one's own one hides, as a crafty fowler conceals himself by camouflage.

He who sees others' faults is ever irritable—his corruptions grow. He is far from the destruction of the corruptions.

*Buddhism*. Dhammapada 252-53

Happy is the person who finds fault with himself instead of finding fault with others.

*Islam*. Hadith

If you want to criticize someone, first criticize yourself more than three times.

*Unification Church*. Sun Myung Moon, 9-30-69

Confucius said, "The gentleman calls attention to the good points in others; he does not call attention to their defects. The small man does just the reverse of this."

*Confucianism*. Analects 12.16

Confucius said, "The good man does not grieve that other people do not recognize his merits. His only anxiety is lest he should fail to recognize theirs."

*Confucianism*. Analects 1.16

Why do you pass judgment on your brother? Or you, why do you despise your brother? For we shall all stand before the judgment seat of God; as it is written,

**Hadith:** Cf. Forty Hadith of an-Nawawi 12, p. 505.
**Analects 12.16:** Cf. Analects 12.21, p. 523; Doctrine of the Mean 14, p. 489; Tao Te Ching 79, p. 702.
**Analects 1.16:** Cf. Analects 15.20, p. 489.

As I live, says the Lord, every knee shall
bow to me
and every tongue shall confess to God.

So each of us shall give account of himself to God.

*Christianity*. Romans 14.10-12

He who treads the Path in earnest
Sees not the mistakes of the world;
If we find fault with others
We ourselves are also in the wrong.
When other people are in the wrong, we
should ignore it,
For it is wrong for us to find fault.
By getting rid of this habit of fault-finding
We cut off a source of defilement.
When neither hatred nor love disturb our mind
Serenely we sleep.

*Buddhism*. Sutra of Hui Neng 2

Why should you try to mend
The failings of the world, sirs?
Correct your bodies first, each one of you!
Correct your minds first, each one!
Lord Shiva does not approve of
Those who shed crocodile tears
To their neighbor's grief.

*Hinduism*. Basavanna, Vacana 124

Censuring others and praising himself, concealing good qualities present in others and proclaiming noble qualities absent in himself, he causes them to have low status. Disparaging himself and praising others, proclaiming qualities which are present in others and not proclaiming those that are absent in himself, with humility and modesty he lifts them to high status. No obstacle should be created in the development of others.

*Jainism*. Tattvarthasutra 6.25-27

Do not judge thy comrade until thou hast stood in his place.

*Judaism*. Mishnah, Abot 2.5

Early in the morning [Jesus] came again to the temple; all the people came to him, and he sat down and taught them. The scribes and the Pharisees brought a woman who had been caught in adultery, and placing her in the midst they said to him, "Teacher, this woman has been caught in the act of adultery. Now in the Law Moses commanded us to stone such. What do you say about her?" This they said to test him, that they might have some charge to bring against him. Jesus bent down and wrote with his finger on the ground. And as they continued to ask him, he stood up and said to them, "Let him who is without sin among you be the first to throw a stone at her." And once more he bent down and wrote with his finger on the ground. But when they heard it, they went away, one by one, beginning with the eldest, and Jesus was left alone with the woman standing before him. Jesus looked up and said to her, "Woman, where are they? Has no one condemned you?" She said, "No one, Lord." And Jesus said, "Neither do I condemn you; go, and do not sin again."

*Christianity*. John 8.2-11

❖

**Sutra of Hui Neng 2:** Cf. Tao Te Ching 79, p. 702; Handbook for Preclears, p. 489.
**Abot 2.5:** A saying of Hillel (lst century B.C.).
**John 8.2-11:** According to tradition, Jesus wrote on the ground the sins of each accuser.

## *Love Your Enemy*

THE PRESCRIPTION TO LOVE YOUR ENEMY and to requite evil with good is sometimes thought of as an impractical and perfectionist ethic, able to be practiced by only a few exceptional souls. But, in fact, this doctrine is widely taught in all religions as a fundamental principle for pursuing relationships with others. The person who insists upon vengeance or retribution is not necessarily committing a crime, but neither will his act of revenge be helpful to spiritual advancement. Revenge, which requites evil with evil, only multiplies evil in the world, while love, by which one strives to overcome evil with good, spreads goodness in the world.

True love is unconditional and impartial—thus the metaphor of the sun that shines down on all life. It is tested and proven by encounters with those who are difficult to love. Where true love prevails, there no enemies are found.

The concluding passages dispute the prescription to love your enemy when it apparently contravenes the principles of justice and right. Sometimes the best way to love an evil person is to make him face justice, or to hinder him from doing wrong. Nevertheless, these corrective actions should be done with a loving heart and with the other person's welfare uppermost in mind.

"He abused me, he beat me, he defeated me, he robbed me!" In those who harbor such thoughts hatred is not appeased.

"He abused me, he beat me, he defeated me, he robbed me!" In those who do not harbor such thoughts hatred is appeased.

Hatreds never cease through hatred in this world; through love alone they cease. This is an eternal law.

*Buddhism*. Dhammapada 3-5

You have heard that it was said, "You shall love your neighbor and hate your enemy." But I say to you, Love your enemies and pray for those who persecute you, so that you may be sons of your Father who is in heaven; for he makes his sun rise on the evil and on the good, and sends rain on the just and on the unjust. For if you love those who love you, what reward have you? Do not even the tax collectors do the same? And if you salute only your brethren, what more are you doing than others? Do not even the Gentiles do the same? You, therefore, must be perfect, as your heavenly Father is perfect.

*Christianity*. Matthew 5.43-48

My Lord! Others have fallen back in showing compassion to their benefactors as you have shown compassion even to your malefactors. All this is unparalleled.

*Jainism*. Vitaragastava 14.5

Of the adage, Only a good man knows how to like people, knows how to dislike them, Confucius said, "He whose heart is in the smallest degree set upon Goodness will dislike no one."

*Confucianism*. Analects 4.3-4

I should be like the sun, shining universally on all without seeking thanks or reward, able to take care of all sentient beings even if they are

**Dhammapada 3-5:** Cf. Jerusalem Talmud, Nedarim 9.4, p. 701.

**Matthew 5.43-48:** Cf. 1 John 4.18-20, pp. 159-60; also Genesis 32.3-20, pp. 459-60, on Jacob's love for Esau; Sun Myung Moon, 10-20-73, p. 702.

bad, never giving up on my vows on this account, not abandoning all sentient beings because one sentient being is evil.

*Buddhism.* Garland Sutra 23

What kind of love is this that to another can shift?
Says Nanak, True lovers are those who are forever absorbed in the Beloved.
Whoever discriminates between treatment held good or bad,
Is not a true lover—he rather is caught in calculations.

*Sikhism.* Adi Granth, Asa-ki-Var, M.2, p. 474

The sage has no fixed [personal] ideas.
He regards the people's ideas as his own.
I treat those who are good with goodness,
And I also treat those who are not good with goodness.
Thus goodness is attained.
I am honest with those who are honest,
And I am also honest with those who are dishonest.
Thus honesty is attained.

*Taoism.* Tao Te Ching 49

It may be that God will ordain love between you and those whom you hold as enemies. For God has power over all things; and God is Oft-forgiving, Most Merciful.

*Islam.* Qur'an 60.7

Aid an enemy before you aid a friend, to subdue hatred.

*Judaism.* Tosefta, Baba Metzia 2.26

Do good to him who has done you an injury.

*Taoism.* Tao Te Ching 63

Do not be overcome by evil, but overcome evil with good.

*Christianity.* Romans 12.21

God said, "Resemble Me; just as I repay good for evil so do you also repay good for evil."

*Judaism.* Exodus Rabbah 26.2

Conquer anger by love. Conquer evil by good. Conquer the stingy by giving. Conquer the liar by truth.

*Buddhism.* Dhammapada 223

Man should subvert anger by forgiveness, subdue pride by modesty, overcome hypocrisy with simplicity, and greed by contentment.

*Jainism.* Samanasuttam 136

May generosity triumph over niggardliness,
May love triumph over contempt,
May the true-spoken word triumph over the false-spoken word,
May truth triumph over falsehood.

*Zoroastrianism.* Yasna 60.5

The good deed and the evil deed are not alike. Repel the evil deed with one which is better, then lo!, he between whom and you there was enmity shall become as though he were a bosom friend.

But none is granted it save those who are steadfast, and none is granted it save a person of great good fortune.

*Islam.* Qur'an 41.34-35

A superior being does not render evil for evil; this is a maxim one should observe; the ornament of virtuous persons is their conduct. One should never harm the wicked or the good or even criminals meriting death. A noble soul will ever exercise compassion even toward those who enjoy injuring others or those of cruel deeds when they are actually committing them—for who is without fault?

*Hinduism.* Ramayana, Yuddha Kanda 115

**Garland Sutra 23:** Cf. Mahaparinirvana Sutra 470-71, pp. 162-63; Perfection of Wisdom in Eight Thousand Lines 321-22, p. 686; Garland Sutra 23, p. 692; Sikshasamuccaya 280-81, p. 692; Digha Nikaya xiii.77, pp. 161-62; Metta Sutta, pp. 160-61.

**Asa-ki-Var, M.2:** Cf. Wadhans, M.1, p. 161; Shalok, Farid, p. 296.

**Dhammapada 223:** Cf. James 1.20, p. 655; Genesis 32.3-20, pp. 459-60.

**Ramayana:** Cf. Yajur Veda 36.18, p. 161.

The reason why God does not punish even though He may see an enemy and have the urge to kill him and get revenge, is that He is thinking of the enemy's parents, wife, and children who all love him. Knowing all too well their unparalleled love toward that person, God cannot strike him with His iron rod. When you really understand such a heart of God, could you take revenge on your enemy? When you know all these things, you would even go and help that person. In this manner one comes closer to the Great Way of heavenly Principle, that Great Way which tries to embrace everything centering on love. When this happens earth will shake and induce even God to shed tears. "You truly resemble me. How happy I am!" He will exclaim. God always looks at things in that perspective. This is how we should understand the teaching to love one's enemy. The source of such a power to love your enemy is neither knowledge, nor money, nor earthly power. It is only true love.

*Unification Church.* Sun Myung Moon, 3-30-90

Someone said, "What do you say concerning the principle that injury should be recompensed with kindness?" The Master said, "With what will you then recompense kindness? Recompense injury with justice, and recompense kindness with kindness."

*Confucianism.* Analects 14.36

According to Anas ibn Malik, the Prophet said, "Help your brother whether he is oppressor or oppressed." Anas replied to him, "O Messenger of God, a man who is oppressed I am ready to help, but how does one help an oppressor?" "By hindering him doing wrong," he said.

*Islam.* Hadith of Bukhari

**Sun Myung Moon, 3-30-90:** See Sun Myung Moon, 10-20-73, p. 702.

**Analects 14.36:** This and the following passage dispute the notion that to love your enemy always means to do kindness, if that would not uphold justice. Confucius is here disputing the proverb from the Tao Te Ching 63, quoted above. Yet Confucius also praises the ideal of universal benevolence in Analects 4.3-4, above. Apparently, even though a man may like an evildoer and want to help him, sometimes doing him a kindness will not be helpful; particularly if that 'kindness' only encourages him to do more evil. Tougher measures may be appropriate, but these, too, should be motivated by genuine love—by a parental concern for the wrongdoer's welfare. See also Yogacarya Bhumi Shastra, p. 341; Sanhedrin 72a, p. 340.

**Hadith of Bukhari:** See the previous note.

# *Turn the Other Cheek*

THE PACIFIST ETHIC TO BEAR INSULTS without complaint and to turn the other cheek is related to the ethic to love one's enemy. Here the emphasis is as much on the individual's internal attitude as it is upon the other's welfare. If a person responds to evil in anger or self-defense, he becomes attached to the evil and it can dominate him. The anger and hatred of his attacker is transmuted into his own anger and resentment at being a victim, and he loses his balance and spiritual poise. But by bearing and accepting insults and abuse without diminution of his own goodwill and mental concentration, he can stay above the hatred and preserve a foundation of spiritual independence and self-possession. Ultimately, it is only by preserving his spiritual subjectivity in the midst of insults that a person can have the strength to love his enemy and win him over. We include several striking examples: the Lotus Sutra's account of a monk who is victorious through never disparaging his abusers and the prophet Isaiah's servant of the Lord.

The concluding passages also deal with the justice of turning the other cheek. They assume an inexorable principle of *Cosmic Justice*, pp. 122-27, which will set things right and even vindicate the victim's passivity. Paul argues that worldly retribution would mitigate the punishment of God, hence, by not acting, the believer will heap burning coals upon the head of his adversary. Buddhist scriptures also speak of the demerit which will come to the evildoer when his insult is accepted without responding. The victim, on the other hand, gains merit through enduring persecution and developing the virtue of patience.

Let there be no injury and no requital.

*Islam*. Forty Hadith of an-Nawawi 32

One should choose to be among the persecuted, rather than the persecutors.

*Judaism*. Talmud, Baba Kamma 93a

Victory breeds hatred, for the defeated live in pain. Happily live the peaceful, giving up victory and defeat.

*Buddhism*. Dhammapada 201

For behold, they had rather sacrifice their lives than even to take the life of their enemy; and they have buried their weapons of war deep in the earth, because of their love toward their brethren.

*Church of Jesus Christ of Latter-day Saints*. Book of Mormon, Alma 26.32

In wars to gain land, the dead fill the plains; in wars to gain cities, the dead fill the cities. This is known as showing the land the way to devour human flesh. Death is too light a punishment for such men who wage war. Hence those skilled in war should suffer the most severe punishments.

*Confucianism*. Mencius IV.A.14

**Forty Hadith of an-Nawawi 32:** On Muhammad's long-suffering and generosity, see Hadith, p. 471.
**Baba Kamma 93a:** Cf. Pesahim 25b, p. 340.
**Dhammapada 201:** Cf. Yogacara Bhumi Sutra 4, pp. 393-94.
**Mencius IV.A.14:** Cf. Tao Te Ching 31, p. 743.

Those who beat you with fists,
Do not pay them in the same coin,
But go to their house and kiss their feet.

*Sikhism.* Adi Granth, Shalok, Farid, p. 1378

You have heard that it was said, "An eye for an eye and a tooth for a tooth." But I say to you, Do not resist one who is evil. But if any one strikes you on the right cheek, turn to him the other also; and if any one would sue you and take your coat, let him have your cloak as well; and if any one forces you to go one mile, go with him two miles.

*Christianity.* Matthew 5.38-41

Those who are insulted but do not insult others in revenge, who hear themselves reproached without replying, who perform good work out of the love of the Lord and rejoice in their sufferings... are "as the sun when he goeth forth in his might."

*Judaism.* Talmud, Yoma 23a

Chi K'ang-tzu asked Confucius about government, saying, "Suppose I were to slay those who have not the Way in order to help those who have the Way, what would you think of it?" Confucius replied saying, "You are there to rule, not to slay. If you desire what is good, the people will at once be good."

*Confucianism.* Analects 12.19

Then they came up and laid hands upon Jesus and seized him. And behold, one of those who were with Jesus stretched out his hand, and drew his sword, and struck the slave of the high priest, and cut off his ear. Then Jesus said to him, "Put your sword back into its place; for all who take the sword will perish by the sword."

*Christianity.* Matthew 26.51-52

Brethren, if outsiders should speak against me, or against the Doctrine, or against the Order, you should not on that account either bear malice, or suffer resentment, or feel ill will. If you, on that account, should feel angry and hurt, that would stand in the way of your own self-conquest.

*Buddhism.* Digha Nikaya i.3

Kuan Chung... could seize the fief of P'ien with its three hundred villages from its owner, the head of the Po family; yet Po, though he lived on coarse food to the end of his days, never uttered a single word of resentment. The Master said, "To be poor and not resent it is far harder than to be rich, yet not presumptuous."

*Confucianism.* Analects 14.11

Monks, even as low-down thieves might be carving you limb from limb with a two-handled saw, even then whoever sets his mind at enmity is not a doer of my teaching. Monks, you should train yourselves thus, "Our minds shall not be perverted, we will not utter evil words, we shall abide cherishing thoughts of good, with minds full of goodwill and with no hatred in our heart. Beginning with that thief, we shall abide suffusing the whole world with thoughts of goodwill that are extensive, exalted, and immeasurable, without hostility and malevolence."

If you, monks, were to attend repeatedly to this exhortation on the parable of the saw, would you see any form of ridicule, subtle or gross, that you could not endure?

*Buddhism.* Majjhima Nikaya i.129

For what reason was he named Never Despise? Because he paid respect to and commended everybody he saw, monks, nuns, men and women disciples; speaking thus, "I deeply revere you. Wherefore? Because you are walking in the bodhisattva way and are to become Buddhas." That monk did not devote himself to reading and reciting the sutras, but only to paying respect, so that when he saw afar off a

**Matthew 26.51-52:** But see also Matthew 10.34, p. 741, and John 2.13-16, p. 745.

**Digha Nikaya i.3:** Cf. Vacana 248, p. 656.

**Analects 14.11:** Kuan Chung had such prestige that no one called him 'presumptuous' when he injured others; it was much harder for the head of the Po family to avoid resentment than it was for Kuan Chung to keep up the air of probity. Cf. Nahjul Balagha, Saying 201, p. 701; I Ching 40, p. 701.

member of the four classes of disciples he would specially go and pay respect to them, saying, "I dare not slight you, because you are all to become Buddhas." Amongst the four classes, there were those who, irritated and angry and low-minded, reviled and abused him, saying, "Where does this ignorant monk come from, who takes it on himself to say, 'I do not slight you,' and who predicts us as destined to become Buddhas? We need no such false predictions." Thus he passed many years, constantly reviled but never irritated or angry, always saying, "You are to become Buddhas." Whenever he spoke thus, they beat him with clubs, sticks, potsherds, or stones. But, while escaping to a distance, he still cried aloud, "I dare not slight you. You are all to become Buddhas." And because he always spoke thus, the haughty monks, nuns, and their disciples dubbed him Never Despise.

*Buddhism*. Lotus Sutra 20

The Lord God has given me
the tongue of a disciple,
that I may know how to sustain with a word
him that is weary.
Morning by morning he wakens,
he wakens my ear to hear as a disciple.
The Lord God has opened my ear,
and I was not rebellious,
I turned not backward.
I gave my back to the smiters,
and my cheeks to those who pulled out the
beard;
I hid not my face
from shame and spitting.
For the Lord God helps me;
therefore I have not been confounded;
therefore I have set my face like a flint,
and I know that I shall not be put to shame;
he who vindicates me is near.

*Judaism* and *Christianity*. Isaiah 50.4-8

If an evil man, on hearing of what is good, comes and creates a disturbance, you should hold your peace. You must not angrily upbraid him; then he who has come to curse you will merely harm himself.

*Buddhism*.
Sutra of Forty-two Sections 7

Beloved, never avenge yourselves, but leave it to the wrath of God; for it is written, "Vengeance is mine, I will repay, says the Lord." No, "if your enemy is hungry, feed him; if he is thirsty, give him drink; for by doing so you will heap burning coals upon his head."

*Christianity*. Romans 12.19-20

❖

**Lotus Sutra 20:** This is recognizably a story about a preacher of Mahayana doctrine being abused and beaten by Theravada monks, but it could apply to any of the many sectarian struggles in the history of Buddhism. The sutra goes on to say that by exercising forbearance upon being beaten and reviled, his accumulated sins were washed away and he ultimately attained the highest goal.

**Romans 12.19-20:** Paul is quoting Deuteronomy 32.35 and Proverbs 25.21-22. In Qur'an 5.27-32, p. 342, Abel refused to strike back when Cain sought to kill him for fear of God and divine punishment; and he recognized that Cain would ultimately be the loser for killing him.

## Good Deeds

GOOD DEEDS are the manifestation of a healthy spiritual life. Good deeds create merit, improve one's relationship with God, and are the best way to annul the effects of past evil deeds.

Heaven is not attained without good deeds.

*Sikhism*. Adi Granth, Ramkali-ki-Var, M.1, p. 952

Many garlands can be made from a heap of flowers. Many good deeds should be done by one born a mortal.

*Buddhism*. Dhammapada 53

For we are his workmanship, created in Christ Jesus for good works, which God prepared beforehand, that we should walk in them.

*Christianity*. Ephesians 2.10

No one who does good deeds will ever come to a bad end, either here or in the world to come. When such people die, they go to other realms where the righteous live.

*Hinduism*. Bhagavad Gita 6.40-41

Be mindful of your duty [to God], and do good works; and again, be mindful of your duty, and believe; and once again: be mindful of your duty, and do right. God loves the doers of good.

*Islam*. Qur'an 5.93

Love covers a multitude of sins.

*Christianity*. 1 Peter 4.8

Good deeds annul evil deeds. This is a reminder for the mindful.

*Islam*. Qur'an 11.114

Whoever, by a good deed, covers the evil done, such a one illumines this world like the moon freed from clouds.

*Buddhism*. Dhammapada 173

I call heaven and earth to witness: Whether Jew or Gentile, whether man or woman, whether servant or freeman, they are all equal in this: that the Holy Spirit rests upon them in accordance with their deeds!

*Judaism*. Seder Eliyyahu Rabbah 10

Anything evil refrain from doing; all good deeds do! So will you be released forever from the influence of evil stars, and always be encompassed by good guardian angels.

*Taoism*. Tract of the Quiet Way

He who carries out one good deed acquires for himself one advocate in his own behalf, and he who commits one transgression acquires one accuser against himself. Repentance and good works are like a shield against calamity.

*Judaism*. Mishnah, Abot 4.13

When the earth is shaken with her earthquake
And the earth yields up her burdens,
And man says, "What ails her?"
That day she will relate her chronicles
Because your Lord inspires her.
That day mankind will issue forth in scattered groups to be shown their deeds.
And whoever has done good, an atom's weight will see it then,

**Ephesians 2.10:** Cf. James 1.25, p. 105.

**1 Peter 4.8:** Cf. Luke 19.2-9, p. 645; Ezekiel 33.14-16, p. 645; Isaiah 1.16-20, p. 520.

**Qur'an 11.114:** Cf. Qur'an 25.71, p. 645; Visparad 15.1, p. 713.

**Tract of the Quiet Way:** Cf. Treatise on Response and Retribution 1-2, pp. 126-27; 5, p. 645; Abot 4.13, p. 238.

And whoever has done ill, an atom's weight
will see it then.

*Islam*. Qur'an 99

Realization of Truth is higher than all else;
Higher still is truthful living.

*Sikhism*. Adi Granth,
Sri Raga Ashtpadi, M.1, p. 62

What does it profit, my brethren, if a man says he has faith but has not works? Can his faith save him? If a brother or sister is ill-clad and in lack of daily food, and one of you says to them, "Go in peace, be warmed and filled" without giving them the things needed for the body, what does it profit? So faith by itself, without works, is dead.

But someone will say, "You have faith and I have works." Show me your faith apart from your works, and I by my works will show you my faith. You believe that God is one; you do well. Even the demons believe—and shudder. Do you want to be shown, you shallow man, that faith apart from works is barren? Was not Abraham our father justified by works, when he offered his son Isaac upon the altar? You see that faith was active along with his works, and faith was completed by works, and the scripture was fulfilled which says, "Abraham believed God, and it was reckoned to him as righteousness"; and he was called the friend of God. You see that a man is justified by works and not by faith alone.... For as the body apart from the spirit is dead, so faith apart from works is dead.

*Christianity*. James 2.14-26

❖

**James 2.14-26:** This argument for good deeds to demonstrate faith relies on the example of Abraham, for it comes as a counterpoint to Galatians 3.1-11, p. 541. Paul's argument in Galatians, that man is saved through faith and not by deeds according to the law, had been misinterpreted by some Christians as advocating antinomianism, the license to do most anything as long as it is not harmful, under the cover of faith. James corrects this misconception by asserting that faith, if it is true, will be substantiated and confirmed by good works.

# Labor and Industry

AN IMPORTANT PRACTICAL FUNCTION OF RELIGION is to encourage the virtues that make for economic success, such as: industry, frugality, concern for home and family, delay of gratification for a future time, honesty in one's dealings, and perseverance in an undertaking. In addition, religion should give positive value to worldly success and the labor required to become prosperous. Max Weber's well-known thesis on the rise of capitalism credits the rise of capitalism in the West to the Calvinist Protestant ethic, which encouraged believers to interpret their success as a sign of God's favor. He doubted that modern industrial societies could arise in cultures of other religions. Today, however, it is imperative that the wealth of advanced economies be enjoyed by all peoples, and this requires that every society develop its own industrial base. And indeed, as the economic rise of the Confucian-based societies of East Asia proves, other religions also possess—or potentially can develop—the foundations necessary to support the development of modern industrial society in their cultural spheres.

We give a few texts from scriptures which support industry and value the accumulation of wealth. They approve of honest work as its own reward, condemning sloth, laziness, and profligacy. But labor is even more sanctified if its wealth, once accumulated and enjoyed, is then devoted to charitable and public ends. Philanthropy is the logical end of capitalist accumulation, and one of its most important religious justifications.

We conclude this section with two versions of the Parable of the Talents, from the New Testament and the Jain scriptures. Though they have different imports, they share in common the theme that a person has the obligation to make the best use of what has been given him.

Work is worship.

*Hinduism*. Virashaiva Proverb

Great is labor; it confers honor on the laborer.

*Judaism*. Talmud, Nedarim 49b

When the blacksmith dies, his hand hangs in the world.

*African Traditional Religions*. Idoma Proverb (Nigeria)

When the prayer is finished, scatter in the land and seek God's bounty, and remember God frequently, that you may prosper.

*Islam*. Qur'an 62.10

Do you keep your feet, hands, intellect ready, O Mazdayasni Zoroastrians, in order to practice lawful, timely, well-done deeds, in order to undo unlawful, untimely, bad-done deeds. Let one practice here good industry; let one make the needy prosperous.

*Zoroastrianism*. Avesta, Visparad 15.1

**Virashaiva Proverb:** This expression, *kayakave kailasa*, means that labor, when done with a selfless attitude (see Bhagavad Gita 3.4-9, below) is equal to self-realization itself. It could also be translated, Service is salvation.

**Qur'an 62.10:** Prayer and spiritual concerns must be the foundation for worldly success.

**Visparad 15.1:** The Parsees in India have long been known for their industry; they occupy much of Bombay's middle class.

And the Lord will make you abound in prosperity, in the fruit of your body, and in the fruit of your cattle, and in the fruit of your ground.... And the Lord will make you the head, and not the tail; and you shall tend upward only, and not downward; if you obey the commandments of the Lord your God.

*Judaism* and *Christianity*. Deuteronomy 28.11-13

Weeping is not the answer to poverty; a lazy man who is hungry has no one to blame but himself.

He who wishes to eat the honey which is under the rock should not be unduly worried about the edge of the axe.

There is no place where one cannot achieve greatness; only the lazy prospers nowhere. There is no place that does not suit me, O divinity!

*African Traditional Religions*. Yoruba Proverbs (Nigeria)

He who says, "It is too hot, too cold, too late!"
Leaving the waiting work unfinished still,
Lets pass all opportunities for good.
But he who reckons heat and cold as straws
And like a man does all that's to be done,
He never falls away from happiness.

*Buddhism*. Digha Nikaya iii.185, Sigalovada Sutta

Go to the ant, O sluggard;
consider her ways, and be wise.
Without having any chief,
officer, or ruler,
she prepares her food in summer,
and gathers her sustenance in harvest.
How long will you lie there, O sluggard?
When will you rise from your sleep?
A little sleep, a little slumber,
a little folding of the hands to rest,
and poverty will come upon you like a vagabond,
and want like an armed man.

*Judaism* and *Christianity*. Proverbs 6.6-11

One who claims to be a saint,
And goes about begging—
Touch not his feet!
He whose livelihood is earned through work,
And part given away in charity—
Such a one, Nanak, truly knows the way of God.

*Sikhism*. Adi Granth, Var Sarang, M.1, p. 1245

We were not idle when we were with you, we did not eat anyone's bread without paying, but with toil and labor we worked night and day, that we might not burden any of you. It was not because we have not that right, but to give you in our conduct an example to imitate. For even when we were with you, we gave you this command: If any one will not work, let him not eat. For we hear that some of you are living in idleness, mere busybodies, not doing any work. Now such persons we command and exhort in the Lord Jesus Christ to do their work in quietness and to earn their own living.

*Christianity*. 2 Thessalonians 3.8-12

He who shirks action does not attain freedom; no one can gain perfection by abstaining from work. Indeed, there is no one who rests even for an instant; every creature is driven to action by his own nature.

**Deuteronomy 28.11-13:** Prosperity is a mandate from God. This passage is often used in lower-class Protestant churches to exhort people to industry, thrift, and ambition, to forswear the fatalism and profligacy of poverty, and adopt a middle-class lifestyle—all with the confidence that they really are meant to succeed in life.

**Digha Nikaya iii.185:** This sutra is addressed to householders and refers to the worldly labors of trade and industry, not merely to spiritual pursuits. Yet the latter also applies, compare Luke 14.16-24, p. 485.

**Var Sarang, M.1:** This passage critiques asceticism which can degenerate into parasitic begging. The religious ideal of ascetic poverty may discourage the sincere believer from striving for economic success. Cf. Dhammapada 308, p. 349.

**2 Thessalonians 3.8-12:** Paul is speaking of how he and his fellow apostles did not rely upon their congregations for support, but earned their own bread.

Those who abstain from action while allowing the mind to dwell on sensual pleasure cannot be called sincere spiritual aspirants. But they excel who control their senses through the mind, using them for selfless service.

Fulfill all your duties; action is better than inaction. Even to maintain your body, Arjuna, you are obliged to act. But it is selfish action that imprisons the world. Act selflessly, without any thought of personal profit.

*Hinduism.* Bhagavad Gita 3.4-9

In the dark night live those for whom the world without alone is real; in night darker still live those for whom the world within alone is real. The first leads to a life of action, the second to a life of meditation. But those who combine action with meditation cross the sea of death through action and enter into immortality through the practice of meditation. So have we heard from the wise.

*Hinduism.* Isha Upanishad 9-11

Rabbi Judah ben Ilai, Rabbi Jose ben Halafta, and Rabbi Simeon ben Yohai were sitting together. Rabbi Judah praised the Roman government for the splendid markets, bridges, and baths they had erected in Palestine. Rabbi Jose kept silent. Rabbi Simeon retorted that they had done so for their own benefit, not for the land's sake.

A disciple incautiously repeated this, and a Roman spy informed the government. An edict was issued that Rabbi Judah be promoted to the headship of Jewish assemblies; that Rabbi Jose be banished to Galilee; and that Rabbi Simeon be executed. Rabbi Simeon and his son, Rabbi Eleazar, hid in a cave for many years and spent their time there in mystical studies, laying the foundation for the Zohar and other works of Kabbalah. When they left the cave, following a change in the administration of Palestine, they beheld several men engaged in agricultural labor. They exclaimed, "These folk neglect eternal affairs and trouble themselves with temporal matters."

Then they returned to the cave until their minds had grown accustomed to the idea that people should engage in material labor as well as in spiritual work, and that such is the will of God.

*Judaism.* Talmud, Shabbat 33b

A clansman has wealth acquired by energetic striving, amassed by strength of arm, won by sweat, lawful and lawfully gotten. At the thought, "Wealth is mine acquired by energetic striving, amassed by strength of arm, won by sweat, lawful and lawfully gotten," bliss comes to him, satisfaction comes to him. This is called "the bliss of ownership."

A clansman by means of wealth acquired by energetic striving... both enjoys his wealth and does meritorious deeds therewith. At the thought, "By means of wealth acquired... I both enjoy my wealth and do meritorious deeds," bliss comes to him, satisfaction comes to him. This is called "the bliss of wealth."

*Buddhism.* Anguttara Nikaya ii.68

Abu Huraira reported God's Messenger as saying, "Among the actions and good deeds for which a believer will continue to receive reward after his death are knowledge which he taught and spread, a good son whom he left behind, or a copy of the Qur'an which he left as a legacy, or a mosque which he built, or a house which he built for the traveller, or a stream which he caused to flow, or a contribution which he gave from his property when he was alive and well, for which he will continue to receive reward after his death."

*Islam.* Hadith of Ibn Majah

It will be as when a man going on a journey called his servants and entrusted to them his property; to one he gave five talents, to another two, to another one, to each according to his ability. Then he went away. He who had received the five talents went at once and traded with them; and he made five talents more. So also, he who had the two talents made two

**Bhagavad Gita 3.4-9:** Krishna does not permit Arjuna to renounce the world as a way to avoid his responsibilities; he is obliged to fight and work for good. Cf. Bhagavad Gita 3.25-26, p. 690.

talents more. But he who had received the one talent went and dug in the ground and hid his master's money. Now after a long time the master of those servants came and settled accounts with them. And he who had received five talents came forward, bringing five talents more, saying, "Master, you delivered to me five talents; here I have made five talents more." His master said to him, "Well done, good and faithful servant; you have been faithful over a little, I will set you over much; enter into the joy of your master." And he also who had the two talents came forward, saying, "Master, you delivered to me two talents; here I have made two talents more." His master said to him, "Well done, good and faithful servant; you have been faithful over a little, I will set you over much, enter into the joy of your master." He also who had received the one talent came forward, saying, "Master, I knew you to be a hard man, reaping where you did not sow, and gathering where you did not winnow; so I was afraid, and I went and hid your talent in the ground. Here you have what is yours." But his master answered him, "You wicked and slothful servant! You knew that I reap where I have not sowed, and gather where I have not winnowed? Then you ought to have invested my money with the bankers, and at my coming I should have received what was my own with interest. So take the talent from him, and give it to him who has the ten talents. For to every one who has will more be given, and he will have abundance; but from him who has not, even what he has will be taken away. And cast the worthless servant into the outer darkness; there men will weep and gnash their teeth."

*Christianity*. Matthew 25.14-30:
Parable of the Talents

Three merchants set out on their travels, each with his capital: One of them gained there much, the second returned with his capital, and the third merchant came home after having lost his capital. This parable is taken from common life; learn to apply it to the Law.

The capital is human life, the gain is heaven; through the loss of that capital man must be born as a denizen of hell or a brute animal.

The slave to his lusts has forfeited [his capital], human life and divine life. Having forfeited them, he will have to endure one of these two states of misery; it will be difficult for him to attain an upward course for a long time...

He who brings back his capital, is to be compared to one who is born again as a man. Those men who through the exercise of various virtues become pious householders will be born again as men; for all beings will reap the fruit of their actions.

But he who increases his capital is like one who practices eminent virtues; the virtuous, excellent man cheerfully attains the state of the gods.

*Jainism*.
Uttaradhyayana Sutra 7.14-21

**Uttaradhyayana Sutra 7.14-21:** This Jain parable, even more than the Parable of the Talents in the Christian Bible, is not really about labor and industry in a worldly sense, but rather uses that theme to illustrate a truth about the spiritual life and the treasure in heaven which is its aim—see Matthew 6.19-21, p. 237. Yet the principles of worldly success and success in the spiritual life are similar: both require investment, ambition, labor, and perseverance.

## *Honesty and Expediency*

THIS SECTION DEALS WITH THE VIRTUES of honesty and expediency. Expediency is not always compatible with honesty, and the tension between these two values creates misunderstandings for the encounter of diverse cultures and religions.

The first group of passages deals with honesty as truth-telling; see also related passages on *Lying and Deceit*, pp. 346-47. The question, What is truth? does not have a simple answer. Truth-telling can sometimes mean to report the facts of a situation, as in the correspondence theory of truth, but most religious truth deals with ideas and realities beyond the level of fact. Hence a second meaning of truth-telling is to be true to the principles and doctrines of religion, and to teach them truly. It is an attribute of truthful words that they be beneficial and instructive, not just factually true. That is probably the sense of truth meant by these passages.

The second group of passages deal with honesty as promise-keeping. In the Abrahamic faiths, promises have often been sealed by oaths, sworn in the name of God. But as Jesus' admonition illustrates, oaths can be abused and sworn falsely, particularly when the person does not truly believe in the God to whom he swears. All religions elevate promise-keeping as a central virtue of human relations.

The last group of passages are on the topic of expediency. Blunt honesty may sometimes conflict with what is most helpful for a person; for example, in time of war it may be necessary to lie to an enemy in order to preserve a life. In leading people to recognize the truth of religion, expediency may also be required, for the truth is sometimes hidden in a package that is outwardly unseemly. Thus when Paul preached the gospel among Jews, he observed the Jewish dietary laws—even though he himself was free from those laws—in order not to cause offense. The Buddhist doctrine of Expedient Devices, or Skill in Means, as expressed in passages from the Lotus Sutra, attempts to reconcile the various schools of Buddhism by showing that Buddha preached various doctrines according to people's temperaments and inclinations. In Nagarjuna this is the doctrine of the Two Truths: relative truth and absolute truth. It is first necessary to grasp the relative truth of worldly phenomena before one can comprehend the absolute truth which is beyond appearances. But once the aspirant has realized the deeper teaching—the absolute truth—and gone beyond to realize enlightenment, the differences among various outward forms of the teaching become insignificant.

The seal of God is truth.

*Judaism*. Talmud, Shabbat 55

Keep your conscience clear.

*Christianity*. 1 Peter 3.16

Straightforwardness and honesty in the activities of one's body, speech, and mind lead to an auspicious path.

*Jainism*. Tattvarthasutra 6.23

Let your conduct be marked by truthfulness in word, deed, and thought.

*Hinduism*. Taittiriya Upanishad 1.11.1

Be honest like Heaven in conducting your affairs.

*Taoism*. Tract of the Quiet Way

May the true-spoken word triumph over the false-spoken word.

*Zoroastrianism*. Yasna 60.5

Putting away falsehood, let everyone speak the truth with his neighbor, for we are members one of another.

*Christianity*. Ephesians 4.25

One should utter the truth.

*Buddhism*. Dhammapada 224

He who utters gentle, instructive, true words, who by his speech gives offense to none—him I call a brahmin.

*Buddhism*. Dhammapada 408

Master Tseng said, "Every day I examine myself.... In intercourse with my friends, have I always been true to my word?"

*Confucianism*. Analects 1.4

One should speak the truth and speak it pleasingly; should not speak the truth in an unpleasant manner nor should one speak untruth because it is pleasing; this is the eternal law.

*Hinduism*. Laws of Manu 4.138

If a lie runs for twenty years, it takes truth one day to catch up with it.

The truth got to market, but it was unsold; lying costs very little to buy.

*African Traditional Religions*. Yoruba Proverbs (Nigeria)

O ye who believe! Stand out firmly for justice, as witnesses to God, even as against yourselves, or your parents, or your kin, and whether it concerns rich or poor: for God can best protect both. Follow not the lusts of your hearts lest you swerve, and if you distort justice or decline to do justice, verily God is well-acquainted with all that you do.

*Islam*. Qur'an 4.135

Run to and fro through the streets of Jerusalem,
look and take note!
Search her squares to see
if you can find a man,
one who does justice
and seeks truth;
that I may pardon her....
O Lord, do not thy eyes look for truth?

*Judaism* and *Christianity*. Jeremiah 5.1-3

When man appears before the Throne of Judgment, the first question he is asked is not, "Have you believed in God," or "Have you prayed and performed ritual acts," but "Have you dealt honorably, faithfully in all your dealings with your fellowman?"

*Judaism*. Talmud, Shabbat 31a

If you plot and connive to deceive men, you may fool them for a while, and profit thereby, but you will without fail be visited by divine punishment. To be utterly honest may have the appearance of inflexibility and self-righteousness, but in the end, such a person will receive the blessings of sun and moon. Follow honesty without fail.

*Shinto*. Oracle of Amaterasu at the Kotai Shrine

Tzu-chang asked about getting on with people. The Master said, "Be loyal and true to your every word, serious and careful in all you do, and you will get on well enough even though you find yourself among barbarians. But if you are disloyal and untrustworthy in your speech, frivolous and careless in your acts, even though you are among your own neighbors, how can you hope to get on well?"

*Confucianism*. Analects 15.5

**Ephesians 4.25:** Cf. Psalm 24.3-6, p. 155; Psalm 101.7, p. 346.

**Dhammapada 408:** Cf. Qur'an 16.125, p. 723.

**Analects 1.4:** Cf. Vacana 440, p. 579; Qur'an 61.2-3, p. 579.

**Yoruba Proverbs:** Cf. Yoruba Proverbs, pp. 184, 346.

**Qur'an 4.135:** Islam does not value expediency or the competing goods of loyalty to family and kindred as highly as it values honesty. Compare Analects 13.18, below.

**Shabbat 31a:** Cf. Psalm 24.3-6, p. 155; Micah 6.6-8, p. 615; Amos 5.23-24, p. 197. Compare Matthew 25.31-45, p. 699.

**Analects 15.5:** Cf. Mihir Yasht 10.2, p. 41.

When a man vows a vow to the Lord, or swears an oath to bind himself by a pledge, he shall not break his word; he shall do according to all that proceeds from his mouth.

*Judaism* and *Christianity*. Numbers 30.2

Fulfil the covenant of God once you have pledged it, and do not break any oaths once they have been sworn to. You have set up God as a Guarantee for yourselves; God knows everything you are doing.

Do not be like a woman who unravels her yarn after its strands are firmly spun. Nor take your oaths in order to snatch at advantages over one another, to make one party more numerous than the other. For God will test you by this.

*Islam*. Qur'an 16.91-92

You have heard that it was said to the men of old, "You shall not swear falsely, but shall perform to the Lord what you have sworn." But I say to you, do not swear at all, either by heaven, for it is the throne of God, or by the earth, for it is his footstool, or by Jerusalem, for it is the city of the great King. And do not swear by your head, for you cannot make one hair white or black. Let what you say be simply "Yes" or "No"; anything more than this comes from evil.

*Christianity*. Matthew 5.33-37

You may modify a statement in the interests of peace.

*Judaism*. Talmud, Yebamot 65b

It is always proper to speak the truth. It is better again to speak what is beneficial than to speak what is true. I hold that this is truth which is fraught with the greatest benefit to all creatures.

*Hinduism*. Mahabharata, Shanti Parva 329.13

Do not give dogs what is holy; and do not throw your pearls before swine, lest they trample them under foot and turn to attack you.

*Christianity*. Matthew 7.6

Do not share this holy truth with anyone who lacks self-control and devotion, lacks the desire to learn, or scoffs at Me.

*Hinduism*. Bhagavad Gita 18.67

The Duke of She addressed Confucius saying, "In my country there was a man called Upright Kung. His father appropriated a sheep, and Kung bore witness against him." Confucius said, "In my country the upright men are of quite another sort. A father will screen his son, and a son his father—which incidentally does involve a sort of uprightness."

*Confucianism*. Analects 13.18

For though I am free from all men, I have made myself a slave to all, that I might win the more. To the Jews I became a Jew, in order to win Jews; to those under the law I became as one under the law—though not being myself under the law—that I might win those under the law. To those outside the law I became as one outside the law—not being without law toward God but under the law of Christ—that I might win those outside the law. To the weak I become weak, that I might win the weak. I have become all things to all men, that I might by all means save some.

*Christianity*. 1 Corinthians 9.19-22

The teaching of the Dharma by the various Buddhas is based on the two truths; namely, the relative [worldly] truth and the absolute [supreme] truth.

Those who do not know the distinction between the two truths cannot understand the profound nature of the Buddha's teaching.

**Qur'an 16.91-92:** Cf. Qur'an 61.2-3, p. 579.

**Matthew 5.33-37:** Jesus said this because oaths sworn on God or the Temple were frequently broken and even used to deceive.

**Mahabharata, Shanti Parva 329.13:** Cf. Mahabharata, Shanti Parva 37.11-14, p. 333.

**Matthew 7.6:** A precious truth, a gift of God, should not be given to those who would treat it with contempt. Teaching should be given in stages, and to those who are open to receive it. Cf. Chuang Tzu 14, p. 513.

**1 Corinthians 9.19-22:** Cf. Doctrine of the Mean 14, p. 507; Lotus Sutra 4, pp. 363-65.

Without relying on everyday common practices [relative truths], the absolute truth cannot be expressed. Without approaching the absolute truth, Nirvana cannot be attained.

A wrongly conceived Sunyata can ruin a slow-witted person. It is like a badly seized snake or a wrongly executed incantation.

The Wise One once resolved not to teach about the Dharma, thinking that the slow-witted might wrongly conceive it.

*Buddhism.* Nagarjuna, Mulamadhyamaka Karika 24.8-12

On a certain occasion the venerable Nanda, brother of the Buddha, the son of the Buddha's aunt, thus addressed a number of monks, "Without zest I follow the Brahma-life. I will give up training and go back to the low."

Someone informed the Buddha... who summoned Nanda and said to him, "How is it, Nanda, that you have no zest for the Brahma-life, that you cannot endure it, that you will give up the training and return to the low?"

"Sir, when I left my home, a Shakyan girl, the fairest in the land, with hair half combed, looked back at me and said this, 'May you soon come back again, young master.' I am always thinking of her, and hence I have no zest for the Brahma-life, I cannot endure the Brahma-life, I will give up training and return to the low."

Then the Exalted One took Nanda by the arm, and together they vanished from the Jeta Grove and appeared among the devas of the Thirty-three. There, as many as five hundred "dove-footed" nymphs had come to minister to Sakka, lord of the devas. The Exalted one said to Nanda, "Nanda, do you see those five hundred dove-footed nymphs?"

"Yes, sir."

"What do you think, Nanda? Which are the more lovely, more worth looking at, more charming, the Shakyan girl, the loveliest in the land, or these five hundred dove-footed nymphs?"

"O, sir, just as if she were a mutilated monkey with ears and nose cut off, even so, sir, the Shakyan girl, the loveliest in the land, if set beside these five hundred nymphs is not worth a fraction of them and cannot be compared with them. Why, these five hundred nymphs are far more lovely, far more worth looking at, far more charming!" Then the Exalted One, taking Nanda by the arm, vanished from the devas of the Thirty-three and reappeared in Jeta Grove.

The monks heard the rumor, "They say that Nanda, brother of the Buddha, leads the Brahma-life for the sake of nymphs. They say the Exalted One has assured him of getting five hundred dove-footed nymphs." Thereupon the monks who were comrades of Nanda called him "hireling" and "menial."...

Now the venerable Nanda, being thus worried, humiliated, and despised since he was called a hireling and a menial by his comrades, living alone, remote, energetic, ardent, making the self strong, in no time attained in this very world, himself realizing it by full comprehension, that for which the clansman rightly goes forth from home to homelessness, even that unsurpassed goal of the Brahma-life, and so abided. He realized, "Ended is birth, lived is the life, done is what was to be done; there is no more of being here." The venerable Nanda had become one of the arahants....

At the end of that night the venerable Nanda came to the Exalted One, and on coming to him saluted him and stood at one side and said, "Sir, as to the Exalted One's standing surety for me for the getting five hundred dove-footed nymphs, I release the Exalted One, sir, from that promise."

"I also, Nanda, grasping your thought with my own, have seen that this is so... Since, Nanda, by not grasping, your heart is released from the cankers, I too am released from my promise."

*Buddhism.* Udana 21-24, Nanda Sutta

**Mulamadhyamaka Karika 24.8-12:** Cf. the Parable of the Raft, Majjhima Nikaya i.134-35, p. 573; Bhagavad Gita 2.42-46, p. 576; Diamond Sutra 21, p. 572; Lankavatra Sutra 61, pp. 454-55; 76, p. 573.

**Udana 21-24:** This is a good example of the Buddha's skill in means, to lead Nanda by means of a small desire to realization of higher truth. For another example, see Digha Nikaya xiii.31-34, 80, pp. 140-41.

"Suppose, for instance, a good physician, who is wise and perspicacious, conversant with the medical art, and skillful in healing all sorts of diseases. He has many sons, say ten, twenty, even up to a hundred. Because of some matter he goes abroad to a distant country. After his departure his sons drink his other poisonous medicines, which send them into a delirium and they lie rolling on the ground. At this moment their father comes back to his home. Of the sons who drank the poison, some have lost their senses, others are sensible.... The father, seeing his sons in such distress, in accordance with his prescriptions, seeks for good herbs altogether perfect in color, scent, and fine flavor, and then pounds, sifts, and mixes them and gives them to his sons to take, saying thus, 'This excellent medicine with color, scent, and fine flavor all perfect, do you take, and it will at once rid you of your distress so that you will have no more suffering.' Those amongst the sons who are sensible, seeing this excellent medicine with color and scent both good, take it immediately and are wholly delivered from their illness. The others, who have lost their senses, seeing their father come, though they are also delighted, salute him, and ask him to heal their illness, yet when he offers them the medicine, they are unwilling to take it. Wherefore? Because the poison has entered deeply, they have lost their senses, and even in regard to this medicine of excellent color and scent they say that it is not good. The father reflects thus, 'Alas for these sons, afflicted by this poison, and their minds all unbalanced! Though they are glad to see me and implore to be healed, yet they are unwilling to take such excellent medicine as this. Now I must arrange an expedient plan so that they will take this medicine.'

"Then he says to them: 'Know, all of you, that I am now worn out with old age and that the time of my death has now arrived. This excellent medicine I now leave here. You may take it and have no fear of not being better.' After thus admonishing them, he departs again for another country and sends a messenger back to inform them, 'Your father is dead.' And now, when these sons hear that their father is dead, their minds are greatly distressed and they thus reflect, 'If our father were alive he would have pity on us, and we should be saved and preserved. But now he has left us and died in a distant country.'

"Deeming themselves orphans with no one to rely on, continuous grief brings them to their senses; they recognize the color, scent, and excellent flavor of the medicine, and thereupon take it, whence their poisoning is entirely relieved. Their father, hearing that the sons are recovered, seeks an opportunity and returns, showing himself to them all.

"Good sons! What is your opinion? Are there any who could say that this good physician had committed the sin of falsehood?"

"No, World-honored One!"

The Buddha then said: "I also am like the father. It has been infinite countless hundred thousand myriad billions of kalpas since I became Buddha. But for the sake of all living beings, I say expediently, 'I must enter Nirvana.' There is none who can lawfully accuse me of falsehood."

*Buddhism.* Lotus Sutra 16:
Parable of the Good Physician

❖

On the use of seemingly evil beings to realize a high purpose, see Holy Teaching of Vimalakirti 6, p. 314; Mahaparinirvana Sutra 424-33, p. 539.

**Lotus Sutra 16:** After having revealed the eternal life of the Buddha, the Lotus Sutra explains the apparent demise of the historic Shakyamuni Buddha as an expedient device. Knowing that if the followers knew of the Buddha's eternal life span, they might become lazy and not vigorously apply themselves to attaining Nirvana, the Buddha uses his power of expedient devices to show his death. The sutra then illustrates this expedient device by a parable. For another expedient device, see the Parable of the Prodigal Son, Lotus Sutra 4, pp. 363-65; on Buddha as the Great Physician, see Garland Sutra 37, p. 373.

## *Witness*

OF ALL THE KINDNESSES WHICH CAN BE CONFERRED upon someone, perhaps the greatest is to lead him to realize the truth and find salvation. The passages which are gathered here describe witnessing to the truth in two forms. First is to witness by example, or to "let your light so shine before men." Through good deeds and a compassionate heart the believer demonstrates his faith as a living reality and naturally draws others to him. Second is to witness by evangelism, by preaching and teaching the doctrine. We include both texts commissioning evangelism and missionary activity and texts describing the standards of good conduct and pure mind which should accompany the preaching.

Master Tseng said, "The gentleman by his culture collects friends about him, and through these friends promotes goodness."

*Confucianism.* Analects 12.24

Whoso is perfect in virtue and insight, is established in the Dhamma, has realized the Truths, and fulfills his own duties—he is respected by all people.

*Buddhism.* Dhammapada 217

You are the light of the world. A city set on a hill cannot be hid. Nor do men light a lamp and put it under a bushel, but on a stand, and it gives light to all in the house. Let your light so shine before men, that they may see your good works and give glory to your Father who is in heaven.

*Christianity.* Matthew 5.14-16

I should be a lamp for the world
Replete with the virtues of Buddhahood,
Their ten powers, their omniscience.
All sentient beings
Burn with greed, anger, and folly;
I should save and free them,
Have them extinguish the pains of the states of woe.

*Buddhism.* Garland Sutra 36

I am the Lord, I have called you in righteousness,
I have taken you by the hand and kept you;
I have given you as a covenant to the peoples,
a light to the nations,
to open the eyes that are blind,
to bring out the prisoners from the dungeon,
from the prison those who sit in darkness.

*Judaism* and *Christianity.* Isaiah 42.6-7

Hillel said, "Be of the disciples of Aaron—one that loves peace, that loves mankind and brings them nigh to the Law."

*Judaism.* Mishnah, Abot 1.12

**Analects 12.24:** Cf. Doctrine of the Mean 33, p. 731.

**Matthew 5.14-16:** Having received the grace of salvation through Christ, the Christian becomes a being of light who should illumine the world. To avoid displaying that light, by refusing to give witness to Christ and God's word or by withholding Christian love, is a sin. Cf. 1 John 4.7-20, pp. 159-60.

**Garland Sutra 36:** Cf. Dhammapada 54, p. 730; Doctrine of the Mean 33, p. 731.

**Isaiah 42.6-7:** Cf. Isaiah 42.1-4, pp. 367-68.

**Abot 1.12:** Judaism no longer encourages missionary activity. But at the time when the Mishnah was compiled Jewish missionaries were active throughout the Roman world.

Believers, be God's helpers. When Jesus the son of Mary said to the disciples, "Who will help me on the way to God?" they replied, "We are God's helpers."

*Islam*. Qur'an 61.14

Asvins, Lords of light, fill me with
the sweetness of the bee-honey,
so I may speak the glorious Word
to the masses of the people.

*Hinduism*. Atharva Veda 6.69.2

Call to the way of your Lord with wisdom and kindly exhortation. Reason with them in the most courteous manner. Your Lord knows best those who stray from His path and those who are rightly guided.

*Islam*. Qur'an 16.125

Those who teach this supreme mystery of the Gita to all who love me perform the greatest act of love; they will come to me without a doubt. No one can render me more devoted service; no one on earth can be more dear to me.

*Hinduism*. Bhagavad Gita 18.68-69

All authority in heaven and on earth has been given to me. Go therefore and make disciples of all nations, baptizing them in the name of the Father and of the Son and of the Holy Spirit, teaching them to observe all that I have commanded you; and lo, I am with you always, even to the close of the age.

*Christianity*. Matthew 28.18-20:
The Great Commission

By discoursing on morality and righteousness, convert both the cunning and the dull. By preaching on the canonical books and histories, enlighten the ignorant and the benighted.... Publish and make known sutras and tracts. Build and repair temples and shrines.... Expound moral maxims to correct the people's faults.

*Taoism*. Tract of the Quiet Way

The Emperor Sujin proclaimed to the assembled lords, "The root of leading the nation's people is education. We are now reverently worshipping the kami, with the result that misfortunes have all disappeared. But as for those people far away from the capital city, they are not yet favored with our imperial grace. Therefore, let us now select from among our assembled lords, some to send to the far provinces in the four directions, to inform the people there of our nation's laws."

*Shinto*. Nihon Shoki 5

If you are aware of a certain truth, if you possess a jewel, of which others are deprived, share it with them in a language of utmost kindliness and goodwill. If it be accepted, if it fulfill its purpose, your object is attained. If anyone should refuse it, leave him unto himself, and beseech God to guide him. Beware lest you deal unkindly with him.

*Baha'i Faith*.
Epistle to the Son of the Wolf, 15

Monks, there are these two gifts, the carnal and the spiritual. Of these two gifts the spiritual gift is preeminent. Monks, there are two sharings together, the sharing of the carnal and the sharing of the spiritual. Of these two sharings together the sharing of the spiritual is preeminent.

*Buddhism*. Itivuttaka 98

**Qur'an 61.14:** See 1 Corinthians 3.9, p. 583.

**Qur'an 16.125:** Cf. Qur'an 6.108, p. 42; 10.99-100, p. 39. Dhammapada 408, p. 718; Laws of Manu 4.138, p. 718.

**Matthew 28.18-20:** The Great Commission is the foundation for Christian missions to the world. Cf. Matthew 10.11-20, pp. 586-87.

**Tract of the Quiet Way:** In keeping with the syncretic nature of religion in China, where the Three Teachings—Confucianism, Taoism, and Buddhism—coexisted, this passage encourages evangelism by means of Confucian books, Buddhist sutras, and Taoist tracts. Evangelism is not to convert people from one religion to another, but rather to bring about a renovation of character and to encourage morality and righteousness. See Tract of the Quiet Way and Commentary, p. 38.

**Epistle to the Son of the Wolf, 15:** Cf. Matthew 10.11-15, pp. 586-87.

**Itivuttaka 98:** cf. Anguttara Nikaya i.61, p. 172; Mulamadhyamaka Karika 24.8-12, pp. 719-20.

There is a traffic in speakers of fine words;
Persons of grave demeanor are accepted as gifts;
Even the bad let slip no opportunity to acquire them.
Therefore on the day of an emperor's enthronement
Or at the installation of the three officers of state,
Rather than send a team of four horses, preceded by a disc of jade,
Better were it, as can be done without moving from one's seat, to send this Tao.
For what did the ancients say of this Tao, how did they prize it?
"Pursuing, they [who have Tao] shall catch; pursued, they shall escape"?
They thought it, indeed, the most precious of all things under heaven.

*Taoism*. Tao Te Ching 62

We are ambassadors for Christ, God making His appeal through us. We beseech you on behalf of Christ, be reconciled to God.... We put no obstacle in anyone's way, so that no fault may be found with our ministry, but as servants of God we commend ourselves in every way: through great endurance, in afflictions, hardships, calamities, beatings, imprisonments, tumults, labors, watching, hunger; by purity, knowledge, forbearance, kindness, the Holy Spirit, genuine love, truthful speech, and the power of God; with the weapons of righteousness for the right hand and for the left; in honor and dishonor, in ill repute and good repute. We are treated as impostors, and yet are true; as unknown, and yet well known; as dying, and behold we live; as punished, and yet not killed; as sorrowful, yet always rejoicing; as poor, yet making many rich; as having nothing, and yet possessing everything.

Our mouth is open to you, Corinthians; our heart is wide. You are not restricted by us, but you are restricted in your own affections. In return—I speak as to children—widen your hearts also.

*Christianity*. 2 Corinthians 5.20-6.13

When the bodhisattva
Enters his quiet room,
And, in perfect meditation,
Sees things in their true meaning,
And, rising from his meditation,
Whether to kings or nations,
Or princes, ministers, and people,
To brahmins or to others,
Opens up, expounds,
And preaches to them this sutra,
His mind shall be at ease
And free from timid weakness.

Let him who would preach this sutra
Renounce an envious, angry, proud,
Deceitful, or false mind,
And ever do upright deeds;
He should disparage none,
Never argue over the Law,
Nor cause others doubts or regret...
But ever be gentle, patient,
And compassionate to all.

*Buddhism*. Lotus Sutra 14

A son or daughter... becomes endowed with that kind of wise insight which allows him to see all beings as on the way to their slaughter. Great compassion thereby takes hold of him. With his heavenly eye he surveys countless beings, and what he sees fills him with great agitation. So many carry the burden of a karma which will soon be punished in the hells, others have acquired unfortunate rebirths which keep them away from the Buddha and his teachings, others are doomed soon to be killed or they are enveloped in the net of false views, or fail to find the path, while others who had gained a rebirth favorable to their emancipation have lost it again.

And he radiates great friendliness and compassion over all those beings, and gives his attention to them, thinking, "I shall become a savior to all those beings, I shall release them from all their sufferings!"

*Buddhism*. Perfection of Wisdom in Eight Thousand Lines 402-3

**2 Corinthians 5.20-6.13:** Cf. 1 Peter 2.12, p. 42; Matthew 10.1-25, pp. 586-87; 1 Corinthians 9.19-22, p. 719.

**Lotus Sutra 14:** This chapter describes rules for correct and effective preaching.

**Perfection of Wisdom in Eight Thousand Lines 402-3:** Here is another expression of the bodhisattva ideal.

To be unsnared by vulgar ways, to make no vain show of material things, to bring no hardship on others, to avoid offending the mob, to seek peace and security for the world, preservation of the people's lives, full provender for others as well as oneself, and to rest content when these aims are fulfilled, in this way bringing purity to the heart—there were those in ancient times who believed that the "art of the Way" lay in these things.... They preached liberality of mind, hoping thereby to bring men together in the joy of harmony, to insure concord within the four seas. Their chief task lay, they felt, in the effort to establish these ideals. They regarded it as no shame to suffer insult, but sought to put an end to strife among the people, to outlaw aggression, to abolish the use of arms, and to rescue the world from warfare. With these aims they walked the whole world over, trying to persuade those above them and to teach those below, and though the world refused to listen, they clamored all the louder and would not give up, until men said, "High and low are sick at the sight of them, and still they demand to be seen!"

*Taoism.* Chuang Tzu 33

❖

**Chuang Tzu 33:** This chapter of the Chuang Tzu describes sages of various schools—Taoists, Mohists, Legalists, Confucianists—who wandered about China during the Chou dynasty, preaching their visions of peace and harmony. See Shih Chi 47, p. 432.

Part Five

# *Providence, Society, and the Kingdom of Heaven*

CHAPTER 20

# GOOD GOVERNMENT AND THE WELFARE OF SOCIETY

BESIDES GENERAL ETHICAL TEACHINGS, THE SCRIPTURES contain specific guidance for building a peaceful and prosperous society. Individual citizens have responsibilities beyond their private lives to contribute to the public good. Rulers and governments are likewise admonished to use their office and authority to promote justice and the common welfare in accordance with divine law. Public authority is not to be taken lightly; the scriptures testify to God's providential hand which controls the destinies of nations and brings them to judgment according to their ways.

The opening sections deal with four roles for individual citizens in fostering the weal of society. These are: the quiet and unheralded work of spiritual guides, the invisible "pillars" of society, who leaven the community by their spirit, teaching, and example; the prophets and reformers who confront the governing authorities with words of admonition and take an active role in correcting injustice; and the soldiers who fight, risking their lives in order to defeat a tyrant and rescue the oppressed. In addition, it is the duty of every citizen to respect and obey the lawfully constituted authorities, who are worthy of support because they preserve peace and order.

The next several sections discuss the standards of good government. Although most of the world's religions were founded in ancient times when the prevailing form of government was monarchy, the principles of government enunciated in the scriptures are still valid for today's democracies. These are universal principles of good government which apply regardless of its form. Topics include: government subject to divine law and responsible to honor the rule of law; the responsibility of government for the welfare of the people and especially for the poor and defenseless among them; honest government and the ruler's standard of conduct; and the role of government to enforce the law and mete out fair punishments.

The last section discusses the providence of God which guides the destinies of nations. Heaven gives prosperity to peoples and nations which promote justice, righteousness, and religion, while nations which oppress the poor and persecute religion are inevitably destroyed. The destinies of nations may be understood to be under the hand of God's providence, or influenced by the blessings and judgments of gods and spirits of the land, or determined by the Mandate of Heaven.

## *The Pillars of Society*

THE PILLARS OF A NATION are those exceptional people who provide its spiritual and moral anchor and bestow its vision and purpose. These are not ordinarily its politicians or rulers. Rather, they are the righteous people, saints, and teachers; ordinary people of courage, principle, and conscience; and people who realize the truth within themselves and are willing to take responsibility for their community. Rarely are they recognized and honored in their lifetime; sometimes they are tolerated as goads and troublemakers and only appreciated after their death; most often they are unsung, anonymous people who, because they are sincere and conscientious, suffer in a world of vanities. These are people who have a deep realization of truth and are called to serve as society's internal leaders. Their example and message has a transforming effect on those who are fortunate to know them. It is often of far greater value than the policies and speeches of the governing authorities.

There are [always] thirty righteous men among the nations, by whose virtue the nations of the world continue to exist.

*Judaism*. Talmud, Hullin 92a

The earth is upheld by the veracity of those who have subdued their passions, and, following righteous practices, are never contaminated by desire, covetousness, and wrath.

*Hinduism*. Vishnu Purana 3.12

Yet I will leave seven thousand in Israel, all the knees that have not bowed to Baal, and every mouth that has not kissed him.

*Judaism* and *Christianity*. 1 Kings 19.18

When the righteous man is in the town, he is its luster, its majesty, and its glory. When he leaves it, its luster, its majesty, and its glory depart.

*Judaism*. Midrash, Genesis Rabbah 68.6

The perfume of flowers blows not against the wind, nor does the fragrance of sandalwood, tagara, and jasmine, but the fragrance of the virtuous blows against the wind; the virtuous man pervades every direction.

*Buddhism*. Dhammapada 54

**Hullin 92a:** God destroyed Sodom and Gomorrah for want of ten righteous men; see Genesis 18.20-33, p. 561. Cf. Berakot 17b, p. 154; Abot 1.2, p. 197; Tanhuma ed. Buber 25a, p. 503.

**1 Kings 19.18:** In God's message to the prophet Elijah on Mount Sinai, we have mention of a righteous remnant that will be spared when God judges Israel. The concept of the remnant is found throughout the prophets: see Isaiah 6.13; 7.3-4; 10.20-23; Amos 5.15.

**Genesis Rabbah 68.6:** Cf. Analects 4.1, p. 221.

Hard to find is a man of great wisdom: such a man is not born everywhere. Where such a wise man is born, that family thrives happily.

*Buddhism*. Dhammapada 193

Surely Allah will raise for this community at the beginning of every century one who shall revive for it its faith.

*Islam*. Hadith of Abu Dawud

The myriad objects owe their existence to the mutual stimulation subsisting between Heaven and earth. Similarly, the holy sage stimulates men's hearts and the whole world is thenceforth at peace.

*Confucianism*. I Ching 31: Attraction

Take responsibility for the most difficult problem in your nation. Take responsibility for the most difficult problem of your church. Take responsibility for the most difficult problem of the world.

*Unification Church*.
Sun Myung Moon, 5-1-81

The bodhisattvas, guardians of the city of Dharma, uphold the true doctrine, and their great teachings resound like the lion's roar throughout the ten directions. Without having to be asked, they are the natural spiritual benefactors of all living beings.

*Buddhism*.
Holy Teaching of Vimalakirti 1

In the Book of Songs it is said,

> He makes no show of his moral worth,
> Yet all the princes follow in his steps.

Hence the moral man, by living a life of simple truth and earnestness, alone can help to bring peace and order in the world.

*Confucianism*.
Doctrine of the Mean 33

My saints are under my protection, and only I know them.

*Islam*. Hadith

The saying goes, "The fish should not be taken from the deep pool; the sharp weapons of the state should not be shown to men." The sage is the sharp weapon of the world, and therefore he should not be where the world can see him.

*Taoism*. Chuang Tzu 10

Confucius remarked, "Among the means for the regeneration of mankind, those made with noise and show are of the least importance."

*Confucianism*. Doctrine of the Mean 33

He will not cry or lift up his voice,
or make it heard in the street;
a bruised reed he will not break,
and a dimly burning wick he will not quench;
he will faithfully bring forth justice.

*Judaism* and *Christianity*. Isaiah 42.2-3

A stranger, however vigilant,
Cannot perceive a locality as clearly as an indigene.
It is the attitude of the indigene to the affairs of his locality
Which determines that of the stranger to the same.
Malofin, the entire town is in your hand.
"Situations do not get spoiled when elders are around,"
This is the age-old wise saying.

*African Traditional Religions*.
Yoruba Song (Nigeria)

Rabbi Assi and Rabbi Ammi, on an educational inspection tour, came to a town and asked for its guardians. The councilmen appeared, but the rabbis said, "These are not guardians, but wreckers of a town! The guardians are the

**Holy Teaching of Vimalakirti 1:** Cf. Lion's Roar of Queen Srimala 4, p. 221.

**Doctrine of the Mean 33:** In Shinto, the emperor is most perfectly in accord with the kami and is set forth as an example for others; see Divine Injunctions, p. 158.

**Hadith:** This is a Sufi tradition; Sufi groups are often secret societies.

**Chuang Tzu 10:** Taoist sages typically live in seclusion; Cf. Tao Te Ching 20, p. 434.

**Isaiah 42.2-3:** This is part of the Servant Song given in full on pp. 367-68.

**Yoruba Song:** Malofin, a village elder, is encouraged to take responsibility for the affairs of his village and not allow them to fall into the hands of the 'stranger,' government officials appointed from the capitol.

teachers of the young, and instructors of the old, as is written: 'Except the Lord keep the city, the watchman wakes but in vain' [Psalm 127.1]."

*Judaism.* Midrash, Lamentations Rabbah, Proem 2

They say, "Why is not this Qur'an sent down to some leading man in either of the two chief cities?"

Is it they who would portion out the Mercy of your Lord? It is We who portion out between them their livelihood in the life of this world: and We raise some of them above others in ranks, so that some may command work from others. But the Mercy of your Lord is better than the wealth which they amass.

*Islam.* Qur'an 43.31-32

## *The Prophet and Reformer*

AS LONG AS THERE IS A CONTRADICTION between the absolute standard of righteousness and the corrupt and evil ways of worldly society, there will be those righteous people who will rise up and call society and their rulers to account. These are the prophets and reformers who put their lives at risk to speak out for the welfare of the community. We do not refer to those specially chosen to bring the revelation of God into the world—those rare founders of religions are covered in another chapter—but to the much larger group of people who arise in every age to call society to practice truth and justice.[1] The prophetic mission in its broadest sense includes all those saints and righteous people who struggle to remind the rulers of their day of the eternal divine message which was first spoken long before. Often they must recast that message into terms with contemporary relevance. The company of those who call for justice includes the prophets of the Old Testament and the Qur'an, the Confucian and Hindu sages, and all those who have followed their examples. In this latter group are many reformers and leaders of moral vision whose righteousness is not recorded in scripture because they came long after the scriptures were written; we might include such people as Martin Luther, Mahatma Ghandi, Martin Luther King, Jr., Muhammad Iqbal, Nichiren, and Simon Kimbangu, to name a few. But a prophetic ministry is not limited to a few saints; in various ways, large and small, it is required of us all.

A second attribute of prophecy is the ability to predict the future. This gift is not used for private ends; it is first and foremost a powerful qualification of the prophet that when he speaks on the affairs of state his words carry authority. The prophet's predictions are accurate because of his or her intimate relationship with Ultimate Reality, in whose hand lies the destinies of nations. Prophecies of the future, selected from various religions, are the subject of the concluding passages of this section.

**Lamentations Rabbah, Proem 2:** Cf. Sutta Nipata 261, p. 564, and related passages on the value of education.

[1] Islam regards Muhammad as the last Prophet, but only in the former, special sense that after him there will be no new revelation.

Every nation has its messenger. Once their messenger comes, judgment will be passed upon them in all fairness and they will not be wronged. They will say, "When will this promise be, if you have been telling the truth?" Say, "I possess no harm nor any advantage by myself, except concerning whatever God may wish. Every nation has a term; whenever their term comes, they will not postpone it for an hour nor advance it."

*Islam*. Qur'an 10.47-49

The word of the Lord came to me, "Son of man, I have made you a watchman for the house of Israel; whenever you hear a word from my mouth, you shall give them warning from me. If I say to the wicked, 'You shall surely die,' and you give him no warning, nor speak to warn the wicked from his wicked way, in order to save his life, that wicked man shall die in his iniquity; but his blood I will require at your hand. But if you warn the wicked, and he does not turn from his wickedness or from his wicked way, he shall die in his iniquity; but you will have saved your life. Again, if a righteous man turns from his righteousness and commits iniquity, and I lay a stumbling block before him, he shall die; because you have not warned him, he shall die for his sin, and his righteous deeds which he has done shall not be remembered; but his blood I will require at your hand. Nevertheless if you warn the righteous man not to sin, and he does not sin, he shall surely live, because he took warning; and you will have saved your life."

*Judaism* and *Christianity*. Ezekiel 3.16-21

Now the word of the Lord came to [Jeremiah], saying,

Before I formed you in the womb I knew you,
and before you were born I consecrated you;
I appointed you a prophet to the nations.

Then I said, "Ah, Lord God! Behold, I do not know how to speak, for I am only a youth." But the Lord said to me,

Do not say, I am only a youth;
for to all to whom I send you you shall go,
and whatever I command you you shall speak.
Be not afraid of them,
for I am with you to deliver you, says the Lord.

Then the Lord put forth his hand and touched my mouth; and the Lord said to me,

Behold, I have put my words in your mouth.
See, I have set you this day over nations and over kingdoms,
to pluck up and to break down,
to destroy and to overthrow,
to build and to plant.

*Judaism* and *Christianity*. Jeremiah 1.4-10

Do Thou give, O Right,
That bliss, that gift of Good Mind;
Do Thou give, O Devotion,
Power to Vishtaspa and my disciples;
Do Thou give, O Wise Ruler,
Whereby Thy Prophet may command a hearing!

*Zoroastrianism*. Avesta, Yasna 28.7

**Qur'an 10.47-49:** Cf. Qur'an 40.78, p. 36.

**Ezekiel 3.16-21:** Thus God holds his prophet responsible to the people for giving timely warning, just as a watchman is responsible to warn of an approaching army.

**Yasna 28.7:** Vishtaspa became Zarathustra's patron, the long-sought ruler whom he convinced to put his doctrine into practice. See Yasna 46.1-3, p. 432.

Our hope is that the world's religious leaders and the rulers thereof will unitedly arise for the reformation of this age and the rehabilitation of its fortunes. Let them, after meditating on its needs, take counsel together and, through anxious and full deliberation, administer to a diseased and sorely afflicted world the remedy it requires.

*Baha'i Faith.* Gleanings from the Writings of Baha'u'llah 110

My mission, today, is the same as it was at the time of the Prophet. I shall strive till I eradicate impiety and injustice, and till I establish a rule of justice and truth, a humane and heavenly regime.

By God! Have the Quraysh given up realizing who or what I am? I have fought against them and defeated them when they were infidels, and now I will fight against them to remove their tyrannous, unjust, and impious rule. Today I am as much their well-wisher as I was during the lifetime of the Holy Prophet, and my courage and determination have not diminished.

*Islam.* Nahjul Balagha, Sermon 38

The most excellent jihad is the uttering of truth in the presence of an unjust ruler.

*Islam.* Hadith of Tirmidhi

Confucius said, "How can he be said truly to love, who exacts no effort from the objects of his love? How can he be said to be truly loyal, who refrains from admonishing the object of his loyalty?"

*Confucianism.* Analects 14.8

"Do not preach"—thus they preach—
"one should not preach of such things;
disgrace will not overtake us."
Should this be said, O house of Jacob?
Is the Spirit of the Lord impatient?
Are these his doings?
Do not my words do good
to him who walks uprightly?
But you rise against my people as an enemy;
you strip the robe from the peaceful,
from those who pass by trustingly with no thought of war....
If a man should go about and utter wind and lies,
saying, "I will preach to you of wine and strong drink,"
he would be the preacher for this people!

*Judaism* and *Christianity.* Micah 2.6-11

A king who does what is not righteous
And not suitable is mostly praised
By his subjects, for it is hard to know
What he will or will not tolerate;
Therefore it is hard to know
What is useful or not to say.

If useful but unpleasant words
Are hard to speak to someone else,
What could I, a monk, say to a king
Who is a lord of the great earth?

But because of my affection for you
And through my compassion for all beings,
I tell you without hesitation
That which is useful but unpleasant....

O steadfast one, if true words
Are spoken without anger,
One should take them as fit to be
Heard, like water fit for bathing.

**Gleanings from the Writings of Baha'u'llah 110:** This passage enunciates Baha'u'llah's prophetic ministry to the nations.

**Nahjul Balagha, Sermon 38:** 'Ali is speaking of his own mission as a Caliph, carrying forward the mission of the Prophet Muhammad.

**Hadith of Tirmidhi:** Cf. Forty Hadith of an-Nawawi 34, p. 741.

**Analects 14.8:** A minister should not hesitate to send admonitions to his superiors in government, sincerely setting forth his advice. For example, see Book of Songs, Ode 254, pp. 769-70. Cf. Chuang Tzu 33, p. 725; Book of History 4.8.1-3, pp. 748-49.

**Micah 2.6-11:** Cf. Jeremiah 19.14-20.16, pp. 633-34.

Realize that I am telling you
What is useful here and later.
Act on it so as to help
Yourself and also others.

*Buddhism.* Nagarjuna,
Precious Garland 301-6

King Hui of Liang said, "I am ready to listen to what you have to say."

"Is there any difference," said Mencius, "between killing a man with a staff and killing him with a knife?"

"There is no difference."

"Is there any difference between killing him with a knife and killing him with misrule?"

"There is no difference."

"There is fat meat in your kitchen and there are well-fed horses in your stables, yet the people look hungry and in the outskirts of cities men drop dead from starvation. This is to show animals the way to devour men. Even the devouring of animals by animals is repugnant to men. If, then, one who is father and mother to the people cannot, in ruling over them, avoid showing animals the way to devour men, wherein is he father and mother to the people?"

*Confucianism.* Mencius I.A.4

After all the kings had been seated and perfect silence had ensued, Krishna, possessing fine teeth and having a voice as deep as that of a drum, began to speak: "In order that, O Bharata, peace may be established between the Kurus and the Pandavas without a slaughter of the heroes, I have come hither. Besides this, O king, I have no other beneficial words to utter.... Know that those wicked sons of yours, headed by Duryodhana, abandoning both virtue and profit, disregarding morality, and deprived of their senses by avarice, are now acting most unrighteously toward their foremost kinsmen. The terrible danger [of universal slaughter thus] has its origin in the conduct of the Kurus. If you become indifferent to it, it will then produce a universal slaughter. If, O Bharata, you are willing, you may be able to allay that danger even yet, for peace, I think, is not difficult of acquisition. The establishment of peace, O king, depends on you and myself. Set right your sons, and I will set the Pandavas right."

*Hinduism.* Mahabharata,
Udyoga Parva 95

Then Amaziah the priest of Bethel sent to Jeroboam king of Israel, saying, "Amos has conspired against you in the midst of the house of Israel; the land is not able to bear all his words. For thus Amos has said,

> Jeroboam shall die by the sword,
> and Israel must go into exile away from his
> land."

And Amaziah said to Amos, "O seer, go flee away to the land of Judah, and eat bread there, and prophesy there; but never again prophesy at Bethel, for it is the king's sanctuary, and it is a temple of the kingdom." Then Amos answered Amaziah, "I am no prophet, nor one of the sons of the prophets; but I am a herdsman, and a dresser of sycamore trees, and the Lord took me from following the flock, and the Lord said to me, 'Go, prophesy to my people Israel.' Now therefore hear the word of the Lord.

> You say, 'Do not prophesy against Israel,
> and do not preach against the house of
> Isaac.'
> Therefore thus says the Lord:

**Mencius I.A.4:** On the ruler as father and mother to the people, see Book of History 5.1.1, p. 753. On other Confucian and Taoist prophetic critiques of courtly extravagance while the poor suffer, see Mencius II.B.4, below; IV.A.3, pp. 767; Book of Songs, Ode 254, pp. 769-70; Tao Te Ching 12, p. 662; 53, p. 755; Chuang Tzu 25, p. 755.

**Mahabharata, Udyoga Parva 95:** Here Krishna takes the part of an honest advisor and mediator in a fruitless effort to prevent war.

'Your wife shall be a harlot in the city,
and your sons and daughters shall fall by the sword,
and your land shall be parceled out by line;
you yourself shall die in an unclean land,
and Israel shall surely go into exile away from its land.'"

*Judaism* and *Christianity*. Amos 7.10-17

Has not the history of those before you reached you: the folk of Noah, and 'Ad and Thamud, and those after them? None save God knows them. Their messengers came to them with clear proofs, but they thrust their hands into their mouths, and said, "Lo! we disbelieve in that with which you have been sent, and lo! we are in grave doubt concerning that to which you call us." Their messengers said, "Can there be doubt concerning God, the Creator of the heavens and the earth? He calls you that He may forgive you your sins and reprieve you until an appointed term." They said, "You are but mortals like us, who would fain turn us away from what our fathers used to worship. Then bring us some clear warrant." Their messengers said to them, "We are but mortals like you, but God gives grace to whom He will of His slaves. It is not ours to bring you a warrant unless by the permission of God. In God let believers put their trust! How should we not put our trust in God when He has shown us His ways? We surely will endure that hurt you do to us. In God let the trusting put their trust!" And those who disbelieved said to their messengers, "Verily we will drive you out from our land, unless you return to our religion." Then their Lord inspired them, "Verily We shall destroy the wrongdoers, and verily We shall make you to dwell in the land after them. This is for him who fears My Majesty and fears My threats." And they sought help from their Lord, and every froward potentate was brought to naught.

*Islam*. Qur'an 14.9-15

Mencius went to P'ing Lu. "Would you or would you not," said he to the governor, "dismiss a lancer who has failed three times in one day to report for duty?"

"I would not wait for the third time."

"But you yourself have failed to report for duty many times. In years of famine close to a thousand of your people suffered, the old and the young being abandoned in the gutter, the able-bodied scattered in all directions."

"It was not within my power to do anything about this."

"Supposing a man were entrusted with the care of cattle and sheep. Surely he ought to seek pasturage and fodder for the animals. If he found that this could not be done, should he return his charge to the owner or should he stand by and watch the animals die?"

"In this I am at fault."

*Confucianism*. Mencius II.B.4

In the spring of the year, the time when kings go forth to battle, David sent Joab, and his servants with him, and all Israel; and they ravaged the Ammonites, and besieged Rabbah. But David remained at Jerusalem.

It happened, late one afternoon, when David arose from his couch and was walking upon the roof of the king's house, that he saw from the roof a woman bathing; and the woman was very beautiful. And David sent and inquired about the woman. And one said, "Is this not Bathsheba, the daughter of Eliam, the wife of Uriah the Hittite?" So David sent messengers, and took her, and she came to him, and he lay with her.... And the woman con-

**Amos 7.10-17:** Israel had its professional prophets who divined for money; Amos denied that he was one of those. He is accused of treason for proclaiming the coming destruction of the dynasty of Jeroboam. Compare Jeremiah 19.14-20.12, pp. 633-34.

**Qur'an 14.9-15:** The Islamic conception of a prophet is one who always preaches faith in the One God as the primary message. But this does not neglect the issues of justice and righteousness, for they are implicit in God's message. Hence those who reject God are inevitably oppressive evildoers. Furthermore, since the prophet places his life in God's hands, he is always vindicated in the end.

**Mencius II.B.4:** See note to Mencius I.A.4, above.

ceived; and she sent and told David, "I am with child."

So David sent word to Joab, "Send me Uriah the Hittite." And Joab sent Uriah to David. When Uriah came to him, David asked how Joab was doing, and how the people fared, and how the war prospered. Then David said to Uriah, "Go down to your house, and wash your feet." And Uriah went out of the king's house, and there followed him a present from the king. But Uriah slept at the door of the king's house with all the servants of his lord, and did not go down to his house. When they told David, "Uriah did not go down to his house," David said to Uriah, "Have you not come from a journey? Why did you not go down to your house?" Uriah said to David, "The ark and Israel and Judah dwell in booths; and my lord Joab and the servants of my lord are camping in the open field; shall I then go to my house, to eat and to drink, and to lie with my wife? As you live, and as my soul lives, I will not do this thing."...

In the morning David wrote a letter to Joab, and sent it by the hand of Uriah. In the letter he wrote, "Set Uriah in the forefront of the hardest fighting, and then draw back from him, that he may be struck down, and die." And as Joab was besieging the city, he assigned Uriah to the place where he knew there were valiant men. And the men of the city came out and fought with Joab; and some of the servants of David among the people fell. Uriah the Hittite was slain also....

When the wife of Uriah heard that Uriah her husband was dead, she made lamentation for her husband. And when the mourning was over, David sent and brought her to his house, and she became his wife, and bore him a son. But the thing that David had done displeased the Lord.

And the Lord sent Nathan to David. He came to him, and said to him, "There were two men in a certain city, the one rich and the other poor. The rich man had very many flocks and herds; but the poor man had nothing but one little ewe lamb, which he had bought. And he brought it up, and it grew up with him and with his children; it used to eat of his morsel, and drink from his cup, and lie in his bosom, and it was like a daughter to him. Now there came a traveler to the rich man, and he was unwilling to take one of his own flock or herd to prepare for the wayfarer who had come to him, but he took the poor man's lamb, and prepared it for the man who had come to him." Then David's anger was greatly kindled against the man; and he said to Nathan, "As the Lord lives, the man who has done this deserves to die; and he shall restore the lamb fourfold, because he did this thing, and because he had no pity."

Nathan said to David, "You are the man. Thus says the Lord, the God of Israel, 'I anointed you king over Israel, and I delivered you out of the hand of Saul; and I gave you your master's wives into your bosom, and gave you the house of Israel and Judah; and if this were too little, I would add to you as much more. Why have you despised the word of the Lord, to do what is evil in his sight? You have smitten Uriah the Hittite with the sword, and have taken his wife to be your wife, and have slain him with the sword of the Ammonites. Now therefore the sword shall never depart from your house, because you have despised me, and have taken the wife of Uriah the Hittite to be your wife.'"

*Judaism* and *Christianity*.
2 Samuel 11.1-12.10

O Lord, your power is greater than all powers.
Under your leadership we cannot fear anything.
It is you who has given us prophetic power,
And has enabled us to foresee and interpret everything.

*African Traditional Religion*.
Dinka Prayer (Sudan)

**2 Samuel 11.1-12.10:** David first tried to conceal his adultery by urging Uriah to sleep with his wife so that there would be no suspicion about who was the child's father. When that failed, he had Uriah killed. Thereupon follows the prophet Nathan's famous oracle. For other biblical prophetic critiques of courtly extravagance at the expense of the poor, see Jeremiah 7.1-15, pp. 768-69; 22.13-16, p. 755; Ezekiel 34.2-10, p. 753; Isaiah 10.1-4, p. 768; Amos 1.3-2.16, pp. 771-72; 8.4-8, p. 345.

And the Lord answered me,
"Write the vision;
make it plain upon tablets,
so that he may run who reads it.
For still the vision awaits its time;
it hastens to the end—it will not lie.
If it seem slow, wait for it;
it will surely come, it will not delay."

*Judaism* and *Christianity*.
Habakkuk 2.2-3

It is an attribute of the possession of the absolute true self to be able to foreknow. When a nation or family is about to flourish, there are sure to be lucky omens. When a nation or family is about to perish, there are sure to be signs and prodigies. These things manifest themselves in the instruments of divination and in the agitation of the human body. When happiness or calamity is about to come, it can be known beforehand. When it is good, it can be known beforehand. When it is evil, it can be known beforehand. Therefore he who has realized his true self is like a celestial spirit.

*Confucianism*.
Doctrine of the Mean 24

Do two walk together,
unless they have made an appointment?
Does a lion roar in the forest,
when he has no prey?
Does a young lion cry out from his den,
if he has taken nothing?
Does a bird fall in a snare on the earth,
when there is no trap for it?
Does a snare spring up from the ground,
when it has taken nothing?
Is a trumpet blown in a city,
and the people are not afraid?
Does evil befall a city,
unless the Lord has done it?
Surely the Lord God does nothing,
without revealing his secret to his servants the prophets.
The lion has roared,
who will not fear?
The Lord God has spoken;
who can but prophesy?

*Judaism* and *Christianity*. Amos 3.3-8

And there the sons of Dhritarashtra enter you,
all of them, together with a host of kings,
Bhishma, Drona, and also the charioteer's son, Karna—
and our own commanders,
even they are with them!

They rush into your awful mouths
with those terrible tusks.
Some can be seen stuck between your teeth,
their heads crushed.

As the many river torrents
rush toward one sea,
those worldly heroes
enter your flaming mouths....

I bow before you, supreme God; be gracious.
You, who are so awesome to see,
tell me, who are you?
I want to know you, the very first Lord,
for I do not understand what you are doing.

I am Time who destroys man's world.
I am the time that is now ripe
to gather in the people here;
that is what I am doing. Even without you,
all these warriors drawn up for battle
in opposing ranks
will cease to exist.

Therefore rise up! Win glory!
When you conquer your enemies,
your kingship will be fulfilled.

**Habakkuk 2.2-3:** Cf. Isaiah 46.9-11, p. 69.
**Doctrine of the Mean 24:** Cf. I Ching, Great Commentary 1.10.1-2, p. 568.

Enjoy it. Be just an instrument,
you who can draw the bow with the left as well
as the right hand!
I myself have slain your enemies long ago.

Do not waver. Conquer the enemies
whom I have already slain—Drona and
Bhishma and Jayadratha,
and Karna also, and the other heroes at arms.
Fight! You are about to defeat your rivals in
war.

*Hinduism*. Bhagavad Gita 11.26-34

Nanak, sitting in this city of corpses, sings the
Lord's praise
And enunciates this principle:
He who raised this creation and in manifold
pleasures engaged it,
Sits apart, watching it.
Holy is the Lord, holy His justice;
True shall be the judgment pronounced by
Him.
As will its body's vesture be torn to shreds,
India shall remember my word.
In 1578 they come; in 1597 they depart—
Another hero shall someday arise.
Nanak utters the word of truth—
Truth he utters; truth the hour calls for.

*Sikhism*. Adi Granth, Telang, M.1, p. 722f.

But you, O Bethlehem Ephrathah,
who are little to be among the clans of Judah,
from you shall come forth for me
one who is to be ruler in Israel,
whose origin is from of old,
from ancient days.

*Christianity*. Micah 5.2

And remember Jesus, the son of Mary, said, "O Children of Israel! I am the apostle of God to you, confirming the Law which came before me, and giving glad tidings of an apostle to come after me whose name shall be Ahmad." But when he came to them with clear signs, they said, "This is evident sorcery."

*Islam*. Qur'an 61.6

❖

**Bhagavad Gita 11.26-34:** Krishna gives Arjuna a vision of the future: His enemies are already defeated and slain. The belief that in giving a prophetic word, God has already acted is characteristic of prophecy in the Bible and the Qur'an (see Qur'an 94, p. 442). For the first part of the theophany, on Krishna's transcendence, see Bhagavad Gita 11.1-25, pp. 66-68.

**Telang, M.1:** Here Guru Nanak is prophesying that the Mughal invaders, who, led by Babur, descended on India in Vikrami year 1578, will leave in 1597. In that year the Mughals were, in fact, routed by Sher Shah. (The Vikrami chronology is one of the classical calendrical systems of India; its reference point is 58 B.C.).

**Micah 5.2:** According to the New Testament (Matthew 2.6), this is a prophecy of the birth of Jesus Christ. There are many similar prophecies in the Old Testament; cf. Deuteronomy 18.15, p. 473; Isaiah 9.6-7, p. 783; 42.1-4, pp. 367-68; 52.13-53.12, pp. 457-58; Daniel 7.13-14, p. 783.

**Qur'an 61.6:** This is a prophecy by Jesus about the coming of Muhammad. *Ahmad* is probably a translation of the Greek word *Parakletos*, Counselor, from John 14.16, p. 462. Since Ahmad and Muhammad are cognates, this is taken to be a prophecy of the future advent of Muhammad by name. For an example of prophecy in the Qur'an about the later career of Muhammad, see Qur'an 94, p. 442.

# *War Against Evil*

WHEN SOVEREIGNTY BELONGS to ruthless tyrants, when neither the force of example nor words of instruction are heeded, those who would maintain a righteous stand may have to fight. The battle against evil is waged sometimes as a spiritual struggle and sometimes as a physical war. Islam recommends the *Jihad,* or Holy War, to suppress evil and advance the cause of God. Roman Catholic tradition speaks of a Just War, which may be undertaken only as a last resort, when all the milder forms of persuasion and struggle have been exhausted. Buddhist and Hindu scriptures praise the struggle against enemies of the Dharma. On the other hand, many scriptures recognize that in a war against evil, the sacrifice of one's own blood, see *Persecution and Martyrdom,* pp. 627-36, is far more precious than shedding the blood of an enemy on the battlefield. Thus Christianity defeated the might of the Roman Empire by the blood of its martyrs. Regardless, the struggle against tyranny demands that we expose ourselves to suffering and torment. In this sense it is said to be superior to a sheltered life of seclusion and contemplation.

A righteous person does not go to war in search of glory or spoils. Neither does he fight from a spirit of vindictiveness, revenge, or to satisfy national honor. The only possible justification for such war is when confronted with manifest tyranny. Unfortunately, religious passions have often been exploited by those who would invoke the name of religion to promote wars for political or economic ends. Therefore, the decision to go to war, even when justified by such doctrines as Just War or Jihad, should be made with the greatest reluctance. It is always better to find peaceful means to reconcile disputes, and the religions of the world have the resources for such reconciliation in almost all cases, if people would only use them.

The foundation for the struggle against tyranny begins with the victory of the individual soul—what in Islam is called the Greater Jihad. The individual struggles to reach the point of absolute faith where he or she has completely vanquished the body and its selfish desires and can purely and absolutely will what is good. A number of well-known passages on the interior life use martial imagery to describe this inner struggle with the lower self. We include a few of them here because of the similarity of theme. However, a spiritualized understanding of warfare threatens to omit the essential social dimension of struggle.

It is a religious duty to fight for justice in the world, while continuing to fight the interior war. The soldier for right arms himself with the virtues of self-control, humility, and willingness to suffer. Through faith, the soldier for God recognizes that God is fighting on his side and is his *Help and Deliverance,* pp. 396-402. He can go forward with absolute firmness, though he knows he may very well be killed. Such warfare is a supreme act of self-sacrifice: to risk one's life for a noble cause.

The first passages in this section define the righteous fight against evil—whether a war with weapons or a peaceful struggle against the spiritual forces of the devil. We learn that death is of no account in the battle for right; the soldier should fight expecting to die and looking forward to his reward in the next life. The next several passages qualify and caution against readiness to fight a physical war; if a good objective can be gained by peaceful means, that is preferred. Bloodshed in war is an evil to be avoided if possible, for all life is sacred. A number of passages use martial imagery to describe the interior warfare against evil spiritual forces and the power of sin within onself. The last passages give historical examples of battles between good and evil.

And if God had not repelled some men by others, the earth would have been corrupted.

*Islam*. Qur'an 2.251

He is the true hero who fights to protect the helpless;
Though cut limb from limb, flees not the field.

*Sikhism*. Adi Granth, Shalok, Kabir, p. 1412

Do not think that I have come to bring peace on earth: I have not come to bring peace, but a sword.

*Christianity*. Matthew 10.34

To come to the relief of the distressed and to help the oppressed, act as amends and expiation of many sins.

*Islam*. Nahjul Balagha, Saying 22

Then the Lord said to Moses, "Go in to Pharaoh and say to him, 'Thus says the Lord, Let my people go, that they may serve me.'"

*Judaism* and *Christianity*. Exodus 8.1

Share in suffering as a good soldier of Christ Jesus. No soldier on service gets entangled in civilian pursuits, since his aim is to satisfy the one who enlisted him.

*Christianity*. 2 Timothy 2.3-4

Whoever of you sees something of which God disapproves, then let him change it with his hand; and if he is not able to do so, then with his tongue; and if he is not able to do so, then with his heart; and that is faith of the weakest kind.

*Islam*. Forty Hadith of an-Nawawi 34

Those are the future saviors of the peoples
Who through Good Mind strive in their deeds
To carry out the judgment which thou hast decreed, O Wise One, as righteousness.
For they were created the foes of Fury.

*Zoroastrianism*. Avesta, Yasna 48.12

The goddess of the sea says goodbye,
She-who-carries-loads-and-never-looks-back.
Since this is how we find the world,
We must fight.
The world has no peace;
This is war.
We must fight to the last man
So that the world may have peace.

*African Traditional Religions*. Yoruba War Song (Nigeria)

King Hsüan of Ch'i asked, "Is it true that T'ang banished Chieh, and King Wu marched against Chou?"

"According to the histories," Mencius replied, "they are true."

"Well," said the king, "then it's alright for a minister to assassinate his ruler?"

"When a man practices violence against the natural human affections, we call him a bandit. When a man practices violence against the common good, we call him a criminal. When a man [in power] practices crime and banditry, we call him a tyrant. I heard that a tyrant named Chou was executed. I didn't hear anything about a ruler being assassinated."

*Confucianism*. Mencius I.B.8

In *Ko*, Revolution, water and fire extinguish each other, behaving as two women who live together but whose wills conflict—such is the nature of revolution. That "faith is not reposed

**Matthew 10.34:** The sword is usually interpreted spiritually as the sword of truth or the sword of divine judgment. Jesus tells his disciples to put away their swords in Matthew 26.51-52, p. 709.

**Nahjul Balagha, Saying 22:** Cf. Hadith of Muslim, p. 627.

**Exodus 8.1:** The slavery and oppression which the Israelites suffered in Egypt was suffering of such magnitude that it called for nothing less than a rebellion, led by Moses, to free the slaves. The Judeo-Christian tradition has always regarded enslavement as intolerable and a proper justification for revolution.

**Forty Hadith of an-Nawawi 34:** Cf. Hadith of Tirmidhi, p. 734; Hadith of Ibn Majah, p. 691.

**Mencius I.B.8:** Mencius' unwillingness to call Chieh and Chou 'rulers' is based upon the Confucian doctrine of Rectification of Names. A person only has the right to be called "king" if his behavior is proper for that office and he fulfills the duties of kingship. See Analects 12.11, p. 507; Mencius I.A.4, p. 735.

in it until the day of its completion" means that revolution must come first, whereafter public faith in it will be established. A civilized and enlightened attitude brings joy; great success makes it possible to put all things to rights. Upon the achievement of a necessary revolution, regret vanishes. The renovating activities of the celestial and terrestrial forces produce the progress of the four seasons. T'ang and Wu rebelled in accordance with Heaven's decree and the people responded to them.

*Confucianism.* I Ching 49: Revolution

For a warrior, nothing is higher than a war against evil. The warrior confronted with such a war should be pleased, Arjuna, for it comes as an open gate to heaven. But if you do not participate in this battle against evil, you will incur sin, violating your dharma and your honor....

Death means the attainment of heaven; victory means the enjoyment of the earth. Therefore rise up, Arjuna, resolved to fight! Having made yourself alike in pain and pleasure, profit and loss, victory and defeat, engage in this great battle and you will be freed from sin.

*Hinduism.* Bhagavad Gita 2.31-38

Good Men! In order to uphold the true dharma, you must arm yourselves with swords and bows and arrows even if you cannot observe the Five Commandments and maintain your dignity. No matter how hard a man preaches, unless he aggressively defeats the evil opponents of Buddhism, he would not be able to save himself and others. You should know that such a person is an idle man. Even if he observes commandments and practices pure conduct, you should know, he will not attain Buddhahood. Should a monk upholding the true dharma aggressively defeat violators of the Buddhist commandments, probably they all would become angry and try to harm him. Even if he were killed, he is worth being called an observer of the commandments and a savior of himself and others.

*Buddhism.* Mahaparinirvana Sutra

On the warpath it is good to die. If you die in war your soul will not become unconscious but pass directly into the next life. You will then be able to decide for yourself the destination of your soul. Your soul will always remain in a happy condition. If you choose to go back to earth as a human being and live again you can do so; you can live a second life on earth or live in the form of those who walk on the light, or in the form of an animal, as you choose. All these benefits will you obtain if you die in battle.

*Native American Religions.* A Winnebago Father's Precepts

Let those fight in the way of God who sell the life of this world for the next. Whoso fights in the way of God, be he slain or be he victorious, on him We shall bestow a vast reward.

How should you not fight for the cause of God, and of the feeble among men and women and children who are crying, "Our Lord! Bring us forth from out of this town whose people are oppressors! Oh, give us from Thy presence some protecting friend! Oh, give us from Thy presence some defender!"

**Bhagavad Gita 2.31-38:** Vv. 31-33, 37-38. Mahatma Gandhi drew upon the Bhagavad Gita as inspiration for his non-violent struggle for Indian independence. While many traditional interpreters regarded the war of the Kurus as symbolic of the war within the individual soul—see Bhagavad Gita 6.5-6, p. 278—Gandhi recognized in these verses a call to a spiritual struggle to build a just society. The spiritual weapon is *satyagraha*, the struggle for truth. According to the Bhagavad Gita 3.10-26, pp. 689-90, it is waged by selfless action in the service of others. Satyagraha is the power of the soul purified by selflessness, willing to endure suffering, and always giving love to the enemy. It is the active application of Jesus' principle to turn the other cheek (Matthew 5.38-41, p. 709), mobilized as a weapon in the struggle for freedom, peace, and justice.

**Mahaparinirvana Sutra:** This passage was quoted by Nichiren, who was so aggressive in his propagation of the Lotus Sutra that many Buddhists of the other schools were incited against him, and some even plotted against his life.

Those who believe do battle for the cause of God; and those who disbelieve do battle for the cause of idols. So fight the minions of the devil. Lo! The devil's strategy is ever weak.

*Islam*. Qur'an 4.74-76

Breaker of hurdles, Finder of light, Thunder-armed,
he triumphs in battle, crushing the foe with his might.
Follow him, brothers! Quit yourselves like heroes!
Emulate Indra in prowess, my comrades!

Ours be Indra when our banners are gathered!
May the arrows that are ours be victorious,
and our heroes rise superior to all!
Protect us, ye gods! in the battle.
Go forward, warriors! and conquer.
May Indra give you protection!
Valiant be your arms, so that
you become invincible.

*Hinduism*. Rig Veda 10.103

How do you pray that sinners die? Rather pray that they should repent, and thus there will be no more wickedness.

*Judaism*. Talmud, Berakot 10a

The force of arms cannot do what peace does. If you can gain your desired end with sugar, why use poison?

*Jainism*. Somadeva, Nitivakyamrita 344

Though we live in the world we are not carrying on a worldly war, for the weapons of our warfare are not worldly but have divine power to destroy strongholds. We destroy arguments and every proud obstacle to the knowledge of God, and take every thought captive to obey Christ.

*Christianity*. 2 Corinthians 10.3-5

In wars to gain land, the dead fill the plains; in wars to gain cities, the dead fill the cities. This is known as showing the land the way to devour human flesh. Death is too light a punishment for such men who wage war. Hence those skilled in war should suffer the most severe punishments.

*Confucianism*. Mencius IV.A.14

Fine weapons are instruments of evil.
They are hated by men.
Therefore those who possess Tao turn away from them....
Weapons are instruments of evil, not the instruments of a good ruler.
When he uses them unavoidably, he regards calm restraint as the best principle.
Even when he is victorious, he does not regard it as praiseworthy,
For to praise victory is to delight in the slaughter of men.
He who delights in the slaughter of men will not succeed in the empire....
For the slaughter of the multitude, let us weep with sorrow and grief.
For a victory, let us observe the occasion with funeral ceremonies.

*Taoism*. Tao Te Ching 31

Whoever, our hostile kin or an outsider, wants to destroy us,
may all the gods discomfit him!
Prayer is my inner coat of mail.

*Hinduism*. Rig Veda 6.75.19

Humility is my mace;
To become the dust under everyone's feet is my dagger.
These weapons no evildoer dare withstand.

*Sikhism*. Adi Granth, Sorath, M.5, p. 628

**Rig Veda 10.103:** Vv. 6, 11, 13. Cf. Bhagavad Gita 11.26-34, pp. 738-39.

**Berakot 10a:** Cf. Jonah 3.3-10, p. 643.

**Mencius IV.A.14:** See Analects 12.19, p. 709; Matthew 26.51-52, p. 340; Dhammapada 201, p. 340; Forty Hadith of an-Nawawi 32, p. 708; and similar passages.

The Prophet declared, "We have returned from the lesser holy war (*al jihad al-asghar*) to the greater holy war (*al jihad al-akbar*)." They asked, "O Prophet of God, which is the greater war?" He replied, "Struggle against the lower self."

*Islam*. Hadith

They that are desirous of victory do not conquer by might and energy so much as by truth, compassion, righteousness, and spiritual discipline. Discriminating then between righteousness and unrighteousness, and understanding what is meant by covetousness, when there is recourse to exertion, fight without arrogance, for victory is there where righteousness is. Under these conditions know, O king, that to us victory is certain in this battle. Indeed, where Krishna is, there is victory.

*Hinduism*. Mahabharata, Bhishma Parva 21

Be strong in the Lord and in the strength of his might. Put on the whole armor of God, that you may be able to stand against the wiles of the devil. For we are not contending against flesh and blood, but against the principalities, against the powers, against the world rulers of this present darkness, against the spiritual hosts of wickedness in the heavenly places. Therefore take the whole armor of God, that you may be able to withstand in the evil day, and having done all, to stand. Stand therefore, having girded your loins with truth, and having put on the breastplate of righteousness, and having shod your feet with the equipment of the gospel of peace; besides all these, taking the shield of faith, with which you can quench all the flaming darts of the evil one. And take the helmet of salvation, and the sword of the Spirit, which is the word of God.

*Christianity*. Ephesians 6.10-17

Having seized the bow whose stick is fortitude and whose string is asceticism, having struck down also with the arrow, which consists of freedom from egotism, the first guardian of the door of Brahman—(for if a man looks at the world egotistically, then, taking the diadem of passion, the earrings of greed and envy, and the staff of sloth, sleep, and sin, and having seized the bow whose string is anger and whose stick is lust, he destroys with the arrow which consists of desires, all beings)—having thereby killed that guardian, he crosses by means of the boat Om to the other side of the ether within the heart, and when the ether becomes revealed as Brahman, he enters slowly, as a miner seeking minerals in a mine, into the Hall of Brahman. After that let him, by means of the doctrine of his teacher, break through the four nets before the shrine of Brahman, until at last he reaches the shrine, that of blessedness and identity with Brahman.

*Hinduism*. Maitri Upanishad 6.28

Invincible is the army of the Saints.
Great warriors are they; humility is their
 breastplate;
The songs of the Lord's glory are their weapons;
The word of the Guru is their buckler.
They ride the horses, chariots, and elephants
Of the understanding of the Divine Path.
Without fear, they advance towards the enemy.

**Hadith:** This is an important Sufi tradition. Muhammad is said to have uttered it at the end of his life, after defeating the pagans and marching victoriously into Mecca. The 'lesser jihad' being finished, the Muslims could reorient their struggle inwardly against the lower self.

**Mahabharata, Bhishma Parva 21:** Cf. Bhagavad Gita 11.26-34, pp. 738-39.

**Ephesians 6.10-17:** Cf. Large Sutra on Perfect Wisdom 431, p. 315. Here the scripture is describing spiritual warfare against the devil and spiritual evil of the heart; it does not refer to physical warfare against tyrants.

**Maitri Upanishad 6.28:** Again, martial imagery is used to describe the spiritual quest, followed by imagery of a traveller seeking buried treasure or a miner seeking gems to describe progress in meditation. The 'four nets' may correspond to the four meditations in the Buddhist Noble Eightfold Path, p. 113, and the four selves of Katha Upanishad 3.13, p. 601, and 2.3.7-8, p. 60. The phrase in parentheses, describing the equipment of the worldly person who, with such weapons as desire, lust, and hatred, destroys all beings, may be compared to James 4.1-3, p. 294; Asa-ki-Var, M.1, p. 323.

They ride into battle singing the Lord's praise.
By conquering those five robber chiefs, the
vices,
They find that they have also conquered the
whole world.

*Sikhism*. Adi Granth,
Shalok Sehskriti, M.5, p. 1356

O Prophet! Exhort the believers to fight. If there be of you twenty steadfast they shall overcome two hundred, and if there be a hundred steadfast they shall overcome a thousand of those who disbelieve, because they are a people without intelligence.

*Islam*. Qur'an 8.65

Jesus went up to Jerusalem. In the temple he found those who were selling oxen and sheep and pigeons, and the money-changers at their business. And making a whip of cords, he drove them all, with the sheep and oxen, out of the temple; and he poured out the coins of the money-changers and overturned their tables. And he told those who sold the pigeons, "Take these things away; you shall not make my Father's house a house of trade."

*Christianity*. John 2.13-16

The Lord said to Joshua, the son of Nun, Moses' minister, "Moses my servant is now dead; now therefore arise, go over this Jordan, you and all this people, into the land which I am giving to them, to the people of Israel.... No man shall be able to stand before you all the days of your life; as I was with Moses, so I will be with you; I will not fail you or forsake you. Be strong and of good courage; for you shall cause this people to inherit the land which I swore to their fathers to give them. Only be strong and very courageous, being careful to do according to all the law which Moses my servant commanded you; turn not from it to the right hand or to the left, that you may have good success wherever you go. This book of the law shall not depart out of your mouth, but you shall meditate on it day and night, that you may be careful to do all that is written in it; for then you shall make your way prosperous, and then you shall have good success. Have I not commanded you? Be strong and of good courage; be not frightened, neither be dismayed, for the Lord your God is with you wherever you go."

*Judaism* and *Christianity*. Joshua 1.1-9

The king said, "Come, you multitudes of the people, listen all to my words. It is not I, the Little Child, who dare to undertake a rebellious enterprise; Heaven has given the charge to destroy the sovereign of Hsia for his many crimes.

"Now, you multitudes, you are saying, 'Our prince does not compassionate us but is calling us away from our husbandry to attack and punish Hsia.' I have indeed heard these words of you all. But the sovereign of Hsia is guilty and, as I fear God, I dare not but punish him.

"Now you are saying, 'What are the crimes of Hsia to us?' The king of Hsia in every way exhausts the strength of his people and exercises oppression in the cities of Hsia. His people have all become idle and will not assist him. They are saying, 'When wilt thou, O sun, expire? We will all perish with thee.'

**Shalok Sehskriti, M.5:** The symbol of Sikhism contains a vertical sword, and Sikh men are required to wear a dagger. Yet these symbols are understood to represent the interior struggle against the 'five robbers' within: lust, wrath, avarice, attachment, and egoism; cf. Sorath, M.3, p. 278.

**Qur'an 8.65:** See p. 400n.

**John 2.13-16:** The cleansing of the temple was the only instance recorded in the gospels when Jesus lifted his hand against others. But in addition, this cleansing of the temple and the triumphal entry were two public demonstrations of Jesus' claim to lordship, which certainly offended the Jewish and Roman authorities and spurred them to have Jesus apprehended. Given the demonstrative nature of this act, many exegetes do not regard it as a sanction for the use of violence.

**Joshua 1.1-9:** Joshua led the Israelites into the Promised Land and made war on the Canaanites. The Bible depicts him as the ideal leader, victorious wherever he went, because his mind was always fixed on the Law of God.

"Such is the course of the sovereign of Hsia. And now I must go punish him. I pray you assist me, the One Man, to carry out the punishment appointed by Heaven."

*Confucianism*. Book of History 4.1: Speech by T'ang

And there came out of the camp of the Philistines a champion named Goliath, of Gath, whose height was six cubits and a span. He had a helmet of bronze on his head, and he was armed with a coat of mail, and the weight of the coat was five thousand shekels of bronze. And he had greaves of bronze upon his legs, and a javelin of bronze slung between his shoulders. And the shaft of his spear was like a weaver's beam, and his spear's head weighed six hundred shekels of iron; and his shield-bearer went before him. He stood and shouted to the ranks of Israel, "Why have you come out to draw up for battle? Am I not a Philistine, and are you not servants of Saul? Choose a man for yourselves, and let him come down to me. If he is able to fight with me and kill me, then we will be your servants; but if I prevail against him, then you shall be our servants and serve us." And the Philistine said, "I defy the ranks of Israel this day; give me a man, that we may fight together." When Saul and all Israel heard these words of the Philistine, they were dismayed and greatly afraid....

And David said to the men who stood by him, "What shall be done for the man who kills this Philistine, and takes away the reproach from Israel? For who is this uncircumcised Philistine, that he should defy the armies of the living God?"...

When the words which David spoke were heard, they repeated them before Saul; and he sent for him. And David said to Saul, "Let no man's heart fail because of him; your servant will go and fight with this Philistine." And Saul said to David, "You are not able to go against this Philistine to fight with him; for you are but a youth, and he has been a man of war from his youth." But David said to Saul, "Your servant used to keep sheep for his father; and when there came a lion, or a bear, and took a lamb from the flock, I went after him and smote him and delivered it out of his mouth; and if he arose against me, I caught him by his beard, and smote him and killed him. Your servant has killed both lions and bears; and this uncircumcised Philistine shall be like one of them, seeing he has defied the armies of the living God." And David said, "The Lord who delivered me from the paw of the lion and from the paw of the bear, will deliver me from the hand of this Philistine."

And Saul said to David, "Go, and the Lord be with you!" Then Saul clothed David with his armor; he put a helmet of bronze on his head, and clothed him with a coat of mail. And David girded his sword over his armor, and he tried in vain to go, for he was not used to them. Then David said to Saul, "I cannot go with these; for I am not used to them." And David put them off. Then he took his staff in his hand, and chose five smooth stones from the brook, and put them in his shepherd's bag or wallet; his sling was in his hand, and he drew near to the Philistine.

When the Philistine looked, and saw David, he disdained him; for he was but a youth, ruddy and comely in appearance. And the Philistine said to David, "Am I a dog, that you come to me with sticks?" And the Philistine cursed David by his gods. The Philistine said to David, "Come to me, and I will give your flesh to the birds of the air and to the beasts of the field." Then David said to the Philistine, "You come to me with a sword and with a spear and with a javelin; but I come to you in the name of the Lord of hosts, the God of the armies of Israel, whom you have defied. This day the Lord will deliver you into my hand, and I will strike you down, and cut off your head; and I will give the dead bodies of the host of the Philistines this day to the birds of the air and to the wild beasts of the earth; that all the earth may know that there is a God in Israel, and that all this assembly may know that the Lord saves not with sword and spear; for the battle is the Lord's and he will give you into our hand."

When the Philistine arose and came and drew near to meet David, David ran quickly toward the battle line to meet the Philistine.

And David put his hand in his bag and took out a stone, and slung it, and struck the Philistine on his forehead; the stone sank into his forehead, and he fell on his face to the ground.... Then David ran and stood over the Philistine, and took his sword and drew it out of its sheath, and killed him, and cut off his head with it.

*Judaism* and *Christianity*. 1 Samuel 17.4-51

## *Respect for Legitimate Government*

THE RESPONSIBILITIES OF THE CITIZEN begin with respect for legitimate government. In some of the passages on this topic, there is an implicit social contract: The people surrender part of their autonomy to the government, which in turn establishes law and order among an unruly and violent population. Other passages distinguish the claims of religion from the claims of government; each is sovereign in its own sphere, and hence we may "render unto Caesar the things that are Caesar's, and unto God the things that are God's." Thus religions teach that the good citizen should respect and cooperate with government, bearing with its policies with which he disagrees, and even enduring occasions when its weight is oppressive. Yet as we have already noted, there are limits to obedience when a government goes against the will of Heaven.

Lack of respect to the constituted authority is the source of most conflicts in the world.

*African Traditional Religions*. Yoruba Proverb (Nigeria)

Rabbi Hanina the deputy of the priests, said, "Pray for the peace of the government; for, except for the fear of that, we should have swallowed each other alive."

*Judaism*. Mishnah, Abot 3.2

Rabbi Simeon ben Lachish said, "'And behold, it was very good' [Genesis 1.4]: this is the kingdom of Heaven; this is also the kingdom of earth. Is then the earthly kingdom good? Yes, for it exacts justice of mankind. As it is said: 'I made the earth and created Rome [reading Edom in place of Adam] upon it' [Isaiah 45.12]."

*Judaism*. Midrash, Genesis Rabbah 9

**Abot 3.2:** This is not a mild platitude suitable for ordinary citizens, but a deliberate choice in the midst of a controversy over how to regard the Roman Empire, which severely oppressed the Jews under its control. Jews who chafed under Roman rule were calling for rebellion, which when it came was disastrous; the Jewish War (68-70 A.D.) ended with the destruction of the Temple, and later the Bar Kochba Rebellion (132-34 A.D.) would be brutally crushed. But the rabbis whose words were compiled in the Mishnah called for resignation to Roman rule.

**Genesis Rabbah 9:** The pun on Adam, 'man' in the verse from Isaiah, is possible because both words are formed from the same Hebrew letters: aleph, dalet, mem. This is in accordance with the interpretive principle that close study of the Hebrew letters can reveal hidden meanings of scripture. The sentiment is the same as in the previous passage.

Ibn 'Umar reported the Prophet as saying, "The sultan is God's shade on earth to which each one of His servants who is wronged repairs. When he is just he will have a reward, and it is the duty of the common people to be grateful; but when he acts tyrannically the burden rests on him, and it is the duty of the common people to show endurance."

*Islam.* Hadith of Baihaqi

Hearing and obeying [those in government] are the duty of a Muslim both regarding what he likes and what he dislikes, as long as he is not commanded to perform an act of disobedience to God, in which case he must neither hear nor obey.

*Islam.* Hadith of Bukhari and Muslim

Let every person be subject to the governing authorities. For there is no authority except from God, and those that exist have been instituted by God. Therefore he who resists the authorities resists what God has appointed, and those who resist will incur judgment. For rulers are not a terror to good conduct, but to bad. Would you have no fear of him who is in authority? Then do what is good, and you will receive his approval, for he is God's servant for your good. But if you do wrong, be afraid, for he does not bear the sword in vain; he is the servant of God to execute his wrath on the wrongdoer. Therefore one must be subject, not only to avoid God's wrath but also for the sake of conscience. For the same reason you also pay taxes, for the authorities are ministers of God, attending to this very thing. Pay all of them their dues, taxes to whom taxes are due, revenue to whom revenue is due, respect to whom respect is due, honor to whom honor is due.

*Christianity.* Romans 13.1-7

Then the people gathered together and lamented, saying, "Evil ways are rife among the people—theft, censure, false speech, and punishment have appeared among us. Let us choose one man from among us, to dispense wrath, censure, and banishment when they are right and proper, and give him a share of our rice in return." So they chose the most handsome, attractive, and capable among them and invited him to dispense anger, censure, and banishment. He consented and did so, and they gave him a share of their rice.

*Mahasammata* means elected (*sammata*) by the whole people (*mahajana*), and hence Mahasammata was the first name to be given to a ruler. He was lord of the fields (*khettanam*) and hence *Khattiya* was his second name. He pleases (*ranjeti*) others by his righteousness, and hence his third name, *Raja.* This was the origin of the nobility, according to the tale of long ago.

*Buddhism.* Digha Nikaya iii.92-93, Agganna Suttanta

And they sent some of the Pharisees and some of the Herodians, to entrap Jesus in his talk. And they came and said to him, "Teacher, we know that you are true, and care for no man; for you do not regard the position of men, but truly teach the way of God. Is it lawful to pay taxes to Caesar, or not? Should we pay them, or should we not?" But knowing their hypocrisy, he said to them, "Why put me to the test? Bring me a coin, and let me look at it." And they brought one. And he said to them, "Whose likeness and inscription is this?" They said to him, "Caesar's." Jesus said to them, "Render to Caesar the things that are Caesar's, and to God the things that are God's."

*Christianity.* Mark 12.13-17

King Wu Ting (c. 1323 B.C.) appointed Yueh prime minister. He gave Yueh his instructions: "Morning and evening, send in your reprimands, and so help me to patch up my personal virtue. Imagine that I am a steel weapon: I will use you for a whetstone. Imagine I have to

**Hadith of Baihaqi:** Cf. Mencius I.B.4, p. 754.

**Hadith of Bukhari and Muslim:** Cf. Hadith of Muslim, p. 750.

**Digha Nikaya iii.92-93:** This is a Buddhist version of the social contract. These etymologies of khattiya (Skt. kshatriya) and raja help signify the meaning of the office, even if they are not historically correct. 'Mahasammata' was the legendary first king of the solar dynasty and ancestor of many lines of kings.

cross a big river: I will use you for a boat and oars. Imagine I am a year of record drought: I will use you as a copious rain...

"You, yes you, teach me what should be my aims. You be the malt that works up the brew. Imagine we are making a good soup, you be the salt and prunes....

"If a talented man is unjust, the ruler should give him no share in the royal responsibility. If the ruler is unjust, the talented man should not eat his food."

*Confucianism.* Book of History 4.8.1-3

## *Government by Divine Law*

THIS SECTION DEALS WITH THE PRINCIPLE that a government is founded upon respect for God and conformity to divine law. In Islamic nations, government is expected to enforce the ordinances of the Shariah. For Hinduism and Buddhism, the way of proper rule is in accordance with the Dharma. For Confucianism, it is the way of propriety *(li)* tempered with benevolence, and for Taoism, in accordance with the Tao. In ancient Israel, the laws of God were written down for the king to study.

Modern Western constitutional governments, as well, are founded on the Judeo-Christian principle that government should be subservient to certain universal laws (e.g., human rights and social duties). In ancient Israel, the Law of Moses was given on Mount Sinai prior to the formation of the state; hence it stood above the state and formed the basis for prophetic critiques of misrule. In the case of the United States, the Constitution came into existence prior to the establishment of a government and forms the legal basis for its authority. A constitution is venerated as a statement of the highest principles of government, and a proper constitution is neither produced by a government to codify its policies nor easily amended by the people to express the will of the majority. Furthermore, modern constitutions contain articles which declare that certain human rights are inalienable and God-given. Governments cannot disregard the rights of the people, because those rights are not the governments' to grant; enshrined in a constitution, they come from a higher Law.

Step beyond what is human,
elect for the Divine Word,
and establish your leadership,
along with all the friends you have.

*Hinduism.* Atharva Veda 7.105

If your kingdom exists for the doctrine
And not for fame or desire,
Then it will be extremely fruitful.
If not, its fruit will be misfortune.

*Buddhism.* Nagarjuna, Precious Garland 327

**Book of History 4.8.1-3:** In the Confucian relation between prince and minister, the able minister serves his lord with good, honest advice and covers for his shortcomings. The prince, in turn, should be attentive and accepting of his minister's wise counsel. Cf. Doctrine of the Mean 20.8, p. 166; Book of Ritual 7.2.19, p. 166; Chuang Tzu 4, pp. 507-8; Analects 14.8, p. 734.

**Atharva Veda 7.105:** Cf. Ramayana, Yuddha Kanda 130, p. 199.

**Precious Garland 327:** Cf. Abot 4.14, p. 763.

A king should abandon his own precious life,
But not the jewel of Righteousness, whereby
the world is gladdened.

*Buddhism*. Golden Light Sutra 12

Warned by a dream, Emperor Sujin reverenced the gods, and therefore was lauded as the wise emperor.

*Shinto*. Kojiki, Preface

If [a ruler] enjoins fear of God, the Exalted and Glorious, and dispenses justice, there will be great reward for him; and if he enjoins otherwise, it redounds on him.

*Islam*. Hadith of Muslim

The Creator... projected that excellent form, justice (*dharma*). This justice is the controller of the ruler. Therefore there is nothing higher than justice. So even a weak man hopes to defeat a stronger man through justice, as one does with the help of a king.

*Hinduism*. Brihadaranyaka Upanishad 1.4.14

No individual is lost and no nation is refused prosperity and success if foundations of their thoughts and actions rest upon piety and godliness, and upon truth and justice.

*Islam*. Nahjul Balagha, Sermon 21

And you will be yourself ruler and president.... You must in everything reverence the statutes and proceed by them to the happy rule of the people. They were the reverence of King Wen and his caution; in proceeding by them to the happy rule of the people, say, "If I can only attain to them."

*Confucianism*. Book of History 5.9.3.8

The Messenger of God said, "The best of your rulers are those whom you love and who love you, who invoke God's blessings upon you and you invoke His blessings upon them. And the worst of your rulers are those whom you hate and who hate you, and whom you curse and who curse you." It was asked, "Should we not overthrow them with the sword?" He said, "No, as long as they establish prayer among you."

*Islam*. Hadith of Muslim

Tao is eternal, but has no fame;
The Uncarved Block, though seemingly of
small account,
Is greater than anything that is under heaven.
If kings and barons would but possess themselves of it,
The ten thousand creatures would flock to do
them homage;
Heaven and earth would conspire
To send Sweet Dew;
Without law or compulsion, men would dwell
in harmony.

*Taoism*. Tao Te Ching 32

When you come to the land which the Lord your God gives you, and you possess it and dwell in it, and then say, "I will set a king over me, like all the nations that are round about me"; you may indeed set a king over you, him whom the Lord your God will choose.... When he sits on the throne of his kingdom, he shall

**Golden Light Sutra 12:** The 'jewel of Righteousness' means the dharma, one of the Three Jewels: Buddha, Dharma, and Sangha. This is from a longer passage, p. 770.

**Kojiki:** In other words, the emperor established harmony with the kami as the basis for his rule.

**Brihadaranyaka Upanishad 1.4.14:** Cf. Atharva Veda 4.1.3, p. 99.

**Nahjul Balagha, Sermon 21:** Cf. Forty Hadith of an-Nawawi 24, p. 197; Abot 4.14, p. 763; Deuteronomy 6.20-8.20, pp. 764-65.

**Book of History 5.9.3.8:** These are the rites and rules of propriety, laid down from ancient times. It includes the principle of benevolence—cf. Mencius IV.A.3, p. 767.

**Hadith of Muslim:** This hadith speaks of the ruler's attitude towards God and the believers. To 'establish prayer' means far more than merely to tolerate religion; it means to uphold the Muslim faith and the laws of the Shariah.

**Tao Te Ching 32:** The 'Uncarved Block' means to dwell without making distinctions or playing favorites, at one with the primal Unity. Cf. Chuang Tzu 7, p. 416; Tao Te Ching 18, p. 201; 80, pp. 198-99; Isaiah 2.2-4, p. 790.

write for himself in a book a copy of this law, from that which is in charge of the Levitical priests, and it shall be with him, and he shall read in it all the days of his life, that he may learn to fear the Lord his God, by keeping all the words of this law and these statutes, and doing them; that his heart may not be lifted up above his brethren, and that he may not turn aside from the commandment, either to the right hand or to the left; so that he may continue long in his kingdom, he and his children, in Israel.

*Judaism* and *Christianity*.
Deuteronomy 17.14-20

The Celestial Wheel is no paternal heritage of yours. You yourself do good, as I did, and earn the Wheel. Act up to the noble ideal of the duty which is set before true world sovereigns.... You, leaning on the Law, honoring, respecting, and revering it, doing homage to it, hallowing it, being yourself a banner of the Law, a signal of the Law, having the Law as your master, should provide the right watch, ward, and protection for your own people, for the army, for the nobles, for vassals, for brahmins, and householders, for town and country dwellers, for the religious world, and for beasts and birds. Throughout your kingdom let no wrongdoing prevail. And whosoever in your kingdom is poor, to him let wealth be given.

*Buddhism*.
Digha Nikaya iii.60-61,
Cakkavatti-Sihanada Suttanta

❖

**Deuteronomy 17.14-20:** This is the Law of the King, part of the Mosaic Law which regulated the conduct of kings—though there was as yet no kingdom when Moses received the Law on Mount Sinai. The king would be responsible to read the Law of Moses and follow it. Cf. Joshua 1.1-9, p. 745; 2 Samuel 23.3-4, p. 757; Jeremiah 18.3-11, p. 764; Deuteronomy 6.20-8.20, pp. 764-65; Isaiah 2.2-4, p. 790.

**Digha Nikaya iii.60-61:** The 'Law' means the Buddha's *Dhamma*. This is an excerpt of the longer passage; see pp. 199-200n.

## *Consideration for the People*

THE CHIEF CONCERN OF ANY GOVERNMENT should be the welfare of its citizens. Therefore the ruler, and hence the government, should be a parent to the people, putting their concerns and needs ahead of his own. He is called the Father and Mother of the People in the Chinese tradition and a Shepherd in the Judeo-Christian and Muslim traditions—titles which express the principle that the ruler should give the people his highest consideration. He should, whenever possible, lighten the people's burdens and abide by the will of the majority. He should give special consideration to the poor and destitute and provide them sufficient means of support. Such a government will be respected by the people, who then will easily submit to its rule.

Governing a large state is like boiling a small fish.

*Taoism*. Tao Te Ching 60

Lay no burden on the public which the majority cannot bear.

*Judaism*. Talmud, Baba Batra 60b

The ruler who submits to democratic ideals,
His rule is lasting.

*Sikhism*. Adi Granth, Maru, M.1

The highest duty of a ruler is to protect his subjects; the ruler who enjoys the rewards of his position is bound to that duty.

*Hinduism*. Laws of Manu 7.144

The duty of rulers: Gladden the people and do not scare them; make things easy and do not make them difficult.

*Islam*. Hadith of Bukhari and Muslim

When loss is above and gain below, the people's joy is boundless. When those above exhibit no pride to the ones below them, their virtue is brightly illumined.

*Confucianism*. I Ching 42: Gain

Emperor Nintoku climbed up a high mountain and, viewing the lands of the four quarters, said, "There is no smoke rising [from fireplaces] in the land. The entire land is impoverished. For a period of three years the people are released from all taxes and conscription." For this reason, the palace became dilapidated; although the rain leaked in everywhere, no repairs were made. The dripping rain was caught in vessels, and the inhabitants moved around to places where it did not leak.

Later, when he viewed the land again, the entire land was filled with smoke. Therefore, realizing that the people were now rich, he reinstated taxes and conscription. For this reason, the common people flourished and did not suffer from his conscription. Thus his reign is praised as being the reign of a saintly ruler.

*Shinto*. Kojiki 110

God weeps... over a leader who domineers over the community.

*Judaism*. Talmud, Hagiga 5b

Guardianship is not to give an order but to give one's self.

*African Traditional Religions*.
Nyika Proverb (Kenya and Tanzania)

**Tao Te Ching 60:** Cf. Mencius I.A.6, p. 187.

**Baba Batra 60b:** Cf. Nupe Proverb, p. 197.

**I Ching 42:** Cf. Tao Te Ching 19, p. 201; 77, p. 387; Analects 20.1.3, p. 459; Great Learning 10.7-9, p. 667.

**Kojiki 110:** Cf. Man'yoshu 1, p. 206; Great Learning 10.7-9, p. 667; Forty Hadith of an-Nawawi 31, p. 679.

Confucius said, "To demand much from oneself and little from others is the way for a ruler to banish discontent."

*Confucianism*. Analects 15.14

Jesus called to them and said, "You know that the rulers of the Gentiles lord it over them, and their great men exercise authority over them. It shall not be so among you; but whoever would be great among you must be your servant, and whoever would be first among you must be your slave; even as the Son of man came not to be served but to serve, and to give his life as a ransom for many."

*Christianity*. Matthew 20.25-28

Desiring to rule over the people,
One must, in one's words, humble oneself before them;
And, desiring to lead the people,
One must, in one's person, follow behind them.
Therefore the sage takes his place over the people yet is no burden;
Takes his place ahead of the people yet causes no obstruction.
That is why the empire supports him joyfully and never tires of doing so.

*Taoism*. Tao Te Ching 66

A sovereign should become one with his people. The sovereign must think that all that he owns is not for himself, but for his country. If that happens, the country will prosper.

*Unification Church*. Sun Myung Moon, 3-17-70

The Caliph is a shepherd over the people and shall be questioned about his subjects.

*Islam*. Hadith of Bukhari and Muslim

Ho, shepherds of Israel who have been feeding yourselves! Should not shepherds feed the sheep? You eat the fat, you clothe yourselves with the wool, you slaughter the fatlings; but you do not feed the sheep. The weak you have not strengthened, the sick you have not healed, the crippled you have not bound up, the strayed you have not brought back, the lost you have not sought, and with force and harshness you have ruled them. So they were scattered, because there was no shepherd; and they became food for all the wild beasts.... Therefore, you shepherds, hear the word of the Lord: Thus says the Lord God, Behold, I am against the shepherds; and I will require my sheep at their hand, and put a stop to their feeding the sheep; no longer shall the shepherds feed themselves. I will rescue my sheep from their mouths, that they may not be food for them.

*Judaism* and *Christianity*. Ezekiel 34.2-10

Heaven and Earth are the father and mother of the ten thousand things. Men are the sensibility of the ten thousand things. It is telling the truth, thinking well, and seeing things clearly that make the principal ruler. The principal ruler is father and mother to the common people.

*Confucianism*. Book of History 5.1.1: The Great Declaration

If the chief has many breasts they are sucked by the people.

*African Traditional Religions*. Akan Proverb (Ghana)

**Analects 15.14:** Cf. Analects 20.1.3, p. 459; Great Learning 10.7-9, p. 667.

**Tao Te Ching 66:** Cf. Tao Te Ching 2, p. 667; 3, p. 758; 7, p. 689; 12, p. 662; 28, p. 648; 77, p. 387; 81, p. 690; Mencius I.A.2, p. 222.

**Hadith of Bukhari and Muslim:** Cf. Hadith of Bukhari, p. 180; Hadith of Baihaqi, p. 766.

**Ezekiel 34.2-10:** On the prophetic critique of excessive courtly extravagance while the poor suffer, see Jeremiah 7.1-15, pp. 768-69; 22.13-16, p. 755; Isaiah 10.1-4, p. 768; Amos 1.3-2:16, pp. 771-72; 8.4-8, p. 345; 2 Samuel 11-12, pp. 736-37.

**Book of History 5.1.1:** This is the central expression of the duties of the ruler in China. Cf. Mencius I.A.4, p. 735; I.B.8, p. 741.

**Akan Proverb:** In other words, the chief is like a parent who properly places himself and his wealth in the service of the people.

To speak ill of those in authority because one is not given a share in such enjoyment [as they are privileged to have] is, of course, wrong. But for one in authority over the people not to share his enjoyment with the people is equally wrong. The people will delight in the joy of him who delights in their joy, and will worry over the troubles of him who worries over their troubles. He who delights and worries on account of the Empire is surely to become a true king.

*Confucianism.* Mencius I.B.4

The government is the guardian of those who have no guardian.

*Islam.* Hadith

Old men without wives, old women without husbands, old people without children, young children without fathers—these four types of people are the most destitute and have no one to turn to for help. Whenever King Wen put benevolent measures into effect, he always gave them first consideration. The Book of Songs says,

> Happy are the rich;
> But have pity on the helpless.

*Confucianism.* Mencius I.B.5

At the end of every seven years you shall grant a release. And this is the manner of the release: every creditor shall release what he has lent to his neighbor; he shall not exact it of his neighbor, his brother, because the Lord's release has been proclaimed.... For there will be no poor among you, for the Lord will bless you in the land which the Lord your God gives you for an inheritance to possess, if only you will obey the voice of the Lord your God, being careful to do all this commandment.

*Judaism* and *Christianity.* Deuteronomy 15.1-5

Give the king thy justice, O God,
and thy righteousness to the royal son!
May he judge thy people with righteousness,
and thy poor with justice!
Let the mountains bear prosperity for the people,
and the hills, in righteousness!
May he defend the cause of the poor of the
people,
give deliverance to the needy,
and crush the oppressor!

*Judaism* and *Christianity.* Psalm 72.1-4

The king's country, sire, is harassed and harried. There are dacoits abroad who pillage the villages and townships and who make the roads unsafe. Were the king, so long as that is so, to levy a fresh tax, verily his majesty would be acting wrongly. But perchance his majesty might think, "I'll soon put a stop to these scoundrels' game by punishments and banishment, fines and bonds and death!" But their license cannot be satisfactorily put a stop to by such a course. The remnant left unpunished would still go on harassing the realm. Now there is one method to adopt to put a thorough end to this disorder. Whosoever there be in the king's realm who devote themselves to keeping cattle and the farm, to them let his majesty give food and seed corn. Whosoever there be in the king's realm who devote themselves to trade, to them let his majesty give capital. Whosoever there be in the king's realm who devote themselves to government service, to them let his majesty give wages and food. Then those men, following each his own business, will no longer harass the realm; the king's revenue will go up; the country will be quiet and at peace; and the populace, pleased with one another and happy, dancing their children in their arms, will dwell with open doors.

*Buddhism.* Digha Nikaya i.135, Kutadanta Sutta

**Mencius I.B.5:** In the Confucian Five Relations, the ethical norm of the ruler towards those below him is benevolence; thus Book of Ritual 7.2.19, p.166. On the Confucian critique of excessive courtly extravagance while the poor suffer, see Mencius I.A.4, p. 735; I.B.8, p. 741; IV.A.3, p. 767; Book of Songs, Ode 254, pp. 769-70.

**Deuteronomy 15.1-5:** The biblical institution of the Sabbatical year granted a reprieve to the poor through a periodic forgiveness of debts. Cf. Leviticus 25.10, p. 197n.

**Psalm 72.1-4:** This is a royal psalm extolling the virtues of the ideal king. Cf. Jeremiah 22.3, p. 197.

Woe to him who builds his house by
unrighteousness,
and his upper rooms by injustice;
who makes his neighbor serve him for nothing,
and does not give him his wages;
who says, 'I will build myself a great house
with spacious upper rooms,'
and cuts out windows for it,
paneling it with cedar,
and painting it with vermillion.
Do you think you are a king
because you compete in cedar?
Did not your father eat and drink
and do justice and righteousness?
Then it was well with him.
He judged the poor and the needy;
then it was well.
Is not this to know me? says the Lord.

*Judaism* and *Christianity*. Jeremiah 22.13-16

The court is corrupt,
The fields are overgrown with weeds,
The granaries are empty;
Yet there are those dressed in fineries,
With swords at their sides,
Filled with food and drink,
And possessed of too much wealth.
This is known as taking the lead in robbery.
Far indeed is this from the Way.

*Taoism*. Tao Te Ching 53

When Po Chü arrived in Ch'i, he saw the body of a criminal who had been executed. Pushing and dragging until he had it laid out in proper position, he took off his formal robes and covered it with them, wailing to Heaven and crying out, "Alas, alas! The world is in dire misfortune, and you have been quicker than the rest of us to encounter it. 'Thou shalt not steal, thou shalt not murder!' they say. But when glory and disgrace have once been defined, you will see suffering; when goods and wealth have once been gathered together, you will see wrangling. To define something that brings suffering to men, to gather together what sets them to wrangling, inflicting misery and weariness upon them, never granting them a time of rest, and yet to hope somehow that they will not end up like this—how could it be possible?

"The rulers of old attributed what success they had to the people and what failures they had to themselves; attributed what was upright to the people and what was askew to themselves. Therefore, if there was something wrong with the body of even a single being, they would retire and take the blame upon themselves. But that is not the way it is done today. They make things obscure and then blame people for not understanding; they enlarge the difficulties and then punish people for not being able to cope with them; they pile on responsibilities and then penalize people for not being able to fulfill them; they make the journey longer and then chastise people for not reaching the end of it. When the knowledge and strength of the people are exhausted, they will begin to piece them out with artifice, and when day by day the amount of artifice in the world increases, how can men keep from resorting to artifice? A lack of strength invites artifice, a lack of knowledge invites deceit, a lack of goods invites theft. These thefts and robberies—who in fact deserves the blame for them?"

*Taoism*. Chuang Tzu 25

**Jeremiah 22.13-16:** Jeremiah addressed this prophetic rebuke to Jehoiakim, son of the good king Josiah. See note to Ezekiel 34.2-10, above.
**Tao Te Ching 53:** Cf. Tao Te Ching 3, p. 758; 12, p. 662.
**Chuang Tzu 25:** Cf. Proverbs 6.30-31, p. 345n.

## *Leadership by Example and Honest Government*

GOVERNMENT SHOULD OPERATE IMPARTIALLY and with integrity. Its leaders should be honest, moral, and virtuous people, who will not take bribes or act corruptly. Because people look up to a nation's leaders as role models, they should set a good example for the people.

The notion that a leader may rule by moral force is widespread in many religions, but it is particularly central to the Confucian ideal of government. On the other hand, the Islamic view of leadership is more pessimistic: People should not expect the ruler to be any different from themselves; they should rather look to God for guidance.

God has promised such of you as believe and do good works that He will surely make them to succeed the present rulers in the earth, even as He caused those who were before them to succeed; and he will surely establish for them their religion which He has approved for them.

*Islam.* Qur'an 24.55

Duke Ai: "May I ask what is the art of government?"

Confucius: "The art of government simply consists in making things right, or putting things in their right places. When the ruler himself is 'right,' then the people naturally follow him in his right course."

*Confucianism.* Book of Ritual 27

Chi K'ang-tzu asked Confucius about government, saying, "Suppose I were to slay those who have not the Way in order to help those who have the Way, what would you think of it?" Confucius replied, saying, "If you desire what is good, the people will at once be good. The essence of the gentleman is that of wind; the essence of small people is that of grass. And when a wind passes over the grass, it cannot choose but bend."

*Confucianism.* Analects 12.19

Concerned alone with the upholding of the world,<br>
you should act.<br>
Whatever the best man does,<br>
others do that also.<br>
The world follows<br>
the standard he sets for himself.

*Hinduism.* Bhagavad Gita 3.20-21

When the king is deceitful, who will not be deceitful? When the king is unrighteous, who will not be unrighteous?

*Jainism.* Somadeva, Nitivakyamrita 17.183

Confucius said, "Those rulers whose measures are dictated by mere expediency will arouse continual discontent."

*Confucianism.* Analects 4.12

Confucius said, "If a ruler himself is upright, all will go well even though he does not give orders. But if he himself is not upright, even though he gives orders, they will not be obeyed."

*Confucianism.* Analects 13.6

**Book of Ritual 27:** The Confucian doctrine of Rectification of Names teaches that people at every position of life should live up to the proper responsibilities of their offices. It should begin with the ruler. See Analects 12.11, p. 506n.; Doctrine of the Mean 14, p. 507; Mencius I.B.8, p. 741.

**Analects 12.19:** On not propagating one's religion by force, see Qur'an 2.256, p. 486. The position that the state has the right and duty to use the sword in order to enforce correct thinking has had a long history in China, from the Legalists of the Ch'in dynasty to Mao Tse-tung in the twentieth century.

**Analects 13.6:** Cf. Analects 4.5, p. 667.

When cattle are crossing, if the old bull
swerves,
They all go swerving, following his lead.
So among men, if he who's reckoned best
Lives not aright, much more do other folk.
If the ruler be unrighteous, the whole land
dwells in woe.

When cattle are crossing, if the bull goes
straight,
They all go straight because his course is
straight.
So among men, if he who's reckoned best
Lives righteously, the others do so too.
The whole land dwells in happiness if the ruler
lives aright.

*Buddhism*. Anguttara Nikaya ii.75

Now a bishop must be above reproach, the husband of one wife, temperate, sensible, dignified, hospitable, an apt teacher, no drunkard, not violent but gentle, not quarrelsome, and no lover of money. He must manage his own household well, keeping his children submissive and respectful in every way; for if a man does not know how to manage his own household, how can he care for God's church?

*Christianity*. 1 Timothy 3.2-5

Emperor Kotoku proclaimed to his ministers, "In governing, let us do truly as was done by the emperors of old in ruling the realm. Let us govern with true sincerity."

*Shinto*. Nihon Shoki 25

The God of Israel has spoken,
the Rock of Israel has said to me:
When one rules justly over men,
ruling in the fear of God,
he dawns on them like the morning light,
like the sun shining forth upon a cloudless
morning,
like rain that makes grass to sprout from the
earth.

*Judaism* and *Christianity*.
2 Samuel 23.3-4

The Emperor Yao was reverent, intelligent, accomplished, sincere, and mild. He was sincerely respectful and capable of modesty. His light covered the four extremities of the empire and extended to Heaven above and the earth below. He was able to make bright his great virtue, bring affection to the nine branches of his family... and harmonize the myriad states. The numerous people were amply nourished and prosperous and became harmonious....

The emperor said, "Oh you Chief of the Four Mountains, I have been on the throne for seventy years. If you can carry out the mandate, I shall resign my position to you." The Chief of the Four Mountains said, "I have not the virtue. I would only disgrace the high position." The emperor said, "Promote someone who is already illustrious, or raise up someone who is humble and mean." They all said to the emperor, "There is an unmarried man in a low position called Shun of Yü." The emperor said, "Yes, I have heard of him. What is he like?" The Chief said, "He is the son of a blind man. His father is stupid, his mother deceitful, his half-brother Hsiang is arrogant. Yet he has been able to live in harmony with them and to be splendidly filial. He has controlled himself and has not come to wickedness." The emperor said, "I will try him; I will wive him and observe his behavior towards my two daughters." He gave orders and sent down his two daughters to the bend of the Kuei River to be wives in the House of Yü. The emperor said, "Be reverent!"...

The emperor said, "Come, you Shun, in the affairs on which you have been consulted, I have examined your words; your words have been accomplished and capable of yielding fine results for three years; do you ascend to the imperial throne." Shun considered himself inferior in virtue and was not pleased. But in the first month, on the first day, he accepted the abdication of Yao in the Temple of the Accomplished Ancestor. Then he made lei sacrifice to the Lord-on-High; he made yin sacrifice to the six Venerable Ones.... He

**Nihon Shoki 25:** Cf. Kojiki, Preface, p. 750.

**2 Samuel 23.3-4:** These are from the last words of King David. Cf. Joshua 1:1-9, p. 745; Deuteronomy 17.14-20, pp. 750-51.

delimited the twelve provinces and raised altars on twelve mountains, and he deepened the rivers.

*Confucianism.* Book of History 1.1.3 and 2.1.2-3

As you are so will you have rulers put over you.

*Islam.* Hadith of Baihaqi

Refrain from exalting the worthy
So that the people will not scheme and contend;
Refrain from prizing rare possessions,
So that the people will not steal;
Refrain from displaying objects of desire,
So that the people's hearts will not be disturbed.
Therefore the sage rules his people thus:
He empties their minds,
And fills their bellies;
He weakens their ambitions,
And strengthens their bones.
He strives always to keep people innocent of knowledge and desires, and to keep the knowing ones from meddling. By doing nothing that interferes with anything, nothing is left unregulated.

*Taoism.* Tao Te Ching 3

By God, any official who takes anything from the public funds without justification will meet his Lord carrying it on himself on the Day of Judgment.

*Islam.* Hadith of Muslim

Bribery is the door through which come all manner of sins. Those who live by bribery cut off their mother's breasts.

*Jainism.* Somadeva, Nitivakyamrita 17.184

He who receives office in order to profit from it is like an adulterer, who gets his pleasure from a woman's body. God says, "I am called holy, you are called holy; if you have not all the qualities which I have, you should not accept leadership."

*Judaism.* Pesikta Rabbati 111a

Neither for the sake of oneself nor for the sake of another, not desiring son, wealth, or kingdom, should a person seek his own success by unjust means. Then only is a man indeed virtuous, wise, and righteous.

*Buddhism.* Dhammapada 84

Do not ask for the position of authority, for if you are granted this position as a result of your asking for it, you will be left to discharge it yourself; but if you are given it without asking you will be helped [by God].

*Islam.* Hadith of Muslim

"Your Majesty," answered Mencius. "What is the point of mentioning the word 'profit'? All that matters is that there should be benevolence and rightness. If Your Majesty says, 'How can I profit my state?' and the counsellors say, 'How can I profit my family?' and the officials and commoners say, 'How can I profit my person?' then those above and those below will be trying to profit at the expense of one another and the state will be imperiled. When regicide is committed in a state of ten thousand chariots, it is certain to be by a vassal with a thousand chariots, and when it is committed in a state of a thousand chariots, it is certain to be by a vassal with a hundred chariots. A share of a thousand in ten thousand or a hundred in a thousand is by no means insignificant, yet if profit is put before rightness, there is no satisfaction short of total usurpation. No benevolent man ever abandons his parents, and no dutiful man ever puts his prince last. Perhaps you will now endorse what I have said: 'All

**Book of History 1.1.3 and 2.1.2-3:** Yao and Shun were revered by Confucius as among the ideal rulers of ancient China because of their personal righteousness.

**Tao Te Ching 3:** This Taoist passage disagrees with the Confucian wisdom that the route to honest government requires that men of ability be sought out and promoted. The Taoist sages recognized that rivalry between 'worthy' advisors was a serious corruption in the state. To feed ambition is to bring out the worst in people and is contrary to the Tao. Cf. Tao Te Ching 12, p.662; 18-19, p. 201.

that matters is that there should be benevolence and rightness. What is the point of mentioning the word "profit"?'"

*Confucianism.* Mencius I.A.1

Rulers lost their senses in levity and frivolity;
[Therefore] Babur's command has gone abroad,
That even princes now go about without a
crust of bread.

*Sikhism.* Adi Granth,
Asa Ashtpadi M.1, p. 417

You will be eager for the office of commander, but it will become a cause of regret on the day of resurrection. It is a good suckler but an evil weaner.

*Islam.* Hadith of Bukhari

## *Judgments and Punishments*

ONE OF THE CHIEF JUSTIFICATIONS of government is that it should preserve law and order, protect the innocent, and punish criminals. Judgments must be made with great care, in order not to punish innocent people mistakenly. The judge should not be partial, but should treat everyone with an equal eye. Many texts enjoin the authorities to be compassionate and prescribe lenient punishments for minor infractions. Punishment should not be prescribed from a vengeful motivation, but always with the criminal's welfare as well as the welfare of society in mind.

Punishment serves as a deterrent to crime and a shield for the innocent. In theistic traditions, the government in meting out punishments is a co-worker with God, who is the final dispenser of justice. In the Hindu and Buddhist traditions, the justice dispensed by the government manifests the fruits of karma on the earth: Justice on earth corresponds to the absolute justice of the cosmos through the operation of karma. Furthermore, since by committing crimes the criminal burdens himself with demerit, which, if not purged by punishment in this life, burdens him in a future life, punishment helps him by reducing the quantity of evil karma which he will have to expiate in the future. Thus a government that vigorously prosecutes and punishes criminals upholds righteousness both in the present, by distinguishing good from evil in the eyes of the people, and in the future, by reducing the quantity of evil karma to be inherited by later generations.

Finally, an important purpose of punishment is rehabilitation. To be effective as a force for rehabilitation and renovation, punishment should elicit sincere repentance. The repentant criminal, by willingly accepting his punishment, is forgiven by God and inherits future blessings.

He who renders true judgments is a co-worker with God.

*Judaism.* Mekilta, Exodus 18.13

Whenever you judge between people, you should do so with justice. How superbly God instructs you to do so; God is Alert, Observant!

*Islam.* Qur'an 4.58

**Mencius I.A.1:** Cf. Book of Ritual 7.1.2, pp. 200-1.

**Asa Ashtapadi M.1:** Nanak attributed the invasion by the Mughal conqueror Babur to God's judgment on the misrule of the kings of India. See Asa, M.1, p. 768.

Governance is the function of the ruler in order to protect the state from the wicked and nourish the good.

*Jainism*. Somadeva, Nitivakyamrita 5.1-2

By justice a king gives stability to the land,
but one who exacts gifts ruins it.

*Judaism* and *Christianity*. Proverbs 29.4

If the thief steals something he takes an oath to decide his fate, but if the oath steals something what will it take?

*African Traditional Religions*. Igala Proverb (Nigeria)

What destroyed your predecessors was just that when a person of rank among them committed a theft they left him alone, but when a weak one of their number committed a theft they inflicted the prescribed punishment on him. I swear by God that even if Fatima daughter of Muhammad should steal, I would have her hand cut off.

*Islam*. Hadith of Bukhari and Muslim

I [Moses] charged your judges at that time, "Hear the cases between your brethren, and judge righteously between a man and his brother or the alien that is with him. You shall not be partial in judgment; you shall hear the small and the great alike; you shall not be afraid of the face of man, for the judgment is God's; and the case that is too hard for you, you shall bring to me, and I will hear it."

*Judaism* and *Christianity*. Deuteronomy 1.16-17

He is not thereby just because he hastily arbitrates cases. The wise man should investigate both right and wrong.

The intelligent person who leads others not falsely but lawfully and impartially, who is a guardian of the law, is called one who abides by righteousness.

*Buddhism*. Dhammapada 256-57

Every person who is tempted to go astray does not deserve punishment.

*Islam*. Nahjul Balagha, Saying 14

The superior man gives careful thought to his judgments and is tardy in sentencing people to death.

*Confucianism*. I Ching 61: Inward Confidence

A sovereign should not inflict excessive punishment, nor should he use harsh words and speak ill of anyone at his back.

*Hinduism*. Matsya Purana 220.10

He who distinguishes good deeds from evil,
Who shows the results of karma—he is called a king.
Ordained by the host of gods, the gods delight in him.
For the sake of himself or others, to preserve the righteousness of his land,
And to put down the rogues and criminals in his domains,
Such a king would give up, if need be, his life and his kingdom.

*Buddhism*. Golden Light Sutra 12

Let the king exert himself to the utmost to punish thieves; for, if he punishes thieves, his fame grows and his kingdom prospers.

A king who thus protects his subjects receives from each and all the sixth part of their spiritual merit; if he does not protect them, the sixth part of their demerit also will fall on him.

**Hadith of Bukhari and Muslim:** On the punishment for theft, see Qur'an 5.38, p. 344.

**Deuteronomy 1.16-17:** Cf. Jeremiah 22.3, p. 197; Exodus 20.16, p. 351; Abot 1.1, pp. 585-86; Isaiah 10.1-4, p. 768.

**I Ching 61:** Cf. I Ching 40, p. 701.

**Golden Light Sutra 12:** To show the results of karma means to enforce justice that the people will recognize that justice is truly enforced, and that the criminals will reap the fruits of their deeds in this life, thereby leaving less demerit to burden their next life. For more of this passage, see p. 770.

A king who protects created beings in accordance with the sacred law and smites those worthy of corporal punishment, [it is as though he] daily offers sacrifices at which hundreds of thousands are given as fees.

A king who does not afford protection, yet takes his share in kind, his taxes, tolls and duties, daily presents and fines, will soon sink into hell.

*Hinduism.* Laws of Manu 8.302-7

Heaven, in its wish to regulate the people, allows us for a day to make use of punishments. Whether crimes have been premeditated, or are unpremeditated, depends on the parties concerned. Let you deal with them to accord with the mind of Heaven and thus serve me, the One Man. Though I would put them to death, do not you therefore put them to death; though I would spare them, do not you therefore spare them. Reverently apportion the five punishments so as fully to exhibit the three virtues. Then shall I, the One Man, enjoy felicity; the people will look to you as their sure dependence; the repose of such a state will be perpetual.

*Confucianism.* Book of History 5.27.4

Punishment alone governs all created beings, punishment alone protects them, punishment watches over them while they sleep; the wise declare punishment to be the law.

If punishment is properly inflicted after due consideration, it makes all people happy; but inflicted without consideration, it destroys everything.

If the ruler did not, without tiring, inflict punishment on those worthy to be punished, the stronger would roast the weaker, like fish on a spit.

All barriers would be broken through, and all men would rage against each other in consequence of mistakes with respect to punishment.

But where Punishment, with a black hue and red eyes, stalks about, destroying sinners, there the subjects are not disturbed, provided he who inflicts it discerns well.

*Hinduism.* Laws of Manu 7.18-25

O king, through compassion you should always
Generate an attitude of help
Even for all those embodied beings
Who have committed appalling sins.

Especially generate compassion
For those murderers, whose sins are horrible;
Those of fallen nature are receptacles
Of compassion from those whose nature is great.

Free the weaker prisoners
After a day or five days;
Do not think the others
Are never to be freed.

For each one whom you do not think
To free you will lose the layman's vow;
Because you will have lost the vow
Faults will constantly be amassed.

As long as the prisoners are not freed,
They should be made comfortable
With barbers, baths, food, drink,
Medicine and clothing.

Just as unworthy sons are punished
Out of a wish to make them worthy,
So punishment should be enforced with compassion
And not through hatred or desire for wealth.

Once you have analyzed the angry
Murderers and recognized them well,
You should banish them without
Killing or tormenting them.

*Buddhism.* Nagarjuna, Precious Garland 331-37

**Laws of Manu 8.302-7:** Vv. 302, 304, 306-7.

**Book of History 5.27.4:** The 'three virtues' are: correctness and straightforwardness in times of peace, strong government in times of disorder, and mild government in times of harmony and order. Cf. Analects 20.1.3, p. 459; Book of History 5.9, pp. 331-32.

**Laws of Manu 7.18-25:** Vv. 18, 20-21, 24-25. Cf. Laws of Manu 9.263, p. 344; Book of History 5.9, pp. 331-32; Golden Light Sutra 12, p. 770.

**Precious Garland 331-37:** Cf. Mencius I.A.6, p. 187.

A thief shall, running, approach the king, with flying hair, confessing that theft, saying, "Thus I have done, punish me."

Whether he is punished or pardoned [after confessing], the thief is freed from the guilt of theft; but the king, if he punishes not, takes upon himself the guilt of the thief.

*Hinduism*. Laws of Manu 8.314, 316

A man came to the Prophet and confessed four times that he had had illicit intercourse with a woman, while all the while the prophet was turning his back to him. Then when he confessed the fifth time, the Prophet turned around... and asked him whether he knew what fornication was, and he replied, "Yes, I have done with her unlawfully what a man may lawfully do with his wife." He then asked him what he wanted by what he had said, and the man replied that he wanted him to purify him, so he gave the command and he was stoned to death. Then God's Prophet heard one of his Companions saying to another, "Look at this man whose fault was concealed by God but who could not leave the matter alone, so that he was stoned like a dog." He said nothing to them but walked on for a time till he came to the corpse of an ass with its legs in the air. He then summoned those Companions, and when they came he said, "Go and eat some of this ass' corpse." They replied, "Prophet of God, who can eat any of this?" whereupon he said, "The dishonor you have just shown your brother is more serious than eating some of this. By Him in whose hand is my soul, he is now among the rivers of Paradise, plunging into them."

*Islam*. Hadith of Abu Dawud

❖

**Laws of Manu 8.314, 316:** Repentance is the key to the thief's successful redemption. Also karma as viewed as a kind of substance. The thief's karma will be destroyed by punishment, otherwise that karma continues to exist and must be transferred to the government. Then it will be manifest in increased crime and social disorder as the people understand that they can steal with impunity.

**Hadith of Abu Dawud:** This man's punishment was truly redeeming because it was submitted to voluntarily with a mind of repentance. Cf. Hadith in Sharh as-Sunna, p. 645.

## *Providence and the Mandate of Heaven*

A PROVIDENCE OF GOD may be discerned in the history of the rise and fall of nations and their rulers. Recognition that God is active in history and guiding the course of nations was a first principle of the revelation to the Jews of ancient Israel. They saw God deliver a band of slaves from the yoke of Pharaoh, and later they recognized God's providence in his dispensing blessings and punishments to the nation of Israel according to whether they were faithful or disobedient to God's will. Similarly, the Classics of Confucianism speak of Heaven's guidance in the affairs of state according to the Mandate of Heaven. Heaven hears the cries of the oppressed and overthrows corrupt regimes, taking the Mandate from them and giving it to new leaders and favoring their revolutions. Comparable notions are also found in the scriptures of Islam, Sikhism, Buddhism, and African traditional religions.

The passages in this section describe God's providence in determining the fate of rulers and nations according to two criteria. First, a nation should be obedient to God's covenant and God's messengers, give reverence to Heaven, and present honor and support to sages and religious teachers. Second, a nation should promote the welfare of the people, ruling them with justice and benevolence, for "Heaven hears as our people see and hear."

Every assembly which is for the sake of Heaven will in the end be established, and every assembly which is not for the sake of Heaven will in the end not be established.

*Judaism.* Mishnah, Abot 4.14

In the land of softly lapping waves, the
Heart of the kami has turned hard.
Leaving the capital in ruins, which
I see, and feel how sad.

*Shinto.* Man'yoshu 1

Have they not travelled in the land to see the nature of the consequence for those who disbelieved before them? They were mightier than those in power [today] and in the traces which they left behind them in the earth. Yet God seized them for their sins, and they had no protector from God.

That was because their messengers kept bringing them clear proofs of God's sovereignty but they disbelieved; so God seized them. Lo! He is Strong, Severe in punishment.

*Islam.* Qur'an 40.21-22

Dishonesty about spoil has not appeared among a people without God casting terror into their hearts; fornication does not become widespread among a people without death being prevalent among them; people do not give short measure and weight without having their provision cut off; people do not judge unjustly without bloodshed becoming widespread among them; and people are not treacherous about a covenant without the enemy being given authority over them.

*Islam.* Hadith of Malik

If there is an evil-minded king who practices wrong teachings, interferes with the disciples of the Buddha, slanders them, speaks ill of them, hurts them with sticks and swords, robs them of

**Abot 4.14:** This is similar to the advice which the New Testament records that Rabbi Gamaliel gave the council of Jewish elders regarding the early Christians in Acts 5.38-39, p. 40. Cf. Precious Garland 327, p. 749.

**Qur'an 40.21-22:** Cf. Nahjul Balagha, Sermon 21, p. 750.

their daily necessities, and bothers those who support them, the king of Brahma Heaven and Indra will immediately send foreign armies to attack him. And also his evil acts will cause several sufferings: civil wars, epidemics, famines, unseasonable storms, fightings, and court fights in this country. They will also cause him to lose his country before long.

*Buddhism*. Great Collection of Sutras

I went down to the potter's house, and there he was working at his wheel. And the vessel he was making of clay was spoiled in the potter's hand, and he reworked it into another vessel, as it seemed good to the potter to do. Then the word of the Lord came to me, "O house of Israel, can I not do with you as this potter has done? says the Lord. Behold, like the clay in the potter's hand, so are you in my hand, O people of Israel. If at any time I declare concerning a nation or a kingdom, that I will pluck up and break down and destroy it, and if that nation, concerning which I have spoken, turns from its evil, I will repent of the evil that I intended to do it. And if at any time I declare concerning a nation or a kingdom that I will build and plant it, and if it does evil in my sight, not listening to my voice, then I will repent of the good, which I had intended to do to it. Now, therefore, say to the men of Judah and the inhabitants of Jerusalem: 'Thus says the Lord, Behold, I am shaping evil against you and devising a plan against you. Return, every one from his evil way, and amend your ways and your doings.'"

*Judaism* and *Christianity*.
Jeremiah 18.3-11

Ananda, so long as the Vajjians assemble in harmony and disperse in harmony; so long as they do their business in harmony; so long as they introduce no revolutionary ordinance, or break up no established ordinance, but abide by the old-time Vajjian Norm, as ordained; so long as they honor, reverence, esteem, and worship the elders among the Vajjians and deem them worthy of listening to; so long as the women and maidens of the families dwell without being forced or abducted; so long as they honor, revere, esteem, and worship the Vajjian shrines, both the inner and the outer; so long as they allow not the customary offerings, given and performed, to be neglected; so long as the customary watch and ward over the arahants that are among them is well kept, so that they may have free access to the realm and having entered may dwell pleasantly therein; just so long as they do these things, Ananda, may the prosperity of the Vajjians be looked for and not their decay.

*Buddhism*. Digha Nikaya ii.73

When your son asks you in time to come, "What is the meaning of the testimonies and the statutes and the ordinances which the Lord our God has commanded you?" then you shall say to your son, "We were Pharaoh's slaves in Egypt; and the Lord brought us out of Egypt with a mighty hand; and the Lord showed signs and wonders, great and grievous, against Egypt and against Pharaoh and all his household, before our eyes; and he brought us out from there, that he might bring us in and give us the land which he swore to give our fathers. And the Lord commanded us to do all these statutes, to fear the Lord our God, for our good always, that he might preserve us alive, as at this day. And it will be righteousness for us, if we are careful to do all this commandment before the Lord our God, as he has commanded us....

For you are a people holy to the Lord your God; the Lord your God has chosen you to be a people for his own possession, out of all the peoples that are on the face of the earth. It was not because you were more in number than any other people that the Lord set his love upon you and chose you, for you were the fewest of all peoples; but it is because the Lord loves you, and is keeping the oath which he swore to your fathers, that the Lord has brought you out with

**Great Collection of Sutras:** This excerpt was quoted by Nichiren in his treatise Daijikkyo on the value of his ministry for the salvation of the nation of Japan. Cf. Precious Garland 327, p. 749.

**Jeremiah 18.3-11:** Cf. 2 Timothy 2.21-22, p. 520; 2 Chronicles 7.14, p. 642; Jonah 3.3-10, p. 643.

a mighty hand, and redeemed you from the house of bondage, from the hand of Pharaoh king of Egypt....

And you shall remember all the way which the Lord your God has led you these forty years in the wilderness, that he might humble you, testing you to know what was in your heart, whether you would keep his commandments, or not. And he humbled you and let you hunger and fed you with manna, which you did not know, nor did your fathers know; that he might make you know that man does not live by bread alone, but that man lives by everything that proceeds out of the mouth of the Lord. Your clothing did not wear out upon you, and your foot did not swell, these forty years. Know then in your heart that, as a man disciplines his son, the Lord your God disciplines you. So you shall keep the commandments of the Lord your God, by walking in his ways and by fearing him. For the Lord your God is bringing you into a good land, a land of brooks of water, of fountains and springs, flowing forth in valleys and hills, a land of wheat and barley, of vines and fig trees and pomegranates, a land of olive trees and honey, a land in which you will eat bread without scarcity, in which you will lack nothing, a land whose stones are iron, and out of whose hills you can dig copper. And you shall eat and be full, and you shall bless the Lord your God for the good land he has given you.

Take heed lest you forget the Lord your God, by not keeping his commandments and his ordinances and his statutes, which I command you this day: lest, when you have eaten and are full, and have built goodly houses and live in them, and when your herds and flocks multiply, and your silver and gold is multiplied, and all that you have is multiplied, then your heart be lifted up, and you forget the Lord.... Beware lest you say in your heart, "My power and the might of my hand have gotten me this wealth." You shall remember the Lord your God, that it is he who gives you power to get wealth; that he may confirm his covenant which he swore to your fathers, as at this day. And if you forget the Lord your God and go after other gods and serve them and worship them, I solemnly warn you this day that you shall surely perish. Like the nations that the Lord makes to perish before you, so shall you perish, because you would not obey the voice of the Lord your God.

*Judaism* and *Christianity*.
Deuteronomy 6.20-8.20

King Wen is on high;
Oh! Bright is he in Heaven.
Although Chou was an old country,
The appointment lighted on it recently.
Illustrious was the House of Chou,
And the appointment of God came at the proper season.
King Wen ascends and descends
On the left and right of God....

Profound was King Wen;
Oh! continuous and bright was his feeling of reverence.
Great is the appointment of Heaven!
There were the descendants of Shang;—
The descendants of the sovereigns of Shang
Were in number more than hundreds of thousands;
But when God gave the command,
They became subject to Chou.

They became subject to Chou;
The appointment of Heaven is not constant.

**Deuteronomy 6.20-8.20:** Deuteronomy 6.20-25, 7.6-8, 8.2-14, 17-20. The Exodus is the first instance of God's activity in history to redeem an oppressed people. It has served as a model for subsequent revolutions, both religious and secular. The politics of the Exodus is not utopian; it remains realistic in its estimation of human weakness and finitude. Even after liberation, people who were once slaves may continue to think and act like slaves until they are educated in the ways of freedom. This is the purpose of the Covenant and the forty years of discipline in the wilderness. Israel must become conscious of its vocation as a people holy to God, set apart from other nations, to exalt God by obeying the commandments and ordinances of the Sinai Covenant. Otherwise there is always the possibility of backsliding, of longing for "the fleshpots of Egypt," as in the incident of the Golden Calf, Exodus 32.1-6, p. 288. The Covenant between God and Israel includes blessings for obedience and curses for disobedience: cf. Deuteronomy 11.26-28, p. 486; 2 Samuel 2.4-9, p. 388; Hosea 4.1-3, p. 222.

The officers of Yin, admirable and alert,
Assist at the libations in our capital;—
They assist at those libations,
Always wearing the hatches on their lower garment and their peculiar cap.
O ye loyal ministers of the king,
Ever think of your ancestor!

Ever think of your ancestor,
Cultivating your virtue,
Always striving to accord with the will of Heaven.
So shall you be seeking for much happiness.
Before Yin lost the multitudes,
Its kings were the assessors of God.
Look to Yin as a beacon;
The great appointment is not easily preserved.

The appointment is not easily preserved;
Do not cause your own extinction.
Display and make bright your righteousness and name,
And look at the fate of Yin in the light of Heaven.
The doings of High Heaven
Have neither sound nor smell.
Take your pattern from King Wen,
And the myriad regions will repose confidence in you.

*Confucianism.*
Book of Songs, Ode 235

The Duke of Chou said, "I make an announcement to all Yin and managers of affairs. Oh, august Heaven, the Lord-on-High, has changed his principal son [the ruler] and this great state Yin's mandate. Now that the king has received the mandate, unbounded is the grace, but also unbounded is the solicitude. Oh, how can he be but careful!

"Heaven has removed and made an end to the great state Yin's mandate. There are many former wise kings of Yin in Heaven, and the later kings and people here managed their mandate. But in the end [under the last king] wise and good men lived in misery so that, leading their wives and carrying their children, wailing and calling to Heaven, they went to where no one could come and seize them. Oh, Heaven had pity on the people of the four quarters, and looking with affection and giving its mandate, it employed the zealous ones [the leaders of the Chou]. May the king now urgently pay careful attention to his virtue.

"Look at the ancient predecessors, the lords of Hsia; Heaven indulged them and cherished and protected them. They strove to comprehend the obedience to Heaven; but in these times they have lost their mandate....

"We do not presume to know and say that the lords of Hsia undertook Heaven's mandate so as to have it for so-and-so many years; we do not presume to know and say that it could not have been prolonged. It was that they did not reverently attend to their virtue, and so they prematurely renounced their mandate. We do not presume to know and say that the lords of Yin received Heaven's mandate for so-and-so many years; we do not know and say that it could not have been prolonged. It was that they did not reverently attend to their virtue, and so they prematurely threw away their mandate. Now the king has succeeded to and received their mandate. We should then also remember the mandates of these two states and in succeeding to them equal their merits."

*Confucianism.* Book of History 5.12.2,
Announcement of the Duke of Chou

Beware of the plea of the oppressed, for he asks God Most High only for his due, and God does not keep one who has a right from receiving what is due.

*Islam.* Hadith of Baihaqi

Heaven hears and sees as our people hear and see; Heaven brightly approves and displays its terrors as our people brightly approve and would fear; such connection is there between

**Book of Songs, Ode 235:** King Wen was the illustrious founder of the Shang dynasty; he was a righteous king who earned the Mandate of Heaven. But when his descendant King Yin brought corruption and troubles to the land, the Mandate of Heaven was lost and a new dynasty, the House of Chou, came to rule. In this poem the rulers of Chou and their subjects, the former retainers of Yin, are admonished to take a lesson from the fate of the previous dynasty. See the following passage.

the upper and lower worlds. How reverent ought the masters of the earth to be!

*Confucianism*. Book of History 2.3.3, Counsels of Kao Yao

I have seen the affliction of my people who are in Egypt, and have heard their cry because of their taskmasters; I know their sufferings, and I have come down to deliver them out of the hand of the Egyptians, and to bring them up out of that land to a good and broad land, a land flowing with milk and honey.

*Judaism* and *Christianity*. Exodus 3.7-8

Whoever vows to tyrannize the humble and the meek
The Supreme Lord burns him in flames.
The Creator dispenses perfect justice,
And preserves His servants.
His majesty is manifest from the primal hour to the end of time!
The traducer is destroyed, afflicted with a great malady.
He is destroyed by Him, against whom no savior exists:
Of such here and hereafter, evil is his repute.
He cherishes His servants, clasping them to His bosom.

*Sikhism*. Adi Granth, Gauri, M.5, p. 199

Have you not seen how your Lord dealt with the people of 'Ad,
With the city of Iram, with lofty pillars,
The like of which were not produced in all the land?
And with the people of Thamud, who cut out huge rocks in the valley?—
And with Pharaoh, Lord of Stakes?
All these transgressed beyond bounds in the lands
And heaped therein mischief on mischief.
Therefore did your Lord pour on them a scourge of diverse chastisements:
For your Lord is as a guardian on a watchtower.

*Islam*. Qur'an 89.6-14

On us shall descend some awful curse,
Like the curse that descended in far-off times.
Thus speaks the Creator of men,
But the men refuse to listen.
On us shall descend some awful curse,
Like the curse that descended in far-off times:
We have but one word to say:
Idle about! Sink in sloth!
Men of such kind will gain nothing from the Father,
For they know not his voice.
He is the one who loves man.

*African Traditional Religions*. Dinka Prayer (Sudan)

Mencius said, "The Three Dynasties won the empire through benevolence and lost it through cruelty. This is true of the rise and fall, survival and collapse, of states as well. An emperor cannot keep the empire within the Four Seas unless he is benevolent; a feudal lord cannot preserve the altars to the gods of earth and grain unless he is benevolent; a minister or a counsellor cannot preserve his ancestral temple unless he is benevolent; a gentleman or a commoner cannot preserve his four limbs unless he is benevolent. To dislike death yet revel in cruelty is no different from drinking beyond your capacity despite your dislike of drunkenness."

*Confucianism*. Mencius IV.A.3

**Book of History 2.3.3:** Cf. Book of History 5.1.1, p. 753; Hagiga 5b, p. 752.

**Exodus 3.7-8:** This is from the call of Moses, Exodus 3.1-4.16, pp. 421-22.

**Gauri, M.5:** Cf. Gauri Sukhmani, M.5, p. 388.

**Qur'an 89.6-14:** 'Ad and Thamud were civilizations whose extensive ruins could still be seen by the people of Muhammad's day. They were a reminder that God's judgment could doom mighty nations. See Qur'an 14.9-15, p. 736; also Obadiah 3-4, p. 290; Isaiah 2.12-17, pp. 290-91.

**Mencius IV.A.3:** Cf. Mencius I.A.6, p. 187; Tao Te Ching 77, p. 387.

Woe to those who decree iniquitous decrees,
and the writers who keep writing oppression,
to turn aside the needy from justice
and to rob the poor of my people of their right,
that widows may be their spoil,
and that they may make the fatherless their
prey!
What will you do on the day of punishment,
in the storm which will come from afar?
To whom will you flee for help,
and where will you leave your wealth?
Nothing remains but to crouch among the
prisoners
or fall among the slain.
For all this his anger is not turned away,
and his hand is stretched out still.

*Judaism* and *Christianity*. Isaiah 10.1-4

God did not make the honey bee
As big as a horse.
Had he made it so big, the bee would be stinging people to death.
God does not elevate
People who would ridicule the unfortunate.
God does not give power
To those who would be wicked to their fellowmen.
No one gains anything through being wicked.

When the wicked are prosperous,
And the righteous are not,
If the situation continues for long
The righteous become frustrated.
Like a small needle,
That is how one first starts the act of falsehood.
The day it becomes as big as a hoe,
It kills.

*African Traditional Religions*
Yoruba Song (Nigeria)

The Lord protected Khorasan from Babur's
invasion
And on Hindustan let loose terror.
The Lord Himself punishes not:
So He sent down the Mughal Babur, dealing
death as Yama.
As the people wailed in their agony of suffering,
Didst Thou feel no compassion for them?
Thou who art Creator of all—
Should a powerful foe molest one equally
powerful,
Little would the mind be grieved;
But when a ferocious tiger falls upon a herd of
kine,
Then must the Master be called to account.
These dogs [profligate rulers] that despoiled the
jewels [India's resources] and wasted them,
Now shameful will be their end.
Thou alone dost join and unjoin—
Such is the greatness of Thy might.
Whoever arrogates to himself greatness,
Tasting all pleasures to satiety,
In the eyes of the Lord is only a worm picking
grain.

*Sikhism*. Adi Granth, Asa, M.1, p. 360

The word that came to Jeremiah from the Lord, "Stand in the gate of the Lord's house, and proclaim there this word, and say, Hear the word of the Lord, all you men of Judah who enter these gates to worship the Lord. Thus says the Lord of Hosts, the God of Israel: Amend your ways and your doings, and I will let you dwell in this place. Do not trust in these deceptive words, 'This is the Temple of the Lord, the Temple of the Lord, the Temple of the Lord.'

"For if you truly amend your ways and your doings, if you truly execute justice one with another, if you do not oppress the alien, the fatherless or the widow, or shed innocent blood in this place, and if you do not go after other gods to your own hurt, then I will let you dwell in this place, in the land that I gave of old to your fathers forever.

"Behold, you trust in deceptive words to no avail. Will you steal, murder, commit adultery, swear falsely, burn incense to Baal, and go after other gods that you have not known, and then come and stand before me in this house, which is called by my name, and say, 'We are deliv-

**Isaiah 10.1-4:** Cf. 1 Samuel 2.4-9, p. 388.

**Asa, M.1:** This is another of Guru Nanak's meditations on the Mughal invasion of India. He concludes that it was justified by the profligacy and corruption of India's rulers. Cf. Asa Ashtpadi, M.1, p. 759.

ered!'—only to go on doing all these abominations? Has this house, which is called by my name, become a den of robbers in your eyes? Behold, I myself have seen it, says the Lord.

"Go now to my place that was at Shiloh, where I made my name dwell at first, and see what I did to it for the wickedness of my people Israel. And now, because you have done all these things, says the Lord, and when I spoke to you persistently you did not listen, and when I called you, you did not answer, therefore I will do to the House which is called by my name, and in which you trust, to the place which I gave to you and to your fathers, as I did to Shiloh. And I will cast you out of my sight, as I cast out all your kinsmen, all the offspring of Ephraim."

*Judaism* and *Christianity*. Jeremiah 7.1-15

God has reversed his usual course of procedure,
And the lower people are full of distress.
The words which you utter are not right;
The plans which you form are not far-reaching.
As there are not sages, you think you have no guidance;
You have no real sincerity.
Your plans do not reach far,
And I therefore carefully admonish you.

Heaven is now sending down calamities;
Do not be so complacent.
Heaven is now producing such movements;
Do not be so indifferent.
If your words were harmonious,
The people would become united.
If your words were gentle and kind,
The people would be settled.

Though my duties are different than yours,
I am your fellow servant.
I come to advise with you,
And you hear me with contemptuous indifference.
My words are about the present urgent affairs;
Do not think them matter for laughter.
The ancients had a saying:
"Consult the gatherers of grass and firewood."

Heaven is now exercising oppression;
Do not in such a way make a mock of things.
An old man, I speak with entire sincerity;
But you, my juniors, are full of pride.
It is not that my words are those of age,
But you make a joke of what is said.
But the troubles will multiply like flames,
Till they are beyond help or remedy.

Heaven is now displaying its anger;
Do not be either boastful or flattering,
Utterly departing from all propriety of demeanor,
Till good men are reduced to personators of the dead.
The people now sigh and groan,
And we dare not examine into the causes of their trouble.
The ruin and disorder are exhausting all their means of living,
And we show no kindness to our multitudes.

Heaven enlightens the people,
As the bamboo flute responds to the earthen whistle;
As two half-maces form a whole one;
As you take a thing, and bring it away in your hand,
Bringing it away, without any more ado.
The enlightenment of the people is very easy.
They have now so many perversities;
Do not you set up your perversity before them.

Revere the anger of Heaven,
And presume not to make sport or be idle.
Revere the changing moods of Heaven,
And presume not to drive about at your pleasure.
Great Heaven is intelligent,
And is with you in all your goings.

**Jeremiah 7.1-15:** In this, the Temple Sermon, Jeremiah castigates those who continued breaking God's covenant secure in the belief that God will never allow his Temple to be destroyed. He points to examples of old: the tabernacle at Shiloh which was destroyed by the Philistines, and the Northern Kingdom of Israel (Ephraim), which was conquered and exiled by Assyria. Note how he accuses them of violating the Ten Commandments: cf. Hosea 4.1-3, p. 222; Exodus 20.1-17, p. 110.

Great Heaven is clear-seeing,
And is with you in your wanderings and indulgences.

*Confucianism.* Book of Songs, Ode 254

The Thirty-three great gods assign the fortune of the king.
The ruler of men is created as son of all the gods,
To put a stop to unrighteousness, to prevent evil deeds,
To establish all beings in well-doing, and to show them the way to heaven.
Whether man, or god, or fairy, or demon,
Or outcaste, he is a true king who prevents evil deeds.
Such a king is mother and father to those who do good.
He was appointed by the gods to show the results of karma....

But when a king disregards the evil done in his kingdom,
And does not inflict just punishment on the criminal,
From his neglect of evil, unrighteousness grows apace,
And fraud and strife increase in the land.

The Thirty-three great gods grow angry in their palaces
When the king disregards the evil done in his kingdom.

Then the land is afflicted with fierce and terrible crime,
And it perishes and falls into the power of the enemy.
Then property, families, and hoarded wealth all vanish,
And with varied deeds of deceit men ruin one another.

Whatever his reasons, if a king does not do his duty
He ruins his kingdom, as a great elephant a bed of lotuses.

Harsh winds blow, and rain falls out of season,
Planets and stars are unpropitious, as are the moon and sun,
Corn, flowers, and fruit and seed do not ripen properly,
And there is famine, when the king is negligent...

Then all the kings of the gods say to one another,
"This king is unrighteous, he has taken the side of unrighteousness!"
Such a king will not for long anger the gods;
From the wrath of the gods his kingdom will perish....

He will be bereft of all that he values, whether by brother or son,
He will be parted from his beloved wife, his daughter will die.
Fire will fall from heaven, and mock-suns also.
Fear of the enemy and hunger will grow apace.
His beloved counselor will die, and his favorite elephant;
His favorite horses will die one by one, and his camels...
There will be strife and violence and fraud in all the provinces;
Calamity will afflict the land, and terrible plague....
Many ills such as these will befall the land
Whose king is partial in justice and disregards evil deeds....

Therefore a king should abandon his own precious life,
But not the jewel of Righteousness, whereby the world is gladdened.

*Buddhism.* Golden Light Sutra 12

**Book of Songs, Ode 254:** This poem is an admonition to the court, written by an elder official whose counsel is no longer being taken. He is evidently a former high official, yet he in humility numbers himself among 'the gatherers of grass and firewood.' Such admonitions were a traditional way of offering loyal, constructive criticism; cf. Book of History 4.8.1-3, pp. 748-49. The writer asserts that Heaven is displaying its anger and signaling its removal of the Mandate from a ruler by bringing floods, earthquakes, rebellions and civil strife, and inauspicious signs in the heavens; cf. Hosea 4.1-3, p. 222; Anguttara Nikaya i.50, p. 222.

**Golden Light Sutra 12:** This sutra is important for the Nichiren schools of Japanese Buddhism, where the teaching of Buddhism has been understood as defending the security of the nation. The Thirty-three

Thus says the Lord:
"For three transgressions of Damascus,
and for four, I will not revoke the punishment;
because they have threshed Gilead
with threshing sledges of iron.
So I will send a fire upon the house of Hazael,
and it shall destroy the strongholds of Ben-Hadad.
I will break the bar of Damascus,
and cut off the inhabitants from the valley of Aven,
and him that holds the scepter from Beth-Eden,
and the people of Syria shall go into exile to Kir," says the Lord.

Thus says the Lord:
"For three transgressions of Gaza,
and for four, I will not revoke the punishment;
because they carried into exile a whole people
to deliver them up to Edom.
So I will send a fire upon the wall of Gaza,
and it shall devour her strongholds.
I will cut off the inhabitants of Ashdod,
and him that holds the scepter from Ashkelon;
I will turn my hand against Ekron;
and the remnant of the Philistines shall perish," says the Lord God.

Thus says the Lord:
"For three transgressions of Tyre,
and for four, I will not revoke the punishment;
because they delivered up a whole people to Edom,
and did not remember the covenant of brotherhood.
So I will send a fire upon the wall of Tyre,
and it shall devour her strongholds."

Thus says the Lord:
"For three transgressions of Edom,
and for four, I will not revoke the punishment;
because he pursued his brother with the sword,
and cast off all pity,
and his anger tore perpetually,
and he kept his wrath forever.
So I will send a fire upon Teman,
and it shall devour the strongholds of Bozrah."

Thus says the Lord:
"For three transgressions of the Ammonites,
and for four, I will not revoke the punishment;
because they have ripped up women with child in Gilead,
that they might enlarge their border.
So I will kindle a fire in the wall of Rabbah,
and it shall devour her strongholds,
with shouting in the day of battle,
with a tempest in the day of the whirlwind;
and their king shall go into exile,
he and his princes together," says the Lord....

Thus says the Lord:
"For three transgressions of Israel,
and for four, I will not revoke the punishment;
because they sell the righteous for silver,
and the needy for a pair of shoes—
they that trample the head of the poor into the dust of the earth,
and turn aside the way of the afflicted;
a man and his father go in to the same maiden,
so that my holy name is profaned;
they lay themselves down beside every altar
upon garments taken in pledge;
and in the house of their God they drink
the wine of those who have been fined.

"Yet I destroyed the Amorite before them,
whose height was like the height of the cedars,
and who was as strong as the oaks;
I destroyed his fruit above,
and his roots beneath.
Also I brought you up out of the land of Egypt,
and led you forty years in the wilderness,
to possess the land of the Amorite.
And I raised up some of your sons for prophets,
and some of your young men for Nazirites.
Is it not indeed so, O people of Israel?" says the Lord.

"But you made the Nazirites drink wine,
and commanded the prophets,
saying, 'You shall not prophesy.'

gods are deities of an intermediate heaven who operate in the world of desires; they are therefore far subordinate to Ultimate Reality as manifest in the Buddha and in enlightened beings. They seem to have a role in manifesting the results of karma. Cf. Anguttara Nikaya i.50, p. 222; Precious Garland 327, p. 749.

"Behold, I will press you down in your place,
as a cart full of sheaves presses down.
Flight shall perish from the swift,
and the strong shall not retain his strength,
nor shall the mighty save his life;
he who handles the bow shall not stand,
and he who is swift of foot shall not save
himself,
nor shall he who rides the horse save his life;
and he who is stout of heart among the mighty
shall flee away naked in that day," says the
Lord.

*Judaism* and *Christianity*.
Amos 1.3-2.16

❖

**Amos 1.3-2.16:** Amos preaches that God's providence applies to all nations; each shall be punished for its sins. But his primary aim is to convict his own country of Israel. By beginning his prophecy with a catalogue of the sins of Israel's neighbors and enemies, this prophet could draw in his audience to approve his words, that is, until the final ironic stanzas where Israel herself receives words of judgment. The Amorites were the earlier inhabitants of Canaan who had been dispossessed by the Israelites; God allowed them to be destroyed because of their sins (see Deuteronomy 9.4-5). The Nazirites were those who devoted themselves to God and vowed not to drink wine or cut their hair; the most famous Nazirite was Samson.

# CHAPTER 21
# ESCHATOLOGY AND MESSIANIC HOPE

MOST RELIGIONS CONTAIN TEACHINGS THAT anticipate a time, beyond the present era of suffering and injustice, when human history will be consummated by a decisive act of God. Evil will be destroyed and goodness will triumph. Typically, the course of events includes three phases: a time of tribulation and confusion when evil and suffering grow more and more rampant; the Last Judgment when God intervenes decisively to destroy all evil; and the coming of a new age of bliss, often called the Kingdom of Heaven. Furthermore, this decisive transformation is often said to require a great leader, a Messiah, who will wield divine authority to destroy evil, establish the saints, and found a new age of unlimited happiness.

Teachings about the Last Days or the End of the World are most characteristic of the Jewish, Christian, and Islamic scriptures. Judaism anticipates the coming of the Messiah who will inaugurate an age of peace and justice on earth. Christianity teaches broadly that Christ, the Messiah, has already come to offer salvation, and he will come again to judge the world. Yet there are a variety of opinions within the Christian family about the details: For some Christ will return to bring judgment (Premillennialism); for some he will come after the progressive decline of evil to consummate the Kingdom of Heaven (Postmillennialism); still others reject millennialism altogether and interpret scriptural passages about the Last Judgment as concerning the spiritual fate of the individual soul. In Islam the Last Judgment is a cardinal doctrine. While it is sometimes understood as a spiritual judgment of the individual soul after death, many passages in the Qur'an clearly describe it as a world-transforming event to occur at the end of time, when the earth will be destroyed and all people will see their just rewards as they are sorted into groups bound for either Paradise or hell.

Hinduism, Buddhism, and Zoroastrianism contain teachings that the world is going through a cosmic cycle in which morals and religion have gradually decayed and have reached a state of dire corruption in this present age, identified as the Kali Yuga or Age of Degeneration of the Dharma. This Kali age will give way to a renovation of faith as the cycle turns and the earth enters a new golden age, the Krita age. Hindu scriptures predict that this cosmic change will be initiated by the advent of the new Avatar; Buddhist scriptures, by the Maitreya Buddha; and Zorastrian scriptures, by the Saoshyant.

Millenarian beliefs are a leavening influence in religion, and they sometimes produce religious or political innovation. Many sectarian movements and new religions began with a fervent belief that the last days had drawn nigh: Christianity itself began as a messianic sect of Judaism; Muhammad preached Islam believing that the Last Judgment was imminent; and the Baha'i Faith began as a messianic movement within Islam, to cite three examples. Millenarian beliefs have inspired oppressed peoples with the hope that the evil system has finally reached its last hour. Bloody rebellions have thus been spawned: The Bar Kochba Rebellion against Roman rule in Palestine (132-35 A.D.) was fought by Jews who believed that their leader was the promised Messiah. European peasants fired with the spirit of the Reformation and convined that the existing church and nobility served the powers of the Antichrist formed revolutionary chiliastic communities at Tabor and Münster. In China in the nineteenth century, the T'ai Ping Rebellion against the British colonizers was organized by secret societies embued with millenarian ideas. African independent churches with millenarian views were significant challenges to the European colonial authorities in the first half of the twentieth century; today these movements are seen as positive forces which foster self-respect and encourage economic and political independence. Considering the unprecedented pace of social change in the nineteenth and twentieth centuries—the unparalleled social dislocations and cultural challenges which have resulted from the world wars, liberation movements, industrialization and technological change, the atomic bomb, the environmental crisis, and the shrinking global village—it is not surprising that a large number of new religions and new sects of old religions have arisen which believe that the present is the time of tribulations preceding the appearance of the Messiah. And some regard their leader as either a forerunner or as the long-awaited Avatar or Messiah who will destroy the evil world-system, establish true religion, and inaugurate a new age.

❖

# *Tribulation*

THE PRELUDE TO THE CONSUMMATION OF HISTORY and the appearance of the Messiah will be a time of tribulation and confusion. Many passages describe how in the Last Days wars, famines, plagues, and natural disasters will abound and civilization will reach its nadir. People will become engrossed in materialism and hedonism, and love will grow cold. Buddhist and Hindu texts affirm that when the consummation is nigh even the civilizations of the contemporary Kali age will plummet to their lowest point.

In some scriptures, the last tribulation will be the appearance of the Beast, the Antichrist, or the Dajjal, who will deny the reality of God and deceive millions with a counterfeit truth. Exactly who the Antichrist might be has been the subject of much speculation, most of it fruitless: it is always possible to view the troubles of one's own time as proof that the tribulations have come, and to identify the Antichrist as a church's favorite opponent.

A number of texts describe the tribulation at the end of the age as primarily due to the decline of religion, as the inspiration of the founder is gradually forgotten and his teachings are corrupted. We record two passages from major religions predicting such a decline, and follow with two passages from new religions which describe the confusion at the turn of the age as due to the ossified teachings the old religions colliding with the inspiration coming with God's new dispensation.

In the evil age to come, living beings will decrease in good qualities and increase in utter arrogance, coveting gain and honors, developing their evil qualities, and being far removed from deliverance.

*Buddhism.* Lotus Sutra 13

But understand this, that in the last days there will come times of stress. For men will be lovers of self, lovers of money, proud, arrogant, abusive, disobedient to their parents, ungrateful, unholy, inhuman, implacable, slanderers, profligates, fierce, haters of good, treacherous, reckless, swollen with conceit, lovers of pleasure rather than lovers of God, holding the form of religion but denying the power of it.

*Christianity.* 2 Timothy 3.1-5

Society will be engulfed by ravaging wars, overflowing with havoc and devastation. In the beginning the conquerors will feel very happy over their successes and booties gathered therein, but it will all have a very sad end. I warn you of the wars of the future; you have no idea of the enormity of evil which they will carry.

*Islam.* Nahjul Balagha, Sermon 141

With the footprints [heralding] the Messiah, presumption shall increase and dearth reach its height; the vine shall yield its fruit but the wine shall be costly; and the empire shall fall into heresy and there shall be none to utter reproof. The academies shall be given to fornication, and... the wisdom of the scribes shall

**Lotus Sutra 13:** Nichiren, Japan's foremost exponent of the Lotus Sutra, believed his own time to be the Age of Degeneration of the Law (Jap. *Mappo*, Skt. *Saddharma-vipralopa*), which demands a restoration at its end. Hence many have expected the coming of the Maitreya, or restorer, who will inaugurate a new age. Some sects of Nichiren Buddhism such as Soka Gakkai and Rissho Kosei Kai identify Nichiren himself as the restorer. A tradition at Daisekiji speaks of a preserved tooth of Nichiren (compare the Tooth of Buddha Temple at Kandy in Sri Lanka), and the claim is that new flesh has grown around the tooth and hence the new age is dawning.

**2 Timothy 3.1-5:** Cf. Hadith of Tirmidhi, p. 316.

become insipid, and they that shun sin shall be deemed contemptible, and truth shall nowhere be found. Children shall shame the elders, and the elders shall rise up before the children. The face of this generation shall be [brazen] as the face of a dog, and the son will not be put to shame by his father. On whom can we stay ourselves? On our Father in heaven.

*Judaism*. Mishnah, Sota 9.15

The seed that was sown by a couple's fornication under the shade of a tree has now reached the season of harvest, and we find youth's immorality prevailing in all cities of the world.... [Adam and Eve's] fallen act sowed the seed of evil. They did it while they were still teenagers, at a premature stage: thus was the seed of evil sown. From this seed, the lineage of evil has come to prevail all throughout human society. Consequently, when the last days come, all youth throughout the world, like Adam and Eve, destroy the ethics of love. It has been forewarned in the Bible that the last days will be Satan's peak years. When this time comes, God's judgment will come with the rod of iron.

*Unification Church*.
Sun Myung Moon, 3-30-90

As Jesus sat on the Mount of Olives, the disciples came to him privately, saying, "Tell us, when will this be, and what will be the sign of your coming and of the close of the age?" And Jesus answered them, "Take heed that no one leads you astray. For many will come in my name, saying, 'I am the Christ,' and they will lead many astray. And you will hear of wars and rumors of wars; see that you are not alarmed; for this must take place, but the end is not yet. For nation will rise against nation, and kingdom against kingdom, and there will be famines and earthquakes in various places: all this is but the beginning of the birth pangs.

"Then they will deliver you up to tribulation, and put you to death; and you will be hated by all nations for my name's sake. And then many will fall away, and betray one another, and hate one another. And many false prophets will arise and lead many astray. And because wickedness is multiplied, most men's love will grow cold. But he who endures to the end will be saved. And this gospel of the kingdom will be preached throughout the whole world, as a testimony to all nations; and then the end will come....

"From the fig tree learn its lesson: as soon as its branch becomes tender and puts forth its leaves, you know that summer is near. So also, when you see all these things, you know that he is near, at the very gates."

*Christianity*. Matthew 24.3-14, 32-33

There will come a time, brethren, when... immoral courses of action will flourish excessively; there will be no word for moral among humans—far less any moral agent. Among such humans, homage and praise will be given to them who lack filial and religious piety, and show no respect to the head of the clan; just as today homage and praise are given to the filial-minded, to the pious and to them who respect the heads of their clans.

Among such humans, there will be no such thoughts of reverence as are a bar to intermarriage with mother, or mother's sister, or teacher's wife, or father's sister-in-law. The world will fall into promiscuity, like goats and sheep, fowls and swine, dogs and jackals.

Among such humans, keen mutual enmity will become the rule, keen ill will, keen animosity, passionate thoughts even of killing, in a mother toward her child, in a child toward its mother, in a father toward his child and a child toward its father, in brother to brother, in brother to sister, in sister to brother. Just as a sportsman feels toward game that he sees, so will they feel.

*Buddhism*.
Digha Nikaya iii.71-72,
Cakkavatti-Sihanada Suttanta

**Matthew 24.3-14, 32-33:** Cf. 1 Thessalonians 5.2-6, p. 528.

**Digha Nikaya iii.71-72:** The sutra faults the failures of early kings to establish the Dhamma as the root cause of humanity's decline; it goes on to state that this decline will be followed by a renewal and new golden age, see Digha Nikaya iii.74-75, pp. 792-93, and the appearance of the Maitreya Buddha, see Digha Nikaya iii.76, pp. 786-87.

Wealth and piety will decrease day by day, until the world will be totally depraved. Then property alone will confer rank; wealth will be the only source of devotion; passion will be the sole bond of union between the sexes; falsehood will be the only means of success in litigation; and women will be objects merely of sensual gratification. Earth will be venerated but for its mineral treasures; the Brahmanical thread will constitute a brahmin; external types will be the only distinction of the several orders of life; dishonesty will be the universal means of subsistence; weakness will be the cause of dependence; menace and presumption will be substituted for learning; liberality will be devotion; simple ablutions will be purification; mutual assent will be marriage; fine clothes will be dignity; and water afar off will be esteemed a holy spring. Amidst all castes he who is the strongest will reign over a principality, thus vitiated by many faults. The people, unable to bear the heavy burdens imposed upon them by their avaricious sovereigns, will take refuge amongst the valleys of the mountains, and will be glad to feed upon wild honey, herbs, roots, fruits, flowers, and leaves: their only covering will be the bark of trees, and they will be exposed to the cold and wind and sun and rain. No man's life will exceed three and twenty years. Thus in the Kali age shall decay constantly proceed, until the human race approaches its annihilation.

*Hinduism.* Vishnu Purana 4.24

And when the Word is fulfilled against the unjust, We shall produce from the earth a Beast to face them: he will speak to them, because that mankind did not believe with assurance in Our signs.

*Islam.* Qur'an 27.82

Let no one deceive you in any way; for that day will not come, unless the rebellion comes first, and the man of lawlessness is revealed, the son of perdition, who opposes and exalts himself against every so-called god or object of worship.... The coming of the lawless one by the activity of Satan will be with all power and with pretended signs and wonders, and with all wicked deception for those who are to perish, because they refused to love the truth and so be saved. Therefore God sends upon them a strong delusion, to make them believe what is false, so that all may be condemned who did not believe the truth but had pleasure in unrighteousness.

*Christianity.* 2 Thessalonians 2.3-12

There is no prophet who has not warned his people about the one-eyed liar [the Antichrist]. I tell you that he is one-eyed, but your Lord is not one-eyed. On his forehead are the letters *k*, *f*, *r* (infidelity).

The Dajjal will come forth having with him water and fire, and what mankind see as water will be fire which burns and what they see as fire will be cold, sweet water. Any of you who live till that time must fall into what they see as fire, for it is sweet, fresh water.

*Islam.* Hadiths of Bukhari and Muslim

And I saw a beast rising out of the sea, with ten horns and seven heads, with ten diadems upon its horns and a blasphemous name upon its heads. And the beast that I saw was like a leopard, its feet were like a bear's, and its mouth was like a lion's mouth. And to it the dragon gave his power and great authority. One of its heads seemed to have a mortal wound, but its mortal wound was healed, and the whole earth followed the beast with wonder. Men worshipped the dragon, for he had given his authority to the beast, and they worshipped the beast, saying, "Who is like the beast, and who can fight against it?"

And the beast was given a mouth uttering haughty and blasphemous words, and it was allowed to exercise authority for forty-two months; it opened its mouth to utter blasphemies against God, blaspheming his name and his dwelling, that is, those who dwell in heaven. Also it was allowed to make war on the saints and to conquer them. And authority was given it over every tribe and people and

**Vishnu Purana 4.24:** Cf. Laws of Manu 1.81-86, pp. 307-8; Bhagavad Gita 8.17-21, p. 78.

tongue and nation, and all who dwell on earth will worship it, every one whose name has not been written before the foundation of the world in the book of life of the Lamb that was slain....

Also it caused all, both small and great, both rich and poor, both free and slave, to be marked on the right hand or the forehead, so that no one can buy or sell unless he has the mark, that is, the name of the beast or the number of its name. This calls for wisdom: let him who has understanding reckon the number of the beast, for it is a human number, its number is six hundred and sixty-six.

*Christianity*. Revelation 13.1-18

The time is near in which nothing will remain of Islam but its name, and of the Qur'an but its mere appearance, and the mosques of Muslims will be destitute of knowledge and worship; and the learned men will be the worst people under the heavens; and contention and strife will issue from them, and it will return upon themselves.

*Islam*. Hadith

[Before the coming of the Maitreya, the holy religion will decline.] How will it occur? After my decease, first will occur the five disappearances. And what are the five disappearances? The disappearance of the attainments, the disappearance of the method, the disappearance of learning, the disappearance of the symbols, the disappearance of the relics. These are the five disappearances that are to occur.

The attainments: Only for a thousand years from the time the Blessed One passes into Nirvana will the priests be able to acquire the analytical sciences. Then as time goes on my disciples will attain only to never-returning, to once returning, to conversion. As long as such exist the disappearance of the attainments will not yet have occurred. But with the death of the last disciple that has attained to conversion, the attainments will have disappeared. This, O Shariputta, is the disappearance of the attainments.

Disappearance of the method: My disciples being unable to realize the trances, the insights, the Paths, and the Fruits, will keep only the four purities of conduct. Then as time goes on they will keep only the commandments forbidding the four deadly sins. As long as there are a hundred or a thousand priests who keep the commandments forbidding the four deadly sins, the disappearance of the method will not have occurred. But when the last priest shall break the precepts, or shall die, the method will have disappeared. This, O Shariputta, is the disappearance of the method.

Disappearance of learning: As long as the text of the Three Baskets, which is the word of the Buddha, and as long as their commentaries are extant, the disappearance of learning will not have occurred. But as time goes on there will be irreligious kings of base extraction, and the courtiers and others in authority will be irreligious, and then the country people throughout the kingdom will be irreligious. On account of their irreligion the god will not rain in due season, and the crops will not flourish properly. And when the crops do not flourish, those who are wont to give the reliances to the congregation of the priests will be unable to do

**Revelation 13.1-18:** The Beast represents human pretension to universal power, and imperial powers in every age have been identified as fulfilling this prophecy. Originally as written, the beast referred specifically to the Roman Empire. The pretensions of the Roman emperor to be a human god, whom all the world worshipped, were seen as a parody of Christ's true kingship. The 'seven heads' probably represent Rome with its seven hills; other features of the Beast: the ten horns, parts like a leopard, a bear, and a lion, resemble the four separate beasts in Daniel 7.2-7. Some scholars identify the miraculous healing of the wounded head to a legend which grew up around Emperor Nero, that he miraculously reappeared after his suicide in 68 A.D. The number 666 is the total numerical value of the letters "Nero Caesar" in the Aramaic langugage. Unbelievers and lapsed Christians worshipped the emperor; thus they were marked with the number of the Beast.

so any more. And the priests, not receiving the reliances, will not teach the novices, and as time goes on learning will disappear.... [and likewise with the disappearance of the symbols and the relics.]

*Buddhism*. Anagatavamsa

Concerning His words—"The sun shall be darkened, and the moon shall not give light, and the stars shall fall from heaven" [Matthew 24.29]... is intended the divines of the former Dispensation, who live in the days of the subsequent Revelations, and who hold the reins of religion in their grasp. If these divines be illuminated by the light of the latter Revelation they will be acceptable to God, and will shine with a light everlasting. Otherwise, they will be declared as darkened, even though to outward seeming they be leaders of men, inasmuch as belief and unbelief, guidance and error, felicity and misery, light and darkness, are all dependent upon the sanction of Him who is the Daystar of Truth....

In another sense, by the terms "sun," "moon," and "stars" are meant such laws and teachings as have been established and proclaimed in every Dispensation, such as the laws of prayer and fasting. These have, according to the law of the Qur'an, been regarded, when the beauty of the Prophet Muhammad had passed beyond the veil, as the most fundamental and binding laws of His dispensation....

Hence, it is clear and manifest that by the words "the sun shall be darkened, and the moon shall not give her light, and the stars shall fall from heaven" is intended the waywardness of the divines, and the annulment of laws firmly established by [prior] divine Revelation, all of which, in symbolic language, have been foreshadowed by the Manifestation of God....

It is unquestionable that in every succeeding Revelation the "sun" and "moon" of the teachings, laws, commandments, and prohibitions which have been established in the preceding Dispensation, and which have overshadowed the people of that age, become darkened, that is, are exhausted, and cease to exert their influence.

*Baha'i Faith*. Book of Certitude, 33-41

The providence of the new age does not start after the complete liquidation of the old age, but is born and grows in the circumstances of the period of consummation of the old age, always appearing to be in conflict with that age. Accordingly, this providence is not easily understood by those who are accustomed to the conventions of the old age. This is why the sages of history who came in charge of the providence of a new age all became victims of the old age. We can give the example of Jesus, who, coming at the close of the Old Testament Age as the center of the new providence of the New Testament Age, appeared to the believers of the Mosaic Law to be a heretic whom they could not understand. Finally, he was rejected because of their disbelief of him, and was crucified. This is why Jesus said, "New wine must be put into fresh wine skins" (Luke 5.38).

Christ will come again at the close of the New Testament Age as the center of the new providence to establish the new heaven and earth, and will give us new words for the building of the new age (Revelation 21.1-7). Therefore, he is apt to be rejected and perse-

**Anagatavamsa:** The Anagatavamsa, or History of Future Events, is a post-canonical text of Theravada Buddhism, written in Pali.

**Book of Certitude, 33-41:** In the Baha'i Faith, the Last Judgment is interpreted as the end of the old dispensations of religion and the beginning of the new dispensation centered on God's messenger Baha'u'llah. This is a typical understanding of many new religions—see also the following passage from the Unification Church—for which the last days are fulfilled not in cosmic cataclysm but in the coming of a new age, new truth, and new Messiah. This passage's teaching on the dimming of the authorities and teachings of the previous religions also parallels texts about traditional founders of religion as revealers of truth surpassing previous truths, such as Udana 73, p. 454, and 2 Corinthians 3.7-16, p. 454. Cf. Matthew 24.29-31, p. 784.

cuted by Christians at the time of the Second Advent just as Jesus was persecuted and derided by the Jews, who said he was possessed by Beelzebul, the Prince of Demons (Matthew 12.24). Therefore, Jesus predicted that first the Lord must suffer many things and be rejected by the generation at the time of the Second Advent (Luke 17.25). Therefore those who, in the transitional period of history, are tenaciously attached to the environment of the old age and comfortably entrenched in it will be judged along with the old age.

*Unification Church.* Divine Principle I.3.5.2

## *The Last Judgment*

HOPE IN A LAST JUDGMENT has always been an answer to the problem of theodicy. Evil will not spoil God's world forever. The dominion of evil in this world will finally be overthrown, and the righteousness of God will be vindicated, when he judges all humankind at the end of days. Evil will be vanquished once and for all, and the glorious realm of God's full sovereignty will appear—the Kingdom of God.

Variations on this theme are represented by the passages in this section. In passages from the Avesta and the Old Testament, the Last Judgment and the emerging Kingdom of God are said to occur on the earth. On the other hand, in the passages from the Qur'an and the New Testament, the earth will be destroyed and the redeemed will live in heaven. Consequently, the Last Judgment may be interpreted either as a supernatural event at the world's end—typically the stance of Islam and most strains of traditional Christianity—or as a social, political, and religious renovation of this world—a view common to Judaism and some new religions, for example in a passage cited below from a scripture of Sekai Kyusei Kyo, a new religion from Japan.

The kingdom of Heaven is like a net which was thrown into the sea and gathered fish of every kind; when it was full, men drew it ashore and sat down and sorted the good into vessels but threw away the bad. So it will be at the close of the age. The angels will come out and separate the evil from the righteous, and throw them into the furnace of fire; there men will weep and gnash their teeth.

*Christianity.* Matthew 13.47-50

And then when retribution
Shall come for their offenses,
Then, O Wise One, Thy Kingdom
Shall be established by Good Thought,
For those who, in fulfilment,
Deliver evil into the hands of Truth!

And then may we be those
Who make life renovated,
O Lord, Immortals of the Wise One,
And O Truth, bring your alliance,

**Divine Principle I.3.5.2:** On the rejection of Christ at the First Advent, see John 1.9-11, p. 428; Mark 6.1-4, p. 428, and related passages. For similar sentiments warning people about confusion surrounding the advent of the Messiah, see Hadith of Muslim, p. 785; Tablets of Baha'u'llah Revealed after the Kitab-i-Aqdas, 231-32, p. 788. On the Lord's suffering, see Sun Myung Moon, 5-1-77, pp. 434-35.

**Matthew 13.47-50:** Cf. Matthew 16.27, p. 126; Lotus Sutra 16, p. 791.

That to us your minds may gather
Where wisdom would be in dispute!

Then, indeed, shall occur
The collapse of the growth of evil,
Then they shall join the promised reward:
Blessed abode of Good Thought,
Of the Wise One, and of Right,
They who earn in good reputation!

*Zoroastrianism*. Avesta, Yasna 30.8-10

For the windows of heaven are opened,
and the foundations of the earth tremble.
The earth is utterly broken,
the earth is rent asunder,
the earth is violently shaken.
The earth staggers like a drunken man,
it sways like a hut;
its transgression lies heavy upon it,
and it falls, and will not rise again.
On that day the Lord will punish
the hosts of heaven, in heaven,
and the kings of the earth, on the earth.
They will be gathered together as prisoners in a pit;
they will be shut up in a prison,
and after many days they will be punished.
Then the moon will be confounded,
and the sun ashamed;
for the Lord of hosts will reign on Mount Zion and in Jerusalem
and before its elders he will manifest his glory.

*Judaism* and *Christianity*. Isaiah 24.18-23

When the Trumpet shall sound one blast
And the earth with its mountains shall be lifted up and crushed with one crash,
Then, on that day, will the Event befall.
Heaven will split asunder, for that day it will be frail,
The angels will be on its sides, and eight will uphold the Throne of their Lord that day, above them.
On that day you will be exposed; not a secret of yours will be hidden.
Then, as for him who is given his record in his right hand, he will say, "Take, read my book!
Surely I knew that I should have to meet my reckoning."
Then he will be in blissful state
In a high Garden
Whose clusters are in easy reach.
[They will say to him,] "Eat and drink at ease for that you sent on before you in past days."
But as for him who is given his record in his left hand, he will say, "Oh, would that I had not been given my book
And knew not what my reckoning!
Oh, would that it had been death!
My wealth has not availed me,
My power has gone from me."
"Take him and fetter him
And then expose him to hellfire.
Then insert him in a chain of seventy cubits' length.
Lo! He used not to believe in God the Tremendous,
And urged not on the feeding of the wretched,
Therefore has he no lover here this day,
Nor any food save filth
Which none but sinners eat."

*Islam*. Qur'an 69.13-37

Scoffers will come in the last days with scoffing, following their own passions and saying, "Where is the promise of [Christ's] coming? For ever since the fathers fell asleep, all things have continued as they were from the beginning of creation." They deliberately ignore this fact, that by the word of God heavens existed long ago, and an earth formed out of water and by means of water, through which the world that then existed was deluged with water and perished. But by the same word the heavens and the earth have been stored up for fire, being kept until the day of judgment and

**Yasna 30.8-10:** 'Good Thought,' 'Truth,' and 'Immortals of the Wise One' are personified attributes of the Wise Lord. See Yasna 43.5, p. 126; 48.4, p. 290; Zamyad Yasht 19.11-12, p. 794. On the triumph of truth, cf. Qur'an 17.85, p. 380; Ramkali-ki-Var, M.1, p. 243.

**Isaiah 24.18-23:** Cf. Isaiah 2.12-17, pp. 290-91.

**Qur'an 69.13-37:** Cf. Qur'an 17.13-14, pp. 242-43; 39.68-75, pp. 244-45; 99, pp. 711-12; also Revelation 20.11-12, p. 243.

destruction of ungodly men. But do not ignore this one fact, beloved, that with the Lord one day is as a thousand years, and a thousand years as one day. The Lord is not slow about his promise as some count slowness, but is forbearing toward you, not wishing that any should perish, but that all should reach repentance. But the the day of the Lord will come like a thief, and then the heavens will pass away with a loud noise, and the elements will be dissolved with fire, and the earth and the works that are upon it will be burned up.

*Christianity*. 2 Peter 3.3-10

Deem not that God is unaware of what the wicked do. He but gives them a respite till a day when eyes shall stare [in terror], as they come hurrying on in fear, their heads upraised, their gaze returning not to them, and their hearts as air. And warn mankind of a day when the doom will come upon them, and those who did wrong will say, "Our Lord! Reprieve us for a little while. We will obey Thy call and will follow the Messengers." [It will be answered,] "Did you not swear before that there would be no end for you? And have you not dwelt in the dwellings of those who wronged themselves of old and has it not become plain to you how We dealt with them, and made examples for you? Verily they have plotted their plot, and their plot is with God, though their plot were one whereby mountains should be moved. So think not that God will fail to keep His promise to His Messengers. Lo! God is Mighty, Able to Requite.

On the day when the earth will be changed to other than the earth, and the heavens likewise, and they will come forth unto God, the One, the Almighty. You will see the guilty on that day linked together in chains, their raiment of pitch, and the Fire covering their faces—that God may repay each soul what it has earned. Lo! God is swift at reckoning.

*Islam*. Qur'an 14.42-51

Civilization as we know it is only transitory; it will finally pass away as the new age dawns and the true civilization is born. That will mark the end of the "provisional" world we live in today. God wills a reckoning for the old civilization and the establishment of a new one, and the time of His reckoning is at last drawing near.

Until now evil forces have had wide latitude in civilization, but in the transition from the old to the new, they will be weeded out. All people will go through an inexorable process of cleansing. The world will be terribly afflicted in payment for untold sins gathered over millennia. The great affliction is the sign that all societies and nations are being purified, and it will lift humankind to a new level of existence where good prevails.

The transition, which is actually upon us now, is the last stage before the beginning of an earthly paradise. In the upheaval, every sphere of life and every corner of civilization will be transformed. Those who believe in God and repent will witness the coming of the new world, and they will be able to start on the road to salvation. But those still heavily burdened with sin and unable to overcome their malicious ways will end this life in absolute misery and may find no salvation in the next.

*Sekai Kyusei Kyo*. Johrei

❖

**2 Peter 3.3-10:** Peter is urging patience to Christians who misunderstood the promise of Christ's Second Coming, thinking that it should have occurred within a few years after his Ascension. Cf. 1 Thessalonians 5.2-6, p. 528; John 12.46-50, p. 454.

# *The Messiah*

THE SCRIPTURES OF MANY RELIGIONS speak of a coming leader who will consummate the fulfillment of the divine will on earth. He will manifest in his person the righteousness and compassion of God, bring about the final defeat of evil, and establish the Kingdom of Heaven on earth. The Hebrew title Messiah—Christ in Greek—means "anointed one," that person who will be specially chosen by God for this mission and empowered to accomplish it. But while the term Messiah is specific to only a few religions, prophecies that a leader will come and accomplish such a mission are nearly universal. Religions call him by various names: Jews long for the promised Messiah; for Christians the Messiah is Jesus of Nazareth, who has already come and ascended to heaven but will reappear (perhaps in a new guise) at his Second Coming. Muslims also expect the second advent of Jesus, who will come as a Muslim Imam, and among Shiite Muslims there are various expectations of a future Imam Mahdi. Buddhist sutras prophesy the coming of the Maitreya Buddha; Vaishnavite Hindu scriptures prophesy the future descent of an avatar named Kalki; Zoroastrian scriptures prophesy the coming of the Saoshyant; and some Confucian texts speak of a future True Man who will finally bring peace to the world by perfectly instituting the Way of Confucius.

"Surely I am coming soon." Amen. Come, Lord Jesus!

*Christianity*. Revelation 22.20

For to us a child is born,
to us a son is given,
and the government shall be upon his shoulder,
and his name shall be called
"Wonderful Counsellor, Mighty God,
Everlasting Father, Prince of Peace."
Of the increase of his government and of peace
there will be no end,
upon the throne of David, and over his kingdom,
to establish it, and to uphold it
with justice and with righteousness,
from this time forth and for ever more.
The zeal of the Lord of hosts will do this.

*Judaism* and *Christianity*. Isaiah 9.6-7

I saw in the night visions,
and behold, with the clouds of heaven
there came one like a son of man.
He came to the Ancient of Days
and was presented before him.
And to him was given dominon
and glory and kingdom,
that all peoples, nations, and languages
should serve him.
His dominion is an everlasting dominion,
which shall not pass away.
And his kingdom one
that shall not be destroyed.

*Judaism* and *Christianity*. Daniel 7.13-14

**Isaiah 9.6-7:** See Isaiah 42.1-4, pp. 367-68.

**Daniel 7.13-14:** The 'son of man' is given dominion after the last beast is slain; see Revelation 13.1-18, pp. 777-78n. Chrisitians identify the son of man with Jesus, and thus is the term used in the Gospels; see the following passage.

Immediately after the tribulation of those days the sun will be darkened, and the moon will not give its light, and the stars will fall from heaven, and the powers of the heavens will be shaken; then will appear the sign of the Son of man in heaven, and then all the tribes of the earth will mourn, and they will see the Son of man coming on the clouds of heaven with power and great glory; and he will send out his angels with a loud trumpet call, and they will gather his elect from the four winds, from one end of heaven to the other.

*Christianity*. Matthew 24.29-31

Then I saw heaven opened, and behold, a white horse! He who sat upon it is called Faithful and True, and in righteousness he judges and makes war. His eyes are like a flame of fire, and on his head are many diadems, and he has a name inscribed which no one knows but himself. He is clad in a robe dipped in blood, and the name by which he is called is The Word of God. And the armies of heaven, arrayed in fine linen, white and pure, followed him on white horses. From his mouth issues a sharp sword with which to smite the nations, and he will rule them with a rod of iron; he will tread the wine press of the fury of the wrath of God the Almighty. On his robe and on his thigh he has a name inscribed, King of kings and Lord of lords.

*Christianity*. Revelation 19.11-16

Rabbi Joshua ben Levi met Elijah at the mouth of the cave of Rabbi Simeon ben Yohai. He asked Elijah, "When will the Messiah come?" Elijah replied, "Go and ask him." "But where is he?" "At the gate of Rome." "And how shall I recognize him?" "He sits among the wretched who are suffering from sores; all the others uncover all their wounds, and then bind them all up again, but he uncovers and binds up each one separately, for he thinks, 'Lest I should be summoned and be detained.'"

Then Rabbi Joshua found him and said to him, "Peace be with you, my Master and Rabbi." The Messiah replied, "Peace be with you, son of Levi." He said, "When is the Master coming?" He replied, "Today."

Then Rabbi Joshua returned to Elijah, who said, "What did he say to you?" He replied, "Peace be with you, son of Levi." Elijah said, "Then he assured to you and your father a place in the world to come." The rabbi said, "He spoke falsely to me, for he said he would come today, and he has not come." Then Elijah said, "He meant 'today, if you hearken to His voice!' [Psalm 95.7]."

*Judaism*. Talmud, Sanhedrin 98a

In the time to come... the Patriarchs will say, "Ephraim, our righteous Messiah, though we are your ancestors, you are greater than we. For you have borne the sins of our children, and you have borne heavy punishments, such as neither the former nor the latter generations have endured, and you became the laughter and the mocking of the nations for Israel's sake, and you sat in darkness, and your eyes saw no light. And your skin shrank upon your bones, and your body withered like a tree, and your eyes grew dark from fasting, and your strength dried up like a potsherd, and all this befell you because of the sins of our children. Is it your will that your children should enjoy the felicity which God has destined to give them in abundance? Perhaps because of the pains which you have endured in overflowing measure for their

**Matthew 24.29-31:** This passage occurs in the context of Jesus' discourse on the Mount of Olives; see Matthew 24.3-14, 32-33, p. 776. For a reinterpretation, see Book of Certitude, 33-41, p. 779.

**Revelation 19.11-16:** This is the image of the conquering Messiah, the King of kings, who brings judgment upon the beast—see Revelation 13.1-18, pp. 777-78—and all wickedness. The sharp sword which issues from his mouth symbolizes the power of the king's decree: that is the Word of God. He has a name known only to himself.

**Sanhedrin 98a:** Rabbinic Judaism learned to live with the seemingly never ending delay of the Bible's messianic promises. It turned inward, having been purged of all political ambition after the disastrous defeats in the Jewish War (68-70 A.D.) and the Bar Kochba Rebellion (132 A.D.). Here the historical promise of the coming of the Messiah is transformed to a personal encounter of faith. Elijah functions as a heavenly interpreter of God's secrets; cf. Baba Metzia 59ab, pp. 561-62. On the Messiah's suffering, see Isaiah 53.1-12, pp. 457-58, and the following passage; also Divine Principle I.3.5.2, pp. 779-80.

sakes, and because you have lain fettered in prison, your mind is not at rest because of them?" Messiah will reply, "Patriarchs, all that I have done, I have done only for your sakes and for your children, and for your honor and theirs, so that they may enjoy the felicity which God has destined for them in abundance." Then they reply, "May your mind be appeased, for you have appeased the mind of your Creator and our mind."

*Judaism.* Pesikta Rabbati 162b-63a

And [Jesus] shall be a Sign of the Hour [of Judgment]; therefore have no doubt about it, but follow Me: this is a straight way.

*Islam.* Qur'an 43.61

The Messenger of Allah observed, "What will be your state when the Son of Mary descends amongst you, and there will be an Imam amongst you? What would you do when the son of Mary would descend and lead you?"

*Islam.* Hadith of Muslim

The Apostle of Allah said, "Were there remaining but one day of the duration of all time, God would send forth a man from the people of my house, who will fill the earth with equity as it has been filled with oppression."

*Islam.* Hadith of Abu Dawud

The Imam who will create a world state will make the ruling nations pay for their crimes against society. He will bring succor to humanity. He will take out the hidden wealth from the breast of the earth and will distribute it equitably amongst the needy deserving. He will teach you simple living and high thinking. He will make you understand that virtue is a state of character which is always a mean between the two extremes, and which is based upon equity and justice. He will revive the teaching of the Holy Qur'an and the traditions of the Holy Prophet after the world had ignored them as dead letters....

He will protect and defend himself with resources of science and supreme knowledge. His control over these resources will be complete. He will know how supreme they are and how carefully they will have to be used. His mind will be free from desires of bringing harm and injury to humanity. Such a knowledge to him will be like the property which was wrongly possessed by others and for which he was waiting for the permission to repossess and use.

He, in the beginning, will be like a poor stranger unknown and uncared for, and Islam then will be in the hopeless and helpless plight of an exhausted camel who has laid down its head and is wagging its tail. With such a start he will establish an empire of God in this world. He will be the final demonstration and proof of God's merciful wish to acquaint man with the right ways of life.

*Islam.* Nahjul Balagha, Sermon 141 and 187

He shall be the victorious Benefactor (*Saoshyant*) by name and World-renovator (*Astavat-ereta*) by name. He is Benefactor because he will benefit the entire physical world; he is World-renovator because he will establish the physical living existence indestructible. He will oppose the evil of the progeny of the biped and withstand the enmity produced by the faithful.

*Zoroastrianism.* Avesta, Farvardin Yasht 13.129

**Pesikta Rabbati 162b-63a:** This rabbinic conception of a suffering Messiah who takes upon himself the sins of Israel stands alongside the older belief that the Messiah would come as a conquering king. This is undoubtedly a midrash on Isaiah 53.1-12, pp. 457-58. Compare the standard Christian interpretation of that prophecy as a description of the vicarious suffering of Jesus Christ for the sins of humankind.

**Qur'an 43.61:** Many Muslims await the Second Coming of Christ, who will come to herald the Last Judgment.

**Hadith of Muslim:** In this tradition, Christ will appear in the flesh as a Muslim Imam. Yet most people will not heed, their faith being corrupt; compare Divine Principle I.3.5.2, pp. 779-80.

**Nahjul Balagha, Sermon 141 and 187:** These are prophecies of the Imam Mahdi, who will come to establish God's kingdom throughout the whole world and restore true faith.

Whenever the Law declines and the purpose of life is forgotten, I manifest myself on earth. I am born in every age to protect the good, to destroy evil, and to reestablish the Law.

*Hinduism.* Bhagavad Gita 4.7-8

When the practices taught by the Vedas and the institutes of law shall nearly have ceased, and the close of the Kali age shall be nigh, a portion of that divine being who exists of his own spiritual nature in the character of Brahma, and who is the beginning and the end, and who comprehends all things, shall descend upon the earth. He will be born as Kalki in the family of an eminent brahmin of Sambhala village, endowed with the eight superhuman faculties. By his irresistible might he will destroy all the barbarians and thieves, and all whose minds are devoted to iniquity. He will then reestablish righteousness upon earth; and the minds of those who live at the end of the Kali age shall be awakened, and shall be as pellucid as crystal. The men who are thus changed by virtue of that peculiar time shall be as the seeds of human beings, and shall give birth to a race who shall follow the laws of the Krita age, the Age of Purity. As it is said, "When the sun and moon, and the luner asterism Tishya, and the planet Jupiter, are in one mansion, the Krita age shall return."

*Hinduism.* Vishnu Purana 4.24

Thus have I heard: At one time the Buddha was staying near Kapilavatthu in the Banyan monastery on the bank of the river Rohani. Then the venerable Sariputta questioned the Lord about the future Conquerer,

The Hero that shall follow you,
The Buddha—of what sort will he be?
I want to hear of him in full.
Let the Visioned One describe him.

When he heard the elder's speech the Lord spoke thus,

I will tell you, Sariputta;
listen to my speech.
In this auspicious eon
Three leaders there have been:
Kakusandha, Konagamana,
and the leader Kassapa too.
I am now the perfect Buddha;
and there will be Maitreya too
before this same auspicious eon
runs to the end of its years.

*Buddhism.* Anagatavamsa

In those days, brethren, there will arise in the world an Exalted One named Metteya. He will be an Arahant, Fully Awakened, abounding in wisdom and goodness, happy, with knowledge of the worlds, unsurpassed as a guide to mortals willing to be led, a teacher for gods and men, an Exalted One, a Buddha, even as I am now. He, by himself, will thoroughly know and see, as it were face to face, this universe, with its worlds of the spirits, its Brahmas and its Maras, and its world of recluses and brahmins, of princes and peoples, even as I now, by myself, thoroughly know and see them. The Law, lovely in its origin, lovely in its progress, lovely in its consummation, will he proclaim, both in the spirit and in the letter; the higher life will he make known, in all its fulness and in all its purity, even as I do now. He will be accompa-

**Bhagavad Gita 4.7-8:** This is the classic verse on the doctrine of Vishnu's incarnations or avatars. Of the ten classical avatars of Vishnu, nine have come in the past: the fish, the tortoise, the boar, the man-lion, the dwarf, Rama, Rama-with-the-Axe, Krishna, and the Buddha. The tenth avatar is the future savior, Kalki (see below). In addition, many leaders of sectarian Hindu movements such as Chaitanya (1486-1533), Ramakrishna (1836-1886), Sri Aurobindo (1872-1950), his wife Mira Richard "the Mother" (1878-1973), Meher Baba (1894-1969), and Satya Sai Baba (1926-) are revered as avatars whose missions will culminate in the coming of a new age for humanity. Cf. Srimad Bhagavatam 1.1, p. 467.

**Anagatavamsa:** The Maitreya (Pali *Metteya*) is predicted to be the future Buddha in the scriptures of both Theravada and Mahayana Buddhism. In both traditions some consider him as the future leader who will usher in the new age of bliss and consummation. On the Anagatavamsa, see pp. 778-79n.

nied by a congregation of some thousands of brethren, even as I am now accompanied by a congregation of some hundreds of brethren.

*Buddhism.* Digha Nikaya iii.76, Cakkavatti-Sihanada Suttanta

Listen attentively with one heart. A man whose spirit shines brightly, a man whose mind is completely unified, a man whose virtue excels everyone—such a man will truly appear in this world. When he preaches precious laws, all the people will totally be satisfied as if the thirsty drink sweet drops of rain from heaven. And each and every one will attain the path of liberation from struggles.

*Buddhism.* Sutra of the Great Accomplishment of the Maitreya

Miroku, the Great God, comes forth, endowed with the great strength of the three in one—Fire, Water, Earth.
Miroku, the Great God, from of old has planted heaven upon earth.
Miroku, the Great God, even as comes a thief, has secretly been born below.
Leaving behind the highly exalted throne to bring salvation, Miroku has been born below.

*Sekai Kyusei Kyo.* Inori-no-Shu

Confucius said, "If a Kingly Man were to arise, within a single generation Goodness would prevail."

*Confucianism.* Analects 13.12

It is only the man with the most perfect divine moral nature who is able to combine in himself quickness of apprehension, intelligence and understanding—qualities necessary for the exercise of command, magnanimity, generosity, benignity, and gentleness—qualities necessary for the exercise of patience, originality, energy, strength of character, and determination—qualities necessary for the exercise of endurance, piety, noble seriousness, order, and regularity—qualities necessary for the exercise of dignity, grace, method, subtlety, and penetration—qualities necessary for the exercise of critical judgment.

Thus all-embracing and vast is the nature of such a man. Profound it is and inexhaustible, like a living spring of water, ever running out with life and vitality. All-embracing and vast, it is like Heaven. Profound and inexhaustible, it is like the abyss.

As soon as such a man shall make his appearance in the world, all people will reverence him. Whatever he says, all people will believe it. Whatever he does, all people will be pleased with it. Thus his fame and name will spread and fill all the civilized world, extending even to savage countries, wherever ships and carriages reach, wherever the labor and enterprise of man penetrate, wherever the heavens overshadow and the earth sustain, wherever the sun and moon shine, wherever frost and dew fall. All who have life and breath will honor and love him. Therefore we may say, "He is the equal of God."

It is only he in this world, who has realized his absolute self, that can order and adjust the great relations of human society, fix the fundamental principles of morality, and understand the laws of growth and reproduction of the universe.

Now, where does such a man derive his power and knowledge, except from himself? How simple and self-contained his true manhood! How unfathomable the depth of his mind! How infinitely grand and vast the moral height of his nature! Who can understand such a nature except he who is gifted with the most perfect intelligence and endowed with the highest divine qualities of character, and who

**Sutra of the Great Accomplishment of the Maitreya:** This is from one of the Six Maitreya Sutras in the Chinese Buddhist canon.

**Inori-no-Shu:** Miroku is the Japanese word for Maitreya, the future Buddha. In the Japanese new religions of the Omoto group, Maitreya is featured as the inaugurator of the new age, the eschatological Kingdom of Heaven on earth.

has reached in his moral development the level of the gods?

*Confucianism.*
Doctrine of the Mean 31-32

O peoples of the earth! By the righteousness of God! Whatever you have been promised in the Books of your Lord, the Ruler of the Day of Return has appeared and been made manifest. Beware lest the changes and chances of the world hold you back from Him who is the Sovereign Truth.

*Baha'i Faith.* Tablets of Baha'u'llah
Revealed after the Kitab-i-Aqdas, 231-32

❖

**Doctrine of the Mean 31-32:** These two chapters express the ideal of the Kingly Man who is to come. On the one hand, they apply to Confucius, and many hold that these chapters were written in praise of him. On the other hand, they anticipate one who has yet to make his appearance in the world.

**Tablets of Baha'u'llah Revealed after the Kitab-i-Aqdas, 231-32:** Many of the messianic religions which have arisen in modern societies have utopian and universalist visions which embrace the entire globe. Thus, in the Baha'i Faith the new Messiah, Baha'u'llah, realizes in his person the missions of all the redemeers prophesied by the various world religions. See also Divine Principle I.3.4.3, p. 796.

# *The Kingdom of Heaven*

THE HOPE FOR THE ADVENT of the millennium, an ideal world, a world without evil, a world in which God's sovereignty is fully manifest, is present to some degree in every world religion. However, this hope is most strongly expressed in the scriptures of Judaism, Christianity, and Islam (and the new religions which stem from them), where it is not only a hope but the firm promise of God. Sometimes the term Kingdom of Heaven denotes a spiritual ideal, a state of bliss beyond death—see *Heaven*, pp. 247-52; but that sense of the term does not do justice to the most thoroughgoing eschatological visions. We are concerned in this chapter with the hope of an ideal future that is to be realized in this world. Furthermore, calling this ideal the Kingdom of Heaven is not necessarily meant to connote that its political system should be a monarchy; it is rather a spiritual vision of God reigning on earth and dwelling with the people.

These passages regard the Kingdom of Heaven from several vantage points. First, it is a world of God's absolute sovereignty; his will alone will be exalted. Righteousness, peace, prosperity, and joy will prevail, gladdening all humanity. Second, human beings will be perfected in character, knowing intimately the heart and will of God and rejoicing in the practice of the heavenly Way. They will have no inward impediments to doing good. Third, death will be no more, or the dead will return in a general resurrection. Fourth, the Kingdom of Heaven will be an ideal community, symbolized by Zion, the Holy City, the New Jerusalem. Finally, we offer passages from several new religions which connect the dawning of this ideal world with the progress of human civilization in this century.

The sovereignty on that day will be God's. He will judge between them.

*Islam*. Qur'an 22.56

The Lord will become king over all the earth; on that day the Lord will be one and his name one.

*Judaism* and *Christianity*. Zechariah 14.9

The seventh angel blew his trumpet, and there were loud voices in heaven, saying, "The kingdom of this world has become the kingdom of our Lord and of his Christ, and he shall reign for ever and ever."

*Christianity*. Revelation 11.15

All Israel shall have part in the World to Come, as it is said, "And the people shall be all righteous; they shall inherit the land forever, the branch of my planting, the work of my hands that I may be glorified" [Isaiah 60.21].

*Judaism*. Mishnah, Sanhedrin 11.1

On the day when We shall roll up heaven as a scroll is rolled for the writings; as We originated the first creation, so We shall bring it back again—a promise binding on Us; so We shall do. For We have written in the Psalms, after the Remembrance, "The earth shall be the inheritance of My righteous servants."

*Islam*. Qur'an 21.104-5

**Qur'an 22.56:** Cf. Qur'an 9.33, p. 367; Hadith of Ahmad, p. 367.
**Zechariah 14.9:** Cf. Isaiah 45.22-23, p. 367; The Lord's Prayer, p. 30.
**Revelation 11.15:** Cf. The Lord's Prayer, p. 30.

Blessed are the meek, for they shall inherit the earth.
Blessed are those who hunger and thirst for righteousness, for they shall be satisfied.
Blessed are the merciful, for they shall obtain mercy.
Blessed are the pure in heart, for they shall see God.
Blessed are the peacemakers, for they shall be called sons of God.
Blessed are those who are persecuted for righteousness' sake, for theirs is the kingdom of Heaven.

*Christianity*. Matthew 5.5-10

We therefore hope in Thee, O Lord our God, that we shall soon behold the triumph of Thy might, idolatry will be uprooted from the earth, and falsehood be utterly destroyed.

We hope for the day when the world will be perfected under the dominion of the Almighty and all mankind learn to revere Thy name; when all the wicked of the earth will be drawn in penitence unto Thee.

O may all the inhabitants of the world recognize that unto Thee every knee must bend, every tongue pledge loyalty. Before Thee, O Lord our God, may they bow in worship, and give honor to Thy glorious name.

May they all acknowledge Thy kingdom, and may Thy dominion be established over them speedily and forevermore. For sovereignty is Thine, and to all eternity Thou wilt reign in glory.

*Judaism*. Daily Prayer Book: Alenu

If kings and barons would but possess themselves of [Tao],
The ten thousand creatures would flock to do them homage;
Heaven and earth would conspire
To send Sweet Dew.
Without law or compulsion, men would dwell in harmony....
To Tao all under heaven will come
As streams and torrents flow into a great river or sea.

*Taoism*. Tao Te Ching 32

It shall come to pass in the latter days
that the mountain of the house of the Lord
shall be established as the highest of the mountains,
and shall be raised above the hills;
and all the nations shall flow to it;
and many peoples shall come, saying,
"Come, let us go up to the mountain of the Lord,
to the house of the God of Jacob;
that he may teach us his ways
and that we may walk in his paths."
For out of Zion shall go forth the law,
and the word of the Lord from Jerusalem.
He shall judge between the nations,
and shall decide for many peoples;
and they shall beat their swords into ploughshares,
and their spears into pruning hooks;
nation shall not lift up sword against nation,
neither shall they learn war any more.

*Judaism* and *Christianity*. Isaiah 2.2-4

Now is the gracious Lord's ordinance promulgated,
No one shall cause another pain or injury;
All mankind shall live in peace together,
Under a shield of administrative benevolence.

*Sikhism*. Sri Raga, M.5, p. 74

This world differs from the days of the Messiah only in respect of servitude to foreign powers.

*Judaism*. Talmud, Sanhedrin 99a

**Matthew 5.5-10:** See p. 155n.

**Alenu:** Cf. Isaiah 2.12-17, pp. 290-91; 45.22-23, p. 367; Kaddish, p. 30.

**Tao Te Ching 32:** Cf. Tao Te Ching 80, pp. 198-99, for a vision of a world at peace and where people will live a simple and contented life.

**Isaiah 2.2-4:** Cf. Isaiah 42.1-4, pp. 367-68; 45.22-23, p. 367; 1 Samuel 2.4-9, p. 388.; Matthew 23.12, p. 387.

**Sanhedrin 99a:** The variety of conceptions about the World to Come in Judaism is evidenced by comparing this conservative statement by Rab Samuel with some of the others in this section which speculate on more radical transformations.

What is the difference between our times and the messianic times? Purity and attainment of knowledge.

*Judaism.* Zohar, Genesis 139a

In the messianic future the Holy One will heal the injury [of Adam's sin]. He will heal the wound of the world.

*Judaism.* Genesis Rabbah 10.4

Beloved, we are God's children now; it does not yet appear what we shall be, but we know that when he appears we shall be like him.

*Christianity.* 1 John 3.2

Some persons asked the Prophet, "Shall we see God on the day of resurrection?" He answered, "Do you feel any trouble in seeing the moon on the night when it is full? Do you feel any trouble in seeing the sun on a cloudless day?" They answered, No. He said, "In the same way you will see your Lord."

*Islam.* Hadith of Muslim

For our knowledge is imperfect and our prophecy is imperfect; but when the perfect comes, the imperfect will pass away. When I was a child, I spoke like a child, I thought like a child, I reasoned like a child; when I became a man, I gave up childish ways. For now we see in a mirror dimly, but then face to face. Now I know in part; then I shall understand fully.

*Christianity.* 1 Corinthians 13.9-12

While the living see, at the kalpa's end,
The conflagration in its burning,
Tranquil remains this realm of mine,
Ever full of gods and men,
Parks and many palaces,
With every sort of gem adorned,
Blooming and fruitful jewel trees,
Where all creatures pleasure take;
The gods strike up their heavenly drums
And music make for evermore,
Showering down celestial flowers
On Buddha and his mighty host.

My Pure Land is not destroyed,
Though all view it as being burned up,
And grief and horror and distress
Thus fill them to the full.
Those creatures, full of sin
By reason of their evil karma,
Throughout kalpas numberless hear not
The name of the most Precious Three.
But those who virtuous deeds shall do,
Are gentle and of upright nature,
These will ever me behold
Here expounding to all the Law.

*Buddhism.* Lotus Sutra 16

"Be holy unto your God" [Numbers 15.40]. As long as you execute the commandments, you are sanctified, but if you separate yourself from the commandments, you are profaned. And God says, "In this world the evil inclination [within every person's heart] separates you from the commandments, but in the world to

**Genesis Rabbah 10.4:** Arguably, the remedy of Torah has already healed the Jews of any injury from Adam's sin—see Shabbat 145b-46a, p. 389; but the Evil Inclination still rages; see Numbers Rabbah 17.6, below. Furthermore, ultimately the entire world must be healed. Cf. 1 Corinthians 15.21-22, p. 388.

**1 John 3.2:** That is, we shall all become perfect and Christ-like at the Second Coming of Christ. Thomas Aquinas described this Beatific Vision as "the ultimate goal for the redeemed." Cf. Romans 8.22-23, p. 222; 2 Corinthians 3.18, p. 415; Sun Myung Moon, 8-26-86, p. 196.

**Hadith of Muslim:** Cf. Berakot 17a, p. 247; Job 19.25-26, p. 415.

**1 Corinthians 13.9-12:** We can expect to gain clearer understanding of truth that can guide us in the Kingdom of Heaven. Cf. John 16.12-13, p. 576; Book of Certitude, 33-41, p. 779; Divine Principle I.3.5.2, pp. 779-80.

**Lotus Sutra 16:** In keeping with the Hindu theory of cycles of cosmic time, 'the kalpa's end' is not a final consummation but rather the end of an age; cf. Bhagavad Gita 8.17-21, p. 78, Linga Purana 1.40, below. Although the entire phenomenal world is apparently consumed in the conflagration, for those with eyes to see, the Buddha's Pure Land remains unharmed. The Buddha's nature is eternal, and similarly the natures of those who realize their own Buddha nature. The 'Precious Three' are the three jewels; Buddha: Dharma and Sargha.

come I will root it out from you, as it is said, 'I will put my Spirit within you, and I will take away the stony heart out of your flesh, and I will give you a heart of flesh, and I will put my Spirit within you, and cause you to walk in my statutes and do them' [Ezekiel 36.26-27]."

*Judaism.* Midrash, Numbers Rabbah 17.6

When God appears, there is goodness, there is justice, there is benevolence, harmony comes of itself, all creatures find their places, and there is not conflict, no preying on each other, no disease, no suffering, no poverty.

*Seicho-no-Ie.* Nectarean Shower of Holy Doctrines

Behold, the days are coming, says the Lord, when I will make a new covenant with the house of Israel and the house of Judah, not like the covenant which I made with their fathers when I took them by the hand to bring them out of the land of Egypt, my covenant which they broke, though I was their husband, says the Lord. But this is the covenant which I will make with the house of Israel after those days, says the Lord: I will put my law within them, and I will write it upon their hearts; and I will be their God, and they shall be my people. And no longer shall each man teach his neighbor and each his brother, saying, "Know the Lord," for they shall all know me, from the least of them to the greatest, says the Lord; for I will forgive their iniquity, and I will remember their sin no more.

*Judaism* and *Christianity.* Jeremiah 31.31-34

In the Kali age, men will be afflicted by old age, disease, and hunger, and from sorrow there will arise depression, indifference, deep thought, enlightenment, and virtuous behavior. Then the age will change, deluding their minds like a dream, by the force of fate, and when the Golden Age begins, those left over from the Kali age will be the progenitors of the Golden Age. All four classes will survive as a seed, together with those born in the Golden age, and the seven sages will teach them all dharma. Thus there is eternal continuity from age to age.

*Hinduism.* Linga Purana 1.40

They will practice these virtues: abstain from taking life, abstain from taking what is not given, abstain from adultery, abstain from lying, abstain from evil speaking, abstain from abuse and from idle talk, abstain from covetousness, from ill will, from false opinions, abstain from the three things—incest, wanton greed, and perverted desires—be filial towards their mothers and fathers, be pious toward holy men, and respect heads of clans. And because of the good they do they will increase in length of life, and in comeliness, so that the sons of them who lived but forty years will come to live eighty years; their sons to 160 years; their sons to 320 years; their sons to 640 years... 2,000 years... 4,000 years... 8,000 years... 20,000 years... 40,000 years; and the sons of those that lived 40,000 years will come to live 80,000 years.

Among such humans there will be only three kinds of disease: appetite, non-assimila-

**Nectarean Shower of Holy Doctrines:** This passage reflects the millenarian hopes in popular Japanese religion, and is given concrete expression in many of the new religions. Cf. Johrei, below.

**Jeremiah 31.31-34:** Christianity regards this prophecy as having been fulfilled with the coming of Jesus Christ, who inaugurated a 'New Covenant'—see 1 Corinthians 11.23-25, p. 609; 2 Corinthians 3.6, p. 574; Galatians 3.21-26, p. 108—from which we get the term New Testament. But the perfect knowledge of God and his law, which would be the full realization of this prophecy, awaits the eschatological future.

**Linga Purana 1.40:** Here the sufferings of the old age beget a process which leads to enlightenment and transfiguration of the age. The 'seven sages' are the traditional teachers of the Veda. Yet the continuity between the ages is required because of the continual operation of the law of karma; the caste system, too, which is a result of karma, also will persist. The image of the survivors as a seed recurs in Vishnu Purana 4.24, p. 786. See also Laws of Manu 1.81-86, pp. 307-8.

tion, and old age. Among such humans, this world will be mighty and prosperous, the villages, towns, and royal cities will be so close that a cock could fly from each one to the next. Among such humans this India—one might think it a Waveless Deep—will be pervaded by mankind even as a jungle is by reeds and rushes.

*Buddhism.*
Digha Nikaya iii.74-75,
Cakkavatti-Sihanada Suttanta

As earthly paradise moves into its advanced stages, people's inner attitudes toward God will directly affect more and more aspects of daily life. Those whose souls are closer to God will be so much of the same heart that they can communicate without verbalizing their thoughts and feelings. By this stage, contemplation will have become the mode of existence for everyone. God will have given them such highly refined powers of spiritual perception that they can at last see his will directly and perfectly understand what is in the hearts and minds of others.

In its ultimate phase, paradise on earth will be so perfect, so unblemished, that it may be called the Crystal World. All evil and hatred will have been cleansed away. The world will have become the final realization of absolute goodness and love. Completely free from even a hint of sin or impurity, humankind at last will dwell in the heavenly abode longed for through the ages. This is the Crystal World of unity with God.

*Sekai Kyusei Kyo.* Johrei

Then comes the end, when he [Christ] delivers the kingdom to God the Father after destroying every rule and every authority and power. For he must reign until he has put all his enemies under his feet. The last enemy to be destroyed is death.

*Christianity.* 1 Corinthians 15.24-26

The holy man told them, "I'll give you something to eat that will kill you, but don't be afraid; I'll bring you back to life again." They believed him. They ate something and died, then found themselves walking in a new, beautiful land. They spoke with their parents and grandparents, and with friends that the white soldiers had killed. Their friends were well, and this new world was like the old one, the one the white man had destroyed. It was full of game, full of antelope and buffalo. The grass was green and high, and though long-dead people from other tribes also lived in this land, there was peace. All the Indian nations formed one tribe and could understand each other. Kicking Bear and Short Bull walked around and saw everything, and they were happy. Then the holy man of the Paiutes brought them back to life again.

"You have seen it," he said, "the new land I'm bringing. The earth will roll up like a blanket with all that bad white man's stuff, the fences and railroads and mines and telegraph poles, and underneath will be our old-young Indian earth with all our relatives come to life again." Then the holy man taught them a new dance, a new song, a new prayer. He gave them sacred red paint.... Now everywhere we are dancing this new dance to roll up the earth, to bring back the dead. A new world is coming.

*Native American Religions.*
Ghost Dance, Sioux Tradition

**Digha Nikaya iii.74-75:** This renovation will be presided over by the Maitreya Buddha; see Digha Nikaya iii.76, pp. 786-87. This description of the ideal world as one of closely packed villages and kingdoms where none will molest its neighbor is similar to the Taoist ideal as presented in Tao Te Ching 80, pp. 198-99.

**Johrei:** The world of daily life is being changed from a state of strife to a 'Crystal World' of purity and harmony. Cf. Vishnu Purana 4.24, p. 786. This transformation is said to have already begun in this century.

**1 Corinthians 15.24-26:** Cf. Job 19.25-26, p. 415; John 11.25, p. 410; 1 Corinthians 15.52-57, pp. 412-13.

**Ghost Dance:** The Native American Ghost Dance, which has incorporated some ideas from Christian eschatology, looks to a divine visitation which will bring judgment upon the white man and vindication to the Native American people. Cf. Yakima Tradition, pp. 233-34.

The wolf shall dwell with the lamb,
and the leopard shall lie down with the kid,
and the calf and the lion and the fatling together,
and a little child shall lead them.
The cow and the bear shall feed;
their young shall lie down together;
and the lion shall eat straw like the ox.
The sucking child shall play over the hole of the asp,
and the weaned child shall put his hand on the adder's den.
They shall not hurt or destroy
in all my holy mountain;
for the earth shall be full of the knowledge of the Lord
as waters cover the sea.

*Judaism* and *Christianity*. Isaiah 11.6-9

The victorious World-renovator and his helpers... shall make the existence renovated—ageless, deathless, unputrifying, uncorruptible, ever-living, ever benefitting, ruling at will. The dead shall rise up, life shall prevail indestructible, and existence shall be renovated at the will of God!

The worlds shall be deathless, by the will of Right, benefitting all! Evil will stand against, but will flee away, here and there causing death to the holy and his progeny and creatures, but running to its death and destruction at the will of the Judge!

*Zoroastrianism*. Avesta, Zamyad Yasht 19.11-12

And the ransomed of the Lord shall return,
and come to Zion with singing;
everlasting joy shall be upon their heads;
they shall obtain joy and gladness,
and sorrow and sighing shall flee away.

*Judaism* and *Christianity*. Isaiah 51.11

In the City Joyful dwell the saints of God;
Neither suffering nor sorrow is found therein;
Neither anxiety to pay tribute nor any imposts;
Neither fear of retribution nor of fall from eminence.
In this happy land where my dwelling is,
Abides unending well-being.
All who therein dwell are blessed with eternal kingship;
None is there reckoned inferior to any.
That city knows no decline;
Its citizens are rich and fulfilled.
Unlimited their freedom—
None are alien there;
All in true liberty abide.
Says Ravidas, the emancipated cobbler,
Only a citizen of that City reckon I my friend.

*Sikhism*. Adi Granth, Gauri, Ravidas, p. 345

Then I saw a new heaven and a new earth; for the first heaven and the first earth had passed away, and the sea was no more. And I saw the holy city, new Jerusalem, coming down out of heaven from God, prepared as a bride adorned for her husband; and I heard a loud voice from the throne saying, "Behold, the dwelling of God is with men. He will dwell with them, and they shall be his people, and God himself will be with them. He will wipe away every tear from their eyes, and death shall be no more, neither shall there be mourning nor crying nor pain any more, for the former things have passed away."

And he who sat upon the throne said, "Behold, I make all things new." Also he said, "Write this, for these words are trustworthy and true." And he said to me, "It is done! I am the Alpha and the Omega, the beginning and the end. To the thirsty I will give from the fountain of the water of life without payment. He who conquers shall have this heritage, and I will be his God and he shall be my son."...

**Isaiah 11.6-9:** Cf. Romans 8.19-23, p. 222.

**Isaiah 51.11:** The promised return to Jerusalem is central to the Jewish messianic hope; it no doubt helped to fuel the Zionist movement and the reestablishment of the State of Israel in this century. Some Christians also expect a return of the Jews to Jerusalem to herald the return of Christ, and have supported the State of Israel for such theological reasons.

**Gauri, Ravidas:** Cf. Suhi Chhant, M.5, p. 196; Sri Raga, M.5, p. 394.

And I saw no temple in the city, for its temple is the Lord God the Almighty and the Lamb. And the city has no need of sun or moon to shine upon it, for the glory of God is its light, and its lamp is the Lamb. By its light shall all the nations walk; and the kings of the earth shall bring their glory into it, and its gates shall never be shut by day—and there shall be no night there; they shall bring into it the glory and the honor of the nations. But nothing unclean shall enter it, nor any one who practices abomination or falsehood, but only those who are written in the Lamb's book of life.

Then [an angel] showed me the river of the water of life, bright as crystal, flowing from the throne of God and of the Lamb through the middle of the street of the city; also, on either side of the river, the tree of life with its twelve kinds of fruit, yielding its fruit each month; and the leaves of the tree were for the healing of the nations. There shall no more be anything accursed, but the throne of God and of the Lamb shall be in it, and his servants shall worship him; they shall see his face, and his name shall be on their foreheads. And night shall be no more; they need no light of lamp or sun, for the Lord God will be their light, and they shall reign for ever and ever.

*Christianity*. Revelation 21.1-22.5

It is our duty in this radiant century to investigate the essentials of divine religion, seek the realities underlying the oneness of the world of humanity, and discover the source of fellowship and agreement which will unite mankind in the heavenly bond of love. This unity is the radiance of eternity, the divine spirituality, the effulgence of God and the bounty of the Kingdom.

*Baha'i Faith*. 'Abdu'l-Baha, The Promulgation of Universal Peace

I give unto you a sign, that you may know the time when these things shall be about to take place—that I shall gather in, from their long dispersion, my people, O house of Israel, and shall establish again among them my Zion....

For it is wisdom in the Father that they should be established in this land [America], and be set up as a free people by the power of the Father, that these things might come forth from them unto a remnant of your seed, that the covenant of the Father may be fulfilled which he has covenanted with his people, O house of Israel....

If they [the Gentiles] will repent and hearken unto my words, and not harden their hearts, I will establish my church among them, and they shall come unto the covenant and be numbered among this the remnant of Jacob, unto whom I have given this land for their inheritance;

And they shall assist my people, the remnant of Jacob, and also as many of the house of Israel as shall come, that they may build a city, which shall be called the New Jerusalem.

And then shall they assist my people that they may be gathered in, who are scattered upon all the face of the land, in unto the New Jerusalem.

And then shall the power of heaven come down among them; and I also will be in the midst. And then shall the work of the Father commence that day, even when this gospel shall be preached among the remnant of this people. Verily I say to you, at that day shall the work of the Father commence among all the dispersed of my people, yea, even the tribes which have been lost, which the Father hath led away out of Jerusalem.

Yea, the work shall commence among all the dispersed of my people, with the Father to prepare the way whereby they may come unto me, that they may call on the Father in my name.

**Revelation 21.1-22.5:** This is the central Christian passage depicting in symbolic terms the coming millennium, the Kingdom of Heaven. Cf. Isaiah 62.4-5, p. 137; Revelation 7.9-17, p. 251. On the Tree of Life as a symbol, see Psalms 1.1-3, p. 106; John 15.4-11, p. 462. On the Church as Bride, see Ephesians 5.22-32, pp. 180-81.

**The Promulgation of Universal Peace:** For more from this text, see p. 198. Cf. Gleanings from the Writings of Baha'u'llah 115, p. 367; 111, p. 188.

Yea, and then shall the work commence, with the Father, among all nations, in preparing the way whereby his people may be gathered home to the land of their inheritance.

And they shall go out from all nations; and they shall not go out in haste, nor go by flight, for I will go before them, says the Father, and I will be their rearward.

*Church of Jesus Christ of Latter-day Saints.*
Book of Mormon, 3 Nephi 21.1-29

The [historical] development of the cultural spheres also shows that a worldwide cultural sphere is now being formed centered on one religion. Nations, too, are moving toward one worldwide structure of sovereignty, starting from the League of Nations, through the United Nations, and reaching today for world government. Regarding economic development, the world is now on the threshold of forming one common market. Extremely well-developed transportation and communication facilities have reduced the limitations of time and space. Men are able to communicate with one another on the earth as easily as if the earth were the garden of a house in which people of all the different races of the East and the West lived as one family. All mankind is crying out for brotherly love.

However, a home is formed around the parents; there alone can true brotherly love occur. Therefore, upon the Second Advent of the Lord as the True Parent of mankind, all men will come to live harmoniously in the garden as one family.

*Unification Church.*
Divine Principle I.3.4.3

❖

**Nephi 21.1-29:** 'My Zion,' the new refuge for the dispersed of God's people, is to be built in America. The New World figures centrally in the Latter-day Saints' expectation of the millennium.

**Divine Principle I.3.4.3:** 'True Parent' is a messianic title, specifying the Messiah's parental love for all humankind and his role as the new Adam, the origin of the new lineage of God that is free from the sin and death which pervades the lineage of the fallen Adam. Cf. Sun Myung Moon, 9-11-77, p. 189; 8-26-86, p. 196; 10-20-73, p. 198; 4-18-87, p. 248; 9-3-89, pp. 442-43; 8-20-89. p. 408.

# INDEX OF SOURCES

Sources are listed by tradition in alphabetical order as follows:

African Traditional Religions
Baha'i Faith
Theravada Buddhism
Mahayana Buddhism
Christian Science
Christianity
Confucianism
Hinduism
Islam
Jainism
Judaism
Korean Religions
Church of Jesus Christ of Latter-day Saints
Mahikari
Maori Traditional Religion
Native American Religions
Omoto Kyo
Perfect Liberty Kyodan
Scientology
Seicho-no-Ie
Sekai Kyusei Kyo and Society of Johrei
Shinto
Sikhism
Tahitian Traditional Religion
Taoism
Tenrikyo
Theosophy
Unification Church
Zoroastrianism

Bibliographical references that repeat will be entered in full when they first appear in each tradition. Page numbers following p. or pp. indicate the page of *World Scripture* on which the passage appears.

## African Traditional Religions

**Akan** (Ghana).
Emefie Ikenga-Metuh, *Comparative Studies of African Traditional Religions* (Onitsha, Nigeria: IMICO Publishers, 1987) [Marked I]; J. H. Nketia, *Drumming in Akan Communities of Ghana* (London: Thomas Nelson, 1963) [Marked N]; Kofi Asare Opoku, *West African Traditional Religion* (Singapore: Far Eastern Publishers, 1978); Kofi Asare Opoku, his own selection submitted to *World Scripture* [Marked O]. All passages are from Opoku's book unless otherwise marked.
pp. 68, 86 [I], 105 [N], 144 [I], 144, 172 [O], 187, 232, 280 [I], 398, 494 [I], 567, 654, 753

**Anuak** (Sudan).
Aylward Shorter, *Prayer in the Religious Traditions of Africa* (London: Oxford University Press, 1975).
p. 54

**Ashanti** (Ghana and Ivory Coast).
Ikenga-Metuh, *Comparative Studies* [Marked I]; R. S. Rattray, *The Ashanti* (London: Oxford University Press, 1923) [Marked R].
pp. 87 [I], 204 [R]

**Banyarawanda** (Tanzania).
E. W. Smith, ed., *African Ideas of God* (Cambridge: Edinburgh House Press, 1961).
p. 69

**Basonge** (Zaire).
Dominique Zahan, *The Religion, Spirituality, and Thought of Traditional Africa*, trans. K.E. Martin and L.M. Martin (Chicago: University of Chicago Press, 1979).
p. 306

**Bette** (Nigeria).
Ryszard Pachocinski, his own translation submitted to *World Scripture*.
p. 505

**Boran** (Kenya).
Shorter, *Prayer in the Religious Traditions*.
pp. 398, 594

**Buji** (Nigeria).
Pachocinski.
pp. 189, 505, 525, 703

**Dinka** (Sudan).
Alfonso M. di Nola, comp., *The Prayers of Man: From Primitive Peoples to Present Times*, ed. Patrick O'Connor; trans. Rex Benedict (New York: Ivan Obolensky, 1961) [Marked D]; Ikenga-Metuh, *Comparative Studies* [Marked I]; Godfrey Lienhardt, *Divinity and Experience: The Religion of the Dinka* (London: Oxford University Press, 1961) [Marked L]; Shorter, *Prayer in the Religious Traditions* [Marked S].
pp. 73 [L], 94 [D], 307 [I], 310 [L], 325 [L], 737 [S], 767 [D]

**Fang** (Gabon).
Smith, *African Ideas of God.*
p. 290

**Fon** (Benin).
Olympe Bhêly-Quénum, *Au Pays des Fons* (Paris).
pp. 243, 530

**Hutu** (Rwanda and Burundi).
Ikenga-Metuh, *Comparative Studies* [Marked I]; Smith, *African Ideas of God* [Marked S].
pp. 307 [I], 518 [S], 726 [S]

**Idoma** (Nigeria).
Wande Abimbola, ed., *Yoruba Oral Tradition* (Ibadan, Nigeria: University Press Ltd., 1975) [Marked A]; Pachocinski [Marked P].
pp. 205 [A], 515 [P], 655 [P], 713 [P]

**Igala** (Nigeria).
Pachocinski.
pp. 344, 513, 530, 582, 652, 660, 691, 760

**Igbo** (Nigeria).
Christopher I. Ejizu, *Ofo: Igbo Ritual Symbol* (Enugu, Nigeria: Fourth Dimension Publishing Co., 1986) [Marked E]; Ikenga-Metuh, *Comparative Studies* [Marked I]; C. K. Meek, *Law and Authority in a Nigerian Tribe* (London: Oxford University Press, 1937) [Marked M].
pp. 125 [I], 170 [E], 238 [I], 260 [M], 491 [I], 493 [I], 495 [I], 495 [I], 550 [E]

**Kalabari** (Nambia).
W.R.C. Horton, "A hundred Years of Change in Kalabari Religion," in *Black Africa: Its Peoples and Their Cultures Today*, ed. John Middleton (New York: Macmillan, 1970), 195, quoted in Ikenga Metuh *Comparative Studies*, 34-35.
p. 288

**Kanufi** (Nigeria).
Pachocinski.
p. 352

**Kikuyu** (Kenya).
Jomo Kenyatta, *Facing Mount Kenya: The Tribal Life of the Gikuyu* (New York: Random House, 1961) [Marked K]; John S. Mbiti, *The Prayers of African Religion* (London: SPCK, 1975; Maryknoll, New York: Orbis Books, 1975) [Marked M].
pp. 550 [M], 612 [K]

## *Baha'i Faith*

*Bahá'u'lláh* (Wilmette, Illinois: National Spiritual Assembly of the Bahá'ís of the United States, 1952, 1976).
27, pp. 215-16
43, p. 289
72, p. 189
81, pp. 234, 260
110, p. 734
111, pp. 35, 188
115, p. 367
127, p. 136
132, p. 147

**Hidden Words of Bahá'u'lláh.**
Bahá'u'lláh, *The Hidden Words of Bahá'u'lláh* (reprint, Wilmette, Illinois: National Spiritual Assembly of the Bahá'ís of the United States, 1985).
Arabic 3, p. 137
Arabic 7, p. 639
Arabic 54, p. 664

**Seven Valleys and the Four Valleys.**
Bahá'u'lláh, *The Seven Valleys and the Four Valleys* (Wilmette, Illinois: National Spiritual Assembly of the Bahá'ís of the United States, 1945, 1973, 1975, 1978).
21, p. 519

**Tablets of Bahá'u'lláh Revealed after the Kitáb-i-Aqdas.**
Bahá'u'lláh, *Tablets of Bahá'u'lláh Revealed after the Kitáb-i-Aqdas* (Wilmette, Illinois: the Universal House of Justice, 1978, 1988).
p. 459; 231-32, p. 788

**'Abdu'l-Bahá, Promulgation of Universal Peace.**
'Abdu'l-Bahá, *The Promulgation of Universal Peace: Talks Delivered by 'Abdu'l-Bahá during His Visit to the United States and Canada in 1912* (Wilmette, Illinois: National Spiritual Assembly of the Bahá'ís of the United States, 1982), 144-45.
pp. 198, 795

# Buddhism

## THERAVADA BUDDHISM

**Anāgatavaṁsa.**
Edward Conze, ed., *Buddhist Texts Through the Ages* (New York: Philosophical Library, 1954) [Marked C]; Henry Clarke Warren, ed., *Buddhism in Translations* (Cambridge: Harvard University Press, 1896; New York: Atheneum, 1982) [Marked W]
pp. 778-79 [W], 786 [C]

**Aṅguttara Nikāya.**
Conze, *Buddhist Texts* [Marked C]; Walpola Rahula, ed., *What the Buddha Taught*, 2d ed. (New York: Grove Press, 1974) [Marked R]; Warren, *Buddhism in Translations* [Marked W]; F. L. Woodward and E. M. Hare, trans., *Gradual Sayings*, 5 vols. (London: Pali Text Society, 1951-65) [Marked WH]; F. L. Woodward, trans., *Some Sayings of the Buddha* (London: Oxford University Press, 1973) [Marked Wo].
i.10, p. 322 [C]
i.50, p. 222 [WH]
i.61, pp. 172 [WH], 556 [WH]
i.137, p. 378 [WH]
i.173-74, p. 490 [Wo]
i.190-91, p. 487 [R]
i.279, p. 249 [Wo]
ii.37-39, p. 468 [C]
ii.68, p. 715 [WH]
ii.75, p. 757 [Wo]
ii.193, p. 431 [WH]
iii.33, p. 499 [W]
iii.368, p. 211 [WH]
iv.41-45, p. 617 [WH]
iv.91, p. 182 [WH]
iv.370, p. 154 [WH]
v.66, p. 517 [WH]
v.322, pp. 88 [WH], 392 [WH]

**Buddhacarita of Ashvaghosha.**
E. B. Cowell, F. Max Müller, and J. Takakusu, trans., *Buddhist Mahâyâna Texts*, Sacred Books of the East, vol. 49 (Oxford: Clarendon Press, 1894) [Marked C]; Wm. Theodore de Bary, ed., *The Buddhist Tradition in India, China and Japan* (New York: Random House, 1969) [Marked D]; E. H. Johnston, trans., *The Buddhacarita; or, Acts of the Buddha*, new enlarged ed. (Delhi, India: Motilal Banarsidass, 1984) [Marked J].
3-5, pp. 425-26 [D]
12.95-101, p. 672 [D]
13, pp. 446-47 [C]
14, p. 437 [D]
15.79-82, p. 456 [C]
27.76-78, p. 609 [J]
28.69, p. 609 [J]

**Buddhaghosa, Parable of the Mustard Seed.**
T. E. Rogers, trans., *Buddhagosa: Buddhist Parables* (London: Trübner & Co., 1870).
pp. 271-72

**Dhammapada.**
Irving Babbitt, trans., *The Dhammapada* (New York: New Directions, 1965) [Marked B]; David J. Kalupahana, trans., *A Path of Righteousness: Dhammapada* (Lanham: University Press of

376, p. 685
379-80, p. 488
383, p. 384
393, p. 191
394, p. 348
396, p. 191
402-22, p. 157
408, p. 718

**Dhammapada Commentary** (Dhammapada Aṭṭhakathā).
*The Teaching of Buddha*, 84th rev. ed. (Tokyo: Bukkyo Dendo Kyokai, 1984).
pp. 431-32

**Dīgha Nikāya**.
Wm. Theodore de Bary, ed., *Sources of Indian Tradition* (New York: Columbia University Press, 1958) [Marked D]; T. W. Rhys Davids and C. A. F. Rhys Davids, trans., *Dialogues of the Buddha (Dīgha Nikāya)*, Parts 1-3, Sacred Books of the Buddhists, vols. 2-4 (London: Pali Text Society, 1956-59) [Marked R]; David Maurice, ed., *The Lion's Roar: An Anthology of the Buddha's Teachings Selected from the Pali Canon* (London: Rider & Co., 1962) [Marked M]; Warren, *Buddhism in Translations* [Marked W]; Woodward, *Some Sayings* [Marked Wo]. *Due to the diversity of translations, readers may find a different numbering system in some sources.
i.115, p. 425 [R]
ii.73, p. 764 [Wo]
ii.88, p. 260 [Wo]
Brahmajāla Sutta.
i, p. 231 [R]
i.3, pp. 655-56 [R], 709 [R]
Samaññaphala Sutta.
i.85, p. 643 [M]
Kūṭadanta Sutta.
i.135, p. 754 [R]
Kassapa-Sīhanāda Sutta.
i.167, p. 672 [R]
Mahāparinibbāna Suttanta.
ii.99-100, p. 488 [W]
ii.155-56, p. 488 [W]
Sakkapañha Suttanta.
ii.276, p. 277 [R]
Cakkavatti-Sīhanāda Suttanta.
iii.59-62, p. 200 [R]
iii.60-61, p. 751 [R]
iii.71-72, p. 776 [R]
iii.74-75, pp. 792-93 [R]
iii.76, pp. 786-87 [R]
Aggañña Suttanta.
iii.92-93, p. 748 [D]
Sigālovāda Sutta.
iii.182-85, p. 355 [M]
iii.185, p. 714 [M]
iii.185-91, pp. 167-68 [R]
iii.187, p. 184 [M]
Kevaddha Sutta.
xi.66, p. 265 [M]
xi.67-83, pp. 264-65 [M]
Tevijja Sutta.
xiii.31-34, pp. 140-41 [R]
xiii.75, p. 394 [R]
xiii.76-77, pp. 161-62 [R]
xiii.80, pp. 140-41 [R]
xiii, pp. 452-53 [R]

**Itivuttaka**.
Nyanaponika Thera, *The Heart of Buddhist Meditation: A Handbook of Mental Training Based on the Buddha's Way of Mindfulness (Satipatthana)* (York Beach, Maine: Samuel Weiser, 1965) [Marked T]; F. L. Woodward, trans., *Minor Anthologies of the Pali Canon: Part 2, Udāna: Verses of Uplift and Itivuttaka: As It Was Said* (London: Pali Text Society, 1948). All passages are from Woodward's translation unless otherwise marked.
11, p. 188
18, p. 695
19, p. 685
36, p. 551
45, p. 278
47, p. 662
53, p. 510
65, p. 698
68-69, p. 185
89, p. 628
98, p. 723
101, p. 406
110, p. 527 [T]
114-15, p. 385

**Jātaka**.
H. T. Francis, trans., *The Jātaka; or, Stories of the Buddha's Former Births*, 6 vols. (London: Pali Text Society, 1895-1907; reprint, 1981).
p. 206

**Khuddaka Pāṭha**.
Bhikkhu Nanamoli, trans., *Khuddaka Pāṭha*, Pali Text Translation Series no. 32 (London: Pali Text Society, 1960) [Marked N]; Woodward, *Some Sayings* [Marked W].
p. 29 [W]; p. 205 [N]
Metta Suttā, pp. 208 [N], 685 [N]
Ten Charges, pp. 111-12 [W]
Tirokudda Sutta, p. 261 [W]

**Majjhima Nikāya**.
I. B. Horner, trans., *Middle Length Sayings (Majjhima Nikaya)*, 3 vols. (London: Pali Text Society, 1954-59) [Marked H]; Maurice, *Lion's*

## MAHAYANA BUDDHISM

(Missoula, Mont.: Scholars Press, 1980) [Marked P]; Alex Wayman and Hideko Wayman, trans., *The Lion's Roar of Queen Śrīmālā* (New York: Columbia University Press, 1974) [Marked W].

3, p. 625 [P]
4, p. 221 [P]
5, p. 466 [P]
13, p. 75 [W]

**Lotus Sutra** (Saddharma-puṇḍarīka).

John Blofeld, *Bodhisattva of Compassion: The Mystical Tradition of Kuan Yin* (Boston: Shambhala, 1978) [Marked B]; Leon Hurvitz, trans., *Scripture of the Lotus Blossom of the Fine Dharma* (New York: Columbia University Press, 1976) [Marked H]; *Lectures on the Sutra* (Tokyo: Nichiren Shoshu International Center, 1978) [Marked L]; Senchu Murano, trans., *The Lotus Sutra* (Tokyo: Nichiren Shu Headquarters, 1974) [Marked M]; W. E. Soothill, trans., *The Lotus of the Wonderful Law* (Oxford: Oxford University Press, 1930) [Marked S].

2, pp. 56 [L], 102 [H], 247 [S], 291 [H], 326 [S], 474 [S], 574 [S], 624 [S]
3, pp. 93 [H], 254 [S], 313-14 [H], 406 [S], 542 [S]
4, pp. 363-65 [S], 557 [M]
5, pp. 91-92 [S], 361 [S], 367 [H], 461 [S]
7, pp. 455-56 [H]
8, p. 382 [S]
10, pp. 88 [S], 566 [S]
12, p. 584 [S]
13, pp. 630 [S], 775 [S]
14, pp. 338 [H], 724 [S]
16, pp. 35 [L], 77 [S], 463 [S], 721 [S], 791 [S]
20, pp. 709-10 [S]
21, p. 137 [H]
25, pp. 35 [H], 402 [B], 592 [S]

**Mahāparinirvāṇa Sūtra.**

Nichiren, *Kaimoku-Shō*, trans. Kyotsu Hori (Tokyo: Nichiren Shū Overseas Propagation Promotion Association, 1987) [Marked N]; *The Teaching of Buddha*, 84th rev. ed. (Tokyo: Bukkyo Dendo Kyokai, 1984) [Marked T]; Kosho Yamamoto, trans., *The Mahaparinirvana Sutra*, 3 vols. (Ube City: Karinbunko, 1973-75) [Marked Y].

p. 274 [N]
p. 742 [N]
214, p. 140 [Y]
214-15, p. 147 [Y]
220, p. 77 [Y]
259, p. 89 [Y]
424-33, pp. 538-39 [T]
470-71, pp. 162-63 [Y]
560, p. 642 [Y]
575-76, p. 375 [Y]

**Mahāratnakūṭa Sūtra.**

Garma C. C. Chang, ed., *A Treasury of Mahāyāna Sūtras: Selections from the Mahāratnakūṭa Sūtra* (University Park: The Pennsylvania State University Press, 1983).

27, p. 347

**Meditation on Buddha Amitāyus** (Amitāyur Dhyāna Sūtra).

E. B. Cowell, F. Max Müller, and J. Takakusu, trans., *Buddhist Mâhâyana Texts*, Sacred Books of the East, vol. 49 (Oxford: Clarendon Press, 1894) [Marked C]; *Shinshū Seiten: Jōdo Shin Buddhist Teaching* (San Francisco: Buddhist Churches of America, 1978) [Marked S].

3.30, p. 370 [S], 597 [C]
9-11, pp. 605-6 [S]
17, p. 462 [C]
27, p. 171 [S]

**Milarepa.**

Garma C. C. Chang, trans., *The Hundred Thousand Songs of Milarepa* (Secaucus, New Jersey: University Books, 1962) [Marked C]; W. Y. Evans-Wentz, ed., *Tibet's Great Yogi, Milarepa,* trans. Lama Kaji Dawa-Samdup (Oxford: Oxford University Press, 1928) [Marked E].

pp. 221 [E], 266 [C], 279 [C], 322 [C], 415 [C]

**Mumonkan.**

Katsuki Sekida, trans., *Two Zen Classics: Mumonkan and Hekiganroku* (Tokyo: Weatherhill, 1977).

1, pp. 572, 601-2
6, p. 585
8, p. 414
17, p. 586
18, p. 417
21, p. 64n
23, p. 383
26, p. 518
30, p. 74
33, p. 640
45, p. 489
46, p. 640

**Myōkōnin.**

D. T. Suzuki, *A Miscellany of Shin Teaching of Buddhism* (Kyoto: Shinshu Otaniha Shumusho, 1949).

p. 553

## Christian Science



## Christianity

## Confucianism

## *Hinduism*

**Bhagavad Gītā.**

Kees W. Bolle, ed., *The Bhagavadgītā: A New Translation* (Berkeley: University of California Press, 1979) [Marked B]; Eknath Easwaran, ed., *The Bhagavad Gita* (Petaluma, Calif.: Nilgiri Press, 1985); Panikkar, *Mantramanjari* [Marked P]; Swami Prabhavananda and Christopher Isherwood, trans., *The Song of God: Bhagavad-Gita* (Hollywood, Calif.: Vedanta Press, 1944, 1972) [Marked Pl]. All passages are from Easwaran's unless otherwise marked.

2.19-25, p. 233
2.31-38, p. 742
2.42-46, p. 576 [B]
2.47-50, p. 667
2.54-61, pp. 155-56
2.66-68, p. 662
2.69, p. 390
2.70, p. 393
2.71, p. 638
3.4-9, pp. 714-15
3.10-26, pp. 689-90
3.20-21, p. 756 [B]
3.31-32, p. 107
3.36-41, p. 294
4.1-3, p. 475
4.7-8, pp. 474, 786
4.11, p. 34
4.19-21, p. 555
4.24-32, p. 621
4.34-35, p. 582
4.36, p. 384
4.37, p. 403
4.37-38, p. 565
4.39-40, p. 543 [P]
5.10-12, p. 554
5.15-16, p. 381 [PI]
5.21-23, p. 133 [B]
5.23, pp. 523 [B], 657 [B]
5.24, p. 379 [B]
6.5-6, pp. 489 [B], 278 [B]
6.7-9, p. 153
6.10-27, p. 603
6.28-32, p. 160
6.35-36, p. 523
6.40-41, p. 711
6.45, p. 510
7.4-7, p. 63 [B]
7.21-23, p. 518
7.25, p. 282
8.5-7, p. 241
8.12-13, p. 241
8.17-21, p. 78 [B]
8.22, p. 544
9.4-10, p. 86 [B]
9.11-12, p. 288 [B]
9.17, p. 95 [B]
9.23-25, p. 266
9.26-28, p. 620
9.29, p. 190
9.30-31, p. 370 [PI]
9.32-33, p. 192
10.14, p. 263 [PI]
10.39, p. 74
10.41, p. 74
11.3-25, pp. 66-68 [B]
11.26-28, pp. 738-39 [B]
11.31-34, pp. 738-39 [B]
11.36-42, p. 467
12.5-7, p. 544 [PI]
12.13, p. 161
12.14-20, p. 156
13.7-8, p. 648 [PI]
13.9-11, p. 676
13.11, p. 569
13.19-22, p. 118
13.26, p. 118
13.32, p. 73
14.3-4, p. 95 [B]
15.1-3, p. 272 [B]
15.9-11, p. 148 [B]
16.6, p. 276 [B]
16.7-16, p. 281
16.21, p. 294
17.3, p. 538 [P]
17.4, p. 265
17.5-6, p. 671
17.17, p. 538 [P]
17.20-21, p. 695
17.20-22, p. 624 [B]
17.28, p. 538 [P]
18.40, p. 272
18.44-48, p. 505
18.55, p. 87 [PI]
18.58, pp. 396 [PI], 492
18.60-61, pp. 495-96 [B]
18.61-62, p. 393 [PI]
18.62, p. 483 [B]
18.63, p. 486
18.65-66, p. 461
18.66, p. 551
18.67, p. 719
18.68-69, p. 723
18.75, p. 451

**Mahābhārata.**

Kisarai Mohan Ganguli, trans., *The Mahabharata of Krishna-Dwaipayana Vyasa* (New Delhi, Munshiram Manoharlal, 1982) [Marked G]; Wendy Doniger O'Flaherty, *The Origins of Evil in Hindu Mythology* (Berkeley: University of California Press, 1976) [Marked O]; Sarvepalli Radhakrishnan, ed., *The Dhammapada* (Madras: Oxford University Press, 1950) [Marked Rad]; V. Raghavan, trans., *The Indian Heritage* (Bangalore: Indian Institute of World Culture, 1963) [Marked Rag]; Pratap Chandra Ray, trans., *The Mahabharata* (Calcutta, Bharata Press, 1890; selections reprinted in S. Radhakrishnan and C. A. Moore, eds., *A*

10.63, p. 112 [M]
11.9, p. 349
11.10, p. 676
11.228-30, p. 643
11.231-34, p. 646
12.3, p. 124
12.8, p. 124
12.9, p. 124

**Nārada Dharma Sūtra.**
Julius Jolly, trans., *The Minor Law-Books*, Sacred Books of the East, vol. 33 (Oxford: Clarendon Press, 1889).
1.210, p. 105

**Vasishtha Dharma Sūtra.**
Bühler, *Sacred Laws of the Aryas.*
28.7, p. 342

**Institutes of Vishnu.**
Julius Jolly, *The Institutes of Vishnu*, Sacred Books of the East, vol. 7 (Oxford: Clarendon Press, 1900).
20.43-46, p. 497

**Puranas.**

**Śrīmad Bhāgavatam** (Bhāgavata Purāṇa).
A. C. Bhaktivedanta, ed., *Kṛṣṇa: The Supreme Personality of Godhead*, vol.1 (Los Angeles: Bhaktivedanta Book Trust, 1970) [Marked B]; Wendy Doniger O'Flaherty, ed., *Hindu Myths: A Sourcebook* (London: Penguin Books, 1975) [Marked O]; Swami Prabhavananda, ed., *Srimad Bhagavatam: The Wisdom of God* (Hollywood: Vedanta Press, 1943). All passages are from Prabhavananda's translation unless otherwise marked.
1.1, p. 467
6.1, pp. 596, 646
9, p. 700
10, pp. 456, 596
10.3, p. 547
10.5, pp. 546-47
10.16, pp. 449 [O]
10.34, pp. 470-71 [B]
11.1, p. 682
11.2, pp. 215, 361
11.3, pp. 40, 179, 323
11.4, p. 291
11.5, pp. 594, 608
11.7, p. 652
11.8, pp. 544-45
11.10, p. 86
11.12, pp. 450, 652
11.13, pp. 220, 639
11.15, pp. 39, 242
11.20, p. 265

**Garuḍa Purāṇa.**
Manmatha Natha Dutt, ed., *The Garuda Purana* (Calcutta: Society for the Resuscitation of Indian Literature, 1908) [Marked D]; Ernest Wood and S. V. Subrahmanyam, eds., *The Garuḍa Purāṇa: Sāroddhārā*, Sacred Books of the Hindus, ed. B. D. Basu, vol. 9 (Allahabad: The Pāṇiṇi Office, Bhuvaneśwarī Āśrama, Bhadurganj, 1911; reprint, New York: AMS Press, 1974) [Marked WS];
2.35, p. 645 [WS]
3.49-71, p. 254 [WS]
5, p. 500 [WS]
112, pp. 185 [D], 703 [D]
115, pp. 564-65 [D]

**Liṅga Purāṇa.**
O'Flaherty, *Origins of Evil.*
1.40, p. 792

**Mārkaṇḍeya Purāṇa.**
Manmatha Natha Dutt, ed., *The Markandeya Puranam* (Calcutta: H.C. Dass, 1896) [Marked D]; F. E. Pargiter, *The Markandaya-Purana* (Calcutta: Asiatic Society, 1904) [Marked P].
10, p. 351 [D]
13-15, p. 693 [P]
Caṇḍī Māhātmya 10, p. 401 [P]

**Matsya Purāṇa.**
*The Matsya Puranam*, Parts 1 & 2, trans. A Taluqdar of Oudh, Sacred Books of the Hindus, ed. B. D. Basu, vol. 17 (Allahabad, 1917; reprint, New York: AMS Press, 1974) [Marked M]; O'Flaherty, *Origins of Evil* [Marked O].
180.5-7, p. 508 [O]
212.25, p. 553 [M]
220.10, p. 760 [M]
221.2, p. 530 [M]

**Parāśara Purāṇa.**
O'Flaherty, *Origins of Evil.*
3, p. 317

**Shiva Purāṇa.**
*The Śiva Purāṇa* (Delhi: Motilal Banarsidass, 1970).
Rudrasaṃhitā
1.16, p. 118
18, p. 257
Vidyeśhvarasaṃhitā
11.22-35, pp. 609-10

**Skanda Purāṇa.**
Wendy Doniger O'Flaherty, *Śiva: The Erotic Ascetic* (Oxford: Oxford University Press, 1973).
1.1.21, p. 297; 5.2.11, p. 672

## *Islam*

Holy Koran Publishing House, 1977) [Marked I]; Jeffery, *Islam* [Marked J].
1, p. 518 [I]
2, pp. 515 [B], 537 [I]
4, p. 496 [J]
6, pp. 147 [B], 653 [B]
12, p. 505 [B]
13, p. 114 [B]
15, p. 700 [I]
24, pp. 197 [B], 493 [B]
26, p. 697 [I]
27, p. 145 [D]
29, p. 353 [I]
31, p. 679 [I]
32, p. 708 [B]
34, p. 741 [B]
36, pp. 186 [B], 699 [I]
38, pp. 152 [B], 414 [B]
40, pp. 639 [B], 679 [B]
41, p. 153 [I]
42, p. 372 [I]

**Sīrat Rasūl Allāh (Ibn Isḥāq)**
A. Guillaume, *The Life of Muhammad: A Translation of Isḥāq's Sīrat Rasūl Allāh* (Oxford: Oxford University Press, 1955).
pp. 423-24, 430-31, 431, 442

**Nahjul Balagha.**
*Nahjul Balagha of Hazrat Ali*, trans. Syed Mohammed Askari Jafery (Pathergatti, India: Seerat-Uz-Zahra Committee, 1965).
Sermon
1, p. 56
21, p. 750
38, p. 734
43, p. 639
54, p. 50
55, pp. 317-18
57, p. 557
67, p. 238
86, pp. 502, 679,
141, pp. 775, 785
187, p. 785
Letter
47, p. 341
Saying
9, p. 684
14, p. 760
21, p. 191
22, p. 741
30, p. 569
32, p. 654
44, p. 642
46, p. 524
52, p. 564
56, p. 296
72, p. 236
90, p. 579
201, p. 701

## *Jainism*

A. B. Athavale and A. S. Gopani, trans., *Sanmatitarka of Siddhasena* (Bombay: Education Board, 1939) [Marked A]; Bhagchandra Jain Bhaskar, his own translation submitted to *World Scripture* [Marked B]; A. Chakravarti, trans., *Pañcāstikāya of Kundakunda* (New Delhi: Bharatiya Jnanapeeth, 1944) [Marked C]; Selwyn Gurney Champion and Dorothy Short, comps., *Readings from World Religions* (London: C. A. Watts & Co., 1951) [Marked CS]; Wm. Theodore de Bary, ed., *Sources of Indian Tradition* (New York: Columbia University Press, 1958) [Marked D]; S. C. Ghosal, trans., *Dravyasaṅgraha of Nemichandra* (Arrah: Central Jain Publishing House, 1917) [Marked G]; Hermann Jacobi, trans., *Jaina Sutras*, 2 vols., Sacred Books of the East, vols. 22, 45 (Oxford: Clarendon Press, 1884, 1895; reprint, New York: Dover, 1968) [Marked Jac]; S. A. Jain, trans., *Reality* (Calcutta: Vira Shasan Sangha, 1960) [Marked Jai]; Padmanabh S. Jaini, *The Jaina Path of Purification* (Berkeley: University of California Press, 1979) [Marked Jaini]; Muni Mahendra Kumar, trans., *Ācārāṅgasūtra* (Delhi, Motilal Banarsidass, 1981) [Marked K]; K. C. Lalwani, trans., *Daśavaikālikasūtra* (Delhi: Motilal Banarsidass, 1973) [Marked L]; Sushil Kumarji Maharaj, *Song of the Soul* (Blairstown, New Jersey: Siddhachalam, 1987) [Marked M]; Muni Nathamal, *Shramana Mahavira*, trans., Sri Dineshchandra Sharma (Calcutta: Mitra Parishad, 1976) [Marked N]; K. C. Sogani, *Ethical Doctrines in Jainism* (Solapur: Jain Sam. Samraksaka Sangh, 1967) [Marked S]; R. H. B. Williams, ed., *Jaina Yoga: A Survey of the Medieval Śrāvakācāras* (Oxford: Oxford University Press, 1963) [Marked W].

**Ācārāṅgasūtra.**
1.6-7, p. 123 [K]
1.28-161, p. 205 [K]
1.35-37, p. 527 [K]
1.147, p. 212 [K]
1.174, p. 154 [K]
2.1-3, pp. 296-97 [K]

## *Judaism*

Schocken Books, 1925, 1962) [Marked H]; Joseph J. Hertz, ed., *Sayings of the Fathers* (New York: Behrman House, 1945) [Marked J]; *Mishnah* (New York: Judaica Press, 1964) [Marked M]; C. G. Montefiore and H. Loewe, eds., *A Rabbinic Anthology* (New York: Schocken Books, 1974) [Marked ML].



**Talmud.**

Baron, *Treasury of Jewish Quotations* [Marked B]; Philip Birnbaum, ed., *The Encyclopedia of Jewish Concepts* (Rockaway Beach, New York: Hebrew Publishing Co., 1964) [Marked Bi]; A. Cohen, ed., *Everyman's Talmud* (New York: E.P. Dutton, 1949) [Marked C1]; A. Cohen, ed., *The Minor Tractates of the Talmud*, 2 vols., 2d ed. (New York: Soncino Press, 1971) [Marked C2]; I. Epstein, trans., *The Babylonian Talmud* (New York: Soncino Press, 1948) [Marked E]; Alexander Feinsilver, trans., *The Talmud for Today* (New York: St. Martin's Press, 1980) [Marked F]; Nahum N. Glatzer, ed., *Hammer on the Rock: A Short Midrash Reader* (New York: Schocken Books, 1948) [Marked G]; Philip Goodman, ed., *The Rosh Hashanah Anthology* (Philadelphia: Jewish Publication Society of America, 1973) [Marked Go]; *Hebrew-English Edition of the Babylonian Talmud* (New York: Traditional Press, 1982) [Marked HE]; Joseph Heinemann, *Prayer in the Talmud: Forms and Patterns* (New York: De Gruyter, 1977) [Marked H]; Montefiore and Loewe, *Rabbinic Anthology* [Marked ML]; George Foote Moore, *Judaism in the First Centuries of the Christian Era*, vol. 1 (Cambridge: Harvard University Press, 1927) [Marked M]; Louis I. Newman and Samuel Spitz, eds., *The Talmudic Anthology* (New York: Behrman House, 1945) [Marked NS]; Jacob J. Petuchowski, *Our Masters Taught: Rabbinic Stories and Sayings* (New York: Crossroad, 1982) [Marked P]; Angelo S. Rappoport, *Ancient Israel: Myths and Legends*, 3 vols. (reprint, Hoboken, New Jersey: Ktav Publishing House, 1987) [Marked R].

**Babylonian Talmud.**

## Korean Religions



## *Church of Jesus Christ of Latter-day Saints*

7.18, p. 196
7.28-37, p. 324
7.48-49, p. 223

## *Mahikari*

**Goseigen.**
Kotama Okada, *Goseigen: The Holy Words*, The English Version (Takayama, Japan: Sukyo Mahikari Honbu, 1982), 20-21.
p. 376

## *Maori Traditional Religion*

Sir George Edward Grey, *Polynesian Mythology and Ancient Traditional History of the New Zealand Race, as Furnished by Their Priests and Chiefs* (London: John Murray, 1855; reprint: *Legends of Aotearoa*, Hamilton, New Zealand: Silver Fern Books, 1988).
pp. 216-17

## *Native American Religions*

**Apache.**
Claire R. Farrer, "Singing for Life: The Mescalero Apache Girls' Puberty Ceremony," in *Southwestern Indian Ritual Drama*, ed. Charlotte J. Frisbie (Albuquerque: University of New Mexico Press, 1980), 145.
p. 531

**Blackfoot.**
Walter McClintock, *The Old North Trail; or, Life, Legends, and Religion of the Blackfeet Indians* (reprint, Lincoln: University of Nebraska Press, 1968).
p. 95

**Cheyenne.**
Truman Michelson, "Notes from Bull Thigh, Sept. 7, 1910," MS 2684-a (Smithsonian Institution, Washington D.C.).
p. 205

**Cree.**
Chief Fine Day, *My Cree People* (Calgary: Northwest Printing and Lithography, Ltd., 1973).
p. 31

**Delaware.**
Elizabeth Tooker, *Native North American Spirituality of the Eastern Woodlands* (New York: Paulist Press, 1979), 115.
p. 570

**Gros Ventres.**
John M. Cooper and Regina Flannery, eds., *The Gros Ventres of Montana, Part Two: Religion and Ritual* (Washington, D.C.: Catholic University of America Press, 1957), 133-36.
pp. 170-71

**Hopi.**
Alice Marriott and Carol Rachlin, comps., *American Indian Mythology* (New York: Crowell, 1968), 197.
p. 244

**Iglulik Eskimo.**
Knud Rasmussen, *Intellectual Culture of the Iglulik Eskimos* (Copenhagen: Gyldendalske Boghandel, 1930), 112-13.
p. 382

**Mohawk.**
Tehanetorens, *Tales of the Iroquois* (Rooseveltown, New York: Awkwesasne Notes, 1976), 16-22.
pp. 277, 311-12

**Nez Perce.**
Helen Addison Howard, *War Chief Joseph* (Caldwell, Idaho: The Caxton Printers, 1941), 85.
p. 173

**Okanogan.**
Ella E. Clark, *Indian Legends of the Pacific Northwest* (Berkeley: University of California Press, 1953), 83-84, quoted in *American Indian Myths and Legends*, ed. Richard Erdoes and Alfonso Ortiz (New York: Pantheon, 1984), 14-15.
p. 207

**Onondaga.**
Erdoes and Ortiz, *American Indian Myths and Legends*, 197.
Hiawatha, pp. 187-88

**Sioux.**
Joseph Epes Brown, ed., *The Sacred Pipe: Black Elk's Account of the Seven Rites of the Oglala Sioux* (Norman: University of Oklahoma Press, 1953) [Marked B]; Frances Densmore, *Teton Sioux Music, Bureau of American Ethnology Bulletin no. 61* (Washington, D.C., 1918) [Marked D]; Erdoes and Ortiz, *American Indian Myths and Legends* [Marked EO]; Joan Halifax, *Shamanic Voices* (New York: E.P. Dutton, 1979) [Marked H]; Frithjof Schuon, *L'Oeil du Coeur* (Paris: Gallimard, 1950) [Marked S]; Ruth Murray Underhill, *Red Man's Religion* (Chicago: University of Chicago Press, 1965) [Marked U]; James R. Walker, *Lakota Belief and Ritual* (Lincoln: University of Nebraska Press, 1980) [Marked W1]; James R. Walker, "The Sun Dance and Other Ceremonies of the Oglala Division of the Teton Dakota," American Museum of Natural History, Anthropological Papers, vol. 16, part 2 (Washington, D.C., 1917) [Marked W2].
pp. 180 [D], 210 [U], 258-59 [D], 610 [W1]
Black Elk, pp. 315 [B], 381-82 [S], 582 [B], 594 [B], 647 [B]
Ghost Dance, p. 793 [EO]
Sun Dance, pp. 53-54 [W2], 693-94 [B]
Vision Quest, pp. 606-7 [H]

**Winnebago.**
Paul Radin, *The Autobiography of a Winnebago Indian* (New York: Dover, 1920) [Marked R1]; Paul Radin, *The Winnebago Tribe, 37th Annual Report of the Bureau of American Ethnology, 1923* (Washington, D.C.; reprint, Lincoln: University of Nebraska Press, 1970) [Marked R2].
pp. 178 [R1], 260-61 [R2], 671 [R1], 700 [R1]

**Yakima.**
Clark, *Indian Legends of the Pacific Northwest*, 143, quoted in *American Indian Myths and Legends*, ed. Erdoes and Ortiz, 118.
pp. 233-34

**Yamana.**
M. Gusinde, *The Yamana* (New Haven: Human Relations Area Files Press, 1932).
p. 689

**Yanomami .**
Jacques Lizot, *Tales of the Yanomami*, trans. Ernest Simon (Cambridge: Cambridge University Press, 1985), 102-3, 105.
pp. 259, 376

**Yuma.**
Erdoes and Ortiz, *American Indian Myths and Legends*, 80-81.
pp. 249-50

**Zuni.**
Ruth Bunzel, "Zuni Ritual Poetry," *47th Annual Report of the Bureau of American Ethnology, 1929-30* (Washington, D.C., 1932), 611-835.
pp. 170, 206

## *Omoto Kyo*

**Michi-no-Shiori.**
Onisaburo Deguchi, *A Guide to God's Way* (Kameoka, Japan: Omoto Kyo, 1957), trans. R. J. Hammer for *World Scripture*.
pp. 36, 53, 515, 549, 641

## *Perfect Liberty Kyodan*

R. J. Hammer, "The Scriptures of 'Perfect Liberty Kyodan': A Translation with a Brief Commentary," *Japanese Religions* 3 (Spring 1963): 18-26.
Precepts.
1-4, p. 134
14, p. 394
18, p. 484
Ritual Prayer.
p. 215

## *Scientology*

**A New Slant on Life.**
L. Ron Hubbard, *A New Slant on Life* (Los Angeles: Bridge Publications, 1988).
p. 231

**Scientology 0-8.**
L. Ron Hubbard, *Scientology 0-8: The Book of Basics* (Los Angeles: Bridge Publications, 1988).
pp. 154, 279

**Handbook for Preclears.**
L. Ron Hubbard, *Handbook for Preclears* (Los Angeles: Bridge Publications, 1989).
p. 489

**Science of Survival.**
L. Ron Hubbard, *Science of Survival* (Los Angeles: Bridge Publications, 1989).
p. 180

## *Seicho-no-Ie*

**Nectarean Shower of Holy Doctrines** (Seikyo Kanro no Hou).
Masaharu Taniguchi, *Holy Sutra Nectarean Shower of Holy Doctrines*, rev. ed. (Gardena, Calif.: Seicho-No-Ie Truth of Life Movement, North American Missionary Hq., 1981).
pp. 231-32, 285, 792
48-49, pp. 142-43

**Holy Sutra for Spiritual Healing.**
Masaharu Taniguchi, *Holy Sutra for Spiritual Healing* (Gardena, Calif.: Seicho-No-Ie Truth of Life Movement, North American Missionary Hq., 1981).
p. 644

## *Sekai Kyusei Kyo and Society of Johrei*

**Inori-no-Shū.**
Mokichi Okada, *Inori-no-Shu* (Atami, Japan: Sekai Kyusei Kyo, 1957), trans. R. J. Hammer for *World Scripture.*
p. 787

**Johrei.**
Mokichi Okada, *Johrei: Divine Light of Salvation* (Kyoto: Society of Johrei, 1984).
pp. 273, 782, 793

## *Shinto*

W. G. Aston, *Shinto: The Way of the Gods* (London: Longmans, Green & Co., 1905) [Marked A]; Harper Havelock Coates and Ryugaku Ishizuka, eds., *Honen the Buddhist Saint: His Life and Teachings* (Kyoto: Chion-in, 1925; reprint, New York: Garland, 1985) [Marked CI]; Selwyn Gurney Champion and Dorothy Short, comps., *Readings from World Religions* (London: Watts & Co., 1951) [Marked CS]; Naofusa Hirai, his own translation [Marked H]; Genchi Kato, *Shinto in Essence* (Tokyo: Nogi Shrine, 1954) [Marked K1]; Passages from Genchi Kato, *Shinto's Terra Incognita to be Explored Yet*, selected and translated by R. J. Hammer for *World Scripture* [Marked K2]; S. Ono, *The Kami Way* (Tokyo: Bridgeway Press, 1960) [Marked O]; Donald L. Philippi, trans., *Kojiki* (Tokyo: University of Tokyo Press, 1959) [Marked P]; *The World of Shinto*, trans. Norman Havens (Tokyo: Bukkyo Dendo Kyokai, 1985) [Marked WS].

**Classics: Literature of the Ancient Period (Before 1191).**
**Kojiki** (Records of Ancient Matters).
Preface, p. 750 [P]
4-6, p. 118 [P]
4.1-6.1, p. 306 [P]
11, pp. 520-21 [P]
19, p. 448 [P]
39.2-3, p. 609 [P]
110, p. 752 [P]
**Nihon Shoki** (Chronicles of Japan).
3, p. 259 [WS]
5, p. 723 [WS]
22, p. 260 [WS]
25, p. 757 [WS]
**Engishiki** (The Engi Formulary).
8, p. 372 [WS]
**Hitachi Fudoki** (Local Gazetteers of Hitachi).
p. 616 [WS]
**Kagura-uta** (Songs of the Divine Dance).
p. 90 [WS],
Offerings (Mitegura), p. 621 [WS]
**Man'yōshū** (A Collection of Myriad Leaves).
1, p. 206 [WS], 763 [WS]
13, pp. 397-98 [WS]
20, pp. 553 [WS], 675 [WS]

**Literature from the Kamakura to Momoyama Periods (1192-1600).**
Arakida, Moritake, One Hundred Poems about the World (Yo No Naka Hyakushu).

## *Sikhism*

M.5, pp. 125, 233, 767
Ravidas, p. 794
Gauri Ashtpadi, M.1, pp. 378, 658
Gauri Bairagāni, M.1, p. 280
Gauri Bāwan Akkharī, M.5, p. 362
Gauri Purabi, Ravidas, p. 284
Gauri Sukhmani, M.5, pp. 57, 157, 289, 292, 388, 397, 495, 584, 596, 650, 672-73, 688
Gauri Vār,
M.4, pp. 122-23
M.5, p. 544
Jaitsari Chhant, M.5, p. 290
Japuji, M.1, pp. 31, 51, 61, 76, 89, 101, 125, 136, 137, 188, 226, 248, 393 [HS], 404 [KS], 493, 519, 522 [HS], 538, 552, 569
Kānara, M.5, pp. 161, 195 [K]
Kīrtan Sohila, M.1, pp. 241, 360-61
Mājh, M.5, pp. 95, 132
Mājh Ashtpadi, M.3, pp. 72, 90 [HS], 204 [HS]
Maru, M.1, pp. 434, 688, 752 [K]
Maru Ashtpadi,
M.1, p. 385
M.5, p. 594 [TS]
Maru Solahe,
M.1, pp. 84-85, 253 [K]
M.3, p. 346 [M]
Maru-ki-Vār, M.1, pp. 292, 639
Rāmkali,
M.1, p. 101
M.5, p. 36 [TS]
Rāmkali Anāndu, M.3, p. 134
Rāmkali Ashtpadi, M.5, p. 581 [M]
Rāmkali Dakhni Onkār, M.1, p. 555
Rāmkali Siddha Goshti, M.1, p. 567
Rāmkali-ki-Vār, M.1, pp. 243, 711
Sārang,
M.1, p. 545
M.4, p. 172 [HS]
Shalok,
M.9, pp. 278 [TS], 323 [TS]
Farid, pp. 271 [TS], 296 [HS], 709 [K]
Kabir, pp. 701, 741
Shalok Sehskriti, M.5, pp. 744-45 [TS]
Shalok Vadhik, M.3, pp. 642-43 [TS]
Sorath,
M.1, p. 322
M.3, p. 278
M.5, pp. 169 [K], 743
Sri Raga,
M.1, pp. 237, 625, 678
M.3, pp. 451, 566 [K]
M.5, pp. 198 [M], 370, 393, 394 [M], 790
Sri Raga Ashtpadi,
M.1, pp. 104, 294, 579, 712
M.3, p. 516
Sri Raga Mahalla, M.1, pp. 192, 495
Sūhi,
M.1, pp. 596, 682
M.5, pp. 282-83, 665, 681
Sūhi Chhant, M.5, pp. 196, 639
Swaiyya Guru, Kala, pp. 474-75
Telang, M.1, p. 739
Vār Mājh, M.1, pp. 344, 422, 462, 506, 520, 615
Vār Sārang, M.1, p. 714
Vār Sorath, M.3, p. 265
Vār Sūhi,
M.1, pp. 348-49
M.3, pp. 174, 180
Wadhans,
M.1, p. 161
M.5, p. 649
Wadhans Alahaniyan Dirges, M.1, p. 629
Wadhans Chhant, M.5, p. 492

## *Tahitian Traditional Religion*

Jean-Marie Loursin, *Tahiti* (Paris: Editions du Seuil, 1957).
p. 83

## *Taoism*

**Chuang Tzu.**
Wing-tsit Chan, comp. and trans., *A Source Book in Chinese Philosophy* (Princeton: Princeton University Press, 1963) [Marked C]; Wm. Theodore de Bary, Wing-tsit Chan, and Burton Watson, comps., *Sources of Chinese Tradition*, vol. 1 (New York: Columbia University Press, 1960) [Marked D]; Herbert A. Giles, trans., *Chuang Tzu: Mystic, Moralist, and Social Reformer*, 2d ed. (Shanghai: Kelly & Walsh, 1926; reprint, New York: AMS Press, 1974) [Marked G]; Burton Watson, trans., *Chuang Tzu: Basic Writings* (New York: Columbia University Press, 1964) [Marked W1]; Burton Watson, trans., *Complete Works of Chuang Tzu* (New York: Columbia University Press, 1968) [Marked W2].
1, pp. 221-22 [W1], 650-51 [D]
2, pp. 40-41 [W1], 120 [W1], 235-36 [D]
4, pp. 274 [W1], 507-8 [W1]

72, p. 126 [W]
73, p. 124 [L]
77, p. 387 [E]
79, pp. 89 [L], 702 [E]
80, pp. 198-99 [D]
81, pp. 570 [W], 690 [C]

**Tract of the Quiet Way** (Yin Chih Wen).
D. T. Suzuki and Paul Carus, trans., *Yin Chih Wen: The Tract of the Quiet Way with Extracts from the Chinese Commentary* (Peru, Illinois: Open Court Publishing Co., 1906; 1950).
pp. 38, 185, 209, 243, 256-57, 336, 346, 524, 527, 697, 711, 717, 723

## *Tenrikyo*

**Ofudesaki** (The Tip of the Divine Writing Brush).
[Miki Nakayama,] *Ofudesaki: The Tip of the Divine Writing Brush* (Tenri City, Japan: The Headquarters of Tenrikyo Church, 1971).
1.1-3, p. 452
2.22, p. 404
3.40, p. 62
3.41, p. 557
3.47, p. 695
4.79, p. 95
7.109-11, p. 137
12.89-94, p. 689
13.43-45, p. 191
14.25, p. 131
14.35, p. 366
17.64-70, p. 326

**Mikagura-uta** (Book of Sacred Songs).
[Miki Nakayama,] *Mikagura-uta: The Songs for the Tsutome* (Tenri City: The Headquarters of Tenrikyo Church, 1976).
p. 174

**Osashizu** (Divine Directions).
[Miki Nakayama,] *Osashizu* (Tenri City: The Headquarters of Tenrikyo Church)
p. 289

## *Theosophy*

H. P. Blavatsky, *The Key to Theosophy: An Abridgment*, ed. Joy Mills (Wheaton, Illinois: Theosophical Publishing House, 1967).
pp. 289-90

## *Unification Church*

**Divine Principle**.
*Divine Principle*, 2d ed. (New York: The Holy Spirit Association for the Unification of World Christianity, 1973).
1.1.2.3.4, p. 175
1.1.3.1, pp. 119-20, 137
1.2.2.2, pp. 304-5
1.3.2.1, p. 389
1.3.4.3, p. 796
1.3.5.2, p. 779-80

**Sun Myung Moon**.
Institute for the Rev. Sun Myung Moon's Sermons and Speeches at Sung Hwa University, its researchers' selection and translation of passages into English from Sun Myung Moon, *Moon Sun Myung Seonsaeng Malseum Seonjip* [Selections from Rev. Sun Myung Moon's Words], more than 100 vols. (Seoul, Korea: Sung Hwa Sa, 1984- ) submitted to *World Scripture*; Sun Myung Moon, *God's Will and the World* (New York: Holy Spirit Association for the Unification of World Christianity, 1985) [Marked G]; Sun Myung Moon, *The Way of God's Will* (New York: Holy Spirit Association for the Unification of World Christianity, 1980) [Marked W]; *Today's World* (New York: Holy Spirit Association for the Unification of World Christianity, 1980- ) [Marked T]; all passages are from the translation of the Institute for the Rev. Sun Myung Moon's Sermons and Speeches unless otherwise marked.
4-14-57, pp. 147, 368
6-28-59, p. 205
10-11-59, p. 325
12-13-59, p. 62
2-21-60, p. 642
2-12-61, p. 74
2-15-67, p. 594
1-1-68, p. 595
8-18-68, p. 411
9-30-69, pp. 171
3-17-70, p. 753
8-9-70, p. 680
10-13-70, pp. 56, 218-19 [G]
11-22-70, p. 522
12-5-71, p. 696
9-11-72, pp. 529 [G], 552 [G], 691 [G]
10-13-72, p. 54
10-20-73, pp. 94 [G], 132 [G], 198 [G], 290 [G], 332 [G], 689 [G], 702 [G]
2-6-77, p. 237

## *Zoroastrianism*

**Avesta.**

James Darmesteter, trans., *The Zend-Avesta, Part 1: The Vendidad,* Sacred Books of the East, vol. 4 (Oxford: Clarendon Press, 1887) [Marked D]; Homi Burjor Dhalla, his own translations submitted to *World Scripture* [Marked Dh]; Jacques Duchesne-Guillemin, *The Hymns of Zarathustra,* trans. from the French by Mrs. M. Henning (London: John Murray, 1963) [Marked Du]; S. Insler, *The Gathas of Zarathustra,* Acta Iranica 8, vol. 1 (Leiden: E.J. Brill, 1975) [Marked I]; H. K. Mirza, his own translations submitted to *World Scripture* [Marked M].

# PRONUNCIATION GUIDE

The languages of the scriptures include Arabic, Hebrew, Greek, Chinese, Japanese, and Indic tongues Sanskrit, Pali, and Prakrit. Pronunciation of proper names and technical terms from these languages presents difficulties for all but the specialist scholar. Here are a few guidelines to aid in pronouncing foreign terms. For diacritical marks, consult the indexes.

Sanskrit, Pali, Hindi, and Prakrit have distinctive consonants, among them: c is pronounced as ch in chair; ś and ṣ are written sh and pronounced as sh in ship. Otherwise the consonant h is distinct from what precedes it: thus th is pronounced as in boathouse, not as in thin; bh as in abhor; ph as in uphill, not as in phase; gh as in log hut. Vowels are pronounced as in Italian or Spanish: long a as in father, short a as in alone, e as in grey, short i as in pin, long i as in police, o as in soft, short u as in pull, long u as in flute. The diphthong au is pronounced ow as in cow. The accent is generally on the next to last syllable or on the nearest long syllable before it. The vowel of the last syllable is generally short, e.g., artha (art-huh), except for feminine names where it is is long, e.g., Sita (seetah), Kali (kalee).

Many Arabic consonants are unfamiliar to speakers of the European languages. '(*'ayn*) is an unaspirated guttural sound made in the throat; kh is pronounced as ch in German ach, th as in that, q as uvular k, and h (ḥ) a soft ch as in German ich. Adjacent vowels are always distinguished as two syllables, separated by a *hamza* or glottal stop before a vowel. It may be written ' or unmarked. Between vowels it is a jerked hiatus, like the Cockney pronunciation of "butter" or "bottle," e.g., Saudi (sa'oodee). Diphthongs are written aw or ay. Generally, the accent falls on the final syllable of a word.

In Hebrew, the consonant *'ayin* is not marked; it is a glottal stop when between vowels. The consonants ch or kh and sometimes h are pronounced as ch in German ach. The vowel e is short, as in end.

Chinese words are rendered according to the Wade-Giles system, which still predominates in scholarly literature in the West, even though some publications use the Pinyin system. Both romanizations only approximate the complex intonations of Chinese. Consonants followed by an apostrophe (ch', k', p', t', ts') are aspirated and sound like the English values ch, k, p, t, ts. Consonants not followed by an apostrophe (ch, k, p, t, ts, tz) are unaspirated and sound like the English values j, g, p, d, dz: e.g., Tao (dow), Ching (jing), Kwan Yin (gwan yin), Po I (bo yee). J is pronounced as r but with the tongue pressed against the palate, e.g., jen (ren); hs is pronounced as sh in ship. Note these vowels: ih is pronounced as ir in sir, e.g., shih (shir); u is long as in flute, but following tz or ss it is barely sounded, e.g., Lao Tzu (lao dz'); i is long as in police, but initial I is Yee. Adjacent vowels are always pronounced as a diphthong: ai as i in bike; ao as ow in cow; ei, eh as ey in grey; ie as in French chien; ou as o in go; ua as wa in want; ui as way.

# SUBJECT INDEX

Wherever possible, the English equivalent for foreign terms has been given in parentheses. The letters a and b have been used after page numbers to denote references to columns.

## A

# C

# E

# H

# I

# J

# M

# O



# P

# Q



# R

# S

# W

# Y



# Z



❖

# ACKNOWLEDGMENTS

Grateful acknowledgment is extended to the following holders of copyright for permission to reprint passages from the works indicated below.

Amana Books (Brattleboro, VT): *The Qur'an*, trans. Thomas B. Irving.

American Oriental Society (New Haven, CT): "Lila" by A. K. Coomaraswamy in *Journal of the American Oriental Society* (June 1941): 98.

Annana Balaga (Sirigere, India): *Vacanas of Basavanna*, ed. H. Deveerappa; trans. L. M. A. Menezes and S. M. Angadi.

Jason Aronson, Inc. (Northvale, NJ): *A Treasury of Jewish Quotations*, ed. Joseph L. Baron.

Asia Publishing House (Bombay) and Ashish Bose: *Hymns from the Vedas*, ed. Abinash Chandra Bose.

Asiatic Society (Calcutta): *The Markandaya-Purana*, ed. F. E. Pargiter.

Astor-Honor, Inc. (New York): *The Prayers of Man*, comp. Alfonso M. di Nola; ed. Patrick O'Connor; trans. Rex Benedict.

Awkwesasne Notes (Rooseveltown, NY): *Tales of the Iroquois*, by Tehanetorens.

Baha'i Publishing Trust (Wilmette, IL): *Epistle to the Son of the Wolf*, by Baha'u'llah. Copyright 1941, 1953, © 1988 by the National Spiritual Assembly of the Baha'is of the United States. *Gleanings from the Writings of Baha'u'llah*, by Baha'u'llah. Copyright 1952, © 1976 by the National Spiritual Assembly of the Baha'is of the United States. *The Hidden Words of Baha'u'llah*, by Baha'u'llah, reprinted 1985 by the National Spiritual Assembly of the Baha'is of the United States. *Kitab-i-Iqan: The Book of Certitude*, by Baha'u'llah. Copyright 1931, 1950 by the National Spiritual Assembly of the Baha'is of the United States. *The Promulgation of Universal Peace: Talks Delivered by 'Abdu'l-Baha during His Visit to the United States and Canada in 1912*, by 'Abdu'l-Baha. Copyright 1982 by the National Spiritual Assembly of the Baha'is of the United States. *The Seven Valleys and the Four Valleys*, by Baha'u'llah. Copyright 1945, 1952, © 1973, 1975, 1978 by the National Spiritual Assembly of the Baha'is of the United States. *Tablets of Baha'u'llah Revealed after the Kitab-i-Aqdas*, by Baha'u'llah. Copyright © 1978, 1988 by the Universal House of Justice.

Behrman House, Inc. (W. Orange, NJ): *Sayings of the Fathers*, ed. Joseph J. Hertz. *The Talmudic Anthology*, ed. Louis I. Newman and Samuel Spitz.

Bhaktivedanta Book Trust—International (Los Angeles): *Krsna: The Supreme Personality of Godhead*, Vol. 1, by A. C. Bhaktivedanta. Copyright © 1970 Bhaktivedanta Book Trust—International.

Bhikkhu Training Center (Maharagama, Sri Lanka): *The Dhammapada*, trans. Narada Maha Thera.

K. H. Bokser: *The Prayer Book: Weekday, Sabbath and Festival*, trans. Ben Zion Bokser.

Georges Borchardt, Inc. (New York): *Tahiti*, by Jean-Marie Loursin.

Ashish Bose: *The Call of the Vedas*, ed. and trans. Abinash Chandra Bose.

Bridge Publications, Inc. (Los Angeles): *Handbook for Preclears*, by L. Ron Hubbard. Copyright © 1989 L. Ron Hubbard Library. All Rights Reserved. *A New Slant on Life*, by L. Ron Hubbard. Copyright © 1988 L. Ron Hubbard Library. All Rights Reserved. *Science of Survival*, by L. Ron Hubbard. Copyright © 1989 L. Ron Hubbard Library. All Rights Reserved. *Scientology 0-8, The Book of Basics*, by L. Ron Hubbard. Copyright © 1988 L. Ron Hubbard Library. All Rights Reserved. Grateful acknowledgement is made to L. Ron Hubbard Library for permission to reprint selections from these copyrighted works of L. Ron Hubbard.

Buddhist Churches of America (San Francisco): *Shinshu Seiten: Jodo Shin Buddhist Teaching.*

The Buddhist Society (London): *The Sutra of Forty-Two Sections*, trans. Chu Ch'an.

Buddhist Text Translation Society of Dharma Realm Buddhist Association (Talmage, CA): *A General Explanation of the Buddha Speaks: The Sutra in Forty-Two Sections*, by Hsuan-hua, trans. Bhikshuni Heng Chih.

Bukkyo Dendo Kyokai (Tokyo): *The Mahayana Mahaparinirvana Sutra*, trans. Kosho Yamamoto. *The Teaching of Buddha*, rev. ed. *The World of Shinto.*

Cambridge University Press (Cambridge): *Tales of the Yanomami*, by Jacques Lizot, trans. Ernest Simon. Copyright © 1985 by Cambridge University Press. Reprinted with the permission of Cambridge University Press.

Carol Publishing Group (New York): *The Hundred Thousand Songs of Milarepa*, trans. Garma C. C. Chang. Copyright © 1977. Published by arrangement with Carol Publishing Group.

Caxton Printers, Ltd. (Caldwell, ID): *War Chief Joseph*, by Helen Addison Howard.

Chaukhambha Orientalia (Varanasi, India): *The Garuda Purana*, trans. M. N. Dutt.

Columbia University Press (New York): *The Awakening of Faith, Attributed to Asvaghosha*, trans. Yoshito S. Hakeda. Copyright © 1967 Columbia University Press. *Chuang Tzu: Basic Writings*, ed. and trans. Burton Watson. Copyright © 1964 Columbia University Press. *Complete Works of Chuang Tzu*, trans. Burton Watson. Copyright © 1968 Columbia University Press. *The Lion's Roar of Queen Srimala*, trans. Alex Wayman and Hideko Wayman. Copyright © 1974 Columbia University Press. *Scripture of the Lotus Blossom of the Fine Dharma*, trans. Leon Hurvitz. Copyright © 1976 Columbia University Press. *Sources of Chinese Tradition*, Vol. 1, ed. Wm. Theodore de Bary, Wing-tsit Chan, and Burton Watson. Copyright © 1960 Columbia University Press. *Sources of Indian Tradition*, Vol. 1, ed. Wm. Theodore de Bary. Copyright © 1958 Columbia University Press. *Sources of Japanese Tradition*, Vol. 1, comp. Ryusaku Tsunoda, Wm. T. de Bary, and D. Keene. Copyright © 1958, 1964 Columbia University Press. Used by permission.

Crossroad Publishing Co. (New York): *Our Masters Taught*, ed. Jacob J. Petuchowski.

Curzon Press Ltd. (London): *A Manual of Hadith*, 2d ed., ed. Maulana Muhammad Ali. *The Sutta-Nipata*, trans. H. Saddhatissa.

Walter de Gruyter & Co. (Berlin): *Prayer in the Talmud*, by Joseph Heinemann.

J. M. Dent & Sons Ltd. (London): *Hindu Scriptures*, trans. and ed. R. C. Zaehner.

Jacques Duchesne-Guillemin: *The Gathas of Zarathustra*, by S. Insler.

E. P. Dutton (New York): *Everyman's Talmud*, trans. Abraham Cohen, Copyright © 1949 by E. P. Dutton. *A Buddhist Bible*, ed. Dwight Goddard. Copyright © 1966 by E. P. Dutton. Reprinted by permission of the publisher, Dutton, an imprint of New American Library, a division of Penguin USA Inc.

Everyman's Library, Ltd. (London): *Hindu Scriptures*, trans. and ed. Nicol Macnicol.

Far Eastern Publishers International (Singapore): *West African Traditional Religion*, by Kofi Asare Opoku.

Claire R. Farrer: "Singing for Life: The Mescalero Apache Girls' Puberty Ceremony," in *Southwestern Indian Ritual Drama*, ed. C. J. Frisbie.

Four Seasons Foundation (San Francisco): *The Perfection of Wisdom in Eight Thousand Lines and Its Verse Summary*, ed. and trans. Edward Conze. Sanskrit language terms were translated into English with permission from the publisher.

Fourth Dimension Publishing Co. (Enugu, Nigeria): *Ofo: Igbo Ritual Symbol*, by Christopher I. Ejizu.

Fay Gaer: *The Lore of the Old Testament*, ed. Joseph Gaer.
Grove Press (New York): *Muntu*, by Janheinz Jahn, trans. Marjorie Grene. *The Way and Its Power*, by Arthur Waley. *What the Buddha Taught*, rev. ed., ed. Walpola Rahula.
Joan Halifax and Richard Erdoes: *Shamanic Voices*, by Joan Halifax.
Raymond Jack Hammer: "The Scripture of 'Perfect Liberty Kyodan': A Translation with a Brief Commmentary" in *Japanese Religion* 3 (Spring 1963): 18-26.
HarperCollins Publishers (New York): *American Indian Mythology*, comp. Alice Marriott and Carol Rachlin. Copyright © 1968 by Alice Marriott and Carol Rachlin. *A New Translation of the Bible Containing the Old and New Testaments*, ed. James Moffatt. Copyright © 1922 by Harper & Row. Reprinted by permission of HarperCollins Publishers.
Harvard University Press (Cambridge, MA): *Judaism in the First Centuries of the Christian Era*, Vol. 1, ed. George Foote Moore, Copyright Vol. 1 © 1927 by the President and Fellows of Harvard College, renewed 1955 by Alfred H. Moore. Reprinted by permission.
Hebrew Publishing Co.: *The Encyclopedia of Jewish Concepts*, ed. Philip Birnbaum, 1964, p. 42. Copyright © 1979. All rights reserved. *Daily Prayer Book*, ed. Philip Birnbaum, 1949, p. 184. Copyright © 1977. All rights reserved. Reprinted by permission of the Publishers, Hebrew Publishing Co., P.O. Box 157, Rockaway Beach, NY 11693.
Heinemann Publishers Ltd. (Oxford): *African Religions and Philosophy*, by John S. Mbiti.
Holy Spirit Association for the Unification of World Christianity (New York): *Divine Principle*, 2d ed. *God's Will and the World*, by Sun Myung Moon. *Today's World*. *The Way of God's Will*, by Sun Myung Moon.
Jeffrey Hopkins: *Compassion in Tibetan Buddhism*.
Charles F. Horne, III: *The Sacred Books and Early Literature of the East*, Vol. 10, ed. Charles F. Horne.
Human Relations Area Files Press (New Haven, CT): *The Yamana*, by M. Gusinde.
Ezzeddin Ibrahim and Denys Johnson-Davies: *An-Nawawi's Forty Hadith*.
Edmund Emefie Ikenga-Metuh: *Comparative Studies of African Traditional Religions*.
Kenneth K. Inada and The Hokuseido Press (Tokyo): *Nagarjuna: Mulamadhyamakakarika*.
Indian Institute of World Culture (Bangalore, India): *The Indian Heritage*, ed. V. Raghavan.
Judaica Press, Inc. (Brooklyn, NY): *Mishnah*.
Kazi Publications (Chicago): *The Translation of the Meanings of Sahih Al-Bukhari*, trans. Muhammad M. Khan.
Khaniqahi-Nimatullahi Publications (New York): *Traditions of the Prophet*, by Javad Nurbakhsh.
Church of Jesus Christ of Latter-day Saints (Salt Lake City, UT): *The Book of Mormon*. *The Doctrine and Covenants*. *The Pearl of Great Price*.
Library of Tibetan Works and Archives (Dharamsala, India): *A Guide to the Bodhisattva's Way of Life*, by Acharya Shantideva, trans. Stephen Batchelor. *Mahayana Purification*, trans. Gonsar Tulku.
Longman Group Ltd. (Harlow, U.K.): *Yoruba Beliefs and Sacrificial Rites*, ed. J. O. Awolalu.
Lutterworth Press (London): *African Ideas of God*, ed. E. W. Smith.
Macmillan Publishing Co. (New York): *Islam: Muhammad and His Religion*, ed. Arthur Jeffery. Copyright © 1958 by Bobbs-Merrill. *Tao-te Ching: The Way of Lao Tzu*, ed. and trans. Wing-tsit Chan. Copyright © 1963 by Bobbs-Merrill. Reprinted by permission of Macmillan Publishing Co.
William McNaughton (Hong Kong): *The Confucian Vision*.
Sushil Kumarji Maharaj: *Song of the Soul*.
Mitra Parishad (Calcutta): *Shraman Mahavir*, by Muni Nathmal, trans. Sri Dineshchandra Sharma.
Motilal Banarsidass (Delhi, India): *The Buddhacarita*, enl. ed., trans. E. H. Johnston. *A Critical Study of Adi Granth*, by Surindar Singh Kohli. *Kularnava Tantra*, by M. P. Pandit. *The Siva Purana*.
Mouton de Gruyter (Berlin): *Korean Shamanistic Rituals*, by Jung Young Lee. Reprinted by permission of Mouton de Gruyter, a Division of Walter de Gruyter & Co.
Munshiram Manoharlal Publishers (New Delhi, India): *The Mahabharata of Krishna-Dwaipayana Vyasa*, trans. Kisarai M. Ganguli.
Senchu Murano: *The Lotus Sutra*, Nichiren Shu Headquarters.
John Murray Publishers Ltd. (London): *Buddhist Psalms*, by Shinran, trans. S. Yamabe and L. Adams Beck. *The Hymns of Zarathustra*, by Jacques Duchesne-Guillemin, trans. from French by M. Henning. *Sayings of Muhammad*, trans. Abdullah Suhrawardy.
The Muslim World, Hartford Seminary Foundation (Hartford, CT): "The Forty Traditions of an-Nawawi,"

by Eric F. F. Bishop, in *The Moslem World* 29 (April 1939): 163-77.

Muslim World League (New York): *The Meaning of the Glorious Qur'an*, trans. Muhammad M. Pickthall.

National Council of the Churches of Christ in the U.S.A., Division of Christian Education (New York): *The Revised Standard Version Apocrypha*. Copyright 1957 by the Division of Christian Education of the National Council of the Churches of Christ in the USA. *The Revised Standard Version Bible*. Copyright 1946, 1952, 1971 by the Division of Christian Education of the National Council of the Churches of Christ in the USA. Used by permission.

New Directions Publishing Corporation (New York): *The Dhammapada*, trans. Irving Babbitt. Copyright 1936 by Edward S. Babbit and Esther B. Howe. Reprinted by permission of New Directions Publishing Corp.

Nichiren Shoshu International Center (Tokyo): *Lectures on the Sutra*, rev. ed.

Nichiren Shu Overseas Propagation Promotion Association (Tokyo): *Hoon-Jo*, by Nichiren, trans. T. Yajima. *Kaimoku-Sho*, by Nichiren, trans. K. Hori.

Nilgiri Press (Petaluma, CA): *The Bhagavad Gita*, trans. Eknath Easwaran. *The Upanishads*, trans. Eknath Easwaran.

Open Court Publishing Co. (Peru, IL): *Treatise on Response and Retribution*, by Lao Tze, trans. D. T. Suzuki and Paul Carus. *Yin Chih Wen: The Tract of the Quiet Way*, trans. D. T. Suzuki and Paul Carus.

The Overlook Press: *Muhammad and the Islamic Tradition*, by Emile Dermenghem, trans. Jean. M. Watt. Copyright 1955 Editions du Seuil, translation copyright 1958 Longmans, Green & Co. Ltd. Published by the Overlook Press, Lewis Hollow Road, Woodstock, NY.

Oxford University Press (Oxford): *The Ashanti*, by R. S. Rattray, 1923. *Divinity and Experience*, by Godfrey Lienhardt, 1961. *The Hevajra Tantra*, Vol. 1, by D. L. Snellgrove, 1959. *Jaina Yoga*, ed. R. H. B. Williams, 1963. *Law and Authority in a Nigerian Tribe*, by C. K. Meek, 1937. *The Life of Muhammad: A Translation of Ibn Ishaq's Sirat Rasul Allah*, trans. A. Guillaume, 1955. *The Lotus of the Wonderful Law*, trans. W. E. Soothill, 1930. *The Mishnah*, trans. and ed. Herbert Danby, 1933. *Nuer Religion*, by E. E. Evans-Pritchard, 1956. *Siva: The Erotic Ascetic*, by Wendy Doniger O'Flaherty, 1973. *Some Sayings of the Buddha*, trans. F. L. Woodward, 1973. *The Thirteen Principal Upanishads*, trans. and ed. R. E. Hume, 1931. *Tibet's Great Yogi, Milarepa*, ed. W. Y. Evans-Wentz, trans. Lama Kaji Dawa-Samdup, 1928. *The Tibetan Book of the Dead*, ed. W. Y. Evans-Wentz, 1927. *The Tibetan Yoga and Secret Doctrines*, ed. W. Y. Evans-Wentz, 1958. Reprinted by permission of Oxford University Press.

Oxford University Press, Indian Branch (Delhi): *The Dhammapada*, trans. and ed. Sarvepalli Radhakrishnan.

Oxford University Press, East African Branch (Nairobi): *Prayer in the Religious Traditions of Africa*, by Aylward Shorter.

Oxford and Cambridge University Presses (Oxford and Cambridge): *The Revised English Bible with the Apocrypha*, © 1989. Reprinted by permission of Oxford and Cambridge University Presses.

Pali Text Society (Oxford): *The Book of the Discipline*, trans. I. B. Horner. *Dialogues of the Buddha (Digha Nikaya)*, Parts 1-3, trans. T. W. Rhys Davids et al. *The Elders' Verses II: Therigatha*, trans. K. R. Norman. *Gradual Sayings (Anguttara Nikaya)*, trans. F. L. Woodward and E. M. Hare. *The Group of Discourses*, trans. K. R. Norman. *The Jataka; or, Stories of the Buddha's Former Births*, Vol. 5, trans. H. T. Francis. *The Minor Readings (Khuddaka Patha)*, trans. Bhikkhu Nanamoli. *Kindred Sayings (Samyutta Nikaya)*, trans. C. A. F. Rhys Davids and F. L. Woodward. *Middle Length Sayings (Majjhima Nikaya)*, trans. I. B. Horner. *The Minor Anthologies of the Pali Canon*, Part 2, Udana and Itivuttaka, trans. F. L. Woodward. *The Minor Anthologies of the Pali Canon*, Part 4, Vimana Vatthu and Peta Vatthu, trans. J. Kennedy and H. S. Gehman. *Psalms of the Early Buddhists*, trans. C. A. F. Rhys Davids.

Pantheon Books (New York): *American Indian Myths and Legends*, ed. Richard Erdoes and Alfonso Ortiz. Copyright © 1984 by Richard Erdoes and Alfonzo Ortiz. Reprinted by permission of Pantheon Books, a Division of Random House, Inc.

Paragon House (New York): *The Tao Te Ching*, by Ellen M. Chen.

Paulist Press (Ramsey, NJ): *Native North American Spirituality of the Eastern Woodlands*, comp. Elizabeth Tooker. Copyright © 1979 Paulist Press.

Penguin Books Ltd. (London): *Confucius: The Analects*, trans. D. C. Lau, Penguin Classics, 1979, pp. 96 and 158. Copyright © D. C. Lau, 1979. *Hindu Myths: A Sourcebook*, trans. Wendy Doniger O'Flaherty, Penguin Books, 1975, pp. 222-26. Copyright © Wendy Doniger O'Flaherty, 1975. *The Lankavatara Sutra: A Mahayana Text*, trans. Daisetz Teitaro Suzuki, first published by Routledge & Kegan Paul, 1932, now published by Penguin Books. Copyright © Daisetz Teitaro Suzuki, 1932. *Tao Te Ching*, by Lao Tzu, trans. D. C. Lau, Penguin Classics, 1963. Copyright © D. C. Lau, 1963. *Mencius*, trans. D. C. Lau, Penguin Classics 1970. Copyright © D. C. Lau, 1970. Reproduced by permission of Penguin Books Ltd.

Penguin USA, Inc. (New York): *The Living Talmud: The Wisdom of the Fathers*, trans. and ed. Judah Goldin. Copyright © 1957 by Judah Goldin. *The Ramayana*, by R. K. Narayan. Copyright © 1972 by R. K. Narayan. Reprinted by permission of Viking Penguin, a division of Penguin USA, Inc.

Pennsylvania State University Press (University Park and London): *The Holy Teaching of Vimalakirti*, trans. Robert A. F. Thurman, 1976. Copyright 1979 by The Pennsylvania State University. *A Treasury of Mahayana Sutras: Selections from the Maharatnakuta Sutra*, ed. Garma C. C. Chang, 1983, pp. 245 and 279. Copyright 1983 by The Pennsylvania State University Press. Reproduced by permission of the publisher.

Philosophical Library, a Division of Allied Books (New York): *Buddhism: Its Essence and Development*, ed. Edward Conze. *Buddhist Texts Through the Ages*, ed. Edward Conze.

Princeton University Press (Princeton, NJ): *The I Ching; or, Book of Changes*, trans. Richard Wilhelm, rendered into English by Cary F. Baynes, Bollingen Series 19. Copyright 1950, © 1967, 1977 renewed by Princeton University Press. *A Source Book in Chinese Philosophy*, trans. Wing-Tsit Chan. Copyright © 1963 by Princeton University Press. Scattered quotes reprinted with permission of Princeton University Press.

Publication Bureau of Punjabi University (Patiala, India): *Sri Guru Granth Sahib*, trans. Gurbachan Singh Talib.

Ramakrishna-Vivekananda Center (New York): *The Upanishads: Volumes I-IV*, trans. Swami Nikhilananda, published by the Ramakrishna-Vivekananda Center of New York. Copyright 1949, 1952, 1956, and 1959, by Swami Nikhilananda.

Random House, Inc. (New York): *The Buddhist Tradition in India, China and Japan*, ed. Wm. Theodore de Bary. Copyright © 1969 by Wm. Theodore de Bary. *Facing Mount Kenya*, by Jomo Kenyatta. Copyright © 1961. *The Wisdom of Confucius*, ed. and trans. Lin Yutang. Copyright © 1938 and renewed 1966 by Random House, Inc. Reprinted by permission of Random House, Inc.

Rider & Co., Random Century Group (London): *The Lion's Roar*, trans. David Maurice. *The Heart of Buddhist Meditation*, trans. and ed. Nyanaponika Thera.

Ronald Press, a Division of John Wiley & Sons (New York): *The Religion of the Hindus*, ed. Kenneth W. Morgan. Copyright © 1953 Ronald Press. Reprinted by permission of John Wiley & Sons, Inc.

Routledge & Kegan Paul (London): *Nupe Religion*, ed. S. F. Nadel.

St. Martin's Press, Inc. (New York): *The Talmud for Today*, trans. Alexander Feinsilver. Copyright © 1980 St. Martin's Press, Inc.

Schocken Books (New York): *Hammer on the Rock: A Short Midrash Reader*, ed. Nahum N. Glatzer, trans. Jacob Sloan. Copyright 1948, 1962 and renewed 1975 by Schocken Books. *Zohar: The Book of Splendor*, ed. Gershom Scholem. Copyright 1949 and renewed 1977 by Schocken Books. Reprinted by permission of Schocken Books, published by Pantheon Books, a division of Random House, Inc.

Scholars Press (Decatur, GA): *The Buddhist Feminine Ideal*, by Diana Y. Paul.

Martin Secker & Warburg (London): *Facing Mount Kenya: The Tribal Life of Gikuyu*, by Jomo Kenyatta.

Seicho-No-Ie Truth of Life Movement North American Missionary Hq. (Gardena, CA): *Holy Sutra for Spiritual Healing*, by Masaharu Taniguchi. *Holy Sutra Nectarean Shower of Holy Doctrines*, rev. ed., by Masaharu Taniguchi.

Sh. Muhammad Ashraf (Lahore, Pakistan): *Mishkat Al-Masabih*, trans. James Robson. *Sahih Muslim*, trans. Abdul Hamid Siddiqi. *Sayings of Muhammad*, trans. Ghazi Ahmad.

Shambhala Publications: *Bodhisattva of Compassion*, by John Blofeld, © 1977. *The Flower Ornament Scripture: A Translation of the Avatamsaka Sutra* (Vols. I and II), trans. and ed. Thomas Cleary, © 1984 (Vol. I), © 1986 (Vol. II). *Selected Sayings from the Perfection of Wisdom*, trans. Edward Conze, © 1955. Reprinted by arrangement with Shambhala Publications, Inc., 300 Massachusetts Ave., Boston, MA 02115.

Shanti Sadan (London): *The Ramayana of Valmiki*, trans. Hari Prasad Shastri.

Shivamurthy Shivacharya Mahaswamiji: *Religion and Society at Cross-roads*.

Harbans Singh: *The Message of Sikhism*, 4th ed., Delhi Sikhi Gurdwara Management Committee.

Smithsonian Institution Press (Washington, DC): "Notes from Bull Thigh, Sept. 7, 1910," *Bureau of American Ethnology*, by Truman Michelson. *Lugbara Religion, Ritual and Authority among an East African People*, by John Middleton, p. 119, © Smithsonian Institution 1988. Reprinted by permission of the Smithsonian Institution Press.

Society of Johrei (Kyoto, Japan): *Johrei*, by Mokichi Okada.

Soncino Press Ltd. (Brooklyn, NY): *The Babylonian Talmud*, trans. and ed. I. Epstein. *Midrash Rabbah*, trans. H. Freedman and Maurice Simon. *The Minor Tractates of the Talmud*, 2d ed, trans. and ed. A. Cohen. *The Zohar*, trans. and ed. Harry Sperling and Maurice Simon.

Sukyo Mahikari Honbu (Takayama, Japan): *Goseigen: The Holy Words*.

Theosophical Publishing House (Wheaton, IL): *The Key to Theosophy: An Abridgment*, by H. P. Blavatsky, ed. Joy Mills.

University of California Press (Berkeley): *The Bhagavadgita: A New Translation*, trans. Kees W. Bolle, © 1979 The Regents of the University of California. *Indian Legends of the Pacific Northwest*, by Ella E. Clark, © 1953 The Regents of the University of California, © renewed 1981 Ella E. Clark. *The Jaina Path of Purification*, by Padmanabh S. Jaini, © 1979 The Regents of the University of California. *The Large Sutra on Perfect Wisdom, with the Divisions of the Abhisamayalankara*, trans. and ed. Edward Conze, © 1975 The Regents of the University of California. *Mantramanjari: The Vedic Experience*, trans. and ed. Raimundo Panikkar, © 1977 Raimundo Panikkar. *The Origins of Evil in Hindu Mythology*, by Wendy Doniger O'Flaherty, © 1976 The Regents of the University of California.

University of Chicago Press (Chicago): *The Mahabharata*, Vol. 1, The Book of the Beginning, trans. and ed. J. A. B. van Buitenen, © 1973 by The University of Chicago. *Red Man's Religion*, comp. Ruth Murray Underhill, © 1965 by The University of Chicago. *The Religion, Spirituality, and Thought of Traditional Africa*, by Dominque Zahan, trans. Kate E. Martin and Lawrence M. Martin, © 1979 by The University of Chicago.

University of Ghana (Accra, Ghana): *Drumming in Akan Communities of Ghana*, ed. J. H. Nketia.

University of Nebraska Press (Lincoln, NE): *Lakota Belief and Ritual*, by James R. Walker, ed. Raymond J. DeMallie and Elaine A. Jahner. Reprinted by permission of University of Nebraska Press, Copyright © 1980 by the University of Nebraska Press.

University of Oklahoma Press (Norman, OK): *The Sacred Pipe: Black Elk's Account of the Seven Rites of the Oglala Sioux*, recorded and ed. Joseph Epes Brown. Copyright © 1953 by the University of Oklahoma Press.

University of Tokyo Press (Tokyo) and Donald L. Philippi: *Kojiki*.

University Press Ltd. (Ibadan, Nigeria): *Yoruba Oral Tradition*, ed. Wande Abimbola.

University Press of America (Lanham, MD): *A Path of Righteousness: Dhammapada*, trans. David J. Kalupahana.

Unwin Hyman Ltd., Part of HarperCollins Publishers (London): *The Analects of Confucius*, trans. Arthur Waley. Copyright © 1938 by George Allen & Unwin Ltd. *Bodhisattva of Compassion: The Mystical Tradition of Kuan Yin*, by John Blofeld. Copyright © 1977 by John Blofeld. *Buddhist Wisdom Books: Containing the Diamond Sutra and the Heart Sutra*, trans. and ed. Edward Conze. Copyright © 1958 by George Allen & Unwin Ltd. *I Ching: The Book of Change*, trans. John Blofeld. Copyright © 1976 by George Allen & Unwin Ltd. *The Koran Interpreted*, trans. Arthur J. Arberry. Copyright © 1955 by George Allen & Unwin Ltd. *The Precious Garland and the Song of the Four Mindfulnesses*, by Nagarjuna, trans. and ed. Jeffrey Hopkins and Lati Rimpoche. Copyright © 1975 by George Allen & Unwin Ltd. *Selections from the Sacred Writings of the Sikhs*, trans. Trilochan Singh et al. Copyright © 1960 by George Allen & Unwin Ltd. *Tantra in Tibet: The Great Exposition of Secret Mantra*, by Tsong-ka-pa, Vol. 1, trans. and ed. Jeffrey Hopkins. Copyright © 1977 by George Allen & Unwin Ltd. Reproduced by kind permission of Unwin Hyman Ltd.

Vedanta Press (Hollywood, CA): *The Song of God: Bhagavad-Gita*, trans. Swami Prabhavananda and Christopher Isherwood. *The Spiritual Heritage of India*, ed. Swami Prabhavananda. *Srimad Bhagavatam: The Wisdom of God*, trans. Swami Prabhavananda. *The Upanishads: Breath of the Eternal*, trans. Swami Prabhavananda and Frederick Manchester.

Samuel Weiser, Inc. (York Beach, ME): *The Heart of Buddhist Meditation*, trans. Nyanaponika Thera, 1965, pp. 145 and 169-70.

Yale University Press (New Haven, CT): *The Midrash on Psalms*, trans. William G. Braude. *Peskita Rabbati*, Vol. 1, trans. William G. Braude.

---

The editor and publishing staff have made every effort to trace the copyright holders but if they have inadvertantly overlooked any, they will be pleased to make the necessary arrangement at the first opportunity.